India Studies in Business and Economics

India is one of the fastest growing economies of the world, with the country being an important G20 member. It is a significant player in the global market with a notable demographic advantage, and an important geo-political and geo-trade position. Additionally, due to its position of being not only the most populous country in the world, but also the world's largest youth population, India has a pivotal role to play in meeting global SDG goals. This makes research from the country to be of immense interest to the global community.

With this backdrop, this series aims to bring forth the latest studies and research specific to India from all areas of economics, finance, business, trade, and management science, often with strong social science and political economy linkages. The titles featured in this series present rigorous research, both empirical and non-empirical in nature, usually accompanied by policy recommendations. They evoke and evaluate various aspects of the economical and/or the business and management landscape in India, with a special focus on India's relationship with the world. The series also tracks research on India's position on social issues, on health, on politics, on agriculture, on rights, and many such topics which directly or indirectly affect sustainable growth of the country.

The series welcomes contributions from scholars or practitioners belonging to the academic community, corporates, think tanks and/or non-governmental organizations, and also policymakers to publish their work in the form of authored monographs, edited volumes or collection of case studies. Each proposal undergoes at least two double blind peer review where a detailed concept note along with extended chapter abstracts and/or a sample chapter is peer reviewed by experienced academics. The reviews may be more detailed if recommended by reviewers. The series follows the Ethics Statement as per Springer Nature's standard guidelines.

Dibyendu Maiti · Bishwanath Goldar ·
K. L. Krishna
Editors

75 Years of Growth, Development and Productivity in India

Issues, Measures, Causes, and Impacts

Springer

Editors
Dibyendu Maiti
Delhi School of Economics
University of Delhi
New Delhi, India

Bishwanath Goldar
Institute of Economic Growth
New Delhi, Delhi, India

K. L. Krishna
Delhi School of Economics
University of Delhi
New Delhi, Delhi, India

ISSN 2198-0012 ISSN 2198-0020 (electronic)
India Studies in Business and Economics
ISBN 978-981-97-8056-3 ISBN 978-981-97-8054-9 (eBook)
https://doi.org/10.1007/978-981-97-8054-9

This Springer imprint is published by the registered company Springer Nature Singapore Pte Ltd.
The registered company address is: 152 Beach Road, #21-01/04 Gateway East, Singapore 189721, Singapore

Preface

After independence, the Indian economy has passed through different phases of economic policy experiments under various economic situations that helped gradually lift its pace of economic growth and address several developmental issues from poverty to well-being during the last 75 years. For an economy with a vast population and regional, cultural, and climatic diversities, the history of economic achievements and challenges therein must be very different from those of others who have already developed in the past and are emerging in different ways. The aim of this edited volume is to document some of them with simple illustrations so that ordinary readers without much knowledge of the subject can understand them easily.

The rise in productivity is one factor that has contributed to the economic growth and development on which the book takes a position. From the classical work of Adam Smith on the *wealth of nations* to the basic development doctrine that is rooted in the Lewisian framework, none could deny the role of technological progress, defined as increases in total factor productivity. Productivity growth, driven by technology, efficiency, and the combination of markets and institutions, plays a prime role in accelerating economic growth, development, and people's welfare. It shifts the domain of production and hence brings opulence to human life. It plays a significant role in pushing up the rate of long-run economic growth. Moreover, the dynamics of productivity growth governing short-run economic activities and business cycles have appeared as a growing research and discussion topic for academics and practitioners. A fair understanding of productivity dynamics is the key to understanding the question of sustained growth and stabilisation strategies of an economy. This apart, the catching-up level of economic development of a nation compared to its frontier, which hinges on the progress of the modern sector in the developing world, is essentially rooted in the question of productivity convergence between the existing sectors. The post-independence period of the Indian economy, commencing from the inception of planning in 1950 to the onset of the pandemic crisis in the 2020s, was characterised by a massive improvement over pre-independence performance coupled with some avoidable inadequacies, particularly in terms of incentives and institutional structures and punctuated with droughts, natural disasters, wars, epidemics, and oil-crisis. The economy witnessed a significant transformation from almost zero growth in the pre-impendence period during 1990-1950 to the Hindu rate of growth of 3.5% in the first three decades of post-independence India to a higher level in the later period. But, the growth rate has seen its ups and downs and has slowed down in recent years. The role of productivity growth in the transition continues to be debated. Though the economy has witnessed a significant improvement in the level of economic development during the past 75 years since independence, still the scholars and policy-makers engaged in the development debate have been bothered about insufficient progress made regarding a number of development outcomes (e.g., poverty, informality, decent employment, and inequality) that seem to have been influenced by the way productivity growth has progressed in India. Therefore, India's productivity growth dynamics continue to engage economists and policy-makers and remain much debated. The trends and patterns of the productivity growth observed in India have accelerated following macroeconomic reforms and policy changes in investment and trade regimes. However, the growing uncertainties in the global market and the changing strategies of financial institutions to cope with the uncertainties affecting investment and trade behaviour must have played detrimental roles in designing productivity growth in recent times. These will be affecting economic growth and stabilisation in the near future. This is another reason why the dynamics of productivity growth in India continue to engage economists and policy-makers and remain much debated.

This book brings together a collection of articles from a set of reputed scholars and policy-makers for in-depth discussions on various issues that are linked with productivity advance having a critical influence on growth and development outcomes. The academic papers, both theoretical and empirical, document the pace and patterns of India's economic growth and productivity since independence, unfolding the issues and factors of the sectors affecting the path of development with a particular focus on productivity growth of the Indian economy that may pave the way for a debate on planning the policy for Vision@2047.

New Delhi, India

Dibyendu Maiti
Bishwanath Goldar
K. L. Krishna

Acknowledgements

While India aims to achieve income levels of a high-income economy by 2047, at the time of 100 years from independence, the history of India's economic transition from very low income under colonial rule to a level of the fastest growing country with all other development challenges must be a good basis to portray the vision accurately, and understand the challenges in attaining the vision. The book aims to fill this gap, with the added advantage that the book can be read without much subject knowledge.

The idea of putting together and editing such a book arose during the final workshop of the India KLEMS project held at the Delhi School of Economics on 16-17 September 2022. Some of the papers presented at the workshop appeared in a special issue of the Indian Growth and Development Review (vol. 17.2), and a few papers were submitted to other journals. As a result, we were left with only a few papers to build on such an important book. Therefore, we extended invitations to others for their contribution to the book. When things were moving slowly, the ICSSR (Indian Council of Social Science Research) stepped in and sanctioned our proposal of financial assistance of Rs 3 Lakhs (F.NoNIS/NS/265/IC/2023-24). This generous support not only helped us hold a workshop but also significantly accelerated the progress towards the book. A group was established, and young scholars agreed to contribute and present at the Delhi School of Economics workshop on 7–9 March 2024. Effectively, this workshop designed the shape of the book.

Our heartfelt gratitude goes out to all the contributors, especially T.C.A. Anant, Pami Dua, Nagesh Kumar, Rajat Acharya, Ajitava Raychaudhuri, and C. Veeramani, for their invaluable time and effort in attending the workshop and contributing their insightful chapters, which significantly enriched the book. Thank is also due to Mr. TCA Ranganathan (Former Chairman & Managing Director, EXIM Bank of India), who attended the workshop and gave valuable inputs to improve each chapter. We also extend our sincere thanks to Mr. Mahesh Madhukar, whose instrumental role in securing financial support from the ICSSR was crucial to the book's progress. We further acknowledge the contributions of Ms. Chinngaineng Haokip and Anjali Gaur, who provided their research assistance, and a special mention to Ms. Chinngaineng Haokip for her unwavering editorial support until the finalisation of all materials for the book. Usual disclaimers apply.

Contents

Editors and Contributors

About the Editors

Dibyendu Maiti is a professor of Economics at the Delhi School of Economics, University of Delhi, India. He specialises in development macroeconomics and international economics, with a specific focus on labour, technology, and the informal sector. Before this, he worked at the University of the South Pacific, Institute of Economic Growth Delhi, and Centre for Studies in Social Sciences Calcutta, as well as held various research positions at the University of Manchester, University of Nottingham, Max Planck Institute of Economics (Jena), Norwegian Institute of International Affairs, University of Oslo. He received the Max Planck India Fellowship, ICSSR-ESRC exchange and ICSSR-CASS exchange fellowship. He publishes research articles in reputed journals, like the Journal of Development Economics, Empirical Economics, Social Research Indicators, Journal of Productivity Analysis, Labour Economics, Economic Modelling, International Review of Economics and Finance, Cambridge Journal of Economics, American Behavioural Scientists, etc. He received the IDRC Young India Social Sciences Award in 2010 and the Global Development Network Award in 2009.

Bishwanath Goldar is a retired professor of Economics at the Institute of Economic Growth (IEG), Delhi. He was a member of the National Statistical Commission and a national fellow of the Indian Council of Social Science Research (ICSSR). He was a professor at the Indian Council for Research on International Economic Relations (ICRIER), New Delhi, during 2003-04 and a visiting professor at the Centre for International Trade and Development, School of International Studies, Jawaharlal Nehru University, New Delhi, during 2012–13. He is currently a non-resident senior fellow at the Institute of Economic Growth. He has many publications in economic journals. His areas of research interest include productivity measurement, industry, trade, foreign direct investment, industrial pollution, energy use of industries, river water pollution, and rural water supply.

K.L. Krishna a founder member of CDE (Centre for Development Economics), at the Delhi School of Economics, has been the principal investigator of the RBI-funded India KLEMS Productivity Project since 2009. With post-graduate qualifications in Statistics from the University of Kerala and the Indian Statistical Institute, Kolkata, and PhD degree in Economics from the University of Chicago, he taught Econometrics and Industrial Economics for four decades. He supervised around 45 PhD and M.Phil. theses in a variety of fields. He served as the head of the Department of Economics and director, Delhi School of Economics, in the 1980s and 1990s. He was the founder and managing editor of the Journal of Quantitative Economics for one decade and the president of the Indian Econometric Society (TIES) for one term. He is a member of the TIES Trust. He was the chairman or member of several official Committees of the Government of India. He held the position of chairman of CESS, Hyderabad, during 2007–13, and MIDS, Chennai during 2013–20. For his contribution on education and economics, he receives *Padma Shri* award, the fourth highest civilian award in India, conferred by the Government of India, in 2025.

Contributors

Rajat Acharyya Department of Economics, Jadavpur University, Kolkata, India

Suresh Chand Aggarwal Institute for Human Development, New Delhi, India

T. C. A. Anant Institute for Studies in Industrial Development, ISID, New Delhi, India

Pulapre Balakrishnan Centre for Development Studies, Thiruvananthapuram, Kerala, India

Samaresh Bardhan Department of Humanities and Social Sciences, Indian Institute of Technology Ropar, Punjab, India

Arpit Barman National Investment and Infrastructure Fund Limited (NIIFL), New Delhi, India

Seema Bathla Centre for the Study of Regional Development, Jawaharlal Nehru University, New Delhi, India

Anup Kumar Bhandari Department of Humanities and Social Sciences, Indian Institute of Technology (IIT), Chennai, India

Garima Chaklader Economics, Masters' Union, Gurgaon, India

Rupa Chanda UN Economic and Social Commission for Asia and the Pacific (UNESCAP), Bangkok, Thailand;
Indian Institute of Management Bangalore, Bangalore, India

Pilu Chandra Das Kidderpore College, University of Calcutta, Kolkata, India

Prabir De Research and Information System for Developing Countries (RIS), New Delhi, India

Pami Dua Department of Economics, Delhi School of Economics, University of Delhi, Delhi, India

Abdul Azeez Erumban University of Groningen, Groningen, The Netherlands

Kausik Gangopadhyay Indian Institute of Management Kozhikode, Kozhikode, India

Shrimoyee Ganguly Centre for Quantitative Economics and Data Science, BIT Mesra, Ranchi, India

Sunetra Ghatak Jindal School of Government and Public Policy, O. P. Jindal Global University, Sonipat, India

Nilabja Ghosh Institute of Economic Growth, Delhi, India

Partha Pratim Ghosh Postgraduate and Research Department of Economics, St. Xavier's College (Autonomous) Kolkata, Kolkata, West Bengal, India

Sudeshna Ghosh Indian Institute of Management Bangalore, Bangalore, India

Bishwanath Goldar Institute of Economic Growth, New Delhi, India

Debajit Jha Jindal School of Government and Public Policy, O. P. Jindal Global University, Sonipat, Haryana, India

Sabyasachi Kar Institute of Economic Growth, University of Delhi Enclave, Delhi, India

K. L. Krishna Delhi School of Economics, University of Delhi, New Delhi, India

Anjani Kumar International Food Policy Research Institute, New Delhi, India

Nagesh Kumar Institute for Studies in Industrial Development (ISID), New Delhi, India

Naveen Kumar Delhi School of Economics, New Delhi, India

Navneet Kumar Centre for the Study of Regional Development, Jawaharlal Nehru University, New Delhi, India

Dibyendu Maiti Delhi School of Economics, University of Delhi, New Delhi, India

Sankar Majumder Visva Bharati University, Santiniketan, India;
GLA University, Mathura, Mathura, India

Debasis Mondal Department of Humanities and Social Sciences, Indian Institute of Technology Delhi, Delhi, India

Chiranjib Neogi Indian Statistical Institute, Kolkata, India

M. Parameswaran Centre for Development Studies, Thiruvananthapuram, Kerala, India

Mayanglambam Rajeshwor Institute of Economic Growth, Delhi, India

Rajesh Ramakrishnan National Institute of Bank Management (NIBM), Pune, India

Ajitava Raychaudhuri Department of Economics, Adamas University, Kolkata, West Bengal, India

Gargi Sanati National Institute of Bank Management (NIBM), Pune, India

C. S. C. Sekhar Agricultural Economics Research Unit, Institute of Economic Growth, Delhi, India

Pooja Sharma Daulat Ram College, University of Delhi, Delhi, India

Namrata Thapa NITI Aayog, Delhi, India

T Thasni Indian Institute of Management Kashipur, Kashipur, Uttarakhand, India

C. Veeramani Centre for Development Studies (CDS), Thiruvananthapuram, India

Abbreviations

ADR	American Depository Receipts
AGCRUPC	Agricultural Credit as a Proportion of Total Credit
AGLCRQN	Agricultural Credit as a Proportion of Agricultural Output
AMIA	Augmented Multiple Indicator Approach
APMC	Agricultural Produce Market Committee
APO	Asian Productivity Organization
ARDL	Autoregressive Distributed Lag
ASI	Annual Survey of Industries
ASUSE	Annual Survey of Unorganised Sector Enterprises
BMPE	Black Money Peso Exchange
BPM	Business Process Management
BRAND	Branch Density
BRE	Business Register of Establishments
BRICS	Brazil, Russia, India, China, and South Africa
CD	Certificate of Deposit
CDR	Credit Deposit Ratio
CDS	Current Daily Status
CEA	Central Electricity Authority
CEPA	Comprehensive Economic Cooperation and Partnership Agreement
CGE	Computable General Equilibrium
CMIE	Center for Monitoring Indian Economy
CONCRUPC	Ratio of Consumer Credit to Total Credit
COVID-19	Coronavirus Disease of 2019
CP	Commercial Paper
CPI	Consumer Price Index
CRR	Cash Reserve Ratio
CSO	Central Statistics Office in the Ministry of Statistics and Programme Implementation
CSSS	Champion Services Sector Scheme
CV	Coefficient of Variation
CWS	Current Weekly Status

DCSSI	Development Commissioner of Small-Scale Industries
DEA	Data Development Analysis
DGFT	Directorate General of Foreign Trade
DIC	District Industries Center
DOCDEX	Documentary Credit Dispute Resolution Export Committee
DPC	District Planning Committee
DTA	Domestic Tariff Area
EC	Economic Census
EDI	Electronic Data Interchange
EDPMS	Export Data Processing and Monitoring System
e-NAM	Electronic National Agriculture Market
EPFO	Employees' Provident Fund Organisation
EPW	Economic and Political Weekly
EPWRFITS	EPW Research Foundation India Times Series
EUS	Employment Unemployment Survey
FATF	Financial Action Task Force
FDI	Foreign Direct Investment
FIT	Flexible Inflation Targeting
FRRR	Fixed Rate Reverse Repo
GATS	General Agreement on Trade in Services (GATS)
GCA	Gross Cropped Area
GDP	Gross Domestic Product
GDR	Global Depository Receipt
GERUPPER	Gross Enrolment Ratio Upper (middle/senior basic school)
GFC	Global Financial Crisis
GFCF	Gross Fixed Capital Formation
GGDC	Groningen Growth and Development Centre
GOI	Government of India
G-SAP	Government Securities Acquisition Programme
GSDPN	Gross State Domestic Product in Nominal Terms
GSDPR	Gross State Domestic Product in Real Terms
G-Sec	Government Securities
GTI	Gross Trading Income
GVA	Gross Value Added
HCE	Household Consumer Expenditure
HDI	Human Development Index
HYV	High-Yielding Varieties
ICC	International Chamber of Commerce
ICRIER	Indian Council for Research on International Economic Relations
ICT	Information and Communication Technology
IDPMS	Import Data Processing and Monitoring System
IHDS	Indian Human Development Survey
IIP	Index of Industrial Production
IKED	India KLEMS Extended Database, Version 2023
INDCRQN	Industrial Credit to Industrial Output

INDCRUPC	Industrial Credit as a Proportion of Total Credit
INGDP	Inward Credit Spillover Expressed as a Proportion of State GDP
INUPC	Inward Credit Spillover Expressed as a Proportion of Total Credit Utilised
IR	Inverse Relationship
IT	Information Technology
JNPA	Jawaharlal Nehru Port Authority
KLEMS	Capital, Labour, Energy, Material and Services
KPSS	Kwiatkowski–Phillips–Schmidt–Shin
KVIB	Khadi and Village Industries Board
KVIC	Khadi and Village Industries Commission
LAF	Liquidity Adjustment Facility
LC	Letters of Credit
LP	Labour Productivity
LTRO	Long-Term Repo Operation
MAKV	Maritime Amrit Kal Vision
MCA	Ministry of Corporate Affairs
MCLR	Marginal Cost of Funds-Based Lending Rate
ME	Measurement Errors
MGNREGS	Mahatma Gandhi National Rural Employment Guarantee Act, 2005
MIA	Multiple Indicator Approach
MOSPI	Ministry of Statistics and Programme Implementation
MPC	Monetary Policy Committee
MPFA	Monetary Policy Framework Agreement
MPR	Monetary Policy Report
MSF	Marginal Standing Facility
MSME	Micro, Small and Medium Enterprises
MSP	Minimum Support Price
NABARD	National Bank for Agriculture and Rural Development
NAS	National Accounts Statistics
NASSCOM	National Association of Software and Service Companies
NFCS	Net Fixed Capital Stock
NFHS	National Family Health Survey
NGO	Non-Governmental Organisation
NHB	National Housing Bank (NHB)
NREGA	National Rural Employment Guarantee Act
NSDP	Net State Domestic Product
NSDP	Net State Domestic Products
NSO	National Statistical Office
NSS	National Sample Survey
NSSO	National Sample Survey Office
NVA	Net Value Added
OAW	Own account workers
OECD	Organisation for Economic Co-operation and Development

OEEC	Organisation for European Economic Co-operation
OLF	Out of Labour Force
OLS	Ordinary Least Squares
OMOs	Open Market Operations
OUTGDP	Outward Credit Spillover Expressed as State GDP
OUTUPC	Outward Cedit spillover Expressed as a Proportion of Total Credit Utilized
PC	Packing Credit or Pre-shipment Credit
PCA	Principal Component Analysis
PCPA	Per cent per annum
PCSI	Credit Sanctioned in jth State but Used in ith State
PCSO	Credit Sanctioned in ith State but Used Elsewhere (Outward spillover)
PDS	Public Distribution System
PIM	Perpetual Inventory Method
PLFS	Periodic Labour Force Survey
PLI	Productivity Linked Incentive
PMJDY	Pradhan Mantri Jan Dhan Yojana
PMLA	Prevention of Money Laundering Act
POB	Place of Birth
POLR	Place of Last Residence
PPI	Port Performance Index
PPS	Probability Proportional to Size
PS	Phillips-Sul
PSU	Public Sector Units
R&D	Research & Development
RBI	Reserve Bank of India
RCA	Revealed Comparative Advantage
RESET	Regression Equation Specification Error Test
RF	Rural Females
RIP	Rural Industries Programme
RM	Rural Males
RNFS	Rural Non-Farm Sector
RWE	Regular Salary and Wage Employees
SCBs	Scheduled Commercial Banks
SD	Standard Deviation
SDF	Standing Deposit Facility
SERCRQN	Service Sector Credit to Services Output
SERCRUPC	Service Sector Credit as a Proportion of Total Credit
SIDBI	Small Industries Development Bank of India
SIDO	Small Industry Development Organisation
SLF-MF	Special Liquidity Facility for Mutual Funds
SLR	Statutory Liquidity Ratio
SLTRO	Special LTRO
SNA	System of National Accounts

SOI	States of India
SSI	Small Scale Industries
STRI	Services Trade Restrictiveness Index
SUT	Supply Use Table
TAC	Technical Advisory Committee
T-Bill	Treasury Bills
TBML	Trade-based Money Laundering
TFP	Total Factor Productivity
TFPG	Total Factor Productivity Growth
TiVA	Trade in Value Added
TLTRO	Targeted Long-Term Repo Operations
TRYSEM	Training Rural Youth for Self-Employment
UCP	Uniform Rules for Customs and Practices
UF	Urban Females
UM	Urban Males
UNCTAD	United Nations Conference on Trade and Development
UPC	Total Bank Credit to Private sector
UPCGDP	Nominal Credit to Nominal GDP
UPS	Usual Principal Status
UPSS	Usual Principal and the Subsidiary Status
URC	Uniform Rules for Collection
URDG	Uniform Rules for Demand Guarantees
US	United States of America
USDA	United States Development Agency
UTs	Union Territories
WACR	Weighted Average Call Money Rate
WALR	Weighted Average Lending Rate
WBES	World Bank Enterprise Survey
WFPR	Work Force Participation Rate
WPI	Wholesale Price Index
WPR	Workforce Participation Rate
WTO	World Trade Organization
YPR	Real GDP Growth Rate

Chapter 1
75 Years of Growth, Development, and Productivity in India—An Overview

Dibyendu Maiti, Bishwanath Goldar, and K. L. Krishna

Abstract When the colonial government handed over the country's rule, the Indian people were abysmally poor. Many countries in the world, specifically in the West, were already developed. During British rule for almost two hundred years, the exorbitant exploitation of resources and its unregulated drain left very little to cycle in the accumulation needed to accelerate economic growth. India was a mostly agrarian economy at the time of the Independence and there was very low economic growth in the first half of the twentieth century (1900-1950). During the last 75 years, the economy has demonstrated significant improvement on many fronts, relying mainly on the service sector expansion, with the manufacturing sector growth playing a critical role. The pace and pattern of economic transformation and lessons drawn from the development path have been documented in the volume.

Keywords Indian growth · Industrialisation debates · Productivity growth · Sectoral dynamics

1.1 Introduction

When the colonial government handed over the country's rule, the Indian people were abysmally poor. Many countries in the world, specifically in the West, were already developed. During British rule for almost two hundred years, the exorbitant exploitation of resources and its unregulated drain left very little to cycle in the accumulation needed to accelerate economic growth. There were only a few non-traditional economic activities run by a handful of rich people serving in the British

D. Maiti (✉) · K. L. Krishna
Delhi School of Economics, University of Delhi, New Delhi, India
e-mail: dibyendu@econdse.org

K. L. Krishna
e-mail: krishna@econdse.org

B. Goldar
Institute of Economic Growth, New Delhi, India

D. Maiti et al. (eds.), *75 Years of Growth, Development and Productivity in India*, India Studies in Business and Economics, https://doi.org/10.1007/978-981-97-8054-9_1

government or owning some industry. The extreme inequalities in income distribution were observed between economic and social classes, the rural and urban sectors and across the states and regions of the economy. A large share of the population was dependent on agriculture for occupation. Agriculture was the principal occupation and economic activity of the Indian economy. About 85% of the population was engaged in agriculture, while the contribution of agriculture to national income was about 50%. The cultivated area for food crop production was only 3/4th of the total cultivable land, and only one-fourth was used for the cultivation of cash crops. On the other hand, only a few industries were existing at that time, concentrated in some areas with no uniformity in production. The mining and cotton textiles were major secondary activities with high regional variation. Tea, coffee, and sugar were the primary exportable products processed in mills. Most industries were engaged in the production of consumption goods, and the only capital goods industry in India was steel, which could produce about 9 lakh tonnes. The service sector was limited to banking, transport, and allied activities with little contribution to employment and limited contribution to income generation. The country possessed an abundant stock of natural resources, but these resources were either underutilised or unutilised. That left the government of independent India to deal with widespread poverty and unemployment, with the vast majority of Indian people dependent on underdeveloped agriculture, resulting in widespread unemployment, poverty, and hunger. Frequent famines and droughts were common, causing a huge shortage of food and starvation. More than 40% of the population was living below the poverty line. Such rampant poverty led to a low standard of living and low human development. The growth of the Indian economy was so low that it was considered 'stagnant'. The biggest fight for the common man was against hunger and widespread diseases. Health, education, and other developmental parameters were all at a very low level.

In contrast to the situation prevailing at the time of India's independence in 1947, the economy is now the fastest-growing major country in the world and has managed to reduce the level of poverty to around 10% of the population (as per the latest national estimates). It demonstrated huge resilience during the phase of the severe financial crisis in 2008. Though service-driven growth and high under-employment and informality remain serious challenges affecting the sustainable development of the country, such an economic transformation becomes a unique experience for less developed economies to learn from. The Indian development experience of the last 75 years offers policy inputs to be drawn by scholars and policymakers to take forward the Indian economy to the level of 'Viksit Bharat' (Developed India) by 2047. After its independence, the Indian economy has gone through various policy experiments under bad to good situations that helped gradually lift its level of economic growth and address a number of development issues, from poverty to well-being, during the last 75 years.

For an economy with a vast population and regional, cultural, and climatic diversities, the history of economic achievements and challenges therein must be very different from those of others who have already developed in the past and are evolving in different ways. One factor that has contributed critically to the economic growth and development of countries is the rise in productivity. The focus on productivity increased much later in India during the 1980s. However, from the classical work of Adam Smith on the wealth of nations to the basic development economics doctrine that is rooted in the Lewisian framework, no one could deny the role of technological progress, defined as total factor productivity. The productivity growth, driven by technology, efficiency, and the combination of market and institutions, plays a prime role in accelerating the economic growth, development, and welfare of an economy.

Though the Indian economy has witnessed significant development during the past 75 years since independence, still several development outcomes (e.g. poverty, informality, inadequate creation of decent employment opportunities, and inequality) that are influenced by the way productivity advancement has progressed are bothering the scholars and policymakers engaged in the development debate. Therefore, the dynamics of the economic transformation, influenced by productivity growth, in India continue to engage economists and policymakers and remain much debated. This chapter aims to highlight the characteristics of different phases of India's economic development over the past 75 years that gave different priorities at different points in the course of economic transformation and summarise the key findings and observations of the following chapters.

1.2 Indian Growth, Development, and Productivity: Paradigm Changes

After independence from the British rule, the country followed strategies from the socialist model to the market-based framework from time to time to deal with the growth and development challenges. Broad shifts of such approaches are summarised here to give an overview of the policy transformation that affected and gave shape to the economic dynamics. The policies were initially implemented through five-year plans in the first six decades, followed by annual plans in later periods.

The government of India constituted a statutory body under the chair of the prime minister of India, known as the Planning Commission, in March 1950 for effective persuasion of the strategic policies of five-year plans. Later on, the National Development Council was established in 1951, including chief ministers of all states, together with the members of the Planning Commission, to cater to the development process of regional states in a federal democratic framework of the country. These two functional bodies played a determining role in bringing changes to the planning process during the 60 years since 1951. While the functional relationship between the centre and state remained the same, the five-year plans were replaced by the annual plan to minimise the influence of the state on efficient outcomes in the market. As the economy gradually developed, the role of the state has been minimised to allow the functioning of the market rule more effectively, with the changing focus of the state subsidiary role. India successfully executed twelve five-year plans in the first 60 years. Let us outline the policy dynamics during the plan periods.

1.2.1 Phase 1: Phase of Nation-Building (1951–1961)

Soon after independence, the government had to get involved in the economic fundamentals in India (commanding heights) to play an instrumental role in investing and running the principal economic activities. Initially, it pursued a socialist approach to planning by emphasising a greater role of state intervention. Since a colonial government had ruled the economy, the classical path of capitalist development of shifting resources from the traditional and subsistence sectors to the industrial and modern sectors could not be followed. Only a few modern sectors (including industrial activities) grew under colonial rule in the country at a slow pace at the hands of a few at the beginning of the nineteenth century and the First World War. Much of the traditional sectors, located in the rural areas, were operated in a subsistence mode. Even agriculture was heavily taxed to provide resources for the colonial government and could not offer sufficient surplus to boost the modern sector. Therefore, the country had to pay much attention to building the economic base by focusing on self-reliance and big industrialisation strategies immediately after independence with an expectation that various forms of small industries and peripheral activities could flourish from its linkage effects. Therefore, the first five-year plan (1951–1956) focused much on the 'Development of agriculture' to solve food security and different problems that formed due to the partition of the nation and the Second World War. The plan was designed to raise the yield of raw materials and food supplied by the rural economy as a linkage for the expansion of non-agricultural activities. The second five-year plan (1956–1961) focused on the development of the public sector and 'rapid industrialisation' to establish large-scale industries, with the assumption that the benefits of such industrialisation would percolate to other sectors and agriculture. The plan stressed industrialisation based on the Industrial Policy Resolution adopted in 1948. The plan emphasised the expansion of the public sector and aimed to frame a socialistic pattern of society, which was grounded on the Harrod-Domer growth model with an emphasis on a rising saving rate for higher growth and equality between saving-investment for balanced growth, which later gave way to the Mahalanobis model, that emphasised the importance of capital goods production in the country.

1.2.2 Phase II: Phase of Self-Reliance (1962–1974)

The severe famine in the last 1950s, along with the rise of petroleum oil and border countries, led to the realisation that the percolation of large-scale industrialisation did not reach other sectors much and pushed them to undertake long-term development strategies that can encourage agriculture and industry for self-reliance. The emphasis was on the long-term development programme by focusing on agricultural development so that the Indian economy could enter into a take-off stage and build the base to construct India as a 'self-reliant' and 'self-generating' economy. Much responsibility was given to the state and grassroots planning for agriculture and rural development. A substantial amount of borrowing has been drawn to the IMF to support development plans, road development, and rural education. The plan adopted the objective of correcting the earlier trend of increased concentration of wealth and economic power. Bank nationalisation was one of the steps that were taken in this direction that could help resource mobilisation in the desired directions and provide financial support to the small-scale industries. To deal with the inflationary pressures and encourage the gains from terms of trade, the currency had been devalued a number of times.

1.2.3 Phase III: Phase of Development and Poverty Alleviation (1974–1985)

The previous emphasis on either large-scale industrialisation or agriculture development did not solve much of the problem of widespread poverty and unemployment in the country. The next two plans (1975–1979 and 1980–1984), therefore, paid greater attention to addressing these problems and proposed objectives of the 'removal of poverty' (Garibi Hatao) and 'attainment of self-reliance'. The key policy priorities were the promotion of growth, with better distribution of income and higher domestic saving rates during these periods. Moreover, various welfare programmes like food for workers, minimum need programmes, and employment guarantee schemes for rural workers were launched. In addition, the national highway system was introduced, and tourism was encouraged to boost activities in rural and remote areas.

From the early 1980s onwards, the economy realised the need to raise the pace of technological progress and productivity growth to achieve these objectives on a priority basis. In particular, the sixth five-year plan pursued technological development policies for efficient use of existing resources and thereby growth acceleration without distorting the employment generation in the country. This approach, perhaps, had been the first serious consideration shown by the national government to improve the productivity and efficiency levels of production in India's planning history. In order to increase productivity growth, it emphasised technological upgradation, efficient use of resources, and capacity utilisation. Realising the importance of the market's role in efficiency gain, the restrictions on industrial practices like licensing systems and reservations for small-scale industries were set to be liberalised gradually. In fact, the growing bureaucracy, corruption, and red tape-ism were the basic ingredients behind the national policymakers' realisation.

1.2.4 Phase IV: Phase of First Generation of Economic Reform (1985–1996)

Technological progress did not improve the economic conditions much because of its adverse effect on employment generation, an issue which has been raised and apprehended by many scholars and policymakers in most state governments. Since then, the Indian economy witnessed a debate on the trade-off between technology and employment. The seventh five-year plan (1985–1990) moved forward and formally started liberalising the economy to replace the strategies of 'import substitution' and 'protection'. This plan initiated the process of trade liberalisation (by reducing the tariff rates). It set a strategy to decentralise the political and economic powers towards more regional and local governments for the sake of effective utilisation of resources and its monitoring mechanism. The attempt to accelerate national income with a gradual drift of technological progress along with the continuous decrease in poverty and unemployment had been retained as major objectives during this plan period. Thereafter, the economy faced severe political uncertainty at the centre during the late 1980s and early 1990s, and this led to the deterioration of the economic condition, both internal and external. Further, a drastic drop in the balance of payment position along with a high rise of the inflation rate during 1990–1991 had urged the economy to gear up and quicken the process of liberalisation during the eighth plan (1992–1997).

The liberalisation included disinvestment in the public sector, withdrawal of licensing policies, reduction of trade barriers, promotion of export sectors, withdrawal of restrictions on capital inflow, banking sector autonomy, etc. The plan undertook these drastic policy changes to deal with these adverse economic situations and to overcome these problems. During the eighth plan period, these changes resulted in a rapid economic expansion due to high growth in agriculture and allied sectors, the manufacturing sector and high growth in exports and imports, leading to improvement in trade and the current account deficit.

1.2.5 Phase V: Phase of the Second Generation of Economic Reform (1997–2007)

The second generation of economic reforms in India, initiated in the late 1990s and early 2000s, progressed to a deeper and more delicate phase in the reform process and aimed at addressing the shortcomings and gaps that were observed in the initial set of reforms launched in the early 1990s. The major components of these second-generation reforms were targeted to the factor markets, public sector, governance and public institutions, and legal sector. The ninth plan (1997–2002), therefore, maintained the same pace of liberalisation with an additional aim of improving quality of life, productive employment, self-reliance, and reduction of regional imbalance, taking advantage of the gradual reform of these areas. The plan ensured the sustained programme of economic reforms and adopted strategies to improve the social development of women and socially disadvantaged groups such as SC/ST (Schedule Caste/ Scheduled Tribe), backward classes, and minorities and by promoting participatory institutions like 'Panchayati Raj' institutions, cooperatives, and self-help groups. The improvement in the spread and accessibility of information technology was also targeted towards more remote and rural areas. Based on this foundation, the tenth plan (2002–2007) further targeted to achieve a higher growth rate and identified some measures to improve efficiency, unleash entrepreneurial energy and proposed major reforms for the agricultural sector, making 'agriculture' the core element of the plan. The eleventh plan targeted 'towards faster and more inclusive growth'.

1.2.6 Phase VI: Phase of De-Globalisation (2008 Onwards)

After the significant progress of economic reforms and the resultant growth, when the economy aimed to improve the social sectors, the Global Financial Crisis of 2008 posed a serious threat to these objectives. Initially, the plan targeted to improve higher education and social sector development and then gradually emphasised the social security provision for the unorganised sector during the early 2010s. When the developed economy started to protect its economic activities to overcome the recession from the financial crisis, the Indian economy initiated strategies to raise skills that could raise productivity for exporting, brought the regulations in the financial sector to reduce the risk and raise resilience, relied on the e-governance to curb down the corruption and improve the investment climate for encouraging the foreign capital inflows, and needed for rapid industrialisation. At the same time, the focus has shifted to sustainable development with a clear target to reduce carbon emissions. Along with these changes, some initiatives were taken to protect domestic industries from global competition and financial risks.

1.3 Contribution of This Book

The book covers chapters that address almost every aspect of the Indian economy. There are 23 chapters focused on nine parts or themes dealing with separate issues. The summary of their findings is given below:

Part I dealt with the economic and productivity growth of the Indian economy and its pace and patterns, and it accommodated two chapters. Chapter 2 by Goldar, Maiti, Aggarwal, Erumban and Das looks at the sources of growth in the Indian economy since independence. India's economic growth was analysed separately for the entire period, 1951–1952 to 2019–2020, and five sub-periods, 1951–1966, 1967–1979, 1980–1993, 1994–2007, and 2008–2019, using the growth accounting framework. The analysis has been undertaken at the aggregate economy level and for major sectors of the economy. It shows that the primary factor influencing sectoral variations in contributing to aggregate TFPG was the weak productivity performance of the manufacturing and non-manufacturing industries during the pre-liberal market reform period. The education, trade openness, structural change, and ICT investments have contributed to TFP growth. The findings suggest that the Indian services sector observed an increase in value-added share from nearly 34 percentage points in 1951 to more than 54 percentage points in 2019. The share of manufacturing and construction increased slightly between 1951 and 2019. The share of agriculture declined over the year, and the remaining sectors' share remained stagnant. Finance, insurance & real estate, and trade, hotels & restaurants observed an improvement in their value-added growth contribution to aggregate economic growth. In contrast, the contribution of agriculture declined over the years. For the remaining sectors, the contributions remained more or less stagnant. The structural shift in employment has been slow in the Indian economy, and the shift took place mainly from agriculture to construction, trade, and transport. The trends in investment rates reveal a consistently low investment rate in the agricultural sector, and the sector's share in the total economy's overall investment has fallen substantially over decades. The capital stock data suggests a consistently growing stock of capital in the economy with the highest growth rate in capital stock in the construction sector. In the first thirty years of India's development, the average annual growth rate in TFP was low, and so was the contribution to TFP growth to the aggregate level of GVA growth. During 1980–1993 and 1994–2007, the rate of growth in TFP exceeded 2% per annum. TFP growth contributed significantly to GVA growth. In the post-GFC period, the growth rate in real GVA has come down slightly, and there has also been a fall in the growth rate in TFP. An analysis of determinants of TFP growth in the Indian economy was undertaken by applying an ARDL model to time series data covering 1951–1952 to 2019–2020. The results indicate that a shift in the industrial structure away from agriculture to the non-agricultural sectors is productivity-enhancing.

In Chapter 3, Parameswaran and Balakrishnan look at the longer term economic growth perspective in India and investigate the trajectory of economic growth in India in the post-independence period. The study identifies various phases of growth of aggregate GDP and its sectors using an updated methodology. The chapter discusses the growth phases of the aggregate economy, thus identifying their origins in terms of sectoral growth changes. It shows that the trend growth rate in aggregate GDP has increased two times, first from 1979 to 1980 onwards and second from 1990 to 1991 onwards. With these two accelerations, the country started catching up with the per capita income of the World and developed regions. As the acceleration in GDP growth from 1979 to 1980 onwards is not correlated with any major policy changes, a number of explanations have been provided for it. The chapter discusses these explanations and, based on the insights drawn from the estimated growth phases of GDP and its sectors, attempts to assess the plausibility of different explanations. Large-scale public investment and an increase in the rate of growth of agricultural production, which commenced in the fifties, enabled the economy to reach a scale necessary for the mechanism of cumulative causation envisaged in the theoretical model to start operating from around the mid-1960s. The Nehru-Mahalanobis Strategy, which had been involved in raising public investment across the economy put the economy on a trajectory of periodically accelerating growth.[1] Further, the acceleration of growth after 1991 fits into the model of accelerating growth through cumulative causation. And, the liberalised policy allowing for greater private sector participation in the infrastructural sectors of the economy since 1991 may be seen as increasing the range of producer services now available to manufacturing. In addition, the deregulation of industrial and trade policy regimes, by easing the entry and exit of firms, must have also lubricated the mechanism of cumulative causation. Though the confidence interval of the last breakpoint of the aggregate GDP is found vast, the year of the onset of the slowdown coincides with the year of demonetisation in the recent past.

Part II of the book is focused on the growth strategies and their pace and patterns. Three chapters address the combination of monetary and fiscal strategies. In Chapter 4, Pami Dua looks at the evolution of monetary policy in India from a global perspective. In 2016, the monetary policy framework moved towards flexible inflation targeting, and a six-member Monetary Policy Committee (MPC) was constituted to set the policy rate. With this step towards modernisation of the monetary policy process, India joined the set of countries that have adopted inflation targeting as their monetary policy framework. The Consumer Price Index (CPI combined) inflation target was set by the Government of India at 4% with $\pm$ 2% tolerance band for the period from 5 August 2016 to 31 March 2021. The target was renewed again for a period of 5 years in March 2021, *i.e.* 1 April 2021 to 31 March 2026. Against this backdrop, the chapter reviews the evolution of monetary policy frameworks in India since the inception of the Reserve Bank of India, especially from the mid-1980s. It also describes the monetary policy transmission process and its limitations in terms of lags and rigidities. It highlights the importance of unconventional monetary policy measures in supplementing conventional tools, especially during the pandemic. Further, it examines the voting pattern of the MPC in India and compares this with that of various developed and emerging economies. The synchronisation of cuts in the policy rate by MPCs of various countries during the global slowdown in 2019 and the COVID-19 pandemic in the early 2020s is also analysed. The subsequent rate increases are also examined, along with the synchronisation in inflation across the globe. In Chapter 5, Thasni, Gangopadhyay and Mondal investigate whether productivity growth explains the unbalanced growth experience of the Indian economy. They have developed a three-sector dynamic general equilibrium model and calibrated its parameters to align with the output and employment share data of the Indian economy from 1983 to 2012. The model's output on employment share indicates that the actual labour share in the secondary and tertiary sectors is relatively lower compared to the model-predicted share. To understand the origins of labour productivity growth, the chapter has presented a shift-share analysis. The findings reveal that within-sector productivity growth is the most significant contributor to overall growth, and the importance of total factor productivities (TFPs) has increased

[1] Interestingly Mahalanobis himself anticipated the acceleration of the economy, see Mahalanobis (1955). See also Parameswaran (2019) for a discussion on historical origins of the idea of cumulative causation and its influence on initial five-year plans in India.

in the post-economic reform period, particularly after 1991. While the contribution of TFP in the manufacturing sector has been moderate, the results emphasise in the book the pressing need for reforms to boost the TFP in this sector. In general, the economic reforms implemented in 1991–1992 have facilitated a more efficient allocation of productive factors across different sectors of the Indian economy.

Part III of the book deals with issues related to agriculture, the primary sector of the economy. Chapter 6 by Ghosh, Neogi and Rajeshwor discusses the factors behind returns from Indian agriculture and the efficiency of resource use. In India's long journey of development and growth, agriculture has played a critical but constraining role. Associated critically with socio-political stability, India's agriculture still occupies large places in employment generation, food security, and land use. Even with the self-sufficiency delivered by the green revolution (GR), Indian agriculture regularly deals with serious and often conflicting problems. Over time, as varied concerns challenged policy, agriculture also encountered new developments. The post-GR period was rich in insightful research and lively debates on the performances of agriculture, transitions in land use, regional disparities, and assessments against other countries. In continuum and as a contribution to the discourse, the chapter assimilates and presents a historical account of Indian agriculture, reinforced by an empirical study of contemporary times covering the base of GR in the Indo-Gangetic belt, seeking to revisit the performance of Indian agriculture with updated perspectives. The analysis indicates that the agriculturally advanced states of the north-west that benefited from the green revolution still yield higher returns due to greater use of inputs but have stable or dipping efficiency. The reason may lie in their use of inputs and entitlement to credit and resultant contribution to sustainability. On the contrary, the water-abundant eastern states lagged behind in value added, but they are performing well in efficiency, and central states are also becoming more efficient in recent times. The small size of the farm, which was unavoidable due to the growth of population, is hampering the attainment of efficiency, but better road connectivity and perhaps the marketing avenues created help them recover the loss of inefficiency relative to larger farms. Higher credit, a landmark policy instrument to support farmers, enhances efficiency. Credit creation has been modernised and expanded with technology, and it has also relaxed and broadened coverage beyond farming over time. In Chapter 7, Bathla, Kumar and Kumar deal with the total factor productivity growth in Indian agriculture and regional convergence. They have estimated total factor productivity (TFP) growth and its contribution to agricultural output growth across 17 major states in India for the period from 1981–1982 to 2019–2020. This is followed by an empirical examination of the convergence of TFP to understand how technology spread in India. The Data Envelopment Analysis Malmquist productivity index is used to estimate the TFP growth, whereas the inter-state convergence is tested using the sigma and beta convergence approaches. The study contributes to the literature by providing TFP estimates at the disaggregate state level over a longer period to assess the increase in public investment in R&D, irrigation, credit flow, and several other policy initiatives taken from the 2000s. The analysis indicates large temporal and spatial variations in the output, input, and TFP indices, validating that the technological diffusion on account of HYVs under the green and yellow revolutions has been uneven. A low TFP growth has been confirmed in several states over time, with the national average being 1.06% from 1981 to 2019. However, the contribution of TFP to output growth was relatively low at 41.4% during the overall study period, but it was found to have increased to 60% during the last decade. The conditional convergence reveals a tendency of productivity in the poorer states to catch up with the richer states, albeit at a very slow speed of 1%. The chapter notes that it is important to enhance expenditure on R&D, extension, technology, and irrigation more in the eastern states to augment and sustain productivity growth and meet the future demand for food. The analysis indicates that technology transmission from the northern states to a few southern states has been uneven. Still, it has enabled India to achieve higher productivity growth and food security. However, wide inter-state differentials in productivity growth may not help maintain the per capita availability of food products. In Chapter 8, Sekhar and Thapa look at rural market imperfections and land productivity in India. Ensuring the viability of farming and increasing farmers' income are the key policy concerns in India at present. To realise these objectives, the functioning of markets is very critical. Market imperfections can increase the production and transaction costs of farmers and have a crucial bearing on farm income. The inverse relationship (IR) between farm size and land productivity is a manifestation of the imperfections and has become a stylised fact in India over time. The study revisits this issue and, using primary data, examines whether market imperfections still prevail in India, particularly in output, input, factor, and credit markets. The results show a prevalence of a strong IR between land productivity and farm size on the output side and farm size and family labour use on the input side. However, intensive use of family labour does not seem to be the only determinant of farm size-productivity relation. The results suggest that Sen's labour dualism theory, together with imperfections in land and credit markets, can offer useful insights. The results of the study point to the prevalence of surplus family labour on small farms even after a decade of enacting a major employment guarantee programme (MGNREGS) and continuing limited access to institutional credit for small farmers. Thus, particularly for marginal and small farmers, reforming land lease markets to enable easier access to land, providing better access to institutional credit, and improving literacy levels to facilitate mobility to other occupations are needed to address some of the observed imperfections.

Part IV dealt with issues related to the service sector and its dynamics. Chapter 9 by Chanda, Chaklader and Ghosh investigates the service-sector dynamics and its role in the Indian economy. Services have been a dynamic sector in the Indian economy, significantly contributing to India's GDP, FDI inflows, and exports. Services have played a key role in India's integration with the world market, particularly due to the performance of segments such as IT and IT-enabled services and business and professional services. The sector has also outperformed manufacturing in terms of growth, productivity, and share in global trade. In large part, its dynamism can be attributed to economic liberalisation and regulatory reforms undertaken in India since 1991. This chapter discusses the growth, development, and productivity dynamics in India's service sector to date and its potential role in shaping India's future growth prospects. It outlines trends in the sector's GDP growth and contribution to the Indian economy, highlighting differences in performance within the service sector and relative to other sectors, and places this performance in the context of the debate surrounding India's services-led growth paradigm in contrast to the traditional primary to secondary sector growth model. The chapter also provides an overview of key regulatory, policy, and other developments in the services sector, with a focus on selected services, and analyses their implications for not only the growth and development of the services sector but also its implications for the larger economy, through direct and indirect linkages with other sectors. The chapter concludes by outlining policy measures that are needed to leverage emerging opportunities as well as address challenges in services.

Part V deals with regional growth and its heterogeneity. Chapter 10 by Jha and Kar focuses on the regional growth dynamics in India since 1960. The Indian economy passed through two distinct regimes in the period after independence. The first regime attempted a heavily regulated mixed-economy model for close to four decades before shifting to a liberalised, privatised, and globalised second regime following the reforms in the early nineties. These two regimes have manifested in the form of two growth episodes—a pre-reform period of relative stagnation and a post-reform period of rapid economic growth. These higher growth outcomes in recent times have also coincided with increased regional inequalities, with some states prospering while others stagnated. This might suggest that the regional growth dynamics have changed drastically as a result of the reforms. Is there any empirical evidence to support this hypothesis? The chapter investigates this question using a long time series of regional data for the pre-reform and post-reform periods. The study finds that there was no qualitative difference in the regional growth dynamics during the two periods, with persistent non-convergence and club formation of per capita income GSDP in both. The individual regions also largely remained in the same clubs across these two episodes. However, there was some quantitative difference between the two periods, mainly in terms of an accelerated divergence between the clubs themselves in the post-reform period. The study concludes with some discussion of the differential policy approaches that are needed for regions in high-income and low-income clubs.

In Chapter 11, Samaresh Bardhan investigates the existence of club convergence in growth and financial development using evidence from Indian states. The paper revisits the issues of convergence in the context of economic growth across Indian states. Unlike the existing body of literature on convergence in the Indian context, an investigation of the possibility of club convergence among Indian states is undertaken. Using state-level data from a sample of 33 states during 1985–2018, Bardhan tests first whether Indian states converge in terms of per capita income. Subsequently, the study examines, among a few other channels of convergence of growth, the role of financial development across Indian states. Unlike most of the existing studies in India, it applies the Phillips and Sul (2007) methodology to detect converging subgroups of states in terms of growth as well as various alternative indicators of financial development. Findings reveal that for the aggregate sample of states, there is no evidence of convergence, which implies that sample states are not converging to a single steady path. However, the study finds evidence of the existence of club convergence. In particular, Indian states are found to diverge in terms of state-level per capita growth as well as alternative indicators of financial development. The empirical findings, however, reveal the formation of clubs in terms of both state-level growth and various indicators of financial development, such as branch density, different compositions of sectoral credit, and credit inflow and credit outflow across states. The study findings point to the prevalence of uneven growth and financial development across Indian states despite several measures taken during the last few decades. The findings also call for concerted policy actions to achieve regional balance in growth and financial development through appropriate reform measures in investment, infrastructure, and financial development.

Chapter 12 by Raychaudhuri and Ghosh addresses the development and change in India's service sector. It analyses the main drivers of growth in India's services sector. The focus is on the interdependence of the services sector on the manufacturing sector and vice versa. Shift-share analysis shows that the change in productivity of services sectors is mainly due to within-sector rather than inter-sector effects. Input–output analysis reveals that although the existing service output levels are heavily dependent on inter-industry intermediate use, the growth of such services depends vitally on final demand in most cases. Technological changes in many sectors have reduced per unit requirement of services, but the scale effect dominates so that a rising final demand has to be supplemented by a larger intermediate demand for services—the latter sometimes labelled as servicification of the manufacturing sector. It emerges from the analysis that while a deliberate push to manufacturing will be a boon to services as well, the growth of the services sector will promote larger use of the same in many manufacturing sectors and at the same time, create more demand for manufacturing goods through inter-industry backward linkage effects.

Part VI looks at issues related to employment, rural non-farm activities, and migration. Chapter 13 by Suresh Chand Aggarwal deals with the status of self-employed and casual Workers in India. During the last fifty years, from 1972 to 2022, the overall workforce participation rate (WPR) in India has stagnated at around 41%. Still, the female WPR has not only been around half of males, it has also declined by 2 percentage points. The average annual growth rate in employment has just been equal to 1.75%, though similar to that of the population (1.8%). However, most of the labour has been employed in labour-intensive sectors of agriculture and construction, mainly as self-employed or casual labour. In India, the share of self-employed in total employment in 2022–2023 is 57%, and another 22% are casual workers. The share of regular workers is thus only 21%. India has a lot of workers in the informal sector who do not have any social security. These workers are the most vulnerable in any catastrophe. As a result, these self-employed and casual workers were and still are the worst sufferers of any catastrophe, e.g. COVID-19. They lost their occupations and jobs due to severe economic lockdowns and restrictions. They did not have alternative employment opportunities. Many of these workers who lost their jobs migrated to rural areas, where many were employed under NREGA. Most workers did not get adequate government support and were forced to take up self-employment for their survival. During COVID-19, not only did the headcount of employment fall, but workers also worked for fewer days per week and for fewer hours per day. The government took a few initiatives. Some more policy initiatives have been recently undertaken in India to increase the formalisation of the economy and provide some social security to the workers through changes in labour laws. The chapter aims to put the status of self-employed and casual workers in perspective. It first provides a brief profile of these workers in India during 1972–2022. Then, the chapter identifies the total loss of employment by the workers during COVID-19 and gives an overview of the policy initiatives that were taken to help the workers during COVID-19. Based on the outcome of the evidence, some policy recommendations have been made to improve the work conditions of the workers.

In Chapter 14, Sankar Majumder gives an overview of the rural non-farm sector in India. Development and growth of the rural non-farm sector is very crucial for providing alternative livelihood in the rural sector. Since the very beginning of her development journey, India has implemented several policies and programmes to enhance non-agricultural livelihood. Data given by different authorities shows that over the last 75 years, this non-farm sector has grown to some extent, but this is far less than the desired one. The focus of the studies and reports on the non-farm sector was mainly on the provision of finance and credit facilities, physical infrastructure and other amenities, institution building for technological graduation, training for skill development and entrepreneurship development. Based on the author's personal experiences as a development practitioner, this chapter presents some other factors that have drawn less attention from both policymakers and academics.

Chapter 15 by Sunetra Ghatak shows the changing dynamics of Inter-state Migration in India. The study of internal migration in India is crucial for understanding population redistribution, labour market dynamics, urbanisation, and regional disparities. Using data from the Census of India and the National Sample Survey Office (NSSO), this chapter explores the trends and patterns of internal migration in India, focusing on both economic and non-economic influencing factors. Aggregate and disaggregate internal migration trends in India are reviewed, highlighting the significant role of non-economic factors, especially in the post-reform period. Most migrations occur within states, influenced by social networks and caste-kinship bonds rather than solely economic opportunities. Education impacts migration patterns, with higher educational attainment leading to longer-distance inter-state migration, while lower-educated individuals tend to migrate within states. Therefore, the analysis in the chapter shows a significant impact of non-economic factors such as education, caste, state administrative borders, etc., along with economic factors such as per capita income and urbanisation. Finally, Ghatak identifies the limitations of official data, emphasising the need for more comprehensive and current data to understand internal migration dynamics in India better.

Part VII deals with some issues related to social sector development in India. Chapter 16 by Sanati, Bhandari and Ramakrishnan focuses on international finance. The field of international finance can be highly complex and challenging to navigate. One of the major issues that individuals and businesses face is the lack of comprehensive documentation that delves into the intricacies of products and processes related to the role of banks and the legal frameworks of international bodies like the International Chamber of Commerce (ICC). To truly gain a deep understanding of the practical applications of international trade, it is essential to study the process and documentation flows that pertain to these transactions. Also, trade-based money laundering is another important aspect of modern day's international trade scenario. The study has touched upon each of these aspects to make it interesting in connection with the overall modern international trade atmosphere. Recently, some literature has been available that bridges the gap between theory and practice related to international trade and finance. These resources cover a wide range of topics, from banking theories to operational procedures relating to the methods of payment and the use of Letters of Credit (LCs), for example, revolving LCs, back-to-back LCs, transferable LCs, standby LCs, with specific applications of documents and documentary compliances. Also, the significance of merchanting trade and the differences between export credit and trade credit have been discussed in the literature. Besides, different types of bank guarantees are discussed, as well as their practical applications. The hedging of foreign exchange risk for merchants has been discussed in detail. On the other hand, the mechanism of interbank cover operation is discussed to elaborate the risk mitigation techniques in the banking book. Also, some empirical literature has been referred to, which highlights the change in operational efficiency of the banks if the credit risk and the market risk become an integral part of the efficiency measure.

Chapter 17 by Pooja Sharma attempts to map skill formation, innovation, and education in determining social capital. Education coupled with skill constitutes a backbone of innovation and economic growth. Skilled individuals not only contribute more efficiently and productively but also improve social welfare. In the chapter, the linkages between education, skill, innovation, and employment are examined. Firstly, it investigates the interlinkages between education, skill, employment, innovation, and inequality. Secondly, the study examines their subsequent impact on social capital and well-being. A panel regression across the 32 (states and union territories) in India for 7 years 1995, 2000, 2005, 2010, 2015, 2020, and 2022 are performed to comprehend the interlinkages between education, employment, innovation, and inequality and also their influence on social capital like crime and suicide. Further, the BRICS countries are also examined concerning these aspects to comprehend how these developing countries are placed in this context. The results reveal that the existing innovations fail to increase employment significantly, while education and expenditure on skill significantly increase employment at the state-level analysis. Increased employment may not increase the income of the state, while human capital, education, or skills do not influence the status of the crime significantly. Among the BRICS countries, education, innovation, and employment levels are much higher in China, while inequality is lower. Inequality is highest in South Africa, while education, innovation, and employment are lowest in South Africa. Though South Africa witnessed better situations of political stability, rule of law, and the absence of terrorism, it witnessed more intentional homicides compared to other countries in BRICS. The results reveal that education and innovation fail to create more employment and are responsible for aggravating inequality. Further, inequality exacerbates suicides, thus deteriorating social capital.

Chapter 18 by Kumar and Maiti investigates the economic impact of global warming in India and policies dealing with it. This chapter reviews empirical methodologies assessing the impact of climate change on economic indicators in India. It begins with an analysis of global climate dynamics, emphasising level and growth effects, using climate econometrics to analyse methodological issues in temperature-GDP econometrics, and summarising methodological discussion on the differentiation between weather and climate change. The chapter then evaluates India's vulnerability to climate shocks, detailing macroeconomic impacts on critical sectors such as agriculture, water resources, and coastal areas, and reviews the evolution of India's environmental policies. It further reviews the role of fiscal, regulatory, and monetary policies in facilitating climate adaptation and mitigation. Additionally, the authors explore diverse econometric approaches for estimating climate change impacts, including cross-sections and panel methods. This review highlights the urgency of coordinated international action and the need for India to implement robust climate policies to ensure sustainable economic growth and fulfil its emission reduction targets.

Part VIII deals with some aspects of industrialisation in India and some data related issues in manufacturing, construction and other sectors of the Indian economy. In Chapter 19, T.C.A. Ananat discusses the methods of compilation of national accounts statistics and the estimation of sectoral contributions, taking cognizance of the fact that the definitions have frequently changed over time. He notes that the India Productivity Report (2022) has a comprehensive introduction and review of productivity measurement and research both in India and globally. This study—which reflects the work of the India KLEMS project—also forms the basis of the KLEMS data now housed at RBI. This database is increasingly being used by many researchers working on the Indian economy. It draws upon National Accounts, Household and Establishment Surveys of the NSS and the Population Census to construct a time series of Capital (K), Labour (L), Energy (E), Material (M), and Services(S). This allows users to do time series analyses on the Indian economy since 1981. However, since the source datasets have seen changes over the years due to improvements in measurement techniques, it creates challenges for time series analysts. The chapter describes the developments in National Accounts after 1981, focusing on issues of estimation of value added in the Informal Sector, Trade, and Construction and examines their implications for productivity studies. The chapter notes that revisions in national accounts have introduced structural breaks in value-added time series at both sectoral levels and in the aggregate. For users of time series data, this poses significant challenges in interpretation, particularly for productivity measurement. Since productivity is measured essentially as a residual (after accounting for growth in inputs), it is a challenge to disentangle the effects of true productivity change from those on account of measurement-induced biases. In the construction sector, for instance, low-productivity growth is built in essentially because of the Leontief type (fixed coefficient) value-added function with constant returns to scale being used. In other sectors (particularly Trade and Manufacturing), part of the Total Factor Productivity (TFP) growth may be spurious due to the measurement bias in the earlier series. One should note that these problems of inter-temporal comparability are likely to occur in all cases where development and technological change have led to improvements in both coverage and quality of statistical data.

Chapter 20 by Nagesh Kumar evaluates 75 years of India's industrial policy, performance, and prospects for a manufacturing-led transformation. Although the Indian economy has emerged from the pandemic as the fastest-growing large economy and also has many other impressive achievements to celebrate the 75 years of its independence, many challenges remain. These include pervasive informality and persisting poverty linked with declining employment elasticity of economic growth. Jobless growth is a major challenge in the context of a country passing through a youth bulge in its demographic transition. The job creation is linked to structural transformation and the failure to industrialise the economy and harness the direct and indirect job-creating potential of manufacturing. In that context, this paper reviews the evolution of the Indian government's approach towards the manufacturing sector, which has changed over the years from a blanket import substitution during the 1960–1980s, followed by economic reforms from 1991, unleashing a process of liberalisation to enable market forces help sharpen the competitiveness of Indian industry for the following three decades. However, the compulsions of job creation, especially for unskilled and semiskilled workers, pushed the government to turn its attention to harnessing the potential of the manufacturing sector through make-in-India and production-linked incentives over the past decade. The chapter also reviews the emerging global trend of a fractured global trading system and the ongoing restructuring of supply chains as a part of the de-risking strategies of global companies, including through friend-shoring and onshoring.

Against the context of India's industrial policy thrust and the changed global context, this chapter reviews India's industrial performance over the 75 years in terms of evolving industrial structure, especially with respect to technology-intensive modern manufacturing sectors and broad productivity trends. The evolving patterns of FDI inflows, trade, and GVC participation landscape are examined, and trends with respect to innovative activity are reviewed. It also reviews the patterns of industrial financing, industrial infrastructure, and MSMEs participation in the manufacturing sector. Another crucial aspect of industrialization examined in the chapter is the prospects of a manufacturing-led transformation in India. It reviews the opportunities available to feed the domestic and export markets. It also focuses on the opportunities emerging in new sunrise sectors, such as digital and green industrialisation, which can be harnessed by the country to leapfrog into an important manufacturing hub while also addressing its global commitments towards sustainability. The chapter concludes with a policy agenda for harnessing India's manufacturing potential to foster inclusive and sustainable prosperity for all its people and the realisation of its developed country vision by 2047.

Part IX looks at the impacts of trade and capital inflows and their impact on the Indian economy. Chapter 21 by Acharyya and Ganguly deals with International Trade and its uneven Gains from theoretical aspects. The Gains from Trade theorem, based on the Ricardian doctrine of comparative advantage, constitutes one of the core propositions in international trade theory. But, while it postulates that the trading nations will experience welfare gains in the aggregate when they specialise according to their comparative advantage, it does not suggest that all economic agents within a trading nation will gain. This chapter reviews the theoretical discourses and country experiences regarding such uneven gains from trade that have pushed policymakers towards trade policy reversals and raised concerns for globalisation's future. Acharyya and Ganguly build an analytical model of politically optimum trade liberalisation based on inequality-driven discontent regarding trade liberalisation to show that the politically optimum choice of tariff rate is larger than the economic optimum rates. Finally, the study reviews India's trade policy paradigm before and after the 1991 Crisis and discuss the changing structure and increasing skill composition of our exports as potential sources of uneven gains and income inequality.

In Chapter 22, C. Veeramani discusses the interaction between trade, FDI, and growth with a particular focus and evidence from the Indian economy. The chapter provides an overview of the evolution of India's trade and FDI policies, emphasising their impacts on economic growth rates. During the post-reform period, India has seen remarkable growth in trade and FDI. However, inward FDI has primarily targeted the domestic market rather than supporting export-oriented growth. A comparative analysis with China reveals India's progress in export diversification but lags in specialisation and global value chain (GVC) participation. Policy reforms are necessary to enhance GVC integration and leverage FDI for export-led growth and job creation, emphasising the need to capitalise on India's comparative advantages for faster export expansion. Veeramani has carried out an econometric analysis of the impact of FDI and trade openness on sector-level economic indicators using panel data from 1999–2000 to 2014–2015. The analysis focuses on the effects of trade openness and FDI on sector-level value added and employment. The findings indicate a positive effect of trade and FDI openness on sector-level real value added and employment. Importantly, import openness positively affects export performance, suggesting that lowering tariffs not only boosts imports but also exports. However, FDI appears to promote imports more than exports, reflecting India's inclination towards domestic market-seeking FDI rather than FDI helping export promotion. This trend aligns with India's low participation in GVCs. The study underscores the need for policy reforms aimed at enhancing India's GVC participation to leverage FDI for export-led growth and job creation.

Chapter 23 by De and Barman portrays the development of ports and its impact on the productivity growth of the economy. Ports are the lifeline of the Indian economy. More than 80% of India's merchandise trade (by volume) is transported via ocean routes. Not only do ports handle trade, but they are also planned to serve the country's strategic needs. However, low productivity and inefficiency of ports in India have been identified as major constraints affecting India's trade. A productive and efficient port has often been a prerequisite for successful growth strategies, particularly those driven by exports. By sharp contrast, a poorly functioning or inefficient port can hinder growth. This chapter analyses the TFP growth (TFPG) of the Indian ports. One of the conclusions is that major ports in India have witnessed significant productivity strides post-inauguration of the Sagarmala project. This study also presents the major determinants of the TFP particularly those which are linked to port's internal and external economies. Improvements in port performance, and in the law and order situation, where the port is located, may lead to an increase in the TFP. The study also suggests that past values of TFP have a significant and positive impact on current TFP in the major ports of India.

Reference

Krishna, K. L., Goldar, B., Das, D. K., Aggarwal, S. C., Erumban, A. A., Das, P. C. (2022). *The India Productivity Report*. Centre for Development Economics, Delhi School of Economics.

Dibyendu Maiti is a professor of Economics at the Delhi School of Economics, University of Delhi, India. He specialises in development macroeconomics and international economics, with a specific focus on labour, technology, and the informal sector. Before this, he worked at the University of the South Pacific, Institute of Economic Growth Delhi, and Centre for Studies in Social Sciences Calcutta, as well as held various research positions at the University of Manchester, University of Nottingham, Max Planck Institute of Economics (Jena), Norwegian Institute of International Affairs, University of Oslo. He received the Max Planck India Fellowship, ICSSR-ESRC exchange and ICSSR-CASS exchange fellowship. He is a member of a technical advisory group of the National Sample Survey Organisation, MoSPI. He publishes research articles in reputed journals, like the Journal of Development Economics, Empirical Economics, Social Research Indicators, Journal of Productivity Analysis, Labour Economics, Economic Modelling, International Review of Economics and Finance, Cambridge Journal of Economics, American Behavioural Scientists, etc. He received the IDRC Young India Social Sciences Award in 2010 and the Global Development Network Award in 2009.

Bishwanath Goldar is a retired professor of Economics at the Institute of Economic Growth (IEG), Delhi. He was a member of the National Statistical Commission and a national fellow of the Indian Council of Social Science Research (ICSSR). He was a professor at the Indian Council for Research on International Economic Relations (ICRIER), New Delhi, during 2003–2004 and a visiting professor at the Centre for International Trade and Development, School of International Studies, Jawaharlal Nehru University, New Delhi, during 2012–2013. He is currently a non-resident senior fellow at the Institute of Economic Growth. He has many publications in economic journals. His areas of research interest include productivity measurement, industry, trade, foreign direct investment, industrial pollution, energy use of industries, river water pollution, and rural water supply.

K. L. Krishna, a founder member of CDE (Centre for Development Economics), at the Delhi School of Economics, has been the principal investigator of the RBI-funded India KLEMS Productivity Project since 2009. With post-graduate qualifications in Statistics from the University of Kerala and the Indian Statistical Institute, Kolkata, and PhD degree in Economics from the University of Chicago, he taught Econometrics and Industrial Economics for four decades. He supervised around 45 PhD and M.Phil. theses in a variety of fields. He served as the head of the Department of Economics and director, Delhi School of Economics, in the 1980s and 1990s. He was the founder and managing editor of the Journal of Quantitative Economics for one decade and the president of the Indian Econometric Society (TIES) for one term. He is a member of the TIES Trust. He was the chairman or member of several official Committees of the Government of India. He held the position of chairman of CESS, Hyderabad, during 2007–2013, and MIDS, Chennai during 2013–2020. He received the Padma Shri Award for his outstanding contribution to education and research in 2025.

Part I
Productivity Growth of Indian Economy—Pace and Patterns

Chapter 2
Sources of Growth in the Indian Economy: Looking Back at the Last 75 Years Since India's Independence

Bishwanath Goldar, Dibyendu Maiti, Suresh Chand Aggarwal, Abdul Azeez Erumban, and Pilu Chandra Das

Abstract Sources of India's economic growth during 1951–1952 to 2019–2020 and five sub-periods, 1951–1966, 1967–1979, 1980–1993, 1994–2007 and 2008–2019 are analysed using the growth accounting framework. The analysis is undertaken at the aggregate economy level and for five major sectors of the economy. The trends in employment and capital formation in the sub-periods and the overall period are examined. The growth in real gross value added and the changes in the sectoral composition are studied. Further, how the sectoral pattern of aggregate TFP has evolved over time is investigated which brings out that the primary factor influencing sectoral variations in contributing to aggregate TFP growth was the relatively weak productivity growth performance of the manufacturing and non-manufacturing industries sector during the period prior to the initiation of liberal market reforms in India. An econometric analysis of determinants of TFP growth is undertaken which shows that education, trade openness, structural change and ICT investments have contributed to TFP growth.

Keywords Indian economy · Long-tem economic growth · Growth accounting · Sources of growth · Employment · Capital formation · Productivity · Structural change · Determinants of TFP growth · Trade openness · ICT investment

B. Goldar (✉)
Institute of Economic Growth, Delhi, India
e-mail: bgoldar49@iegindia.org

D. Maiti
Delhi School of Economics, Delhi, India

S. C. Aggarwal
Institute for Human Development, New Delhi, India

A. A. Erumban
University of Groningen, Groningen, The Netherlands

P. C. Das
Kidderpore College, University of Calcutta, Kolkata, India

D. Maiti et al. (eds.), *75 Years of Growth, Development and Productivity in India*, India Studies in Business and Economics, https://doi.org/10.1007/978-981-97-8054-9_2

2.1 Introduction

2.1.1 Study Objective

The purpose of the chapter is to analyse trends in the sources of India's economic growth Over the last 75 years since India's Independence in 1947. From a mostly agrarian economy at the time of the Independence and very low growth over the first half of the twentieth century (1900–1950)[1] India has come a long way on the development path in the last 75 years. Today, India is one of the major industrial and economic powers in the global economy, with a large services sector capable of offering low-cost, high-quality services to the world. This long period of 75 years saw major development efforts being made by the Indian government aiming to improve the standards of living of the country's population. According to Conference Board estimates, India's per capita income increased from 876 international $ (in 2021 PPP terms) in 1950 to 6,919 international $ in 2020 (The Conference Board Total Economy Database, April 2022). That is an eightfold increase in 75 years. This increase in the per capita income level can be attributed to several factors, some of which are given attention to in this chapter. In particular, the chapter considers the roles of capital accumulation, technology, improved education and worker skills and better allocation of resources among sectors arising from structural changes in the economy.

The analysis of sources of growth is carried out in this chapter by focussing on the supply-side of the economy. An analysis of the demand-side of growth in terms of the role played and contribution made by import substitution and export expansion will provide additional useful insight into the process of growth. Considering the roles of income inequality and the problem of finding enough domestic demand for domestically produced products are also important for such an analysis. The demand-side analysis is, however, outside the scope of this chapter.

The analysis of sources of growth is undertaken by applying the growth accounting methodology (see the discussion on methodology in *India Productivity Report* (Krishna et al., 2022a)). This methodology, rooted in neoclassical economic theory, has found wide application, including applications for analysis of economic growth in emerging economies. The methodology helps in separating the contributions of factor accumulation and total factor productivity (TFP) growth to output growth. The core methodology of growth accounting, as developed further by Jorgenson and associates (see Jorgenson et al., 2005), makes it possible to measure the contributions to growth made by reallocations of factor inputs—labour and capital—across sectors over time.

There has been a good deal of research on productivity trends in the Indian economy in the past using the growth accounting methodology. Some of the studies

[1] According to Maddison database, India's per capita income grew barely during 1900–1950. The average growth during 1900–1950 was 0.07%. With close to half a percentage population growth, that implies just above 0.5 percentage GDP growth in half a century. See Bolt and van Zanden (2020) and Broadberry et al. (2015).

on this topic include Dholakia (2002) covering the period 1960 to 2000, Sivasubramonian (2004) covering the period 1950 to 1999, Virmani (2004) covering the period 1950 to 2003 and Bosworth et al. (2007) covering the period 1960 to 2004. Productivity trends in the Indian economy in the period 1950 to 2015 have been analysed in Das et al. (2021a) and the trends in the period 1980–2011 have been analysed in Das et al. (2016). A recent study on productivity trends in the Indian economy is the *India Productivity Report* (Krishna et al., 2022a) which has covered the period 1980 to 2017. Another study covering by and large the same period is Krishna et al. (2022b). This is probably the first study in which productivity trends in the Indian economy are analysed covering a period of 75 years since India's Independence.[2]

2.1.2 India's Development Experience and Periodization Adopted in the Study

In 2022, India completed three-quarters of a century after its Independence in 1947 from British colonialization. It is important to look back at the developmental effort made by the country over the last 75 years and how these efforts contributed to the growth in GDP, a measure, albeit crude, of the improvements in the economic well-being of the people. It is also important to study the trends in productivity in the Indian economy over this period since productivity bears a close connection with the earning of the households and hence their welfare.[3] Also, an analysis of the long-term trends in factor accumulation and productivity may help gain a good understanding of the sources of India's economic growth.

India's development efforts through a planned economic development began from the First Five Year Plan in 1951. In this study, therefore, the period since 1951 is studied. The Second Five Year Plan bore the imprint of the well-known Mahalanobis model. The path chosen in the Second Five Year Plan with emphasis of import-substituting industrialization and development of heavy chemicals, metals and machinery continued in the Third Five Year Plan which ended in 1966. There was emphasis on establishment of state-run public sector industrial units to capture the commanding heights of the economy. This period, 1951 to 1966, has thus been taken as the first phase of India's economic development for the analysis presented in the chapter.

In the next 13 years, i.e., the period 1967 to 1979, there was consolidation of the development gains made in the first phase of India's economic development. This was also a period when there was some re-thinking on the development priorities and accordingly a shift was there towards equity in the growth-equity trade-off. This

---

[2] For a recent review of productivity studies covering the overall economy, broad sectors, and detailed organized manufacturing industries, as well as more recent research using the KLEMS framework for disaggregated industries, see the *India Productivity Report* (Krishna et al., 2022a).

[3] See Basu et al. (2022) for a recent discussion on how measures of total factor productivity are related to welfare in open and closed economies.

period contained the three years of Plan Holidays, and the Fourth and the Fifth Five Year Plans. Concerns for employment generation, development of small-scale industries and the need to take care of the poor in the development process received due consideration. Also, self-reliance received a priority in view of the balance of payment difficulties faced. The Fifth Five Year Plan (1974–1979) focussed, *inter alia*, on employment generation, poverty alleviation and reducing income inequalities. The reservation policy for small-scale industries, entailing the production of certain products exclusively reserved for small-scale industries, began in 1967 with 47 items which was later increased to 504 items in 1978. In 1972–1973, of the total output of small-scale units, about a quarter were of the reserved items (Bala Subramanya, 1995). This period of 13 years is thus taken as the second phase of India's economic development.

The third phase of India's economic development includes the 1980s when there was a change in policy-thinking in India towards creating a business-friendly environment. This is an important change from a development strategy guided by socialist thinking to a pro-business leaning. This period has been called a period of pro-business reforms by Rodrik and Subramanian (2004) as against pro-market reforms of the 1990s. According to them, in the 1980s, there was an attitudinal shift in the Indian government favouring business, and they note further that this favoured the interest of the existing business rather than the new entrants or consumers. Accordingly, the phase 1980 to 1993 may be taken as the third phase of India's economic development, and this is so done in the analysis in the chapter. While significant policy changes (including industrial policy and trade-tariff policy) were made in 1991 coupled with exchange rate depreciation, it is appropriate to include 1991 to 1993 in the third phase of India's development, called pre-reform phase, as these were the years of transition and economic turmoil. In the study undertaken by Panagariya and associates (2014), they have taken a cut-off in 1993 to compare the growth performance in different phases. This is an additional reason why in this study too, the cut-off year for defining the pre-reform era has been taken as 1993. Accordingly, the third phase of India's economic development has been taken as 1980 to 1993 which is mainly characterized by pro-business reforms.

The fourth phase of India's economic development may be delineated as 1994 to 2007 and the fifth phase as 2008 onwards. The cut-off in 2008 is right to adopt to separate the post-GFC (global financial crisis) period during which there was a marked slowdown in global trade and India's development was majorly influenced by the process of coping with this slowdown in the global trade.

The fourth phase, i.e., 1994 to 2007, was marked by: (1) liberalization of industrial policies, (2) lowering of tariff rates from one of the highest in the world to very low levels and (3) removal of quantitative restrictions on imports of industrial goods—intermediate and capital goods were freed from quantitative restrictions in 1991 and almost all consumer goods freed in 2000 and 2001. By the end of the 1980s, India's exchange rate was substantially over-valued and with the depreciation of the real effective exchange rate in the 1990s, the extent of over-valuation was considerably reduced. The result of the economic reforms of the 1990s and those undertaken later was that the prices of industrial goods in India got aligned by and large with the international prices.

On considerations of data availability (at the time of writing this chapter), the fifth phase for the present study is confined to 2008–2019. Apart from the issue of data availability, there is also the huge impact of Covid pandemic which impacted the economy in 2020 with some recovery made in 2021. In the study of long-term trends in India's economic growth, it seems it is better to confine to the period up to 2019 and consider the developments in 2020 and 2021 separately.

2.1.3 Organization of the Chapter

The chapter is organized as follows. The next section, i.e., Sect. 2.2 briefly outlines the growth accounting methodology. Section 2.3 analyses trends in the growth rates in real GVA (gross value added) in different sectors of the Indian economy and at the aggregate economy level. Structural changes that have taken place over time in terms of sectoral shares in aggregate GVA are studied in this section. Section 2.4 deals with trends in employment and labour productivity (LP) in various sectors of the Indian economy and at the aggregate level. An international comparison of trends in labour productivity at the aggregate economy level, comparing India with some of the other major economies, is made. Section 2.5 deals with capital accumulation, capital intensity and capital productivity. The analysis is undertaken at the sectoral level and for the aggregate economy. In Sect. 2.6, an analysis of trends in total factor productivity (TFP) and its contribution to GVA growth is undertaken for major sectors of the economy and at the aggregate level. An estimate of the contribution of factor reallocation to productivity growth at the aggregate level is also made. Section 2.7 contains an analysis of sectoral pattern of the aggregate TFP growth based on Harberger diagrams. Section 2.8 presents an econometric analysis of determinants of the aggregate economy–level TFP growth. Finally, Sect. 2.9 of the chapter summarizes the key findings of the study and concludes.

The chapter has several annexures at the end. These deal with construction of the series on labour and capital inputs and the factor income shares.

2.2 Basics of Growth Accounting Methodology and Database

The growth accounting methodology is widely used across advanced and emerging economies to study the sources of economic growth. The contributions of factor inputs and productivity to the aggregate-level economic growth are ascertained by this method. The methodology allows for assessment of the gains in the aggregate-level productivity arising from reallocation of primary inputs, labour and capital, among different sectors of the economy.

The basics of the methodology lie in neoclassical economics, particularly the concept of production function and the neoclassical theory of the firm. To explain briefly the basic methodology, let us assume that for each industry there is a five-input production function. The inputs are Capital (K), Labour (L), Energy (E), Materials (M) and Services (S). The production function may be written as:

$$Q = f(K, L, E, M, S, t). \tag{2.1}$$

Q denoted gross output in this equation and t denoted time, representing technological progress. Under the assumption of constant returns to scale and factors of production being paid according to their marginal product, the rate of technological change or TFP growth can be derived by taking logarithmic derivation with respect to time.

$$\frac{dlnQ}{dt} = \sum s_x \frac{dlnx}{dt} + \frac{\partial lnQ}{\partial t}, x = K, L, E, M, S, \tag{2.2}$$

where, s_x is the elasticity of Q with respect to input x,

$$s_x = \frac{\partial lnQ}{\partial lnx} \tag{2.3}$$

The rate of technical change is the second term (i.e., ∂lnQ/∂t) on the right hand side of Eq. (2.2) which can be obtained from other terms in the equation. To apply this empirically, an approximation is taken, a Tornqvist index is applied. This involves the assumption that the underlying production is of translog form. For this reason, the discrete approximation to Eqs. (2.2) and (2.3) provides the translog index of TFP.

While the above description indicates how the growth accounting methodology can be applied at the level of individual industries, difficulties arise when an estimate of TFP growth has to be made at the economy level. The gross output production function is not meaningful at the economy level and the appropriate concept to use is the value added which can be aggregated across industries to yield the aggregate-level value added. The production function at the aggregate economy level may be written as (V denotes value added):

$$V = g(K, L, t). \tag{2.4}$$

The existence of an aggregate value-added function when production technology at the industry level is represented by a gross output function requires a number of highly restrictive assumptions. Estimation of TFP growth at the economy level can be done with imposing the assumption that an aggregate economy production (value added) function exists. Aggregation of industry level TFP growth to the economy level can be done using alternate framework/procedure: production possibility frontier approach or direct aggregation of industry level TFP growth rates.

At the time, the dataset on output and inputs were prepared for this study, the latest available India KLEMS database (version 2021) covered the period 1980–1981 to 2019–2020. The database contained data on gross output, value added and the five inputs mentioned above, K, L, E, M and S along with factor income shares. Therefore, the framework described above could be applied to the India KLEMS database.[4] However, the present study covers the period since 1951 and there are considerable difficulties in extending all variables in the India KLEMS database backwards to 1951. Only the value-added series, employment series, capital stock series and the series on the income share of labour in value added could be extended backward to 1951. This database, constructed for this study (details in Annexures) covering the period 1951–1952 to 2019–2020, is hereafter called India KLEMS database, version 2021 (extended to 1951). At the time the chapter was finalized, more recent versions of the India KLEMS database had become available, covering 2020–21 and 2021–22. However, as explained above, the study period was not extended beyond 2019–20, as it is more appropriate to confine the analysis to this timeframe and consider developments in 2020–21 and 2021–22 separately.

Since, in the database constructed for the study, data on only two inputs are available, the value-added function framework is used for the analysis at the industry/sector level. At the economy level, it is assumed that an aggregate value-added production function exists, consistent with the sector/industry level value-added production function.

The assumption that a value-added function exists at the industry/sector level involves the assumption of separability. The form of the gross output production function that is assumed may be written as:

$$Q = h(V(K, L, t), E, M, S). \tag{2.5}$$

The assumption of separability imposes restrictions on the elasticity of substitution between inputs. Equation (2.5) implies that the elasticity of substitution between capital and labour is independent of the quantities of E, M and S used. When it is assumed that there is an aggregate-level value-added function for the economy, one requires the assumption that each type of labour input gets the same wage rate in different industries and the same applies to each type of capital input, getting the same rental price in each industry. Obviously, these are highly restrictive assumptions on which the economy-level growth accounting in this study is based, since a two-input framework is applied at the industry/sector level and the economy level.

[4] For an overview of the KLEMS approach to measuring productivity in Indian industries, see the first chapter of the *India Productivity Report* (Krishna et al., 2022a).

2.3 Growth in GVA and Structural Change

The analysis presented in this section of the chapter uses the sector-wise estimates of GVA (gross value added) at current and constant prices drawn from the *National Accounts Statistics* (National Statistics Office, Ministry of Statistics and Programme Implementation, Government of India) including the back series. The period covered in the study is 1951–1952 (hereafter written also as 1951) to 2019–2020 (2019).

The analysis begins with the changes in the structure of the economy over the period 1951 to 2019. In Fig. 2.1 and Appendix Table 2.22, we provided the value-added shares (at current prices) since 1951 for select industry aggregates. We observe that except for a slight increase during the 1960s, the value-added share of agriculture & allied activities has declined steadily since Independence until 2008 and then it remained stagnant. It has declined from 49.5% in 1951 to 18% in 2008. By contrast, the share of services sector increased from 34% in 1951 to 54.8% in 2019. However, the share of services remained stable during the first three decades since Independence.

The share of transport, storage & communication in the aggregate GVA increased from 3.1% in 1951 to 7.7% in 2005 and then fell to 6.3% in 2019. The share of finance, insurance & real estate has declined steadily since 1955 until 1980, then remained stagnant for next twenty years and then increased gradually, whereas the share of trade, hotels & restaurants and social & community services (which include public administration and defense, health services, education services, etc.) has increased over the entire period. However, increases in the share of these sectors were not sufficient to offset the decline in the share of finance, insurance & real estate, resulting in no improvement in the share of overall services until 1980.

There has been an improvement in the share of construction—it increased from 3.1% in 1951 to 9.7% in 2008 and then fell to 7.5% in 2019. The share of the utilities sector (electricity, gas & water supply) and the mining sector increased slightly during the first three decades after Independence and then remained stable over the last four decades.

Let us consider next the growth rate of the Indian economy and its major sectors over the last seven decades, spanning 1951 to 2019 (growth rates are from 1952 to 2019). The aggregate economy growth rates are obtained as Tornqvist aggregates of industry value-added growth rates. In a Tornqvist aggregation approach, the growth rate of each industry's real value added is weighted by the nominal value-added share of that industry while calculating the aggregate value-added growth rate.[5]

Figure 2.2 makes a graphic presentation of the annual growth rate of aggregate (real) value added during 1952–2019, and Table 2.1 provides the average growth rates for the aggregate economy and broad sectors for the five sub-periods (previously mentioned) and the entire period, 1952–2019. During the first 30 years after Independence, the average annual value-added growth rate of the Indian economy

[5] For a discussion on the application of the Divisia Index (approximated by the Tornqvist index) for measuring aggregate-level GVA growth based on industry level GVA growth, see Oulton (2022).

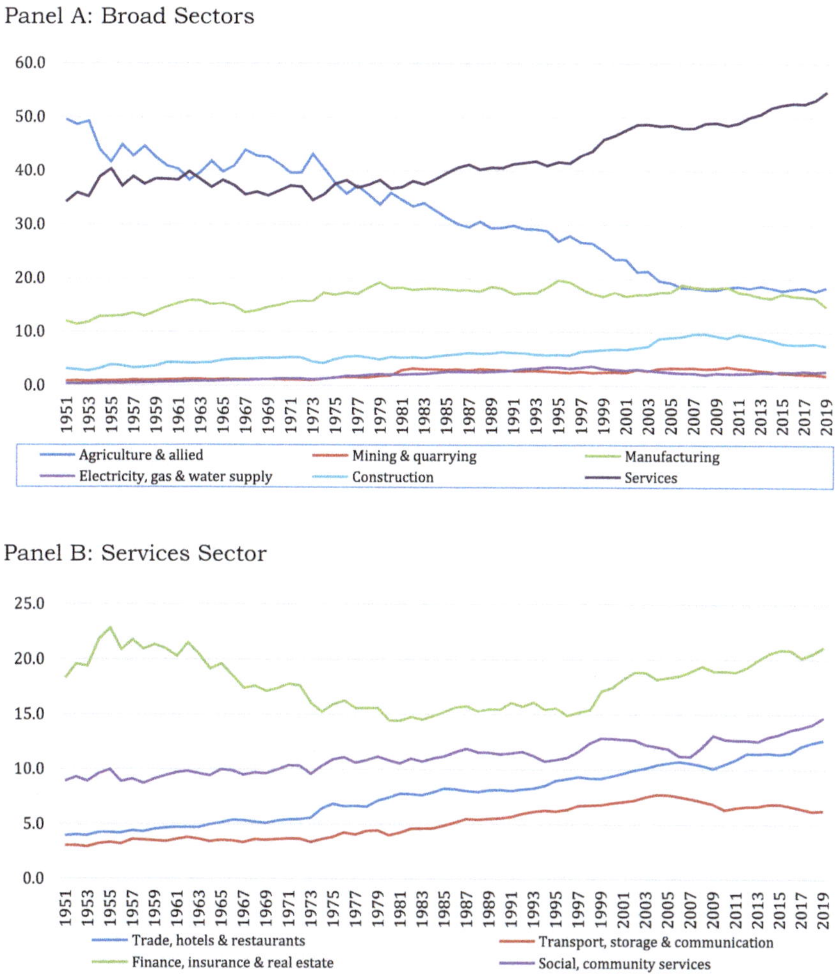

Fig. 2.1 Sectoral GVA shares at current prices (in per cent). *Source* Authors' computations based on India KLEMS database, 2021 (extended to 1951)

was slightly less than 3.5%. During 1980–1993, pro-business policies were implemented in India, and as a result, the annual average GDP growth rate rose to 5.3% and subsequently pro-market reforms consisted of dismantling of licence-permit-raj, freeing the trade of industrial goods and reducing the tariff to very low levels by Indian standards, which further escalated the growth rate to 6.3% during 1994–2007. Growth rate declined to 5.7% in the post-global financial crisis period.

The average annual growth rate in real gross value added of the Indian economy was 4.8% during 1952–2019. The average annual growth rate in Gross Value Added (GVA) for manufacturing; utility sector; construction; trade, hotels & restaurants; transport, storage & communication; finance, insurance & real estate and social &

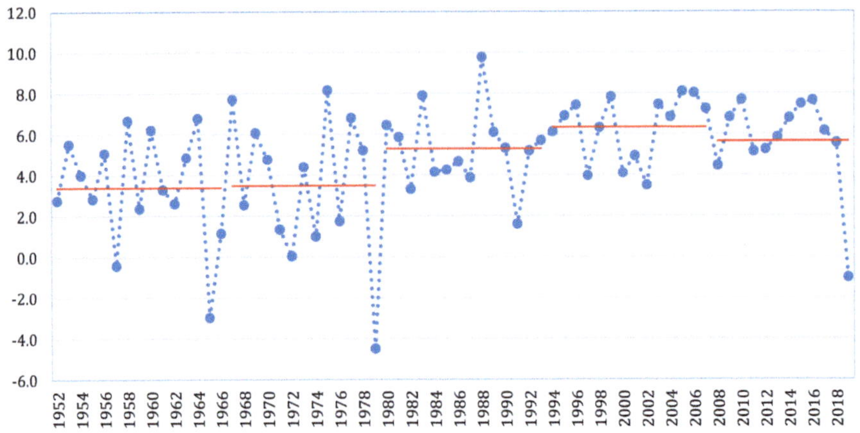

Fig. 2.2 Growth Rate of aggregate Indian economy (%). *Source* Authors' computations based on India KLEMS database, 2021 (extended to 1951)

Table 2.1 Real gross value-added growth rate, broad sectors (% per year)

Sectors	1952–1966	1967–1979	1980–1993	1994–2007	2008–2019	1952–2019
Agriculture & allied	1.63	2.27	3.80	2.88	3.71	2.82
Mining & quarrying	5.16	3.05	7.00	4.92	0.71	4.30
Manufacturing	5.88	4.42	4.94	7.38	6.01	5.74
Electricity, gas & water supply	10.45	7.48	7.94	5.93	5.80	7.61
Construction	6.36	2.36	4.52	8.22	4.30	5.24
Trade, hotels & restaurants	5.16	4.19	5.42	8.35	5.95	5.82
Transport, storage & communication	5.67	5.62	5.77	9.57	5.04	6.37
Finance, insurance & real estate	2.83	3.71	7.97	7.03	7.19	5.69
Social & community services	4.66	4.39	5.29	6.21	7.53	5.57
Total economy	3.38	3.48	5.30	6.34	5.65	4.80

Source Authors' computations based on India KLEMS database, 2021 (extended to 1951)

community services was more than 5%, whereas it was 2.8% for agriculture & allied activities and 4.3% for mining & quarrying.

During 1952–1966, electricity, gas & water supply grew the fastest at 10.5% per annum. The other sectors which grew at a rate of more than 5% per year are construction; manufacturing; transport, storage & communication; trade, hotels & restaurants and mining & quarrying. At the other end, GVA growth has been quite slow in agriculture & allied activities and finance, insurance & real estate. During 1967–1979, GVA growth rate improved slightly, with agriculture & allied and finance, insurance & real estate seeing a rise, even though all other sectors registered a fall. Between 1980 and 1993 all the broad sectors depicted improvement in GVA growth rate, three sectors that registered very impressive growth were agriculture & allied; mining & quarrying and finance, insurance & real estate. During the 1994–2007 period, when the aggregate economy witnessed a growth acceleration, the sectors that registered very impressive growth were manufacturing; construction; trade, hotels & restaurants and transport, storage & communication. However, agriculture & allied and mining & quarrying registered a fall in growth rate. Except agriculture & allied and social & community services all other sectors witnessed a growth slowdown after the global financial crisis in 2007–2008.

In Table 2.2 and Fig. 2.3, we provide the sectoral contributions to the aggregate economy value-added growth. We have calculated the contribution of each industry to total economy GVA growth by multiplying individual industry growth rate by its value-added share. During 1952–2019, out of the aggregate value-added growth rate of 4.8%, services sectors contributed about 2.44 percentage points. Within the services sector, finance, insurance & real estate contributed most (1.00 percentage point) followed by social & community services (0.63 percentage point). The contribution of manufacturing sector for the whole period has been around 0.95 percentage point. Agriculture has contributed slightly less than 0.9 percentage points to the total economy GVA growth. Comparing industry contribution among different sub-period, we found that finance, insurance & real estate; and trade, hotels & restaurants recorded an improvement in their value-added growth contribution to aggregate economy growth, while the contribution of agriculture declined over the year. As regards the remaining sectors, their contributions more or less remained stagnant.

2.4 Employment, Employment Elasticity and Labour Productivity in India: 1951–2019

A structural change in an economy is a part of the process of economic development characterized by the large productivity gaps between different parts of the economy. An economy's overall productivity depends on what happens within industries and the reallocation of resources across sectors. The structural change in labour productivity (LP) at the level of the economy will thus occur whenever labour is reallocated from low-productive to high-productive sectors. In view of the importance of

Table 2.2 Sectoral contribution to aggregate economy GVA growth (% points)

Sectors	1952–1966	1967–1979	1980–1993	1994–2007	2008–2019	1952–2019
Total economy (% per year)	3.38	3.48	5.30	6.34	5.65	4.80
Contribution of:						
Agriculture & allied	0.75	0.99	1.22	0.68	0.67	0.87
Mining & quarrying	0.05	0.04	0.19	0.14	0.02	0.09
Manufacturing	0.81	0.70	0.88	1.32	1.04	0.95
Electricity, gas & water supply	0.07	0.10	0.20	0.18	0.14	0.14
Construction	0.25	0.12	0.26	0.61	0.38	0.32
Trade, hotels & restaurants	0.23	0.25	0.43	0.80	0.65	0.47
Transport, storage & communication	0.19	0.21	0.29	0.67	0.34	0.34
Finance, insurance & real estate	0.58	0.62	1.22	1.20	1.44	1.00
Social & community services	0.44	0.45	0.60	0.74	0.96	0.63

Source Authors' computations based on India KLEMS database, 2021 (extended to 1951)

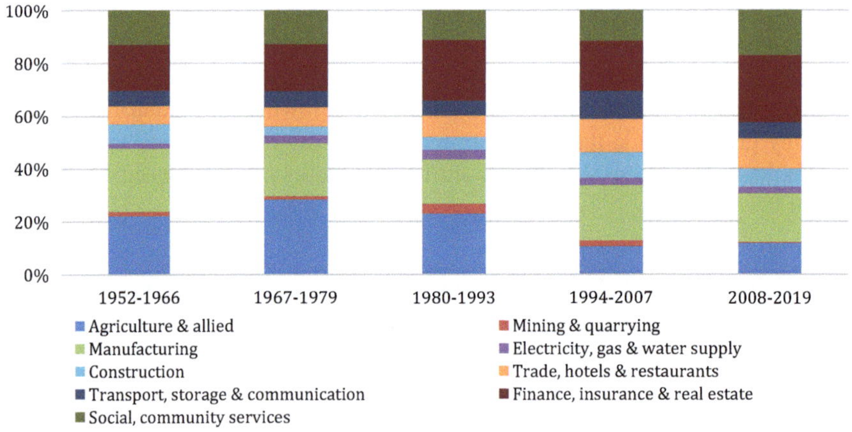

Fig. 2.3 Sectoral contribution to aggregate economy GVA growth (in per cent). *Source* Authors' computations based on India KLEMS database, 2021 (extended to 1951)

labour productivity, we examine, in this section, India's labour productivity growth to understand the proximate process of growth.

APO (2018) considers labour productivity and its drivers important because of its close links to GDP per capita. OECD (2016) and Dieppe (2020) have emphasized the need to focus on labour productivity. That labour productivity is essential to study also emerges from the wring of Krugman (1994), who said, 'Productivity isn't everything, but in the long run it is almost everything'. Labour productivity shows the volume of output produced per unit of labour input (OECD, 2016). It is a key indicator of economic performance and an essential driver of changes in living standards.

For our analysis of labour productivity growth in India's economy, we define labour productivity as real gross value-added per person employed which is a common practice in studies on labour productivity (see, for instance, *India Productivity Report* (Krishna et al., 2022a)),

$$\text{i.e., } \mathrm{LP}_i = V_i/L_i \tag{2.6}$$

where, LP_i is labour productivity in the ith broad sector; V_i and L_i are the real gross value added and employment for the ith broad sector.

However, the discussion on labour productivity is preceded by the discussion on structure and trends in employment along with employment elasticity to have a full understanding of the underlying trend in LP.

2.4.1 Employment—Structure, Growth and Employment Elasticity

The structure of employment and trend in growth in employment for the broad sectors is provided in Tables 2.3 and 2.4, and the estimates of employment elasticity are summarized in Table 2.5.

From Table 2.3 and 2.4, we find that there has been a structural shift of employment from agriculture to mainly construction, trade and transport. Manufacturing and social & community services have also experienced a small increase in the share of employment. While the structural change was slow in the pre-reform period up to 1993, it has picked up pace in the post-reform period from 1994 onwards.

How the structural change has occurred is evident from Table 2.4 in which we observe that the average growth in employment in agriculture and allied activities has fallen significantly in the period of post market reforms, i.e., after 1993. While earlier the average growth rate was more than or equal to 1.5% in the pre-1993 period, it has now been decelerating to a pace of 0.4% per annum during the post-financial crisis period of 2008–2019. As a result of the slow growth in employment in the sector, we observe the displacement of labour from agriculture and the falling employment elasticity in agriculture (Table 2.5) which has now become negative, and the sector is no longer contributing to the growth in employment. In line with the change in the structure of employment, we notice a significant average growth in employment of more than 3% per annum in the sectors of construction, trade, transport and electricity, gas and water supply. However, for the total economy the growth in employment has been faster in the pre-reform period of 1951–1993 as compared to the post-reform period of 1994–2019.

The impact of a slow growth in employment is also visible from Table 2.5, where we notice that after 1967–1979, the employment elasticity of the total economy has been consistently declining in all the sub-periods of the study. While the elasticity was high in agriculture during the first sub-period, it has been relatively high in the sectors of construction, trade and transport in the post 1993 period. The three sectors, mining, electricity and financial services, have contributed a steady but small share in total employment with employment elasticity to be either less than or almost equal to that of the total economy. The manufacturing sector has experienced higher employment elasticity in the pre-reform period and its capacity to generate employment in the economy has eroded especially after the global financial crisis in 2008 and was almost zero during the period of 2008–2019. But in line with the new manufacturing policy and the emphasis on the sector, the sector would have to create many more jobs in the future. Financial services & real estate, and public administration, social

Table 2.3 Structure of employment in India-1951–2019

Sectors	1951–1966 (%)	1967–1979 (%)	1980–1993 (%)	1994–2007 (%)	2008–2019 (%)
Agriculture & allied	72.2	72.6	66.5	59.0	47.4
Mining & quarrying	0.5	0.4	0.6	0.5	0.5
Manufacturing	9.7	9.5	10.8	11.4	12.3
Electricity, gas & water supply	0.3	0.2	0.3	0.3	0.5
Construction	1.2	1.7	3.0	4.9	10.6
Trade, hotels & restaurants	4.4	5.3	6.8	9.2	11.5
Transport, storage & communication	1.6	1.9	2.6	3.7	5.2
Finance, insurance & real estate	1.5	1.3	1.4	1.6	1.9
Social & community services	8.6	7.0	7.9	9.3	10.1
Total economy	100.0	100.0	100.0	100.0	100.0

Source Authors' computations based on India KLEMS database, 2021 (extended to 1951)

Table 2.4 Average annual growth rates of employment in broad sectors of Indian economy

Sectors	1952–1966 (%)	1967–1979 (%)	1980–1993 (%)	1994–2007 (%)	2008–2019 (%)	1952–2019 (%)
Agriculture & allied	1.7	1.9	1.5	0.1	−0.4	1.0
Mining & quarrying	−0.2	2.3	5.2	0.1	−4.1	0.8
Manufacturing	2.2	2.8	2.2	2.6	0.3	2.1
Electricity, gas & water supply	1.6	4.0	4.1	1.1	5.0	3.0
Construction	3.4	4.2	6.1	7.3	5.0	5.2
Trade, hotels & restaurants	0.8	4.6	3.4	3.9	3.0	3.1
Transport, storage & communication	2.4	4.3	3.7	4.7	3.2	3.7
Finance, insurance & real estate	0.7	1.5	3.6	3.1	1.4	2.1
Social & community services	0.7	1.5	3.6	2.0	1.8	1.9
Total economy	**1.6**	**2.2**	**2.1**	**1.5**	**1.0**	**1.7**

Source Authors' computations based on India KLEMS database, 2021 (extended to 1951)

Table 2.5 Employment elasticity in India (=growth rate in employment/growth rate in real GVA)

Sectors	1952–1966	1967–79	1980–93	1994–2007	2008–2019	1952–2019
Agriculture & allied	1.05	0.84	0.40	0.03	−0.11	0.36
Mining & quarrying	−0.03	0.74	0.74	0.02	−5.78	0.17
Manufacturing	0.37	0.63	0.45	0.36	0.06	0.36
Electricity, gas & water supply	0.15	0.53	0.51	0.18	0.86	0.40
Construction	0.53	1.78	1.35	0.89	1.17	0.99
Trade, hotels & restaurants	0.15	1.10	0.64	0.46	0.51	0.53
Transport, storage & communication	0.43	0.76	0.65	0.49	0.64	0.57
Finance, insurance & real estate	0.26	0.40	0.45	0.44	0.20	0.36
Social & community services	0.16	0.34	0.68	0.33	0.24	0.35
Total economy	0.50	0.67	0.41	0.24	0.18	0.36

Source Authors' computations based on India KLEMS database, 2021 (extended to 1951)

and community services had relatively higher employment elasticity during 1980–1993 but the elasticity declined in the post-reform era mainly due to competition and the impact of financial crisis during 2008–2019 further reduced significantly the employment generating potential of the two sectors.

2.4.2 *Labour Productivity in the Broad Sectors: Level and Growth*

The average level of labour productivity, which is defined as real value added per unit of employment, is presented in Table 2.6. We find that though for the all the sectors there has been an increase in the average level of LP in all the sub-periods, but there is a lot of disparity in the level of productivity among these broad sectors. While the finance, insurance and real estate sector has observed a consistent increase in average labour productivity in all the sub-periods and is a high of Rs. 897 thousand (per person) during 1951–2019, the agricultural sector has an average LP of only Rs. 40 thousand, i.e., just around 4% of finance, insurance and real estate. Manufacturing, trade, transport and communication, and social & community services (which include public administration & defense, health and education services) also have low level of average LP. Mining and electricity sectors have moderate levels of average LP. Plausible explanations for labour not to move from agriculture to manufacturing in India during its journey of economic growth could be its inability to generate employment and a similar level of LP in manufacturing as in the services sector where it was easier to take a job—may be as a casual labour or self-employed.

The trends in growth in labour productivity at broad sector level for the period 1952 to 2019 are summarized in Table 2.7. It shows that the average annual growth rate of labour productivity for the total economy has an upward trend during all the sub-periods except the second one of 1967–1979 and while it has increased at an average annual growth rate of less than two per cent before 1993; the growth rate was more than 4.5% during the later period of 1994 to 2019. It is also seen from the table that all the broad sectors of the economy, except the electricity sector, show acceleration in labour productivity growth during the period from 1994 to 2019 as compared to the period of 1951 to 1993. The sector of electricity shows deceleration in growth in the later periods, but overall, it still achieved a positive and higher (than the total economy) growth in labour productivity at more than 4.5%. The construction sector, on the other hand has experienced a lot of volatility and an overall negligible productivity growth.

The major contribution to the growth in LP in the total economy during 1952–2019 has been made by four broad sectors despite some volatility during the sub-periods (Table 2.8). These are agriculture (17.6%), manufacturing (23.1%), finance, insurance & real estate (24.9%) and social & community services (16.3%). The contribution to growth in the aggregate-level LP is mainly determined by the average size of the sector in total GVA and its growth in LP. Thus, either a higher share in GVA

Table 2.6 Average labour productivity in broad sectors of Indian economy (Rs. 000, at 2011–12 prices)

Sectors	1951–1966	1967–79	1980–93	1994–2007	2008–2019	1951–2019
Agriculture & allied	27.6	28.9	33.2	44.1	72.8	40.2
Mining & quarrying	241.6	415.4	453.0	914.4	1352.5	647.0
Manufacturing	41.3	65.5	81.5	141.7	297.4	118.9
Electricity, gas & water supply	80.0	240.8	365.6	733.2	862.6	436.9
Construction	196.9	207.0	148.1	152.6	163.7	174.2
Trade, hotels & restaurants	50.6	61.7	69.1	109.3	207.8	95.7
Transport, storage & communication	50.6	72.5	86.8	141.9	254.8	116.1
Finance, insurance & real estate	269.6	403.7	601.7	1183.7	2277.4	896.9
Social & community services	32.5	60.9	76.9	116.0	249.5	101.6
Total economy	37.6	47.1	61.0	102.4	204.7	86.3

Source Authors' computations based on India KLEMS database, 2021 (extended to 1951)

Table 2.7 Average annual growth rate of labour productivity in broad sectors of Indian economy

Sectors	1952–1966 (%)	1967–1979 (%)	1980–1993 (%)	1994–2007 (%)	2008–2019 (%)	1952–2019 (%)
Agriculture & allied	−0.1	0.4	2.3	2.8	4.1	1.8
Mining & quarrying	5.3	0.8	1.8	4.8	4.8	3.6
Manufacturing	3.7	1.6	2.7	4.8	5.7	3.7
Electricity, gas & water supply	8.8	3.5	3.9	4.9	0.8	4.6
Construction	3.0	−1.8	−1.6	0.9	−0.7	0.0
Trade, hotels & restaurants	4.4	−0.4	2.0	4.5	2.9	2.7
Transport, storage & communication	3.3	1.3	2.0	4.9	1.8	2.7
Finance, insurance & real estate	2.1	2.2	4.4	4.0	5.8	3.6
Social & community services	3.9	2.9	1.7	4.2	5.7	3.6
Total economy	1.6	1.1	3.1	4.7	4.6	3.0

Source Authors' computations based on India KLEMS database, 2021 (extended to 1951)

Table 2.8 Contribution of broad sectors to growth in LP of the Indian economy

Sectors	1952–1966 (%)	1967–1979 (%)	1980–1993 (%)	1994–2007 (%)	2008–2019 (%)	1952–2019 (%)
Agriculture & allied	1.2	20.9	30.8	17.1	18.4	17.6
Mining & quarrying	3.0	0.5	2.1	3.5	3.0	2.4
Manufacturing	28.2	20.7	20.0	22.9	23.9	23.1
Electricity, gas & water supply	3.1	3.6	3.8	4.3	0.6	3.5
Construction	5.9	−8.5	−3.1	2.2	−1.6	−0.6
Trade, hotels & restaurants	10.0	−2.3	6.4	11.6	7.2	6.9
Transport, storage & communication	6.0	4.2	4.3	9.2	3.1	5.9
Finance, insurance & real estate	22.9	34.9	27.7	16.1	27.7	24.9
Social & community services	19.8	26.0	8.0	13.1	17.7	16.3
Total economy	100.0	100.0	100.0	100.0	100.0	100.0

Source Authors' computations based on India KLEMS database, 2021 (extended to 1951)

or a high growth in LP may lead to higher contribution to the aggregate level growth in LP. So, a sector like agriculture despite low average growth in LP contributed more to the overall average growth in LP because of its large share in GVA.

2.4.3 Employment and Labour Productivity in Total Economy

To get a composite picture about the employment situation in India, its basic characteristics are summarized in Table 2.9. We find from the table that during the period of heavy industrialization (1952–1966), the growth in employment in India was lower than the growth in population with low average growth in LP of 1.6% per annum and an employment elasticity of 0.50. In the subsequent two sub-periods before the pro-market reforms started in 1994, the growth in employment has been equal to the growth in population and the employment elasticity remained stable because of stagnant growth in GVA. However, the LP growth started to accelerate especially in the period of beginning of pro-business reforms (1980–1993). In the post-reform period after 1994, we witness not only a deceleration in the growth of population but also in the growth of employment, resulting in a gradual fall in employment

Table 2.9 Average annual growth in population, employment, real GVA, labour productivity and employment elasticity in India during 1952–2019

Indicator	1952–1966	1967–1979	1980–1993	1994–2007	2008–2019	1952–2019
Average annual growth in Population (%)	2.1	2.2	2.1	1.8	1.4	1.9
Average annual growth in Employment (%)	1.6	2.2	2.1	1.5	1.0	1.7
Average annual growth in real GVA (%)	3.3	3.3	5.2	6.1	5.6	4.7
Employment elasticity	0.50	0.67	0.41	0.24	0.18	0.36
Average annual growth in LP (%)	1.6	1.1	3.1	4.7	4.6	3.0

Source Authors' computations based on India KLEMS database, 2021 (extended to 1951). For source of population data, refer to Annexure B.

elasticity. However, the accelerated growth in GVA led to a significant acceleration in the growth of LP. The same behaviour is also seen in Figs. 2.4 and 2.5. Figure 2.4 depicts that growth in employment was lower than the growth in population in the first and the last two sub-periods but was almost same in the second and the third sub-periods of 1967–1979 and 1980–1993, respectively. In Fig. 2.5, we observe that the average growth in GVA has consistently increased over the period till the financial crisis started (2008–2019) but the growth in employment increased in the first two sub-periods and it started decelerating beginning the sub-period of 1980–1993. While the employment elasticity has almost followed the trends in the growth in employment, the growth in LP has followed the pattern of growth in GVA.

2.4.4 A Cross-Country Comparison of Labour Productivity

It is now worth exploring to see how India, having achieved a more than five-fold increase in the level of labour productivity for the aggregate economy during 1951–2019 (Table 2.6) and an annual average growth rate of 3% in LP (Table 2.7, last row), compares with some of the other selected countries. The comparison would help to view the India's labour productivity growth trajectory in the right perspective. The following discussion focusses on that objective.

The section compares India's record on employment growth and labour productivity growth during 1952–2019 and the average level of LP at different points of time, with a select number of countries that include the BRICS countries, a few other fast-growing economies in the region and the selected advanced economies (Japan

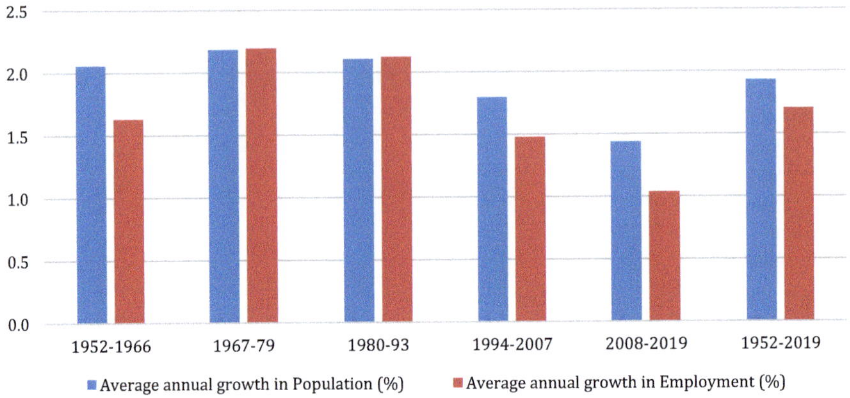

Fig. 2.4 Average annual growth in population and employment. *Source* Authors' computations based on India KLEMS database, 2023 (extended to 1951). For source of population data, refer to Annexure B.

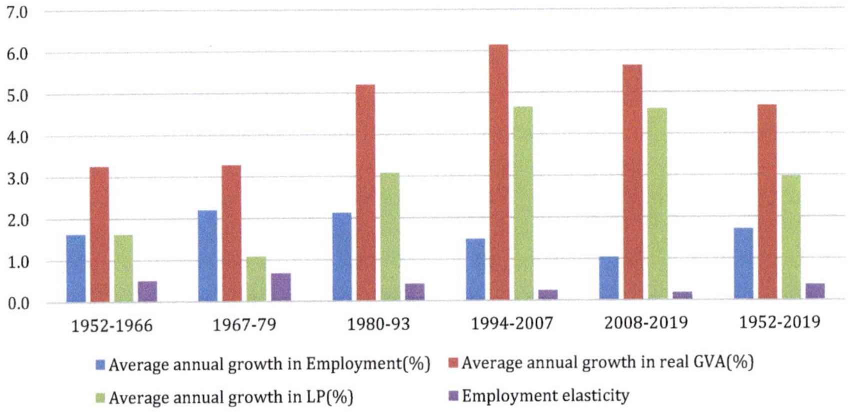

Fig. 2.5 Average annual growth in employment, real GVA, LP and employment elasticity. *Source* Authors' computations based on India KLEMS database, 2021 (extended to 1951)

and United States). India's record on employment growth is not bright and is among the countries with low growth in employment. Despite India achieving one of the highest average annual growth rates among the selected countries, both in GDP and labour productivity during 1952–2019 (Table 2.10), India had the lowest level of labour productivity in 2019 among the countries considered for the analysis with the exception of Vietnam and Bangladesh.

It is evident that in 2019, despite its labour productivity increasing by more than ten times between 1951 and 2019, India's labour productivity was only two-thirds of that of China, three-fourths of that in Indonesia and around one-half of that in Brazil and Thailand (Table 2.10). It can also be seen from the table that the labour productivity

Table 2.10 A cross-country comparison of growth in GDP, growth in employment, growth in LP* and the level of LP* (Internatioal $)

Country	Average annual Growth in GDP (1952–2019) (%)	Average annual Growth in employment (1952–2019) (%)	Average annual Growth in LP (1952–2019) (%)	LP in 1951	LP in 1967	LP in 1980	LP in 1994	LP in 2008	LP in 2019
				($)	($)	($)	($)	($)	($)
Brazil	4.5	2.6	1.8	10,982	19,033	35,834	30,790	34,853	36,248
Russian Federation	2.7	0.7	2.0	17,106	32,039	44,581	34,864	55,030	61,127
India	5.2	1.6	3.6	1,925	2,781	3,128	4,885	10,226	20,439
China	6.1	1.8	4.3	2,063	2,707	3,606	6,275	15,737	31,640
South Africa	3.2	1.6	1.5	19,572	35,441	51,099	40,391	51,786	53,945
Bangladesh	3.9	2.1	1.8	4,618	5,689	4,962	6,081	9,059	15,390
Indonesia	5.1	2.3	2.7	4,598	5,245	9,693	14,261	18,790	26,977
Malaysia	5.9	2.8	3.0	9,159	12,799	23,765	40,010	56,420	65,952
Philippines	4.6	2.8	1.8	7,650	11,014	15,232	12,193	16,459	25,250
Thailand	5.9	2.1	3.8	3,173	6,143	9,083	20,068	26,894	37,527
Vietnam	5.1	2.5	2.6	3,724	4,745	4,231	6,242	11,654	19,648
Japan	4.4	0.8	3.5	8,224	24,926	48,587	69,730	81,941	84,320
United States	3.1	1.4	1.7	45,995	68,533	78,271	97,031	126,117	140,590

* Labour productivity per person employed in 2021 international dollars, converted using Purchasing Power Parities

Notes The Chinese estimates are based on alternative GDP estimates by the Conference Board and will not be consistent with China's official data. The official data would suggest Chinese labour productivity levels are slightly higher

Source Authors' calculations from the Total Economy Database: Conference Board, April, 2022

in India in 2019 was only 24% of that in Japan and 14.5% of that in United States. However, a comparison of India's labour productivity with that of China reveals that while China had almost the same level of labour productivity as India in 1951, India's labour productivity in 2019 was only 67% of that of China.[6] China, because of rapid growth in labour productivity during 1980 to 2019, has not only surpassed Bangladesh, Philippines and Vietnam but has also narrowed down its gap with the other selected countries (Brazil, Indonesia, Russia, South Africa and Thailand). India has to narrow down the relative gap in labour productivity by adopting suitable policies so as to increase its labour productivity at a faster pace for not only to grow in size but also to improve the per capita income of its population.

2.5 Trends in Investment and Capital Stock, 1952–2019

The accumulation of capital, especially equipment capital, which is expected to augment worker productivity, is considered to have an important role in determining the speed and course of economic growth and development. However, the measurement of capital to understand sources of growth is cumbersome, as the magnitude of services delivered by different capital assets is often not directly observable (see Harper et al., 1989; Erumban, 2008). Machines and buildings, which are generally the components of total tangible capital assets,[7] deliver their services during their lifetime, and the actual hours these assets are used in any given year are hardly known. Therefore, empirical analysis on growth and development often relies on measures of capital stock and capital services (Caselli, 2005; Jorgenson, 1988). This section looks into the trends in investment rates (i.e., investment to GDP ratio), growth rates of capital stock and the trends in capital intensity measured in terms of capital-to-output ratio and capital per worker ratio, in nine broad sectors of the Indian economy since Independence.

2.5.1 Investment to GDP Ratio

Tables 2.11 and 2.12 provide the industry-wise investment rates (the ratio of total GFCF (gross fixed capital formation) to gross value added), respectively, in nominal and real terms, averaged over the five sub-periods during 1952–2019. We note the main trends in investment rates by sector below.

[6] In 1967, labour productivity in India was higher than China but the gap started widening up since 1980.

[7] More recently, the importance of intangible capital has gained much attention in the literature, and studies suggest that these assets often have a higher role in driving worker productivity in advanced economies (Corrado et al., 2009, 2022). In this study, we consider only tangible assets as capital stock. Information on intangible assets for India is still scanty.

Table 2.11 Average investment rates (current prices) by industry

Sector	1952–1966	1967–1979	1980–1993	1994–2007	2008–2019	1952–2019
Agriculture & allied	0.06	0.09	0.11	0.14	0.17	0.11
Mining & quarrying	0.17	0.32	0.45	0.28	0.29	0.30
Manufacturing	0.21	0.26	0.40	0.52	0.39	0.35
Electricity, gas & water supply	1.87	1.72	1.83	1.07	1.41	1.59
Construction	0.09	0.09	0.09	0.21	0.24	0.14
Trade, hotels & restaurants	0.03	0.08	0.07	0.08	0.26	0.10
Transport, storage & communication	0.98	0.80	0.65	0.40	0.54	0.68
Finance, insurance & real estate	0.18	0.27	0.34	0.58	0.51	0.37
Social & community services	0.25	0.27	0.44	0.39	0.44	0.36
Total economy	0.17	0.22	0.31	0.36	0.38	0.28

Note Nominal investment rates are obtained as the ratio of total nominal investment and total nominal value added

Source Authors' computations based on India KLEMS database, 2021 (extended to 1951)

Agriculture: The average nominal investment rate in agriculture had consistently improved since 1950, from a mere 6% during the 1952–1966 period, when the focus was primarily on heavy industrialization, to 17% in the post-GFC decade. However, the relative price dynamics of investment to output seemed to have lowered the pace of the real investment rate from the late 1960s till the early 1990s. Despite this rising trend, two other important dynamics are worth noting. The first, in general, the relative investment rate in India's agricultural sector (along with trade, hotels & restaurant sectors) remained the lowest among the nine sectors considered in Tables 2.11 and 2.12 throughout the last seven decades. The second, the share of agriculture in total investment in the national economy fell from 16 to 17% range in the first and second periods, which covered more than 25 years, to just above 10% during the 1980s, and further to 9% in the 1990s, and 8% in the post-crisis period (Appendix Table 2.23). One possible factor behind the fall in agricultural investment share could be the low levels of public investment. Often studies have argued that the priority of the government to focus on subsidies rather than enhancing public sector investments in agriculture affects the agricultural sector in India (Fan et al., 2008).

Manufacturing: Investment rates in India's manufacturing sector is relatively higher than other sectors, barring three service industries, transport, storage &

Table 2.12 Average investment rates (at constant prices) by industry

Sector	1952–1966	1967–1979	1980–1993	1994–2007	2008–2019	1952–2019
Agriculture & allied	0.07	0.10	0.10	0.11	0.16	0.11
Mining & quarrying	0.03	0.07	0.16	0.12	0.24	0.12
Manufacturing	0.18	0.24	0.33	0.44	0.38	0.31
Electricity, gas & water supply	2.33	1.71	1.79	1.06	1.48	1.69
Construction	0.04	0.04	0.05	0.16	0.25	0.10
Trade, hotels & restaurants	0.02	0.06	0.06	0.07	0.24	0.08
Transport, storage & communication	1.44	0.86	0.58	0.42	0.55	0.79
Finance, insurance & real estate	0.54	0.62	0.36	0.49	0.47	0.50
Social & community services	0.37	0.32	0.39	0.36	0.45	0.38
Total economy	0.19	0.23	0.24	0.30	0.37	0.26

Note Real investment rates are obtained as the ratio of total real investment and total real value added

Source Authors' computations based on India KLEMS database, 2021 (extended to 1951)

communication, social & community services (which include government services), and finance, insurance & real estate, and the heavily capital-intensive utility (electricity, gas & water supply) sector. Although the investment to GDP ratio in the manufacturing sector showed only little improvement in the second period over the first, it improved substantially during the pro-business reform periods of the 1980s and the pro-market reforms of the 1990s. However, it has seen a massive decline to the 1980s levels in the post-crisis decade. This intense fall in manufacturing investment rate is documented by Krishna et al. (2022b), and we also note that the fall was more intense in nominal terms than the real investment rate. Apparently, on average, the investment price in manufacturing grew faster than the sector's output price.

Other industries: The average nominal investment to GDP ratio in the mining & quarrying sector showed a rising trend from the 1952–1966 period until the 1980–1993 period. Nonetheless, it fell drastically in the 1990s and has remained flat since then. However, in real terms, the post-crisis period shows improvement, suggesting that investment prices grew slower than output prices in the sector. Although the utility sector maintains a relatively very high investment rate than other sectors of the economy, the investment to GDP ratio in the sector was somewhat flat until the 1980s. Moreover, it dropped massively in the 1994–2007 period before slightly picking up again in the post-crisis. This trend is common in both real and nominal rates. Finally, the construction sector shows interesting dynamics within the other industries group. The average investment rate in this sector was relatively stagnant at 9% during the first three periods, which covered the first four decades after India's Independence. However, the average investment rate in the sector had jumped significantly to more than 1/5th of the sector's value added during the pro-market reforms period of the 1990s. That rising trend continued, although at a slower pace in the post-crisis period.

Services: In our broad industry categories presented in Tables 2.11 and 2.12, we have three different market services sectors. The trade, hotels & restaurants sector had the lowest investment rate among all sectors in the first period, at 2%. The sector generally shows a relatively low investment rate in the range of 2 to 7%, except for the last period. Yet, the average investment rate improved during the second period, 1967–1979, from the previous period. It may be noted that the second period was a phase of consolidated efforts to create jobs and promote small and medium industries and reduce poverty. However, after that initial pick in the average investment rate, it stayed flat until the economic reforms kicked off in the 1990s and moved up quite impressively in the post-crisis period. Yet, it still has one of the lowest investment rates among the nine sectors we compare in Table 2.11.

The transport, storage and communication sector shows a unique pattern, with a consistently falling average investment rate throughout the different phases of India's economic reforms until 2007 and a minor improvement in the post-crisis period. This was the sector with the second-highest investment rate in the first period.

Among the services, the finance and insurance (including real estate) sector has shown uninterrupted improvement in nominal investment rate until the 1994–2007 period, with faster progress in the mid-1990s. Interestingly, however, the real investment rate fell drastically in the 1980–1993 period, compared to the 1967–1979 period, indicating a faster increase in the relative price of investment. The post-crisis period has shown a decline in the investment rate—both real and nominal.

The social and community services, which is primarily the non-market services sector that includes government, health, education and all other services, have seen moderate improvement in the 1967–1979 period over the previous period but notable improvement in the 1980–1993 period. However, the average investment to GDP ratio in the sector fell during the 1994–2007 period, although it could regain the averages in the 1980–1993 period again during the post-global financial crisis period.

Aggregate economy: Overall, with ups and downs across industries, the economy-wide investment rate has improved substantially from the import-substituting heavy industrialization phase of 1952–1966 to the pro-market reform period of 1994–2007. However, in the post-crisis period, it has only enhanced moderately, as the annual investment rate has invariably been falling since 2008 (Fig. 2.6). It is evident from Fig. 2.6 that the national economy has never faced such a drastic decline in investment to GDP ratio in its history as it has been undergoing since the global financial crisis. Although it had episodes of falling investment rates in the mid-1960s and the early 1990s, they were relatively smaller. Although the global headwinds in the post-financial crisis period might be an important reason for the weak investment rates, the stress in the domestic financial market, currency pressure and weaknesses in public

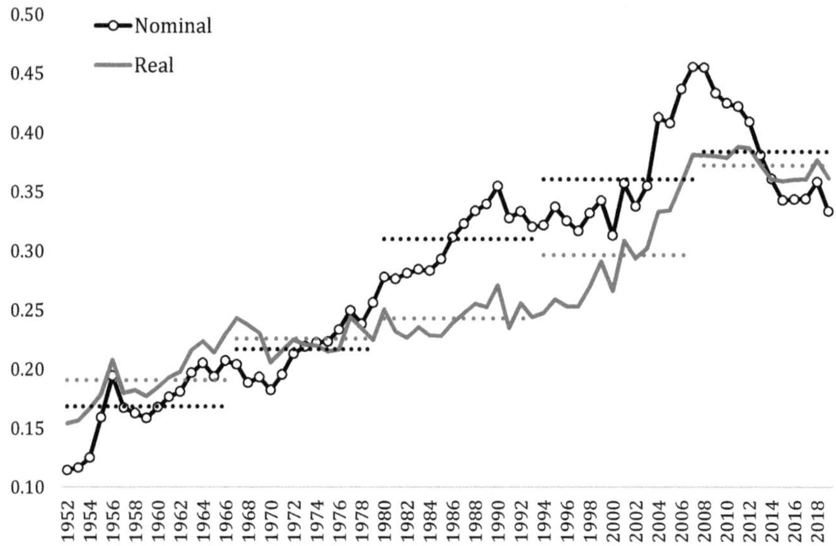

Fig. 2.6 Annual investment rates, aggregate economy. *Notes* Investment rates are obtained as the ratio of nominal (real) GFCF to nominal (real) value added in the aggregate economy. The dotted lines are the average investment rates for the five consecutive periods, as provided in Tables 2.11 and 2.12. *Source* Authors' computations based update on India KLEMS database, 2021 (extended to 1951)

investment are all indispensable factors contributing to it. Developing economies, including India, face several global challenges, including the changing dynamics of globalization and rapid advances in manufacturing technology that facilitates re-shoring and near-shoring, casting a shadow over their investment attractiveness. Yet, the potential for attracting foreign investment, especially in the manufacturing sector, is very high in India. However, India's infrastructural and institutional weaknesses are still acting as adverse factors. Domestically, private sector investment constitutes three-fourths of all investment as of 2019, but more than half of that comes from the household or informal sector. The poor share of public investment is another major challenge that India needs to address, which adds to its infrastructural weakness.

2.5.2 *Growth Rates of Capital Stock*

We obtained estimates of capital stock for each of the nine sectors using the perpetual inventory method (Eq. 2.9 in Annexure C). Table 2.13 provides the average growth rate of capital stock by sectors, measured as log changes in the estimated real capital stock.

On average, the capital stock grew at slightly above 5% in the aggregate economy, with agriculture showing the lowest growth at 3.4% and construction the highest, at

Table 2.13 Average growth rates of capital stock by industry

Sector	1952–1966	1967–1979	1980–1993	1994–2007	2008–2019	1952–2019
Agriculture & allied	2.6	3.7	2.9	3.4	4.4	3.4
Mining & quarrying	11.6	9.8	10.6	5.1	7.3	9.0
Manufacturing	10.1	6.8	7.4	8.1	5.7	7.7
Electricity, gas & water supply	23.6	7.7	7.3	4.1	7.0	10.3
Construction	18.1	6.0	5.6	14.9	10.2	11.2
Trade, hotels & restaurants	4.2	12.0	5.9	8.4	16.4	9.0
Transport, storage & communication	6.7	3.2	3.1	4.5	9.0	5.3
Finance, insurance & real estate	2.8	3.5	2.9	7.3	6.2	4.5
Social & community services	12.6	4.9	5.5	5.8	8.0	7.4
Total economy	4.6	4.3	4.4	6.2	7.1	5.3

Note The aggregate capital stock is obtained as the sum of capital stock in three assets—construction, machinery and transport equipment. Asset-wise capital stock is calculated using the perpetual inventory approach with asset-specific depreciation rates and investment price deflators. The depreciation rates used are consistent with the India KLEMS database (see Das et al., 2021b)
Source Authors' computations based on India KLEMS database, 2021 (extended to 1951)

just above 11%. The economy-wide capital stock growth rate was relatively stable, hovering around 4.5% during the first three periods (1952 to 1993). Nevertheless, the post-reform period has seen a substantial improvement to above 6% during the post-reform period prior to the global financial crisis and further improvement to 7% during the post-crisis period.

In the early self-reliance and industrialization regime of the 1952–1966 period, the faster growth in capital stock was observed in utility, mining, manufacturing and construction sectors, along with social and community services, which included public administration and defense along with the health and education sectors. Except for a major improvement in the pace of capital expansion in trade, hotels & restaurants, and moderate upticks in agriculture, and finance, insurance & real estate sectors, the capital stock growth rate has dropped in all other sectors in the subsequent 1967–1979 period. However, the trade, hotels & restaurants sector lost that momentum in the 1980s. In contrast, all other sectors somewhat sustained, with a margin of one per cent up or down in the growth rate, leading the economy-wide capital stock growth rate to remain slightly stable in the 1980s.

During the period that followed India's pro-market reforms until the global financial crisis, 1994–2007, all sectors of the economy witnessed an improvement in capital stock growth rate, ranging from 0.4% point increase in the social and community service sector to 9.3% increase in the construction sector. Only two sectors, mining and utilities, have seen a fall in capital stock growth rate, thus helping the aggregate economy improve capital growth by nearly two percentage points from the previous period.

In the post-crisis period, the growth rate further improved in all sectors except the manufacturing, construction and finance, insurance and real estate sectors. These sectors have seen a drop from their high growth in the previous period yet sustained a sound capital growth rate during the post-crisis period.

2.5.3 *Trends in Capital Intensity*

We look at the capital intensity in the Indian economy in terms of capital-to-output ratios (i.e., the amount of capital required to produce one unit of output) and capital-to-worker ratios, or capital deepening (i.e., the amount of capital available to the worker). The ratio of capital stock to real output is an important ingredient of classic growth theories, as it is considered to be informative of the growth rate an economy can attain with a given rate of investment. A rising capital-to-worker ratio can help improve productivity on the one hand, while it can be challenging for labour-abundant economies like India if the capital-intensive industries grow overly faster, keeping the labour-intensive sectors behind.

The capital-output ratios provided in Table 2.14 suggest clear evidence of an increase in capital per unit of output at the aggregate level in the second period over the first. However, throughout the pro-business and pro-market reforms periods, it remained rather stable at just above three. It improved in the post-crisis period. The real capital-output ratio at the aggregate level was higher than the nominal ratios in the first two periods (the nominal ratios are provided in Appendix Table 2.24). In contrast, it was low by over half a percentage point in the 1980s and 1990s, and the difference was relatively minimal in the post-crisis period cases. Overall, India's current capital-output ratio is quite comparable to advanced economies like the United States. To put this in perspective, the nominal (real) capital-output ratio in the United States was 3.3 (3.2) during the post-crisis period until 2019.

There are indeed differences across industries. Three sectors that had consistently high capital-output ratios are the utility sector, transport, storage & communication sector and finance, insurance & real estate sector. The last sector is merely a reflection of buildings in the real estate sector. Agriculture, mining, construction, trade, hotels & restaurants are among those that generally sustained relatively lower capital-output ratios.

The improvement in the aggregate capital-output ratio during the second period, when the policy efforts were diverted substantially to welfare objectives, is reflected in a rise in social and community services, but also in manufacturing and utility

Table 2.14 Average real capital-output ratios by industry

Sector	1952–1966	1967–1979	1980–1993	1994–2007	2008–2019	1952–2019
Agriculture & allied	1.4	1.7	1.8	1.8	2.2	1.8
Mining & quarrying	0.2	0.4	1.0	1.0	1.8	0.8
Manufacturing	1.3	2.2	2.9	3.6	3.6	2.7
Electricity, gas & water supply	11.3	15.5	16.0	12.4	12.7	13.5
Construction	0.2	0.4	0.5	0.9	1.8	0.7
Trade, hotels & restaurants	0.2	0.4	0.6	0.6	1.4	0.6
Transport, storage & communication	14.3	12.6	8.4	5.1	4.0	9.1
Finance, insurance & real estate	10.3	10.5	7.2	5.2	5.3	7.8
Social & community services	2.6	4.2	4.6	4.0	4.0	3.8
Total economy	2.6	3.1	3.2	3.1	3.5	3.1

Note Capital output ratios are obtained as the ratio of total capital stock and total value added, both in real terms

Source Authors' computations based on India KLEMS database, 2021 (extended to 1951)

sectors. The only sector that had a decline was transport, storage & communication. In the pro-business reform phase of the 1980s, most sectors had moderate improvements in capital-output ratios, but massive reductions in two sectors, viz. transport, storage & communications, and finance, insurance & real estate, have resulted in somewhat stable ratios at the aggregate level. The capital-output ratio remained stable in several sectors during the pro-market reform phase of the 1990s, and in some sectors, like manufacturing and construction, it increased moderately. But utility, transport, storage & communication, and finance, insurance & real estate sectors have witnessed substantial erosion, followed by moderate declines in social & community service. Finally, in the post-crisis period, except for a decline in the transport, storage & communication sector and a stable capital-output ratio in manufacturing and social & community services sectors, the ratios increased in other sectors, albeit moderately, leading to an overall rise in capital-output ratio.

A more remarkable story of India's capital deepening is evident in Table 2.15, where we provide the ratio of capital stock (in Rs crore at 2011–12 constant prices, where one crore equals ten million) to the number of workers (in thousand persons). At the aggregate level, the average capital stock per worker ratio has increased more than seven times from 1952–1966 to 2008–2019. This increase has been consistent over different phases of reforms, as capital accumulation has been happening faster across various sectors.

While looking at the composition of capital stock in terms of equipment vs. buildings, the high capital-worker ratio in most sectors is primarily a reflection of construction assets. Yet, the mechanization of the Indian economy has also been happening so rapidly. For instance, the equipment capital per worker ratio has increased more than 30 times from the first period 1952–1966 to the post-crisis period 2008–2019, from a mere 0.6 to nearly 20 (Table 2.16, see also Fig. 2.7).

In the first period, during the phase of import substitution and heavy industrialization, the sectors with high equipment dependence were utilities, transport, storage & communication, manufacturing, construction and mining. In the second period, in addition to the utility and mining sectors, we see substantial improvement in the manufacturing, and transport, storage & communication sectors. In general, except in agriculture, all sectors had more equipment per worker in the second period.

While agriculture still remained less equipment intensive during the pro-business phase of Indian reforms, manufacturing, along with social & community services and finance, insurance & real estate services, increased their equipment capital per worker ratios, along with a continued rise in equipment capital per worker in

Table 2.15 Average capital deepening (capital per worker ratios) by industry, all capital assets

Sector	1952–1966	1967–1979	1980–1993	1994–2007	2008–2019	1952–2019
Agriculture & allied	3.9	4.7	5.9	7.8	15.4	7.3
Mining & quarrying	4.2	16.4	41.3	83.3	244.9	72.9
Manufacturing	5.2	13.6	22.9	48.2	100.2	36.1
Electricity, gas & water supply	94.2	345.6	537.1	844.8	1034.2	553.9
Construction	3.6	7.1	6.5	12.1	27.8	10.9
Trade, hotels & restaurants	1.0	2.5	4.1	6.1	28.1	7.8
Transport, storage & communication	69.5	85.8	68.2	63.1	98.5	76.2
Finance, insurance & real estate	271.9	407.3	385.2	571.1	1120.3	532.4
Social & community services	8.6	24.6	33.3	43.0	93.8	38.9
Total economy	9.7	14.3	18.7	30.1	68.2	27.0

Note Capital deepening is obtained as the ratio of total capital stock (in constant prices) and total employment

Source Authors' computations based on India KLEMS database, 2021 (extended to 1951)

Table 2.16 Average capital deepening (capital per worker ratios) by industry, equipment assets

Sector	1952–1966	1967–1979	1980–1993	1994–2007	2008–2019	1952–2019
Agriculture & allied	0.1	0.1	0.1	0.5	2.1	0.5
Mining & quarrying	3.2	13.8	37.1	74.0	214.1	64.0
Manufacturing	2.3	5.4	8.8	20.9	51.0	16.6
Electricity, gas & water supply	17.7	91.3	193.6	352.2	535.0	228.1
Construction	2.0	3.6	2.8	5.2	12.4	5.0
Trade, hotels & restaurants	0.2	0.4	0.6	1.0	5.4	1.4
Transport, storage & communication	12.4	15.3	14.7	17.0	49.5	20.9
Finance, insurance & real estate	0.3	1.1	2.6	15.5	103.2	22.2
Social & community services	0.8	2.6	6.2	8.7	20.1	7.3
Total economy	0.6	1.4	3.0	6.3	19.7	5.8

Note Capital deepening in equipment assets is obtained as the ratio of capital stock in the sum of machinery and transport equipment (in constant prices) and total employment
Source Authors' computations based on India KLEMS database, 2021 (extended to 1951)

utility and mining sectors. Interestingly, the construction and transport, storage & communication sectors witnessed a decline in equipment capital deepening during this period.

During the pro-market reform phase, all sectors of the economy embraced more capital per worker, albeit agriculture and trade sectors remained the sectors with the least rise in capital deepening. The manufacturing and finance, insurance & real estate sectors were the two that witnessed rapid rises in capital deepening, in addition to the utilities and mining sectors during this period.

For the first time during the past seven decades, it was in the post-crisis period that the agricultural sector showed a faster rise in capital deepening. While the capital per worker in agriculture increased only sixfold between 1952–1967 and 1994–2007 and remained less than 1 throughout, it increased to 2.1, i.e., nearly 30-fold from the initial period, in the post-crisis period. The two heavily capital-intensive sectors, mining and utilities, remained the sectors with the highest rise in capital-worker ratio, but also many other sectors, including finance, insurance & real estate, transport, storage & communication and manufacturing, have also seen a notable increase in capital deepening during this period.

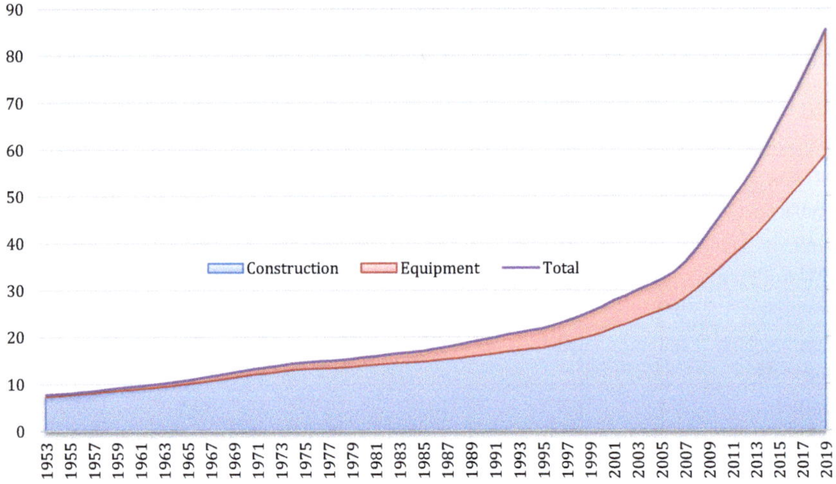

Fig. 2.7 Annual capital deepening (capital per worker ratios) by asset, aggregate economy. *Note* Capital deepening is obtained as the ratio of total capital stock (in constant prices) and total employment. *Source* Authors' computations based on India KLEMS database, 2023 (extended to 1951)

2.6 Trend in Total Factor Productivity

2.6.1 Methodology

Computations of TFP have been done by using the value-added function framework (see Sect. 2.2). The changes in labour and capital quality are not taken into account. Thus, in our computations, the gains in labour quality and capital quality (composition effect) form a part of the TFP estimates, and productivity growth is therefore slightly exaggerated in which the quality aspect is incorporated in the analysis of sources of growth (see India Productivity Report (Krishan et al., 2022a)). This has, however, an advantage in terms of comparability of our estimates with such estimates in previous studies. Several earlier studies of productivity growth in the Indian economy have used capital stock as the measure of capital input and the number of workers employed as the measure of labour input without paying attention to changes in labour quality. Although some studies on productivity growth in the Indian economy did adjust the labour input series by considering the changes in the level of education (e.g., Sivasubramonian, 2004), none of the studies took into account the distinction between capital stock and capital services by incorporating the changes in capital composition. Thus, by adhering to a simple measure of labour and capital inputs, disregarding the impact of quality changes, greater comparability in the productivity estimates between this study and the earlier studies is obtained.

Estimation of TFP growth has been done by applying the translog index. For making computations of TFP growth for the agriculture sector, three inputs are considered: labour, capital and land. The income accruing to land constituted a significant part of GVA in agriculture especially in the first two decades of India's planned economic development. Thus, the inclusion of land input in the computation of TFP growth is important. For the computation of TFP growth at the economy level, again, three inputs are considered (since the agriculture sector is a part of the economy), namely, labour capital and land. However, for computing TFP growth rates in other major sectors of the economy, such as manufacturing, only two inputs are considered: labour and capital.

In the three-input framework, the growth rate in TFP in sector j, denoted by $\Delta lnAj$, is obtained as (V denotes real gross value added, L labour, K capital and N land input):

$$\Delta lnV_j = \bar{s}_j^K.\Delta lnK_j + \bar{s}_j^L.\Delta lnL_j + \bar{s}_j^N.\Delta lnN_j + \Delta lnA_j \tag{2.7}$$

In this equation, s^K, s^L and s^N are the income shares of capital, labour and land input, adding to unity. The bars over s indicate that an average of the current year and the previous year has to be taken. When the two-input framework is used, the growth rate in TFP is obtained as:

$$\Delta lnV_j = \bar{s}_j^K.\Delta lnK_j + \bar{s}_j^L.\Delta lnL_j + \Delta lnA_j \tag{2.8}$$

In this case, the incomes shares of labour and capital add to unity.

While the analysis of labour productivity, capital intensity and capital-output ratio (inverse of capital productivity) was undertaken in the previous two sections at the level of nine sectors of the Indian economy, for the analysis of TFP trends some of the sectors have been combined into groups. Thus, the analysis in this section is undertaken for the following broad sectors or groups: (i) agriculture and allied activities, (ii) manufacturing, (iii) non-manufacturing industry (includes mining and quarrying, electricity and water supply, and construction), (iv) market services-I (includes trade, hotels and restaurants, transport, storage and communication), (v) market services-II (includes banking, finance and insurance, real estate, ownership of dwellings and business services) and (vi) social and community services (includes public administration and defence, education and health services and other personal services). The first group of market services includes several services such as trade and transport that provide support to businesses. This group is therefore called business supporting market services. The second group includes certain services such as banking and finance and development of real estate that help in the creation of new businesses or expansion of existing businesses. Thus, despite its heterogeneous nature, this group is hereafter called business promoting market services. The group including various social and community services, which dominated by public administration and defence and includes education and health, is hereafter called non-market services.

The rates of TFP growth in various major sectors of the Indian economy during 1951 to 2019 and the sub-periods within this overall period is discussed in Sect. 6.2. The TFP growth rates at the aggregate economy level are discussed in Sect. 6.3.

2.6.2 TFP Growth, Major Sectors of the Economy

2.6.2.1 Agriculture and Allied Activities

In the period 1952 to 1979, TFP growth rate in agriculture and allied activities was low (Fig. 2.8). The performance was relatively much better in the periods 1980–1993, 1994–2007 and 2008–2019. TFP growth rate in agriculture during 2008–2019 was high at about 2.5% per annum and it contributed about two-thirds of the GVA growth. Thus, in the recent period, GVA growth in agriculture was mostly driven by productivity improvements.

Table 2.17 presents a comparison of TFP growth rates in the agriculture and allied activities sector obtained in this study with the estimates presented in Sivasubramonian (2004). There is considerable similarity between the two sets of estimates. It should be noted that the estimates of Sivasubramonian (2004) include the growth in 1951 over 1950 which is excluded in the present study. The series on land input used in this study is the same as in Sivasubramonian (2004) up to 1997. For 1998 and 1999, new data have been used, which have been used to extend the series till 2019.

It is important to draw attention to the fact that the average rate of TFP growth in the period 1951 to 1964 was about one and a half per cent per annum. This does not match the pattern observed in Fig. 2.8. The reason is that there was a large fall in TFP in 1965. India was hit by droughts in 1965 and 1966. If these two years are removed from the first sub-period and are included in the second period, the average

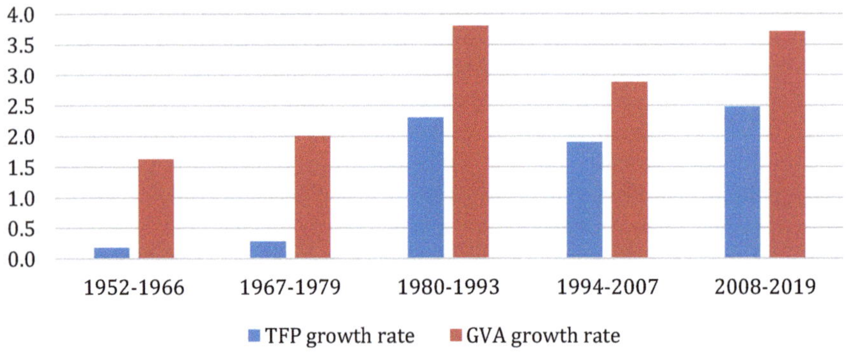

Fig. 2.8 TFP and GVA growth, Agriculture and allied activities (% per annum). *Source* Authors' computations based on India KLEMS Database, 2021 (extended to 1951)

Table 2.17 Source of growth, agriculture and allied sector, comparison of two studies

Period	TFP growth rate	GVA growth rate	Labour input contribution	Capital input contribution	Land input contribution
	Estimates in the present study				
1952–1964	1.48	2.89	0.91	0.34	0.16
1965–1980	0.07	1.78	1.14	0.50	0.08
1981–1999	1.98	3.19	0.60	0.60	0.01
	Estimates made by Sivasubramonian (2004)				
1951–1964	1.47	2.83	0.94	0.18	0.24
1965–1980	0.08	1.80	1.07	0.50	0.14
1981–1999	1.77	3.20	0.73	0.62	0.08

Source Authors' computations based on India KLEMS Database, 2023 (extended to 1951). The estimates of Sivasubramonian are taken from his study

rate of TFP growth for the period 1952 to 1964 is found to be 1.5% per annum which compares well with the average growth rate in TFP during 1994–2007.

It is interesting to note that that green revolution began in India in 1968 which brought in new technology, but this did not get reflected in an enhanced rate of TFP growth. Rather, the rate of TFP growth in agriculture during 1965–1980 or 1967–1979 was low if not negligible. This is the finding not only of the present study, but also that of Sivasubramonian (2004). The estimate of TFP growth in agriculture during 1960 to 1980 made by Bosworth et al. (2007) is (−) 0.1% per annum. This is broadly consistent with the estimates obtained in this study.

2.6.2.2 Manufacturing

The rate of TFP growth Indian manufacturing was negligible in the period from 1951 to 1993 (Fig. 2.9). There was improvement in the post-reform period and a marked improvement in TFP growth in the post–GFC period. In the post-GFC period (2008–2019), nearly one-third of GVA growth in manufacturing arose from productivity improvements.

In Table 2.18 a comparison is made between the TFP growth estimates for manufacturing obtained in this study and those in Bosworth et al. (2007). The estimates of TFP growth rates are relatively higher in the study by Bosworth and associates. The main reason is that in the study by Bosworth and associates labour input has been given weight of 0.6 and capital input has been given a weight of 0.4 whereas in this study, based on the computations of factor income shares made (see Annexure D), labour has been given a weight of 0.4 to 0.5 and capital has been given a weight of 0.5 to 0.6 (in different years). Interestingly, in both studies, the TFP growth rate during1984 to 2004 is found to be greater than that during 1974–1983.

The finding that the rate of TFP growth in the manufacturing sector during 1951 to 1979 was negligible is at variance with the estimates of TFP grown in organized

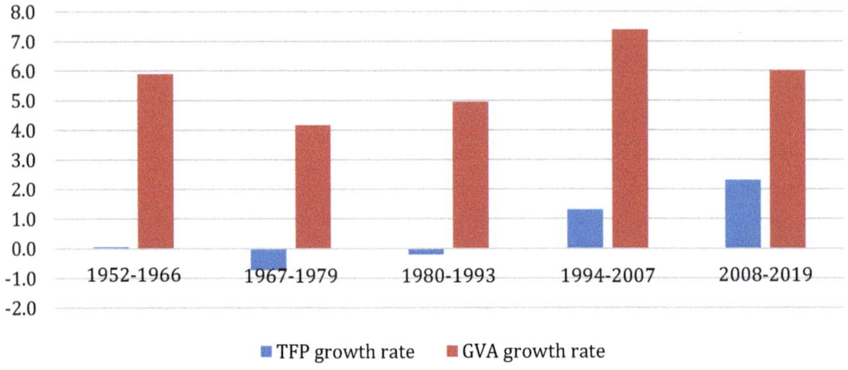

Fig. 2.9 TFP and GVA growth, Manufacturing (% per annum). *Source* Authors' computations based on India KLEMS Database, 2021 (extended to 1951)

Table 2.18 Comparison of estimated TFP growth rates in manufacturing (per cent per annum) among two studies

Period	This study	Bosworth et al. (2007)
1961–1973	0.14	1.1
1974–1983	−0.73	−0.3
1984–1993	0.06	2.1
1984–2004	0.28	1.5

Source Authors' computations based on India KLEMS Database, 2021 (extended to 1951). The growth rates obtained in the study undertaken by Bosworth et al. (2007) have been taken from that study

manufacturing presented in Goldar (1986), although this is line with the estimates of Ahluwalia (1991) who reported that the growth rate in TFP in organized manufacturing during 1965–1979 was (−)0.3% per annum. In Goldar (1986), the rate of TFP growth in organized manufacturing was reported as 1.27% per annum for 1952–1965 (aggregate of 29 industries of *Census of Indian Manufactures*) and 1.31% per annum during 1960 to 1979 (aggregate of Census sector of *Annual Survey of Industries*). For 1965–1979, the estimated growth rate in TFP is, again, about 1.3% per annum.[8]

For the 1980s and later period, there are several estimates of TFP growth in India's organized manufacturing (see Goldar, 2022). Estimates of TFP growth rate in organized manufacturing in the 1980s based on single deflated GVA range from 1.4% per annum to 4.5% per annum (estimate reported in Goldar, 2006). The median out of nine estimates listed in Goldar (2022) is 3.1% per annum (estimate reported in Trevedi et al., (2000)). This may be contrasted with the estimate for the period 1980–1993 obtained in this study which is (−)0.2% per annum. One possible reason for this divergence in TFP growth estimates is that TFP growth in the unorganized

[8] Why the estimates of TFP growth for the period 1965 to 1979 in Goldar (1986) and Ahluwalia (1991) differ is not discussed here.

segment of manufacturing was negative and this brought down TFP growth in the aggregate manufacturing sector to a negligible level. According to the estimates of Unni et al. (2001), the rate of TFP growth in unorganized manufacturing during 1978–1990 was (−)2.66% per annum.

Interestingly, in the period 2008–2019, the growth rate in TFP in organized manufacturing was low (assessment based on data drawn from *Annual Survey of Industries*; an average growth rate of (−)0.4% per annum during 2008–2017 according to Goldar (2024)). Thus, in this period, it is the TFP improvements in the unorganized manufacturing sector that contributed positively to TFP growth at the aggregate level of manufacturing.

2.6.2.3 Non-Manufacturing Industry

TFP growth performance of the non-manufacturing industry sector has been negative or low positive in various sub-periods during the period under study (Fig. 2.10). The average growth rate was minus two per cent per annum in the first 30 years of planned development in India. The performance was only marginally better during 1994–2007. In the more recent period, 2008–2019, there has been a fall in TFP in non-manufacturing industry sector; possibly the source of this fall in TFP level lies in productivity decline in the construction sector. There was a marked increase in employment in the construction sector, but there was no commensurate increase in real GVA, leading to significant fall in labour productivity (see Sect. 2.4, Table 2.7).

That there was a negative growth in TFP in the non-manufacturing industry during the 1960s through 1980s is evident from the estimates of TFP growth presented in Bosworth et al. (2007). For the periods, 1961–1973, 1974–1983 and 1984–1993, the growth rates in TFP in the industry sector (including manufacturing) was less than the TFP growth rate in the manufacturing sector by 0.5 to 1.2 percentage points. This implies that in all these periods, the rate of TFP growth in the non-manufacturing

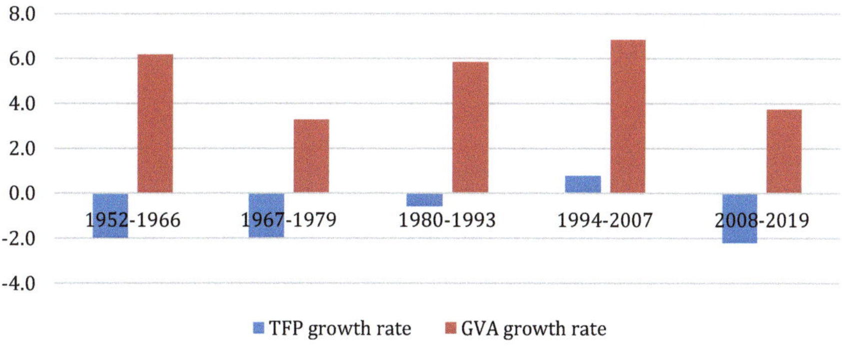

Fig. 2.10 TFP and GVA growth, non-manufacturing industry (% per annum). *Source*: Authors' computations based on India KLEMS Database, 2021 (extended to 1951)

industry sector was negative, which is consistent with the estimates obtained in this study (as presented in Fig. 2.10). For the period 1961 to 1980, the growth rate in TFP in manufacturing is reported as (−)0.2% per annum, and that for the industry sector is reported as (−)0.6% per annum. This means that the TFP growth rate in the non-manufacturing was less than (−)0.6% per annum, probably about (-)0.9 or (-) 1.0% per annum. In this study, the average growth rate in TFP in non-manufacturing industry during 1961 to 1980 is found to be (−)1.5% per annum. This is broadly consistent with the estimates of Bosworth et al. (2007).

2.6.2.4 Services

The rate of growth in TFP in business supporting market services (market services-I) was close to two per cent per annum or more during 1952–1966, 1980–1993 and 1994–2007 (Fig. 2.11). During 1994–2007, the growth rate in TFP in this sector was about four per cent per annum and it accounted for nearly half of the GVA growth. There was, however, a significant fall in TFP growth rate in business supporting market services in the post-GFC period, when it turned negative. This was accompanied by a marked fall in the growth rate of real GVA.

TFP growth rate in the business promoting market services (market services-II) which includes banking, finance and real estate, was low in the initial three decades on India's economic development (Fig. 2.12). The growth rate in TFP rose to a high level at about five per cent per annum during 1980–1993 accounting for a large part of the growth in GVA. The TFP growth rate was low again during 1994–2007 which was the post-reform period including the high growth phase of the Indian economy, 2003–2007. In the more recent period, the rate of TFP growth was higher than one per cent per annum and it accounted for about a fifth of the growth in GVA.

Rates of TFP growth and real GVA growth in social and community services or non-market services were relatively low in the first thirty years of India's economic

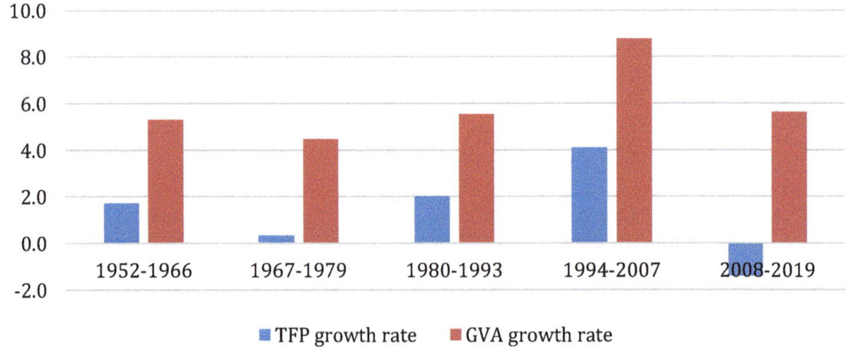

Fig. 2.11 TFP growth rate and GVA growth rate in market services-I (% per annum). *Source* Authors' computations and based on India KLEMS Database, 2021 (extended to 1951)

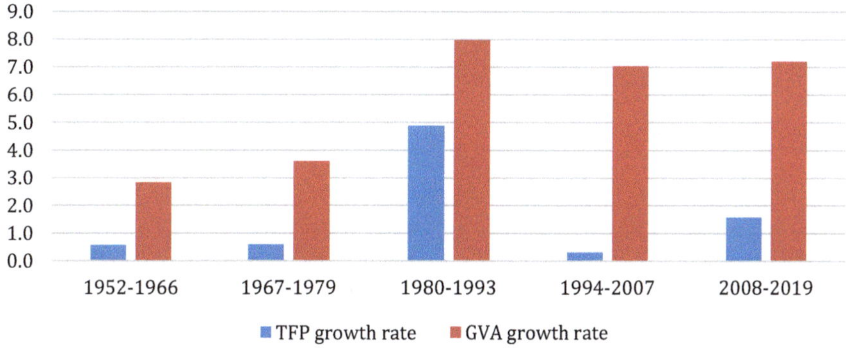

Fig. 2.12 TFP growth rate GVA growth rate in market services-II (% per annum). *Source* Authors' computations based on India KLEMS Database, 2021 (extended to 1951)

development (Fig. 2.13). In the period since 1980, the rate of TFP growth has been about four per cent per annum or more and the rate of growth in real GVA has been seven per cent per annum or more. TFP growth accounted for more than half of the real GVA growth. Deeper analysis reveals that the high rates of TFP growth in this sector is mainly driven by public administration and defence (see Krishna et al., (2022b), Fig. 2).

Rates of TFP growth and real GVA growth in services sector, combining market and non-market services, are shown in Fig. 2.14. The growth rates in TFP were relatively low in the first thirty years of India's economic development. In the period 1980 to 2007, the rate of TFP growth has been more than two per cent per annum. In the post-GFC period, the rate of TFP growth has come down. This reflects the marked fall that has occurred in the growth rate in TFP in business supporting market services (see Fig. 2.11).

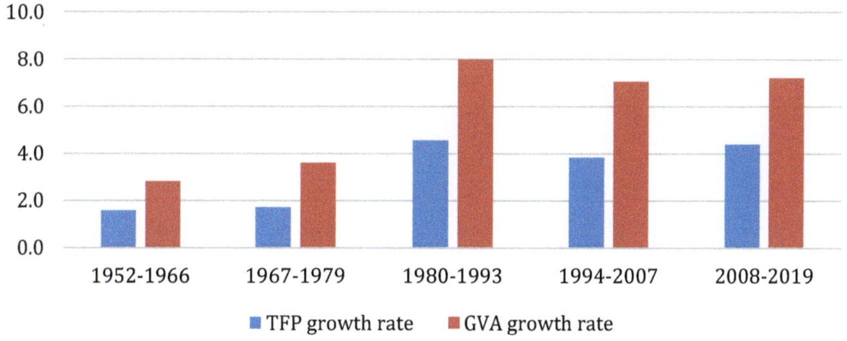

Fig. 2.13 TFP and GVA growth, social and community services (% per annum). *Source* Authors' computations based on India KLEMS Database, 2021 (extended to 1951)

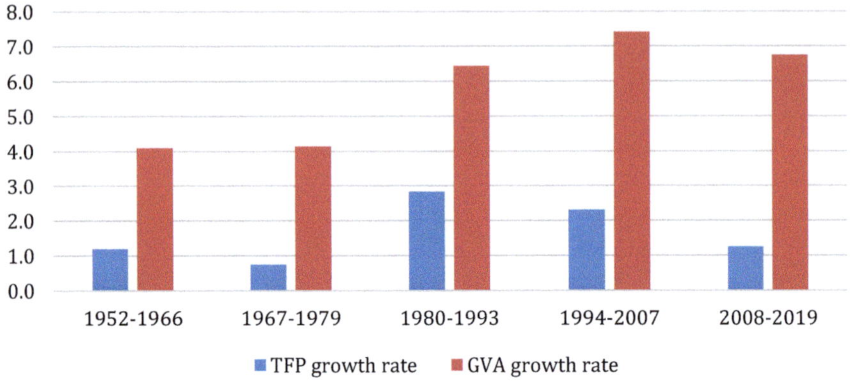

Fig. 2.14 TFP and GVA growth, services sector (% per annum). *Source* Authors' computations based on India KLEMS Database, 2021 (extended to 1951)

Table 2.19 Comparison of estimated TFP growth rates in the services sector (per cent per annum)

Period	This study	Bosworth et al. (2007) after adding back the contribution of education
1961–1973	1.07	0.9
1974–1983	1.26	1.0
1984–1993	3.02	2.4
1994–2004	2.23	4.5

Source Authors' computations based on India KLEMS Database, 2021 (extended to 1951). The growth rates for the Bosworth et al. (2007) have been taken from that study

Comparing the growth rate in TFP in the services sector obtained in this study with such estimates in Bosworth et al. (2007), it is found that the estimates for the period 1961 to 1993 are similar (Table 2.19). However, for the more recent period 1994 to 2004, the estimate of TFP growth obtained in this study is much lower than the estimate in Bosworth et al. (2007). It is difficult to provide the reason for the difference. This might have arisen because of the differences in the weights based on the income share of factors used in the two sets of estimates.

2.6.3 TFP Growth Estimate at the Aggregate Economy Level

The estimates of TFP growth and real GVA growth for aggregate economy is shown in Fig. 2.15. In the first thirty years of India's development, the average annual growth rate in real GVA was a little above three per cent per annum. The growth rate in TFP was low and so was the contribution to TFP growth to the aggregate-level GVA growth. In the period 1980–1993, the GVA growth rate rose to about five per cent per annum. The growth rate in TFP was about two per cent per annum accounting for about 40% of the GVA growth. The acceleration in GVA growth during 1980–1993 is mostly attributable to substantially increased TFP growth rate. In the post-reform period, the growth rate in real GVA rose to about six per cent per annum, and the growth rate in TFP was about two per cent per annum, accounting for about a third of the real GVA growth. In the post-GFC period, the growth rate in real GVA has come down slightly and there has been a fall also in the growth rate in TFP.

The relative contribution of labour input to real GVA growth at aggregate economy level was about 20% or more during 1952–1966, 1967–1979 and 1980–1993 (Fig. 2.16). In the more recent period 1994 to 2019, the contribution of labour input to aggregate-level GVA growth came down to about 10%. In the post-reform period, capital accumulation has been the main contributor to the aggregate real GVA growth. The contribution of TFP growth to the aggregate-level GVA growth was over 40% during 1980–1993. During 1994–2007 and 2008–2019 the relative contribution of TFP growth to GVA growth came down. However, despite this decline, the relative contribution of TFP growth to GVA growth was more than 25% during 2008–2019.

Compared to the estimates made by Sivasubramonian (2004), the estimates of TFP growth in the Indian economy during 1952–1979 obtained in this study (about 0.6% per annum) is slightly low. The average annual growth rate in TFP for the period 1951–1980 is about one per cent per annum in the estimates made by Sivasubramonian (2004).

For the period, 1981 to 2007, the average annual growth rate in TFP is found to be about two per cent per annum in this study. This by and large matches the estimates obtained in several earlier studies (see Table 2.20).

If the entire period under study, 1952 to 2019 is divided into two parts, 1952–1979 and 1980–2019, the contribution of TFP growth to GVA growth was rather limited during 1952–1979, and the small contribution that TFP growth made to GVA growth came from the services sector. In the period, 1980–2019, on the other hand, the contribution of TFP growth to the aggregate economy-level GVA growth was

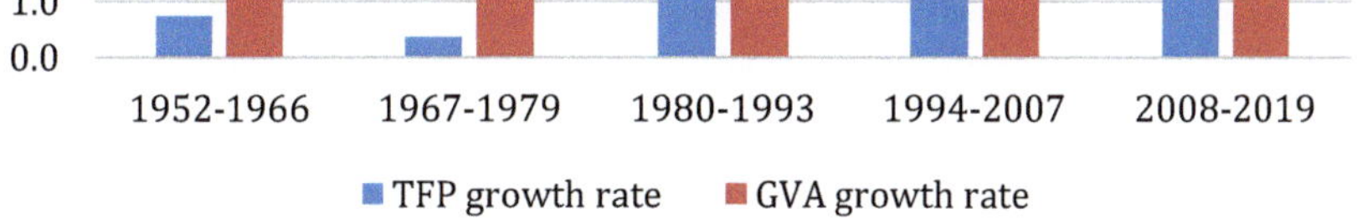

Fig. 2.15 TFP growth rate and GVA growth rate in the Indian economy (% per annum). *Source* Authors' computations based on India KLEMS Database, 2021 (extended to 1951)

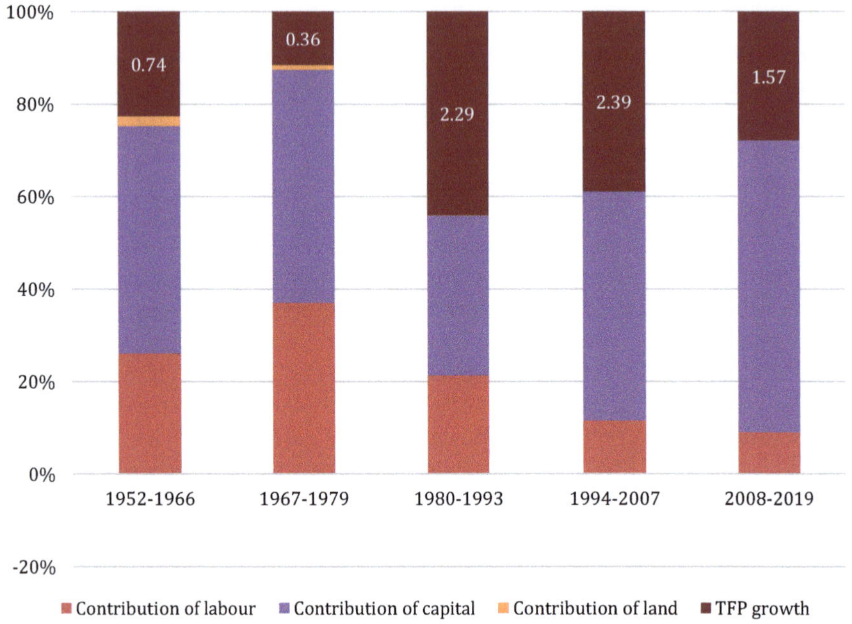

Fig. 2.16 Relative contributions of inputs and TFP to GVA growth, Indian economy. *Source* Authors' computations based on India KLEMS Database, 2021 (extended to 1951)

substantial, and these gains in TFP mainly emanated from the agriculture and allied activity, manufacturing and services.

Figure 2.17 shows the contribution of different broad sectors to the aggregate-level TFP growth. Sectoral TFP growth rates have been multiplied by their share in aggregate GVA to compute the contribution of different sector. The gap that remains between weighted aggregation of sector-level TFP growth rates and the directly computed TFP growth rate from the aggregate economy data is taken as the contribution of factor reallocation among sectors.[9]

It is seen in Fig. 2.17 that the services sector contributed majorly to the aggregate-level TFP growth during periods 1980–1993, 1994–2007 and 2008–2019. The contribution of the manufacturing sector has been relatively smaller. Only in the post-GFC

[9] The concept may be explained the following way. Aggregate input growth rates (labor and capital) can be calculated as the sum of output-weighted industry input growth (labor and capital) and the output-weighted growth of industry input shares within the aggregate economy. Thus, we have two components, industry-specific input growth (within effect)—assuming input growth is proportional to the sector's size; and reallocation effect (if input shares increase in sectors with high output shares, it generates positive reallocation effects). When this idea is integrated into aggregate growth accounting, assuming aggregate value-added growth is a Tornqvist index, we can find that aggregate TFP is the difference between industry value-added growth and industry input growth, both weighted by industry output shares, plus reallocation effects (of both capital and labor). This concept should not be confused with aggregation of TFP growth from micro enterprise level which involves a different framework and methods of computation of within effect and reallocation effect.

Table 2.20 Estimates of TFP growth in the Indian economy, select earlier studies

Author(s)	Method	Period	Estimated TFP growth rate (% per annum)
Dholakia (2002)	Value-added function (land included as an input)	1960–1985	0.8
		1985–2000	2.9
Sivasubramonian (2004)	Value-added function (land included as an input); estimates for non-residential sectors of the economy	1950–1960	1.8
		1960–1970	1.2
		1970–1980	0.2
		1980–1990	2.0
		1990–1999	2.0
		1950–1999	1.4
Virmani (2004)	Value-added function	1950–1964	1.9
		1965–1979	0.1
		1980–1991	2.5
		1992–2003	3.6
Jorgenson and Vu (2005)	Value-added function (contribution of ICT investment taken into account)	1989–1995	2.1
		1995–2003	2.5
Bosworth et al. (2007)	Value-added function (land included as an input)	1960–1980	0.2
		1980–2004	2.0
		1983–1993	1.7
		1993–1999	2.8
		1999–2004	2.0
Bosworth and Collins (2008)	Value-added function (land included as an input)	1978–1993	1.1
		1993–2004	2.3
		1978–2004	1.6
Bosworth and Maertens (2010)	Value-added function (land included as an input)	1980–1990	2.2
		1990–2000	1.8
		2000–2005	2.1

Source and *Note* This table was a part of the Report of the India KLEMS project at ICRIER submitted to the RBI in 2014. It is seen in the table that several studies have found a low rate of TFP growth in the period 1951–1979 compared to the growth rate achieved during the 1990s and later

period, the manufacturing sector has made a significant contribution to the aggregate-level TFP growth. It may be pointed out here that although services contributed significantly to TFP growth during 2008–2019, it is mostly traceable to non-market services (see Figs. 2.11, 2.12 and 2.13). The agriculture sector contributed significantly to the aggregate-level TFP growth during the periods 1980–1993, 1994–2007 and 2008–2019. Interestingly, a significant part of the aggregate-level TFP growth arose from factor reallocation among sectors. This was particularly important during 1980–1993 and 1994–2007.

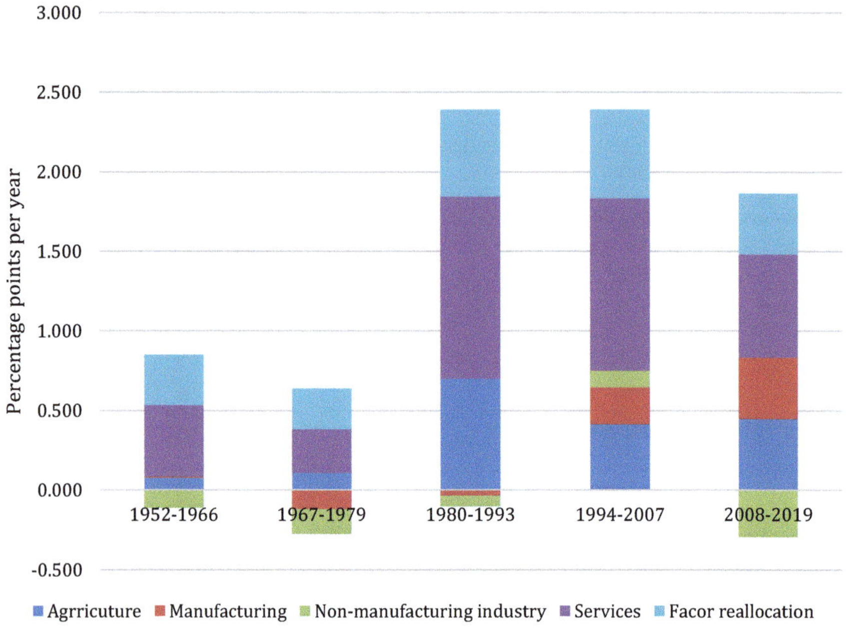

Fig. 2.17 Sector-wise contribution to the aggregate-level TFP growth. *Source* Authors' computations based on India KLEMS Database, 2021 (extended to 1951)

2.7 Sectoral Pattern of Aggregate TFP Growth

In Fig. 2.18, we present a Harberger diagram (Harberger, 1998) that plots the cumulative contributions of six major sectors to aggregate TFP growth against the cumulative shares of these sectors in total value added. Harberger diagrams, presented for all five periods under consideration, help us discern sectoral patterns of TFP growth, distinguishing between a broad-based or 'yeast' type versus a more concentrated 'mushroom' type pattern and whether these patterns change over different periods. The grey horizontal line in the diagram represents aggregated TFPG (TFP growth) excluding reallocation effects. The shaded area beneath the concave-shaped Harberger curve provides insights into the equality of TFP growth distribution across sectors. A lower area indicates broad-based growth ('yeast-like'), while a larger area suggests concentration in a few sectors ('mushroom-like').

The number of sectors considered in our analysis is too small to draw robust conclusions regarding the sectoral patterns of TFP. Nevertheless, we discern that the growth pattern leaned more toward a 'mushroom-like' trajectory in the 1950s and 1960s, a period when the aggregate TFPG was very minimal in the Indian economy.

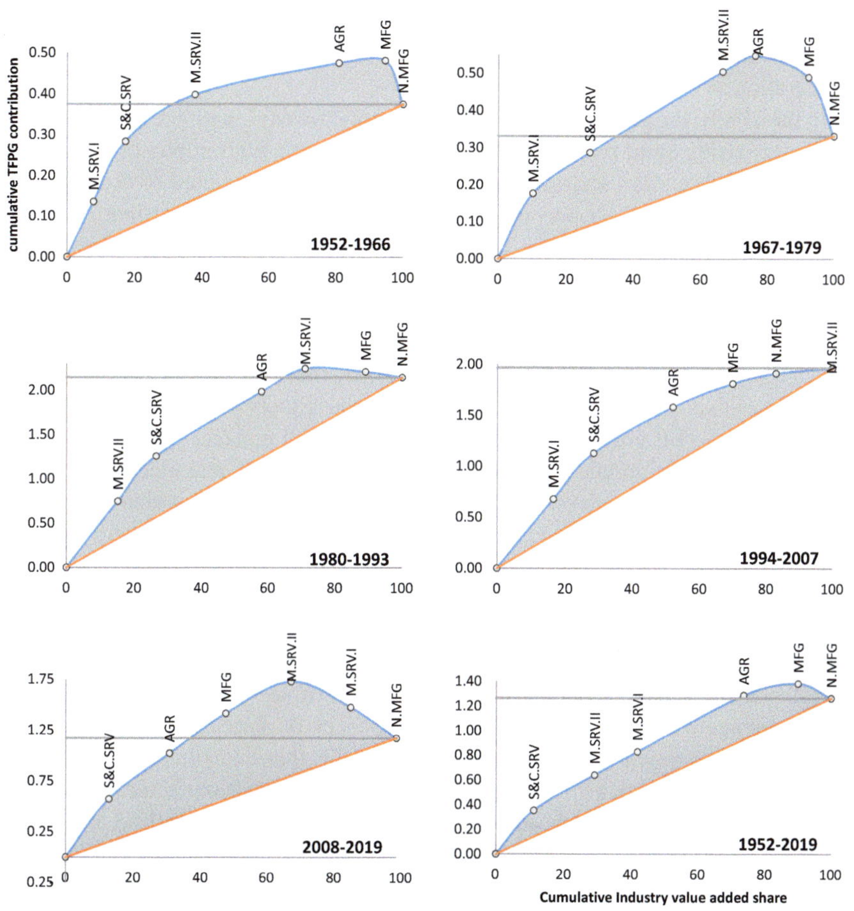

Fig. 2.18 Harberger diagrams of aggregate total factor productivity growth in India. *Note* AGR = Agriculture & allied; N.MFG = Non-manufacturing industries; MFG = Manufacturing; M.SRV.I = Market Services-I (trade, hotels & restaurants, transport, storage & communication); M.SRV.II = Market Services-II (banking, finance & insurance, real estate, ownership of dwellings & business services) and S&C.SRV = Social & Community Services (public administration & defence, education & health services and other personal services). The grey area delineates the space beneath the Harberger diagram and the diagonal line. The grey line represents the aggregated TFPG, calculated as the sum of sectoral TFPG weighted by the respective sector's value-added share. *Source* Authors' computations based on India KLEMS Database, 2021 (extended to 1951)

The relative area under the Harberger curve was elevated during this period, as indicated by the shaded grey area.[10] During this time, two of the major sectors—manufacturing and non-manufacturing industries—contributed to lowering aggregate TFP

[10] The relative area under the Harberger curve is the curvature measured by the space between the Harberger diagram and the diagonal line, an indicator of equal distribution (see Das et al., 2016; Timmer et al., 2010).

growth, whereas services and agriculture, constituting more than 80% of total value added, added up to half a percentage point in TFP growth before it lowered due to deceleration in the industrial sector.

In the 1980s, the pattern becomes slightly more 'yeasty', with the area under the curve decreasing amid rising overall TFP growth, along with improvements in the agriculture and services sectors. Together, these sectors contributed 70% of all value added in the economy on average and attained a TFP growth contribution of 2.2 percentage points. However, the manufacturing and non-manufacturing industrial sectors continued to exhibit weak performance, contributing to reducing aggregate TFP growth.

A more evenly distributed sectoral productivity contribution is evident from the 1990s until the financial crisis, during which the TFP pattern becomes more 'mushroom-like'. During this period, the industrial sectors of the economy experienced positive TFP growth, contributing to the overall enhancement of aggregate TFP. The relative importance of both manufacturing and non-manufacturing sectors for aggregate TFP growth overrode that of market services-II, which consists of banking, finance and insurance, real estate, ownership of dwellings and business services sectors.

In the post-crisis period, the area under the Harberger diagram increases again, reflecting the losses in TFP growth in market services-I (i.e., the aggregate of trade, hotels and restaurants, transport, storage and communication sectors) and non-manufacturing industry. The positive contribution of sectoral TFPG amounted to 1.7 percentage points, coming from market services-II, agriculture, manufacturing and social & community services—sectors that together constituted close to 70% of value added. The two sectors, market services-I and non-manufacturing, together constituting the rest of value added, experienced productivity decline, evoking a lowering effect on aggregate TFPG.

Thus, while the sectoral pattern of aggregate TFP has evolved over periods, the primary factor influencing sectoral variations in contributing to aggregate TFPG was the weak productivity performance of the manufacturing and non-manufacturing industries during the pre-liberal market reform period. While TFPG contributions of services and agriculture sectors somewhat conformed to the general trend in the aggregate economy, whether during periods of rapid productivity growth or slow growth, the industrial sectors tended to deviate, particularly in the pre-reform period.

2.8 What Determines TFP Growth in India: A Time Series Analysis

Although TFP growth is commonly viewed as a measure of changes in disembodied technical change, the residual measure obtained from growth accounting can reflect many unmeasured factors, particularly in long time series data, and our understanding of what it consists of is still limited.[11] For example, it could reflect mismeasurement in prices, input (especially capital input) and output. It could also capture improvements in management practices, better organization of production, general advancements in education, reallocation of resources across industries, economies of scale or changes in the institutional quality of the economy. Therefore, it is imperative to have a broader understanding of the factors that drive TFP growth in our long time series data. While a comprehensive analysis of the determinants of TFP is beyond the scope of this study, we attempt to examine the determinants of TFP in India's aggregate economy over 1951–2019 period, using an Autoregressive Distributed Lag series (ARDL) model, similar to the analysis in Goldar et al. (2023).

In their study using an ARDL model, Goldar et al. (2023) consider a greater number of explanatory variables to explain TFP, including ICT investment, infrastructure investment and FDI, based on data from the period 1990 to 2019. Due to our long historical time series, conducting such a comprehensive analysis is challenging. In the analysis presented here, we consider the following seven factors which could potentially influence TFP: (i) annual rainfall, (ii) trade openness measured by the ratio of exports plus imports to GDP, (iii) the average years of education of the working age population, (iv) the share of agriculture and allied sector in the total capital stock, (v) the ratio of structure to equipment in the capital stock, (vi) the share ICT capital stock in total fixed capital stock and (vii) the growth rate of GDP of the OECD countries. The first six factors are obtained for the aggregate Indian economy and are reflective of factors enhancing productivity such as weather conditions, integration with the global economy, the composition of the capital stock and improvements in the overall education of workers in the Indian economy. The share of agricultural sector capital stock is included to capture the impact of structural change in the economy in terms of shift away from agriculture. Since the employment numbers are interpolated between benchmark years, capital stock might be a better measure, which may also help limit endogeneity problem, as most of the capital stock already exists because of the decisions taken in the past. The seventh factor considered represents the global economic conditions.

The annual all-India rainfall data for 1951 to 2016 are taken from a report of the Indian Institute of Tropical Meteorology, Pune (Kothawale & Rajeevan, 2017). We extend the series to 2019 using data from the databases of the EPW Research Foundation. The measure of trade openness (the ratio of exports plus imports to GDP) have been obtained from the World Development Indicator of the World Bank since 1960. To extend these series backward till 1951, we rely on *Economic Survey* (Ministry of Finance, Government of India), 2022–2023 (Table 6.1 B, p. 110). Data on average years of schooling among person of age of 15–64 years have been taken from a document prepared by Ritchie et al. (2023). These are quinquennial estimates,

[11] For example, Abramowitz (1956) referred to the residual TFP as "some sort of measure of our ignorance about the causes of economic growth", indicating the limitations of the current understanding of the concept. Similarly, Prescott (1998), who underlined the role of input utilization and business cycles in driving TFP in his earlier works, emphasized the limitations of existing economic theories in understanding TFP and called for a comprehensive understanding of the concept.

from 1950 to 2020, which have been interpolated to derive the annual series from 1950 to 2020. The share of agriculture and allied sector in total fixed capital stock of the economy has been computed from the sector-wise capital series prepared for the present study (discussed in Sect. 2.5). The ratio of structure to equipment in India's capital stock is based on the computations made for capital stock discussed in Sect. 2.5. The share of ICT assets in total fixed assets is taken from the Total Economy Database of the Conference Board.[12] Finally, the GDP growth of OECD member countries have been primarily taken from the World Development Indicator of the World Bank which is available from 1960 (growth rate from 1961). This has been extended backward using GDP data for two major country groups taken from Maddison (2006), namely Western Europe and Western Offshoots (which includes Australia, New Zealand, Canada and the United States), This is strictly not OECD countries but includes by and large the OEEC countries which preceded the OECD. There is a slight inter-temporal data comparability issue, which can be ignored.

The dependent variable in the model being estimated is the TFP index for the aggregate economy, with the base year set as 1951–1952 for which the index value is set at 1.0.[13] To generate the series of indices for subsequent years, we extrapolate the base year using the growth rates in TFP computed using the methods discussed earlier in this chapter. This approach is similar to the one used in the analysis of determinant of TFP in Indian manufacturing undertaken by Krishna et al. (2020).

We expect a positive effect of rainfall on TFP because a good rainfall will raise the agricultural yields and deficient rainfall will lower the yields, which will in turn have effect on the rest of the Indian economy (see Goldar et al., 2023 in this context). We expect a positive effect of education on TFP because education raises the labour quality (see Liu & Bi, 2019, in this context, who have found a positive effect of higher education on TFP in China). There are many studies that have found that exports and imports lead to productivity enhancement in Indian manufacturing (see, for example, Ranjan & Raychaudhuri, 2011; Narayanan & Sahu, 2020; Goldar, 2020, 2022; Goldar et al., 2020; Rijesh, 2019, 2024). A positive effect of trade openness on productivity is therefore expected.

The share of agriculture and allied sector in total capital stock captures the effects of the changes in the structure of the economy on aggregate-level productivity. Since the level of productivity is relatively higher in the non-agricultural sector than in the agriculture sector, a fall in the share of the agricultural sector in the economy

---

[12] While the series for other variables used for the analysis is from 1951 to 2019, for this variable, i.e., the series on ICT share, data could be obtained for the years 1960 to 2019. The ICT share in capital stock in India was very low in the 1960s. After studying the properties of the series by carrying out unit root tests, the data for 1960 to 1967 was dropped, the series from 1968 to 2019 has been used for the analysis.

[13] The TFP index is for financial years, i.e., from 1 April of the current year to 31 March of the next year. In the analysis undertaken all previous sections of the chapter, data for financial years were used. However, data on the explanatory variables are in most cases in calendar year. This causes a slight mismatch in the data. However, this problem cannot be addressed satisfactorily by any adjustments made to the data series. This issue has therefore been ignored. This problem, in our opinion, does not seriously affect the results of econometric analysis.

will lead to an increase in the aggregate-level TFP because of inter-sectoral resource reallocation effect. Hence, a negative coefficient for the variable in the estimated model is expected, i.e., a fall in the share in agriculture will raise aggregate-level TFP.

As regards the share of ICT assets in total fixed assets and the structure to equipment ratio in capital assets, a positive effect of the former on TFP and a negative effect of the latter is expected. The basis for these expectations is the findings reported in several earlier studies and the theoretical discussion presented therein (see, for example, Erumban & Das, 2016, 2020; Krishna et al., 2020; Goldar, 2020; Goldar et al., 2023; Li & Tian, 2023 among others). Note that an increase in the share of ICT assets and a decrease in the structure to equipment ratio raises in a certain sense the 'quality of capital assets' and thus contributes to TFP growth.

The growth rate in GDP of OECD countries may be treated as an indicator of the global economic conditions and thus is expected to have a positive effect on India's aggregate-level productivity through various channels including trade and FDI. In the study undertaken by Goldar et al. (2023), a positive effect of the growth rate of OECD countries' GDP on the growth rate of TFP in India was found. Accordingly, a positive effect of this variable in India's aggregate-level TFP is hypothesized.

Before applying the ARDL model it is essential that the variable be subjected to unit root tests to check for stationarity of the series. The results of the unit root tests are shown in Annexure E. The test results provide justification for using the ARDL model.[14]

The estimates of the ARDL model are shown in Table 2.21. The estimated long-run coefficients are shown in the table, along with the results of some diagnostic tests. The results of the Pesaran et al. (2001) bounds test done for all five model results indicate co-integration.

The results indicate a significant positive effect of rainfall on TFP, implying that rainfall deficiencies can adversely impact TFP in India. A significant positive effect of education and trade openness on TFP is found, as expected. The trade-to-GDP variable serves also as a proxy for the economic reforms in the Indian economy.[15] The finding of a positive effect of trade-GDP ratio on TFP captures in part the beneficial effect of economic reforms. The negative coefficient of the share of agriculture and allied activities in total capital stock reflects the productivity gains accruing from a shift in the structure of the economy from agricultural to non-agricultural activities. The results show that an increase in the share of equipment in capital stock relative to structure increases TFP. This finding matches the results of analysis presented in Krishna et al. (2020). A significant positive effect of ICT investment on TFP is found, corroborating the finding of Goldar et al. (2023). Although the coefficient of

[14] Both the augmented Dickey-Fuller and the Phillips-Perron tests have been performed, and the results show that the dependent variable (TFP index) is integrated of order one, denoted as I(1), and the explanatory variables consist of a combination of I(0) and I(1) variables.None the variables can be strictly considered I(2). Thus, the use of an ARDL model for analysis is justified.

[15] Trade-GDP ratio was about 11% during 1951–1979, about 14% during 1980–1990, the period of early economic reforms, and 36% during 1991–2019. The high value for 1991–2019 is primarily attributable to a more liberal trade and tariff policy.

Table 2.21 Estimates of the ARDL model explaining TFP index (1951 = 1.0) at the economy level. Study Period: 1951–2019

Explanatory variables	Long-run coefficients				
	Model-1	Model-2	Model-3	Model-4	Model-5
Rainfall (in milli meters) × 10^3	0.143 (2.38)**	0.365 (2.11)**	0.376 (2.01)**	0.343 (1.95)*	0.022 (2.91)***
Average years of schooling among working-age population	0.121 (1.93)*	0.230 (11.19)***	0.265 (3.17)***	0.261 (3.32)***	0.242 (2.01)**
Trade to GDP ratio (%)	0.011 (3.03)***	0.009 (2.90)***	0.007 (1.55)	0.008 (1.73)*	0.004 (1.78)*
Share of agriculture and allied activities in total economy capital stock (%)	−0.033 (1.89)*				−0.097 (−3.36)***
Structure-equipment ratio (%)					−0.082 (−2.99)***
Share of ICT assets in total capital stock (%)					0.439 (8.26)***
Growth rate in GDP of OECD countries (computed by taking log difference)		1.424 (1.22)		1.355 (1.18)	
Trend	Not included	Not included	Included	Included	Included
ARDL lag structure	(1,0,0,3,1)	(1,0,0,3,0)	(1,3,0,0)	(1,0,0,3,0)	(1,0,0,3,0,0,4)
Adjustment coefficient	−0.33 (5.67)***	−0.34 (−5.49)***	−0.34 (−4.98)***	−0.36 (−5.11)***	−0.83 (−5.42)***
R^2 of error correction model	0.46	0.43	0.41	0.43	0.83
Pesaran et al. (2001) bounds test	$F = 9.34$; $t = (-)5.68$	$F = 8.24$; $t = (-)5.49$	$F = 8.19$; $t = (-)4.98$	$F = 6.85$; $t = (-)5.11$	$F = 16.54$; $t = (-)5.42$
Inference about the existence of level relationship: Null hypothesis is no level relationship	Rejected at a 1% level	Rejected at a 1% level	Rejected at a 1% level	Rejected at a 1% level	Rejected at a 1% level
No. of observations and sample	66 (1954–2019)	66 (1954–2019)	66 (1954–2019)	66 (1954–2019)	52 (1968–2019)

Note t-values in parentheses. *** prob. < 0.01; ** prob. < 0.05; * prob. < 0.1
The optimal lag length has been determined on the basis of Bayesian information criteria. The sample in the last row is less than the study period because of lags, except the last column where data for a shorter period is used in order to use the ICT share variable
Source Authors' computations using data explained in the text

the GDP growth in OECD countries is not statistically significant, it is positive as expected. In the analysis presented in Goldar (2023), a significant positive effect of GDP growth in OECD countries on TFP growth in the Indian economy was found.

In summary, the results of the regression analysis show that the estimated TFP indices have a statistically significant relationship with the variables we identified as determinants of TFP. The findings indicate a positive effect of education, trade openness, ICT investments and rainfall on TFP, which aligns with theoretical expectations. While we do not entirely dismiss the possibility of measurement issues, our results emphasize that the measured TFP indices are not merely reflective of such errors and lend credence to the aggregate TFP measure we use, rather than being solely reflective of biases arising from assumptions about product and factor markets.

2.9 Summary of Findings and Concluding Remarks

The main findings of the analysis presented in the chapter are summarized below. The discussion follows the order in which the analysis was presented above.

2.9.1 GVA Growth and Structural Change

In Sect. 2.3 we analysed value-added growth and sectors' contribution to aggregate economy growth rate. Aggregated TFPG (TFP growth) suggest that India's services sector recorded an increase in value-added share from nearly 34 percentage points in 1951 to more than 54 percentage points in 2019. Share of manufacturing and construction increased slightly between 1951 and 2019. The share of agriculture declined over the years and remaining sectors' share remained stagnant.

The Indian economy grew at 4.8% per annum during 1952 to 2019 and the growth has improved over different sub-periods until 2007–2008. At disaggregate level, the growth rates show wide heterogeneity across industries and over time. In terms of broad sectors, services sectors and electricity, gas & water supply achieved growth at a faster rate than others, while agriculture grew at a much slower rate. During 1967 to 1979 and 2008 to 2019, except for agriculture & allied activities; and finance, insurance & real estate, all other sectors experienced a fall in growth rate. We also found that finance, insurance & real estate; and trade, hotels & restaurants observed an improvement in its value-added growth contribution to aggregate economy growth, while contribution of agriculture declined over the year. For the remaining sectors, the contributions remained more or less stagnant.

2.9.2 Employment Growth and Changes in Labour Productivity

In Sect. 2.4, we analysed the structure and growth of employment along with elasticity of employment and labour productivity. We found that the structural shift in employment has been slow in the Indian economy, and the shift took place mainly from agriculture to construction, trade and transport. The growth in employment in agriculture decelerated faster after the 1993 reforms with a negative employment elasticity during 2008–2019. The growth in employment in the total economy was, however, faster in the pre-reform period than the post-reform period of 1994–2019. The employment elasticity in the manufacturing sector was higher in the pre-reform period and it eroded especially after the global financial crisis in 2008 and has been almost zero during the period of 2008–2019. We observe a high employment elasticity only in the broad sectors of construction, transport and trade. Though the level of labour productivity (LP) increased for all the broad sectors, its growth rate varied between sectors and the sub-periods. The growth rate in LP was above average in electricity, manufacturing, financial services, mining and public administration but was quite low in other sectors, especially the labour-intensive sectors of construction and agriculture.

It is also observed that for the total economy, the growth in employment mainly kept pace with the growth in population till 1993, but later on, it started lagging behind and the gap further increased during 2008–2019. It also resulted in a declining employment elasticity in the post-reform period. However, due to a rapid growth in GVA, the growth in LP accelerated in the post-reform period. But despite a ten times increase in the level of LP between 1951 and 2019, India's overall LP in 2019 was lower than China and other selected countries considered for the study. India will have to focus on increasing its employment growth as well as growth in LP to come to the levels achieved by its international competitors.

2.9.3 Investment Rate and Changes in Capital Intensity

Our analysis of trends in investment rates (Sect. 2.5) reveals a consistently low investment rate in the agricultural sector, and the sector's share in the total economy's overall investment has fallen substantially over decades. This observation is consistent with previous studies that attributed the fall in agricultural investment to low levels of public investment. In the manufacturing sector, where investment to GDP ratios are generally higher than in other sectors, investment rates have improved in the pro-business and pro-market reform periods. Still, the sector has seen massive erosions in investment rates post-crisis. The efforts to boost manufacturing investment need to continue if India has to achieve its aspirations to become a global manufacturing production hub in the coming years. Among services, trade, hotels & restaurants services generally sustained a low yet improving investment rate. On the contrary, the transport, storage & communication sector witnessed a high investment rate at the beginning, but it consistently fell over the years, barring a minor improvement in the post-crisis period. The non-market services (i.e., social, community services sector) also showed an improvement in investment rate in the post-crisis period, after a fall in the 1990s through the late 2000s from a notable gain in the 1980s. Overall, although the economy-wide investment rate has improved from the early import-substituting heavy industrialization regimes of the 1950s to the pro-market reforms in the 1990s, the improvement in the average investment rate has been much more modest in the post-crisis period. The pace of decline in the post-crisis annual investment rate in the economy has been historically fast, both due to global headwinds and domestic challenges. The potential for attracting investment in the manufacturing sector is still high for India, but to tap that potential, several weaknesses in infrastructure, human capital and institutional spheres need to be addressed.

Our analysis of capital stock suggests a consistently growing stock of capital in the economy with the highest growth rate in capital stock in the construction sector. During the period that followed India's pro-market reforms until the global financial crisis, 1994–2007, all sectors of the economy witnessed an improvement in capital stock growth rate. In the post-crisis period, although some important sectors, including manufacturing, have seen a drop in the growth rate of capital stock, almost all sectors sustained a sound growth rate. The sustained growth in capital stock has also resulted in a consistent increase in the capital-to-worker ratio across the board. Although the capital-to-output ratio remained somewhat stable, the capital deepening (capital per worker) has grown quite substantially over the years. It has increased by more than seven times over the last 7.5 decades. Although the Indian economy generally sees rapid mechanization, the high and rapid increase in capital workers ratio is primarily driven by construction assets and not equipment. Among the broad sectors, while agriculture remained relatively less equipment intensive throughout, manufacturing and services (except trade and hotels & restaurants) have increased their capital per worker ratios substantially. Almost all sectors of the economy have seen a massive increase in capital stock per worker ratios in the post-crisis period. For the first time during the past seven decades, it was in the post-crisis period that the agricultural sector also showed a faster rise in capital deepening. Thus, our results clearly indicate that the Indian economy has been increasingly shifting towards a capital-intensive economy. The uninterrupted shift towards a capital-intensive economy is visible across all major sectors of the economy.

2.9.4 TFP Growth and Its Contribution to GVA Growth

The analysis of trends in total factor productivity (TFP) in Sect. 2.6 revealed that in the first thirty years of India's development, the average annual growth rate in TFP was low and so was the contribution to TFP growth to the aggregate-level GVA growth. During 1980–1993 and 1994–2007, the rate of growth in TFP exceeded two per cent per annum. TFP growth contributed significantly to GVA growth. In the post-GFC period, the growth rate in real GVA has come down slightly and there has been a fall also in the growth rate in TFP.

Analysis of different inputs to the aggregate-level GVA growth showed that the relative contribution of labour input to real GVA growth at aggregate economy level was about 20% or more during 1952–1993. In the more recent period 1994 to 2019, the contribution of labour input to aggregate-level GVA growth came down to about 10%. In the post-reform period, capital accumulation has been the main contributor to the aggregate real GVA growth. The contribution of TFP growth to the aggregate-level GVA growth was over 40% during 1980–1993. During 1994–2007 and 2008–2019 the relative contribution of TFP growth to GVA growth came down. However, despite this decline, the relative contribution of TFP growth to GVA growth was more than 25% during 2008–2019.

Among the major sectors, the growth rate in TFP was generally relatively higher in services than in other major sectors. The relatively high TFP growth in services is to a large extent traceable to the social and community services which registered a high growth rate in TFP during 1980 to 2019. TFP growth rate in manufacturing was relatively better during 1994–2007 than during 1952–1993. The rate of TFP growth increased further during the post-GFC period. Another interesting finding is that the average rate of TFP growth in agriculture was about two per cent per annum during 1980–2019 accounting for the dominant part of GVA growth in agriculture. It is surprising to find that GVA growth in agriculture was mostly productivity driven rather than input driven which goes against a common impression about this sector.

The differences in performance among different sectors are reflected in the sectoral contribution to the aggregate-level TFP growth. The services sector contributed majorly to the aggregate-level TFP growth during periods 1980–1993, 1994–2007 and 2008–2019.[16] The contribution of the manufacturing sector has been relatively smaller. Only in the post-GFC period, the manufacturing sector has made a significant contribution to the aggregate-level TFP growth. The agriculture sector contributed significantly to the aggregate-level TFP growth during the periods 1980–1993, 1994–2007 and 2008–2019. Interestingly, a significant part of the aggregate-level TFP growth arose from factor reallocation among sectors. This was particularly important during 1980–1993 and 1994–2007.

The Harberger diagrams in Sect. 2.7, illustrating sectoral patterns of TFP growth, revealed variations across different periods despite the limited number of sectors analysed. The TFP growth pattern took on a 'mushroom-like' trajectory in the 1950s and 1960s, primarily influenced by the weak productivity performance of the industrial sector (both manufacturing and non-manufacturing industries). In the 1980s and 1990s, the sectoral TFP growth exhibited a more evenly distributed, 'yeasty' pattern, which, however, reverted to a 'mushroom-like' pattern in the post-global financial crisis period. This shift indicates an increase in the area under the Harberger diagram,

---

[16] The *India Productivity Report* (Krishna et al., 2022a) noted that the substantial contribution of service growth to the aggregate economy TFP growth was a combination of its high output shares and impressive growth rates.

reflecting losses in TFP growth in some market services and non-manufacturing industrial sectors. Overall, the evolution of sectoral patterns underscores the significant impact of industrial sectors, particularly during the pre-liberal market reform period.

2.9.5 Determinants of TFP Growth in the Indian Economy

In Sect. 2.8, an analysis of determinants of TFP growth in the Indian economy was undertaken by applying an ARDL model to time series data covering 1951–1952 to 2019–2020. Seven explanatory variables were considered. Regression analysis showed that the estimated TFP indices have a statistically significant relationship with the variables we identified as determinants of TFP. The findings indicate a positive effect of education, trade openness, ratio of equipment to structure in the capital stock, ICT investments and rainfall on TFP, which aligns with theoretical expectations. We also found that a shift in the industrial structure away from agriculture to the non-agricultural sectors is productivity enhancing.

Annexure A: Additional Tables

See Tables 2.22, 2.23 and 2.24.

Annexure B: Construction of Employment Series

The employment series has been obtained by extending backward the employment data in the India KLEMS database (2021). The KLEMS (2021) database provides data on employment from 1980–1981 to 2019–2020 for the total economy and the selected 27 industries. The database uses the major rounds of the Employment-Unemployment Surveys from 38th round (1983) to 68th round (2011–2012) and the PLFS (Periodic Labour Force Survey) of 2017–2018 to 2019–2020 by NSO. The workforce participation rates (WPR) for Rural Male, Rural Female, Urban Male and Urban Female from EUS are used along the respective Census populations to obtain the total number of persons employed for each category separately and the final total employment. The distribution of employment in the different for 27 KLEMS industries and broad sectors is also obtained from EUS and the PLFS and

Table 2.22 GVA share (at current prices)

Industry	1951–1952	1967–1968	1980–1981	1994–1995	2008–2009	2019–2020
Agriculture & allied	49.5	43.9	35.9	28.8	17.9	18.3
Mining & quarrying	0.9	1.1	1.9	2.7	3.2	2.0
Manufacturing	12.0	13.6	18.2	18.3	18.2	14.7
Electricity, gas & water supply	0.3	1.0	2.1	3.5	2.1	2.7
Construction	3.1	4.9	5.3	5.7	9.7	7.5
Trade, hotels & restaurants	3.9	5.3	7.4	8.5	10.4	12.7
Transport, storage & communication	3.1	3.3	4.0	6.3	7.1	6.3
Finance, insurance & real estate	18.3	17.4	14.4	15.5	19.4	21.1
Social & community services	8.9	9.5	10.8	10.7	12.0	14.7

Source Authors' computations based on India KLEMS database, 2021 (extended to 1951)

the distribution is applied to the total employment to obtain the employment for each broad sectors.[17]

To build employment series for the present study, the estimate of total employment from 1980–1981 to 2019–2020 is taken from the India KLEMS database. To extend the data series backwards from 1980 to 1950–1951, we have used the other published sources for WPR and the Census population. While the Census population data for 1951, and 1961 is taken from Visaria (1996), the number of persons employed for 1951 and 1961 are used from Sivasubramonian (2004). The population and employment for the four segments for the 27th NSSO round (1972–1973) and 32nd round (1977–1978) are also based on estimates by Visaria. From 38th round to 2019–2020, the population and employment numbers are taken from the India KLEMS database. We thus finally use the total number of persons employed by UPSS for 1951, 1961, 1973–1974, 1977–1978, 1983, 1987–1988, 1993–1994, 1999–1900, 2004–2005, 2011–2012, 2017–2018, 2018–2019 and 2019–2020.

[17] It may be mentioned that the industrial classification under KLEMS do not completely match with the industrial classification under NAS. In the analysis presented here, the broad industrial classification we adopted matches with the NAS classification so that there is consistency between the earlier data and the later data (covered in India KLEMS database). Therefore, if one considers the employment numbers for broad sectors from KLEMS data, these may not completely match with the NAS based broad sectors employment estimates we have made.

Table 2.23 Average sectoral share in aggregate nominal investment

Industry	1952–1966	1967–1979	1980–1993	1994–2007	2008–2019	1952–2019
Agriculture & allied	16.4	16.9	11.3	8.9	7.9	12.4
Mining & quarrying	1.0	1.9	4.1	2.2	2.1	2.3
Manufacturing	16.9	18.8	23.4	25.6	17.7	20.5
Electricity, gas & water supply	6.5	10.6	14.5	9.1	8.7	9.9
Construction	2.0	2.1	1.7	4.0	5.4	3.0
Trade, hotels & restaurants	0.7	2.1	1.9	2.2	7.7	2.7
Transport, storage & communication	20.1	13.8	10.4	7.7	9.5	12.5
Finance, insurance & real estate	23.1	20.9	16.8	27.8	26.0	22.9
Social & community services	13.4	12.9	16.1	12.5	14.9	13.9
Total Economy	100.0	100.0	100.0	100.0	100.0	100.0

Note The values are the share of each sector in total economy GFCF, calculated in current prices
Source Authors' computations based on India KLEMS database, 2021 (extended to 1951)

The broad sector distribution of employment for the corresponding years has also been obtained from different sources. While the employment distribution for 1951 and 1961 has been taken from Agrawal (1999, p. 122), that for 1972–1973 to 1993–1994 is taken from Visaria (1996). Sundaram (2007, p. 3125) provides the estimates of employment distribution for the survey rounds of 1999–1900 and 2004–2005 and the authors have computed the distribution for the other rounds from the unit-level data. The employment distribution among the broad sectors is then used with total employment to obtain the employment in each of the broad sectors for each of the benchmark year.

The estimates of employment for the intervening years have been obtained by simple interpolation of the (i) total employment, and of (ii) broad sectors. The interpolated numbers for the broad sectors are finally adjusted with the total employment of the year. However, while the estimates from the major rounds are centred around the mid-year of the Census and survey rounds, i.e., January for Census and July for 38th round and 1st January for the other rounds; the interpolation has been centred around 1st October for both the total employment and the sectoral distribution so as to coincide with the mid-year of the national income estimates which refer to the financial year and are used for GVA and capital stock. The base is thus shifted to October of each year while interpolating the persons employed.

Table 2.24 Average nominal capital-output ratios by industry

Industry	1952–1966	1967–1979	1980–1993	1994–2007	2008–2019	1952–2019
Agriculture & allied	1.2	1.5	2.0	2.2	2.3	1.8
Mining & quarrying	1.0	2.0	2.8	2.4	2.1	2.1
Manufacturing	1.5	2.4	3.6	4.2	3.7	3.0
Electricity, gas & water supply	9.4	15.7	16.4	12.4	11.9	13.1
Construction	0.5	0.8	0.9	1.1	1.7	1.0
Trade, hotels & restaurants	0.3	0.6	0.8	0.7	1.4	0.8
Transport, storage & communication	9.9	11.7	9.5	4.8	4.0	8.1
Finance, insurance & real estate	3.5	4.6	6.6	6.2	5.8	5.3
Social & community services	1.7	3.6	5.1	4.3	4.0	3.7
Total economy	2.1	2.9	3.9	3.8	3.6	3.2

Note Capital output ratios are obtained as the ratio of total capital stock and total value added, both in nominal terms

Source Authors' computations based on India KLEMS database, 2021 (extended to 1951)

Annexure C: Construction of Capital Stock Series

This annexure briefly outlines the methodology employed to estimate capital stock for the nine broad sectors. Unlike the India KLEMS database, which uses capital services to calculate the contribution of capital input and total factor productivity to value-added growth, this study relies on capital stock. Although capital services are a better measure to use in growth accounting, the longer time series used for the analysis of productivity in this chapter makes it tedious to calculate the user cost of capital, which is an essential ingredient to capital service calculation (see Erumban, 2008). The total capital stock in each sector used in this study is obtained by adding estimates of capital stocks for different capital assets. The methodology used to obtain asset-specific capital stock is the standard perpetual inventory method (PIM), similar to the India KLEMS database (see Das et al., 2021b). Assuming time-invariant asset-specific geometric depreciation rate, capital stock in asset i in year t for any given sector can be constructed as:

$$K_{i,t} = K_{i,t-1}(1 - \delta_i) + I_{i,t} \tag{2.9}$$

where $K_{i,t}$ is the volume of capital stock in asset i in year t, δ_i is the geometric depreciation rate for asset type i that is constant over time, $I_{i,t}$ is real investment in asset i in year t.

To estimate sectoral capital stock by asset type, we require real values of sector-asset investment matrices. Asset-wise nominal capital formation by broad sectors of the economy, separately for public and private sectors, are obtained from the National Statistics Office (NSO) of the Government of India for the India KLEMS database. This is the data underlying the published aggregate gross fixed capital formation by broad industry groups in the National Accounts Statistics (NAS). Such detailed asset-sector data are collected for the period 1950–2016, and the years after 2016, the data has been extended using the published NAS series. While doing this, we take the most recent NAS as the benchmark series and extrapolate the entire investment series for any given asset-sector combination, using the growth rates in the older series. To construct the real investment series, the current price investment values are deflated using asset-specific GFCF (gross fixed capital formation) deflators. The asset-wise investment price deflators are constructed as a ratio of current price investments to constant price investments in the NSO series, which are then converted to the base 2011–2012. Following the India KLEMS approach, in our calculations, we consider three different asset types: construction, machinery & equipment and transport equipment. For the detailed asset groups available in the asset-sector database provided by the NSO, and the corresponding asset categories we used in our calculation (i.e., construction, machinery & equipment and transport equipment), see Das et al. (2021b).

Since our series started in 1951, an estimate of the initial capital stock has been obtained for 1950 from the NAS. For the depreciation rate, following the India KLEMS approach, we rely on estimates of asset lifetimes provided by the NSO, assuming a double declining balance rate. We assume 80 years of lifetime for buildings, 20 years for transport equipment and 25 years for machinery and equipment, resulting in respective depreciation rates of 2.5%, 10% and 8%. Once the asset-specific capital stock volumes are constructed using the equation above, we aggregate them across assets to obtain the total capital stock. More details on the basic investment, investment prices and asset-specific initial capital stock data can be found in Das et al. (2021b).

Annexure D: Construction of Time Series on Factor Income Shares

In Sect. 2.6, estimates of TFP have been presented for the economy as a whole and for five broad sectors, namely, (i) agriculture and allied activities, (ii) manufacturing, (iii) non-manufacturing industry (including mining and quarrying, electricity and water supply and construction), (iv) market services-I (including trade, hotels and restaurants, transport, storage and communication), (v) market services-II (banking, finance and insurance, real estate, ownership of dwellings and business services) and (vi) social and community services (including public administration and defence, education and health services and other personal services).

The computation of TFP requires series on real GVA, employment and capital stock. The methodology of construction on these series have been discussed above including Annexures B and C. Also, time series on factor incomes share were needed. The method of construction of factor income shares is discussed in this annexure.

The India KLEMS database, 2021 which we used for this study contains data on output, input, factor income shares and productivity for 27 sectors of the Indian economy covering the period 1980–1981 to 2019–2020. The factor income share series provided in this database have been computed by using several pieces of information the most important of which is the data on factor incomes shares provided in the NAS. Other important pieces of information used for the construction of this series includes the decomposition of employment in different sectors of the economy into regular, casual and self-employed and the wages rates of these three categories of workers for different sectors. An estimate of the wage rate applicable to self-employed workers is derived from an estimated Mincer equation. It is not possible to apply this methodology for making estimates for the 1950s and 1960s because the unit-level data of employment surveys are not available. Therefore, for constructing factor incomes share series for the six major sectors listed above, covering the period 1951–1952 to 2019–2020, a simple method has been applied. The methodology differs among the sectors. This is explained below.

Agriculture and allied: Income share of labour and combined total of land and capital have been taken from India KLEMS data for the years 1980 to 1999. To extend the series to 1951, the labour income share in agriculture sector in Sivasubramonian (2004) has been used. Sivasubramonian (2004) has provided income shares of labour, land and capital in value added. This information is used to split the combined total income share of capital and land into their respective shares. This has been done for the years 1951 to 1997. Sivasubramonian (2004) has provided the current prices and constant prices value of land for 1950–1999 and along with land used in agriculture (net sown area plus fellow lands) in thousand hectares. The series on land used in agriculture has been extended to 2019–2020, and the value of the land has been derived in the same way as done in Sivasubramonian (2004), i.e., using the wholesale prices index for agricultural products. The ratio of the nominal income from land to the value of land has increased over time according to the computations made by Sivasubramonian (2004). The ratio was about 16% in 1993, and about 17% in 1997–1998. For all subsequent years, this ratio has been taken as 18%. Then applying this ratio to the value of land at current prices, the income accruing to land in agriculture has been computed. These data have been used to compute the shares of labour, capital and land in gross value added in agriculture and allied activities in different years between 1998 to 2019.

Manufacturing: From different NAS series, i.e., NAS with different base years, data on factor income shares have been obtained for registered and unregistered manufacturing. For the registered manufacturing sector, the factors incomes are divided into compensation of employees and operating surplus, and therefore the incomes shares of labour and capital (including land on which the factories are built) are directly obtained. For the unregistered manufacturing sector, the labour and capital components of the income are not given separately in NAS. Instead, data on mixed income is provided. This has been split into labour and capital income in the same proportion as in the registered manufacturing sector (labour and capital income out of net value added, NVA), except when the share of labour in NVA is less than 60%. In those cases, the splitting of the mixed income into labour and capital income has been done in the proportion of 60:40.

Using NAS data and applying the above procedure, the incomes shares of labour and capital in GVA in manufacturing have been computed for different years from 1960 to 1985. The series has been extrapolated to 2019 using the income share data in India KLEMS database. The series has been extended backward to 1951 on the basis of the time series in labour income share in aggregate non-agriculture sector during 1951 to 1960 in Sivasubramanion (2004). An assumption made here that the trends observed for the non-agriculture sector for 1951–1960 was applicable to each of the major components in the non-agriculture sector.

A word is needed on the choice of the 60:40 ratio applied to NVA of unregistered manufacturing. Since labour and capital incomes are not available separately for the unorganized sector, earlier studies have often used some ad hoc methods. Dholakia (2002), for instance, used three alternatives: labour income component is half, two-thirds or three-fourths of the mixed income. Sivasubramonian (2004) has computed the labour income share for the organized sector and applied it to the unorganized sector to separate labour and capital income components out of mixed income. Bosworth et al. (2007) recognized the difficulties making a right estimate of labour and capital income components out of NVA of the unorganized sector and they assumed that income share of labour for the aggregate manufacturing sector and the aggregate of other major sectors except agriculture is 60%. For agriculture, the shares were taken as: 0.5 for labour, 0.25 for capital and 0.25 for land input.

Other sectors: For computing labour component out of net value added other non-agricultural sectors, the share of labour component out of mixed income of the unorganized sector has been taken as 60%, except for real estate and ownership of dwelling (which is discussed later). The share of labour income out of GVA has been computed for 1960 to 1974, 1970 to 1981 and 1980 to 1985 using NAS data with different base years. These have then been spliced to yield series from 1960 to 1985. The series has been extrapolated forward to 2019 making use of the income share data in India KLEMS database. The series has been extrapolated backward to 1951 using the series on labour income share in non-agriculture sector reported in Sivasubramonian (2004).

The 60:40 factor applied to the mixed income of unorganized sector enterprises in non-agricultural activities cannot be applied to the NAS sector called real estate, ownership of dwellings and business services. The imputed rent from self-occupied house is a major part of this sector which is included probably in the unorganized segment. To quote from National Accounts Statistics, sources and methods (2012): 'The economic activities covered in this sector are ownership of dwellings (occupied residential houses) including imputed value of owner-occupied dwellings also.

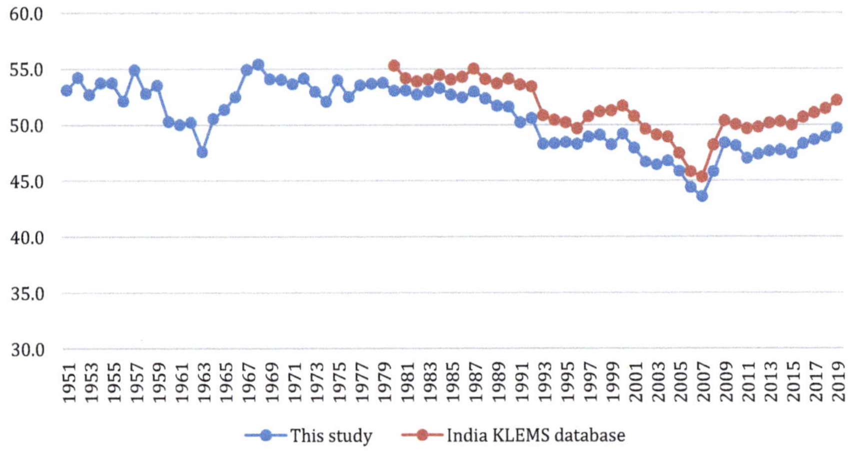

Fig. 2.19 Labour income share in GVA (%), Indian economy. *Source* Authors' computations as explained in the text

Services rendered by non-residential buildings are considered to be a subsidiary activity of the industries, which occupy the buildings and therefore, are not included in this sector'. For owner-occupied houses and the cases where individuals have given their houses on rent, there are two components: an opportunity cost of the amount invested in the house and the annual cost repair and maintenance which generate in part some labour income. Out the mixed income of unorganized sector within NAS sector called real estate, ownership of dwellings and business services, rent is the dominant component. The 60:40 factor applied in other non-agricultural sector is not applicable in this case. For this sector, the ratio of labour income to capital income out of mixed income has been taken as 20:80. Labour income share has been computed separately for banking and insurance, and real estate, ownership of dwellings and business services and then these have been combined using GVA weights.

Table 2.25 shows the mean income share of capital in different major sectors of the economy for different sub-periods. For the agriculture sector, the shares of capital and land are both shown. Table 2.26 shows the income shares of labour, capital and land for the aggregate economy for different sub-periods. The economy-level factor income shares are based on the sector-level income shares (the economy-level factor shares in different years are shown in Fig. 2.19).

Annexure E

See Table 2.27.

Table 2.25 Income shares (%) of capital input and land in GVA, by major sectors and sub-periods, 1951 to 2019

Period	Agriculture		Manufacturing	Non-manufacturing industry	Market services-I	Market services-II	Non-market services
	Capital share (%)	Land share(%)	Capital share (%)	Capital share (%)	Capital share (%)	Capital share (%)	Capital share (%)
1951–1966	13.2	31.5	45.6	33.3	45.6	70.8	25.2
1967–1979	13.6	26.5	51.0	33.7	48.3	74.8	24.4
1980–1993	21.1	21.6	56.8	40.2	45.4	75.6	22.2
1994–2007	27.0	17.0	63.2	41.8	47.8	87.7	22.2
2008–2019	33.7	10.9	61.8	37.7	46.7	85.1	22.2

Source Authors' computations using methodology explained in the text

Table 2.26 Factor income shares in GVA, Indian economy, by sub-periods

Period	Labour share (%)	Capital share (%)	Land share (%)
1951–1966	52.1	34.3	13.6
1967–1979	53.6	35.9	10.5
1980–1993	52.0	41.2	6.8
1994–2007	47.3	48.7	4.0
2008–2019	47.9	50.1	2.0

Source Authors' computations using methodology explained in the text

Table 2.27 Unit root test, augmented Dickey-Fuller test and Phillips-Perron test, 1951–2019

	Augmented Dickey-Fuller test		Phillips-Perron test	
Variable	Levels	1st difference	Levels	1st difference
TFP index, Indian economy (1951–1952 = 1.0)	1.324	−5.516	1.361	−5.566
Rainfall	−8.866	−15.688	−8.854	−19.330
Trade to GDP ratio (%)	−0.301	−7.324	−0.454	−7.417
Share of agriculture and allied activities in total economy capital stock (%)	−2.901	−2.750	−1.765	−2.678
Structure-equipment ratio (%)	−3.389	−2.988	−2.414	−3.229
Share of ICT assets in total capital stock (%) (series from 1968 to 2019 used)	6.033	−1.848	3.648	−2.167
Growth rate in GDP of OECD countries (computed by taking log difference)	−5.541	−12.014	−5.542	−15.172

Notes

(1) The critical value at the 1% level is −3.75, at a 5% level, it is −3.00 and at 10% level it is −2.59 for the Augmented Dickey-Fuller test and the Phillips-Perron test

(2) Since the results of Dickey-Fuller test and Phillips-Perron test for the ICT share variable (which uses data for 1968–2019 and allow for trend) do not indicate that the series is stationary, the (Kwiatkowski–Phillips–Schmidt–Shin) KPSS test has been applied for verification. The results of KPSS test show that the series is trend stationary

(3) The series on average years of schooling among working age population has been formed by applying interpolation to quinquennial estimates. Hence, the unit root tests for this variable have been done by applying the (Kwiatkowski–Phillips–Schmidt–Shin) KPSS test. From the results obtained, we find that the series on education is not stationary in levels or in the first difference. Also, the series in levels is not trend stationary (i.e., not stationary around a trend). However, when the first difference of the variable is taken, the series is found trend stationary if the test statistic is compared with the critical value for one per cent level of statistical significance (i.e., the test statistic is less than the critical value). This justifies the inclusion of the educational attainment variable in the ARDL model

Source Authors' computations

References

Abramowitz, M. (1956). Resource and output trends in the United States since 1870. *American Economic Review, 46*(2), 5–23.

Agrawal, A. N. (1999). *Indian economy: Problems of development and planning*. Wishwa Prakashan.

Ahluwalia, I. J. (1991). *Productivity and growth in Indian manufacturing*. Oxford University Press.

APO. (2018). *APO productivity databook*. Asian Productivity Organization.

Bala Subramanya, M. H. (1995). Reservation Policy for small scale industries: Has it delivered the goods? *Economic and Political Weekly,* 30(21).

Basu, S., Pascali, L., Schiantarelli, F., & Serven, L. (2022). Productivity and the welfare of nations. *Journal of the European Economic Association, 20*(4), 1647–1682.

Bolt, J., & van Zanden, J. L. (2020). *Maddison style estimates of the evolution of the world economy. A new 2020 update.*

Bosworth, B., & Collins, S. M. (2008). Accounting for Growth: Comparing China and India. *Journal of Economic Perspectives*, 22 (1), 45–66.

Bosworth, B., Collins, S. M., & Virmani, A. (2007). *Sources of growth in the Indian economy* (Working Paper No. 2901). National Bureau of Economic Research.

Bosworth, B., & Maertens, A. (2010). Economic Growth and Employment Generation: The Role of the Service Sector. In E. Ghani (Ed.), *The Service Revolution in South Asia*. (pp. 103–146). Oxford University Press .

Broadberry, S. N., Custodis, J., & Gupta, B. (2015). India and the great divergence: An Anglo-Indian comparison of GDP per capita, 1600–1871. *Explorations in Economic History, 55*, 58–75.

Caselli, F. (2005). Accounting for cross-country income differences. In P. Aghion & S. N. Durlauf (Eds.), *Handbook of Economic Growth* (Vol. 1A, pp. 679–741). Elsevier.

Corrado, C., Haskel, J., Jona-Lasinio, C., & Iommi, M. (2022). Intangible capital and modern economies. *Journal of Economic Perspectives, 36*(3), 3–28.

Corrado, C., Hulten, C., & Sichel, D. (2009). Intangible capital and US economic growth. *Review of Income and Wealth, 55*(3), 661–685.

Das, D. K., Erumban, A., Aggarwal, S., & Sengupta, S. (2016). Productivity growth in India under different policy regimes. In D. W. Jorgenson, K. Fukao, & M. P. Timmer (Eds.), *The world economy: Growth or stagnation?* (pp. 234–280). Cambridge University Press.

Das, D. K., Erumban, A. A., & Mallick, J. (2021a). Economic growth in India during 1950–2015: Nehruvian socialism to market capitalism. *Journal of Economic Surveys, 35*(3), 926–951.

Das, D. K., Erumban, A. A., Aggarwal, S., & Das, P. C. (2021b). *Measuring productivity at the industry level, the India KLEMS database*. Data Manual, Reserve Bank of India. https://rbi.org.in/Scripts/PublicationReportDetails.aspx?UrlPage=&ID=1186

Dholakia, B. H. (2002). Sources of India's accelerated growth and the vision of the Indian economy in 2020. *Indian Economic Journal, 9*(4), 27-46.

Dieppe, A. (Ed.). (2020). *Global productivity: Trends, drivers, and policies*. Advance Edition. Washington, DC: World Bank. License: Creative Commons Attribution CC BY 3.0 IGO.

Erumban, A. A. (2008). Rental prices, rates of return, capital aggregation and productivity: Evidence from EU and US. *Cesifo Economic Studies, 54*(3), 499–533.

Erumban, A. A., & Das, D. K. (2016). Information and communication technology and economic growth in India. *Telecommunications Policy, 40*(5), 412–431.

Erumban, A. A., & Das, D. K. (2020). ICT investment and economic growth in India: An industry perspective. In D. Maiti, F. Castellacci, & A. Melchior (Eds.), *Digitalisation and development* (pp. 89–117). Springer.

Fan, S., Gulati, A., & Thorat, S. (2008). Investment, subsidies, and pro-poor growth in rural India. *Agricultural Economics, 39*(2), 163–170.

Goldar, B. (1986). *Productivity growth in Indian Industry*. Allied Publishers.

Goldar, B. (2006). Productivity growth in Indian manufacturing in the 1980s and 1990s. In S.D. Tendulkar, A. Mitra, K. Narayanan, & D. K. Das (Eds.), *India: Industrialisation in a reforming economy: Essays for K.L. Krishna* (pp. 31–54). Academic Foundation.

Goldar, B. (2020). Services input and productivity in Indian manufacturing plants. *Indian Growth and Development Review, 13*(1), 99–124.

Goldar, B. (2022, Fall). Did trade liberalization boost total factor productivity growth in manufacturing in India in the 1990s? *International Productivity Monitor.*

Goldar, B. (2024). Total factor productivity growth in india manufacturing in the post-reform period. Available at SSRN: https://ssrn.com/abstract=4681660 or https://doi.org/10.2139/ssrn.4681660

Goldar, B., Chawla, I., & Behera, S. R. (2020). Trade liberalization and productivity of Indian manufacturing firms. *Indian Growth and Development Review, 13*(1), 73–98.

Goldar, B., Chattopadhyay, S. K., Nath, S., Sengupta, S., & Das, P. C. (2023). Determinants of Total Factor Productivity Growth in India. *Theoretical Economics Letters, 13*, 683–718. https://doi.org/10.4236/tel.2023.133041

Harper, M. J., Berndt, E. R., & Wood, D. O. (1989). Rates of return and capital aggregation using alternative rental prices. In D. W. Jorgenson & R. Landau (Eds.), *Technology and capital formation* (pp. 331–372). MIT Press.

Harberger, A. C. (1998). A vision of the growth process. *The American Economic Review, 88*(1), 1–32.

Jorgenson, D. W. (1988). Productivity and postwar US economic growth. *Journal of Economic Perspectives, 2*(4), 23–41.

Jorgenson, D. W., Ho, M., & Stiroh, K. (2005). *Information technology and the American growth resurgence.* The MIT Press.

Jorgenson, D. W. & Vu, K. (2005). Information technology and the world economy. *Scandinavian Journal of Economics*, 107(4), 631–650.

Kothawale, D. R., & Rajeevan, M. (2017). *Monthly, seasonal and annual rainfall time series for all-India, homogeneous regions and meteorological subdivisions: 1871–2016* (Research Report No. RR-138). Indian Institute of Tropical Meteorology, Pune.

Krishna, K. L., Goldar, B., Das, D. K., Aggarwal, S. C., Erumban, A. A., & Das, P. C. (2020). Manufacturing productivity in India: The role of foreign sourcing of inputs and domestic capacity building. In Fraumeni, B. (Ed.), *Measuring economic growth and productivity: Foundations, KLEMS production models, and extensions* (pp. 95–116) Academic Press.

Krishna, K. L., Goldar, B., Das, D. K., Aggarwal, S. C., Erumban, A. A., & Das, P. C. (2022a). *India productivity report*. Centre for Development Economics, Delhi School of Economics, available at the Website of the Reserve Bank of India. https://rbidocs.rbi.org.in/rdocs/PublicationReport/Pdfs/INDIAPRODUCTIVITYREPORT26D0A735C8B4411FBD4513A11532FA51.PDF

Krishna, K. L., Goldar, B., Erumban, A. A., Das, P. C., & Aggarwal, S. C. (2022b). Sources of India's post-reform economic growth: An Analysis based on India KLEMS database. *Economic and Political Weekly, 57*(31), 36–43.

Krugman, P. 1994. *The age of diminishing expectations: U.S. economic policy in the 1990s.* MIT Press.

Li, S., & Tian, Y. (2023). How does digital transformation affect total factor productivity: Firm-level evidence from China. *Sustainability, 15*(12), 9575.

Liu, J., & Bi, C. (2019). Effects of higher education levels on total factor productivity growth. *Sustainability, 11*, 1790.

Maddison, A. (2006). *The world economy, development centre studies.* OECD Publishing.

Narayanan K., & Sahu, S. K. (2020). Firm-level productivity and exports; The case of manufacturing sector in India. In: S. C. Aggarwal, D. K. Das & R. Banga (Ed.), *Accelerators of India's growth—Industry, trade and employment, India studies in business and economics* (pp. 159–175). Springer.

OECD. (2016, July), *OECD Employment outlook.* OECD.

Oulton, N. (2022). *The Divisia approach to measuring output and productivity: with an application to the BEA-BLS integrated industry-level production account, 1987–2020* (Discussion paper No. 2217). Centre for Macroeconomics, London School of Economics and Political Science.

Panagariya, A., Chakraborty, P., & Rao, M. G. (2014). *State level reforms, growth, and development in Indian states* (Vol. 3). Oxford University Press.

Pesaran, M. H., Shin, Y., & Smith, R. J. (2001). Bounds testing approaches to the analysis of level relationships. *Journal of Applied Econometrics*, 16(3), 289–326.

Prescott, E. C. (1998). Needed: A theory of total factor productivity. *International Economic Review, 39*(3), 525–551.

Ranjan, P., & Raychaudhuri, J. (2011). Self-selection vs learning: Evidence from Indian exporting firms. *Indian Growth and Development Review, 4*(1), 22–37.

Rijesh, R. (2019). International trade and productivity growth in Indian industry: Evidence from the organized manufacturing sector. *Journal of South Asian Development, 14*(1), 1–39.

Rijesh, R. (2024). Trade, labour reallocation and productivity growth in the Indian manufacturing sector. *Indian Economic Review*. https://doi.org/10.1007/s41775-024-00210-6

Ritchie, H., Samborska, V., Ahuja N., Ortiz-Ospina, E., & Roser, M. (2023). Global education. Published online at OurWorldInData.org. https://ourworldindata.org/global-education [Online Resource].

Sivasubramonian, S. (2004). *The sources of economic growth in India: 1950–51 to 1999–2000.* Oxford University Press.

Sundaram, K. (2007). Employment and poverty in India, 2000–2005. *Economic and Political Weekly, 42*(30), 3121–3131.

Rodrik, D., & Subramanian, A. (2004). *From "Hindu growth" to productivity surge: The mystery of the Indian growth transition* (IMF working paper, no. WP/04/77, 2004), International Monetary Fund.

Timmer, M. P., Inklaar, R., O'Mahony, M., & Van Ark, B. (2010). *Economic growth in Europe: A comparative industry perspective.* Cambridge University Press.

Total Economy Database (2022, April). https://conference-board.org/data/economydatabase/total-economy-database-productivity.

Trevedi, P., Prakash, A., & Sinate, D. (2000). *Productivity in major manufacturing industries in India: 1973–74 to 1997–98.* Development Research Group Study No. 20, Department of Economic Analysis and Policy, Reserve Bank of India, Mumbai.

Unni, J., Lalitha, N., & Rani, U. (2001). Economic reforms and productivity trends in Indian manufacturing. *Economic and Political Weekly, 36*(41), 3914–3922.

Virmani, A. (2004). *Economic reforms: Policy and institutions - Some lessons from Indian reforms* (Working Paper No. 121). Indian Council for Research on International Economic Relations, New Delhi.

Visaria, P. (1996). Structure of Indian workforce, 1961–1994, *Indian Journal of Labour Economics*, 725–739.

Bishwanath Goldar is a retired professor of Economics at the Institute of Economic Growth (IEG), Delhi. He was a member of the National Statistical Commission and a national fellow of the Indian Council of Social Science Research (ICSSR). He was a professor at the Indian Council for Research on International Economic Relations (ICRIER), New Delhi, during 2003–2004 and a visiting professor at the Centre for International Trade and Development, School of International Studies, Jawaharlal Nehru University, New Delhi, during 2012–2013. He is currently a non-resident senior fellow at the Institute of Economic Growth. He has many publications in economic journals. His areas of research interest include productivity measurement, industry, trade, foreign direct investment, industrial pollution, energy use of industries, river water pollution, and rural water supply.

Dibyendu Maiti is a professor of Economics at the Delhi School of Economics, University of Delhi, India. He specialises in development macroeconomics and international economics, with a specific focus on labour, technology, and the informal sector. Before this, he worked at the University of the South Pacific, Institute of Economic Growth, Delhi, and Centre for Studies in Social Sciences, Calcutta, as well as held various research positions at the University of Manchester, University of Nottingham, Max Planck Institute of Economics (Jena), Norwegian Institute of International Affairs, University of Oslo. He received the Max Planck India Fellowship, ICSSR-ESRC exchange and ICSSR-CASS exchange fellowship. He publishes research articles in reputed journals, like the Journal of Development Economics, Empirical Economics, Social Research Indicators, Journal of Productivity Analysis, Labour Economics, Economic Modelling, International Review of Economics and Finance, Cambridge Journal of Economics, American Behavioural Scientists, etc. He received the IDRC Young India Social Sciences Award in 2010 and the Global Development Network Award in 2009.

Suresh Chand Aggarwal retired as Professor and Head of the Department of Finance and Business Economics (earlier known as Business Economics), University of Delhi. Prof. Aggarwal is currently a Visiting Professor at the Institute for Human Development, Delhi. He was an ICSSR's Senior Fellow for two years, 2018–19, and has been the Principal Investigator in E-Content Development for Post Graduate Courses in Business Economics under E–PGpathshala by UGC. He has worked for ILO and has been an external Consultant to Reserve Bank of India and ICRIER. He contributed as a Lead Researcher on labour in an RBI funded project on India KLEMS database from 2010 to 2021. Prof Aggarwal has guided research to a number of students and has published extensively in national and international Journals. Most of his published work are on labour,industry and inclusive growth.

Abdul Azeez Erumban is an assistant professor at the Faculty of Economics and Business (FEB) and a fellow at the FEB's Research Institute, University of Groningen, the Netherlands. His research focuses on productivity, technological change, structural change, digital transformation, globalisation, global value chains, and international comparisons of economic development. He maintains an interest in economic issues within emerging markets, notably India, China, Latin America, and the Middle East. Actively engaged in World-KLEMS initiatives, Erumban maintains strong relationships with international productivity research networks. He has contributed to the Reserve Bank of India's India KLEMS project and the European Commission's World Input–Output Database project. He has corporate experience as a Senior Economist at the Conference Board and has been involved in several consulting for international organisations, including the OECD, the World Bank, and the ILO. His key publications are in the Journal of Economic Perspectives, World Development, Review of Income and Wealth, Journal of Comparative Economics, Industrial and Corporate Change, and Structural Change and Economic Dynamics.

Pilu Chandra Das is an assistant professor in the economics department at Kidderpore College, University of Calcutta. He has an MA in economics and M.Phil. from the Delhi School of Economics, University of Delhi. His M.Phil. thesis was on "Total Factor Productivity in Indian Organised Manufacturing: the story of the Noughties", dealing with productivity in the Indian registered manufacturing sector. He has been associated with the India KLEMS project since 2012. His research interest is mostly in productivity, and he has been a co-author of several papers prepared under the India KLEMS project. He has several published papers. Earlier, he was associated with ICRIER as a research assistant in a project named "Estimating Domestic Value Added and Foreign Content in India's Exports" sponsored by the Department of Economic Affairs, Ministry of Finance, Government of India.

Chapter 3
Economic Growth in India: A Longer View

M. Parameswaran and Pulapre Balakrishnan

Abstract This chapter investigates the trajectory of economic growth in India in the post-independence period. The study identifies various phases of growth of aggregate GDP and its sectors using the methodology of Bai and Perron (*Econometrica* 66:47–78, 1998). The methodology has the advantage that it is immune to the researcher's prior beliefs. The chapter discusses the growth phases of the aggregate economy, thus, identifies their origins in terms of sectoral growth changes. In the last section, the chapter discusses the significance of the growth accelerations of the economy and the different explanations provided.

Keywords Economic growth · Growth regimes · Indian economy

3.1 Introduction

India, being home to the largest population in the world, faster economic growth and consequent prosperity has the potential to make it one of the largest markets with all its associated benefits. Further, as India also has the highest number of poor people in the world, faster growth can also lift them out of poverty (see Nitnaware, 2022; UNDP & OPHI, 2022). Mainly, these two considerations have attracted the attention of the scholars and general public to the performance of the Indian economy and its underlying factors, including the policy regime. This chapter explores the trajectory of economic growth in India in the post-independence period. The focus is on identifying the different phases of economic growth and discussing the explanations provided for the observed growth transition.

M. Parameswaran (✉) · P. Balakrishnan
Centre for Development Studies, Thiruvananthapuram, Kerala, India
e-mail: parameswaran@cds.edu

D. Maiti et al. (eds.), *75 Years of Growth, Development and Productivity in India*, India Studies in Business and Economics, https://doi.org/10.1007/978-981-97-8054-9_3

To identify the growth regimes of aggregate GDP and its sectors, we use a methodology based onBai and Perron (1998).[1] The methodology has the advantage that the identification of different growth phases is independent of the researcher's beliefs and, therefore, satisfies the maxim of 'allowing the data to speak freely' (Hoover et al., 2008). This chapter is organized as follows. Section II explains the methodology and data, Section III discusses the results and Section IV discusses the significance of each shift in GDP growth rate. Then, the various explanations provided for growth accelerations. The last section concludes the chapter.

3.2 Identifying Growth Phases: Methodology

We estimate the trend growth rate of aggregate GDP and its sectors using the specification

$$lnY_t = a + gt + u_t$$

where, lnY, g, t and u denote the log of GDP, the growth rate, the time trend and a random disturbance term, respectively. The subscript t denotes time. As we are considering 73 years of data—from 1950–1951 to 2022–2023—the parameters, a and g need not be constant, varying across different growth regimes, making it necessary to identify the breakpoints of the above regression model. Therefore, we first estimate the break dates of the above regression model for aggregate and sectoral GDP. Next, based on these estimated break dates, we estimate period-wise growth rates.

The above regression model containing $m + 1$ growth regimes and therefore m break dates ($T_1, \ldots, T_m$) can be written as follows:

$$\begin{aligned} nY_t &= a_1 + g_1 t + u_t, & t &= 1, \ldots, T_1 \\ lnY_t &= a_2 + g_2 t + u_t, & t &= T_1 + 1, \ldots, T_2 \\ &\vdots \\ lnY_t &= a_{m+1} + g_{m+1} t + u_t, & t &= T_m + 1, \ldots, T \end{aligned} \quad (3.1)$$

We adopt the convention that $T_0 = 0$ and $T_{m+1} = T$, the total number of observations. The number of breakpoints m and the break dates ($T_1, \ldots, T_m$) are treated as unknown and estimated from the data. The Bai and Perron (1998) method allows for the simultaneous estimation of multiple breaks in a time series. The break dates are estimated as global minimizers of the sum of squared residuals from an OLS regression of (1) using a dynamic programming algorithm (Bai & Perron, 2003). The procedure is as follows. Given the number of breaks m, for each partition ($T_1, \ldots, T_m$) denoted $\{T_P\}$,

[1] Balakrishnan and Parameswaran (2007) uses this methodology to identify the growth regimes of aggregate GDP and the description of the methodology in this chapter closely follows that one given in that paper.

the associated least squares estimates $\beta_p = (a, g)_p$ are obtained by minimizing the sum of squared residuals $\sum_{j=1}^{m+1} \sum_{t=T_{j-1}+1}^{T_j} [lnY_t - a_j - g_j t]^2$. The resulting estimates $\hat{\beta}_P$ are used to compute the sum of squared residuals—denoted $S_T(T_1, ..., T_m)$—associated with the partition $\{T_P\}$. Now the estimated breakpoints $(\hat{T}_1, ..., \hat{T}_m)$ are such that $(\hat{T}_1, ..., \hat{T}_m) = argmin_{(T_1,...,T_m)} S_T(T_1, ..., T_m)$, , where the minimization is done over all possible partitions $(T_1, ..., T_m)$ subject to $T_i - T_{i-1} \geq h$. Note that h is the minimum length assigned to a segment and T_i is the ith break point. The procedure considers all possible combination of segments and selects the partition that minimizes the sum of squared residuals. Thus, the least squares estimates of break dates are those that minimize the full-sample sum of squared residuals in (3.1).

The above procedure sequentially computes optimal breakpoints starting from one to the maximum permitted by T and h. In Bai and Perron (1998), if the number of breakpoints is unknown, a test based on the *supF* statistic is proposed to choose the number of breakpoints. As this testing procedure assumes non-trending regressors, it is inapplicable in the present context. An alternative approach which accommodates trending regressors is to use the Bayesian Information Criteria (BIC) (Bai & Perron, 2003; Uctum et al., 2006). Here, the number of breaks selected is that for which BIC is at a minimum. We adopt this procedure to choose the number of breaks. This criterion is particularly appropriate when multiple breaks are considered because it introduces a penalty factor for additional breakpoints, which necessarily reduces the sum of squared residuals,[2] as is apparent from below:

$$BIC(m) = \ln \hat{\sigma}^2(m) + p^* \ln(T)/T$$

$$p^* = (m+1)q + m + p$$

$$\hat{\sigma}^2 = T^{-1} \sum_{t=1}^{T} \hat{u}_t^2$$

where. m is the number of breaks, q is the number of explanatory variables whose coefficients are subject to shift and p is the number of explanatory variables whose coefficients are constant.

3.3 Data and Estimation

We use data on aggregate GDP and its sectors, at factor cost, obtained from National Account Statistics, MOSPI. The GDP series are in 2011–2012 prices and cover the period 1950–1951 to 2022–2023. The data for the year 2021–2022 are second

[2] See Bai and Perron (2003) for a comparison of the performance of BIC and *supF* statistic.

Table 3.1 List of sectors

No	Sector	Short name
1	Agriculture, forestry and fishing	AFF
2	Mining and quarrying	MINE
3	Manufacturing	MANU
4	Electricity, gas, water supply & other utility services	EGW
5	Construction	CON
6	Trade, repair, hotels and restaurants	THR
7	Transport, storage, communication & services related to broadcasting	TSC
8	Financial services	FINANCE
9	Real estate, ownership of dwellings & professional services	REALESTATE
10	Public administration and defence	PUBLICADMIN
11	Other services	OTHERSERVICES
12	Aggregate GDP	GDP

revised estimates and that for the year 2022–2023 are first revised estimates. Table 3.1 presents the list of the sectors with their name in short form.

As in Balakrishnan and Parameswaran (2007), in the estimation of break dates, the minimum length of a segment, h. Given the length of the time series, this implies a maximum number of 8 breakpoints and 9 growth regimes. Further, a minimum length of eight for a segment also implies that the search for break dates is now confined to the period 1958–1959 to 2014–2015. The break dates have been estimated allowing for a shift in both intercept (a) and slope coefficient (g)—the case of 'pure structural change'. The growth rates across regimes are estimated using the methodology given by Boyce (1986). Boyce's procedure imposes continuity at the breakpoints while estimating the above regression model in order to avoid certain anomalies that could emerge in the estimation of kinked exponential growth models. While estimating the growth rates, we also noted that the year 2020–2021, the year of the COVID-19 epidemic, was 'influential' in most of the cases.[3] Therefore, we included a dummy variable in the growth regression that takes the value 1 for the year 2020–2021 and zero for all the other years. Now, the coefficient of the dummy variable estimates the rate of decline in GDP from its trend value in the year 2020–2021.

[3] We computed DFBETA values for all the regressions, i.e., GDP and its sectors, and found that the absolute value of DFBETA is highest in the year 2020-21, and also either close to or more than the cut off value of 1 suggested by Bollen and Jackman (1990).

3.4 Results and Discussion

The estimated break dates are presented in Table 3.2. The parenthesis below the reported breakpoint contains the 95% confidence interval of the estimated breakpoint. The following points can be drawn from the Table. Aggregate GDP has three breaks: 1978–1979, 1990–1991 and 2014–2015. The confidence intervals of the first two break dates are quite narrow, suggesting a precise estimation of the break dates. Different from the first two breakpoints, the confidence interval of the last breakpoint is wide—between 2009-2010 and 2015–2016. The first break date of the aggregate GDP, 1978–1979, is also identified in earlier studies by Wallack (2003), Hatekar and Dongre (2005) and Balakrishnan and Parameswaran (2007). The number of breakpoints in the sectors vary from six break dates in Mining and Quarrying (MINE) and three break dates in Agriculture, Forestry and Fishing (AFF), Trade, Hotels and Restaurants (THR) and Transport, Storage and Communication (TSC).

Table 3.3 presents the estimated growth rates, and the brackets below contain the period of the reported growth rates. The row named D20 reports the coefficient of the dummy variable for the year 2020–2021. The coefficient is multiplied by 100, so the reported numbers are the percentage decline in GDP in the year 2020–2021 from its trend value. The following points can be inferred from the growth rate estimates.

Aggregate GDP growth has four different phases during the 73 years of the post-independence period. In the first phase, covering the period 1950–1951 to 1978–1979, the economy recorded a growth rate of 3.5%. In the second and third phases, covering the periods 1979–1980 to 1990–1991 and 1991–1992 to 2014–2015, the GDP growth rate increased continuously, from 4.3% to 6.2%, respectively, in periods II and III. However, in the last phase, 2015–2016 to 2022–2023, the growth rate declined to 5.8%. The acceleration in growth from 1991 to 1992 (1.95 percentage points) is much higher than that from 1979 to 1980 (0.76 percentage points). This result contradicts the argument of Rodrik and Subramanian (2005:195) that the growth acceleration in the early 1980s is more than that due to the genuine liberalization in 1991, which, according to them, 'added very little to aggregate economic performance'. Note, however, that they had far fewer observations in post-1991 (up to 2000–2001) to work with than we do today.

It is difficult to trace the shift in GDP growth rate in a particular year to shifts in the growth rate of particular sectors in years close to the shifts in aggregate GDP. Some sectors record shifts in their growth rate long before and some long after the shifts in the growth rate of aggregate GDP, and both these shifts can, respectively, generate and sustain shifts in GDP growth rate. Regarding the sectoral sources of shifts in the growth rate of aggregate GDP from 1979 to 1980, five sectors, namely Agriculture, Forestry and Fishing, Mining and Quarrying, Construction, Financial Services and Real estate, Ownership of Dwellings and Professional Services recorded an increase in their growth rate in the years near 1979–1980. Regarding the second shift in GDP growth from 1990 to 1991, the sectors that registered higher growth rates around this year are Manufacturing, Trade, Repair, Hotels and Restaurants and Transport, Storage, Communication and Services related to Broadcasting. Similarly, the sectors

Table 3.2 Estimated breakpoints

Break	ALFF	MINE	MANU	EGW	CON	THR
1	1694–1665 (–) [1958/59 – 1965/66]	1959–1960 (+) [1958/59 – 1960/61]	1965–1966 (–) [1964/65 – 1966/67]	1957–1958 (+) [1956/57 – 1959/60]	1969–1970 (–) [1968/69 – 1970/71]	1970–1971 (+) [1969/70 – 1971/72]
2	1978–1979 (+) [1974/75 – 1980/81]	1969–1970 (–) [1968/69 – 1970/71]	1994–1995 (+) [1993/94 – 1996/97]	1967–1968 (–) [1966/67 – 1968/69]	1981–1982 (+) [1980/81 – 1983/84]	1994–1995 (+) [1993/94 – 1995/96]
3	2001–2002 (+) [1999/00 – 2002/03]	1979–1980 (+) [1978/79 - 1982/83]	2005–2006 (+) [2004/05 – 2006/07]	1985–1986 (+) [1984/85 – 1991/92]	2000–2001 (+) [1999/00 – 2001/02]	2014–2015 (–) [1999/00 – 2015/16]
4		1987–1988 (–) [1986/87 – 1988/89]	2014–2015 (–) [2010/11 – 2015/16]	1999–1900 (–) [1998/99 – 2000/01]	2008–2009 (–) [2007/08 – 2009/10]	
5		2006–2007 (–) [2004/05 – 2007/08]				
6		2014–2015 (–) [2013/14 – 2015/16]				
Break	TSC	FINANCE	REALESTATE	PUBLICADMIN	OTHERSERVICES	GDP
1	1993–1994 (+) [1992/93 – 1994/95]	1965–1966 (–) [1960/61 – 1966/67]	1964–1965 (+) [1963/64 – 1965/66]	1961–1962 (+) [1960/61 – 1963/64]	1984–1985 (+) [1983/84 – 1985/86]	1978–1979 (+) [1977/78 – 1979/80]
2	2003–2004 (–) [2002/03 – 2004/05]	1979–1980 (+) [1978/79 – 1980/81]	1979–1980 (+) [1978/79 – 1980/81]	1972–1973 (–) [1971/72 – 1974/75]	2003–2004 (+) [2002/03 – 2004/05]	1990–1991 (+) [1989/90 – 1991/92]
3	2014–2015 (–) [2012/13 – 2015/16]	1999–1900 (–) [1998/99 – 2000/01]	1990–1991 (–) [1989/90 – 1991/92]	1985–1986 (+) [1982/83 – 1986/87]	2014–2015 (–) [2013/14 – 2015/16]	2014–2015 (–) [2009/10 – 2015/16]
4		2014–2015 (–) [2013/14 – 2015/16]	1998–1999 (–) [1997/98 – 1999/00]	1997–1998 (+) [1996/97 – 1998/99]		
5			2013–2014 (+) [2012/13 – 2014/15]	2007–2008 (–) [2006/07 – 2008/09]		

Notes (1) 95% confidence intervals of break dates are given in brackets. (2) The signs + and –, in parentheses, indicate acceleration and deceleration, respectively

Table 3.3 Estimated growth rates (in per cent)

Period	ALFF	MINE	MANU	EGW	CON	THR
1	2.19 1950/51 – 1964/65]	4.78 [1950/51 – 1959/60]	5.95 [1950/51 – 1965/66]	8.70 [1950/51 – 1957/58]	6.56 [1950/51 – 1969/70]	4.74 [1950/51 – 1970/71]
2	2.12 [1965/66 – 1978/79]	5.55 [1960/61 – 1969/70]	4.74 [1966/67 – 1994/95]	12.10 [1958/59 – 1967/68]	2.19 [1970/71 – 1981/82]	5.01 [1971/72 – 1994/95]
3	2.86 [1979/80 – 2001/02]	2.79 [1970/71 – 1979/80]	6.86 [1995/96 – 2005/06]	7.33 [1968/69 – 1985/86]	4.68 [1982/83 – 2000/01]	8.13 [1995/96 – 2014/15]
4	3.22 [2002/03 – 2022/23]	8.53 [1980/81 – 1987/88]	7.82 [2006/07 – 2014/15]	7.45 [1986/87 – 1999/00]	10.70 [2001/02 – 2008/09]	6.49 [2015/16 – 2022/23]
5		5.08 [1988/89 – 2006/07]	5.24 [2015/16 – 2022/23]	5.70 [2000/01 – 2022/23]	5.27 [2009/10 – 2022/23]	
6		1.99 [2007/08 – 2014/15]				
7		1.34 [2015/16 – 2022/23]				
D20	3.64	−10.30	−3.91	−6.02	−14.00	−18.70

Period	TSC	FINANCE	REALESTATE	PUBLICADMIN	OTHERSERVICES	GDP
1	5.67 1950/51 – 1993/94]	6.58 [1950/51 – 1965/66]	2.42 [1950/51 – 1964/65]	5.88 [1950/51 – 1961/62]	3.25 [1950/51 – 1984/85]	3.49 [1950/51 – 1978/79]
2	9.41 [1994/95 – 2003/04]	6.06 [1966/67 – 1979/80]	2.69 [1965/66 – 1979/80]	7.23 [1962/63 – 1972/73]	6.03 [1985/86 – 2003/04]	4.25 [1979/80 – 1990/91]
3	8.75 [2004/05 – 2014/15]	9.63 [1980/81 – 1999/00]	7.32 [1980/81 – 1990/91]	5.19 [1973/74 – 1985/86]	10.10 [2004/05 – 2014/15]	6.20 [1991/92 – 2014/15]
4	4.25 [2015/16 – 2022/23]	7.78 [2000/01 – 2014/15]	6.93 [1991/92 – 1998/99]	5.80 [1986/87 – 1997/98]	6.03 [2015/16 – 2022/23]	5.76 [2015/16 – 2022/23]

(continued)

Table 3.3 (continued)

Period	TSC	FINANCE	REALESTATE	PUBLICADMIN	OTHERSERVICES	GDP
5		4.73 [2015/16 – 2022/23]	6.62 [1999/00 – 2013/14]	5.86 [1998/99 – 2007/08]		
6			7.85 [2014/15 – 2022/23]	5.78 [2008/09 – 2022/23]		
D20	−20.30	0.45#	−5.25	−2.86#	−13.10	−7.65

Notes All growth rates and coefficient of the D20-21 dummy are statistically significant, except those marked with #

that recorded a decline in their growth rate in years near to 2014–2015 are Mining and Quarrying, Manufacturing, Trade, Repair, Hotels and Restaurants and Transport, Storage, Communication and Services related to Broadcasting, Financial Services and Other Services.

Using the methodology explained in the Appendix, Table 3.4 presents the average contribution of sectors to change in the GDP growth rate in a period over the previous period.[4] The table also gives the standard aggregation of sectors, namely Primary, Secondary and Tertiary. The table shows that Period II (1979–1980 to 1990–1991) recorded 0.76 percentage point increase in the growth rate compared to the Period I. This increase in the growth rate is overwhelmingly contributed by the tertiary sector, with substantial contributions from Real Estate, Ownership of Dwellings and Professional Services (35.3%), Financial Services (16%) and Public Administration and Defence (15%). Period III (1990–1991 to 2014–2015) recorded a 1.95 percentage point increase in the trend growth rate, and this increase is contributed by both the Secondary and Tertiary Sectors. The negative contribution of the Primary Sector (-33.9%) is more than offset by the positive contribution of the Secondary and Tertiary Sectors. In this phase, the major contributors to the increase in growth are Manufacturing, Trade, Repair, Hotels and Restaurants, Transport, Storage, Communication and Services Related to Broadcasting, Real estate, Ownership of Dwellings and Professional Services and Other Services. In Period IV (2015–2016 to 2022–2023) the GDP growth rate recorded a decline of −0.44 percentage points, and both secondary and Tertiary sectors contributed to this decline with greater contribution from Trade, Repair (34.5%), Transport, Storage, Communication and Services related to Broadcasting (46%), Financial Services (33.7) and Manufacturing (17%). Three sectors, namely Real estate, Ownership of Dwellings and Professional Services, Agriculture, Forestry and Fishing and Electricity, Gas, Water Supply and Other Utility Services contributed to reducing the decline in the growth rate of GDP.

Another notable result is the estimated decline in GDP from its trend value in the COVID-19 year, which is −7.7%. This rate of decline in GDP is higher (in absolute

[4] Note that this decomposition of the change in the growth rate of aggregate GDP into sectoral contributions captures only the direct contribution of the sectors.

Table 3.4 Contribution by sectors to change in GDP growth rate (in per cent)

Sectors	Period II	Period III	Period IV
Change in growth rate#	0.76	1.95	−0.44
ALFF	−24.6	−23.8	−7.0
MINE	14.7	−10.1	8.4
Primary Sector	**−9.9**	**−33.9**	**1.5**
MANU	5.1	23.4	17.0
EGW	6.2	−0.1	−1.2
CON	−4.5	13.2	2.2
Secondary	**6.8**	**36.6**	**18.0**
THR	11.5	33.7	34.5
TSC	10.2	23.0	46.6
FINANCE	16.1	15.4	33.7
REALESTATE	35.3	13.0	−64.5
PUBLICADMIN	15.0	−2.7	6.8
OTHERSERVICES	14.9	14.9	23.5
Tertiary Sector	**103.1**	**97.3**	**80.6**
Total	**100.0**	**100.0**	**100.0**

Notes # Change in growth rate in a period over its previous period is in percentage points

value) than the one based on annual growth rates, which is equal to −4.3%. This discrepancy between the rate of change from the trend value of GDP and the annual growth rate arises because the annual growth rate is being computed in the case of an economy whose growth rates have been declining.

The following paragraphs discuss some notable results related to the growth of various sectors of India's economy.

1. Up to 2001–2002 growth rate of Agriculture, Forestry and Fishing (AFF) remained between 2 and 3%. However, during the last period (2002–2003 to 2022–2023) its growth rate exceeded 3%. As Table 3.3 reveals, the relatively higher growth rate of AFF enabled the sector to lower the decline in GDP growth from 2015 to 2016 onwards.
2. During the first 15 years of the post-independence period, the manufacturing sector recorded a growth rate of 6%, and thereafter, for a long period of time till 1994–1995, the sector grew at less than 5%. However, from 1995 to 1996 onwards, the manufacturing sector recorded a two percentage points increase in the growth rate—growing at 6.9%. The sector registered a further increase in its growth rate during the period 2006–2007 to 2014–2015. This acceleration in the manufacturing growth rate may be reflecting the effects of the policy reforms introduced from 1991 onwards that mainly focused on the liberalization of trade and industrial policy regimes to accelerate manufacturing growth. This growth acceleration also enabled the sector to contribute to the higher growth rate of

aggregate GDP in Period III, as seen in Table 3.4. However, the superior performance of agriculture from 2002 to 2023 should also be factored in. However, from 2015 to 2016 onwards, the manufacturing sector recorded a decline of more than two percentage points in its growth rate. This decline in the growth rate of manufacturing coincides with that of the aggregate GDP, and as seen from Table 3.4, the contribution of manufacturing to the decrease in aggregate GDP is 17%. Notably, this drastic decline in the growth rate happened in the context of many policy initiatives like 'Make in India' directed at manufacturing.

3. Attesting the services-led nature of Indian economic growth, most services sectors recorded relatively higher growth rates in most of the phases. As shown in Table 3.4, both accelerations and deceleration of aggregate GDP growth are majorly contributed to by the tertiary sector. The direct contribution of the tertiary sector to the increase in GDP growth in Period II (1979–1980 to 1990–1991) is 103.1% and 97% for Period III (1991–1992 to 2014–2015). The decline in GDP growth after 2015–2016 is also mainly contributed to by the tertiary sector (80.6%).

3.5 Explaining the Growth Transitions

In this section, we first discuss the significance of the growth transitions in the Indian economy in the post-independence period as depicted in Fig. 3.1. It is important to note that the major growth transition in the Indian economy happened in 1952–1953. Using 120 years' GDP data for the period 1900–1901 to 2019–2020, Balakrishnan et al. (2020) show that the growth transition in 1952–1953 is major in terms of the extent of increase in the growth rate—trend growth rate increased by 5.5 percentage points.

Figures 3.2 and 3.3, respectively, plot the evolution of per capita income of India relative to that of the world and developed regions, namely OECD and North America. The figures show that until 1979–1980, the per capita income of India relative to that of the world and developed regions was declining. From 1979 to 1980 onwards, the per capita income of the country relative to the world increased, and relative to developed regions, was constant in the 1980s. This implies that during the 20 years from 1960 to 1980, the per capita income of India was growing at a rate less than that of the world and developed countries, resulting in the deteriorating relative position of the country. However, the first growth transition of 1979–1980 enabled the country to grow faster than the world and almost equal with respect to developed regions. The second growth transition in 1991–1992, which witnessed an increase in the GDP growth rate by two percentage points, is much more significant in terms of relative performance. From 1991 to 1992 onwards, the per capita income of the country relative to that of the world and developed regions increased—implying that the Indian economy was growing faster than the developed regions, marking the beginning of a catching-up process.

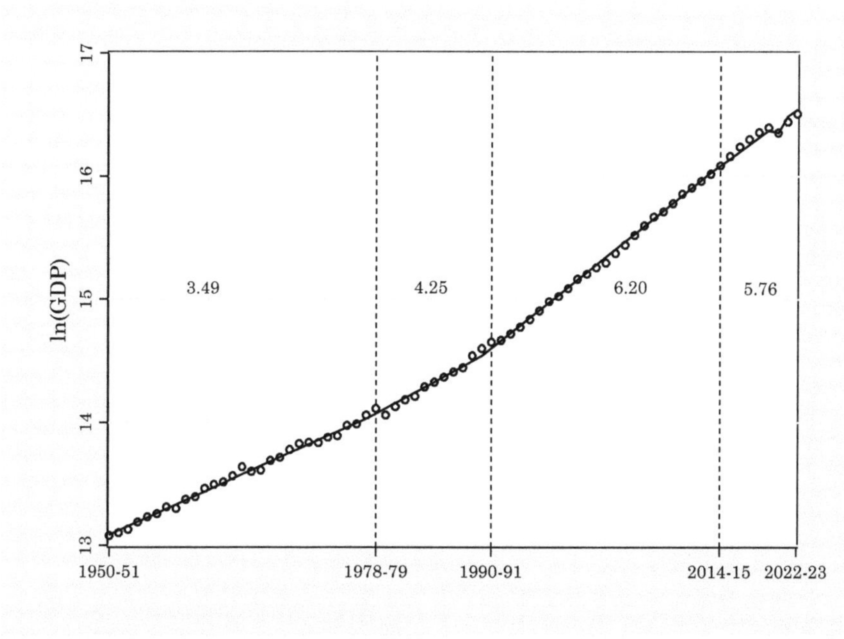

Fig. 3.1 Growth phases of the Indian economy

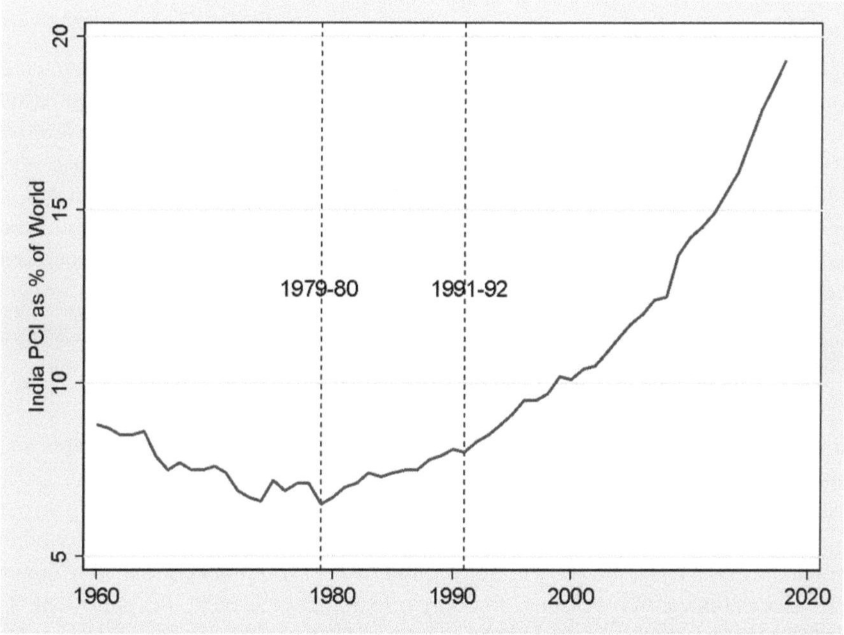

Fig. 3.2 Per capita income (PCI) of Indian as per cent of world PCI. *Source* World Development Indicators Database

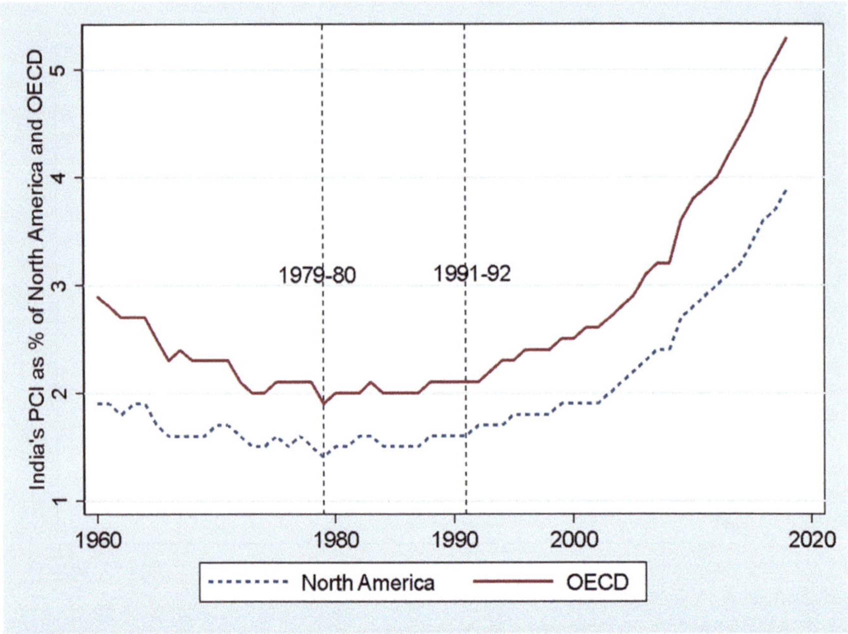

Fig. 3.3 Per capita income of India as per cent of OECD and North America. *Source* World Development Indicators Database

A story of India's post-independence economic growth commonly encountered runs as follows. The policy regime in the early stages consisted of detailed regulation of the private sector, wider public sector participation and industrialization behind tariff walls. Consequently, India had inefficient industries. The outcome was a very moderate growth of the economy. It required the policy of liberalization initiated in 1991, following a balance of payments crisis, which led to the dismantling of the licence-permit raj to usher in faster economic growth. For instance, to quote Sen et al., (2017: 250):

> After a prolonged period of low economic growth since independence (famously known as the "Hindu rate of growth"), India has transitioned to a high growth trajectory since the early 1990s.

However, as we have seen above, the first acceleration in economic growth happened more than a decade before the beginning of the economic policy reforms in 1991, and this acceleration is significant as it enabled the country to start improving its per capita income vis-a-vis the rest of the world. Unlike the acceleration in economic growth in 1990–1991, the acceleration around 1979–1980 is not correlated with any serious economic policy reforms, prodding researchers to search for explanations. In the following paragraphs, we review three papers that try to provide an explanation for the observed growth trajectory of the Indian economy. The first two papers attempt to explain the first acceleration around 1979–1980, and the last one tries to explain the repeated periodic acceleration of the economy. The last part of this section discusses different explanations provided for the deceleration in growth since 2015–2016.

Rodrik and Subramanian (2005) and political scientists Kohli (2006a, 2006b) have argued that the acceleration in India's economic growth occurred primarily due to a change in the attitude of the national government under Prime Minister Indira Gandhi towards India's private sector. Rodrik and Subramanian (2005) (henceforth RS) further elaborated this argument and tested its empirical validity. RS drew a distinction between the *pro-market* and *pro-business* orientation of the government. A pro-market orientation focuses on enabling the full-fledged functioning of the market and aims to achieve this through economic liberalization. A pro-business orientation, in contrast, favours existing industries aiming to raise their profitability. Easing restrictions on capacity expansion for incumbents, removing price controls and reducing corporate taxes are examples of pro-business policies. RS observe that all of these happened in India in the 1980s and are best described as pro-business rather than pro-market policies. According to RS, the attitudinal change became a powerful trigger because of India's good initial conditions in terms of economic and political institutions. They argued that India's per capita income was several times lower than what is warranted by its relatively superior economic and political institutions. In this way, they describe India as an under-performer in the 1960s and 1970s, and hence relatively minor changes in the policy environment can produce a large growth impact. The registered manufacturing sector is argued to be the major beneficiary of the attitudinal shift, as this segment is subjected to detailed rules and regulations, and therefore, this sector is postulated to play a key role in accelerating economic growth. Therefore, in the empirical testing of the attitudinal shift argument, RS focused on the growth of registered manufacturing and showed that its growth was higher in the 1980s and 1990s in those states which were ruled by the Congress party or its allies. One serious problem with the attitudinal shift argument is that, even if it is true, its potential to generate an economy-wide growth acceleration is doubtful. The registered manufacturing sector accounted for around 8.5% of aggregate GDP in the 1970s, and hence its ability to lift the aggregate GDP growth is questionable, as the implied multiplier effect is very high. Further, as shown in Table 3.4, there was no acceleration in the growth of manufacturing either in the 1970s or in the 1980s. Manufacturing growth registered an acceleration only from 1995 to 1996. Table 3.4 also reveals that the acceleration in GDP growth from 1979 to 1980 was overwhelmingly contributed by the services sectors, and the contribution of the secondary sector, which consists of manufacturing, was very low.

Sen (2007) re-examined the underlying reasons for the acceleration of the Indian economic growth around the early 1980s. The study shows that after 1975, there was a significant increase in the rate of equipment investment by the private corporate sector, helping the sector to absorb the latest technology. Sen shows that the rate of equipment investment has a statistically significant positive effect on per capita GDP growth. The increase in the rate of equipment investment was attributed to the decline in the relative price of capital goods due to the liberalization of its import and financial deepening owning to bank nationalization. Similar to the attitudinal shift argument, Sen (2007) also traces the sources of growth acceleration to a tiny part of the manufacturing sector, namely the corporate sector and hence subject to all the weaknesses of the attitudinal shift argument.

A notable weakness of the attitudinal shift argument and equipment investment explanations of Indian growth acceleration is the omission of an important feature of India's growth story—that is, most of the early growth accelerations were largely driven by the services sector. Balakrishnan et al. (2017) present a model which generates increasing growth rates over time through cumulative causation arising from the positive feedback relationship between the manufacturing and services sectors.[5]

The theoretical model focuses on *producer services* which enter manufacturing production as intermediate inputs. Though there is no explicit modelling of the agriculture sector, the implicit assumption is that agriculture is characterized by surplus labour with a constant marginal product of labour. Hence, labour migrates from agriculture to manufacturing over time as long as the wage rate in manufacturing is higher than the constant wage rate in agriculture. The manufacturing sector uses labour and a variety of specialized services as complementary inputs (along the lines of Dixit & Stiglitz, 1977). Manufacturing production is carried out by perfectly competitive firms, which are price takers. Therefore, each of the inputs entering into manufacturing production gets paid its marginal product. Also, the complementarity between labour and specialized inputs in manufacturing production means that greater employment of one input increases the marginal productivity of the other.

The specialized inputs for manufacturing production are supplied by the service sector firms, which operate as local monopolists. A fixed set-up cost is associated with the production of each variety of service input. Hence, the production of specialized inputs is not viable until the manufacturing production reaches a certain scale and there is sufficient demand for these inputs. However, once the minimum scale requirement is met, higher manufacturing production generates higher demand and, therefore, higher profits for the services sector. Excess profits generated in the service sector are reinvested in the same sector to produce newer varieties of producer services. As these newer varieties are employed in manufacturing production in the next period, the productivity of labour in manufacturing goes up, thereby drawing more labour to manufacturing. This increase in the scale of manufacturing makes the production of newer varieties of services profitable and this leads to further increase in manufacturing productivity.

Two interrelated and dynamic mechanisms drive growth in Balakrishnan, Das and Parameswaran model. These are (a) the dynamics associated with augmented varieties (i.e., increasing specialization in production) and (b) the dynamics associated with the movement of labour from agriculture to manufacturing (i.e., the process of migration). Let n denote the number of varieties, and L denote the number of workers employed in manufacturing production at any point in time. Notice that n captures the degree of specialization, while L is a proxy for the scale of manufacturing production. One can then derive the following laws of motion that govern the dynamics of n and L, respectively:

[5] This part of the discussion draws largely on Balakrishnan et al. (2021).

i. Given the fixed cost associated with production of specialized inputs, the growth rate of n is a positive function of the scale of manufacturing production;
ii. Given the constant wage rate in agriculture, the growth rate of L is a positive function of the productivity of labour in manufacturing production.[6]

Noting that the scale of manufacturing is represented by L and that labour productivity in manufacturing production is positively related to n (due to the assumed complementarity in manufacturing production), these two dynamic mechanisms now create a positive feedback loop such that as n increases, the growth rate of L goes up, and as L increases, the growth rate of n goes up. Indeed, this positive feedback loop (capturing a process of cumulative causation) generates accelerating growth in the model.

To understand how the mechanics of cumulative causation works here, let us begin with some (n, L) combinations. Now, suppose L goes up (due to some external reason). This would now set in motion a chain of events as follows. An increased flow of labour into manufacturing production will raise demand for the complementary specialized inputs. This, in turn, will raise the profitability of each of the existing specialized inputs. Higher profits are then invested in augmenting the variety of specialized inputs, which means more such inputs would be available for manufacturing production in the next period. This would raise the productivity of labour in manufacturing production. The higher marginal product of labour and the concomitant higher wages in manufacturing relative to agriculture will then draw in more labour from agriculture, expanding the scale of operation of the manufacturing sector even further.

This virtuous cycle of ever-increasing varieties and ever-expanding productivity of labour generates a process of *accelerating* growth in manufacturing production. To see how note that the growth rate of manufacturing is the sum of the growth rate of L and the growth rate of n. Now consider a one-shot increase in L, which raises the growth rate of n (by the law of motion specified in (i)). Had there been no other effect, then this one-shot increase in L would have raised the growth rate of manufacturing once and for all, and there would have been no continued acceleration. However, the rise in n now activates the law of motion for L (as specified in (ii)) such that L grows further and at a higher rate. This way, the growth of manufacturing *accelerates* not just because both n and L keep increasing but because as they increase, they feed into each other's growth rate, thereby *increasing* the growth rates of L and n simultaneously! The increasing growth rate of manufacturing is accompanied by an increasing growth rate of the producer services as well (since higher manufacturing growth implies increasing demand for specialized inputs). In other words, the cumulative causation implied in the model will result in an accelerating growth rate for the non-agricultural sector.

---

[6] The fact that these laws of motion are defined as growth rates, and not as absolute changes, indicate presence of knowledge externalities in production of newer varieties (ceteris paribus, higher existing varieties imply greater production of new varieties) and presence of network externalities in the migration process (ceteris paribus, greater number of workers employed in manufacturing draws in more labourers from agriculture to manufacturing).

Two caveats apply. First, due to the existence of a fixed cost in the production of specialized inputs, the process of cumulative causation leading to accelerating growth does not operate until the size of manufacturing production is large enough. Secondly, the process of cumulative causation will stop working if the flow of labour from agriculture to the manufacturing sector dries up. The labour migration process could come to a halt either because the surplus labour in agriculture has been exhausted or because the productivity in agriculture has risen. Both will lower the relative wage gap between manufacturing and agriculture, thereby slowing down the labour absorption rate in manufacturing production.

The model is actually characterized by multiple possible equilibrium trajectories in the long run. There exists a lower equilibrium where the manufacturing and services sectors stagnate at a very low level and a higher equilibrium with large and growing manufacturing and services sectors. In the absence of any external stimulus, a poor economy can remain stuck at the lower equilibrium permanently. This creates the scope for state intervention in the form of massive investment in manufacturing and services sectors, thereby activating the positive feedback mechanism and generating accelerating growth.

Balakrishnan et al. (2017) empirically tested the implications of the model using data for the period 1950–1951 to 2009–2010. As the presence of positive feedback between the two sectors of the non-agricultural economy implies a long-run equilibrium relationship among them, the study used a cointegration methodology. The paper shows that the time series of the GDP of manufacturing and producer services—they together account for around 85% of total GDP—display 'segmented cointegration', i.e., the series are co-integrated but for a segment of this period, namely from 1965–1966 to 2009–2010.

Our interpretation of the finding of segmented cointegration between the manufacturing and services sectors of the Indian economy was as follows. Large-scale public investment and an increase in the rate of growth of agricultural production, which commenced in the fifties, enabled the economy to reach a scale necessary for the mechanism of cumulative causation envisaged in the theoretical model to start operating from around the mid-1960s. It is plausible that the Nehru-Mahalanobis Strategy, which had been involved in raising public investment across the economy put the economy on a trajectory of periodically accelerating growth.[7] Further, the acceleration of growth after 1991 fits into the model of accelerating growth through cumulative causation. In the model, positive exogenous shocks like greater public investment or faster agricultural growth can alter the growth of manufacturing and, thereby, the overall economic growth. In fact, shocks like these were likely to have been at work during the growth transitions of the early fifties and the late seventies. Similarly, the liberalized policy allowing for greater private sector participation in the infrastructural sectors of the economy since 1991 may be seen as increasing the

[7] Interestingly Mahalanobis himself anticipated the acceleration of the economy, see Mahalanobis (1955). See also Parameswaran (2021) for a discussion on historical origins of the idea of cumulative causation and its influence on initial five-year plans in India.

range of producer services now available to manufacturing. In addition, the deregulation of industrial and trade policy regimes, by easing the entry and exit of firms, must have also lubricated the mechanism of cumulative causation.

Growth Slowdown Since 2015–2016: A few authors have explored the possible reasons for the growth slowdown since 2015–2016. However, as not many years have elapsed since the onset of the slowdown, and it is also intertwined with the COVID-19 shock, a detailed and rigorous analysis of the factors behind the slowdown is yet to come. We provide a snapshot of the various explanations, starting with examining the trends in investment in India during the past decade, as it is the proximate determinant of economic growth, particularly in developing countries. Table 3.5 shows that, over the past decade, the investment rate has not increased in India. Now, unless the productivity of capital has increased, no increase in the rate of growth may be expected. Subramanian and Felman (2019) attribute the stagnation in investment to a homegrown twin-balance-sheet crisis, which came in two waves. In the first wave, the infrastructure investment made during India's investment boom of the mid-2000s began to sour—putting the balance sheets of the banks and infrastructure companies in trouble. According to Subramanian and Fellman, still, the economy continued to grow due to a large fall in international oil prices, increased government spending and a credit boom financed by Non-Bank Financial Companies (NBFCs). This credit boom financed unsustainable real estate inventory accumulation that finally burst in 2019—putting the balance sheet of both NBFCs and real estate companies in red. Consequently, consumption, too, has sputtered, causing growth to collapse. Other factors arguably contributing to the slowdown in growth include demonetization (Chodorow-Reich et al., 2019) and monetary tightness (Balakrishnan, 2022). Chodorow-Reich et al. (2019) show that demonetization resulted in a reduction in economic activity and a contraction in employment. Here, it is also important to note that, though the confidence interval of the last breakpoint of the aggregate GDP is vast, the year of the onset of the slowdown coincides with the year of demonetization.

3.6 Concluding Remarks

This chapter explored the growth trajectory of the Indian economy in the post-independence period. The study uses a methodology, according to Bai and Perron (1998), that allows the identification of the growth phases of aggregate GDP and its sectors without being influenced by the researcher's beliefs. The chapter shows that aggregate GDP has increased its trend growth rate two times, first from 1979 to 1980 onwards and second from 1990 to 1991 onwards. With these two accelerations, the country started catching up with the per capita income of the world and developed regions. As the acceleration in GDP growth from 1979 to 1980 onwards is not correlated with any major policy changes, a number of explanations have been provided for it. The chapter discussed these explanations and, based on the insights

Table 3.5 Gross Fixed Capital Formation (GFCF) (as per cent of GDP)

Sector	2013–2014	2014–2015	2015–2016	2016–2017	2017–2018	2018–2019	2019–2020	2020–2021	2021–2022
Public	7.3	7.3	8.0	7.6	7.3	7.6	7.7	7.4	7.7
Private	25.3	23.9	22.7	23.2	23.7	24.3	24.8	23.6	25.0
Corporate	12.6	11.5	12.7	12.0	11.3	11.4	11.9	11.6	11.8
Household	12.6	12.3	10.0	11.2	12.4	12.9	12.9	12.0	13.2
GFCF	32.6	31.1	30.7	30.8	31.0	31.9	32.5	31.0	32.7

Source Author's calculation from *Estimates of National Income, Consumption Expenditure, Saving and Capital Formation*, published online periodically by the National Statistical Office; https://www.mospi.gov.in/sites/default/files/press_release/PressNoteNAD_28feb23final.pdf, accessed 11.9.23

drawn from the estimated growth phases of GDP and its sectors, attempted to assess the plausibility of different explanations. We believe that the insights emerging from this study are useful inputs both in devising policy and judging which of the many suggestions for quickening growth currently being made are likely to work.

Acknowledgements We thank K. L. Krishna, Bishwanath Goldar and Dibyendu Maiti for giving us an opportunity to present this study in a workshop held at the Delhi School of Economics. We thank the discussant, Sabyasachi Kar and other seminar participants for their useful comments and suggestions. We also thank Mausumi Das for earlier co-authorship on this topic. Pulapre Balakrishnan acknowledges financial support from Ashoka University. Errors and omissions, if any, would be ours.

Appendix

Decomposition of Change in Aggregate Growth Rate

Consider two periods 1 & 2, respectively, consisting of *n1* and *n2* years. Denote aggregate GDP, primary, secondary and tertiary sector incomes by *Y*, *P*, *S* and *T*. Let w_{it} denote the share of sector *i* ($i = P, S, T$) in *Y* in year *t* and *g* denote the growth rate. Y in year *t* can be written as follows:

$$Y_t = P_t + S_t + T_t \tag{3.2}$$

From (3.2), the growth rate of *Y* can be written as:

$$g_{Yt} = w_{Pt} g_{Pt} + w_{St} g_{St} + w_{Tt}\, g_{Tt} \tag{3.3}$$

where $g_{Yt} = \left(\frac{Y_t - Y_{t-1}}{Y_{t-1}}\right)$ is the growth rate of *Y* in year *t* and g_{Pt}, g_{St} and g_{Tt} are defined similarly. Using (3.3), the average annual growth rate for the period 1 ($\overline{g}_{Y1}$) can be written as follows. Where a bar over notations has been used to denote average value.

$$\overline{g}_{Y1} = \overline{w_{P1} g_{P1}} + \overline{w_{S1} g_{S1}} + \overline{w_{T1} g_{T1}} \tag{3.4}$$

where,

$$\overline{g}_{Y1} = n1^{-1}\left(\sum_{t=1}^{n1} g_{Yt}\right), \text{ and } \overline{w_{i1} g_{i1}} = n1^{-1}\left(\sum_{t=1}^{n1} w_{it} g_{it}\right).$$

Similarly, $\overline{g}_{Y2}$ can be written as below,

$$\overline{g}_{Y2} = \overline{w_{P2} g_{P2}} + \overline{w_{S2} g_{S2}} + \overline{w_{T2} g_{T2}} \tag{3.5}$$

In (3.5), averages are taken over $n2$ observations in period two. Subtracting (3.4) from (3.5),

$$(\overline{g}_{Y2} - \overline{g}_{Y1}) = (\overline{w_{P2}g_{P2}} - \overline{w_{P2}g_{P1}}) + (\overline{w_{S2}g_{S2}} - \overline{w_{S1}g_{S1}}) + (\overline{w_{T2}g_{T2}} - \overline{w_{T1}g_{T1}}) \quad (3.6)$$

Dividing (3.6) throughout by the left-hand side value and multiplying it by 100 gives the percentage contribution of each sector to the change in the average growth rate of Y in period two over that in previous period.

References

Bai, J., & Perron, P. (1998). Estimating and testing linear models with multiple structural changes. *Econometrica, 66*(1), 47–78.

Bai, J., & Perron, P. (2003). Computation and analysis of multiple structural change models. *Journal of Applied Econometrics, 18*(1), 1–22.

Balakrishnan, P., & Parameswaran, M. (2007). Understanding economic growth in India: A prerequisite. *Economic and Political Weekly, 62*(27), 2915–2922.

Balakrishnan, P., Das, M., & Parameswaran, M. (2017). The internal dynamic of Indian economic growth. *Journal of Asian Economics, 50*, 46–61.

Balakrishnan, P., Das, M., & Parameswaran, M. (2021). Growth transitions in India: Myth and reality. *Economic and Political Weekly, 56*, 43–49.

Balakrishnan, P. (2022). *India's economy from Nehru to Modi: A brief history*. Permanent Black.

Bollen, K. A., & Jackman, R. W. (1990). Regression diagnostics: An expository treatment of outliers and influential cases. In J. Fox & J. Scott Long (Ed.), *Modern methods of data analysis*, (pp. 257–291). Sage Publications.

Boyce, J. K. (1986). Kinked exponential models for growth rate estimation. *Oxford Bulletin of Economics and Statistics, 48*(4), 385–391.

Chodorow-Reich, G., Gopinath, G., Mishra, P., & Narayanan, A. (2019). Cash and the economy: Evidence from India's demonetization. *The Quarterly Journal of Economics, 135*(1), 57–103.

Dixit, A. K., & Stiglitz, J. E. (1977). Monopolistic competition and optimum product diversity. *The American Economic Review, 67*(3), 297–308.

Hatekar, N., & Dongre, A. (2005). Structural breaks in India's growth: Revisiting the debate with a longer perspective. *Economic and Political Weekly, 40*(14), 1432–1435.

Hoover, K. D., Johansen, S., & Juselius, K. (2008). Allowing the data to speak freely: The Macroeconometrics of the Cointegrated Vector Autoregression. *The American Economic Review, 98*(2), 251–255.

Kohli, A. (2006a). Politics of economic growth in India, 1980–2005. Part II: The 1990s and beyond. *Economic and Political Weekly, 41*(14), 1361–1370.

Kohli, A. (2006b). Politics of economic growth in India, 1980–2005– Part I: The 1980s. *Economic and Political Weekly, 41*(13), 1251–1259.

Mahalanobis, P. C. (1955). The approach of operational research to planning in India. *Sankhyā: The Indian Journal of Statistics, 16*(1/2), 3–130.

Nitnaware, H. (2022, October 17). India has pushed back poverty, still home to most poor people in world: UNDP index. *Down To Earth.*

Parameswaran, M. (2019). Virtuous cycle and economic growth in India. *Economic and Political Weekly, 54*(41), 16–18.

Rodrik, D., & Subramanian, A. (2005). From "Hindu growth" to productivity surge: The mystery of the Indian growth transition. *IMF Staff Papers, 52*(2), 193–228.

Sen, K. (2007). Why did the elephant start to trot? India's growth acceleration re-examined. *Economic and Political Weekly, 42*(43), 37–47.

Sen, K., Kar, S., & Sahu, J. P. (2017). The stroll, the trot, and the sprint of the elephant. In L. Pritchett, K. Sen, & E. Werker (Eds.), *Deals and development: The political dynamics of growth episodes* (pp. 250–284). Oxford University Press.

Subramanian, A., & Felman, J. (2019). *India's great slowdown: What Happened? What is the way out?* (Working Paper, No. 370). Centre for International Development at Harvard University.

Uctum, M., Thurston, T., & Uctum, R. (2006). Public debt, the unit root hypothesis and structural breaks: A multi-country analysis. *Economica, 73*(289), 129–156. Wiley.

UNDP and OPHI. (2022). *Global Multidimensional Poverty Index 2022: Unpacking deprivation bundles to reduce multidimensional poverty*. United Nations Development Programme and Oxford Poverty and Human Development Initiative.

Wallack, J. S. (2003). Structural breaks in Indian macroeconomic data. *Economic and Political Weekly, 38*(41), 4312–4315.

M. Parameswaran is a professor at the Centre for Development Studies. His areas of research include economic development and macroeconomics. He has published research articles on economic growth in India, trade and technological progress, inflation, and trade and productivity growth.

Pulapre Balakrishnan works in the areas of macroeconomics and development. He has published articles on inflation, growth and the measurement of productivity. His book "India's Economy from Nehru to Modi: A Brief History" appeared in 2022. He is a recipient of the Malcolm Adiseshaiah Award for Distinguished Contribution to Development Studies (2014). Balakrishnan is an honorary visiting professor of the Centre for Development Studies. His published work is listed on www.pulaprebalakrishnan.in.

Part II
Growth Strategies—Pace and Patterns

Chapter 4
Monetary Policy in India: A Global Perspective

Pami Dua

Abstract In 2016, the monetary policy framework moved towards flexible inflation targeting and a six-member Monetary Policy Committee (MPC) was constituted for setting the policy rate. With this step towards modernization of the monetary policy process, India joined the set of countries that have adopted inflation targeting as their monetary policy framework. The Consumer Price Index (CPI combined) inflation target was set by the Government of India at 4% with ± 2% tolerance band for the period from August 5, 2016 to March 31, 2021. The target was renewed again for a period of 5 years in March 2021, i.e. April 1, 2021 to March 31, 2026. In this backdrop, the paper reviews the evolution of monetary policy frameworks in India since the inception of the Reserve Bank of India, especially from the mid-1980s. It also describes the monetary policy transmission process and its limitations in terms of lags and rigidities. It highlights the importance of unconventional monetary policy measures in supplementing conventional tools, especially during the pandemic. Further, it examines the voting pattern of the MPC in India and compares this with that of various developed and emerging economies. The synchronization of cuts in the policy rate by MPCs of various countries during the global slowdown in 2019 and the COVID-19 pandemic in the early 2020s is also analysed. The subsequent increases in the rates are also examined along with the synchronization in inflation across the globe.

Keywords Inflation targeting · Monetary policy committee · Monetary transmission process · Unconventional monetary policy measures

JEL Classification E4 · E5

This is an extended version of the paper published in the Indian Economic Review, Vol 55, 117–154 titled 'Monetary Policy Framework in India', Dua (2020).

Disclaimer: The views expressed in this paper are of the author and not of the Monetary Policy Committee (MPC), of which she was a member.

P. Dua (✉)
Department of Economics, Delhi School of Economics, University of Delhi, Delhi, India
e-mail: dua@econdse.org

D. Maiti et al. (eds.), *75 Years of Growth, Development and Productivity in India*, India Studies in Business and Economics, https://doi.org/10.1007/978-981-97-8054-9_4

4.1 Introduction

The monetary policy framework in India has evolved over the past few decades in response to financial developments and changing macroeconomic conditions. The operational framework of monetary policy has also gone through significant changes with respect to instruments and targeting mechanisms. The preamble of the Reserve Bank of India (RBI) Act, 1934 was also amended in 2016, which now clearly provides the mandate of the RBI. It reads as follows:

> To regulate the issue of Bank notes and keeping of reserves with a view to securing monetary stability in India and generally to operate the currency and credit system of the country to its advantage; to have a modern monetary policy framework to meet the challenge of an increasingly complex economy; to maintain price stability while keeping in mind the objective of growth.

The aim of monetary policy in the initial years of inception of RBI was mainly to maintain the sterling parity, with exchange rate being the nominal anchor of monetary policy. Liquidity was regulated through open market operations (OMOs), bank rate and cash reserve ratio (CRR). Soon after independence and through the late 1960s, the role of the central bank was aligned with the planned development process of the nation in accordance with the five-year plans. Thus, it played a major role in regulating credit availability, employing OMOs, bank rate and reserve requirement towards this end. At the same time, the statutory liquidity ratio (SLR) requirement was a secure source for government borrowing as well as an additional instrument of monetary and liquidity management.

With the nationalization of major banks in 1969, the main objective of monetary policy through the 1970s till the mid-1980s was the regulation of credit in accordance with the developmental needs of the country. This period was marked by monetization of fiscal deficit while inflationary consequences of high public expenditure necessitated frequent recourse to CRR.

In 1985, on the recommendation of the Committee set up to Review the Working of the Monetary System (Chairman: Dr. Sukhamoy Chakravarty), a new monetary policy framework, monetary targeting with feedback was implemented based on empirical evidence of a stable demand for money function. However, financial innovations in the 1990s implied that demand for money may be affected by factors other than income. Further, interest rates were deregulated in the mid-1990s and the Indian economy was getting increasingly integrated with the global economy. Therefore, the RBI began to deemphasize the role of monetary aggregates and implemented a multiple indicator approach (MIA) to monetary policy in 1998 encompassing all economic and financial variables that influence the major objectives outlined in the preamble of the RBI Act. This was done in two phases—initially MIA and later augmented MIA (AMIA) which included forward looking variables and time series models.

Based on RBI's Report of the Expert Committee to Revise and Strengthen the Monetary Policy Framework (2014, Chairman: Dr Urjit R Patel), a formal transition was made in 2016 towards flexible inflation targeting and a six-member Monetary

Policy Committee (MPC) was constituted for setting the policy repo rate. The Monetary Policy Framework Agreement (MPFA) was signed between the Government of India and the RBI in February 2015 to formally adopt the flexible inflation targeting (FIT) framework. This was followed up with the amendment to the RBI Act, 1934 in May 2016 to provide a statutory basis for the implementation of the FIT framework. With this step towards modernization of the monetary policy process, India joined the set of countries that adopted inflation targeting, starting from 1990 by New Zealand, as their monetary policy framework. The Central Government notified in the Official Gazette dated August 5, 2016, that the Consumer Price Index (CPI) inflation target would be 4% with ±2% tolerance band for the period from August 5, 2016 to March 31, 2021. The target was again renewed for a period of 5 years in March 2021, i.e. April 1, 2021 to March 31, 2026. At the time of writing (June 2024), this period would end in less than two years. Further, at the end of the four-year term in September 2020 of three external members serving on the first MPC, three new external members were appointed to the MPC in October 2020. Since their term is also due to end in September 2024, this would require the re-constitution of the MPC and establishment of the third MPC. In this backdrop, this paper discusses the evolution of the monetary policy framework in India and describes the workings of the current framework.

The paper is divided into the following sections. Section 4.2 presents a schematic representation of the main components of a general monetary policy framework and describes its key features. Section 4.3 describes the genesis of the monetary policy framework in India since 1985 covering the Monetary Targeting Framework, Multiple Indicator Approach and Flexible Inflation Targeting. The main recommendations of RBI's Report of the Expert Committee to Revise and Strengthen the Monetary Policy Framework (2014, Chairman: Dr Urjit R Patel) are also discussed. Composition, workings and voting pattern of the Monetary Policy Committee from October 2016 to June 2024 are also provided. Further, a comparison of voting patterns with various countries across the globe is undertaken.

Section 4.4 discusses a general framework for monetary policy transmission and applies the framework to India. It also describes interest rate linkages at the global level. Section 4.5 examines unconventional monetary policy measures adopted in late 2019 and early 2020. Section 4.6 concludes the paper.

4.2 Schematic Representation of a Monetary Policy Framework

The specification of the monetary policy framework facilitates the conduct of monetary policy. The general framework comprises well-defined objectives/goals of monetary policy along with instruments, operating targets and intermediate targets that aid

Instruments → Operating Targets → Intermediate Targets → Goals of Monetary Policy

Fig. 4.1 Key components of a monetary policy framework

in the implementation of monetary policy and achievement of the ultimate objectives. A schematic representation of a monetary policy framework is shown in Fig. 4.1 (Laurens et al., 2015; Mishkin, 2016).

Instruments are tools that the central bank has control over and are used to achieve the operational target. Examples of instruments include open market operations, reserve requirements, discount policy, lending to banks, policy rate. Operational targets are the financial variables that can be controlled by the central bank to a large extent through the monetary policy instruments and guide the day-to-day operations of the central bank. These can impact the intermediate target and thus help in the delivery of the final goal of monetary policy. Examples of operational targets include reserve money and short-term money market interest rates.

Intermediate targets are variables that are closely related with the final goals of monetary policy and can be affected by monetary policy. Intermediate targets may include monetary aggregates and short-term and long-term interest rates. Goals refer to the final policy objectives. These may include price stability, economic growth, financial stability and exchange rate stability.

This general framework is applied to the monetary targeting framework with feedback that prevailed from 1985 to 1998 and to the inflation targeting framework that exists from 2016 onwards. The multiple indicator approach that was operational from 1998 to 2016 was based on a number of financial and economic variables and was not exactly specified on the basis of this framework although broad money was treated as an intermediate target and the goals of monetary policy are the same across the various frameworks.

4.3 Genesis of Monetary Policy in India Since 1985

4.3.1 Monetary Targeting with Feedback: 1985–1998

In the 1970s through the mid-1980s, monetization of the fiscal deficit exerted a dominant influence on monetary policy with inflationary consequences of high public expenditure necessitating frequent recourse to CRR. Against this backdrop, in 1985, on the recommendation of the Committee set up to Review the Working of the Monetary System (RBI, 1985; Chairman: Dr. Sukhamoy Chakravarty), a new monetary policy framework, monetary targeting with feedback was implemented based on empirical evidence of a stable demand for money function. The recommendation of the committee was to control inflation within acceptable levels with desired output growth. Further, instead of following a fixed target for money supply growth,

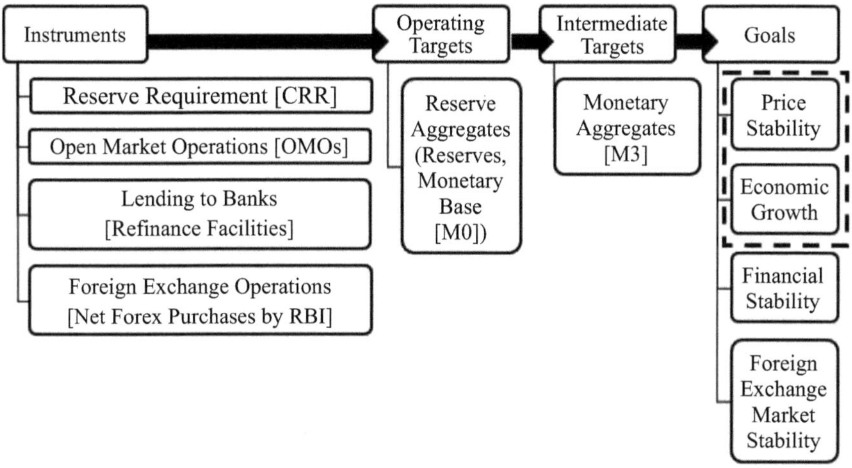

Fig. 4.2 Monetary policy linkages—Monetary targeting in India. Operating framework: 1985–1998. *Notes* (1) Primary objective of monetary policy in India is to maintain price stability, while keeping in mind the objective of growth. (2) Definitions of variables are given in Annexure 1

a range was followed which was subject to mid-year adjustments. This framework was termed "Monetary Targeting with Feedback" as it was flexible enough to accommodate changes in output growth.

This operational framework is depicted in Fig. 4.2. (Definitions of variables shown in Fig. 4.2 are given in Annexure 1.) The main instruments in this framework were cash reserve ratio (CRR), open market operations (OMOs), refinance facilities and foreign exchange operations. Broad money (M3) was chosen as the intermediate target while reserve money (M0) was the main operating target. However, an analysis of money growth outcomes during the monetary targeting framework reveals that targets were rarely met (RBI, 2009–2012). Even with increases in CRR, money supply growth remained high and fueled inflation.

Further, financial innovations in the 1990s implied that demand for money may be affected by factors other than income. Since the mid-1990s, with global integration, factors such as swings in capital flows, volatility in the exchange rate and global growth also impacted the economy. Moreover, interest rates were deregulated allowing for changing interest rates and a market determined management system of exchange rates was also adopted.

4.3.2 Multiple Indicator Approach: 1998–2016

Against the backdrop of changing domestic and global dynamics, RBI implemented a multiple indicator approach (MIA) to monetary policy in 1998 encompassing various economic and financial variables based on the recommendations of RBI's Working

Group on Money Supply (RBI, 1998; Chairman: Dr YV Reddy). These variables included several quantity variables such as money, credit, output, trade, capital flows, fiscal indicators as well as rate variables such as interest rates, inflation rate and the exchange rate. The information on these variables provided a broad-based monetary policy formulation, which not only encompassed a diverse set of information but also accorded flexibility to the conduct of monetary management.

The MIA was conceptualized when Dr. Bimal Jalan was Governor and was implemented in two stages—MIA and later Augmented MIA, by including forward looking variables and a panel of time series models, in addition to the economic and financial variables (Mohanty, 2010; Reddy, 1999). Forward looking indicators were drawn from RBI's industrial outlook survey, capacity utilization survey, inflation expectations survey and professional forecasters' survey. All the variables together with time series models provided the projection of growth and inflation while RBI provided the projection for broad money (M3) and treated this as the intermediate target.

The operational framework of AMIA is illustrated in Fig. 4.3. Compared to the monetary targeting framework, the goals of monetary policy remained the same and broad money continued to serve as the intermediate target while the underlying operating mechanism of MIA evolved over time. In May 2011, the weighted average call money rate (WACR) was explicitly recognized as the operating target of monetary policy while the repo rate was made the only one independently varying policy rate. These measures improved the implementation and transmission of monetary policy along with enhancing the accuracy of signalling of monetary policy stance (Mohanty, 2011).

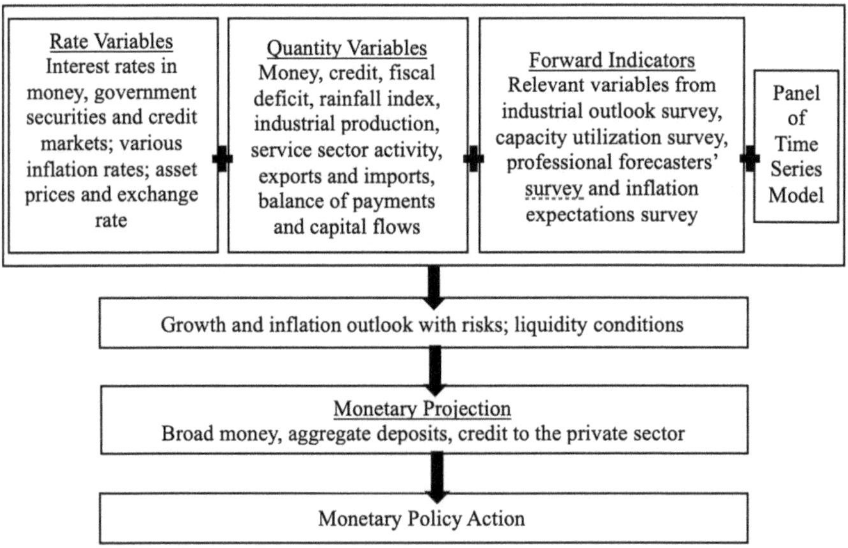

Fig. 4.3 Augmented Multiple Indicator Approach (AMIA). Operating framework: 1998–2016. *Source* RBI Bulletin, December 2011

4.3.2.1 Shift Towards Inflation Targeting

The importance of focusing on inflation was first highlighted in the Report of the Committee on Financial Sector Reforms (Government of India, 2009; Chairman: Dr Raghuram Rajan) constituted by the Government of India. The report recommended that RBI can best serve the cause of growth by focusing on controlling inflation and intervening in currency markets only to limit excessive volatility. The report pointed out that the cause of inclusion can also be best served by maintaining this focus because the poorer sections are least hedged against inflation. Further, the report recommended that there should be a single objective of staying close to a low inflation number, or within a range, in the medium term, moving steadily to a single instrument, the short-term interest rate to achieve it.

Former RBI Governor, Dr. Raghuram Rajan set up an Expert Committee in 2013 to Review and Strengthen the Monetary Policy Framework (RBI, 2014; Chairman: Dr Urjit R Patel). The mandate of the Committee, amongst others, was to review the objectives and conduct of monetary policy in a globalized and highly inter-connected environment. The committee was also required to review the organizational structure, operating framework and instruments of monetary policy, liquidity management framework, to ensure compatibility with macroeconomic and financial stability, as well as market development. The impediments to monetary policy transmission were to be identified and measures along with institutional pre-conditions to improve transmission across financial markets and real economy were to be suggested.

Some issues central to the report were selecting the nominal anchor for monetary policy, defining the inflation metric and specifying the inflation target. A nominal anchor is central to a credible monetary policy framework as it ties down the price level or the change in the price level to attain the final goal of monetary policy. It is a numerical objective that is defined for a nominal variable to signal the commitment of monetary policy towards price stability.

Generally, five types of nominal anchors have been used, namely, monetary aggregates, exchange rate, inflation rate, national income and price level. The Expert Committee recommended inflation to be the nominal anchor of the monetary policy framework in India as flexible inflation targeting recognizes the existence of growth-inflation trade-off in the short run and stabilizing and anchoring inflation expectations is critical for ensuring price stability on an enduring basis. Further, low and stable inflation is a necessary precondition for sustainable high growth and inflation is also easily understood by the public.

Regarding the inflation metric, the Committee recommended that RBI should adopt the all India CPI (combined) inflation as the measure of the nominal anchor. This is to be defined in terms of headline CPI inflation, which closely reflects the cost of living and influences inflation expectations relative to other available metrics. CPI is also easily understood as it is used as a reference in wage contracts and negotiations. Headline inflation was preferred against core inflation (headline inflation excluding food and fuel inflation) since food and fuel comprise more than 50% of the consumption basket and cannot be discarded.

The Committee recommended the target level of inflation at 4% with a band of ±2% around it. The tolerance band was formulated in the light of the vulnerability of the Indian economy to supply and external shocks and the relatively large weight of the food in the CPI basket.

The Expert Committee also recommended that decision making should be vested in a Monetary Policy Committee (MPC).

4.3.3 Flexible Inflation Targeting: 2016 Onwards

With the signing of the Monetary Policy Framework Agreement (MPFA) between the Government of India and the RBI on Feb 20, 2015, Flexible Inflation Targeting (FIT) was formally adopted in India. In May 2016, the Reserve Bank of India (RBI) Act, 1934 was amended to provide a statutory basis for the implementation of the FIT framework. The amended RBI Act, 1934 also provided that the Central Government shall, in consultation with the Bank, determine the inflation target in terms of the Consumer Price Index, once in every 5 years.

Accordingly, the Central Government has notified in the Official Gazette 4% Consumer Price Index (CPI) inflation as the target for the period from August 5, 2016 to March 31, 2021 with the upper tolerance limit of 6% and the lower tolerance limit of 2%. The amended RBI Act, 1934 also provides that RBI shall be seen to have failed to meet the target if inflation remains above 6% or below 2% for three consecutive quarters. In such circumstances, RBI is required to provide the reasons for the failure and propose remedial measures and the expected time to return inflation to the target.

In 2016, India thus joined several developed and emerging market economies that have implemented inflation targeting. Figure 4.4 shows the timeline for implementation of inflation targeting for countries in this category, starting in 1990.

4.3.3.1 Monetary Policy Committee: Composition, Monetary Policy Framework and Voting Patterns

The amended RBI Act, 1934 provides for a statutory and institutionalized framework for a six-member Monetary Policy Committee (MPC) to be constituted by the Central Government by notification in the Official Gazette. The Central Government in September 2016 thus constituted the MPC with three members from RBI including the Governor as Chairperson and three external members (with a four-year term) as per Gazette Notification dated September 29, 2016. The second MPC became operational in October 2020. (Details of the composition of the MPCs are given in Annexure 3.) The Committee is required to meet at least four times a year although it has been meeting on a bi-monthly basis since October 2016. Each member of the MPC has one vote, and in the event of equality of votes, the Governor has a second or casting vote. The resolution adopted by the MPC is published after conclusion of

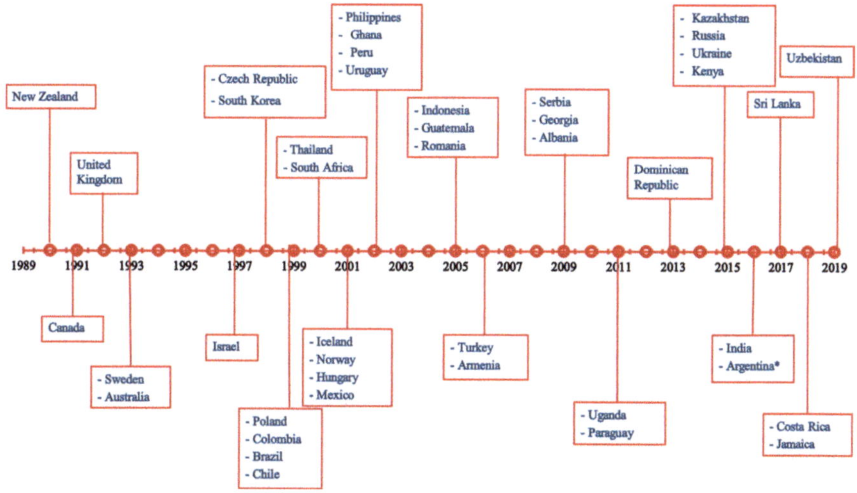

Fig. 4.4 Inflation targeting regime adoption. *Notes* (1) See Annexure 4 for details. (2) * Inflation Targeting ended in 2018 in Argentina. (3) *Source* International Monetary Fund (2023); Dua (2020); Agénor and da Silva (2019); Various Central Bank websites

every meeting of the MPC. On the fourteenth day, the minutes of the proceedings of the MPC are published which includes the resolution adopted by the MPC, the vote of each member on the resolution, and the statement of each member on the resolution.

It may be noted that before the constitution of the MPC, a Technical Advisory Committee (TAC) on Monetary Policy was set up in 2005 which consisted of external experts from monetary economics, central banking, financial markets and public finance. The role of this committee was to enhance the consultative process of monetary policy by reviewing the macroeconomic and monetary developments in the economy and advising RBI on the stance of monetary policy. With the formation of MPC, the TAC on Monetary Policy ceased to exist.

The MPC is entrusted with the task of fixing the benchmark policy rate (repo rate) required to contain inflation within the specified tolerance band. The framework entails setting the policy rate on the basis of current and evolving macroeconomic conditions. Once the repo rate is announced, the operating framework looks at liquidity management on a day-to-day basis with the aim to anchor the operating target—the weighted average call rate (WACR)—around the repo rate. This is illustrated in Fig. 4.5, where the intermediate targets are the short-term and long-term interest rates and the goals of price stability and economic growth are aligned with the primary objective of monetary policy to maintain price stability, keeping in mind the objective of growth. In addition to the repo rate, the instruments include liquidity facility, CRR, OMOs, lending to banks and foreign exchange operations (RBI, 2018).

It is imperative here to note some of the key elements of the revised framework for liquidity management (RBI, 2019) that are particularly relevant for the operating

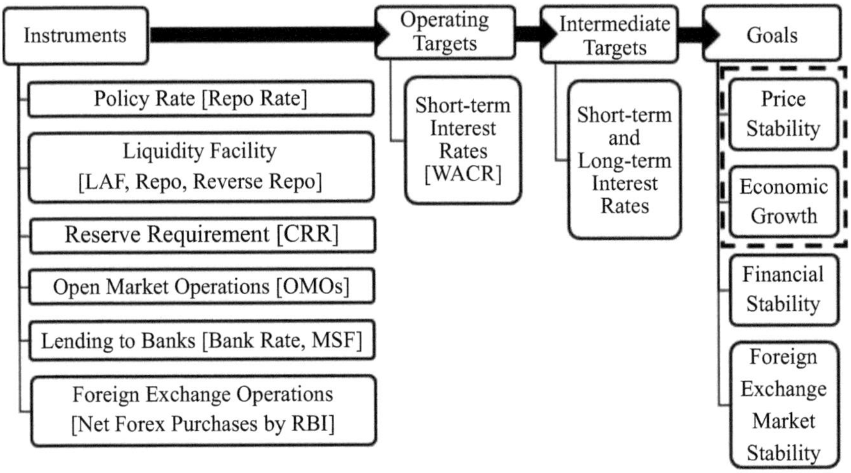

Fig. 4.5 Monetary policy linkages—Interest rate targeting in India. Operating framework: 2016 onwards. *Notes* (1) Primary objective of monetary policy in India is to maintain price stability, while keeping in mind the objective of growth. (2) Definitions of variables are given in Annexure 1

framework shown in Fig. 4.5. As noted in the RBI Monetary Policy Report (MPR), April 2020 (RBI, 2020d):

- Liquidity management remains the operating procedure of monetary policy; the weighted average call rate (WACR) continues to be its operating target.
- The liquidity management corridor is retained, with the marginal standing facility (MSF) rate as its upper bound (ceiling) and the fixed reverse repo rate as the lower bound (floor), with the policy repo rate in the middle of the corridor.
- The width of the corridor is retained at 50 basis points—the reverse repo rate being 25 basis points below the repo rate and the MSF rate 25 basis points above the repo rate. (The corridor width was asymmetrically widened on March 27 and April 17, 2020.)
- Instruments of liquidity management continue to include fixed and variable rate repo/reverse repo auctions, outright open market operations, forex swaps and other instruments as may be deployed from time to time to ensure that the system has adequate liquidity at all times.
- The current requirement of maintaining a minimum of 90% of the prescribed CRR on a daily basis will continue. (This was reduced to 80% on March 27, 2020 but restored subsequently in September 2020.)

Some key elements of the liquidity management framework such as the 14-day main repo/reverse repo auction conducted every fortnight remained suspended during March 2020 till mid-January 2021 but resumed thereafter. Moreover, the width of the LAF corridor was asymmetrically widened to 90 basis points—the MSF remaining above the repo rate by 25 basis points while the reverse repo was placed at 65 basis points below the repo rate (MPR, October 2020). The asymmetric downward adjustment of the reverse repo was done to discourage banks from passively parking surplus liquidity with the RBI; instead, banks were urged to explore credit opportunities. Moreover, the floor rate of interest was lowered through the reduction in the reverse repo rate which facilitated in lowering borrowing costs in the economy. With the return of normalcy after the pandemic, the Reserve Bank fully restored the liquidity management framework instituted in February 2020, albeit with some refinements in April 2022. For instance, the uncollateralized standing deposit facility (SDF) was introduced as the floor of the LAF corridor, replacing the reverse repo rate on April 8, 2022. With the removal of the collateral constraint associated with reverse repo operations, the SDF provides greater operational flexibility and autonomy to the Reserve Bank in liquidity management. Moreover, it acts as a hard lower bound on overnight interest rates in the economy. The SDF rate was institutionalized at 25 bps below the policy rate. The MSF rate continued to be 25 bps above the policy repo rate. Thus, the width of the LAF corridor was restored to the pre-pandemic configuration of 50 bps, symmetrically around the policy repo rate. The fixed rate reverse repo (FRRR) rate was retained at 3.35% and remains a part of the RBI's toolkit and its operation will be at the discretion of the RBI for purposes specified from time to time. The FRRR along with the SDF imparts flexibility to the RBI's liquidity management framework. Both the MSF and the SDF are available on all days of the week, throughout the year (MPR, April 2022; RBI, 2022).

The first meeting of the MPC was held in October 2016. Between October 2016 and June 2024, the MPC has met 48 times. Table 4.1 shows the voting patterns for each meeting with respect to the direction of change in the policy rate, magnitude of change and the stance of monetary policy. Table 4.2, on the other hand, provides an overall summary of the voting of all the meetings. It is interesting to note in Table 4.2, that with respect to direction of change/status quo of the policy rate, consensus was achieved in 32 meetings out of 48. Of these 32 meetings, there were 5 meetings where there were differences in the magnitude of the change voted for although there was consensus regarding the direction of change. The diversity in voting of the MPC members reflects the differences in the assessment and expectations of individual members as well as their policy preferences.

To examine if this diversity exists in MPCs of other countries as well, we analyse the voting patterns of 13 countries across the globe during October 2018 to June 2024 in Table 4.3. For some countries, we find dissents in certain meetings, similar to the lack of consensus in some of the meetings of the Indian MPC.

It merits mention that the committee approach towards the conduct of monetary policy has gained prominence across globe. The advantages of this approach include confluence of specialized knowledge and expertise on the subject domain, bringing together different stakeholders and diverse opinions, improving representativeness and collective wisdom, thus making the whole greater than the sum of parts (Blinder & Morgan, 2005; Maier, 2010). Further, Rajan (2017) notes that MPC would bring more minds to bear on policy setting, preserve continuity in case a member has to quit or retire, and be less subject to political pressures.

Table 4.1 RBI MPC policy repo rates (October 2016–June 2024)

Date	Policy repo rate voting and decision	Stance decision and voting
October 2016	Reduce 25 bps [6–0] 6.50 to 6.25	Accommodative 6–0
December 2016	Maintain 6.25 bps [6–0]	Maintain Accommodative 6–0
February 2017	Maintain 6.25 bps [6–0]	Change to Neutral 6–0
April 2017	Maintain 6.25 bps [6–0]	Maintain Neutral 6–0
June 2017	Maintain 6.25 bps [5–1] Reduce 50 bps [1]	Maintain Neutral 6–0
August 2017	Reduce 25 bps [4–2] 6.25 to 6.00 bps Reduce 50 bps [1] Maintain 6.25 bps [1]	Maintain Neutral 6–0
October 2017	Maintain 6.00 bps [5–1] Reduce 25 bps [1]	Maintain Neutral 6–0
December 2017	Maintain 6.00 bps [5–1] Reduce 25 bps [1]	Maintain Neutral 6–0
February 2018	Maintain 6.00 bps [5–1] Increase 25 bps [1]	Maintain Neutral 6–0
April 2018	Maintain 6.00 bps [5–1] Increase 25 bps [1]	Maintain Neutral 6–0
June 2018	Increase 25 bps [6–0] 6.00 to 6.25 bps	Maintain Neutral 6–0
August 2018	Increase 25 bps [5–1] 6.25 to 6.5 Maintain 6.25 bps [1]	Maintain Neutral 6–0
October 2018	Maintain 6.50 bps [5–1] Increase 25 bps [1]	Change to Calibrated Tightening 5–1
December 2018	Maintain 6.50 bps [6–0]	Maintain Calibrated Tightening 5–1
February 2019	Reduce 25 bps [4–2] 6.5 to 6.25 bps Maintain 6.5 bps [2]	Change to Neutral 6–0
April 2019	Reduce 25 bps [4–2] 6.25 to 6.0 bps Maintain 6.25 bps [2]	Maintain Neutral 5–1
June 2019	Reduce 25 bps [6–0] 6.0 to 5.75 bps	Change to Accommodative 6–0
August 2019	Reduce [6–0] Reduce 35 bps [4] 5.75 to 5.40 bps Reduce 25 bps [2]	Maintain Accommodative 6–0

(continued)

Table 4.1 (continued)

Date	Policy repo rate voting and decision	Stance decision and voting
October 2019	Reduce [6–0] Reduce 25 bps [5] 5.40 to 5.15 Reduce 40 bps [1]	Maintain Accommodative 6–0
December 2019	Maintain 5.15 bps [6–0]	Maintain Accommodative 6–0
February 2020	Maintain 5.15 bps [6–0]	Maintain Accommodative 6–0
March 2020	Reduce [6–0] Reduce 75 bps [4] 5.15 to 4.40 bps Reduce 50 bps [2]	Maintain Accommodative 6–0
May 2020	Reduce [6–0] Reduce 40 bps [5] 4.40 to 4.00 bps Reduce 25 bps [1]	Maintain Accommodative 6–0
August 2020	Maintain 4.0 bps [6–0]	Maintain Accommodative 6–0
October 2020	Maintain 4.00 bps [6–0]	Maintain Accommodative 6–0
December 2020	Maintain 4.00 bps [6–0]	Maintain Accommodative 6–0
February 2021	Maintain 4.00 bps [6–0]	Maintain Accommodative 6–0
April 2021	Maintain 4.00 bps [6–0]	Maintain Accommodative 6–0
June 2021	Maintain 4.00 bps [6–0]	Maintain Accommodative 6–0
August 2021	Maintain 4.00 bps [6–0]	Maintain Accommodative 5–1
October 2021	Maintain 4.00 bps [6–0]	Maintain Accommodative 5–1
December 2021	Maintain 4.00 bps [6–0]	Maintain Accommodative 5–1
February 2022	Maintain 4.00 bps [6–0]	Maintain Accommodative 5–1
April 2022	Maintain 4.00 bps [6–0]	Maintain Accommodative 6–0
May 2022	Increase 40 bps [6–0] 4.00 to 4.40 bps	Maintain Accommodative 6–0
June 2022	Increase 50 bps [6–0] 4.40 to 4.90 bps	Withdrawal of Accommodation 6–0

(continued)

Table 4.1 (continued)

Date	Policy repo rate voting and decision	Stance decision and voting
August 2022	Increase 50 bps [6–0] 4.90 to 5.40 bps	Withdrawal of Accommodation 5–1
September 2022	Increase 50 bps [5–1] 5.40 to 5.90 bps Increase 35 bps [1]	Withdrawal of Accommodation 5–1
December 2022	Increase 35 bps [5–1] 5.90 to 6.25 bps Maintain 5.90 [1]	Withdrawal of Accommodation 4–2
February 2023	Increase 25 bps [4–2] 6.25 to 6.50 bps Maintain 6.25 [2]	Withdrawal of Accommodation 4–2
April 2023	Maintain 6.50 bps [6–0]	Withdrawal of Accommodation 5–1
June 2023	Maintain 6.50 bps [6–0]	Withdrawal of Accommodation 5–1
August 2023	Maintain 6.50 bps [6–0]	Withdrawal of Accommodation 5–1
October 2023	Maintain 6.50 bps [6–0]	Withdrawal of Accommodation 5–1
December 2023	Maintain 6.50 bps [6–0]	Withdrawal of Accommodation 5–1
February 2024	Maintain 6.50 bps [5–1]	Withdrawal of Accommodation 5–1
April 2024	Maintain 6.50 bps [5–1]	Withdrawal of Accommodation 5–1
June 2024	Maintain 6.50 bps [5–2]	Withdrawal of Accommodation 5–2

Source Reserve Bank of India Monetary Policy Committee Meeting Press Releases and Minutes of Meetings

4.4 Monetary Policy Transmission Framework

This section presents a stylized representation of a framework for monetary policy transmission and also applies this framework to India.

Monetary policy transmission is the process through which changes in monetary policy affect economic activity in general as well as the price level. With developments in financial systems, the world over, and growing sophistication of financial markets, most central banks use the short-term interest rate as the policy instrument for the conduct of monetary policy. Monetary policy transmission is thus the process through which a change in the policy rate is transmitted first to the short-term money market rate and then to the entire maturity spectrum of interest rates covering the money and bond markets as well as banks' deposit and lending rates. These impulses,

Table 4.2 RBI MPC voting summary (October 2016–June 2024)

Total Meetings	Meetings with decision to increase rates	Meetings with decision to decrease rates	Meetings with decision to maintain rates	Meetings with Consensus regarding direction of change/status quo
48	8	9	31	32
	June 2018 Aug 2018 May 2022 June 2022 Aug 2022 Sept 2022 Dec 2022 Feb 2023	Oct 2016 Aug 2017 Feb 2019 Apr 2019 June 2019 Aug 2019 Oct 2019 Mar 2020 May 2020	Dec 2016 Feb 2017 Apr 2017 June 2017 Oct 2017 Dec 2017 Feb 2018 Apr 2018 Oct 2018 Dec 2018 Dec 2019 Feb 2020 Aug 2020–Apr 2022 (11 meetings) Apr 2023–June 2024 (8 meetings)	Oct 2016 Dec 2016 Feb 2017 Apr 2017 June 2018 Dec 2018 June 2019–Aug 2022 (21 meetings) Apr–Dec 2023 (5 meetings)

Source Reserve Bank of India Monetary Policy Committee Press Releases and Minutes of Meetings

in turn, impact consumption (private and government), investment and net exports, which affect aggregate demand and hence output and inflation.

There are five channels of monetary transmission—interest rate channel; exchange rate channel; asset price channel; credit channel and expectations channel. The *interest rate channel* is described above. Monetary transmission takes place through the *exchange rate channel* when changes in monetary policy impact the interest rate differential between domestic and foreign rates leading to capital flows (inflow or outflow) which in turn affects the exchange rate and hence the relative demand for exports and imports. Transmission through the *asset price channel* occurs when changes in monetary policy influence the price of assets such as equity and real estate that lead to changes in consumption and investment. A change in prices of assets can lead to a change in consumption spending due to the associated wealth effect. For example, if interest rates fall, people may consider purchasing assets that are non-interest bearing such as real estate and equity. A rise in demand for these assets may result in higher prices, a positive wealth effect and thus higher consumption. Further if equity prices rise, firms may increase investment spending. Transmission through the *credit channel* happens if monetary policy influences the quantity of available credit. This may happen if the willingness of financial institutions to lend changes due to a change in monetary policy. Further, debt obligations of businesses may also change due to a change in the interest rate. For instance, if the policy rate

Table 4.3 Monetary policy committees: voting patterns in various countries (October 2018–June 2024)

Continent	Country	Meetings statistics				
		Total	Consensus	Dissent	Meetings with rate cut	Meetings with rate increase
AFRICA	South Africa	35	14	21	July 2019, Jan 2020, Mar 2020, Apr 2020, May 2020, July 2020	November 2018, November 2021–May 2023
ASIA	China	25	N/A	N/A	Nov 2019, Feb 2020, April 2020, Jan 2022, Aug 2022, June 2023, Aug 2023	–
	India	48	32	16	Feb 2019, Apr 2019, June 2019, Aug 2019, Oct 2019, April 2020, Mar 2020, May 2020	May 2022, June 2022, August 2022, September 2022, December 2022, February 2023
	Indonesia	68	NA	NA	July 2019, August 2019, September 2019, Oct 2019, Feb 2020, Mar 2020, June 2020, November 2020, Feb 2021	September 2018, November 2018, August 2022, September 2022, October 2022, November 2022, December 2022, October 2023, April 2024
	Japan	47	14	33	Maintain Status Quo	Maintain Status Quo
EUROPE	ECB	49	N/A	N/A	Sep 2019, June 2024	July 2022, Sep 2022, Oct 2022, Dec 2022, Feb 2023, Mar 2023, May 2023, June 2023, July 2023, Sep 2023
	UK	48	23	25	Mar 2020, Mar 2020	Dec 2021, Feb 2022, Mar 2022, May 2022, June 2022, Aug 2022, Sep 2022, Nov 2022, Dec 2022, Feb 2023, Mar 2023, May 2023, June 2023, August 2023

(continued)

Table 4.3 (continued)

Continent	Country	Meetings statistics				
		Total	Consensus	Dissent	Meetings with rate cut	Meetings with rate increase
EUROPE/ ASIA	Russia	49	N/A	N/A	June 2019, July 2019, Sep 2019, Oct 2019, Dec 2019, Feb 2020, Apr 2020, June 2020, July 2020, April 8 2022, Apr 29 2022, May 2022, June 2022, July 2022, Sep 2022	Sep 2018, Dec 2018, Mar 2021, Apr 2021, June 2021, July 2021, Sep 2021, Oct 2021, Dec 2021, Feb 11 2022, Feb 28 2022, July 2023, Aug 2023. Sep 2023, Oct 2023, Dec 2023
NORTH AMERICA	Canada	47	N/A	N/A	Mar 4 2020, Mar 16 2020, Mar 27 2020, June 2024	Oct 2018, Mar 2022, Apr 2022, June 2022, July 2022, Sep 2022, Oct 2022, Dec 2022, Jan 2023, Mar 2023, Apr 2023, June 2023, July 2023
	Mexico	48	24	24	August 2019–September 2020, February 2021, March 2024	November 2018, December 2018, June 2021–March 2023
	US	59	49	0	May 2019, July 2019, Sep 2019, Oct 2019, Mar 3 2020, Mar 15 2020	Sep 2018, Dec 2018, Jan 2020, June 2021, Mar 2022, May 2022, June 2022, July 2022, Sep 2022, Nov 2022, Dec 2022, Jan 2023, Mar 2023, May 2023, July 2023
OCEANIA	Australia	63	N/A	N/A	June 2019, July 2019, Oct 2019, Mar 3 2020, Mar 18 2020, Nov 2020	May 2022, June 2022, July 2022, Aug 2022, Sep 2022, Oct 2022, Nov 2022, Dec 2022, Feb 2023, Mar 2023, May 2023, June 2023, Nov 2023,
SOUTH AMERICA	Brazil	45	41	4	July 2019, Sep 2019, Oct 2019, Dec 2019, Feb 2020, Mar 2020, May 2020, June 2020, Aug 2020, Aug 2023, Sep 2023, Nov 2023, Dec 2023, January 2024	Mar 2021, May 2021, June 2021, Aug 2021, Sep 2021, Oct 2021, Dec 2021, Feb 2022, Mar 2022, May 2022, May 2022, June 2022, Aug 2022

Source Central Bank Websites

falls, debt obligations of firms may decrease, strengthening their balance sheets. As a result, financial institutions may be more willing to lend to businesses, thus increasing investment spending. Monetary policy changes can impact public's expectations of output and inflation and accordingly, aggregate demand can be impacted via the *expectations channel.* For instance, expected future changes in the policy rate can impact medium-term and long-term expected interest rates through market expectations and thus affect aggregate demand. Further, if inflation expectations are firmly anchored by the central bank, this would imply price stability.

A stylized representation of the monetary policy transmission framework of a change in the policy rate is shown in Fig. 4.6. Figure 4.7 depicts the monetary transmission through the interest rate channel with specific reference to India. (Definitions of all variables shown in Fig. 4.6 are given in Annexure 2.) This shows that a change in the policy rate (repo rate) first impacts the call money rate (weighted average call money rate—WACR) and in turn all other money market rates as well as bond market rates including the repo market, certificates of deposit (CD) and commercial paper (CP) markets, Treasury Bill (T-Bill) market, Government Securities (G-Sec) market and the Bond Market. The lending rate of banks also changes as depicted by the marginal cost of funds-based lending rate (MCLR). This further impacts consumption and investment decisions as well as net exports and through these, aggregate demand and ultimately the goals of monetary policy. Details of the monetary transmission process are given in RBI (2020c).

The transmission mechanism is beset with lags. As explained in simple terms in Rangarajan (2020), there are two components of the transmission mechanism. The first is how far the signals sent out by the central bank are picked by the banks and the

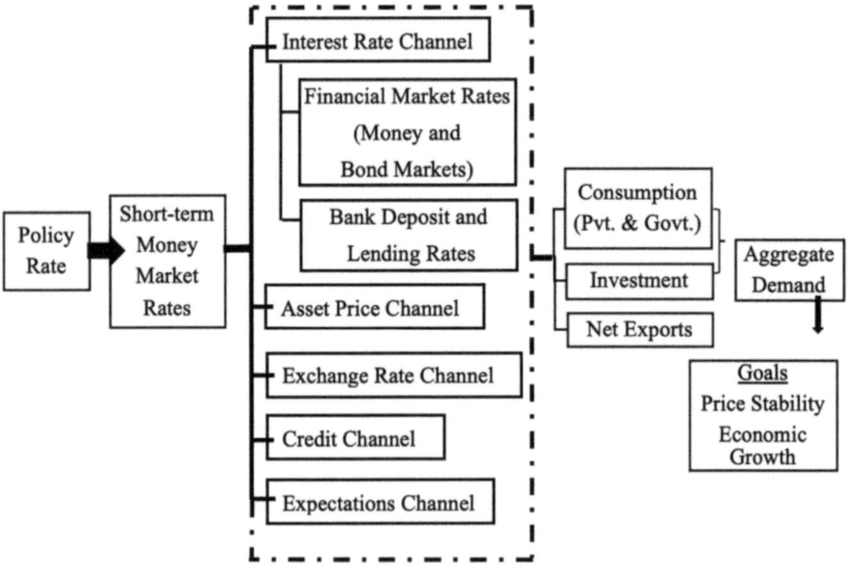

Fig. 4.6 Monetary policy transmission framework

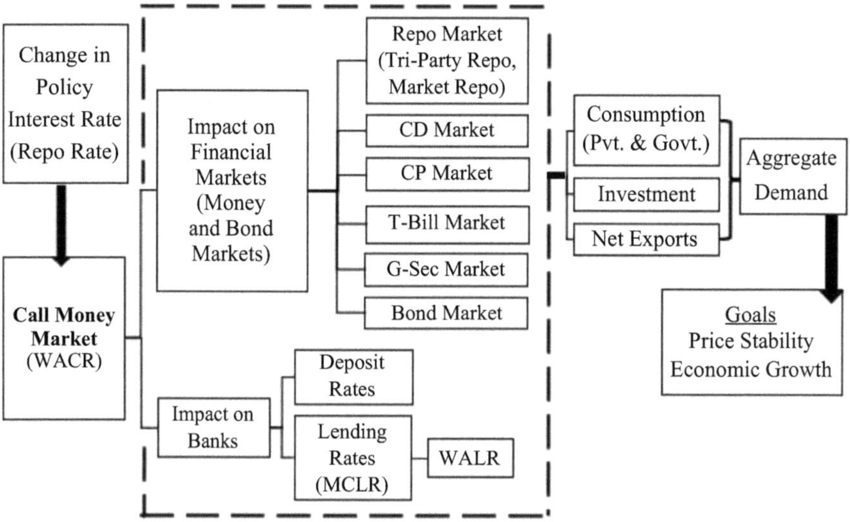

Fig. 4.7 Monetary policy transmission in India—Interest rate channel. *Note* Definitions of variables are given in Annexure 2

second is how far the signals sent out by the banking system impact the real economy. Rangarajan (2020) labels the first component as "inner leg" and the second as "outer leg".

To illustrate monetary transmission of the first kind, we examine the impact of policy rate changes on financial market rates. During the last easing phase, i.e. February 7, 2019 to April 7, 2022, in response to 250 bps decrease in policy repo rate, transmission to various money and bond markets ranged from 320 basis points in the overnight call money market to 81 basis points in the market for 5-year government securities to 41 basis points in the market for 10-year government securities. In the tightening period, i.e. April 8, 2022 to April 30, 2024, in response to 250 bps increase in policy repo rate, transmission to various money and bond markets ranged from 333 basis points in the overnight call money market to 59 basis points in the market for 5-year government securities.

Transmission to the credit market was also significant. In the last easing period, the 1-year median marginal cost of funds-based lending rate (MCLR) declined by 155 bps during February 2019 and March 2022. The weighted average lending rate (WALR) on fresh rupee loans sanctioned by banks fell by 232 bps while the WALR on outstanding rupee loans declined by 150 bps during February 2019 to March 2022. In the current tightening period, the 1-year median marginal cost of funds-based lending rate (MCLR) increased by 167 bps during April 2022 and March 2024. The weighted average lending rate (WALR) on fresh rupee loans sanctioned by banks increased by 185 bps while the WALR on outstanding rupee loans increased by 111 bps during May 2022 to February 2024.

Monetary transmission in various markets is depicted in Figs. 4.8, 4.9 and 4.10. Figure 4.8 shows the policy corridor with the MSF rate as the ceiling and the reverse repo rate/SDF as the floor for the daily movement in the weighted average call money rate. The figure shows that the WACR moved closely in tandem with the policy rate (repo rate). Figure 4.9 shows that the G-Sec market rates followed the movements in the policy rate. Figure 4.10 shows that the direction of change of MCLR was more or less in synchronization with that of the repo rate. The WALR for fresh rupee loans tracked the repo rate much more than the WALR on outstanding loans.

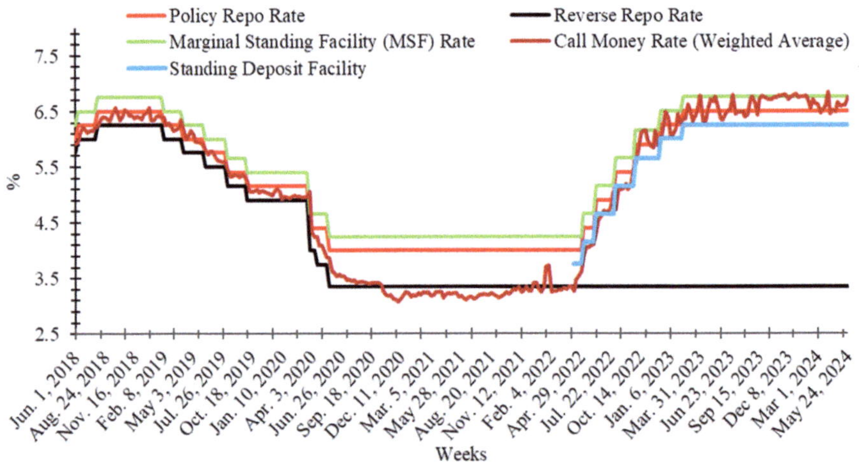

Fig. 4.8 Policy corridor and WACR. *Source* RBI Database on Indian Economy, RBI Weekly Statistical Supplement

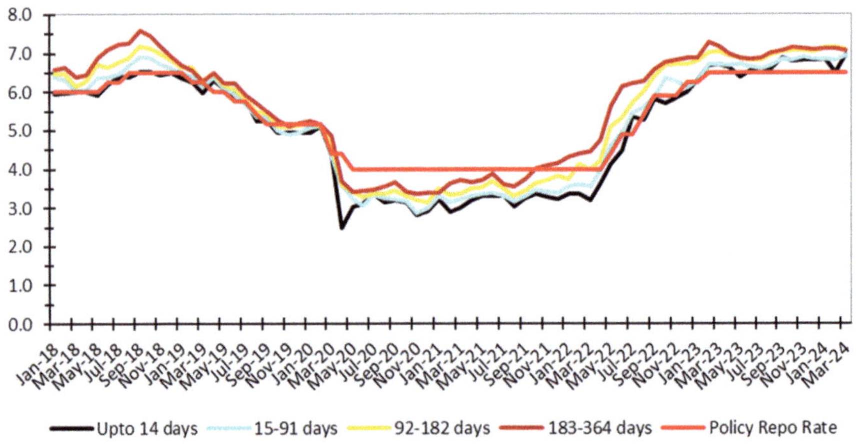

Fig. 4.9 Government security market and repo rate. *Source* RBI Database on Indian Economy

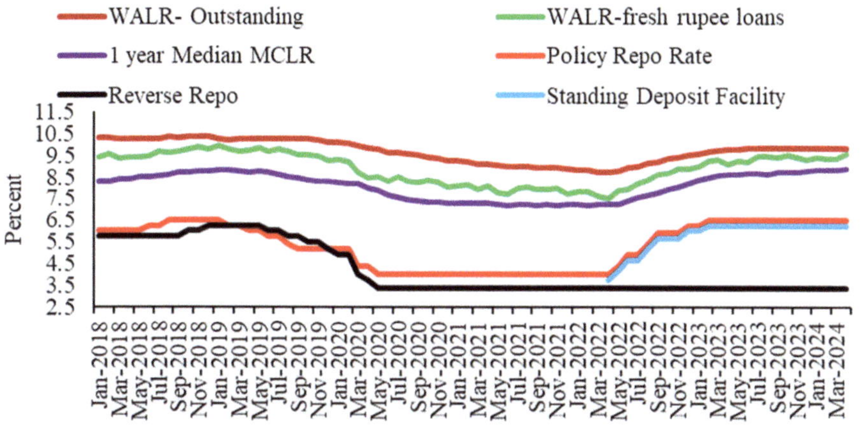

Fig. 4.10 Lending rates of scheduled commercial banks. *Source* RBI Website

Figure 4.11 shows the 4% target inflation rate with the ±2% tolerance band along with the headline inflation rate. This shows that the headline inflation stayed within the band up to November 2019 averaging around 3.6% but rose after that and continued rising during the pandemic before returning to 6% in December 2020. It also exceeded 6% during most of 2022. The GDP growth dropped sharply during the pandemic to −23.4% (2020–2021 Q1) (Fig. 4.12). Growth before and after the pandemic averaged around 5.5% (2018–2019 Q1 to 2019–2020 Q3) and 8.6% (2021–2022 Q1 to 2023–2024 Q2), respectively.

An interesting phenomenon, worldwide is the synchronization in the movements in interest rates across the globe in both advanced and emerging economies. Table 4.4 shows the change in interest rates in two phases—October 2018 to March 2022 and

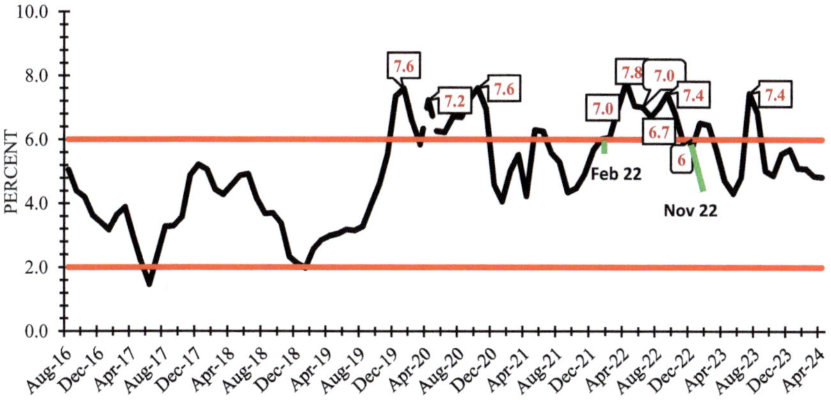

Fig. 4.11 CPI combined inflation (2012 = 100) with 2%, 4% and 6% bands. *Source* Ministry of Statistics and Programme Implementation, GOI

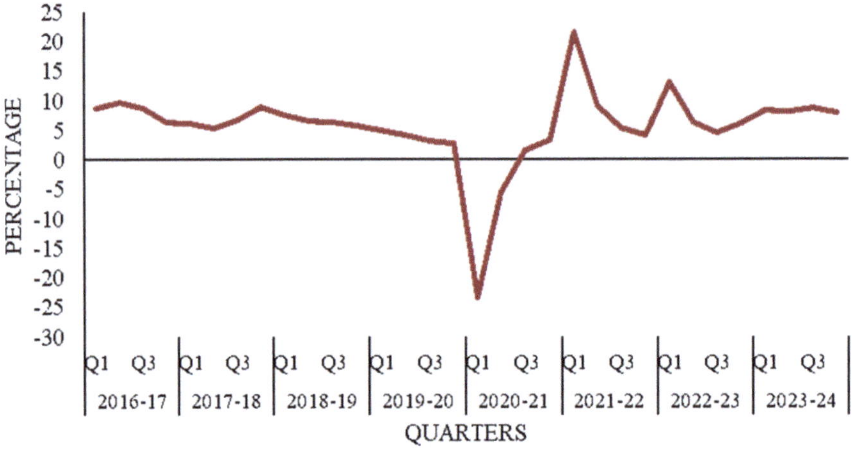

Fig. 4.12 Growth Rate of Indian GDP at Constant Prices (2011-12 = 100) *Source* Ministry of Statistics and Programme Implementation, GOI

April 2022 to June 2024 for both sets of countries. Taken along with Table 4.3, Table 4.4 shows that that MPCs in various countries voted for a cut in their policy rate in 2019 at a time when many countries were simultaneously experiencing a slowdown. Further, due to the pandemic, some countries cut the policy rate sharply. This was followed by hikes in the interest rate as shown in the last column of Tables 4.3 and 4.4. This is further elaborated in Figs. 4.13A and 4.13B that show the easing in interest rates in 2020 and the hikes in 2022 and 2023 for advanced and emerging economies, respectively. In these figures, the first quarter denotes January to March.

This global pattern of rate cuts in 2019 and subsequent hikes is aligned with the movements in the repo rate (policy rate) in India. These global patterns are illustrated in Figs. 4.14A and 4.14B that show that the policy rates for advanced and emerging economies, respectively, moved in tandem from 2017 to 2024 (June). Figures 4.15A, 4.15B, 4.16A and 4.16B show the synchronization of inflation rates and GDP growth, respectively, across the globe.

4.5 Unconventional Monetary Policy Measures

We have so far discussed conventional monetary policy. As already described, monetary transmission of conventional monetary policy entails a change in the policy rate impacting financial markets from short-term interest rates to longer-term bonds and bank funding and lending rates. A change in the policy rate is thus expected to permeate through the entire spectrum of rates that further translates into affecting

Table 4.4 Monetary policy committees: Change in policy rate in various countries (October 2018–June 2024)

Advanced country	Current policy rate (June 2024)	Total rate cuts (bps) (Oct 2018–Mar 2022)	Total rate hike (bps) (Apr 2022–June 2024)
US	5.4	−235	500
ECB	3.75	−10	450
UK	5.25	−65	450
JAPAN	−0.1	0	0
Australia	4.35	−140	425
Canada	4.75	−150	450
Emerging country	**Current policy rate (June 2024)**	**Total rate cuts (bps) (Oct 2018–Mar 2022)**	**Total rate hike (bps) (Apr 2022–June 2024)**
Brazil	10.5	−450	200
Russian Federation	16	−350	850
India	6.5	−250	250
China	2.5	−45	0
South Africa	8.25	−325	400
Indonesia	6.25	−250	275
Mexico	11.0	−425	475

Source Central Bank Websites

interest sensitive spending and thus economic activity. However, if there are problems in the monetary policy transmission mechanism or if additional monetary stimulus is required in the circumstances that the policy rate cannot be reduced further (or in addition to a change in the policy rate), then the central banks may employ unconventional monetary policy tools. Unconventional monetary measures target financial variables other than the short-term interest rate such as term spreads (e.g. interest rates on risk-free bonds), liquidity, credit spreads (e.g. interest rates on risky assets) and asset prices. The objective of unconventional tools is to supplement the conventional monetary policy tools, especially during crisis periods to reinvigorate economic activity. For instance, as shown in Fig. 4.17, while the Indian policy rate was at a low of 4% from May 2020 to April 2022, unconventional measures were adopted by the Reserve Bank of India to revive the economy.

Thus, in the recent past, RBI has utilized various unconventional tools in addition to conventional monetary policy measures. To better understand the use of unconventional tools in the Indian economy, examples of unconventional monetary policy tools are first analysed and their applications to the Indian scenario are described. Broadly, unconventional measures can be classified into four categories—large scale asset purchases, lending operations, forward guidance and negative interest rates (BIS, 2019). The key features of the measures and their applications in India are described in Table 4.5.

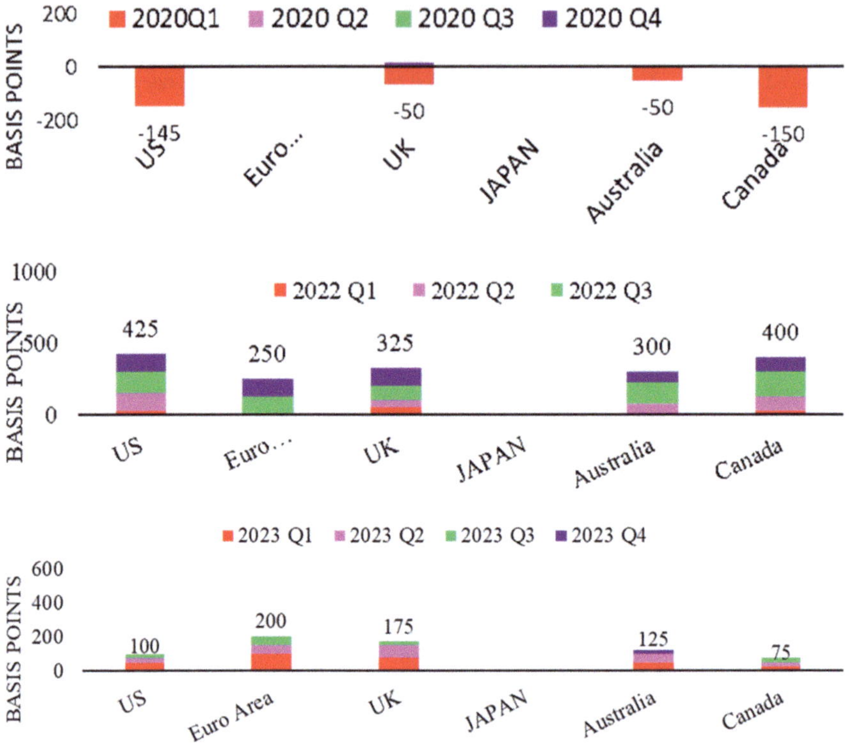

Fig. 4.13A Advanced economies: Policy easing and tightening

- Large scale asset purchases (also referred to as quantitative easing) by a central bank involve purchase of long-term government securities financed by crediting reserve accounts that commercial banks hold at the central bank. This purchase would lower government bond yields and serve as a signal that the policy rate will stay at a lower level for a longer period. Sellers of government bonds may, in turn, change their investment portfolios and invest in more risky assets (e.g. corporate bonds) leading to a decrease in the relevant interest rate and higher asset price and thus boost economic growth. Central banks can also purchase assets from the private sector.
- Lending operations entail provision of liquidity to financial institutions by the central bank through the creation of new or extension of existing lending facilities. This mechanism is different from conventional lending since this is undertaken at looser or specific conditions, e.g. expanding the set of eligible collateral, extending maturity of the loan, providing funding at lower cost and channel/target lending to desired areas or activities with explicit conditions on loans. This lending increases the credit flows to the private sector and helps to restart flow of credit to credit-starved sectors. It can also lead to lower borrowing costs for the financial and real economy sectors.

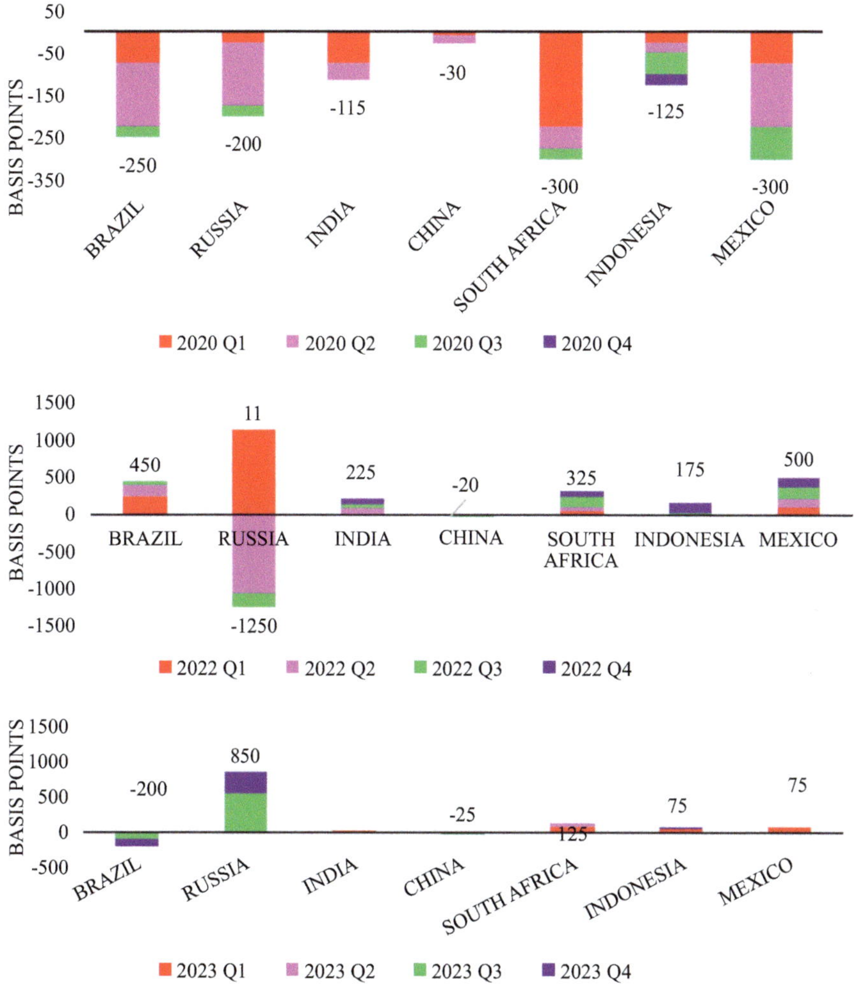

Fig. 4.13B Emerging economies: Policy easing and tightening. *Source* Central Bank Websites

- Forward guidance involves central banks communicating future policy intentions and commitments regarding the policy rate in order to influence policy expectations. Forward guidance is given routinely by most central banks. Its use as an unconventional tool implies that a central bank uses this to signal that it is open to undertaking extraordinary policy actions for a longer duration. Forward guidance can be 'time specific' or 'state specific'. Under the former, the central bank makes a commitment to keep interest rates low for a specified period. Under the latter, the central bank maintains low rates until specific economic conditions are met.

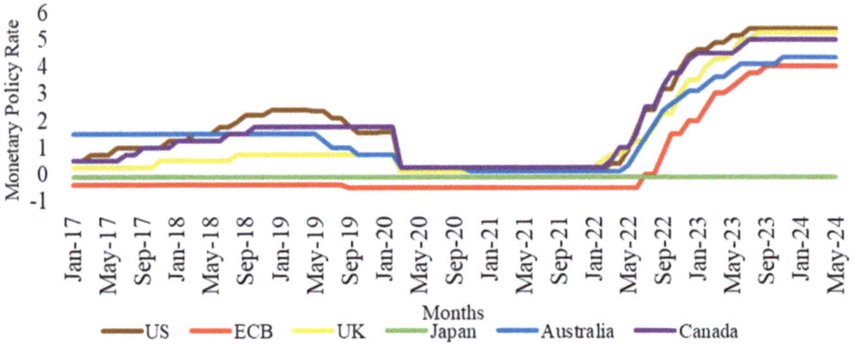

Fig. 4.14A Comparison of advanced economies monetary policy interest rates 2017–2024. *Notes* (1) US: Fed Funds Rate; ECB: Interest Rate on Deposit Facility; UK: Bank Rate; Japan: Policy Rate; Australia: Cash Target Rate; Canada: Target Overnight Rate (2) *Source* Central Bank Websites

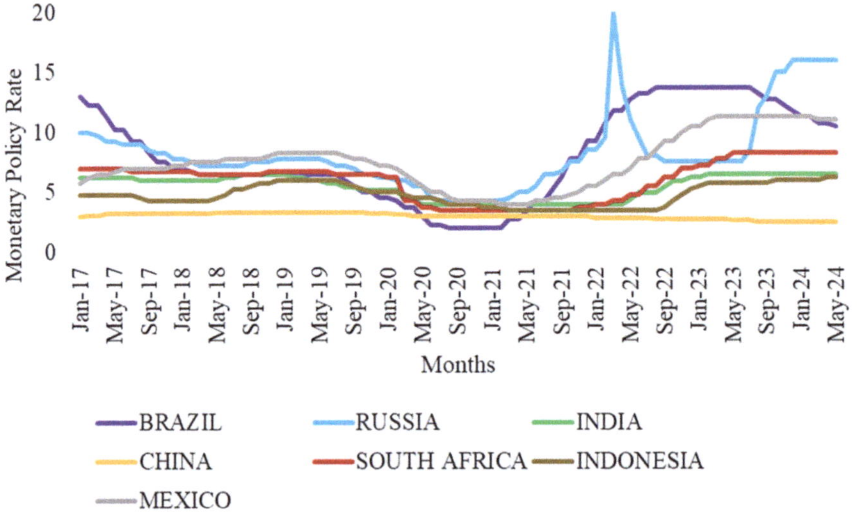

Fig. 4.14B Comparison of emerging economies monetary policy interest rates 2017–2024. *Notes* (1) Brazil: Selic Rate; Russia: Key Rate; India: Repo Rate; China: Medium-Term Lending Facility; South Africa: Repo Rate; Indonesia: BI 7-Day (Reverse) Repo Rate; Mexico: Target overnight interbank funding rate. *Source* Central Bank Websites

- The rationale of a negative interest rate is that if an interest rate is charged on the reserves that commercial banks hold at the central bank, the banks may be induced to reduce their excess reserves by increasing lending.

The first three of these have been applied to India and are reported in Table 4.4. These include Operations Twist in December 2019 and January as well as April 2020, long-term repo operation (LTRO) in February 2020, targeted long-term repo operations (TLTRO) in March and April 2020 and special refinance facilities to

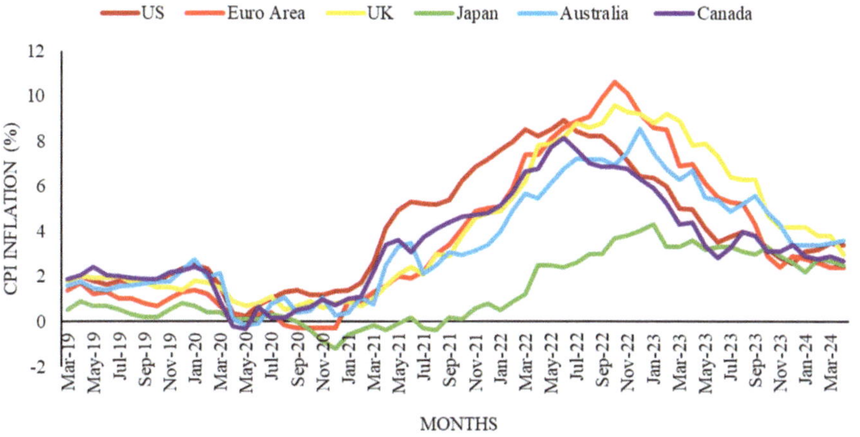

Fig. 4.15A Inflation (CPI) in advanced economies 2019–2024. *Sources* FRED, OGD Platform India, Ministry of Statistics and Programme Implementation, Moody's Analytics, OECD

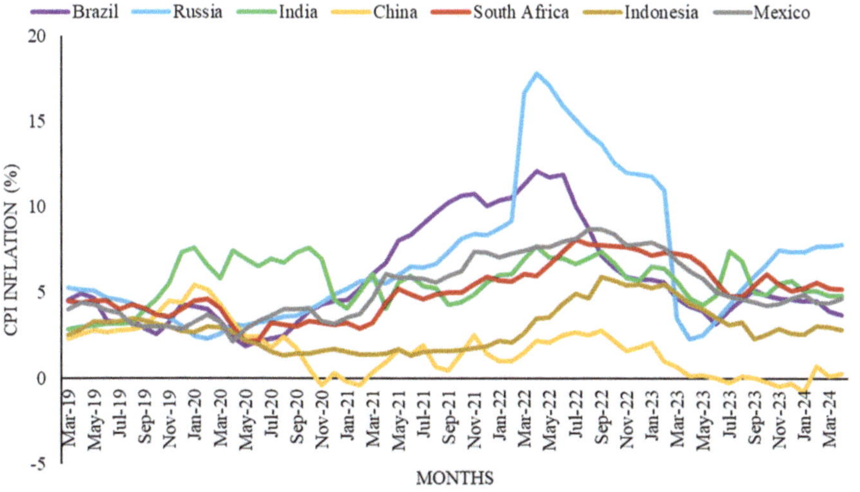

Fig. 4.15B Inflation (CPI) in emerging economies 2019–2024. *Sources* FRED, OGD Platform India, Ministry of Statistics and Programme Implementation, Moody's Analytics, OECD

National Bank for Agriculture and Rural Development (NABARD), Small Industries Development Bank of India (SIDBI) and National Housing Bank (NHB) in April 2020. Further, G-SAP was announced in April 2021, followed by another round in June 2021, Special Liquidity Facility for Mutual Funds (SLF-MF) in April 2020, on tap TLTRO in October 2020, term liquidity facility for healthcare infrastructure and services in May 2021, Special LTRO (SLTRO) for SFBs and on tap liquidity window for certain contact-intensive sectors (Monetary Policy Reports and Governor's Statement, various issues).

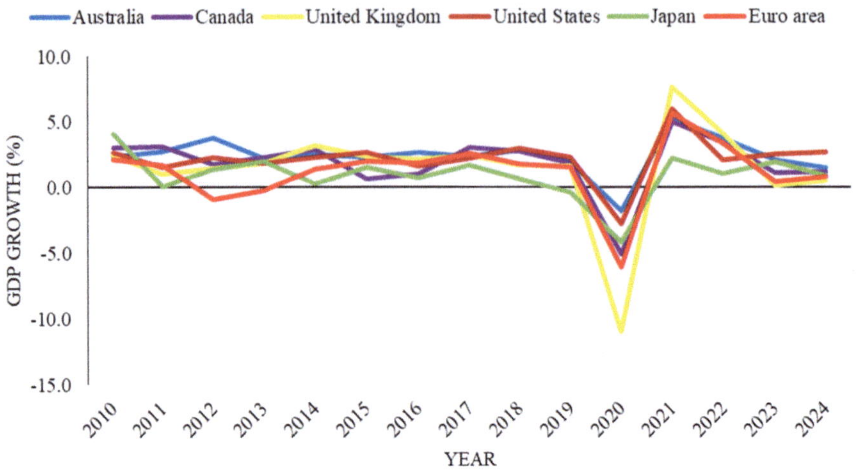

Fig. 4.16A Real GDP growth (Annual %) in advanced economies 2010–2024

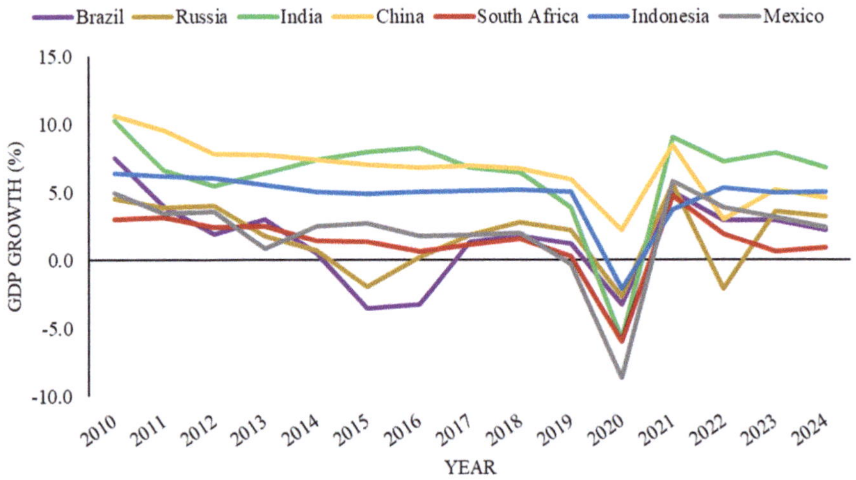

Fig. 4.16B Real GDP growth (Annual %) in emerging economies 2010–2024

From time to time, the RBI Governor and MPC provide forward guidance. In October 2020, the MPC provided both state-contingent and time-contingent forward guidance by continuing "... *with the accommodative stance of monetary policy as long as necessary—at least during the current financial year and into the next year—to revive growth on a durable basis and mitigate the impact of COVID-19, while ensuring that inflation remains within the target going forward*" (MPC Resolution, October 2020; RBI, 2020g). In April 2021, the evolving role and nature of forward guidance came to the fore as the MPC shifted to state-based rather than time-based guidance, recognizing the difficulty of perfectly anticipating how the economy would

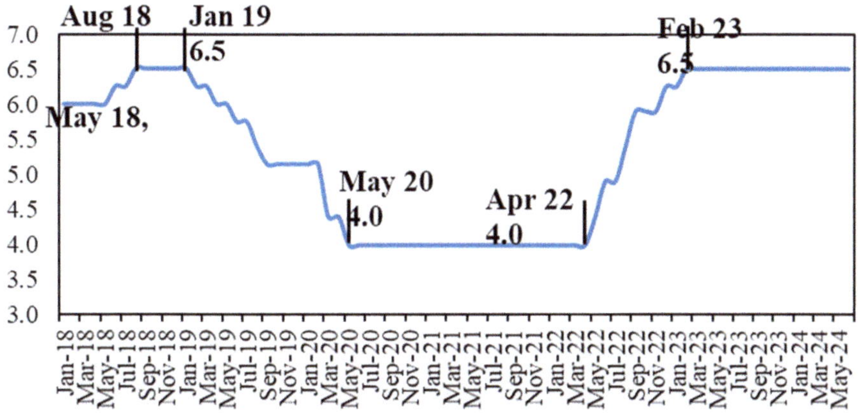

Fig. 4.17 Policy repo rate

progress and when the recovery would get firmly entrenched amid the ongoing pandemic. According to the MPC Resolution, April 2021 (RBI, 2021b), "… *the MPC decided to continue with the accommodative stance as long as necessary to sustain growth on a durable basis and continue to mitigate the impact of COVID-19 on the economy, while ensuring that inflation remains within the target going forward*". While the utility of forward guidance at very low policy rates is unambiguously proven, its efficacy at higher rates is questionable.[1] The Governor has noted: "…*Recognising that explicit guidance in a rate tightening cycle is inherently fraught with risks, the MPC has also eschewed from providing any future guidance on the timing and level of the terminal rate*[2]".

The application of these unconventional monetary tools was necessitated, first by the slowdown in the Indian economy in 2019, and second, by the impact of COVID-19 pandemic due to which economic activity and financial markets, the world over, came under severe stress. It was thus necessary for the Reserve Bank to employ measures to mitigate the impact of COVID-19, revive growth and preserve financial stability. Thus, the unconventional monetary policy tools supplemented the conventional monetary policy measures to revive growth and restore market confidence in the economy.

---

[1] Patra et al. (2023).

[2] Das (2023).

Table 4.5 Unconventional policy measures

UMP measure	Financial indicators	Mechanism	Intermediate goals	Application for India
Large scale asset purchases	- Long-term yields - Asset prices - Financial system liquidity	- Purchase of long-term government securities financed by crediting reserve accounts that commercial banks hold at the central bank, lowering government bond yields - Induce sellers of government bonds to purchase riskier assets (e.g. corporate bonds), leading to lower cost of debt, i.e. reduction in relevant interest rates and higher asset prices - Central banks can also purchase assets from the private sector - Purchases lead to large increases in central banks' balance sheets	- Lower interest rates on risk-free assets (e.g. government securities) across different terms to maturity - Lower interest rates across various markets - Signalling device that policy rate will stay lower for longer and thus, stabilize interest rate expectations - Easing financial conditions	- Simultaneous buying and selling of long-term and short-term G-Secs have been used to 'twist' and flatten the yield curve (Operation Twist) in December 2019, January and April 2020 - Secondary market G-Sec acquisition programme (G-SAP) was announced in April 2021, followed by a second round in June 2021. Aim was to ensure orderly evolution of the yield curve to facilitate monetary transmission across financial instruments. An upfront commitment was provided on size of G-Sec purchases in contrast to regular purchases through OMOs, which are driven by systemic liquidity considerations. Both liquid and illiquid securities were purchased, bulk of which were in 5–10-year segment of the G-Sec yield curve, imparting liquidity to this segment. G-SAP thus reinforced softening impact on yields

(continued)

Table 4.5 (continued)

UMP measure	Financial indicators	Mechanism	Intermediate goals	Application for India
Lending operations	- Credit growth - Corporate yield spreads - Financial system liquidity	- Provision of liquidity to financial institutions through creation of new or extension of existing lending facilities - Different from conventional lending due to looser or specific conditions, e.g. expanding set of eligible collateral, extending maturity of loan, provide funding at lower cost, channel lending to desired areas or activities with explicit conditions on loans	- Increase credit flows to private sector - Restart flow of credit to credit-starved sectors - Lower borrowing costs for financial and real economy sectors - Stabilize interest rate expectations - Easing financial conditions	- To augment credit flows to productive sectors at reasonable cost, RBI announced LTROs on Feb 6, 2020 - TLTRO and TLTRO 2.0 were announced on Mar 27 & April 17, 2020, respectively, to stimulate targeted lending wherein banks access liquidity at lower costs from RBI to be lent to targeted sectors - Provision of special refinance facilities to NABARD, SIDB and NHB were announced on April 17, 2020 to enable them to meet sectoral credit needs - To reduce liquidity pressures on mutual funds, RBI opened a Special Liquidity Facility for Mutual Funds (SLF-MF) in April 2020 - To revive specific sectors, 'on tap TLTRO' was announced in October 2020 for five specific sectors. In December 2020, 26 stressed sectors were brought under this scheme, which was subsequently expanded to include bank lending to NBFCs in February 2021 - Term liquidity facility (TLF) for healthcare infrastructure and services was introduced in May 2021 - Special LTROs (SLTRO) were started for small finance banks (SFBs) - On tap liquidity window for certain contact-intensive sectors was initiated to face second wave of pandemic

(continued)

Table 4.5 (continued)

UMP measure	Financial indicators	Mechanism	Intermediate goals	Application for India
Forward guidance	- Policy Rate - Stance of monetary policy - Policy space	- State central banks' intentions and commitment regarding policy rate - Typically, can be 'time specific' or 'state specific' - Under time specific, central bank makes a commitment not to increase interest rates for a specified time period - Under state specific, central bank maintains low rates until specific economic conditions are met	- Signalling device that policy rate will stay lower for longer	- RBI Governor and MPC resolutions regularly offer forward guidance on the trajectory of policy direction, policy stance (accommodative, neutral and tightening) and policy space - As an unconventional tool, RBI signals extraordinary policy actions for a longer duration - In October 2020, MPC provided both state-specific and time-specific forward guidance - In April 2021, MPC shifted to state-based rather than time-based guidance

(continued)

Table 4.5 (continued)

UMP measure	Financial indicators	Mechanism	Intermediate goals	Application for India
Negative interest rate	- Policy Rate - Long-term yields - Financial conditions	- Banks reduce their excess reserves by increasing lending and purchasing other financial assets	- Adjustment of long-term yields downwards in line with expectations of future short-term rates - Easing financial conditions	NA

Notes

The final goals of unconventional monetary policy are to boost economic growth and supplement conventional monetary policy tools especially during the easing cycle

1. Operation Twist, RBI Monetary Policy Report (MPR), April 2020 (RBI, 2020d)
2. G-SAP, RBI MPR, April 2022 (RBI, 2022); Patra and Bhattacharyya (2022)
3. Long-Term Repo Operations, RBI Governor's Statement, February 6, 2020; RBI MPR, April 2020 (RBI, 2020a, 2020d)
4. Targeted Long-Term Repo Operations, RBI Governor's Statement, March 27 and April, 17, 2020; RBI MPR, April 2020 (RBI, 2020b, 2020d, 2020e)
5. National Bank for Agriculture and Rural Development (NABARD), Small Industries Development Bank of India (SIDBI) and National Housing Bank (NHB), RBI Governor's Statement, April 17, 2020 (RBI, 2020e)
6. SLF-MF, RBI Governor's Statement, April, 17, 2020 (RBI, 2020e)
7. On tap TLTRO, RBI and MPR October 2020 (RBI, 2020f)
8. TLF, SLTRO, Liquidity Window, RBI Governor's Statement, October 2021 (RBI, 2021c); RBI Annual Report, 2021–2022 (RBI, 2021a)
9. Policy stance—Accommodative: interest rates stay the same or decrease; Tightening: interest rates stay the same or increase; Neutral: interest rates can decrease, increase or stay the same

4.6 Conclusion

This paper reviews the evolution of monetary policy frameworks in India since the mid-1980s. It also describes the monetary policy transmission process and its limitations in terms of lags in transmission as well as the rigidities in the process. It also highlights the importance of unconventional monetary policy measures in supplementing conventional tools, especially during periods of crisis such as the COVID-19 pandemic.

At the time of writing (June 2024), seven and a half years have passed since the implementation of the Flexible Inflation Targeting Framework and the constitution of the Monetary Policy Committee. With the implementation of FIT, India joined the group of various developed, emerging and developing countries that have implemented inflation targeting since 1990.

The inflation target specified by the Central Government was 4% for the Consumer Price Index (CPI) inflation for the period from August 5, 2016 to March 31, 2021 with the upper tolerance limit of 6% and the lower tolerance bound of 2%. This was subsequently renewed for a further 5-year period (April 1 2021 to March 31, 2026). As shown in Fig. 4.11, from August 2016 through March 2020, the headline inflation generally stayed within the tolerance band with the average inflation rate slightly less than 4% during this period. Subsequently, however, there were episodes of high/unusual inflation in 2020 and 2022 due to supply shocks (food inflation, oil prices) but these were suitably integrated in the policy decisions.

The Monetary Policy Committee has also been in existence since October 2016. The mandate of the MPC is to set the policy repo rate while taking cognizance of the primary objective of monetary policy—to maintain price stability while keeping in mind the objective of growth—as well as the target inflation rate within the tolerance band. Once the policy repo rate is set, the monetary transmission process facilitates the percolation of the change in the policy rate to all financial markets (money and bond markets) as well as the banking sector which further impacts interest sensitive spending in the economy and eventually increases aggregate demand and output growth.

In practice, however, there are rigidities as well as lags in the transmission process that impede the speed and magnitude of the transmission and thus question the efficacy of monetary policy with respect to the policy repo rate. Nevertheless, the external benchmarking system introduced by RBI in October 2019 and extended in April 2020 has strengthened the monetary transmission process. As per this, all new floating rate personal or retail loans (housing, auto, etc.) and floating rate loans extended by banks to Micro and Small Enterprises from October 01, 2019 and floating rate loans to Medium Enterprises from April 01, 2020 are benchmarked to one of the following, viz., (i) Reserve Bank of India policy repo rate; (ii) Government of India 3-Months and 6-Months Treasury Bill yield published by the Financial Benchmarks India Private Ltd (FBIL) and (iii) any other benchmark market interest rate published by the FBIL. Banks are free to offer such external benchmark linked loans to other types of borrowers as well but cannot adopt multiple benchmarks within a loan category.

Of course, the policy repo rate is not a panacea for all ills but serves well as a signalling rate. The RBI routinely brings out the Statement on Developmental and Regulatory Policies[3] that is released simultaneously with the resolution of the MPC. RBI has also taken recourse to unconventional measures to supplement the conventional tools to restore market confidence and revive economic activity. With the slowdown in 2019 followed by the extraordinary slump in economic activity due to COVID-19 pandemic, RBI has been compelled to use rather innovative and unconventional tools starting in December 2019 as discussed in Table 4.5. These helped to supplement the low policy rate of 4% between March 2020 and April 2022.

Needless to say, in the unprecedented times of the global pandemic (and, in general, in periods of severe crises), a multi-pronged approach comprising monetary, fiscal and other policy measures is required to protect economic activity and minimize the negative impact of the pandemic (crisis) on economic growth. The importance of monetary-fiscal coordination is highlighted in the resolution of the Monetary Policy Committee dated March 27, 2020 (available on the RBI website) that states the following: "*Strong fiscal measures are critical to deal with the situation*". Thus, in addition to monetary policy, fiscal policy had a major role in combating the economic effects of the COVID-19 pandemic. In response to the need of the hour, the Government of India implemented various fiscal measures to provide a boost to the economy. In fact, while central banks across the globe responded to the global pandemic with monetary and regulatory measures, various governments reinforced the monetary measures by deploying massive fiscal measures to shield economic activity from the effect of the COVID-19 pandemic.

Further, the synchronization of movements in policy rates, inflation rate and GDP growth across the globe during the crisis period (Tables 4.3 and 4.4, Figs. 4.13–4.16) highlights the strong integration of India with the rest of the world. This also brings to the fore the importance of innovative and unconventional policy measures to tackle crises and for building resilience of the economy. The monetary policy measures adopted by RBI show that India is equipped to handle such crises, to the extent possible. In fact, the Reserve Bank has played a major role in mitigating the impact of the COVID-19 pandemic on the Indian economy, reviving growth and preserving financial stability through implementation of a plethora of policy measures.

A few words about the workings of the MPC are also warranted. As discussed in the paper, the voting pattern of the Indian MPC is comparable to international standards, reflecting the healthy diversity in the assessment of the members. The workings of the MPC are transparent with the resolution being made available soon after the end of the meetings. Furthermore, each member of the Committee has to submit a statement that is made available in the public domain on the 14th day after

[3] Statement on Developmental and Regulatory Policies sets out various developmental and regulatory policy measures and macroprudential policies for strengthening financial markets and systems, regulation and supervision, banking sector, etc. from time to time.

the meeting. Thus, each member is individually accountable, making the process perhaps more stringent than that of MPCs in other countries.

Finally, recent work by Blanchard and Bernanke (2024) on the post-pandemic global inflation that was primarily caused by supply disruptions and increase in prices of food and fuel, merits mention. The study shows that unlike the 1970s, the inflationary impact of these supply shocks has not been persistent, which may be attributed to the credibility of central bank inflation targets. This provides support for inflation targeting.

Acknowledgements I am indebted to Rajiv Ranjan, Executive Director, Reserve Bank of India for invaluable feedback and support in updating and extending my earlier work (Dua, 2020). I also gratefully acknowledge immense help and useful suggestions from Deepika Goel, Associate Professor, Aryabhatta College, University of Delhi.

Annexure 1: Glossary—Figures 4.2 and 4.5

Repo rate is the interest rate at which the RBI provides liquidity under the liquidity adjustment facility (LAF) to all participants against the collateral of government and other approved securities.
Standing Deposit Facility (SDF) Rate: The rate at which the Reserve Bank accepts uncollateralized deposits, on an overnight basis, from all LAF participants. With its introduction in April 2022, the SDF rate replaced the fixed reverse repo rate as the floor of the LAF corridor.
Reverse Repo Rate: Following the introduction of the SDF, the fixed rate reverse repo is used at the discretion of the RBI for purposes specified from time to time. Earlier it was the (fixed) interest rate at which the RBI absorbed liquidity, on an overnight basis, from banks against the collateral of eligible government securities under the LAF.
Liquidity Adjustment Facility (LAF) refers to the Reserve Bank's operations through which it injects/absorbs liquidity into/from the banking system. It consists of overnight as well as term repo/reverse repos operations at variable rates (conducted through auctions), SDF and MSF.
LAF Corridor has the marginal standing facility (MSF) rate as its upper bound (ceiling) and the standing deposit facility (SDF) rate as the lower bound (floor), with the policy repo rate in the middle of the corridor.
Marginal Standing Facility (MSF) Rate: The penal rate at which banks can borrow, on an overnight basis, from the Reserve Bank by dipping into their Statutory Liquidity Ratio (SLR) portfolio up to a predefined limit (2%). This provides a safety valve against unanticipated liquidity shocks to the banking system.
Main Liquidity Management Tool: A 14-day term repo/reverse repo auction operation at a variable rate conducted to coincide with the cash reserve ratio (CRR) maintenance cycle is the main liquidity management tool for managing frictional liquidity requirements.
Fine Tuning Operations: The main liquidity operation is supported by fine-tuning operations, overnight and/or longer tenor, to tide over any unanticipated liquidity changes during the reserve maintenance period. In addition, the Reserve Bank conducts, if needed, longer-term variable rate repo/reverse repo auctions of more than 14 days.

(continued)

(continued)

Bank Rate acts as the penal rate charged on banks for shortfalls in meeting their reserve requirements (cash reserve ratio and statutory liquidity ratio). This rate has been aligned with the MSF rate and, changes automatically as and when the MSF rate changes alongside policy repo rate changes.
Cash Reserve Ratio (CRR): The average daily balance that a bank is required to maintain with the Reserve Bank as a per cent—stipulated by the RBI—of its net demand and time liabilities (NDTL) as on the last Friday of the second preceding fortnight.
Statutory Liquidity Ratio (SLR) is the share of NDTL that the scheduled commercial banks are required to maintain on a daily basis in safe and liquid assets, such as unencumbered government securities and other approved securities, cash and gold.
Open Market Operations (OMOs) are conducted by the RBI by way of sale/purchase of government securities to/from the market with an objective to adjust the rupee liquidity conditions in the market on a durable basis.
Market Stabilization Scheme (MSS) was introduced as an instrument for monetary management in April 2004. Surplus liquidity of a more enduring nature arising from large capital inflows is absorbed through sale of short-dated government securities and treasury bills. The cash so mobilized is held in a separate government account with the RBI.
Monetary Base (Reserve Money/ M0) = Currency in circulation + Bankers' deposits with the RBI + 'Other' deposits with the RBI.
M1 = Currency with the public + Demand deposits with the banking system + 'Other' deposits with the RBI.
M2 = M1 + Saving deposits of post office saving banks.
M3 = M1 + Time deposits with the banking system.
Call money rate is the rate at which money are lent and borrowed overnight in the uncollateralized money market.
Weighted average call money rate (WACR) is volume-weighted average of rates at which overnight money or money at short notice are lent and borrowed in the money market.
Refinance facility under Monetary Targeting Framework was provided by RBI as an additional source of reserves. The two types of refinance facility provided to banks included export credit refinance (extended against bank's outstanding export credit eligible for refinance) and general refinance (provided to banks to tide over their temporary liquidity shortages).

Source Handbook on RBI's Weekly Statistical Supplement; Reserve Bank of India Website

Annexure 2: Glossary—Figure 4.7

Marginal Cost of Funds-Based Lending Rate (MCLR): An internal benchmark rate for determining the interest rate on all floating rate rupee loans.[4] It was introduced on April 1, 2016 after replacing the base rate system. MCLR comprises of marginal costs of funds (92% share of Marginal Cost of Deposits and Other Borrowings + 8% share of return on net worth)[5] + negative carry-on account of CRR + operating costs + tenor premium.
External Benchmark-Based Lending Rate (EBLR): All new floating rate personal or retail loans (housing, auto, etc.) and floating rate loans extended by banks to Micro and Small Enterprises from October 01, 2019 and floating rate loans to Medium Enterprises from April 01, 2020 are benchmarked to one of the following, viz., (i) Reserve Bank of India policy repo rate; (ii) Government of India 3-Months and 6-Months Treasury Bill yield published by the Financial Benchmarks India Private Ltd (FBIL) and (iii) any other benchmark market interest rate published by the FBIL. Banks are free to offer such external benchmark linked loans to other types of borrowers as well but cannot adopt multiple benchmarks within a loan category.
Weighted Average Lending Rate (WALR): The weighted average of the lending rates of all SCBs (excluding RRBs, payment banks and small finance banks) on the outstanding rupee loans and fresh rupee loans sanctioned by the banks. It is based on lending rates to different sectors with weights based on credit extended to different sectors.
Money Market: Market for lending and borrowing of short-term funds which are highly liquid. It covers money and financial assets that are close substitutes for money including call money, repo, Tri-party repo, T-bills, Cash Management Bills, Commercial Paper and Certificate of Deposit.
Call Money Market: **Instrument:** Overnight money and money at short notice (up to a period of 14 days) is lent and borrowed without collateral. Call money is liquid and can be turned into money quickly at low cost and provides an avenue for equilibrating the short-term surplus funds of lenders and the requirements of borrowers. **Borrowers**: Scheduled Commercial Banks (excluding RRBs), Co-operative Banks (other than Land Development Banks) and Primary Dealers (PDs). **Lenders**: Same as borrowers.
Market Repo: **Instruments:** Repurchase agreement (Repo) which is used for borrowing funds by selling securities with an agreement to repurchase the said securities on a mutually agreed future date at an agreed price which includes interest for the funds borrowed. Government securities, CPs, CDs, Units of Debt ETFs, listed corporate bonds and debentures are eligible securities for repo. Repo against corporate bonds are called repo in corporate bond. **Participants:** Banks, PDs, Mutual Funds, listed corporates, All India Financial Institutions, any other entity approved by the RBI.

(continued)

[4] Interest rates on fixed rate loans of tenor below 3 years shall not be less than the benchmark rate for similar tenor.

[5] In case of newly set up banks (either domestic or foreign banks operating as branches in India) where lending operations are mainly financed by capital, the weightage for this component may be higher in proportion to the extent of capital deployed for lending. This dispensation will be available for a period of three years from the date of commencing operations.

(continued)

Tri-Party Repo Market: **Instrument:** Tri-party repo, a repo contract where a third entity (apart from the borrower and lender), called a Tri-Party Agent, acts as an intermediary between the two parties to the repo to facilitate services like collateral selection, payment and settlement, custody and management during the life of the transaction. **Participants:** Scheduled commercial banks, recognized stock exchanges and clearing corporations of stock exchanges or clearing corporations authorized under PSS Act and any other entity regulated by RBI or SEBI are eligible subject to certain criterion. All the repo market eligible entities are permitted to participate in Tri-party repo market.
Treasury Bills Market: **Instrument:** Short-term debt instruments issued by the GOI and sold by RBI on an auction basis. Treasury bills are zero coupon securities that pay no interest, issued at a discount and redeemed at the face value at maturity. They are currently issued in three tenors, namely, 91 day, 182 day and 364 day. They are also traded in the secondary market. **Investors:** Any person resident of India, including firms, companies, corporate bodies, institutions and Trusts along with Non-Resident Indians and Foreign Investors (subject to approval by government) can invest through a competitive route.
Certificate of Deposits Market: **Instrument: A** negotiable money market instrument issued in dematerialized form or as a usance promissory note against funds deposited at a bank or other eligible financial institution for a specified time period. Maturity ranges from 7 days to three years. CDs can be traded in the secondary market. **Issuers**: Banks and Financial Institutions. **Investors**: Individuals, Corporations, Companies (including banks and PDs), Trusts, Funds, Associations and Non-Resident Indians (but only on non-repatriable basis).
Commercial Paper Market: **Instrument: A**n unsecured money market instrument issued in the form of a promissory note. They are issued for the maturities between a minimum of 7 days and a maximum of up to one year from the date of issue (given that the credit rating of the issuer is valid in the period). CPs can be traded in the secondary market. **Issuers**: Corporates, PDs and All India Financial Institutions (FIs) **Investors:** Individuals, Banks, Other corporate bodies (registered and incorporated in India), Non-Resident Indians.
Bond Market: **Instrument: A** debt instrument whereby an investor loans money to an entity (typically corporate or government) which borrows the funds for a defined period of time at a variable or fixed interest rate. Bonds are used by companies, municipalities, states and sovereign governments to raise money to finance a variety of projects and activities **Issuers:** Government or Corporates. **Investors:** Banks, Mutual Funds, Foreign Institutional Investors, Provident Funds, Pension Funds.
Government Securities Market: **Instrument:** A tradeable instrument issued by the Central or the State Governments. It acknowledges the government's debt obligation. Securities issued by State Governments in India are known as State Development Loan (SDL). The short-term G-Secs (Treasury Bills) have original maturities of less than one year while long-term G-Secs (Government Bonds or dated securities) have original maturity of one year or more. There is an active secondary market in G-Secs. **Participants**: Commercial banks, PDs, Institutional investors like insurance companies, Other banks including cooperative banks, regional rural banks, Mutual funds, Provident and Pension funds, Foreign Portfolio Investors (allowed with quantitative limits prescribed from time to time) and Corporates.

(continued)

(continued)

Corporate Bond Market: **Instrument:** Debt securities issued by private and public corporations. Companies issue corporate bonds to raise money for a variety of purposes, such as building a new plant, purchasing equipment or growing the business. The stock exchanges have a dedicated debt segment in their trading platforms to facilitate the needs of retail investors. A corporate bond is generally priced on the basis of price of G-Sec of comparable tenure with a spread added to it. They are also traded in secondary market. **Participants:** Corporates, banks, retail investors and institutional investors including insurance companies and mutual funds, foreign investors.

Source Handbook on RBI's Weekly Statistical Supplement; Reserve Bank of India Website

Annexure 3: Constitution of the Monetary Policy Committee

The Gazette Notification of the Ministry of Finance dated September 29, 2016 notes the following:

"In exercise of the powers conferred by Section 45ZB of the Reserve Bank of India Act, 1934 (2 of 1934), the Central Government hereby constitutes the Monetary Policy Committee of the Reserve Bank of India, consisting of the following, namely: -

i. The Governor of the Bank—Chairperson, ex officio;
ii. Deputy Governor of the Bank, in charge of Monetary Policy—Member, ex officio;
iii. One officer of the Bank to be nominated by the Central Board—Member, ex officio;
iv. Shri Chetan Ghate, Professor, Indian Statistical Institute (ISI)—Member;
v. Professor Pami Dua, Director, Delhi School of Economics (DSE)—Member; and
vi. Dr. Ravindra H. Dholakia, Professor, Indian Institute of Management, Ahmedabad, Member."

(continued)

(continued)

The three external members served on the Committee since October 2016 till September 2020. They were replaced by the following external members who are currently serving the Committee from October 2020 onwards.

(i) Dr. Shashanka Bhide, Senior Advisor, National Council of Applied Economic Research, Delhi;
(ii) Prof. Ashima Goyal, Professor, Indira Gandhi Institute of Development Research;
(iii) Prof. Jayanth R. Varma, Professor, Indian Institute of Management, Ahmedabad.

There have been some changes in the RBI members as follows:

- Former Governor, Dr. Urjit Patel chaired the Committee from October 2016 to December 2018. Governor, Shri Shaktikanta Das has presided from the February 2019 meeting onwards.
- Shri R. Gandhi, Former Deputy Governor attended the October and December meetings in 2016.
- Dr. Viral Acharya, Former Deputy Governor in charge of Monetary Policy attended the meetings from February 2017 to June 2019.
- Shri Bibhu Prasad Kanungo, Deputy Governor attended the meetings from August to December 2019.
- Dr. Michael Patra has attended all the meetings till date, first as Executive Director till December 2019 and then as Deputy Governor in charge of Monetary Policy from February 2020 onwards.
- Dr. Janak Raj attended meetings from February–June 2020 as Executive Director.
- Dr. Mridul Saggar attended meetings from August 2020 till April 2022 as Executive Director.
- Dr. Rajiv Ranjan has been attending meetings from June 2022 onwards as Executive Director.

Annexure 4: Inflation Targeting Regime Adoption

Year of IT adoption	Countries	Classification	Band/Interval/Point target (2024)
1990	New Zealand	AE	2.00% ± 1.0%
1991	Canada	AE	2.00% ± 1.0%
1992	UK	AE	2.00%
1993	Sweden	AE	2.00%
1993	Australia	AE	2.00%–3.00%
1997	Israel	AE	1.00%–3.00%
1998	Czech Republic	AE	2.00% ± 1.0%
1998	South Korea	AE	2.00%
1999	Poland	EME	2.50% ± 1.0%
1999	Colombia	EME	3.00% ± 1.0%
1999	Brazil	EME	3.00% ± 1.5%
1999	Chile	EME	3.00% ± 1.0%

(continued)

(continued)

Year of IT adoption	Countries	Classification	Band/Interval/Point target (2024)
2000	Thailand	EME	1.5%–3.5%
2000	South Africa	EME	3.00%–6.0%
2001	Iceland	AE	2.50%
2001	Norway	AE	2%
2001	Hungary	EME	3.00% ± 1.0%
2001	Mexico	EME	3.00% ± 1.0%
2002	Philippines	EME	3.0% ± 1.0%
2002	Ghana	EME	8.00% ± 2.0%
2002	Peru	EME	2.0% ± 1.0%
2002	Uruguay	EME	3.00%–7.00%
2005	Indonesia	EME	2.5% ± 1%
2005	Guatemala	EME	4.00% ± 1%
2005	Romania	EME	2.5% ± 1.0%
2006	Turkey	EME	5.00% ± 2%
2006	Armenia	EME	4.00% ± 1.5%
2009	Serbia	EME	3.00% ± 1.5%
2009	Georgia	EME	3.00%
2009	Albania	EME	3%
2011	Uganda	EME	5.00% ± 2.0%
2011	Paraguay	EME	4.00% ± 2.0%
2012	Dominican Republic	EME	4.0% ± 1.0%
2013	Japan	AE	2.00%
2013	Moldova	EME	5.00% ± 1.5%
2015	Kazakhstan	EME	5.00%
2015	Russia	EME	4.00%
2015	Ukraine	EME	5.00%
2015	Kenya	EME	5.0% ± 2.5%
2016	India	EME	4.00% ± 2%
2016	Argentina	EME	Ended IT in 2018
2017	Sri Lanka	EME	5%
2018	Costa Rica	EME	3.0% ± 1%
2018	Jamaica	EME	4%–6%
2019	Uzbekistan	EME	5%

Notes

1. Countries are classified on the basis of the IMF classification (https://www.imf.org/en/Publications/WEO/weo-database/2023/April/groups-and-aggregates)
2. AE: Advanced Economy, EME: Emerging Market Economy

References

Agénor, P. R., & da Silva, L. A. P. (2019). *Integrated inflation targeting-another perspective from the developing world*. Bank for International Settlements.

Bank for International Settlements. (2019). *Unconventional monetary policy tools: A cross-country analysis*. Report by Working Group, Committee on the Global Financial System.

Blanchard, O. J., & Bernanke, B. S. (2024). *An analysis of pandemic-era inflation in 11 economies* (No. w32532). National Bureau of Economic Research.

Blinder, A., & Morgan, J. (2005). Are two heads better than one? An experimental analysis of group versus individual decision-making. *Journal of Money, Credit and Banking, 35*(5), 789–811.

Das, S. (2023, June 13). *Central banking in uncertain times: The Indian experience, opening plenary address delivered at the summer meetings organized by central banking*. London, UK.

Dua, P. (2020). Monetary policy framework in India. *Indian Economic Review, 55*(1), 117–154.

Government of India. (2009). *A hundred small steps: Report of the committee on financial sector reforms* (Chairman: Raghuram Rajan). Planning Commission, New Delhi.

International Monetary Fund. (2023). *Annual report on exchange arrangements and exchange restrictions 2022*. IMF.

Laurens, B. J., Eckhold, K., King, D., Maehle, N., Naseer, A., & Durré, A. (2015). *The Journey of inflation targeting: Easier said than done—The case for transitional arrangements along the road, WP 136*. International Monetary Fund.

Maier, P. (2010). How central banks take decisions: An analysis of monetary policy meetings. In P. L. Siklos, M.T. Bohl, & M. E. Woher (Eds.), *Challenges in central banking: The current institutional environment and forces affecting monetary policy*. Cambridge University Press.

Mishkin, F. S. (2016). *The economics of money, banking, and financial markets*. Pearson.

Mohanty, D. (2010). *Monetary policy framework in India: Experience with multiple-indicators approach*. Speech delivered at the Conference of the Orissa Economic Association in Baripada, Orissa on 21st February 2010. Orissa.

Mohanty, D (2011). *Changing contours of monetary policy in India*. Reserve Bank of India Bulletin. Mumbai.

Patra, M. D., & Bhattacharyya, I. (2022). Priming monetary policy for the pandemic. *Economic and Political Weekly, LVII*(20).

Patra, M. D., Bhattacharyya, I., & John, J. (2023). *When circumspection is the better part of communication*. RBI Bulletin, July, Mumbai.

Rajan, R (2017). *I do what I do*. Harper Collins.

Rangarajan, C. (2020). *The new monetary policy framework—What it means*. Prof. Sukhamoy Chakravarty Memorial Lecture. Delivered at Annual Conference of the Indian Econometric Society at Madurai Kamaraj University in January 2020. https://www.nipfp.org.in/media/medialibrary/2020/02/WP_297_2020.pdf

Reddy, Y. V. (1999). *Monetary policy operating procedures in India, in monetary policy operating procedures in emerging market economies, Bank for International Settlement* (Paper No. 5, 99–109).

Reserve Bank of India. (1985). *Report of the committee to review the working of the monetary system* (Chairman: Dr. Sukhamoy Chakravarty). Mumbai.

Reserve Bank of India. (1998). *Report of the working group on money supply: Analytics and methodology of compilation* (Chairman: Dr. Y. V. Reddy). Mumbai.

Reserve Bank of India. (2013). *Report on currency and finance 2009–2012: Fiscal-monetary co-ordination*. Mumbai.

Reserve Bank of India. (2014). *Report of the expert committee to revise and strengthen the monetary policy framework* (Chairman: Dr. Urjit Patel). January, Mumbai.

Reserve Bank of India. (2017). *Report of the internal study group to review the working of the marginal cost of funds based lending rate system* (Chairman: Dr. Janak Raj), September. Mumbai.

Reserve Bank of India. (2018). *Forex market operations and liquidity management* (by—Janak Raj, Sitikantha Pattanaik, Indranil Bhattacharya and Abhilasha), RBI Bulletin, August, Mumbai.

Reserve Bank of India. (2019). *Report of the Internal Working Group to Review the Liquidity Management Framework*. September, Mumbai.

Reserve Bank of India. (2020a, February). *Governor's statement, sixth bi-monthly monetary policy statement*. Mumbai.

Reserve Bank of India. (2020b, March). *Governor's statement, seventh bi-monthly monetary policy statement*. Mumbai.

Reserve Bank of India. (2020c, March). *Monetary Policy Transmission in India—Recent Trends and Impediments* (by—Arghya Kusum Mitra and Sadhan Kumar Chattopadhyay). RBI Bulletin, Mumbai.

Reserve Bank of India. (2020d, April). *Monetary policy report*. Mumbai.

Reserve Bank of India. (2020e, April). *Governor's statement*. Mumbai.

Reserve Bank of India. (2020f, October). *Monetary policy report*. Mumbai.

Reserve Bank of India. (2020g, October). *Monetary policy committee resolution*. Mumbai.

Reserve Bank of India. (2021a). *Annual report,* 2020–21. Mumbai.

Reserve Bank of India. (2021b, April). *Monetary policy committee resolution*. Mumbai.

Reserve Bank of India. (2021c, October). *Governor's statement*. Mumbai.

Reserve Bank of India. (2022, April). *Monetary policy report*. Mumbai.

Vasudevan, A. (2017). Reflections on analytical issues in monetary policy: The Indian economic realities. *Economic and Political Weekly, 52*(12), 45–52.

Chapter 5
Does the Productivity Growth Numbers Explain the Unbalanced Growth Experience of the Indian Economy?

T Thasni, Kausik Gangopadhyay, and Debasis Mondal

Abstract We have developed a three-sector dynamic general equilibrium model and calibrated its parameters to align with the output and employment share data of the Indian economy from 1983 to 2012. The model's output on employment share indicates that the actual labour share in the secondary and tertiary sectors is relatively lower compared to the model-predicted share. To understand the origins of labour productivity growth, we have conducted a shift-share analysis. Our findings reveal that within-sector productivity growth is the most significant contributor to overall growth, and the importance of total factor productivities (TFPs) has increased in the post-economic reform period, particularly after 1991. While the contribution of TFPs in the manufacturing sector has been moderate, our results emphasize the pressing need for reforms to boost the TFP in this sector. In general, the economic reforms implemented in 1991–92 have facilitated a more efficient allocation of productive factors across different sectors of the Indian economy.

This paper was presented at the workshop titled 'Growth, Development, and Productivity: 75 Years of Indian Experiences', held at the Delhi School of Economics from 7 to 9 March 2024. We extend our gratitude to all workshop participants for their valuable comments and suggestions. We would specially like to thank our discussant, Debajit Jha, for his insightful comments and dedicated efforts in enhancing our manuscript. Parts of this article are adapted from the thesis work by Thasni T. at the Indian Institute of Management Kozhikode. An earlier version of this work, titled "A Dynamic General Equilibrium (DGE) Model of Structural Transformation for India," can be found in the IIMK Working Paper series (Thasni et al. (2021)). The current version has been significantly refined and enhanced based on feedback from seminar participants, editors, and the discussant. Any remaining errors are solely our responsibility

T. Thasni
Indian Institute of Management Kashipur, Kashipur, Uttarakhand, India
e-mail: thasni.t@iimkashipur.ac.in

K. Gangopadhyay
Indian Institute of Management Kozhikode, Kozhikode, India
e-mail: kausik@iimk.ac.in

D. Mondal (✉)
Department of Humanities and Social Sciences, Indian Institute of Technology Delhi, Delhi, India
e-mail: debasis@hss.iitd.ac.in

D. Maiti et al. (eds.), *75 Years of Growth, Development and Productivity in India*, India Studies in Business and Economics, https://doi.org/10.1007/978-981-97-8054-9_5

Keywords Agricultural productivity · Structural transformation · Sectoral productivity · Calibration · Multi-sector growth model · General equilibrium

JEL Classification C15 · C53 · C68 · O11 · O41

5.1 Introduction

India is one of the fastest growing emerging economies in the world averaging almost 4.62% rate of growth of real GDP per capita during the years 2012 to 2022. According to world GDP ranking 2024, it has become the fifth largest economy in terms of aggregate GDP in recent times and is on its way to becoming the third largest one in the present decade.[1] The growth experience across various sectors of the economy has been diverse and it is often referred to as a services-led economic growth as this sector has been one of the major contributors to the overall economic growth of the Indian economy. Sectoral employment and sectoral output, as a percentage of overall employment and GDP of the economy, respectively, have also remained unequal for a long period potentially indicating the existence of an unbalanced growth. Our paper sheds light on this important topic of unequal sectoral division of various aggregate economic outcomes in a framework of structural change and economic growth that India has enjoyed over the past several decades since 1983.

Since 1983 and till the year 2012, the annual average rate of growth of per capita real (value added) GDP of the Indian economy was about 4.06%.[2] Along with this high growth rate of per capita output, aggregate labour productivity in India was growing at a rate of 4.55% during 1983–2012.[3] It is well known that the service sector is the main growth generator of the Indian economy. The growth rate of the service sector was at 4.80% annually for the same period. The other two major sectors, agriculture and industry, were growing at a rate of 2.93% and 3.73%, respectively.

In this paper, we model a three-sector dynamic economy that could closely replicate the uneven growth experience of the Indian economy for the period 1983–2012. Our work is a contribution to the large literature in this area that takes the task of generating data from a model economy by calibrating the parameters. We show that

---

[1] See the report by Shan (2022) in this connection.

[2] Data source: World Bank data on the annual percentage growth rate of GDP per capita based on constant local currency.

[3] We define labour productivity by taking a ratio of aggregate GDP to workers. The workforce participation rate, defined as the ratio of the total workforce in an economy over the total population, declined by 0.49% annually for the years 1983 to 2012. To see this, write $\frac{Y}{P} \equiv \frac{Y}{L}\frac{L}{P}$, where $\frac{Y}{P}$ is the per capita GDP, $\frac{Y}{L}$ is the labour productivity, and $\frac{L}{P}$ is the fraction of workforce in the population. The variables Y, P, and L are aggregate GDP, total population, and workforce, respectively. We know the growth rate of $\frac{Y}{P}$ is 4.06% and the growth rate of $\frac{Y}{L}$ is 4.55%. Therefore, the growth rate of $\frac{L}{P}$ must be -0.49%. This matches closely with the data from the World Bank which shows that the labour force participation rate for India (as % of the total population ages 15+) was declining at a rate of 0.45% annually from 1983 to 2012.

our model can generate similar growth rates of the major sectors of the economy as observed in data for the years 1983–2012. Regarding sectoral employment share, our model could not perform well. The reason could be that we have not modelled various distortions in the real world including taxes and subsidies and any labour market-related rigidity hindering the free flow of labour across sectors.

We have performed a simple growth accounting exercise following a Cobb-Douglas production function and compared our results with the previous work along this line. The (real value added) growth in the service sector turned out to be the highest at 7.87% over the years 1983–2012. Within individual sectors, the contribution of TFPs and other factors in the sectoral value added has been calculated. TFPs play the most prominent role in agriculture where almost 70% of the growth of the agriculture sector has been explained by its TFP growth and the remaining 30% is explained by the accumulation of physical capital, labour, and land. In Bosworth et al. (2007), almost 61% of the agriculture sector value added has been explained by the TFP growth for the period 1980–2004. In Verma (2012a), the contribution of TFP in agriculture is 59% for the years 1980–2005. Thus, the importance of TFPs in agriculture has seen a marked increase in the period following 2004.

We have conducted a shift-share analysis to highlight the sources of sectoral labour productivity growth. Our findings reveal that within-sector productivity growth has been the most important factor in comparison with the growth arising out of structural change. In our , out of the average productivity growth of 4.55% over the years 1983–2013, structural change-related components explain about 29% of this growth. This result is consistent with other studies in the literature. In De Vries et al. (2012), the contribution of structural change (or, sectoral relocation effect) in aggregate productivity growth was about 19% during the period 1991–2008.[4]

5.1.1 Literature Review

There is now a large and growing body of work that analyses structural change and growth in a non-balanced growth framework. Our theoretical model is close to the work of Ngai and Pissarides (2007); Acemoglu and Guerrieri (2008) and Verma (2012a). In Ngai and Pissarides (2007), the authors built a multi-sector growth model without any fixed factor and having equal factor intensities across sectors. Their model can generate balanced growth while having differences in TFP growth rates across sectors. In Acemoglu and Guerrieri (2008)'s two-sector model, the sectors can have differential capital intensities and differential TFP growth. The consumption goods turn out to be compliment in their calibration of the elasticity of substitution parameter.

We have drawn inspiration from Verma (2012a), who built a theoretical model and calibrated it utilizing Indian data spanning from 1980 to 2005. Additionally, she

[4] See Table 5.7 of their paper.

undertook analysis incorporating tax-financed public capital to better align employment share data with model outputs. Our study builds upon hers, extending the analysis up to the latest available data point in 2013, as capital data are not accessible beyond this period. However, labour data are available until 2018. In our framework, the matching of the employment share data is relatively poor compared to the output share data. Our data sources are different from that of Verma (2012a) and hence, the calibrated parameter values turn out to be different. The growth rate of TFP in agriculture is 2.59% in our data while this is 1.91% in Verma (2012a). While TFP growth alone explains around 70% of the agricultural value added in our data, it is about 59% there. This difference is primarily due to the higher contribution of TFP in the post-reform period.

In a related study focusing on India, Ghate et al. (2016) examined the role of distortions in an overlapping generations (OLG) growth model featuring two sectors: agriculture and the modern sector. Their analysis involved calibrating the model to investigate the impacts of sector-specific tax policies, infrastructure investments, and labour market distortions on the allocation of labour and capital across sectors. They also explored how increasing the allocation of tax-financed public capital to agriculture could affect private capital, contingent upon the substitutability between private and public capital. Notably, their findings underscored that removing labour market frictions enhances aggregate growth. In contrast, our model operates under frictionless conditions where the allocation of capital and labour is determined by competitive forces in both the product and labour markets. In the appendix, we incorporate various distortions (or 'wedges') following Hsieh and Klenow (2009) to explore potential outcomes in our framework. However, our analysis does not formally demonstrate any results regarding the removal of distortions and its impact.

The empirical literature analysing the growth and structural change in India is large. Bosworth et al. (2007) empirically examined the origins of productivity growth in the service sector of the Indian economy for the period 1960–2004. During the 1980–2004 period, agricultural output per worker has grown at a rate of 1.8% in their work and about 61% of this growth is explained by TFP growth in agriculture.[5] In our work, agricultural value added has grown at a rate of 2.87% during 1983–2012 and nearly 70% of this growth is explained by the TFP growth in agriculture. In Bosworth and Collins (2008), they have analysed the growth experiences of India and China during 1978–2004. They emphasized the role of (sectoral) reallocation in the growth accounting framework.[6] In our work too, it has been shown that sectoral reallocation has contributed to overall productivity improvement. However, within-sector productivity improvement turns out to be the major source of productivity growth in India as shown in our present work.

Eichengreen and Gupta (2011) analysed the role of the service sector for the years 1950 to 2008. They decomposed the service sector into three subgroups and showed that modern services (communication, business, and banking services) experienced the highest value-added growth rate during the post-liberalization period

[5] See Table 5.4 of their paper.

[6] See Table 5.5 of their paper.

(see Table 5.2 of their paper). However, the sectoral share of these three categories of services in the aggregate service sector was only 9.1% in the year 2000. Verma (2012b) explore reasons for services-led growth and identify that sectoral TFP growth rates are the major source for tertiary sector-led growth in India. Lahiri and Yi (2009) have computed the capital and labour allocation wedge for two Indian states, namely Maharashtra and West Bengal. Erumban et al. (2019) study the effect that structural change has had on the aggregate productivity of the Indian economy for the years 1980 to 2011. They identified a stagnant manufacturing sector that could not create enough job opportunities due to its heavy reliance on the within-sector productivity change.

The study Krishna et al. (2022) reveals that India's manufacturing sector contributed to the country's economic expansion during the high-growth period (2003–2007) and after the Global Financial Crisis. It has been the driving force behind India's improving total factor productivity since 2003. It also makes it clear that the manufacturing sector still has significant problems to solve, notwithstanding recent productivity gains. Employment, investment, and return on investment all fell after the Great Financial Crisis. Therefore, India's manufacturing sector continues to play a significant role in the country's economic expansion, but India's underlying difficulties must be addressed if the country is to continue growing.

Using two-sector models, Mondal (2019) and Gangopadhyay and Mondal (2021) analysed the role of agricultural productivity and the relative price of agriculture in the context of structural change and growth. When goods are gross substitutes in consumption, then resources move to the sector that has the highest TFP growth. This is because relative price declines at a higher rate for the sector witnessing higher growth of TFPs. Share of consumption expenditure increases and resources is attracted towards the sector with relatively higher growth. Opposite takes place when goods are complemented. This intuitive reasoning has played out in previous theoretical works. In our paper too, the service sector has attracted resources from other sectors of the economy due to its highest TFP growth and the fact that goods are substitutes in consumption.

The rest of the paper is organized as follows: Section 5.2 lays out a model of a three-sector economy with homothetic preference and competitive market structure. Section 5.3 deals with data construction and measurement-related issues. The method to measure sectoral contribution has also been presented in this section. Results and discussions have been provided in section 5.4. Finally, Section 5.5 provides concluding remarks.

5.2 The Economic Environment

In our model, there is a continuum of agents of measure L, each endowed with one unit of labour. The economy comprises three sectors: agriculture, manufacturing, and services. Labour is fully mobile across these sectors, which ensures that the wage rate is equalized among them. Each unit of labour earns a competitive wage denoted by ω. Product and factor markets are perfectly competitive across all sectors. In our setup, manufacturing goods serve as both consumption goods and capital goods capable of accumulation over time, while the other two goods exclusively serve as consumption goods.

5.2.1 Households and Preferences

The utility function of the representative household can be represented as follows:

$$U(c_{at}, c_{mt}, c_{st}) = \ln \left(\alpha c_{at}^{\theta} + \gamma c_{mt}^{\theta} + (1-\alpha-\gamma) c_{st}^{\theta}\right)^{\frac{1}{\theta}}; \quad \theta \in (-\infty, 1). \tag{5.1}$$

where c_{at}, c_{mt}, and c_{st} represent the consumption of agriculture, manufacturing, and service goods by the representative household. We denote the elasticity of substitution between any two goods in the preference as $\phi \equiv \frac{1}{1-\theta} \in (0, \infty)$. The relative bias for consumption of the agricultural good and the manufacturing good as opposed to the service good is denoted by the parameters α and γ, both of which are assumed to be positive such that $(1-\alpha-\gamma) \in (0, 1)$.

A representative agent maximizes an infinite horizon dynamic optimization problem given by

$$\underset{\{c_{at}, c_{mt}, c_{st}\}}{\text{Max}} \sum_{n=0}^{\infty} \beta^{t} \ln\left[\alpha c_{at}^{\theta} + \gamma c_{mt}^{\theta} + (1-\alpha-\gamma) c_{st}^{\theta}\right]^{\frac{1}{\theta}} \tag{5.2}$$

,

subject to $p_{at}c_{at} + p_{mt}c_{mt} + p_{st}c_{st} + K_{t+1} - (1-\delta)K_t = w_t L_t + r_{Kt} K_t + R_{lt} L_{at}$.

Here, $\beta \in (0, 1)$ is a discount factor. R_{lt} and r_{Kt} represent the returns to land and capital at time t. The left-hand side of the budget equation represents expenditure on consumption and investment, while the right-hand side denotes the agent's income. We normalize the price of the manufacturing good to unity, $p_{mt} \equiv 1$. Under this normalization, p_{at} and p_{st} indicate the relative prices of the agricultural and service goods, respectively. These prices can alternatively be referred to as the terms-of-trade for agriculture and services.

5.2.2 Production

We establish a standard three-sector competitive model featuring constant returns to scale across all sectors. The agriculture sector utilizes three factors of production: capital (K), labour (L), and land (l). The manufacturing and service sectors, on the other hand, employ two factors of production: labour and capital. The output of the three sectors follows a Cobb-Douglas production function and can be expressed as follows:

$$
\begin{aligned}
Y_{at} &= A_{at} K_{at}^{\phi_a} l_{at}^{\sigma_a} L_{at}^{1-\phi_a-\sigma_a}, \\
Y_{mt} &= A_{mt} K_{mt}^{\phi_m} L_{mt}^{1-\phi_m}, \\
Y_{st} &= A_{st} K_{st}^{\phi_s} L_{st}^{1-\phi_s}.
\end{aligned} \tag{5.3}
$$

Market clearing conditions for the output market can be shown as follows:

$$
\begin{aligned}
c_{at} &= Y_{at}, \\
c_{mt} + K_{t+1} - (1-\delta)K_t &= Y_{mt}, \\
c_{st} &= Y_{st}.
\end{aligned} \tag{5.4}
$$

Equation (5.4) implies that both the agriculture good and the service good are consumed completely, whereas the manufacturing sector output can be both consumed and invested, where δ is the constant rate of depreciation of capital.

Market clearing conditions for the input markets can be shown as follows:

$$
\begin{aligned}
K_{at} + K_{mt} + K_{st} &= K_t, \\
L_{at} + L_{mt} + L_{st} &= L, \\
l_{at} &= l.
\end{aligned} \tag{5.5}
$$

Product and factor markets are competitive and the firms from different sectors solve the following optimization problems:

$$
\begin{aligned}
&\underset{K_{at}, L_{at}, l_{at}}{\text{Max}} \; p_{at} Y_{at} - r_{kt} K_{at} - \omega_t L_{at} - R_{lt} l_{at}; \quad s.t. \\
&Y_{at} = A_{at} K_{at}^{\phi_a} l_{at}^{\sigma_a} L_{at}^{1-\phi_a-\sigma_a},
\end{aligned} \tag{5.6}
$$

$$
\underset{K_{mt}, L_{mt}}{\text{Max}} \; Y_{mt} - r_{kt} K_{mt} - \omega_t L_{mt}; \quad s.t. \quad Y_{mt} = A_{mt} K_{mt}^{\phi_m} L_{mt}^{1-\phi_m}, \tag{5.7}
$$

$$
\underset{K_{st}, L_{st}}{\text{Max}} \; p_{st} Y_{st} - r_{kt} K_{st} - \omega_t L_{st}; \quad s.t. \quad Y_{st} = A_{st} K_{st}^{\phi_s} L_{st}^{1-\phi_s}. \tag{5.8}
$$

5.2.3 Defining the Equilibrium

The equilibrium of our model at any period t is defined as follows:

1. Given the productivity shocks $\{A_{at}, A_{mt}, A_{st}\}_{t=0}^{T}$, the representative household maximizes the infinite horizon dynamic utility noted in Eq. (5.2).

2. Given the productivity shocks $\{A_{at}, A_{mt}, A_{st}\}_{t=0}^{T}$ and given the stocks of the existing capital K_{at}, K_{mt}, and K_{st}, the firms from all the three sectors solve their respective profit maximization problem given by Eqs. (5.6), (5.7), and (5.8).
3. The output and input markets are clear as outlined in Eqs. (5.4) and (5.5).

The equilibrium in our model is known by decisions by the households about their contemporaneous consumption and tomorrow's capital stock. The firms solve their problems by deciding on the capital stock to be employed in the firm. The market clearing process decides the contemporaneous output prices and the rents for the inputs of labour, capital, and land.

5.2.4 *Solving the Model*

We have normalized the amount of labour and land to unity, that is, $L = 1$ and $l = 1$, respectively, for all the periods.

5.2.4.1 Solution to Firms' Problems

We substitute the value for Y_{at} from the production function into the firm's maximization problem. The maximization problem in Eq.(5.6) then gives us the following first-order conditions.[7] The FOC concerning $K_{a,t}$ yields the following:[8]

$$r_{kt} = p_{at} A_{at} \phi_a k_{at}^{\phi_a - 1} L_{at}^{-\sigma_a}, \tag{5.9}$$

where $k_{at} = \frac{K_{at}}{L_{at}}$ and we set $l_{at} = 1$.

Similarly, the maximization problems of firms from manufacturing and service sectors will yield the following expressions of r_{kt}:

$$r_{kt} = A_{mt} \phi_m K_{mt}^{\phi_m - 1} L_{mt}^{1-\phi_m} = A_{mt} \phi_m k_{mt}^{\phi_m - 1}, \tag{5.10}$$

where $k_{mt} = \frac{K_{mt}}{L_{mt}}$,

$$r_{kt} = p_{st} A_{st} \phi_s K_{st}^{\phi_s - 1} L_{st}^{1-\phi_s} = p_{st} A_{st} \phi_s k_{st}^{\phi_s - 1}, \tag{5.11}$$

where $k_{st} = \frac{K_{st}}{L_{st}}$.

In the same manner, we can derive the equations for wage rate by equating it to the marginal productivity of labour in all sectors:

$$\omega_t = p_{at} A_{at} (1 - \phi_a - \sigma_a) K_{at}^{\phi_a} l_{at}^{\sigma_a} L_{at}^{-\phi_a - \sigma_a}$$

[7] See appendix 5.6.1 for the detail derivations.

[8] This is a reduced form of Eq. (5.62) in the appendix with no distortions.

$$= p_{at}A_{at}(1 - \phi_a - \sigma_a)k_{at}^{\phi a}L_{at}^{-\sigma a}, \tag{5.12}$$

$$\omega_t = A_{mt}(1 - \phi_m)K_{mt}^{\phi_m}L_{mt}^{-\phi_m} = A_{mt}(1 - \phi_m)k_{mt}^{\phi_m}, \tag{5.13}$$

$$\omega_t = p_{st}A_{st}(1 - \phi_s)K_{st}^{\phi_s}L_{st}^{-\phi_s} = p_{st}A_{st}(1 - \phi_s)k_{st}^{\phi_s}. \tag{5.14}$$

As labour and capital can freely move across sectors, we have the no-arbitrage condition where wages and rentals are equalized across sectors. Since the sectors are competitive, the wage-rental ratio, $\frac{\omega_t}{r_{kt}}$, will be equal across sectors. Therefore,

$$\frac{\omega_t}{r_{kt}} = \frac{(1 - \phi_a - \sigma_a)}{\phi_a}k_{at} = \frac{(1 - \phi_m)}{\phi_m}k_{mt} = \frac{(1 - \phi_s)}{\phi_s}k_{st}. \tag{5.15}$$

The above equation implies the following relation on sectoral capital intensity:

$$k_{at} = \frac{\phi_a}{(1 - \phi_a - \sigma_a)}\frac{(1 - \phi_m)}{\phi_m}k_{mt}, \tag{5.16}$$

$$k_{st} = \frac{\phi_s}{(1 - \phi_s)}\frac{(1 - \phi_m)}{\phi_m}k_{mt}. \tag{5.17}$$

The marginal product of capital across sectors are equal and equating the marginal products of the manufacturing sector and service sector will yield the following relation:

$$r_{kt} = A_{mt}\phi_m k_{mt}^{\phi_m - 1} = p_{st}A_{st}\phi_s k_{st}^{\phi_s - 1}, \tag{5.18}$$

$$\Rightarrow p_{st} = \frac{\phi_m}{\phi_s}\frac{A_{mt}}{A_{st}}\frac{k_{mt}^{\phi_m - 1}}{k_{st}^{\phi_s - 1}}. \tag{5.19}$$

The last equation can be simplified by substituting the value for k_{st}.

$$p_{st} = \Big(\frac{\phi_m}{\phi_s}\Big)^{\phi_s}\Big(\frac{1 - \phi_s}{1 - \phi_m}\Big)^{\phi_s - 1}\frac{A_{mt}}{A_{st}}k_{mt}^{\phi_m - \phi_s}. \tag{5.20}$$

Equating the marginal products of the manufacturing sector and the agriculture sector will yield the following relations:

$$r_{kt} = p_{at}A_{at}\phi_a k_{at}^{\phi_a - 1}L_{at}^{-\sigma_a} = A_{mt}\phi_m k_{mt}^{\phi_m - 1}, \tag{5.21}$$

$$\Rightarrow p_{at} = \frac{A_{mt}\phi_m k_{mt}^{\phi_m - 1}}{A_{at}\phi_a k_{at}^{\phi_a - 1}L_{at}^{-\sigma_a}},$$

$$\Rightarrow p_{at} = \frac{A_{mt}\phi_m k_{mt}^{\phi m-1}}{A_{at}\phi_a k_{at}^{\phi a-1} L_{at}^{-\sigma a}},$$

$$\Rightarrow p_{at} = \frac{A_{mt}}{A_{at}} \frac{k_{mt}^{\phi_m-\phi_a}}{L_a^{-\sigma_a}} \left(\frac{\phi_m}{\phi_a}\right)^{\phi_a} \left(\frac{1-\phi_m}{1-\phi_a-\sigma_a}\right)^{1-\phi_a} \tag{5.22}$$

Equations (5.20) and (5.22) show that relative price of service and agricultural good depends on the capital-labour ratio in the manufacturing sector (k_{mt}) and the intensity of capital share between the sectors. For example, if capital share intensities are everywhere the same, i.e. $\phi_m = \phi_s = \phi_a$, then relative price of service would be invariant to factor movements across the sectors. Similarly, relative price of agriculture would be invariant to capital movements across the sectors. Relative price of agriculture would still depend on the labour allocation in the agriculture sector as long as $\sigma_a \neq 0$.

It can be shown that if $\phi_m = \phi_s = \phi_a$, i.e. values of capital and labour shares are equal across sectors, then sectoral output share will be equal to sectoral employment share. This is result of balanced growth. Under this balanced growth condition, all sectoral $\frac{K}{Y}$ ratios would just be equal if TFPs are all equal. This is a result from Ngai and Pissarides (2007).[9]

The existence of unbalanced growth in our work, therefore, depends on two crucial assumptions: (i) capital intensities are different across sectors and (ii) there is land in the production of agriculture such that $\sigma_a \in (0, 1)$.

5.2.4.2 Household

The Lagrangian for the household's utility maximization problem can be written as follows:

$$\begin{aligned}
&\mathcal{L}(c_{at}, c_{mt}, c_{st}, \lambda_1, \lambda_2, \ldots, \lambda_t, \ldots) \\
&= \sum_{n=0}^{\infty} \beta^t \ln\left[\alpha c_{at}^{\theta} + \gamma c_{mt}^{\theta} + (1-\alpha-\gamma) c_{st}^{\theta}\right]^{\frac{1}{\theta}} \\
&- \sum_{n=0}^{\infty} \lambda_t \begin{bmatrix} p_{at}c_{at} + c_{mt} + p_{st}c_{st} + K_{t+1} \\ -(1-\delta)K_t - w_t L_t - r_{Kt}K_t - R_{lt} \end{bmatrix}.
\end{aligned} \tag{5.23}$$

The above maximization problem has been solved in appendix 5.6.2. Here we report the first-order conditions (FOC) only. Using the FOCs and substituting for the expression of λ yield the relations for c_{at} and c_{st} as follows:

$$c_{at} = \left(\frac{\gamma p_{at}}{\alpha}\right)^{\frac{1}{\theta-1}} c_{mt},$$

[9] See the technical appendix in Verma (2012a) who has derived detailed results along this line.

$$c_{st} = \left(\frac{\gamma p_{st}}{1-\alpha-\gamma}\right)^{\frac{1}{\theta-1}} c_{mt}. \tag{5.24}$$

Using these two equations in (5.24), we get,

$$c_{st} = (\frac{\alpha}{1-\alpha-\gamma}\frac{p_{st}}{p_{at}})^{\frac{1}{\theta-1}} c_{at}. \tag{5.25}$$

We know that the inter-temporal Euler equation is

$$U^{'}(c_t) = \beta U^{'}(c_{t+1}).f^{'}(K_{t+1}),$$

where β is the discounting factor and $U(.)$ is the instantaneous utility function as given in equation (5.1). Using eq. (5.1), we can write the inter-temporal Euler equation in a simplified form as follows:[10]

$$\left(\frac{c_{mt+1}}{c_{mt}}\right)^{\theta-1}\frac{C_t}{C_{t+1}} = \frac{1}{\beta(1+r_{kt+1}-\delta)}, \tag{5.26}$$

where $C_t \equiv \alpha c_{at}^{\theta} + \gamma c_{mt}^{\theta} + (1-\alpha-\gamma)c_{st}^{\theta}$ and $C_{t+1} \equiv \alpha c_{at+1}^{\theta} + \gamma c_{mt+1}^{\theta} + (1-\alpha-\gamma)c_{st+1}^{\theta}$.

5.2.4.3 Unbalanced Growth

We substitute the values of consumption derived from household's optimization in the utility function by appealing to the market clearing conditions as noted in Eq. (5.4) and to the production functions as described in Eq. (5.3).[11]

We rewrite the inter-temporal Euler equation and substitute the market clearing conditions for capital, labour, land inputs, and sectoral goods consumption with those for output markets. This approach yields the inter-temporal Euler equations for the agriculture, manufacturing, and service sectors.[12]. Here, we focus solely on the steady-state conditions.

1. The steady-state condition for the agriculture sector can be written as follows:

$$\begin{aligned}\big[(1-\phi_a)\alpha(A_a K_a^{\phi_a})^{\theta} L_a^{\theta(1-\phi_a)-1} - \\ (1-\alpha-\gamma)(1-\phi_s)(A_s K_s^{\phi_s})^{\theta}(1-L_a-L_m)^{\theta(1-\phi_s)-1}\big] = 0.\end{aligned} \tag{5.27}$$

---

[10] See appendices 5.6.2 and 5.6.3 for detail derivations. The equation (5.26) is a reduced form of eq. (5.42) in appendix 5.6.2.

[11] See the detailed derivations in appendix 5.6.3. We substitute the values of K_t and K_{t+1} in the utility function to have Eq. (5.44) in the appendix.

[12] We have noted these equations in Appendix 5.6.4 as Eq. (5.45), Eq. (5.46), and Eq. (5.47). See Attanasio and Low (2004) in this connection.

2. The steady-state condition for the manufacturing sector can be written as follows:

$$\Big[\gamma(1-\phi_m)\Big(A_m K_m^{\phi_m} L_m^{1-\phi_m} + (1-\delta)(K_a + K_m + K_s) - K_a - K_m - K_s\Big)^{\theta-1}$$
$$\Big(A_m K_m^{\phi_m} L_m^{-\phi_m}\Big) - (1-\alpha-\gamma)(1-\phi_s)A_s K_s^{\phi_s}(1 - L_a - L_m)^{\theta(1-\phi_s)-1}\Big] = 0 \tag{5.28}$$

3. Finally, for the service sector, we substitute $L_s = 1 - L_a - L_m$ in the steady-state equation of the service sector market clearing. This yields the following equation:

$$(1-\beta+\beta\delta)\left[\gamma\theta\begin{pmatrix} A_m K_m^{\phi_m} L_m^{1-\phi_m} + (1-\delta) \\ (K_a + K_m + K_s) - K_a - K_m - K_s \end{pmatrix}^{\theta-1}\right]$$
$$= \beta(1-\alpha-\gamma)\theta\phi_s\big(A_s(1-L_a-L_m)^{1-\phi_s}\big)^{\theta} K_s^{\theta\phi_s-1}\Big]. \tag{5.29}$$

Along with the above three equations, the steady-state inter-temporal Euler equations of the household optimization yield the following two equations:

$$(1-\beta+\beta\delta)\left[\gamma\theta\begin{pmatrix} A_m K_m^{\phi_m} L_m^{1-\phi_m} + (1-\delta) \\ (K_a + K_m + K_s) - K_a - K_m - K_s \end{pmatrix}^{\theta-1}\right]$$
$$= \beta * \Big[\alpha\theta\phi_a\big(A_a l_a^{\sigma_a} L_a^{1-\phi_a-\sigma_a}\big)^{\theta} K_a^{\phi_a\theta-1}\Big], \tag{5.30}$$

$$1 = \beta * \big[(\phi_m A_m L_m^{1-\phi_m} K_m^{\phi_m-1} + (1-\delta))\big]. \tag{5.31}$$

This will result in a system of five equations, eqs, (5.27)-(5.31), in five unknowns, namely K_a, K_m, K_s, L_a, L_m. Solving this system yields the optimal allocations of labour capital across sectors. Finally, we can compute the value of L_s using the relation $L_s = 1 - L_a - L_m$.

5.2.4.4 A Value Function-Based Formulation

The same formulation may be done by a value function approach. The state variables are the capital levels for the sectors, K_a, K_m, K_s. The technology levels are also parameters although they are not necessarily the state variables. The value function equation is given below:

$$V(K_a, K_m, K_s) = \max_{K_a, K_m, K_s, L_a, L_m, L_s} \ln\Big(\alpha\big(A_a K_a^{\phi_a} l_a^{\sigma_a} L_a^{1-\phi_a-\sigma_a}\big)^{\theta}$$
$$+\gamma\big(A_m K_m^{\phi_m} L_m^{1-\phi_m} + (1-\delta)K - K'\big)^{\theta} + (1-\alpha-\gamma)$$

$$\left(A_{st}K_s^{\phi_s}L_s^{1-\phi_s}\right)^{\theta}\Big)^{\frac{1}{\theta}} + \beta \cdot V\left(K_a', K_m', K_s'\right) \tag{5.32}$$

In this equation, the notations have been used in the usual sense with K_a, K_m, and K_s denoting the level of capital in different sectors and L_a, L_m, and L_s denoting the labour employed in those sectors in the contemporary period. The capital stock for the next period is given by K_a', K_m', and K_s'. The usual constraints on the movement of capital and labour apply.

We can use the first-order conditions as well as the envelop theorem to end up getting the same equations we obtained earlier.

5.2.5 *Numerical Solution of the Model*

5.2.5.1 Finding a Root of an Equation

For the simulation of the model, we need to find the solutions numerically to create a grid around the fixed-point solution of the steady-state equations of the policy variables. We have used a fixed-point algorithm to reach the fixed-point solution for the policy variables. One such algorithm is the Newton-Raphson method, named after Isaac Newton and Joseph Raphson, which is a root-finding algorithm used in numerical analysis. It produces successively better approximations to the roots (or zeroes) of a real-valued function. It all starts with a single-variable function f, which is defined for a real variable x, the function's derivative f' and an initial guess x_0 for the root of f in the most fundamental version. If the function meets all of the necessary assumptions and the initial guess is within reasonable bounds, then

$$x_1 = x_0 - \frac{f(x_0)}{f'(x_0)}.$$

Note that x_1 is a more accurate approximation of the root than the value x_0. In general,

$$x_{n+1} = x_n - \frac{f(x_n)}{f'(x_n)}.$$

We carry out this updating iteratively until a sufficiently precise value is obtained.

The issue in this case is finding a good initial guess. Initially, we considered a two-sector economy (which means the function is a variable function) and considered the steady-state equations of the two-sector economy. The solution for the policy variables of the two sectors is treated as the initial guesses that are reasonably close to the true root of the three-sector steady-state equations. We use the fixed-point solution for the simulation of the model.

5.2.6 Discrete State Space Method Algorithm

The value function for the three-sector model is solved using a numerical method called the discrete state space method (Burnside (1999), Fliegner et al. (1994), Baxter et al. (1990)) as it helps to solve dynamic optimization programming problems. It requires the creation of a grid of the state variables around the steady-state values of the state variables. We created a grid spanning from $0.5 \times \overline{K_a}$ to $1.5 \times \overline{K_a}$ in the case of agriculture sector capital, $0.5 \times \overline{K_m}$ to $1.5 \times \overline{K_m}$in the case manufacturing sector capital, $0.5 \times \overline{K_s}$ to $1.5 \times \overline{K_s}$ in the case of a service sector capital, $0.5 \times \overline{L_a}$ to $1.5 \times \overline{L_a}$ in the case of agriculture sector labour, and $0.5 \times \overline{L_m}$ to $1.5 \times \overline{L_m}$ in the case manufacturing sector labour where the $\overline{K_a}$, $\overline{K_m}$, $\overline{K_s}$, $\overline{L_a}$, and $\overline{L_m}$ are the steady-state fixed-point solution of the state variables obtained as the output of the fixed-point algorithm.

The state variables K_{at}, K_{mt}, K_{st} values are taken from the grid values. Each time the values of the state variables are increased a nominal increase is given as follows:

The next step is to find out the value for the function in the Bellman equation format with the initial guess. We defined two temporary grids to store the value functions that we generate each time using the grid values of the policy variables and compare the values to get the maximum value of the value function and store it in a third grid for the maximum value function. The corresponding values for the policy variables are also stored. The difference between the current value of the function and the previous value is computed to generate the difference value and the same procedure until the difference value reaches a negligibly small value. The grid values stored for the policy variables corresponding to the maximum value of the Bellman equations are used for the simulation of the model.

For each year, there are five policy variable grids and these grids are used for finding the state variables of the economy for the current period. Corresponding to the state variable using the policy variable grids, we interpolated the policy variable values for the five policy variables for each year. These policy variables are used to compute the output and employment of the economy. The output and labour values are then used for further analysis.

5.3 Measurements of Variables and Calibration

5.3.1 Construction of Variables

Our study requires the following variables:

1. Land
2. Labour

3. Capital
4. Output—GDP (constant prices)
5. Output—GDP (current prices)

5.3.1.1 Output—GDP

For the output variable, we have considered GDP at constant prices in the 2011–12 back series. The data are available in EPWRFITS under the National Accounts Statistics of India and Domestic Product of States of India links. The data are presented in Lakhs of INR values. We have considered data from 1983–84 to 2012–13. We restrict the period from 1983–34 to 2012–13 due to the non-availability of the labour and capital stock data. The labour data are available from 1983–84 to 2017–18, but the capital stock data are available until 2012–13. We have considered the 10 major sectors based on the Groningen Growth and Development Centre (GGDC) sectoral definition and combined the sectors into three sectors forming the three-sector definition. The mapping of three sectors from EPW (NAS) data has been shown in appendix 5.6.5.[13]

5.3.1.2 Labour

For the calculation of labour employed for different sectors in different Indian states, we have used different National Sample Survey Office (NSSO) datasets: 9 different rounds of Employment Unemployment Survey (EUS) during 1983–2012, 11 different rounds of Household Consumer Expenditure (HCE) during 1990–2002, and the solitary round of Periodic Labour Force Survey (PLFS) for 2017–18.[14] Apart from NSSO data, we have exploited the census data for the years 1991, 2001, and 2011.

5.3.1.3 Land

We have taken into account the measure of total cropped area for the land variable. The total cropped area data are available from different sources such as RBI, CMIE (Centre for Monitoring Indian Economy), World Bank indicators, and EPWRFITS. We have accessed multiple sources to ensure data triangulation. The total cropped area data are available for all of India as well as statewide till 2015–16. We considered the total cropped area data from 1983–84 to 2012–13 for all India.

---

[13] See Figure 5.4 in appendix 5.6.5 which shows the conversion from 10 sector to 3 sector.

[14] This is similar to the work by Gangopadhyay et al. (2024).

5.3.1.4 Capital

The data on Capital, net fixed capital stock (NFCS) in the 2004–05 price series, as constructed in the NAS, are employed for our analysis. The NFCS data are available industry-wise. The NFCS data are available annually for different sectors as an all-India figure.

5.3.1.5 Price Index

There are no explicit data available for the price indices for the different sectors, even at the all-India level. We have used the notion of price deflator to construct price indices across sectors. First, we have converted the Net Domestic Product (NDP) data at the constant price into the constant 2011–12 price. Second, we have calculated the price index for a specific sector in a particular year by dividing the NDP at current prices for that sector by the NDP at constant 2011–12 prices corresponding to the same period.

5.3.2 *Growth Accounting*

For the growth accounting, we followed the Solow residual methodology to compute the Total Factor Productivity (TFP) growth rates for each period.

$$\begin{aligned}\frac{\partial Y_{At}/\partial t}{Y_{At}} &= \frac{\partial A_{at}/\partial t}{A_{at}} + \phi_a \frac{\partial K_{at}/\partial t}{K_{at}} + \sigma_a \frac{\partial l_{at}/\partial t}{l_{at}} \\ &+ (1-\phi_a-\sigma_a)\frac{\partial L_{at}/\partial t}{L_{at}}.\end{aligned} \tag{5.33}$$

From the above equation, we can compute the value for the agriculture sector TFP as follows:

$$\begin{aligned}\frac{\partial A_{at}/\partial t}{A_{at}} &= \frac{\partial Y_{At}/\partial t}{Y_{At}} - \phi_a \frac{\partial K_{at}/\partial t}{K_{at}} - \sigma_a \frac{\partial l_{at}/\partial t}{l_{at}} \\ &- (1-\phi_a-\sigma_a)\frac{\partial L_{at}/\partial t}{L_{at}}.\end{aligned} \tag{5.34}$$

Likewise, we computed the TFP of the manufacturing and service sector as follows:

$$\frac{\partial A_{mt}/\partial t}{A_{mt}} = \frac{\partial Y_{mt}/\partial t}{Y_{mt}} - \phi_m \frac{\partial K_{mt}/\partial t}{K_{mt}} - (1-\phi_m)\frac{\partial L_{mt}/\partial t}{L_{mt}}, \tag{5.35}$$

$$\frac{\partial A_{st}/\partial t}{A_{st}} = \frac{\partial Y_{st}/\partial t}{Y_{st}} - \phi_s \frac{\partial K_{st}/\partial t}{K_{st}} - (1-\phi_s)\frac{\partial L_{st}/\partial t}{L_{st}}. \tag{5.36}$$

The Eqs.(5.34), (5.35), and (5.36) give the growth of TFP of agriculture, manufacturing, and service sectors, respectively.

In Table 5.1, we have reported the results from a growth accounting exercise using equations (5.34), (5.35), and (5.36). The factor share values, as reported in Table 5.1 ($\phi_a = 0.22$, $\phi_m = 0.50$, $\phi_s = 0.35$, $\sigma_a = 0.20$), are all calibrated in Table 5.2 later. Based on these parameters, we analyse the sector-wise contributions of TFP in Table 5.1. We find that TFP contributes 70% to the aggregate value-added growth of the agriculture sector. In industry and services, TFP contributes 23.3% and 47.5%, respectively. These figures can be compared with those reported in Verma (2012a) (51.3% for agriculture, 12.7% for industry, and 40.4% for services) and Bosworth et al. (2007) (61% for agriculture, 34% for industry, and 72% for services) during the period 1980–2004.[15] The discrepancies in TFP contributions across these works may stem from differences in data coverage and sources of data.

Note that post-liberalization, TFP contributions have increased for agriculture and services, but have decreased for manufacturing. This suggests that, in the post-liberalization era, growth in the manufacturing sector relies more on the expansion of factor inputs rather than on advancements in knowledge and R&D. This trend is concerning. Conversely, the contribution of labour to manufacturing growth has more than doubled in the post-liberalization period. This is positive news as it indicates a faster expansion of employment opportunities in manufacturing compared to the pre-liberalization era.

5.3.3 *Calibration*

We aim to examine whether the model can replicate the structural transformation observed in the Indian economy during the period from 1983 to 2012. Since data on capital are available only until 2012, our analysis is confined to the years 1983 to 2012. Our primary objective is to evaluate whether the employment and output shares generated by the model align with their counterparts in the actual data. The baseline accounting method will provide annual TFP growth rates for each of the three sectors across the entire Indian economy. Each period in the dataset corresponds to one year.

To calibrate the initial TFP for each sector, we set the initial TFP of the manufacturing sector to one. Additionally, we assumed that the ratios $\frac{p_a Y_A}{p_s Y_S}$ and $\frac{p_m Y_M}{p_s Y_S}$ in the model are the same to those observed in the data for the initial year. The nominal output values used for this calibration are based on the initial period, specifically from 1983–84.

[15] This is taken from their Table 5.4 with heading 'Sources of Economic Growth, Major Sectors, 1960–2005'. We have considered their calculation for 1980–2004.

Table 5.1 Growth accounting: baseline results

	Agriculture	Industry	Service
Factor Share			
Capital	0.22	0.50	0.35
Labour	0.58	0.50	0.65
Land	0.20		
Decomposition of average annual changes in real value added (%)			
Entire period 1983–2012			
Growth in real value added	2.87	7.11	7.87
Due to Capital	1.01	3.88	2.39
	(35.2)	(54.6)	(30.3)
Due to Labour	−0.12	1.57	1.74
	(−4.2)	(22.1)	(22.1)
Due to Land	−0.03		
	(−1.0)		
Due to TFP	2.01	1.66	3.74
	(70.0)	(23.3)	(47.5)
Pre liberalization period 1983–1991			
Growth in real value added	2.21	7.66	6.54
Due to Capital	0.85	3.72	1.51
	(38.5)	(48.6)	(23.1)
Due to Labour	0.55	0.88	2.48
	(24.9)	(11.5)	(37.9)
Due to Land	0.20		
	(9.0)		
Due to TFP	0.61	3.06	2.55
	(27.6)	(39.9)	(39.0)
Post liberalization period 1991–2012			
Growth in real value added	3.12	6.91	8.38
Due to Capital	1.07	3.94	2.73
	(34.3)	(57.0)	(32.6)
Due to Labour	−0.37	1.84	1.46
	(−11.9)	(26.6)	(17.4)
Due to Land	−0.12		
	(−3.8)		
Due to TFP	2.54	1.13	4.19
	(81.4)	(16.4)	(50.0)

The number in parenthesis is the % contribution of the factor to the real value-added growth

5.3.3.1 Discount Factor and Depreciation Rate

We considered the world bank data on real interest rate for India for the period 1983–2013. We took the average of the real interest rate which is approximately 6.38% per annum. For discount factor calculation, we considered the following equation:

$$\beta = \frac{1}{1+r} = 0.94,$$

where we set $r = 0.0638$ as the real interest rate. We have taken the depreciation rate (δ) as 5% which is standard in the literature.

5.3.3.2 Parameters of the Utility Function

The calibration of the parameters θ, α, γ, and $(1-\alpha-\gamma)$, representing the elasticity of substitution and the weights of agriculture, manufacturing, and service sector goods in the utility function, followed the methodology outlined by Acemoglu and Guerrieri (2008). Ensuring market clearing, the household's utility maximization in the agriculture and service sectors implies:

$$\frac{p_s Y_S}{p_a Y_A} = \frac{(1-\alpha-\gamma)}{\alpha}\left(\frac{Y_S}{Y_A}\right)^{\theta}.$$

Taking the logarithm on both sides and regressing real value-added data against the ratio of nominal value-added data yields:

$$\log \frac{p_s Y_S}{p_a Y_A} = \log \frac{(1-\alpha-\gamma)}{\alpha} + \theta \cdot \log\left(\frac{Y_S}{Y_A}\right).$$

Similarly, for manufacturing and the service sector:

$$\log \frac{p_s Y_S}{p_m Y_M} = \log \frac{(1-\alpha-\gamma)}{\gamma} + \theta \cdot \log\left(\frac{Y_S}{Y_M}\right).$$

From these regressions, we derived the parameters for the elasticity of substitution ($\frac{1}{1-\theta}$) and the weights of consumption goods across the three sectors in the utility function. These values are reported in Table 5.2 below.

5.3.3.3 Parameters of the Production Functions

In the production functions described by Equation (5.3), the parameters ϕ_a, ϕ_m, and ϕ_s represent the factor income shares of capital in the agriculture, manufacturing, and service sectors, respectively. We followed the methodology outlined in Gollin

(2002) to calibrate these factor income shares for both labour and capital in each sector.

We used data from the EPWRFITS dataset as discussed in Section 5.3, covering the period from 2004 to 2013. This dataset includes components such as compensation of employees, operating surplus/mixed income, and consumption of fixed capital, disaggregated for organized and unorganized sectors. We have adopted two adjustment procedures that are discussed in Gollin (2002).

Initially, we computed the factor income shares of labour by following the equation:

$$\text{Labour Income Share} = \frac{\text{Employee Compensation}}{\text{Employee Compensation} + \text{operating surplus} + \text{Consumption of Fixed Capital}}.$$

This exercise resulted in labour income shares of magnitude 0.17, 0.39, and 0.32 for the agriculture, manufacturing, and service sector, respectively. These numbers are less, particularly in the context of a developing country such as India. One possibility of correcting the number is through the omission of self-employment incomes as they may not be precise about segregating capital and labour incomes. Considering a large proportion of the Indian workers are self-employed, dropping all the self-employed is rather drastic. As a compromise, we have adopted two adjustments out of the three adjustments that Gollin (2002) has proposed in his work.

In the first adjustment, we considered the operating surplus/mixed income of the unorganized sector as part of the employee compensation and followed the following equation:

$$\text{Labour Income Share} = \frac{\text{Employee Compensation} + \text{Unorganised sector operating surplus}}{\text{Employee Compensation} + \text{operating surplus} + \text{Consumption of Fixed Capital}}.$$

This adjustment of the operating surplus from the unorganized sector resulted in the labour income shares from each of the sectors as follows: 0.64 (after adjusting for income share to land), 0.54, and 0.74 for agriculture, manufacturing, and service sectors, respectively.

When accounting for the entire operating surplus from the unorganized sector within employee compensation, there is a tendency to overestimate national income allocated to labour. This overestimation occurs because self-employed labour in developing countries often utilizes a significant amount of capital. To mitigate this issue of overestimating labour income share, we implemented a second adjustment to factor in self-employment income. In this adjustment, we assumed that the operating surplus from the unorganized sector reflects the same mix of labour and capital as seen in the broader economy. We applied the following approach:

$$\begin{aligned}\text{Labour Income Share} &= \text{Employee Compensation/(Employee} \\ &\text{Compensation} + \text{operating surplus} + \text{Consumption of} \\ &\text{Fixed Capital} - \text{Unorganised sector operating surplus).}\end{aligned}$$

Table 5.2 Calibrated parameters

Parameters	Description	Values
ϕ_a	Capital share in agriculture	0.22
σ_a	Land share in agriculture	0.20
ϕ_m	Capital share in industry	0.50
ϕ_s	Capital share in services	0.35
A_{a0}	Initial TFP level in agriculture	2.30
A_{m0}	Initial TFP level in industry	1.00
A_{s0}	Initial TFP level in services	2.25
A_a	Growth rate of TFP in agriculture	2.01
A_m	Growth rate of TFP in industry	1.66
A_s	Growth rate of TFP in services	3.74
β	Discount factor	0.94
δ	Depreciation rate	0.05
α	Weight on agricultural good	0.45
γ	Weight on industrial good	0.24
$1-\alpha-\gamma$	Weight on service good	0.31
$1/(1-\theta)$	Elasticity of substitution	1.8847

The resulting labour income shares from this adjustment are 0.51, 0.46, and 0.55 for the agriculture, manufacturing, and service sectors, respectively. We averaged the values obtained from the first and second adjustments to determine the labour income shares used in our model. Thus, the calibrated values for the labour income share in the agriculture, manufacturing, and service sectors are 0.58, 0.50, and 0.65, respectively. As for the rent attributed to land used in the agriculture sector, we adopted the reported value of 0.2 as documented by Sivasubramonian (2004).

As far as the technological growth parameters are concerned, the values for the initial TFP level are computed so that the sectoral output level calculated in the model matches the correspondent figure from the data. From then on, the TFPs of the sectors are calculated by multiplying the initial TFP by a factor based on the growth rate. We have calculated the growth rates from the data by the method of Solow residuals as described in Section 3.2. The growth rates for the sectors are calibrated going by these actual growth rates of the sectors over time. Table 5.2 tabulates all the calibrated values for the parameters.

For the initial level TFP in agriculture and manufacturing sectors calibration, we kept the initial level TFP of manufacturing sector as one. Then, as mentioned in section 5.3.3, we computed the initial TFP for the two sectors. The initial level TFP in agriculture sector shows a sharp decline from that of Verma (2012a) and that of service sector is more or less similar.[16] The difference in initial TFP for agriculture sector may arise out of the datasets and the time period that we considered.

[16] In Verma (2012a), initial TFP in agriculture and services was set as 5.25 and 2.57 per cent, respectively.

5.4 Results and Discussion

5.4.1 Results

5.4.1.1 Sectoral Output and Labour Share

The trends in the sectoral output and labour shares from the model vis-à-vis their data counterparts are displayed in Figure 5.1. While understandably the model output and the observed data show modest differences in the values, the trends over time are the same in both cases. The initial period output shares from the model for agriculture, manufacturing, and service sectors are as follows 38.93%, 21.38%, 39.70%, respectively, and the observed data of the output shares for the three sectors are 43.57%, 21.75%, and 34.68%, respectively. The final period output shares from the model are 33.15%, 19.31%, and 47.54%, whereas the corresponding figures from the observed

Fig. 5.1 Sectoral shares of output and employment: baseline results. We have presented a three-year moving average after interpolating the data for the missing years

data are 21.62%, 28.90%, and 49.48%, respectively. Both model and observed data show similar trends in the output share of the sectors.

The model overestimates the agriculture sector output share and underestimates the output share of the manufacturing sector. The model can track the service sector output share as the observed data, almost perfectly. The agriculture output shares of both model output and the observed data show a decreasing trend. In the case of manufacturing sector output share, the model and the observed data show slight differences. Though both are showing a decreasing trend, the observed data of manufacturing output show an increase and then show a decreasing trend. The model output of the manufacturing output share shows a decreasing trend throughout our study. The service sector output shares of model output and the observed data are more or less similar value-wise and both show an increasing trend.

The sectoral labour shares from the model are 40.00%, 23.65%, and 36.36% for agriculture, manufacturing, and service sectors, respectively, for the initial period. However, the observed data of the initial period sectoral labour shares are 68.53%, 13.43%, and 18.04%, respectively. Except for the agriculture sector, the model overestimates the sectoral labour share in the initial period. The final period sectoral labour shares from the model output are 38.42%, 21.75%, and 39.83%, respectively. The observed data for the same are 47.10%, 24.00%, and 28.90%, respectively. The model underestimates the labour share of the agriculture and manufacturing sectors.

The labour shares of the three sectors from the model as well as from the observed data are plotted in Figure 5.1. The model underestimates the labour share of the agriculture sector, however overestimates that of the manufacturing and the service sectors. The employment share of agriculture from the model output shows a stagnated trend, while the observed employment share shows a slightly decreasing trend. In the case of the manufacturing sector, labour shares in the model output show a decreasing trend, while the observed share shows an increasing trend. The service sector labour shares from the model and the observed data show similar trends.

5.4.2 Intuitive Discussions

The elasticity of substitution parameter plays an important role in generating structural change in models with differential TFP growth across sectors. If consumption goods are complements, then, in the presence of differential TFP growth across sectors, resources are transferred to the sector experiencing the lowest TFP growth. Conversely, if consumption goods are substitutes, then resources move to the sector witnessing highest TFP growth.

The intuitions are straightforward. The sector witnessing highest TFP growth also experiences the most rapid decline in the price of the good it produces. We obtained the value of the elasticity of substitution greater than one, implying that the goods are substitutes in the preferences.

Table 5.3 Growth rate of three sectors: Model output

Sector	Growth rate in different periods				
	1983–2013	1983–1991	1991–1999	1998–2008	2007–2013
Economy	3.81	4.13	3.73	3.48	4.00
Agriculture	3.54	3.87	2.56	3.78	3.98
Manufacturing	3.66	3.37	3.55	1.94	7.47
Services	3.92	4.59	5.58	3.07	2.12

Table 5.4 Growth rate of three sectors: Data

Sector	Growth rate in different periods				
	1983–2013	1983–1991	1991–1999	1998–2008	2007–2013
Economy	4.55	3.03	4.69	4.64	6.64
Agriculture	2.93	1.24	1.52	3.16	7.33
Secondary	3.73	5.80	7.29	1.65	−0.59
Tertiary	4.80	2.50	6.77	4.62	6.10

5.4.2.1 Labour Productivity Growth

We have computed the compounded annual growth rate (henceforth CAGR) of labour productivity from the model output during 1983–2013 (Table 5.3) and that from the actual data (Table 5.4). The model output shows a growth rate of 3.81% for the entire period for the economy as a whole. In contrast, the data give a growth rate of 4.55%. Among the three sectors, the services sector and the agriculture sector show the highest and lowest growth rate, respectively, in both model output and data.

We have divided the time horizon into four sub-periods: 1983–1991 (pre-economic reform period), 1991–1998 (early economic reform period), 1998–2007 (pre-global slump period), and 2007–2013 (post-global slump period).[17] Essentially, the year 1991 is a watershed moment for India as the beginning of economic reform. It makes sense to consider the pre-1991 years as a separate sub-period. The second wave of reforms effectively began in 1998 when India got a stable government at the centre after a few years of political instability. We take 1998 as the second break point. The year 2007 gives a natural break to compare the pre- and post-global economic crisis period.

During 1983–1991, the model's growth rate and data show differing results. For the second sub-period during 1991–1998, the model shows the lowest growth rate in the primary sector, which is in line with the figures from the data. For the third sub-period, 1998–2007, the model and the data arrive at the same labour productivity growth rate in the manufacturing sector which shows the lowest growth rate among the three sectors. During the final sub-period, 2007–2013, the model output growth rate and its data counterpart were at variance.

[17] We have discussed this division of sub-periods in Gangopadhyay et al. (2024).

5.4.2.2 Structural Transformation Index

After computing the growth rate, we decompose the growth into three effects: ‘within the sector’, ‘between sector’, and ‘interaction’ effects, using the canonical decomposition method. The decomposition of the labour productivity into three effects facilitates us to compute the Structural Transformation Index (*STI*) for the data (in Table 5.5) and the model output (in Table 5.6).

The economy shows an *STI* of 0.04 for the model output (Table 5.6) from the entire study period, while its data counterpart is 0.29 (Table 5.5). As in the case of data, the second sub-period also shows a negative *STI* value for the model output. In other words, the *STI* of the Early Years of the economic reform period is negative as is the case with the *STI* from the data. The maximum amount of *STI* is observed during the pre-global slump period (1998–2007) as in the case of data. In the decomposition of the productivity growth into three effects, we observe that like the case of data, the model output also has the within-sector component as the largest component. Figure 5.2 is the graphical version of Table 5.6 and Figure 5.3 is the graphical version for Table 5.5.

Finally, Table 5.7 shows the contribution of structural transformation and within-sector productivity towards the growth in labour productivity for the period 1983–2013. From Table 5.7, we can note that the contribution of ST is nominal at 4%, and the growth is almost entirely contributed by the within-sector productivity changes. Out of the three sectors, the services sector is the largest contributor.

Table 5.5 Decomposition of the aggregate labour productivity growth and *STI* calculation: Data

Period	Within sector effect	Between sector effect	Interaction effect	Productivity growth rate (%)	STI (%)
1983–2013	3.25	0.29	1.01	4.55	0.29
1983–1991	2.57	0.34	0.12	3.03	0.15
1991–1998	4.91	−0.11	−0.11	4.69	−0.05
1998–2007	3.15	1.18	0.31	4.64	0.32
2007–2013	4.40	2.16	0.07	6.64	0.34

Table 5.6 Decomposition of the aggregate labour productivity growth and *STI* calculation: model output

Period	Within sector effect	Between sector effect	Interaction effect	Productivity growth rate (%)	STI (%)
1983–2013	3.66	0.03	0.12	3.81	0.04
1983–1991	4.01	0.07	0.04	4.13	0.03
1991–998	4.14	−0.17	−0.23	3.73	−0.11
1998–2007	3.05	0.32	0.11	3.48	0.12
2007–2013	3.73	0.32	−0.05	4.00	0.07

Table 5.7 Contribution of structural transformation and sectoral output in aggregate productivity growth from 1983 to 2013: model output

Growth Rate (%)	3.81
Structural Transformation (%)	4.00
Sectoral Productivity (%):	96.00
(1) Agriculture (%)	36.24
(2) Manufacturing (%)	21.04
(3) Services (%)	38.71

Fig. 5.2 Canonical decomposition of growth rate: model output

Fig. 5.3 Canonical decomposition of growth rate: data

5.4.3 Departure from the Perfect Market Condition

Understandably, India may not have the economic environment conducive to the concept of a non-intervened market. Instead, India experiences misallocation and various distortions at multiple stages. Hsieh and Klenow (2009) have compared the US manufacturing productivity to that of India and found a huge cost on account of misallocation of resources for the Indian economy.

We have introduced wedges in the capital market and profits, following the approach of Buera and Kaboski (2009) and Cai (2015), to account for market imperfections. Appendix 5.6.4 presents the detailed calculations. It is important to note that the wedge on capital does not affect the relative prices of sectoral goods. However, we expect a relative decrease in the real interest rate compared to wages, potentially resulting in slower growth for the capital-intensive manufacturing sector.

In the absence of any wedge in the capital market, if the wedge on the profit is uniform across sectors, then the impact of the wedges will not change our conclusion, at all. This is because of the fact that the wedges shall cancel out to favour one sector over the other.

The wedge at the agriculture sector could explain the persistent gap between the model and the data in our bench line model. If agriculture sector has a wedge, it would reduce the profit and therefore, disguised unemployment in that sector may be explained to an extent.

We need some assumption on the values of the wedges to make it more interesting. Suppose the manufacturing sector has a higher wedge compared to the services sector. In other words, $\tau_m > \tau_s$. Then, the prices of the manufacturing good relative to the agricultural and service goods would rise. The greater cost of capital would mean a slowing down of overall growth. Naturally, to explain the growth, we need to have a greater share of labour allocated to manufacturing. However, such a reallocation may not necessarily align with observed data patterns.

5.4.4 Discussion

The performance of our model to closely track the employment data comes with mixed success and this needs some discussion. Manufacturing employment share data has shown a slight upward turn in recent years, especially since 1997. Our model could not capture this upward trend. In previous works in the literature, as in Verma (2012a), similar divergences between data and model predictions have been observed concerning employment share. There, to overcome this limitation, public capital has been introduced in the model. We have not included any tax-transfer policies or any publicly financed capital. However, we would like to point out the role of various distortions that might be introduced in the theoretical model to better capture the time trend of sectoral employment shares.

A similar analysis has been carried out in Mondal (2019) for India in a two-sector model with agriculture and non-agriculture which is a combination of manufacturing and services. The presence of higher distortion between these two sectors results into slower pace of structural transformation. In Ghate et al. (2016), the impact of sector-specific taxes has been introduced to show the relative desirability of moving capital across sectors. It is possible to quantify relative (sector-specific) distortions in our three-sector model by way of matching the employment share data.

Several works in the literature have quantified the potential rate of growth of aggregate productivity by eliminating any distortions from the model. These counterfactual exercises inform us about the relative importance of sectors in accelerating the overall growth of an economy.[18] In India, the slow growth of manufacturing TFPs has often been blamed for its stagnant employment share. There are multiple arguments behind this inadequate performance of the manufacturing sector. Strict and rigid labour laws, unfavourable industrial policies ignoring the small-scale industry, and excessive institutional requirements to start a business are a few of the commonly cited reasons.[19]

A caveat may be given against any premature general conclusion to hold these causes responsible towards slowdown of the manufacturing sector without sufficient evidence about the channel. Maiti (2019) and Bhattacharjea (2021) have shown that the labour market reforms to make it more flexible and pro-employer is ineffective because most of the industries may be exempted from the purview of the laws due to having less than 100 formal workers. Therefore, it is important to specify both the mechanism and the channel by which any labour market reform to make it more flexible can improve the performance of the manufacturing sector.

5.5 Conclusion

The present study is an attempt to understand the underlying factors causing the unbalanced growth of the Indian economy using a general equilibrium model for a period from 1983 to 2013. The three-sector model simulates the output and employment share of the country to compute labour productivity. The model output of employment share shows that the actual labour share of the secondary sector and the tertiary sector is relatively very less compared to the model determined share. However, the labour share of the agriculture sector from data is much higher compared to the model output. Since our model does not include any distortion, to begin with, we posited that these mismatches are caused by real-world distortions.

[18] See, for example, Duarte and Restuccia (2010); Üngör (2017), etc. For a 10-sectoral disaggregation without counterfactual analysis, see Thasni et al. (2024).

[19] The bottlenecks discussed here can be integrated into the calibration exercise to generate various scenarios. For instance, one might explore questions such as the potential outcomes if the labour market transitions from rigidity to flexibility. However, to simulate these structural issues lies beyond the purview of our present work. Quantifying these bottlenecks using a three-sector model can be a very fruitful research agenda for the future.

We determined the average labour productivity using the model output and then decomposed the productivity growth using the standard shift-share-based method. We measured the contribution of structural change to the aggregate productivity of the economy. It reveals that the maximum contribution of structural transformation in economic growth took place during the period 1998 to 2007. The economic reforms introduced in the country during the years 1991-92 may have helped the country to reallocate the production factories across different sectors causing the economy to grow at a higher rate due to the reallocation of factors of production.

Our theoretical work, like other works in the literature, is based on simple assumptions of perfect competition and the free movement of factors of production across sectors. These assumptions can be questioned and one may like to introduce various barriers in the movement of labour and capital. These barriers can play a very important role in hindering aggregate productivity growth. We have also assumed away from the important role of human capital in promoting growth, especially in the service sector of an economy. Taking into account all these important factors in a model and deriving quantitative predictions for the economy can be a very promising future research agenda.

Appendix

General Equilibrium: Solving the Model

Solution to Firms' Problems

$$\pi\left(K_{a,t+1}, L_{at}, l_{at}\right) = p_{at}A_{at}K_{at}^{\phi_a} l_{at}^{\sigma_a} L_{at}^{1-\phi_a-\sigma_a} - r_{kt}K_{at} - \omega_t L_{at} - R_{lt}l_{at} \tag{5.37}$$

The FOC concerning $K_{a,t}$ yields the following:

$$\frac{d\pi}{dK_{at}} = -r_{kt} + p_{at}A_{at}\phi_a K_{at}^{\phi_a-1} l_{at}^{\sigma_a} L_{at}^{1-\phi_a-\sigma_a} = 0 \tag{5.38}$$

where $k_{at} = \frac{K_{at}}{L_{at}}$ and we set $l_{at} = 1$.

Household

$$\begin{aligned}
\frac{dL}{dc_{at}} &= \frac{1}{\theta}\left[\alpha c_{at}^{\theta} + \gamma c_{mt}^{\theta} + (1-\alpha-\gamma)c_{st}^{\theta}\right]^{\frac{1}{\theta}-1}\theta\alpha c_{at}^{\theta-1} - \lambda \cdot p_{at} \\
\frac{dL}{dc_{mt}} &= \frac{1}{\theta}\left[\alpha c_{at}^{\theta} + \gamma c_{mt}^{\theta} + (1-\alpha-\gamma)c_{st}^{\theta}\right]^{\frac{1}{\theta}-1}\theta\gamma (c_{mt})^{\theta-1} - \lambda \\
\frac{dL}{dc_{st}} &= \frac{1}{\theta}\left[\alpha c_{at}^{\theta} + \gamma c_{mt}^{\theta} + (1-\alpha-\gamma)c_{st}^{\theta}\right]^{\frac{1}{\theta}-1}\theta(1-\alpha-\gamma)(c_{st})^{\theta-1} - \lambda p_{st}
\end{aligned} \tag{5.39}$$

$$U'(c_t) = \frac{dU}{dc_{mt}} = \frac{\gamma c_{mt}^{\theta-1}}{\alpha c_{at}^{\theta} + \gamma c_{mt}^{\theta} + (1-\alpha-\gamma)c_{st}^{\theta}}; \tag{5.40}$$

and

$$U'(c_{t+1}) = \frac{dU}{dc_{mt+1}} = \frac{\gamma c_{mt+1}^{\theta-1}}{\alpha c_{at+1}^{\theta} + \gamma c_{mt+1}^{\theta} + (1-\alpha-\gamma)c_{st+1}^{\theta}}. \tag{5.41}$$

Substituting these values we get the following inter-temporal Euler equation:

$$\frac{\gamma c_{mt}^{\theta-1}}{\alpha c_{at}^{\theta} + \gamma c_{mt}^{\theta} + (1-\alpha-\gamma)c_{st}^{\theta}} = \beta \frac{\gamma c_{mt+1}^{\theta-1}}{\alpha c_{at+1}^{\theta} + \gamma c_{mt+1}^{\theta} + (1-\alpha-\gamma)c_{st+1}^{\theta}} \\ ((1-\delta) + r_{Kt+1}). \tag{5.42}$$

Unbalanced Growth

We substitute the values of consumption in the utility function by appealing to the market clearing conditions as noted in Eq. (5.4) and to the production functions as described in Eq. (5.3).

$$U(C_t) = \ln\left[\alpha(A_{at}K_{at}^{\phi_a} l_{at}^{\sigma_a} L_{at}^{1-\phi_a-\sigma_a})^{\theta} + \gamma(A_{mt}K_{mt}^{\phi_m} L_{mt}^{1-\phi_m} + \\ (1-\delta)K_t - K_{t+1})^{\theta} + (1-\alpha-\gamma)(A_{st}K_{st}^{\phi_s} L_{st}^{1-\phi_s})^{\theta}\right]^{\frac{1}{\theta}}. \tag{5.43}$$

We substitute the values of K_t and K_{t+1} in the utility function to have:

$$U(C_t) = \ln\Big[\alpha\Big(A_{at}K_{at}^{\phi_a} l_{at}^{\sigma a} L_{at}^{1-\phi_a-\sigma_a}\Big)^{\theta} + \lambda\Big(A_{mt}K_{mt}^{\phi_m} L_{mt}^{1-\phi_m} + (1-\delta)$$

$$(K_{at} + K_{mt} + K_{st}) - K_{at+1} - K_{mt+1} - K_{st+1})^{\theta}(1-\alpha-\gamma)\Big(A_{st}K_{st}^{\phi_s} L_{st}^{1-\phi_s}\Big)^{\theta}\Big]^{\frac{1}{\theta}}$$

$$U(C_{t+1}) = \ln\Big[\alpha\Big(A_{at+1}K_{at+1}^{\phi_a} l_{at+1}^{\sigma_a} L_{at+1}^{1-\phi_a-\sigma_a}\Big)^{\theta}$$

$$+\gamma\Big(A_{mt+1}K_{mt+1}^{\phi_m} L_{mt+1}^{1-\phi_m} + (1-\delta)(K_{at+1} + K_{mt+1} + K_{st+1}) - K_{at+2} - K_{mt+2} - K_{st+2}\Big)^{\theta}$$

$$+(1-\alpha-\gamma)\Big(A_{st+1}K_{st+1}^{\phi_s} L_{st+1}^{1-\phi_s}\Big)^{\theta}\Big]^{\frac{1}{\theta}} \tag{5.44}$$

The inter-temporal Euler equation can be re-written as

$$\frac{\partial U(C_t)}{\partial C_t}\cdot\frac{\partial C_t}{\partial K_{t+1}} = -\beta\frac{\partial U(C_{t+1})}{\partial C_{t+1}}\cdot\frac{\partial C_{t+1}}{\partial K_{t+1}}$$

where

$$C_t = \left[\alpha(A_{at}K_{at}^{\phi_a}l_{at}^{\sigma_a}L_{at}^{1-\phi_a-\sigma_a})^{\theta} + \gamma(A_{mt}K_{mt}^{\phi_m}L_{mt}^{1-\phi_m} + (1-\delta)(K_{at}+K_{mt}+K_{st}) \right.$$
$$\left. -K_{at+1} - K_{mt+1} - K_{st+1})^{\theta} + (1-\alpha-\gamma)(A_{st}K_{st}^{\phi_s}L_{st}^{1-\phi_s})^{\theta}\right]$$

and

$$C_{t+1} = \left[\alpha\left(A_{at+1}K_{at+1}^{\phi_a}l_{at+1}^{\sigma_a}L_{at+1}^{1-\phi_a-\sigma_a}\right)^{\theta} + \gamma\left(A_{mt+1}K_{mt+1}^{\phi_m}L_{mt+1}^{1-\phi_m}\right.\right.$$
$$\left.+(1-\delta)(K_{at+1}+K_{mt+1}+K_{st+1}) - K_{at+2} - K_{mt+2} - K_{st+2}\right)^{\theta}$$
$$\left.+(1-\alpha-\gamma)\left(A_{st+1}K_{st+1}^{\phi_s}L_{st+1}^{1-\phi_s}\right)^{\theta}\right]$$

The FOCs of $U(C_t)$, $U(C_{t+1})$, and $f(k_{t+1})$ with respect to K_{at}, K_{mt}, K_{st} are given by:

$$\frac{\partial U(C_t)}{\partial C_t} * \frac{\partial C_t}{\partial K_{at+1}} = -\beta\frac{\partial U(C_{t+1})}{\partial C_{t+1}} * \frac{\partial C_{t+1}}{\partial K_{at+1}}$$

$$\frac{\partial U(C_t)}{\partial C_t} = \frac{\frac{1}{\theta}}{C_t}$$

$$\frac{\partial C_t}{\partial K_{at+1}} = \gamma\theta\left(A_{mt}K_{mt}^{\phi m}L_{mt}^{1-\phi_m} + (1-\delta)(K_{at}+K_{mt}+K_{st})\right.$$
$$\left.-K_{at+1} - K_{mt+1} - K_{st+1}\right)^{\theta-1}(-1)$$

$$\frac{\partial U(C_{t+1})}{\partial C_{t+1}} = \frac{\frac{1}{\theta}}{C_{t+1}}$$

$$\frac{\partial C_{t+1}}{\partial K_{at+1}} = \alpha\theta\phi_a(A_{at+1}l_{at+1}^{\sigma_a}L_{at+1}^{1-\phi_a-\sigma_a})^{\theta}K_{at+1}^{\phi_a\theta-1} + \gamma\theta(A_{mt+1}K_{mt+1}^{\phi_m}L_{mt+1}^{1-\phi_m}+$$
$$(1-\delta)(K_{at+1}+K_{mt+1}+K_{st+1}) - K_{at+2} - K_{mt+2} - K_{st+2})^{\theta-1}(1-\delta)$$

Therefore, the inter-temporal Euler equation for the agriculture sector can be written as:

$$\frac{\frac{1}{\theta}}{C_t} * \Big[\gamma\theta\Big(A_{mt}K_{mt}^{\phi_m}L_{mt}^{1-\phi_m} + (1-\delta)(K_{at}+K_{mt}+K_{st})$$
$$-K_{at+1} - K_{mt+1} - K_{st+1}\Big)^{\theta-1}(-1)\Big] = (-)\beta\frac{\frac{1}{\theta}}{C_{t+1}}$$
$$*\Big[\alpha\theta\phi_a\Big(A_{at} + 1l_{at+1}^{\sigma_a}L_{at+1}^{1-\phi_a-\sigma_a}\Big)^{\theta}K_{at+1}^{\phi_a\theta-1} + \gamma\theta\Big(A_{mt+1}K_{mt+1}^{\phi_m}L_{mt+1}^{1-\phi_m}$$
$$+(1-\delta)(K_{at+1}+K_{mt+1}+K_{st+1}) - K_{at+2} - K_{mt+2} - K_{st+2}\Big)^{\theta-1}(1-\delta)\Big]$$

Substituting the market clearing conditions for the input market for capital, labour, and land and the consumption of goods of the sectors by the market clearing conditions for the output market and writing the inter-temporal Euler equations (Attanasio and Low, 2004) concerning the capitals of agriculture, manufacturing, and service sectors will yield the following three expressions:

1. For agriculture sector:

$$\frac{\frac{1}{\theta}}{C_t} * \Big[\gamma\theta\Big(A_{mt}K_{mt}^{\phi_m}L_{mt}^{1-\phi_m} + (1-\delta)(K_{at}+K_{mt}+K_{st}) - K_{at+1}$$
$$-K_{mt+1} - K_{st+1}\Big)^{\theta-1}(-1)\Big] = (-)\beta\frac{\frac{1}{\theta}}{C_{t+1}} * \Big[\alpha\theta\phi_a\Big(A_{at+1}l_{at+1}^{\sigma_a}L_{at+1}^{1-\phi_a-\sigma_a}\Big)^{\theta}$$
$$K_{at+1}^{\phi_a\theta-1} + \gamma\theta\Big(A_{mt+1}K_{mt+1}^{\phi_m}L_{mt+1}^{1-\phi_m} + (1-\delta)(K_{at+1}+K_{mt+1}+K_{st+1}) - K_{at+2}$$
$$-K_{mt+2} - K_{st+2}\Big)^{\theta-1}(1-\delta)\Big] \tag{5.45}$$

2. For manufacturing sector:

$$\frac{\frac{1}{\theta}}{C_t} * \Big[\gamma\theta\Big(A_{mt}K_{mt}^{\phi_m}L_{mt}^{1-\phi_m} + (1-\delta)\ (K_{at}+K_{mt}+K_{st}) - K_{at+1}$$
$$-K_{mt+1} - K_{st+1}\Big)^{\theta-1}(-1)\Big] = (-)\beta\frac{\frac{1}{\theta}}{C_{t+1}} * \Big[\gamma\theta\Big(A_{mt+1}K_{mt+1}^{\phi_m}L_{mt+1}^{1-\phi_m} + (1-\delta)$$
$$(K_{at+1}+K_{mt+1}+K_{st+1}) - K_{at+2} - K_{mt+2} - K_{st+2}\Big)^{\theta-1}$$
$$\Big(\phi_m A_{mt+1}L_{mt+1}^{1-\phi_m}K_{mt+1}^{\phi_{m-1}} + (1-\delta)\Big)\Big] \tag{5.46}$$

3. For service sector:

$$\frac{\frac{1}{\theta}}{C_t} * \Big[\gamma\theta\Big(A_{mt}K_{mt}^{\phi_m}L_{mt}^{1-\phi_m} + (1-\delta)(K_{at}+K_{mt}+K_{st}) - K_{at+1}$$
$$-K_{mt+1} - K_{st+1}\Big)^{\theta-1}(-1)\Big] = (-)\beta\frac{\frac{1}{\theta}}{C_{t+1}} * \Big[\gamma\theta\Big(A_{mt+1}K_{mt+1}^{\phi_m}L_{mt+1}^{1-\phi_m}$$
$$+(1-\delta)(K_{at+1}+K_{mt+1}+K_{st+1}) - K_{at+2} - K_{mt+2} - K_{st+2}\Big)^{\theta-1}(1-\delta)$$
$$+(1-\alpha-\gamma)\theta\phi_s\Big(A_{st+1}L_{st+1}^{1-\phi_s}\Big)^{\phi}K_{st+1}^{\theta\phi_s-1}\Big] \tag{5.47}$$

At the steady state, these three equations reduce to the following form:

1. For agriculture sector The inter-temporal Euler equation for the agriculture sector can be written as follows:

$$\begin{aligned}\big[\gamma\theta(A_m K_m^{\phi_m} L_m^{1-\phi_m} + (1-\delta)(K_a+K_m+K_s) - K_a - K_m - K_s)^{\theta-1}\big] = \\ \beta * \big[\alpha\theta\phi_a(A_a l_a^{\sigma_a} L_a^{1-\phi_a-\sigma_a})^{\theta} K_a^{\phi_a\theta-1} + \gamma\theta(A_m K_m^{\phi_m} L_m^{1-\phi_m} + \\ (1-\delta)(K_a+K_m+K_s) - K_a - K_m - K_s)^{\theta-1}(1-\delta)\big]\end{aligned} \tag{5.48}$$

2. For the manufacturing sector

   The inter-temporal Euler equation for the manufacturing sector can be written as follows:

$$\begin{aligned}\big[\gamma\theta(A_m K_m^{\phi_m} L_m^{1-\phi_m} + (1-\delta)(K_a+K_m+K_s) - K_a - K_m - K_s)^{\theta-1}\big] = \\ \beta * \big[\gamma\theta(A_m K_m^{\phi_m} L_m^{1-\phi_m} + (1-\delta)(K_a+K_m+K_s) - K_a - K_m - K_s)^{\theta-1} \\ (\phi_m A_m L_m^{1-\phi_m} K_m^{\phi_m-1} + (1-\delta))\big]\end{aligned} \tag{5.49}$$

3. For service sector

   The inter-temporal Euler equation for the service sector can be written as follows:

$$\Big[\gamma\theta\big(A_m K_m^{\phi_m} L_m^{1-\phi_m} + (1-\delta)(K_a+K_m+K_s) - K_a - K_m - K_s\big)^{\theta-1}\Big]$$
$$= \beta * \Big[\gamma\theta\big(A_m K_m^{\phi_m} L_m^{1-\phi_m} + (1-\delta)(K_a+K_m+K_s) - K_a - K_m - K_s\big)^{\theta-1}$$
$$(1-\delta) + (1-\alpha-\gamma)\theta\phi_s\big(A_s L_s^{1-\phi_s}\big)K_x^{\theta\phi_s-1}\Big] \tag{5.50}$$

Along with these steady-state inter-temporal Euler equations, the intra-temporal equation will give rise to two more equations concerning the agriculture sector and manufacturing sector labour. For the intra-temporal equations, we can differentiate the utility function concerning the labour force of each sector. The utility function can be re-written as follows:

$$U(C_t) = \ln\Big[\alpha\left(A_{at}K_{at}^{\phi_a}l_{at}^{\sigma_a}L_{at}^{1-\phi_a-\sigma_a}\right)^{\theta} + \gamma\left(A_{mt}K_{mt}^{\phi_m}L_{mt}^{1-\phi_m}\right)$$
$$+(1-\delta)(K_{at}+K_{mt}+K_{st}) - K_{at+1} - K_{mt+1} - K_{st+1})^{\theta} + (1-\alpha-\gamma) \tag{5.51}$$
$$\left(A_{st}K_{st}^{\phi_s}(1-L_{at}-L_{mt})^{1-\phi_s}\right)^{\theta}\Big]^{\frac{1}{\theta}}$$

where we substituted $L_{st} = 1 - L_{at} - L_{mt}$. Differentiating the utility function concerning the labour force of each sector will yield the following equations:

1. Concerning Agriculture labour force:

$$\frac{\partial U(C_t)}{\partial L_{at}} = \frac{\frac{1}{\theta}}{C_t}\big[(1-\phi_a)\alpha\theta A_{at}^{\theta}K_{at}^{\phi_a\theta}L_{at}^{\theta(1-\phi_a)-1} + \\ (1-\alpha-\gamma)(1-\phi_s)\theta(A_{st}K_{st}^{\phi_s})^{\theta}(1-L_{at}-L_{mt})^{\theta(1-\phi_s)-1} * -1\big] = 0 \tag{5.52}$$

   It can be re-written as follows:

$$\big[(1-\phi_a)\alpha A_{at}^{\theta}K_{at}^{\phi_a^{\theta}}L_{at}^{\theta(1-\phi_a)-1} - \\ (1-\alpha-\gamma)(1-\phi_s)(A_{st}K_{st}^{\phi_s})^{\theta}(1-L_{at}-L_{mt})^{\theta(1-\phi_s)-1}\big] = 0 \tag{5.53}$$

2. Concerning Manufacturing labour force:

$$\frac{\partial U(C_t)}{\partial L_{mt}} = \frac{\frac{1}{\theta}}{C_t}\big[\gamma\theta(A_{mt}K_{mt}^{\phi_m}L_{mt}^{1-\phi_m} + (1-\delta)(K_{at}+K_{mt}+K_{st}) - \\ K_{at+1} - K_{mt+1} - K_{st+1})^{\theta-1}((1-\phi_m)A_{mt}K_{mt}^{\phi_m}L_{mt}^{-\phi_m}) + \\ (1-\alpha-\gamma)(1-\phi_s)\theta A_{st}K_{st}^{\phi_s}(1-L_{at}-L_{mt})^{\theta(1-\phi_s)-1} - 1\big] = 0 \tag{5.54}$$

   It can be re-written as follows:

$$\big[\gamma(1-\phi_m)(A_{mt}K_{mt}^{\phi_m}L_{mt}^{1-\phi_m} + (1-\delta)(K_{at}+K_{mt}+K_{st}) - \\ K_{at+1} - K_{mt+1} - K_{st+1})^{\theta-1}(A_{mt}K_{mt}^{\phi_m}L_{mt}^{-\phi_m}) - \\ (1-\alpha-\gamma)(1-\phi_s)A_{st}K_{st}^{\phi_s}(1-L_{at}-L_{mt})^{\theta(1-\phi_s)-1}\big] = 0 \tag{5.55}$$

At steady state, this equation reduces to the following form:

1. For the agriculture sector

$$\big[(1-\phi_a)\alpha(A_aK_a^{\phi_a})^{\theta}L_a^{\theta(1-\phi_a)-1} - \\ (1-\alpha-\gamma)(1-\phi_s)(A_sK_s^{\phi_s})^{\theta}(1-L_a-L_m)^{\theta(1-\phi_s)-1}\big] = 0 \tag{5.56}$$

2. For the manufacturing sector

$$(1-\beta+\beta\delta)\big[\gamma\theta\left(A_mK_m^{\phi_m}L_m^{1-\phi_m}\right) + (1-\delta)(K_a+K_m+K_s)$$
$$-K_a - K_m - K_s)^{\theta-1}\big] = \beta(1-\alpha-\gamma)\theta\phi_s \tag{5.57}$$
$$\left(A_s(1-L_a-L_m)^{1-\phi_s}\right)^{\theta}K_S^{\theta\phi_s-1}\big]$$

Substituting the $L_s = 1 - L_a - L_m$ in the steady-state equations of the inter-temporal Euler equations will yield the following equation for the service sector:

$$\begin{aligned}&(1-\beta+\beta\delta)\big[\gamma\theta\big(A_m K_m^{\phi_m} L_m^{1-\phi_m} + (1-\delta)(K_a+K_m+K_s)\\&-K_a-K_m-K_s\big)^{\theta-1}\big] = \beta(1-\alpha-\gamma)\theta\phi_s\\&\big(A_s(1-L_a-L_m)^{1-\phi_s}\big)^{\theta} K_s^{\theta\phi_s-1}\big]\end{aligned} \tag{5.58}$$

Along with the above equations, the steady-state inter-temporal Euler equations of the agriculture sector and the manufacturing sector are as follows:

$$\begin{aligned}&(1-\beta+\beta\delta)\big[\gamma\theta\big(A_m K_m^{\phi_m} L_m^{1-\phi_m} + (1-\delta)(K_a+K_m+K_s)\\&-K_a-K_m-K_s\big)^{\theta-1}\big] = \beta * \Big[\alpha\theta\phi_a\big(A_a l_a^{\sigma_a} L_a^{1-\phi_a-\sigma_a}\big)^{\theta} K_a^{\phi_a\theta-1}\Big]\end{aligned} \tag{5.59}$$

$$1 = \beta * \big[(\phi_m A_m L_m^{1-\phi_m} K_m^{\phi_m-1} + (1-\delta))\big] \tag{5.60}$$

Introducing Misallocation into the Model

Here we introduce wedges in our model as presented in the main text to cater to the idea of departure from the perfectly competitive market. Wedges in profit could indicate systematic misallocation as analysed by Hsieh and Klenow (2009). After the introduction of wedges as in Buera and Kaboski (2009); Cai (2015), the profit function can be written as follows:

$$\begin{aligned}\pi\big(K_{a,t}, L_{at}, l_{at}\big) &= (1-\tau_a)p_{at}A_{at}K_{at}^{\phi_a} l_{at}^{\sigma_a} L_{at}^{1-\phi_a-\sigma_a}\\&-\big(1+\tau^r\big)r_{kt}K_{at} - \omega_t L_{at} - R_{lt} l_{at};\end{aligned} \tag{5.61}$$

where τ means the wedges. The FOC concerning $K_{a,t}$ yields the following:

$$\frac{d\pi}{dK_{at}} = -r_{kt}(1+\tau^r) + (1-\tau_a)p_{at}A_{at}\phi_a K_{at}^{\phi_a-1} l_{at}^{\sigma_a} L_{at}^{1-\phi_a-\sigma_a} = 0 \tag{5.62}$$

$$\Rightarrow (1+\tau^r)r_{kt} = (1-\tau_a)p_{at}A_{at}\phi_a k_{at}^{\phi_a-1} L_{at}^{-\sigma_a}, \tag{5.63}$$

where $k_{at} = \frac{K_{at}}{L_{at}}$ and we set $l_{at} = 1$.

Similarly, denoting for $k_{mt} = \frac{K_{mt}}{L_{mt}}$ and $k_{st} = \frac{K_{st}}{L_{st}}$, the maximization problems of firms from manufacturing and service sectors yield the following expressions:

$$(1+\tau^r)r_{kt} = (1-\tau_m)A_{mt}\phi_m K_{mt}^{\phi_m-1} L_{mt}^{1-\phi_m} = (1-\tau_m)A_{mt}\phi_m k_{mt}^{\phi_m-1}. \tag{5.64}$$

$$(1+\tau^r)r_{kt} = (1-\tau_s)p_{st}A_{st}\phi_s K_{st}^{\phi_s-1}L_{st}^{1-\phi_s} = (1-\tau_s)p_{st}A_{st}\phi_s k_{st}^{\phi_s-1}. \tag{5.65}$$

In the same manner, we can derive the equations for wage by equating it to the value marginal productivity of labour in different sectors. This leads to the following expressions:

$$\begin{aligned}\omega_t &= (1-\tau_a)p_{at}A_{at}(1-\phi_a-\sigma_a)K_{at}^{\phi_a}l_{at}^{\sigma_a}L_{at}^{-\phi_a-\sigma_a}\\ &= (1-\tau_a)p_{at}A_{at}(1-\phi_a-\sigma_a)k_{at}^{\phi_a}L_{at}^{-\sigma_a}\end{aligned} \tag{5.66}$$

$$\omega_t = (1-\tau_m)A_{mt}(1-\phi_m)K_{mt}^{\phi_m}L_{mt}^{-\phi_m} = (1-\tau_m)A_{mt}(1-\phi_m)k_{mt}^{\phi_m} \tag{5.67}$$

$$\omega_t = (1-\tau_s)p_{st}A_{st}(1-\phi_s)K_{st}^{\phi_s}L_{st}^{-\phi_s} = (1-\tau_s)p_{st}A_{st}(1-\phi_s)k_{st}^{\phi_s} \tag{5.68}$$

As labour and capital can freely move across sectors, we have the no-arbitrage condition where wages and rentals are equalized across sectors. Since the sectors are competitive, the wage-rental ratio, $\frac{\omega_t}{r_{kt}}$, will be equal across sectors. Therefore,

$$\begin{aligned}\frac{\omega_t}{r_{kt}} &= \frac{(1-\phi_a-\sigma_a)(1+\tau^r)}{\phi_a}k_{at} = \frac{(1-\phi_m)(1+\tau^r)}{\phi_m}\\ k_{mt} &= \frac{(1-\phi_s)(1-\tau^r)}{\phi_s}k_{st}.\end{aligned} \tag{5.69}$$

The above equation implies the following relation on sectoral capital intensity:

$$k_{at} = \frac{\phi_a}{(1-\phi_a-\sigma_a)}\frac{(1-\phi_m)}{\phi_m}k_{mt} \tag{5.70}$$

$$k_{st} = \frac{\phi_s}{(1-\phi_s)}\frac{(1-\phi_m)}{\phi_m}k_{mt} \tag{5.71}$$

The marginal product of capital across sectors is equal and equating the marginal products of capital for manufacturing and service sector yields the following relation:

$$p_{st} = (\frac{1-\tau_m}{1-\tau_a})\frac{\phi_m}{\phi_s}\frac{A_{mt}}{A_{st}}\frac{k_{mt}^{\phi_m-1}}{k_{st}^{\phi_s-1}}. \tag{5.72}$$

Similarly, equating the marginal products of capital between manufacturing and agriculture sector yields the following relation:

$$r_{kt} = (\frac{1-\tau_m}{1-\tau_a})p_{at}A_{at}\phi_a k_{at}^{\phi_a-1}L_{at}^{-\sigma_a} = A_{mt}\phi_m k_{mt}^{\phi_m-1}; \tag{5.73}$$

Sr. no	10 sector disaggregation	Three Sector Disaggregation
1	**Agriculture and Allied Activities**	Primary
2	Agriculture	Primary
3	Livestock	Primary
4	Forestry and Logging	Primary
5	Fishing	Primary
6	**Mining and Quarrying**	Primary
7	**Manufacturing**	Secondary
8	Registered	Secondary
9	Unregistered	Secondary
10	**Construction**	Secondary
11	**Electricity,Gas and Water supply**	Secondary
12	**Transport Storage and Communication**	Tertiary
13	Railways	Tertiary
14	Transport by other means	Tertiary
15	Road Transport	Tertiary
16	Water Transport	Tertiary
17	Air Transport	Tertiary
18	Services Incidental to Transport	Tertiary
19	Storage	Tertiary
20	Communication	Tertiary
21	**Trade,Hotels and Restaurants**	Tertiary
22	Trade and Repair Services	Tertiary
23	Hotels and Restaurants	Tertiary
24	**Banking and Insurance**	Tertiary
25	Real Estate,Ownership of Dwellings and Business Services	Tertiary
26	**Public Administration**	Tertiary
27	**Other Services**	Tertiary

Fig. 5.4 Mapping of three sectors from EPW (NAS) data

$$\Rightarrow \quad p_{at} = (\frac{1-\tau_m}{1-\tau_a})\frac{A_{mt}\phi_m k_{mt}^{\phi_m-1}}{A_{at}\phi_a k_{at}^{\phi_a-1} L_{at}^{-\sigma_a}}. \tag{5.74}$$

Mapping of Three Sectors from EPW (NAS) Data

This appendix has reference to subsection 5.3.1.1 and footnote 13. In Figure 5.4, we mapped EPW (NAS) data from ten sectors into three sectors. The sectoral aggregation is done following the GGDC 10 sector database. See De Vries et al. (2012) for similar sectoral aggregation.

References

Acemoglu, D., & Guerrieri, V. (2008). Capital deepening and nonbalanced economic growth. *Journal of Political Economy, 116*(3), 467–498.

Attanasio, O. P., & Low, H. (2004). Estimating euler equations. *Review of Economic Dynamics, 7*(2), 406–435.

Baxter, M., Crucini, M. J., & Rouwenhorst, K. G. (1990). Solving the stochastic growth model by a discrete-state-space, Euler-equation approach. *Journal of Business & Economic Statistics, 8*(1), 19–21.

Bhattacharjea, A. (2021). Labour market flexibility in Indian manufacturing: A critical survey of the literature. *International Labour Review, 160*(2), 197–217.

Bosworth, B., & Collins, S. M. (2008). Accounting for growth: Comparing China and India. *Journal of Economic Perspectives, 22*(1), 45–66.

Bosworth, B., Collins, S. M., & Virmani, A. (2007). *Sources of growth in the Indian economy* (NBER Working Paper [w12901]).
Buera, F. J., & Kaboski, J. P. (2009). Can traditional theories of structural change fit the data? *Journal of the European Economic Association, 7*(2–3), 469–477.
Burnside, C. (1999). Matlab code for discrete state-space methods for the study of dynamic economies. *QM &RBC Codes 77, Quantitative Macroeconomics & Real Business Cycles.*
Cai, W. (2015). Structural change accounting with labor market distortions. *Journal of Economic Dynamics and Control, 57*, 54–64.
De Vries, G. J., Erumban, A. A., Timmer, M. P., Voskoboynikov, I., & Wu, H. X. (2012). Deconstructing the brics: Structural transformation and aggregate productivity growth. *Journal of Comparative Economics, 40*(2), 211–227.
Duarte, M., & Restuccia, D. (2010). The role of the structural transformation in aggregate productivity. *The Quarterly Journal of Economics, 125*(1), 129–173.
Eichengreen, B., & Gupta, P. (2011). *The service sector as India's road to economic growth* (Working Paper 16757). National Bureau of Economic Research.
Erumban, A. A., Das, D. K., Aggarwal, S., & Das, P. C. (2019). Structural change and economic growth in India. *Structural Change and Economic Dynamics, 51*, 186–202.
Fliegner, T., Nijmeijer, H., & Kotta, Ü. (1994). Some aspects of nonlinear discrete-time descriptor systems in economics. In *Predictability and nonlinear modelling in natural sciences and economics* (pp. 581–590). Springer.
Gangopadhyay, K., & Mondal, D. (2021). Productivity, relative sectoral prices, and total factor productivity: Theory and evidence. *Economic Modelling, 100*, Article 105509.
Gangopadhyay, K., Mondal, D., & Thasni, T. (2024). The decomposition of productivity growth for India: Before and after 1991. *IIM Kozhikode Society & Management Review.*
Ghate, C., Glomm, G., & Streeter, J. L. (2016). Sectoral infrastructure investments in an unbalanced growing economy: The case of potential growth in India. *Asian Development Review, 33*(2), 144–166.
Gollin, D. (2002). Getting income shares right. *Journal of Political Economy, 110*(2), 458–474.
Hsieh, C.-T., & Klenow, P. J. (2009). Misallocation and manufacturing tfp in China and India. *The Quarterly Journal of Economics, 124*(4), 1403–1448.
Krishna, K., Goldar, B., Erumban, A. A., Das, P. C., & Aggarwal, S. C. (2022). Sources of India's post-reform economic growth: An analysis based on India KLEMS database. *Economic and Political Weekly, 57*(31), 36–43.
Lahiri, A., & Yi, K.-M. (2009). A tale of two states: Maharashtra and West Bengal. *Review of Economic Dynamics, 12*(3), 523–542.
Maiti, D. (2019). Trade, labor share, and productivity in India's industries. *Labor income share in Asia: Conceptual issues and the drivers*(pp. 179–205). Springer.
Mondal, D. (2019). Structural transformation and productivity growth in India during 1960–2010. *Economic Modelling, 82*, 401–419.
Ngai, L. R., & Pissarides, C. A. (2007). Structural change in a multisector model of growth. *American Economic Review, 97*(1), 429–443.
Shan, L. (2022). India may become the third largest economy by 2030, overtaking Japan and Germany. *CNBC-Asia Economy.*
Sivasubramonian, S. (2004). *The sources of economic growth in India 1950–1 to 1999–2000.* Oxford University Press.
Thasni, T., Gangopadhyay, K., & Mondal, D. (2021). *A dynamic general equilibrium (dge) model of structural transformation for India* (Working Paper IIMK/WPS/467/ECO/2021/10). Indian Institute of Management Kozhikode.
Thasni, T., Gangopadhyay, K., & Mondal, D. (2024). Structural transformation of the Indian states: Heterogeneity among them in a ten-sector economy. *Indian Growth and Development Review, 17*(2), 232–259.
Üngör, M. (2017). Productivity growth and labor reallocation: Latin America versus east Asia. *Review of Economic Dynamics, 24*, 25–42.

Verma, R. (2012a). Can total factor productivity explain value added growth in services? *Journal of Development Economics, 99*(1), 163–177.

Verma, R. (2012b). Structural transformation and jobless growth in the Indian economy. In *The Oxford Handbook of the Indian Economy*.

Part III
Agriculture

Chapter 6
Indian Agriculture Through the Decades: Returns and Efficiency of Resource Use

Nilabja Ghosh, Chiranjib Neogi, and Mayanglambam Rajeshwor

Abstract In India's long journey of development and growth, agriculture has played a critical but constraining role. Associated critically with socio-political stability, India's agriculture still occupies large places in employment generation, food security and land use. Even with the self-sufficiency delivered by the Green Revolution (GR), Indian agriculture regularly deals with serious and often conflicting problems. Over time, as varied concerns challenged policy, agriculture also encountered new developments. The post-GR period was rich in insightful research and lively debates on the performances of agriculture, transitions in land use, regional disparities and assessments against other countries. In continuum and as a contribution to the discourse, this paper assimilates and presents a historical account of Indian agriculture, reinforced by an empirical study of contemporary times covering the base of GR in the Indo-Gangetic belt seeking to revisit the performance of Indian agriculture with updated perspectives.

Keywords Agricultural productivity · Farm income · Efficiency · Input elasticity

6.1 Background

In India's long journey of development, agriculture played a critical but constraining role. To start with, at the end of the second five-year plan, as planners became preoccupied with large industries, agriculture hit back on the success of the first one when droughts further tested dilution of their focus. Between the 1960s and early 1970s, trapped in severe food shortage, the nascent industrialization process drew relief from a public law passed in the USA (PL480) that allowed food shipments to India on rupee payment partly as a grant and partly as a long-term loan (Rakshit,

N. Ghosh (✉) · M. Rajeshwor
Institute of Economic Growth, Delhi, India
e-mail: nila@iegindia.org

C. Neogi
Indian Statistical Institute, Kolkata, India

D. Maiti et al. (eds.), *75 Years of Growth, Development and Productivity in India*, India Studies in Business and Economics, https://doi.org/10.1007/978-981-97-8054-9_6

2008, Hooda & Gulati, 2013) helping to build up vital food stocks and enabling deficit financing for industrialization. On the contrary, it discouraged investment in agriculture. The pressure on foreign policy created by this basic external dependence forced the government to try other policies and finally to discontinue the contract in 1971.

A life-saving technological advancement made in Mexico and later amplified in Manila came to the support of India when the Green Revolution (GR) was launched in the 1960s. Under the leadership of an esteemed scientist, M. S. Swaminathan, exotic hybrid seeds were tried out on Indian soils. Along with chemical fertilizers and pesticides, high-yielding variety (HYV) seeds constituted a bio-chemical package of inputs. Supported by necessary irrigation, legislated land reforms, price incentives, and credit and marketing privileges backed by public procurement at Minimum Support Price (MSP), GR saved the country from starvation but left its marks to be garnered and managed through history to this day.

While agriculture was meeting the food demands of Indian consumers who had started enjoying growing incomes, by and by, its significance also for the growth of the country's GDP gained visibility. While before GR, PL 480 was creating a market for industrial goods in urban India by depressing food prices, GR gradually steered the rural sector to emerge as a market for industrial products, thus empowering the growth of both the agriculture and manufacturing sectors.

Although India moved beyond food sufficiency and became a food exporter, the sustainability of agriculture, growth of agricultural GDP (GDPAG), management of food prices, and finally, the welfare of farmers appeared as continuous challenges. The government also had to address many historical repressions on agriculture with limited success.

By its own design, GR crafted regional and class disparities in the Indian economy (Frankel, 2006). The perfectly divisible bio-chemical inputs were size-neutral but not resource-neutral when only larger farmers had access to finances. The National Commission on Agriculture, 1976, had foreseen the coexistence of a large subsistence sector of small farmers with a progressive sector of large farmers who had acquired investible surplus (GOI, 1976). Already privileged with perennial rivers and irrigation, the north-west, along with a few deltaic basins of the east became the base of GR but they were only pockets of growth (Rao, 1983). While regional imbalances generated by GR have been well documented since the 1970s, loss of sustainability arising from intense input use soon added to the discourse.

Food price was proving to be a double-edged sword with contrary effects on producers and consumers (Mellor, 1966, Benjamin & Brandt, 2002). Moreover, the liberalization of 1991 made the price policy in consistent and the widening gap in incomes between agriculture and the rest of the economy become more conspicuous. At a time when the government's role was meant to shrink, a policy drawn from the years of food scarcity entitled farming to profuse budgetary support. Open procurement of rice and wheat, which is then produced in abundance, was expensive. Grain stocks to be maintained by the government became Voluminous, raising contradictions between the interests of farmers and the government's commitment to budgetary prudence and investment obligations. MSP was said to distort the market price that was expected to equate demand and supply. Over the 1980s, concerns also grew about the misuse and leakages of government funds from their legitimate uses.

The biased incentive to grow the beneficiary food crops rice and wheat across the country became untenable with sustanability. Even parts of the northern plains marked as the heart of GR are allured to grow rice in a departure from their traditional cropping pattern. The rotation of Kharif season rice with winter wheat began to degenerate their ecological balance even as traditional crops like millets, pulses and oilseeds lost share across the country. The food habits of the people (Baviskar, 2012) moved in tandem. In a changing paradigm, to rationalize cropping patterns away from food crops, the central government proposed wide ranging marketing reforms in which private and corporate sectors, especially the food processors, could join as buyers. Such changes in long-prevailing and adapted systems of infrastructure and skills are not politically easy to implement in federal India, where agriculture is a State subject under the Constitution.

In a new development, natural disasters became more evident, justifying fears of climate change (CC) raised by scientists at the theoretical level. An open-air activity, agriculture began to cope with serious rainfall anomalies in monsoon-dependent India. As CC portends to be a hard test on agricultural systems of the world (Del Buono, 2021), the urgency to adapt to more sustainable and climate-resilient forms grew. Post-2010, geo-political relations, growing inter-country dependencies, WTO agreements on fair trade and wars elsewhere encroached upon the economics of Indian agriculture and even revived food insecurity threats. The Russia-Ukraine war compromised India's access to edible oils and fertilizer. Trade itself became insecure in the conflict-ridden high seas. Timely trade negotiation, monitoring of the weather and production outlook, continual planning and management of surplus are now policy imperatives.

A move away from an exclusive focus on consumer interest was manifest when India added 'Farmers Welfare' to the name of the agriculture ministry in the year 2015 (15th August), making household earning from agriculture a major policy target. Another outstanding transformation in the early days of the new century was the entry of information and communication technology (ICT) into the vast and scattered rural economy. The ICT revolution raised hopes of bringing the rural economy to the mainstream and bridging the gulf between farmers and other members of agricultural value chains without excessive intermediation of powerful third-party agents (Ghosh et al., 2020). Computerization can aid fair efficient marketing with information dissemination. Price discovery, monitoring of practices, direct payments of public benefits, recording of agrarian structure, access to technology and advancement of institutional credit are likely to be beneficial.

The objectives of agricultural policy in contemporary times are broader than ever before, blending national food security with greater farm incomes even as the sector itself diversifies. Backed by an empirical assessment of contemporary times, this chapter is a review of the progress and broadenings of India's agriculture, taking up from the pre-GR days delving through the problems, achievements and left-overs of GR and focusing in particular on the post-GR period to trace the performance of India's agriculture and its various dimensions with a perspective departing from earlier studies only to capture current concerns. The discourse has two components. In the first part, the problems that Indian agriculture inherited from earlier regimes are discussed based mostly on a broad review of literature on agriculture that often focused on the inter-relations among environment, production and social and cultural features (Thorner, 1976). The second part is confined to contemporary India with a regional perspective on Indo-Gangetic plains (IGP) to find out the relative performances of the production, value added, inputs used and efficiency of input use also trying to explain the performance with empirical data analysis.

6.2 Indian Agriculture Over the Years: Performance, Challenges and the Transition

Challenges have accompanied Indian agriculture's long journey from the days of distressful food crises to the times of abundance in a dynamic and uncertain world. Problems either persisted in unchanged or mutated forms or gave way to new ones. Before stepping into the muddy track of Indian agriculture, it may be worth having a broad glimpse at the achievements.

6.2.1 Progress of Agriculture Under the Green Revolution

At the dawn of independence, Indian farmers were not only poor but also thought to be illiterate, superstitious (Haydock et al., 2021) and static in practice. The apprehension about their resistance to GR, however, proved unfounded as successful demonstrations by lead farmers and government encouragement led to widespread adoption of the new farm technology. The irrationality of farmers also proved to be an oversimplification when responses to incentives (Krishna, 1963) brought increasing area under the new seeds at a time when food prices were rising. A public extension system with field workers helped the technology to reach the fields.

GR undoubtedly served in tiding over India's food crisis, but even in the 1950 and 1960s, driven by acreage and irrigation expansion, the gross cropped area (GCA) had been rising fast (Fig. 6.1). Irrigation was a historical legacy from pre-colonial times. The colonial government applied the evolving engineering technology to build dams on the snow-fed Himalayan rivers, the Ganga and the Indus. In South India, local rulers managed rivers that were not perennial. GR replaced land and labour as sources of growth by land-augmenting bio-chemical inputs and, to a lesser extent, by labour-substituting machinery (Rao, 1983).

Between 1951 and 2020, India's population nearly quadrupled (Table 6.1). The annual growth rate tapered down from a high of 2.15% from 1951 to 1991 to 1.6% per year from 1991 to 2020. Although the figures for the 2020s are estimates, the latest Census being awaited, India's population is reaching saturation. Crop production,

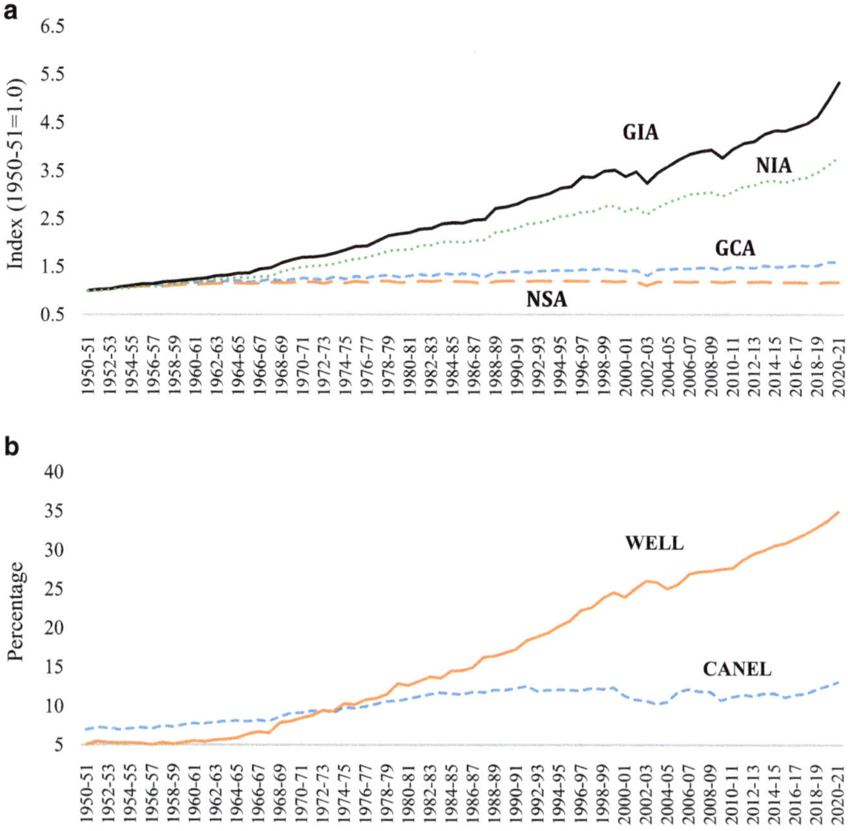

Fig. 6.1 **a** Land use in Indian agriculture from 1950–51. **b** Irrigation by source in Indian agriculture from 1950–51

too, rose, though constrained by limited land area (NSA) that stagnated at around 140 million hectares in recent decades. The initial land expansion came at the cost of forests, but from the 1990s, urbanization, housing, environment and infrastructure, especially highways, became contenders with agriculture for land. Fortunately, a consistent increase in cropping intensity (CI) in both periods kept GCA moving as expanding irrigation and short-duration crops (HYV) enabled multiple cropping of land. GCA reached 211 million hectares in 2020, compared to 132 million hectares in 1951.

From a mere 17% in 1950–51, irrigation intensity doubled by 1990–91 (Table 6.1). Though dwindling in drought years like 1987–88, 2002–03, 2009–10 and 2015–16, the expansion of GIA by 2020–21 in the face of a largely stable NSA was remarkable even as structurally, irrigation shifted sharply from surface to groundwater (Fig. 6.1a and b). Wells took over canals in irrigated acreage in 1973–74. By 2020–21 canals accounted only for 13% of NIA. Dams have since been rather discredited for failing to redirect natural flows of water (Ghosh et al., 2016). Nevertheless, water stored

Table 6.1 Transitions in Indian agriculture 1950–51 to 2020–21

Year	Population	Area (GCA)	Farm size	Fertilizer	GDPAG	Cropping intensity	Net irrigation	Rice and wheat share in GCA
	Million	Million hectare	Hectare	Kg./Hectare	Rs.'000 / Hectare	%		
1950–51	361.2	131.9	2.96	0.5	23.49	111.1	17.1	31.1
1960–61	439.2	152.8	2.60	1.9	27.67	114.7	18.3	30.8
1970–71	548.2	165.8	2.28	13.1	32.35	117.7	23.0	33.6
1980–81	683.3	172.6	1.84	32.0	36.97	123.1	28.8	36.2
1990–91	846.4	185.7	1.55	67.5	50.58	130.0	34.0	36.0
2000–01	1028.7	185.3	1.33	90.1	67.74	131.1	41.1	38.1
2010–11	1210.8	198.1	1.15	141.9	87.22	140.1	45.1	37.2
2020–21	1347.1	211.4	1.08*	153.9	110.81	151.1	53.1	36.4
CAGR%	1.93	0.68	–1.54	8.53	2.24	0.44	1.63	0.23

Source DES (Website), MoA&FW (Website), Census of India (Website), DEA (2023). Population figures are for 1951 to 2011 from decennial Census of India but for 2020–21 figure is Census estimate. * India's latest farm-size figure in 2015–16

in reservoirs is monitored keenly for farming. Depletion of live storage in a major dam is an alert for water scarcity, and pressure on its capacity forces sudden release, which creates upstream or downstream floods. Groundwater irrigation, too, is not without its costs. It is blamed for water-table recession, land subsidence, inequity and electricity consumption. A conjunctive use drawing advantage of groundwater enriched by seepage in synergy with power generated at dams is recommended (Dhawan, 1988). Indian agriculture before GR hardly consumed chemical fertilizer, but growing phenomenally, it became the prime source of success. Despite the rapid intensification in the 1980s and 1990s, the paucity of its intake compared to countries like China and the USA was blamed for the relatively low crop yield rates (Table 6.2). By 2000, India, however, surpassed other countries in fertilizer consumption per unit NSA.

Staple cereals, rice and wheat together gained a share in the strained GCA up to 38% in 2001 (Table 6.1), while millets and pulses lost area. The contrast reflected the selective success of seed technology and all the biased government support for 'food' as perceived (Fig. 6.2a). Because of ecological adversities of mono-cropping and shortage of nourishing crops, crop diversification (Sivaraman, 2023) was promoted, perhaps as a result of which rice and wheat together lost share from 2000–01. Though rice, jowar and lentils failed to catch up to the world's best, physical productivity increased for all study crops, not excluding pulses and millets that lost acreage (Fig. 6.2b).

Table 6.2 Country wise crop productivity (tones/hectare) and Fertilizer intake (Kg./Hectare)

		1961	1970	1980	1990	2000	2010	2020
Rice	India	1.5	1.7	2.0	2.6	2.9	3.4	4.1
	China	–	–	–	–	6.3	6.5	7.0
	USA	3.8	5.2	4.9	6.2	7.0	7.5	8.5
Wheat	India	8.5	1.2	1.4	2.1	2.8	2.8	3.4
	China	–	–	–	–	3.7	4.7	5.7
	USA	1.6	2.1	2.3	2.7	2.8	3.1	3.3
Jowar	India	0.4	0.5	0.7	0.8	0.8	0.9	1.0
	China	–	–	–	–	2.9	4.4	8.1
	USA	2.7	3.1	2.9	4.0	3.8	4.5	4.6
Lentil	India	0.5	0.5	0.4	0.6	0.7	0.7	0.8
	China	–	–	–	–	1.2	2.0	2.5
	USA	0.7	1.0	1.1	1.0	1.6	1.5	1.6
Rapeseed Mustard	India*	0.4	0.6	0.6	0.9	0.9	1.2	1.5
	China	–	–	–	–	0.6	0.7	0.8
	USA	0.95	1.0	0.94	0.95	0.95	0.97	1,0
Fertilizer consumption of Agricultural Land (NSA)	India	2.6	–	–	53.6	–	–	181.7
	China	NA	–	–	69.3	–	–	85.9
	USA	16.7	–	–	42.7	–	–	51.7

Source FAOSTAT (Website), DES (Website)

The crop yield gains, however, did not come without cost. While not all costs are quantifiable, financial costs in terms of input costs can be subtracted to measure the income generated from farming activity. India's national income measured by GDP at constant price picked up speed in the 1970s, more remarkably in 1991–2010, falling in 2021, the year of pandemic but the slow-moving GDPAG barely remained above the plateauing population (Fig. 6.3). GDPAG per hectare at 2011–12 price reached Rs. 111 thousand in 2020–21 growing at 2.24% annually when real GDP per hectare grew at 4.07%.

6.2.2 *Waking up to Post-GR Problems*

When GR, antibiotics and other medical technologies defeated the Malthusian predicament, the rapid march of population in the twentieth century did not economically help India's farm sector that was languishing in poverty since independence. An inefficient feudal framework, further reinforced by the British land revenue system, generated highly unequal rural power equations with unproductive intermediaries in institutions that operated in complex ways. Independent India's government had to

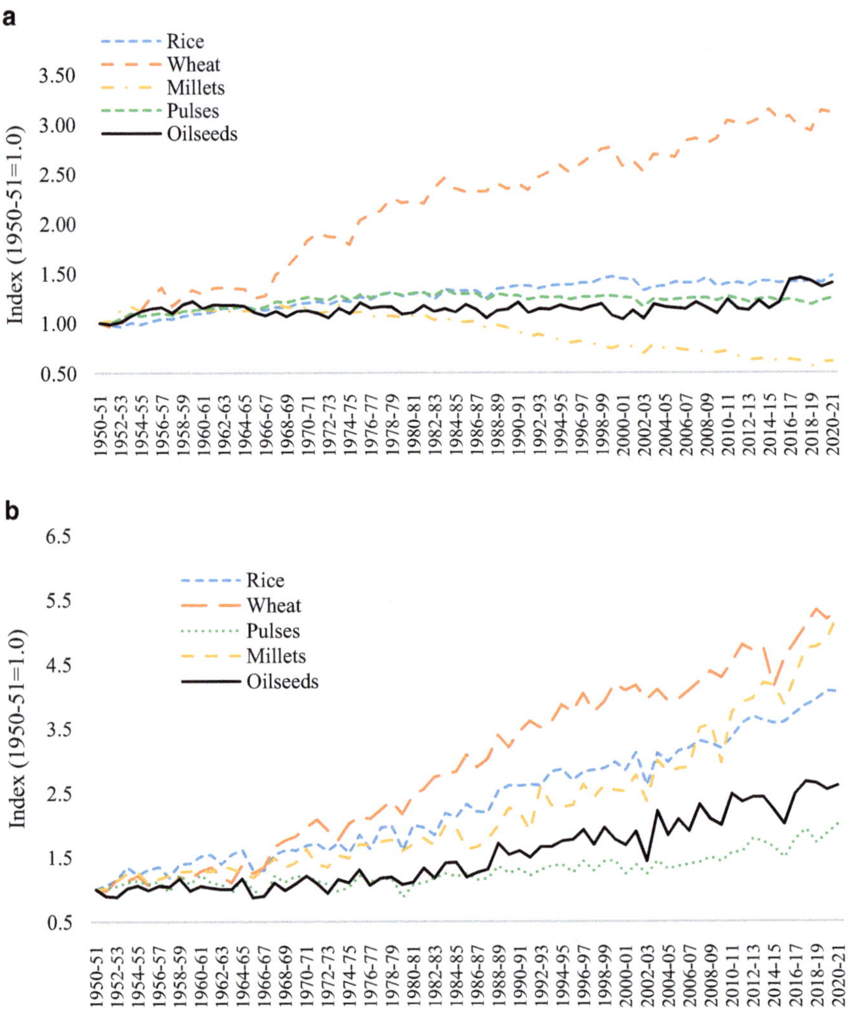

Fig. 6.2 **a** Area under major crops in India. **b** Crop yield progress

legislate land reform measures like abolition of the established zamindary system, land ceiling and their distribution of attached surplus land to prevent land holdings from becoming too large. Regulation of rent and restraints on tenant eviction aimed to empower farmers to take risk.

Market imperfections, commonly described by the 'interlocking' of markets, entitled powerful entities to appear before the farmer in different markets that were entangled without distinction (Bhaduri, 1984). A landed rich farmer would not just lease out land but double up as a trader to dictate the crops to be grown and become suppliers of inputs. Appearing as money lenders charging high rates of interest on capital, they often entrapped farmers in debt. In cases of extreme default, by attaching

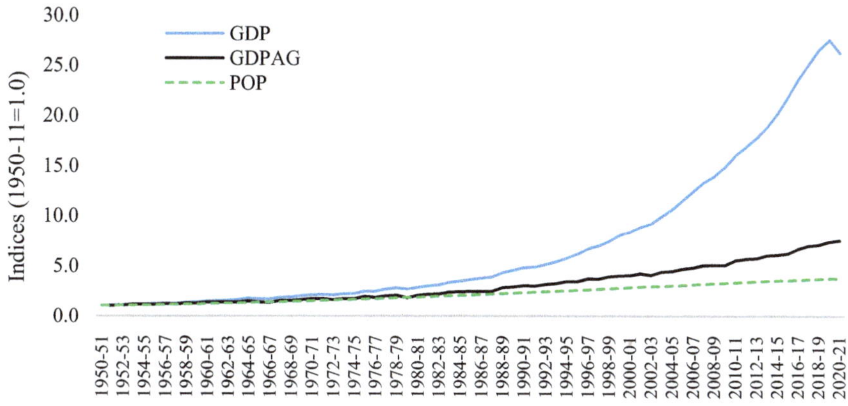

Fig. 6.3 Agricultural growth in India

all of their land they reduced marginal holders to join the ranks of farm labour class. On the contrary many 'absentee landlord would not even cultivate land'.

The small and continuously diminishing average farm size impeded mechanization and commercialization yielding little product surplus for sale. Large sections of peasants with small (up to 2 hectares) or marginal (up to 1 hectare) holdings lingered at subsistence levels though they had utilized family labour to their advantage (Tripp, 2006) during GR while banking support and subsidies helped them adopt the bio-chemical technology. Due to cultural inhibitions to manual work (Waite, 2005), large holders resorted to hiring labour and further to purchasing machines in response to rising wages. However, as population grew, income generation capacity of agriculture was stunted by the fragmentation of farms reinforced by a dysfunctional land market abetted by the cultural value attached to holding land (Ghatak & Roy, 2007). Still grappling with an over 86% share of small and vulnerable farms, India is exploring ways to develop small industries, accommodate a large informal sector and generate off-farm rural employment opportunities.

Indian agriculture depends strongly on monsoon which has always been errant. River valley projects contributed to canal irrigation and flood control services. They also generated electricity that powered well irrigation. Although, the independent government of India vastly expanded the infrastructure, irrigation itself depends on rainfall and its expansion has limits. Many agro-climatic regions have to subsist in water scarcity. Expansion of irrigation had to be accompanied by effective water management. Soil organic content was degraded as chemicals leached into the water and air. Relentless use of bio-chemical inputs needed restraint as sustainability became a component of agricultural policy objective.

Towards a more competitive product market, in colonial times, the Agriculture Produce Marketing Committee (APMC) was instituted with auctions where traders were licensed. To entitle farmers to fair prices and escape unscrupulous agents, this legislation was reinforced by the independent government. To curb distress sales a dual market was created where the government conducted with open procurement at minimum support prices. Although MSP was not a legal commitment, administratively it assured farmers of sale at remunerative prices and also influenced the price in the open market. To free farmers from the clutches of local exploitative money lenders, the new government of the 1950s also regulated money lending while expanding the banking network across rural India. Widely nationalizing banks in 1969 and committing them to a priority loan-share to farmers were further steps. A tiered cooperative credit structure was constituted going down to the grassroot level with their apex body NABARD formed in 1982 for regulation. Subsidies on food and inputs were accommodated in public budgets. Machines were made cheaper with import policy. Economic, administrative and judicial means were deployed to make irrigation projects, their command area development and water distribution efficient. Deficiencies in the measures were widely and critically researched.

6.2.3 Misgivings that Lingered

Misgivings shrouded GR from the start but redressals were incomplete. Dilution of the objectives of agricultural Census for designing land ceiling, tolerance of oral tenancy, false titling of land (benami) and other evasive strategies of land owners limited the success of land reforms. Described as kulaks (Singh, 1987) a class of capitalist farmers who were progressive enough to drive the GR emerged but by and large the legislations could hardly battle the entrenchment of caste and class relations with land ownership. Prevalence of informal tenancy permitted evasion of tenurial laws. Even the progressiveness of endowed commercial farmers was questioned (Nair, 1983). Nair attributed the differences in input use and growth rate evidenced between Bihar and Punjab despite their similar soils and land laws to the risky ambience in eastern India leading to the small holder dominance and choice of share-cropping practices. Soon the same land laws began obstructing the formation of land markets and inhibited even legal leasing of land that could have replaced disinterested landlords by enthusiastically practicing tenants.

The number of smaller farmers swelled with land fragmentation. Being historically privileged with irrigation (Khushro, 1964) and family labour, they were argued to be more productive as evident from FMS data of the time. Evidences even suggested an inverse relation of productivity with farm size raising one of the liveliest and sustained historical debates (Sen, 1964). Over time, as population grew the average farm size came down in size and viability (Table 6.1). Household members had to resort to off-farm economic activities to supplement farm incomes and even migrate to distant states to make a living and survive. Migration could be theoretically an equilibrating process signalling progress (Todaro & Smith, 2020) but the rural migration from eastern villages is said to be a distress driven 'push' the weakness of which was glaringly exposed by the pandemic crisis marked by 'reverse migration' (Naregal, 2021). Creating local employment began to be seen as a way to prevent distress migration (Borah, 2022).

Burdened with prudential norms formal bankers soon began showing reluctance to lend to a risky sector. Rural credit repeatedly led to defaults and faced setbacks especially following droughts when distress of farmers compelled loan waivers by the governments. Despite a crop insurance scheme operating since 1999 to enable banks continue with lending, informal money lenders, found to be timelier and simpler in procedures, persisted. Market regulations too reached their own limits generating a kind of monopsony of local licensed traders who remained backward in methods (Ghosh, 2013), barring entry of more efficient new agents and depriving farmers of new markets, alternative products and higher prices. The MSP was seen to hinder market reform and equity. The market remained highly fragmented by various formal and informal barriers to grain flows within the country and in fact, advocates of globalization claimed that farmers were 'dis-protected' in the global market (Gulati, 2009). To take care of farmer's income and equity, procurement was extended to crops beyond rice and wheat and MSP was announced for 22 crops committing 50% profit over cost and a price stabilization fund was formed mainly for pulses. But the benefits continue to bypass small and subsistence peasants with little surplus.

A model marketing act was circulated in 2004. Largely a failure with states differing widely in their reactions, the event did set in motion a slow progress in the opening up of markets to private operators, emergence of innovative market channels and formation of farmers' collectives (Ghosh, 2013). In 2021 (November) the Union government under a majority rule took Constitutional advantage to pass but soon withdraw three market reform laws[1] even while a clamour for legalized MSP arose. Amendments to an established system tied to livelihood of large sections obviously proves politically difficult.

6.2.4 Contemporary Challenges and Paradoxes

Independence found Indian agriculture constrained by backwardness, technological deficiencies, climatic debacles, poor institutions and the miserable poverty of small farmers. Low productivity translating to low production and national food insecurity in a land-scarce nation was historically the primary problem addressed. Achievement in the GR and in post-GR times can best be summarized by greater land utilization from fast growth of CI and yield from a hectare of cropped acreage accompanying expanding irrigation and use of fertilizer and HYV seeds. Yet, GR exacted higher costs not always quantified. Certain external effects and developments also turned the situation.

[1] Agreement on Price Assurance and Farm (Empowerment and Protection) Services Act 2020, Produce Trade and Commerce (Promotion and Facilitation) Act 2020 and the Essential Commodities (Amendment) Act 2020.

6.2.5 Climate Change

Climate change (CC) is probably the most outstanding intrusion into policy space in recent times. Emissions and rise of global temperatures, as recorded by the Stevenson screen, strengthened by subsequent instrumentation, and a meeting at Rio in 1992, culminated in successive negotiations and commitments to limit emissions (Ghosh, 2011). Severe and extreme weather anomalies and events like heat waves, storms, droughts or excessive rainfall with little predictability could arguably result in CC. Harm already inflicted by past emissions is not easy to reverse. Indian agriculture has always depended on a capricious monsoon, but as its anomalies became a regular feature, policy had to impart climate resilience to agriculture, an activity most exposed to nature.

Analysis of meteorological data (IMD, Website) suggests that monsoon is regionally diverse in pattern and may be diminishing (IMD, Website) with rainfall deficits increasing (Pandey & Sengupta, 2018) in some places. The government has responded with legislated disaster management, climate-sensitive research and information dissemination. Farmers, known to be adaptive to nature, may also be adjusting practices to the transition (Ghosh et al., 2022). Drought and flood management by continually forecasted and monitored, weather and production.

6.2.6 Information and Communication

Poor communication in dispersed Indian villages traditionally inhibited the flow of goods, money and information, leading to frequent food scarcity. India's development policy today lays great emphasis on infrastructure creation. While the farm population stands to benefit from physical connectivity and from the employment generated by construction, it is not enough. Data itself has become a fuel for powering the economy. The most outstanding development is brought by the information and communication technology (ICT) that started to invade the rural economy in the early years of the current century. The average farmer, as part of the rural population, is far more educated than in GR days and ICT with its multiple language outreach overcomes much of the limitations faced by farmers in connecting to technology and the market.

Extension, which had begun floundering after GR, switched to an online and more interactive mode for problem-solving, information sharing and early warning as both extension and crop insurance became more privatized. ICT has made money transfers simpler and safer. At the root of this revolution lies the authentication by JAM, which involves a bank account (JanDhan), Unique identity (Aadhar) and mobile connectivity. Direct-benefit transfers from government (DBT) are making subsidization simpler and more secure from malpractices. In a token measure of income redistribution, a DBT known as PM-Kisan (PIB, 2023) credits the accounts of small farmers. Credit allows farmers to access inputs and better technology in time. It has always been important, but in its long evolutionary history, farm credit is revolutionized by the issue of the Kisan credit card (KCC). Further strengthening and simplification by computerization of land records (Samantara, 2010). ICT still holds immense potential for agriculture.

6.2.7 *Farmer's Income*

A promise of doubling the farmer's income heralded a shift in focus from production to producer income. Large sections of Indian workers who depend on agriculture in some way include landed farmers, lessors of cultivable land, hired farm labourers, unpaid workers of family farms, suppliers of animal services, water and machine power. Expenses made for production accrue either to them or flow out to manufacturers of material inputs in other sectors. The price rise of material inputs constrains farmers' income. As the importance of supplementary off-farm incomes grew, the government placed emphasis on agro-processing and many welfare measures, reforms in MSP targeted towards a wider range of crops and reducing corruption with innovative methods. PM-Kisan was an additional pay-out over farmers' income to mitigate the hardship of farmers.

6.3 Contemporary Scene

We now come to focus on the contemporary period, i.e., the new century and millennium, Indo-Gangetic belt (IGB), the prime beneficiary region from GR and major food crops grown in IGB states. The data covers 11 states in the IGB over a time period of 16 years and includes 12 crops. Based on climate, soils, river basin projects and history, three broad sub-regions (Table 6.3) are also delineated from among the select states in the IGB: Eastern (E), Central (C) and North Western (NW). Data for the analysis are taken from official sources. MOA&FW provide data on crop yield, area and prices (wholesale price) as well as total irrigation by sources are collected from DES, Website and inputs and costs from cost of cultivation (COC) since DES does not report cost data. However, from the sample surveys, COC is the only credible source in the public domain on inputs in values and physical measures (for many inputs) and cost per hectare. For each state, a number of food crops constituting at least 70% of its total GCA and 87% in foodgrain and oilseed areas are considered in the study. Their share exceeds 85% of the food crop area in all the regions, though in some diversified states such as Gujarat and Rajasthan, horticulture and cash crops have a substantial share in GCA.

Total state-level use of individual inputs, composite input cost and the composite output price are all derived as averages across only select crops (from COC) weighted by crop acreages in the states (from DES). We sum up the value of all crops (price (P) x yield (Y) x area(A)) and divide this total by the sum of the area under all these crops to obtain the value of crops (VO) in Rs per hectare. From this we subtract

Table 6.3 Study regions and study crop share in Area (%)

Regions	State name	Crop name	GCA	Foodgrain and oilseed area
Eastern Region (ER)	Bihar (BH)	Maize, Rapeseed, Paddy, Wheat, Gram	81.2	91.0
	Jharkhand (JH)	Maize, Paddy, Wheat	86.6	86.3
	Orissa (OD)	Paddy, Arhar, Moong, Urad	76.1	85.8
	West Bengal (WB)	Rapeseed, Paddy	62.0	84.8
	State total		71.6	86.3
Central Region (CR)	Chhattisgarh (CH)	Maize, Paddy, Wheat, Gram, Urad, Soybean	78.0	82.1
	Madhya Pradesh (MP)	Jowar, Maize, Rapeseed, Paddy, Wheat, Arhar, Gram, Urad, Soybean	81.1	88.5
	Uttar Pradesh (UP)	Bajra, Maize, Rapeseed, Paddy, Wheat, Arhar, Gram, Urad	73.6	90.6
	State total		77.2	88.9
North Western Region (NWR)	Gujarat (GJ)	Bajra, Groundnut, Maize, Rapeseed, Paddy, Wheat, Arhar	42.4	72.2
	Haryana (HY)	Bajra, Rapeseed, Paddy, Wheat, Gram	64.7	96.7
	Punjab (PJ)	Paddy, Wheat	80.5	96.5
	Rajasthan (RJ)	Bajra, Jowar, Maize, Rapeseed, Wheat, Gram, Moong, Urad, Soybean	65.1	84.4
	State total		62.0	85.2
All region			70.2	86.9

the sum of all material cost (MC) across the study crops in Rs/hectare to obtain the value added (VA) in Rs/hectare in the state farming. VA includes farm profit and remuneration from farm, animal and machine labour. All the data are expressed at per-hectare level of study crops, and all value measures are further divided by CPI for an agricultural labourer (CPIAL) of the state and year for temporal comparability to control for the effect of inflation. The assessment of performance is made tracking land use, the use of inputs, the output and the efficiency. Simple graphs are major methods of tracking, but regression models with Stochastic Frontier Analysis (SFA) and efficiency are also part of the methodology.

Conceptually,

$$VA = VO - MC \tag{1a}$$

$$VO = P \times A \times Y \tag{1b}$$

Table 6.4 Mean of the variables in the equation (Sample Average)

	Unit	Eastern region	Central region	North western region	State average
VA	Rs'000./ Hectare	28.4	23.7	39	30.3
Fertilizer	Kg./Hectare	103.3	105.8	145.9	118.3
Irrigation	Ratio	0.6	0.6	0.7	0.6
Tractor purchase	unit/'000 Hectare	2.9	2.6	2.9	2.8
Rent	Rs.'000/ Hectare	8.9	9.4	13.5	10.6
Human Labour	Hours/ Hectare	809.7	449.6	386.3	548.5
Reservoir volume	BCM	3.7	8.5	6.4	6.2
Monsoon rainfall;	centimeter	118	1065	48	906
Farm Size	Hectare	0.8	1.3	2.8	1.6
Credit	Rs. Cr/'000 Hectare	2.0	1.4	3.5	2.3

where Material Cost (MC) is the sum of costs of material inputs, which includes Fertilizer costs, Manure costs, Owned machine labour costs, Seed costs, Insecticides costs and Owned animal labour costs. By excluding from the real value of output (VO), the component that moves away to the industrial sector as material cost (MC), VA is derived as the residual output that accrues as incomes to the agents who serve agriculture (Eqs. 1). Under the contemporary priorities, the performance of agriculture would be better represented by VA than the production and farmer's profit. Although the VA is fairly low at Rs. 30 thousand on average, not surprisingly, it is highest in the GR beneficiary NWR at Rs. 39 thousand, followed closely by ER (Table 6.4).

6.3.1 *Explaining the Productivity*

The performance of agriculture is believed to be an outcome of many factors like nature-ordained soil fertility and climate, the use of material inputs as decided by supervising farmers, labour hired or from family members, past investments made by farming agents on assets like machines for cultivation and irrigation services from public and private assets and above all the efficiency of use of all inputs and technology that reflects the managerial competence. Despite falling behind in rainfall, water in reservoir storage and labour use, NWR, with a larger average farm size (3.8

hectares), has a lead in outcome as well as inputs. Over time, however, things have not been static.

Technological relations between inputs and output can be comprehended with production functions analysis (PFA) of empirical data. In agriculture PFA is conducted using linear, log-linear, Cobb–Douglas, quadratic and Translog functions in structural form for years but price-based reduced form and use of instrumental variables (IV) help avoid endogeneity in an equilibrating market (Heady, 1952, 1957, Nathan, 1971, Narayana et al., 1991, Ghosh & Neogi, 1995). Among examples is a predicted rise in demand for farm machinery, with farm-level strawberry data analysis showing that machines complemented labour and were highly productive.

Multiplicatively, production function is given by Eq. 2a.

$$y_i = f(x_i;\, \beta)e^{(v_i)}[i = 1, 2, \ldots ..n] \tag{2a}$$

Or in explicit firm production is modelled as

$$\text{Log Y} = a_0 + \Sigma a_1(\text{Log X}_i) + (1/2)\Sigma a_2(\text{Log X}_i)\left(\text{Log X}_j\right) + u_{it} \tag{2b}$$

where the dependent variable is Y and Xi are the inputs in a non-linear relation and Y is a stochastic variable While for X_i non-stochasticity in some cases doubtful, instrumetal variable are use overcome endogeneity. The term X_iX_i is the interaction term between the same inputs when i = j. The squared input variable will expectedly suggest a negative coefficient depicting the adversity of excess input use. Between two different inputs, the interaction term can carry a positive (complementarity) or a negative (substitution) coefficient. VA is modelled with Eq. 2b using several intuitively plausible explanatory variables. Pooled data gives observations that are subjected to panel data regression, pooled (POLS), random effect (RE) and fixed effect (FE).

6.3.2 Stochastic Frontier Models and Measuring Inefficiency

In a seminal study, Battese and Coelli (1992) set a wave of empirical research to estimate the possible frontier of production possibility and measure the inefficiency of firms, both of which exercises would be useful for policymakers in adjudging, monitoring and comparing production performances in a sector and identifying the factors that can be modulated to improve the performances holistically. Voluminous work (Aigner et al., 1977, Battese & Coelli, 1992, 1995, Jondrow et al., 1982, Kumbhakar & Lovel, 2000, Greene, 2005, Ghosh & Neogi, 1995, Neogi & Ghosh, 1995; Neogi et al., 2014) make up the literature on stochastic function model with efficiency measurement. Results on farm size, mechanization, input use, crop choice and biodiversity (Larsen & McComb, 2021, MacDonald et al., 2014, Muyanga & Jayne, 2019, Noack & Larsen, 2019, Geiger et al., 2010, Hautier et al., 2011) flowed from the limited application of the method to agriculture.

The basic premise behind the approach is that the efficiency of practices under the given natural conditions can account for production differences between similar units that use the same inputs. Stochastic Production Frontier (SPF) is the means to measure the maximum output possible with the given inputs in an ideal case, though in reality, the producing unit may not be perfectly efficient, and the observed output will fall short of the frontier. Further, the unit's inefficiency measured by the shortfall can be modelled as a component of the residual whose other part is the usual random iid that can be both positive and negative. Ideally, a producer can be assumed to exert effort to attain complete efficiency and thereby reach the frontier output (Batteste et al., 1989; Battese & Coelli, 1992, Coeli et al., 2003).

The conventional representations of SPF function multiplicatively and logarithmically are respectively,

$$y_i = f(x_i;\beta)e^{(v_i - \mathrm{u})}[i = 1, 2, \ldots..n] \tag{3a}$$

and

$$\mathrm{Log\ Y} = \mathrm{a_0} + \Sigma \mathrm{a_1}(\mathrm{Log\ X_i}) + (1/2)\ \Sigma \mathrm{a_2}(\mathrm{Log\ X_i})\left(\mathrm{Log\ X_j}\right) + \mathrm{v_{it}} - \mathrm{u_{it}} \tag{3b}$$

where $\mathrm{v_{it}}$ is random iid following N(0, σ_2v), and is independent of $\mathrm{u_{it}}$ while $\mathrm{u_{it}}$, a non-negative random variable independently distributed N($\mathrm{m_{it}}$, σ_2u) truncated at zero is assumed to account for the technical inefficiency in production. The technical efficiency is given by Eq. (6.4)

$$TE = \frac{Y_i}{Y_i^*} = \frac{f(x_i;\beta)e^{(V_i - U_i)}}{f(x_i;\beta)e^{(V_i)}} = e^{-U_i} \tag{6.4}$$

Estimation in SFA using maximum likelihood (ML) has been developed in the literature (Kumbhakar, 2000, Battese & Coelli, 1992, Greene, 2005) with varying approaches. To disentangle time-varying inefficiency from unit-specific time-invariant unobserved heterogeneity, Greene's method, termed the 'True time-varying model', is used employing panel data following 'Fixed effect' or 'Random effect' depending on the visualization of the case and the assumptions on the unobserved unit-specific heterogeneity. Specifications used in modelling are pooled Ordinary Least Square (POLS) and Radom effect (RE) are examined and their results presented.

The variation of efficiency or inefficiency is then explained with exogenous variables. Taking $\mathrm{u_i}$ as a function of relevant variables and an intercept term the equation is

$$u_i \sim N^+(\mu_i, \sigma_u^2)$$

$$\mu_i = z_i{}'\varphi$$

where $u_i$is a realization from a truncated (or half) normal random variable, $\mathbf{z}_i$is a vector of exogenous variables (including a constant term), and φ is the vector of unknown parameters to be estimated.

Such influences may include the average farm size decided by demography. Credit disbursal by the organized financial system measured by crop loan value deflated by CPIAL per hectare of GCA shaped by the country's financial system and government policy of crop insurance and subsidies can be another effect on efficiency. Infrastructural assets like roads could matter.

6.3.3 Model

In Indian agriculture, the exercise would be particularly relevant for policy-making to achieve aims like enhancing farmer incomes (DFI[2]), achieving regional balance, especially for the rain-fed eastern region (RADP[3]) and the emerging Central region, attaining sustainable development with resource use efficiency especially in the Western belt of Indo-Gangetic basin (IGB) and addressing farmers' welfare. With a broad dataset, the cross-section units can be comprehensively described by nature, policy and decision variables some of which are quantitative while others are more qualitative represented by dummy variables.

All analysis for inputs and outcomes is done at the per-hectare level with real values using methods PFA as well as SFA. The RE model with IV is preferred based on a Hausman test and to accommodate the dummy variables for characterization without treating the units as distinct with their fixed effects. The robustness of the model is indicated by the RE and POLS, producing largely comparable results with the same signs of the coefficients. Application of input j that is decision of the farmer is given by

$$X_{jst} = f\left(P_{jst}, Z_{jst} \right)$$

where P is the relative price of input relative to composite crop price and Z is any other relevant variable, both variables being crop neutral.

---

[2] Government had constituted an Inter-Ministerial Committee in April 2016 to examine issues relating to 'Doubling of Farmers Income (DFI)' and recommended strategies to achieve the same. The final report in 14 volumes was submitted to the government in September 2018 suggesting various policies, reforms and programmes.

[3] Rainfed Area Development Programme (RADP) is launched in the year 2011–12 as a sub-scheme under Rashtriya Krishi VikasYojana (RKVY) for improving quality of life of farmers' especially, small and marginal farmers by offering a complete package of activities to maximize farm returns. RADP focuses on Integrated Farming System (IFS) for enhancing productivity and minimizing risks associated with climatic variabilities.

6.3.4 Variables

For each cross-section unit, a varying number (n) of crops (i) are covered depending on their dominant cropping pattern. Corrected for price rice VA for a state(s) is expressed as

$$VA_{st} = \frac{\frac{\sum_i P_{ist} Y_{ist} A_{ist}}{\sum A_{ist}} - \frac{\sum_{ist} MC_{ist}}{\sum A_{ist}}}{CPIAL_{st}} \tag{6.5}$$

Among natural explanatory variables is the land, which is measured by its productive power considering the three most dominant soil types of India, namely, alluvial (AVL), Black (BLK), and Red (RED), ranked in each state by their shares in the GCA to construct corresponding dummy variables. For example, if AVL ranks first in states, the dummy is AVL1 (AVL1 = 1 if it ranks first and zero otherwise).[2] The economic contribution of land depends on its location near a road, railway station, town, market or other facilities and other attributes like elevation or depression, rockiness, soil organic matter (SOM[4]) richness, proneness to waterlogging, etc. In the absence of such profound characterization in the data, rent on owned land (RENT) as given by COC is used as a proxy, assuming that the reported rent takes account of superiority over marginal land as classically postulated (Ricardo, 1963).

Climate is a natural attribute but is expected to be interactive with other water variables. Appearing as ratios of dams and irrigation variables in the model representing past investment in structures and equipment (motors, pumps) by public and private agents. Water supply for irrigation in the desired amount depends on the average storage in the reservoirs (RSV) in river basins in the respective sub-regions holding managed water from past natural rainfall. The river projects incur huge budgetary costs for administration. Irrigation facility helps to make use of the natural and stored water.

Soil fertility can be modulated by the use of chemical fertilizer whose application (FERT) is decided based on prices and constrained by working capital and water available. Fertilizer use, associated with target production, can ingrain endogeneity. Labour (LAB) used of both by family and attached labour (FLAB) and by casual labour (HLAB) can be seen as an endogenous decision too, depending on wage relative to crop price and available machine and other ingredients both exogenous to farmer's decision. Although farm implements like threshers, tillers and pumps also substitute for human labour, animals and ploughs, tractor remains the most dominant machine. It is acquired by a one-time large investment, but the practice of leasing machines has grown, crossing over local and district boundaries even to inter-state lending (Singh, 2017; Mehta et al., 2023). In the burgeoning machine service market, larger farmers are likely to invest primarily for their own use and small farmers to hire their extra capacity, but with long-term easy credit available,

[4] Soil organic matter is the fraction of the soil that consists of plant or animal tissue in various stages of breakdown (decomposition). Most of our productive agricultural soils have between 3 and 6% organic matter. Soil organic matter contributes to soil productivity in many different ways.

any reversal of the roles and emergence of a professional class of service providers is not improbable. Measured using two alternative specifications, as number of tractors sold (TRAC) and as cost of machine services (MACH), mechanization of farming (TMA, Website, COC) will be influenced by economics and farm size. Covering all machines (MACH) allows the state of income accrual and ownership to differ.

6.4 Contemporary Scene

Empirical evidence on the outcome and input of Indian agriculture are elicited from data from the reference period 2005–06 to 2020–21 in the three regions East/ Northeast (ENE), Central (C) and North-Western (NW) region.

6.4.1 Land Use

As a total cropped area, which is net land area (NSA) times CI, grew, cropping patterns moved in different ways. Among the major field crops, rice gained area shares in E and NW but lost share in C. Cropping patterns moved away from pulses and oilseeds in region E, but wheat and millets (mostly maize) gained. C moved away from rice, millets and even pulses it was once known for. Also, strangely, wheat lost share in NW along with millets and oilseeds but moved towards pulses and rice. The most remarkable in improved cropping intensity was C (Fig. 6.4a), while NW recovered only in 2018–19 after a long slump. The laggardness of the East in land utilization can be attributed to the slow growth of irrigation intensity (Fig. 6.4b). Association between irrigation and cropping intensities seem clear with C winning the race in both and NW lying in slump between 2011 and 2018. Analogously, canal irrigation increased in tandem with reservoir storage in E but canals lost share in the other two regions.

As can be expected the average farm size decreased in the time period but the reduction was relatively low or even minimal in Haryana and West Bengal while farm size came down by 8% in Punjab, 22% in Madhya Pradesh and 19% in Rajasthan (Fig. 6.5).

Rainfall appears uneven in the study period but behaved dissimilarly (Fig. 6.6a). Temporally, all three regions encountered swings annually creating temporary crisis but giving space for reservoir storage while spatially, the trends did not necessarily merge. Reservoir levels increased in all regions It may be noted that higher levels in May augurs well for Kharif cultivation but actual impact would depend on the water management performance (Figs. 6.6b and 6.7).

Represented by the value-added per hectare, output from agriculture accruing as incomes in the sector grew fastest in E over the entire period. VA in region NW increased in sync with E till 2007–08 but C moved sower. Towards the end of sample period NW and C moved in sync but E was growing faster in VA (Fig. 6.8).

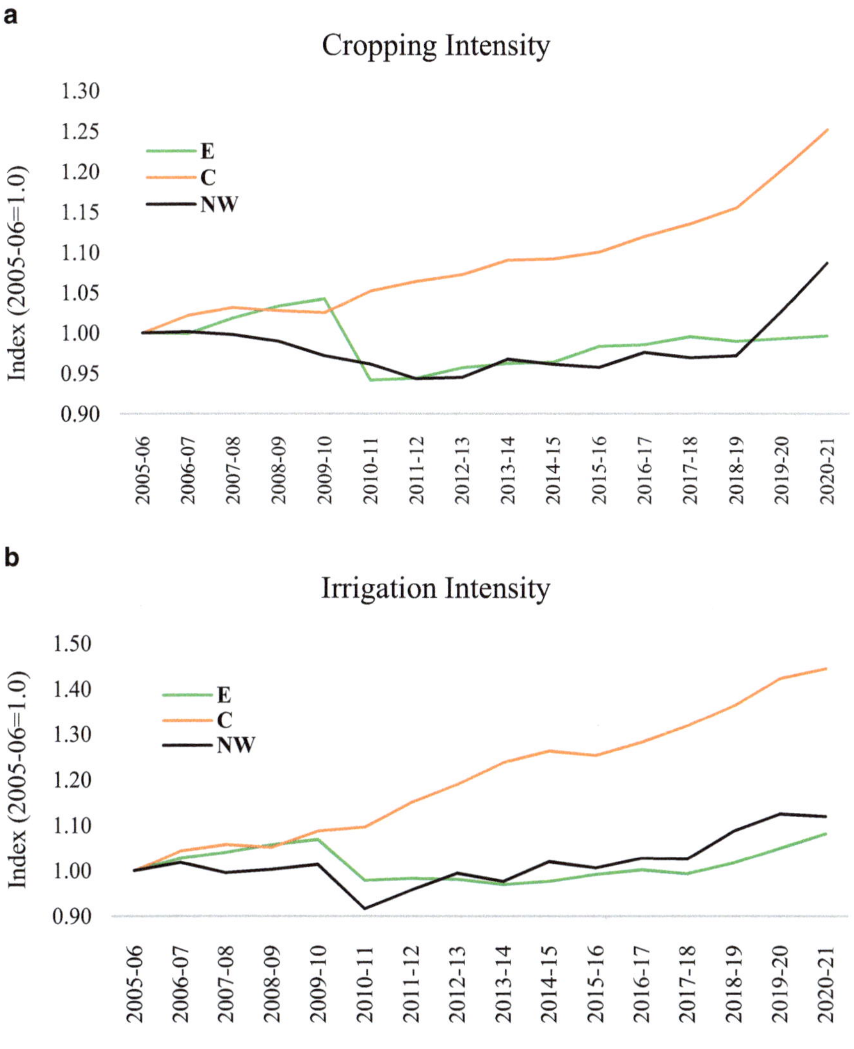

Fig. 6.4 Crops and irrigation

6.4.2 Input Use

Among the major input variables (Table 6.5) in physical units, fertilizer use increased by highest amounts and interestingly, while NW started with high intake and grew, the other regions tended to catch up as seen in the plots in logarithms in Fig. 6.8. Labour inputs came down in all three regions but remained highest in E. All three regions exhibited healthy growth in mechanization measured by machine services but moved conversely with labour use by both indicators (Fig. 6.9).

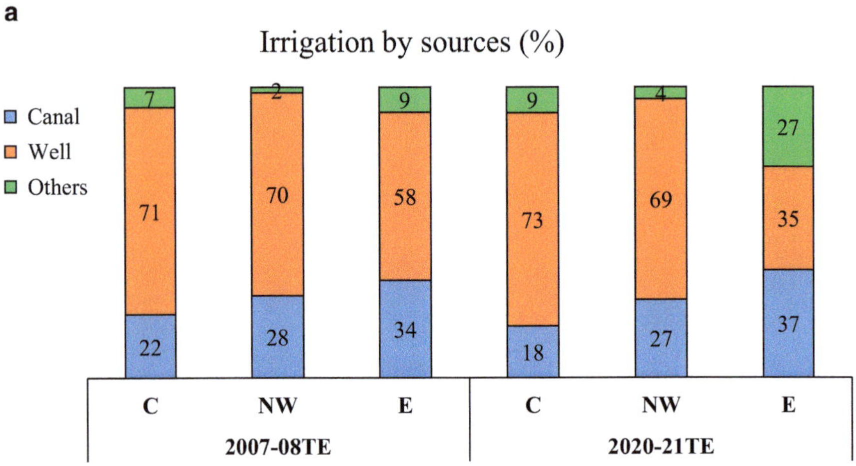

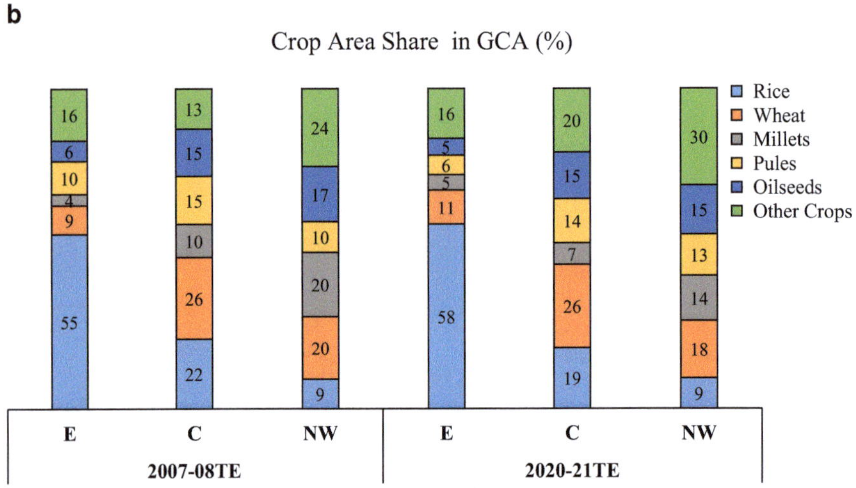

Fig. 6.4 (continued)

6.5 Productivity Analysis

Value added for the model, estimated using panel data with simple Pooled OLS and stochastic methods, brings out similar results. While the auxiliary equation with IV (Table 6.6) suggests that the price of fertilizer relative to the average crop price determines its use with a significant negative effect, working capital and irrigation facilities of all types available have positive effects. Fertilizer used as IV is an important contributor to VA, for which alluvial soil appeared as the dominant factor. Other useful attributes of land signified by the rent also emerge as statistically significant. Water, of course, shows a supportive role of higher average rainfall incidence and the

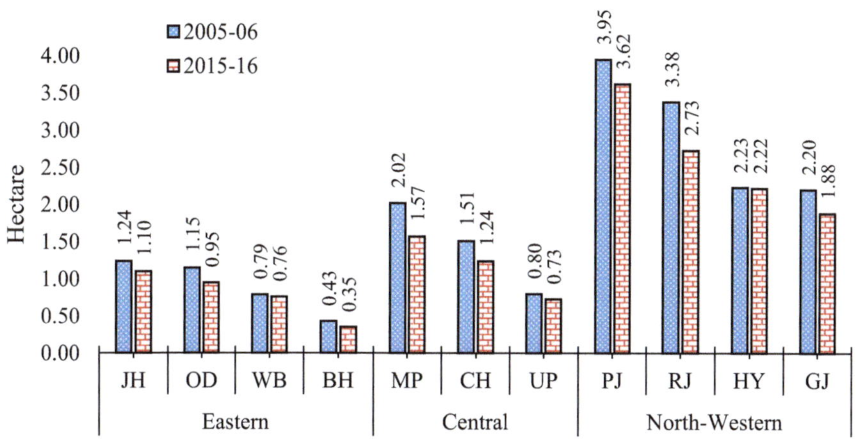

Fig. 6.5 Region-wise farm size (Hectare)

artificial controllability of water with reservoirs, but irrigation intensity helps only in the presence of fertilizer. Reservoir level itself has a significant positive effect. Total labour hours become unproductive in the analysis of efficiency variation of SFA model and while mechanization by both specifications is beneficial for VA, the productivity is lower in alluvial soil. Inputs uses of fertilizer, labour and machines are all affected by economic factors such as their prices relative to crop price and credit and working capital are also important for fertilizer and mechanization. Larger farms seem to use less labour and buy fewer tractors.

6.6 Efficiency Analysis

Inefficiency derived from the SFA has been varied over the sample period, with eastern states like Bihar making enormous improvements while some western states like Punjab, Haryana and Rajasthan became more inefficient. While NW remained most efficient at levels, both E and C gained efficiency over time, and NW became relatively inefficient. The regressions (Table 6.6) show that small farms may be more inefficient, but the negative interaction of farm size and roads suggests that the difference in efficacy effect of farm size may narrow with greater road intensity. Credit has helped to make agriculture more efficient.

Returns from resources treated as an outcome due to east-oriented development policies increased in the lagging states of the east with sustainable and judicious use of resources, making less increasingly wasteful use of the same resources. In fact, behaviours suggest that advanced agricultural states retain a lead but have been generating returns from resources making increasingly wasteful use of them benchmarked by East and Central, whereas arguably, due to east-oriented development

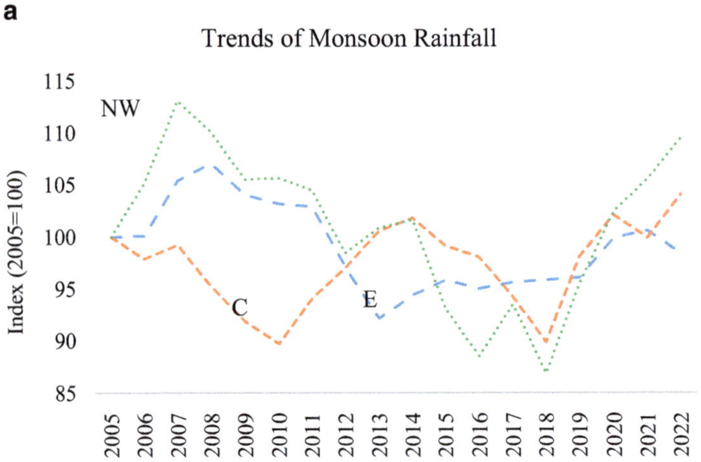

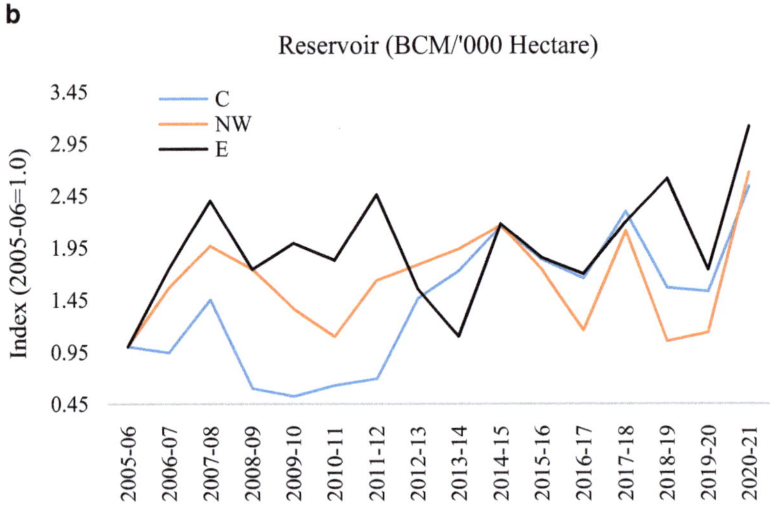

Fig. 6.6 **a** Rainfall average of 5 years. **b** Reservoir water availability in end of the May month

policies, the lagging East is picking up pace, even surpassing NW by judicious use of resources (Figs. 6.10 and 6.11) and (Tables 6.7 and 6.8).

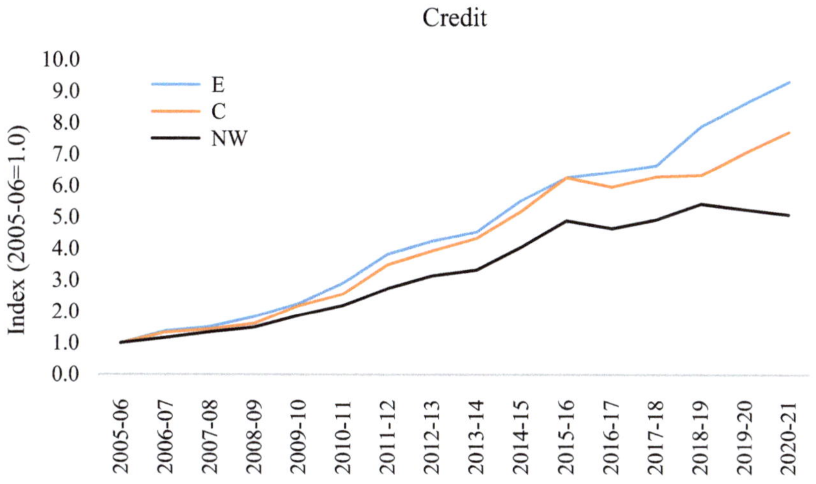

Fig. 6.7 Credit allocation

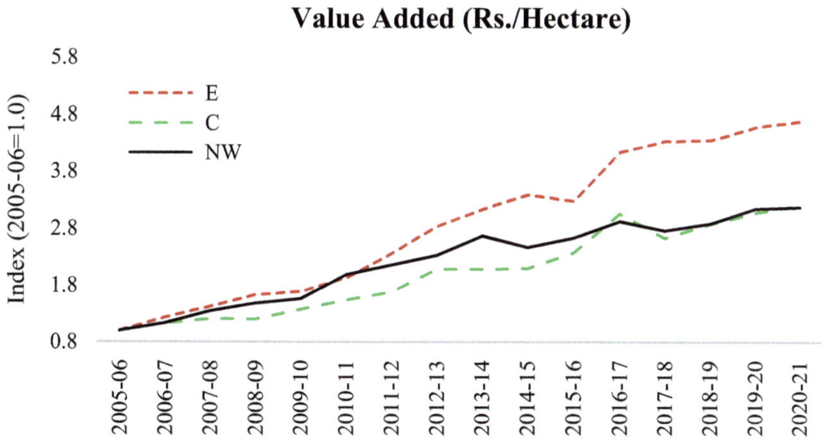

Fig. 6.8 Indices of VA in region wise. *Note* Eastern—BH, OD, JH, WB, Central—MP, CH, UP and North Western—PJ, HY, RJ, GJ

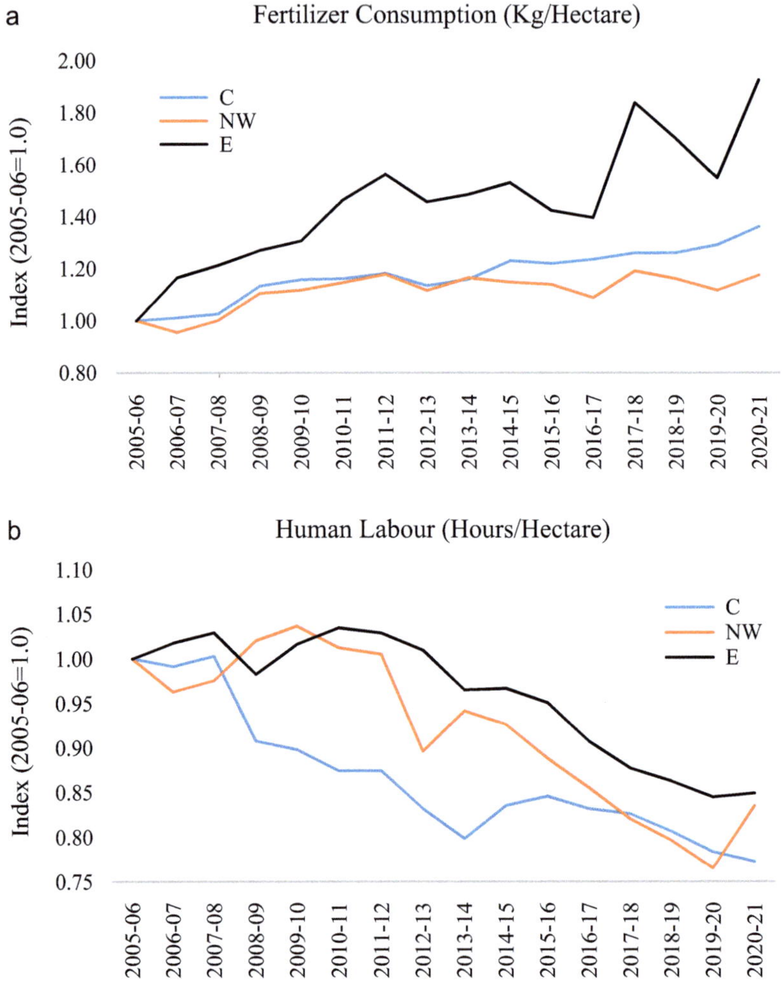

Fig. 6.9 Input use indices

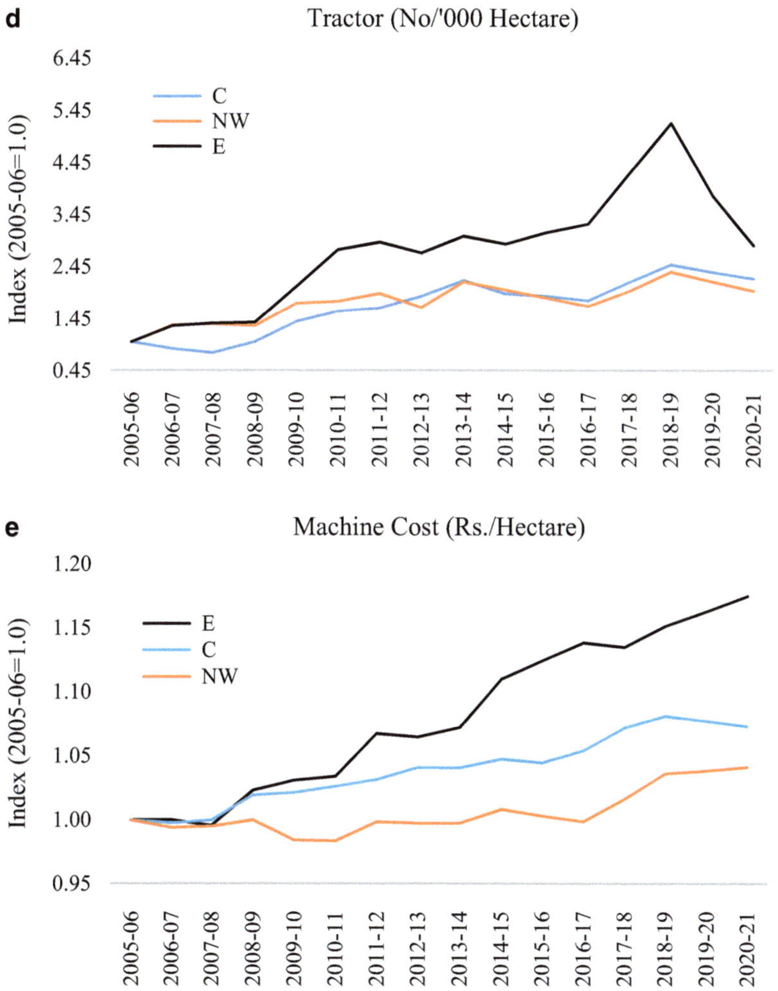

Fig. 6.9 (continued)

6.7 Conclusion

Indian agriculture has come a long way from resource shortage, backward technology, poverty and marker imperfections despite some initiation of infrastructure, irrigation and marketing policy in pre-colonial and colonial status. Independent India, faced with food insecurity, embarked on developments on many fronts to overcome import dependence. India launched the green revolution that delivered the much-sought food sufficiency but, in turn, created many problems like unsustainability, inequity, fiscal burden and political dilemmas that remain to be dealt with even as new developments like the concern for climate change with monsoonal anomalies and the introduction

Table 6.5 Progress in Input use by regions

Year (TE)	Fertilizer consumption (Kg./Hectare)			Human labour (Hours/Hectare)			Well/NSA (Ratio)			RBANK (No./'000 Hectare)		
	C	NW	E	C	NW	E	C	NW	E	C	NW	E
2007–08	96	159	95	542	509	822	0.42	0.45	0.21	0.14	0.11	0.16
2008–09	100	165	102	525	512	817	0.43	0.46	0.21	0.14	0.11	0.16
2009–10	105	173	106	508	525	817	0.44	0.47	0.21	0.14	0.11	0.16
2010–11	109	181	113	485	532	819	0.44	0.48	0.22	0.14	0.12	0.17
2011–12	111	185	121	479	529	831	0.45	0.48	0.23	0.14	0.13	0.18
2012–13	110	185	125	467	505	829	0.47	0.48	0.20	0.15	0.14	0.20
2013–14	110	186	126	453	492	810	0.48	0.48	0.17	0.16	0.17	0.21
2014–15	112	184	125	446	479	794	0.50	0.48	0.13	0.18	0.19	0.22
2015–16	114	186	124	448	477	778	0.51	0.49	0.13	0.19	0.22	0.24
2016–17	117	182	121	454	463	763	0.52	0.49	0.13	0.20	0.23	0.26
2017–18	118	184	130	453	444	738	0.53	0.50	0.13	0.21	0.24	0.28
2018–19	119	185	138	446	428	715	0.55	0.50	0.14	0.21	0.24	0.29
2019–20	121	187	142	437	413	698	0.57	0.50	0.14	0.21	0.24	0.29
2020–21	124	186	145	427	415	690	0.58	0.50	0.14	0.20	0.24	0.29
CAGR (%)	2.0	1.2	3.3	-1.8	-1.5	-1.3	2.5	0.9	-3.0	3.0	6.2	4.7

Source DES, Website, RBI, Website

of ICT promise to transform practices, opportunities and ways we deal with the problems.

Agricultural performance, best approximated by economic returns to farmers or service providers in the farm sector at large in the current perspective, is determined by factors and natural endowments as can be expected, including good soil and water, but further analysis showed how the efficiency of the use of resources also made a difference to the performances across states. While productive use of individual inputs is an important step towards prosperous agriculture, greater efficiency reflects gain from all inputs used in conjunction to deliver more output from the same amount of input or the same output from less input in entirety. Farm income thus depends on conventional inputs, which is influenced by economic factors.

The analysis indicated that the agriculturally advanced states of the north-west that benefitted from the green revolution still yield higher returns due to greater use of inputs but have stable or dipping efficiency. The reason may lie in their use of inputs and entitlement to credit and resultant contribution to sustainability. On the contrary, the water-abundant eastern states lagged behind in value added, but they are performing well in efficiency, and central states are also becoming more efficient in recent times. The small size of the farm, which was unavoidable due to the growth of population, is hampering the attainment of efficiency, but better

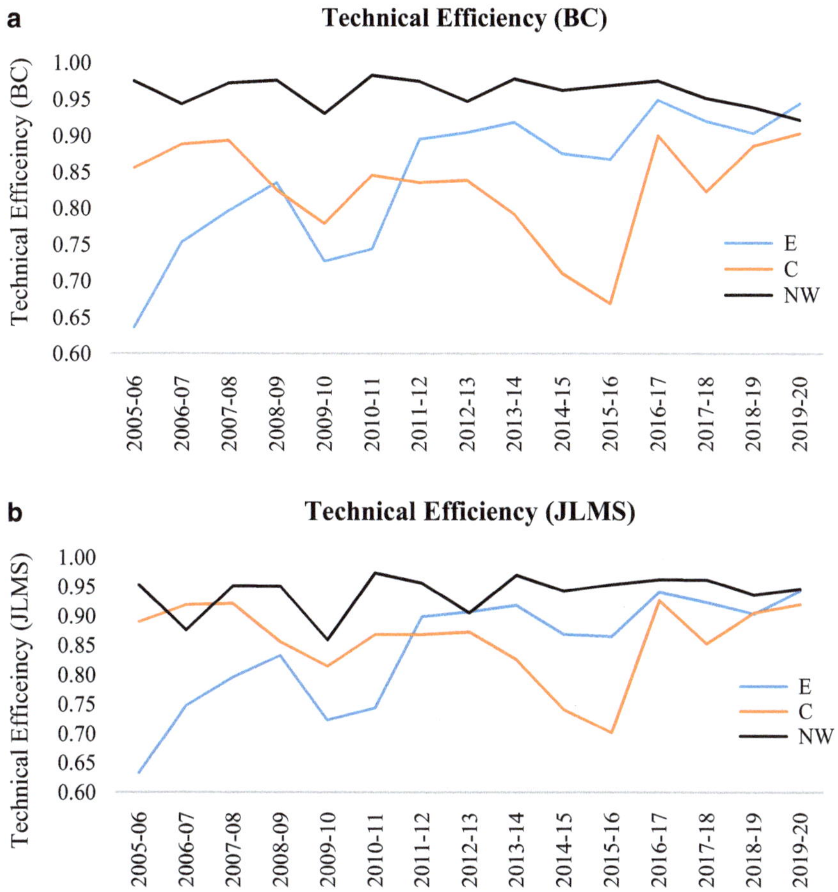

Fig. 6.10 Technical efficiency for region wise based on TRE model (Tractor)

road connectivity and perhaps the marketing avenues created help them recover the loss inefficiency relative to larger farms. Higher credit, a landmark policy instrument to support farmers enhances efficiency. Credit creation has been modernized and expanded with technology and also relaxed and broadened in coverage beyond farming over time.

Table 6.6 Regression to explain Real Value Added (Rs/Hect) in agriculture (VAF)

Variable	Model 1 POOLED	Model 2 (Panel)		Model 3 (Frontier)		Model 4 (Frontier with inefficiency)	
		SPEC: 1	SPEC: 2	SPEC: 1	SPEC: 2	SPEC: 1	SPEC: 2
				Instrumental (IV)			
Irrigation (NIA/NSA)	–	–	1.696*** (3.30)	–		–	
Fert X Irrigation	0.33*** (4.50)	0.25*** (3.15)	–	0.311*** (4.70)	0.303*** (4.67)	0.311*** (4.84)	0.244*** (3.48)
RESV X Irrigation	0.21*** (4.1)	0.154*** (2.92)	0.233*** (3.15)	0.224*** (4.85)	0.223*** (4.81)	0.219*** (4.87)	0.171*** (3.31)
RESV	0.16*** (3.44)	0.137** (2.55)	0.145** (2.58)	0.130*** (3.79)	0.259*** (6.10)	0.128*** (4.25)	0.186*** (4.47)
Tractor (No/hectare)	0.21*** (3.75)	0.163*** (2.99)	0.157*** (2.92)	0.403*** (4.25)	–	0.328*** (3.42)	-
Machine (Rs./Hectare)	–	–	–	–	0.418*** (4.47)	–	0.139 (1.39)
Land Rent	0.71*** (11.74)	0.735*** (10.41)	0.755*** (10.33)	0.352*** (5.97)	0.436*** (6.87)	0.317*** (5.82)	0.353*** (5.31)
Total Labour (hours/hect)	0.08* (1.83)	0.092** (2.07)	0.059 (1.33)	–0.07*** (–6.54)	–0.065*** (–5.50)	–0.07*** (–6.61)	–0.067*** (–4.45)
Rainfall (mm) (3Y M.A.)	–0.00 (–1.18)	–0.000 (–0.55)	–	0.001*** (5.52)	0.001*** (5.22)	0.001*** (6.70)	0.001*** (5.13)
DUM-ALV x Tractor	–0.23*** (–3.61)	–0.113* (–1.72)	–0.096 (–1.49)	–0.28*** (–2.83)	–	–0.28*** (–2.86)	–
DUM-ALV x Machine	–	–	–	–	–0.418*** (–3.30)	–	–0.250* (–1.84)
DUM-ALV	0.56*** (6.04)	0.421*** (3.75)	0.32*** (3.18)	0.953*** (8.50)	4.140*** (3.96)	0.94*** (8.72)	2.738** (2.42)
Constant	2.83*** (5.18)	2.501*** (4.16)	2.66*** (4.11)	5.886*** (12.47)	3.121*** (3.75)	6.01*** (12.81)	5.325*** (5.75)
R^2 Within	–	0.44	0.42	–		–	
Between	–	0.92	0.90	–		–	
Overall	0.79	0.78	0.75	–		–	
Wald chi^2	–	275.3	272.47	637.74	650.15	892.41	645.47
No. of Observation	165	165	176	165	165	165	165
No. of Groups	11	11	11	11	11	11	11

Note Model 1: used POLS Model, Model 2: used panel regression with two different specification, Model 3: used stochastic frontier in two specification (SPEC), (i) SPEC: 1—tractor used and (ii) SPEC: 2—Machine service used and Model 4: Estimated stochastic frontier model with USIGMA option to allows for modelling how inefficiency varies with other variables

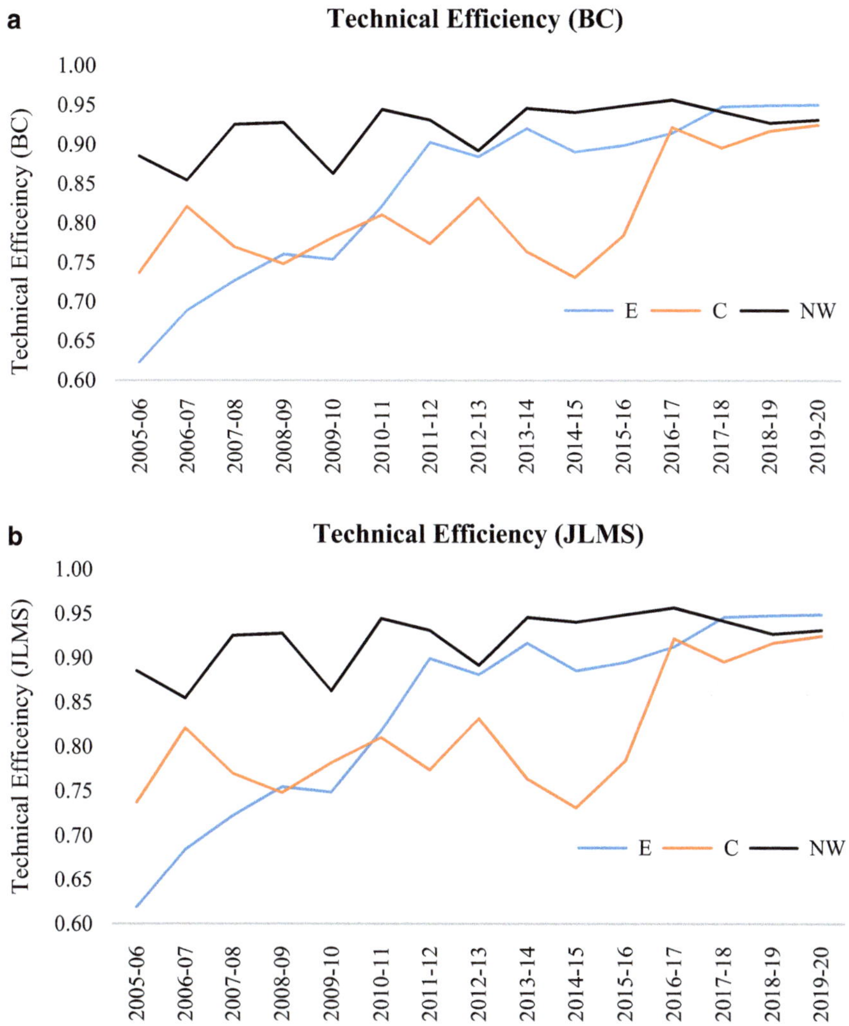

Fig. 6.11 Technical efficiency for region wise based on TRE model (Machine service)

Table 6.7 Regression to explain Input use in agriculture

Variables		Tractor (No./hect)	Machine services (Rs./hect)	Fertilizer (Kg./hect)	Family labour (Hours/hect)	Casual labour (Hours/hect)
Wage/Crop Price		0.31*** (2.80)	–	–	–0.21*** (–4.78)	–0.28*** (–4.92)
Irrigation		–	0.37** (2.10)	0.26*** (3.71)	–	–
Fert Price/Farm Price		–	–	–0.18*** (–4.22)	–	–
Tractor*Farm Size		–	–	–	–	0.17*** (3.71)
Farm Size		–0.31* (–1.96)	–	–	–0.59*** (–4.07)	–0.45*** (–2.96)
Farm Price		–	0.40* (1.74)	–		–
Family labour		–0.36** (–2.01)	–	–		–
RESV		0.23*** (2.72)	–	–		–
RESV X Irrigation		–	–	–	–0.05*** (4.98)	–
Rainfall		–	–	–	–0.12** (–2.02)	–
Rainfall (3y M.A.)		–	–	–	–	0.38** (2.38)
Credit		0.79*** (4.23)	1.17*** (9.49)	–	–	–
Working Capital		–	–	0.81*** (14.12)	–	–
Constant		6.00*** (4.56)	7.12*** (11.60)	2.74*** (11.07)	5.87** (14.03)	2.20** (2.11)
R^2	Within	0.53	0.41	0.65	0.2578	0.21
	Between	0.26	0.48	0.79	0.48	0.59
	Overall	0.40	0.45	0.76	0.47	0.57
Wald chi^2		183.1	121.11	322.82	62.67	57.89
No. of Observation		176	176	176	176	165
No. of Groups		11				
Sample period		2005–06 to 2020–21				

Note Parenthesis figures are z-statistics and ***, **, * denotes the level of significance at 1, 5 and 10%

Table 6.8 Efficiency equation

Variables	Efficiency			
	Model 1		Model 2	
	BC	JLMS	BC	JLMS
Farm size	0.17*** (3.17)	0.17*** (3.17)	0.06** (2.13)	0.07** (2.15)
Credit	0.08** (2.47)	0.08** (2.46)	0.04* (1.83)	0.04* (1.84)
Road x farm size	–0.06*** (–2.99)	–0.06*** (–3.00)	–0.02** (–2.07)	–0.02** (–2.09)
Constant	0.84*** (94.7)	0.84*** (93.2)	0.89*** (176.0)	0.89*** (170.0)

Note Parenthesis figures are z-statistics and ***, **, * denotes the level of significance at 1, 5 and 10%. Model 1: used tractor and Model 2: used Machine service. BC-Battese and Coelli (1992) method for efficiency and JLMS: Jondrow et al. 1982 method for efficiency

References

Aigner, D., Lovell, C. A. K., & Schmidt, P. (1977). Formulation and estimation of stochastic production models. *Journal of Econometrics, Journal of Econometrics, 6*, 21–37.

Battese & Coelli. (1992). Frontier production functions, technical efficiency and panel data: With application to paddy farmers in India, Vol. 3, pp. 153–169.

Battese, G., & Coelli, T. (1995). A model for technical inefficiency effects in a stochastic frontier production function for panel data. *Empirical Economics, 20*, 325–332.

Battese, G. E., Coelli, T. J., & Colby, T. C. (1989). Estimation of frontier production functions and the efficiencies of Indian farms using panel data from ICRISAT's village level studies. *Journal of Quantitative Economics, 5*, 327–348.

Baviskar, A. (2012). Food and agriculture. In V. Dalmia & R. Sadana (Eds.), *Cambridge companion to contemporary Indian culture* (pp. 49–66). Cambridge University Press.

Benjamin, Dwayne, & Loren Brandt. (2002). Agriculture and income distribution in rural Vietnam under economic reforms: A tale of two regions. Working Papers benjamin-02-01, University of Toronto, Department of Economics.

Bhadhuri, A. (1984). *Economic structure of backward agriculture.* Macmillan Indian Ltd.

Borah, G. (2022). Distress migration and involuntary return during pandemic in Assam: Characteristics and determinants. *Ind. J. Labour Econ., 65*, 801–820. https://doi.org/10.1007/s41027-022-00392-8

Census of India (Website). https://censusindia.gov.in/census.website/. Office of the Registrar General & Census Commissioner, India, Ministry of Home Affairs. Government of India.

Del Buono, D. (2021). Can biostimulants be used to mitigate the effect of anthropogenic climate change on agriculture? It is time to respond. *Sci Total Environ. Jan 10;751*, 141763.

Department of Economic Affairs (DEA). (2023). Economic Survey, 2022–23. Ministry of Finance, Government of India.

Dhawan, B. D. (1988). *Irrigation in India's agricultural development: Productivity, stability.* Institute of Economic Growth, Sage Publications, Delhi.

Directorate of Economic and Statistics (DES) (Website). Department of Agriculture and Farmers Welfare, Ministry of Agriculture and Farmers Welfare, Government of India. https://eands.dacnet.nic.in/

FAOSTAT (Website). https://www.fao.org/faostat/en/#data/RFN

Frankel, F. R. (2006). *India's political economy: The gradual revolution (1947–2004).* Oxford University Press.

Geiger, Flavia & Bengtsson, Jan & Berendse, Frank & Weisser, Wolfgang & Emmerson, Mark & Morales, Manuel & Ceryngier, Piotr & Liira, Jaan & Tscharntke, Teja & Winqvist, Camilla & Eggers, Sönke & Bommarco, Riccardo & Pärt, Tomas & Bretagnolle, Vincent & Plantegenest, Manuel & Clement, Lars & Dennis, Chris & Palmer, Catherine & Oñate, Juan & Inchausti, Pablo. (2010). Persistent negative effects of pesticides on biodiversity and biological control potential on European farmland. *Basic and Applied Ecology*, 97-105. https://doi.org/10.1016/j.baae.2009.12.001

Ghatak, M., & Sanchari, R. (2007). Land reform and agricultural productivity in India: A review of the evidence. *Oxford Review of Economic Policy, 23*(2), 251–269.

Ghosh Nilabja, Amarnath Tripathi, Mayanglambam Rajeshwor, Ruchin Verma, & Kumar Shankar. (2016). Problems of water and food insecurity in the Indian part of the Kosi river basin: A study on agriculture. Report submitted to ICIMOD, Nepal.

Ghosh, Nand C. Neogi. (1995, April-June). Supply response of food grains and policy actions: A model with rational expectation hypothesis. *Indian Journal of Agricultural Economics.*

Ghosh, Nilabja. (2011). Role of climate change and agricultural performance. Submitted to Ministry of Agriculture & Farmers Welfare.

Ghosh, N. (2013). *India's agricultural marketing: Market reforms and emergence of new channels (India Studies in Business and Economics.* Springer.

Ghosh, Nilabja, Mayanglambam Rajeshwor, Parmeet Kumar Vinit. (2020). Towards one agricultural market in India: Does the ICT Help? Book (eds) by Dibyendu Maiti, Dr. Fulvio Castellacci, Arne Melchior. Digitalisation and Development Issues for India and Beyond. Springer Singarpore.

Ghosh, Nilabja, Mayanglambam Rajeshwor, & Amritanshi Preeti. (2022, November 19). Climatic trends, cropping pattern shifts, and migration of rice in India. *Economic & Political Weekly* (EPW), *LVII*(47), 35–45.

Government of India (GOI). (1976). Crop production, sericulture and apiculture. Report of the national commission on agriculture, Ministry of agriculture and irrigation.

Greene, W. (2005). Reconsidering heterogeneity in panel data estimators of the stochastic frontier model. *Journal of Econometrics, 126*, 269–303.

Gulati, Ashok. (2009). Emerging trends in Indian agriculture: What can we learn from these? *Agricultural Economics Research Review, 22.*

Hautier, Y., Seabloom, E. W., Borer, E. T., Adler, P. B., Harpole, W. S., Hillebrand, H., Lind, E. M., MacDougall, A. S., Stevens, C. J., Bakker, J. D., Buckley, Y. M., Chu, C., Collins, S. L., Daleo, P., Damschen, E. I., Davies, K. F., Fay, P. A., Firn, J., Gruner, D. S., Jin, V. L., Klein, J. A., Knops, J. M., La Pierre, K. J., Li, W., McCulley, R. L., Melbourne, B. A., Moore, J. L., O'Halloran, L. R., Prober, S. M., Risch, A. C., Sankaran, M., Schuetz, M., & Hector, A. (2014, April 24). Eutrophication weakens stabilizing effects of diversity in natural grasslands. *Nature, 508*(7497), 521–525. https://doi.org/10.1038/nature13014. Epub 2014 Feb 16. PMID: 24531763

Haydock Karen, Abhijit Sambhaji Bansode, Gurinder Singh, & Kalpana Sangale. (2021). Learning and sustaining agricultural practices the dialectics of cultivating cultivation in Rural India. Springer Nature Switzerland.

Hoda, A., & Gulati, A. (2013). India's agricultural trade policy and sustainable development. Issue Paper 49, International Centre for Trade and Sustainable Development (ICTSD) International Environment House 2 7 Chemin de Balexert, 1219 Geneva, Switzerland.

Indian Meteorological Department (IMD) (Website). Ministry of Earth Science, Government of India. https://mausam.imd.gov.in/

Indian Meteorological Department (IMD) (Website). Ministry of Earth Science, Government of India. https://mausam.imd.gov.in/

Khusro, A. M. (1964). Returns to scale in Indian Agriculture. Agricultural and food sciences, economics. *Indian Journal of Agricultural Economics 19*(3). Bombay, *PP51.*

Krishna, Raj. (1963, September). Farm supply response in India-Pakistan: A case study of the Punjab Region. *Economic Journal, 477–487*.
Kumbhakar, S. C., & Lovell, K. C. A. (2000). *Stochastic frontier analysis*. Cambridge University Press.
Larsen, A., & McComb, S. (2021). Land cover and climate changes drive regionally heterogeneous increases in US insecticide use. *Landscape Ecology., 36*, 1–19. https://doi.org/10.1007/s10980-020-01130-5
MacDonald, James M., Penni Korb, & Robert a Hoppe. (2014). Farm size and the organization of U.S. Crop Farming. USDA Economic Research Report, 2014, ERR-152.
Maps of India (MoI) (Website). Maps of Major Soil Types of India. https://www.mapsofindia.com/maps/schoolchildrens/major-soil-types-map.html
Mehta, Bangale, Chandel, & Kumar. (2023). Farm Mechanization in India: Status and way forward. Agricultural Mechanization in Asia, Africa and Latin America, Vol. 54, No. 2, Springer.
Mellor, J. W. (1966). *The economics of agricultural development*. Cornell University Press.
Ministry of Road Transport and Highways (MoRTH) (Website). Basic Road Statistics of India (various). Government of India. https://morth.nic.in/
Muyanga, Milu, & Thomas S. Jayne. (2019). Revisiting the farm size-productivity relationship based on a relatively wide range of farm sizes: Evidence from Kenya. *American Journal of 49Agricultural Economics, 101*(4), 1140–1163.
Nair, Kusum. (1983). Transforming traditionally: Land and labor in agriculture in Asia and Africa. Riverdale Co Pub.
Naregal, Bina. (2021, August 21). Labour 'Invisibility' during COVID-19 Times. *Economic and Political Weekly, 56*(34), 37–43.
Neogi, C., & Ghosh, B. (1994, October). Intertemporal efficiency variations in Indian manufacturing industries. *Journal of Productivity Analysis, 5*(3).
Neogi, N., Kamiike, A., & Sato, T. (2014, December 27). Factors behind performance of pharmaceutical industries in India. *Economic and Political Weekly, XLIX*.
Noack, Frederik, & Ashley Larsen. (2019). The contrasting effects of farm size on farm incomes and food production. *Environmental Research Letters, 14*(8), 084024.
Pandey Kiran, & Rajit Sengupta. (2018, October 1). India had a deficit monsoon in 13 of the last 18 years. Downtoearth.
Press Information Bureau (PIB). (2023, August 8). Pradhan Mantri KisanSamman Nidhi Scheme.
Purushothaman, S., Patil, S., Purushothaman, S., & Patil, S. (2019). Family farms in agrarian literature—A critique. *Agrarian Change and Urbanization in Southern India: City and the Peasant*, 25–52.
Rakshit, M. (2008). Food policy in India: Some longer-term issues. Book (Eds) by Uma Kapila "*Indian Economy Since Independence*", Academic Foundation, New Delhi.
Rao, V. K. R. V. (1983). *India's national income 1950–80: An analysis of economic growth and change*. SAGE Publications Pvt.
Reserve Bank of India (RBI) (Website). India's Central Bank, Government of India. https://www.rbi.org.in/Scripts/Publications.aspx?publication=Annual
Ricardo, David. (1963). Principles of political economy and taxation. Rpt. Homewood, Illinois: Richard D. Irwin Inc.
Sen, Amritya. (1964). Size of holdings and productivity. *The Economic Weekly, Annual Number Ferbruary, 323326*.
Shamantara, Samir (2010). Kisan Credit Card- A Study. Occational paper 52, NABARD.
Singh, Charan. (1987). Land reforms in UP and the Kulaks. Vikas Publishing House Pvt Ltd., 5 Ansari Road, New Delhi.
Singh, Sukhpal. (2017). How inclusive and effective are farm machinery rental services in India? Case studies from Punjab. *Ind. Jn. of Agri. Econ., 72*(3), 230–250.
Sivaraman, K., Thankamani, C. K., & Srinivasan, V. (2023). Crop diversification: Cropping/system approach for enhancing farmers' income. In *Handbook of Spices in India: 75 Years of Research and Development* (pp. 3847–3926). Singapore: Springer Nature Singapore.

Thorner, D. (1976). *The agrarian prospect in India: Five lectures on land reform delivered in 1955 at the Delhi school of economics*. University Press.

Todaro Michael, P., & Stephen, C. Smith. (2020). Economic Development. Pearson Education Limited, UK.

Tractor and Mechanization Association (TMA) (Website). Indian Tractor Industry. https://www.tmaindia.in/

Tripp, R. (2006). *Self-sufficient agriculture: Labour and knowledge in small-scale farming*. Routledge.

Waite, L. (2005). How is labouring enabled through the body? A case study of manual workers in rural India. *Contemporary South Asia, 14*(4), 411–428.

Chapter 7
Total Factor Productivity Growth in Indian Agriculture and Regional Convergence

Seema Bathla, Anjani Kumar, and Navneet Kumar

Abstract The present study has estimated total factor productivity (TFP) growth and its contribution to agricultural output growth across 17 major states in India for the period from 1981–82 to 2019–20. This is followed by an empirical examination of the convergence of TFP to understand how technology spread in India. The Data Envelopment Analysis Malmquist productivity index is used to estimate the TFP growth, whereas the inter-state convergence is tested using the sigma and beta convergence approaches. The study contributes to the literature by providing TFP estimates at the disaggregate state level over a longer period to make an assessment on account of an increase in public investment in R&D, irrigation, credit flow, and several other policy initiatives taken from the 2000s. The analysis indicates large temporal and spatial variations in the output, input, and TFP indices, validating that the technological diffusion on account of HYVs under the green and yellow revolutions has been uneven. A low TFP growth is confirmed in several states over time, the national average being 1.06% from 1981 to 2019. However, the contribution of TFP to output growth was low at 41.42% during the overall study period, but it was found to have increased to 60% during the last decade. The conditional convergence reveals a tendency of productivity in the poorer states to catch up with the richer states, albeit at a very slow speed of 1%. It is important to enhance expenditure on R&D, extension, technology, and irrigation more in the eastern states to augment and sustain productivity growth to meet the future demand for food.

Keywords Agricultural output · Total factor productivity · Spatial model · Productivity convergence · India

S. Bathla (✉) · N. Kumar
Centre for the Study of Regional Development, Jawaharlal Nehru University, New Delhi, India
e-mail: seema.bathla@gmail.com

N. Kumar
e-mail: navneetkumar2095@gmail.com

A. Kumar
International Food Policy Research Institute, New Delhi, India
e-mail: Anjani.Kumar@cgiar.org

D. Maiti et al. (eds.), *75 Years of Growth, Development and Productivity in India*, India Studies in Business and Economics, https://doi.org/10.1007/978-981-97-8054-9_7

JEL Classification F43 · O13 · O47 · R12

7.1 Background and Objectives

7.1.1 Background

Development economists perceive productivity growth in agriculture as very important to ensure adequate output growth to meet the escalating demand for food (see, for example, Hayami & Ruttan, 1985; Mellor, 1976). India has made remarkable progress in agriculture during the past five decades, transforming herself from a food deficit to a net food exporter country. This transformation is largely attributed to the developments in agricultural research, effective dissemination of research output, public investment in infrastructure, and appropriate institutional and policy support. Agricultural growth began to increase in the mid-sixties following the adoption of high-yielding varieties (HYVs) of wheat and paddy under the green revolution. The development of HYVs is accompanied by increased levels of input use, particularly fertilisers, irrigation, tractors, and a package of research, policies, and institutional reforms (e.g. procurement of foodgrains at minimum support price, access to credit and wholesale markets). These initiations significantly contributed to augmenting foodgrain production and agricultural growth by more than 3% per annum, considerably higher than the rate of growth in population. According to Parikh et al. (2016), India has fallen short of the targeted 4% per annum, which is required to sustain the GDP growth rate of at least 8% per annum. This may imply that the decline in agriculture's contribution to national income has been much faster than its decline as a provider of employment.[1] Increasing and maintaining productivity growth is, therefore essential to ensure food security for the population at large.[2]

Kumar and Rosegrant (1994) estimated low growth in total factor productivity (TFP) at 1.1 to 1.4% from 1971 to 1988. Nevertheless, its contribution was found to be half of the agricultural output growth, and the remaining half was contributed by labour, capital, and other inputs. From the mid-eighties, a deceleration in the productivity growth of cereals was identified. Studies maintained that if gains from the green revolution were attained and returns to public research had declined, it would mean that future production growth could only be input-based. It implied that future productivity gains in rice production would have to be achieved from the eastern and southern regions compared to the northern and western regions. Therefore, public investment in research, irrigation, and rural infrastructure should be targeted towards these potential areas.[3] The study reported a much higher increase

[1] The share of agriculture in GDP has declined from 41% in 1980-81 to about 16% 2022–23, while its employment share in aggregate employment has fallen from 70 to only 41% during this period.

[2] If agricultural output is high, food prices will not tend to rise and poor people will be able to afford food and have nutritious diet.

[3] The returns from public investment in rice research were estimated to be more than 55%.

in TFP in the northern states—Punjab and Haryana, the early adopters of HYVs. Though the HYVs technology eventually spread to the southern states and then to the western, and the eastern parts of the country, the gains in the latter were relatively more from two revolutions—yellow (oilseeds) and white (milk).

Chand, Kumar, and Kumar (2011) maintained that India would require a minimum 1.4% growth in the food output to maintain the current level of per capita availability of food products. The level of per capita consumption of most of the food items was found to be significantly below the minimum requirement of a healthy diet, necessitating higher growth of agriculture to meet the future demand. This would require a paradigm shift from an increase in productivity from a single resource (partial productivity) to TFP, i.e. the entire set of resources used in production. Their findings were based on a quantification of the role of R&D, extension, and other factors in output growth from 1971 to 2006. Kannan (2011) highlighted an uneven spread and gains from green revolution technology across states and crops, perhaps due to diverse agro-climatic conditions and natural resource endowments. He confirmed that most of the crops grown in Karnataka had registered a low productivity growth since the eighties. A relatively higher growth identified from 2000–01 to 2007–08 was attributable to government expenditure on research, education and extension, canal irrigation, rainfall, and the balanced use of fertilisers.

In a cross-country analysis from 1961 to 2015, Fuglie and Rada (2018) found stagnancy in agricultural TFP growth in the Southeast Asian economies viz. Cambodia, Bangladesh, Myanmar, Nepal, and Vietnam. A much higher rate of TFP growth (in the range of 1 to 4.6%) from the early 1990s up to 2010 was explained by investments in research, wider adoption of new technologies, trade policy reforms, farmers' education, and availability of irrigation water. In the subsequent period, the average rate of productivity growth was close to 1.5% in most of the countries, including India. From 2011 to 2015, only Myanmar and the Philippines showed a negative rate of growth in it. As per Bathla and D'Souza (2015), TFP growth in Indian agriculture is less than 1% from 1993 to 2011, thus pointing towards little chance of its catching up with the other economic sectors. However, an improvement in TFP was visible through its higher contribution to agricultural growth than that of labour and capital from 48% in 1993–94 to 52% in 2011–12. The inter-sectoral productivity gaps could be bridged by accelerating investment in agriculture, especially given the large differences in the rural–urban incomes and levels of poverty.

For the more recent period, Krishna and Meenakshi (2022) revealed an increase in both TFP and labour productivity growth. The TFP was estimated from 1981–82 to 2018–19 based on two different data sources—the USDA and KLEMS model. The contribution of TFP to agricultural output growth was nearly one-third over the 38 years and rose to the maximum of 58% during 2010–11 to 2018–19. Further, the contribution of labour was much lower in comparison to capital and TFP. The authors maintained that the recent output growth was driven more by technology than by prices and men exiting agriculture.[4]

Sengupta et al. (2023) found an increase in the TFPG from 0.8% to around 2.0% upon inclusion of land and land quality—irrigated, rainfed, and fallow. The growth accounting decomposition shows an increase in the contribution of TFPG to agricultural output growth from 48% in the 1980s to 78% in the 2010s. The study found productivity improvement to be driven by public gross capital formation stock, research and development, mechanisation in agriculture, and favourable terms of trade.

Literature validates that the growth performance of Indian agriculture has shown large variations over time. This, along with wide inter-state differentials in TFP growth, continues to be an important cause for concern. Fewer studies have estimated TFP across all the states and for each of the agri-subsectors. It is important to delve into a disaggregate analysis of TFP as several states have increased investments in research, irrigation, and rural infrastructure from early 2000 to trigger agricultural growth and arrest a decline in cereal productivity growth. Bathla, Joshi, and Kumar (2020) found an increase in public capital formation along with easy availability of institutional credit from the early 2000s, which have '*crowded in*' private household investment and revived agricultural growth. Policy support and technological innovations have also encouraged farmers to diversify to horticulture and livestock activities, thereby contributing to high productivity (Singh, 2023). A notable progress in the development of allied activities is reported from Maharashtra, North East region, Himachal Pradesh, Madhya Pradesh, Odisha, and Bihar.

7.1.2 *Objectives*

Against this backdrop, we undertake a state-wise estimation of TFP in agriculture (crop sector) to analyse its contribution to output growth and subsequently address the question of whether technological advancements have contributed to regional convergence. Given large inter-state differentials in the endowment of natural resources (land, soil, rainfall), labour and capital use and public priority to invest in irrigation and technology, we hypothesise that technology diffusion may be slow across the states. The analysis can offer new insights into the technological spread and constraints that farmers face. It may also underline the importance of technological diffusion over capital accumulation, as the latter is considered a prime factor in achieving higher growth. According to Miller and Upadhyaya (2002), the test for convergence in TFP may also be useful in providing evidence on the public and private nature of the technology. In case it is a public good, then it can transit boundaries fast and we find convergence in TFP.

[4] According to Pattanayak et al. (2021), the two databases showed consistent results but a re-look is required due to serious omissions in the results viz. failure to capture an increased reliance on irrigation adequately and the effects of climatic variations (rainfall) on TFP growth.

The extant literature on the convergence hypothesis shows mixed results. Regional convergence is tested based on either partial productivity measures (land or labour productivity) or per capita income. To quote, Balaji and Pal's (2014) found a narrowing of land productivity gaps, whereas labour productivity showed little regional convergence from 1990 to 2011. However, the average speed of convergence remained unchanged during the 1990 and 2000s, with some improvement in its speed from 2005 to 2011. A few states that were initially lagging showed catching up with more productive states. The persistence of productivity gaps is explained by different agro-climatic conditions, access to irrigation and levels of farm mechanisation in each state. The study suggested that regions that are way behind should be identified so that a targeted public policy can be adopted. The policy should be supportive of marginal and small farmers and encourage sustainable practices for faster convergence. Increased investments and technology adoption are a must for the lagging states.

Based on Net State Domestic Product, Kaur and Dhillon (2016) found that out of 24 states in India, only seven displayed a tendency towards convergence, and the remaining showed considerable divergence. From 1980–81 to 2011–12, the agriculture income has risen faster in northern states viz. Punjab, Haryana, and Western Uttar Pradesh, mainly due to the Central and respective state governments' initiatives in providing irrigation water, use of high-yielding varieties at subsidised rates, consolidation of land holdings, and foodgrain procurement. These factors explained a widening of regional disparities in farm income during the seventies and eighties. Again, large inter-state differentials in farm income were reported in Basu and Misra (2022) based on a consistent time series of average real farm income per cultivator across 18 major Indian states for 1987–88, 1993–94, 1999–2000, 2004–05, 2007–08, 2009–10, and 2011–12. Similar results are noted in Balaji and Gopinath (2023) based on household income across 599 districts from three pan-India NSS situation assessment surveys (2003, 2013, and 2019). The authors found that among states, Punjab, Haryana, Kerala, West Bengal, and Tamil Nadu held the top position in terms of real farm income per cultivator in 2011–12. In terms of the average annual growth rate of real farm income per cultivator between 2004–05 and 2011–12, the top five states were Rajasthan, Tamil Nadu, Kerala, West Bengal, and Haryana. The average annual farm income in the top five states in 2011–12 was Rs. 1,04,831 in real terms. The corresponding figure for the bottom five states was only Rs. 26,408. The authors found some evidence for farm income convergence, but this tendency did not change state rankings drastically, especially at the top of the ranked list of states. Other than Haryana, none of the states at the top of the ranked list, initiated market-oriented reforms, suggesting that the agriculture marketing system reforms might not have been beneficial to average farmers.

The conditional convergence model used to capture spatial spillovers shows farm incomes have been converging but at slower rates and among farmers in the left tail of the income distribution. The farm income growth from agriculture and livestock is explained by irrigation infrastructure, crop diversification, and distance to the urban market, thus explaining spatial income disparities. Returns to these factors are higher for middle-income farmers than for the rich or poor. Another important finding is that the spatial spillovers, likely from technological change, captured in the residuals also had a positive impact on farm incomes. According to the authors, connecting the poorest to the markets, strengthening infrastructure, promoting diversification for the middle-income groups, and nudging high-income farmers towards value chains can improve growth convergence.

We use the TFP estimate, which is a better measure to test regional convergence. Following is the structure of the paper. In section II, we delineate the methodological approach to the estimation of TFP and its spatial convergence along with details on the database utilised. Section III provides historical trends and patterns in TFP across 17 major states along with its contribution to output growth for the overall period from 1981–82 to 2019–20. Section IV presents results and discussions on inter-state convergence in TFP and provides estimates on the speed of convergence over the select time period. The last section concludes and draws policy implications.

7.2 Methodological Approach and Database

7.2.1 Total Factor Productivity

Estimation of TFP in agriculture involves various methodological approaches. Researchers often choose methods based on the availability of data, the nature of the agricultural system, and the specific objectives taken. Quite often, the estimates fail to match due to the use of different methodologies and sources of data but they are useful in capturing the trends. We have used the Data Envelopment Analysis (DEA)-based Malmquist productivity index, which has been widely used in the literature for estimating the TFP change over time of various economic activities (Ray, 2004; Watkins et al., 2014). In brief, the DEA approach is a non-parametric method under the frontier approach. It is extensively found useful because it makes (a) the productivity and efficiency estimates easy to compute and parameter-free, (b) does not involve restrictive assumptions regarding economic behaviour, such as cost minimisation or profit maximisation as found in other techniques viz. growth accounting approach, and (c) does not execute any functional form on the production function (Charnes et al., 1978).

The methodology is directed to frontiers rather than central tendencies (Seiford & Thrall, 1990) and attempts to measure the productivity and efficiency of Decision-Making Units (DMUs)/firms through linear programming techniques, which 'envelop' observed input–output vectors as tightly as possible (Boussofiane et al., 1991). The original model was applicable when technologies were characterised by constant returns to scale and all firms operate at an optimal scale (Coelli, 1996). However, imperfect competition may cause a firm not to operate at optimal scale. The best production frontier is derived using the observed input–output points and then the firms/regions are compared to the best practice frontier. It's another important advantage is that it does not require data on prices of input (or output). DEA can also be applied in the case of a small sample size. However, its main limitation is that the results are highly sensitive to outliers and measurement errors. The productivity estimates are sensitive to data noise and outliers and can suffer from the problem of 'unusual' weights that are higher or lower than expected when aggregating inputs to measure TFP. Results are also affected by data characteristics and quality issues. The output-oriented model is estimated under the assumption of constant returns to scale. The state-wise analysis is undertaken from 1981–82 to 2019–20. The output index is constructed using the value of output from the crop sector (foodgrains, pulses, oilseeds, fibres, horticulture, sugarcane, etc.). The selected inputs include power consumption in agriculture, net irrigated area, fertiliser consumption, and labour employed. Annexure Table 7.1 provides a description of inputs used and output to measure the TFP index in each of the 17 major states of India.

7.2.2 *Regional Convergence*

As mentioned, the use of HYVs was uneven, adopted in the northern states from mid-sixties, and in due course penetrated to the southern and western parts of the country. To what extent does technology spread pan India is tested using the convergence hypothesis based on the neo-classical growth models, propounded by Solow (1956) and Swan (1956). Following Barro (1991), Barro, and Sala-i-Martin (1995), the following models are used.

7.2.3 *Sigma (Σ) Convergence*

Sigma convergence is when the cross-sectional variance of the log value of TFP or income per capita falls over time. A declining trend in the standard deviation indicates the presence of sigma convergence, and if otherwise, it is a case of sigma divergence, i.e. more dispersion.

7.2.4 *Absolute Beta (B) Convergence*

Following Solow (1957), β-convergence is when poor countries grow faster on average than rich countries. Under the hypothesis of unconditional (absolute beta convergence), all countries or regions tend to converge to a common steady state. In other words, countries or regions converge to the same level of income per worker or TFP in the long run. In contrast, conditional beta convergence may imply that a country or a region is converging to different steady states, but a country further below its steady state will grow faster (Gutierrez, 2000b).

The unconditional absolute beta convergence is estimated using a cross-sectional regression of time-averaged growth rates on initial levels of TFP. An inverse relationship points to the fact that the poorer states/regions grow faster than the richer ones. The following model explains it.

$$\frac{\left[lnln\left(y_{i,t+T}\right) - lnln\left(y_{i,t}\right)\right]}{T} = \alpha - \left(1 - e^{-T}\right)\left(\frac{1}{T}\right)\left[ln\left(y_{i,t}\right)\right] + u_{t,i}$$

where $y_{i,t}$ and $y_{i,t+T}$ are the initial and last year's values of TFP, T is the length of the period, and i represents different states. The absolute beta convergence is tested for the overall period and four sub-periods. The equation can be represented as:

$$\Delta y_{i,t,t+T} = \alpha + blnY_{i,t} + \in_{i,t}$$

where,

$$\Delta y_{i,t,t+T} = \frac{\left[lnln\left(y_{i,t+T}\right) - lnln\left(y_{i,t}\right)\right]}{T}$$

And,

$$b = -(1 - e^{-T})(1/T)$$

If the regression coefficient turns out to be negative and is statistically significant, i.e. if b < 0, it is the case of absolute beta convergence. This may indicate that the states with lower initial levels of TFP are growing faster than the ones having higher initial levels of it. Equating the coefficient of $lnln\left(y_{i,t}\right)$ with $-(1 - e^{-T})$ (1/T) and solving for β, we estimate the speed of convergence. It is β = -(1/T) ln (bT + 1), where 'b' represents the value of the slope coefficient in the regression model.

7.2.5 *Conditional Beta (Β) Convergence*

Existing tests for conditional beta convergence regress the growth rate of real TFP onto the initial value of real TFP and other control variables viz. fertiliser use, trade intensity, public investment, etc. According to Miller and Upadhyay (2002), the use of panel data allows the estimation of convergence to different steady states since the intercept responds to fixed effects. It may, therefore, not require additional explanatory variables. In other words, the panel data approach controls for state and time-fixed effects. It accommodates differences across regions and allows different steady states for each region, hence transforming into a test of conditional convergence, conditional on those fixed effects across regions. The estimated regression model has the following form.

$$g_{tfp\,it} = lntfp_{it} - lntfp_{it-1} = \alpha + \beta_{tfp} lntfp_{it-1} + \epsilon_{tfp\,it}$$

where, $g_{tfp\,it}$ is the annual growth rate in TFP from (t-1) to t across the states. The tfp_{it-1} is TFP in the previous period (t-1) in each state, and $\epsilon_{tfp\,it}$ is the error term. The annual rate of growth in the pooled (time series—cross-section) regression estimates $g_{tfp\,it}$ as the logarithmic difference in TFP between 1990–1999 and 1981–1989; 2000–2009 and 1990–1999; 2019–2009 and 2000–2009 at the state level. The corresponding lagged logarithms of TFP are for 1981–1989, 1990–1999, and 2000–2009. The Modified Wald test is done to check the presence of heteroskedasticity. The model did not show the presence of heteroskedasticity. The analysis is done for the overall period and the four sub-periods: 1981–1989, 1990–1999, 2000–2009, and 2010–2019. The 17 states included in the analysis are grouped into four regions. The northern region includes Punjab, Haryana, Himachal Pradesh, Uttar Pradesh, Jammu and Kashmir. The southern region consists of Andhra Pradesh, Karnataka, Kerala, and Tamil Nadu. The western region includes Gujarat, Madhya Pradesh, Maharashtra, and Rajasthan and the eastern region comprises Assam, Bihar, Odisha, and West Bengal.

7.3 Results and Discussions

7.3.1 Inter-State Trends in TFP

Table 7.1 presents the decadal growth rates in the output, inputs, and TFP, along with the share of TFP in output growth at all of India and across 17 major states over the past four decades. In India, the GVO per NSA (crop sector) registered a growth rate of 2.27 and 3.07% during the first and second decades, i.e. 1981–1989 and 1990–99. However, the average growth rate declined to 2.62% during the third decade (2000–2009), followed by a decline to 1.81% from 2010 to 2019. In the case of the input, we observe a lower rate of growth at 0.92% during the eighties and negative during the nineties decades, followed by an increase to 0.44% during the 2000s and then a significant decline to 2.48%.

During the last four decades, the average annual rate of growth in TFP has hovered around 1.05% only. Literature indicates an increase in TFP growth during the 2010 is due to a significant increase in horticulture and livestock activities. Since we have considered only the crop sector in the analysis, our estimates may not be strictly comparable with Sengupta et al. (2023), Krishna and Meenakshi (2022), and Fuglie and Rada (2018). However, we find one commonality in the literature, i.e. the share of TFP in output growth remains high, varying from 30 to 100% across the states, averaging at 41.42%.

The state-level analysis reveals significant variations in the share of TFP in output growth. The contribution of TFP to output growth is almost 100% in Kerala, very high in Assam, and J&K, (71% each), Odisha (68%), Punjab (61.0%), Tamil Nadu (59),

Table 7.1 Average annual growth in the output, input and TFP indices and % share of TFP in output growth from 1981–82 to 2019–20

State	Output growth	Input growth	TFP growth	%Contribution of TFP to output growth
ANDHRA PRADESH	2.71	–0.52	1.10	40.49
ASSAM	1.45	–0.25	1.04	71.61
BIHAR	3.29	0.60	1.01	30.59
GUJARAT	3.51	0.02	1.06	30.25
HARYANA	2.70	–0.36	1.05	38.88
HIMACHAL PRADESH	3.18	0.67	1.06	33.24
JAMMU & KASHMIR	1.52	1.79	1.08	71.26
KARNATAKA	2.57	–0.15	1.11	42.99
KERALA	0.63	–2.03	1.05	100.0
MADHYA PRADESH	3.42	–0.17	1.08	31.55
MAHARASHTRA	3.53	0.60	1.07	30.17
ODISHA	1.56	0.61	1.06	68.29
PUNJAB	1.73	–0.98	1.05	61.07
RAJASTHAN	3.25	0.09	1.04	32.10
TAMILNADU	1.77	–1.60	1.05	59.43
UTTAR PRADEH	1.91	–0.04	1.05	54.93
WEST BENGAL	2.48	0.27	1.09	43.87
All INDIA	2.56	–0.01	1.06	41.42

Note The variables in TFP estimation are taken per NSA

and Uttar Pradesh (54.93%), respectively. Among all the states, these states, along with Andhra Pradesh, Karnataka, and West Bengal, have more than 40% contribution of TFP to output growth, between 20 and 40% in Bihar, Gujarat, Haryana, and Himachal Pradesh. The fluctuating trends, along with the lower rate of TFP growth at the disaggregate level, do not augur well for sustainable growth of agriculture. It is essential to increase investment in agricultural R&D (in both public and private sectors) to accelerate TFP and its growth. An improvement in TFP in Indian agriculture is crucial to meet the sustainable development goals of zero hunger and no poverty by 2030. Among the states, Assam, Jammu & Kashmir, Kerala, Odisha, Punjab, and Tamil Nadu experienced lower growth rates in the output index from 1981 to 2019. Andhra Pradesh and Madhya Pradesh had the highest growth rate (2.60 to 5.73%) during 2010–2019. The progress was not satisfactory during the nineties as most of the states showed a declining trend. The revival in growth was visible in the 2000s in Gujarat, Odisha, and Rajasthan, respectively. Like the output index, growth in the input index too depicted significant inter-state differences and fluctuating trends over time. By and large, the growth in input index in most states exhibits either stagnating or declining trends, indicating efficiency in the input use and, hence, scope to attain higher productivity levels.

As shown in Fig. 7.1, a higher contribution of TFP to output growth is found in the recent decade at 60%, which indicates that technological change is the key driver behind the growth in Indian agriculture. It was much higher during the eighties when technological diffusion was at its peak, followed by a decline during the nineties. The 1990s coincided with a massive cutdown in public investment in agriculture (including irrigation), which negatively impacted private investment and culminated in an agrarian crisis in many states. Significant increase in budgetary outlays towards agriculture and R&D from the mid-2000s along with various flagship programmes such as the National Horticulture Mission, National Food Security Mission, and adequate flow of institutional credit revived private investment and growth (Kumar et al., 2023). These initiatives helped to revive Indian agriculture in later years.

It is important to highlight the contribution of maize, fruits-vegetables, and fibres in accelerating the growth in the crop sector. The gross value of output (GVO) in agriculture (crop sector) in total GVO from agriculture and allied activities has gradually declined from 70 to 54% over the period. This decline in the share is mainly on account of a gradual decline in the share of some coarse cereals and an increase in the share of livestock activities. A bifurcation of the GVO within the crop sector shows that, for various crops, there is a high share of fruits and vegetables at 28%, almost equivalent to the share of cereals in GVO. The remaining share (45%) is that of pulses, oilseeds, sugarcane, spices, and medicinal plants. The area share of cereals in the total cropped area has also declined by 10 percentage points from 59.2% in TE 1952 to 49.4% in TE 2021 (Annex Table 7.2).

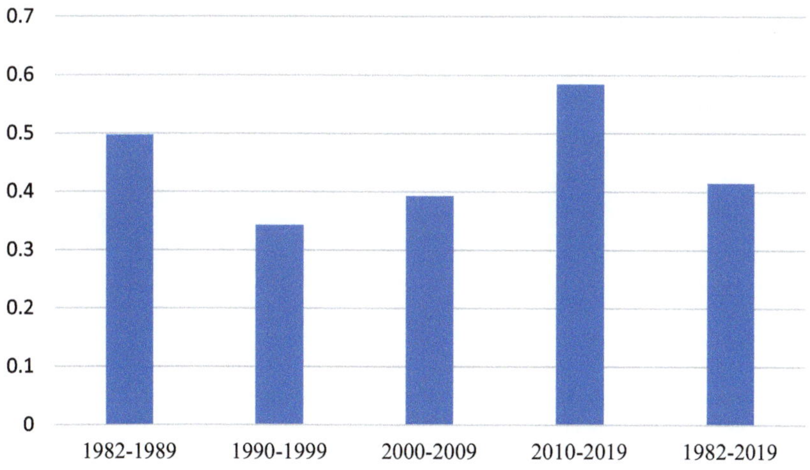

Fig. 7.1 Contribution of TFP to output growth in India (%)

In value terms at 2011–12 prices, fruits-vegetables were valued at Rs. 30,752 crores in TE 1952, which jumped to Rs. 381,364 crores in TE 2020–21. A significant increase in the value of fruits and vegetables as compared to the value of wheat and paddy has been noticed since the early nineties. In terms of the share of fruits-vegetables in the value of crop output, it has more than doubled from 12.7 to 27.8%, while that of coarse grains and pulses have decreased from 9.5% and 11.7% to 3.8% and 5.3%, respectively. The share of cereals in GVO has declined from 33.6% during the early nineties to 27.4% by TE 2020–21, mainly on account of paddy.

Rising per capita income, changing dietary patterns, growing urbanisation and health awareness have led to a significant increase in the consumption of fruits-vegetables. A market-driven change led by private sector investments in R&D and government initiatives under the National Horticulture Mission may have encouraged farmers to diversify cropping pattern towards high-value horticulture crops. Figure 7.2 shows the average annual rate of growth in the value of output of major crop categories over five periods from 1950–51 to 2020–21. There has been an increase in growth in gross value of output (GVO) of maize and horticulture from 1.75 and 3.06% during the seventies-eighties to 3.6% each during the 2010s, respectively. The maximum growth is identified in fibres from 2.09 to 11.2% over the same period followed by negative growth during the last decade.

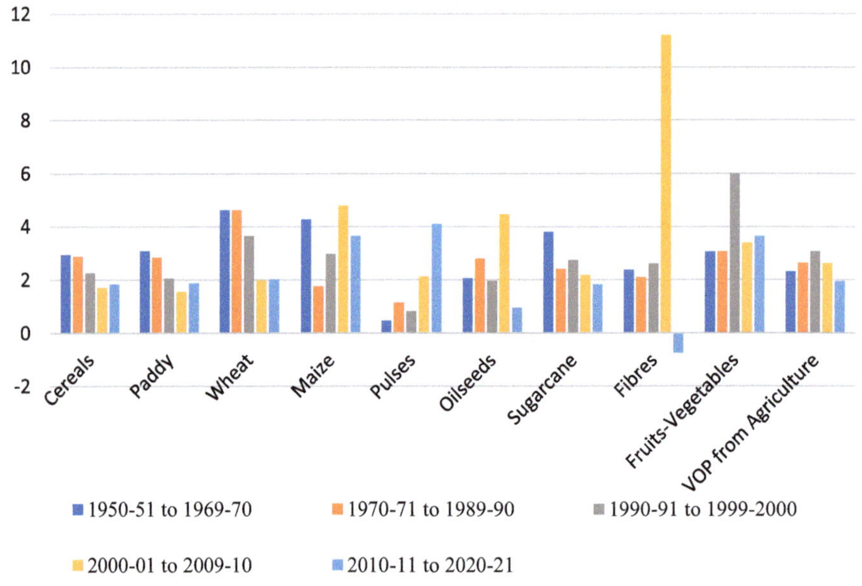

Fig. 7.2 Average annual rate of growth in value of agriculture output (Crop sector) at 2011–2 prices (CAGR %) from 1950–51 to 2020–21

7.3.2 *Empirical Results of Inter-State Productivity Convergence*

Figure 7.3 reveals trends in the value of sigma convergence in the TFP index across 17 Indian states. The study period from 1981 to 2019 shows large inter-state differences in TFP. When divided into four sub-periods of 10 years each, it shows an increasing trend in TFP during the eighties followed by a declining trend in it during the nineties. The decade 2000s again showed large variations, and after that, an increase from 0.46 in 2010 to 0.60 in 2016 followed by a decline to 0.20 by 2019. This may imply that there has been a sigma divergence in TFP across the states during the eighties and nineties and, subsequently, a tendency towards convergence. Compared to 2000–09, no definite pattern in productivity convergence is visible during 2010–19.

Another way of testing initial indications of beta convergence is unconditional beta convergence. Table 7.2 presents results from cross-section regression results for each sub-period and for the overall period. A negative and statistically significant coefficient represents convergence during this period. Results show negative and significant coefficients during all periods, from 1981 to 2019, implying that states with low TFP did catch up with those with higher productivity. An improvement is visible from 2000s as the coefficient is negative with a slight improvement in the annual speed of convergence from 0.077 to 0.093. In each period, the speed of convergence is considerably low, close to 1%. The analysis provides some evidence of unconditional convergence in TFP in Indian states, as the coefficient is negative and statistically significant, albeit at a slow rate. The overall period from 1981 to 2019 fails to show a high speed of convergence, though the coefficient is negative and significant (–0.031).

The conditional convergence result is like the unconditional beta convergence result. As shown in Table 7.3, the regression coefficient is negative (0.12) and statistically significant at a 1% level of significance.[5] These results validate Balaji and Gopinath (2023) that the spatial spillovers, likely from technological change and other factors, positively impact farm incomes. The inter-state disparities can be lessened if the government invests in R&D, irrigation infrastructure and connects the poorest (mainly eastern states) to the markets.

7.4 Summing up and Implications

This study estimates total factor productivity (TFP) in agriculture and its contribution to output growth in all of India and in each of the major 17 states from 1981–82 to 2018–19. This analysis is followed by an estimation of inter-state convergence in TFP to analyse the spatial impact of technology diffusion. TFP estimations are based

[5] It is expected that the early adopters of technology viz. northern and southern states would have higher level of convergence in comparison to the western and eastern regions. A separate analysis is not undertaken due to fewer number of observations in the panel.

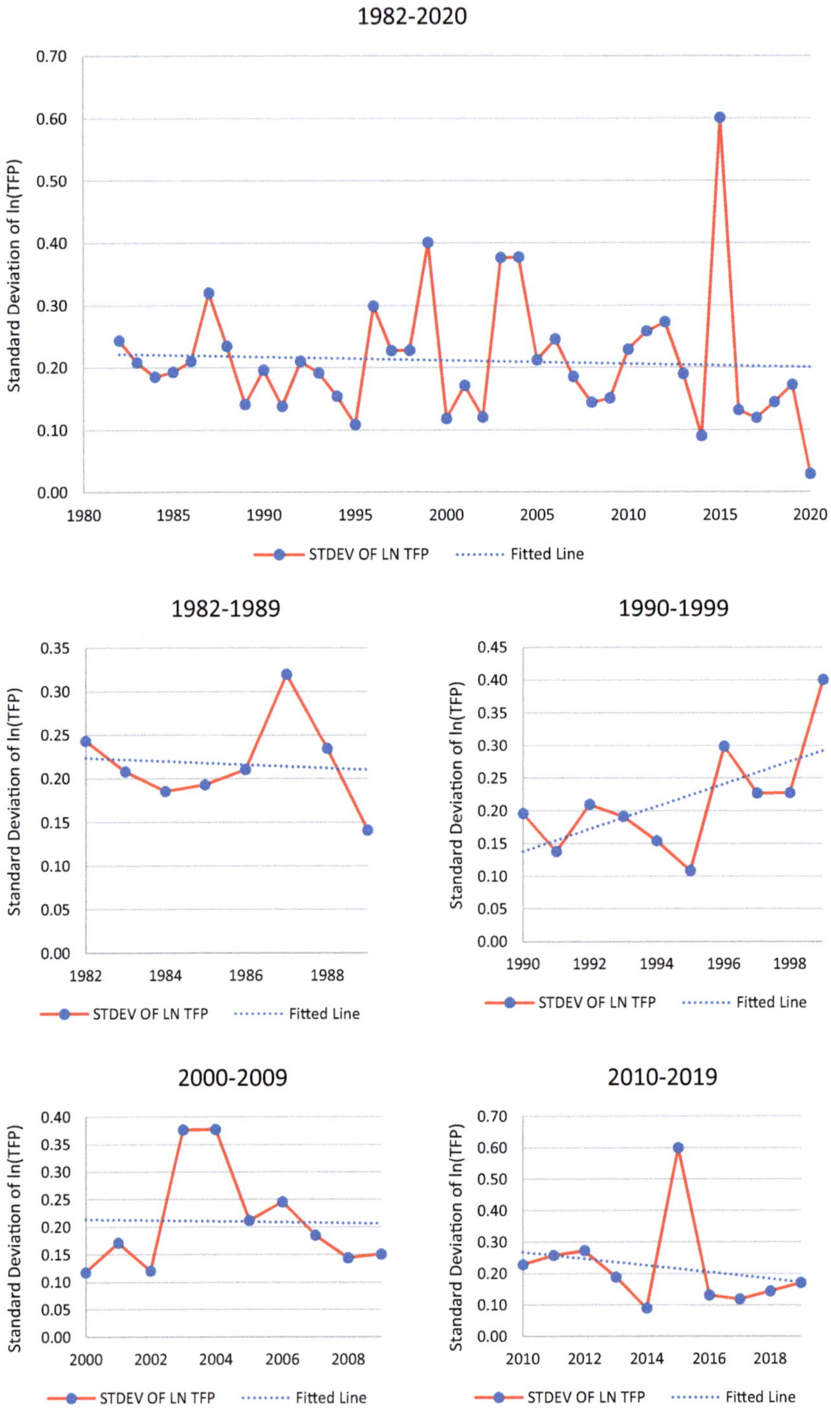

Fig. 7.3 Convergence in TFP based on sigma convergence for overall period and decade wise

Table 7.2 Unconditional beta convergence in TFP (Cross-section model)

Time period	Constant	Coefficient	Speed of convergence	R-Square	No. of observations
1982–1989	0.022* (0.006)	–0.141* (0.018)	0.094	0.80	17
1990–1999	–0.011 (0.010)	–0.117* (0.019)	0.077	0.25	17
2000–2009	0.015* (0.004)	–0.154* (0.029)	0.093	0.64	17
2010–2019	–0.004 (0.004)	–0.136* (0.008)	0.085	0.81	17
1982–2019	0.000 (0.002)	–0.031* (0.004)	0.021	0.73	17

Note Values in parentheses represent robust standard errors. *, **, and *** denote significance at 1%, 5%, and 10% levels, respectively

Table 7.3 Conditional beta convergence in TFP (1981–2019)

Dependent variable: Annual Rate of Growth in TFP		
Variables	Fixed effects	Std. Err.
β_{tfp}	–0.12* (–91.2)	0.013
Constant	0.005* (5.48)	0.001
Sigma_u	0.003	
Sigma_e	0.005	
rho	0.214	
F test that all u_i = 0: F(16, 33)	0.81	Prob > F = 0.66
R-square (within, between, overall)	0.99, 0.62, 0.99	
No. of observations	51	
No. of groups	17	

Note Values in parentheses represent the t-values. *, **, and *** denote significance at 1%, 5%, and 10% levels, respectively

on the Malmquist Index, while inter-state convergence is analysed using the sigma and beta convergence approaches.

The trends in the output, input, and TFP index exhibit large temporal as well as spatial variations. The TFP growth is estimated at 1.06% per annum from 1981–2019 but its contribution to agricultural output is low at 41.42% during this period. Several states exhibit higher TFP growth and its significant contribution (more than 40%) to output growth. A higher contribution (60%) of TFP to output growth during the recent decade has been made possible due to government support through the adoption of HYVs, increase in public investments in irrigation, research, and extension services, rural infrastructure, procurement of foodgrains at pre-announced prices, and demand driven growth in horticulture crops.

The analysis indicates that technology transmission from the northern states to a few southern states has been uneven but it has enabled India to achieve higher productivity growth and food security. However, wide inter-state differentials in productivity growth may not help maintain the per capita availability of food products. Policy interventions should be designed and targeted as per the requirements of technology, infrastructure development, and research to augment TFP growth and its contribution to output growth. Concerted efforts are needed to promote practices that enhance productivity growth without much impact on natural resources. Fluctuations in public outlays towards R&D constrain the delivery of consistent research output. There is a need to maintain smooth growth in the allocation of research resources and minimise regional imbalances Also, efforts are needed to attract private investment in agricultural R&D, and a sound framework for public–private partnership in agricultural research and extension needs to be developed and promoted. A sound policy environment that promotes technological innovations and their adoption by farmers in each state is essential to foster higher productivity and sustainable agricultural growth. Further, the evidence on the convergence of TFP growth across states is not much visible, with a low speed of convergence at 1%. The analysis points towards a need to promote inclusive and sustainable growth, prioritise investments, infrastructure development, and technological advances and their wider spread in the lagging states.

Acknowledgements The authors are grateful to Prof. K L Krishna and Mr. Naveen Kumar for providing critical comments. We also thank the workshop participants for their suggestions on improving the paper.

Annexure Tables

See Annexure Tables 7.4, 7.5 and 7.6.

Table 7.4 Definitions, sources, and descriptive statistics of variables used for TFP measurement

Outputs and Inputs used to measure total factor productivity (TFP)				
Variable	Description	Source	Mean	Std-Deviation
Value of output from crop sector Rs. crores at 2011 prices	Crops include all cereals, pulses, oilseeds, fibres, fruits, and vegetables	National Accounts Statistics, MOSPI	51,195.36	3,175,141.7
Electricity consumption	Consumption of electricity in agriculture in gigawatts	State-wise Consumption of Electricity for Agriculture purposes; Agricultural Statistics at a Glance, various issues; state-wise land use statistics, Directorate of Economics and Statistics, Ministry of Agriculture & Farmers Welfare, GoI	5,493.67	6,567.55
Net irrigated area	Net irrigated area in '000 hectares	State-wise land use statistics, Directorate of Economics and Statistics, Ministry of Agriculture & Farmers Welfare, GoI	3,218.74	2,966.13
Fertiliser consumption	Fertiliser consumption in '000 tonnes	Agricultural Statistics at a Glance, various issues, Directorate of Economics and Statistics, GoI	1,002.52	918.06
Labour	Number of persons employed in agriculture in 000's	Annual reports of Periodic Labour Force Survey (PLFS) for 2017/2018, 2018/2019, 2019/2020; NSSO reports on key indicators of employment and unemployment in India (2011/2012); Employment and Unemployment Situation in India 2004/2005; and NSS surveys/reports of previous rounds/years, Ministry of Statistics &Programme Implementation, GoI	10,951	7,947

Table 7.5 Value of output, cropped area, and percentage share of crops at all India

Year	VOP at 2011–12 price (INR Crore)						Share (%)					
	TE 1952–53	TE 1969–70	TE 1989–90	TE 1999–00	TE 2009–10	TE 2020–21	TE 1952–53	TE 1969–70	TE 1989–90	TE 1999–00	TE 2009–10	TE 2020–21
1. cereals	66,945	1,21,029	2,10,843	2,70,051	2,98,622	3,76,453	27.7	31.9	33.6	32.0	28.5	27.4
1.a. paddy	36,180	65,651	1,11,171	1,42,878	1,54,926	1,91,670	15.0	17.3	17.7	16.9	14.8	14.0
1.b. wheat	8,984	23,249	63,239	90,949	1,01,591	1,32,889	3.7	6.1	10.1	10.8	9.7	9.7
1.c. coarse cereals	23,055	33,734	37,216	36,231	42,203	51,894	9.5	8.9	5.9	4.3	4.0	3.8
1.c.1. jowar	11,131	15,971	18,548	13,257	11,415	7,030	4.6	4.2	3.0	1.6	1.1	0.5
1.c.2. bajra	2,782	4,843	5,899	6,898	8,088	9,452	1.2	1.3	0.9	0.8	0.8	0.7
1.c.3. maize	3,080	6,544	8,872	12,302	19,635	31,251	1.3	1.7	1.4	1.5	1.9	2.3
2. pulses	28,244	35,055	40,250	44,463	47,319	72,181	11.7	9.2	6.4	5.3	4.5	5.3
3. oilseeds	20,417	30,680	58,081	78,352	93,070	1,15,897	8.5	8.1	9.3	9.3	8.9	8.4
4. sugarcane	10,557	19,298	30,807	42,617	49,094	67,761	4.4	5.1	4.9	5.0	4.7	4.9
5. fibres	10,979	17,413	26,587	36,274	64,897	74,546	4.5	4.6	4.2	4.3	6.2	5.4
6. fruits & vegetables	30,752	51,624	1,03,984	1,73,488	2,43,970	3,81,364	12.7	13.6	16.6	20.5	23.3	27.8
Value of output from agriculture (crop sector)	2,41,622	3,79,693	6,26,875	8,44,762	10,47,184	13,73,220	100.0	100.0	100.0	100.0	100.0	100.0

	Cropped area (million hectare)						Share (%)					
Year	TE 1952–53	TE 1969–70	TE 1989–90	TE 1999–00	TE 2009–10	TE 2020–21	TE 1952–53	TE 1969–70	TE 1989–90	TE 1999–00	TE 2009–10	TE 2020–21
1. cereals	79.6	99.8	102.1	101.6	99.7	98.4	59.2	61.7	57.2	53.5	51.6	49.4
1.a. paddy	30.2	37.0	40.9	44.5	43.8	44.3	22.5	22.9	22.9	23.4	22.7	22.2
1.b. wheat	9.7	15.9	23.6	27.2	28.1	30.8	7.2	9.8	13.2	14.3	14.5	15.4
1.c. coarse cereals	39.7	46.9	37.6	29.9	27.9	23.3	29.5	29.0	21.1	15.7	14.4	11.7
1.c.1. jowar	16.4	18.6	15.1	10.3	7.7	4.4	12.2	11.5	8.5	5.4	4.0	2.2
1.c.2. bajra	9.8	12.5	10.6	9.4	9.1	7.4	7.3	7.7	5.9	4.9	4.7	3.7
1.c.3. maize	3.4	5.7	5.8	6.3	8.2	9.5	2.5	3.5	3.2	3.3	4.2	4.8
2. pulses	19.2	22.0	22.6	22.5	23.0	28.7	14.3	13.6	12.7	11.8	11.9	14.4
3. oilseeds	11.2	15.0	21.6	25.5	26.7	26.9	8.3	9.3	12.1	13.4	13.8	13.5
4. sugarcane	1.8	2.4	3.4	4.1	4.6	4.8	1.3	1.5	1.9	2.1	2.4	2.4
5. fruits & vegetables				9.6	12.6	17.2				5.0	6.5	8.6
Gross cropped area (GCA)	134.3	161.8	178.4	190.0	193.2	199.2	100.0	100.0	100.0	100.0	100.0	100.0

Note for TE: * Fourth Advance Estimate of cropped area; GCA for 2020–21 relates to 2018–2019 as latest estimates for land utilisation are available till 2018–19.
Source Agricultural Statistics at a Glance, Minister of Agriculture and Farmers Welfare, GoI

Table 7.6 Annual rate of growth in the value of output in agriculture (crop sector) 2011–12 prices (%)

Year	1. cereals	1.a. paddy	1.b. wheat	1.c. coarse cereals	1.c.1. jowar	1.c.2. bajra	1.c.3. maize	2. pulses	3. oilseeds	4. sugarcane	5. fibres	6. fruits & vegetables	Value of output from agriculture
1950–51 to 1969–70	2.94	3.08	4.62	1.74	1.76	2.59	4.27	0.46	2.05	3.79	2.37	3.05	2.30
1970–71 to 1989–90	2.87	2.83	4.62	0.55	1.69	–0.05	1.75	1.14	2.79	2.40	2.09	3.06	2.63
1990–91 to 1999–2000	2.25	2.05	3.64	–0.17	–2.83	1.06	2.96	0.83	1.96	2.74	2.61	6.00	3.07
2000–01 to 2009–10	1.71	1.54	1.98	1.67	–0.86	0.80	4.79	2.11	4.46	2.17	11.21	3.39	2.62
2010–11 to 2020–21	1.84	1.87	2.01	1.31	–3.97	0.14	3.65	4.10	0.94	1.82	–0.74	3.63	1.94
1950–51 to 2020–21	2.47	2.34	4.13	0.86	–0.69	1.59	3.15	0.96	2.66	2.62	2.81	4.00	2.57

References

Bathla, S., & D'souza, A. (2015). Inter-sectoral productivity differentials in India: Is convergence achievable? *South Asia Economic Journal, Sage Publications, 16*(1), 82–102.

Bathla, S., Joshi, P.K., Kumar, A. (2020). Agricultural growth and rural poverty reduction in India: Targeting investments and input subsidies, Springer Nature, Singapore (p. 132).

Balaji, S. J., & Pal, S. (2014, December 27). *Agricultural Productivity Growth, Economic and Political Weekly, 49*(52).

Balaji, S. J., & Gopinath, M. (2023). Spatial growth and convergence in Indian agriculture. *Agricultural Economics, 54,* 761–777. https://doi.org/10.1111/agec.12807 Also presented in the Annual Meeting, Agricultural and Applied Economics Association, July 28–30, 2024, New Orleans, LA **335564**.

Barro, R. J. (1991). Economic growth in a cross section of countries. *Quarterly Journal of Economics, 106*, 407–443.

Barro, R. J., & Sala-i-Martin, X. X. (1995). *Economic growth.* McGraw Hill.

Basu, Deepankar, & Misra, Kartik. (2022). An empirical investigation of real farm incomes across Indian states between 1987–88 and 2011–12. *Economics Department Working Paper Series, 320.*

Boussofiane, A., Dyson, R. G., & Thanassoulis, E. (1991). Applied data envelopment analysis. *European Journal of Operations Research, 52*, 1–15.

Chand, Ramesh, Kumar, Praduman, & Kumar, Sant. (2011). Total factor productivity and contribution of research investment to agricultural growth in India. Policy Paper 25, National Centre for Agricultural Economics and Policy Research, New Delhi.

Charnes, A., Cooper, W. W., & Rhodes, E. (1978). Measuring the efficiency of decision making units. *European Journal of Operational Research, 2*, 429–444.

Coelli, T. J. (1996). A guide to DEAP version 2.1: A Data Envelopment Analysis (computer) Program. Working paper no. 8/96. CEPA working papers. Department of Econometrics, University of New England, Australia.

Fuglie, Keith O., & Nicholas, E. Rada. (2018). https://www.ers.usda.gov/data-products/international-agricultural-productivity/

Gutierrez, L. (2000b). Why is agricultural labour productivity higher in some countries than others? Selected paper 2000 Annu¬ al Forida. Meeting of the American Agricultural Economics Association, Tampa, Florida.

Hayami, Y., & Ruttan, V. W. (1985). *Agricultural development: An international perspective* (2nd ed.). Johns Hopkins University Press.

Kannan, E. (2011). Total factor productivity growth and its determinants in Karnataka agriculture, Working Paper 265, Institute for Social and Economic Change, Bangalore.

Kaur and Dhillon. (2016). Disparities in agriculture income across the Indian States, chapter 8 in S. Bathla and A.Dubey (ed) Changing Contours of Indian Agriculture, Investment, Income and Non-farm Employment, Springer 2016.

Krishna, K. L., & Meenakshi, J. V. (2022, September). Agricultural productivity growth and structural transformation in rural India: Some recent evidence. *Journal of Quantitative Economics,* Springer; *The Indian Econometric Society, 20*(1), 277–302.

Kumar, Anjani, Bathla, Seema, & Verma, Smriti. (2023). Revisiting the relationship between Public and Private Capital Formation in Indian Agriculture: A Disaggregated Analysis. *Economic and Political Weekly 58*(32).

Kumar, P., & Rosegrant, M. W. (1994). Productivity and sources of growth for rice in India. *Economic and Political Weekly, 29*, A183–A188.

Mellor, J. W. (1976). The new economics of growth: A strategy for India and the developing world. A Twentieth Century Fund Study. Cornell University Press.

Miller, S. M., & Upadhyay, M. P. (2002). Total factor productivity and the convergence hypothesis. *Journal of Macroeconomics, 24*(2), 267–286.

Parikh, K. S., Ghosh, P. P., & Binswanger-Mkhize, H. P. (2016). Rapid economic growth in India: Technical change in agriculture, irrigation and food security. *The Indian Economic Journal, 64*(1–4), 115–136.

Pattanayak, A., Kumar, K., & Anneboina, L. (2021). Distributional impacts of climate change on agricultural total factor productivity in India. *Journal of the Asia Pacific Economy., 26*, 381–401.

Rada, N. E., & Fuglie, K. O. (2018). New perspectives on farm size and productivity. Food Policy.

Ray, S. C. (2004). *Data envelopment analysis: Theory and techniques for economics and operations research.* Cambridge University Press.

Sedithippa Janarthanan, Balaji & Munisamy, Gopinath. (2023). Spatial growth and convergence in Indian Agriculture, Annual Meeting, July 23–25, Washington D.C. 335564, Agricultural and Applied Economics Association.

Seiford, L. M., & Thrall, R. M. (1990). Recent developments in DEA: The mathematical programming approach to frontier analysis. *Journal of Econometrics, 46*, 7–38.

Sreerupa Sengupta, S., Suganthi, D., & Goldar, B. (2023). Total factor productivity growth in Indian agriculture: Accounting for land quality. *Reserve Bank of India Occasional Papers, 44*(1)

Singh, P. (2023, October 10–13). Challenges in Indian agriculture, memorial lecture presented at the XVI agricultural science congress, National Academy of Agricultural Sciences jointly with the Central Marine Fisheries Research Institute at Kochi.

Solow, R. (1956). A contribution to the theory of economic growth. *Quarterly Journal of Economics, 70*, 65–94.

Solow, R. (1957). Technical change and the aggregate production function. *Review of Economics and Statistics, 39*, 312–320.

Watkins, K. B., Hristovska, T., Mazzanti, R., Wilson, C. E., Jr., & Schmidt, L. (2014). Measurement of technical, allocative, economic, and scale efficiency of rice production in Arkansas using data envelopment analysis. *Journal of Agriculture Applied Economics, 46*(1), 89–106.

Seema Bathla is a professor at the Centre for the Study of Regional Development, Jawaharlal Nehru University.

Chapter 8
Rural Market Imperfections and Land Productivity in India

C. S. C. Sekhar and Namrata Thapa

Abstract Ensuring the viability of farming and increasing farmers' income are the key policy concerns in India at present. For realizing these objectives, the functioning of markets is very critical. Market imperfections can increase the production and transaction costs of farmers and have a crucial bearing on farm income. The inverse relationship (IR) between farm size and land productivity is a manifestation of the imperfections and has become a stylized fact in India over time. The study revisits this issue and, using primary data, examines whether market imperfections still prevail in India, particularly in output, input, factor and credit markets. The results show a prevalence of a strong IR between land productivity and farm size on the output side and farm size and family labour use on the input side. However, intensive use of family labour does not seem to be the only determinant of farm size-productivity relation. The results suggest that Sen's labour dualism theory, together with imperfections in land and credit markets, can offer useful insights. Results of our study point to the prevalence of surplus family labour on small farms even after a decade of enacting a major employment guarantee program (MGNREGS) and continuing limited access to institutional credit of small farmers. Thus, particularly for marginal and small farmers, reforming land lease markets to enable easier access to land, providing better access to institutional credit and improving literacy levels to facilitate mobility to other occupations are needed to address some of the observed imperfections.

Keywords Farm income · Farm profitability · Farm size-productivity relation · India · Market imperfections · Rural markets

This is a modified version of "Rural market imperfections in India: Revisiting old debates with new evidence" by Sekhar, C. S. C. & Thapa, N. (2023). *Development Policy Review*, 41, 12,708. https://doi.org/10.1111/dpr.12708

C. S. C. Sekhar (✉)
Agricultural Economics Research Unit, Institute of Economic Growth, Delhi, India
e-mail: csekhar@iegindia.org

N. Thapa
NITI Aayog, Delhi, India
e-mail: nmrtthapa@gmail.com

D. Maiti et al. (eds.), *75 Years of Growth, Development and Productivity in India*, India Studies in Business and Economics, https://doi.org/10.1007/978-981-97-8054-9_8

JEL Codes Q12 · Q13 · Q18

8.1 Introduction

Ensuring a decent level of income for farmers is a current policy priority in India. Some of the pathways for realizing this objective are increasing productivity, reducing the cost of production and ensuring higher output prices. These pathways can be used in combination with one another. Most of the policy initiatives adopted from the mid-1960s till 2017 belonged to the first two categories. This resulted in decent agricultural growth. However, the recent thrust of the policy turned, in addition to output price support and some direct income transfers, to allow an increased role for the market.

The economic reforms of the 1990s largely ignored agriculture. As a result, the gap between the income of agricultural and non-agricultural workers increased from Rs 25,398 in 1993–94 to Rs 54,377 by 1999–2000 (NITI Aayog, 2020). In the next ten years, this gap increased further to Rs 1.42 lakh. The small and marginal farmers were largely excluded from the operation of the Agricultural Produce Market Committees (APMC) and output marketing has been a key constraint. The Electronic National Agricultural Market (e-NAM) and the now repealed 'Farm Laws' aim to enable a free play of markets in Indian agriculture. Given this recent policy thrust on the output markets, the functioning of factors (land, labour, capital) and input markets also assumes renewed significance. Any imperfection in these markets will manifest in the form of an imperfection in the output markets, which will have a crucial bearing on farm income.

The inverse relationship (IR) between land size and land productivity on one hand and the direct relationship between land size and labour productivity on the other have now become *stylized facts* in India. However, many changes have occurred in Indian agriculture since the mid-1990s. A severe stagnation had set in during the mid-1990s, followed by a revival from 2004 (Chand et al., 2007). Many policy changes, particularly relating to the labour market, have also occurred during this period. A large rural employment program, MGNREGS, was launched in 2007 to provide legally guaranteed employment for a minimum of 100 days in a year to each adult at a statutorily fixed wage rate. In spite of such major changes, there have been very few studies in the last two and a half decades exploring the effect of these changes on the functioning of agricultural markets.

In the backdrop of these changes in agricultural performance and policies, what is the current status of IR? What are the possible factors driving the change, if any? We attempt to address these issues by drawing upon an in-depth primary survey in four major states of India. The chapter is organized as follows: Sect. 8.2 discusses the various dimensions and interconnectedness of imperfections in rural markets through a detailed review of the literature. Section 8.3 discusses the objectives, materials and methods of the present study. Section 8.4 presents an overview of the sample region.

In Sect. 8.5, the analysis and the main results of the study are presented, followed by conclusions in the last section.

8.2 Rural Market Imperfections in India: Review of Past Literature

Rural markets in developing countries are complex and function far less effectively than what the standard textbook models assume (Barrett & Mutambatsere, 2008; De Janvry et al., 1991; Harriss-White, 1999; Holden et al., 2001). The inverse relationship (IR) between land size and land productivity and the direct relationship between land size and labour productivity have become *stylized facts* in India (Khusro, 1964; Sen, 1962, 1966; Rudra, 1968; Bhagawati-Chakravarthy, 1969; Srinivasan, 1972; Bardhan, 1973, 1989; Heltberg, 1998; Basu, 1983; Bhalla, 1986; Bhalla & Roy, 1988; Chand et al., 2011, Deininger et al., 2018). The IR was initially puzzling as there was considerable evidence in favour of constant returns to scale of farm production in different countries (e.g., Hayami & Ruttan, 1970; Berry & Cline, 1979; Fulginiti & Perrin, 1993). If IR existed and factor markets were perfect, would not farmers be able to subdivide their lands, improve land productivity and eventually eliminate IR (Heltberg, 1998)? Thus, *imperfections* in other factor markets emerged as possible explanations for IR (in land productivity). The first strand of this literature focussed on imperfections only in the labour market. Chayanov (1966), Sen (1962), Carter (1984), Carter and Wiebe (1990) found that peasant households applied family labour more intensively because the opportunity cost of their time is low. Sen (1962) proposed 'labour dualism' to explain this phenomenon. Missing labour markets for women and children, non-clearing labour markets (resulting from wages lower than the reservation wage) and lower skill endowments of rural labour (that prevent them from moving to more productive urban occupations) are some of the factors proposed as possible reasons for the intensive use of family labour on small farms. This, *ceteris paribus,* leads to *higher land productivity*, because of better 'quality' and 'commitment' of family labour (compared to hired labour). However, given the limits to increasing land productivity beyond a certain threshold and, due to better access of large farmers to credit, which results in higher farm investment and mechanization, the *output or income per capita* is expected to be higher on large farms. *Thus, the output per unit of land is inversely proportional, while output per capita is directly proportional to the land size.*

A question then arises as to why the small farmers cannot augment their land through leasing and purchasing, and realize higher per capita incomes? If land and credit markets are efficient, even if there are imperfections in labour markets, the small landholdings with an excess supply of family labour should be able to lease in land and absorb this excess supply (Brandt, 1987). This led to the hypothesis of multiple market failures, as a single market failure is not sufficient to explain the IR. Failure in land markets and possibly credit markets is also necessary, in addition to labour market failure. Thus, theories of multiple market failures evolved (Braverman & Stiglitz, 1982; Heltberg, 1998; Holden & Binswanger, 1998; Skoufias, 1995; Basu, 1983; Feder, 1985; Barrett, 1996; Lamb, 2003; Foster & Rosenzweig, 2010; Binswanger & Deininger, 1997; Wineman & Jayne, 2021; Sheng et al., 2019).

Land market imperfections arise due to sticky operational holdings from imperfections in both lease and sales markets. Imperfections in the lease market may arise due to restrictive land lease legislations, Marshallian inefficiency[1] and transaction costs (Skoufias, 1995 as cited in Heltberg, 1998). On the other hand, imperfections in the land sale market may arise due to legal restrictions on sale; distress sales due to crop failure owing to poor credit and insurance markets; and high land values relative to expected returns from land.[2] Credit markets are also plagued by a number of imperfections in developing countries. Due to the risk and asymmetric information inherent in agriculture, the credit supply to the farm sector is often rationed by formal financial institutions (Heltberg, 1998). There are also issues of moral hazard and adverse selection. Due to either a lack of assets or assets that are hard to collaterize, the lenders deem small farmers to be less creditworthy (Holden & Binswanger, 1998).

The predominant effect of all this is to make the production and consumption decisions of the farm household non-separable (Singh et al., 1986; Holden & Binswanger, 1998; De Janvry, 2006)[3] and lead to interlocking of markets. Under this system, two or more markets are locked together in an inter-temporal contract by binding distinct transactions into one contract (Jan & Harriss-White, 2012). This results in arrangements such as extended family system, labour exchange or share contracts (Holden & Binswanger, 1998; Holden et al., 2001; Binswanger & Mcintire, 1987 as cited in De Janvry et al., 1991).

Several other factors were further added as possible reasons for IR. These include labour supervision costs (Bardhan, 1973; Bhalla, 1986; Eswaran & Kotwal, 1986; Feder, 1985); distress sales by small farmers (Bhagwati & Chakravarty, 1969); land quality (Khusro, 1964: Carter, 1984; Bhalla & Roy, 1988, Assunção & Braido, 2007; Benjamin, 1995; Lamb, 2003; Barrett et al., 2010) and risk (Srinivasan, 1972; Rosenzweig & Binswanger, 1993). In the more recent literature, ‘edge effects’ (Bevis & Barrett, 2020), measurement errors (ME) and improved measures of productivity have emerged as important factors to explain IR. Lamb (2003) first suggested that ME in farm size might account for IR. Some of the later studies examined the implication of improved measurement of plot size (Holden & Carletto et al., 2013, 2015; Cohen, 2019; Fisher, 2013) and the possible effect of measurement errors in

[1] Marshallian inefficiency theorizes that sharecropping is inefficient as compared to fixed rent (Marshall, 1920) since sharecroppers tend to undersupply effort in terms of the application of inputs in crops, particularly quality of labour.

[2] This results from the several additional functions of land in rural societies such as insurance, inflation-hedge, savings, prestige and collateral value (Binswanger and Deininger, 1997; Heltberg, 1998; Sekhar and Thapa, 2021).

[3] Non-separability implies that consumption needs and asset distribution may have significant effect on production decisions. This will have an adverse effect on production of some households (Foltz 2004).

self-reported crop output on IR using crop-cuts (Desiere & Jolliffe, 2018; Gourlay et al., 2019). These studies find that MEs in self-reported output drive a spurious IR, provided the plot size is measured without error, and this IR disappears if a more reliable measure from crop-cuts is used.

Although there was a plethora of literature on IR in India during the 1960 and 1970s, there have been very few studies in the last two and a half decades. This was despite a severe stagnation in agricultural growth in the mid-1990s, followed by a revival from 2004–05 (Chand et al., 2007). To our knowledge there are only three studies related to India during this period (Foster & Rosenzweig, 2010; Chand et al., 2011; Deininger et al., 2018).

Foster and Rosenzweig (2010) show that the large farms in India are more efficient, more mechanized, use less labour per acre, including supervisory labour, and, most importantly, have higher profitability per acre. Large landowners also appear to have an advantage in the credit market. In fact, Foster and Rosenzweig's findings are interesting. They find that the profitability is U-shaped, with farms at the lower end reaping higher returns due to intensive use of family labour, while those at the higher end benefit from better mechanization and access to credit. The turning point, as per their estimates, is 20 acres. This is four times the maximum size of the land holding, which is 5 acres, of the small farmers in India (marginal and small farmers)! This implies that there is significant scope for improvement in outcomes from land consolidation and moving labour force out of agriculture. Deininger et al. (2018), using a large national farm panel (1982, 1999 and 2008), find that the IR has weakened significantly over time due to the substitution of capital for labour in response to non-agricultural labour demand; declining efficiency of family labour vis-à-vis hired labour in 2008 (but not in 1982 and 1999!) and a decline in imperfections in labour market around 2008. Both studies use data only up to 2008. Using NSS 59th round data for the agricultural year 2002–03, Chand et al. (2011), find that the inverse relationship between farm size and land productivity was quite pronounced even with the advancement of technology or modernization of agriculture.

Many policy changes, particularly related to labour market, have occurred in India since these studies were conducted. A large rural employment program (MGNREGS) was launched in 2007, which provides legally guaranteed employment for a minimum of 100 days in a year for each adult at a statutorily fixed wage rate. This has the effect of raising the reservation wage and labour supply. Although there is some evidence of an increase in mechanization, there is little evidence of the declining efficiency of family labour vis-à-vis hired labour or a decline in imperfections in labour market, as claimed by Deininger et al. (2018). Further, despite an increase in the flow of institutional credit to agriculture (NABARD, 2018), the percentage of outstanding loans from institutional sources was a mere 28% for agricultural households with less than 0.01 ha of land, as against 68% for households possessing greater than 10 ha of land (NSSO, 2021). This shows that the access to institutional credit for small farmers in India is still quite limited.

In view of the paucity of the latest evidence on IR in India that factors in the changes in labour markets, the present study proposes to examine the issue of IR using more recent and disaggregated data. Further, since the IR may also result from an intensive use of factors or inputs on small farms, we also test these pathways for any observed IR.

8.3 Study Objectives, Materials and Methods

8.3.1 Objectives

It is clear from the literature that imperfections in labour and land markets mostly manifest in the form of decreasing land productivity and increasing labour productivity (per capita output) with farm size. It is also likely that larger farms face supervision constraint; use more land and inputs and; possess better access to mechanization and credit, all of which could have a positive impact on per capita output (or labour productivity).

Thus the following specific hypotheses have been tested using primary household data.

(1) Does an inverse relation (IR) between land productivity and farm size and; a direct relation between per capita output (labour productivity) and farm size still exist?
(2) Does the intensity of use of family labour, fertilizer consumption, cropping intensity and access to bank credit vary with land size?

8.3.2 Materials and Methods

Following the tradition in the previous literature, neoclassical framework with constant returns to scale and rational behaviour of farmers form the theoretical underpinnings of our model. A brief explanation of these assumptions is in order here. Households maximize their consumption subject to a budget constraint. Given the absence of or imperfections in the credit market, production is the main mode of financing consumption needs. In this way, production gets linked with consumption, and the rigidities in the factor markets on the production side become important. The imperfection in the labour market and lack of skill endowments generate surplus labour on small farms, leading to *higher land productivity* on small farms. Similarly, limited labour and higher capital lead to *higher labour productivity* on large farms. In the credit market, the rigidities on the supply side, in the form of the requirement of collateral (owned land), lead to *higher credit uptake* on large farms.

Village-specific differences in the agro-climatic conditions, infrastructure and institutions, are likely to affect the land productivity. Thus, we have used village-level effects to control for the unobserved heterogeneity due to climate, soil type, infrastructure and market access. Although some of the recent studies have advocated the use of total factor productivity (Rada & Fuglie, 2019), we have used land and labour productivity as regressands to be able to posit the study in the extant literature. Since market failure is a feature of the household and is not crop-specific (De Janvry et al., 1991: pp. 1401), we have focussed on aggregate productivity (not crop-specific) and aggregate input use in our analysis.

Tabular analysis and econometric methods (ordinary least squares or OLS and Tobit) are the main analytical tools used. While OLS has been used for testing all the hypotheses, the Tobit model has been used for testing the hypothesis on bank credit. This is because a large number of farmers have nil borrowings from the bank. This makes the distribution of borrowings left-censored and lumped at zero. Since the distribution does not have a conditional normal distribution, OLS is not appropriate and therefore, maximum likelihood estimation (Tobit) has been used. The complete empirical strategy is outlined in the following schematic diagram (Fig. 8.1).

We control for state and village-specific effects through the use of dummies. It is possible that, due to village-specific differences, not only the *levels* of productivity (intercept) are different across farmers in different villages, but also the *slope* (marginal effect of farm size on productivity) may also differ. To account for this, we test the differences in marginal effects of farm size across villages through appropriate interactions. Since we do not have panel data or plot-level data, we are unable to control for the household-level effects. However, the inclusion of owned land, which does not vary from year to year and is closely correlated with technology adoption, networks and access to markets, indirectly accounts for time-invariant household-level fixed effects. We have also included some of the household-specific socio-economic variables like the education of the head and caste, in our model. These are expected to account (at least partially) for the household's adoption of improved technology and access to credit markets, which, in turn, are expected to influence productivity.

The general model is $y_{ij} = \alpha' x_{ij} + \beta a_{ij} + \gamma_j + \varepsilon_{ij}$ where y_{ij} denotes the explained variable in household i and village j; x_{ij} is the set of explanatory variables; a_{ij} is the variable of interest (operated area); γ_j is the jth village dummy; ε_{ij} is the error term, and α, βand γ are parameters to be estimated. To correct for heteroscedasticity, we have used White's heteroscedasticity-robust standard errors in the model.[4] The six estimated equations of the model are as follows.

[4] The error term is heteroscedastic when the variance of the error term is not constant. This leads to violation of efficiency (minimum variance) property and hence affect the standard errors and ultimately the t-statistic and hypothesis testing. One of the ways of overcoming this is by using Whites' modified standard errors which results in standard errors being robust even in the presence of heteroscedasticity.

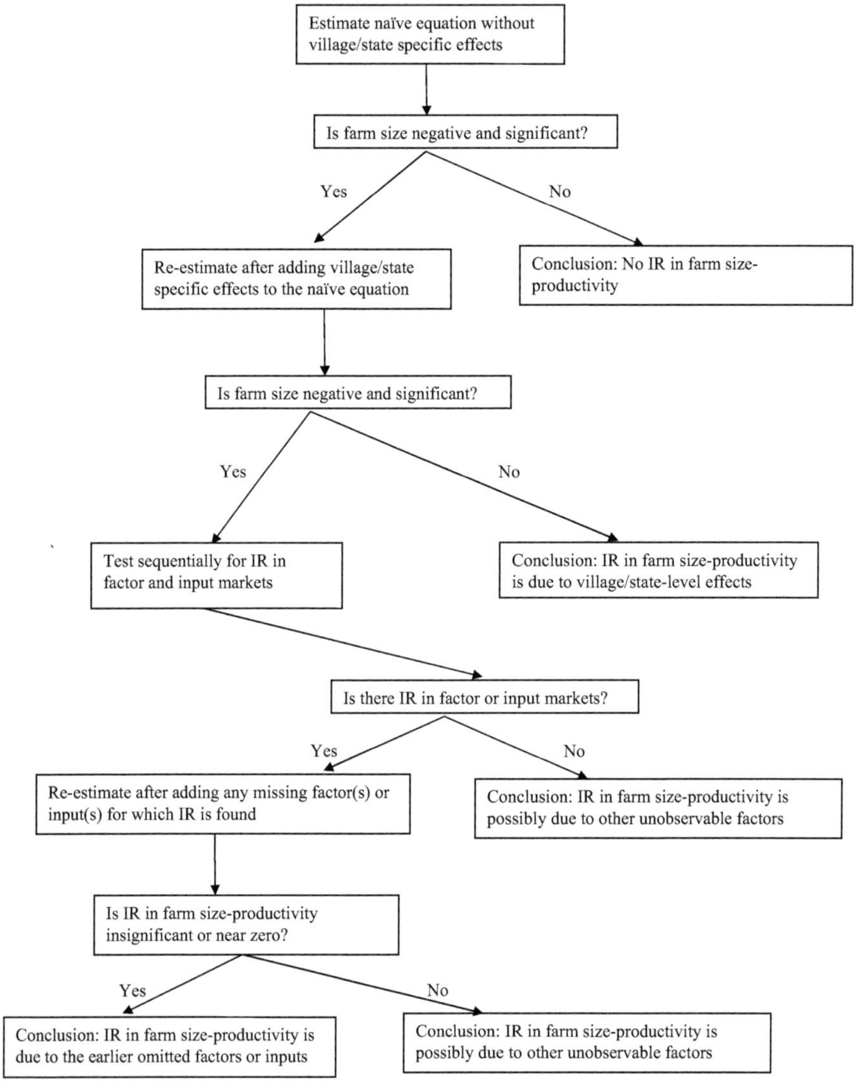

Fig. 8.1 Schematic diagram—Econometric model

8.3.2.1 Econometric Model

1. Land productivity and farm size relationship
   va1perha = f(SD, VD, CD, ED; opa,opa^2, flpd/hlpd, owa, %IA, %arwhtricsug, fert/opa, interaction of SD/VD with OPA)

   +/ − − + / − + + + + + + /−

2. Labour productivity (Output per capita) and farm size relationship
   va1percapita = f(SD, VD, CD, ED, opa, opa^2, flpdhlpd, owa, %IA, %arwhtricsug, fertopa, interactions of SD/VD with OPA)

   +/ − + + +/ − + + + + +/−

3. Family labour use and farm size relationship (supervision constraint)
   flpd/hlpd = f(SD, VD, CD, ED; opa, opa^2, CI, interactions of SD/VD with OPA)

   +/ − − + / − + + /−

4. Fertilizer consumption and farm size relationship (input intensity)
   fert/opa = f(SD, VD, CD, ED; opa, opa^2, %IA, %arwhtricsug, interactions of SD/VD with OPA)

   +/ − +/ − +/ − + + +/−

5. Cropping intensity and farm size relationship (intensive use of land)
   CI = f(SD, VD, CD, ED; opa, opa^2, %IA, flpdhlpd, interactions of SD/VD with OPA)

   +/ − +/ − +/ − + + +/−

6. Bank credit and farm size relationship (credit constraint)
   bancre = f(SD,VD,CD,ED; owa, interactions of SD/VD with OPA)

   +/ − + + /−

In the above model, the first two equations denote the output and the rest denote the factor markets. This way we can assess the IR, if any, and also the possible pathways through the factor use.

Notation

L_ denotes natural log. The corresponding variable names in the later tables are also indicated in parentheses.

va1perha (L_VA1PERHA): value-added per hectare (Rs/ha).

va1percapita (L_VA1PERPRN): value-added per capita or person (Rs/capita).

SD, VD, CD, ED: Dummy variables for state, village, caste and education of the head respectively.

opa (L_OPAREA): operated area (ha).

opa^2: square of the operated area.

owa (L_OWN_LAND): owned land (ha).

%IA (PER_IRR_OP): percentage of irrigated area to operated area (%).

%arwhtricsug (PER_AR_PDWHSUG): percentage of area under paddy, wheat and sugarcane to total area (%).

fert/opa (L_EXP_FERT_HA): expenditure on fertilizer consumption (Rs/ha).

flpd/hlpd (RATIO_FL_HL_DAYS): ratio of person-days of family labour to hired labour (%).

CI (CI_CROP_INTEN): cropping intensity (GCA/operated area).

bancre (AMT_GOVBNK): amount borrowed from Bank (Rs/ha).

8.3.2.2 Data and Sampling Methodology

Primary data has been collected through multi-stage sampling from four states—Bihar, Gujarat, Madhya Pradesh and Punjab—in the eastern, western, central and northern regions of the country respectively. Although data has been collected for one southern state, Andhra Pradesh, the state had to be eventually dropped due to data quality issues. One district each was selected to represent the distinct agro-climatic conditions of the state. From each district, two non-contiguous villages were selected with sufficient geographic spread. From each village, a sample of 50 farmers was selected with representation from each land size category of marginal (<1 hectare), small (1–2 hectares), medium (2.1–4 hectares), large (4.1–10 hectares) and very large (>10 hectares) using stratified random sampling with PPS (probability proportional to size). A total of 1800 households have been covered across four states, 21 districts and 45 villages. A structured questionnaire was used to collect information. The reference year of the study was July 2018 to June 2019.

Table 8.1 Distribution of households across the landholding categories

Landholding_categories	Percentage of households				
	Bihar	Gujarat	MP	Punjab	Overall
Marginal	43	39	20	27	34
Small	29	30	28	31	30
Medium	17	20	30	23	22
Large	9	10	14	15	11
Very Large	2	2	7	4	3
Total	100	100	100	100	100
Total number of households	300	800	400	300	1800

8.4 Overview of the Sample Region

The majority of the sample households belong to the marginal and small landholding categories, constituting 34% and 30% respectively (Table 8.1). The principal occupation is cultivation (97%). While cultivation is the predominant occupation for medium, large and very large categories, the marginal and small farmers seem to supplement cultivation with other sources of income (Table 8.2). All the farm categories are more engaged in paddy and wheat cultivation, possibly owing to lower yield risk (Chatterjee et al., 2020) (Table 8.3). This is more in Punjab because of extensive irrigation and assured price support. No clear relationship is evident at first between the net value of output per hectare and the farm size when family labour is not factored in (Table 8.4).[5] But when the cost of family labour is included using market wage rates, the net value-added per hectare increases with farm size. This indicates that the main advantage small landholdings possess are cheap family labour, which probably disappears when market wage rates are imputed for family labour. However, imputing market wages to family labour may not be totally appropriate because of missing or incomplete markets, particularly for women. The use of appropriate shadow price instead of market wage is more appropriate. The income per capita (value-added) showed no such differences though, which increased with farm size in all the states, whether or not the family labour is imputed at the market wage rate (Table 8.5). In all four states, the smaller landholdings appear to use more family labour, as reflected in the average person-days per ha of family labour and farm servants (Table 8.6).

[5] Labour input is the person-days per hectare and is calculated as follows.

Average person-days per hectare = (average number of labour employed × average number of days × average number of hours per day) / (8*operated area in ha).

Table 8.2 Distribution of households by principal occupation across the landholding categories

Landholding_ Categories	Percentage of households						
	Cultivation	Agricultural labour	Dairy	Non-agricultural wage labour	Others	Total	Total number of households
Marginal	93	0	1	1	5	100	606
Small	97	0	1	0	2	100	533
Medium	99	0	0	0	0	100	398
Large	100	0	0	0	0	100	204
Very Large	98	0	2	0	0	100	59
Total	97	0	1	0	2	100	1800

Table 8.3 Percentage of gross cropped area under paddy and wheat

Landholding_Categories	Bihar	Gujarat	MP	Punjab
Marginal	44	48	48	73
Small	44	27	43	77
Medium	45	24	38	89
Large	46	32	38	86
Very Large	47	19	37	89
Total	45	29	39	85

8.5 Econometric Analysis and Results

The econometric model has been outlined in Sect. 8.3.2.1. The main variable of interest is the operated area, except in the bank credit equation. In the bank credit equation, the variable of interest is the owned area, since the operated area cannot be used as collateral. We first look at the summary statistics (Table 8.7) and plots of important variables. The summary statistics show that almost all the variables have higher skewness and fatter tails (leptokurtic), which is indicative of some outliers. The bank credit variable also shows high skewness and kurtosis in the full sample because of a large number of zero values, but the truncated sample appears satisfactory. In the frequency distribution plots of log values (Fig. 8.2), fertilizer consumption expenditure (l_exp_fert_ha) shows a narrow distribution, while others, such as hired labour (l_tot_hiredlab_pdays) appear to be widely distributed. A closer look at the granular data in the dot plots (Fig. 8.3) shows that fertilizer consumption expenditure (l_exp_fert_ha) is more dispersed for households from 200 to 1100. Similarly, 'hired labour use' is distinctly higher for households from 1100 to 1500. This indicates that some villages (or even states) are different from the rest. This supports our use of village-level dummies and interactions to account for this inter-village heterogeneity. With these brief insights about our data, we turn to our estimation results.

Table 8.4 Value-added per hectare (Rs/ha)

Landholding_ Categories	Bihar	Gujarat	MP	Punjab
Only paid-out costs included				
Marginal	22,819 (286.75)	27,046 (339.87)	48,156 (605.15)	106,211 (1334.69)
Small	24,631 (309.52)	25,795 (324.15)	50,790 (638.25)	108,784 (1367.02)
Medium	25,069 (315.03)	45,018 (565.71)	67,566 (849.06)	132,891 (1669.96)
Large	26,483 (332.80)	60,886 (765.12)	74,640 (937.95)	117,102 (1471.55)
Very large	23,055 (289.72)	28,768 (361.51)	75,167 (944.58)	122,893 (1544.32)
Total	24,807 (311.73)	40,980 (514.97)	69,237 (870.06)	119,677 (1503.90)
Paid-out costs plus family labour imputed using market wage rate				
Marginal	–36,339 (–456.65)	–44,604 (–560.51)	13,250 (166.50)	–115,939 (–1456.93)
Small	511 (6.42)	–11,763 (–147.82)	26,604 (334.32)	–18,266 (–229.54)
Medium	11,360 (142.75)	20,398 (256.33)	47,945 (602.49)	58,700 (737.65)
Large	19,930 (250.45)	48,458 (608.94)	45,643 (573.57)	84,393 (1060.51)
Very Large	20,150 (252.21)	22,967 (288.61)	60,883 (765.08)	103,626 (1302.20)
Total	4822 (60.60)	14,027 (176.27)	48,148 (605.05)	50,493 (634.51)

Note Value-added is computed as the value of output minus the paid-out costs. Figures in parentheses are in USD. 1USD = INR 79.58 (as of September 14, 2022; *source* RBI)

8.5.1 Relationship Between Farm Size and Productivity[6]

(A) Land Productivity (value-added Per Hectare)

As discussed in Sect. 8.2, small farms show higher intensity of family labour due to factors like non-clearing labour markets because of a lower wage than the reservation wage; lower skill endowments and, missing markets for women and children. The better quality and commitment of family labour on small farms compared to hired labour and the higher supervision costs of the hired labour on large farms are expected to lead, *ceteris paribus,* to decreasing value-added per hectare (output net of costs) with an increase in farm size.

Specification 1 is the naïve specification with only the operated area, owned area and inputs such as irrigated area, fertilizer consumption, area under MSP crops etc. In specification 2, two variables are added—the village dummy and its interactions with the operated area. Household-specific variables such as education (of the head), caste and a squared term of the operated area to account for any possible non-linearity are also included. Higher education of the head is expected to positively influence adoption of technology and access to credit. Caste, which is an important social

[6] For detailed results and various model specifications, see Sekhar et al. (2021), Sekhar and Thapa (2021, 2023).

Table 8.5 Value-added per person (Rs/capita)

Landholding_ Categories	Bihar	Gujarat	MP	Punjab
Only paid-out costs included				
Marginal	2551 (32.06	4192 (52.68)	7202 (90.50)	20,733 (260.54)
Small	6872 (86.36)	8308 (104.40)	14,348 (180.30)	36,874 (463.37)
Medium	12,099 (152.04)	24,659 (309.87)	36,272 (455.81)	82,258 (1033.68)
Large	27,331 (343.45)	76,083 (956.09)	82,566 (1037.55)	136,817 (1719.29)
Very Large	46,549 (584.95)	73,165 (919.42)	205,156 (2578.07)	266,767 (3352.29)
Overall	8251 (103.69)	18,976 (238.46)	46,658 (586.32)	74,152 (931.82)
Paid-out costs plus family labour imputed using market wage rate				
Marginal	–4063 (–51.06)	–6913 (–86.87)	1982 (24.91)	–22,632 (–284.40)
Small	142 (1.78)	–3788 (–47.60)	7516 (94.45)	–6192 (–77.81)
Medium	5483 (68.90)	11,173 (140.40)	25,739 (323.45)	36,335 (456.60)
Large	20,569 (258.48)	60,552 (760.92)	50,490 (634.48)	98,602 (1239.07)
Very Large	40,682 (511.22)	58,410 (734)	166,170 (2088.15)	224,945 (2826.74)
Overall	1604 (20.16)	6495 (81.62)	32,446 (407.73)	31,286 (393.15)

Note (1) Value-added per person is computed by dividing the total value-added by number of adults in a family. Figures in parentheses are in USD. 1USD = INR 79.58 (as of September 14, 2022; *source* RBI)
(2) Two children (below 18 years) are considered equal to one adult

Table 8.6 Average annual person-days per hectare: Family labour & farm servants

Landholding_Categories	Bihar	Gujarat	MP	Punjab
Marginal	69	178	81	76
Small	72	86	56	78
Medium	39	75	45	59
Large	30	41	34	26
Very Large	15	29	26	10
Total	48	65	121	40

attribute in rural India, is expected to influence access to inputs, services and credit. The village dummies are expected to control for the unobserved heterogeneity due to climate, soil type, market infrastructure and governance. The interaction terms help to discern slope differences across the villages, if any. The proportion of irrigated areas and fertilizer consumption per hectare are included to account for higher yields that might result from the intensive use of these inputs. Proportion of area under

Table 8.7 Summary statistics of important variables

Variables	Unit	Mean	Median	Max	Min	Std. dev	Skewness	Kurtosis	Obs
VA1PERHA	INR	51,304 (645)	37,050 (466)	2,059,276 (25,878)	–344,734 (–4332)	93,966 (1181)	9.4	174.2	1800
VA1PERPRN	INR	33,766 (424)	11,552 (145)	2,015,350 (25,326)	–112,963 (–1420)	83,006 (1043)	10.5	204.3	1800
OPAREA	hectare	2.4	1.5	52.6	0.1	3	6.5	72.3	1800
OWN_LAND	hectare	2.1	1.4	52.6	0	2.9	7.3	94.8	1800
IRRIG_LAND	hectare	2.3	1.4	44.5	0	3.1	5.6	55.3	1800
CI_CROP_INTEN	%	151	145	600	25	51.1	0.6	6.1	1800
TOT_FAMLAB_PDAYS	person-days	1476	1040	25,600	0	1666	4.9	45.2	1800
TOT_HIREDLAB_PDAYS	person-days	5127	720	119,680	0	11,598	4.0	24.6	1800
EXP_FERT_HA	INR per ha	8266 (104)	7500 (94)	137,500 (1728)	0	5505 (69)	8.3	174.7	1800
AMT_GOVBNK	INR	79,399 (998)	0	250,000 (3142)	0	203,063 (2552)	5.6	46.5	1800
L_AMT_GOVBNK (log value)		12.05	12.21	14.73	9.21	0.89	–0.02	3.3	556

Note Figures in parentheses are in USD. 1USD = INR 79.58 (as of September 14, 2022; *source* RBI)

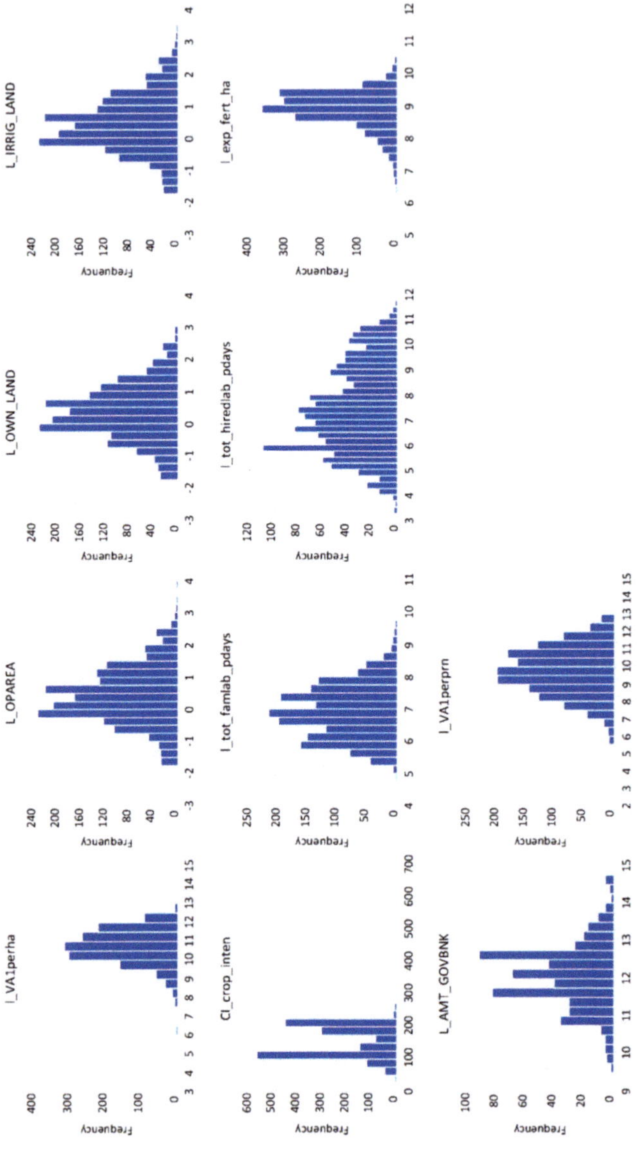

Fig. 8.2 Frequency distributions of important variables

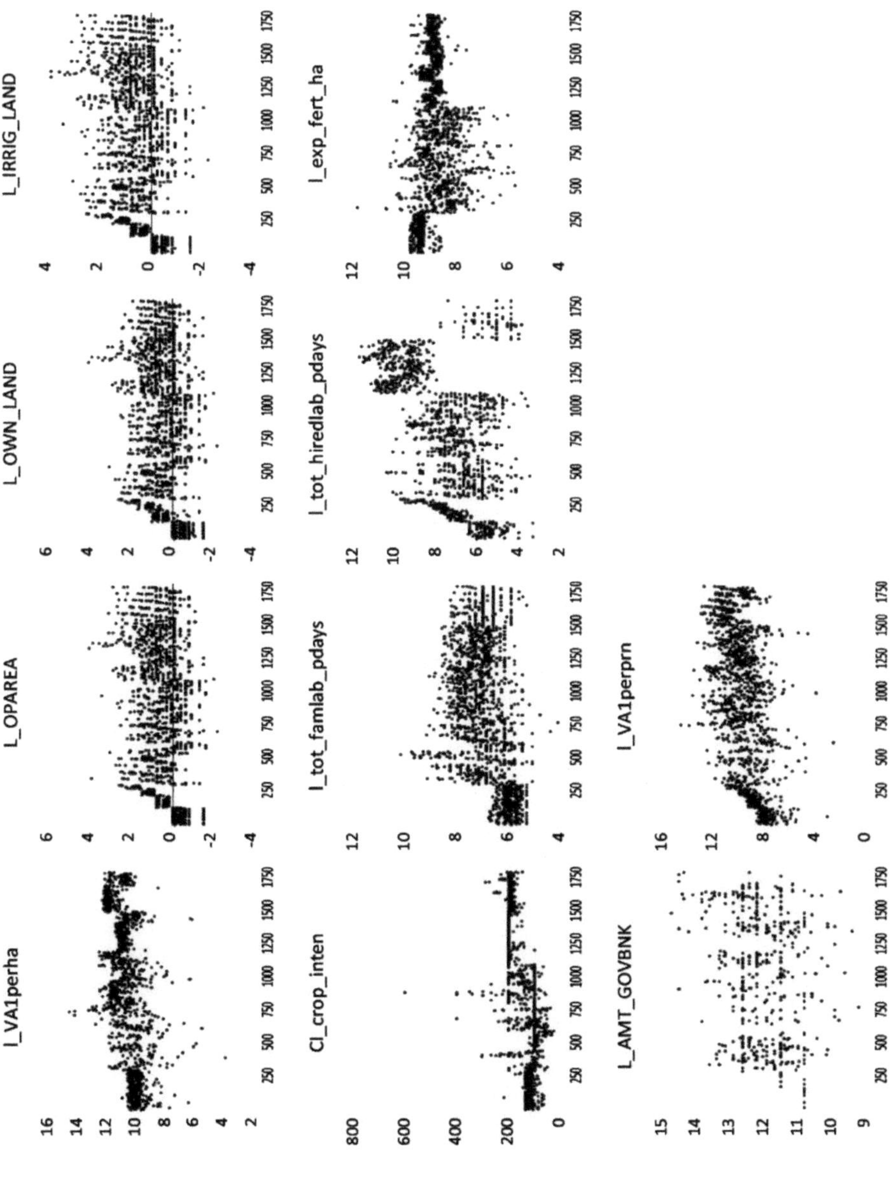

Fig. 8.3 Dot plots of important variables

Table 8.8 Effect of farm size on productivity

Explanatory variables	Land productivity (value-added per hectare)		Labour productivity (value-added per person)	
	Specification 1	Specification 2	Specification 1	Specification 2
Log(operated area)	–0.13** (0.07)	–0.52*** (0.10)	0.72*** (0.08)	0.48*** (0.11)
Log(owned land)	0.36*** (0.07)	0.49*** (0.07)	0.43*** (0.09)	0.49*** (0.08)
%irrigated area to operated area	0.006*** (0.002)	0.002 (0.002)	0.007*** (0.002)	0.002 (0.002)
%area under paddy, wheat & sugarcane to total area	0.012*** (0.001)	0.003** (0.002)	0.01*** (0.001)	0.004*** (0.002)
Log(exp on fertilizer consumption per ha)	0.041 (0.05)	0.23*** (0.06)	0.09* (0.06)	0.20*** (0.06)
Ratio of person-days of family to hired labour	–	–	–	–
State/Village dummies and interactions	–	**Village**	–	**Village**
Whether significant (p-values) of dummies and interactions	–	Yes (0.000)	–	Yes (0.000)
Caste and education dummies (household effects), and non-linearity in operated area	–	Yes	–	Yes
Adjusted R sq	0.19	0.50	0.53	0.72
Log-likelihood	–1961.76	–1554.91	–2147.63	–1719.35
Ramsey RESET test (p-values)	34.48 (0.00)	2.46 (0.12)	0.00 (0.97)	1.89 (0.06)
No. of included observations	1503	1503	1503	1503

Note 1 Level of significance- *,**,*** denote significance at 10%, 5% and 1% respectively. Values in parentheses of coefficients indicate standard errors
Note 2 1-Naïve specification; 2- specification1 plus village effects plus caste, education and non-linearity effects

MSP-supported crops[7] captures the effect of better price from MSP, which may help in realizing higher value-added per hectare (Desiere & Joliffe, 2018). Owners of large farms (not mere cultivators) are expected to have better access to credit and technology, which in turn can have a positive effect on the output. The results are presented in Table 8.8.

Looking at Table 8.8, specification 1 of land productivity, operated area (farm-size) shows a negative and statistically significant effect. A 1% increase in farm size leads to a decrease in land productivity of 0.13%. However, this effect increases to 0.52%

[7] MSP refers to statutory minimum support price, which is the assured price announced by the central (federal) government, effective mainly for wheat and rice.

in specification 2. This is strongly suggestive of the presence of IR when village-specific factors are controlled. The owned area also shows the expected positive and significant coefficient of 0.36% in the naïve specification, showing the favourable effect of better access to credit and technology/mechanization on land productivity (Table 8.8). This effect increases further to 0.49% in specification 2 when village-level effects are controlled. All the intercept and slope dummies are jointly significant in this specification. The individual village interaction terms are significant in nearly 21 out of the 44 villages, implying that the marginal effect varies across villages. The effect of irrigation, although positive, is statistically insignificant when village-level heterogeneity is accounted for, suggesting that intra-village differences in irrigation are perhaps not very important. The squared term of the operated area has been found to be insignificant, suggesting the absence of non-linearity in the relationship.

(B) Labour Productivity (value-added Per Capita)

Due to better access to inputs and credit of the large farmers and the resulting farm investment and mechanization, *output per capita (income per capita)* is expected to be higher on large farms. We test this hypothesis using the same specifications and explanatory variables used in the previous set of regressions (of value-added per hectare). The only difference is that the dependent variable is 'value-added per capita'.

As expected, the operated area shows a highly positive and significant effect in the naïve specification (Table 8.8). This is in agreement with the results in the section on tabular analysis (Table 8.5). All other explanatory variables, except irrigation, show a significant positive effect. Irrigation, as in the previous set of regressions, is insignificant when village-level heterogeneity is controlled for. The intercept and slope dummies are jointly significant in specification 2. The interaction term (slope dummy) is found to be significant in 18 villages, indicating that the marginal effect varies across villages. The results of the Ramsey RESET test[8] indicates that all the regressions are satisfactory, ruling out model mis-specification.

8.5.2 Relationship Between Farm Size and Factor Use

It is clear from the above results that IR exists between farm size and land productivity. But is the inverse relation a result of intensive use of some factor(s) or input(s) on small farms? To understand this, we now test the relation between farm size and use of factors like family labour, land, fertilizer use and credit using Eqs. (3) to (6) of the model outlined in Sect. 3.2.1. State and village level effects are controlled. Bihar state and Kesabe village (Bihar) constitute the base group.

Intensive use of family labour on small farms and supervision constraints faced by large farmers are hypothesized to be the main factors behind IR. If true, this

[8] RESET test (Regression Equation Specification Error Test) is a general test for checking specification errors including omitted variables, incorrect functional form and correlation between the error term and the explanatory variables.

implies that the ratio of family labour to hired labour is highest in the smallest land category and should decline with farm size. We test this with Eq. 3, wherein the ratio of person-days[9] of family labour to hired labour is regressed on farm size. We control for cropping intensity (ratio of the total area cropped to the operated area) to factor in the intensive use of land. We also included state & village dummies; and their interactions with operated area and household-level variables such as caste and education as before. The results support the hypothesis regarding family labour use. The farm size (operated area) negatively and significantly affects labour use intensity (Table 8.9). The coefficient is significant in all three specifications and increases from –0.98 in specification 1 to –1.17 in specification 3, when village-specific factors and household-level variables are included. This result is in agreement with the results of other studies (Desiere and Joliffe, 2018, Ali & Deininger, 2015 for Rwanda; Larson et al., 2014 for several African countries).

To test for intensive use of fertilizers on small farms, we regress fertilizer consumption expenditure per hectare on the operated area. Since fertilizer consumption expenditure is expected to be more for irrigated farms and for crops like rice, wheat and sugarcane, we control for percentage of irrigated area and area under these crops. The results do not seem to support the hypothesis that fertilizer consumption is higher on small farms (Table 8.9). The coefficient of the operated area which is statistically significant in specification 1 (0.06) becomes less than half in magnitude and insignificant once village-level factors are controlled for in specification 2 and 3. The percentage of irrigated area and area under paddy, wheat and sugarcane show positive and statistically significant effects, though. Overall, there seems to be hardly any evidence of intensive use of fertilizer on small farms.

To test for intensive use of land by small farms, we next regress cropping intensity on farm size. Since cropping intensity is expected to be higher on farms with better irrigation and with committed and quality labour, we control for these variables. The results do not seem to support the hypothesis of more intensive use of land on small farms (Table 8.9). As in the case of fertilizer use, the coefficient of the operated area becomes less than half in magnitude and insignificant once village-specific factors are included. Irrigated area has a significant positive coefficient but family labour doesn't show a significant effect.

Access to formal credit from banks is expected to affect the value of the output through higher use of inputs and complementary investment. Small farmers, because of the lower collateral value of their land, may not be considered credit-worthy and have relatively less access to bank credit than larger farmers. We test this by regressing the amount of bank credit per hectare on the owned area. We use owned land here since only owned land can be used as collateral and not the operated land. Since a large number of farmers in our sample had zero borrowings, we have only 556 sample observations after censoring at zero. Because of this small number of observations, we could not test for the village-specific effects. We could only test for the state-level effects (not interactions). The results show a positive and significant coefficient of owned land in both linear and log-linear specifications (Table 8.9) which shows

[9] Calculated as (number of labourers $\times$ number of days worked $\times$ number of hours worked) $\div$ 8.

Table 8.9 Relationship of input use and factor use with farm size

Explanatory variables	Intensity of family labour use			Fertilizer consumption			Cropping intensity			Bank credit			
Specification	1	2	3	1	2	3	1	2	3	1	2	3	4
										Log-linear		linear	
Log(operated area)	−0.98*** (0.09)	−0.71*** (0.15)	−1.17*** (0.11)	0.06*** (0.02)	0.03 (0.05)	0.014 (0.05)	3.94** (1.72)	−1.76 (5.35)	−1.41	–			
Log(owned land)	–	–	–	–	–	–	–	–	–	0.12*** (0.02)	0.11*** (0.02)	114,182.4*** (33,065.8)	101,791** (26,512.7)
%irrigated area to operated area	–	–	–	0.005*** (0.001)	0.003*** (0.001)	0.003*** (0.001)	0.28*** (0.05)	0.09** (0.05)	0.09** (0.05)	–	–	–	–
%area under paddy, wheat & sugarcane to total area	–	–	–	0.001 (0.005)	0.005*** (0.001)	0.005*** (0.001)	–	–		–	–	–	–
Log(exp on fertilizer consumption per ha)	–	–	–	–	–	–	–	–	–	–	–	–	–
Ratio of person-days of family to hired labour	–	–	–	–	–	–	−0.27 (0.28)	0.06 (0.21)	0.09 (0.20)	–	–	–	–
Cropping intensity	−0.003 (0.004)	0.001 (0.004)	−0.005 (0.004)	–	–	–	–	–		–	–	–	–
State/Village dummies and interactions	State	Village	Village	State	Village	Village	State	Village	Village	State	State	State	State

(continued)

Table 8.9 (continued)

Explanatory variables	Intensity of family labour use			Fertilizer consumption			Cropping intensity			Bank credit			
Specification	1	2	3	1	2	3	1	2	3	1	2	3	4
Whether significant (p-values)	–	Yes (0.000)	Yes (0.000)	Yes (0.000)	Yes (0.000)	Yes (0.000)	Yes (0.000)	Yes (0.000)	Yes (0.000)	Yes (0.000)	Yes (0.000)	Yes (0.000)	Yes (0.000)
Caste and education dummies (household effects), and non-linearity in operated area	–	–	Yes	–	–	Yes	–	–	Yes	–	Yes	–	Yes
Adjusted R sq	0.22	0.38	0.24	0.24	0.44	0.44	0.47	0.70	0.70	–	–	–	–
Log-likelihood	–4080.4	–3889.41	–4061.43	–1452.21	–1150.14	–1142.24	–7145.24	–6709.88	–6706.91	–628.57	–614.67	–7411.506	–7399.44
Ramsey RESET test (p-values)	3.09 (0.09)	4.06 (0.04)	6.21 (0.00)	2.09 (0.14)	2.49 (0.10)	5.58 (0.00)	0.02 (0.90)	3.14 (0.08)	6.53 (0.02)	–	–	–	–
No. of included observations	1420	1420	1420	1797	1797	1797	1420	1420	1420	556	556	556	556

Note Level of significance- *,**,*** denote significance at 10%, 5% and 1% respectively. Values in parentheses of coefficients indicate standard errors that the large farmers have much better access to formal credit. State dummies are positive and significant indicating that credit availability is significantly higher in the relatively developed states of Gujarat, MP and Punjab than in Bihar (Table 8.9). However, due to absence of interaction terms, it is difficult to assess differences in marginal effects across states, if any.

8.5.3 Is Family Labour Use a Determinant of Farm Size-Productivity Relationship?

It was seen from the foregoing analysis that farm size bears an IR with land productivity on the output side and family labour use on the input side. Can it be inferred then that family labour use is driving the observed IR in land productivity, as suggested by the labour dualism theory? To explore this further, we return back to the model we estimated in Table 8.8. We reestimate specification 2 of the 'land productivity' equation by augmenting it with the 'family labour use' variable. If family labour is indeed the sole determinant of IR between farm size and productivity, then with the inclusion of this variable the IR should become zero or insignificant. The results are presented in Table 8.10. As can be seen, the effect of farm size remains almost the same, as in Table 8.8 and is significant at 1%. The coefficients of other variables also remain almost unchanged. The coefficient of family labour even becomes insignificant. Thus, it appears that the IR in family labour use may not be the only determinant of IR in land productivity but there could be other unobserved factors at work.

This result is consistent with many recent studies in countries such as Ethiopia, Tanzania, Malawi, Uganda, Peru, Bangladesh, Madagascar and Brazil (Abay et al., 2019; Aragon et al., 2021; Helfand & Taylor, 2021; Barrett et al., 2010; Desiere & Joliffe, 2018). Two possible explanations for IR, other than family labour, are measurement errors (ME) and intra-household allocative inefficiency. Desiere and Joliffe (2018), after a systematic and careful analysis, also reject all previous explanations of the IR, and conclude that systematic measurement error in self-reported production is the possible explanation for the IR.

Another important explanation for the observed IR is the 'edge effect' (Bevis & Barrett, 2020). Edge effect is a phenomenon of higher yields along a plot's perimeter than on the plot's interior. This is because crops along the edges (perimeter) face less competition for nutrients, water, space and sunlight than crops on the plot's interior (area). Hence, yields on small plots will be higher than on the large ones, since the ratio of perimeter to the area of smaller plots is larger.[10] However, our study includes a number of large and very large farms, constituting about 14% of the total sample size. Thus, any IR due to 'edge effect' should be moderated by this somewhat large proportion of large and very large farms.

---

[10] If the length and breadth of the plot are 'a' and 'b' respectively, then the ratio of its perimeter to area 'r' is given by $r = 2(a+b)/(a*b) = 2(1/b + 1/a)$. This implies that smaller 'a' and 'b' are, larger is 'r'.

Table 8.10 Effect of family labour on farm size-productivity relation

Explanatory variables	Land productivity (value-added per hectare)	Labour productivity (value-added per person)
Log(operated area)	–0.50*** (0.12)	0.51*** (0.13)
Log(owned land)	0.46*** (0.08)	0.43*** (0.09)
%irrigated area to operated area	0.001 (0.002)	–0.00 (0.002)
%area under paddy, wheat & sugarcane to total area	0.003* (0.002)	0.004* (0.002)
Log(exp on fertilizer consumption per ha)	0.26*** (0.07)	0.22*** (0.07)
Ratio of person-days of family to hired labour	–0.011 (0.01)	–0.02** (0.01)
State/Village dummies and interactions	**Village**	**Village**
Whether significant (p-values) of dummies and interactions	Yes (0.000)	Yes (0.000)
Caste and education dummies (household effects), and non-linearity in operated area	Yes	Yes
Adjusted R sq	0.44	0.71
Log-likelihood	–1286.65	–1395.82
Ramsey RESET test (p-values)	3.12 (0.08)	1.89 (0.06)
No. of included observations	1186	1186

Note 1 Level of significance- *,**,*** denote significance at 10%, 5% and 1% respectively. Values in parentheses of coefficients indicate standard errors

Limitations of the Study

A limitation of the study is that it is based on cross-section data. A panel data set can help in controlling for household-level fixed effects. Inclusion of data on improved measures of plot size and production (crop cuts) can also help in a better understanding of the effect of MEs and edge effect.

8.6 Conclusions

The study reveals a strong inverse relationship between farm size and land productivity when village-level heterogeneity is controlled for. There is evidence of a more intensive use of family labour on small farms. There is little or no evidence of IR in case of any other factor or input use. There is evidence of scale effect in case of credit. The imperfections in labour market appear to be compounded by those in the land and credit markets and skill endowments of small & marginal farmers.

As most of the land market imperfections arise from lease market restrictions, reforming tenancy laws/regulations, are therefore, urgently needed, to enable easier access to land, particularly for marginal and small farmers (Haque, 2001, 2013; Deininger et al., 2012, GoI, 2016). Imperfections in the credit market are particularly binding for small & marginal farmers which need to be addressed through better access to formal credit (NSSO, 2021). More than half of the farm workforce in India is illiterate while this percentage in the non-farm sector is only 30% (Himanshu et al., 2011). Such low levels of literacy in the farm sector severely impair their ability to move to other occupations, leading to surplus family labour on small farms (Dreze & Sen, 1995; Sekhar, 2005). This requires a long-term emphasis on improving primary education. Thus, reforming land lease markets; increasing access to credit and improving literacy levels of small farmers are necessary to address some of the imperfections observed.

References

Abay, K. A., Abate, G. T., Barrett, C. B., & Bernard, T. (2019). Correlated non-classical measurement errors, 'Second best' policy inference, and the inverse size-productivity relationship in agriculture. *Journal of Development Economics, 139*, 171–184.

Ali, D. A., & Deininger, K. (2015). Is there a farm size–productivity relationship in African agriculture? Evidence from Rwanda. *Land Economics, 91*(2), 317–343.

Aragon, F. M., Restuccia, D., & Rud, J. P. (2021). Are small farms really more productive than large farms? *Food Policy*, 102168.

Assunção, JulianoJ., & Braido, L. H. B. (2007). Testing household-specific explanations for the inverse productivity relationship. *American Journal of Agricultural Economics, 89*(4), 980–990.

Bardhan, P. K. (1973). Size, productivity and returns to scale: An analysis of farm level data in Indian agriculture. *Journal of Political Economy* (November-December, 1973), 1370–1386 1973a.

Bardhan, P. (Ed.). (1989). *The economic theory of agrarian institutions*. Clarendon Press.

Barrett, C. B. (1996). On price risk and the inverse farm size-productivity relationship. *Journal of Development Economics, 51*(2), 193–215.

Barrett, C. B., & Mutambatsere, E. (2008). *Agricultural markets in developing countries.*

Barrett, C. B., Bellemare, M. F., & Hou, J. Y. (2010). Reconsidering conventional explanations of the inverse productivity-size relationship. *World Development, 38*(1), 88–97.

Basu, K. (1983). The emergence of isolation and interlinkage in rural markets. *Oxford Economic Papers, 35*(2), 262–280.

Benjamin, D. (1995). Can unobserved land quality explain the inverse productivity relationship? *Journal of Development Economics, 46*(1), 51–84.

Berry, A. R., & Cline, W. R. (1979). *Agrarian structure and productivity in developing countries* (p. 1979). Johns Hopkins University Press.

Bevis, L. E., & Barrett, C. B. (2020). Close to the edge: High productivity at plot peripheries and the inverse size-productivity relationship. *Journal of Development Economics, 143*, Article 102377.

Bhagwati, J. N., & Chakravarty, S. (1969, September). Contributions to Indian economic analysis: A Survey, *American Economic Review* (supplement).

Bhalla, Surjit, S. (1986, August). *Size determination of farms-theory and evidence*, World Bank.

Bhalla, Surjit S., & Roy, P. (1988, March). Mis-Specification in farm productivity analysis: The role of land quality, *Oxford Economic Papers*, Mar., 1988, New Series, *40*(1), 55–73.
Binswanger, H. P., & McIntire, J. (1987). Behavioral and material determinants of production relations in land-abundant tropical agriculture. *Economic Development and Cultural Change, 36*(1), 73–99.
Binswanger, H. P., & Deininger, K. (1997). Explaining agricultural and agrarian policies in developing countries. *Journal of Economic Literature, 35*, 1958–2005.
Brandt, L. (1987). Farm household behavior, factor markets, and the distributive consequences of commercialization in early twentieth-century China. *The Journal of Economic History, 47*(3), 711–737.
Braverman, A., & Stiglitz, J. E. (1982). Sharecropping and the interlinking of agrarian markets. *The American Economic Review, 72*(4), 695–715.
Carletto, C., Savastano, S., & Zezza, A. (2013). Fact or artifact: The impact of measurement errors on the farm size–productivity relationship. *Journal of Development Economics, 103*, 254–261.
Carletto, C., Gourlay, S., & Winters, P. (2015). From guesstimates to GPStimates: Land area measurement and implications for agricultural analysis. *Journal of African Economies, 24*(5), 593–628.
Chand, R., Raju, S. S., & Pandey, L. M. (2007). Growth crisis in agriculture: Severity and options at national and state levels. *Economic and Political Weekly, 42*(26), 2528–2533.
Chand, R., Prasanna, P. L., & Singh, A. (2011). Farm size and productivity: Understanding the strengths of smallholders and improving their livelihoods. *Economic and Political Weekly, 46*(26/27), 5–11.
Chatterjee, S., Krishnamurthy, M., Kapur, D., & Bouton, M. (2020). A study of the agricultural markets of Bihar, Odisha and Punjab, Final Report, *Center for the Advanced Study of India, University of Pennsylvania: Philadelphia.*
Chayanov, A. V. (1966). *The theory of peasant economy*, ed. Daniel Thorner, B. Kerblay, R. E. F. Smith (Homewood: R. D. Irwin).
Carter, M. R. (1984). Identification of the inverse relationship between farm size and productivity: An empirical analysis of peasant agricultural production. *Oxford Economic Papers, 36*(1), 131–145.
Carter, M. R., & Weibe, K. D. (1990). Access to Capital and its impact on agrarian structure and productivity in Kenya. *American Journal of Agricultural Economics, 72*(5), 1146–1150.
Cohen, A. (2019). Estimating farm production parameters with measurement error in land area. *Economic Development and Cultural Change, 68*(1), 305–334.
Deininger, Klaus, Songqing Jin, & Hari K Nagarajan. (2012). Equity and efficiency impacts of rural land rental restrictions: Evidences in India. In *Land Policies for Inclusive Growth* (Ed.), T. Haque, Concept Publishing Co., New Delhi.
Deininger, S. Klaus, Songqing Jin, Yanyan Liu, & Sudhir K. Sing. (2018, May). Can labor-market imperfections explain changes in the inverse farm size–productivity relationship? Longitudinal evidence from Rural India. *Land Economics 94*(2), 239–258.
De Janvry, A., & Sadoulet, E. (2006). Progress in the modeling of rural households' behavior under market failures. In *Poverty, inequality and development* (pp. 155–181). Springer, Boston, MA.
De Janvry, A., Fafchamps, M., & Sadoulet, E. (1991). Peasant household behaviour with missing markets: Some paradoxes explained. *The Economic Journal, 101*(409), 1400–1417.
Desiere, S., & Jolliffe, D. (2018). Land productivity and plot size: Is measurement error driving the inverse relationship? *Journal of Development Economics, 130*, 84–98.
Dreze, J., & Sen, A. K. (1995). *India: Economic development and social opportunity*. Oxford University Press.
Eswaran, M., & Kotwal, A. (1986). Access to capital and agrarian production organisation. *The Economic Journal, 96*(382), 482–498.
Feder, G. (1985). The relation between farm size and farm productivity: The role of family labor, supervision and credit constraints. *Journal of Development Economics, 18*(2–3), 297–313.

Foster, A., & Rosenzweig, M. R. (2010). Barriers to farm profitability in India: mechanization, scale and credit markets. In *Conference Agriculture for Development-Revisited, University of California at Berkeley. October* (Vol. 24, pp. 1–2).

Fulginiti, Lilyan E., & Richard K. Perrin. (1993, August). Prices and productivity in agriculture. *The Review of Economics and Statistics, 75*(3), 471–482.

GoI. (2016, March 31). *Report of the Expert Committee on Land Leasing*, NITI Aayog, Government of India, New Delhi.

Gourlay, S., Kilic, T., & Lobell, D. B. (2019). A new spin on an old debate: Errors in farmer-reported production and their implications for inverse scale-productivity relationship in Uganda. *Journal of Development Economics, 141*, Article 102376.

Haque, T. (2001). Impact of tenancy reforms on productivity improvement and socio-economic status of poor tenants. *NCAP Policy Paper No.13*, ICAR, New Delhi.

Haque, T. (2013, November). Agricultural land leasing in India – Policy, practice and impact. *Yojana*, New Delhi, Vol. 57.

Harriss-White, B. (Ed.). (1999). Agricultural markets from theory to practice: Field experience in developing countries. Springer.

Hayami, Yujiro, & Vernon W. Ruttan. (1970, December). Agricultural productivity differences among countries. *American Economic Review*, 895–911.

Helfand, S. M., & Taylor, M. P. (2021). The inverse relationship between farm size and productivity: Refocusing the debate. *Food Policy, 99*, Article 101977.

Heltberg, R. (1998). Rural market imperfections and the farm size—Productivity relationship: Evidence from Pakistan. *World Development, 26*(10), 1807–1826.

Himanshu, H., Lanjouw, P., Mukhopadhyay, A., & Murgai, R. (2011). Non-farm diversification and rural poverty decline: A perspective from Indian sample survey and village study data. LSE Asia Research Centre working paper 44.

Holden, S. T., & Binswanger, H. P. (1998). Small-farmer decision-making, market imperfections, and natural resource management in developing countries. *Agriculture and the environment: perspectives on sustainable rural development*, 50–71.

Holden, S., Shiferaw, B., & Pender, J. (2001). Market imperfections and land productivity in the Ethiopian highlands. *Journal of Agricultural Economics, 52*(3), 53–70.

Holden, S. T., & Fisher, M. (2013). Can area measurement error explain the inverse farm size productivity relationship? https://nmbu.brage.unit.no/nmbu-xmlui/bitstream/handle/11250/2478787/clts_wp12_2013.pdf?sequence=1

Jan, M. A., & Harriss-White, B. (2012). The three roles of agricultural markets: a review of ideas about agricultural commodity markets in India. *Economic and Political Weekly*, 39–52.

Khusro, A. M. (1964). Returns to scale in Indian agriculture. *Indian Journal of Agricultural Economics, 19*(3 & 4), 51–80.

Lamb, R. L. (2003). Inverse productivity: Land quality, labor markets, and measurement error. *Journal of Development Economics, 71*(1), 71–95.

Larson, D. F., Otsuka, K., Matsumoto, T., & Kilic, T. (2014). Should African rural development strategies depend on smallholder farms? An exploration of the inverse-productivity hypothesis. *Agricultural Economics, 45*(3), 355–367.

Marshall, Alfred. (1920). *Principles of Economics*. Macmillan.

NABARD. (2018). All India rural financial inclusion survey 2016–17. National Agricultural Bank for Agricultural and Rural Development, Government of India. Retrieved from https://www.nabard.org/auth/writereaddata/tender/1608180417NABARD-Repo-16_Web_P.pdf

NITI Aayog. (2020). New Farm Acts: Understanding the implications. NITI Aayog working paper series 1/2020.

NSSO. (2021, September). *Situation assessment of agricultural households and land and livestock holdings of households in Rural India, 2019*, NSS 77th Round (January 2019-December 2019), Ministry of Statistics and Programme Implementation, Government of India.

Rada, N. E., & Fuglie, K. O. (2019). New perspectives on farm size and productivity. *Food Policy, 84*, 147-152.

Rosenzweig, M. R., & Binswanger, H. P. (1993). Wealth, weather risk and the composition and profitability of agricultural investments. *The Economic Journal, 103,* 56-78.
Rudra, A. (1968). More on returns to scale in Indian agriculture. *Economic and Political Weekly, 26*, 1968.
Sekhar, C. S. C. (2005). Economic growth, social development and interest groups. *Economic and Political Weekly., 40*(50), 5338–5346.
Sekhar, C. S. C, Namrata Thapa, & Vikas Singh. (2021). Agricultural market imperfections and farm profitability. *Report submitted to the Ministry of Agriculture & Farmers Welfare, Government of India.* https://desagri.gov.in/aer-report/
Sekhar, C. S. C., & Thapa, N. (2021). Agricultural market imperfections and farm profitability. *Working Paper 440,* Institute of Economic Growth https://iegindia.org/working-paper/agricultural-market-imperfections-and-farm-profitability-in-india/
Sekhar, C. S. C., & Thapa, N. (2023). Rural market imperfections in India: Revisiting old debates with new evidence. *Development Policy Review, 41*, 12708. https://doi.org/10.1111/dpr.12708
Sen, A. K. (1962). An aspect of Indian agriculture. *Economic Weekly, 14*, 243–266.
Sen, A. K. (1966). Peasants and dualism with or without surplus labor. *Journal of Political Economy, 74*(5), 425–450.
Sheng, Y., Ding, J., & Huang, J. (2019). The relationship between farm size and productivity in agriculture: Evidence from maize production in Northern China. *American Journal of Agricultural Economics, 101*(3), 790–806.
Singh, I., Squire, L., & Strauss, J. (Eds.). (1986). *Agricultural household models.* The Johns Hopkins University Press.
Skoufias, E. (1995). Household resources, transaction costs, and adjustment through land tenancy. *Land Economics, 71*, 42–56.
Srinivasan, T. N. (1972). Farm size and productivity-implications of choice under uncertainty. *Indian Journal of Statistics,* Series B, Vol. 34, part 4.
Wineman, A., & Jayne, T. S. (2021). Factor market activity and the inverse farm size-productivity relationship in Tanzania. *The Journal of Development Studies, 57*(3), 443–464.

C S C Sekhar is a professor at Agricultural Economics Research Unit, Institute of Economic Growth, Delhi. He works on agricultural markets (market structure, price formation, exports, and imports), food security, agricultural growth, rural development, political economy of development and governance. Other important interests include applied econometrics, econometric modelling, WTO issues related to agriculture, development economics and law & economics.

Namrata Thapa is engaged as a consultant at NITI Aayog, Delhi. She has a diverse academic and professional background, and has worked as an Assistant Professor in Economics at the Birla Institute of Management Technology and as a Senior Research Analyst at the Institute of Economic Growth. She holds a Ph.D. degree in Economics from the Centre for Development Studies (CDS), Trivandrum. Her broad research interests include Development Economics, Innovation Studies, Agriculture and Rural Development, Gender Economics.

Part IV
Service Sector

Chapter 9
Service Sector Dynamics and Role in the Indian Economy

Rupa Chanda, Garima Chaklader, and Sudeshna Ghosh

Abstract Services have been a dynamic sector in the Indian economy, significantly contributing to India's GDP, FDI inflows, and exports. Services have played a key role in India's integration with the world market, particularly due to the performance of segments such as IT and IT-enabled services and business and professional services. The sector has also outperformed manufacturing in terms of growth, productivity, and share in global trade. In large part, its dynamism can be attributed to economic liberalization and regulatory reforms undertaken in India since 1991. This chapter discusses the growth, development, and productivity dynamics in India's service sector till date and its potential role in shaping India's future growth prospects. It outlines trends in the sector's GDP growth and contribution to the Indian economy, highlighting differences in performance within the service sector and relative to other sectors, and places this performance in the context of the debate surrounding India's services-led growth paradigm in contrast to the traditional primary to secondary sector growth model. The chapter also provides an overview of key regulatory, policy, and other developments in the services sector, with a focus on selected services, and analyzes their implications for not only the growth and development of the services sector but also its implications for the larger economy, through direct and indirect linkages with other sectors. The chapter concludes by outlining policy measures that are needed to leverage emerging opportunities as well as address challenges in services.

R. Chanda (✉)
UN Economic and Social Commission for Asia and the Pacific (UNESCAP), Bangkok, Thailand
e-mail: rupa@iimb.ac.in

R. Chanda · S. Ghosh
Indian Institute of Management Bangalore, Bangalore, India

G. Chaklader
Economics, Masters' Union, Gurgaon, India

D. Maiti et al. (eds.), *75 Years of Growth, Development and Productivity in India*, India Studies in Business and Economics, https://doi.org/10.1007/978-981-97-8054-9_9

9.1 Introduction

Services have been a dynamic sector of the Indian economy, serving as an engine of growth over the past few decades and consistently outperforming other sectors of the economy. Services grew at 7.5% on average per year during the 1993–2018 period (Goldar et al., 2024), accounting for about half of aggregate economic growth. Today, services inclusive of construction services account for over 60% of India's GDP, up from less than 40% a few decades ago (UNCTADstat Data Centre). Their share in employment has also risen consistently, doubling from 17% in 1980 to 34% in 2017, contributing 60% of the additional employment generated during this period (Krishna et al., 2022), helping to reduce the economy's employment dependence on agriculture.

India's integration with the global market have also been facilitated by the services sector, particularly due to competitive segments such as information technology (IT) and IT-enabled services (ITeS). India features among the ten leading exporters in the world. Its services exports today amount to over $300 billion and have consistently grown as a share of global services exports to nearly 4%, considerably surpassing the share of India's manufacturing exports in the world market. The contribution of services to India's trade basket has risen to over 40% and is expected to rise to over 50% in future. Services are also the largest recipient of FDI inflows in the Indian economy and in some services, India has emerged as a source of FDI. Further, successful technological advancements in services and growing tradability of these services have contributed to India's improved Global Innovation ranking. Evidence also suggests that the growing integration of India's service sector with world markets has contributed positively to productivity, efficiency, and overall competitiveness both within the service sector as well as in other sectors of the economy.

A range of factors, including India's economic liberalization and regulatory reforms since the 1990s, policy incentives, rising incomes, technological advancements especially in information and communication technology (ICT), demographics, and global market dynamics, among others, have shaped the sector's growth trajectory, its rising contribution to the Indian economy, as well as India's global performance. Notwithstanding these developments, however, there have been concerns about the sector's growth trajectory and contribution. One key issue that has been highlighted is whether the leapfrogging from agriculture to services with a stagnant manufacturing sector, is desirable and sustainable. Questions have also been raised about the pattern and orientation of India's services growth, its services exports which remain dominated by segments such as and IT services, the extent and nature of the sector's integration with the rest of the Indian economy, and the growth of informal services and related employment in the sector. In addition to these structural considerations, there remain many regulatory, infrastructural, human capital, financial, and other constraints which hamper the sector's growth and competitiveness and its wider contribution and spillovers to the Indian economy. An understanding of these issues and challenges warrants a closer examination of India's service sector, the role played by the regulatory and policy environment in shaping its development and identifying areas for intervention.

This chapter aims to provide a better understanding of the growth, development, and productivity dynamics in India's service sector and how services could play a greater role in the future growth prospects of the Indian economy. Following the introduction, Sect. 9.2 provides an overview of the key characteristics of India's service sector growth. It outlines trends in the sector's GDP growth and contribution to the Indian economy in terms of output, employment, trade, and FDI. This section also presents the sector's linkages with other sectors of the economy in terms of its value-added contribution to both output and exports, and highlights differences in performance across different segments within services and across other sectors. Section 9.3 builds on the broader macro-overview of trends and presents the debate surrounding India's services-led growth paradigm in contrast to the traditional primary to secondary sector growth model and the implications for development. Section 9.4 focuses on the productivity dynamics of India's service sector. It provides an empirical analysis of India's productivity dynamics using KLEMS 2021 data. It also presents the results at the industry level. Section 9.5 discusses key regulatory, policy, and other developments in the services sector, with a focus on selected services, and analyzes their implications for not only the growth and development of the sector itself but also its implications for the larger economy, through direct and indirect linkages between services and other sectors. The concluding section summarizes the main findings regarding the service sector's contribution to the Indian economy and outlines policy measures that would be needed to leverage emerging opportunities as well as address challenges in services.

9.2 Macroeconomic Overview of India's Services Sector

The services sector has been a leading source of growth in India and an important part of India's trade and investment flows. The following discussion highlights salient trends and characteristics of services growth and contribution to the Indian economy.

9.2.1 Services Contribution to Value-Added

Services growth has consistently outpaced growth in overall GDP and in other sectors of the economy since independence. The compound annual growth rate (CAGR) of services in the decades upto 2000 ranged between 5 and over 8% compared to manufacturing and agriculture, whose CAGRs were below 6% and around 3%, respectively. During the 2000–19 period, services registered a compound annual growth rate (CAGR) of nearly 8%, compared to less than 7% for overall GDP and industry. Although services growth fell sharply in 2020 to –7.6% due to Covid, when key subsectors such as trade and transport were severely affected by the lockdown, the sector recovered in 2021, along with manufacturing (Fig. 9.1).

Services have also shown considerable resilience in growth, withstanding several shocks that affected the global and Indian economy over the past few decades. As illustrated in Fig. 9.2, between 1980 and 2020, for the most part, the sector exhibited average annual growth rates of around 7% (excepting the period marked by Covid most recently), reaching an average of 8% growth per annum during the 2003–11 period despite the global financial crisis of 2008–09. Further, through most of this period, services growth exceeded that of manufacturing.

The sector's robust growth performance has resulted in its consistently rising contribution to the Indian economy, from around 25% of GDP in 1950 to 49% of GDP in 2000 to 62% in 2019 (inclusive of construction), almost mirroring the simultaneous decline in the share of agriculture in India's economy from around 60% of GDP in 1950 to less than 20% in 2022. India's experience in this regard stands in contrast to that of many other developing countries in that it has leapfrogged from the primary to the tertiary sector, with a stagnant secondary sector, raising concerns about its growth paradigm (Fig. 9.3).

A disaggregated overview of the service sector, however, reveals that this growth performance has not been uniform across services subsectors. The growth driver within the services sector has been market services. As reflected in Table 9.1, the contribution of market services to GDP has more than doubled over the 1990–2020 period. In particular, ICT-intensive services, especially business services, have significantly grown in importance, recording a tenfold increase in their contribution between 1990 and 2020. In contrast, non-ICT based market services have exhibited a stagnant share of around 4.5% while nonmarket services have overall experienced a decline in their contribution to the service sector. This strong growth in ICT-intensive

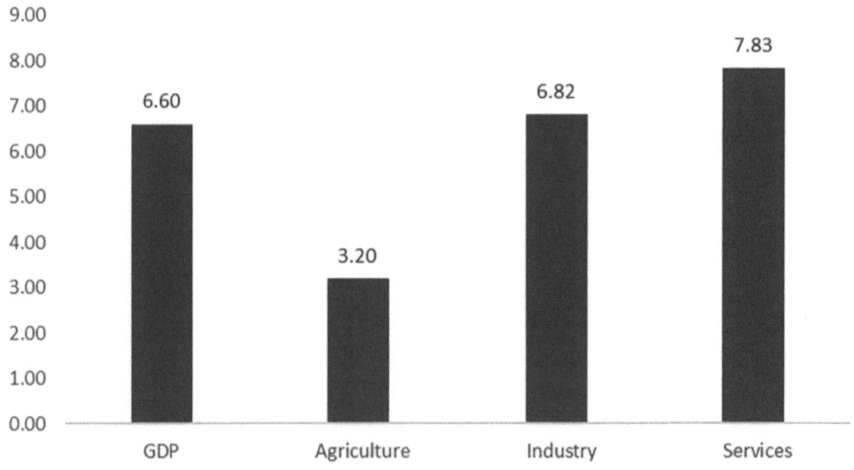

Fig. 9.1 CAGR of India's overall and sector-wise output (%), 2000–19. *Source* https://unctadstat.unctad.org/datacentre/ accessed: 24-04-2024

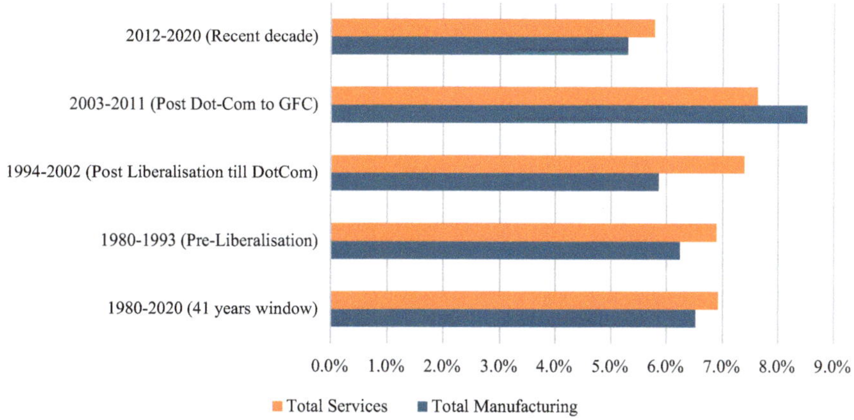

Fig. 9.2 Average annual growth in manufacturing and services value-added (%), 1980–2020. *Source* Authors' computation from KLEMS database 2021

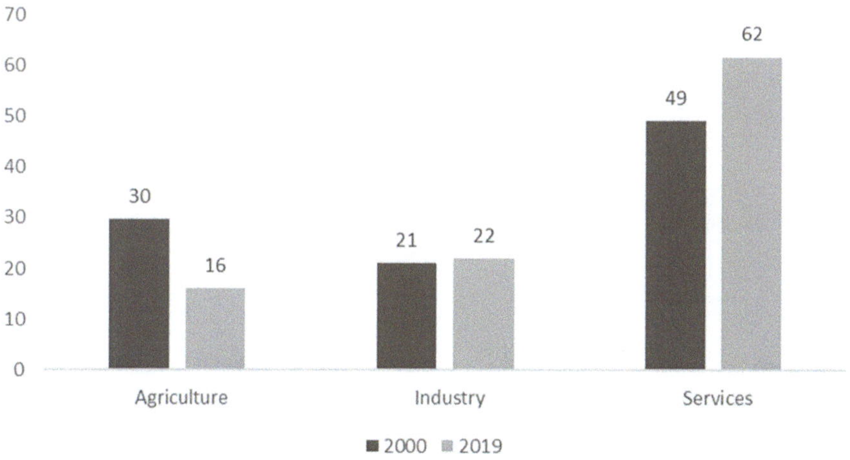

Fig. 9.3 Sectoral composition of India's GDP, selected years (%). *Source* https://unctadstat.unctad.org/datacentre/ accessed: 24-04-2024

business services largely reflects the impact of liberalizing telecom services in 1994, which allowed the entry of private players into the market, as well as advancements in ICT technologies which have made possible the fragmentation and delivery, including cross-border delivery, of many business activities.

Disaggregated growth estimates provided in Table 9.2 confirm the role of ICT-intensive market services in driving the service sector's growth in India. Telecommunication as well as business services registered average annual growth rates of over 15% during the 1994–2002 period, with business services consistently growing at around 10% or more between 1990 and 2020. Even financial services experienced

Table 9.1 Value-added share by industry (%), selected years

Description	1980 (%)	1990 (%)	2000 (%)	2010 (%)	2020 (%)
Total	100.00	100.00	100.00	100.00	100.00
Agriculture, hunting, Forestry, and fishing	41.10	33.27	26.14	18.33	16.27
Mining and quarrying	4.04	5.25	4.65	4.11	2.34
Total manufacturing	**12.73**	**14.76**	**15.49**	**17.72**	**17.86**
Food products, beverages, and tobacco	1.37	1.80	1.98	1.86	2.05
Textiles, textile products, leather, and footwear	1.90	1.74	1.75	1.97	1.90
Wood and products of wood	1.71	0.79	0.44	0.25	0.24
Pulp, paper, paper products, printing, and publishing	0.46	0.60	0.34	0.52	0.37
Coke, refined petroleum products, and nuclear fuel	0.60	1.57	1.32	1.42	1.51
Chemicals and chemical products	1.11	1.76	2.50	2.36	2.65
Rubber and plastic products	0.20	0.38	0.73	0.73	0.78
Other non-metallic mineral products	0.62	1.07	1.11	1.09	1.12
Basic metals and fabricated metal products	2.59	2.54	2.63	3.08	2.61
Machinery, nec	0.89	1.01	0.94	1.38	1.25
Electrical and optical equipment	0.23	0.38	0.44	1.04	1.04
Transport equipment	0.75	0.86	0.95	1.55	1.90
Manufacturing, nec; recycling	0.29	0.25	0.37	0.45	0.46
Electricity, gas, and water supply	1.55	2.05	2.36	2.23	2.30
Construction	7.73	7.02	6.86	8.92	7.65
Total services	**32.86**	**37.65**	**44.49**	**48.69**	**53.58**
Market services	14.48	16.59	23.14	28.80	33.91
ICT services	10.40	12.36	18.15	22.84	29.35
Trade	6.90	7.09	8.54	9.75	10.73
Financial services	2.19	3.49	5.14	6.03	6.55
Business service	0.97	1.43	3.56	5.52	10.29
Post and telecommunication	0.34	0.34	0.92	1.55	1.77
Non-ICT services	4.08	4.22	4.98	5.96	4.56
Hotels and restaurants	0.60	0.65	0.96	1.10	0.53
Transport and storage	3.47	3.58	4.02	4.86	4.02
Non-market services	18.38	21.07	21.36	19.89	19.67
Public administration and defense	5.34	5.89	6.37	6.11	6.17
Education	1.65	1.89	2.45	3.04	3.93

(continued)

Table 9.1 (continued)

Description	1980 (%)	1990 (%)	2000 (%)	2010 (%)	2020 (%)
Health and social work	0.59	0.74	0.95	1.42	1.54
Other services	10.80	12.55	11.59	9.31	8.02

Source Authors' computation from KLEMS database 2021

rapid growth through most of this period, notwithstanding the impact of the 2008 global financial crisis. In comparison, most other services such as transport, trade, health, and education services, have grown on average at around 5% or less through this period, highlighting the heterogenous nature of growth dynamics within the service sector.

9.2.2 *Services Role in Employment*

The service sector's contribution to overall employment has also risen steadily, though perhaps not commensurate to its rising contribution to value-added. Table 9.3 provides the relative employment shares of different industries over the 1980–2020 period. As highlighted, services accounted for nearly 33% of all jobs in 2020, up significantly from just 16% in 1980. As with value-added growth, market services have been the main contributor to employment, with their employment share rising from 9 to 22% while that of nonmarket services increased only modestly from 8 to 11% during the 1980–2020 period. Within market services, ICT-intensive services have exhibited stronger employment growth. In contrast to services, the manufacturing sector's incremental contribution to employment has been minimal through most of this period, in fact declining from 12 to 10% between 2011 and 2020 and confirming the long-standing concerns about the manufacturing sector's inability to create jobs.

A comparative overview of employment growth in the services and manufacturing sectors in Fig. 9.4 confirms the relatively stronger role of the service sector in job creation in India. Services have consistently registered higher employment growth than manufacturing over the entire past four decades, though the rate of job creation has decelerated over time. A closer examination across different service sector activities indicates that job growth has been particularly significant in specific business services activities, such as consulting, data analysis, and professional services, which have been expanding and creating employment opportunities. Segments such as financial and health services have also exhibited relatively strong employment growth. On the other hand, some services such as post and telecommunications which have performed well in terms of value-added growth have, however, experienced a decline in employment growth, indicating that employment and value-added

Table 9.2 Average annual growth in value-added by industry (%), 1981–2020

Description	1981–90 (%)	1991–2000 (%)	2001–2010 (%)	2011–20 (%)	2020 (%)
Agriculture, hunting, forestry, and fishing	3.26	3.30	2.50	3.51	3.32
Mining and quarrying	7.86	4.08	5.64	1.33	–8.62
Total manufacturing	7.20	6.51	8.65	5.32	–0.60
Food products, beverages, and tobacco	7.54	6.98	6.60	4.89	3.71
Textiles, textile products, leather, and footwear	5.54	6.27	8.97	5.09	–18.45
Wood and products of wood	–2.59	–0.20	2.54	3.54	–18.84
Pulp, paper, paper products, printing, and publishing	8.36	–0.97	12.07	2.04	–17.24
Coke, refined petroleum products, and nuclear fuel	18.60	4.16	6.83	10.30	48.94
Chemicals and chemical products	9.73	9.77	5.98	5.62	12.32
Rubber and plastic products	15.46	12.95	6.27	8.91	6.05
Other non-metallic mineral products	11.92	5.68	6.94	4.35	–5.87
Basic metals and fabricated metal products	5.13	5.86	9.10	4.08	1.79
Machinery, nec	7.11	6.17	13.28	2.56	–5.68
Electrical and optical equipment	11.49	9.63	16.90	5.29	–0.74
Transport equipment	6.43	7.18	12.35	6.70	–9.52
Manufacturing, nec; recycling	2.78	11.98	10.07	5.64	–23.64
Electricity, gas, and water supply	8.48	6.47	6.43	5.01	–3.63
Construction	4.49	5.36	10.03	2.41	–7.30
Total services	7.20	7.22	7.67	6.06	–7.82
Market services	7.11	9.21	8.89	6.89	–9.83
ICT services	7.50	9.83	8.90	7.99	–6.17
Trade	5.85	8.01	7.79	6.09	–19.32
Financial services	11.01	8.73	8.32	6.19	5.11
Business service	9.78	16.47	11.20	12.49	2.92
Post and telecommunication	5.60	17.18	11.48	6.56	1.75
Non-ICT services	6.04	7.21	8.87	1.69	–27.95
Hotels and restaurants	7.37	10.49	8.04	–3.18	–56.41
Transport and storage	5.81	6.56	9.06	2.55	–21.11
Non-market services	7.27	5.41	6.11	4.77	–4.14

(continued)

Table 9.2 (continued)

Description	1981–90 (%)	1991–2000 (%)	2001–2010 (%)	2011–20 (%)	2020 (%)
Public administration and defense	7.13	6.56	6.51	5.23	2.26
Education	7.41	8.58	9.51	7.06	–2.33
Health and Social work	8.34	8.67	11.35	6.55	–3.99
Other services	7.25	4.09	4.42	3.22	--9.35

Source Authors' computation from KLEMS database 2021

performance have not always moved in tandem across all service subsectors and activities.

9.2.3 Services Role in Trade

India's service sector has also exhibited its dynamism in the international market. Services trade as a share of India's GDP has increased over time, reflecting the growing trade orientation of the sector. In 2022, India ranked as the 5th largest exporter and 6th largest importer of commercial services (excluding intra-EU trade). Its share in world services exports increased from only 0.8% in 1980 and quadrupled between 2000 and 2022 from 1.1 to 4.4%. In comparison, its share in global merchandise exports stood at less than 2%. Likewise, reflecting India's greater presence in global services as opposed to goods trade, its share in global services imports stood at 3.8% in 2022 up from 0.7% in 1980 and compared to less than 3% in case of global merchandise imports (WTO, 2023). This is also evident from revealed comparative advantage (RCA)[1] estimates where services consistently exhibit greater competitiveness than goods (Fig. 9.5).

India's competitiveness in services and growing integration with the global services market is reflected in its increased services trade over the past two decades, with services exports experiencing a CAGR of 10.6% over the 2005–19 period and average annual growth rates exceeding that of global services exports as well as those of some leading services exporters. As shown in Table 9.4, India's services exports have risen manifold, from $2.8 billion in 1980 to around US$ 50bn in 2005 to over US$ 300bn in 2022 while its services imports have grown from $2.9 billion in 1980 to US$ 60bn to nearly US$ 250bn over this same period. The growing trade surplus in services over the past decade plus has been an important contributor to India's balance of payments stability. Although Covid severely impacted services

[1] RCA is the ratio of a sector's share in a country's exports to the same sector's share in world exports.

RCA > 1 in a sector means that the concerned country has a revealed comparative advantage in that sector.

Table 9.3 Employment share by industry (%), selected years

Description	1980 (%)	1990 (%)	2000 (%)	2010 (%)	2020 (%)
Total	100.00	100.00	100.00	100.00	100.00
Agriculture, hunting, forestry, and fishing	69.83	64.59	59.30	49.27	43.80
Mining and quarrying	0.52	0.71	0.64	0.55	0.31
Total manufacturing	**10.43**	**10.68**	**10.93**	**11.71**	**10.08**
Food products, beverages, and tobacco	2.23	2.34	2.51	2.39	1.84
Textiles, textile products, leather, and footwear	3.70	3.42	2.93	2.99	2.11
Wood and products of wood	0.94	0.90	1.13	0.87	0.56
Pulp, paper, paper products, printing, and publishing	0.25	0.28	0.32	0.34	0.33
Coke, refined petroleum products, and nuclear fuel	0.02	0.03	0.03	0.03	0.04
Chemicals and chemical products	0.36	0.43	0.45	0.43	0.49
Rubber and plastic products	0.08	0.14	0.18	0.24	0.23
Other non-metallic mineral products	0.92	0.89	0.86	1.04	0.76
Basic metals and fabricated metal products	0.72	0.77	0.86	0.95	1.05
Machinery, nec	0.19	0.18	0.31	0.38	0.51
Electrical and optical equipment	0.17	0.23	0.26	0.48	0.67
Transport equipment	0.18	0.23	0.24	0.32	0.42
Manufacturing, nec; recycling	0.67	0.86	0.83	1.25	1.08
Electricity, gas, and water supply	0.28	0.32	0.28	0.33	0.46
Construction	1.99	3.73	4.52	9.46	11.94
Total services	**16.94**	**19.98**	**24.33**	**28.67**	**33.41**
Market services	9.12	11.81	15.14	18.52	22.26
ICT services	6.43	8.33	10.63	12.81	15.90
Trade	5.80	7.34	9.08	10.02	11.83
Financial services	0.31	0.51	0.57	0.91	1.13
Business service	0.18	0.30	0.65	1.50	2.64
Post and telecommunication	0.14	0.18	0.33	0.38	0.29
Non-ICT services	2.70	3.49	4.50	5.71	6.36
Hotels and restaurants	0.80	0.91	1.17	1.64	1.80
Transport and storage	1.90	2.57	3.34	4.06	4.57
Non-market services	7.81	8.16	9.19	10.15	11.15
Public administration and defense	2.75	2.84	2.47	1.79	1.63
Education	1.58	1.62	2.15	2.95	3.24

(continued)

Table 9.3 (continued)

Description	1980 (%)	1990 (%)	2000 (%)	2010 (%)	2020 (%)
Health and social work	0.58	0.56	0.72	0.97	1.41
Other services	2.90	3.14	3.86	4.44	4.87

Source Authors' computation from KLEMS database 2021

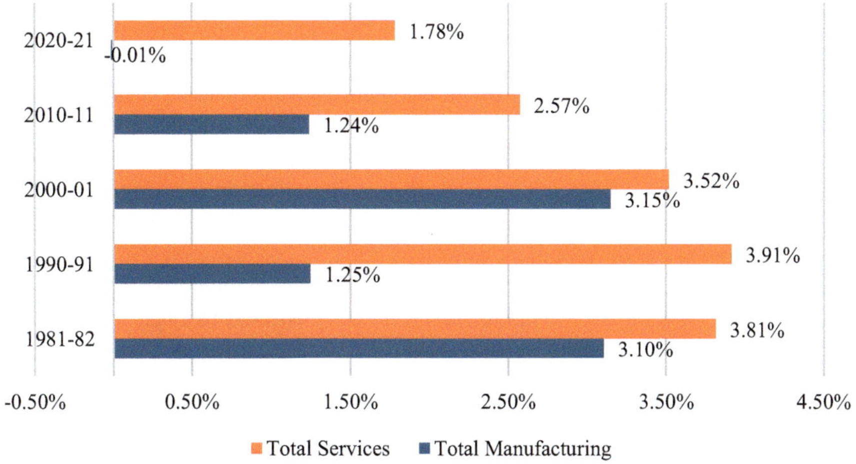

Fig. 9.4 Employment growth in manufacturing and services, 1980–2020 (% per annum). *Source* Authors' computation from KLEMS database 2021

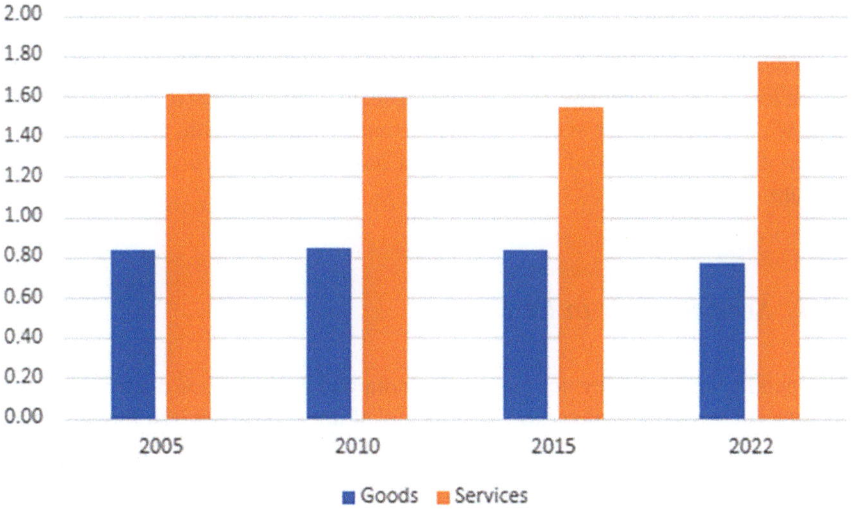

Fig. 9.5 India's Revealed Comparative Advantage (RCA) for goods and services. *Source* https://unctadstat.unctad.org/datacentre/ accessed: 24-04-2024

trade, causing a decline of 5.4% in India's services exports between 2019 and 2020, with travel services exports declining sharply by 57% in 2020, services trade was resilient and recovered by 2022.

As shown in Table 9.4, among the main services trade categories, other services exports have increased in importance over time, mirroring the growth and employment dynamics in these services discussed earlier. Other services exports experienced a CAGR of 10.9% over the 2005–19 period and an average annual growth rate of nearly 20% during the 2005–10 period. Other services have also increased their importance in overall services imports. Further disaggregation of other services trade provided in Table 9.5 highlights the dominance of computer services as well as the growing role of professional and management consulting services and research and development (R&D) services in India's services exports and the importance of Technical, trade-related & other business services in India's services imports. These trends reflect the impact of factors such as services liberalization, growing demand for services, technology, and the role of business and professional services in supporting economic growth and development as well as trade.

Thus the trends in India's services exports reflect its comparative advantage in other services, specifically computer services, as illustrated in Figs. 9.6 and 9.7, respectively.

As shown in Fig. 9.6, other services have consistently exhibited RCAs of over 1 over the 2005–20 period, though there is a declining trend in their competitiveness over time. Within other services, Computer services as well as Professional & Management Consulting services have maintained their comparative advantage with RCAs over 1, for the past two decades. Technical, trade-related & other business services have lost their comparative advantage post 2005, making India's services export competitiveness mostly dependent on Computer and Professional & Management Consulting over the past decade and half. However, a point of concern is the steady decline in comparative advantage for computer services, suggesting that India may be losing its competitive edge in this subsector. Thus, trends in India's services trade, while reflecting the sector's strengths and dynamic growth, also indicate the need to diversify and broad base the export basket given its current concentrated structure.

9.2.4 Services Role in FDI

The opening up of the services sector in India and its increased contestability in the domestic services market has led to its global integration through foreign direct investment (FDI) flows, alongside trade. Over the past few decades, there has been a structural shift in FDI inflows towards the service sector. The average share of services in FDI rose from 10.5% for the 1990–94 period to 28.3% during the 1995–99 period and by 2016–17, services accounted for nearly 62% of FDI inflows in India. Cumulative FDI inflows into services for the January 2000-March 2018 period stood at \$222.9 billion or roughly 60% of total cumulative FDI inflows for this entire

Table 9.4 India's services trade values and shares by key categories (USD mn and %), selected years

Categories	2005		2010		2015		2020		2022	
Exports										
	Value	Share	Value	Share	Value	Share	Value	Share	Value	Share
Total services	52,179	100	117,068	100	156,278	100	203,145	100	309,374	100
Goods-related services	n/a	n/a	0	0	324	0.21	406	0.20	1595	0.52
Transport	6537	12.53	13,275	11.34	14,319	9.16	20,791	10.23	37,536	12.13
Travel	7493	14.36	14,490	12.38	21,013	13.45	13,036	6.42	21,360	6.90
Other	38,149	73.11	89,303	76.28	120,622	77.18	168,912	83.15	248,883	80.45
Imports										
Services	60,636	100	114,928	100	123,567	100	153,737	100	249,522	100
Goods-related services	n/a	n/a	0	0	336	0.27	963	0.63	1857	0.74
Transport	33,009	54.44	46,705	40.64	52,257	42.29	53,813	35.00	108,944	43.66
Travel	6187	10.20	10,490	9.13	14,838	12.01	12,574	8.18	25,881	10.37
Other	21,440	35.36	57,733	50.23	56,136	45.43	86,387	56.19	112,840	45.22

Source https://unctadstat.unctad.org/wds/ReportFolders/reportFolders.aspx?sCS_ChosenLang=en accessed: 22-11-2023. *Notes* Total services include construction. Goods-related services cover manufacturing services on physical inputs owned by others and maintenance and repair services not included elsewhere

Table 9.5 Composition of India's "Other" services exports and imports by key categories (%)

Flow	Other services categories	Year				
		2005	2010	2015	2020	2022
Exports	Construction	0.91	0.59	1.23	1.66	1.34
	Insurance & pension	2.47	1.99	1.65	1.39	1.35
	Financial	3.00	6.53	4.43	2.43	2.95
	Telecommunications	2.05	1.69	1.73	1.62	1.35
	Computer	41.72	43.00	43.74	38.67	38.38
	R&D	0.63	1.15	1.32	3.96	5.50
	Professional & management consulting	22.81	26.05	30.71	35.04	38.57
	Technical, trade-related, & other business services	24.05	11.61	9.71	8.37	7.02
	Audiovisual & related	n/a	0.26	0.29	0.46	0.64
	Personal, cultural, & recreational (other than audiovisual & related)	0.29	0.83	0.76	0.84	0.90
Imports	Construction	2.81	2.80	1.75	2.98	2.92
	Insurance & pension	17.15	14.20	9.58	6.52	9.80
	Financial	4.05	19.18	5.71	5.29	6.04
	Telecommunications	0.97	3.07	1.54	1.59	1.47
	Computer	4.89	6.15	4.72	10.42	15.24
	R&D	0.42	0.90	0.61	0.72	0.71
	Professional & management consulting	10.11	34.06	17.75	13.54	13.58
	Technical, trade-related, & other business services	52.78	37.10	36.22	41.45	44.24
	Audiovisual & related	n/a	0.44	0.32	0.59	1.18
	Personal, cultural, & recreational (other than audiovisual & related)	0.49	11.37	2.18	2.56	4.22

Source https://unctadstat.unctad.org/wds/ReportFolders/reportFolders.aspx?sCS_ChosenLang=en accessed:22-11-2023

period. Service sector FDI has grown more rapidly than manufacturing FDI (based on DPIIT website and RBI Handbook of Statistics).

In recent years, although global FDI flows have declined, falling by 12% in 2022 due to overlapping crises, FDI inflows into India have remained resilient, increasing by 11.6% that same year. The top 10 sectors that attracted the most cumulative

Table 9.6 Top 10 sectors attracting FDI inflows in India, USD mn

Rank (Apr 2000-Sept 2023)	Sector	2021–22 (April-March)	2022–23 (April-March)	2023–24 (April-Sept)	Cumulative equity inflow (April 2000-Sept 2023)	% of cumulative Equity inflow Apr 2000-Sept 2023 (in terms of USD)
1	Services **	7131	8707	3853	106,709	16.29
2	Computer software & hardware	14,461	9394	2401	97,312	14.86
3	Trading	4538	4792	920	40,451	6.18
4	Telecommunications	668	713	271	39,315	6.00
5	Automobile industry	6994	1902	664	35,408	5.41
6	Construction (infrastructure) activities	3248	1703	2402	32,088	4.90
7	Construction development*	125	146	66	26,422	4.03
8	Chemicals (other than fertilizer)	966	1850	411	21,714	3.32
9	Drugs & pharmaceuticals	1414	2058	117	21,581	3.30
10	Metallurgical industries	2272	219	172	17,405	2.66

Source https://dpiit.gov.in/publications/fdi-statistics accessed: 27-11-23

* Townships, housing, built-up infrastructure and construction-development projects

** Services sector includes Financial, Banking, Insurance, Non-Financial / Business, Outsourcing, R&D, Courier, Tech. Testing and Analysis, Other

Notes FDI inflow received through Government Route + Automatic Route + acquisition of existing shares only. Figures are provisional

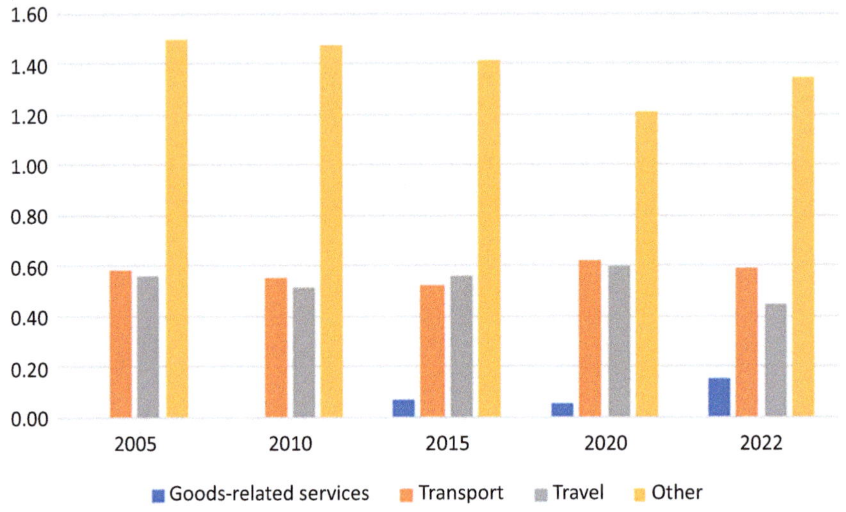

Fig. 9.6 RCAs for service trade categories, selected years. *Source* https://unctadstat.unctad.org/datacentre/ accessed: 24-04-2024. *Notes* Goods-related services cover manufacturing services on physical inputs owned by others and maintenance and repair services not included elsewhere. Goods-related services n/a for 2005

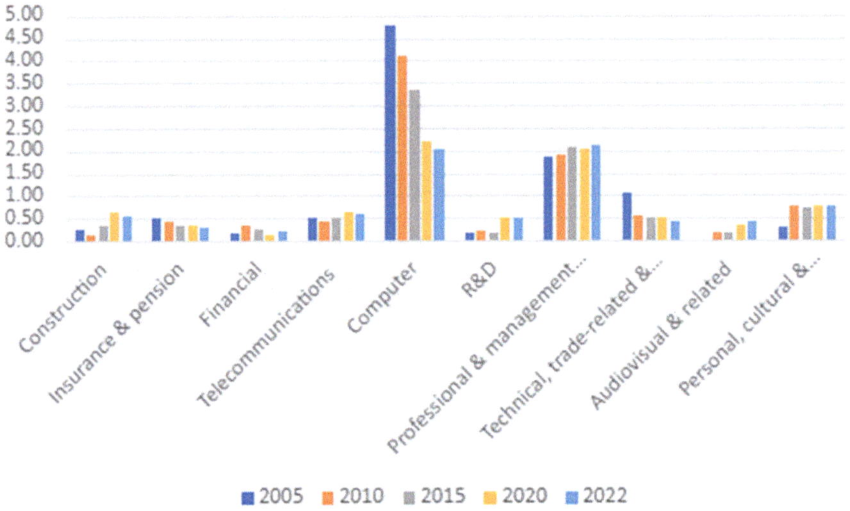

Fig. 9.7 RCAs for Key "Other" services categories. *Source* https://unctadstat.unctad.org/datacentre/ accessed: 24-04-2024

equity inflow[2] from April 2000 to September 2023 in India include, computer software and hardware, telecommunications, trading and construction while hotel and tourism, information and broadcasting (including print media), hospital and diagnostic centres, education and consultancy services feature among the top 20 sectors receiving FDI.

Liberalization of FDI regulations in most services through the automatic route coupled with regulatory reforms undertaken since 1991 has driven FDI growth in India's services sector. Important recent FDI reforms include the permitting of 100% FDI under automatic route for Single Brand Retail Trading, Construction Development; Telecom Services (including Telecom Infrastructure Providers in specified category) (DPIIT, 2021a) and allowing 74% foreign investment under automatic route in insurance companies and 100% through the automatic route in insurance intermediaries (DPIIT, 2021b), among others.

Although systematic data is not available to gauge the evolving role of the service sector in India's outward FDI flows, some studies point to the growing share of services in these outflows. During the 2000–14 period, services outward FDI accounted for 53% of approved equity, of which the majority were in IT and ITeS, construction, and communication services (Chaudhry et al., 2018). In IT services, overseas investments have taken the form of greenfield ventures, such as the setting up of R&D centres for work on new technologies like blockchain application and artificial intelligence or the form of acquisitions of overseas firms in areas like cloud services, analytics and business process outsourcing. The service sector accounts for a significant share of India's growing outward FDI in Africa in segments such as financial, transport, communication, and business services (Chaudhry et al., 2018, Fig. 9.7). The growth in India's outward FDI flows in services is a result of the government's liberalization of guidelines for overseas investments (India Brand Equity Foundation, 2018).

9.2.5 Services Linkages with the Economy

It is increasingly recognized that services are an important input for production and trade processes. From R&D and product design in the initial stages to transport and distribution following production to retailing, repair and maintenance in the final stages, with services such as telecommunications and finance intermediating these processes, services are present all through the value chain. The preceding discussion has highlighted the growing direct contribution of services to both value-added and exports. However, an examination of the indirect contribution of services as an input to production as well as to exports is important to gauge the sector's wider linkages with the economy and implications for growth and competitiveness.

---

[2] Cumulative FDI inflow consists of Equity inflow + "Re-invested earnings" + "Other capital", where equity inflow is the largest component.

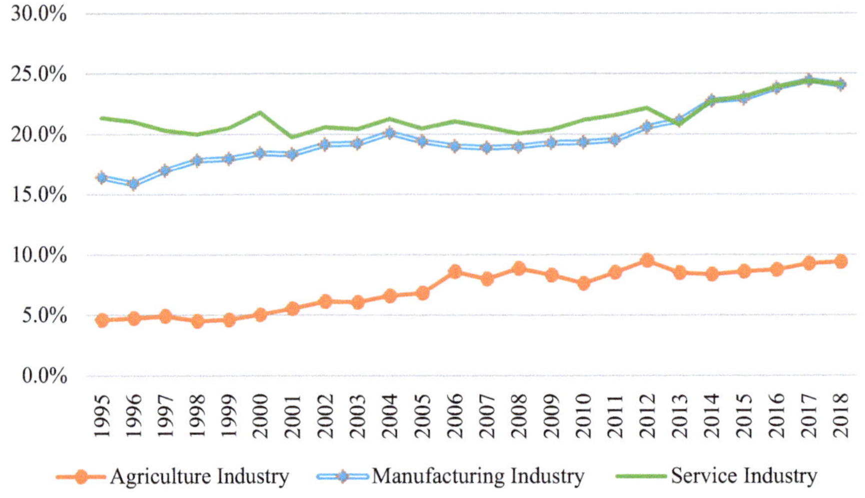

Fig. 9.8 Services input as a share of output, 1995–2018. *Source* OECD.Stat, Symmetric Input–Output Tables[3] (2021 edition)

9.2.5.1 Input Contribution of Services

An analysis of the consumption of intermediate services indicates growing reliance on services inputs across all sectors of the economy, though reliance has been greater in the case of manufacturing and services. As shown in Fig. 9.8, the contribution of services to manufacturing output increased from 15% in 1995 to 24% in 2018 while its contribution to services output rose from a little over 20% to around 25% during this same period. Services input contribution to agriculture has been comparatively low, but has witnessed a rising trend, doubling its value-added share in agricultural output from 4.7% in 1995 to 9.4% in 2018. The contribution of services value-added to the service sector has generally been higher than in other sectors, as would be expected, and has increased modestly from around 20% to 25% over the 1995–2018 period.

Growing services intensity, even if at relatively low levels in some sectors suggests changes in production approach and structure over time, with a growing role for supporting services. For example, the rising contribution of services in agricultural output possibly reflects the growing importance of services such as logistics, storage and distribution, marketing and extension, financial, and technical services, among others in supporting agricultural activities, though the trend also suggests that the pace of this integration has been slow. The increase in the contribution of services inputs to the manufacturing sector similarly indicates the growing interdependence

[3] The Symmetric Input–Output Tables (2021 edition) report the sale or purchase of goods of one industry from another. The reported transactions refer to the value of intermediate goods and services used by sector *i* which are produced in sector *j*. This transaction value of intermediate expenditures indicates the direct reliance of different industries on services.

of the two sectors. The trends in the services sector not only reflect intra- service sector linkages, but also the dependence of services on other parts of the economy.

These trends clearly have implications for growth and productivity given the recognized importance of services for competitiveness, efficiency, costs, diversification and structural transformation strategies, and value chain upgradation, among others. In order to better understand the implications of the increased value-added role of services in the economy, we examine the source of this growing contribution, whether this is stemming from modern services such as IT, finance, professional services, or traditional ones such as logistics, transport, and distribution.[4] Figure 9.9a to c provide a breakdown for the relative contributions of modern as well as traditional services to agriculture, manufacturing, and services, respectively.

The trends in the nature of services usage across the three sectors provide some useful insights. First, in both agriculture and manufacturing, traditional services have dominated over the entire period, likely reflecting the role of segments such as transport and distribution services. Second, the share of modern services, albeit still low, is on the rise in agriculture. This is a trend worth investigating to understand the nature and causes, such as whether this stems from use of more specialized and technical services in agriculture in recent years (as this would have implications for agricultural productivity and performance in the long run). Third, in the manufacturing sector, there is much greater reliance on traditional services than in the other sectors, and although the role of modern services is on the rise, it remains modest. The latter indicates that the integration of services such as IT, R&D, technical, and business/professional services, remains limited. This in turn might reflect a combination of factors such as lack of scale, technology, and modernization in the manufacturing sector which constrains the uptake of modern services, alongside factors such as the high cost of traditional services. Fourth, in the case of the services sector, modern services account for a much larger share than in other sectors of the economy, reflecting the role of segments such as IT, financial, and business and professional services. Furthermore, services such as education, human health, and arts and entertainment, have also increased their contribution to services output. These trends suggest growing diversification of the services sector and its linkages within the service sector.

A closer look at the usage of services within the manufacturing sector and trends in the use of modern versus traditional services, reveals considerable heterogeneity across manufacturing industries as well as evolution over the 1995 and 2018 period.

---

[4] Several earlier studies have split services into traditional services and modern services (Sahoo and Dash, 2014; Mishra et al., 2011; Benz et al., 2017; Ghani and Kharas, 2010; Eichengreen and Gupta, 2013). While the former can be stored and exchanged digitally, the latter rely mostly on face-to-face interactions (Mishra et al., 2011). In this chapter, traditional services cover Transportation and storage service expenses; Construction services; Wholesale and retail trade and repair of motor vehicles; Accommodation and food services; and Real Estate services. Modern services include Publishing, audio-visual, and broadcasting activities; Telecommunications; IT and other information services; Financial and insurance activities and other business sector services. Remaining services such as public services, education, human health, arts and entertainment, and other services activities are categorized as social services. Total services are defined as the sum of modern services output, traditional services output, and social services output.

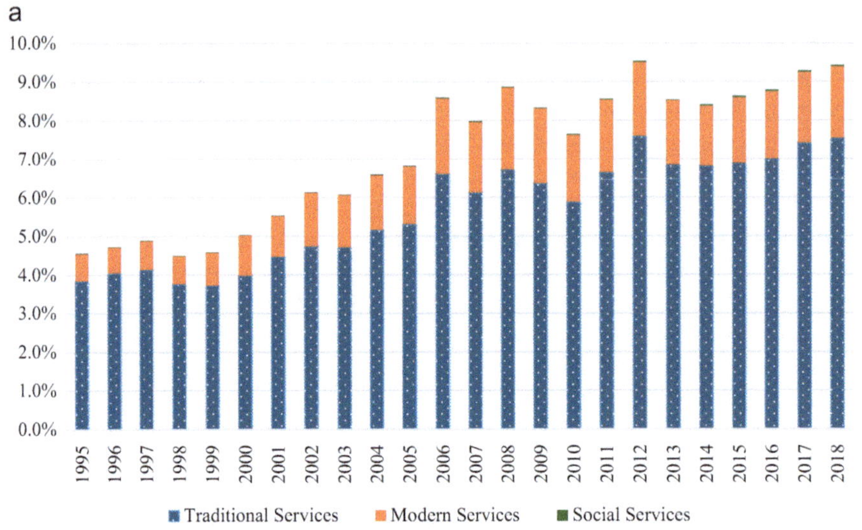

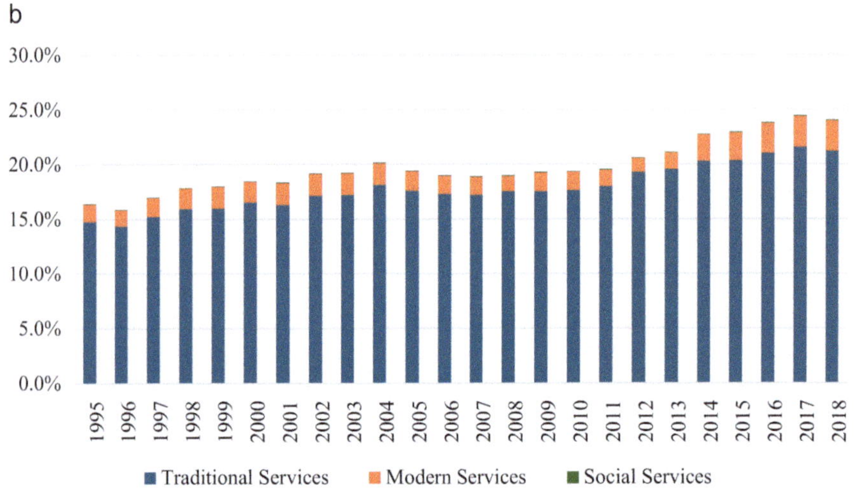

Fig. 9.9 **a** Services content as a share in Agriculture Output of India, 1995–2018. **b** Services content as a share in Manufacturing Output of India, 1995–2018. **c** Services content as a share in Services Output of India, 1995–2018. *Source* OECD.Stat, Symmetric Input–Output Tables (2021 edition)

As shown in Fig. 9.10, across manufacturing industries, there is a growing role of services inputs, for instance from 15 to 30% in the textiles industry, from a little over 15% to over 35% in the computer and electronics industry, from a little over 20% to over 30% in the food and beverages industry, and from 13 to 26% in the basic metals industry. The only industry which has seen a decline in its services consumption is the coke and petroleum industry. Thus, across manufacturing industries, there is growing

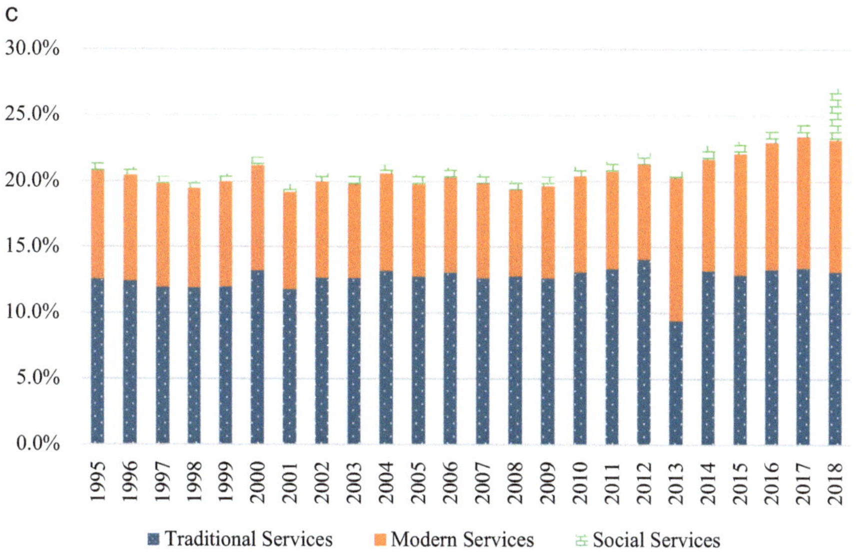

Fig. 9.9 (continued)

integration of services into their operations, with some industries experiencing more pronounced shifts than others.

Although across industries, traditional services dominate in terms of their contribution to manufacturing output, in several industries, there is growing reliance on modern services. This increase is particularly visible in the computer and electronics, textiles, electrical equipment, and food and beverage industries, indicating growing services contribution to both emerging and traditional manufacturing industries. The computer and electronics sector in particular shows a significant increase in the integration of services over time. This can be attributed to technological advancements which are pushing companies within this sector to rely more heavily on services such as software development, maintenance, and technical support to enhance their products and maintain competitiveness. Further, the increasing complexity of modern computer and electronic devices necessitates specialized services for design, installation, and troubleshooting, further driving the need for service integration. Many companies in this sector are transitioning from traditional product-based models to service-oriented models, offering subscription-based services, cloud computing, and software as a service (SaaS). This strategic shift naturally leads to higher absorption of services within the sector.

An examination of the source traditional services that are consumed across different manufacturing industries reflects the dominance of logistics and distribution services and their growing role over time, followed by construction services, across most industries. Among source segments of modern services, financial services emerge as the most important intermediate services, followed by administrative and support services and in the case of some industries such as computer and electronic

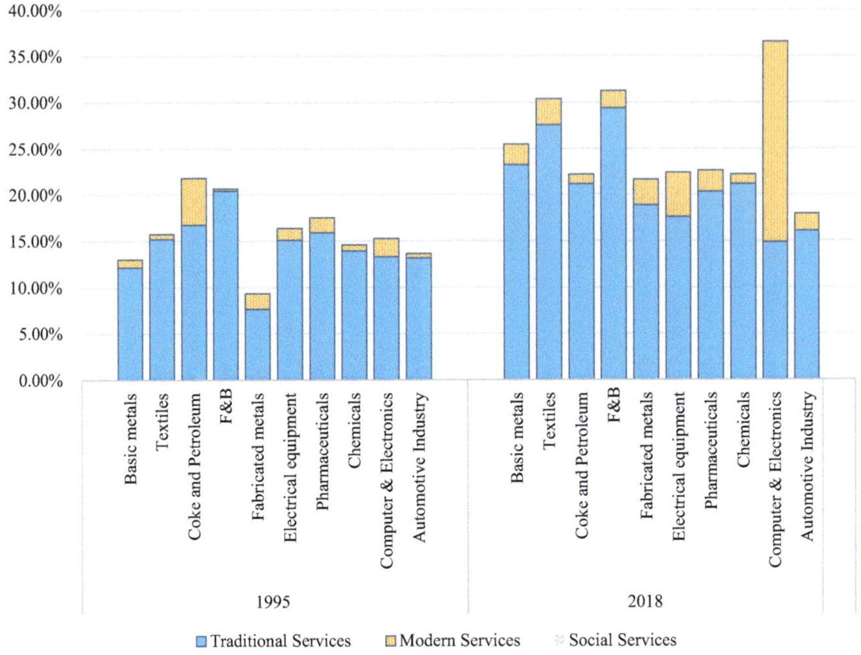

Fig. 9.10 Composition of Services Usage Across Manufacturing Industries, 1995 & 2018. *Source* OECD.Stat, Symmetric Input–Output Tables (2021 edition)

and optical equipment, professional, technical and scientific services have grown in importance. But overall, the contribution of modern services, despite showing a rising trend, remains modest across all manufacturing industries.

The overall takeaway from these trends is that the service sector's integration with the economy has increased over the past two decades. However, this is predominantly driven by a few services such as transport and distribution. Services linkages are greatest within the sector itself. Moreover, although segments such as IT, business, communication, and professional services have grown in importance in the economy, their widespread adoption and linkages with other sectors, and even within the services sector, remain limited. The trends further reflect the fact that services themselves are dependent on other sectors of the economy as a significant part of its own value-added arises outside the service sector. Hence, the input–output analysis clearly underscores the interdependence of sectors and the fact that continued services growth in part rests on growth in the rest of the economy.

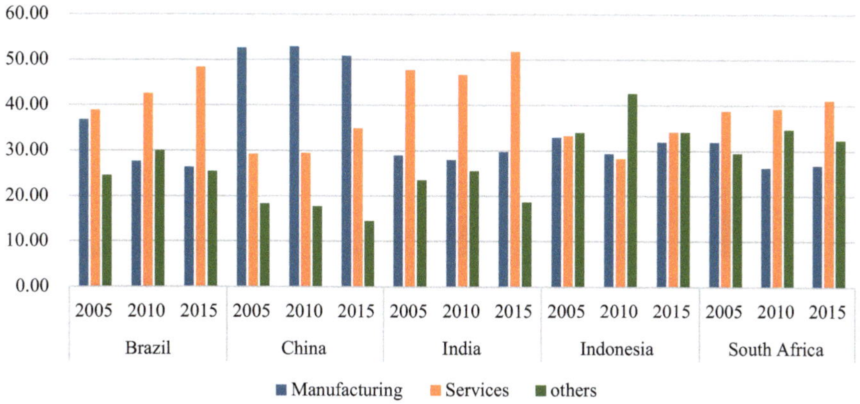

Fig. 9.11 Decomposition of value-added (VAD) Content of Gross Exports by Sectors (%), Selected Years. *Source* Authors' construction based on https://stats.oecd.org/Index.aspx?DataSetCode=TIVA_2018_C2# accessed: 29-3-2019. *Note* Others include Agriculture, Hunting, Forestry, Fishing, mining, and utilities

9.2.5.2 *Services Value-Added Contribution to Exports*[5]

Along similar lines, the role of services value-added contribution in India's exports requires examination. Analysis shows that services contributed to over 50% of value-added in India's gross exports in 2015, higher than that in other developing countries and significantly greater than the Balance of Payments (BoP) based share of services exports in India's total exports. Further, services value-added contribution has consistently exceeded that of manufacturing and most of this content has been of domestic origin. Figure 9.11 shows the decomposition of value-added content in India's overall gross exports across the three sectors of the economy, while Figs. 9.12 and 9.13 highlight the relative importance of traditional versus modern services and the significance of specific service segments in India's gross exports, respectively.

Figures 9.14 and 9.15 illustrate that modern services such as IT and information services contribute more than traditional segments such as transport and distribution services in India's gross exports. This is consistent with the shift in the pattern of India's services exports towards ICT-intensive market services, noted earlier. However, as illustrated in Fig. 9.14, the value-added contribution of these market services to manufacturing exports is quite small. It is traditional services such as trade and distribution and to a lesser extent transport and storage that contribute most of the value-added to manufacturing exports. Thus, competitive segments such as IT and information services or other business services (R&D services and other business support activities) which can potentially create more value, increase business sophistication, and raise technological depth in manufacturing, show very low levels of contribution to manufacturing exports. These services mainly contribute to

[5] Much of the discussion in this section is based on Chakraborty and Chanda (2019) and Chanda (2017)

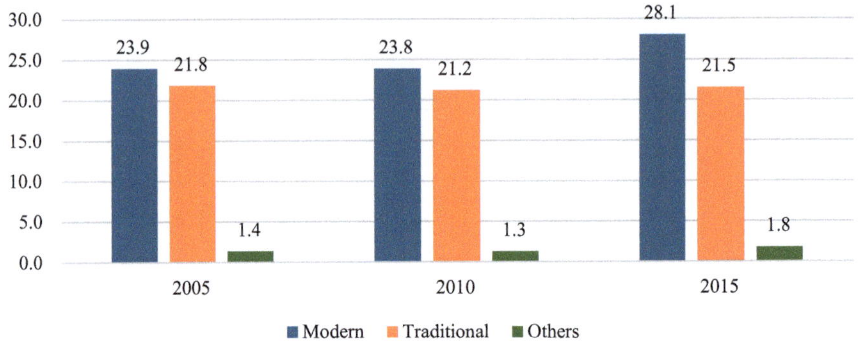

Fig. 9.12 Traditional vs Modern Services VAD in Gross Exports (%). *Source* Author's construction based on https://stats.oecd.org/Index.aspx?DataSetCode=TIVA_2018_C2# accessed: 29-3-2019. *Note* Modern services include D58T63, D64T66, D68, D69T82 in the OECD TiVA database (which include other business services, financial services, communication, computer and information, among others), traditional services include D45T56 in the OECD TiVA database, others include Public administration, education and health, social and personal services

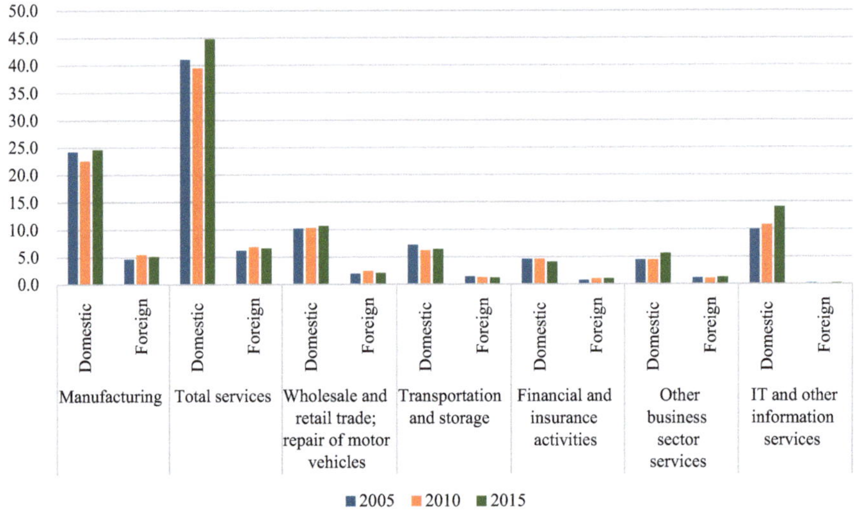

Fig. 9.13 Value-added Contribution by Source Industries in Gross Exports. *Source* Authors' construction based on https://stats.oecd.org/Index.aspx?DataSetCode=TIVA_2018_C2# accessed: 29-3-2019

India's services exports as shown in Fig. 9.15, indicating that within services linkages are stronger than services-manufacturing linkages in the case of the modern, fast-growing services.

These servicification trends raise several questions about the extent to which the rapid growth in services output, employment, and trade is creating spillovers for

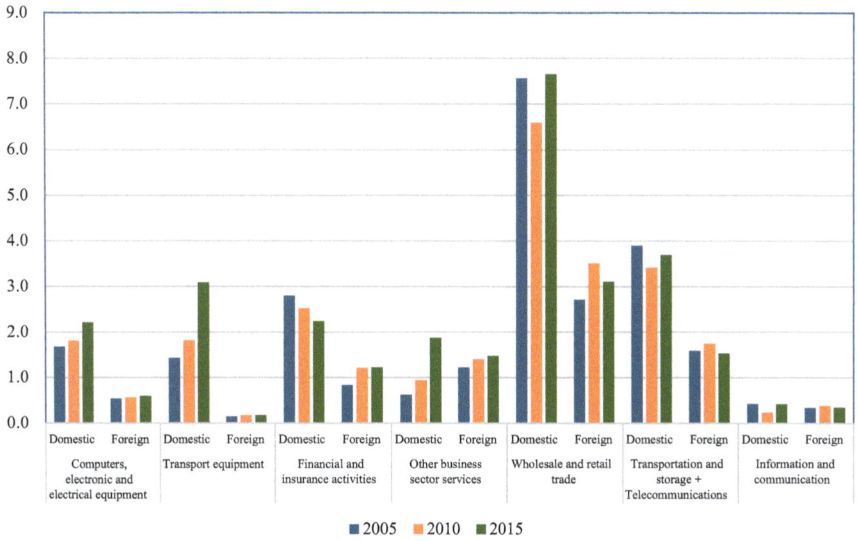

Fig. 9.14 Value-added Contribution by Source Sectors (Services and Industries) in Gross Manufacturing Exports. *Source* Author's construction based on https://stats.oecd.org/Index.aspx?DataSetCode=TIVA_2018_C2# accessed: 29-3-2019

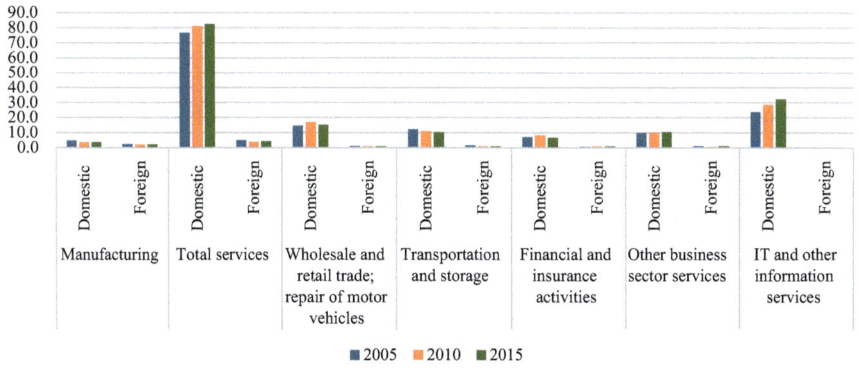

Fig. 9.15 Value-Added Contribution by Source Industries in Total Services Exports, %. *Source* Author's construction based on https://stats.oecd.org/Index.aspx?DataSetCode=TIVA_2018_C2# accessed: 29-3-2019

sectors such as manufacturing. Globally competitive segments like IT services are not contributing in any significant way to India's manufacturing exports as India's IT services exports are largely being directly exported (given the high share of within segment exports) than being embedded within manufacturing exports (Chanda, 2017). To what extent then are IT services being leveraged in India to improve manufacturing processes and raise efficiency. Are these reflective of problems in

Indian manufacturing with regard to scale, fragmentation, infrastructure, and regulations that result in low absorption of IT in manufacturing exports or might this reflect the nature of India's manufacturing export basket and constraints to integrating IT services in these exports. To what extent is pattern of growth in India's service sector and its orientation possibly limiting services integration with manufacturing? Further, does the very low contribution of R&D and business services in India's manufacturing exports reflect the currently limited role of innovation in India's manufacturing sector and the potential to move up the value chain into more R&D intensive manufacturing? Might the weak services to manufacturing link also reflect challenges affecting the service sector, including those related to capacity, quality, regulation, the degree of liberalization, and modernization in services.[6] As the regulatory environment in services, the degree of contestability in services markets, and policies which affect quality, productivity, efficiency, and capacity in services have a bearing on other sectors, according to several studies (Escaith, 2014; Miroudot et al., 2013; USITC, 2013), do these trends suggest the need for service sector-related policy reforms and initiatives to strengthen the linkages?

Overall, the discussion on growth dynamics in India's services sector and the latter's contribution to GDP, employment, trade, FDI, and linkages with manufacturing, not only highlights the growing importance of services in the economy but also certain gaps and concerns regarding its growth orientation. The following section discusses the sources of growth in India's services and manufacturing sectors, with a focus on the productivity dynamics in the two sectors and their related implications.

9.3 Understanding India's Services-Led Growth Paradigm

India's growth trajectory, in particular its services-led growth experience, leap frogging from the primary to the tertiary sector, with a relatively stagnant manufacturing sector stands in contrast to that of most other countries, which have seen a structural shift in their economies from the primary to the secondary to the tertiary sector. As established in the literature (See, Fisher, 1935, 1952; Clark, 1940, 1949; Kuznets, 1972 and other studies) with a rise in per capita income, there is an initial shift from an agricultural to an industrial economy due to industrialization, which implies an increase in the share of the secondary sector in output and employment, combined with a decline in the share of the primary sector.With further rise in per capita income, there is a structural shift towards the tertiary sector. According to this traditional development paradigm of "agriculture to manufacturing to services" (Kaldor, 1966; Kuznets, 1959; Pack & Westphal, 1986) manufacturing is central to the developmental transition and necessary for sustained productivity growth. This shift has been attributed to several factors as highlighted in Kaldor, 1967; Baumol, 1967; Fuchs, 1968, and Rowthorn and Ramaswami, 1997, among other studies. An

[6] See, Chanda (2017) for further discussion on servicification of Indian manufacturing.

increasingly important service sector is viewed as a symptom of a mature economy and slower growth (Baumol, 1967).

There is, however, some debate whether such a structural shift in output and employment is an inevitable part of economic growth and whether the patterns can be different for countries making their transitions at different points of time and against different backdrops in terms of technological, trade, and other contexts. Although the historical experience of both developed and developing countries confirms the pattern noted in the literature (Chenery & Syrquin, 1975; UNCTAD, 2003; United Nations, 2006), the employment potential of industrialization might differ in the case of late industrializing developing countries in comparison to developed countries if there is access to high-productivity capital-intensive technology from developed countries (UNCTAD, 2003). Thus, the shift in employment away from agriculture might be slower in developing countries, while de-industrialization and tertiarization of employment might begin at lower levels of income than in the case of developed countries.

The debate about the universality of the pattern of growth and structural shifts as well as the implications of an alternate trajectory for employment and productivity, among others is pertinent to the case of India. The rapid growth of India's services sector, as highlighted in preceding sections, makes the Indian case of structural change an exception to the general rule. Moreover, certain features of India's services growth experience stand out. First is the premature nature of the transition to a services-driven economy, at a very low level of per capita income without achieving full-fledged industrialization. The second is that the large share of services in India's GDP is not matched by a corresponding share in employment, although the services sector has created jobs and helped reduce poverty.[7] Third, the Indian experience is quite different from that of both developed and developing countries. Unlike in the case of developed countries, the attainment of high levels of industrialization and a shift in employment towards services in India has not preceded the tertiarization of output. Unlike in the case of other Asian developing countries, the manufacturing sector has not occupied a significant share of the economy and the dominance of services in the economy is much larger. India's shift towards services is also not comparable to that of developing countries in Latin America, where higher levels of per capita income and the shift towards services was associated with a slowing down of growth while in India, this shift coincided with a higher growth path (Mazumdar, 2010).[8]

---

[7] Services sector growth has been an important contributor to poverty reduction in India, with a one percentage increase in service growth associated with a 1.5% decrease in the poverty rate. According to Ghani (2022), services growth has reduced poverty through two channels in India, first as the largest source of job growth and second by providing income which has further driven demand for goods and services and for the jobs to produce them.

[8] The beginnings of the structural shift towards services in India have been placed at different points of time by different authors. In the mid-1970s by Mitra (1988), in the mid-1990s by Rakshit (2007), and some others.

Given India's different growth trajectory, it is but natural that there are concerns about the nature, sustainability, and replicability of its development pattern and questions about its dependence on the service sector. The following discussion provides a brief overview of the literature surrounding some of these issues for India, focusing on the nature and causes of India's services-led growth, the observed impact on employment, and the implications for productivity.

9.3.1 Explaining India's Services-Led Growth

There is substantial literature on India's growth experience, both empirical and otherwise, including attempts to identify structural breaks in its growth process, the role of services, and to explain the causal factors. Based on an examination of the growth in output and change in its composition, Mazumdar (2010) identifies three turning points, in the mid-1960s, 1980, and the mid-1990s which separate the entire post-independence period into sequential phases of growth and structural change. Based on his analysis, we can infer that the period before 1980 was characterized by a relatively slower pace of aggregate growth than the one after, but at the same time it was the period in which the industrial (including manufacturing) sector was the driver of growth and structural change in output. This was a more pronounced feature of the phase from independence to the mid-1960s. The period of accelerated growth after 1980 was accompanied by the replacement of industry by services as the sector with the most prominent role. The expansion of the public sector mainly explained the increased importance of services in the process of growth and structural change during this phase. From the mid-1990s, the services-oriented trajectory was reinforced by the private organized sector which replaced the public sector as the engine of growth. The pattern of growth which began in the 1980s was more sharply reinforced following liberalization from the mid-1990s.

Studies largely attribute the striking growth of India's services sector and its rising contribution to GDP since the 1990s to policy changes and initial conditions. Panagariya (2005) concludes that the 1991 market reforms and subsequent liberalizing policy changes helped sustain growth in the Indian economy. The case of IT services illustrates the positive impact of the 1990s market reforms, with telecommunications liberalization providing the impetus. The Software Technology Parks of India (STPI) initiative of India in 1991 which aimed to overcome infrastructural and procedural constraints by providing data communication facilities, office space, and "single window" statutory services contributed to the growth of IT services. India's telecommunications policies of 1994 and 1999 allowed private sector investments into the sector and cleared the path for the establishment of alternative international gateways that were also critical to development of IT and ITeS. Along similar lines, Gordon and Gupta (2004), cite the rapid growth of the communications subsector in the 1990s coincident with deregulation, the corresponding increase in the private sector's share in the services sector and the positive correlation between India's FDI inflows and services growth. Liberalized services such as business and telecommunications services have attracted significant domestic and foreign investment. Services growth has also been attributed to domestic factors such as the structure of indirect taxation in India with historically light taxation of services due to the nature of India's constitutional tax provisions.

The growing role of services in India's exports has been attributed to a combination of domestic and external factors. Domestic liberalization and related FDI inflows in services, along with external forces such as the globalization of services and their growing role in global trade and FDI flows, India's large diaspora, and Y2K are seen as drivers of India's services exports, particularly in IT and ITeS where India has emerged as a leading player. In contrast, services which face high trade or domestic barriers have generally witnessed slower growth. There have also been spillover effects of services such as financial services exports which have contributed to the development of other export-oriented services, creating more jobs while globalization of services has provided opportunities for developing countries like India to find new segments and niches within the service sector.

Overall, the premature shift in the Indian economy towards services can be seen to be an outcome of policy changes, economic liberalization, the reinforcing effects of deregulation and liberalization across certain sectors, initial conditions, and various external forces.

9.3.2 Examining the Implications of Services-Led Growth

The question that follows is whether services can continue to be an engine of growth for India and can India's services-led growth paradigm counter the established pattern of development. Further, what are its welfare and distributional consequences? What are the consequences of this growth path for employment and productivity, and what are the related challenges of education and skilling to support and sustain such a development trajectory?

To answer these questions, one of the key issues to examine is the relationship between services growth and employment. As highlighted earlier in Sect. 9.2, the service sector's share in employment has risen over time. However, this increase has not been commensurate to the growing share of services in the economy and the experience of other countries where services occupy a dominant position. The relatively low absorption of employment in services lack of corresponding growth in employment is a potential concern as it has implications for welfare and distribution. But a review of the literature indicates that the explanations lie both within and outside the service sector. There are three broad explanations.

The first is the performance of other sectors, in particular the low productivity in agriculture combined with lack of job growth and low employment absorption capacity in manufacturing due to a sluggish industrial sector and use of relatively capital-intensive technology. The latter features have resulted in the continued large share of the labour force in agriculture (See, Singh, 2006; Gordon & Gupta, 2004).

According to Planning Commission (2001), the total employment impact for the economy was determined more by changes in employment growth in agriculture than by slowdown in services employment growth. Non-commensurate employment growth in services can thus be reposed as reflecting factors outside the services sector.

A second explanation concerns the broader issues plaguing India's labour market and related issues of skilling and productivity which can explain the pattern and pace of employment shifts seen in India, including the failure of the service (and manufacturing) sector to significantly absorb labour from the primary sector. Most studies attribute this feature to long-run structural and policy constraints in the labour market, including restrictive labour regulations and incomplete labour reforms which are reflected in low employment elasticities across sectors since the 1980s. Further, the weak link between employment growth and the structural shift in the economy towards services can also be attributed to the fact that labour reallocation associated with structural change was mainly through the movement of labour across sectors within the unorganized economy, resulting in growth of the informal sector, rather than through shifts from the unorganized to the organized part of the economy (D'Costa, 2023).

A third explanation relates to productivity and skill bias. The fact that employment growth has consistently lagged GDP growth indicates rising labour productivity (Mazumdar, 2010). The point of concern here is that this increase in labour productivity has not translated into a stronger and wider demand for labour, which can be attributed to India's pattern of skill development and its educational system that has led to a skill bias in both the manufacturing and services sectors. Studies such as Kochhar et al. (2006) which focus on skill intensity suggest that the nature of the economic policies followed by India since independence created a pattern of specialization distinct from the typical developing country at comparable income levels. This shaped the country's development pattern in the post-1980 reform period resulting in a manufacturing sector that was more diversified, more skill-intensive, and less (unskilled) labour-intensive than in comparable developing countries. This skill bias is also evident in India's services sector and its subsectoral drivers. Services in India, particularly the faster growing segments such as IT and business services are relatively more skill-intensive than is commensurate with India's level of income and development.[9]

What then are the implications of the skill-intensive growth pattern in services for development? First, as skills such as fluency in non-accented English, or a good quality undergraduate engineering degree are entry barriers to these services, instead of drawing in new job seekers and increasing employment, the growth of these

[9] According to Kocchar et al. (2006), cross-country level regressions for the year 2000 suggest that India's services share of GDP was significantly higher than the norm in that year but only when a country size variable was included. Services employment, however, was always significantly lower than the norm. This result is consistent with the kind of skill-biassed development observed in India pre-1980.

segments is likely to push up the earnings of the skilled workers, often towards developed country levels, potentially widening income inequality.[10] The second implication for development is on the demand side, with the pattern of goods and services being skewed towards the demand pattern of the upper end of the income distribution.[11] In this case, there may not be the kinds of spillovers that would occur in manufacturing, where expertise developed for mass produced goods for the middle classes in rich countries can be transferred to an array of goods that also satisfy the needs of the masses in the developing country. The same degree of spillovers may not be available for call centres and BPO operations and the wider efficiency benefits that can arise from low/medium skill labour-intensive manufacturing, may not arise from the growth of such service segments.

But there is also evidence to suggest that the growth of India's services sector, including its skill-intensive segments such as IT services, has had significant direct and indirect employment impact and wider multiplier effects in the economy. For instance, as per the National Skills Mission's estimates, in 2016, the Indian IT–BPM Industry employed about 3 million people directly and about 9 million indirectly. As of 2023, direct employment in the Indian IT and Business Process Management industry numbers was estimated at over 5.4 million (Statista, 2023). The NASSCOM Perspective Report 2020 estimated that this industry could potentially contribute as much as 30 million in employment opportunities (direct and indirect) by 2020. These estimates are indicative of the sector's huge employment potential, notwithstanding its skill intensity, with employment being created in many less skill-intensive ancillary services such as security, housekeeping, transport, training, and hospitality services. Growth in segments such as IT, financial, communication, and business services, which have been among the most dynamic performers within the service sector, has also had economy-wide multiplier effects through FDI inflows, increased demand for ICT products, and related infrastructure development. Evidence indicates that an increase in tradable services employment, such as in IT services, has positively affected non-tradable services employment (Avdiu et al., 2023). Analysis by Bhagwati, Panagariya, and Srinivasan (2004) supports the view that trade in emerging services, as experienced by India, provides positive welfare gains.

In the context of consumer services, Fan et al. (2021) find that productivity growth in segments such as retail, restaurants, and residential real estate services, which serve the final consumer, accounted for almost one-third of the increase in welfare between 1987 and 2011 and was an important driver of structural transformation and rising living standards during this period. Employment in such services has also risen in recent decades. The welfare gains from the growth of these services have, however, been skewed towards high-income urban dwellers mainly due to the availability of better and cheaper goods and from the growing supply of local services.

---

[10] See, Mazumdar (2010) for discussion on industry and services growth and structural transformation in India.

[11] Sarkar (1998) shows how demand thresholds can matter for growth and how a sufficiently large middle class can be crucial in enabling growth. This idea is also broadly related to the "big push" view of development advanced in the 1940s by Rosenstein-Rodan.

The rise of the service sector more generally has also enabled the growth of the non-farm economy which involves a wide range of ancillary services and activities that have a direct bearing on poverty eradication in rural areas. The service sector's growth is also seen as contributing to increased participation of women in the labour force, particularly in organized segments such as IT and ITeS.

In addition to the linkages between services growth and employment, questions about the sustainability of a service sector-led growth pattern in India also relate to the impact of services growth on overall as well as sectoral productivity in India. This is particularly important given the significance of productivity for sustaining long-run growth. The evidence in this regard is favourable. Banga and Goldar (2004) find a significant and positive impact of services input on industrial productivity and a favourable impact of greater use of services in manufacturing in the 1990s on total factor productivity (TFP). The analysis also finds that trade reforms played an important role in increasing the use of services in the manufacturing sector, thus corroborating the earlier discussion on the role of policy changes and economic liberalization in enabling India's service sector growth. Other studies have also highlighted the positive spillovers from services growth to manufacturing through income and demand (Mazumder 2010), or through organizational learning (as occurred in India from IT services to ITeS), although some studies also note that India's manufacturing sector may have been partly constrained by weaknesses in service subsectors such as transportation and logistics (Singh, 2006).

In sum, the implications of India's services-driven growth model are mixed. There are clearly positive implications of the service sector's strong growth and trade performance. But there are also areas of concern. However, these impacts have been conditioned by a wide range of structural, regulatory, institutional, and external factors. Hence, services growth needs to be underpinned by continued reforms and economic liberalization, along with targeted policies in services to enable more equitable distribution of the welfare gains from services growth.

9.4 Productivity Dynamics in India's Services Sector

The preceding discussion has highlighted the various causes underlying the services growth experience. The following discussion builds on the earlier analysis by providing an empirical analysis of the sources of growth in India's manufacturing and services sector, focusing on the productivity dynamics in the two sectors. Such an empirical decomposition of the sources of growth is important to assess the sustainability and quality of growth as well as identify areas for policy intervention. In this context, in addition to capital deepening and labour expansion, total factor productivity TFP plays a key role in sustaining long-run growth as there are limitations to growth through labour and capital accumulation.[12]

[12] TFP is a measure of the efficiency with which human and material resources are converted into goods and services.

We use the Indian KLEMS (2021) dataset (sourced from the National Accounts Statistics), which is part of a global initiative to promote and simplify the analysis of growth and productivity patterns, to estimate TFP in India's manufacturing and services sectors for the 1980–81 to 2020–21 period. We further analyze the sources of value-added growth within the two sectors, for 13 industry groups which comprise manufacturing and 10 industry groups which comprise services.

We adopt the aggregate product function approach as outlined by Jorgenson et al. (2007) for this estimation. The methodology makes certain assumptions. It assumes a uniform value-added function for each industry as a function of labour (L), capital (K), and technology, thus enabling aggregation across industries. The approach also assumes that the returns to labour and capital are the same across industries. The aggregate value-added using the aggregate production function approach is expressed as:

$$V = \sum V_i$$

where

V = aggregate value-added using aggregate production approach.

V_i = value-added in industry *i*.

The computed aggregate growth in Total Factor Productivity (TFP) represents the residual obtained from aggregate value-added after adjusting for changes due to capital and labour. It is expressed as:

$$TFP = \Delta \ln(V) - \overline{v}_k \, \Delta \ln(K) - \overline{v}_l \, \Delta \ln(L)$$

where

K = aggregate capital stock in the economy.

L = quality adjusted employment in the economy.

$\overline{v}_k$ = two-year averages of the compensation share of capital in total nominal output.

$\overline{v}_l$ = two-year averages of the compensation share of labour in total nominal output.

The estimated trends in Total Factor Productivity (TFP) growth using this methodology for the manufacturing and services sectors, are presented in Fig. 9.16.

The trends in TFP growth indicate a distinct shift pre and post 2000. Before 2000, TFP growth in the manufacturing sector underwent significant fluctuations, marked by notable crests and troughs, while the service sector exhibited a relatively stable trend. The two sectors also followed quite divergent paths during the pre-2000 period. Post-2000, however, the two sectors show a converging trend in their TFP growth, which might indicate strengthening of linkages between the two sectors and greater commonality in policy and other factors affecting their performance. Figure 9.16 also highlights the significantly more stable trend in productivity growth in the services sector compared to that in manufacturing and the severe impact of Covid-19 on both.

Fig. 9.16 Trends in TFP Growth in Manufacturing and Services (1980–2020). *Source* Authors' calculations based on KLEMS (2021)

Tables 9.7 and 9.8 provide a breakdown for the sources of value-added growth across various subsectors of manufacturing and services for the 1980–2020 period. Table 9.7 shows significant variations in value-added growth across different manufacturing industries. During the period 1980–2020, electrical and optical equipment, rubber and plastic products, the transport sector, coke and petroleum products, and the chemical sector contributed to the overall growth rate of the manufacturing sector. Growth in TFP was the primary source of value-added growth in four industries: Electrical and Optical Equipment, Chemicals and Chemical Products, Food Products, Beverages and Tobacco, and the Manufacturing nec industries. An examination of the contributions from the input side shows that capital made the highest contribution in the coke and petroleum products sector, accounting for 12.5%, while labour made a minimal contribution across all manufacturing industries, remaining below 2%.[13]

Table 9.8 shows large variations in value-added growth across service subsectors with highest growth exhibited in business, financial and telecom services. An examination of the role of factor inputs in this growth shows that capital was the main driver across a spectrum of services, including trade, telecom, financial services, health, and business services. Labour contributed less than capital, though more than in the case of manufacturing, with its highest contribution observed in the business services sector (3.36%).

Several useful insights emerge from a comparison of the two sectors and their sources of growth. First, on average, services have experienced higher TFP growth than manufacturing, which may reflect the impact of liberalization, greater competition in many services, and regulatory reforms. Second, though capital deepening

[13] The contribution of labour or capital input is defined as the product of the value share of the input and its corresponding growth rate.

Table 9.7 Sources of growth in Indian manufacturing, 1980–2020 (% per annum)

Manufacturing industry	VA growth (%)	Contribution of labour input (%)	Contribution of capital input (%)	TFPG (%)
Food products, beverages, and tobacco	6.48	0.54	3.71	2.24
Textiles, textile products, leather, and footwear	5.47	0.09	4.39	1.00
Wood and products of wood	0.51	–0.08	4.00	–3.40
Pulp, paper, paper products, printing, and publishing	4.90	1.06	2.11	1.73
Coke, refined petroleum products, and nuclear fuel	7.75	0.29	12.50	–5.04
Chemicals and chemical products	7.63	0.77	4.10	2.76
Rubber and plastic products	8.84	0.84	8.10	–0.10
Other non-metallic mineral products	6.94	0.35	6.70	–0.12
Basic metals and fabricated metal products	5.48	0.71	5.06	–0.29
Machinery, nec	6.33	1.14	6.25	–1.06
Electrical and optical equipment	9.26	1.93	3.94	3.38
Transport equipment	7.77	1.11	6.18	0.48
Manufacturing, nec; recycling	6.60	1.45	2.94	2.21
Manufacturing sector	6.31	0.51	4.70	1.10

Source Authors' calculations based on KLEMS (2021)

as opposed to labour accumulation has contributed more to value-added growth in both manufacturing and services, its relative contribution has been greater in the case of manufacturing, reflecting the sector's failure to create jobs. This corroborates the earlier discussion regarding the employment dynamism exhibited by services compared to manufacturing. Third, subsectors such as telecommunications, financial, and business services, i.e., ICT-intensive market services have experienced capital deepening reflecting the growing role of technology in driving their growth. Fourth, several services such as education and health, have experienced relatively balanced contribution across all sources of growth. This is also true for services as a whole compared to manufacturing. These trends indicate that there may be more binding constraints in manufacturing compared to services, preventing the contribution of components, particularly with respect to labour. Fifth, the relatively lower contribution of TFP growth in case of business services suggests that alongside the role of technological advancements, the subsector's growth has been driven by availability of skilled and low-cost labour, and thus the scope to move up the value chain through innovation and higher productivity growth if the subsector is to remain competitive.

Table 9.8 Sources of growth in India's services sector, 1980–2020 (% per annum)

Service industry	VA growth (%)	Contribution of labour input (%)	Contribution of capital input (%)	TFPG (%)
Trade	6.57	1.63	5.28	–0.34
Hotels and restaurants	5.15	2.05	3.90	–0.80
Transport and storage	5.83	2.03	2.10	1.70
Post and telecommunication	9.61	1.29	5.94	2.38
Financial services	8.20	1.93	3.75	2.52
Business service	11.37	3.36	7.46	0.56
Public administration and defense; compulsory social security	5.83	0.25	1.09	4.49
Education	7.64	2.51	2.89	2.24
Health and social work	7.86	2.57	3.72	1.57
Other services	4.72	1.61	2.04	1.07
Service sector	6.69	1.84	2.70	2.14

Source Authors' calculations based on KLEMS (2021)

This latter inference is corroborated by the segment's declining competitiveness and its limited integration with manufacturing. Overall, the analysis of the sources of growth suggests that there is much scope to broad base growth in the service sector and to create employment as well as boost productivity across a wide range of services.

9.5 Policy Environment in Services

The variable performance across different services indicates the role of different influencing factors. An understanding of these facilitating and constraining policies and regulations is important given ample evidence that indicates the many positive spillovers from a fast growing, productive, and competitive services sector to the rest of the economy. For instance, infrastructure services such as transport and logistics, telecommunications are indispensable for driving economic growth. Empirical analysis (Saidi et al., 2020) shows the role of better infrastructure services in attracting FDI and for enabling trade and employment creation. Khanna and Sharma (2021) find a positive and sizeable effect of infrastructure services on manufacturing productivity in India. Hence, initiatives such as PM Gatishakti have significant implications for productivity and expansion of not only logistics services, but also other activities that are supported by these services. Likewise, Gulati et al. (2020) find that industries which have adopted ICT have been key drivers of overall aggregate productivity. Hence, policies affecting the growth of ICT services and their absorption by other sectors of the economy are important for determining overall growth and productivity dynamics in the economy.

The following discussion focuses on the policy environment, both in terms of regulatory and other barriers which constrain the service sector, directly or indirectly, as well as specific initiatives that have been undertaken to facilitate the service sector's growth and competitiveness in recent decades. It provides an overview of the general evolution of policies and reforms in the services sector over the past three decades and presents a few initiatives in recent years which highlight the government's increased attention to services and recognition of the economy-wide implications of a strong and competitive services sector. The discussion also highlights the growing importance of services in India's trade negotiations and strategic partnerships with other countries.

9.5.1 Broad Trends in Services Policies and Regulations

Since 1991, the general trend in the policy environment for services has been to liberalize and streamline regulatory processes, strengthen regulatory institutions in key services, enhance contestability in the domestic market by allowing private players as well FDI, and to encourage innovation and competitiveness. The earlier discussion on FDI growth in India's services sector highlighted the role of services liberalization in terms of the easing of FDI regulations and allowing 100% foreign equity participation through the automatic route across a range of services. The elimination of government monopoly and the establishment and strengthening of independent regulators in several services, such as telecom, financial and insurance services, has also been an important feature of service sector reforms in India. Some examples of further liberalization in recent times include the lifting of several restrictions on cabotage in maritime transport in 2018, approval of self-handling for air cargo operators in 2019, and introduction of regulations on non-discriminatory interconnection rates in the telecommunications sector. Amendments in archaic Acts governing many services have been another important step. For instance, the Companies Act 2013 replaced the Companies Act 1956 and eliminated some earlier restrictions such as on the maximum number of partners permitted in a partnership formed by professionals. Such legislative changes have implications for the efficiency and competitiveness of several professional services which were earlier constrained by regulatory restrictions on the size and scope of firms.

9.5.1.1 Selected Initiatives

Several initiatives have also been taken in recent years to boost the service sector, recognizing its significant contribution to overall growth and competitiveness. One key initiative is the Champion Services Sector Scheme (CSSS) that was launched in 2018–29, under which the Central Government has earmarked a sum of Rs.

5,000 crores for the 2019–20 to 2023–24 period with the objective of promoting growth, creating more jobs, and promoting exports in selected services sectors. These include IT & ITeS, Tourism & Hospitality Services, Medical Value Travel, Transport & Logistics Services, Accounting and Finance Services, Audio Visual Services, Legal Services, Communication Services, Construction and Related Engineering Services, Environmental Services, Financial Services and Education Services. The CSSS focuses on implementing reforms in each of these selected subsectors, based on 5 pillars, namely: (1) new processes to improve the ease of doing business; (2) new infrastructure to strengthen physical and digital connectivity; (3) new sectors to identify untapped areas for value addition; (4) new mindset to shifting from an approval to partnership mindset between government and business; and (5) new standards to strengthen export competitiveness of various services. A key thrust area under this scheme is to promote trade in services, by negotiating meaningful market access, addressing domestic constraints within services through periodic consultations with stakeholders, through the formulation of standards in various services to ensure quality in global markets (143 standards on services have been published by the Bureau of Indian Standards (BIS) as of Jan 2023), and the development of districts as export hubs through institutional mechanisms at the state and district levels to facilitate exports.

Within services, a key focus area has been the development of transport and logistics infrastructure, given the latter's huge multiplier effects. Government initiatives include building large highway systems in India (expressways and freight corridors), inland waterways (Jalmarg Vikas project), port modernization, and new port development (Sagarmala project) with a focus on sustainability. One major initiative in this context is PM Gatishakti National Master Plan, which was launched in October 2021 to provide multimodal connectivity infrastructure to various economic zones. The objective is to reduce logistics costs and turnaround time, increase cargo handling capacity, and overall increase economic efficiency. The plan encompasses railways, roads, ports, waterways, airports, mass transport, and logistics infrastructure and is expected to bring together central and state government as well as private sector efforts and the use of digital tools and technologies to integrate geospatial data across different ministries on a digital platform in order to enable planning, monitoring, reviewing, and implementation of infrastructure projects. While there remain challenges to implementing this scheme, it has the potential to transform India's infrastructure and significantly enhance the role of transport and logistics services in India's growth process.

Many other schemes and programs launched in recent years highlight the growing recognition of services and their role in the economy. These include initiatives such as Startup India initiative, which offers support to innovative startups in both manufacturing and services and can provide a significant boost to innovation and growth in new services, Ayushman Bharat to develop India's health infrastructure, Digital India and several measures related to the digital economy, including data privacy and e-commerce regulations. Such policies have a bearing on the wider economy, not just services.

9.5.1.2 Challenges and Limitations

Notwithstanding such liberalization and reform measures, both border and behind-the-border regulations continue to exist in India's services sector, hampering growth, efficiency, and contestability in services. The Organisation for Economic Co-operation and Development (OECD) Services Trade Restrictiveness Index (STRI) which classifies India as a restrictive economy in the service sector, albeit flawed in its methodology in the sense that it fails to capture the significant extent of liberalization that has occurred in India's services, does reveal some important characteristics of India's service sector restrictions. The first is that lack of regulatory transparency, i.e., information and implementation related barriers affect India's services trade, possibly undermining liberalization undertaken at the border. The second characteristic is that business and professional services remain the most protected services in India, with implications for standards and competitiveness of such supporting services. Legal services, for example, remain closed to FDI.[14] There are also competitiveness and regulatory indices for India which suggest that there are constraints to the service sector's efficiency and capacity to contribute effectively to other parts of the economy in India. For instance, India ranks poorly on transport and communications infrastructure under the "Enabling Trade Index" (by World Economic Forum (WEF)) and on the "Logistics Performance Index" (by World Bank). On the innovation and sophistication sub index, which reflects a country's capacity and quality in R&D services, it shows a declining performance ("Global Competitiveness Report" by WEF). Indices which capture the incidence of regulatory barriers highlight the fact that services FDI in India remains more restricted than manufacturing FDI and that the overall protection level in services remains high compared to that in other countries.

A few examples highlight the variety of barriers that still plague the service sector. In the health services sector for example, although 100% FDI is permitted, there remain barriers to provision of medical services by non-nationals, except for specific purposes. Education services fall under the jurisdiction of both state and central governments and are faced with a plethora of regulations that constrain the setting up of establishments and the entry of foreign education providers. Difficulties in repatriating salaries and income from research and limitations on employing foreign faculty adversely affects the sector. Some professional services suffer from non-uniformity of standards and absence of market and reform-oriented professional councils. Many services are also constrained by infrastructural and human resource constraints. The audiovisual services sector, for example, suffers from poor infrastructure in terms of lack of well-equipped studios and erratic power supply as well as lack of skilled manpower in areas such content production, editing, postproduction and digital media. Publishing services are constrained by the lack of industry

---

[14] The OECD STRI quantifies various regulatory barriers affecting services trade, taking a value of 0 for a completely open service sector and 1 for a completely closed service sector. See Grosso et al. (2015) for further details.

status which in turn enables unregulated distribution and a grey market in books that undermines business.

9.5.2 *Services in India's Economic Diplomacy*[15]

Given the growing importance of services in India's domestic economy as well as in international trade, India has been strategically negotiating for increased market access in services through broad-based and comprehensive free trade agreements (FTAs) that cover goods, services, investment and other issues. Thus far India has signed several comprehensive free trade agreements. These include the India-Singapore Comprehensive Economic Co-operation Agreement (CECA) (2005), the India-Korea Comprehensive Economic Partnership Agreement (CEPA) (2010), the India Malaysia CECA (2011), the India-Japan CEPA (2011), India-ASEAN (Association of Southeast Asian Nations) Trade in Services Agreement (2014), India-Mauritius Comprehensive Economic Cooperation and Partnership Agreement (2021), India-United Arab Emirates (UAE) CEPA (2022), and India-Australia Economic Cooperation and Trade Agreement (2022). India is also in the process of negotiating services inclusive free trade agreements with Canada, the UK, and the EU.

The FTA partner countries of India have given market access preferences in various services that go beyond their General Agreement on Trade in Services (GATS) commitments under the World Trade Organization (WTO). Several other agreements involving services, are currently under negotiation. However, analysis suggests that services trade with these partner countries has not grown significantly and that their share in India's services exports remain low. This is mainly due to the continued presence of regulatory and cultural barriers that make it difficult for Indian service providers to penetrate their partner countries' markets. Issues pertaining to mobility of service providers, discriminatory standards, non-recognition of qualifications continue to constrain India's services exports in its sectors of interest.

Through its recently signed and prospective agreements, India hopes to gain market access in services across modes[16] and sectors and has also offered many

---

[15] See, Chanda (2020) for further discussion.

[16] As per the modal classification of supply of services under the General Agreement on Trade in Services (GATS) there are four modes by which services can be traded. These are mode 1 or the cross border supply of services wherein a service crosses borders as in the case of transport services or information, data processing, and BPO services; mode 2 or consumption abroad wherein the consumer moves to the country of the service provider as in the case of tourism, healthcare and education services; mode 3 or commercial presence where a juridical entity is set up in another country in the form of a subsidiary, joint venture, franchise, affiliate office, etc. to provide the service as in the case of banking or telecommunication services; and mode 4 or movement of natural persons wherein the service provider moves temporarily to provide the service in another country without seeking permanent residence or citizenship in the host country, as in the case of software professionals working on the client site or doctors and nurses who work temporarily in other markets.

services. Under the India-UAE CEPA, for example, India has offered market access to the UAE in around 100 subsectors, while Indian service providers will have access to around 111 subsectors from 11 broad service sectors (PIB, 2022). The Agreement is also expected to foster people to people linkages between the two countries. The India-Europan (EU) Bilateral Trade and Investment Agreement promises potential gains through greater market access for India's professional services in the EU and increased investment inflows from the EU in areas such as financial and R&D services. However, there are sensitivities surrounding the mobility of Indian professionals to the EU, data protection regulations in the EU and liberalizing investments in certain services in India.

Overall, to what extent the expected gains from services agreements will materialize for India depends on three factors, namely, the nature of commitments India is able to secure from its FTA partners, the extent to which these commitments are undermined by domestic regulations in partner countries, and India's own competitive strengths and ability to leverage these agreements. In particular, India's focus on areas such as movement of professionals and sectors such as IT, ITeS, and professional services may need to change given sensitivities about immigration, job losses, as well as data protection. A more strategic approach might be to focus on gaining market access through overseas investments (mode 3) in the service sector, which would facilitate the movement of service providers and cross-border delivery from India, while supporting this approach with domestic reforms and regulatory measures to address issues of standards and data security, among others.

Beyond the ratification of agreements, services are also featuring in India's bilateral cooperation and other initiatives with many countries in areas such as Science and Technology, R&D, education, skilling, startups, and digital economy. Services are likely to feature importantly in the context of new alliances such as the Indo-Pacific Economic Framework for Prosperity (IPEF) given their membership. These trends indicate that services have become and will increasingly become more and more integrated into India's formal and informal economic diplomacy arrangements.

9.6 Concluding Thoughts and Way Forward

The discussion in this chapter highlights the strong performance of India's services sector across many dimensions but also the variety of constraints that continue to hold it back. It is also evident that the government increasingly recognizes this sector's contribution to the economy, through its domestic as well as external initiatives. The main message that emerges from this discussion is that India's services sector should be viewed not in isolation but as one which is both dependent on and contributes to other sectors of the economy. The state of physical infrastructure in areas such as communication and logistics services, the quality of services such as health and education which are critical for growth in human capital and productivity, FDI policies which shape the degree of competition and efficiency in services, and the level of standards in services, all have a direct bearing on economy-wide competitiveness.

Similarly, income and employment opportunities in other sectors generate demand for and create new opportunities in services, resulting in a mutually reinforcing relationship between services and the rest of the economy. These interlinkages must be reflected in the way services are integrated into national initiatives for skilling, entrepreneurship, manufacturing and the like.

Alongside such efforts, India can also strategically use its trade and investment agreements to strengthen its services sector and realize its potential. This would require moving beyond a simple focus on securing commitments in certain modes and services to explore new possibilities that capture the synergies that exist between services and other sectors, between different services and across different modes of services supply. This could involve leveraging outward investments by Indian manufacturing and services firms in FTA partner countries to expand business, IT and other supporting services or facilitating manufacturing and services investments from FTA partners to realize its objectives under the "Make in India" and other government initiatives. But to achieve this, India would have to go beyond the mechanics of services commitments and rule-making under its FTAs and encourage Business to Business (B2B) dialogue and understanding so as to address firm-level and organizational barriers and mindsets which currently impede India's export prospects in services. Thus, promoting services growth and competitiveness will require a broad perspective of the sector in terms of its linkages with the economy, the stakeholders who shape its performance and the many macro, micro and institutional level impediments to its growth.

Specifically, more attention to one particular area, would enable the service sector to sustain its growth momentum in the long run as well as capitalize on emerging opportunities, namely skilling. The sector today faces a shortage of skilled and trained workers across a range of services, especially in high value and knowledge-intensive services with rapidly evolving technologies. More comprehensive skill development and an education system that can adapt to the changing demands of the labour market and promotes lifelong learning and upskilling. Without more investment in skills and training across a wide range of services, it will be hard to maintain growth, raise productivity, improve competitiveness, expand exports, attract investments, and realize the intersectoral spillovers. All other interventions and initiatives, whether it is investments in physical and digital infrastructure, technology adoption in services, and digitalization initiatives, supporting innovation and entrepreneurship programs, and even regulatory oversight, will ultimately require human resource capacity, making skilling and education, the underlying foundation for long term development of the services as well as manufacturing sectors.

References

Avdiu, B., Pela, K., & Froy, C. A. (2023, December 12). What we're reading about productivity growth and jobs. *World Bank Blogs*. Retrieved from https://blogs.worldbank.org/en/jobs/what-were-reading-about-productivity-growth-and-jobs

Banga, R., & Goldar, B. N. (2004, August). Contribution of services to output growth productivity in Indian manufacturing: Pre and post reform. ICRIER Working Paper, No. 139.

Baumol, W. J. (1967). Macroeconomics of unbalanced growth: The anatomy of urban crisis. *American Economic Review, 57*(3), 415–426.

Benz, S., Khanna, A., & Nordas, H. K. (2017). Services and performance of the Indian economy: Analysis and policy options. *OECD Trade Policy Papers*, No. 196, Paris: OECD publishing.

Bhagwati, J., Panagariya, A., & Srinivasan, T. N. (2004). The muddles over outsourcing. *Journal of Economic Perspectives*, Fall.

Chakrabarty, S., & Chanda, R. (2019, December). Services Contribution to Manufacturing Exports and Value-Added: Evidence from India and China", IIMB Working Paper No. 602.

Chanda, R. (2020). India's services trade: Opportunities, challenges and international engagements, Chapter 3 in P. De, A. Raychaudhuri and S. Gupta (eds.), *World Trade and India: Multilateralism, Progress and Policy Response*, Sage Publishers.

Chanda, R. (2017). Services for manufacturing, in S. Mahendra Dev (Ed.), *India Development Report 2017*, Oxford University Press, New Delhi, pp. 209–223.

Chaudhry, D., Tomar, P., & Joshi, P. (2018). Deconstructing Indian Overseas Foreign Direct Investments: Historical & Contemporary Trends, Oxfam Discussion Paper. Retrieved from https://icrier.org/others/deconstructing-indian-overseas-foreign-direct-investments-historical-contemporary-trends/

Chenery, H., & Syrquin, M. (1975). *Patterns of development 1950–1970.* World Bank and Oxford University Press.

Clark, C. (1940). *Revised and reprinted in 1951.* MacMillan & Co., Ltd.

Clark, C. (1949). Theory of economic growth. *Econometrica*, 17(Supplement).

D'Costa, A. P. (2023, April 10). India's workforce woes. East Asia Forum. Retrieved May 9, 2024, from https://eastasiaforum.org/2023/04/10/indias-workforce-woes/

Department for Promotion of Industry and Internal Trade (DPIIT). (2021a). 'Review of Foreign Direct Investment (FDI) Policy on Telecom Sector', Press Note No. 4 (2021 Series), Ministry of Commerce and Industry, Government of India. Retrieved from https://dpiit.gov.in/sites/default/files/pn4-2021.PDF

DPIIT. (2021b). Review of Foreign Direct Investment (FDI) policy on Insurance Sector, Press Note No. 2 (2021 Series), Ministry of Commerce and Industry, Government of India. Retrieved from https://dpiit.gov.in/sites/default/files/pn2-2021.pdf

Eichengreen, B., & Gupta, P. (2013). The two waves of service-sector growth. *Oxford Economic Papers, 65*(1), 96–123.

Escaith, H. (2014). Participating and upgrading in trade in value-added: The services perspective, presented at the Third Conference of Latin America Network for Research in Services:Innovation and internationalization in services: New sources of economic development in Latin America, March 13–14, Mexico City: Mexico.

Fan, T., Peters, M., & Zilibotti, F. (2021). *Growing like India: The unequal effects of service-led growth* (Working Paper No. 28551). National Bureau of Economic Research. Retrieved from http://www.nber.org/papers/w28551

Fisher, A. G. B. (1935). *The clash of progress and security.* MacMillan & Co., Ltd.

Fisher, A. G. B. (1952). A note on tertiary production. *The Economic Journal, 62*(248), 820–834.

Fuchs, V. R. (1968). *The service economy.* National Bureau of Economic Research and Colombia University Press.

Ghani, E. (2022). India's New growth model, reinventing India: PIC policy Paper #31, Pune International Centre. Retrieved from https://puneinternationalcentre.org/wp-content/uploads/2022/06/Indias-New-Growth-Model_Policy-Paper-31_compressed-1.pdf

Ghani, E., & Kharas, H. (2010). The service revolution. *World Bank - Economic Premise*, (14), 1–5. Retrieved from https://econpapers.repec.org/article/wbkprmecp/ep14.htm

Goldar, B., Das, P. C., & Dutta, S. (2024). The role of services in India's post-reform economic growth. *Structural Change and Economic Dynamics, 68*, 355–370. https://doi.org/10.1016/j.strueco.2023.10.016

Gordon, J. & Gupta, P. (2004, September). Understanding India's Services Revolution, IMF Working Paper WP/04/171.

Grosso, G. M., Gonzales, F., Miroudot, S., Nordås, H. K., Rouzet, D., & Ueno, A. (2015). Services Trade Restrictiveness Index (STRI): Scoring and weighting methodology. *OECD Trade Policy Papers*, No. 177. Paris: OECD Publishing.

Gulati, S., Saksena, U., Shukla, A. K., Dhanya, V., & Sonna, T. (2020). Trends and dynamics of productivity in India: Sectoral analysis. *Reserve Bank of India Occasional Papers, 41*(1), 77–108.

India Brand Equity Foundation. (2018). Indian Investment Abroad - Overseas Direct Investment by Indian Companies. Retrieved from https://www.ibef.org/economy/indian-investments-abroad

Jorgenson, D. W., Ho, M. S., Samuels, J. D., & Stiroh, K. J. (2007). Industry origins of the American productivity resurgence. *Economic Systems Research, 19*(3), 229–252.

Kaldor, N. (1966). *Causes of the slow rate of economic growth of the United Kingdom*. Cambridge University Press.

Kaldor, N. (1967). *Strategic factors in economic development*. Cornell University.

Khanna, R., & Sharma, C. (2021). Does infrastructure stimulate total factor productivity? A dynamic heterogeneous panel analysis for Indian manufacturing industries. *The Quarterly Review of Economics and Finance, 79*, 59–73.

Kochhar, K., Kumar, U., Raghuram, R., Subramanian, A. & Tokatlidis, I. (2006). India's Pattern of Development: What Happened, What Follows?, IMF Working Paper WP/06/22.

Krishna, K. L., Goldar, B., Das, D. K., Aggarwal, S. C., Erumban, A. A., & Das, P. C. (2022). *India Productivity Report*. Centre for Development Economics, Delhi School of Economics.

Kuznets, S. (1959). *Six lectures on economic growth*. The Free Press of Glencoe.

Kuznets, S. (1972). *Modern economic growth: Rate, structure, and spread* (Indian). Oxford and IBH Publishing Co., Pvt. Ltd.

Mazumdar, S. (2010). Industry and services in growth and structural change in India: Some unexplored features. Institute for Studies in Industrial Development.

Miroudot, S., Rouzet, D., & Spinelli, F. (2013). Trade policy implications of global value chains: Case studies, Organisation for Economic Co-operation and Development (OECD) Trade Policy Paper No. 161.

Mishra, S., Lundström, S., & Anand, R. (2011). Service export sophistication and economic growth. World Bank Policy Research Working Paper, (5606). Retrieved from https://ssrn.com/abstract=1816582

Mitra, A. (1988, April). "Disproportionality and the Services Sector: A Note", Social Scientist.

National Association of Software and Service Companies (NASSCOM). (2020). *NASSCOM Perspective Report 2020*. Retrieved from https://nasscom.in/perspectives

Pack, H., & Westphal, L. (1986). Industrial strategy and technological change: Theory versus reality. *Journal of Development Economics, 22*, 87–128.

Panagariya, A. (2005). The triumph of India's market reforms: The record of the 1980s and 1990s, policy analysis, November 7, No. 554. Retrieved from https://www.cato.org/policy-analysis/triumph-indias-market-reforms-record-1980s-1990s

Press Information Bureau (PIB). (2022). Comprehensive Economic Partnership Agreement (CEPA) between India and the United Arab Emirates (UAE) Unveiled. Retrieved from https://pib.gov.in/PressReleasePage.aspx?PRID=1810279

Planning Commission. (2001). Report of the task force on employment opportunities, chaired by M. S. Ahluwalia, New Delhi, Government of India.

Rakshit, M. (2007, February). Services-led growth: The Indian experience, Money & Finance.

RBI. (various years). Handbook of Statistics on Indian Economy. Mumbai: Reserve Bank of India (RBI).

Rowthorn, R., & Ramaswamy, R. (1999). Growth, trade and deindustrialization. *IMF Staff Papers, 46*(1), 18–41.

Rosenstein-Rodan, P. (1943). Problems of industrialization of eastern and south-eastern Europe. *Economic Journal, 53*(210/211), 202–211.

Sahoo, P., & Dash, R. K. (2014). India's surge in modern services exports: Empirics for policy. *Journal of Policy Modeling, 36*(6), 1082–1100.

Saidi, S., Mani, V., Mefteh, H., Shahbaz, M., & Akhtar, P. (2020). Dynamic linkages between transport, logistics, foreign direct investment, and economic growth: Empirical evidence from developing countries. *Transportation Research Part a: Policy and Practice, 141*, 277–293.

Sarkar, A. (1998). Endogenous growth and the size of the market. *Keio Economic Studies, 35*(1), 29–44.

Singh, N. (2006). Services-led industrialization in India: Assessment and lessons. Retrieved from https://www.un.org/esa/sustdev/publications/industrial_development/2_3.pdf

Statista. (2023). *India: IT industry direct and indirect employment*. Retrieved June 11, 2023, from https://www.statista.com/statistics/320729/india-it-industry-direct-indirect-employment/

UNCTAD. (2003). Trade and development report 2003, New York and Geneva: United Nations Conference for Trade and Development.

UN. (2006). World economic and social survey 2006. Geneva: United Nations.

United States International Trade Commission (USITC). (2013). The economic effects of significant US import restraints (8th update) - Special Topic: Services' Contribution to Manufacturing, Investigation Number, pp. 332–325.

WTO. (2023). *World trade statistical review 2023*. World Trade Organization.

Online Data Sources

DPIIT FDI statistics. (2023). Retrieved November 27, 2023, from https://dpiit.gov.in/publications/fdi-statistics

INDIA KLEMS database. (2021). Retrieved April 2024, from https://rbi.org.in/Scripts/KLEMS.aspx

OECD TiVA database. (2019). Retrieved March 29, 2019, from https://stats.oecd.org/Index.aspx?DataSetCode=TIVA_2018_C2

OECD IOT database. Retrieved May 8, 2024, from https://stats.oecd.org/Index.aspx?DataSetCode=IOTS_2021

UNCTADstat Data Centre. Retrieved from https://unctadstat.unctad.org/wds/ReportFolders/reportFolders.aspx?sCS_ChosenLang=en, (2019, November 23; 2023, November 22)

WB (various years). *Logistics Performance Index Report*. World Bank.

WEF (various years). *The Global Competitiveness Report*. World Economic Forum.

WEF (various years). *The Global Enabling Trade Report.* World Economic Forum.

Part V
Growth Heterogeneity

Chapter 10
Regional Growth Dynamics in India Since Independence

Debajit Jha and Sabyasachi Kar

Abstract The Indian economy passed through two distinct regimes in the period after independence. The first regime attempted a heavily regulated mixed-economy model for close to four decades, before shifting to a liberalized, privatized, and globalized second regime following the reforms in the early nineties. These two regimes have manifested in the form of two growth episodes—a pre-reform period of relative stagnation and a post-reform period of rapid economic growth. These higher growth outcomes in recent times has also coincided with increased regional inequalities, with some states prospering while others stagnated. This might suggest that the regional growth dynamics has changed drastically as a result of the reforms. Is there any empirical evidence to support this hypothesis? This paper investigates this question using a long time series of regional data for the pre-reform and post-reform period. The study finds that there was no qualitative difference in the regional growth dynamics during the two periods, with persistent non-convergence and club formation of per capita GSDP in both. The individual regions also largely remained in the same clubs across these two episodes. There was some quantitative difference between the two periods however, mainly in terms of an accelerated divergence between the clubs themselves in the post-reform period. The study concludes with some discussion of the differential policy approaches that are needed for regions in high-income and low-income clubs.

Keywords Economic growth · Convergence dynamics · Convergence club · Economic reforms · India

D. Jha (✉)
Jindal School of Government and Public Policy, O. P. Jindal Global University, Sonipat, Haryana, India
e-mail: jhadebajit@gmail.com

S. Kar
Institute of Economic Growth, University of Delhi Enclave, Delhi, India

D. Maiti et al. (eds.), *75 Years of Growth, Development and Productivity in India*, India Studies in Business and Economics, https://doi.org/10.1007/978-981-97-8054-9_10

10.1 Introduction

The Indian economy has undergone significant transformations since gaining independence in 1947. Initially characterized as a mixed-economy model with heavy government intervention and planning, the 1991 economic reforms marked a pivotal shift towards liberalization, privatization, and globalization. Over the decades, sectors such as agriculture, manufacturing, and services have evolved, with services emerging as a dominant contributor to GDP. Despite challenges like unemployment, income inequality, infrastructure gaps, and poor bureaucratic capability, India has shown resilience and sustained economic growth, becoming one of the world's fastest-growing major economies.

This was not always the case, however. In the pre-reform period, India experienced significant challenges in achieving robust economic growth, both at the aggregate and sectoral levels. Aggregate economic growth was hampered by a heavily regulated economy, characterized by bureaucratic controls, import substitution policies, and a dominant public sector. This led to inefficiencies, resource misallocation, and stagnant productivity across various sectors. Agriculture, which employed a substantial portion of the population, faced issues such as low yields, inadequate infrastructure, and fragmented landholdings, contributing to persistent rural poverty. The industrial sector, while protected from foreign competition, struggled with outdated technology, low economies of scale, and limited access to capital. Services, though relatively less regulated, were constrained by infrastructure bottlenecks and a lack of skilled manpower.

Overall, poor economic growth in the pre-reform period reflected the need for structural changes to unlock India's economic potential and integrate it into the global economy. After some limited changes during the 1980s, India embarked on a transformative journey of economic reforms in the early 1990s that shifted its trajectory from a predominantly closed, centrally planned economy to one characterized by liberalization, privatization, and globalization. These reforms, driven by the urgency to revitalize a stagnating economy, aimed to dismantle bureaucratic controls, reduce government intervention, and encourage private enterprise and foreign investment. Key measures included slashing industrial licencing requirements, opening up various sectors to competition, and devaluing the currency to boost exports. These changes not only sparked rapid economic growth but also modernized infrastructure, expanded consumer choices, and integrated India more deeply into the global economy. Despite initial challenges, the reforms laid the foundation for India's emergence as a dynamic economy in the subsequent decades, significantly altering the country's economic landscape and global standing.

India experienced significant economic growth, marked by both aggregate expansion and sectoral diversification, in this post-reform period. Following the liberalization reforms of the early 1990s, the Indian economy shifted gears from a largely closed, centrally planned system to a more market-oriented approach. Aggregate economic growth soared, with GDP expanding rapidly, bolstered by robust industrialization, services sector growth, and increasing foreign investment inflows. The services sector, particularly IT services and business outsourcing, emerged as a powerhouse, contributing substantially to GDP and employment. Meanwhile, agriculture, though less dynamic, saw improvements in productivity and infrastructure. The manufacturing sector also made strides, driven by investments and technological advancements. Overall, India's post-reform economic landscape witnessed a diversified growth trajectory.

Despite this success in aggregate terms, economic growth in India has increasingly been facing certain challenges that may jeopardize its sustainability in the long run. One particular problem has been the rising regional inequality in the economy, manifested in terms of the divergence of state per capita incomes over time and documented in the academic literature. The economic liberalization policies initiated in the early 1990s have spurred rapid growth in certain regions, particularly urban and industrialized areas, while rural and less-developed regions have struggled to keep pace. This has exacerbated pre-existing regional disparities, leading to a widening gap between prosperous states like Maharashtra, Gujarat, and Karnataka, and lagging states such as Bihar, Uttar Pradesh, and Odisha. Studies highlight that factors such as differential access to infrastructure, education, healthcare, and institutional support play crucial roles in perpetuating these disparities. Moreover, while some states have successfully leveraged reforms to attract investment and foster growth, others have faced challenges related to governance, infrastructure deficits, and social inequalities, reinforcing the divergence in economic outcomes across regions. Addressing these inequalities remains a pressing challenge for policymakers aiming to achieve inclusive and sustainable development across India.

There are two issues related to regional inequality in post-independence India, that has not been sufficiently addressed in our opinion. The first is related to the underlying growth process—whether it is generating a growth dynamic of absolute divergence or is it rather leading to the formation of convergence clubs. It is important to understand this distinction, mainly because the policy implications for regional dynamics manifesting absolute divergence are quite different from those for convergence clubs. Appropriate research into this question requires the adoption of a methodology that can distinguish between these two alternative possibilities. The second issue that has not been addressed adequately is whether these trends in rising inequality have been a result of long-run characteristics of the pre-reform growth experience that have also persisted in the post-reform period or is it that the reforms have drastically changed the underlying regional growth dynamics resulting in such rising inequality. Research into this issue requires taking a critical look at the differences in growth dynamics in the pre and post-reform periods.

In this paper, we attempt to address these issues. The methodology and data section describe in detail how we attempt to fulfil the requirements of this analysis. The rest of the paper is organized as follows. In Sect. 10.2, we briefly discuss the convergence literature in two parts—the cross-country convergence literature and the regional convergence literature in the Indian context. The methodology and the data used in the present study have been discussed in Sect. 10.3. We present the results of our analysis in Sect. 10.4. Section 10.5 concludes the study.

10.2 The Convergence Debate in Cross-Country Studies and in Indian States

There are two broad streams of the empirical growth literature that are relevant for this study. The first one is the literature based on cross-country data looking for evidence in favour of or against convergence of national economies over time. The second literature is that of regional convergence across Indian states. In this section we will discuss them one by one.

The neoclassical growth theory posits that less affluent countries tend to narrow the income gap with richer ones over time, a phenomenon termed convergence. Two main tests were initially employed in empirical literature to assess convergence: σ-convergence, which examines the reduction in income disparities among economies, and β-convergence, focusing on economies with lower initial incomes experiencing accelerated growth rates to catch up with richer counterparts. Criticism arose against these cross-sectional methods, citing their failure to consider unobservable differences between countries (cross-sectional heterogeneity) and susceptibility to measurement errors, endogeneity biases, and spatial autocorrelation (Temple, 1999). Notably, not all economies converge; they may form convergence clubs, reaching distinct steady states based on initial conditions (Baumol, 1986).

To address these shortcomings, various dynamic methods were developed to test the club convergence hypothesis, including regression-tree procedures (e.g. Durlauf & Johnson, 1995), time series and panel data approaches (e.g. Bernard & Durlauf, 1995, 1996; Evans & Karras, 1996; Hobijn & Franses, 2000), and the distribution dynamics approach (e.g. Quah, 1997). The Phillips and Sul approach (2007, 2009) represents a significant breakthrough in identifying club convergence by addressing previous limitations, allowing differentiation between absolute convergence, transitional divergence with long-run convergence, club convergence, and absolute divergence. Empirical studies on club convergence have primarily focused on variables like income, GDP, and total factor productivity. Empirical studies in club convergence have focused on variables such as income (e.g. Ghosh et al., 2013; Aksoy et al., 2019; Cutrini, 2019; Cavallaro & Villani, 2021; Zhang et al., 2019; Espoir, 2022), gross domestic product (GDP) (e.g. Hamit-Haggar, 2013; Monfort et al., 2013; Choi & Wang, 2015; Tian et al., 2016; Bergeaud et al., 2020; Desli & Gkoulgkoutsika, 2020; Gonzalez et al., 2020; Mazzola & Pizzuto, 2020; Gunawan et al., 2021; Ursavaş & Mendez, 2022), or total factor productivity (e.g. You et al., 2019). Many studies have tried to identify club convergence beyond macroeconomic variables such as in the field of ecology and energy, health expenditure, covid-19 infections etc.

In the context of India, a significant portion of the literature has predominantly relied on conventional regression-based and distribution-based methods to examine the long-term distribution of per capita incomes across states. From the regression-based and distribution-based studies on regional convergence in India we can identify two broad trends—(a) except Cashin and Sahay (1996), all the regression-based studies have shown evidence of either divergence or conditional convergence of state per capita income in both pre-reform and post-reform period (e.g. Nagaraj et al., 1998; Aiyar, 2001; Baddeley, 2007; Purfield, 2006; Rao et al., 1999, Ghosh, 2008). Cashin and Sahay (1996) found evidence of absolute convergence in state per capita income of Indian states between 1960 to 1991 across 20 Indian states. (b) all the distribution-based studies have indicated that although the divergence between per capita income of the states was increasing slowly in the pre-reform period, the speed of divergence has increased in the post-reform period (e.g. Dasgupta et al., 2000, Ahluwalia, 2000, 2002; Bhattacharya & Sakthivel, 2004; Kar & Sakthivel, 2007; Ghate & Wright, 2012; Rangarajan et al., 2014; Clark & Wolcott, 2003; Chikte, 2011; Cherodian & Thirlwall, 2013).

Although a large number of studies within this framework have indicated that per capita income among Indian states have diverged in recent times, only a few have compared the growth dynamics in the pre-reform and the post-reform period. Among the limited literature on this issue, some have shown that divergence characteristics have been stronger in the post-reform period (e.g., Ahluwalia, 2002; Bhattacharya & Sakthivel, 2004; Rao et al., 1999; Sachs et al., 2002) while others have reported findings of absolute convergence among Indian states in the pre-reform period (e.g., Cashin & Sahay, 1996). All of these studies are also limited by the lack of back-data that was available earlier for the pre-reform period.

A very small number of studies have also looked at the possibility of club convergence or polarization in India. These studies employ different methodologies, such as the time series method (e.g. Ghosh, 2008), generalized regression-tree-based approach (e.g. Chaudhuri & Marimoutou, 2007), distribution dynamics approach (e.g. Kar et al., 2011; Bandyopadhyay, 2012), or Phillips-Sul approach (e.g. Ghosh et al., 2013) in analyzing the distribution of per capita income among states. However, these studies have also ignored the comparative role of the reforms in driving the growth dynamics of Indian sub-national regions.

The above discussion shows that a broad trend has emerged in the literature on Indian states that shows divergence of state per capita incomes in the post-reform period. Methodologically, most of the contributions to this literature have applied summary measures such as β- and σ-convergence that consider only two possibilities—convergence and divergence (non-convergence). On the other hand, the cross-country empirical growth literature discussed above has become increasingly critical of these summary measures and moved on towards club convergence, a possibility that most of the literature on Indian states (using β- or σ-convergence) is unable to even consider. Clearly, the convergence debate in the context of Indian states has a long way to go. The literature (or the lack of it) also highlights the insufficient analysis of the role of the reforms underlying the growth dynamics in India. Whatever little literature exists on this issue is also not very robust, as it is based on very limited back-data for the pre-reform period that was available earlier. These gaps in the literature provide the motivation for this paper. Our objective is to understand the growth dynamics of sub-national regions in India in the period after independence, particularly in terms of club formation, and looking for similarities and differences in such dynamics in the pre-reform and post-reform period. In terms of data, we use a much longer pre-reform time series data compared to existing studies, and this allows us to undertake a more robust comparison of pre-reform and post-reform growth dynamics in India. Methodologically, we differentiate between absolute convergence, club convergence and absolute divergence (using the Phillips-Sul technique) adding much more nuance to the existing literature.

10.3 Methodology and Data

This section describes the methodology used in our analysis and the data used for the same.

10.3.1 Philips-Sul Test for Club Convergence

In the present study we use the Phillips-Sul (2007, 2009) method (henceforth PS) to endogenously identify convergence clubs in the distribution of state per capita income in India for the period 1960 to 2021. This method can differentiate between growth dynamics exhibiting absolute convergence, absolute divergence or club convergence. We discuss the method briefly here.

Let's assume X_{it} represents panel data of per capita NSDP of Indian states. The common factor representation of X_{it}

$$X_{it} = \left(\frac{g_{it} + a_{it}}{u_t}\right) u_t = \delta_{it} u_t \tag{10.1}$$

where δ_{it} is the time-varying-idiosyncratic component (measures the distance between an individual observation X_{it} and the common component) and μ_t is the common component.

However, we cannot directly fit the model without imposing some restrictions on δ_{it} and μ_t. Thus, Phillips and Sul (2007) proposed removing the common factor and calculated relative per capita NSDP as -

$$h_{it} = \frac{X_{it}}{\frac{1}{N}\sum_{i=1}^{n} X_{it}} = \frac{\delta_{it}}{\frac{1}{N}\sum_{i=1}^{n} \delta_{it}} \tag{10.2}$$

In this framework, convergence is achieved when $h_{it} \to 1$ as $t \to \infty$, *or* the cross-section variance of h_{it} satisfies the condition:

$$H_t = \frac{1}{N}\sum_{i=1}^{n} (h_{it} - 1)^2 \to 0 \text{ if } \lim_{t\to\infty} \delta_{it} = \delta \text{for all } i. \tag{10.3}$$

Phillips-Sul is a two-step method. In the first step, we test the null hypothesis of convergence using a *log t* test, while in the second step, it tries to identify the presence of club convergence using a clustering algorithm and *log t* test of the form

$$log\left(\frac{H_1}{H_t}\right) - 2log\{log(t)\} = a + blog(t) + \varepsilon_t \tag{10.4}$$

The null hypothesis of convergence is rejected at 5% if the test statistics is < –1.65. Conversely, 0 < b < 2 implies convergence in growth rate and b ≥ 2 implies convergence in levels.

The PS method has several advantages over the traditional regression-based and distribution-based methods. The traditional cross-section and panel data regressions are inefficient methods in the presence of technological heterogeneities. The PS method addresses this by employing a non-linear time-varying factor model which allows heterogeneity across panel units and over time. Second, in the PS methods, there is no need to assume trend stationarity or stochastic non-stationarity of time series in the panel. Thirdly, since the method is based on the OLS regression method, it is easy to employ. Finally, the PS approach remains robust in the presence of structural breaks in time series (Antonakakis et al., 2017).

10.3.2 Data

As discussed in Sect. 10.2, most of the studies on regional growth dynamics in India have focused on the post-reform period. Even for the studies that compared the regional growth dynamics in the pre-reform and the post-reform periods, the pre-reform sample was too limited because of the unavailability of state per capita incomes before the 1980s. As a result, the pre-reform growth dynamics remained mostly unexplored. However, in recent years, a substantial amount of new data has come to study the pre-reform growth dynamics from 1960 onward which can provide a much richer understanding of the regional growth dynamics in India. In this study we have used per capita NSDP data of Indian states at 2011–12 base for the period 1960 to 2021. Based on the availability of data we have used two different samples of states for both the pre- and post-reform periods. The first sample consists of 16 states. For this sample data was available from 1960 onward. The second sample consists of 18 states starting from the year 1965.

10.4 Testing for Convergence in the Pre-Reform and Post-Reform Periods

In this section, we present the results of the log t test and the clustering algorithm for different samples of Indian states in the pre- and post-reform period. In the pre-reform period, we present results from two samples, the first includes sixteen states (data available from 1960 to 1992) while the second includes eighteen states (data available from 1965 to 1992). To keep the results of the post-reform period comparable with the results of the pre-reform period, we estimate the results for the post-reform period based on the same two samples used in the pre-reform estimation.

10.4.1 Growth Dynamics in the Pre-Reform Period, 1960–1992

First, we present the results of the log t test of PS for per capita NSDP of 16 Indian states and UTs for the period between 1960 and 1992. The results of the PS log t test for the pre-reform period have been presented in the first row of Table 10.1. The test statistics (t_b), presented in the first row and the last column, is –36.19 which rejects the null hypothesis of convergence at 5% level. The coefficient of log t has been found to be –0.69 and the speed of convergence is –0.345.

Since the null hypothesis of convergence has been rejected in the first step of the PS method, we run the club convergence test in the second step. The test identified three convergence clubs and two divergent states. The relative transition paths of these three convergence clubs and two divergent states have been presented in panel (a) of Fig. 10.1. The figure shows that the three clubs and the two divergent states are mildly diverging from each other for the entire pre-reform period. The relative transition paths for each state in the three convergence clubs have been presented respectively in Fig. 10.1 (b), 1(c), and 1(d). The speed of convergence is the highest (0.681) in club 3 and the lowest (0.112) in club 1.

Next, we present the results of the PS log t test for an augmented sample—the sixteen states and UTs above, plus two more states, Punjab and Haryana, whose data is available only from 1965. Hence, the period for this analysis is between 1965 and 1992, and the sample size is 18. The results are presented in Table 10.2 and Fig. 10.2. The test statistics (t_b) of log t test for the entire sample has been found to be –61.461, representing non-convergence of the entire sample. The estimated speed of convergence is –0.789. The test identified four convergence clubs and two divergent states. The three clubs and two divergent states remained the same as in the case of 16 states and UTs, with the addition of a new high-income club (the first club in this estimation, consisting of the two additional states, Haryana and Punjab). This result of Haryana and Punjab forming the highest-income convergence club is expected. This is because these two states were experiencing the benefits of green revolution and following higher growth trajectories compared to other Indian states

Table 10.1 PS results (1960–1992) for 16 Indian states & UTs

Clubs	States	Coefficient ($\hat{b} = 2\hat{\alpha}$)	Speed of convergence ($\hat{\alpha}$)	Test statistics (t_b)
Entire sample	AP, BI, DL, GU, JK, KA, KE, MAN, MH, MP, RAJ, TEL, TN, TRI, UP, WB	–0.6916	–0.3458	–36.1917
First club	GUJ, JK, KA, KE, MAN, MH, RAJ, TEL, TN	0.224	0.112	2.858
Second club	AP, UP, WB	0.479	0.239	8.512
Third club	MP, TRI	1.362	0.681	11.693
Divergent group	BI, DL	–0.862	–0.431	–80.562

Note Results are significant at 5% level of significance

in the pre-reform period. The speed of convergence was the highest for the club 4 while it was lowest for the club 1.

The above results of the PS test presented in Table 10.1 and 10.2 together with the relative transition paths (presented in Figs. 10.1 and 10.2) show that the Indian states were diverging from each other in an absolute sense, even in the pre-reform period. In terms of growth dynamics, the states were converging towards more than one steady state, indicating club convergence.

10.4.2 *Growth Dynamics in the Post-Reform Period, 1993–2021*

We study the convergence behaviour of the states in the post-reform period using the same states that were there in the two samples used in the previous section. This ensures that the results of the post-reform period are comparable with the results of the pre-reform period. The results of the PS log t test for the case of sixteen Indian states in the post-reform period have been presented in Table 10.3. The test statistics (t_b) for the entire sample, presented in the first row and last column, is found to be –1054.11. This rejects the null hypothesis of absolute convergence at 5% level. The coefficient of log t has been found to be –0.98 and the speed of convergence is –0.49.

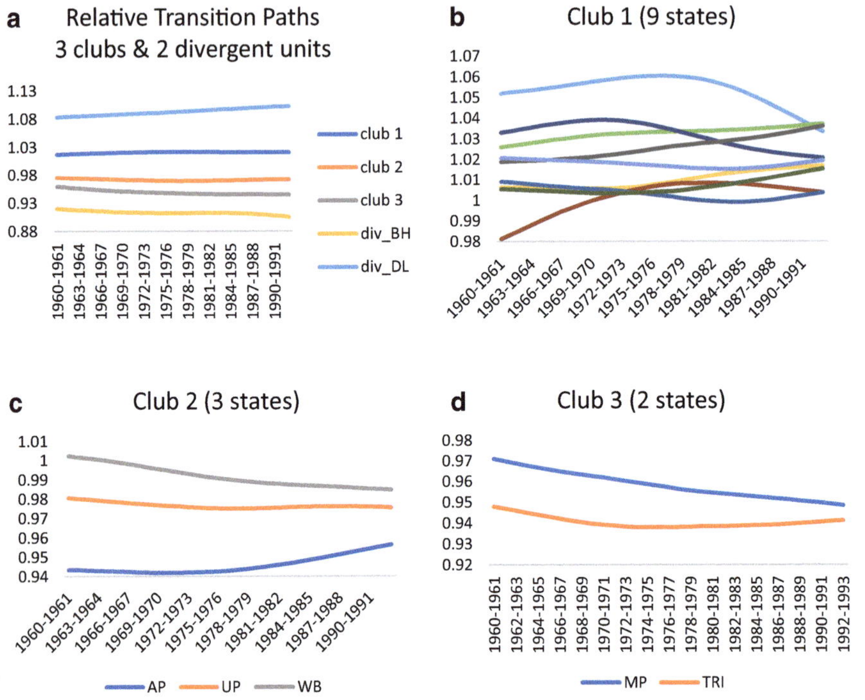

Fig. 10.1 Relative transition paths of 3 convergence clubs and 2 divergent states for 16 Indian states in the pre-reform period

Table 10.2 PS results (Pre-Reform, 1965–1992) for 18 Indian States & UTs

Clubs	States	Coefficient ($\hat{b} = 2\hat{\alpha}$)	Speed of convergence ($\hat{\alpha}$)	Test statistics (t_b)
Entire sample	AP, BI, DL, GU, HAR, JK, KA, KE, MAN, MH, MP, PUN, RAJ, TEL, TN, TRI, UP, WB	–0.7890	–0.3945	–61.4614
First club	HAR, PUN	0.089	0.0445	0.789
Second club	GUJ, JK, KA, KE, MAN, MH, RAJ, TEL, TN	0.181	0.0905	2.177
Third club	AP, UP, WB	0.315	0.1575	5.491
Fourth club	MP, TRI	1.162	0.581	9.331
Divergent group	BI, DL	–0.888	–0.444	–104.399

Note Results are significant at 5% level of significance

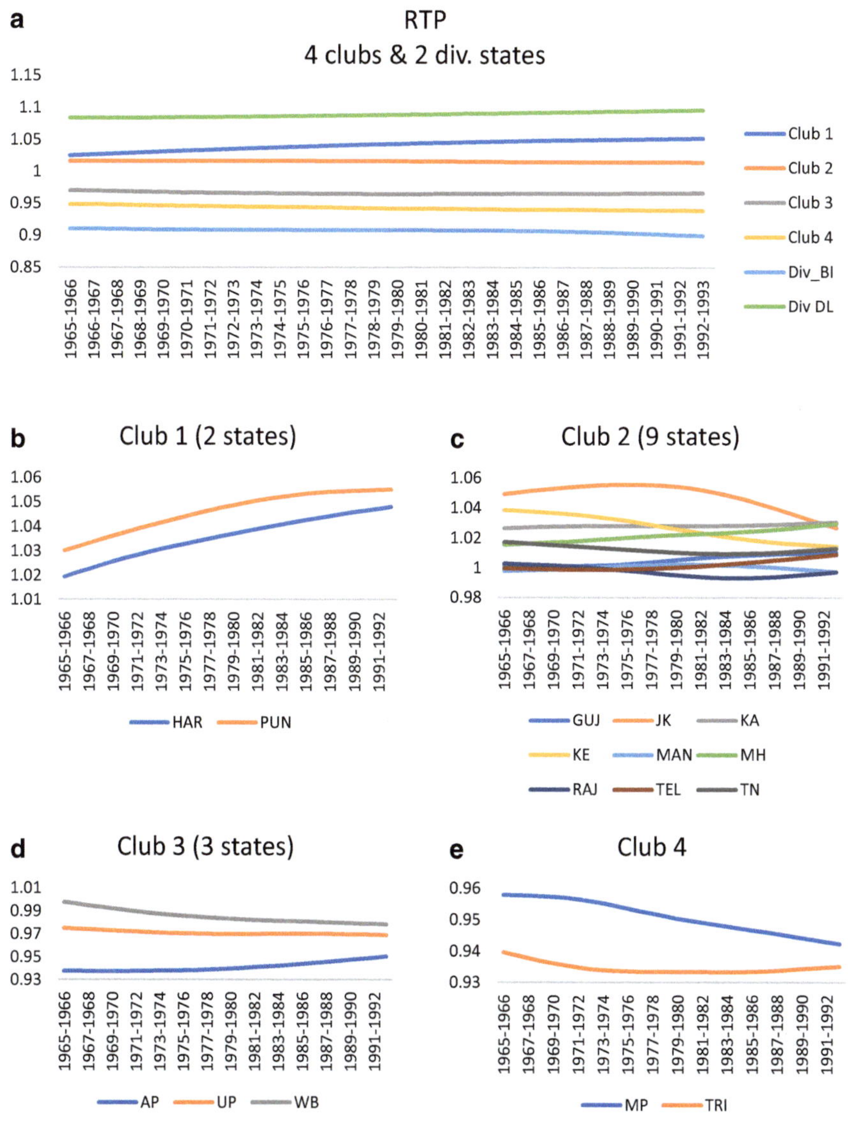

Fig. 10.2 Relative transition paths of 4 convergence clubs and 2 divergent states for 18 Indian states in the pre-reform period

The results of the club convergence algorithm have also been presented Table 10.3. The test identified three convergence clubs. The relative transition paths of these three convergence clubs have been presented in panel (a) of Fig. 10.3. The figure shows that the three convergence clubs were clearly diverging from each other for the entire post-reform period. The relative transition paths for the members of the

Table 10.3 PS results (Post-Reform, 1993–2021) for 16 Indian States & UTs

Clubs	States	Coefficient ($\hat{b} = 2\hat{\alpha}$)	Speed of convergence ($\hat{\alpha}$)	Test statistics (t_b)
Entire sample	AP, BI, DL, GU, JK, KA, KE, MAN, MH, MP, RAJ, TEL, TN, TRI, UP, WB	–0.9863	–0.4931	–1054.1118
First club	AP, DL, GU, KA, KE, MH, TEL, TN, TRI	0.101	0.050	4.336
Second club	JK, MP, RAJ, WB	0.782	0.391	6.494
Third club	BI, MAN, UP	0.388	0.194	6.118

Note Results are significant at 5% level of significance

three identified clubs have been presented respectively in Fig. 3b, c, and d. The speed of convergence was the highest (0.39) in club 2 and the lowest (0.05) in club 1.

Next, we present the results of the PS log *t* test for the period 1993 to 2021 for eighteen Indian states (Haryana and Punjab have been included along with the initial 16 states). The results have been presented in Table 10.4 and Fig. 10.4 (a to d). The full sample tend to be diverging from each other. The test statistics (t_b) of log *t* test for the entire sample has been found to be –746.075, supporting non-convergence. The estimated speed of convergence is –0.485. The results of the club convergence test identified four convergence clubs. The results of the club convergence test for the two samples (sixteen and eighteen states respectively) have more differences compared to those two in the pre-reform period. However, these differences are in terms of the club-membership of a few individual states, while the overall result between the two samples are broadly similar.

10.4.3 A Comparison of the Pre-Reform and Post-Reform Periods

It is useful to compare the results for the pre-reform and post-reform period at this stage. We start with the similarities among these two episodes. First, both episodes have shown evidence of non-convergence among the sub-national regions within India. Moreover, both have shown evidence of club formation, rather than absolute divergence. Interestingly, the number of clubs (ignoring divergent members) have also remained the same in these two periods—three clubs if we use data from 16

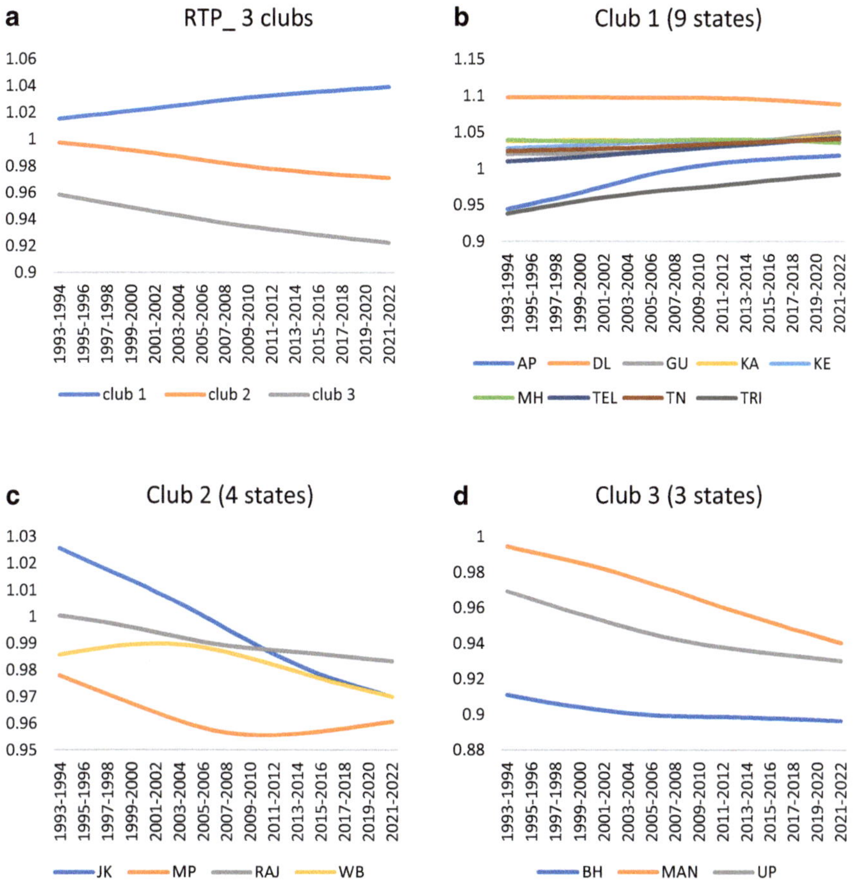

Fig. 10.3 Relative transition paths of 3 convergence clubs for 16 Indian states in the post-reform period

Table 10.4 PS results (Post-Reform, 1993–2021) for 18 Indian States & UTs

Clubs	States	Coefficient ($\hat{b} = 2\hat{\alpha}$)	Speed of convergence ($\hat{\alpha}$)	Test statistics (t_b)
Entire sample	AP, BI, DL, GU, HAR, JK, KA, KE, MAN, MH, MP, PUN, RAJ, TEL, TN, TRI, UP, WB	–0.9702	–0.4851	–746.0754
First club	AP, DL, GU, HAR, KA, KE, MH, TEL, TN	0.269	0.1345	13.626
Second club	PUN, RAJ, TRI, WB	0.123	0.0615	3.857
Third club	JK, MAN, MP	0.342	0.171	4.984
Fourth club	BI, UP	0.022	0.011	1.827

Note Results are significant at 5% level of significance

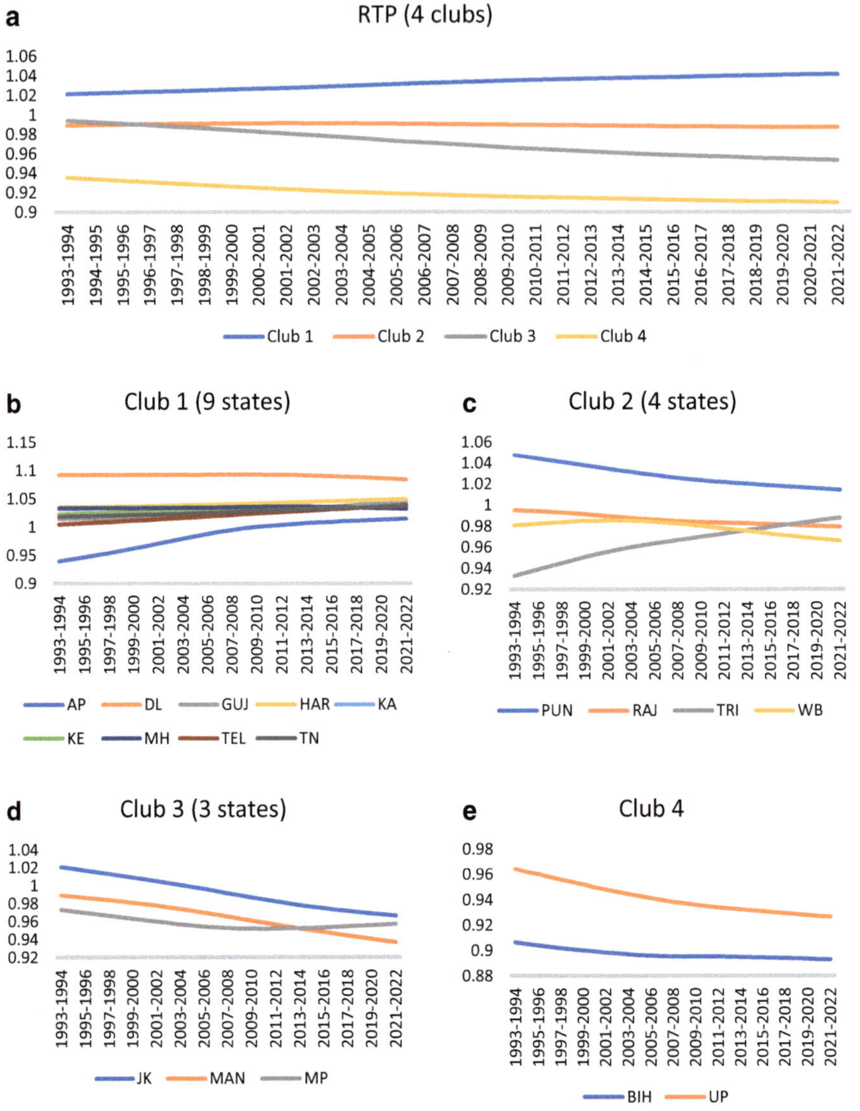

Fig. 10.4 Relative transition paths of 4 convergence clubs for 18 Indian states in the post-reform period

states and four clubs if we use data from 18 states. The membership of the states in the higher income clubs and the lower income clubs across both the periods have also remained broadly similar.

There are some differences as well during these two episodes. The speed of divergence has increased in the post-reform period compared to the pre-reform period (e.g., in the case of 16 states, the speed of convergence coefficient $(\widehat{\alpha})$ has decreased from –0.34 to –0.49). From a visual analysis of the transition paths, it is also clear that the clubs are moving away from each other at a faster rate in the post-reform period, compared to the pre-reform period. Moreover, the membership of some of the states have shown rapid transition from one club to another following the reforms. For example, although Jammu & Kashmir was in the first club (in the case of 16 states) and second club (in the case of 18 states) in the pre-reform period, it has transitioned to a lower club (in the second club in the case of 16 states and third club in the case of 18 and 32 states) in the post-reform period. Similarly, Manipur has transitioned from a higher convergence club (in the first club in the case of 16 states and in second club in the case of 18 states) in the pre-reform period to a lower club (lowest club) in the post-reform period. Punjab is another state where we can observe a transition towards a lower convergence club. These results are possibly due to the fact that these states were facing problems of insurgency during some of these periods. In contrast, Andhra Pradesh and Tripura have transitioned from a lower club in the pre-reform period to a higher club in the post-reform period. The result of Andhra Pradesh is again not surprising as the states has shown growth in industry and service sectors, especially IT sector. To sum up, while the broad dynamics of the states in terms of the membership of clubs remain unchanged from the pre-reform to the post-reform period, some transitions have been observed in the post-reform period.

10.5 Robustness of the Results

Robustness of the results are important for any empirical analysis. We undertake three exercises to provide further support to our results. The first exercise is to make the study comparable to the current literature on this issue. Here, the main concern is whether taking a truncated sample for the post-reform period has biassed the study. More specifically, would the results be similar if we took all states and UTs for which post-reform data is available (providing a sample of 32 states and UTs) instead of the smaller sample (16 and 18 states, respectively)? To answer this question, we apply the PS test using all the states and UTs (32) for which per capita NSDP data is available in the for the period 1993 to 2021.

The results remain broadly similar to those based on either sixteen or eighteen states used in the previous section. These results have been presented in Table 10.5 and Fig. 10.5. The club convergence test identified four convergence clubs and one divergent state. Similarity of the results with the case of 18 states for the same period can be easily observed once we compare the members of the two upper and two lower convergence clubs. All the states those are in the two upper convergence clubs (i.e., first and second club) in the case of 18 states in the post-reform period remained in the upper two convergence clubs in the case of 32 states. Similarly, the states in the lower two clubs in the case of 18 states also remained in the lower two clubs in the case of 32 states. Therefore, we can conclude that the club convergence dynamics of the Indian states in the post-reform period remained broadly similar, whether it was from the full sample available or the smaller sample that has been used in the previous section.

The second robustness exercise addresses the critic that understanding growth dynamics of regions based only on their per capita GDP may be misleading as the latter is too narrow a concept to fully describe the development of a country or a region (Streeten, 1994). According to this view, development is a multi-dimensional concept which can only be captured by different factors like health, education etc. along with per capita GDP. If a region performs well in terms of per capita GDP, but not so much in terms of other indicators like education, health etc., it may not achieve broad-based development. To address this, we study whether the growth dynamics of Indian states remain the same, if we substitute per capita GSDP of the states with a more multi-dimensional measure of development. Specifically, we explore the possibility of club convergence using the Human Development Index (HDI) for 36 Indian States and UTs using data from Global Data Lab. Due to unavailability of HDI data before 1990, our analysis is based on the period between 1990 and 2021. The results have been presented in Table 10.6.

The test statistics (t_b), presented in the first row and the last column, is –23.52 which rejects the null hypothesis of absolute convergence at 5% level. The coefficient of log t has been found to be –0.33 and the speed of convergence is –0.16. Since the null hypothesis of convergence has been rejected in the first step of the PS method, we run the club convergence test in the second step. The test identified

Table 10.5 PS results (Post-Reform, 1993–2021) for 32 Indian States & UTs

Clubs	States	Coefficient ($\hat{b} = 2\hat{\alpha}$)	Speed of convergence ($\hat{\alpha}$)	Test statistics (t_b)
Entire sample	AN, AP, ASS, AUR, BI, CHAN, CHAT, DL, GO, GU, HAR, HP, JK, JH, KA, KE, MAN, MEG, MH, MP, NAG, ODI, PUN, PUDU, RAJ, SIK, TEL, TN, TRI, UK, UP, WB	–1.0390	–0.5195	–241.9671
First club	AN, AP, CHAN, DL, GO, GU, HAR, SIK, TEL, TN, UK	0.127	0.0635	4.811
Second club	HP, KA, KE, MH, PUDU, PUN, TRI	0.469	0.2345	6.369
Third club	CHAT, JK, MP, NAG, ODI, RAJ, WB	0.513	0.2565	7.197
Fourth club	ASS, BI, JH, MAN, MEG, UP	–0.006	–0.003	–0.118
Divergent group	AUR			

Note Results are significant at 5% level of significance

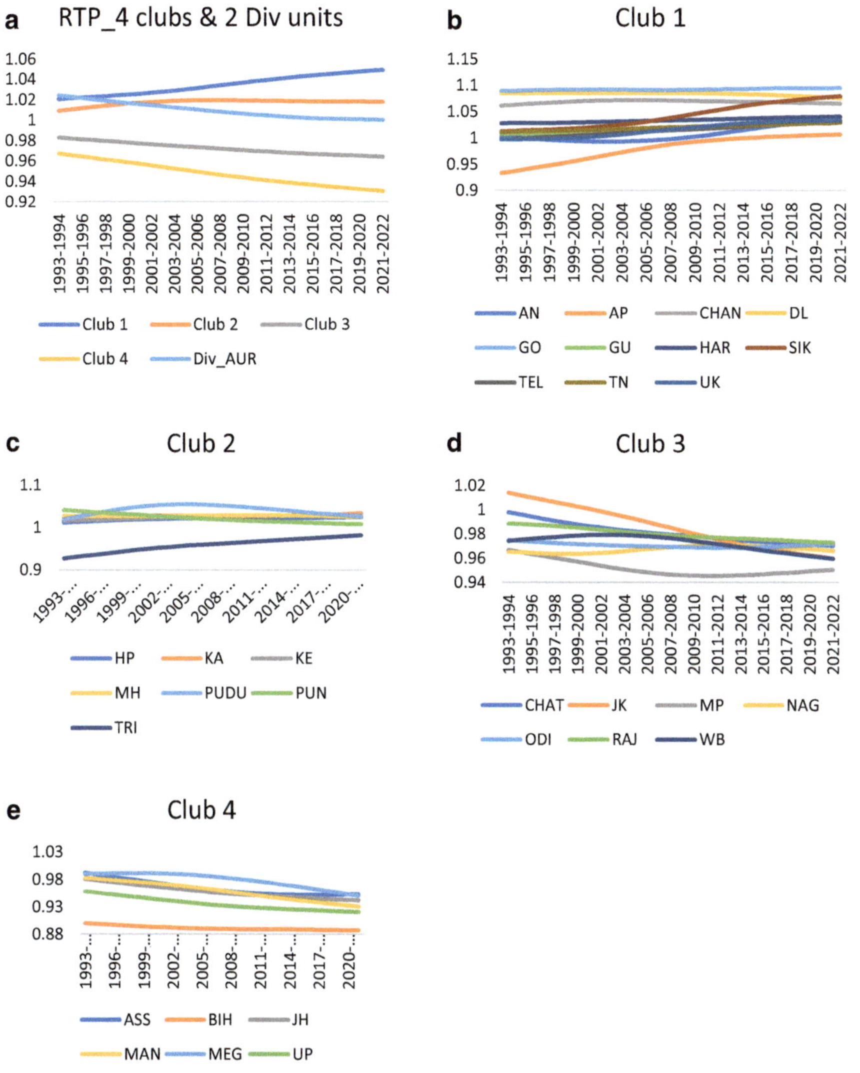

Fig. 10.5 Relative transition paths of 4 convergence clubs and 1 divergent state for 32 Indian states in the post-reform period

two convergence clubs. The relative transition paths of these two convergence clubs have been presented in panel (a) of Fig. 10.6. The figure shows that the two clubs are clearly diverging from each other for the entire period. The relative transition paths for each state in the two convergence clubs have been presented respectively in Fig. 10.1 (b), and 1(c). The speed of convergence is higher in Club 2 than in Club 1.

Table 10.6 PS results (1990–2021) for 36 Indian states and UTs using human development index

Clubs	States	Coefficient ($\hat{b} = 2\hat{\alpha}$)	Speed of convergence ($\hat{\alpha}$)	Test statistics (t_b)
Entire sample	A&N, AP, AP, AS, BI, CHAN, CHAT, DL, D&N, D&D, GO, GUJ, HAR, HP, JHR, JK, KA, KE, MAN, LAK, MH, MP, MEG, MIZ, NAG, ODI, PUDU, PUN, RAJ, SIK, TEL, TN, TRI, UK, UP, WB	–0.33	–0.16	–23.52
First club	A&N, AP, AP, CHAN, DL, D&N, D&D, GO, GUJ, HAR, HP, JK, KA, KE, MAN, LAK, MH, MEG, MIZ, NAG, ODI, PUDU, PUN, RAJ, SIK, TEL, TN, TRI, UK, WB	0.078	0.039	2.11
Second club	AS, BI, CHAT, JHR, MP, UP	2.39	1.19	10.49

Note Results are significant at 5% level of significance

These results using HDI are broadly similar to the results discussed earlier in this section using per capita GSDP of Indian states for the post-reform period. The states those performed poorly in terms of per capita income and situated in club 3 or 4, are also performed poorly in terms of HDI and situated in club 2. Hence, the broad dynamics in terms of club formation doesn't change much when we shift from per capita GSDP to a broad-based definition of regional development captured by state human development index.

The third robustness exercise is related to the debate about the timing of the initiation of economic reforms in India. Some studies claim (e.g., DeLong, (2001)) that gradual economic reforms had started in India not in the early nineties but from the mid-eighties, and hence the second episode had been initiated earlier than was popularly understood. In order to test whether our results are sensitive to the date of the initiation of the second episode, we have re-estimated our results based on a sample starting from 1985 rather than 1993. We restricted the number of states to 18 to compare the results with the benchmark results of post-1993 for 18 Indian states. The results of this exercise have been presented in Table 10.7 and Fig. 10.7.

The results remain broadly similar. The club convergence test identified three convergence clubs and one divergent state. Similarity of the results with the case of 18 states for the 1993–2021 (Table 10.4) can be easily observed once we compare the members of the upper and two lower convergence clubs in Table 10.4 and Table 10.7. Except Tripura, all the states belonging to convergence club 1 based on 18 states for the period 1993–2021, remained in convergence club 1 in the case of 18 states and

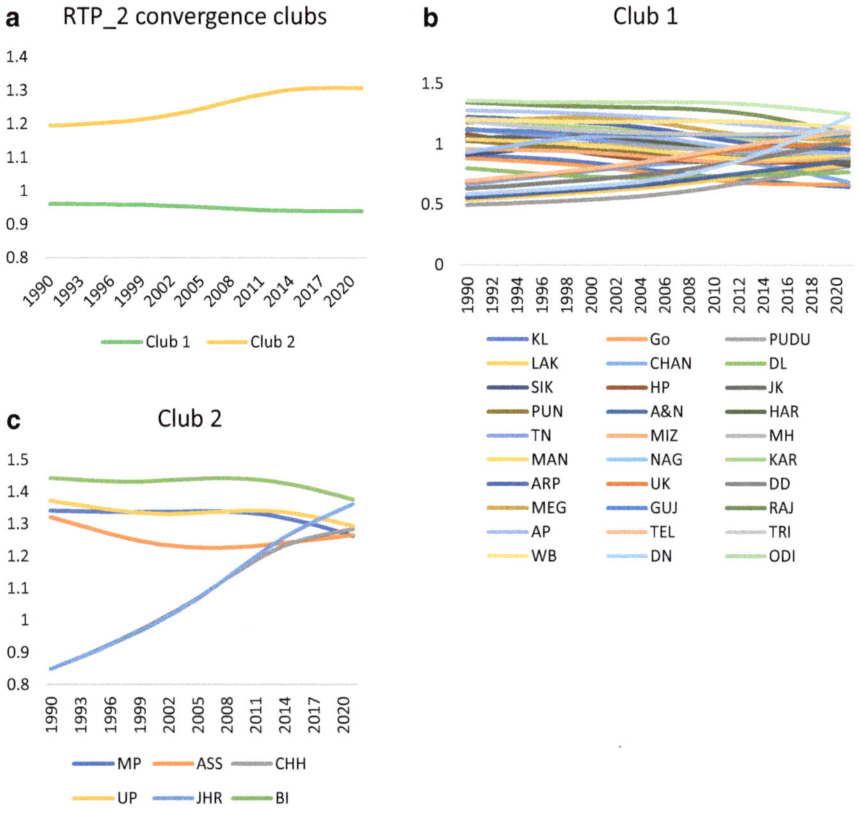

Fig. 10.6 Relative transition paths of 2 convergence clubs for 36 Indian states, 1990–2021

Table 10.7 PS results (1985–2021) for 18 Indian States and UTs using GSDP per capita

Clubs	States	Coefficient ($\hat{b} = 2\hat{\alpha}$)	Speed of convergence ($\hat{\alpha}$)	Test statistics (t_b)
Entire sample	AP, DL, GU, HAR, JK, KA, KE, MH, MP, PUN, RAJ, TEL, TN, TRI, UP, WB	–0.92	–0.46	–44.00
First club	AP, BI, DL, GU, HAR, KA, KE, MAN, MH, TEL, TN, TRI	0.44	0.22	11.78
Second club	JK, RAJ, MP, WB	0.85	0.42	17.27
Third club	BI, MAN, UP	0.56	0.28	7.36
Divergent group	PUN			

Note Results are significant at 5% level of significance

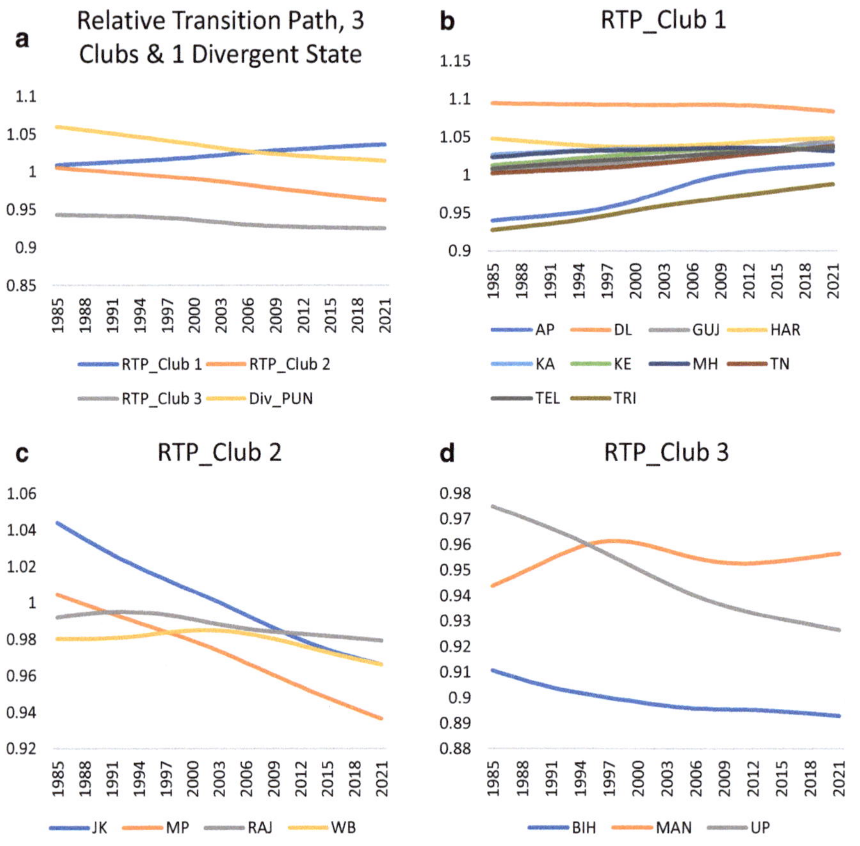

Fig. 10.7 Relative transition paths of 3 convergence clubs and 1 divergent state for 18 Indian states, 1985–2021

the period 1985–2021. Similarly, all the states in the lower three clubs in the 1993–2021 period also remained in the lower two clubs and one divergent group in the 1985–2021 period. Therefore, we can conclude that the club convergence dynamics of the Indian states in the post-reform period remained broadly similar, irrespective of the initial date of the economic reforms.

10.6 Conclusion

The economic reforms initiated in the 1990s marked a watershed moment for the Indian economy, fundamentally transforming its trajectory from a heavily regulated and closed system to one characterized by liberalization, privatization, and globalization. These reforms dismantled the Licence Raj, liberalized trade and investment policies, and opened up various sectors to private and foreign participation. This shift unleashed unprecedented growth opportunities, spurred technological advancements, and integrated India more deeply into the global economy. As a result, the reforms catalyzed higher GDP growth rates, enhanced productivity, and attracted significant foreign investment.

The reforms, however, have also been associated with rising inequalities, and one of the forms in which this has manifested itself is the divergence of regional per capita incomes. Conversely, there has been a belief that the policy regime in the pre-reform period may have been weak on its growth impetus, but it was not inequalizing by nature. This belief is partly based on the fact that the policy regime during the pre-reform period had specific initiatives that attempted to bring down regional inequalities. How far are these beliefs supported by evidence? There have been a few academic studies mostly supporting these hypotheses. However, these studies are not very robust as they suffered from limited data availability and use of inappropriate econometric techniques. In this study, we have attempted to rectify these shortcomings and undertake a comparative analysis of growth dynamics among Indian sub-national regions in the pre-reform and post-reform period.

The results of our analysis reveal both similarities and differences in the growth dynamics for the pre-reform and post-reform periods. Both periods exhibit non-convergence among sub-national regions, indicating persistent disparities. Interestingly, club convergence is observed in both periods, where states tend to cluster into distinct income groups rather than exhibiting absolute divergence. Membership within these clubs remains stable over time, with states largely maintaining their relative income positions. Thus, there does not seem to be much qualitative difference in the underlying growth dynamics during the two episodes.

Quantitative differences, however, emerge in the speed of divergence, which has been accelerating significantly in the post-reform era as indicated by a more negative convergence coefficient. Visual analysis further underscores this trend, showing faster separation between income clubs post-reform compared to the more gradual moving apart observed in the pre-reform period. These findings highlight the complex dynamics of regional economic disparities in India, emphasizing both continuity and change between the pre-reform and post-reform period. This also provides some evidence against the belief that the pre-reform period was not inequalizing. What we find instead is that both periods have been inequalizing—with the formation of convergence clubs—but the post-reform period has seen an acceleration in this trend.

The results also show that most regions showed dynamic persistence over time. States such as Haryana, experiencing the benefit of green revolution, remained in the highest-income club in both the pre-reform and the post-reform period. Other states such as Gujarat, Karnataka, Kerala and Telangana remained in the high-income convergence club, probably due to the growth in their industrial sectors. On the other hand, Bihar was a low-income divergent club in the pre-reform period and in the lowest convergence club in the post-reform period. Another state that has been stuck in a low-income trap since the pre-reform period was Madhya Pradesh. There was significant mobility in some states however. For these states, there was rapid transitions from one club to another, suggesting a dynamic economic landscape influenced by economic or policy shocks. For example, Andhra Pradesh was one of the poorly performing states in the pre-reform period that accelerated to the highest-income convergence club in the post-reform period. This result is possibly due to the many policy reforms and development of a strong base of industry and service sector in this state, with Hyderabad emerging as one of the IT hubs in the country in the post-reform period. On the other hand, states like Jammu and Kashmir, Punjab etc. which were stuck with insurgencies, stagnated and joined poorer clubs in the post-reform period.

What policy implications can we draw from our finding? The policy implication of club convergence is complicated as we need different policy packages to tackle the challenges of the regional economies stuck in different convergence clubs. For example, the policy challenge for the economies in the high-income convergence clubs is to maintain their trajectory in order to remain in the high-income state. The policy challenge for the economies stuck in the low-income trap is to ignite economic growth so that they can join a high-income club. Policies for such growth acceleration usually involve correcting for either government or market failures, or both failures in some cases. For the economies in the high-income convergence clubs that have already achieved significant growth acceleration, policies addressing government and market failures may not have much impact. Instead, they need to implement deep institutional reforms as the absence of such institutional capacity may result in these economies running out of steam and the possibility of a growth slowdown, dragging them down to lower clubs.

References

Ahluwalia, M. S. (2000, May). Economic performance of states in post-reforms period. *Economic and Political Weekly.*

Ahluwalia, M. S. (2002). State-level performance under economic reforms in India, in A. O. Krueger (Ed.), *Economic Policy Reforms and the Indian Economy*, Oxford University Press.

Aiyar, S. (2001). Growth theory and convergence across Indian states: a panel study. *India at Crossroads: Sustaining Growth and Reducing Poverty. International Monetary Fund, Washington*, pp. 143–169.

Antonakakis, N., Christou, C., Cunado, J., & Gupta, R. (2017). Convergence patterns in sovereign bond yield spreads: Evidence from the Euro Area. *Journal of International Financial Markets, Institutions and Money, 49*, 129–139. https://doi.org/10.1016/j.intfin.2017.03.002

Aksoy, T., Taştan, H., & Kama, O. (2019). Revisiting income convergence in Turkey: Are there convergence clubs? *Growth and Change, 50*(3), 1185–1217. https://doi.org/10.1111/grow.12310

Aslund, A., & Johnson, S. (2003). Small enterprises and economic policy. Working Paper. Sloan School, MIT.

Azariadis, C., & Drazen, A. (1990). Threshold externalities in economic development. *The Quarterly Journal of Economics, 105*(2), 501–526.

Baumol, W. (1986). Productivity growth, convergence, and welfare: What the long-run data show. *The American Economic Review, 76*(5), 1072–1085.

Bergeaud, A., Cette, G., & Lecat, R. (2020). Convergence of GDP per capita in advanced countries over the twentieth century. *Empirical Economics, 59*(5), 2509–2526. https://doi.org/10.1007/s00181-019-01761-x

Bernard, A. B., & Durlauf, S. N. (1995). Convergence in international output. *Journal of Applied Econometrics, 10*(2), 97–108. https://doi.org/10.1002/jae.3950100202

Bernard, A. B., & Durlauf, S. N. (1996). Interpreting tests of the convergence hypothesis. *Journal of Econometrics, 71*(1–2), 161–173. https://doi.org/10.1016/0304-4076(94)01699-2

Besley, T., & Burgess, R. (2002). Can labor regulation hinder economic performance? Evidence from India. CEPR Discussion Paper No. 3260.

Bhattacharya, B. B., & Sakthivel, S. (2004, March). Regional growth and disparity in India. *Economic and Political Weekly.*

Cashin, P., & Sahay, R. (1996). International migration, centre-state grants, and economic growth in the states of India. *IMF Staff Papers, 43*(1).

Cavallaro, E., & Villani, I. (2021). Club convergence in eu countries: A sectoral perspective. *Journal of Economic Integration, 36*(1), 125–161. https://doi.org/10.11130/jei.2021.36.1.125

Chaudhuri, B., & Marimautou, V. (2007). Growth and convergence clubs in Indian States, 1965–2002, unpublished mimeo.

Choi, C. Y., & Wang, X. (2015). Discontinuity of output convergence within the United States: Why has the course changed? *Economic Inquiry, 53*(1), 49–71. https://doi.org/10.1111/ecin.12129

Cutrini, E. (2019). Economic integration, structural change, and uneven development in the European Union. *Structural Change and Economic Dynamics, 50*, 102–113. https://doi.org/10.1016/j.strueco.2019.06.007

DeLong, J. (2001, July). India since independence: An analytical growth narrative.

Desli, E., & Gkoulgkoutsika, A. (2020). World economic convergence: Does the estimation methodology matter? *Economic Modelling, 91*, 138–147. https://doi.org/10.1016/j.econmod.2020.05.027

Durlauf, S. N., & Quah, D. T. (1999). The new empirics of economic growth. In J. Taylor & M. Woodford (Eds.), *Handbook of Macroeconomics*, North-Holland.

Durlauf, S. N., Johnson, P. A., & Temple, J. (2005). "Growth Econometrics", handbook of economic growth, in: P. Aghion, & S. Durlauf (Eds.), *Handbook of economic growth* (1 edn.), Vol. 1, chapter 8, pp. 555-677, Elsevier.

Durlauf, S. N., & Johnson, P. A. (1995). Multiple regimes and cross-country growth behaviour. *Journal of Applied Econometrics, 10*(4), 365–384. https://doi.org/10.1002/jae.3950100404

Espoir, D. K. (2022). Convergence or divergence patterns in income distribution across countries: A new evidence from a club clustering algorithm. *Cogent Economics and Finance, 10*(1), 2025667. https://doi.org/10.1080/23322039.2022.2025667

Evans, P., & Karras, G. (1996). Convergence revisited. *Journal of Monetary Economics, 37*(2), 249–265.

Friedman, E., Johnson, S., Kaufmann, D., & Zoido-Lobaton, P. (2000). Dodging the grabbing hand: The determinants of unofficial activity in 69 countries. *Journal of Public Economics, 76*, 459–493.

Ghosh, M. (2008). Economic reforms, growth and regional divergence in India. *Margin: The Journal of Applied Economic Research, 2*, 265–285.

Ghosh, M., Ghoshray, A., & Malki, I. (2013). Regional divergence and club convergence in India. *Economic Modelling, 30*(1), 733–742. https://doi.org/10.1016/j.econmod.2012.10.008

Gonzalez, M. C. B., Tierney, H. L. R., Nazarov, Z., & Kim, M. H. (2020). Divided: The two Americas-examining club convergence in the U.S. *Applied Economics, 52*(53), 5783–5796. https://doi.org/10.1080/00036846.2020.1776832

Gunawan, A. B., Mendez, C., & Otsubo, S. (2021). Provincial income convergence clubs in Indonesia: Identification and conditioning factors. *Growth and Change, 52*(4), 2540–2575. https://doi.org/10.1111/grow.12553

Hamit-Haggar, M. (2013). A note on convergence across Canadian provinces: New insights from the club clustering algorithm. *Annals of Regional Science, 50*(2), 591–601. https://doi.org/10.1007/s00168-012-0500-x

Hobijn, B., & Franses, P. H. (2000). Asymptotically perfect and relative convergence of productivity. *Journal of Applied Econometrics, 15*(1), 59–81. https://doi.org/10.1002/(SICI)1099-1255(200001/02)15:1<59::AID-JAE544>3.0.CO;2-1

Islam, N. (2003). What have we learned from the convergence debate? *Journal of Economic Surveys, 17*, 309–362.

Kar, S., & Sakthivel, S. (2007). Reforms and regional inequality in India. *Economic and Political Weekly, 42*(47), 69–77.

Kar, S., Jha, D., & Kateja, A. (2011). Club-convergence and polarisation of states: A nonparametric analysis of post-reform India. *Indian Growth and Development Review, 4*(1), 53–72.

Matsuyama, K. (1992, December). Agricultural productivity, comparative advantage, and economic growth. *Journal of Economic Theory*, 317–334.

Mazzola, F., & Pizzuto, P. (2020). Great recession and club convergence in Europe: A cross country, cross-region panel analysis (2000–2015). *Growth and Change, 51*(2), 676–711. https://doi.org/10.1111/grow.12369

Monfort, M., Cuestas, J. C., & Ordonez, J. (2013). Real convergence in Europe: A cluster analysis. *Economic Modelling, 33*, 689–694. https://doi.org/10.1016/j.econmod.2013.05.015

Nagaraj, R., Varoudakis, A., & Veganzones, M. (1998). Long-run growth trends and convergence across Indian States, Technical Paper No 131, *OECD Development Centre, Paris, France.*

Streeten, P. P. (1994). Human development: Means and ends. *American Economic Review, 84*, 232–237.

Phillips, P. C. B., & Sul, D. (2007). Transition modeling and econometric convergence tests. *Econometrica, 75*(6), 1771–1855. https://doi.org/10.1111/j.1468-0262.2007.00811.x

Phillips, P. C. B., & Sul, D. (2009). Economic transition and growth. *Journal of Applied Econometrics, 24*(7), 1153–1185. https://doi.org/10.1002/jae.1080

Quah, D. T. (1997). Empirics for growth and distribution: Stratification, polarization, and convergence clubs. *Journal of Economic Growth, 2*(1), 27–59.

Rao, M. G., Shand, R. T., & Kalirajan, K. P. (1999). Convergence of incomes across Indian States. *Economic and Political Weekly, 34*(13), 769–778.

Rodriguez-Clare, A. (1996). The division of labor and economic development. *Journal of Development Economics, 49*(April), 3–32.

Rodrik, D., & Subramanian, A. (2004). Why India can grow at 7 percent a year or more: projections and reflections, *IMF Working Papers. 04/118, International Monetary Fund, Washington, DC.*

Rodrik, D. (1996a). Coordination failures and government policy: A model with applications to East Asia and Eastern Europe. *Journal of International Economics, 40*, 1–22.

Rodrik, D. (1996b, March). Understanding economic policy reform. *Journal of Economic Literature, XXXIV*, 9–41.

Rodrik, D. (2005). "Growth Strategies", in P. Aghion & S. Durlauf (Eds.), *Handbook of Economic Growth*, Vol. 1A, Elsevier.

Sachs, J. D., Bajpai, N., & Ramiah, A. (2002). Understanding regional economic growth in India. *Asian Economic Papers, 1*(3), 32–62.

Temple, J. (1999). The new growth evidence. *Journal of Economic Literature, 37*(1), 112–156.

Tian, X., Zhang, X., Zhou, Y., & Yu, X. (2016). Regional income inequality in China revisited: A perspective from club convergence. *Economic Modelling, 56*, 50–58. https://doi.org/10.1016/j.econmod.2016.02.028

Trindade, V. (2003). *The big push, industrialization, and international trade: The role of exports.* Syracuse University, March.

Ursavaş, U., & Mendez, C. (2022). Regional income convergence and conditioning factors in Turkey: Revisiting the role of spatial dependence and neighbor effects. *Annals of Regional Science.* https://doi.org/10.1007/s00168-022-01168-0

You, K., Dal Bianco, S., Lin, Z., & Amankwah-Amoah, J. (2019). Bridging technology divide to improve business environment: Insights from African nations. *Journal of Business Research, 97*, 268–280. https://doi.org/10.1016/j.jbusres.2018.01.015

Zhang, W., Xu, W., & Wang, X. (2019). Regional convergence clubs in China: Identification and conditioning factors. *Annals of Regional Science, 62*(2), 327–350. https://doi.org/10.1007/s00168-019-00898-y

Chapter 11
Club Convergence in Growth and Financial Development: Evidence from Indian States

Samaresh Bardhan

Abstract The paper revisits the issues of convergence in the context of economic growth across Indian states. Unlike existing body of literature on convergence in Indian context, we investigate the possibility of club convergence among Indian states. Using state level data of a sample of 33 states during 1985–2018, we first test whether Indian states converge in terms of per capita income. Subsequently, we examine, among few other channels of convergence of growth, the role of financial development across Indian states. Unlike most of the existing studies in India, we apply (Phillips & Sul, 2007) methodology to detect converging subgroups of states in terms of growth as well as various alternative indicators of financial development. Findings reveal that for the aggregate sample of states, there is no evidence of convergence, which implies that sample states are not converging to a single steady. However, we find evidence of the existence of club convergence. In particular, Indian states are found to diverge in terms of state level per capita growth as well as alternative indicators of financial development. Our empirical findings, however, reveal the formation of clubs in terms of both state level growth as well as various indicators of financial development such as branch density, different composition of sectoral credit and also indicators of credit inflow and credit outflow across states. Findings point to the prevalence of uneven growth and financial development across Indian states, despite several measures taken during the last few decades. Findings also call for concerted policy actions for achieving regional balance in growth and financial development through appropriate reform measures in investment, infrastructure and financial development.

Keywords Indian states · Economic growth · Financial development · Club convergence · Panel Data

S. Bardhan (✉)
Department of Humanities and Social Sciences, Indian Institute of Technology Ropar, Punjab, India
e-mail: samaresh@iitrpr.ac.in

D. Maiti et al. (eds.), *75 Years of Growth, Development and Productivity in India*, India Studies in Business and Economics, https://doi.org/10.1007/978-981-97-8054-9_11

11.1 Introduction

In India, since independence, there has been increasing concerns among economists and policy makers about the growing regional disparities and greater emphasis is placed on the issues of convergence of per capita incomes in the context of Solow-Swan neoclassical growth model. Most of the existing studies reveal that Indian states diverge in terms of per capita state domestic product (SDP) due to reasons such as inter-state variations in size, demographic features, sectoral activities, production structures, human capital, and infrastructure (Cashin & Sahay, 1996a; Dasgupta et al., 2000; Ahmed & Varshney, 2009). Along with the above probable sources of regional disparity, financial development is also projected as a potential factor both for the determination of economic development and for the explanation of the lack of convergence of income, as we observe in the large body of existing literature in cross-country context on the role of financial development on economic growth (Beck et al. 2000). In cross-country context, Aghion et al. (2005), in the framework of Schumpeterian growth model, investigate empirically that a country will converge to the growth rate of the world technological frontier once it surpasses a critical level of financial development. The study also reveals that financial development exerts a positive, but gradually 'vanishing effect' on steady state per capita real GDP in relation to the frontier and this argues that financial development significantly determines growth divergence across countries. Fung (2009) considers the interaction of the financial and real economic sectors into a traditional test for convergence to examine whether financial development and economic development converge to or diverge from each other. Findings of the study indicate that middle and high-income countries conditionally converge in terms of both economic and financial development. Several subsequent cross-country studies on the role of finance on growth observe similar vanishing effect on growth, in developed economies, attributed to either decreasing marginal returns, highest credit flow to the private sector and fundamental change in the transmission mechanism of finance across different levels of economic and financial development (Arcand et al., 2015; De la Torre et al., Gründler, 2015; 2011; Rousseau & Wachtel, 2011). However, these studies observe that countries with less developed financial markets benefit from an increase in the size of the financial sector. Apergis et al. (2012) uses the Phillips and Sul (2007) methodology to alternative indicators of financial development and analyze the degree of convergence of financial development for a panel of 50 countries. Findings of the study indicate that all countries do not converge to a single equilibrium state in financial development and there is strong evidence of club convergence.

Similar to the cross-country context, differences across states/regions within a country in terms of the level of overall financial development, availability of credit to the borrowers, deposit mobilization, expansion of bank branch network etc. appear to be relevant in the discussions of income divergence in recent decades. The issue that has received relatively less attention than the cross-country finance-growth relationship is the importance of promoting geographically diffuse banking sector development across regions/states within a country (Kendall, 2012). It is argued that the least financially developed regions/states in a country suffer from disproportionately greater penalty in terms of suppressed economic growth. In fact, states/regions within a country such as India diverge in terms of financial development for various reasons. First, inequality in financial development in terms of distribution of credit among Indian states is mainly driven by demand and supply of credit conditional on economic development. In particular, it depends on a number of factors, including economic and financial growth, mobilization of deposits, and the banking network. Larger states/regions are characterized by comparatively large banking expansion with greater branch network, compared to smaller states. Until the financial sector reforms introduced in India in 1991, policies mandated that banks must open branches into poor and rural areas, and lend on favourable terms to the so-called priority sectors including agriculture and small-scale industry and to traditionally disadvantaged groups within these sectors. However, post reform of 1991, the rural branch licencing mandate was discontinued and new regulations encouraged lending based on market forces. This led to persistence divergence in financial development across states/regions. Second, there is the possibility that credit sanctioned in one state, may well be utilized in a different state owing to the differences in the stages of development in a state/region, infrastructural facilities, investment climate and general governance. As the financing of investment involves transaction cost, borrowers generally prefer to have finance made available at the place of utilization. It might lead to the divergence in financial development across states and hence lead to the uneven financial development across states/regions.

Against this background, this paper revisits issues of convergence of growth as well as financial development across Indian states, both at aggregate level as well as across different sectors such as agriculture, industry, services and explores the possibility of clustering of states (club convergence) unlike full convergence. The paper has the following motivations.

First, while existing empirical evidence on growth convergence is considerably large in cross-country context and also at the provincial level within a developed country with mixed evidence of convergence as well as divergence due to vanishing effect of finance, empirical evidence at sub-national level, in a developing economy such as India is considerably less. In general, while there is evidence of convergence in developed countries, developing countries mostly exhibited divergence. In India, states diverge in terms of economic background, geographic, demographic and cultural features, stock of human capital, level of infrastructure, financial development, public expenditure, despite commonly shared national economic policies and also certain institutional features (Cashin & Sahay, 1996a; Basu and Maertens, 2007). Therefore, it appears important to investigate whether such divergences still prevails across Indian states despite several national policies and state-specific measures of development are put in place during last few decades.

Second, existing cross-country and intra-country analysis of growth convergence mostly use two commonly used measures, sigma convergence and beta convergence. Observe, a fall in dispersion of real per capita income over time across a group of economies or a set of regions/states in a country, is considered to be an evidence of σ-convergence. On the otherhand, negative and statistically significant coefficient of initial per capita income in the regression of growth rate of real per capita income with or without conditioning variables, is considered to be an evidence of beta convergence. The rejection of the σ convergence, however, does not necessarily indicate that there is no convergence. In fact, the presence of *transitional dynamics* in the data can result in rejection of null hypothesis of σ convergence. On the otherhand, β-convergence is considered to be necessary, but not sufficient for σ-convergence (Quah, 1993). Ideally, the dispersion of income should wither away in the long run if all the economies with common technologies and similar structures converge to a common real per capita income. However, the dispersion of real per capita income may not approach zero if the economies converge to *convergence clubs* or to their own unique equilibrium. Given these, we use a relatively new methodology proposed by Phillips and Sul (2007) for testing the convergence hypothesis that helps us to identify the *convergence clubs* among Indian states. It is claimed to be an improvement over existing methods in that it uses a nonlinear time varying factor model and provides the framework for modelling transitional dynamics as well as long run behaviour. Furthermore, this methodology can be used to test for convergence in other relevant economic variables.

Third, existing literature on convergence mostly measures growth convergence based on per capita income using per capita net state domestic product and estimates the standard growth convergence equation where the average annual growth of per capita income is regressed on initial per capital income (Raju, 2012). However, given the positive role of financial development in economic growth discussed above, and given the fact that financial development receives relatively less attention in the discussion of growth convergence/divergence, we also test convergence of states in terms of various financial development indicators across Indian states. It would help us conjecture whether pattern of convergence in growth across states conforms to the pattern of convergence in terms of financial development. It would also provide us newer insights into the role of financial development and hence financial intermediation in potential explanation for income divergence across states or group of states or convergence among some other states. Unlike previous studies in Indian context, we investigate whether Indian states form convergence clubs, in terms of financial development along with the possibility of convergence clubs in growth variable.

Finally, existing recent studies in Indian context mostly carry out the analysis of growth convergence considering the decade of 1980s 1990s and 2000s (for example, see Kalra & Sodsriwiboon, 2010; Lolayekar & Mukhopadhyay, 2020; Raju, 2012). Unlike existing studies in Indian context, we further extend our data period and use a very large and comprehensive database during 1985–2018, covering 34 years which encompasses both pre liberalization period and post liberalization period and also covers the four decades of 1980s, 1990s, 2000s and 2010s.

Given these motivations, the basic research question addressed in this paper is whether Indian states form convergence clubs in terms of indicator of growth despite the fact that, in general, there is divergence across states. We also address the same for various alternative financial development indicators. Given that financial development is an important factor explaining economic development, income convergence (divergence) among certain states may reflect the convergence (divergence) in financial development between those states. In particular, convergence in terms of financial development and income divergence across states at the same time, would lead to the possibility that financial development hardly contributes to mitigation of income divergence across states. On the otherhand, divergence of states in term of financial development and hence transmission of the process of financial intermediation and growth divergence across states or groups of states may explain the continuing income inequality.

Section 11.2 presents the review of literature. Section 11.3 presents a brief overview of growth and financial development in India. Section 11.4 presents details of data used. Section 11.5 describes the details of methodologies used. Section 11.6 presents our empirical findings on convergence and also of club convergence for growth as well as financial development. Section 11.7 concludes the paper.

11.2 Relevant Literature: Growth Convergence

The issues of convergence (divergence) in the literature of economic growth centre on the negative relationship between the growth of per capita income and initial level of income (Barro & Sala-i-Martin, 1991). It is based on the argument that countries/regions within a country may experience unequal incomes and hence uneven growth rates in the short run, but will eventually converge to a steady state (Solow, 1956). Evidence of absolute as well as conditional convergence and σ-convergence are mixed (Barro & Sala-i-Martin, 1991; Sala-i-Martin 1996; Laurini et al., 2005). It appears that most of the earlier studies on convergence focused on the developed countries with relatively less attention to the developing countries. However, existing studies on the developing countries mainly exhibited divergence. For instance, while in Chinese context, economic reforms during the 1980s and 1990s led to the economic disparity, growing inequalities in Mexico during the period 1980–2000 are found to be related to trade reforms (Kanbur & Zhang, 2004; Sanchez-Reaza & Rodrıguez-Pose, 2002). In the context of Brazilian municipalities, however, there is found to be an evidence of convergence clubs (Laurini et al., 2005).

In India, issues related to convergence have drawn great deal of attention since last few decades because of the persistence of regional disparities and we observe mixed evidence. Few earlier studies based on the data until the 1990s have found evidence of convergence across Indian states (Bajpai & Sachs, 1996; Cashin & Sahay, 1996b; Dholakia, 1994; Sarkar, 1994). On the otherhand, Rao et al. (1999), Ahluwalia (2001), Sachs et al. (2002), Bhattacharya & Sakthivel (2004) found evidence in support of divergence hypothesis among Indian states. Marjit and Mitra (1996) present a critic of the approach of Barro-Sala-I-Martin (1995) and find evidence of divergence across Indian states based on the data preceding liberalization. Nagaraj et al. (2000), Aiyar (2001), Kochhar et al. (2006) and Misra (2007) observe absolute divergence and conditional convergence with control variables of share of agriculture, price shocks, infrastructure, literacy rate, and private investment in states. Sachs et al.

(2002) find evidence of income divergence across 14 Indian states during 1980–1998. Bandyopadhyay (2003) finds evidence of convergence clubs based on estimates of non-parametric stochastic kernels and transition probability matrices.

Subsequent studies on convergence across Indian states covering subsequent decade of 2000s (2001–10), revealed that Indian states have experienced higher growth at the cost of increasing divergence across all major states during 2001–09 as compared to the periods of 1993–2001 and 1971–2009 (Kumar & Subramanian, 2012). Using per capita net state domestic product across 21 Indian states during 2001–09, the study estimates the standard growth convergence equation where the average annual growth of per capita income for 2001–09 is regressed on log of initial per capita income of 2001. Purfield (2006) finds evidence of both absolute and conditional convergence in growth during 1975–2003, considering the roles of state's economic policies in 1990s, private sector investment, size of government, and institutions. Kalra and Sodsriwiboon (2010) investigate convergence and spillover across Indian states using non-stationery panel data techniques using a sample of 15 Indian states during 1960–2004 and find evidence of income divergence for the entire sample period, convergence in sub-periods characterized by structural breaks and evidence of club convergence for low and high income states. Raju (2012) examines the issue of convergence/divergence in growth rates across states based on both sigma and beta convergence for the period 2001–10. Lolayekar and Mukhopadhyay (2020) used instrumental variable and distribution dynamics for empirical tests of growth convergence across Indian states during 1981–2010 and found that the ratio of working age group to total population, political stability and alliance, and development expenditure exert a positive and significant impact on growth. These studies, however, largely used either smaller sample of states or restricted the period of analysis until the 1990s, except few recent studies. Moreover, existing studies mostly used both cross-sectional regression and panel estimation techniques and find evidence of conditional convergence or divergence.

We have also reviewed the related literature on the role of financial development in economic growth. Empirical literature on growth finance nexus in cross-country context as well as in regional context within a country documents that financial intermediaries facilitate the pace of mobilization of savings that leads to economic growth. Findings of these studies, in general, observe positive effects of financial development on economic growth (King & Levine, 1993; Bhattacharya & Sivasubramanian, 2003; Levine et al., 2000). Across Indian states, few studies observe mixed evidence on the causality and uni-directional causality (Misra, 2003; Nain & Kamaiah, 2014).

We observe few studies which applied club convergence test in the context of other countries. Martin and Vazquez (2015) employed the regression based convergence test of Phillips and Sul (2007) and identified three convergence clubs of Latin American countries where per capita income dispersion decreased over time. Fufa and Kim (2018) found evidence of convergence clubs in the study of the finance-growth nexus applying the nonlinear transitional dynamics. Findings revealed that stages of economic growth of each country play a significant role in formation of convergence clubs and financial development plays a significant role in the process of economic growth of each convergence club. Apergis et al. (2012), applied Phillips and Sul (2007) methodology in cross-country context to various indicators of financial development and per capita output and found evidence of convergence clubs for both. The study also observed some association between the convergence clubs of both financial development of per capita GDP. Basturk et al. (2010) studied the effect of financial development indicators on GDP for a large panel of countries and identifies convergence clubs for groups of countries with similar GDP structure. It also investigated both short run and long run effects of financial development on GDP and the composition of convergence clubs while in long run, the indicators have a positive effect of GDP.

Few studies investigated formation of club convergence in Indian context. Ghosh et al. (2013) used the Phillips and Sul (2007) methodology in Indian context and found evidence of club convergence both at the aggregate as well as sectoral level, in a sample of 15 Indian states. Hembram and Halder (2019) used Markov chain and stochastic kernel in their study and observed that the major states support the process of club convergence and economies that are similar in structural characteristics and initial per capita income, converge in per capita terms in long run. A recent study by Nag and Pradhan (2023) used the club convergence technique proposed by Phillips and Sul (2007) to investigate the convergence hypothesis in a different context of Human Development Index (HDI) across Indian states and union territories (UTs) during 1990–2019 and find that states with the lowest HDI converge faster than those with higher HDI. However, in this chapter, we investigate club convergence in both per capita gross state domestic product (GSDPR) in real terms and various financial development indicators, following Phillips and Sul (2007).

We observe very few studies on the convergence across Indian states on the issues of financial development, in general, except few existing studies address the heterogeneity in credit distribution across Indian states. Herwadkar and Ghosh (2013), using a sample of 22 states for 2004–2012, evaluates whether credit inequality across Indian states can be explained by state-specific factors representing credit demand and supply and infrastructure facilities. The paper finds that the differences in credit distribution can be explained by factors such as financial deepening and physical infrastructure development which indicates that states which attract higher deposits, have better banking networks and infrastructure facilities attract more credit as compared to other states. In a more recent study, Haider and Adil (2024) examine, under given heterogeneities, whether credit accessibility among states converges over time, particularly in industrial and agricultural lending. Employing club convergence tests (Phillips & Sul, 2007), authors find evidence of substantial heterogeneities and multiple transition paths for industrial credit convergence across states; while agriculture credit is relatively less heterogeneous as compared with industry. However, unlike the existing studies, we carry out the club convergence tests and examine the possibility of multiple transition paths for several indicators of financial development, along with growth indicator for a large sample of 32 states and for the period 1985–2018 that encompasses both pre liberalization as well as post liberalization periods.

11.3 Growth and Financial Development: Indian Scenario

In India, scheduled commercial banks (SCBs) play a pivotal role in the financial intermediation and constitute the primary source of savings mobilization and financing investments. Indian financial market was highly regulated prior to reforms and government mostly resorted to financial repressionist policies in order to finance increasing government deficit. Public sector banks which mostly dominated Indian banking during pre-reform period, hardly focused on the expansion of credit to wider range of borrowers such as industries and retail customers. During 1980s, a shift in credit distribution in favour of a vast range of informal sector activities and underdeveloped regions and states helped widen the economy's demand base and contributed to a more dispersed sectoral and regional growth. With reforms measures since early 1990s, following recommendations of the Narsimham Committee (GOI, 1991, 1998), private and foreign owned banks also started operating, leading to an apparent increase in competition and operational efficiency. Increased financial intermediation is also thought to cater to the needs of credit by micro, small and medium scale enterprises (MSMSE) sector, services sector and also agriculture sector towards the broader objectives of achieving sustainable growth rates which are likely to generate higher growth and mitigate divergence across states. However, contrary to expectations, during 1990s, even with financial sector reforms, banks were faced with weaknesses in operations following enormous growth of banking activities which continued until 2002–03. In fact, banks were found to be reluctant to extend credit to agriculture, small-scale industries, and individual borrowers.

During last few decades, there had been significant surge in credit to household and services sector, following a notable increase in demand for housing, other retail loans, and also a significant growth of service sector (RBI, 2006). During first half of 2000s, long-term loans increased only for household credit, and half of the household credit was meant for housing and rest to meet the demand of consumer durables, excluding education loans (EPWRF, 2008). Agricultural credit significantly increased during 1980s, followed by a sharp deceleration in 1990s, and gained momentum again during first half of 2000, following a series of policy initiatives taken by Reserve Bank of India (EPWRF, 2008). Bank credit to agriculture had increased following bank nationalization and reached 18% towards the end of 1980s and declined to less than 10% by late1990s. Consequently, the number of farm loan accounts with SCBs reduced from 27.74 million in March 1992 to 20.84 million in March 2003 (Shetty, 2004); however, bank credit to the industrial sectors reduced during mid-1990 following demand slowdown due to recession in industrial sector.

The distribution of growth across sectors also appeared to be uneven. The growth rates of agricultural and industrial sectors declined from 3.54% and 7.10% to 2.69% and 5.68%, respectively, during 1980s and 1990s (Bhattacharya & Kar, 2004). In contrast, the service sector registered a sharp increase from 6.76% to 7.69 % during 1980s and 1990s, respectively (Bhattacharya & Kar, 2004). With these different growth episodes across sectors, noticeable changes in sectoral composition of output are also observed, with agriculture share declining from 40% in 1980 to 24% in 2000, and share of industry going up from 24% to 28% (Bhattacharya & Kar, 2004). In contrast, share of services sector rose remarkably from 31% to 47%. These shifts in financial intermediation and sectoral composition in aggregate GDP over recent decades are supposed to have significant implications for changing role of financial intermediation in sectoral growth and hence aggregate growth and divergence in Indian economy.[1]

11.4 Data

For our analysis of convergence, we have used a sample of 33 states over the period of 1985–86 to 2018–19. As growth indicator of a state, we use gross state domestic product in real terms (GSDPR) and sectoral GSDPR of a state. We also define a set of state level financial indicators. These include branch density, sectoral (agriculture, industry, services and household) credit as proportions of total credit utlilized as well as sectoral GDP. (See appendix for details of variable definitions.). Statistical data of GSDP (base: 2004–05) is collected from States of India (SOI) database, Center for Monitoring Indian Economy, (CMIE). Statistical information for state level credit, deposit and branches for different sectors, is retrieved from RBI data sources as well as from SOI, CMIE. (see appendix for details of definitions).

11.5 Econometric Methodology

11.5.1 Beta Convergence and Sigma Convergence

We first apply the conventional techniques of convergence viz. β-convergence and σ-convergence in our empirical analysis. In classical convergence analysis, we conventionally measure β-convergence by estimating Barro-type regression model (Barro & Sala-I Martin, 1991) of the rate of growth on initial per capita income as follows:

$$\mathrm{Log}\left(y_{it}/y_{i,t-1}\right) = \alpha + \beta \log y_{i,t-1} + \varepsilon, \tag{11.1}$$

where

$\mathrm{Log}(y_{it}/y_{i,\,t-1})$ stands for rate of growth of real per capita real income and y_{t-1} is income per capita at period t−1. We test the null hypothesis H_0: $\beta \geq 0$ (there is no absolute convergence) against the alternative hypothesis H_A: $\beta < 0$ (there is absolute convergence). Equation (11.1) measures absolute convergence considering all other factors to be homogenous across the states. In absolute convergence, we assume that factors such as the rate of growth of population, saving rate, technological

[1] Certain parts of the description of the movement of sectoral credit and sectoral growth, presented in this section, is similar to that discussed in Bardhan and Sharma (2022).

progress, depreciation are same across the states and examine whether the income gap between two economies/states increases without these additional control variables. However, all these above factors may not be uniform across the states and hence states may not converge to a common steady state but may converge to different levels of steady state determined by the different state-specific relevant factors. This leads to hypothesize the conditional convergence where we scrutinize whether the gap between two states narrows down or widens over time, with additional control variables. If there are persistent differences in technologies or other determinants of production, long run convergence takes place but these steady states can differ, their characteristics being conditional on differences in productive capital. In conditional convergence, we estimate the following growth equation:

$$\mathrm{Log}\left(y_{it}/y_{i,t-1}\right) = \alpha + \beta \log y_{i,t-1} + \mu z_{it} + \varepsilon \quad (11.2)$$

Equation (11.2) measures conditional convergence where the factors are heterogeneous among the economies/states. Log difference of income per capita stands for the annual growth rate between dates t and $t-1$, y_{t-1} is per capita income at $t-1$, and zt is a vector of variables that the regression is conditioning with coefficient vector μ. These variables are included as the potential factors determining the steady-state income. In our study, we have carried out the test of both absolute and conditional convergence using OLS. We have estimated it using a cross-sectional regression and the hypothesis for β-convergence is as follows:

$$H_o : \beta > 0 \text{ against } H_1 : \beta < 0$$

Under the null hypothesis there is no beta convergence while under the alternative hypothesis there is beta convergence. A negative coefficient of beta in equation1 states that poorer states catch up with the richer states, given the homogenous factors across the states. Non negative coefficient of beta, on the other hand, indicates that there exists divergence.

While beta convergence seeks to answer whether poorer economies/states grow faster than richer ones and also examines the speed of convergence and whether the convergence process is conditional or unconditional, sigma convergence predicts whether the aggregate cross-sectional variance increases/decreases over time (Raju, 2012). Barro and Sala-i-Martin (1995) point out that beta convergence is a necessary condition but not sufficient for sigma convergence and both are complementary to each other. Accordingly, in our convergence test, we have used both. For estimating sigma convergence, we estimate the following linear equation:

$$Y_t = a + bt + u_t \quad (11.3)$$

where Y_t is the value of standard deviation (SD)/coefficient of variation (CV) in year t, a is the constant term, b is the linear trend rate for SD/CV, t denotes time (year) and goes from 1 to 32, and u's are the stochastic error terms. Sigma convergence only depicts the cross-sectional dispersion. In the absence of shocks in per capita income and with a common steady state, beta convergence tends to result in sigma convergence.

11.5.2 Club Convergence

In this sub-section, we apply the novel econometric technique proposed by Phillips and Sul (2007), which formulates the convergence patterns of groups of economies/states as a nonlinear time varying factor model and allows for both the varying time paths as well as individual heterogeneity. Unlike other approaches in which economies are grouped a priori, this methodology allows the endogenous determination of convergence clubs.

Contrary to conventional measures, club convergence is defined as the tendency of the economies/states to converge to multiple steady-state equilibrium, given that per capita income of the economies/states with similar characteristics and similar initial conditions, converge to each other or they are grouped as 'clubs' as they fall in different regimes (Canova, 2004; Durlauf & Johnson, 1995; Galor, 1996; Quah, 1993). This methodology used in this chapter aims to test whether a panel of economies converge or diverge. It differs from the commonly used tests of convergence discussed above in that unlike beta convergence, it helps us to identify convergence clubs in one or more subgroups, even if states diverge, as a whole. This improved methodology introduces a procedure of clustering to detect the probable convergence clubs, endogenously. It allows for heterogeneous behaviour of economies/states, transition paths as well as transitional divergence. Phillips and Sul (2007) employ the nonlinear time varying factor model that can capture the transitional dynamics and long run behaviour. The methodology uses the following time varying common factor representation of yit for state i:

$$\mathrm{Y}_{\mathrm{it}} = \delta_{\mathrm{it}}.\boldsymbol{\mu}_{\mathrm{t}} \tag{11.4}$$

where $\boldsymbol{\mu}_t$ is the common factor and δ_{it} is the time varying idiosyncratic factor that takes into account the transition dynamics i.e. deviation of state i from the common path. Given this, all N states/economies converge to a steady state if $\lim_{k\to\infty} \delta i\,(t+k) = \delta$ for all i = 1…N, irrespective of whether states/economies are near the steady state or in transition. Equation (11.4) justifies that the paths to steady states can differ across sample states. Test of convergence, following this method, is carried out by scrutinizing the temporal behaviour of $\delta_{i,t}$. While doing that, panel data decomposition of the variable (output, for example) is used following the method. Y_{it} is usually decomposed as follows:

$$\mathrm{Y}_{\mathrm{it}} = \mathrm{g}_{\mathrm{it}} + \mathrm{a}_{\mathrm{it}} \tag{11.5}$$

where git stands for systematic factor (including the permanent common component) and ait indicates transitory component. For temporal transitional heterogeneity, eq. (11.5) is modified as follows:

$$\mathrm{Y}_{\mathrm{it}} = \left(\frac{\mathrm{g}_{\mathrm{it}} + \mathrm{a}_{\mathrm{it}}}{\mu_{\mathrm{t}}}\right)\mu_{\mathrm{t}} = \delta_{\mathrm{it}}\mu_{\mathrm{t}} \tag{11.6}$$

where δ_{it} absorbs a_{it}, and μ_t refers to the common factor. Here, idiosyncratic components are separated from common such that δit is the transition path of the economy to the common steady-state growth path determined by μ_t. The common growth component μ_t may follow either a trend-stationary process or a non-stationary stochastic trend with drift, since no specific assumption regarding the behaviour of μ_t is made according to method used for test of club convergence. To test whether different states in our sample converge, the estimation of δit plays the significant role and for that, the following relative transition component is suggested:

$$\mathrm{h}_{\mathrm{it}} = \frac{Y_{it}}{\frac{1}{N}\sum_{i=1}^{N} Y_{it}} = \frac{\delta_{it}}{\frac{1}{N}\sum_{i=1}^{N} \delta_{it}} \tag{11.7}$$

h_{it} is the relative transition parameter which measures the loading coefficient relative to the panel average at time t. It can be directly computed from the given data such that the common steady-state trend μ_t can be removed and an individual trajectory for each state, i in relation to the panel average, can be detected. The relative measure, hit captures the transition path with respect to panel average and it traces the relative individual behaviour as well as the relative departure of the ith (state) from the common growth path, μ_t. With convergence, there should be a common limit in the transition path of each state and the coefficient h_{it} should converge towards unity ($h_{it} \rightarrow 1$) for all $i = 1.....N$, as $t \rightarrow \infty$. Equation 11.7 indicates that cross-sectional mean of h_{it} is unity and the cross-sectional variance of h_{it} (H_{it}) can be computed as follows:

$$\mathrm{H}_{\mathrm{it}} = \frac{1}{N}\sum (\mathrm{h}_{\mathrm{it}} - 1)^2 \rightarrow 0 \text{ as } \mathrm{t} \rightarrow \infty, \mathrm{i} = 1, 2 \ldots \mathrm{N} \tag{11.8}$$

Now, for the econometric test of convergence and the setting the empirical procedure of defining club convergence, Phillips and Sul (2007, 2009) consider the following semi- parametric form of time varying coefficient, δ_{it} :

$$\delta_{\mathrm{it}} = \delta_{\mathrm{i}} + \sigma_{\mathrm{it}}\zeta_{\mathrm{it}}, \tag{11.9}$$

where

$$\sigma_{\mathrm{it}} = \frac{\sigma_i}{L(t)t^{\alpha}}, \sigma_{\mathrm{i}} > 0, \mathrm{t} \geq 0,$$

δ_i is fixed (time invariant), ζ_{it} are i.i.d. N(0, 1) random variables across i, but weakly dependent over t, L(t) is a slowly changing increasing function (L(t) → ∞ as t → ∞), α is the rate of convergence. Given these specifications, a regression t test is used for test of the null hypothesis of convergence as follows:

$$H_0 : \delta_i = \delta, \quad \alpha \geq 0$$
$$H_1 : \delta_i \neq \delta, \quad \alpha < 0$$

In order to test convergence among different cross section unit (e.g. states), Phillips and Sul (2007) estimate the following regression equation by ordinary least squares (OLS) technique:

$$\log\left(\frac{H_1}{H_2}\right) - 2\log(\log(t)) = a + b\log(t) + \varepsilon_t \tag{11.10}$$

where t = [rT],[rT] + 1,….T and r > 0.[2] In the above regression, $H_t = \frac{1}{N}\sum(H_{it} - 1)^2$ and (H_1/H_t) is the cross-sectional variance ratio, b is the speed of convergence parameter of δ_{it}. The null hypothesis of convergence is tested through a one-sided t-test robust to both heteroskedasticity and autocorrelation of the inequality $\alpha \geq 0$ (using the estimated $b = 2\alpha$) and specifically it is rejected at 5% level if $t_b < -1.65$. The one-sided t test is as follows:

$$t_b = \frac{\hat{b} - b}{sb} \rightarrow N(0, 1)$$

This test is called log t test. In the presence of multiple equilibrium or multiple steady states, the rejection of null of convergence doesn't rule out the formation of convergence within some states in our sample known as Clubs. In case, the log t test is rejected for the entire sample, this methodology suggests repeating the test procedures according to a clustering mechanism.

11.6 Empirical Findings

11.6.1 Descriptive Statistics

Table 11.1 presents the average movement of real GDP growth per capita (GSDPR) as well as real GDP growth rates (YPR) at aggregate level across all states in our sample for different sub-periods. We observe that there is a significant spurt in average

---

[2] −2 log (log t) is a penalization function that improves the performance of the test under the alternative; r assumes a positive value in the interval (0, 1] in order to discard the first block of observation from the estimation, and [rT] is the integer part of rT. Phillips and Sul suggest using r ∈ [0.2, 0.3] for small sample size (T < 50) as a result of Monte Carlo simulations.

growth rate across states between pre-reform period and the post reform period. In particular, average per capita real GDP growth rate has increased from 3.6% to 6.2% for all 32 states taken together during 1985–86 to 2018–19. We also observe from the Table 11.1 that for less developed states such as Bihar, Orissa and Assam, per capita real GDP growth rates during the initial periods has been quite low as compared to the later periods compared to the relatively more developed states like Kerala, Maharashtra and Punjab. We also observe that most of the states experience wide fluctuation in the growth rate of real GDP per capita during 1990–99 to 2000–09. Table 11.1 also reveals that the average real per capita growth rate increased since the post reform period.

Table 11.2 presents the average movement of components of bank credit across various sectors such as personal (household) credit, industrial credit, service sector credit and agricultural credit, as a proportion of sectoral credit. We observe that post liberalization, disbursement of personal credit has significantly increased. On an average, for all the states taken together, personal credit as a percentage of total credit outstanding (UPC) has significantly increased from 4.7% to 28% during the period of 1985–89 to 2010–15. In contrast, industrial credit has registered a decline from around 40% to around 30% during the same period. In so-called developed states like Punjab, Maharashtra, Kerala, Tamil Nadu, there has been an upward trend in the disbursement of personal credit. For Kerala, it has increased from 8.46% to 34.56% during the per reform and post reform periods. For less developed states, there has also been an increase in the disbursement of personal credit. Services sector credit as a percentage of total credit outstanding, on an average, across all states, has also registered a decline from 30% to 25%. Agricultural credit as a proportion of total credit has registered a decline for all states taken together during the pre-liberalization period and the periods of post liberalization. However, in all other sectors, sectoral credit as a proportion of sectoral output has registered an increase.

We also compute average movement of the growth of sectoral credit as a proportion of sectoral output across all states in our sample (see Table 11.3). We observe that agricultural credit as a percentage of agricultural output in the pre-reform period was recorded to be about 11.47% during 1985–89, it gradually increased to 21.06% during 1990–99 and further in subsequent sub-periods. In the beginning of the 2000s, RBI initiated several measures for steady inflow of credit towards the agricultural sector. In developed states such as Andhra Pradesh, Kerala, Maharashtra, there have been an upward trend in sectoral credit as a proportion of sectoral output between pre and post reform periods. For example, in Kerala, it increased from 14.74% to 65.67% during 1985–89 to 2010–2015 (Table 11.3). In the relatively less developed states like Bihar, Jharkhand and Manipur, we also observe similar trend. As far as industrial credit is concerned, we observe that taking all the states taken together, the share of industrial credit in total industrial output has increased from 63 to 97% during 1985–90 and 1991–1999. On the other hand, the proportion of services sector credit in total services output has increased from 11.6% to 22.1% during 1985–90 to 2010–15.

We also present the movement of branch density across Indian states as another relevant indicator of financial development (Table 11.4). It is worthy to mention that

Table 11.1 Periodic growth rates of per capita income (GDP) and real GDP across States of India

	Real per capita growth Rate (GSDPR)					Real GDP growth rate (YPR)				
States	1985–89	1990–99	2000–09	2010–15	2016–2018	1985–89	1990–99	2000–09	2010–15	2016–2018
1. AP	0.058 (0.072)	0.035 (0.042)	0.057 (0.033)	0.056 (0.018)	0.061 (0.031)	0.090 (0.102)	0.054 (0.042)	0.067 0.033)	0.069 (0.019)	0.253 (0.319)
2. ARP	0.030 (0.016)	0.036 (0.068)	0.055 (0.065)	0.035 (0.045)	0.039 (0.025)	0.100 (0.042)	0.053 0.062)	0.076 0.060)	0.057 (0.045)	–
3. Assam	0.007 (0.043)	0.008 (0.014)	0.032 (0.020)	0.051 (0.019)	–	0.039 (0.045)	0.025 0.014)	0.051 0.018)	0.065 (0.02)	0.075 (0.012)
4. Bihar	0.010 (0.069)	0.004 (0.101)	0.043 (0.080)	0.055 (0.068)	–	0.054 (0.064)	0.033 (0.107)	0.064 (0.079)	0.061 (0.078)	0.239 (0.283)
5. Jharkhand	–	–	0.026 (0.086)	0.037 (0.080)	0.073 (0.007)	–	0.024 (0.117)	0.071 (0.073)	0.048 (0.071)	–
6. Goa	0.065 (0.056)	0.067 (0.068)	0.057 (0.043)	0.106 (0.067)	0.089 (0.028)	0.115 (0.057)	0.063 (0.074)	0.085 (0.031)	–	−0.605 (1.22)
7. Gujarat	0.047 (0.169)	0.044 (0.094)	0.065 (0.054)	0.058 (0.017)	0.082 (0.005)	0.053 (0.099)	0.051 (0.035)	0.086 (0.015)	0.161 (0.286)	−0.079 (0.268)
8. Haryana	0.029 (0.099)	0.026 (0.035)	0.066 (0.016)	0.062 (0.028)	0.068 (0.012)	0.075 (0.104)	0.050 (0.034)	0.085 (0.015)	0.084 (0.028)	0.050 (0.045)
9. HP	0.054 (0.047)	0.038 (0.024)	0.058 (0.014)	0.057 (0.011)	0.055 (0.002)	0.082 (0.091)	0.058 0.023)	0.073 (0.013)	–	0.045 (0.039)
10. J&K	–	0.023 (0.004)	0.027 (0.014)	0.023 (0.034)	–	0.047 (0.007)	0.051 (0.006)	0.053 (0.046)	–	–
11. Karnataka	0.054 (0.013)	0.050 (0.034)	0.046 (0.040)	0.060 (0.030)	0.090 (0.021)	0.076 (0.052)	0.067 (0.034)	0.069 0.037)	0.080 (0.035)	0.521 (0.750)
12. Kerala	0.033 (0.043)	0.047 (0.023)	0.065 (0.022)	0.056 (0.005)	0.061 (0.010)	0.063 (0.066)	0.054 (0.024)	0.074 (0.016)	–	−0.116 (0.324)

(continued)

Table 11.1 (continued)

	Real per capita growth Rate (GSDPR)					Real GDP growth rate (YPR)				
States	1985–89	1990–99	2000–09	2010–15	2016–2018	1985–89	1990–99	2000–09	2010–15	2016–2018
13. MP	0.024 (0.066)	0.039 (0.050)	0.030 (0.062)	0.052 (0.031)	0.062 (0.035)	–	–	0.083 (0.055)	0.053 (0.030)	0.026 (0.056)
14. Chhattisgarh	–	–	0.048 (0.070)	0.037 (0.034)	0.056 (0.026)	–	0.017 (0.038)	0.083 (0.055)	0.053 (0.030)	0.026 (0.056)
15. Maharashtra	0.058 (0.054)	0.044 (0.043)	0.056 (0.048)	0.053 (0.022)	0.062 (0.018)	0.092 (0.101)	0.058 (0.050)	0.085 (0.034)	0.065 (0.017)	0.060 (0.003)
16. Manipur	0.017 (0.027)	0.030 (0.039)	0.028 (0.051)	0.037 (0.042)	0.039 (0.033)	0.056 (0.023)	0.041 (0.054)	0.052 (0.037)	0.065 (0.017)	–
17. Meghalaya	0.037 (0.055)	0.031 (0.044)	0.042 (0.023)	0.015 (0.11)	0.048 (0.044)	0.092 (0.056)	0.052 (0.041)	0.070 (0.023)	0.034 (0.110)	–
18. Mizoram	–	–	0.053 (0.035)	0.049 (0.075)	0.040 (0.035)	–	–	0.085 0.042)	–	−0.296
19. Nagaland	–	–	0.072 (0.020)	0.060 (0.034)	0.013 0.080)	–	–	0.075 (0.021)	0.055 (0.031)	0.204 (0.250)
20. Odisha	0.043 (0.089)	0.010 (0.084)	0.057 (0.054)	0.046 (0.032)	0.078 (0.045)	0.020 (0.171)	0.040 (0.054)	0.080 (0.044)	0.070 (0.047)	–0.525 (1.018)
21. Punjab	0.035 (0.019)	0.025 (0.017)	0.041 (0.025)	0.044 (0.007)	0.048 (0.006)	0.056 (0.052)	0.046 (0.013)	0.058 (0.023)	0.057 (0.008)	0.087 (0.047)
22.Rajasthan	0.058 (0.163)	0.037 (0.081)	0.038 (0.096)	0.060 (0.032)	0.047 (0.011)	0.119 (0.145)	0.045 (0.079)	0.074 0.094)	0.074 (0.017)	0.195 (0.229)
23. Sikkim	–	–	0.115 (0.152)	0.072 (0.013)	0.066 (0.058)	–	–	0.131 (0.150)	–	−0.102 (0.349)

(continued)

Table 11.1 (continued)

	Real per capita growth Rate (GSDPR)					Real GDP growth rate (YPR)				
States	1985–89	1990–99	2000–09	2010–15	2016–2018	1985–89	1990–99	2000–09	2010–15	2016–2018
24.Tamilnadu	0.036 (0.038)	0.050 (0.028)	0.057 (0.049)	0.060 (0.029)	0.070 (0.015)	0.068 (0.061)	0.061 (0.027)	0.078 (0.052)	0.066 (0.016)	0.233 (0.266)
25. Tripura	0.060 (0.032)	–	0.065 (0.024)	0.072 (0.015)	0.094 (0.020)	0.109 (0.055)	–	0.081 (0.023)	–	0.252 (0.271)
26. UP	0.036 (0.038)	0.016 (0.030)	0.033 (0.022)	0.041 (0.009)	0.061 (0.022)	0.073 (0.049)	0.035 (0.029)	0.058 (0.017)	0.064 (0.020)	0.322 (0.452)
27. Uttarakhand	–	–	0.099 (0.036)	0.060 (0.020)	0.0676 (0.009)	–	0.036 (0.044)	–	0.077 0.020)	−0.565 (1.102)
28. WB	0.022 (0.006)	0.047 (0.014)	0.047 (0.016)	0.031 (0.047)	0.051 (0.005)	0.057 (0.017)	0.062 (0.016)	–	0.041 (0.052)	–
29. A & N Islands	0.0153 (0.031)	0.025 (0.093)	0.072 (0.058)	0.062 (0.013)	0.114 (0.002)	0.055 (0.041)	0.051 (0.089)	0.090 (0.043)	–	–
30. Chandigarh	–	–	0.076 (0.025)	0.027 (0.035)	0.051 (0.019)	–	0.090 (0.030)	0.085 (0.035)	–	0.279 (0.354)
31. Delhi	0.039 (0.008)	0.024 (0.070)	0.061 (0.038)	0.055 (0.016)	0.048 (0.010)	0.092 (0.055)	0.063 (0.070)	0.087 (0.028)	0.075 (0.016)	–
32. Puducherry	0.012 (0.019)	0.057 (0.119)	–	0.015 (0.119)	0.075 (0.028)	0.056 (0.034)	0.085 (0.118)	–	0.041 (0.120)	0.163 (0.129)
Average	**0.037**	**0.033**	**0.054**	**0.050**	**0.062**	**0.072**	**0.050**	**0.076**	**0.065**	**0.030**

Note values within bracket denote standard deviation of growth rate for the period. Growth rates are calculated as average annual (YTY) growth rate

Table 11.2 Sector-wise composition of credit as a proportion of total bank credit

	CONCRUPC				INDCRUPC			
State	1985–89	1990–99	2000–09	2010–15	1985–89	1990–99	2000–09	2010–15
1	0.057 (0.013)	0.128 (0.018)	0.238 (0.045)	0.212 (0.024)	0.352 (0.029)	0.393 (0.025)	0.335 (0.033)	0.357 (0.096)
2	0.022 (0.006)	0.120 (0.070)	0.319 (0.078)	0.473 (0.083)	0.556 (0.096)	0.472 (0.181)	0.179 (0.057)	0.231 (0.150)
3	0.0278 (0.005)	0.111 (0.037)	0.331 (0.115)	0.350 (0.068)	0.451 (0.056)	0.403 (0.078)	0.289 (0.010)	0.229 (0.079)
4	0.044 (0.013)	0.126 (0.034)	0.280 (0.047)	0.279 (0.025)	0.359 (0.022)	0.320 (0.025)	0.257 (0.042)	0.153 (0.044)
5	–	–	0.261 (0.065)	0.293 (0.013)	–	–	0.373 (0.071)	0.326 (0.022)
6	0.058 (0.021)	0.141 (0.025)	0.264 (0.059)	0.295 (0.121)	0.570 (0.040)	0.512 (0.033)	0.413 (0.035)	0.267 (0.153)
7	0.048 (0.005)	0.079 (0.007)	0.145 (0.037)	0.150 (0.006)	0.614 (0.024)	0.602 (0.027)	0.545 (0.034)	0.545 (0.002)
8	0.037 (0.013)	0.092 (0.015)	0.195 (0.049)	0.174 (0.023)	0.452 (0.035)	0.505 (0.036)	0.394 (0.077)	0.361 (0.022)
9	0.047 (0.019)	0.150 (0.037)	0.233 (0.030)	0.257 (0.022)	0.367 (0.012)	0.354 (0.017)	0.374 (0.042)	0.306 (0.055)
10	0.042 (0.012)	0.098 (0.038)	0.211 (0.040)	0.329 (0.006)	0.339 (0.041)	0.246 (0.062)	0.232 (0.092)	0.190 (0.010)
11	0.061 (0.015)	0.121 (0.021)	0.247 (0.042)	0.243 (0.012)	0.418 (0.005)	0.420 (0.015)	0.362 (0.027)	0.344 (0.006)
12	0.085 (0.019)	0.174 (0.039)	0.343 (0.066)	0.346 (0.010)	0.332 (0.020)	0.310 (0.030)	0.189 (0.038)	0.135 (0.012)
13	0.044 (0.017)	0.097 (0.015)	0.221 (0.044)	0.203 (0.009)	0.387 (0.014)	0.399 (0.029)	0.321 (0.050)	0.287 (0.040)
14	–	–	0.210 (0.048)	0.200 (0.006)	–	–	0.397 (0.063)	0.371 (0.007)
15	0.033 (0.009)	0.061 (0.004)	0.123 (0.038)	0.109 (0.004)	0.516 (0.072)	0.543 (0.031)	0.448 (0.016)	0.439 (0.010)
16	0.054 (0.001)	0.117 (0.028)	0.488 (0.132)	0.542 (0.037)	0.275 (0.0663)	0.349 (0.052)	0.150 (0.063)	0.092 (0.014)
17	0.047 (0.005)	0.176 (0.071)	0.300 (0.080)	0.359 (0.033)	0.238 (0.083)	0.231 (0.069)	0.390 (0.124)	0.324 (0.030)
18	0.035 (0.006)	0.131 (0.098)	0.528 (0.108)	0.586 (0.030)	0.295 (0.072)	0.265 (0.065)	0.107 (0.047)	0.075 (0.018)
19	0.039 (0.006)	0.119 (0.046)	0.421 (0.123)	0.519 (0.103)	0.387 (0.044)	0.358 (0.082)	0.184 (0.042)	0.150 (0.029)
20	0.047 (0.014)	0.133 (0.038)	0.275 (0.041)	0.219 (0.005)	0.351 (0.042)	0.325 (0.025)	0.328 (0.028)	0.332 (0.018)

(continued)

Table 11.2 (continued)

	CONCRUPC				INDCRUPC			
State	1985–89	1990–99	2000–09	2010–15	1985–89	1990–99	2000–09	2010–15
21	0.041 (0.019)	0.093 (0.016)	0.189 (0.055)	0.134 (0.008)	0.373 (0.064)	0.414 (0.025)	0.355 (0.048)	0.393 (0.042)
22	0.049 (0.014)	0.118 (0.024)	0.226 (0.038)	0.166 (0.012)	0.349 (0.014)	0.384 (0.020)	0.322 (0.038)	0.385 (0.023)
23	0.027 (0.007)	0.144 (0.071)	0.482 (0.128)	0.375 (0.053)	0.228 (0.103)	0.305 (0.086)	0.164 (0.084)	0.404 (0.076)
24	0.057 (0.012)	0.105 (0.014)	0.212 (0.044)	0.193 (0.009)	0.480 (0.012)	0.484 (0.015)	0.405 (0.036)	0.385 (0.014)
25	0.080 (0.066)	0.092 (0.032)	0.383 (0.073)	0.423 (0.012)	0.212 (0.034)	0.198 (0.033)	0.106 (0.020)	0.090 (0.010)
26	0.042 (0.011)	0.105 (0.020)	0.229 (0.051)	0.190 (0.011)	0.403 (0.012)	0.393 (0.015)	0.284 (0.032)	0.313 (0.007)
27	–	–	0.297 (0.043)	0.295 (0.015)	–	–	0.295 (0.025)	0.272 (0.037)
28	0.043 (0.005)	0.089 (0.017)	0.172 (0.035)	0.118 (0.010)	0.607 (0.010)	0.586 (0.019)	0.457 (0.030)	0.492 (0.029)
29	0.039 (0.025)	0.130 (0.032)	0.251 (0.122)	0.480 (0.0310)	0.250 (0.133)	0.215 (0.058)	0.165 (0.035)	0.082 (0.010)
30	0.046 (0.010)	0.063 (0.012)	0.135 (0.063)	0.116 (0.010)	0.403 (0.100)	0.432 (0.105)	0.301 (0.077)	0.516 (0.080)
31	0.049 (0.016)	0.072 (0.017)	0.122 (0.029)	0.086 (0.009)	0.466 (0.050)	0.559 (0.049)	0.460 (0.025)	0.529 (0.060)
32	0.056 (0.014)	0.146 (0.041)	0.325 (0.072)	0.364 (0.010)	0.464 (0.043)	0.474 (0.047)	0.267 (0.080)	0.165 (0.004)
Av	**0.047**	**0.115**	**0.270**	**0.280**	**0.396**	**0.395**	**0.308**	**0.304**
	SERCRUPC				AGLCRUPC			
State	1985–89	1990–99	2000–09	2010–15	1985–89	1990–99	2000–09	2010–15
1	0.194 (0.081)	0.167 (0.021)	0.166 (0.015)	0.185 (0.053)	0.316 (0.031)	0.214 (0.021)	0.176 (0.007)	0.256 (0.081)
2	0.259 (0.150)	0.195 (0.081)	0.334 (0.088)	0.273 (0.173)	0.159 (0.118)	0.127 (0.035)	0.088 (0.021)	0.610 (0.012)
3	0.351 (0.140)	0.267 (0.029)	0.214 (0.025)	0.289 (0.099)	0.164 (0.043)	0.143 (0.028)	0.082 (0.019)	0.159 (0.041)
4	0.318 (0.096)	0.242 (0.086)	0.130 (0.011)	0.130 (0.011)	0.251 (0.007)	0.230 (0.039)	0.147 (0.029)	0.313 (0.097)
5	–	–	0.207 (0.033)	0.267 (0.073)	–	–	0.087 (0.014)	0.122 (0.019)
6	0.136 (0.124)	0.226 (0.025)	0.240 (0.037)	0.249 (0.165)	0.073 (0.012)	0.0567 (0.020)	0.026 (0.007)	0.0404 (0.023)

(continued)

Table 11.2 (continued)

	SERCRUPC				AGLCRUPC			
State	1985–89	1990–99	2000–09	2010–15	1985–89	1990–99	2000–09	2010–15
7	0.154 (0.074)	0.138 (0.014)	0.155 (0.013)	0.180 (0.029)	0.145 (0.012)	0.121 (0.028)	0.108 (0.016)	0.106 (0.005)
8	0.182 (0.059)	0.130 (0.009)	0.155 (0.036)	0.258 (0.019)	0.282 (0.024)	0.222 (0.035)	0.202 (0.018)	0.181 (0.010)
9	0.389 (0.162)	0.295 (0.015)	0.217 (0.054)	0.26 (0.064)	0.177 (0.011)	0.130 (0.023)	0.127 (0.024)	0.195 (0.026)
10	0.530 (0.234)	0.518 (0.089)	0.456 (0.104)	0.338 (0.090)	0.118 (0.015)	0.074 (0.015)	0.057 (0.015)	0.133 (0.033)
11	0.226 (0.084)	0.199 (0.012)	0.198 (0.033)	0.257 (0.073)	0.240 (0.013)	0.189 (0.022)	0.138 (0.014)	0.159 (0.015)
12	0.311 (0.131)	0.266 (0.012)	0.247 (0.021)	0.321 (0.119)	0.177 (0.014)	0.147 (0.015)	0.135 (0.021)	0.211 (0.013)
13	0.285 (0.108)	0.193 (0.069)	0.128 (0.010)	0.209 (0.049)	0.290 (0.104)	0.210 (0.020)	0.189 (0.016)	0.247 (0.049)
14	–	–	0.192 (0.038)	0.233 (0.045)	–	–	0.129 (0.033)	0.185 (0.028)
15	0.430 (0.290)	0.287 (0.026)	0.351 (0.023)	0.389 (0.009)	0.070 (0.007)	0.046 (0.008)	0.042 (0.006)	0.0402 (0.004)
16	0.489 (0.235)	0.335 (0.063)	0.173 (0.047)	0.208 (0.224)	0.192 (0.057)	0.147 (0.092)	0.125 (0.025)	0.200 (0.027)
17	0.373 (0.038)	0.285 (0.065)	0.176 (0.072)	0.218 (0.109)	0.289 (0.109)	0.188 (0.068)	0.073 (0.025)	0.121 (0.034)
18	0.391 (0.227)	0.363 (0.064)	0.193 (0.061)	0.262 (0.255)	0.315 (0.040)	0.173 (0.053)	0.118 (0.043)	0.152 (0.016)
19	0.331 (0.177)	0.249 (0.032)	0.192 (0.028)	0.196 (0.125)	0.211 (0.073)	0.183 (0.027)	0.110 (0.022)	0.102 (0.042)
20	0.278 (0.108)	0.248 (0.017)	0.199 (0.025)	0.250 (0.042)	0.217 (0.113)	0.049 (0.067)	0.132 (0.022)	0.181 (0.019)
21	0.2867 (0.185)	0.229 (0.020)	0.197 (0.057)	0.195 (0.014)	0.281 (0.020)	0.208 (0.027)	0.206 (0.018)	0.248 (0.040)
22	0.263 (0.116)	0.206 (0.012)	0.173 (0.017)	0.172 (0.038)	0.295 (0.011)	0.231 (0.024)	0.222 (0.013)	0.259 (0.026)
23	0.110 (0.115)	0.319 (0.072)	0.251 (0.098)	0.231 (0.102)	0.098 (0.014)	0.152 (0.051)	0.060 (0.019)	0.036 (0.012)
24	0.192 (0.146)	0.218 (0.015)	0.216 (0.020)	0.254 (0.049)	0.135 (0.076)	0.126 (0.022)	0.105 (0.020)	0.166 (0.018)
25	0.380 (0.130)	0.437 (0.055)	0.293 (0.032)	0.341 (0.118)	0.271 (0.051)	0.218 (0.021)	0.151 (0.027)	0.181 (0.018)

(continued)

Table 11.2 (continued)

	SERCRUPC				AGLCRUPC			
State	1985–89	1990–99	2000–09	2010–15	1985–89	1990–99	2000–09	2010–15
26	0.279 (0.105)	0.187 (0.067)	0.165 (0.017)	0.205 (0.036)	0.218 (0.015)	0.207 (0.013)	0.223 (0.020)	0.259 (0.031)
27	–	–	0.194 (0.016)	0.240 (0.072)	–	–	0.156 (0.016)	0.486 (0.742)
28	0.249 (0.104)	0.194 (0.014)	0.249 (0.034)	0.276 (0.017)	0.080 (0.006)	0.057 (0.012)	0.064 (0.012)	0.078 (0.005)
29	0.455 (0.089)	0.448 (0.060)	0.354 (0.107)	0.367 (0.092)	0.160 (0.061)	0.084 (0.019)	0.149 (0.094)	0.655 (0.028)
30	0.390 (0.269)	0.324 (0.133)	0.412 (0.137)	0.264 (0.041)	0.183 (0.054)	0.086 (0.054)	0.117 (0.043)	0.080 (0.039)
31	0.450 (0.170)	0.261 (0.030)	0.322 (0.032)	0.328 (0.039)	0.024 (0.021)	0.019 (0.010)	0.048 (0.013)	0.029 (0.007)
32	0.199 (0.123)	0.164 (0.016)	0.231 (0.028)	0.295 (0.112)	0.229 (0.041)	0.148 (0.050)	0.108 (0.020)	0.198 (0.019)
Av	**0.306**	**0.262**	**0.231**	**0.254**	**0.195**	**0.144**	**0.123**	

Note Number appearing in first column of this table denotes the serial number of a state as mentioned in Table 11.1 Values within bracket denote standard deviation

branch expansion policies undertaken by the government over the last three decades played a pivotal role in state's financial intermediation process, in an attempt to alleviate regional disparities and poverty especially in the underdeveloped rural areas (See Burgess & Pande, 1995). In 2014, government introduced Pradhan Mantri Jan Dhan Yojana (PMJDY) in order to provide greater access of banking facilities in rural areas through opening of new bank accounts. Following the nationalization of commercial banks, there were about 30,000 bank branches in the rural unbanked locations. In 1977, a new branch licencing policy was put in place under which, a bank was required to open 4 branches in an unbanked location, in order to open a new branch. Our observations in Table 11.4 reveal certain reflections on the inclusive nature of financial development and the effects of policy changes mentioned above. We observe that during our period of investigation, number of branches per lakh population has increased from 9 to 12 approximately. From Table 11.4, we also observe that developed states like Maharashtra, Haryana have witnessed fluctuating trend in branch density (BRAND) over the periods, while Kerala had witnessed an increasing trend in branch density during the same periods. Underdeveloped states like Bihar, Rajasthan, however, witnessed a fluctuating trend in branch density during the periods of investigation.

In Table 11.5, we have presented the movement of few select indicators of credit inflow/outflow, in order to understand spatial distribution scenario of credit disbursement across states. We have defined two alternative indicators of outward and inward migration (spillover) of credit, in level. First, we define outward migration as the credit sanctioned in ith state but used elsewhere (PCSO) and inward migration as the

Table 11.3 Sectoral credit as a proportion of sectoral output

	INDCRQN				SERCRQN	
States	1985–89	1990–99	2000–09	2010–15	1985–89	1990–99
AP	0.327 (0.046)	0.356 (0.024)	0.829 (0.425)	1.611 (0.724)	0.093 (0.035)	0.077 (0.010)
ARP	0.254 (0.119)	0.182 (0.140)	0.088 (0.037)	0.177 (0.180)	0.062 (0.013)	0.036 (0.010)
Assam	0.191 (0.029)	0.199 (0.072)	0.211 (0.118)	0.282 (0.257)	0.087 (0.031)	0.058 (0.008)
Bihar	0.091 (0.017)	0.349 (0.178)	0.504 (0.118)	0.211 (0.105)	0.073 (0.016)	0.082 (0.016)
Jharkhand	–	–	0.139 (0.039)	0.198 (0.030)	–	–
Goa	0.623 (0.071)	0.362 (0.088)	0.258 (0.041)	0.187 (0.021)	0.157 (0.003)	0.113 (0.018)
Gujarat	0.346 (0.054)	0.317 (0.046)	0.440 (0.060)	0.601 (0.058)	0.073 (0.027)	0.068 (0.0042)
Haryana	0.314 (0.026)	0.289 (0.029)	0.340 (0.081)	0.581 (0.044)	0.113 (0.031)	0.063 (0.009)
HP	0.162 (0.014)	0.116 (0.025)	0.223 (0.065)	0.210 (0.032)	0.141 (0.056)	0.098 (0.016)
J&K	–	0.113 (0.017)	0.258 (0.147)	0.209 (0.045)	–	0.170 (0.063)
Karnataka	0.445 (0.041)	0.401 (0.027)	0.668 (0.143)	0.875 (0.075)	0.168 (0.054)	0.127 (0.013)
Kerala	0.396 (0.030)	0.316 (0.050)	0.285 (0.010)	0.305 (0.044)	0.136 (0.043)	0.107 (0.004)
MP	0.204 (0.022)	0.277 (0.063)	0.389 (0.064)	0.419 (0.076)	0.085 (0.022)	0.071 (0.026)
Chatisgarh	–	–	0.178 (0.030)	0.266 (0.026)	–	–
Maharashtra	0.481 (0.045)	0.602 (0.095)	1.132 (0.262)	1.685 (0.123)	0.366 (0.289)	0.223 (0.024)
Manipur	0.055 (0.024)	0.078 (0.016)	0.037 (0.015)	0.048 (0.008)	0.068 (0.020)	0.045 (0.012)
Meghalaya	0.090 (0.039)	0.078 (0.061)	0.339 (0.283)	0.186 (0.019)	0.060 (0.017)	0.037 (0.007)
Mizoram	0.136 (0.066)	0.081 (0.032)	0.085 (0.031)	0.076 (0.018)	0.056 (0.007)	0.036 (0.006)
Nagaland	0.221 (0.029)	0.167 (0.077)	0.099 (0.064)	0.144 (0.019)	0.049 (0.021)	0.029 (0.013)
Odisha	0.200 (0.043)	0.144 (0.019)	0.248 (0.052)	0.269 (0.021)	0.102 (0.024)	0.075 (0.012)

(continued)

Table 11.3 (continued)

	INDCRQN				SERCRQN	
States	1985–89	1990–99	2000–09	2010–15	1985–89	1990–99
Punjab	0.363 (0.036)	0.356 (0.034)	0.514 (0.157)	0.920 (0.088)	0.193 (0.135)	0.138 (0.013)
Rajasthan	0.181 (0.020)	0.177 (0.015)	0.293 (0.112)	0.500 (0.033)	0.085 (0.044)	0.061 (0.006)
Sikkim	0.157 (0.069)	0.126 (0.049)	0.138 (0.117)	0.158 (0.071)	0.070 (0.038)	0.045 (0.022)
Tamilnadu	9.573 (20.56)	0.458 (0.051)	0.715 (0.116)	0.932 (0.020)	0.138 (0.046)	0.140 (0.007)
Tripura	0.181 (0.050)	0.134 (0.057)	0.045 (0.021)	0.070 (0.009)	0.084 (0.017)	0.084 (0.024)
UP	0.240 (0.023)	0.229 (0.019)	0.296 (0.062)	0.499 (0.044)	0.078 (0.026)	0.064 (0.008)
Uttarakhand	–	–	0.212 (0.028)	0.171 (0.024)	–	–
WB	0.471 (0.077)	0.606 (0.037)	0.738 (0.160)	1.250 (0.119)	0.108 (0.032)	0.089 (0.014)
A&N Islands	0.083 (0.029)	0.091 (0.062)	0.140 (0.078)	0.048 (0.004)	0.045 (0.011)	0.047 (0.020)
Chandigarh	–	3.001 (1.345)	3.356 (1.542)	8.454 (1.715)	–	0.500 (0.197)
Delhi	1.101 (0.129)	1.829 (0.511)	3.871 (1.011)	8.716 (1.559)	0.334 (0.148)	0.246 (0.038)
Puducherry	0.149 (0.046)	0.228 (0.089)	0.102 (0.015)	0.143 (0.016)	0.105 (0.038)	0.078 (0.013)
Average	**0.631**	**0.402**	**0.536**	**0.971**	**0.116**	**0.104**
	SERCRQN		AGLCRQN			
States	2000–09	2010–15	1985–89	1990–99	2000–09	2010–15
AP	0.205 (0.121)	0.378 (0.193)	0.216 (0.025)	0.147 (0.013)	0.376 (0.187)	0.769 (0.148)
ARP	0.157 (0.138)	0.144 (0.082)	0.019 (0.016)	0.015 (0.004)	0.033 (0.016)	0.022 (0.002)
Assam	0.078 (0.025)	0.139 (0.061)	0.058 (0.018)	0.042 (0.012)	0.053 (0.022)	0.149 (0.033)
Bihar	0.068 (0.015)	0.083 (0.023)	0.064 (0.014)	0.089 (0.013)	0.143 (0.073)	0.259 (0.037)
Jharkhand	0.099 (0.030)	0.137 (0.039)	–	–	0.088 (0.023)	0.154 (0.018)
Goa	0.149 (0.013)	0.194 (0.070)	0.117 (0.021)	0.084 (0.024)	0.095 (0.036)	0.232 (0.045)

(continued)

Table 11.3 (continued)

	SERCRQN		AGLCRQN			
States	2000–09	2010–15	1985–89	1990–99	2000–09	2010–15
Gujarat	0.116 (0.032)	0.177 (0.038)	0.114 (0.028)	0.098 (0.026)	0.212 (0.075)	0.228 (0.032)
Haryana	0.098 (0.040)	0.206 (0.018)	0.146 (0.018)	0.096 (0.015)	0.242 (0.087)	0.388 (0.034)
HP	0.133 (0.026)	0.165 (0.051)	0.074 (0.013)	0.057 (0.013)	0.137 (0.068)	0.233 (0.014)
J&K	0.283 (0.050)	0.196 (0.028)	–	0.028 (0.003)	0.070 (0.039)	0.171 (0.069)
Karnataka	0.220 (0.090)	0.309 (0.096)	0.182 (0.006)	0.143 (0.016)	0.404 (0.142)	0.614 (0.071)
Kerala	0.139 (0.021)	0.267 (0.095)	0.147 (0.014)	0.111 (0.016)	0.284 (0.128)	0.657 (0.091)
MP	0.096 (0.025)	0.163 (0.033)	0.093 (0.020)	0.101 (0.014)	0.249 (0.0861)	0.293 (0.037)
Chatisgarh	0.105 (0.033)	0.170 (0.033)	–	–	0.119 (0.070)	0.256 (0.030)
Maharashtra	0.466 (0.128)	0.690 (0.033)	0.137 (0.011)	0.114 (0.019)	0.284 (0.098)	0.384 (0.070)
Manipur	0.036 (0.010)	0.055 (0.051)	0.039 (0.011)	0.033 (0.021)	0.048 (0.028)	0.120 (0.012)
Meghalaya	0.065 (0.031)	0.081 (0.039)	0.084 (0.045)	0.044 (0.017)	0.060 (0.032)	0.119 (0.043)
Mizoram	0.048 (0.0156)	0.097 (0.086)	0.070 (0.030)	0.026 (0.014)	0.093 (0.060)	0.161 (0.020)
Nagaland	0.026 (0.013)	0.052 (0.049)	0.078 (0.039)	0.049 (0.021)	0.028 (0.019)	0.053 (0.021)
Odisha	0.111 (0.032)	0.154 (0.021)	0.070 (0.039)	0.018 (0.025)	0.135 (0.051)	0.263 (0.026)
Punjab	0.173 (0.042)	0.241 (0.031)	0.155 (0.015)	0.109 (0.018)	0.240 (0.079)	0.483 (0.099)
Rajasthan	0.102 (0.025)	0.138 (0.033)	0.111 (0.014)	0.083 (0.013)	0.246 (0.083)	0.316 (0.036)
Sikkim	0.124 (0.067)	0.192 (0.129)	0.050 (0.010)	0.044 (0.010)	0.097 (0.071)	0.066 (0.014)
Tamilnadu	0.206 (0.049)	0.305 (0.071)	0.231 (0.044)	0.210 (0.033)	0.495 (0.189)	0.942 (0.158)
Tripura	0.059 (0.017)	0.113 (0.040)	0.082 (0.012)	0.063 (0.012)	0.063 (0.024)	0.116 (0.018)

(continued)

Table 11.3 (continued)

	SERCRQN		AGLCRQN			
States	2000–09	2010–15	1985–89	1990–99	2000–09	2010–15
UP	0.087 (0.020)	0.136 (0.026)	0.072 (0.008)	0.079 (0.006)	0.194 (0.073)	0.299 (0.037)
Uttarakhand	0.083 (0.016)	0.111 (0.033)	–	–	0.180 (0.077)	0.867 (1.214)
WB	0.152 (0.054)	0.207 (0.019)	0.053 (0.008)	0.040 (0.013)	0.091 (0.040)	0.148 (0.013)
A&N Islands	0.113 (0.040)	0.103 (0.026)	0.021 (0.008)	0.012 (0.004)	0.217 (0.233)	0.104 (0.052)
Chandigarh	0.838 (0.248)	0.650 (0.145)	–	3.256 (1.47)	26.46 (19.95)	44.32 (11.27)
Delhi	0.567 (0.152)	0.804 (0.113)	0.298 (0.251)	0.652 (0.538)	7.611 (4.558)	6.698 (1.503)
Puducherry	0.114 (0.036)	0.200 (0.091)	0.320 (0.059)	0.264 (0.138)	0.468 (0.225)	1.284 (0.189)
Average	**0.166**	**0.221**	**0.115**	**0.211**	**1.235**	**1.911**

extent of credit sanctioned in jth state but used in ith state (PCSI). Based on these two basic credit migration variables (in level) defined, we have defined four ratios: INUPC, OUTUPC, INGDP and OUTGDP (see appendix for details). Table 11.5 reveals that during 1990–99 to 2010–15, the average outward migration of credit across states, as a percentage of total credit (UPC) has increased from 2.9% to 8.7%. On the other hand, average inward migration of credit has been recorded to be have substantially decreased from 13.3% to 1.9% during the same period. We have also calculated the extent of both outward as well as inward migration of credit during the same period, as a proportion of SGDP. Observe, outward migration of credit is recorded to be around 1%, on an average and there is no visible change during 1990–99 to 2010–15. As far as inward migration of credit as proportion of SGDP is concerned, we observe that it has increased from around 1.3% to 3% during the same period.

11.6.2 Tests of Beta Convergence

First, we present our findings based on the beta convergence. We carry out all the convergence tests for 32 sample states in India for the period, 1985–2018. In Table 11.6, we report both the tests of absolute beta convergence as well as conditional beta convergence based on OLS estimates. We have considered the growth rate of per capita gross state domestic product (GSDPR) as the dependent variable. The independent variable of equation

Table 11.4 State-wise bank branch density

	BRAND (Branch Density)								
States	1985–89	1990–99	2000–09	2010–15	States	1985–89	1990–99	2000–09	2010–15
AP	7.222 (0.055)	7.094 (0.056)	7.347 (0.583)	9.267 (1.709)	WB	5.989 (0.204)	6.125 (0.209)	5.712 (0.156)	7.155 (0.647)
ARP	7.666 (0.201)	7.349 (0.521)	5.993 (0.233)	8.036 (1.276)	A&N Islands	6.808 (0.932)	9.443 (0.685)	9.339 (0.568)	14.052 (2.064)
Assam	5.128 (0.238)	5.291 (0.239)	4.663 (0.137)	5.830 (0.659)	Chandigarh	24.27 (1.092)	22.003 (0.996)	26.10 (3.343)	36.396 (2.719)
Bihar	5.552 (0.080)	5.324 (0.325)	4.468 (0.151)	4.305 (0.567)	Delhi	14.33 (0.581)	11.983 (0.693)	12.374 (1.499)	18.137 (1.374)
Jharkhand	–	–	5.450 (0.202)	7.195 (0.732)	Puducherry	9.297 (0.179)	8.807 (0.188)	9.383 (1.315)	15.231 (1.684)
Goa	23.66 (0.612)	23.337 (0.846)	26.648 (2.219)	39.855 (5.054)	**Average**	**9.107**	**9.036**	**8.757**	**12.185**
Gujarat	8.535 (0.093)	8.088 (0.305)	7.416 (0.330)	10.218 (1.205)					
Haryana	8.045 (0.162)	7.694 (0.139)	8.093 (0.883)	14.046 (2.457)					
HP	12.966 (0.948)	14.000 (0.383)	13.43 (0.819)	18.742 (2.057)					
J&K	10.715 (0.312)	10.250 (0.612)	8.189 (0.187)	10.856 (1.603)					
Karnataka	9.965 (0.059)	9.638 (0.172)	9.554 (0.475)	13.057 (1.648)					
Kerala	10.266 (0.035)	10.374 (0.214)	11.551 (0.898)	16.190 (1.677)					

(continued)

Table 11.4 (continued)

	BRAND (Branch Density)								
States	1985–89	1990–99	2000–09	2010–15	States	1985–89	1990–99	2000–09	2010–15
MP	6.680 (0.157)	6.339 (0.338)	5.543 (0.211)	5.810 (0.495)					
Chatisgarh	–	–	4.977 (0.225)	7.244 (1.133)					
Maharashtra	7.373 (0.121)	7.154 (0.173)	6.847 (0.340)	9.230 (0.873)					
Manipur	4.152 (0.067)	4.390 (0.261)	3.255 (0.223)	4.216 (0.825)					
Meghalaya	8.684 (0.229)	9.074 (0.524)	7.529 (0.239)	8.713 (0.825)					
Mizoram	9.372 (1.026)	10.338 (0.593)	8.821 (0.347)	11.677 (1.822)					
Nagaland	6.774 (0.312)	4.999 (0.752)	3.864 (0.338)	6.424 (1.122)					
Odisha	6.304 (0.229)	6.537 (0.174)	6.296 (0.358)	8.889 (1.22)					
Punjab	11.153 (0.062)	10.817 (0.106)	11.417 (0.897)	17.206 (2.570)					
Rajasthan	7.161 (0.104)	6.758 (0.311)	6.006 (0.216)	7.979 (0.968)					
Sikkim	6.027 (0.964)	8.600 (0.803)	10.255 (1.508)	16.977 (2.633)					

(continued)

Table 11.4 (continued)

	BRAND (Branch Density)								
States	1985–89	1990–99	2000–09	2010–15	States	1985–89	1990–99	2000–09	2010–15
Tamilnadu	7.936 (0.122)	8.053 (0.038)	8.0949 (0.544)	11.691 (1.442)					
Tripura	5.921 (0.248)	6.319 (0.281)	5.796 (0.287)	8.755 (1.587)					
UP	6.173 (0.098)	5.872 (0.296)	5.269 (0.308)	6.614 (0.512)					
Uttarakhand	–	–	10.55 (0.815)	15.886 (2.092)					

Table 11.5 State level credit inflow and outflow (as proportion of total Credit and GDP) and Credit-GDP ratio

	OUTUPC (PCSO/UPC)			INUPC (PCSI/UPC)			OUTGDP (PCSO/GSDPN)		
State	1990–99	2000–09	2010–15	1990–99	2000–09	2010–15	1990–99	2000–09	2010–15
1	0.006 (0.002)	0.038 (0.036)	0.013 (0.008)	0.024 (0.003)	0.104 (0.040)	0.056 (0.020)	0.001 (0.0003)	0.027 (0.029)	0.014 (0.001)
2	0.003 (0.008)	0.025 (0.002)	0.007 (0.006)	0.301 (0.131)	0.355 (0.124)	0.177 (0.151)	0.0001 (9.146E)	0.007 (0.0161)	0.001 (0.001)
3	0.025 (0.025)	0.007 (0.008)	0.025 (0.014)	0.148 (0.033)	0.218 (0.172)	0.062 (0.035)	0.002 (0.002)	0.001 (0.002)	0.005 (0.003)
4	0.010 (0.004)	0.012 (0.008)	0.006 (0.006)	0.044 (0.022)	0.090 (0.096)	0.062 (0.048)	0.002 (0.001)	0.004 (0.003)	0.001 (0.001)
5	–	0.014 (0.009)	0.012 (0.008)	–	0.095 (0.067)	0.055 (0.033)	–	0.002 (0.002)	0.003 (0.002)
6	0.009 (0.003)	0.015 (0.028)	0.012 (0.019)	0.053 (0.019)	0.126 (0.049)	0.054 (0.031)	0.002 (0.001)	0.004 (0.007)	0.004 (0.006)
7	0.011 (0.003)	0.012 (0.007)	0.009 (0.004)	0.094 (0.009)	0.222 (0.071)	0.107 (0.018)	0.002 (0.0004)	0.004 (0.002)	0.004 (0.001)
8	0.019 (0.015)	0.020 (0.019)	0.028 (0.030)	0.221 (0.009)	0.206 (0.029)	0.158 (0.034)	0.003 (0.002)	0.006 (0.007)	0.012 (0.013)
9	0.026 (0.007)	0.015 (0.021)	0.007 (0.005)	0.160 (0.029)	0.243 (0.061)	0.112 (0.058)	0.003 (0.001)	0.004 (0.006)	0.002 (0.002)
10	0.050 (0.034)	0.027 (0.041)	0.022 (0.041)	0.012 (0.011)	0.069 (0.034)	0.016 (0.008)	0.008 (0.006)	0.008 (0.011)	0.006 (0.010)
11	0.011 (0.002)	0.014 (0.008)	0.011 (0.007)	0.034 (0.007)	0.125 (0.065)	0.069 (0.005)	0.003 (0.0004)	0.008 (0.005)	0.007 (0.005)
12	0.005 (0.001)	0.001 (0.008)	0.017 (0.008)	0.011 (0.004)	0.039 (0.017)	0.022 (0.005)	0.001 (0.0001)	0.003 (0.002)	0.009 (0.004)

(continued)

Table 11.5 (continued)

	OUTUPC (PCSO/UPC)			INUPC (PCSI/UPC)			OUTGDP (PCSO/GSDPN)		
State	1990–99	2000–09	2010–15	1990–99	2000–09	2010–15	1990–99	2000–09	2010–15
13	0.009 (0.007)	0.013 (0.011)	0.024 (0.043)	0.077 (0.006)	0.073 (0.015)	0.060 (0.015)	0.002 (0.001)	0.005 (0.005)	0.008 (0.013)
14	–	0.006 (0.004)	0.010 (0.003)	–	0.160 (0.057)	0.068 (0.038)	–	0.001 (0.001)	0.003 (0.001)
15	0.048 (0.008)	0.212 (0.077)	0.123 (0.010)	0.009 (0.001)	0.015 (0.008)	0.015 (0.010)	0.020 (0.004)	0.165 (0.071)	0.132 (0.010)
16	0.019 (0.012)	0.005 (0.004)	0.003 (0.002)	0.021 (0.007)	0.028 (0.017)	0.041 (0.023)	0.001 (0.001)	0.0003 (0.0002)	0.0004 (0.0002)
17	0.057 (0.052)	0.016 (0.017)	0.040 (0.048)	0.130 (0.173)	0.249 (0.166)	0.114 (0.065)	0.003 (0.003)	0.003 (0.002)	0.007 (0.009)
18	0.013 (0.012)	0.030 (0.060)	0.007 (0.010)	0.150 (0.111)	0.139 (0.104)	0.078 (0.019)	0.0004 (0.0004)	0.003 (0.005)	0.002 (0.002)
19	0.010 (0.006)	0.007 (0.012)	0.001 (0.002)	0.155 (0.095)	0.110 (0.104)	0.145 (0.183)	0.0004 (0.0002)	0.0003 (0.0003)	0.0002 (0.0003)
20	0.004 (0.001)	0.004 (0.003)	0.009 (0.005)	0.037 (0.010)	0.114 (0.044)	0.068 (0.022)	0.0004 (0.0001)	0.001 (0.0007)	0.003 (0.001)
21	0.009 (0.003)	0.045 (0.038)	0.022 (0.031)	0.056 (0.011)	0.074 (0.041)	0.063 (0.068)	0.002 (0.0004)	0.018 (0.015)	0.013 (0.017)
22	0.021 (0.041)	0.011 (0.006)	0.004 (0.003)	0.079 (0.012)	0.112 (0.035)	0.065 (0.025)	0.002 (0.004)	0.003 (0.002)	0.002 (0.001)
23	0.065 (0.086)	0.037 (0.043)	0.005 (0.009)	0.025 (0.027)	0.135 (0.114)	0.343 (0.073)	0.004 (0.006)	0.008 (0.008)	0.001 (0.003)
24	0.021 (0.004)	0.043 (0.019)	0.117 (0.182)	0.017 (0.002)	0.066 (0.016)	0.042 (0.010)	0.007 (0.001)	0.024 (0.013)	0.079 (0.121)

(continued)

Table 11.5 (continued)

	OUTUPC (PCSO/UPC)			INUPC (PCSI/UPC)			OUTGDP (PCSO/GSDPN)		
State	1990–99	2000–09	2010–15	1990–99	2000–09	2010–15	1990–99	2000–09	2010–15
26	0.005 (0.005)	0.016 (0.033)	0.003 (0.004)	0.024 (0.014)	0.019 (0.012)	0.030 (0.036)	0.0004 (0.0005)	0.001 (0.002)	0.001 (0.001)
27	0.016 (0.026)	0.021 (0.016)	0.016 (0.012)	0.095 (0.008)	0.129 (0.029)	0.107 (0.054)	0.002 (0.003)	0.006 (0.005)	0.005 (0.004)
28	–	0.012 (0.006)	0.010 (0.007)	–	0.139 (0.036)	0.0692 (0.0401)	–	0.003 (0.001)	0.002 (0.002)
29	0.047 (0.015)	0.039 (0.017)	0.017 (0.012)	0.015 (0.004)	0.090 (0.024)	0.044 (0.005)	0.009 (0.003)	0.013 (0.007)	0.008 (0.006)
30	0.014 (0.011)	0.016 (0.018)	0.011 (0.014)	0.198 (0.143)	0.439 (0.184)	0.026 (0.029)	0.0006 (0.0004)	0.003 (0.004)	0.001 (0.002)
31	0.098 (0.025)	0.060 (0.033)	0.041 (0.029)	0.067 (0.026)	0.088 (0.053)	0.041 (0.008)	0.101 (0.022)	0.010 (0.051)	0.105 (0.061)
32	0.158 (0.010)	0.115 (0.038)	0.056 (0.043)	0.028 (0.021)	0.060 (0.024)	0.043 (0.005)	0.115 (0.004)	0.155 (0.027)	0.126 (0.089)
33	0.025 (0.015)	0.036 (0.027)	0.038 (0.035)	0.219 (0.058)	0.138 (0.059)	0.044 (0.009)	0.004 (0.003)	0.008 (0.006)	0.014 (0.014)
Average	**0.028**	**0.030**	**0.023**	**0.086**	**0.133**	**0.077**	**0.010**	**0.019**	**0.018**

	INGDP(PCSI/GSDPN)			UPCGDP(Credit/GDP)			
State	1990–99	2000–09	2010–15	1985–89	1990–99	2000–09	2010–15
1	0.005 (0.0005)	0.065 (0.042)	0.058 (0.031)	0.216 (0.016)	0.211 (0.010)	0.589 (0.300)	0.960 (0.319)
2	0.016 (0.008)	0.057 (0.052)	0.033 (0.037)	0.078 (0.029)	0.067 (0.023)	0.148 (0.079)	0.165 (0.036)

(continued)

Table 11.5 (continued)

	INGDP(PCSI/GSDPN)			UPCGDP(Credit/GDP)			
State	1990–99	2000–09	2010–15	1985–89	1990–99	2000–09	2010–15
3	0.013 (0.003)	0.039 (0.036)	0.013 (0.006)	0.107 (0.015)	0.098 (0.019)	0.174 (0.043)	0.251 (0.104)
4	0.008 (0.004)	0.032 (0.040)	0.014 (0.009)	0.081 (0.015)	0.148 (0.032)	0.288 (0.085)	0.239 (0.066)
5	–	0.016 (0.011)	0.013 (0.009)	–	0.170 (0.039)	0.226 (0.013)	0.226 (0.013)
6	0.012 (0.004)	0.036 (0.015)	0.018 (0.002)	0.343 (0.018)	0.247 (0.041)	0.285 (0.023)	4.584 (8.619)
7	0.019 (0.003)	0.073 (0.034)	0.044 (0.007)	0.196 (0.023)	0.194 (0.021)	0.321 (0.068)	0.412 (0.036)
8	0.0356 (0.003)	0.055 (0.009)	0.070 (0.015)	0.203 (0.022)	0.163 (0.015)	0.274 (0.072)	0.438 (0.015)
9	0.017 (0.003)	0.056 (0.015)	0.034 (0.014)	0.131 (0.010)	0.119 (0.016)	0.235 (0.061)	0.257 (0.015)
10	0.001 (0.001)	0.019 (0.009)	0.004 (0.002)	–	0.140 (0.034)	0.298 (0.074)	0.290 (0.045)
11	0.009 (0.002)	0.074 (0.054)	0.046 (0.004)	0.278 (0.020)	0.254 (0.019)	0.554 (0.166)	0.664 (0.013)
12	0.002 (0.0007)	0.014 (0.007)	0.011 (0.002)	0.236 (0.022)	0.208 (0.011)	0.345 (0.069)	0.487 (0.011)
13	0.014 (0.001)	0.025 (0.007)	0.0221 (0.005)	0.123 (0.016)	0.164 (0.024)	0.343 (0.089)	0.371 (0.070)
14	–	0.030 (0.013)	0.020 (0.012)	–	–	0.191 (0.046)	0.286 (0.018)

(continued)

Table 11.5 (continued)

	INGDP(PCSI/GSDPN)			UPCGDP(Credit/GDP)			
State	1990–99	2000–09	2010–15	1985–89	1990–99	2000–09	2010–15
15	0.004 (0.001)	0.012 (0.009)	0.016 (0.011)	0.351 (0.033)	0.382 (0.041)	0.769 (0.1984)	1.070 (0.023)
16	0.0011 (0.0004)	0.003 (0.003)	0.006 (0.003)	0.058 (0.011)	0.059 (0.006)	0.092 (0.041)	0.127 (0.007)
17	0.009 (0.013)	0.073 (0.096)	0.021 (0.012)	0.084 (0.018)	0.070 (0.030)	0.215 (0.137)	0.184 (0.008)
18	0.006 (0.004)	0.017 (0.008)	0.016 (0.003)	0.082 (0.031)	0.052 (0.012)	0.162 (0.071)	0.195 (0.008)
19	0.008 (0.006)	0.010 (0.014)	0.025 (0.038)	0.090 (0.010)	0.067 (0.024)	0.078 (0.047)	0.138 (0.034)
20	0.004 (0.001)	0.028 (0.013)	0.019 (0.007)	0.132 (0.022)	0.118 (0.0112)	0.240 (0.056)	0.282 (0.009)
21	0.013 (0.002)	0.030 (0.020)	0.038 (0.043)	0.230 (0.015)	0.211 (0.018)	0.3738 (0.091)	0.580 (0.030)
22	0.009 (0.001)	0.031 (0.017)	0.024 (0.010)	0.128 (0.009)	0.119 (0.009)	0.270 (0.086)	0.365 (0.014)
23	0.002 (0.002)	0.034 (0.032)	0.080 (0.038)	0.158 (0.025)	0.080 (0.021)	0.254 (0.127)	0.217 (0.060)
24	0.005 (0.001)	0.037 (0.013)	0.029 (0.008)	6.573 (14.08)	0.305 (0.019)	0.546 (0.118)	0.701 (0.028)
26	0.002 (0.001)	0.002 (0.002)	0.006 (0.007)	0.113 (0.0277)	0.097 (0.020)	0.104 (0.039)	0.168 (0.011)
27	0.012 (0.001)	0.033 (0.012)	0.036 (0.019)	0.120 (0.010)	0.132 (0.008)	0.249 (0.063)	0.335 (0.008)

(continued)

Table 11.5 (continued)

State	INGDP(PCSI/GSDPN)			UPCGDP(Credit/GDP)			
	1990–99	2000–09	2010–15	1985–89	1990–99	2000–09	2010–15
28	–	0.031 (0.012)	0.016 (0.009)	–	–	0.221 (0.030	0.226 (0.001)
29	0.003 (0.001)	0.030 (0.011)	0.020 (0.002)	0.197 (0.026)	0.215 (0.022)	0.330 (0.086)	0.443 (0.018)
30	0.012 (0.013)	0.086 (0.051)	0.005 (0.005)	0.047 (0.006)	0.050 (0.020)	0.185 (0.052)	0.163 (0.003)
31	0.067 (0.019)	0.148 (0.078)	0.083 (0.018)	–	1.109 (0.242)	1.794 (0.307)	2.128 (0.147)
32	0.020 (0.016)	0.092 (0.046)	0.091 (0.009)	0.540 (0.045)	0.711 (0.104)	1.441 (0.357)	2.110 (0.112)
33	0.040 (0.016)	0.027 (0.008)	0.016 (0.003)	0.190 (0.040)	0.205 (0.041)	0.212 (0.060)	0.355 (0.029)
Average	**0.013**	**0.041**	**0.0302**	**0.410**	**0.205**	**0.369**	**0.613**

Note Spill-over variables could not be calculated for the sub-period, 1985–89 as the required data for the same is not available

Table 11.6 Beta Convergence Tests

Beta convergence (1985–2018)			Beta convergence (1985–1990)		Beta convergence (1991–2000)		Beta convergence (2001–2010)		Beta convergence (2011–2018)	
Growth	OLS(1)	OLS(2)	Absolute convergence	Conditional convergence	Absolute convergence	Conditional convergence	Absolute convergence	Conditional convergence	Absolute convergence	Conditional convergence
Lnper	0.01245***	0.0055	−0.0080	−0.0697**	0.004496	−0.00441	0.0188345***	0.0006026	0.0040485	0.020704
capita(t−1)	(0.00266)	(0.0061)	(0.0113)	(0.000328)	(0.0073509)	(0.01461)	(0.0055366)	(0.0113853)	(0.0048746)	(0.0109141)
GOV		9.95e–09		5.70e–07		−4.07e–08		2.26e–08		1.85e–09
		(8.92e–09)		(6.35e–07)		(1.03e–07)		(2.72e–08)		(1.12e–08)
Infra		−3.15e–08		−3.88e–07		3.21e–08		−6.99e–08		−2.75e–08
		(3.42e–08)		(2.91e–07)		(9.42e–08)		(6.68e–08)		(4.48e–08)
Gerupper		0.000039		−0.00022		0.0003284		0.0000374		−0.0007707***
		(0.000149)		(0.0006819)		(0.0003087)		(0.0002495)		(0.0002657)
CDR		0.00013		0.0007098		−0.0000625		0.0001922		0.0000392
		(0.00011)		(0.0006798)		(0.0002947)		(0.0002236)		(0.0001619)
Brand		0.00024		0.0080983**		0.000376		0.0015436		−0.0009503
		(0.0006)		(0.0037146)		(0.0016539)		(0.0010392)		(0.0008583)
Constant	−0.08133*** (0.0273)	−0.01871 (0.0543)	0.1136964 (0.1096855)	0.6436918** (0.2927401)	−0.0129882 (0.0729844)	0.0491815 (0.1321195)	−0.1343909 (0.0572858)	0.0317866 (0.1047054)	0.0087876 (0.0531079)	−0.0869116 (0.1031634)
R^2	0.0249	0.0207	0.0039	0.1143	0.0014	0.0117	0.0429	0.0465	0.0033	0.0820

Note *** implies 1% level of significance** implies 5% leve lof significance* implies 10% level of significance. Values in parentheses denote standard error

(Table 11.1) is lagged GSDPR per capita. Column (2) in Table 11.6 reports absolute beta convergence and column (3) reports conditional convergence. Column 2 reveals that coefficient of lagged GSDPR is positive and significant and, therefore, we fail to reject the null hypothesis of divergence. It only indicates absolute divergence in terms of per capita GDP across Indian states. In column (3) of Table 11.6, we report the results of estimated conditional convergence. In this case also, we find the estimated coefficient of lagged GSDPR is found to be positive but statistically insignificant, even after incorporating financial development indicators such as branch density, credit-deposit ratio (CDR) and also few other indicators of development across states such as government expenditure, infrastructure as controls for conditional convergence test, which are heterogeneous across the states. We have also carried out convergence test of growth across sample states for different sub-periods. Subsequent columns of Table 11.6 present the beta-convergence test results for different sub-periods in our sample. Columns 4–5 depict the same for 1985–90 and observe evidence of conditional growth convergence as coefficient of lagged GSDPR is negative and significant in case of conditional convergence. For absolute convergence, however, coefficient of lagged GSDPR is negative but insignificant. During the sub-period 1991–2000, which corresponds to the liberalization period in Indian economy, our tests of beta convergence do not reveal significant coefficients of lagged GSDPR although we find desired signs of the coefficients for both absolute convergence as well as conditional beta convergence. We argue that during this period, several reform measures might have been instrumental in growth convergence across states. During 2001–2010, we find the evidence of absolute divergence as the coefficient of lagged GSDPR is positive and significant. However, during 2011–2018, we observe both coefficients of lagged initial GDP are positive but insignificant.

For sigma (σ) convergence, we alternatively consider standard deviation (SD) as well as coefficient of variation (CV) as the dependent variable while the independent variables are linear time trend and constant (see Table 11.7). For all the states taken together, we calculate SD and regress it on time to check whether it falls over time. Our findings reveal that the coefficient of SD is positive but insignificant which is indicative of σ-divergence for all the states taken together. However, with CV as the dependent variable, coefficient of time is negative and significant which reveals that CV declines over time and it is significant.

Table 11.7 Sigma convergence (Robustness Test) 1985–2018

SD/CV	OLS (SD as dependent variable)	OLS (CV as dependent variable)
Time	10.14872 (5.859753)	−0.0884875** (0.0398162)
constant	−118.3494 (117.5607)	3.226907*** (0.7758197)
R^2	0.0857	0.1374

Note values in parentheses denote Standard error. SD and CV denote standard deviation and coefficient of variation respectively

11.6.3 Club Convergence Tests: Growth Variables

B convergence measures are claimed to have limitations as these represent an 'average' measures. However, in the presence of heterogeneity in a state, these measures may not capture individual heterogeneity. Therefore, these measures may not address the possibility of some specific clusters (Hembram & Halder, 2019). This section presents our findings of club convergence of real per capita GSDP and various financial development indicators. First, we test whether real per capita GSDP converges or diverges across states in our sample. In the next step, we test the presence of converging subgroups. Here, we test the null hypothesis (H0) of convergence against the alternative hypothesis (H1) of absence of convergence. In the first stage, we test the null of convergence for the overall sample, H0: $\delta i=\delta$ and $\alpha \geq 0$, against the alternative of no convergence, H1: $\delta i \neq \delta$ for all i, or $\alpha < 0$. In Table 11.8, the first row measures the full convergence of per capita SGDP which includes the full sample. Values in column 2 indicate the estimated t statistics based on log t regression described by Eq. (11.7). Finding reveals that convergence test rejects the null hypothesis of full convergence across Indian states as the estimated log t-statistic is less than -1.65 for per capita income. We fail to reject the null of convergence as long as estimated t-statistic is larger than -1.65 at 5% level of significance.[3] Values in bold refer to the non-rejection of this hypothesis.

At the aggregate level, the statistic $t_b = -40.69$ is below the critical value (i.e. t_b $-1{:}65$) at 5% level of significance and thus the null of full convergence is rejected. It indicates significant divergence in per capita income among states in our sample over the study period. This finding of divergence of per capita incomes is also consistent with the findings of the existing literature. This does not, however, preclude the possibility of convergence clubs. Following Phillips and Sul (2007), we investigate the formation of club convergence in terms of real GDP per capita (GSDPR) across states. Rows 3–6 confirm the formation of four convergence clubs of Indian states (Table 11.8). Club 1 consists of eight states. The log t-statistic of this subgroup is 4.46, which is well above the critical value. Hence, we accept the null of convergence within this cluster. The second club that appears in our club convergence test includes six states with the estimated log t-statistic equal to -0.892 (>-1.65), which implies the acceptance of the null of convergence within this cluster. Club 3 consists of six states in our sample where the value of the log t statistic is equal to 10.19 which indicate the null hypothesis of convergence within this cluster of states, is accepted. Similarly, we observe the formation of club 4 which consists of four states in our sample in terms of real GDP per capita. Row 7 of Table 11.8 shows the evidence of a non-convergent group of states consisting of Goa and Manipur.

We also observe from Table 11.8 that club 1 consists of both high income states (Maharashtra, Gujarat, Delhi Haryana) as well as few low income states (Tripura, Sikkim, Pudecherry, Andaman & Nicobar Islands). Club 2 consists of states which have similar growth rates except Nagaland. Club 3 consists of few low income states (Meghalaya, Arunachal Pradesh, Odisha, Rajasthan) and middle income states (West

[3] Here, convergence is checked by one-sided t test.

Table 11.8 Club convergence: per capita GSDP (whole sample)

States	t-statistic	beta coefficient
Full Sample	−40.69[a]	−0.964
Club 1: Andaman & Nicobar Islands, Delhi, Haryana, Gujarat, Maharashtra, Pondicherry, Sikkim, Tripura	**4.46**	0.129
Club 2: Himachal Pradesh, Karnataka, Kerala, Nagaland, Punjab, Tamil Nadu	**−0.892**	−0.019
Club 3: AndhraPradesh, ArunachalPradesh, Meghalaya, Odisha, Rajasthan, West Bengal	**10.19**	1.116
Club 4: Assam, Bihar, Madhya Pradesh, UP	**−1.323**	−0.074
Non-Convergent Group: Goa, Manipur	−262.959	−1.330

[a]The value of t-statistic is less the critical value of −1.65 at 5% level of significance and hence, we reject the null hypothesis of convergence

Bengal and Andhra Pradesh). Club 4 consists of mostly low income states (Assam, Bihar, Madhya Pradesh and Uttar Pradesh). We argue that evidence of different clubs in terms of SGDP per capita may be attributed largely to the regional divergence in financial development as well as infrastructure development across sample states.

11.6.4 Club Convergence (Per Capita GSDPR): Different Sub-Periods

We have bifurcated the full sample period, 1985–2018 into four sub-periods and re-run the club convergence test for each of the different sub-period in order to investigate how the compositions of various clubs formed change over the sub-periods (Tables 11.9–11.12). In particular, we compare the pre and post reform periods and identify the transitions of various states in formation of clubs, according to PS methodology (2007). The sub-period 1985–1990 marks the pre-reform period, as we have defined. Observe, from Table 11.9 that in this sub-period, state such as Andaman & Nicobar Islands did not belong to any club in terms of GSDP per capita. However, in the post reform period 1991–2000, we observe that Andaman & Nicobar Islands forms a club along with Delhi and Puducherry in club 1 (See Table 11.10). It is also evident from Tables 11.9 and 11.10 that Goa appears to be a member of Club 1 in Table 11.9, which marks the period before reforms. However, in post reform period, Goa becomes a part of the non-convergent group. **Secondly**, we observe that certain states belong to certain clusters in both the pre and post reform periods. For example, Himachal Pradesh and Gujarat belong to the same clubs, i.e. Club 3 and Club 2 during the two sub-periods respectively (see Tables 11.9 and 11.10). Similarly, Haryana and Maharashtra belong to the same clubs in both the periods (Tables 11.9 and 11.10). Andhra Pradesh and Meghalaya also belong to the same group in both the periods. **Thirdly**, comparing Tables 11.9 and 11.10, we observe that so-called highly developed states of Maharashtra, Gujarat, Tamil Nadu and Karnataka exhibit their presence in both the sub-periods. However, there is greater tendency of convergence, observed among these states in the post liberalization period. It appears that the effect of economic liberalization on growth across states which was less observed in early 1990s, appeared to be prominent later in the decade. Ghosh et al. (2013) also observed that the states that implemented reforms in various market segments were found to have performed better than other states. Kochhar et al. (2006) observed that the states with weaker institutions and poorer infrastructure experienced lower income and industrial growth. While AP, Gujarat, Karnataka, Maharashtra and Tamil Nadu are classified as the most reform-oriented states, and Haryana, Orissa, and WB as the intermediate reformers, Assam, Bihar, Kerala, MP, Punjab, Rajasthan and UP are considered as the slowest reformers (Bajpai & Sachs, 1996; Sachs et al., 2002).

We have also investigated the formation of convergence clubs in terms of GSDP per capita for the subsequent sub-periods. In Tables 11.11 and 11.12, we present the club convergence results for the sub-periods 2001–2010 and 2011–2018, respectively. We observe that although poorer states such as of Bihar, appears to be a member state in club 4 (see Table 11.8) along with few relatively less developed states for the aggregate sample, it does not form part of any convergence club in terms of real GSDP per capita in different sub-periods and appear to be the members of non-convergent group of states, along with few other relatively less developed states such as Madhya Pradesh, UP and few states in north- eastern region. Interestingly, these poorer states did not even exhibit sustained development since the introduction of liberalization measures in Indian economy initiated in early 1990s. In contrast, while smaller states like Manipur, which belonged to the non-convergent group in the sub-period of 1991–2000, joins the club 6 with Assam and Andhra Pradesh, in subsequent periods of 2000–2010 and 2011–2018 (Tables 11.11 and 11.12).

Table 11.9 Club Convergence: Per Capita GSDPR (1985–1990)

States	t-statistic	beta coefficient
Full Sample	−25.82[a]	−1.3412
Club 1: Delhi, Goa	**3.226**	2.510
Club 2: Haryana, Maharashtra, Puducherry, Punjab	**0.216**	0.044
Club 3: Gujarat, Himachal Pradesh, Nagaland	**8.415**	1.322
Club 4: Kerala, TamilNadu	**2.276**	10.172
Club 5: Arunachal Pradesh, Assam, Karnataka, Meghalaya, Rajasthan, Sikkim	**1.396**	0.105
Club 6: Manipur, Odisha, Tripura, West Bengal	**0.904**	0.177
Club 7: Andhra Pradesh, MP	**8.522**	4.502
Non-Convergent Group: Andaman & Nicobar Island, Bihar, UP	−21.333	−1.328

[a]The value of t-statistic is less the critical value of −1.65 at 5% level of significance and hence, we reject the null hypothesis of convergence

Table 11.10 Club convergence: per capita GSDPR (1991–2000)

States	t-statistic	β coefficient
Full Sample	−16.1029[a]	−1.2414
Club 1: Andaman & Nicobar Island, Delhi, Puducherry	**5.203**	0.439
Club 2: Gujarat, Haryana, Himachal Pradesh, Karnataka, Kerala, Maharashtra, Punjab, Tamil Nadu	**−1.553**	−0.160
Club 3: Arunachal Pradesh, Meghalaya, Nagaland, Rajasthan, Sikkim, Tripura, West Bengal	**3.698**	0.574
Club 4: Andhra Pradesh, Assam, MP, Odisha, UP	**−0.745**	−0.083
Non-Convergent Group: Bihar, Goa, Manipur	−49.194	−1.319

[a]The value of t-statistic is less the critical value of −1.65 at 5% level of significance and hence, we reject the null hypothesis of convergence

Table 11.11 Club convergence: per capita GSDPR (2000–2010)

States	t-statistic	β coefficient
Full Sample	−28.5388[a]	−1.2570
Club 1: Andaman & Nicobar Island, Gujarat, Haryana, Maharashtra, Puducherry, Sikkim	**−0.119**	−0.010
Club 2: Himachal Pradesh, Kerala, Punjab, Tamil Nadu	**1.247**	0.503
Club 3: Karnataka, Nagaland	**2.376**	4.593
Club 4: Arunachal Pradesh, Tripura	**2.909**	0.915
Club 5: Meghalaya, Odisha, Rajasthan, West Bengal	**1.865**	0.262
Club 6: Andhra Pradesh, Assam, Manipur	**2.856**	0.351
Non-Convergent Group: Bihar, Delhi, Goa, MP, UP	−36.351	−1.189

[a]The value of t-statistic is less the critical value of −1.65 at 5% level of significance and hence, we reject the null hypothesis of convergence

11.6.5 Club Convergence Tests: Measures of Financial Development

In this section, we present our findings of clustering of states, in terms of various alternative indicators of financial development. We hardly observe any study in Indian context which investigates the club convergence of states in terms of various financial development indicators. As a first step to that attempt, we carry out club convergence test for eight alternative state level financial development indicators. These include branch density per lakh population (BRAND), ratio of agricultural credit to agricultural output (AGLCRQN), ratio of industrial credit to industry output (INDCRQN), services sector credit to services output (SERCRQN), agricultural credit to total

Table 11.12 Club convergence per capita GSDPR (2011–2018)

States	t-statistic	β coefficient
Full Sample	−25.7826[a]	−1.3229
Club 1: Andaman & Nicobar Island, Delhi	**−1.347**	−0.152
Club 2: Gujarat Haryana, Puducherry, Sikkim	**5.149**	0.349
Club 3: Karnataka, Kerala, Tamil Nadu, Tripura	**1.124**	0.158
Club 4: Arunachal Pradesh, Odisha	**2.344**	0.418
Club 5: AndhraPradesh,Rajasthan,WestBengal	**2.899**	0.504
Club 6: Assam, MP, Manipur, Meghalaya, UP	**−0.041**	−0.004
Non−Convergent Group: Bihar, Goa, Himachal Pradesh, Maharashtra, Nagaland, Punjab	−34.980	−1.183

[a]The value of t-statistic is less the critical value of −1.65 at 5% level of significance and hence, we reject the null hypothesis of convergence

credit (AGLCRUPC), ratio of industrial credit to total credit (INDCRUPC), ratio of consumer credit to total credit (CONCRUPC) and ratio of service sector credit to total credit (SERCRUPC). Some of these indicators are aggregate by construction such branch density and the rest are the indicators of sectoral credit.

Apart from above indicators of financial intermediation across Indian states, we also carry out club convergence test of few additional variables which mainly capture the magnitudes of inflow and outflow of credit from one state to another. In fact, credit disbursed by a bank branch located in one state may, well be, utilized in another state. In other words, there may be inflow or outflow of credit from one state to another (Das & Maiti, 1998). For that purpose, we define four new credit variables expressed as proportions of total credit utilized and total nominal GDP of a state: INUPC, OUTUPC, INGDP and OUTGDP (see section 6.1 for details of definition). INUPC and OUTUPC indicate inward and outward credit spillover/migration expressed as a proportion of total credit utilized in a state respectively. INGDP and OUTGDP, alternatively define inward and outward credit spillover/migration expressed as a proportion of state GDP respectively (See appendix for definitions). We carry out the club convergence tests of all these four alternative credit spillover/migration variables to test whether states also form clustering in terms of migration of credit from one state to another. We first present the club convergence test results for few select aggregate indicators of financial development. Subsequently, we present club convergence results for sectoral indicators of financial development and club convergence results for the credit spillover/migration variables as explained above.

11.6.5.1 Club Convergence: Aggregate Variables

In Table 11.13, we present our findings of the convergence pattern of branch density (BRAND) across states. We reject the null hypothesis of full convergence for BRAND as the estimated value of log t test is less than −1.65. However, for branch density,

Table 11.13 Club convergence: branch density

States	t-statistic	β coefficient
Full Sample	−32.88[a]	−1.2580
Club 1: Andaman Nicobar, Delhi, Haryana, Himachal Pradesh, Karnataka, Kerala, Puducherry, Punjab, Sikkim	**6.526**	0.420
Club 2: Andhra Pradesh, Arunachal Pradesh, Gujarat, Maharashtra, Meghalaya, Nagaland, Odisha, Rajasthan, Tripura	**0.017**	0.002
Club 3: Assam, Madhya Pradesh, Manipur	**4.046**	0.636
Non-Convergent Group: Bihar, Goa, Tamil Nadu, UP	−113.045	−1.218

[a] The value of t-statistic is less the critical value of −1.65 at 5% level of significance and hence, we reject the null hypothesis of convergence

we observe the formation of 3 clubs and one non-convergent club. Under the non-convergent club, we have Bihar, Goa, Tamil Nadu and Uttar Pradesh. We have few important observations from Table 11.13 about the clustering of states in terms of branch density. While Club 1 and club 2 comprise of a mix of both financially more developed states as well as less developed states, club 3 consists of only financially less developed states. The central objective of state-led branch expansion program in India since bank nationalization in 1969 was to accelerate the flow of formal credit and also saving opportunities to the rural poor, towards achieving the broader objectives of social banking. However, banks mostly favoured opening branches in developed regions, while state-led bank branch expansion programs tend to target poorer regions, leading to unambiguous effect on broader social objective of poverty alleviation (Burgess & Pande, 1995). Prior to the reforms initiated in 1990s, banks were highly regulated in terms of branch licencing policy and entry in financial system. These restrictions were thought to adversely affect the efficiency of financial intermediation across states. However, with reforms initiated in 1991, following recommendations of the Narsimham Committee (GOI, 1991, 1998), domestic private banks, including foreign banks were allowed to operate along with public sector banks leading to an expansion of branch network across states. Of late, government laid more emphasis on the bank-based transfer of various subsidies and proceeds of various welfare schemes to the intended beneficiaries (GOI, 2016). Consequently, the so- called poorer states also received considerable expansion of branches during the last couple of decades. Our findings of formation of clubs support these observations where richer states are found to form clubs along with less developed states.

11.6.5.2 Club Convergence: Sectoral Variables

Here, we present the club convergence results for four select sectoral credit variables. Table 11.14 presents the pattern of club convergence of agricultural credit as a proportion to agricultural GSDP (AGLCRQN). We reject the null hypothesis of full convergence in Table 11.14 as the estimated log t test is less than −1.65. However, we observe the formation of four clubs for this variable. In club 1, club 2, club 3, club 4, there are clustering of three states, 6 states, 7 states, and 7 states, respectively. We also observe the formation of a divergent group consisting of Nagaland and Sikkim which do not converge with any of the states.

Table 11.15 reports the convergence pattern of states in terms of Industrial Credit to Industrial GSDPN (INDCRQN). We reject the null hypothesis of full convergence. However, we observe the formation of only two clubs and the states belonging to each of these clubs are mostly homogenous. Club 1 consists of 15 states, while the club 2 consists of 11 states. Club1 consists of a mix of both highly developed states as well as moderately developed states such as West Bengal. However, club 1 consists of all the agriculturally developed states such as Punjab, Uttar Pradesh, Haryana, West Bengal and Andhra Pradesh. On the other hand, club 2 consists of mostly less developed states having less industrial development. In fact, higher level of industrial activities in a state seems to attract greater credit flow. However, it also brings in the possibility of further polarization of states. Therefore, effective government policy interventions might address this problem and thereby mitigate the possibility of further inequality. These policies may include creating favourable environment for industrial expansion in the form of building strong infrastructure, favourable investment climate in states, easing the rules and regulations related to the industrial sector and expediting the decision making process (Herwadkar & Ghosh, 2015).

Table 11.16 presents our finding of club convergence results for services sector credit expressed as a proportion of services output (SERCRQN). Null hypothesis of full convergence is rejected as the value of log t test is less than −1.65. However, we find the formation of four clubs for services sector credit as a proportion of services GDP. Club1 consists of Maharashtra and Andhra Pradesh, considered to be the states with higher growth of services sector given that these states are financially more developed compared to others states. Club 2 and club 3 consist of 5 and 13 states

Table 11.14 Club convergence: agricultural credit as a proportion to agricultural GSDP

States	t−statistic	β coefficient
Full Sample	−2.623[a]	0.5458
Club 1: Delhi, Puducherry, Tripura	**0.467**	0.058
Club 2: Andhra Pradesh, Himachal Pradesh, Karnataka, Kerala, Punjab, Tamil Nadu	**−0.577**	−0.045
Club 3: Assam, Bihar, Haryana, Maharashtra, Odisha, Rajasthan, UP	**4.479**	0.561
Club4: Andaman Nicobar Island, Goa, Gujarat, MP, Manipur, Meghalaya, West Bengal	**1.416**	0.198
Non-Convergent Group: Nagaland, Sikkim	**−1.140**	−0.907

[a] The value of t-statistic is less the critical value of −1.65 at 5% level of significance and hence, we reject the null hypothesis of convergence

Table 11.15 Club convergence: industrial credit as a proportion to industrial GSDP

States	t-statistic	β coefficient
Full Sample	−3.7544[a]	−0.6832
Club 1: Andhra Pradesh, Delhi, Gujarat, Haryana, Karnataka, Madhya Pradesh, Maharashtra, Meghalaya, Odisha, Punjab, Rajasthan, Tamil Nadu, Tripura, UP, West Bengal	**0.587**	0.029
Club 2: Andaman & Nicobar Island, Arunachal Pradesh, Assam, Bihar, Goa, Himachal Pradesh, Kerala, Manipur, Nagaland, Puducherry, Sikkim	**−0.236**	−0.046

[a]The value of t-statistic is less the critical value of −1.65 at 5% level of significance and hence, we reject the null hypothesis of convergence

respectively, which are mix of both more developed as well as less developed states. Club 4 consists of 5 less developed states including three north-eastern states, Bihar and Andaman and Nicobar Islands. We also find the formation of a non-convergent group for this variable. Since services sector output consists of professional and other services, transport operators, trade and finance, output generated out of these activities are assumed to be comparatively more prevalent in financially developed states compared to those in less developed states. Accordingly, credit extended to support these activities is also likely to be higher in those developed states. This argument justifies the formation of convergence clubs in this case.

Tables 11.17–11.20 present the club convergence results of sectoral credit to total credit. Table 11.17 shows that the null of full convergence is rejected for agricultural credit to total credit utilized. Four convergence clubs are formed while we consider the share of agricultural credit in total credit. Club 1 consists of two under developed states Bihar, Tripura. In club 2, we have 13 states and some of the states (such as Punjab, Uttar Pradesh, Andhra Pradesh) in this club are predominantly agriculturally

Table 11.16 Club convergence: services credit as a proportion to services sector GSDP

States	t-statistic	β coefficient
Full Sample	−7.3711[a]	−1.2989
Club 1: Andhra Pradesh, Maharashtra	**0.641**	0.058
Club 2: Arunachal Pradesh, Haryana, Karnataka, Sikkim, Tamil Nadu	**15.530**	0.842
Club 3: Assam, Goa, Gujarat, Himachal Pradesh, Kerala, Madhya Pradesh, Mizoram, Odisha, Puducherry, Punjab, Rajasthan, UP, West Bengal	**0.005**	0.000
Club 4: Andaman & Nicobar Is, Bihar, Meghalaya, Nagaland, Tripura	**1.337**	0.147
Non-Convergent group: Delhi, Manipur	−25.937	−1.052

[a]The value of t-statistic is less the critical value of −1.65 at 5% level of significance and hence, we reject the null hypothesis of convergence

developed states which have greater access to agricultural credit as compared to other states.

In Table 11.18, we present the club convergence results for industrial credit to total credit. We reject the null hypothesis of full convergence at 1% level of significance. However, 6 clubs are formed for this indicator of industrial credit. Observe, less developed states like Bihar, Manipur form the non-convergent group, as they diverge from all other states, due to their least access to industrial credit as a proportion to total credit utilized. States such as Karnataka, Maharashtra and Tamil Nadu belong to the same club given that access to industrial credit in these states is quite similar and higher than many other states in the sample. Clubs 5 and 6 consist of those states having lesser share of industrial credit.

Table 11.17 Club convergence: agricultural credit as a proportion to total credit

States	t-statistic	β coefficient
Full Sample	−2.9601[a]	−2.1294
Club 1: Bihar, Tripura	**−0.288**	−0.475
Club 2: Andhra Pradesh, Assam, Haryana, Himachal Pradesh, Kerala, MP, Manipur, Odisha, Puducherry, Punjab, Rajasthan, Tamil Nadu, Uttar Pradesh	**1.381**	0.077
Club 3: Karnataka, Meghalaya, West Bengal	**5.451**	0.532
Club 4: Gujarat, Maharashtra, Nagaland	**3.071**	0.089
Club 5: Andaman & NicobarIs, Arunachal Pradesh, Delhi, Goa, Sikkim	**3.597**	0.358

[a]The value of t-statistic is less the critical value of −1.65 at 5% level of significance and hence, we reject the null hypothesis of convergence

Table 11.18 Club convergence: industrial credit as a proportion to total credit

States	t-statistic	β coefficient
Full sample	−4.8137[a]	−2.3963
Club 1: Delhi, Sikkim, Tripura	**0.253**	0.079
Club 2: Gujarat, WestBengal	**0.845**	0.265
Club 3: Goa, Haryana, HP, Karnataka, Maharashtra, Odisha, Punjab, Tamil Nadu, UP	**−1.059**	−0.169
Club 4: Andhra Pradesh, Rajasthan	**0.921**	1.606
Club 5: Andaman & Nicobar Island, Arunachal Pradesh, Assam, Kerala, Nagaland, Puducherry	**1.869**	0.354
Club 6: MP, Meghalaya	**−0.474**	−0.900
Non-Convergent Club: Bihar, Manipur	−8.268	−3.514

[a]The value of t-statistic is less the critical value of −1.65 at 5% level of significance and hence, we reject the null hypothesis of convergence

In Table 11.19 we report the club convergence results of consumer (household) credit as a share of total credit utilized. We reject the null hypothesis of full convergence as the log t-statistic is −13.336 < −1.65 at 5% level of significance. However, we observe the formation of four clubs for consumer credit. Notably, the member states of club 3 comprise of a combination of developed states and few less developed states. Other clubs formed mostly consist of less developed states. Since consumer credit consists of credit extended to housing, consumer durables, education vehicles etc., financially more developed states are likely to account for larger share of consumer credit compared to less developed states.

In Table 11.20, we present our findings of club convergence result for services sector credit as a share of total credit. For service sector credit, we carry out the estimation for the period of 1985–2015. We reject the null hypothesis of full convergence for SERCRTUPC and we observe the formation of only two convergence clubs. Table 11.20 depicts that there is almost convergence for this variable because majority of the states (23) are the member of Club 1 except Manipur, Nagaland and Rajasthan. Until the mid-1990s, expansion of services sector credit across Indian states was negligible. However, with the introduction of financial liberalization, since

Table 11.19 Club convergence: household credit as a proportion to total credit

States	t-statistic	β coefficient
Full Sample	−13.3306[a]	−1.6594
Club 1: Andaman & Nicobar Island, Arunachal Pradesh, Manipur, Meghalaya, Nagaland, Sikkim	**0.833**	0.184
Club 2: Assam, Goa, Kerala, Puducherry, Tripura	**4.004**	1.379
Club 3: Andhra Pradesh, Bihar, Gujarat, Haryana, HP, Karnataka, MP, Odisha, Rajasthan, Tamil Nadu, UP	**−1.409**	−0.100
Club 4: Maharashtra, Punjab, West Bengal	**9.660**	1.804

[a]The value of t-statistic is less the critical value of −1.65 at 5% level of significance and hence, we reject the null hypothesis of convergence

Table 11.20 Club convergence: services sector credit as a proportion to total credit

States	t-statistic	β coefficient
Full Sample	−2.2466[a]	−0.4260
Club 1: Andaman & Nicobar Islands, Andhra Pradesh, Arunachal Pradesh, Assam, Bihar, Delhi, Goa, Gujarat, Haryana, HP, Karnataka, Kerala, MP, Maharashtra Meghalaya, Mizoram, Odisha, Puducherry, Punjab, Tamil Nadu, Tripura, UP West Bengal	**1.288**	0.048
Club 2: Manipur, Nagaland, Rajasthan	**8.820**	4.364

[a]The value of t-statistic is less the critical value of −1.65 at 5% level of significance and hence, we reject the null hypothesis of convergence

Table 11.21 Club convergence: outward migration of credit as a proportion of GSDP

States	t-statistic	β coefficient
Full Sample	−3.6269[a]	−1.4593
Club 1: Maharashtra, TamilNadu	**5.261**	0.617
Club 2: Andaman & Nicobar Island, Andhra Pradesh Arunachal Pradesh, Assam, Bihar, Goa, Gujarat, Haryana, Himachal Pradesh, Karnataka, Kerala, MP, Manipur, Meghalaya Mizoram, Nagaland, Odisha, Puducherry, Punjab, Rajasthan, UP, West Bengal	**0.548**	0.092
Non-Convergent Group: Delhi, Sikkim, Tripura	−128.893	−0.983

[a] The value of t-statistic is less the critical value of −1.65 at 5% level of significance and hence, we reject the null hypothesis of convergence

the mid-1990s, services sector credit significantly increased and it gained momentum in post-2000 period, because of a sharp rise in credit demand from households, education, communication, medical and health services. It happened in most of the states in our sample and perhaps, it justifies the formation of a larger convergence club consisting of most of the Indian states.

11.6.5.3 Club Convergence: Migration of Credit

In Tables 11.21–11.24, we report the club convergence results of four alternative indicators of credit spillover/migration in order to assess the spatial divergence of distribution of credit across Indian states.[4] As we have discussed, there is the possibility that credit sanctioned in one state, may well be utilized in a different state for various factors such as stages of development in a state, infrastructural facilities, investment climate and general governance. As the financing of investment involves transaction cost, borrowers generally prefer to have finance made available at the place of utilization. Therefore, the extent of migration of credit from it's place of sanction to it's place of utilization is likely to diminish with the improvement in financial infrastructure and investment climate across states. There are very few studies which previously looked into the issues of credit migration across Indian states. Existing evidence is, however, mixed. Das and Maiti (1998) found no significant evidence of credit migration. On the otherhand, Tyagarajan and Saoji (1977) observed that credit migration was largely restricted to four major metropolitan cities. Chatterjee et al. (1997) observed uniformity in-migration of credit in the major states during 1974 and 1994.

Tables 11.21 reports the club convergence results of OUTGDP which is defined as a measure of credit sanctioned in the ith state but utilized in the jth state as a

[4] Findings reported in Tables in this section are based on available data for the period 1995–96 to 2014–15.

proportion of GSDPN. We reject the null hypothesis of convergence as estimated value of log t-statistic, −3.6269 < −1.65. However, two clubs are formed, along with one non-convergent club for this measure of credit migration variable. Club 1 comprises of two developed states of Maharashtra and Tamil Nadu. This observation reveals that outflow of credit commonly happens in case of few financially developed states. On the otherhand, 22 other states in our sample belong to club 2, in case of which outflow of credit are also found to occur and this convergent cluster comprises of both developed as well as less developed states.

Table 11.22 reports the findings of INGDP, a measure of credit sanctioned in the jth state but utilized in the ith state, expressed as a proportion of GSDPN. Null hypothesis is rejected for INGDP as the value of log t test is less than −1.65. Here, we observe the formation of 3 clubs. Club1 comprises of two states of Gujarat and Haryana. Club 2 comprises of 9 states and club 3 consists of 15 sample states in terms of INGDP. Table 11.22 reveals that in-migration of credit takes place in almost all the states. Comparing Tables 11.21 and 11.22, we observe that in case of out-migration of credit, there is greater tendency towards convergence among states compared to that in case of in-migration of credit.

Tables 11.23–11.24 present club convergence results for the remaining two alternative indicators of migration of credit, expressed as a proportion of total credit: INUPC (credit sanctioned in j^{th} state but utilized in ith state, where i = home state, j = non home state) and OUTUPC (credit sanctioned in ith state but utilized in jth state). Table 11.23 presents the results of Club Convergence of INUPC. We find that apart from Haryana and Tamil Nadu which form part of club 1, all the remaining states converge in Club 2, so there is a tendency of full convergence in case of INUPC. Table 11.24 presents the club convergence result of OUTUPC. We find the rejection of null hypothesis of full convergence for OUTUPC. However, we observe the formation of two clubs. Club 1 consists of Haryana, Maharashtra, Manipur and Tripura. The remaining states in our sample form the club2. The null hypothesis of full convergence is rejected as the value of log t (−2.4807) is less than −1.96.

Table 11.22 Club convergence: inward migration of credit as a proportion of GSDP

States	t-statistic	β coefficient
Full Sample	−3.0254[a]	−3.0110
Club 1: Gujarat, Haryana	**−1.296**	−2.744
Club 2: Andhra Pradesh, Goa, Karnataka, Punjab, Rajasthan, Sikkim, Tamil Nadu, UP, West Bengal	**0.743**	0.132
Club 3: Andaman & Nicobar Island, Arunachal Pradesh, Assam, Bihar, Himachal Pradesh, Kerala, MP, Maharashtra, Manipur, Meghalaya, Mizoram, Nagaland, Odisha, Puducherry, Tripura	**3.251**	0.469

[a]The value of t-statistic is less the critical value of −1.65 at 5% level of significance and hence, we reject the null hypothesis of convergence

Table 11.23 Club convergence: inward migration of credit as a proportion of total credit

States	t-statistic	β coefficient
Full Sample	−1.9614[a]	−0.5514
Club 1: Haryana, TamilNadu	**−1.286**	−2.687
Club 2: Andaman & Nicobar Island, Andhra Pradesh Arunachal Pradesh Assam, Bihar, Delhi, Goa, Gujarat, Himachal Pradesh, Karnataka, Kerala, MP, Maharashtra, Manipur Meghalaya, Mizoram, Nagaland, Odisha, Puducherry, Punjab, Rajasthan, Sikkim, Tripura, UP, West Bengal	**1.692**	0.274

[a]The value of t-statistic is less the critical value of −1.65 at 5% level of significance and hence, we reject the null hypothesis of convergence

Table 11.24 Club convergence: outward migration of credit as a proportion of total credit

States	t-statistic	β coefficient
Full Sample	−2.4807[a]	−1.3252
Club 1: Haryana, Maharashtra, Manipur, Tripura	**−0.643**	−0.033
Club 2: Andaman & Nicobar Island, Andhra Pradesh, Arunachal Pradesh, Assam, Bihar, Delhi, Goa, Gujarat, Himachal Pradesh, Karnataka, Kerala, MP, Meghalaya, Mizoram, Nagaland, Odisha, Puducherry, Punjab, Rajasthan, Sikkim, UP, West Bengal	**0.868**	0.089

[a]The value of t-statistic is less the critical value of −1.65 at 5% level of significance and hence, we reject the null hypothesis of convergence

Table 11.24 reveals that apart from few states, all the remaining states tend to converge and form a single club in terms of OUTUPC.

11.7 Concluding Remarks

In this paper, we revisit the issues of convergence in the context of economic growth and financial development across Indian states, given considerable inter-state variation across all states. We first test whether Indian states converge in terms of per capita income, using the standard measures of beta convergence and sigma convergence. However, unlike the large body of existing literature on the issues of convergence in Indian context, we have scrutinized the possibility of club convergence among Indian states, even if the states diverge in terms of economic growth, in general. Phillips and Sul (2007) methodology employed in this paper allows us to identify regional club convergence. We have used state level real per capita gross domestic product for a sample of 32 states during the period 1985–86 to 2018–19. For examining club convergence, along with growth indicator we also consider several alternative indicators of financial development across Indian states, given the fact that Indian financial market has undergone several reforms during the last three decades. It is also relevant in view of the fact that in a bank-based financial system such as India, availability of bank credit, in particular, plays a pivotal role in facilitating economic growth. Our findings reveal that in general, Indian states diverge in terms of income as well as alternative indicators of financial development. However, these do not preclude the possibility of formation of convergence clubs (clustering of states). Our findings of club convergence, in general, show that we did not find evidence of convergence for the whole sample, which implies that the selected sample of states is not converging to a single steady state, however, find the existence of club convergence. The result of estimating the convergence club endogenously identified several clubs for growth and indicators of financial development in our sample states. We observe that in most of the cases, developed states such as Maharashtra, Gujarat, Karnataka form the convergence clubs in terms of both growth indicators as well as various indicators of financial development. However, interestingly, many of the less developed states as Bihar, Madhya Pradesh also form convergence clubs along with so-called developed states, in certain cases. Perhaps, following the introduction of various liberalizations measures, many of the so-called less developed states during the last three decades have been able to manage better infrastructural development, expansion of banking activities through greater branch network and financial inclusion, which in turn, helped those states to 'catch-up' to the developed states. North-eastern states which are comparatively less developed are found to form clubs in several cases of growth and financial development indicators. We find evidence of the formation of convergence clubs in terms of various indicators of inflow as well as outflow of credit.

Our findings on state level convergence of growth and financial development offer important implications from policy perspectives, for achieving regional balance in growth and financial development. The observed divergence in state level per capita income and the formation of different convergence clubs are attributable to varying steady-state levels of per capita income across different states. In particular, the divergence in per capita income across states occurs perhaps due to the varying levels of physical, social and economic infrastructure, varying investments in economic and social sectors, policy reforms executed at state level etc. Previous studies on this issue in the context of Indian states also make similar predictions (for example, see Kalra & Sodsriwiboon, 2010; Kumar & Subramanian, 2012; Ghosh et al., 2013). Unlike previous studies in Indian context, we also conduct convergence test in terms of alternative measures of financial development across states and we observe evidence of convergence clubs for different indicators of financial development, as well. Therefore, considering both these aspects of growth and financial development, from policy perspectives it appears pertinent to focus more on balanced financial development, augmenting investments in physical and social sectors across states and maintaining balanced development in agriculture, industry and services sectors across states. These are supposed to be instrumental in mitigating divergence across states in the long run (see Ahluwalia, 2001; Ghosh et al., 2013 for similar discussions). Our findings of state level divergence in income as well as financial development and the formation of convergence clubs also have certain implications regarding the role of economic reforms initiated in 1990s. While it is argued that economic reforms led to high growth performance in many states, many other states did not manage to grow in tandem, perhaps because of the lack of favourable environment to implement the reform policies (See Ahluwalia, 2001, Kalirajan et al., 2009, for more discussions). Therefore, it appears that poorer states can catch up the relatively richer states by implementing various reform programs in investment and infrastructure. Favourable credit policies of the central bank should also be adopted simultaneously to support and achieve sector specific growth objectives across states with the broader goals of achieving regional balance.

Phillips and Sul (2007) methodology, however, can also be used to investigate whether the observed convergence of growth variable is associated with the convergence of financial development indicators. In fact, growth convergence across a group of states may not drive the observed convergence in terms of financial development indicators of the same group of states. We also may not exclude financial development as an explanatory factor leading to the growth convergence. On the other hand, if a financial development indicator diverges for the aggregate sample, but converges across several subgroup of states, and also real per capita income converges across several sub-samples, we may (or may not) predict that this financial development indicator is associated with per capita income. The Fisher's exact test of independence can be appropriately used to scrutinize whether club convergence of two variables (growth and financial development) with respect to the number of clubs and their composition share some association. This exercise of testing the hypothesis of whether financial development measures explain convergence of real per capita income in convergence clubs is kept as future agenda of research.

Acknowledgements Samaresh Bardhan acknowledges the financial support received from ICSSR, New Delhi under the Scheme of Impactful Research on Social Sciences (IMPRESS), for carrying this research as a part of the research project 'Growth Convergence among Indian states: Role of credit spillovers and social banking' (grant number: F. No.IMPRESS/P2929/135/18-19/ICSSR). The excellent research assistance of Ms Anushka Mullick, research assistant of the said research project at the Indian Institute of Technology Ropar, is also gratefully acknowledged.

Appendix

Variables	Definition	Data source
GSDPR	Growth rate of real per capita gross domestic product at 2004–05 prices (in rupees)	CMIE, States of India
GSDPN	State-wise nominal gross domestic product at 2004–05 prices (in rupees)	CMIE, States of India

(continued)

(continued)

Variables	Definition	Data source
YPR	Growth rate of real state domestic product (SGDP), aggregate level	CMIE, States of India
GOV	Ratio of state Government expenditure(at current prices) to GSDP at current prices	CMIE, States of India
Infra	Road + Rail Length in Km per 100,000 population	CMIE, States of India
UPC	Total bank credit to Private sector credit (utilized)	CMIE, States of India
PCSO	Credit sanctioned in ith state but used elsewhere (Outward spillover)	CMIE, States of India
PCSI	Credit sanctioned in jth state but used in ith state = PCS (Inward spillover)	CMIE, States of India
UPCGDP	Nominal credit to nominal GDP	Author's Calculations
OUTUPC	PCSO/UPC	Author's Calculations
INUPC	PCSI / UPC	Author's Calculations
OUTGDP	PCSO/GSDPN (nominal GDP)	Author's Calculations
INGDP	PCSI/GSDPN(nominal GDP)	Author's Calculations
AGLCRQN	Agricultural credit as a proportion of agricultural output (nominal)	CMIE, States of India
INDCRQN	Industrial credit/industrial output (nominal), refers to credit disbursed to 17 industries in India	CMIE, States of India
SERCRQN	Service sector credit/services output (nominal), services credit refers to bank credit to Professional and other services, trade, finance and transport operators	CMIE, States of India
AGLCRUPC	Agricultural credit/Total credit utilized	CMIE, States of India
INDCRUPC	Industrial credit/Total credit utilized	CMIE, States of India
CONCRUPC	Consumer credit/Total credit utilized (consumer credit includes loans disbursed to households for housing, consumer durables, vehicles, education, personal credit card and other)	CMIE, States of India
SERCRUPC	Services credit/Total credit utilized	CMIE, States of India
BRAND	Branches per 100,000 population (Branch density)	CMIE, States of India
GERUPPER	Gross Enrollment ratio upper (middle/senior basic school: upper primary)	CMIE, States of India

(continued)

(continued)

Variables	Definition	Data source
CDR	Credit Deposit ratio (Total Credit/ total Deposit)	Author's Calculations

References

Aghion, P., Howitt, P., & Mayer-Foulkes, D. (2005). The effect of financial development on convergence: Theory and evidence. *Quarterly Journal of Economics, 120*, 173–222.

Ahluwalia, M. S. (2001). *State level performance under economic reforms in India.* Centre for Research on Economic Development and Policy Reform (Working Paper No 96). Stanford University.

Ahmed, S., & Varshney, A. (2009). *Battles half won: The political economy of India's growth and economic policy since independence.* Commission on Growth and Development (Working Paper No. 15).

Aiyar, S. (2001). *Growth theory and convergence across Indian states, in India at the crossroads: Sustaining growth and reducing poverty* (T. Callen & P. Reynolds, & C. Towe, Eds.) (pp. 143–169). International Monetary Fund.

Apergis, N., Christou, C., & Miller, S. (2012). Convergence patterns in financial development: Evidence from club convergence. *Empirical Economics, 43*, 1011–1040.

Arcand, J.-L., Berkes, E., & Panizza, U. (2015). Too much finance? *Journal of Economic Growth, 20*, 105–148.

Bajpai, N., & Sachs, J. (1996). *Trends in inter-state inequalities of income in India.* Harvard Institute for International Development (Development Discussion Paper No. 528).

Bandyopadhyay, S. (2003). *Convergence club empirics: Some dynamics and explanations of unequal growth across Indian states* (WIDER Working Paper Series DP2003–77). UNU-WIDER.

Bardhan, S., & Sharma, R. (2022). Sectoral growth and sectoral credit: Panel evidence from Indian States. In P. Mukherjee (Ed.), *Revisiting the Indian financial sector*. India Studies in Business and Economics. Springer. https://doi.org/10.1007/978-981-16-7668-0_7

Barro, R., & Sala-i, X. (1991). Convergence across states and regions. *Brookings Papers on Economic Activity, 1*(1), 107–182.

Barro, R., & Sala-i-Martin, X. (1995). *Economic growth.* McGraw-Hill, Inc.

Basturk, N., Paap, R., & van Dijk, D. J. C. (2010). *Financial development and convergence clubs* (Econometric Institute Research Papers EI 2010-52). Erasmus University Rotterdam, Erasmus School of Economics (ESE), Econometric Institute.

Basu, K., & Maertens, A. (2007). The pattern and causes of economic growth in India. *Oxford Review of Economic Policy, 23*(2), 143–167.

Beck, T., Levine, R., & Loayza, N. (2000). Finance and the sources of growth. *Journal of Financial Economics, 58*(1–2), 261–300.

Bhattacharya, B. B., & Kar, S. (2004). Long run growth prospects for the Indian economy. In R. K. Sinha (Ed.), *Macroeconomic projections, India 2025: Social economic and political stability.* Shipra Publications.

Bhattacharya, B. B., & Sakthivel, S. (2004, January). Regional growth and disparity in India. *Economic and Political Weekly, 39*(10), 1071–1077.

Bhattacharya, B. B., & Sivasubramanian, M. N. (2003). Financial development and economic growth in India: 1970–1971 to 1998–1999. *Applied Financial Economics, 13*(2), 925–929.

Burgess, R., & Pande, R. (1995). Do rural banks matter? Evidence from the Indian social banking experiment. *American Economic Review, 95*(3), 780–795.

Canova, F. (2004). Testing for convergence clubs in income per capita: A predictive density approach. *International Economic Review, 45*, 49–77.

Cashin, P., & Sahay, R. (1996a). Internal migration, Centre-state grants and economic growth in the States of India. *IMF Staff Papers, 43*(1), 123–171.

Cashin, P., & Sahay, R. (1996b). Regional economic growth and convergence in India. *Finance and Development, Economic and Political Weekly*, (2006), 'Special Banking Statistics'.

Chatterjee, A., Bhattacharya, K., & Gayen, S. (1997). *Migration of credit across states: An empirical investigation with some new measures.* Banking Statistics Division, Department of Statistical Analysis and Computer Services, Reserve Bank of India. https://www.rbi.org.in. Accessed 12 August 2020.

Dasgupta, D., Maiti, P., Mukherjee, R., Sarkar, S., & Chakrabarti, S. (2000, July 1). Growth and interstate disparities in India. *Economic and Political Weekly*, 2413–2422.

Das, P. K., & Maiti, P. (1998). Bank credit, output and bank deposits in West Bengal and selected states. *Economic and Political Weekly*, 3081–3088.

De la Torre, A., Feyen, E., & Ize, A. (2011). *Financial development: Structure and dynamics* (Policy Research Working Paper Series 5854). The World Bank.

Dholakia, R. (1994, August 21). Spatial dimension of acceleration of economic growth in India. *Economic & Political Weekly, 29*(35).

Durlauf, S. N., & Johnson, P. A. (1995). Multiple regimes and cross-country growth behavior. *Journal of Applied Econometrics, 10*, 365–384.

EPW Research Foundation. (2008). *Agricultural credit in India: Changing profile and regional imbalances.* EPW Research Foundation.

Fufa, T., & Kim, J. (2018). Financial development, economic growth and convergence clubs. *Applied Economics, 50*(60), 6512–6528.

Fung, M. K. (2009). Financial development and economic growth: Convergence or divergence? *Journal of International Money and Finance, 28*(1), 56–57.

Galor, O. (1996). Convergence? Inferences from theoretical models. *The Economic Journal, 106*, 1056–1069.

Ghosh, M., Ghoshray, A., & Malki, I. (2013). Regional divergence and club convergence in India. *Economic Modelling, 30*, 733–742.

Government of India. (1991). *Report of the Committee on the financial system (Narasimham Committee I).* Ministry of Finance.

Government of India. (1998). *Report of the Narasimham Committee on the banking sector reforms (Narasimham Committee II).* Ministry of Finance.

Government of India. (2016). *Economic Survey 2015–16.* Ministry of Finance

Gründler, K. (2015). *The vanishing effect of finance on growth* (Discussion Paper Series, No. 133). Julius Maximilian University of Würzburg, Chair of Economic Order and Social Policy, Würzburg.

Haider, S., & Adil, M. H. (2024). Credit accessibility across Indian states: Evidence from club convergence. *Asian Economic Letters, 5*(2), 1–6.

Hembram, S., & Halder, S. K. (2019). Beta, sigma and club convergence: Indian experience from 1980 to 2015. *Indian Economic Review, 54*, 343–366.

Herwadkar, S., & Ghosh, S. (2013). What explains credit inequality across Indian states: An empirical analysis. *Reserve Bank India Occasional Papers, 34*(1&2), 112–137.

Herwadkar, S., & Ghosh, S. (2015). Does industrial activity explain regional dispersion in credit: Empirical evidences across Indian states. *The Journal of Industrial Statistics, 4*(1), 76–90.

Kalirajan, K., Bhide, S., & Singh, K. (2009). *Development performance across Indian states and the role of the governments* (ASARC Working Paper, 2009/05). Australian National University.

Kalra, S., & Sodsriwiboon, P. (2010). *Growth convergence and spillovers among Indian states: What matters? What does not?* (IMF Working Paper, WP/10/96).

Kanbur, R., & Zhang, X. (2004). *Fifty years of regional inequality in China: A journey through central planning, reform, and openness* (WIDER Research Paper, No. 2004/50). ISBN 9291906395, UNU-WIDER, Helsinki. Accessed on July 1, 2024.

King, R. G., & Levine, R. (1993). Finance and growth: Schumpeter might be right. *The Quarterly Journal of Economics, 108*(3), 717–737.

Kendall, J. (2012). Local financial development and growth. *Journal of Banking and Finance, 36*(5), 1548–1562.

Kochhar, K., Kumar, U., Rajan, R., Subramanian, A., & Tokatlidis, I. (2006). *India's pattern of development: What happened, what follows* (IMF Working Paper No. 06/22). 22

Kumar, U., & Subramanian, A. (2012, January 21). Growth in India's states in the first decade of the 21st century: Four facts. *Economic & Political Weekly, 67*(3).

Laurini, M., Andrade, E., Pedro, L., & Pereira, V. (2005). Income convergence clubs for Brazilian Municipalities: A non-parametric analysis. *Applied Economics, 37*, 2099–2118.

Levine, R., Loayza, N., & Beck, T. (2000). Financial intermediation and growth: Causality and causes. *Journal of Monetary Economics, 46*(1), 31–77.

Lolayekar, A. P., & Mukhopadhyay, P. (2020). Understanding growth convergence in India (1981–2010): Looking beyond the usual suspects. *PLoS One, 15*(6), Article e0233549.

Marjit, S., & Mitra, S. (1996, August). Convergence in regional growth rates: Indian research agenda. *Economic and Political Weekly, 31*(33), 2239–2242.

Martin, V., & Vazquez, G. (2015). Club convergence in Latin America. *The B.E. Journal of Macroeconomics, De Gruyter, 15*(2), 791–820.

Misra, B. S. (2003). Analytics of credit-output nexus in India. *Reserve Bank of India Occasional Papers, 24*(1& 2), 145–171.

Misra, B. S. (2007). *Regional growth dynamics in India in the post-economic reform period*. Palgrave Macmillan.

Nag, A., & Pradhan, J. (2023). Does club convergence matter? Empirical evidence on inequality in the human development index among Indian states. *Humanities and Social Sciences Communications, 10*(25), 1–12.

Nagaraj, P., Varoudakis, A., & Véganzonès, M. A. (2000). Long-run growth trends and convergence across Indian states. *Journal of International Development, 12*(1), 45–70.

Nain, M. Z., & Kamaiah, B. (2014). Financial development and economic growth in India: Some evidence from non-linear causality analysis. *Economic Change and Restructuring, 47*(4), 299–319.

Phillips, P. C., & Sul, D. (2007). Transition modeling and econometric convergence tests. *Econometrica, 75*, 1771–1855.

Purfield, C. (2006). *Mind the gap-is economic growth in India leaving some states behind?* (IMF Working Paper No. 06/103).

Quah, D. (1993). Exploiting cross section variation for unit root inference in dynamic data. *International Economic Studies Paper, 549*.

Rao, M. G., Shand, R. T., & Kalirajan, K. P. (1999). Convergence of incomes across Indian states: A divergent view. *Economic and Political Weekly, 34*(13), 769–778.

Raju, S. (2012). Growth across states in the 2000s: Evidence of convergence. *EPW, 47*(23), 76–79.

RBI. (2006). *Credit market*. Report on Currency and Finance 2005–06 (pp. 119–163). India

Rousseau, P. L., & Wachtel, P. (2011). What is happening to the impact of financial deepening on economic growth? *Economic Inquiry, 49*(1), 276–288.

Sachs, J., Bajpai, N., & Ramiah, A. (2002). Understanding regional economic growth in India. *Asian Economic Papers, 1*, 3.

Sala-i-Martin, X. (1996). Regional cohesion: Evidence and theories of regional growth and convergence. *European Economic Review, 40*(6), 1325–1352.

Sánchez-Reaza, J., & Rodríguez-Pose, A. (2002). The impact of trade liberalization on regional disparities in Mexico. *Growth and Change, 33*, 72–90.

Sarkar, P. C. (1994). Regional imbalances in Indian economy over plan periods. *Economic & Political Weekly, 29*(2), 621–633.

Shetty, S. L. (2004). Distributional issues in bank credit: Multi-pronged strategy for correcting past neglect. *Economic and Political Weekly, 39*(29), 3265–3269.

Solow, R. (1956). A contribution to the theory of economic growth. *The Quarterly Journal of Economics, 70*, 65–94.

Tyagarajan, M., & Saoji, S. H. (1977). *Migration of credit: An aspect of banking in Metropolitan centres* Reserve Bank of India Bulletin (December), (pp. 802–813).

Chapter 12
Development and Change in Services Sector of India: The Drivers and the Users

Ajitava Raychaudhuri and Partha Pratim Ghosh

Abstract The present paper analyzes the main drivers of growth of the services sector in India. The focus is on the interdependence of the services sector on manufacturing sector and vice versa. Shift-share analysis shows that the change in productivity of services sectors is mainly due to within-sector rather than inter-sector effects. Input–Output analysis reveals that although the existing service output levels are heavily dependent on inter-industry intermediate use, the growth of such services depends vitally on final demand in most cases. Technological changes in many sectors has reduced per unit requirement of services but the scale effect dominates so that a rising final demand has to be supplemented by larger intermediate demand for services—the latter sometimes labelled as servicification of manufacturing sector. It emerges that while a deliberate push to manufacturing will be a boon to services as well, the growth of the services sector will promote larger use of the same in many manufacturing sectors and at the same time create more demand for manufacturing goods through inter-industry backward linkage effect.

Keywords Productivity · Servicification · Shift-share analysis · Input–output analysis · Linkages · Structural decomposition

JEL Classification D24 · D57 · J24 · E24 · O11

A. Raychaudhuri (✉)
Department of Economics, Adamas University, Kolkata, West Bengal, India
e-mail: ajitava1@gmail.com

P. P. Ghosh
Postgraduate and Research Department of Economics, St. Xavier's College (Autonomous) Kolkata, Kolkata, West Bengal, India

D. Maiti et al. (eds.), *75 Years of Growth, Development and Productivity in India*, India Studies in Business and Economics, https://doi.org/10.1007/978-981-97-8054-9_12

12.1 Introduction

The services sector in India has drawn attention for a couple of important reasons. One is that the services sector has done much better than the goods sector in India's export performance. The other is the fact that services have made strong inroads as intermediate inputs in the manufacturing sector of India.Thus, from both aspects, it is really important to understand the recent strong growth performance of several services sectors in India as well as its changing composition. The sources of this growth and compositional changes in the services sector in India are not free from debates. One finding on which there is largely a consensus is the fact that growth in the services sector is mainly caused by "within" factors which imply that technological and organizational changes in the services sector itself are the main causal factors of growth. At the same time, there are significant compositional changes in the services sector, which requires a clearer understanding of the main drivers of growth of that sector. The controversy lies in the conjecture whether manufacturing (or the industrial sector, to be more precise) has played a more significant role in the last couple of decades than what one had observed before. This obviously requires identification of the main drivers and users of the services sector in India with a particular eye on manufacturing (and broadly, the industrial sector). The present paper is an effort to highlight the important strand of research focused on these issues, along with some original findings.

The paper proceeds in the following way—Sect. 12.2 gives both an overview of the dependence of the services sector on the manufacturing sector as well as a discussion on the "servicification" of the Indian economy in Sect. 12.2.1 along with a discussion on the compositional change within the services sector in Sect. 12.2.2. A shift-share analysis of growth of the services sector vis-à-vis the other sectors appears in Sect. 12.2.3. The interlinkage between services and other sectors is shown in Sect. 12.3, with a compositional change in the demand for the services sector in Sect. 12.3.1 and sources of change in Sect. 12.3.2, all carried out in an input–output framework. A linkage analysis is shown in Sect. 12.3.3 using detailed input–output matrices. A decomposition analysis of the services sector growth in an input–output framework is shown in Sect. 12.4 and 12.4.1. Section 12.5 has the concluding section.

12.2 Services Sector and its Dependence on Manufacturing Sector

Eichengreen and Gupta (2011) claim—"The results show that the correlation between growth in manufacturing and services has been falling over time. These correlations confirm the pattern that we see in the input–output matrices and imply that growth momentum in services in recent years has been largely independent of that in manufacturing. The next table *(Table 12.1—italics authors')* shows the correlation between the growth of specific services and manufacturing. For traditional services such as trade and hotels, the correlation is relatively high, though it has declined over time. Interestingly, the growth of modern services such as communications, business services and financial services is not correlated with the growth of value-added to manufacturing. Again, this implies that these services have a growth momentum of their own which does not simply derive from outsourcing by manufacturing (p. 13)." Further, the same paper (ibid., 2011) claims—"Calculating the use of services per unit of value-added in agriculture and industry using the three input–output matrices, *(presented here as Table 12.2)* does not suggest that the intensity with which services are used in industry has changed much over time. The implication is that growth in the intermediate demand for services from industry is due mainly to increasing output rather than increasing outsourcing of in-house manufacturing-sector activities to the service sector (p. 11)".

On the other hand, a recent book suggests that most of the outputs of services sector are inputs and not final demand. Hence such programmes like "Make in India" should utilize business services to promote local production of intermediate inputs. In other words, the complementarity between the manufacturing and services sectors is key to the development of India (Balasubramanyam & Balasubramanyam, 2021, p. 18). The same is reiterated in the introduction of the book edited by Bhide et al. (2021, p. 9). This is also the line of thought in a working paper written by Krishna et al. (2015, p. 37) and we quote—"It is hard to imagine that India can sustain a high GDP growth in the longer term, and achieve a higher level of per capita income, without focusing on developing a solid manufacturing sector and thereby increasing opportunities for its young population".

The increasing role of services in economic activity is also reflected in the growing importance of services in global trade and India's trade. Government Economic Survey acknowledges it too and we quote—"India has maintained its impressive

Table 12.1 Correlation between growth in services sub-sectors and manufacturing in India

Year	Trade	Transport	Hotels	Communication	Business Services	Banking
1951–1965	0.86***	0.33	0.67***	0.45*	0.31	−0.14
1966–1980	0.52**	0.01	0.49*	−0.15	−0.05	0.59*
1981–1995	0.82***	0.39	0.37	0.41	0.53**	−0.16
1996–2008	0.01	0.71***	0.43	0.27	−0.43	0.06

Note *, **, *** Indicate that the correlations are significant at 1, 5, and 10% levels respectively

Table 12.2 Service input per unit of output in agriculture and industry in India

	1993	1998	2003
Agriculture	0.07	0.06	0.08
Industry: Weighted	0.84	0.55	0.72
Industry: Unweighted	0.79	0.55	0.73

Source For both Tables 12.1 and 12.2, Eichengreen and Gupta (2011, p. 46)

performance in world services trade in the post COVID-19 period. This is mainly on account of the top three namely computer, business and transportation services that constitute more than 80 % of total services exports (Economic Survey, 2021–2022, p. 98)".

12.2.1 *"Servicification" in Indian Economy*

The above is supported by Chanda (2021, pp. 45–46), and she has calculated the disaggregated picture of the growth of other commercial services components and shares of selected services in total services exports in the following table (relabelled as Table 12.3 here and taken from Chanda, ibid., p. 50):

As rightly explained by her—"India's competitiveness in 'other services' is mainly on account of two segments, namely, computer and information services and professional and management consulting services (with RCA values consistently greater than 1) (Chanda, ibid., p. 51)". This is also supported by later analysis using WBES (World Bank Enterprise Survey) data by Pant and Chakraborty (2024). So exports did play a role, albeit in a few concentrated sectors, in the growth of services. However, the most important observation she made is on "servicification", which implies that intermediate input usage of services in manufacturing exports has gone up since 2005 and contributed to the growth of business and commercial services. However, the domestic segment contributed much more to the growth of these services (Chanda, ibid., p. 55). Specifically, IT and information technology did not play that important a role in the manufacturing export, implying the fragmentation and smaller scale

Table 12.3 Value of "other" commercial services exports ($mn) and shares of selected categories in total services exports (%), selected years

Category	1990	2000	2005	2017
Other commercial services ($mn)	2,107	11,247	38,149	139,301
Communication(%)	–	2.98	–	–
Construction(%)	–	0.66	0.67	1.25
Insurance(%)	2.51	1.79	1.81	1.34
Financial(%)	–	2.18	2.20	2.45
Computer and information(%)	–	30.61	31.01	28.74
Royalties and licence fees(%)	0.01	0.39	–	–
Other business services(%)	31.29	35.33	35.12	32.16
Personal, cultural, recreational(%)	–	0.21	–	–
R&D(%)	–	–	0.65	1.64

Source http://unctadstat.unctad.org/wds/ReportFolders/reportFolders.aspx?sCS_ChosenLang=en (accessed October 1, 2018), Taken from Chanda (2021, p. 50)
Note 1990, 2000 figures are based on BPM5; 2005, 2010 and 2017 figures are based on BPM6. Blanks indicate that data are not available for these disaggregated categories.

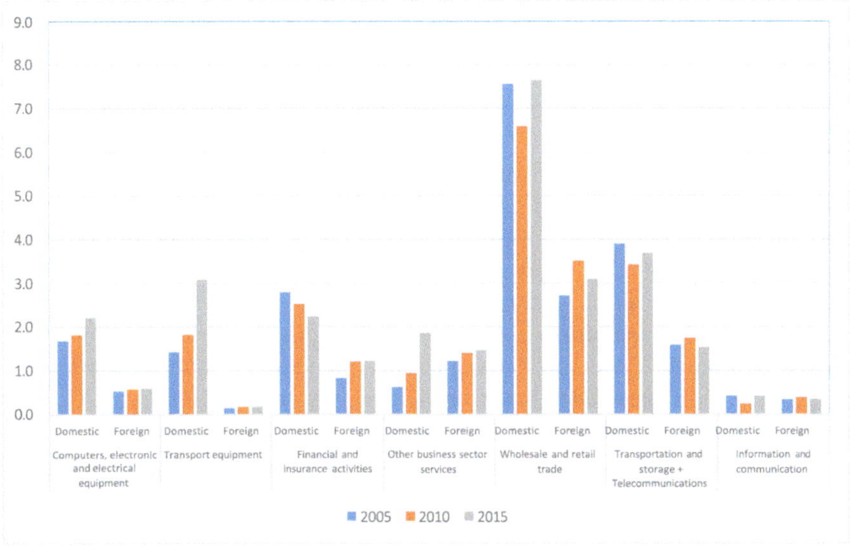

Fig. 12.1 Value added contribution by source sectors (services and industries) in gross manufacturing exports. *Source* Author's construction based on https://stats.oecd.org/Index.aspx?DataSetCode=TIVA_2018_C2# (accessed March 29, 2019), taken from Chanda (ibid., p. 55)

of the manufacturing units involved in exports. The following quote from Chanda's paper and table from the TiVA database of OECD and quoted by Chanda (ibid., p. 55) succinctly clarifies the issue: "The contribution of the service sector to overall manufacturing exports is concentrated in traditional services such as trade and distribution services and to a lesser extent in transport and storage services. However, segments such as IT and information services or other business services (which include R&D services and other business support activities), which can potentially increase business sophistication and raise technological depth in production, show very low levels of contribution to manufacturing exports. The value-added content from IT and information services in manufacturing exports was barely 1% in 2015, and that of other business services was just a little over 3% (Chanda, ibid., p. 56)" (Fig. 12.1).

12.2.2 Compositional Change in the Services Sector

It is clear from the previous discussion that although business and other commercial services have rapidly grown in India, they depend more on the domestic markets. The question is, how far this depends on the growth of the manufacturing sector in India? Eichengreen and Gupta (2011) believe the answer is "very little" while Bhide et al. (2021) think otherwise. One should note Eichengreen and Gupta did not go beyond 2009 using only the 2003 input–output table, while Bhide et al. (2021)

based their arguments more on conjecture looking at the broad picture of growth and composition of the services sector till late in the decade of 2010s. The present paper tries to understand this aspect more clearly.

The following tables are taken from the KLEMS database (Reserve Bank of India 2024).

The Tables 12.4, 12.5, 12.6 show the relative change of value-added share as well as share in employment of the three major sectors in the Indian economy. It is now well accepted that many emerging economies, including India, did not follow the so-called Kuznets law of structural change. The declining share of the primary sector in real value-added is largely captured by the services sector. The same is not true for employment shares—the share of the primary sector in employment has not declined much. Table 12.7 shows that the relative share of the services sector in aggregate real value-added has risen significantly between 1980 and 2020, but the rise is steep during the decade of 2010–2020. The same is true for employment in the services sector but the rise is less spectacular compared to that in the real value-added. Clearly, the value-added share of the services sector has risen much faster than employment between 2020–2021 and 1980–1981, and the acceleration is much faster during the last 10 years in the decade starting in 2010–2011.The biggest rise is in business services, financial services, health and social work and transport and storage services (Table 12.6). The only decrease is in public administration and defence and compulsory social security. Nonetheless, services sector has performed significantly differently than both the primary and secondary sectors.

12.2.3 *Shift-Share Analysis of Change in the Services Sector vis à vis Other Sectors*

In an excellent paper, Basu and Veermani (2021) have gone into a detailed analysis of employment in the services sector, especially its growth and composition. The following is a quote from that paper—"….the change in aggregate labour share (ΔLS) between years $t-k$ and t can be decomposed into within (shift) and between (share) components using the following equation:

$$\Sigma_i(\overline{w}_i\Delta \mathrm{LS}_i) + \Sigma(\overline{LS}_i\Delta wi)$$

where the bar above the variables stands for the average value of the given variable for period t and $t-k$ and the subscript i represents sector. The first term on the RHS of the above equation $\Sigma_i(\overline{w}_i\Delta \mathrm{LS}_i)$ is the "within sector" (shift) component, which captures the contribution of changes in labour share within each sector, keeping the share of value-added in each sector constant at its average value. The second term $\Sigma(\overline{LS}_i\Delta wi)$ is the "between sector" (share) component, which gives the contribution of the changes in the value-added shares of each sector, keeping the share of labour value-added constant at its average value. The within and between components

Table 12.4 Value added at constant 2011–2012 prices (in Crores of ₹)

Sectors	1980–1981	1990–1991	2000–2001	2010–2011	2020–2021
Agriculture total	**581,113 (41.10)**	**811,417 (33.27)**	**1,065,837 (26.15)**	**1,411,634 (18.33)**	**2,076,327 (16.37)**
Agriculture, hunting, forestry and fishing	581,113	811,417	1,065,837	1,411,634	2,076,327
Industry	368,239 (26.06)	709,249 (29.08)	1,197,070 (29.36)	2,529,862 (32.98)	3,886,718 (30.65)
Mining and quarrying	57,053	128,109	189,727	316,533	289,905
Food products, beverages and tobacco	19,306	43,853	80,833	143,233	215,731
Textiles and products, leather and f-wear	26,853	42,487	71,367	151,416	274,353
Wood and products of wood	24,191	19,388	17,924	19,479	34,745
Pulp, paper and products, printing	6511	14,546	13,956	40,430	47,710
Coke, refined petroleum products etc	8539	38,392	53,627	109,714	183,434
Chemicals and chemical products	15,725	42,966	101,887	181,646	345,443
Rubber and plastic products	2848	9343	29,676	56,397	108,029
Other non-metallic mineral products	8765	26,063	45,094	84,073	148,068
Basic metals and fabricated products	36,691	61,996	107,070	237,422	375,853
Machinery, nec	12,539	24,532	38,409	106,527	167,479
Electrical and optical equipment	3228	9250	17,817	80,210	134,025
Transport equipment	10,658	21,064	38,772	119,113	214,942
Manufacturing, nec; recycling	4125	6097	15,063	34,651	75,625
Electricity, gas and water supply	21,929	49,964	96,385	171,947	287,757
Construction	109,278	171,198	279,465	687,072	983,619
Services	**464,580 (32.86)**	**918,412 (37.65)**	**1,813,854 (44.49)**	**3,749,902 (48.69)**	**6,718,437 (52.98)**
Trade	97,527	173,017	348,000	750,536	1,369,375
Hotels and restaurants	8553	15,779	39,035	84,433	70,938
Transport and storage	49,134	87,248	164,007	374,304	498,281
Post and telecommunication	4775	8403	37,597	119,347	220,902

(continued)

Table 12.4 (continued)

Sectors	1980–1981	1990–1991	2000–2001	2010–2011	2020–2021
Financial services	30,977	85,097	209,411	464,305	824,562
Business service	13,712	34,984	145,113	425,074	1,289,357
Public admin, defence and social security	75,526	143,540	259,566	470,839	757,616
Education	23,297	46,142	99,794	234,291	482,051
Health and social work	8374	18,014	38,753	109,654	196,000
Other services	152,706	306,187	472,578	717,118	1,009,356
Aggregate value added	**1,413,932**	**2,439,078**	**4,076,761**	**7,761,398**	**12,681,482**

Note The figures in the parentheses are sectoral shares in the aggregate

capture the contribution of intra and inter-sectoral changes, respectively, in aggregate labour share changes. The analysis is done for two sub-periods: Pre-liberalization (1980–1993) and post-liberalization (1993–2016)" (Basu & Veermani, 2021, p. 11).

The shift-share analysis is a popular analytical tool that focuses on the composition of growth in any sector. Again, quoting from Veermani and Basu (ibid., 2021, p. 12)—"During the pre-liberalization period, the aggregate labour share declined by 3.75 percentage points, of which 78 per cent (2.93 percentage points) was contributed by the within component while the remaining 22 per cent (0.82 percentage points) was contributed by the between component. During the post-liberalization period (1993–2016), the decline in labour share is fully explained by the 'between sector' component (Basu & Veermani, 2021, p. 12)", and although 2007–2016 figures re-establish the primacy of the "within" factor (Table 12.8).

The major jump in the 10 years of the last decade is in business services, which is a basket of various services, including audit, legal, insurance, technical, consultancy, architectural etc., whose demand may originate from domestic and/or foreign sources. But how much of these are from the industrial (or to be specific, manufacturing) sector in the form of intermediate demand? Eichengreen and Gupta (2011), supported by some others, do believe it is due to final demand and not intermediate demand. However, their data uses the latest 2003 input–output tables, and their analysis stopped in 2009. The major impetus to business services (and to some extent to telecommunication services, especially from 2000 onwards) came after 2010, and this is not analyzed quantitatively. Some positive trend is noted for Trade and education services also after 2000 onwards. On the other hand some of the traditional services like Public Administration and Defence, Transport and storage, as well as other services have continuously declining shares in the real value-added from 1980–1981 to 2020–2021.

Following Rodrik et al. (2011, pp. 12–13) and Majid (ILO, 2019), one can try to understand the change in the services sector through a shift-share analysis of labour productivity in the services sector. The formula for this is well known as: $\Delta Y_t = \sum_{i=1}^{n} \omega_{i,t-k} \Delta y_{i,t} + \sum_{i=1}^{n} \overline{y}_{i,t} \Delta \omega_{i,t}$, where ΔY_t is growth in the aggregate labour

Table 12.5 Employment in different sectors of the Indian economy

Number of persons employed (in 1000s)

Sectors	1980–1981	1990–1991	2000–2001	2010–2011	2020–2021
Agriculture	**198,022 (69.83)**	**223,726 64.59)**	**242,985 (59.30)**	**230,132 (49.27)**	**238,218 (43.80)**
Agriculture, hunting, forestry and fishing	198,022	223,726	242,985	230,132	238,218
Industry	**37,516 (13.23)**	**53,452 (15.43)**	**67,089 (16.37)**	**103,041 (22.06)**	**123,969 (22.79)**
Mining and quarrying	1487	2446	2619	2590	1708
Food products, beverages and tobacco	6315	8094	10,304	11,185	10,002
Textiles, textile products, leather and footwear	10,504	11,853	11,993	13,987	11,476
Wood and products of wood	2667	3107	4629	4048	3057
Pulp, paper, paper products, printing and publishing	714	957	1322	1566	1769
Coke, refined petroleum products and nuclear fuel	46	93	110	146	238
Chemicals and chemical products	1020	1476	1862	2028	2649
Rubber and plastic products	240	471	741	1101	1273
Other non-metallic mineral products	2597	3082	3544	4858	4148
Basic metals and fabricated metal products	2047	2662	3530	4415	5705
Machinery, nec	542	616	1262	1798	2750
Electrical and optical equipment	481	797	1077	2225	3628
Transport equipment	514	781	995	1500	2273
Manufacturing, nec; recycling	1897	2988	3418	5851	5861
Electricity, gas and water supply	797	1110	1151	1554	2475
Construction	5646	12,919	18,533	44,187	64,957
Services	**48,024 (16.93)**	**69,197 (19.98)**	**99,696 (24.33)**	**133,887 (28.67)**	**181,716 (33.41)**
Trade	16,439	25,411	37,210	46,804	64,353
Hotels and restaurants	2268	3167	4780	7683	9768
Transport and storage	5387	8918	13,674	18,973	24,832
Post and telecommunication	398	638	1361	1793	1604
Financial services	882	1757	2335	4235	6133

(continued)

Table 12.5 (continued)

Number of persons employed (in 1000s)					
Business service	502	1032	2660	6988	14,381
Public administration and defence; compulsory social security	7802	9834	10,127	8379	8852
Education	4493	5625	8793	13,765	17,635
Health and social work	1641	1935	2938	4518	7663
Other services	8214	10,881	15,818	20,748	26,493
Aggregate employment	**283,562**	**346,374**	**409,770**	**467,060**	**543,902**

Table 12.6 Disaggregated share in service sector employment

Sectors	1980–1981 share	1990–1991 share	2000–2001 share	2010–2011 share	2020–2021 share	Ratio of 2020–2021 share to 1980–1981
Trade	0.342	0.367	0.373	0.350	0.354	1.034
Hotels and restaurants	0.047	0.046	0.048	0.057	0.054	1.138
Transport and storage	0.112	0.129	0.137	0.142	0.137	1.218
Post and telecommunication	0.008	0.009	0.014	0.013	0.009	1.065
Financial services	0.018	0.025	0.023	0.032	0.034	1.837
Business service	0.010	0.015	0.027	0.052	0.079	7.570
Public administration and defence; compulsory social security	0.162	0.142	0.102	0.063	0.049	0.299
Education	0.094	0.081	0.088	0.103	0.097	1.037
Health and social work	0.034	0.028	0.029	0.034	0.042	1.234

Table 12.7 Relative change in output and employment shares of three major sectors

Real value added			Employment		
Sector	Ratio of share of 2020–2021 over 1980–1981	Ratio of share of 2010–2011 over 1980–1981	Sector	Ratio of share of 2020–2021 over 1980–1981	Ratio of share of 2010–2011 over 1980–1981
Agriculture	0.40	0.41	Agriculture	0.63	0.76
Industry	1.18	1.08	Industry	1.72	1.48
Services	2.32	1.54	Services	1.97	1.59

Table 12.8 Disaggregated share in service sector real value-added (at 2011–2012 prices)

	1980–1981 share	1990–1991 share	2000–2001 share	2010–2011 share	2020–2021 share	Ratio of 2020–2021 share to 1980–1981	Ratio of 2010–2011 share to 1980–1981
Trade	0.210	0.188	0.192	0.200	0.204	0.970934	0.9534265
Hotels and restaurants	0.018	0.017	0.022	0.023	0.011	0.573526	1.223022
Transport and storage	0.106	0.095	0.090	0.100	0.074	0.701269	0.9438065
Post and telecommunication	0.010	0.009	0.021	0.032	0.033	3.199031	3.096554
Financial services	0.067	0.093	0.115	0.124	0.123	1.840671	1.856969
Business service	0.030	0.038	0.080	0.113	0.192	6.502264	3.840647
Public administration and defence; compulsory social security	0.163	0.156	0.143	0.126	0.113	0.693657	0.7723542
Education	0.050	0.050	0.055	0.062	0.072	1.430821	1.245937
Health and social work	0.018	0.020	0.021	0.029	0.029	1.61851	1.622303
Other services	0.329	0.333	0.261	0.191	0.150	0.457068	0.5818019

productivity of the services sector in the economy in time period *t*, Δy_{it} stands for growth in sectoral productivity, $\Delta\omega_{i,t}$ stands for change in the labour share of *ith* sector between two time periods $t-k$ and *t*, $\sum$ stands for summing over *n* number of sectors, $\omega_{i,t-k}$ stands for share of employment of the specific *ith* sector in total employment in the initial period $t-k$, and $\overline{y}_{i,t}$ stands for average of productivity between two time periods *t and* $t-k$. Thus, *k* in the subscript which is subtracted from *t* denotes locating the initial time point from where the change in share is to be calculated. However, it is better to take averages of the two periods while calculating the changes in weights or changes in sectoral labour productivity. The expression above denotes two things—"The first term in the decomposition is the weighted sum of productivity growth within individual sectors, where the weights are the employment share of each sector at the beginning of the time period. We will call this the 'within' component of productivity growth. The second term captures the productivity effect of labour reallocations across different sectors. It is essentially the inner product of productivity levels (at the end of the time period) with the change in employment shares across sectors. We will call this second term the 'structural change' term. When changes in employment shares are positively correlated with productivity levels, this term will be positive, and structural change will increase economy-wide productivity growth (Rodrik, 2011, p. 13)".

Table 12.9 shows labour productivities in various sub-sectors of services, as given in the previously mentioned KLEMS database. Given the rising role of business services, financial services, other services, and post and telecommunication in the last decade of this century, let us have a shift-share analysis for the services sector comparing 1980–1981 with 2020–2021. Results are shown in Table 12.10.

Table 12.9 Labour productivity in the services sector from KLEMS database (in rupees 10,000)

Sectors	1980–1981	1990–1991	2000–2001	2010–2011	2020–2021
Trade	5.93266	6.808744	9.352324	16.03572	21.27912
Hotels and restaurants	3.771164	4.982317	8.166318	10.98959	7.262285
Transport and storage	9.120847	9.78336	11.99408	19.72824	20.06608
Post and telecommunication	11.99749	13.17085	27.62454	66.56274	137.7195
Financial services	35.12132	48.43312	89.68351	109.6352	134.4468
Business service	27.31474	33.89922	54.55376	60.82914	89.65697
Public administration and defence; compulsory social security	9.680338	14.5963	25.63108	56.19275	85.58698
Education	5.185177	8.203022	11.34926	17.02078	27.3349
Health and social work	5.102986	9.309561	13.19027	24.27047	25.57745
Other services	18.59094	28.1396	29.87596	34.56324	38.09897

Table 12.10 Labour productivity change decomposition for 10 sectors services economy as mentioned above

Period	Within (Capital accumulation)	Between (Labour transfer or structural change)	Change in labour productivity
1980–2020	$\Sigma\omega_{i,t-k}\Delta y_{i,t}$	$\Sigma\overline{y}_{i,t}\Delta\omega_{i,t}$	ΔY_t
Economy	1.068	-0.038	1.030
Percentage share	103.7%	-3.7%	100%

Source Authors' calculation from previous tables

The data above shows the overwhelming dominance of intra-sectoral technological or organizational change within the existing sectors. In fact labour productivity had an overall decline for inter-sectoral transfer of labour force. This implies that within growing sectors like business services, telecommunications, etc., technological change or capital accumulation in general play the most important role in changing the production and employment scenario. In fact, this does not show any convergence of labour productivity across sectors, thereby leading to more inequality within the services sector.

12.3 The Inter-Sectoral Linkages and the Role of Manufacturing Sector

However, the above discussion does not show conclusively the drivers and users of development and change in the services sector in India over the years. This can only be deciphered through an analysis using input–output tables. The use of the services table will show in clear terms which sectors are really driving the growth of the services sector in India. The so-called "service-led growth" is certainly not an autonomous phenomenon. In this context, one needs to understand the inter-linkages between the services and the manufacturing sectors for the simple reason that the services sector's demand originates either in the inter-industry-input-usage or final demand. If final demand drives the story, then such stress on the manufacturing sector in terms of "make in India" programme, executed mainly through the productivity-linked incentive (PLI) schemes, will be primarily a story confined to that sector alone. However, if intermediate i.e. inter-industry-input-usage of the output of services shows an equal, if not better, role vis-à-vis the final demand, then these efforts and schemes to invigorate the manufacturing sector will simultaneously lead to a service sector stimulus too. This is the cornerstone of a long-standing discussion on the role of the manufacturing sector in India's "service-led growth" story (Eichengreen & Gupta, 2011 mentioned at the beginning of this paper).

Any sector of an economy does not grow in isolation. It affects and is affected by other sectors of the economy. A simple analysis of CSO data reveals that between

Table 12.11 Correlation between the growth rates of net value-added in the manufacturing sector and service sectors

Electricity, gas, water supply, and other utilities	0.46
Construction	0.57
Railways	0.63
Road transport	0.49
Air transport	0.46
Hotels and restaurants	0.47
Trade and repair services	0.34
Real estate, ownership of dwellings and professional services	0.23
Public administration and defence	0.18
Financial services	0.04
Other services	0.40

Source Computed from CSO data sourced from the website mospi.gov.in

the years 2012–2013 and 2021–2022, there has been a positive correlation between the growth rates of the net value-added in the services sectors and those of the manufacturing sector. The correlation coefficients are given in Table 12.11.

The figures reveal that during the period 2012–2013 to 2021–2022, the correlation between the growth rate of manufacturing and various services sectors ranged from 0.63 (with railway transport) to 0.04 (Financial Services). This led to two questions on the outputs of the services sectors:

(i) How are these outputs used in the economy? and
(ii) How are the outputs generated or supplied?

12.3.1 *Composition of Demand for Services Sector in the Last Decade*

We analyzed the latest available Supply-Use Tables published by the Ministry of Statistics for the years 2011–12, 2015–16 and 2019–2020, the last one comprising 140 products (sectors) and 66 industries. The following results emerged:

These outputs are used as inter-industry inputs and as final demand. Table 12.12 gives the details of inter-industry use of outputs of the service sectors.

For the year 2019–2020, the share of output of services sectors used as inter-industry-inputs is quite high for Electricity (81%), Water Supply (63%), Repair and Maintenance of Motor Vehicles (66%), Railway Transport (53%), Air Transport (49%), Supportive and Auxiliary Transport Activities (84%), Storage and Warehousing (100%), Communication Services (57%), Financial Services (66%), Insurance Services (41%), Real Estate Services (40%), Legal Services (54%), and Other Business Services (65%). A similar pattern existed for the years 2015–2016 and

Table 12.12 Inter-industry-use of outputs of the services sectors

Sl. No	All service sectors	2011–2012 (%)	2015–2016 (%)	2019–2020 (%)
1	Construction and construction services	12.48	11.02	19.75
2	Electricity	**79.37**	**76.11**	**80.67**
3	Gas	17.31	12.16	26.81
4	Water supply	**84.10**	**83.29**	**62.72**
5	Trade	0.00	0.00	0.00
6	Repair & maintenance of motor vehicle	**75.28**	**73.54**	**66.29**
7	Hotels and restaurant	**43.05**	**35.55**	**26.49**
8	Railway transport	20.01	17.56	53.01
9	Land transport	23.24	12.73	21.70
10	Air transport	**60.38**	**61.64**	**48.51**
11	Water transport	3.20	0.64	2.11
12	Supportive and auxiliary transport activities	**99.97**	**99.94**	**83.56**
13	Storage and warehousing	**100.00**	**100.00**	**100.00**
14	Communication services	**57.22**	**53.23**	**57.00**
15	Financial services	**67.27**	**64.78**	**66.39**
16	Insurance services	29.25	23.47	41.45
17	Ownership of dwellings	0.00%	0.00	0.00
18	Real estate services	**100.00**	**100.00**	**40.49**
19	Renting of machinery and equipment	**100.00**	**100.00**	**32.38**
20	Research & development services	0.00	0.00	33.68
21	Legal services	**49.55**	**48.67**	**53.73**
22	Other business services	**38.09**	**73.83**	**65.09**
23	Computer related services	2.92	0.71	8.80
24	Public administration and defence	0.00	0.00	0.00
25	Education services	1.57	5.74	8.51
26	Human health and social care services	0.49	0.35	7.42
27	Community, social and personal services	0.33	0.57	12.69
28	Recreation, entertainment and radio & TV broadcasting and other services	5.84	5.76	35.80

Source results of the present study, computed from SUTs

2011–2012. However, a significant increase was there for other business services while a significant decrease is observed for hotels and restaurant services.

For the Business Services, the share of output used as inter-industry-inputs during 2011–2012, 2015–2016 and 2019–2020 are shown in Table 12.13.

For the rest of the services sectors, the dominant share of output was used to meet final demand. For example, in 2019–2020, among the various categories of

Table 12.13 Inter-industry-use of business services output

Sl. No	Business services	2011–2012 (%)	2015–2016 (%)	2019–2020 (%)
1	Electricity	79	76	81
2	Water supply	84	83	63
3	Repair & maintenance of motor vehicle	75	74	66
4	Railway transport	20	18	53
5	Air transport	60	62	49
6	Supportive and auxiliary transport Activities	100	100	84
7	Storage and warehousing	100	100	100
8	Communication services	57	53	57
9	Financial services	67	65	66
10	Insurance services	29	23	41
11	Legal services	50	49	54
12	Other business services	38	74	65

Source Results of the present study, computed from SUTs

final demand, exports played an important role for the use of Water Transport (93%), Renting of Machinery and Equipment (67%), Computer related Services (48%), and Recreational Services (39.5%). For the remaining services sectors domestic final demand absorbed the output to a large extent.

Thus, analysis of the use of services sector outputs showed that both inter-industry-input as well as final demand (domestic and exports) played important roles for the utilization the outputs of the services sectors. Notably for the sectors that have the fastest growth in recent years, inter-industry demand played the dominant role, especially for other business services.

12.3.2 *Sources of Change in Service Sector Output*

Regarding the supply of output, it was found that the service sector outputs were largely supplied by service industries during each of the years 2011–2012, 2015–2016, and 2019–2020.

The only caveat here is that the supply use table (SUT) does not follow the exact same classification of services as in the KLEMS table. However, our focus will be on those sectors that have (i) high shares in the services economy in India and (ii) those sectors which have very rapid growth. Trade falls in the first category, while business and financial services fall in both categories. Thus the drivers of growth in the services sector can be said to be the business and financial services, which also have shown significant technological and organizational innovations.

We observe that the Growth of the services sector can definitely occur through increases in the final demand for services. However, it is also undoubtedly connected with the demand for services as inputs that go into the production of other sectors of the economy. Similarly, as the services sector expands, it facilitates the growth of other sectors of the economy, reinforcing the sector-level interdependencies in the economy. Now, two fundamental questions that come up are:

(1) how does service-led growth affect the rest of the economy?
(2) how much have the other sectors of the economy contributed to the growth of the services sector?

Together, these questions enquire about the relationship between the services sector and the rest of the economy. To proceed further in this direction, we need an appropriate framework for the study. The issue of service-led growth has been analyzed using various other approaches, such as multi-sector neoclassical growth models, computable general equilibrium (CGE) models, econometric studies and descriptive statistical tools. Mainstream models focus on technology and primary inputs as the alternative sources of growth in an economy. Although there have been developments that incorporate underutilized resources in CGE models, very little work has been done in a demand-constrained framework that integrates sector-wise interrelationships at detailed disaggregate levels.

Input–Output Analysis is a versatile methodology well suited for addressing the above mentioned queries. Well-established techniques in the Input–Output tradition such as linkage analysis and structural decomposition analysis are especially suited for answering questions pertaining to detailed sector-level causes and effects of growth in the service sectors or for that matter any chosen sector of an economy.

Recently published Input–Output tables and Supply-Use tables of the Indian economy provide well over a hundred disaggregated sectors of the economy, allowing the researcher substantial room to enquire about the input sources for producing services as well the sector-level destinations of the services that are produced. Final demand categories are available not just at the macroeconomic level but also at the detailed product mix levels corresponding to the hundred-plus sectors of the economy. The distribution of final demand is also calculable. Such a vast repository of information available over time helps to perform several analytical exercises, such as:

i. Quantifying the inter-sectoral linkages, especially the linkages between services and manufacturing sectors.
ii. Decomposing the sources of growth of the service sectors (by pair-wise comparison of the data from successive Input–Output tables) into effects of changes in technology and changes in final demand level, final demand mix, and final demand distribution.

12.3.3 Linkage Analysis in the Input–Output Framework

Linkage analysis is a widely used technique for measuring the degree of interconnectedness of the various sectors of an economy. For an economy with a large number of sectors, the gross output vector is given by

$$\boldsymbol{x} = \boldsymbol{A}\boldsymbol{x} + \boldsymbol{f} \tag{12.1}$$

where $\boldsymbol{x}$ is the $(n \times 1)$ vector of sector-level outputs, $\boldsymbol{A}$ is the $(n \text{ x } n)$ matrix of technical coefficients and $\boldsymbol{f}$ is the $(n \times 1)$ vector of sector-level final demands. With this behavioural equation, we can now solve the model for the sector-level outputs as follows. From Eq. (12.1),we obtain $(\boldsymbol{I} - \boldsymbol{A})\boldsymbol{x} = \boldsymbol{f}$, which implies

$$\boldsymbol{x} = (\boldsymbol{I} - \boldsymbol{A})^{-1}\boldsymbol{f} = \boldsymbol{L}\boldsymbol{f} \tag{12.2}$$

where $\boldsymbol{L} = (\boldsymbol{I} - \boldsymbol{A})^{-1}$ is the Leontief inverse, denoted by $[l_{ij}]$, which exists provided that the Hawkins Simon condition is satisfied. In our example of a three-sector economy, the Leontief inverse and backward linkages is shown in Appendix 1.

Out of the economy-wide backward linkages of the services sectors, the contribution or share of the manufacturing sectors was segregated to obtain a clear view of the interdependence between services and manufacturing. The Input–Output Tables of 2003–2004, 2007–2008, 2011–2012, 2015–2016, and 2019–2020 were considered for this exercise.[1] Results are shown in Tables 12.16 and 12.17 in Appendix 2.

Table 12.16 shows that between 2003–2004 and 2007–2008, the share of manufacturing sector linkages in the economy-wide backward linkages of the services sectors has ranged from 4% to almost 87%. The service sectors that show more than 10% of their backward linkages attributable to the manufacturing sectors in both these years are Construction, Electricity, Water Supply, Transport (Rail, Land, Water, Air, and Auxiliary), Storage and warehousing, Communication, Trade, Hotels and Restaurants, Banking, Insurance, Medical and Health, Business Services, Computer and related Activities, Other Commercial Social & Personal Services and Other Services. There were nineteen and twenty-one such sectors in 2003–04 and 2007–08 respectively. In addition, during 2007–2008, Legal Services and Renting of Machinery and Equipment also shows 10% or more of its backward linkage coming from the manufacturing sectors.

Results of similar analysis for the years 2011–2012, 2015–2016, and 2019–2020[2] are shown in Table 12.17 in Appendix 2. In 2011–2012 we found twenty-two service sectors (all except Ownership of Dwellings) with more than 10% of their backward linkages attributable to the manufacturing sectors. For 2015–2016 and 2019–2020, the number of such services were fifteen and fourteen respectively. The services

[1] The Input–Output Tables for 2011–2012, 2015–2016 and 2019–2020 were constructed from the Supply-Use Tables available in the website mospi.gov.in.

[2] The number of services sectors in the Input–Output tables of 2003–2004 and 2007–2008 were 25 (sectors 106 to 130) whereas those in the rest of the years were 23 (sectors 113–135).

sectors that have more than 10% of their backward linkages arising from the manufacturing sectors in all three years are—Construction and Construction Services, Electricity, Gas, Water Supply, Trade and Transport, Repair and Maintenance of Motor Vehicles, Storage and Warehousing, Communication Services, Real Estate, Renting of Machinery and Equipment, Other Business Services, and Human Health & Social Care Services.

The reverse channel of interdependence between the services and manufacturing sectors was also explored in detail. The share of service sectors in the backward linkages of the manufacturing sectors for the same five years (2003–2004, 2007–2008, 2011–2012, 2015–2016, and 2019–20) was analyzed. The Input–Output Tables for the years 2003–2004 and 2007–2008 show 60 manufacturing sectors (sectors 46 to 105), while the years 2011–2012, 2015–2016, and 2019–2020 show 57 manufacturing sectors (sectors 56 to 112). The results are summarized in Tables 12.18 and 12.19 in Appendix 3.

It is observed that in 2003–2004 and 2007–2008, about 54 manufacturing sectors had 10% or more of their respective backward linkages attributable to the services sectors. Similarly, in the years 2011–2012, 2015–2016, and 2019–2020, the number of manufacturing sectors that owed 10% or more of their backward linkages to the services sectors was 27, 34, and 60, respectively. Although the percentage shares are lesser than in the case of the service sectors, the number of relevant sectors has increased over the period of study.

Thus our analysis of linkages shows the importance of the manufacturing-share of backward linkages of the services sectors, the services-share of backward linkages of manufacturing sectors and the number of manufacturing sectors with 10% or more of their backward linkages emanating from the services sectors over time. We next move on to structural decomposition analysis of the sources of growth of the services sectors in the economy.

12.4 Structural Decomposition Analysis

Using this technique, we decomposed the growth of each of the services sectors of the economy into two broad components—changes due to inter-industry-input usage and changes in final demand. The change due to inter-industry-input usage was further decomposed into changes in the inter-industry-inputs coming from the primary, secondary (manufacturing) sector and services sectors. In the literature, the change in inter-industry input is known as change in technology. Further, the change due to final demand was decomposed into changes in overall final demand (GDP), final demand mix (sector-level shares of each component of final demand) and final demand distribution (shares of C, I, G, NX in GDP). A technical note is provided in Appendix 4.

Four pairs of Input–Output Tables were considered to calculate the sector-level growth rates during the periods 2003–2004 to 2007–2008, 2007–2008 to 2011–2012, 2011–2012 to 2015–2016, and 2015–2016 to 2019–2020. We denote these as Phase

1, 2, 3, and 4 respectively, shown in Table 12.14. Table 12.14 has four parts, which present the following results. Part I shows whether inter-industry input usage or use as final demand is the dominating factor underlying the growth of the Services Sectors. Part II presents those service sectors where inter-industry-input usage has increased. It also pinpoints whether such an increase has been generated by the manufacturing/primary/services sectors. Part III gives us the Services Sectors where final demand usage has increased via the level/mix/distribution effect. Part IV shows those sectors where inter-industry-input usage of sector output has decreased.

The main findings are summarized with reference to the rows of Table 12.14 as follows.

(1) The Growth of a few service sectors has been majorly driven by the use of inter-industry inputs. Among these, manufacturing sectors have contributed in some cases to the changes in inter-industry inputs, as evident from rows 1 and 4.
(2) Primary and Services sectors have also increased their contribution as inter-industry-inputs going to the Services Sectors. This is evident from row-5 and row-6.
(3) Final demand, in particular, the level of final demand, has been the major driver of the growth of most service sectors, as shown in row-2 and row-7.
(4) In a few cases, final demand mix and distribution effects have contributed to the growth of some service sectors. This is shown in row-8 and row-9.
(5) In many of the sectors where final demand had been the major force, inter-industry—input usage has been a supporting factor. Furthermore, the changes in inter-industry-inputs have sometimes been contributed by the manufacturing sectors. These are shown in row-3 and row-4.
(6) In those sectors where inter-industry-input has played a dominant role, final demand level effect has also played a supportive role in the growth process, as shown in row-7.
(7) In those instances, where inter-industry-input usage has decreased, growth has been sustained through changes in final demand level, mix and distribution. This is true by the logic of overall growth of the concerned services sectors.
(8) In each phase, some of services sectors have experienced a reduction in their usage as inter-industry-input while the other service sectors have experienced an increase in their usage as inter-industry input. We may say that for the latter, there has been servicification throughout the economy.

12.4.1 Tying up the Results

Analysis of Supply-Use tables (results shown in Tables 12.12 and 12.13) clearly shows that the outputs of many Services Sectors, particularly the Business Services Sectors have been used intensively as inter-industry inputs in the economy. This in itself shows the importance of the services sector as a major factor in the overall production structure of the economy. Since the demand for services originates largely

Table 12.14 Results of structural decomposition analysis of the growth of services sectors

Serial no	Characteristic feature	Phase-1: 2003–2004 to 2007–2008	Phase-2: 2007–2008 to 2011–2012	Phase-3: 2011–2012 to 2015–2016	Phase-4: 2015–16 to 2019–2020
Part-1					
1	Sectors where inter-industry-inputs formed the major or at least an important source of growth	Construction (11.41%), trade (12.65%), hotels and restaurants (38.53%), business services (40%), legal services (28.28%), real estate activities(18.47%)—in all, six sectors out of twenty five sectors	Water supply (38.8%), real estate activities (78.37%), renting of machinery and equipment (84.52%), other services (42.1%)—in all, four sectors out of eighteen sectors	Repair and maintenance of motor vehicles (54.16%), real estate services (26.41%), Legal services (14%), other business services (98.74%)—in all, four out of twenty-three sectors	Gas (71.7%), storage and warehousing (65.41%), insurance services (61.39%), renting of machinery and equipment (34.64%), research and development services (82.84%), recreational services (92.95%)—in all, six out of twenty-three sectors
2	Sectors where final demand formed the major source of growth	All the other nineteen services sectors	All the other fourteen services sectors	All the other nineteen services sectors	All the other seventeen services sectors
Part-2					

(continued)

Table 12.14 (continued)

Serial no	Characteristic feature	Phase-1: 2003–2004 to 2007–2008	Phase-2: 2007–2008 to 2011–2012	Phase-3: 2011–2012 to 2015–2016	Phase-4: 2015–16 to 2019–2020
3	Sectors whose use as inter-industry-inputs has increased	Construction, air transport, trade, hotels and restaurants, education and research, medical and health, business services, legal services, real estate activities	Water supply, banking, business services, legal services, real estate activities, renting of machinery and equipment, other services	Electricity, repair and maintenance of motor vehicles, real estate services, legal services, other business services, education services, community/social and personal services	Construction & construction services, electricity, gas, trade and transport, storage and warehousing, financial services, insurance services, renting of machinery and equipment, research and development services, computer related services, education services, human health and social care services, community/social and personal services, recreational services
4	Sectors where manufacturing has been the dominant or an important source within the inter-industry-input effect	Construction (99.45%), trade (57.59%), hotels and restaurants (58.98%), business services (120.89%), legal services (72.22%), real estate activities(73.6%)	Renting of machinery and equipment (27.06%)	Electricity (263.62%), repair and maintenance of vehicles (57.45%), other business services (28.69%),	Construction & construction services (27.31%), electricity (255.01%), gas (21.2%), financial services (250.36%), insurance services (148%), renting of machinery and equipment (22.85%), research and development services (9.41%), education services (18.25%), education services, human health and social care services (57.69), recreational services (8.66%)

(continued)

Table 12.14 (continued)

Serial no	Characteristic feature	Phase-1: 2003–2004 to 2007–2008	Phase-2: 2007–2008 to 2011–2012	Phase-3: 2011–2012 to 2015–2016	Phase-4: 2015–16 to 2019–2020
5	Sectors where inter-industry-inputs into services from primary sectors has increased	Construction, water supply, storage and warehousing, trade, hotels and restaurants, banking, education and research, business services, computer related activities, legal services, real estate services, other commercial/personal/social services	Construction, renting of machinery and equipment	Construction and construction services, electricity, financial services, renting of machinery and equipment, legal services, other business services, computer related services, education services, human health and social care services, community / social / personal services	All sectors except electricity, ownership of dwellings, real estate services, legal services, other business services, public administration and defence
6	Sectors where inter-industry-inputs into services from services sectors has increased	Construction, trade, hotels and restaurants, education and research, medical and health, legal services, real estate services, other services	Electricity, water supply, banking, business services, legal services, real estate activities, renting of machinery and equipment, other services	Repair & maintenance of motor vehicles, real estate services, legal services, other business services, education services, community/social/personal services, recreational services	Construction, gas, trade & transport, storage and warehousing, renting of machinery and equipment, research and development services, legal services, computer-related services, educational services, human health & social care services, community/social/personal services, recreational services
Part-3					

(continued)

Table 12.14 (continued)

Serial no	Characteristic feature	Phase-1: 2003–2004 to 2007–2008	Phase-2: 2007–2008 to 2011–2012	Phase-3: 2011–2012 to 2015–2016	Phase-4: 2015–16 to 2019–2020
7	Sectors where final demand level effect dominated within the final demand effect	All services sectors except real estate activities	All services sectors except water supply, real estate activities, renting of machinery and equipment and other services	All services sectors	All services sectors except real estate services and community / social / personal services
8	Sectors where final demand mix effect dominated or was important within the final demand effect	Real estate activities	Construction, electricity, water supply, insurance, ownership of dwellings, medical & health, business services, other commercial/social/ personal services, other services, public administration	Trade and transport, repair and maintenance of motor vehicles, storage and warehousing, communication services, research & development, legal services, computer related services, education services, community/social /personal services	Water supply, real estate services, renting of machinery & equipment, legal services, other business services, computer-related services, education services, community/social/personal services
9	Sectors where final demand distribution effect dominated within the final demand effect	None	Hotels & restaurants, computer and related activities	Gas, hotels & restaurants, repair and maintenance of motor vehicles, renting of machinery and equipment, other business services	Gas, insurance services, ownership of dwellings, public administration & defence, human health & social care services, recreational services

(continued)

Table 12.14 (continued)

Serial no	Characteristic feature	Phase-1: 2003–2004 to 2007–2008	Phase-2: 2007–2008 to 2011–2012	Phase-3: 2011–2012 to 2015–2016	Phase-4: 2015–16 to 2019–2020
Part-4					
10	Sectors where inter-industry input usage has decreased	Electricity, water supply, railway transport, water transport, supporting and auxiliary transport, storage and warehousing, communication, banking, insurance, computer & related activities, renting of machinery & equipment, other commercial/ social/ personal services, other services—in all twelve sectors out of twenty five	Construction, trade & transport services, hotels & restaurants, insurance, education and research, medical and health, computer and related activities, other commercial/ social/personal services—in all, seven sectors out of eighteen	Construction & construction services, gas, water supply, trade and transport, hotels & restaurants, storage & warehousing, communication services, financial services, insurance services, renting of machinery & equipment, computer related services, human health & social care services, recreational services—in all, thirteen sectors out of twenty three	Water supply, repair & maintenance of motor vehicles, hotels & restaurants, communication services, real estate services, other business services—in all, six sectors out of twenty three

Source Results from the present study

in the form of inter-industry inputs, it is clear that the level of output of the services sectors depends on the production of each sector of the economy.

Backward Linkage of the Services Sectors with the Manufacturing Sectors and vice versa (results shown in Tables 12.16, 12.17, 12.18 and 12.19 in the Appendix below) also quantify and underscore the interdependence between the Services and Manufacturing sectors.

A Structural Decomposition of the growth rates of the Services Sectors reveals the importance of both inter-industry-input usage and final demand in the growth process of the Services Sectors with a dominant role played by final demand.

Drawing an analogy from neoclassical growth models, one may dare to state that the inter-industry-input factor creates a "level effect" on the outputs of the Service Sectors. At the same time, there is undoubtedly a "growth effect" on the services sector originating from final demand.

12.5 Conclusions

This paper has tried to unravel the underlying dynamics and interdependence behind the so-called "supply-led growth" hypothesis that is discussed in the context of India. The real issue lies between the contending questions of how far this growth is self-propelled and how much of this depends on the inter-industry demand emanating mainly from the manufacturing sector. The data shows uneven growth within the services sector, where the main push has come through various types of business services. Also, the change in productivity in the services sector is not inter-sectoral through labour transfer but rather through capital accumulation and technological change. To get a clear idea, one needs some idea about the inter-sectoral dependence of the services sector on other sectors in the economy through backward and forward linkages (and multipliers). A detailed input–output analysis clearly shows two things—in some sectors, especially the fastest growing ones like business services, including communications and IT, the existing output levels are heavily dependent on inter-industry intermediate use of such services. However, the growth of such services, when decomposed, shows the importance of final demand in most cases. Further, technological changes in many sectors, especially manufacturing, have reduced per the unit requirement of services, but the scale effect dominates so that a rising final demand (including that from exports) has to be supplemented by greater inter-industry demand for services—the latter sometimes labelled as servicification of the manufacturing sector.

So, the final conclusion is that a deliberate push to the manufacturing sector will be a boon to the services sector as well. Despite the technological adverse change in some cases, the scale of enhanced service production requires more demand for manufacturing sector inputs. In addition, although not yet highly significant, more services are used in some manufacturing sectors, which is known as the servicification of manufacturing-sector production processes. This servicification may well be due to the substitution of other inputs by services due to changes in technology, but the result is an additional demand for services in the economy. So even though recent growth of services seems to be largely driven by final demand, the dependence of existing levels of services sector output on the manufacturing sector is well beyond doubt. Thus, the growth of the services sector will promote larger use of the same in many manufacturing sectors and, at the same time, will create more demand for manufacturing goods through the inter-industry backward linkage effect.

Appendix 1: Concept of Backward Linkage

See Table 12.15.

The elements of the Leontief Inverse, denoted by $l_{ij,}$ have very important economic interpretation.

For the three-sector economy characterized by the Leontief inverse given in Table 12.15, we obtain, using Eq. (12.2),

$$x_i = l_{i1}f_1 + l_{i2}f_2 + l_{i1}f_1 + l_{i3}f_3 \quad i = 1, 2, 3$$

For the n-sector economy, we obtain

$$\begin{aligned} x_i &= l_{i1} + l_{i2}f_2 + l_{i1}f_1 + \ldots + l_{in}f_n \quad i = 1, 2, \ldots, n \\ &= \sum\nolimits_{j=1}^{n} l_{ij}f_j \qquad i, j = 1, 2, \ldots, n \end{aligned} \tag{12.3}$$

Thus, the (i, j)th element l_{ij} of the Leontief inverse matrix $\boldsymbol{L}$ gives the total (direct and indirect) effect of a unit change in the final demand of the jth sector on the output of the ith sector (or industry). The direct effects are given by the technical coefficients a_{ij}. The indirect effects arise due to the repeated interactions between the industries during the process of production.

The backward linkage (Chenery & Watanabe, 1958) of any sector is the total value of production of all sectors of the economy required to sustain unit-level final demand for the output of the jth sector. This value of total required production is measured by the value of the total inputs required from all sectors of the economy to satisfy a unit of final demand for the output of the jth sector. The backward linkage of the jth sector with the entire economy is conceptually the same as the simple output multiplier of the jth sector. The backward linkage for any sector j is mathematically expressed

Table 12.15 A simple illustration of the Leontief inverse

	Agriculture	Manufacturing	Services
Agriculture	l_{11}	l_{12}	l_{13}
Manufacturing	l_{21}	l_{22}	l_{23}
Services	l_{31}	l_{32}	l_{33}

as the sum of all the elements of the jth column vector of the Leontief inverse $\boldsymbol{L}$. Considering a unit increase in the final demand of sector j alone, we express $\Delta \boldsymbol{f}$ as a column vector with 1 (one) in the jth position and zeroes everywhere else. Therefore, $\boldsymbol{L}\Delta \boldsymbol{f}$ picks out the jth column of the matrix $\boldsymbol{L}$. Now the sum of all these elements of the jth column of the Leontief inverse $\boldsymbol{L}$ represents the simple output multiplier for the jth sector and is given by BL = $\sum_{i=1}^{n} l_{ij}$; $j= 1, 2, \ldots ,n$

Appendix 2: Backward Linkages of the Services Sectors

See Tables 12.16 and 12.17

Appendix 3: Backward Linkages of Manufacturing Sectors

See Tables 12.18 and 12.19.

Appendix 4: A Technical Note on Structural Decomposition

We express the change in the sector-level output as:

$\Delta x =$ change due to Δ Technology + change due to Δ FD.

Δ Technology arises from (i) Δ Tech (1) due to inputs from primary sectors (ii) Δ Tech (2) due to inputs from secondary or manufacturing sectors, and (iii) Δ Tech (3) due to inputs from services sectors.

Δ FD arises due to(a) Δ FD level (b) Δ FD mix, and (c) Δ FD distribution.

The Final Results for Computation (Miller & Blair, 2009) are

$$\begin{aligned}\Delta \boldsymbol{x} = {} & (1/2)\boldsymbol{L_1} * (\boldsymbol{\Delta A}^{(1)} + \Delta \boldsymbol{A}^{(2)} + \ldots + \boldsymbol{\Delta A}^{(n)}) \\ & * \boldsymbol{L_0}(\boldsymbol{f}_0 + \boldsymbol{f}_1) + (1/2)(\boldsymbol{L_0} + \boldsymbol{L_1})\,[(1/2)\,(\Delta f_{\text{level}})\,(\boldsymbol{B_0 d_0} + \boldsymbol{B_1 d_1}) \\ & + (1/2)\{f_{\text{level0}}(\Delta \boldsymbol{B})\boldsymbol{d_1} + f_{\text{level1}}(\Delta \boldsymbol{B})\boldsymbol{d_0})\} \\ & + (1/2)\,(f_{\text{level0}}\boldsymbol{B_0} + f_{\text{level1}}\boldsymbol{B_1})\Delta \boldsymbol{d}]\end{aligned} \tag{12.4}$$

=Effect of change in Technology

+ Effect of change in Final Demand Level

+ Effect of change in Final Demand Mix

+ Effect of change in Final Demand Distribution.

Table 12.16 Backward linkages of services in 2003–2004 and 2007–2008

Sector no	Service sector name	BL 2003–2004	Share of Mfg sectors 2003–2004	BL 2007–2008	Share of Mfg sectors 2007–2008
106	Construction	2.23	**80.23%**	2.34	**80.69%**
107	Electricity	2.58	**77.04%**	2.20	**77.38%**
108	Water supply	1.73	**87.71%**	1.92	**85.13%**
109	Railway transport services	2.31	**86.97%**	1.93	**87.54%**
110	Land transport including via pipeline	2.25	**75.98%**	2.29	**72.02%**
111	Water transport	1.83	**84.99%**	2.24	**86.87%**
112	Air transport	2.17	**83.01%**	2.22	**80.51%**
113	Supporting and aux. transport activities	1.97	**28.78%**	1.99	**25%**
114	Storage and warehousing	1.92	**33.10%**	1.94	**31%**
115	Communication	1.58	**26.01%**	1.60	**27%**
116	Trade	1.36	**14.43%**	1.41	**16%**
117	Hotels and restaurants	2.24	**15.16%**	2.33	**14%**
118	Banking	1.37	**10.41%**	1.31	**11%**
119	Insurance	1.61	**20.39%**	1.50	**17%**
120	Ownership of dwellings	1.11	7.93%	1.10	7%
121	Education and research	1.21	8.57%	1.21	9%
122	Medical and health	1.78	**30.89%**	1.90	**27%**
123	Business services	2.08	**20.53%**	2.02	**21%**
124	Computer & related activities	1.52	**13.34%**	1.49	**14%**
125	Legal services	1.28	3.24%	1.39	**16%**
126	Real estate activities	1.48	6.37%	1.43	5%

(continued)

Table 12.16 (continued)

Sector no	Service sector name	BL 2003–2004	Share of Mfg sectors 2003–2004	BL 2007–2008	Share of Mfg sectors 2007–2008
127	Renting of machinery & equipment	1.29	4.27%	1.62	**25%**
128	O.com, social & personal services	1.49	**20.35%**	1.49	**18%**
129	Other services	1.68	**15.67%**	1.68	**19%**
130	Public administration	1.00	0.00%	1.00	0%

Source Results of the present study

Table 12.17 Backward linkages of services in 2011–2012, 2015–2016, and 2019–2020

Sector no	Service sector name	BL 2011–2012	Share of Mfg sectors 2011–2012	BL 2015–2016	Share of Mfg sectors 2015–2016	BL 2019–2020	Share of Mfg Sectors 2019–2020
113	Construction and construction services	2.30	**38.27%**	2.03	**25.59%**	2.16	**28%**
114	Electricity	2.34	**38.15%**	2.04	**20.24%**	2.07	**19%**
115	Gas	2.60	**46.20%**	2.44	**27.96%**	2.40	**22%**
116	Water supply	1.99	**23.15%**	1.83	**13.48%**	1.90	**20%**
117	Trade and transport	2.02	**29.02%**	1.85	**17.82%**	1.92	**16%**
118	Repair & maintenance of motor Vehicle	1.95	**26.53%**	1.78	**14.95%**	1.87	**15%**
119	Hotels & restaurant	2.01	**18.43%**	1.74	2.78%	2.14	8%
120	Storage and warehousing	2.19	**38.19%**	2.01	**22.84%**	3.12	**20%**
121	Communication services	2.44	**29.46%**	2.09	**16.74%**	2.24	**13%**
122	Financial services	1.65	**17.25%**	1.59	7.64%	1.68	7%
123	Insurance services	1.75	**13.23%**	1.87	8.76%	2.20	**12%**
124	Ownership of dwellings	1.10	3.35%	1.07	1.43%	1.07	2%
125	Real estate services	2.35	**32.48%**	2.00	**18.11%**	1.80	**17%**
126	Renting of machinery & equipment	1.94	**25.03%**	2.14	**18.53%**	2.05	**14%**
127	Research & development services	1.79	**20.56%**	1.84	**11.95%**	1.46	8%
128	Legal services	2.56	**26.12%**	2.21	**16.37%**	1.61	8%
129	Other business services	1.80	**20.56%**	1.84	**11.95%**	1.98	**12%**
130	Computer related services	1.62	**10.44%**	1.54	4.99%	1.74	9%

(continued)

Table 12.17 (continued)

Sector no	Service sector name	BL 2011–2012	Share of Mfg sectors 2011–2012	BL 2015–2016	Share of Mfg sectors 2015–2016	BL 2019–2020	Share of Mfg Sectors 2019–2020
131	Public administration and defence	1.75	**16.20%**	1.49	5.49%	1.45	5%
132	Education services	1.50	**12.15%**	1.49	7.09%	1.46	8%
133	Human health and social care services	1.71	**31.42%**	1.64	**30.08%**	1.69	**15%**
134	Community, social and personal services	2.01	**28.88%**	1.88	**18.82%**	1.58	8%
135	Recreation, entertainment and radio & TV broadcasting and other services	1.93	**14.27%**	1.90	8.26%	1.91	**15%**

Source Results of the present study

Table 12.18 Backward linkages of manufacturing in 2003–2004 and 2007–2008

Sector no	Manufacturing sector name	BL 2003–2004	Share of services sectors 2003–2004	BL 2007–2008	Share of services sectors 2007–2008
46	Khadi, cotton textiles(handlooms)	2.31	**13.57%**	2.06	**12.86%**
47	Cotton textiles	2.60	**12.45%**	2.71	**13.93%**
48	woollen textiles	2.57	**13.76%**	2.49	**14.01%**
49	Silk textiles	2.47	**15.19%**	2.83	**16.35%**
50	Art silk, synthetic fibre textiles	2.74	**13.50%**	2.87	**14.24%**
51	Jute, hemp, mesta textiles	2.15	**14.47%**	2.24	**15.63%**
52	Carpet weaving	2.33	**14.34%**	2.34	**14.99%**
53	Readymade garments	2.59	**14.76%**	2.57	**15.82%**
54	Miscellaneous textile products	2.53	**13.60%**	2.73	**15.43%**
55	Furniture and fixtures-wooden	2.03	**11.37%**	2.12	**12.41%**
56	Wood and wood products	1.87	**10.01%**	2.02	**10.87%**
57	Paper, paper prods. & newsprint	2.54	**10.27%**	2.59	**10.80%**
58	Printing and publishing	2.43	9.76%	2.66	**10.92%**
59	Leather footwear	2.28	**13.11%**	2.60	**14.04%**
60	Leather and leather products	2.36	**13.00%**	2.49	**13.75%**
61	Rubber products	2.60	**10.95%**	2.49	**10.77%**
62	Plastic products	2.70	**10.06%**	2.95	**11.03%**
63	Petroleum products	2.26	6.01%	2.42	5.82%
64	Coal tar products	2.44	**10.54%**	2.17	8.96%
65	Inorganic heavy chemicals	2.53	**10.79%**	2.91	**10.78%**
66	Organic heavy chemicals	2.52	**10.78%**	2.78	**10.47%**

(continued)

Table 12.18 (continued)

Sector no	Manufacturing sector name	BL 2003–2004	Share of services sectors 2003–2004	BL 2007–2008	Share of services sectors 2007–2008
67	Fertilizers	2.59	9.91%	3.34	9.44%
68	Pesticides	2.45	**11.31%**	2.80	**11.96%**
69	Paints, varnishes and lacquers	2.57	**10.83%**	2.50	**10.62%**
70	Drugs and medicines	2.38	9.12%	2.78	**11.07%**
71	Soaps, cosmetics & glycerin	2.50	**10.47%**	2.75	**12.24%**
72	Synthetic fibres, resin	2.55	9.82%	2.75	**10.78%**
73	Other chemicals	2.48	**10.82%**	2.53	**11.03%**
74	Structural clay products	2.32	**10.54%**	2.17	**10.43%**
75	Cement	2.36	**10.99%**	2.32	**10.91%**
76	Other non-metallic mineral prods	2.29	9.32%	2.56	**10.60%**
77	Iron, steel and ferro alloys	2.42	**11.82%**	2.45	**12.62%**
78	Iron and steel casting & forging	2.60	**11.38%**	2.67	**11.83%**
79	Iron and steel foundries	2.60	**10.79%**	2.71	**11.67%**
80	Non-ferrous basic metals	2.56	**11.15%**	2.71	**11.92%**
81	Hand tools, hardware	2.41	**10.16%**	2.68	**11.91%**
82	Miscellaneous metal products	2.53	**11.09%**	2.71	**11.82%**
83	Tractors and agri. implements	2.64	**13.84%**	2.73	**13.04%**
84	Industrial machinery(F & T)	2.62	**11.30%**	2.96	**11.22%**
85	Industrial machinery(others)	2.52	**11.67%**	2.72	**11.86%**
86	Machine tools	2.54	**11.83%**	2.76	**12.33%**

(continued)

Table 12.18 (continued)

Sector no	Manufacturing sector name	BL 2003–2004	Share of services sectors 2003–2004	BL 2007–2008	Share of services sectors 2007–2008
87	Other non-electrical machinery	2.58	**12.31%**	2.86	**11.73%**
88	Electrical industrial Machinery	2.77	**12.35%**	2.94	**12.26%**
89	Electrical wires & cables	2.85	**10.29%**	3.00	**10.95%**
90	Batteries	2.83	**12.34%**	2.78	**13.38%**
91	Electrical appliances	2.70	**14.68%**	2.77	**15.59%**
92	Communication equipments	2.98	**15.64%**	2.89	**16.14%**
93	Other electrical Machinery	2.71	**11.31%**	2.80	**12.00%**
94	Electronic equipments(incl.TV)	2.97	**13.28%**	2.92	**13.63%**
95	Ships and boats	2.71	**11.34%**	5.16	4.88%
96	Rail equipments	2.48	**11.17%**	2.74	**10.49%**
97	Motor vehicles	2.62	**15.13%**	3.02	**12.54%**
98	Motor cycles and scooters	2.57	**14.85%**	2.98	**13.06%**
99	Bicycles, cycle-rickshaw	2.68	**12.82%**	2.97	**14.40%**
100	Other transport equipments	2.52	**14.69%**	2.74	**13.37%**
101	Watches and clocks	2.10	**13.03%**	1.93	**11.03%**
102	Medical, precision & optical instruments	2.30	**13.47%**	2.58	**14.01%**
103	Jems & jewellery	2.47	**11.91%**	2.76	**11.22%**
104	Aircraft & spacecraft	2.20	**23.46%**	4.68	6.23%
105	Miscellaneous manufacturing	2.60	**11.35%**	2.70	**12.79%**

Source Results of the present study

Table 12.19 Backward linkages of manufacturing in 2011–2012, 2015–2016, and 2019–2020

Sector no	Manufacturing sector name	BL 2011–2012	Share of services sectors 2011–2012	BL 2015–2016	Share of services sectors 2015–2016	BL 2019–2020	Share of services sectors 2019–2020
56	Cotton yarn and cotton textiles	2.15	5%	2.06	8%	2.20	**12%**
57	Synthetic yarn and synthetic textiles	2.18	6%	2.07	8%	2.22	**12%**
58	Wool yarn and woollen textiles	2.15	5%	2.07	8%	2.20	**12%**
59	Silk yarn and silk textiles	2.15	5%	2.07	8%	2.20	**12%**
60	Carpet weaving	2.15	5%	2.07	8%	2.20	**12%**
61	Ready made garments	2.11	5%	1.98	8%	2.17	**12%**
62	Misc. Textile products	2.12	5%	2.06	8%	2.20	**12%**
63	Leather footwear	1.94	2%	1.94	4%	2.21	**13%**
64	Leather and leather products, except footwear	1.96	3%	1.95	4%	2.21	**13%**
65	Wood and wood products except furniture	2.06	**12%**	1.99	7%	1.83	**11%**
66	Paper, paper products and newsprint	2.54	**13%**	2.35	12%	2.14	**15%**
67	Publishing, printing and allied activities	2.40	8%	2.13	11%	2.14	**14%**
68	Furniture & fixtures	2.11	11%	2.08	7%	2.05	**10%**
69	Rubber products	2.45	9%	2.24	10%	2.38	**14%**
70	Plastic products	2.43	9%	2.25	9%	2.38	**14%**
71	Petroleum products	2.77	8%	2.48	12%	2.64	**13%**
72	Coal tar products	2.77	8%	2.48	12%	2.63	**13%**

(continued)

Table 12.19 (continued)

Sector no	Manufacturing sector name	BL 2011–2012	Share of services sectors 2011–2012	BL 2015–2016	Share of services sectors 2015–2016	BL 2019–2020	Share of services sectors 2019–2020
73	Inorganic chemicals	2.66	7%	2.39	8%	2.38	**10%**
74	Organic chemicals	2.59	7%	2.35	7%	2.50	**12%**
75	Fertilizers	2.63	5%	2.35	5%	2.38	**10%**
76	Pesticides	2.62	5%	2.33	5%	2.38	**10%**
77	Paints, varnishes and lacquers	2.63	5%	2.35	5%	2.38	**10%**
78	Drugs and medicine	2.16	5%	1.89	4%	1.96	**13%**
79	Soaps, cosmetics and glycerin	2.58	5%	2.32	5%	2.36	**10%**
80	Synthetic fibres, resin	2.43	5%	2.17	7%	2.32	**11%**
81	Other chemicals and chemical products	2.40	5%	2.14	6%	2.47	**11%**
82	Cement	2.07	**13%**	1.92	**11%**	2.18	**18%**
83	Non-metallic mineral products	2.08	**13%**	1.94	**11%**	2.18	**18%**
84	Iron and steel Ferro alloys	2.56	**13%**	2.38	**13%**	2.61	**16%**
85	Iron and steel casting and forging	2.48	**13%**	2.37	**12%**	2.60	**16%**
86	Iron and steel foundries	2.51	**13%**	2.36	**12%**	2.61	**16%**
87	Non-ferrous basic metals (including alloys)	2.51	**13%**	2.47	**14%**	2.49	**17%**
88	Hand tools, hardware	2.44	**12%**	2.25	**11%**	2.39	**11%**
89	Miscellaneous metal products	2.42	**12%**	2.34	**13%**	2.41	**12%**
90	Tractors and other agricultural implements	2.37	**11%**	2.21	**15%**	2.30	**13%**
91	Industrial machinery for food and textile industry	2.35	**11%**	2.22	**14%**	2.30	**13%**

(continued)

Table 12.19 (continued)

Sector no	Manufacturing sector name	BL 2011–2012	Share of services sectors 2011–2012	BL 2015–2016	Share of services sectors 2015–2016	BL 2019–2020	Share of services sectors 2019–2020
92	Industrial machinery (except food and textile)	2.40	**11%**	2.22	**15%**	2.30	**13%**
93	Machine tools	2.42	**11%**	2.23	**14%**	2.30	**13%**
94	Other non-electrical machinery	2.44	**11%**	2.25	**15%**	2.34	**12%**
95	Electrical industrial machinery	2.55	**13%**	2.33	**15%**	2.30	**13%**
96	Electrical cables, wires	2.57	**12%**	2.33	**14%**	2.47	**12%**
97	Batteries	2.59	**13%**	2.34	**15%**	2.47	**12%**
98	Electrical appliances	2.53	**12%**	2.31	**13%**	2.46	**12%**
99	Communication equipment	2.63	**13%**	2.42	**23%**	2.51	**14%**
100	Other electrical machinery	2.59	**11%**	2.38	**18%**	2.45	**13%**
101	Electronic equipment including T.V	2.53	**11%**	2.23	**21%**	2.52	**14%**
102	Medical precision, optical instrument	2.49	**10%**	2.33	**14%**	2.34	**13%**
103	Watches and clocks	2.20	6%	1.90	**11%**	2.24	**12%**
104	Ships and boats	2.53	**10%**	2.30	**12%**	2.34	**11%**
105	Rail equipment	2.58	**10%**	2.30	**12%**	2.34	**11%**
106	Motor vehicles	2.59	9%	2.30	**12%**	2.34	**11%**
107	Motor cycles and scooters	2.60	9%	2.30	**12%**	2.34	**11%**
108	Bicycles, cycle-rickshaw	2.58	9%	2.30	**12%**	2.34	**11%**
109	Aircrafts & spacecrafts	2.60	9%	2.30	**11%**	2.34	**11%**
110	Other transport equipment	2.59	9%	2.29	**12%**	2.34	**11%**
111	Gems & jewellery	3.02	9%	3.31	6%	2.57	**14%**
112	Miscellaneous manufacturing	2.52	**11%**	2.41	9%	2.36	**13%**

Source Results of the present study

References

Balasubramanyam, V. N., & Balasubramanyam, A. (2021). Can services lead the Indian economy? In S. Bhide, V. N. Balasubramanyam & K. L. Krishna (Eds.), *Deciphering India's services sector growth*. Routledge.

Basu, A., & Veermani, C. (2021). *Labour share in Indian economy: An exploratory analysis of the role of trade, technology and structural transformation* (Working Paper 2021–27). Indira Gandhi Institute of Development Research.

Bhide, S., Balasubramanyam, V. N., & Krishna, K. L. (Eds.). (2021). Introduction. In S. Bhide, V. N. Balasubramanyam & K. L. Krishna (Eds.), *Deciphering India's services sector growth*. Routledge.

Chanda, R. (2021). India's services trade: Opportunities, challenges and international engagements. In A. Raychaudhuri, P. De & S. Das (Eds.), *World trade and India: Multilateralism, progress and policy response*. Sage Publications Private Ltd.

Chenery, H. B., & Watanabe, T. (1958). International comparisons of the structure of production. *Econometrica, 26*(4), 487–521.

Eichengreen, B., & Gupta, P. (2011, October). *The service sector as the road to India's economic growth* (NBER Working Paper 16757). National Bureau of Economic Research.

Krishna, K. L., Erumban, A. A., Das, D. K., Aggarwal, S., & Das, P. C. (2015). *Industry origins of economic growth and structural change in India. Centre for development economics, Delhi school of economics* (Working Paper No. 273). Available at. http://www.cdedse.org/pdf/work273

Majid, N. (2019). *Structural change and employment in India, Geneva: International labour office*. Accessed on February 10, 2024. Available at https://www.ilo.org/emppolicy/projects/sida/18-19/WCMS_735166/lang--en/index.htm

McMillan, M., & Rodrik, D. (2011). *Globalization, structural change and productivity growth* (NBER Working Paper 17143). National Bureau of Economic Research.

Miller, R. E., & Blair, P. D. (2009). *Input output analysis foundations and extensions*. Cambridge University Press.

Pant, S., & Chakraborty, D. (2024). Is service orientation benefitting manufacturing exports from low-middle income countries? Firm-level empirical evidence from WBES data. *Global Business Review*, 1–22. https://doi.org/10.1177/09721509241245544

Reserve Bank of India. (2024). *KLEMS database*. Available at https://www.rbi.org.in/scripts/klems.aspx

Part VI
Labour, Rural Non-farm and Migration

Chapter 13
The Status of Self-Employed and Casual Workers in India

Suresh Chand Aggarwal

Abstract During the last fifty years during 1972 to 2022, the overall workforce participation rate (WPR) in India has stagnated at around 41% but the female WPR has not only been around half of males, it has also declined by 2 percentage points. The average annual growth rate in employment has just been equal to 1.75%, though similar to that of population (1.8%). However, most of the labour has been employed in labour intensive sectors of agriculture and construction mainly as self-employed workers or casual labour. In India, the share of self-employed in total employment in 2022–23 is 57% and another 22% are casual workers. The share of regular workers is thus only 21%. India, has a lot of workers in the informal sector without any social security. These workers are the most vulnerable in any catastrophe. As a result, these self-employed, and casual workers were and still are the worst sufferers of any catastrophe, e.g. COVID-19 (Aggarwal, 2023b). They lost their occupations, and jobs due to severe economic lock downs and restrictions. They did not have alternative employment opportunities. Many of these workers who lost their jobs migrated to rural areas where many took employment under NREGA. Most workers did not get adequate financial support from the governments and were forced to take up self-employment for their survival. During COVID, not only the headcount employment fell but workers worked for less number of days per week and also for less number of hours per day. Government took few initiatives but they were perhaps not enough. Some more policy initiatives have been recently undertaken in India to increase the formalization of the economy and provide some social security to the workers through changes in the labour laws. The chapter aims to put the status of self-employed and casual workers in perspective. It first provides the brief profile of these workers in India during 1972–2022. Then the chapter identifies the total loss in employment by the workers during COVID-19, and gives an overview of the policy

The paper is an updated and revised version of the unpublished papers 'The status of Self-employed, Contract, and Gig Workers in India: Some recent Changes' presented at the 37th IARIW general conference held at Luxemburg from 22–26th August 2022, and a version of the same paper 'The status of Self-employed and Casual Workers in India: Some recent changes due to COVID19,' which is available on SSRN, WPS no 4517644, July 2023.

S. C. Aggarwal (✉)
Institute for Human Development, New Delhi, India
e-mail: suresh.aggarwal@ihdindia.com

D. Maiti et al. (eds.), *75 Years of Growth, Development and Productivity in India*, India Studies in Business and Economics, https://doi.org/10.1007/978-981-97-8054-9_13

initiatives which were taken to help the workers during COVID-19. Based on the outcome of the evidence, some policy recommendations have been made to improve the work condition of the workers.

Keywords Employment · Self-employed workers · Casual workers · Feminization · COVID-19 · Days worked · Hours worked

JEL Code J21

13.1 Introduction

The measurement of labour input has always been a challenge before the economists aiming to study the contribution of labour in output and productivity. The issue of measurement is also important to understand how the national income is distributed between different inputs, especially labour and capital. The issue of distribution of national income has once again occupied the centre stage due to rising inequality in recent decades and the recent shocks to the economies due to Global financial crisis in 2008 and the COVID-19 pandemic in 2019. Both of these events have led to the waves of anti-globalization and anti-immigration. In all these happenings, the labour has been the most severally affected and it is the vulnerable among these the self-employed, and the casual workers who have borne the maximum brunt of external shocks like COVID-19.

India has a lot of workers in the informal sector without any social security. These workers are the most vulnerable in any catastrophe. As a result, these self-employed, and casual workers were and still are the worst sufferers of COVID-19. They lost their occupations, and jobs due to severe economic lock downs and restrictions. They did not have alternative employment opportunities. Many of the casual workers lost their jobs and did not get adequate financial support from the governments. Despite some economic revival, their economic status is still below the pre-COVID-19 period. However, some policy initiatives were taken during COVID and have also been undertaken in recent years to increase the formalization of the economy and provide some social security to the workers through changes in the labour laws.

The chapter provides in section two a brief discussion about the data and concepts used in the chapter. While in section three we first provide an overview of the exact magnitude and status of the workers in India, the recent status of self-employed and casual workers is discussed in section four. Then, in section five the chapter evaluates the impact of COVID-19 on the employment status of workers, and section six highlights the policy initiatives which were taken to improve the delicate economic status of the vulnerable workers. Based on the outcome of the evidence, policy recommendations have been made in section seven to improve the job and income security of these workers.

13.2 Data and Concepts

The main data sources used for estimating employment are the different rounds of Employment and Unemployment Survey (EUS) by National Statistical Survey Office (NSSO) and the annual Periodic labour force surveys (PLFS)[1] by National Statistical Office (NSO), Ministry of Statistics and Programme Implementation (MOSPI), Government of India (GOI).

Based on the activity status of the persons, EUS/PLFS groups them into (i) either in the labour force either actually working (employed) or are seeking work or being available for work if the work is available (unemployed), or (ii) out of labour force (OLF). Those persons who are working are categorized by EUS/PLFS into three broad categories of (i) self-employed which includes those who (a) worked in household enterprises as -own account workers, or (b) as an employer, or (c) as helper or unpaid family worker, (ii) worked as wage/salaried employee, (iii) casual labour (a) in public work or (b) in other works. The EUS /PLFS also provides several concepts of employment, depending upon the reference period it uses (one year, one week, and each day of the reference week) to determine the activity status. These activity statuses are thus defined as Usual status consisting of only the principal status (UPS) or both the principal and the subsidiary status (UPSS), current weekly status (CWS) and the current daily status (CDS). According to EUS (2011–12) 'The usual activity status relates to the activity status of a person during the reference period of 365 days preceding the date of survey and the current weekly activity status of a person is the activity status obtaining for a person during a reference period of 7 days preceding the date of survey.'

13.3 Profile of Workers in India

Though the main objective of the chapter is to focus on the recent changes in the status of the self-employed, and casual workers in India, but a brief background of the total workforce in India during the last fifty years-1972–73 to 2022–23 is provided for a better understanding. However, a more detailed discussion about the status is restricted to only the recent years from 2017–18 to 2022–23.

Table 13.1 summarizes the workforce participation rate (WPR) of male and female workers in rural and urban sectors employed in usual principal and subsidiary status (UPSS) from 1972–73 to 2022–23. It can be observed that during the fifty years, while there has been only a marginal increase in workforce participation rate (WPR) from 537 to 544 per thousand for total males (TM), but there has been a substantial decline of 19 points in the WPR for total females (TF) from 289 to 270 during the

[1] The PLFS have been started with an aim to bring out high frequency data on employment. It may be mentioned that the annual Survey results which are provided under PLFS covers employment-unemployment from the respective July to June, thus includes four quarters of July–Sept, Oct–Dec, Jan–March, and April–June. Hence, the year 2017–18 covers July 2017 to June 2018.

same period.[2] As a consequence of this decline, a decline in WPR for total persons (TP) also took place—from 418 to 411 per thousand persons. Though there has been some fluctuations in the WPR for both rural and urban sectors but the substantial decline in WPR happened more in the rural sector and that too in the female WPR between 2004–05 and 2017–18. Incidently, this was a high growth phase of the Indian economy, especially from 2004 to 2014, and the trend in employment indicates that growth has been employment neutral. The decline in female WPR during 2004–05 to 2017–18 may have happened, because it is argued that females generally exit the labour force during prosperity and join the labour market during econmic distress. In between 2011–12 and 2017–18, the WPR for total persons had declined to as low as 347 in 2017–18 from 386 in 2011–12. Even the absolute employment fell for the first time during this period from 472.9 million in 2011–12 (2011) to 458 million in 2017–18 (2017) and the decrease was only in female employment by 25 million. Since 2017, there has been a continuous increase in the WPR in all the subsequent PLFS rounds and the WPR rate has now reached 411 in 2022–23 (2022) for total[3] persons and has also gone up for both total males and total females. However, in general, the WPR has been much lower among females than among their male counterparts. It was only 165 for females against 521 per 1000 for males in 2017–18, but has increased to 270 for females and 544 for males in 2022. As a result of which total 106 million persons 73 million in rural (70% of total) and 32 million in urban, and 35 million males (16 in rural and 19 in urban) and 71 million females (60% of the total) (57 million in rural alone), have joined the workforce between 2017 and 2022 (Appendix Table A1). Thus, there has been 'feminization' and 'ruralization' of the increase in workforce.

The compound annual growth rate of employment over the same period-divided into few sub-periods is depicted in Appendix Table A2. The Table shows that the long-term annual growth rate in employment has been 1.75% with corresponding growth in male employment of 1.82% and of the females as 1.61%. However, there has been a tendency of a declining trend in growth rate from one sub-period to another except the last four years from 2018–2022. The growth rate was 2.38% during 1972–73 to 1983, 2.02% during 1983 to 1993–94, 1.85% during 1993–94 to 2004–05, a stagnant rate of only 0.46% during 2004–05 to 2011–12, and a negative growth of 0.05% during 2011–12 to 2018–19. However the annual growth rate in employment during 2018–19 to 2022–23 has been phenomenal at 4.6%. This 4.6% annual employment growth has been mainly induced by 11.63% growth in the employment of total females of which rural female employment grew by 12.7% and urban female employment by 8.64%.

A number of explanations have been put forward in the literature for significantly lower WPR among females as compared to males in India. Predominant among them is the 'distressed employment' hypothesis. The studies argue that females have many household responsibilities—they are the care givers to both the children and

[2] In 2022–23, the WPR for TF is less than one-half of TM.

[3] Total includes both rural and urban sectors.

Table 13.1 Work participation rate (per thousand persons of all ages) by gender and sector by UPSS

Year	RM	RF	RP	UM	UF	UP	TM	TF	TP
1972–73	545	318	435	501	134	353	537	289	418
1977–78	552	331	444	508	156	341	543	297	423
1983	547	340	445	512	151	340	538	296	420
1987–88	539	323	434	506	152	337	531	285	412
1993–94	553	328	444	521	155	347	545	286	420
1999–00	531	299	417	518	139	337	527	259	397
2004–05	**546**	**327**	**439**	549	166	365	547	**287**	**420**
2011–12	**543**	**248**	**399**	546	147	355	544	**219**	**386**
2017–18	**517**	**175**	**350**	530	142	339	521	**165**	**347**
2018–19	**521**	**190**	**358**	527	145	341	523	**176**	**353**
2019–20	538	240	392	542	169	359	539	218	382
2020–21	549	271	413	549	170	363	549	242	398
2021–22	547	266	408	550	173	366	548	240	396
2022–23	540	300	423	556	187	377	544	270	411

Source EUS and PLFS, different rounds
Note RM is rural males, RF is rural females, and UM and UF are urban males and urban females respectively

the elderly in the family[4] and tender to many other unpaid household chores. They take up work only during economic hardships and if the economy and the family is doing well, they tend to withdraw from the workforce (Ghose, 2016; Mehrotra & Sinha, 2017). The WPR of women thus move anti-cyclically to the performance of the economy. Another plausible explanation especially for decline in female WPR since 2004 is that an increasing number of females are joining and staying in schools and colleges (Ghose, 2016; Mehrotra et al., 2014; Thomas, 2015) or attending to domestic duties (Thomas, 2015). Few studies (Kapoor, 2023; State of Working India, 2023) have attributed the surge in female employment during 2018 to 2022 to distress employment and the shift of females from domestic duties to unpaid family labour, while others (Goldar & Aggarwal, 2024) explain it by increase in work opportunities to women in agriculture and due to better access to water, cooking gas, etc. giving them more time to devote to work. Whatever the reasons, the WPR of females (age 15+) is still relatively very low in India—a mere 36% in 2022, as compared with 80% in Nepal (2016), 65% in Bhutan (2021), 51% in South Africa (2022), 54% in Brazil (2022), and 61% in China (2021).[5] Such a huge gender gap in WPR is not

[4] The Niti Aayog is now working closely with ILO to develop the fine print for a care economy and with the Bill & Melinda Gates Foundation as well as with V. V. Giri National Labour Institute to increase the participation of women in the labour force (The Economic Times, 16th May 2022).

[5] https://genderdata.worldbank.org/indicators/sl-tlf-acti-zs/?estimate=National.

observed in many countries of the World, may be except Turkey, and few countries of Middle East and North Africa (Viswanathan et al., 2021).

The structure of employment by industry reveals (Table 13.2) that India initially followed the traditional pattern of growth with decreasing share of employment in agriculture from 74% in 1972–73 to only 42.5% in 2018–19, with a simultaneous increase in the share of other sectors including manufacturing. Since 2018–19 however, the share of employment in agriculture has increased by more than 3 percentage points to 45.8% in 2022–23. Out of 93 million addition to employment between 2018–19 and 2022–23, 63% i.e. 58 million have joined agriculture, and 16 million (18%) joined construction, and only 7 million (8%) are employed in other industrial activities of mining, manufacturing and utilities. The services sector provided employment to only 11 million (12%) workers. The employment in agriculture during this phase of the economy (2018–2022) grew by an annual growth rate of 6.6% followed by 6.5% in construction, 2.8% in mining, manufacturing and utilities, and only 1.8% in services. So, agriculture and the construction sectors, which are both labour intensive with generally low level of labour productivity and low earnings, have absorbed four-fifth of the additional employment. The huge addition to employment in agriculture since 2018–19 seems not only to imply a reversal of the structural transformation that took place till 2017–18,[6] but also signify a huge dearth of employment opportunities in other sectors, especially industry. However, over the 50 years the long-term growth in employment in agriculture has been a modest 0.79% per year and the overall employment growth of 1.75% per year has been induced mainly by a high growth of 5.8% in construction, 3.1% in services, and a 2.28% by mining, manufacturing and utilities. So, the current trend may be just a temporary setback and could be reversed with suitable policies. The fast changing technology is however a threat and an opportunity for India to create jobs in non-agriculture sectors to provide employment to the newly educated workforce and face international competition.

The reason for increased participation by workers in agriculture in the recent years may also be attributed to a fall in rate of growth of GDP in India. The Indian economy has been slowing since 2016–17 with a continuous fall in its GDP growth rate from 8.26% in 2016–17 to 6.8% per annum during 2017–18, 6.53% in 2018–19, 4.04% in 2019–20 and −8% in 2020–21, the last two years being affected by the spread of COVID-19. During the two years of COVID-19, out of 51 million additional rural workers, 50 million joined agriculture possibly due to reverse migration from urban to rural sector. The share of females in it was 36 million. However, there has been some recovery in the growth rate since 2020–21 with growth in real GDP being above 6%. But despite the recovery in economic growth, out of a total 24 million additional workers in 2022–23 over 2020–21 who joined the workforce, 14 million (58%) have been rural female workers.

[6] The absolute number of persons employed in agriculture had reduced by 30 million between 2011–12 and 2017–18.

Table 13.2 Percentage distribution of employment by broad industry sectors

Year↓/ Broad sectors →	Agriculture and allied activities	Construction	Mining, manufacturing and utility	Services
1972–73	73.9	1.8	9.5	15.0
1983	68.6	2.2	11.6	17.6
1993–94	64.0	3.2	11.7	21.1
2004–05	56.3	5.7	13.1	24.9
2011–12	48.9	10.6	13.8	26.7
2017–18	44.1	11.7	13.1	31.1
2018–19	42.5	12.1	13.1	32.3
2019–20	45.6	11.6	12.1	30.7
2020–21	46.5	12.1	11.8	29.6
2021–22	45.5	12.4	12.5	29.6
2022–23	45.8	13.0	12.2	28.9

Source Author's computations from EUS and PLFS, MOSPI, NSO

In a poor economic growth environment, persons, especially poor and unemployed, cannot afford to wait for 'good' jobs and tend to take any job for their sustenance as they have families to support and their chances of getting any alternative and regular employment are absent. It could be a case of 'distress' employment where employment rate may increase and the unemployment rate may decrease. Thus, the total unemployment rate by usual status among all ages above 15 years, which was at a high of 6.1% for total persons in 2017–18, fell to a low of only 3.2% in 2022–23 (Table 13.3), and it fell for both males and females by almost half to just 2.9% for females and 3.3% for males. But during the same period, the youth unemployment rate (15–29 years), though has declined in recent years, but still is very high among both males and females at around 11 and 10% and is a great cause of worry because it indicates that India is not able to take full advantage of its 'demographic dividend'. The unemployment rate among the educated persons (with education of secondary and above) follows a similar trend and is much higher among females in all the years as compared to males. In 2022–23, it is 10.3% for females as compared to 6.4% for males. The trend may be in sync with the overall employment trend. So, around 60% of the population is out of the labour force and a large number is idle and unemployed.

It is however not only the level and the structure of employment which is the key to understand the growth process, but the quality of employment also plays a crucial role. It is true that in India even among those who are employed, there are many who are poor, illiterate, employed as casual labour with relatively low wages, and who are predominantly in the informal sector of the economy where not only they earn lower wages, but have little social security and few days of employment in a year. Basu and Maertens (2009) have raised the issue of insufficient creation of 'good jobs' which could help in reducing poverty. Nayyar (2012) and Ghose (2015) have defined quality of employment on the basis of the three parameters—wages, the availability of

Table 13.3 Unemployment rate (%) for youth (15–29 years), all ages and educated* by UPSS

	Youth 15–29			All ages-15 and above			Educated		
Year	TM	TF	TP	TM	TF	TP	TM	TF	TP
2017–18	17.8	17.9	17.8	6.2	5.7	6.1	9.9	18.5	11.4
2018–19	17.2	17.7	17.3	6.0	5.2	5.8	9.7	17.1	11.0
2019–20	15.1	14.6	15.0	5.1	4.2	4.8	9.0	14.1	10.1
2020–21	13	12.5	12.9	4.5	3.5	4.2	8.1	12.6	9.1
2021–22	12.6	11.8	12.4	4.4	3.3	4.1	7.8	11.8	8.6
2022–23	9.7	10.6	10.0	3.3	2.9	3.2	6.4	10.3	7.3

Source Author's computations from EUS and PLFS, MOSPI, NSO
*Secondary (10 years of schooling) and above

written job contracts, and the availability of social security benefits. However, wages themselves depend among others, on skills and experience. So, education plays an important role in the quality of employment and one may say that labour with higher educational level is of better quality. Written job contracts and availability of social security benefits are associated with the nature of employment. In regular and salaried jobs, one generally has both, whereas in casual employment especially in informal sector both are missing. Since the quality of employment has been defined on the basis of nature of employment, the written job contract availability, and the social security benefits available in the job (Ghose, 2015; Nayyar, 2012; Papola & Sharma, 2015), based on these parameters it is perceived that the 'best' jobs are regular and salaried ones especially in the formal sector, and the worst ones are the casual jobs in the informal sectors. Some discussion on quality of jobs in India is presented below from 2004–05, when the reversal of trend in WPR happened.

While Table 13.4 highlights the distribution of employment in India in the informal sector, Table 13.5 provides the distribution on the basis of status of employment. Table 13.4 shows that almost three-fourth of the total employment has been in the informal sector during 2004–05 to 2022–23. There has been some decrease in the share till 2018–19 but since then it is on a continuous increase. The increase in the share of the informal sector employment in recent years is evident for both males and females. In 2022–23, more than three-fourth of the total employed males are engaged in the informal sector. Most of the labour in the informal sector is contract labour which has the advantage of low cost and flexibility in hiring and firing to the employers. Detailed analysis by Goldar (2022) shows that most of the contract workers are hired by plants of size 100–300 workers/or more than 300 workers. The contract workers' share is also high in plants which hire more regular workers. Earlier Singh et al (2019) also found evidence that the large firms, and also the firms producing for export markets are more likely to hire contract workers, whose wages are lower than the regular workers. Chandrasekhar and Ghose (2014) also found that 'contractualization of work has become a pervasive feature of both public and private sectors in all three major sectors, and is particularly marked in mining, manufacturing industry and some services.'

Table 13.4 Percentage of workers engaged in proprietary and partnership (P & P) enterprises among workers engaged in non-agriculture and AGEGC sectors (UPSS)

Year	TM	TF	TP
2004–05	76.7	79.7	77.5
2011–12	73.4	69.2	72.4
2017–18	71.0	54.7	68.2
2018–19	71.5	54.1	68.4
2019–20	72.9	56.5	69.5
2020–21	75.3	56.7	71.4
2021–22	75.2	58.4	71.8
2022–23	77.9	60.8	74.3

Source Prepared by author using EUS and PLFS reports, MOSPI, NSO

Note PLFS defines informal sector enterprises as proprietary and partnership type enterprises within the non-agriculture and AGEGC sectors. (PLFS, p. 58)

Table 13.5 Percentage distribution of workers (UPSS) by Status in employment

Employment status →	Self-employed			Regular employees			Casual workers		
Year↓	Males	Females	Persons	Males	Females	Persons	Males	Females	Persons
2004–05	54.7	61.4	56.9	17.2	8.3	14.3	28.1	30.3	28.9
2011–12	50.7	56.1	52.2	19.8	12.7	17.9	29.4	31.2	29.9
2017–18	52.3	51.9	52.2	23.4	21.0	22.8	24.3	27.0	25.0
2018–19	51.7	53.4	52.1	24.4	21.9	23.8	24.0	24.7	24.1
2019–20	52.4	56.3	53.5	24.0	20.0	22.9	23.6	23.7	23.6
2020–21	53.9	59.4	55.6	22.7	17.4	21.1	23.3	23.2	23.3
2021–22	53.2	62.1	55.8	23.6	16.5	21.5	23.2	21.4	22.7
2022–23	53.6	65.3	57.3	23.2	15.9	20.9	23.2	18.8	21.8

Source Author's computations from EUS and PLFS, MOSPI, NSO

Table 13.5 displays another characteristics of labour on the basis of which one may infer about the quality of employment[7] in an economy. Table 13.5 shows that the share of workers as regular wage/salaries employees was just 14% in 2004–05 and the share increased continuously to almost 24% in 2018–19 but declined to 21% in 2022–23. During the last five years, the decline is substantial among females almost by one-third of the percentage points. On the other hand, the share of workers in self-employment has decreased for all the workers by around five percentage points between 2004–05 and 2018–19 (a normal year before the onset of COVID), but since

[7] The quality of employment is described in terms of the share of employment as regular employees with social security and job contract. The higher is the share better is the employment quality. The higher share of self-employed and casual labour thus is an indication of 'poor' quality of employment.

then the entirely opposite trend of an increase in the share of self-employed persons has been observed. The increase in the share is very substantial for female self-employment—a 12 point increase, than the 2 point increase for male counterparts. The trend is an indication of poor quality employment, especially for females. An opposite trend is observed for casual labour where the share has declined for both males (5 percentage points) and females (12 percentage points) between 2004–05 and 2022–23. Overall, out of total 106 million addition to jobs in 2022–23 over 2017–18, around 80%, i.e. 84 million have been added to self-employed, 9 million by casual labour and only 13 million (i.e. just 14% of the total) by regular employees. One may thus say that some degree of informalization has taken place during the recent period especially among female workers.

A plausible explanation for the recent reversal in trend of increase in share of regular employees and of a decrease in share of the self-employed is found in the increasing informalization of the formal sector of the economy. Within formal sector, employment of workers have been taking place without any concomitant social security associated with it. The employees without any written contract or paid leave or other social security have been substantial (Table 13.6) and they are rendered vulnerable. Lot of sub-contracting and outsourcing have also been going on in the formal sector, as a result of which employment is shifting from large enterprises to small ones where informality and lack of social security is higher and informalization of the formal sector is taking place. Also, with a significant increase in the role and number of 'gig' workers,[8] accentuated by COVID-2019, the regular employees share started falling and that of self-employed started increasing.[9] According to ILO (2024, p. 25) 'the recent decline in the share of regular workers without a written contract (from 69.8% in 2018–19 to 58.6% in 2022–23) and the increase in workers having a long-term contract (from 21.5% in 2018–19 to 26.4% in 2021–22) indicate a reduction of jobs for vulnerable regular workers during the pandemic period.'

Thus, taken together the employment in the informal sector and in the casual and self-employment categories, one may infer that the quality of employment in India is still poor and conscious efforts are to be made to further improve it.

Though regular employees are expected to enjoy security of jobs, but a view of the wage/salaried employees in recent years, however reveals that a very large proportion of them also do not enjoy the same security of jobs which is generally expected. Viswanathan et al. (2021) has also linked nature of employment formal or informal with employment contract and found relatively weak employment contract in agriculture, manufacturing, and electricity & construction but strong in financial services, and public & other services. Table 13.6 however shows that even in 2022–23, 58.6% of the wage/salaried employees do not have any written job contract. The proportion is even higher for males than the females. The proportion has however, observed a declining trend—it declined from 71% in 2017–18 to 58% in 2022–23.

[8] Refer to Aggarwal (2023) for an overview of 'gig' workers.

[9] With emergence of e-commerce, and a boost during COVID, many of the vulnerable regular employees had to forego their jobs and are now replaced by temporary or 'gig' workers who are mainly treated as self-employed and not counted as employees by the companies but.

Table 13.6 Percentage of regular wage/salaried employees who had no written job contract, not eligible for paid leave and not eligible for any social security benefit among regular wage/salaried employees in usual status (UPSS) in non-agriculture sector

	percentage of regular wage/salaried employees who had no written job contract					
Year →	(2017–18)	(2018–19)	(2019–20)	(2020–21)	(2021–22)	(2022–23)
Males	72.3	70.3	68.1	65.2	62.9	59.6
Females	66.8	66.5	65.0	61.5	59.1	55.8
Total Persons	71.1	69.5	67.3	64.3	62.0	58.6
	percentage of regular wage/salaried employees not eligible for paid leave					
Males	55.2	54.7	53.1	49.3	50.5	47.8
Females	50.4	50.6	49.8	43.7	44.6	43.5
Total Persons	54.2	53.8	52.3	47.9	49.2	46.8
	percentage of regular wage/salaried employees not eligible for any social security benefit					
Males	49.0	51.2	53.6	53.1	52.2	53.1
Females	51.8	54.4	56.0	55.8	55.7	56.5
Total Persons	49.6	51.9	54.2	53.8	53.0	53.9

Source PLFS, MOSPI, NSO, different years

Not only this, more than half of the wage/salaried employees were not eligible for paid leave in 2017–18 and around 47% are still not eligible for paid leave. In regard to the access to social security benefits, the PLFS reports show that in 2022–23 more than half-54% of the wages/salaried employees are not eligible for any social security benefit[10] and the proportion has increased since 2017–18 and is even higher for females than males. Thus, it is observed that a lower proportion of females are eligible for any social security benefit. It is clear that more than half of the regular workers have no written contract, or paid leave or access to social security in 2022–23. The reason for this observed decline in the share of workers with no written contract and eligible for paid leave and increase in social security benefits, as mentioned above, is the emergence of 'gig' economy leading to informalization of the formal sector. Now the workers are part of the formal sector but are informal with no written job contracts or eligible for paid leave but are now contributing to EPFO, a social security benefit, due to change in the eligibility to contribute to it.

[10] For PLFS (2020–21, p. 59) survey the following social security benefits were only considered:

(i) only PF/ pension (i.e. GPF, CPF, PPF, pension, etc.), (ii) only gratuity, (iii) only health care & maternity benefits,

(iv) only PF/ pension and gratuity, (v) only PF/ pension and health care & maternity benefits,

(vi) only gratuity and health care & maternity benefits, (vii) PF/ pension, gratuity and health care & maternity benefits.

Those who were not covered under any of the above social security schemes were considered as not eligible for any social security benefits.

We thus find that (i) in 2022–23, there is a wide disparity in the WPR for males and females WPR has been very low in India especially for females, (ii) increase in employment has been driven significantly by rural sector and by females, (iii) 63% of the additional employment between 2018–19 and 2022–23 has been in agriculture, (iv) there has been 'femalization' of the increase in workforce, and (v) more than half of the employed are working as self-employed, 22% as casual labour and only 21% of the workers are in wage/regular employment. Over the period of 2017–18 to 2022–23, there has been a decline in the share of casual and regular wage/salaried employees but the share of self-employed has further increased by almost 5 percentage points.

13.4 Recent Status of Self-Employed and Casual Workers

In this section, we explore in more details the recent status of self-employed and casual workers since 2017–18 to 2022–23, two years before and two years after the COVID-19 during 2019 and 2020. We analyze the trend in employment through the lens of gender, sector, industry, days worked in a week, hours worked per day, and the earnings of the workers.

(I) **Employment Status of Workers by Gender and Sector—2017–18 to 2022–23**

From Table 13.7, we observe that the change in the share of workers by activity has changed very marginally between 2017 and 2022. Overall the share of self-employed (OAW + helper) is more than 50% for both males and females but whereas the share of own account workers (OAW) is higher among males, the share of unpaid labour (helpers in household enterprises) is higher among females.

With minor changes between the two years 2017 and 2022, the own account workers are around 48% among rural males, 35% for urban males, only around 28% for rural females and urban females in 2022. On the other hand unpaid family members are present predominantly among rural females with a share of around 40% and the share among rural males and urban females is just around 11–12% and is only 4.7% for urban males.

For casual workers, there is a five point difference between total males and total females but in general the share is higher in the rural sector than in the urban sector. However among regular employees, the share among males (23–24%) is higher than the females which itself has declined by 2022—to only 16%. It seems therefore, that employment as regular employees is more of an urban phenomenon than the rural one because of large differences in the two proportions. The driver to increased employment of females between 2017–18 and 2022–23 is their higher and increasing participation in unpaid work (helper) and own account work, and lower in wage/regular employee and casual employment. Kapoor (2023) also attributes the increase in females WPR to more unpaid family work.

Table 13.7 Employment status of workers by gender and sector (%)

	Year	OAW	helper	RWE	CL	All workers
Rural Male	2017–18	48.0	9.8	14.0	28.2	100.0
	2018–19	48.2	9.2	14.2	28.3	100.0
	2019–20	48.0	10.4	13.8	27.8	100.0
	2020–21	48.6	11.0	13.6	26.8	100.0
	2021–22	47.3	11.3	14.7	26.8	100.0
	2022–23	47.8	11.0	14.3	26.8	100.0
Rural Female	2017–18	19.0	38.7	10.5	31.8	100.0
	2018–19	21.8	37.9	11.0	29.3	100.0
	2019–20	20.6	42.3	9.5	27.5	100.0
	2020–21	21.9	42.8	9.1	26.2	100.0
	2021–22	25.1	42.7	8.1	24.1	100.0
	2022–23	27.9	43.1	8.0	21.0	100.0
Urban Male	2017–18	34.9	4.3	45.7	15.1	100.0
	2018–19	34.6	4.1	47.2	14.2	100.0
	2019–20	34.6	4.1	47.2	14.1	100.0
	2020–21	35.4	4.5	45.3	14.9	100.0
	2021–22	35.0	4.6	46.2	14.3	100.0
	2022–23	34.7	4.7	47.1	13.6	100.0
Urban Female	2017–18	23.7	11.0	52.1	13.1	100.0
	2018–19	24.9	9.6	54.7	10.7	100.0
	2019–20	23.5	11.1	54.2	11.1	100.0
	2020–21	26.0	12.4	50.1	11.5	100.0
	2021–22	26.7	12.7	50.3	10.3	100.0
	2022–23	27.6	12.8	50.8	8.9	100.0
Total Males	2017–18	44.1	8.2	23.4	24.3	100.0
	2018–19	44.0	7.6	24.4	24.0	100.0
	2019–20	43.9	8.5	24.0	23.6	100.0
	2020–21	44.8	9.2	22.7	23.3	100.0
	2021–22	43.8	9.4	23.6	23.2	100.0
	2022–23	44.3	9.3	23.2	23.2	100.0
Total Females	2017–18	20.2	31.7	21.0	27.0	100.0
	2018–19	22.5	30.9	21.9	24.7	100.0
	2019–20	21.3	35.0	20.0	23.7	100.0
	2020–21	22.8	36.6	17.4	23.2	100.0

(continued)

Table 13.7 (continued)

	Year	OAW	helper	RWE	CL	All workers
	2021–22	25.4	36.7	16.5	21.4	100.0
	2022–23	27.8	37.5	15.9	18.8	100.0

Source Author's computations from PLFS unit data
Note OAW = own account workers and employers, helper is helper or unpaid family worker in household enterprises, RWE is regular salary and wage employees, and CL is casual labour

So, self-employment exists more in rural areas-both males and females, with high share of own account workers among rural males and unpaid family workers among rural females. Share of casual workers is highest among rural males and rural females. Since regular employees are more of an urban phenomenon, so increasing urbanization could be a step to increase its share.

(ii) **Percentage Distribution of Employment by Industry and Employment Status-2017–18 and 2022–23**

The gender wise distribution of employment by employment status and industry is presented for 2017 and 2022 in Table 13.8. It is observed from the table that though there is no significant change in the structure of male employment between 2017 and 2022, the share of own account workers and helpers has increased for female workers along with a decline in the share of casual workers in other work. A wide divergence is also noticed between different industrial sectors in terms of the nature of employment it provides to males and females in both 2017–18 and 2022–23. Agriculture employs mainly own account workers, helpers and casual labour. However, while the share of own account workers is the highest for rural and urban males (around 59%), it is the helpers who account for the highest share for females (48 to 51%). On the contrary, in manufacturing while around 50% of males have employment as regular employees and one-third as self-employed, but 65% of the females are employed as self-employed labour and only 17–19% as regular employees. It is also noticed that construction employs more than 80 and 90% of male and female workers as casual labour. Trade sector also has pre-dominance of self-employed labour more among females (70–72%) than males (67–68%). It is however noteworthy that female employment as helpers is very significant in trade. On the other hand, transport and other services employ females majorly as regular employees and males as both regular and own account workers.

So, despite a similarity at the aggregate level we find much divergence in the composition of employment status between both males and females. While own account male workers exist predominantly in agriculture and trade, followed by transport, manufacturing, and other services, own account female workers are employed mainly in manufacturing, trade, and construction followed by agriculture. On the other hand, employers are found among males in a small proportion in agriculture and trade and among females in trade. Male Unpaid family workers/helpers are mostly in agriculture and a small share in trade but females work as unpaid family

Table 13.8 Percentage distribution of employment by industry and employment status -2017–18 and 2022–23

Broad sectors	Own-account worker	Employer	Helper	Regular/ Wage earners	Casual labour in public works	Casual lab in other work	Total
Total males-2017–18							
Agriculture	59.1	2.3	15.6	1.2	0.0	21.8	100.0
Manufacturing	26.8	3.0	4.6	48.5	0.0	17.0	100.0
Construction	9.7	1.8	0.4	5.8	3.5	78.8	100.0
Trade	56.6	4.0	7.6	27.0	0.0	4.9	100.0
Transport	37.8	1.4	0.9	48.9	0.0	11.0	100.0
Other services	23.4	1.7	1.4	69.3	0.0	4.2	100.0
Total	41.7	2.4	8.2	23.4	0.5	23.8	100.0
Total females-2017–18							
Agriculture	15.98	0.54	48.00	1.27	0.00	34.21	100.00
Manufacturing	50.43	0.56	16.08	19.01	0.00	13.92	100.00
Construction	0.34	0.06	0.20	2.58	42.62	54.20	100.00
Trade	40.55	1.10	30.58	23.49	0.00	4.28	100.00
Transport	4.48	1.33	0.33	93.21	0.00	0.66	100.00
Other services	9.19	0.45	2.25	85.04	0.00	3.06	100.00
Total	19.67	0.54	31.71	21.03	2.14	24.90	100.00
Total males-2022–23							
Agriculture	58.81	4.57	19.24	1.22	0.06	16.11	100.00
Manufacturing	24.13	4.96	4.56	55.34	0.00	11.01	100.00
Construction	9.99	3.05	0.47	4.55	0.91	81.03	100.00
Trade	52.21	6.76	8.80	27.93	0.00	4.30	100.00
Transport	42.25	1.90	0.69	46.23	0.00	8.92	100.00
Other services	24.47	3.47	1.81	67.15	0.00	3.11	100.00
Total	39.94	4.32	9.31	23.19	0.18	23.06	100.00
Total females-2022–23							
Agriculture	26.16	0.55	51.08	0.64	0.60	20.98	100.00
Manufacturing	61.50	0.72	15.02	17.08	0.00	5.68	100.00
Construction	0.08	0.47	0.39	3.22	45.02	50.82	100.00
Trade	32.36	1.21	43.55	20.51	0.00	2.37	100.00
Transport	3.11	0.30	2.71	93.17	0.00	0.70	100.00
Other services	11.70	0.56	1.81	84.03	0.32	1.58	100.00
Total	27.25	0.60	37.48	15.89	2.22	16.56	100.00

Source Author's computations from PLFS, MOSPI, NSO

labour in large proportion in agriculture and trade and in a small share in manufacturing also. In the service sector, a duality in employment is observed. While transport and other services employ more regular employees both male and female, but trade sector has more of informal employment—self-employed and casual.

Male casual labour are found mainly in construction but also in agriculture, manufacturing, and transport. The female casual labour also has similar industrial distribution and works in construction, agriculture and manufacturing but the share is relatively less in construction and more in agriculture as compared to males. We thus find higher level of informalization for females than more males.

(iii) Days and Hours Worked by Employment Status-2017–18 and 2022–23

Days: The average number of days worked in a week between 2017–18 and 2022–23 has marginally declined for total males (8%) and for females (11%) and also in all employment status categories (Table 13.9). It is an indication of higher level of underemployment by both males and females in 2022–23. It is also evident that females work for less average number of days in a week than males-another indication of underemployment by females. It could be due to the supply side-their added responsibility of domestic duties and family care, or demand side-the less demand for female labour due to many inherent bias of employers. It is also noticed that casual labour both in public work and other work -both male and female, gets employment for fewer number of days in a week. Surprisingly, in both the years while number of days worked by males in other employment status is almost similar to regular employees but females work much less as casual labour in public works (only for 3 days a week in 2017–18 and 2.4 days in 2022–23), in 'other casual work' (for around 4.5 days in 2017–18 and only 3.8 days in 2022–23), and as employer (6 days in 2017–18 and 5.2 days in 2022–23) as compared to around 6.8 and 5.8 days respectively as regular employee.

Hours: Another source of underemployment of workers is working for less number of hours in a day than the full day (assuming average eight hours of work per day). While the number of hours worked per day has reduced by 11% for male workers, it has reduced by whopping 35% among female workers between 2017–18 and 2022–23. The reduction in hours worked for males and females has been observed across almost all employment status. It is clear that females also work less average number of hours than their male counterparts in all employment status. The females work relatively less number of hours per day as casual worker and as helper in family enterprises. The hours of work per day by males is less as casual worker and self –employed worker than regular employees.

(iv) Days Per Week and Hours Per Day Worked by Employment Status-2017–18 and 2022–23 (Regular Worker = 1)

To understand the relative change in the structure of employment and the status of self-employed and casual workers, we also analyze the days worked per week and the hours worked per day by them vis. a vis. regular workers (Table 13.10). It gives us an idea about the extent of underutilization of these workers. Since regular wage/

Table 13.9 Days and Hours Worked by Employment Status-2017–18 and 2022–23

Average number of hours worked in a day					Average number of days worked in a week				
Year →	2017–18	2022–23	2017–18	2022–23	Year	2017–18	2022–23	2017–18	2022–23
Employment Status↓	Males	Males	Females	Females	Employment Status	Males	Males	Females	Females
OAW	7.4	6.7	6.7	4.4	OAW	6.7	6.4	6.2	5.9
Employer	7.8	6.9	6.8	4.8	Employer	6.8	6.1	6.0	5.2
Helper	6.4	5.2	6.3	3.5	Helper	6.3	5.5	5.2	4.5
RWE	8.4	7.3	6.9	6.0	RWE	6.9	6.0	6.8	5.8
CL in public works	6.4	5.4	5.7	2.4	CL in public works	5.7	3.6	3.1	2.4
CL in other work	6.0	5.5	5.2	3.8	CL in other work	5.2	5.1	4.5	3.8
Total	7.2	6.4	6.4	4.2	Total	6.4	5.9	5.5	4.9
Change in %		−11%		−35%	Change in %		−8%		−11%

Source Author's computations from PLFS, MOSPI, NSO
Note OAW-own account worker, helper-unpaid family workers, RWE is regular salary and wage employees, CL in PW is Casual labour in public works, and CL in OW is Casual lab in other work

salaried employment is considered to be the best among all employment status, we take the category as the benchmark and compare others with it.

Relative Days: While for all the males the average number of days worked in a week are close to the days worked by males as regular employees, but total females work for 17–18% less number of days in a week in both 2018 and 2021 than *female regular employees*. The male casual labour and self-employed works only at around 80% and 90% respectively of the days worked by a regular employee. So, the underutilization of the male workers is marginal at 10–20%. While female workers always work relatively more days as self-employed workers, their days worked as casual worker has reduced between the two years. They work the minimum number of average days as casual labour in public works 40% of the regular employees, followed by casual work in other works, and as unpaid family helper. We thus find a lot of underemployment among female workers.

Relative Hours Worked Per Day: Another source of underutilization of workers is working for less than the full day (assuming of eight hours per day). The number of hours worked in a day relative to hours worked by regular employees is shown on the left hand panel of Table 13.10. In 2022–23, the relative number of hours has increased for males in own account work, employer and as casual work in other work. It is also clear that females work relatively less average number of hours in 2022 than in 2017 in all employment status. Females work much less number of hours per day as casual worker and as helper in family enterprises as compared to the regular employees. The hours of work per day by males is also relatively less as casual worker and self-employed worker.

(V) Earnings Per Day Worked by Employment Status-2017–18 and 2022–23

From the data on nominal earnings per day for different employment status for males and females for 2017–18 and 2022–23 (Appendix Table A3), two trends are observed. *First*, is that females receive an average of just 62% and 56% respectively of the male's earnings in 2017 and 2022. It is true across all employment status but the gap in earnings by females is less for regular employees and casual labour in public work because of basic wage regulations in both types of status (Table 13.11). The *second* trend is that there is a significant gap in the earnings of regular employees and all other workers. Own-account workers, unpaid family labour (helpers) receive the minimum earnings followed by casual labour in public works among both males and females. While male casual workers in other works receive an average of 50% of the earnings of regular employees in 2017–18, the proportion is 62% in 2022–23. The proportions are even lower for females (41 and 51 respectively). Within self-employed workers, while the male helpers received 40–48%, the female helpers just receive 29–37% of the earnings of a regular employee. On the contrary, an own account male worker get around 47% (only 1/3rd for female) and a male employer around three-fifth (only ½ for females) to that of a regular employee in 2017–18 (Table 13.11). In 2022–23, the trend is similar to 2017–18 except that the employers are able to earn more than the regular wage employees, which could be due to adoption of emerging technologies and the scaling up of the firms.

Table 13.10 Days per week and hours per day worked by employment status-2017–18 and 2022–23 (regular worker = 1)

Average number of hours worked in a day (Regular = 1)					Average number of days worked in a week (Regular = 1)				
Year →	2017–18	2022–23	2017–18	2022–23	Year	2017–18	2022–23	2017–18	2022–23
Employment Status↓	Males	Males	Females	Females	Employment Status	Males	Males	Females	Females
OAW	0.88	0.92	0.98	0.73	OAW	0.98	1.07	0.91	1.01
Employer	0.93	0.94	0.98	0.79	Employer	0.98	1.03	0.88	0.90
Helper	0.77	0.71	0.91	0.58	Helper	0.91	0.93	0.76	0.78
RWE	**1.00**	**1.00**	**1.00**	**1.00**	RWE	**1.00**	**1.00**	**1.00**	**1.00**
CL in PW	0.76	0.75	0.82	0.39	CL in PW	0.82	0.60	0.45	0.41
CL in OW	0.72	0.75	0.76	0.62	CL in OW	0.76	0.85	0.66	0.65
Total	0.86	0.88	0.92	0.69	Total	0.92	0.99	0.81	0.85
Change in %		2%		−25%	Change in %		7%		5%

Source Author's computations from PLFS, MOSPI, NSO

Note OAW-own account worker, helper-unpaid family workers, RWE is regular salary and wage employees, CL in PW is Casual labour in public works, and CL in OW is Casual lab in other work

Table 13.11 Earnings per day worked by employment status-2017–18 and 2022–23

Females to Males earnings ratio			Relative earnings of others vis a vis regular workers				
				Males	Females	Males	Females
Employment status↓/Year →	2017–18	2022–23	Employment status↓/Year →	2017–18		2022–23	
OAW	0.56	0.37	OAW	0.47	0.34	0.67	0.32
Employer	0.56	0.69	Employer	0.61	0.45	1.36	1.24
Helper	0.56	0.59	Helper	0.40	0.29	0.48	0.37
RWE	0.76	0.76	RWE	1.00	1.00	1.00	1.00
CL in PW	0.90	0.79	CL in PW	0.31	0.37	0.44	0.45
CL in OW	0.62	0.63	CL in OW	0.50	0.41	0.62	0.51
All workers	0.62	0.56					

Source Author's computations from PLFS, MOSPI, NSO
Note OAW-own account worker, helper-unpaid family workers, RWE is regular salary and wage employees, CL in PW is Casual labour in public works, and CL in OW is Casual lab in other work

So, the females are the worst sufferers and get lowest earnings as they mostly work as helpers, own account workers and as casual workers. Not only the earnings are the lowest for these employment status but the earnings of females even in these status are almost half of the males. For, females it is therefore a double whammy they work in low paying job and get half of their counterpart males even in these employment (Appendix Table A3).

13.5 Impact of COVID-19 on the Employment Status of Workers

In this section, we investigate the impact of a recent catastrophe of COVID-19 on employment and evaluate if its bruises have fully healed. COVID-19, caused by severe acute respiratory syndrome coronavirus was detected by China in 2019 and reported to WHO on 31st December 2019 so the name COVID-19. In India, the first case of COVID-19 was detected in Kerala, a southern region of India, on 30th January 2020 and then it started spreading to other parts of the country. To restrict the spread of the pandemic, on the evening of 24 March 2020, with 519 confirmed cases and 9 deaths in the country, the Prime Minister of India announced that the entire country would be placed under a 'total lockdown' for at least three weeks as a preventive measure against the COVID-19 pandemic. All non-critical businesses and services were ordered closed except for hospitals, grocery stores, and pharmacies, and there was a 'total ban' on leaving the home for non-essential purposes. All public transport was suspended. The immediate impact of the lockdown was a complete collapse of economic opportunities and jobs, except for few resulting in a mass exodus of persons on the next day from all the major towns to their native places.

It was humungous and was the largest since partition in 1947. With no work and no money, thousands of migrant workers were seen walking or bicycling hundreds of kilometres to go back to their native villages. There was a mass exodus of reverse migration from urban to rural homes. The lockdown was again extended on 14th April till 3rd May, and then again extended till 17th May and subsequently till 31st May 2020. So, the total national lockdown remained for 58 days.

The unlocking was gradually and cautiously started from 1st June 2020 and continued till 30th November. The infection rates had started to drop by the end of September 2020 and the daily cases which had peaked in mid-September with over 90,000 cases reported per day, dropped to below 15,000 in January 2021. However, in February end 2021, India got hit by the second wave of COVID-19.[11] This second wave was very severe from early April 2021 and caused a rapid surge in cases and deaths. Cases started to rise resulting in state-wide lockdowns from April to June 2021. The situation was even worse in US, Europe, and few other countries. Russia, Mexico, Peru, UK, Italy, and Indonesia are the other countries with a heavy death toll.[12] After the widespread use of vaccines in US, Europe, China, Russia, India and few more, the severity of the tolls had reduced but COVID-19 with different strains continued for long and still exists in some parts. However, despite the presence of COVID-19, by late 2021 the unlocking of the economies had gradually been done by most of the countries with very few restrictions.

As a result of the COVID-19 restrictions and lockdowns, the disruption was more in the jobs with more physical proximity. Consequently, the most visible impact of COVID-19 was the dramatic increase in employees working remotely. Most impacted industries were education,[13] construction, trade, leisure & travel, tourism, manufacturing, transport, storage, & communication. The impact among the rural non-farm self-employed workers was more on the unskilled workers than the skilled workers (Bairagya, 2022). The informal workers, which form 90% of the workers, and working in MSMEs were the most hit by the disruption (Ghosh, 2022). According to Ghosh (2022, pp. 200–201) 'self-employed persons faced multiple whammies: their markets collapsed, the supply chain that enabled them to access inputs broke down, they could not get credit to keep afloat, and then they were forced to repay interest on loans once the moratorium on repayment ended by September 2022.'

According to a report by McKinsey Global Institute (MGI) (2020), the females faced more disruption—1.8 times more than the males due to COVID-19 and left the workforce. Over 52% of the pandemic job losses in India were females and more than 22% of the female workforce in the unorganized sector were out of the jobs post lockdown (Srinivasan-Mint 26th July 2022, p .6). Using panel data from India, Abraham et al. (2022) also found that 'conditional on being in the workforce

[11] It is cited that due to the decline in the number of cases and the beginning of the vaccination Programme, people started becoming careless, not wearing masks and not following social distancing.

[12] For a review of COVID-19 in the world, refer to Ghosh (2022).

[13] It may however be mentioned that the educational institutions-schools and colleges, remained shut for almost two years starting on 24th March 2020. As per the UN estimates the number of crises affected children in the world has increased significantly.

prior to the pandemic, females were seven times more likely to lose work during the nationwide lockdown, and conditional on losing work, eleven times more likely to not return to work subsequently, compared to men.' From the analysis based on the data of a World Bank survey during September 2020, Dutta and Kar (2022) found that 'on average, females in rural areas did not have an occupation relative to males in most of the surveyed States.' Goldin (2022) also found evidence of female employment and WPR being affected more than male due to COVID in US. The reasons cited by the experts for the females leaving the workforce are the burden of both work from home and care giving responsibilities and the fear that if go out for work then they may carry COVID and infect other members of the household. Also, more females were employed in the industries that were more severely affected by COVID-19—education, trade, tourism, traditional manufacturing, financial services, etc.

The initially economic impact of the complete lockdown of the economy resulted in the fall in the GDP growth in India to just 3.1% in the fourth quarter of 2019–20 as compared to around 6% in the corresponding quarter of 2018–19. India was probably facing the worst recession since Independence. India experienced the highest fall in GDP growth rate of (−) 23.9% during April–June 2020. All the crucial sectors like manufacturing, construction, trade, hotel industry saw a decline and slid into negative growth with manufacturing growth at −39.3%, Mining growth at −23.3%, Construction growth at −50%, Trade & hotel industry growth at −47%. With factories and workplaces shut down, millions of migrant workers had to deal with the loss of income, food shortages, and uncertainty about their future. Unemployment went up and millions lost employment, while salaries were cut for many others. The incomes just reduced to nil, and it was free food that ensured the survival of the people. Based on a survey of 5000 respondents during the first wave of the pandemic, April and May 2020, the study by Kesar et al. (2021) also found that during the lockdown nearly two-thirds of the respondents lost their job and those in job experienced a sharp decline in earnings. A report by ILO states that over 400 million informal workers in India may have been pushed further into poverty due to the pandemic. While manufacturing, especially the informal, was the most affected by the strict lockdowns and the migration of labour, the impact on the services sectors varied among different services.[14] Many workers, especially males in the workforce, who could not return to work, moved to self-employment or daily wage work in agriculture, trade or construction, whereas the females had limited options to come back to work (Abraham et al., 2022).

The rural sector in India had to face the pressure of the migrant labour and it provided shelter to them, mainly through the National Rural employment Guarantee Act (NREGA) scheme.[15] In the absence of any meaningful social security, NREGA

---

[14] Based on their analysis from a survey of 2396 respondents in Ethiopia, Mamo et al. (2022) found that females more than males, rural persons more than urban, and persons in industry, services, and trade more than agriculture were likely to be unemployed due to COVID.

[15] The objective of NREGA Act is 'to provide for the enhancement of livelihood security of the households in rural areas of the country by providing at least one hundred days of guaranteed

Table 13.12 Employment under MNREGA (million)

Period	No of HHs	No of person-days
March 2020	15.9	182.8
May 2020	37.3	542.5
November 2020	27.7	289.2
March 2021	29.3	451.9
November 2021	17.5	228.7
March 2022	20.0	245.0
June 2022	27.6	422.0
December 2022	18.3	240.0

Source Author's compilations from NREGA website

acted as buffer to the migrant labour for the loss of job and income in the cities.[16] During the COVID-19, the demand and the actual employment under NREGA, which acts as a shelter for rural labour and an alternative employment opportunity, went up significantly despite workers facing implementation problems of getting adequate work and in accessing their wages. Those who got employment, didn't get for the promised 100 days. A household got employment only for average 48.4 days during 2019–20, 51.5 days in 2020–21, 50.1 days in 2021–22, 47.8 days in 2022–23 and 52.1 days in 2023–24. Since, the NREGA programme is basically demand driven, hence with increase in demand for work under the scheme the employment is generated and provided. Still, all those who seek work under MNREGA don't get it and the unmet demand[17] has been 15.6% in FY2020, 16% in FY2021, and 10.5% in FY2024 (*Mint*, 21st May 2024). So, there has been no significant improvement either during COVID period or after that in providing employment for the promised period and a large gap still exists.

While the employment generated under the scheme in March 2020, just before the COVID-19 was to 15.9 million households with number of person-days work generated at 182.8 million (NREGA web site, July 2022) (Table 13.12), the figures went up immediately after COVID-19 in May 2020 to 37.3 million households and 542.5 million person-days. The increase in rural employment in May was more than 100% and it was made possible by a substantial increase, almost by 60%, in actual expenditure under the scheme.

The demand and employment under the scheme fell with the economic recovery and with migration of labour again from rural to urban centres. In November 2020,

wage employment in every financial year to every household whose adult members volunteer to do unskilled manual work' and 'Every person who has done the work given to him under the Scheme shall be entitled to receive wages at the wage rate for each day of work.'

[16] In view of the important role played by NREGA during the COVID crisis, the Economic Advisory Council to the Prime Minister of India suggested in May 2022, to the government to launch a guaranteed employment scheme for the urban unemployed also so that the surplus labour is rehabilitated.

[17] The unmet demand varies between States-it has been high in UP, MP, AP, Bihar, and Maharashtra among others and relatively low in TN, Odisha, and Karnataka.

the employment generated under the scheme was only to 22.7 million households and the person-days of work provided was only 289.2 million. However, these numbers were still much higher than the pre-COVID-19 levels. The same trend continued again with the onset of the second wave of COVID-19 in March–April 2021, which was very severe till at least June 2021 but continued till October 2021. The employment under NREGA was again very high in March–April 2021 with employment for 29.3 million households and 451.9 million person-days of work but it declined in November 2021 to only 17.5 million of households and 228.7 million person-days, which was respectively almost 23 and 21% less than November 2020. The NREGA programme thus not only acted as an employer of the last resort for the rural workers but it provided them a job and income security. The employment under it fluctuated with the severity of COVID-19 but because of slow recovery in urban jobs, the employment under it even in March 2022 and June 2022 at 20 and 27.6 million for households and 245 and 422 million person-days respectively is significantly higher than the pre-COVID-19 days. But due to gradual recovery since then and the reverse migration from rural to urban centres, the numbers have come down to 18.3 million households and 240 million person-days by Dec 2022, which is however still higher than the pre-COVID-19 days of March 2020. Meanwhile, the real average wages have seen a slow but gradual increase since 2020–21 (FY21)—from Rs. 200.71 to Rs.208.84 in FY 22, Rs. 217.9 in FY23 and Rs. 237.59 during FY24.

Thus, its importance as an employment generation scheme continues till the total economy including the rural economy become 'normal' and is almost on the growth trajectory of the pre-COVID-19 years once again. However, there are regional variations and States like Maharashtra, Arunachal Pradesh, HP, Tripura, etc. still have much higher demand for NREGA work in 2023–24 than in 2020–21. On the other hand it is lower in States of Gujarat, Odisha, UP, MP, Goa, etc. The work demand under NREGA was expected by the government to decline in FY2024 on the back of improved economic activities and it had accordingly reduced the budgeted amount under the scheme for FY2024 to Rs. 86 thousand crores but the actual spending has come to Rs. 1.06 trillion. Interestingly, the budgeted amount has generally been lower than the actual expenditure since 2016–17.

13.5.1 Estimates of Loss in Employment Due to COVID-19

Different estimates have been shared by many researchers about the exact extent of the impact of COVID-19 on the labour market i.e. on the structure of employment and unemployment.[18] There are however, no direct official estimates of this impact on labour. Besides the use of employment in NREGA as an indicator of hardships

[18] Among other individuals, CMIE has been bringing out very high frequency estimates on employment and unemployment in India both before and during COVID, but many including the Ministry of Labour and Employment have expressed doubts on its methodology and coverage. Refer to The Economic Times, 27th April 2022 for the detailed criticism by the Ministry of the methodology used by CMIE.

among the rural labour, we have tried to assess the impact of COVID-19 on urban and rural labour through the use of quarterly estimates from the annual PLFS 2019–20 (July 2019 to June 2020) and 2020–21 (July 2020 to June 2021). The two survey rounds thus cover the first and the second wave of the pandemic. However, it may be mentioned that no survey was done during April and May 2020 and April and May 2021.[19] Thereafter, the surveys were resumed as usual and the information was asked with respect to the actual reference period which would have been adopted if there were no pandemic. However, it involved a long recall period responses from the households. There was thus a mismatch of the recall period for the earlier pre-pandemic period survey and the post pandemic period survey. Thus, any estimates we obtain from the 2019–20 and 2020–21 surveys for the relevant quarters must have been underestimated because of long recall responses from the households for the COVID-19 affected period. So, adjustment for these estimates must be made. However, we have no actual information on the extent of the impact and the exact adjustment which must be made. Therefore, to gauge the real impact of COVID-19 on employment we must not only examine the impact on employment by head count alone, i.e. number of persons but also must look in to the impact on number of days actually worked and the number of hours worked each day.[20] In this context, we first explore the workforce participation rates (WPR) and the unemployment rates by CWS[21] for persons of age 15 and above,[22] which are presented in Table 13.13.

It is evident that during the first wave of COVID-19 in April 2020, the WPR declined for all-RM, RF, UM, and UF. However, the decline is steeper in urban sector for UM (eight percentage points from 67.5% to 59.2%) and UF (five points

[19] 'In the *Annual Report, Period Labour Force Survey, July 2020-June 2021,*' the following is stated (Chapter 1, p. 1): 'The fieldwork of PLFS was suspended first time from 18.03.2020 due to COVID-19 pandemic, and was resumed in June 2020 with the pending samples for this period. This, therefore, had a spill-over effect in completion of field work allotted for the survey period July 2020 to June 2021. Subsequently, there was another spill-over effect due to the second wave of Covid-19 when the field work of PLFS was again suspended in April 2021 in most parts of the country. The field work was gradually resumed in the first week of June 2021 with COVID-19 related restrictions.' In the *Annual Report, Period Labour Force Survey, July 2021-June 2022*, the following is stated (Chapter 1, p. 1): 'Due to the second wave of COVID-19 pandemic related restrictions, the field work of PLFS was suspended for the second time in April 2021 in most parts of the country. The field work was gradually resumed in the first week of June 2021.'

[20] For a broader perspective of the impact of COVID and how much recovery has now taken place, a comparison of pre-COVID quarter of April–June 2019 is also made with the two COVID year quarters and the post-COVID quarter of April–June 2022 and April–June 2023. The results are presented and briefly described in the Annexure.

[21] Labour force, according to CWS, is the number of persons either employed or unemployed on an average in a week preceding the date of the survey. LFPR is defined as the percentage of the population in the labour force. According to the PLFS, under CWS a person is considered as unemployed in a week if he/she did not work even for one hour on any day during the reference week but sought or was available for work at least for one hour on any day during the reference week.

[22] The WPR under quarterly estimates are not strictly comparable with annual WPR because quarterly estimates are, (i) by CWS instead of UPSS, (iii) for age 15 and above instead of all ages, and (iii) some seasonality in employment.

Table 13.13 Percentage Distribution of persons (of age 15 and above) by WPR, Unemployed and OLF by CWS—before and during COVID-2019–20 and 2020–21

2019–20								
	RM		RF		UM		UF	
Period →	Jan–March 2020	April–June 2020	Jan–March 2020	April–June 2020	Jan–March 2020	April–June 2020	Jan–March 2020	April–June 2020
WPR	71.2	65.9	27.5	23.9	67.5	59.2	20.8	16.0
Unemployed	5.8	10.3	1.5	2.1	6.8	12.9	2.4	4.2
Out of labour force (OLF)	23.1	23.8	71.0	74.1	25.7	27.9	76.8	79.8
2020–21								
	Jan–March 2021	April–June 2021	Jan–March 2021	April–June 2021	Jan–March 2021	April–June 2021	Jan–March 2021	April–June 2021
WPR	72.7	69.7	30.4	26.8	68.8	64.7	21.3	17.1
Unemployed	4.5	7.0	1.5	1.7	5.8	8.5	2.2	2.8
Out of labour force (OLF)	22.8	23.3	68.1	71.5	25.4	26.9	76.5	80.1

Source Author's compilations from PLFS, MOSPI, NSO

from 20.8 to 16%) and it is five points (from 71 to 66%) for RM and more than three points (from 27.5 to 24%) for RF. COVID-19 not only impacted the WPR but also Unemployment—the share of unemployed has increased for all the categories of sector and gender. The pace of increase in unemployment is faster for males-rural and urban as compared to females. The out of labour force (OLF) share has increased marginally for males but faster for females by more than three percentage points.

In second wave of COVID-19 from April to June 2021 the WPR again declined for all-RM, RF, UM, and UF. The decline is again steeper for UM (four percentage points from 68.8 to 64.7%) and UF (four percentage points from 21.3 to 17.1%) and is three percentage points for RM and RF. The share of unemployed also increased significantly among urban workers. As a result, OLF share moved similar to the first wave in 2020, i.e. increased marginally for males but faster for females at more than three percentage points.

We thus find from Table 13.13 that during both wave of COVID, the WPR for both sectors and genders of employment fell, more significantly in the first wave than the second wave and the impact has been more severe in urban sector. However, to ascertain if the fall in WPR is due to COVID or due to the seasonality of employment during the two quarters, we present the economy's WPR for the same two quarters (Jan–March and April–June) for five years starting from 2018–19 (a year before COVID), two COVID years and for 2021–22 and 2022–23 (i.e. 2 years after COVID) in Table B1 of Annexure. It confirms that the WPR fell (and unemployed increased) significantly, by five and three percentage points, in the two COVID years (2019–20 and 2020–21) as compared to the other years. So, the change in WFP during the two COVID quarters of 2019–20 and 2020–21 may not have occurred only due to the seasonality of employment but also due to the adverse impact of COVID.

A noteworthy point is that if we compare April–June 2020, a period of first wave of COVID-19 when WPR had declined with Jan–March 2021—a period just before the second wave of COVID-19, then we observe that not only WPRs have recovered for both males and females, but are slightly higher than the corresponding period of 2020. It shows that the recovery in the subsequent quarters was almost as quick as the setback to employment due to COVID-19.

However, for a better understanding of the impact of COVID on employment, the number of persons affected by COVID-19 in first wave in 2020 and in second wave[23] in 2021 are summarized in Fig. 13.1. It shows that

(i) as compared to Jan–March 2020, the total employment in April–June 2020 (first wave period) fell by 52 million out of which 32 million males (17 in rural and 15 in urban) and 20 million females (12 million in rural and 8 in urban) lost their job.
(ii) While the overall loss in jobs is 11%, the loss in job is **more in urban areas** at 15% as compared to just 9% in rural sector.

---

[23] Change during first wave was between Jan–March 2020 and April–July 2020 which are part of PLFS 2019–20, similarly change during second wave was between Jan–March 2021 and April–May 2021 which are part of PLFS 2020–21.

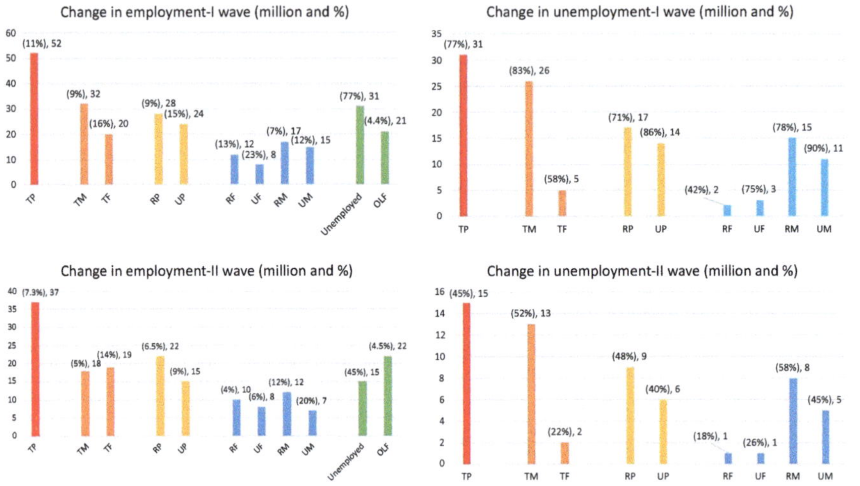

Fig. 13.1 Change in persons employed, unemployed and OLF due to COVID-19-first & second wave (in million and %) (*Source* Author's computations from PLFS, MOSPI, NSO)

(iii) The decline is 9% for males (7% in rural and 12% in urban) and **16% for females** (13% for rural and 23% for urban), supporting the earlier contention that more females were adversely affected than males.

(iv) The loss in employment is thus more severe in urban sector and among females.

(v) Out of 52 million who left the workforce, 31 million are rendered unemployed and 21 million went out of the labour force.

(vi) Among the 31 million addition to unemployment, the addition by males is 26 million and only 5 million by female workers. While the rural sector has added 17 million (2 million females and 15 million males) more to the unemployed, the urban sector added 14 million (3 million females and 11 million males) persons to it.

(vii) The second COVID-19 wave, as is known was less severe because the experience of the first wave had made us more prepared and careful. Still, 37 million-18 million males (10 million in rural and 8 million in urban) and 19 million females (12 in rural and 7 in urban sector) lost their employment.

(viii) The loss is more severe among females-a decline of 14% as compared to 4% for males.

(ix) However this time, only 15 million (40%) have joined the unemployed army-13 million males (8 million rural males and 5 million urban males) and 2 million females (1 million each in rural and urban sector) and the rest of 22 million have gone out of the labour force. The rural sector thus have experienced higher exodus to the unemployed and to OLF.

13.5.2 Impact of COVID on Workers by Employment Status

The adverse impact of COVID-19 has not, however, been same for all labour and it has varied by employment status. Table 13.14(a) and 13.14(b) summarize the distribution of persons by CWS in employment for the pre-COVID-19 and COVID-19 period in 2020 and 2021 and shows that the severely affected by COVID-19 are the urban self-employed—own account workers, the employers and the unpaid family labour and the impact on rural persons is relatively moderate except on employers. For urban males, there is a fall of almost one-third in own account workers, around 60% as employer and around 30% as unpaid family labour. For urban females, the corresponding decline is almost half for own account workers, 75% among employers and 40% for unpaid family worker. Among rural males and females, the adverse impact on regular employees is a fall of around 35%, and a fall of 37% for urban males and 44% for urban females. On the other hand while employment as casual labour in other works has fallen by almost 20% in all categories, but employment as casual work in public works and in MGNEGA have increased due to shift of labour from other employments. It is also noticed that those who had the regular job or casual job but could not work increased sharply for both rural and urban males and females. It happened perhaps due to strict lockdowns and closure of working places.

The share of the population joining the ranks of OLF has increased for all the four groups and a significant number of the females have joined domestic duties. The change in other status is marginal. Females perhaps prefer to join domestic duties as they are required to devote more time to domestic duties and family care, especially when schools for the children and factories for the menfolk are shut down.

Though the second COVID-19 wave was more severe but the impact on labour in this wave was similar to the first wave except the severity was slightly mild due to better preparedness and less stringent restrictions on the movement of persons.

The results of the PLFS surveys thus point out how the labour market experienced a lot of shock and changes during the two waves of COVID-19. It seems that during a shock, while males prefer to being at work rather than being unemployed, the females prefer to leave the labour force and join domestic duties.

13.5.3 Impact of COVID on Workers by Industrial Distribution

We next examine the change in the industrial structure of employment due to COVID-19 and analyze how the workers had to move from one industrial sector to another during the period of COVID-19 in 2020 and in 2021. The results of the surveys of PLFS are reported in Table 13.15. It is observed that due to the two COVID-19 waves, rural male workers moved from manufacturing and construction to agriculture, thus increasing the share of agriculture in employment. While construction is the most severely affected for urban males, they have moved to a sector which could

Table 13.14 (a): Percentage distribution of persons (of age 15 years and above) working according to CWS by status in employment-2019–20 (b) Percentage distribution of persons (of age 15 years and above) working according to CWS by status in employment-2020–21

2019–20	RM		RF		UM		UF	
Employment Status↓/Period →	Jan–March 2020	April–June 2020	Jan–March 2020	April–June 2020	Jan–March 2020	April–June 2020	Jan–March 2020	April–June 2020
(a) WFPR	71.2	65.9	27.5	23.9	67.5	59.2	20.8	16.0
own account workers	31.8	29.4	5.8	5.1	19.0	13.1	4.5	2.4
Employer	1.8	0.8	0.1	0.1	2.9	1.2	0.2	0.1
helper/unpaid family worker	6.6	6.8	10.9	9.0	2.6	1.8	2.2	1.4
regular salaried/ wage employee	10.0	6.5	2.6	1.8	31.7	19.8	11.1	6.2
worked as casual wage labour in public work	0.1	0.4	0.4	0.4	0.1	0.0	0.1	0.1
worked as casual wage labour in MGNREG works	0.1	0.5	0.4	0.7	0.0	0.0	0.1	0.0
worked as casual wage labour in other works	18.1	13.6	6.6	4.7	8.3	4.8	1.9	1.0
had work in HH enterprise but did not work due to sickness	0.2	0.1	0.1	0.0	0.1	0.1	0.0	0.0

(continued)

Table 13.14 (continued)

2019–20	RM		RF		UM		UF	
Employment Status↓/Period →	Jan–March 2020	April–June 2020	Jan–March 2020	April–June 2020	Jan–March 2020	April–June 2020	Jan–March 2020	April–June 2020
had work in HH enterprise but did not work due to other reasons	1.9	5.3	0.5	1.2	1.8	9.1	0.3	2.0
had regular salaried/wage employment but did not work due to sickness	0.0	0.0	0.0	0.0	0.0	0.1	0.0	0.0
had regular salaried/wage employment but did not work due to other reasons	0.5	2.6	0.2	0.9	1.0	9.2	0.4	2.9
(b) OLF	23.1	23.8	71.0	74.1	25.7	27.9	76.8	79.8
at educational institution	13.1	13.4	10.7	10.4	14.1	13.4	11.9	11.3
Domestic duties only	0.9	1.8	33.1	37.5	1.2	2.3	50.8	55.0
Domestic duties and goods collection, etc	0.5	0.5	19.9	18.4	0.1	0.2	6.5	5.8

(continued)

Table 13.14 (continued)

2019–20	RM		RF		UM		UF	
Employment Status↓/Period →	Jan–March 2020	April–June 2020	Jan–March 2020	April–June 2020	Jan–March 2020	April–June 2020	Jan–March 2020	April–June 2020
rentiers, pensioners, remittance recipients, etc	4.6	4.2	4.1	4.7	7.4	8.3	5.1	4.8
Disability	1.4	1.3	1.0	1.0	1.2	1.1	0.9	0.7
Others (Begging, prostitution, etc.)	2.6	2.6	2.2	2.1	1.7	2.7	1.6	2.2
2020–21	RM		RF		UM		UF	
Employment Status↓/Period →	Jan–March 2021	April–June 2021	Jan–March 2021	April–June 2021	Jan–March 2021	April–June 2021	Jan–March 2021	April–June 2021
(a) WFPR	72.7	69.7	30.4	26.8	68.8	64.7	21.3	17.1
own account workers	33.3	31.8	7.3	6.4	21.0	19.1	5.5	3.8
employer	1.9	1.1	0.1	0.1	2.5	1.8	0.1	0.1
helper/unpaid family worker	6.6	7.0	11.9	9.7	2.9	2.5	2.3	1.7
regular salaried/ wage employee	10.0	9.2	3.1	2.8	31.2	25.9	10.9	8.0
worked as casual wage labour in public work	0.2	0.2	0.2	0.3	0.1	0.1	0.0	0.0

(continued)

Table 13.14 (continued)

2020–21	RM		RF		UM		UF	
Employment Status↓/Period →	Jan–March 2021	April–June 2021	Jan–March 2021	April–June 2021	Jan–March 2021	April–June 2021	Jan–March 2021	April–June 2021
worked as casual wage labour in MGNREG works	0.2	0.3	0.5	0.7	0.0	0.0	0.0	0.0
worked as casual wage labour in other works	19.5	17.0	6.9	5.9	9.8	7.7	2.0	1.6
had work in HH enterprise but did not work due to sickness	0.1	0.1	0.0	0.0	0.1	0.1	0.0	0.0
had work in HH enterprise but did not work due to other reasons	0.8	2.0	0.2	0.4	0.7	3.9	0.2	0.7
had regular salaried/wage employment but did not work due to sickness	0.0	0.0	0.0	0.0	0.1	0.1	0.0	0.0
had regular salaried/wage employment but did not work due to other reasons	0.2	1.0	0.1	0.5	0.3	3.6	0.3	1.3
(b) OLF	22.8	23.3	68.1	71.5	25.4	26.9	76.5	80.1

(continued)

Table 13.14 (continued)

2020–21	RM		RF		UM		UF	
Employment Status↓/Period →	Jan–March 2021	April–June 2021	Jan–March 2021	April–June 2021	Jan–March 2021	April–June 2021	Jan–March 2021	April–June 2021
at educational institution	13.9	14.4	11.2	11.1	13.6	14.2	12.1	12.8
Domestic duties only	0.7	1.0	29.5	32.5	1.1	1.2	50.8	53.4
Domestic duties and goods collection, etc	0.7	0.6	20.6	21.1	0.2	0.1	6.2	6.4
rentiers, pensioners, remittance recipients, etc	4.3	4.3	4.4	4.7	7.6	8.1	5.3	5.3
Disability	1.3	1.3	0.8	0.8	1.2	1.4	0.6	0.8
Others (Begging, prostitution, etc.)	2.0	1.7	1.7	1.3	1.7	1.9	1.4	1.5

Source Author's computations from PLFS, MOSPI, NSO

possibly provide them employment. But the employment for rural females is severely affected in the manufacturing sector and for urban females in the construction and services sector. However, surprisingly the share of manufacturing in employment has increased for RM, RF, and UM during the second wave. The services sector—both market and non-market is impacted during both the COVID-19 waves of 2020 and 2021.

It seems that the data does not fully support the popular perception and finding of several surveys and articles that the manufacturing activities had almost completely stopped during COVID-19 and manufacturing employment was severely impacted. The PLFS data indicates that the share of workers in manufacturing shrank mainly for rural males and females in the first wave and only for urban males in the second wave. Between 2019–20 and 2020–21, in fact as per the PLFS, the employment in manufacturing increased from 60 to 63 million, i.e. by 5%. So, what led to the increase in the number of workers in the manufacturing?[24]

13.5.4 *Impact of COVID on Non-Agriculture Employment by Size of Enterprises*

It is also pertinent to find out the impact of COVID-19 on the industry by size of persons in an enterprise to understand how the workers moved from one enterprise to another. It can be observed from Table 13.16 that during the first wave, many workers have moved from relatively bigger firms to micro firms with less than six persons. The movement away from bigger firms especially from the medium (6–10 workers) and big firms (20 and above workers) to micro firms is a signal of distress in the labour market and a move towards more informalization. These small firms are generally household enterprises with family helpers. The movement during the second wave did take place but it was relatively of small magnitude and the large firms are not affected as they were better prepared than before.

It is obvious that we are not able to capture the real impact of COVID-19 by just analyzing the number of persons employed in manufacturing. We therefore investigate it by looking at the data for number of days worked in a week and the number of hours worked per day during both the COVID-19 waves and the results are reported in Table 13.17.

13.5.5 *Impact of COVID on Days Worked in a Week and Hours Worked Per Day*

It can be viewed from Table 13.17 (the upper panel showing actual average number of days worked in a week and the average number of hours worked in a day and Fig. 13.2

[24] Refer to Goldar and Aggarwal (2023) for a discussion on it.

Table 13.15 Percentage distribution of workers (of age 15 years and above) in CWS by selected broad sectors-2019–20 and 2020–21

2019–20	**RM**		**RF**		**UM**		**UF**	
Broad Sectors↓/ Period →	Jan–March 2020	April–June 2020	Jan–March 2020	April–June 2020	Jan–March 2020	April–June 2020	Jan–March 2020	April–June 2020
Agriculture	54.3	57.1	74.1	75.5	4.6	5.8	6.9	8.8
Manufacturing	7.9	6.6	6.0	4.6	18.7	19.3	13.7	16.6
Construction	14.1	12.6	4.2	4.6	12.0	9.3	4.9	2.9
Market Services	16.9	16.6	5.7	5.5	48.2	49.6	34.3	32.6
Non-market Services	6.0	6.4	10.0	9.7	14.9	14.1	40.0	38.9
Total	100	100	100	100	100	100	100	100
2020–21	**RM**		**RF**		**UM**		**UF**	
Broad Sectors	Jan–March 2021	April–June 2021	Jan–March 2021	April–June 2021	Jan–March 2021	April–June 2021	Jan–March 2021	April–June 2021
Agriculture	52.1	52.3	73.6	73.4	4.8	5.3	8.7	9.5
Manufacturing	7.0	7.5	5.5	5.8	19.9	19.2	15.3	16.2
Construction	15.3	15.1	4.5	4.1	12.8	12.3	5.3	3.3
Market Services	18.6	18.0	5.2	4.9	46.7	47.7	25.3	25.6
Non-market Services	6.3	6.3	11.1	11.7	14.2	14.1	45.1	45.1
Total	100	100	100	100	100	100	100	100

Source Author's computations from PLFS, MOSPI, NSO

Table 13.16 Distribution of non-agriculture employment by size of enterprises

No. of workers in an enterprise↓/Period →	Jan–March 2020	April–June 2020	Jan–March 2021	April–June 2021
less than 6	58.4	60.7	62.0	62.6
6 to less than 10	13.4	11.0	11.4	11.1
10 to less than 20	6.3	6.1	6.5	5.9
20 and above	18.3	17.0	18.0	18.2
Total	100.0	100.0	100.0	100.0

Source Author's computations, PLFS, MOSPI, NSO

showing the percentage change between the pre-COVID-19 quarter to COVID-19 affected quarter) that there is a drastic fall in the number of days and number of hours worked in the Indian economy, especially during the first wave of 2020 in the urban sector where the average days worked have reduced by a huge 27% for urban males and 26% for urban females as compared to just 8% and 4% for rural males and rural females. The corresponding decline in the number of hours worked per day is 31% for urban males, 28% for urban females, and only 12% and 5% for rural males and rural females.

As observed earlier, the results again indicate that the impact of COVID was more severe in the urban sector than the rural sector but the second wave was relative mild on the number of persons employed. The same impact is seen here also where the fall in the number of days worked as well as in number of hours worked is lower than in 2020. We find that the number of days have reduced by 14% and 11% respectively for urban males and females during the second wave. The corresponding change is 7% and 1% for rural males and females. The change in the average number of hours worked per day is, on the other hand, 11,10,3 and 1% respectively for urban males, urban females, rural males, and rural females. So, the fall in both days and hours is observed to be *more in the urban sector* and among males and must be adjusted with head count employment to gauge the full impact of COVID-19. How much correction is needed on this count?

The correction on account of loss in the average number of days worked per week and hours per week has been calculated by the joint loss on both the counts and are reported in Table 13.18. We find that the required downward correction in 2019–20 in the head count number will be to the order of 19% for rural males (RM), 9% for rural females (RF), a huge 49% and 47% for urban males (UM) and urban females (UF). The corresponding adjustments for second wave of 2020–21 are 10, 2, 23 and 20% respectively.

A similar total correction which is required due to loss of weekdays and hours worked can be computed for different employment status and for different broad sector industries from the computations of the respective losses as reported in Table 13.19 and Table 13.20. However, this correction in the head count numbers to obtain person-days and person hours worked in an economy would take care of the changes which took place between Jan–March and April–June of 2020 and 2021.

Table 13.17 Average number of days worked per week and hours worked per day

	RM		RF		UM		UF	
Period →	Jan–March 2020	April–June 2020	Jan–March 2020	April–June 2020	Jan–March 2020	April–June 2020	Jan–March 2020	April–June 2020
total hours worked per day	6.6	5.8	5.4	5.1	7.3	5.1	6.0	4.3
total days worked per week	6.2	5.7	6.0	5.8	6.0	4.4	6.0	4.4
Period →	Jan–March 2021	April–June 2021	Jan–March 2021	April–June 2021	Jan–March 2021	April–June 2021	Jan–March 2021	April–June 2021
total hours worked per day	6.2	6.0	6.1	6.0	6.1	5.4	6.1	5.4
total days worked per week	6.7	6.3	5.3	5.2	7.4	6.3	5.8	5.2

Source Author's computations from PLFS, MOSPI, NSO

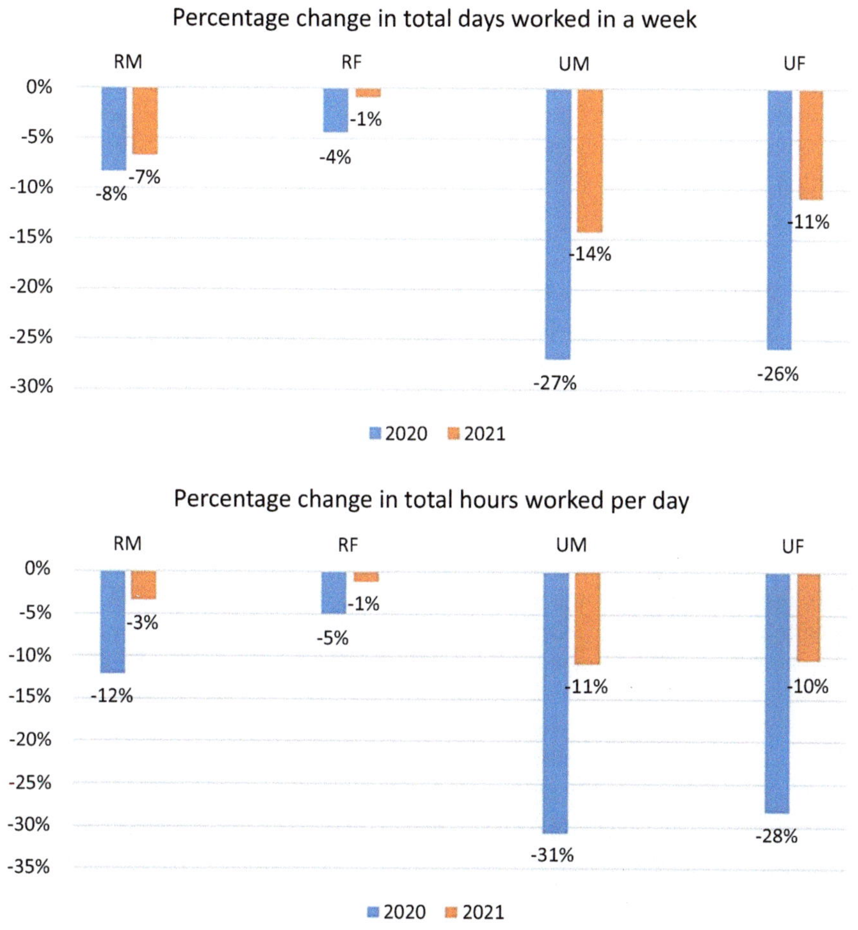

Fig. 13.2 Percentage change in total days worked in a week and total hours worked per day. *Source* computations by the author from PLFS, MOSPI, NSO

Table 13.18 Total correction required in the head count employment numbers

Year	2019–20	2020–21
RM	−19%	−10%
RF	−9%	−2%
UM	−49%	−23%
UF	−47%	−20%

Source Author's computations, PLFS, MOSPI, NSO

But, as mentioned earlier also, one perhaps cannot ascribe all these changes to only COVID-19, and other factors including seasonality may also be at play, as is evident from a casual look at Annexure Table B1. So, if it is possible to find this seasonality etc. from an analysis of more quarters, then we may be able to find the exact impact of COVID-19 from the adjustments. Perhaps, this may be an interesting research question and may be attempted in future research.

13.6 Policy Initiatives to Meet the Challenges Faced by Workers Due to COVID-19—A Brief Overview

Governments around the World took different initiatives to protect their workers including the platform workers from the disruptive impact of COVID-19. The countries generally adopted the liberal monetary policies by injecting huge amount of liquidity in the economies and used their active fiscal policies to transfer income to the vulnerable population. The income and health security were provided to the workers including the platform workers.[25] In India, with the detection of COVID-19 in Jan 2020, over twenty States announced relief packages including free and increased ration to the card holders. Just two days after the 'total lockdown' announcement, the central government[26] announced an economic package of Rs. 1.7 lac crores (US$22million) which included food security scheme, and cash transfer primarily for migrant labour and daily wage labour. Free cooking gas cylinder was also released for three months. This was followed by RBI, the Central Bank of the country, cutting repo rates, injecting liquidity of Rs. 3.74 lac crores, and permitting banks to provide a moratorium on all loans for three months. India, under the Atmanirbhar Bharat Abhiyan, also announced an Rs. 20 lakh crore package on May 12th, 2020, to cater to various sections including cottage industry, MSMEs, labourer, middle class, among others. Subsequently more financial packages were announced in October and November 2020, with the total stimulus package at Rs. 29.87 lac crores. Periodically, the RBI also announced more measures to meet the COVID-19 challenges. The RBI Governor announced more measures on 17th April 2020 to counter the economic impact of the pandemic which also included Rs. 50 thousand crore (US$6.6 billion) special finance to NABARD, SIDBI, and NHB. The government also supported the NREGA scheme to provide employment to the migrants who had moved from urban centres to the rural areas because of lockdowns, and increased the outlay on the scheme from Rs. 75 thousand crores in 2019–20 to more than Rs. 1.18 lac crores in 2020–21 an increase of more than 50%, but sensing the fall in the demand for work under NREGA because of the gradual unlocking of the economy, the government

---

[25] For more details on global best practices, please refer to Niti Aayog Report (2022, Box 6.2.2).

[26] The government adopted a four pronged strategy aimed to protect initially the life and later on both the life and livelihood of the population (for details refer to the GOI (2021): Economic Survey-2020–21, Vol II).

Table 13.19 Average number of days worked per week and hours worked per day–by employment status—in rural and urban sectors 2019–20 and 2020–21

	Total days worked in a week				Total hours worked per day			
	Rural		Urban		Rural		Urban	
Employment Status↓/ Period →	Jan–March 2020	April–June 2020	Jan–March 2020	April–June 2020	Jan–March 2020	April–June 2020	Jan–March 2020	April–June 2020
Self-Employed	6.4	6.0	6.2	4.4	6.1	5.6	7.0	4.6
Regular-wage employees	6.1	4.7	6.1	4.3	7.0	5.2	7.2	5.0
Casual labour	5.6	5.5	5.2	4.9	6.2	5.9	6.1	5.6
	Jan–March 2021	April–June 2021	Jan–March 2021	April–June 2021	Jan–March 2021	April–June 2021	Jan–March 2021	April–June 2021
Self–Employed	6.4	6.3	6.4	5.6	6.2	5.9	7.1	6.0
Regular–wage employees	6.2	5.6	6.1	5.4	7.0	6.4	7.2	6.3
Casual labour	5.5	5.5	5.3	5.2	6.2	6.0	6.1	5.9

Source Author's computations, PLFS, MOSPI, NSO

Table 13.20 Average number of days worked per week and hours worked per day by selected broad sectors in rural and urban sectors

	Total days worked in a week				Total hours worked per day			
	Rural		Urban		Rural		Urban	
Broad Sector↓/ Period →	Jan–March 2020	April–June 2020	Jan–March 2020	April–June 2020	Jan–March 2020	April–June 2020	Jan–March 2020	April–June 2020
Agriculture	6.2	6.1	6.0	5.8	5.9	5.7	5.7	5.6
Manufacturing	6.1	4.6	6.1	3.9	6.8	5.0	7.4	4.4
Electricity	6.4	5.8	6.1	5.0	7.1	6.5	7.2	6.0
Construction	5.7	5.3	5.3	4.6	6.5	5.9	6.3	5.4
Market Services	6.2	5.1	6.1	4.4	7.3	5.7	7.3	5.0
Non-market Services	5.9	4.7	6.0	4.3	6.1	4.7	6.6	4.5
	Jan–March 2021	April–June 2021	Jan–March 2021	April–June 2021	Jan–March 2021	April–June 2021	Jan–March 2021	April–June 2021
Agriculture	6.2	6.2	6.1	6.0	5.9	5.7	5.7	5.5
Manufacturing	6.2	5.7	6.1	5.3	6.9	6.2	7.2	6.1
Electricity	6.3	6.3	5.9	6.0	7.3	7.3	7.0	6.8
Construction	5.6	5.5	5.5	5.2	6.4	6.2	6.5	6.1
Market Services	6.4	6.0	6.2	5.5	7.6	7.0	7.6	6.3
Non-market Services	6.2	5.6	6.1	5.5	6.3	5.6	6.4	5.7

Source Author's computations, PLFS, MOSPI, NSO

reduced its outlay on the scheme to Rs. 1.08 lac crores in 2022–23. With the expectation that demand for NREGA work will further reduce, the budgetary allocation has been further cut to only Rs. 73 thousand crores with a promise that if the demand for NREGA work goes up, the allocation may be revised upward.[27] As a result of the measures taken by the active fiscal and liberal monetary policies, a gradual recovery of the economy was witnessed and by December 2021 India has been almost back to the pre-COVID-19 level of GDP.

Many initiatives were also taken by individual firms to protect the workers against COVID-19. Some of the measures taken by businesses included:

a. The businesses supported the livelihood of workers and their families by providing health access and expanding paid leave including paid sick leave,
b. They helped in securing income and livelihood of workers and small businesses by extending financial help and delaying the pay-back periods.
c. The firms also extended many safety and health measures like use of hand sanitizers and masks, dissemination of information, etc. They helped the workers in adapting to the new work environment and practices, e.g. going digital, cashless payments, and contactless deliveries.

COVID-19 affected not only economically but also physically—the health of the people. The government immediately provided an emergency health fund of Rs. 150 billion. Temporary medical infrastructure was created to save lives and liberal financial assistance was provided to develop and administer vaccine programme. To provide better access to the health facilities, the Indian government announced in April 2022 to extend the Ayushman Bharat health cover to over 40 crores more people who are currently not covered under any government or private health insurance scheme. With it, almost 70% of the population is expected to be protected by some health insurance but existing government health insurance plans need to be further expanded to include the hitherto left out persons-the so called 'missing' middle. The scheme will now be a great boon to all the workers who earn between Rs. 15,000–25,000 per month, as the government wants to include them in the Ayushman Bharat scheme. Another decision which would greatly help the 'part time' workers known as Anganwadi[28] workers is a landmark decision by the Supreme Court (SC) of India on 25th April 2022, to extend the benefits of gratuity under the Payment of Gratuity Act, 1972, to all Anganwadi workers. The decision will provide some social security to these workers as and when implemented, and will also help many other similarly placed workers when the same benefit is also extended to them.

---

[27] The actual spending has generally been higher than the budgeted amount since 2016 and is Rs. 1.06 trillion in FY 2024.

[28] Anganwadi workers are mainly the health workers but are assigned all pervasive duties, which include the identification of the beneficiaries, cooking nutritious food for school children, conducting pre-schools for children, etc. Therefore, while the Governments consider them as part time workers, the SC rejected this plea and accepted them as full-time workers.

13.7 Few Policy Recommendations for Improving the Work Conditions of Workers

On the basis of the discussion, one may infer that the worst impact of COVID, due to lockdowns and other restrictions, were felt by informal workers who constitute 90% of the total employment in the Indian economy. They faced loss in jobs, wages and incomes if self-employed. On the other hand the formal workers got some legal and social protection if were not able to go to work. This suggest that though there is a need, and may be scope, for increasing formalization instead of informalization of the economy, but it may be limited due to fast changing technology in which the nature of work is bound to change. It is therefore imperative that social security benefits are provided to all the workers.

The government of India has taken few steps to extend the social security benefits to all the workers, especially under the Code on Social Security (Ministry of Labour and Employment, 2020)[29] but it has to ensure an effective implementation of the Code with an assurance of minimum wages to all workers. However, beside minimum wages and access to basic nutrition, the social protection programme may also have to include access to good quality health, sanitation and education. The government, along with incentivizing the private sector, has to undertake employment generation programme, and the NREGA scheme may be strengthened and expanded in coverage and scope.

It is obvious that gender gap exist in all labour market characteristics, which has strong implications for overall GDP growth (Viswanathan, p. 143) and if female WPR is increased then it would add substantial amount to India's GDP. Concrete steps, therefore need to be undertaken to remove any bias and hesitancy towards the employment of female workers so that their participation in the labour force goes up. For it to happen, removing the many existing barriers and biases is crucial in facilitating the movement of female workers in the workforce. A conducive work atmosphere also needs to be created where females have both digital and physical safety and feel as equal partner in the growth of the firms and the economy. MSMEs, which suffered the most during COVID, need to be provided with adequate support, especially financial needs through liberal credit packages from microfinance and other institutions.

As also suggested by the Economic Advisory Council to the Prime Minister of India in May 2022, 'the government must allocate more percentage of the expenditure towards social services and the social sector to make the most vulnerable population resilient to sudden shocks and stop their descent into poverty' (The Economic Times, 19th May 2022). Ghosh (2022) has also emphasized the need for a proactive fiscal policy so that strong fiscal response and adequate public spending is available in the case of such a humongous disaster facing the economy and the subsequent recovery

---

[29] It has been passed by the Indian Parliament but has not been implemented so far.

from it. Due to very slow recovery in the level of employment, wages, self-employed incomes, and mass consumption she advocated to raise public spending, especially in employment-intensive sectors. However, it will require raising enough public resources, which could be done by adopting suitable policies to raise more of both tax and non-tax revenue.

Appendix

See Tables A1, A2, and A3.

Table A1 Employment in India-1972–73 to 2022–23 (000)

Year	RM	RF	RT	UM	UF	UT	TM	TF	Total workers
1972–73	126,000	70,000	196,000	31,600	9400	41,000	158,000	79,000	237,000
1977–78	140,000	80,000	220,000	37,100	9800	46,900	177,000	90,000	267,000
1983	153,865	90,657	244,521	46,703	12,147	58,850	200,568	102,804	303,371
1987–88	164,665	92,992	257,656	52,826	14,106	66,932	217,491	107,097	324,588
1993–94	187,822	104,767	292,589	64,620	17,221	81,841	252,442	121,988	374,430
1999–00	198,823	105,782	304,605	75,565	18,243	93,808	274,388	124,025	398,413
2004–05	218,872	123,966	342,839	90,438	24,623	115,061	309,310	148,589	457,900
2011–12	234,600	101,800	336,400	109,200	27,300	136,500	343,800	129,100	472,900
2017–18	232,358	74,828	307,186	120,801	30,027	150,828	353,159	104,855	458,014
2018–19	235,488	81,801	317,289	122,701	31,387	154,088	358,188	113,188	471,376
2019–20	244,438	104,052	348,491	128,656	37,221	165,877	373,095	141,273	514,368
2020–21	250,901	118,110	369,010	133,068	38,311	171,380	383,969	156,421	540,390
2021–22	251,018	116,509	367,527	135,824	39,723	175,547	386,843	156,232	543,075
2022–23	248,745	132,022	380,767	139,837	43,726	183,563	388,582	175,748	564,330

Source Author's computations, EUS, and PLFS, MOSPI, NSO

Table A2 Annual growth in employment in India-1972–73 to 2022–23

Period	RM	RF	RT	UM	UF	UT	TM	TF	Total workers
1972–1983	1.92%	2.49%	2.13%	3.79%	2.47%	3.50%	2.30%	2.54%	2.38%
1983–1993	1.92%	1.39%	1.72%	3.14%	3.38%	3.19%	2.21%	1.64%	2.02%
1993–2004	1.40%	1.54%	1.45%	3.10%	3.30%	3.15%	1.86%	1.81%	1.85%
2004–2011	1.00%	−2.78%	−0.27%	2.73%	1.49%	2.47%	1.52%	−1.99%	0.46%
2011–2018	0.05%	−3.08%	−0.83%	1.68%	2.01%	1.75%	0.59%	−1.86%	−0.05%
2018–2022	1.38%	12.71%	4.66%	3.32%	8.64%	4.47%	2.06%	11.63%	4.60%
1972–2022	1.37%	1.28%	1.34%	3.02%	3.12%	3.04%	1.82%	1.61%	1.75%

Source Author's computations from Table A1

Table A3 Nominal Earnings per day (Rs.) by employment status for males and females in 2017–18 and 2022–23

	2017–18		2022–23	
Employment Status	Male	Females	Male	Females
Own-account work	256	144	468	173
Employer	335	189	954	661
Helper	219	122	333	195
Regular-Wage employees	547	417	700	535
Casual labour in public works	170	154	305	241
Casual lab in other work	276	170	431	273
All workers	327	202	543	306

Source Author's computations, PLFS, MOSPI, NSO

Annexure

Status of Employment in Pre-COVID-19 Quarter of 2019 to Post-COVID-19 Quarter of 2023

In the annexure, we present briefly the summary results for the quarter of April–June[30] for the five years-two years of COVID-19, i.e. 2019–20 and 2020–21 along with one year prior to COVID-19 (2018–19) and two years (2021–22 and 2022–23) after the COVID-19 to ascertain the current status of employment to gauge the recovery after COVID-19 and ascertain that the change during the two quarters of Jan–March 2020 and April–June 2021 is not only cyclical but due to COVID.

[30] It may again be mentioned that the annual Survey results which are provided under PLFS covers employment-unemployment from the respective July to June, thus includes four quarters of July–Sept, Oct–Dec, Jan–March, and April–June. Hence, the year 2017–18 covers July 2017 to June 2018.

It is seen from Table B1 that WPR in each of the April–June quarter is not significantly different to that of Jan–March except the two COVID years. Thus one may attribute that the WPR changes in the two COVID years is mainly due to it and not due to major cyclical fluctuations. Table B1 shows that the first wave of COVID-19 affected the workers very badly due to the strict lockdowns and reduced the WPR in April–June 2020. The workers were forced to leave the labour market and become unemployed. However due to better preparedness, the WPR in April–June 2021 was higher than the COVID-19 and the pre-COVID-19 period of April–June 2019, and the WPR in April–June 2023 is even higher. Taking a longer view, the CMIE data shows that while the joblessness averages 6.6% during Jan 2016 to Feb 2020, it averaged 8.5% from March 2020 to Feb 2024 (Sabnavis, 2024) indicating that the recovery in employment is still to take place.

However, Table B2 shows that, though the WPR in 2022–23 is higher than in 2019–20, but the total days per week worked by workers, which had reduced during the COVID-19 years more in the first wave, has not fully recovered in 2022–23 from the pre-COVID-19. Similar is situation for average number of hours worked by a person in a day. In 2022–23, it is less than the average in 2019. It can also be observed that the real earnings per worker in 2022–23 are less than in 2019. Thus, one may conclude that while the WPR has returned to the pre-COVID-19 levels, but the workers have not been able to recover completely from the shock of COVID-19.

Table B3 shows that the shock to real earnings was felt by all types of workers except the casual workers, because the wages of casual workers are generally fixed on the basis of minimum wages administered by the State. So, while the casual workers did experience a marginal increase in their real earnings, but that of self-employed and regular employees is still lower than the pre-COVID-19 period.

Another feature that is noted from Table B4 is that due to COVID-19, more and more workers in non-agricultural economic activities have shifted from medium and large size firms to small firms, generally the household enterprises with less than 6 workers, and the share of workers in these small firms had gone up during both the waves.

Table B1 Percentage Distribution of persons of age 15 and above by CWS in last two quarter of the PLFS round

	2018–19		2019–20		2020–21		2021–22		2022–23	
Period	Jan–March 19	April–June 19	Jan–March20	April–June 20	Jan–March 21	April–June 21	Jan–March 22	April–June 22	Jan–March 23	April–June 23
WPR	43.8	44.6	47.8	42.9	49.4	46.1	48.4	48.1	52.7	52.1
Unemployed	4.0	4.2	4.0	7.0	3.3	4.8	3.4	3.2	2.7	3.0
OLF	52.2	51.2	48.3	50.2	47.3	49.1	48.2	48.6	44.5	44.9

Source Author's computations, PLFS, MOSPI, NSO

Table B2 Total hours worked per day, days worked in a week and real earnings of workers of age 15 and above by CWS in last quarter of the PLFS round

	2018–19	019–20	2020–21	2021–22	2022–23
Period	April–June 2019	April–June 2020	April–June 2021	April–June 2022	April–June 2023
Total hours worked per day	6.65	5.43	6.02	6.24	6.1
Total days worked per week	6.13	5.34	5.85	6.03	5.96
Real Earnings per day (2001 = 100) (Rs.)	109	113	97	105	101

Source Author's computations, PLFS, MOSPI, NSO

Table B3 Real Earnings per day (Rs.) of workers of age 15 and above by CWS in last quarter of the PLFS round

	2018–19	2019–20	2020–21	2021–22	2022–23
Period	April–June 2019	April–June 2020	April–June 2021	April–June 2022	April–June 2023
Own-account work	86	103	78	83	77
Employer	121	140	109	111	111
Helper	59	74	50	56	51
Regular-Wage employees	188	183	174	180	180
Casual labour in public work	52	70	59	67	65
Casual labour-other work	97	90	97	105	105
All workers	109	113	97	105	101

Source Author's computations, PLFS, MOSPI, NSO

Table B4 Distribution of employment by size of the enterprises in non-agriculture activities by CWS and age 15+

no of workers in an enterprise	April–June 2019	April–June 2020	April–June 2021	April–June 2022	April–June 2023
less than 6	59.1	60.7	62.6	60.8	61.8
6 to less than 10	11.8	11.0	11.1	12.8	12.2
10 to less than 20	7.1	6.1	5.9	7.1	7.1
20 and above	17.6	17.0	18.2	17.4	18.2
Total	100	100	100	100	100

Source Author's computations, PLFS, MOSPI, NSO

References

Abraham, R., Basole, A., & Kesar, S. (2022). Down and out? The gendered impact of the Covid-19 pandemic on India's labour market. *Economia Politica, 39*, 101–128. https://doi.org/10.1007/s40888-021-00234-8

Aggarwal, S. C. (2023a). Gig workers in India: An overview, on *Research Gate*, https://doi.org/10.13140/RG.2.2.29650.32964

Aggarwal, S. C. (2023b). *The status of self-employed and casual workers in India: Some recent changes due to COVID19.* SSRN, WPS no 4517644, July.

Bairagya, I. (2022). Effects of COVID-19 pandemic on the rural non-farm self-employed in India. *Economic and Political Weekly, 57*(26–27), 39–47.

Basu, K., & Maertens, A. (2009). The growth of industry and services in South Asia. In E. Ghani & S. Ahmed (Eds.), *Accelerating growth and job creation in South Asia.* Oxford Univeristy Press.

Chandrasekhar, C. P., & Ghosh, J. (2014). *Contract workers in manufacturing.* https://www.researchgate.net/publication/315768208

Dutta, N., & Kar, S. (2022). An analysis of rural shocks in India during the pandemic. *Economic and Political Weekly, 29*, 18–21.

Ghose, A. K. (2015). Service-led growth and employment in India. In K. V. Ramaswamy (Ed.), *Labour, employment and economic growth in India.* Cambridge University Press, Delhi.

Ghose, A. K. (2016). *India employment report 2016*, Institute for Human Development. Oxford University Press.

Ghosh, J. (2022). *The making of a catastrophe.* Aleph Book Company.

Goldar, B. (2022). *Export participation and employment of contract workers in organized manufacturing plants in India.* SSRN, April.

Goldar, B., & Aggarwal, S. C. (2023, June). Trends in employment, productivity, real wages and labour standards in Indian manufacturing in recent years. *Indian Journal of Labour Economics.*

Goldar, B., & Aggarwal, S. C. (2024). *Explaining the significant hikes in female workforce participation rate in India in recent years and some thoughts on how to raise it further* (IEG Working Paper No. 462). Delhi

Goldin, C. (2022, April). *Understanding the economic impact of COVID-19 on females* (NBER WP 29974). http://www.nber.org/papers/w29974

Government of India. (2021). *Economic survey- 2020–21* (Vol. II). GOI, Ministry of Finance, New Delhi.

ILO. (2024). *India employment report 2024: Youth employment, education and skills.* ILO and IHD, New Delhi

Kapoor, R. (2023, April 25). *More unpaid family work may be driving up India's employment statistics. Mint.*

Kesar, S., Abraham, R., Lahoti, R., Nath, P., & Basole, A. (2021). Pandemic, informality, and vulnerability: Impact of COVID-19 on livelihoods in India. *Canadian Journal of Development Studies, 42*(1–2), 145–164. https://doi.org/10.1080/02255189.2021.1890003

Mamo, W. B., Feyisa, H. L., Yitayaw, M. K., & Tereda, S. N. (2022). Employment status during the COVID-19 pandemic: Evidence from Ethiopia. *Indian Journal of Labour Economics, 65*(1), 123–135.

McKinsey Global Institute. (2020, June). *COVID-19 and gender equality: Countering the regressive effects.*

Mehrotra, S., Parida, J., Sinha, S., & Gandhi, A. (2014). Explaining employment trends in the Indian economy: 1993–94 to 2011–12. *Economic and Political Weekly, 49*(32), 49–57.

Mehrotra, S., & Sinha, S. (2017). Explaining falling female employment during a high growth period. *Economic and Political Weekly, 52*(39), 54–62.

Ministry of Labour and Employment. (2020). *The code on social security, 2020*, Government of India. https://labour.gov.in/sites/default/files/SS_Code_Gazette.pdf

National Commission for Enterprises in the Unorganised Sector (NCEUS). (2007, August). *Report on conditions of work and promotion of livelihoods in the unorganised sector.* http://dcmsme.gov.in/Condition_of_workers_sep_2007.pdf
National Sample Survey Office. *Employment and unemployment in India*, 2011–12.
National Statistical Office. *Annual survey, periodic labour force survey*, MOSPI, Different reports.
Nayyar, G. (2012). *The service sector in India's development.* Cambridge University Press.
Papola, T. S., & Sharma, A. N. (2015). Labour and employment in fast growing India: Issues of employment and inclusiveness. In U. Kapila (Ed.), *Indian Economy Since Independence*, pp. 523–560. Academic Foundation.
Sabnavis, M. (2024, April 25). A decade's data shows that India is yet to recover fully from COVID. *Mint.*
Singh, J., Das, D. K., Abhishek, K., & Kukreja, P. (2019). Factors influencing the decision to hire contract labour by Indian manufacturing firms. *Oxford Development Studies, 47*(4), 406–419. https://doi.org/10.1080/13600818.2019.1624705
Srinivasan, S. (2022, July 26). Charcha 2022: The power of covening. *MintMint*, p. 6.
State of Working India. (2023). *Social identities and labour market outcomes.* Centre for Sustainable Development, Azim Premji University, Bengaluru, Karnataka.
Thomas, J. J. (2015). India's labour market during the 2000s. In K. V. Ramaswamy (Ed.), *Labour, employment and economic growth in India.* Cambridge University Press.
Viswanathan, B. (2021). Diversity in services sector employment in India: Evidence from India human development survey, 2011–12. In Shashanka Bhide et al. (Eds.), *Deciphering India's service sector growth.* Routledge.

Suresh Chand Aggarwal retired as Professor and Head of the Department of Finance and Business Economics (earlier known as Business Economics), University of Delhi. Prof. Aggarwal is currently the Visiting Professor at Institute for Human Development, New Delhi. He was ICSSR's Senior Fellow for two years - 2018-19 and has been the Principal Investigator in E-Content Development for Post Graduate Courses in Business Economics under E-PGpathshala by UGC. He has worked for ILO and has been an external Consultant to Reserve Bank of India and ICRIER. Contributed as a Lead Researcher on labour in an RBI funded project on India KLEMS from 2010 to 2021. Prof Aggarwal has guided research to a number of students and has published extensively in National and international Journals. His most of the published work has been related to labour, industry and inclusive growth.

Chapter 14
Rural Non-farm Sector: Development Perspective

Sankar Majumder

Abstract Development and growth of the rural non-farm sector is very crucial for providing alternative livelihood in the rural sector. India, since the very beginning of its development journey, has taken several policies and programmes for enhancing the non-agricultural livelihood. Data given by different authorities shows that over the last 75 years this non-farm sector has grown to some extent but this is far less than the desired one. Focus of the studies and reports on non-farm sector was mainly on the provision of finance and credit facilities, physical infrastructure and other amenities, institution building for technological up gradation, training for skill development and entrepreneurship development. Based on the author's personal experiences as development practitioner this paper presents some other factors which have drawn less attention of both the policy makers and academics.

Keywords Non-Farm Sector · Enterprises · Entrepreneur · Registered Units · Unregistered Units

14.1 Section 1

The majority of the Indian population resides in the rural sector. The contribution of the agricultural sector towards GDP has considerably gone down during the last 75 years, but the composition of the occupational structure shows that the majority of the rural population is still dependent on agricultural activities for their livelihood. Following the standard development theories, India, since the very beginning of its development journey, has taken several policies and programmes for enhancing the non-agricultural livelihood. This non-agricultural sector has a high degree of heterogeneity consisting of Small Scale Industries, Small Scale Business Sector Enterprises, Village & Cottage Industries and so on. Numerous economic activities

S. Majumder (✉)
Visva Bharati University, Santiniketan, India
e-mail: sankar.majumder@gla.ac.in

GLA University, Mathura, Mathura, India

D. Maiti et al. (eds.), *75 Years of Growth, Development and Productivity in India*, India Studies in Business and Economics, https://doi.org/10.1007/978-981-97-8054-9_14

in a tiny and informal manner, even at a very low level and low scale of operation dominate the scenario and are sources of livelihood for a section of the Indian population, especially in rural areas. In the background of the declining contribution of agriculture, the development and growth of the non-agricultural sector is very crucial for providing alternative livelihood in the rural sector. Analysis of the performances of this sector over the years has been undertaken by many researchers from various angles: in terms of growth of units, employment and output, contribution to GDP, contribution to exports, deepening of capital, adoption of new products and new technologies, rejection of traditional items, changing pattern of composition, impact of liberalization and globalization, changing pattern of organizational pattern, problems of production, infrastructure, finance, marketing and so on.

14.2 Section 2

This section presents the scenario of non-agricultural activities in terms of their units and employment over the last 75 years. Important sources of time series data are the Annual Survey of Industries, Economic Census, NSS Survey on Unincorporated Non-Agricultural Enterprises, SSIs and MSME Census and publications of different authorities responsible for the Registration of MSMEs. Each source has its own criterion for the classification and coverage of units, time period of survey and area. Data from these sources are not comparable. Moreover, due to various reasons none of these four sources are exhaustive.

14.2.1 Annual Survey of Industries

Since 1959 following the Collection of Statistics Act, 1953, ASI has been conducted covering the entire industrial units, called factories, registered under the Sects. 2(m)(i) and 2(m)(ii) of the Factories Act, 1948. The ASI frame is revised every year. Presently, the survey also covers Bidi and Cigar manufacturing establishments registered under the Bidi and Cigar Workers (Conditions of Employment) Act 1966. All electricity undertakings engaged in the generation, transmission and distribution of electricity, not registered with the Central Electricity Authority (CEA) are also covered under ASI. However, defence establishments, oil storage and distribution depots and departmental units such as railway workshops, RTC workshops and Govt. Mints, sanitary, water supply, gas storage etc., are excluded from the purview of the survey. Since 2014–15, the units with 100 or more employees not registered under Sect. 2 m (i) and 2 m (ii) of the Factories Act, 1948 but registered under any of the seven Acts/Board/Authority viz., Companies Act. 1956, Factories Act. 1948, Shops and Commercial Establishment Act, Societies Registration Act, Cooperative Societies Act, Khadi and Village Industries Board, Directorate of Industries (District Industries Center) in the Business Register of Establishments (BRE) prepared and

Table 14.1 Number of factories and employees in rural and urban sector

Year	Number of Factories					Number of Employees				
	Rural		Urban		Total(in '000)	Rural		Urban		Total(in lakhs)
	No (in '000)	%	No (in '000)	%		No (in lakhs)	%	No (in lakhs)	%	
1999–2000	46.04	35.0	85.52	65.0	131.56	29.99	36.7	51.73	63.3	81.73
2009–10	59.44	38.2	99.43	61.8	158.88	48.12	40.8	69.8	59.2	117.92
2019–20	103.29	41.9	143.22	58.1	246.5	72.98	43.9	93.26	56.1	166.24
2021–22	104.99	42.0	144.99	58.0	249.99	76.99	44.7	95.17	55.3	172.15

Source Reports of Annual Survey of Industries

maintained by the State Governments are also considered. As the coverage of the surveys in different years is different, it is difficult to make a definite statement; but from Table 14.1, it can be grossly said that there were increasing trends in the number of factories and employment. During the period 1999–2000 to 2021–22, number of factories increased by 2.28 times and employment increased by 2.57 times in rural areas.

14.2.2 Economic Census

Central Statistical Organisation (CSO), Government of India started 'Economic Census and Follow Up Surveys' in 1976. It conducts a census of all economic activities (excluding those engaged in crop production and plantation) followed by detailed sample surveys of unorganized segments of different sectors of the non-agricultural economy. The First Economic Census (1977) considered only the registered units of non-agricultural establishments employing at least one hired worker on a fairly regular basis. Economic Censuses undertaken in the years 1980, 1990, 1998, 2005, 2013, provide data on all the registered and unregistered units of agricultural and non-agricultural sectors (except those involved in crop production and plantation, public administration, defence and compulsory social security), engaged in production and/or distribution of goods and/ or services other than for the sole purpose of own consumption. Table 14.2 shows that during the period between the 2nd Economic Census (1980) and the 6th Economic Census (2013) the number of enterprises increased by 3.11 times, but the total employment increased by 2.78 times in rural areas. In urban areas enterprises increased by 3.28 times, but the total employment increased by 2.17 times.

Table 14.2 Number of establishments and employment as per 2nd and 6th economic census

Type of Establishments	Rural		Urban		Total (in lakhs)
	No(in lakhs)	%	No(in lakhs)	%	
2nd Economic Census (1980)					
All Enterprise Units	111.91(100)	60.77	72.24	39.23	184.14(100)
Own Account Enterprises	86.94(77.68)	64.72	47.38	35.42	134.32(100)
Establishments with at least one hired worker	24.97(22.32)	50.12	24.85	49.88	49.83(100)
Total Employment	244.26(100)	45.59	291.57	54.41	535.83(100)
Hired Workers	100.19(41.01)	33.91	195.28	66.09	295.46(100)
6th Economic Census(2013)					
All Enterprise Units	347.96(100)	59.48	236.99	40.52	584.95(100)
Own Account Enterprises	275.64(79.22)	65.69	144.00	34.31	419.64(100)
Establishments with at least one hired worker	72.32(20.78)	43.75	92.99	56.25	165.31(100)
Total Employment	678.95(100)	51.71	633.98	48.10	1312.94(100)
Hired Workers	286.16(42.15)	39.12	445.29	60.88	731.45(100)

Source Reports of Economic Census

14.2.3 NSS Survey on Unincorporated Non-Agricultural Enterprises

Enterprise surveys as follow-up surveys of the Economic Census (EC) are conducted by NSSO. So far, 15 such follow-up surveys on non-agricultural enterprises have been conducted by NSSO starting from the NSS 33rd round (July 1978–June 1979) to the Survey on Unincorporated Non-Agricultural Enterprises (Excluding Construction) of NSS 73rd round (July 2015–June 2016) and covered the entire unincorporated non-agricultural sector (excluding construction). During the period 1999–2000 to 2021–22, number of enterprises increased by 1.3 times whereas number of total employment increased by 1.26 times in rural areas. During the same period, number of enterprises increased by 1.6 times and the number of total employment increased by 1.54 times in urban areas (Table 14.3).

14.2.4 Census of Small Scale Industries/MSME Census

The First All-India Census of Small Scale Industrial Units was conducted in 1973–74 by Small Industry Development Organisation (SIDO), covering units registered with

Table 14.3 Number of unincorporated non-agricultural enterprises and workers engaged as per economic surveys of NSSO during 1999–2000 and 2015–16

Year	Number of Factories					Number of Employees				
	Rural		Urban		Total(in '000)	Rural		Urban		Total(in lakhs)
	No (in '000)	%	No (in '000)	%		No (in lakhs)	%	No (in lakhs)	%	
1999–2000	46.04	35.0	85.52	65.0	131.56	29.99	36.7	51.73	63.3	81.73
2009–10	59.44	38.2	99.43	61.8	158.88	48.12	40.8	69.8	59.2	117.92
2019–20	103.29	41.9	143.22	58.1	246.5	72.98	43.9	93.26	56.1	166.24
2021–22	104.99	42.0	144.99	58.0	249.99	76.99	44.7	95.17	55.3	172.15

Figures under the % columns indicate the percentages of rural and urban sector out of the combined
Figures within the brackets indicate the % within the rural sector and within the urban sector separately
Source Reports of NSS 55th round (1999–2000) and 73rd round (July 2015- June 2016)

the State Directorate of Industries and falling in the purview of SIDO. The Office of DCSSI conducted the Second All-India Census of Registered SSI units to collect complete data on the working of all registered SSI Units in 1990–91 with reference year as 1987–88. The Third Census of SSI units aimed to cover both registered and unregistered units in the SSI sector for the first time. The Fourth Census (2006–07) also covered both the Registered and Unregistered sectors. Under the Registered sector, in addition to DIC-registered enterprises, units under the coverage of KVIC, Coir Board and identified MSMEs registered under the Factories Act 1948 were covered. All non-agricultural enterprises subject to the definitions as per the MSME Development Act, 2006, were eligible for registration but not registered. Activities excluded were Retail/Wholesale Trade Establishments, General Merchandized Stores, Sale Outlets for industrial components, Legal Services, Educational Services, Social Services, Hotels & Restaurants, Transport Storage & Warehousing (except Cold Storage) (Table 14.4).

The changes in the classification of SSIs/MSMEs and the coverages of units of SSIs/MSMEs restrict the precise temporal comparison in the growth of units or of the corresponding contribution. However, the data given by the 3rd and 4th Census show that over the 5 years this non-farm sector has grown to a great extent. Both the number of units (rural–urban combined) and the total employment (rural–urban combined) increased by 2.01 times each. However, this increase was not enough to absorb the surplus labour of the rural/agricultural sector. Data given by the Labour Bureau Survey Reports and Periodic Labour Force Survey (PLFS) reports shows continuation of high rate of rural and urban unemployment (Table 14.5).

Table 14.4 Number of units of MSMEs and number of employment according to the 3rd and 4th SSI/MSME Census

Characteristics	Rural Units(in lakhs)		Urban Units(in lakhs)		Rural + Urban Units(in lakhs)		Employment in Rural + Urban Units(in lakhs)	
	3rd Census	4th Census	3rd Census	4th Census	3rdCensus	4th Census	3rdCensus	4th Census
	(2001–02)	(2006–07)	(2001–02)	(2006–07)	(2001–02)	(2006–07)	(2001–02)	(2006–07)
Unregistered	52.00	120.00	40.00	78.74	92	198.74	187.69	408.84
	[56.52%]	[60.38%]	[43.48%]	[39.62%]	[100]	[100]	[75.28%]	[81.45%]
Registered	6.09	7.07	7.65	8.57	13.74	15.64	61.63	93.09
	[44.32%]	[45.2%]	[55.68%]	[54.8%]	[100]	[100]	[24.72%]	[18.55%]
Total	58.09	127.07	47.65	87.31	105.74	214.38	249.32	501.93
							[100]	[100]

Figures within the brackets indicate the percentages of rural and urban sector out of the combined sectors for 3rd and also for 4th SSI/MSME Census
Source Reports of 3rd and 4th SSI/MSME Census

Table 14.5 Unemployment rate according to usual status for persons (age group 15 years and above) since 2011–12 to 2021–22 (in percentage)

Sector	2011–12	2012–13	2013–14	2015–16	2016–17	2017–18	2018–19	2019–20	2020–21	2021–22
Rural	2.9	3.5	2.9	3.4	3.5	5.3	5.0	3.9	3.3	3.2
Urban	4.7	5.3	4.9	4.4	5.3	7.7	7.6	6.9	6.7	6.3
Total	3.3	4.0	3.4	3.7	3.9	6.0	5.8	4.8	4.2	4.1

Source (i) Labour Bureau Survey Reports for 2011–12 to 2016–17, and (ii) Annual PLFS Survey reports for 2017–18 to 2021–22
(*Note* the results of Labour Bureau Survey are not comparable with the results of PLFS results due to the different survey methodologies).

14.3 Section 3

This section presents a very brief note on the policies and programmes over the last 75 years.

Both at the Centre and in the States, policies, programmes and procedures were initiated immediately after independence in 1947 to protect this non-farm sector. A number of changes in policies and programmes have taken place over the last 75 years. There were a few distinct phases of this 75 years: from independence to 1977, when the first non-congress government came to power at the centre; from this time to the adoption of new economic policy in 1991; from 1991 to the enactment of the MSME Act 2006; from 2006 onwards. Policies were related to various issues like classification and definition of the sector, protection, reservation, provision of financing, marketing, infrastructural facilities, skill and technology development, consideration of the sector as a priority sector and so on.

Academics, policy makers and various committees have investigated the factors responsible for the slow growth of RNFS and made recommendations for better results. The focus of these studies and reports was mainly on the provision of finance and credit facilities, physical infrastructure and other amenities, institution building for technological upgradation, training for skill development and entrepreneurship development. Based on these studies and recommendations, various measures have been taken from time to time.

14.4 Section 4

This section presents the experience gathered during the ground level work of the author as development practitioner and draws the attention of the policy makers towards some crucial factors for the development of enterprises in rural areas.

For a better understanding of the causes behind the slow/less-than-desired growth, there is a need to look at factors other than the provision of physical infrastructure, marketing infrastructure, credit, administrative procedure, etc. The availability of persons to undertake entrepreneurial activities, their quality, strength, entrepreneurial ambience, etc. are important issues. These factors have drawn less attention from both the policy makers and academics. Development of entrepreneurial activities in the non-farm sector requires persons have the capabilities to taking risks and working under uncertainties and persons have the capabilities of decision-making and thinking differently in innovative ways. Creation of this band of persons demands long-term holistic planning involving the whole process of bringing up the children, our higher education system and the long-standing social attitude towards business and entrepreneurship.

To deal with these issues, the first step is to attract and identify the persons interested in undertaking entrepreneurial activities. At the district and sub-district levels, the government machinery available for promoting industries is the District Industries

Center with two/three project managers, one Industrial Development Officer at the Block level, the Office of the KVIB at the district level, District Rural Development Agency and Standing Committee of Industries at the district panchayat. These bodies coordinate and implement ongoing industry-related programmes and schemes. My experiences of working as a member of the District Planning Committee for a period over two decades and more and as Coordinator of the Rural Industries Programme of SIDBI at the district level show that these bodies and the programmes had no mechanism and financial provision for identification of the persons interested in undertaking entrepreneurial activities, and also for making them aware about the potential entrepreneurial activities in their locality. The local NGOs and panchayats take the initiative to build awareness about the schemes and programmes. As a result, only a few persons usually come for these schemes and programmes.

Another important aspect towards which policy makers' concern need be drawn is the problem of' selection of enterprises faced by the potential entrepreneurs. Choosing an enterprise requires exposure to and knowledge about the ongoing and potential enterprises in their locality, their own understanding of their personal capacities (physical, technical and financial), and the availability of government schemes and assistance.

It was observed that many of the people, who were coming forward for undertaking entrepreneurial activities, even didn't know what enterprise to venture into. Rather, they said, 'I do not know what to do, tell me what I shall do'. The above-mentioned district level bodies in many places had prepared a reports on potential industries and the shelves of schemes in the district. But these 'Shelf of Schemes' were kept on the shelf show piece and rarely for implementation. For instance, in a particular year, one district authority in West Bengal was going to engage an agency to prepare the 'Shelf of Schemes'. During the meeting at the final round, one district official (who was not present in the earlier meeting) said that some 8–10 years back, the district authority got the 'Shelf of Schemes' of the district prepared by 'WEBCON' (a consultancy firm). It shows the state of administrative machinery for the promotion of industries at the district level.

After selecting the type of enterprise, the potential entrepreneur has to prepare a scheme or a project for submission to the financial bodies or to any government office. This requires the assistance of professional (specialized) persons and/or agencies/ institutions. These services are available mainly in the cities and rarely at the district and sub-district levels.

Once the scheme of the enterprise is prepared/formulated of, comes the issue of the capacity of the potential entrepreneur to communicate and follow up with the officers of the government, financial institutions, and also the ruling political and panchayat personnel. Creation of a smooth working environment demands long-term holistic planning for communication capacity building among the potential entrepreneurs and changing the long-standing social attitude of the other stakeholders towards business and entrepreneurship.

Skill development training is another venture that promotes employment and self-employment. Equipping the youths with skills is the first step. Let me consider the experience of organizing TRYSEM training. A large number of youths received training for skill development in different trades. To start one's own commercial production after training, one needs the materials work environment; one has to purchase equipment, tools, raw materials, etc. After production, he/she has to sell the product. In both cases, he/she has to deal with the business sections, and in this case, his/her skill is very poor. Unless he/she is skilled in participating in the input and output markets, it would be difficult to survive of these, most of the TRYSEM-trained youths failed to start their own units. Thus, only technical training is not sufficient to promote the entrepreneur. There is the necessity of generating a bundle of skills in them so that they can bargain to stay in the market.

In the background of the above discussion, it can be said that along with the provision of infrastructure, finance and technology, what is needed is long-term holistic planning for creating a band of persons with all the entrepreneurial qualities. On one side, this requires a change in mindset to change the long-standing social attitude towards business and entrepreneurship on the other.

Abbreviations:

ASI	Annual Survey of Industries
BRE	Business Register of Establishments
CEA	Central Electricity Authority
CSO	Central Statistical Organisation
DCSSI	Development Commissioner of Small Scale Industries
DIC	District Industries Center
DPC	District Planning Committee
EC	Economic Census
GDP	Gross Domestic Product
KVIB	Khadi and Village Industries Board
KVIC	Khadi and Village Industries Commission
MSME	Micro Small and Medium Enterprises
NSSO	National Sample Survey Organisation
NGO	Non-Governmental Organisation
RIP	Rural Industries Programme
RNFS	Rural Non-Farm Sector
SSI	Small Scale Industries
SIDO	Small Industry Development Organisation
SIDBI	Small Industries Development Bank of India
TRYSEM	Training Rural Youth for Self-Employment

References

Annual Survey of Industries. (Reports of the years 1999–2000, 2009–10, 2019–20,2021–22). *National Data Archives*. https://microdata.gov.in

Bhattacharjee, M., Chakrabarti, S., & Rajeev, M. (2024). An inclusive transformation of the rural non-farm economy leveraging farm–non-farm linkages. *EPW, 59*(15)

GOI, Reports of the SSIs/MSMEs Censuses. https://www.dcmsme.gov.in

GOI, Reports of the Economic Censuses: Second Economic Census. https://www.mospi.gov.in. All India Report of Sixth Economic Census.

Government of India, Annual Reports of MSME for different years. https://msme.gov.in

Labour Bureau Survey Reports for the years 2011–12 to 2016–17, https://labourbureau.gov.in

NSS 55th Round 1999–2000. Informal non-agricultural enterprises survey. National Data Archive. https://microdata.gov.in

NSS 73rd Round, 2015–16. Economic characteristics of unincorporated non-agricultural enterprises (excluding construction) in India National Data Archive. https://microdata.gov.in

Periodic Labour Force Survey. Annual Reports for the years 2017–18 to 2021–22. https://www.mospi.gov.in

Ramesh, C., Srivastava, S. K., & Jaspal, S. (2017). Changes in rural economy of India, 1971 to 2012: Lessons for job-led growth. *Economic & Political Weekly*, 52.

RBI. (2019). Report of the expert committee on micro, small and medium enterprises. https://dcmsme.gov.inof Expert Committee

Sajeevan, G. (2012). Present status of MSME statistics. *The Journal of Industrial Statistics, 1*(2), 269–282.

Surbhi, K., & Snehashish, B. (2019). Dualism and structural transformation: The informal manufacturing sector in India. *The European Journal of Development Research*

Sankar Majumder M.A in Economics from the University of Calcutta and Ph.D from Indian Institute of Technology, Kharagpore. Worked as Lecturer and Reader in the Department of Economics, Vidyasagr University (1987 to 2007). Worked as Professor in Economics at Visva-Bharati (a Central University) from 2007 to 2022. Dean and Proctor at Visva-Bharati. Fellow at Indian Institute of Advanced Study, Shimla (1991–93). Presently working as Professor and Head of the Department of Economics, GLA University, Mathura, Uttar Pradesh. Beside academic assignments in the universities worked as a member of different statutory government bodies (District Planning Committee, Urban Development Body, etc.), State Level Advisory Committee on decentralized planning. Worked as the Secretary of a development society(MPDS) for more than 20 years and was directly involved in action research, policy formulation and program implementation of Development Programmes at the state and district levels and undertook project works from NABARD, SIDBI and various government departments. **Areas of Research Interest:** Research and Action research in the areas of development specially decentralized participatory planning, entrepreneurship development, field study based research work in the areas of environmental economics, MSMEs, NGO activities, environmental economics, agricultural economics, public economics. Publications: 02 Books, 01 edited Book, several articles in journals and edited books.

Chapter 15
Changing Dynamics of Internal Migration in India

Sunetra Ghatak

Abstract The study of internal migration in India is crucial for understanding population redistribution, labour market dynamics, urbanisation, and regional disparities. Using data from the Census of India and the National Sample Survey Office (NSSO), this paper explores the trends and patterns of internal migration in India, focusing on both economic and non-economic influencing factors. This paper reviews aggregate and disaggregate internal migration trends in India, highlighting the significant role of non-economic factors, especially in the post-reform period. Most migrations occur within states, influenced by social factors rather than solely economic opportunities. Finally, the paper also identifies limitations of official data, emphasising the need for more comprehensive and current data to better understand internal migration dynamics in India.

Keywords Census · Economic and non-economic factors · India · Internal migration · NSSO · Post-reform periods

15.1 Introduction

The central issue in the study of the internal migration process is the redistribution of a country's population, which can either overpopulate or depopulate an area independently of natural population growth. In the case of India, the study of internal migration is not only significant from the demographic point of view but also sheds light on labour market forces, urbanisation, regional disparities, social and political processes that have a bearing on the area of origin and destination of migrants. The last few decades' rising per capita income, increasing regional disparities, and improvements in transportation and communication facilities have created social and economic changes, and migration has been considered an integral part of the development process. Furthermore, India is the most populous country in the world, having the advantage of a 'demographic dividend' (almost 60% in the 15–59 age group)

S. Ghatak (✉)
Jindal School of Government and Public Policy, O. P. Jindal Global University, Sonipat, India
e-mail: sunetraghatak@gmail.com; sunetra.ghatak@jgu.edu.in

D. Maiti et al. (eds.), *75 Years of Growth, Development and Productivity in India*, India Studies in Business and Economics, https://doi.org/10.1007/978-981-97-8054-9_15

and a median age of about 24 years as per the 2011 census, where migration driven by economic reasons could be a significant phenomenon. While several economic, social, cultural, and political factors simultaneously play an important role in the process of internal migration, the effects of these factors vary over time and regions. Therefore, the analysis of internal migration patterns considering demographic and economic diversity between regions and states has significance in understanding how increasing economic growth has influenced migration over time, especially in the post-reform period. A proper understanding of the changing dynamics of internal migration would help in the estimation of future population redistribution and labour market dynamics responding to urbanisation and regional income disparities.

Theories of migration based on developing countries have explained internal migration in a dual-economy structure (e.g., Harris & Todaro, 1970; Lewis, 1954; Todaro, 1969). In a dual economy, a modern industrial sector and a subsistence agriculture sector exist simultaneously. Given the unlimited supply of rural labour force with their zero marginal productivity, on the one hand, and the higher modern sector wages, on the other, the rural labour force is faced with an incentive to migrate to more promising urban sectors where they can earn positive returns from migration leading to capital accumulation and economic growth in the urban-centric modern sectors (Pandey, 2015). According to these dual-economy models, the early empirical studies have explained migration in dual terms of 'supply push' and 'demand-pull' factors i.e., 'push' from the area of their origin to the place of destination and the 'pull' of the destination from the place of the origin (Mahapatro, 2012; Nair & Narain, 1985; Premi, 1990; Srivastava, 2012; Zachariah, 1963, 1964). These models agreed to the point that migrants often respond strongly to economic incentives.

However, it has been observed that some individuals migrate given similar labour market conditions, while others do not.[1] This indicates a role of other factors which is not adequately captured by economic incentives. More recent migration theories tried to address this issue with the help of individual decisions to migrate from different angles such as human capital, socio-cultural factors, social structures, and caste/kinship bonds and contact fields. Explaining the behaviour of a potential migrant, the literature highlights that variations in educational status and skill sets can influence migration decisions. It argues that only individuals with the necessary skills will likely migrate to urban areas (Sjaastad, 1962). Rather than a human endowment, socio-cultural factors can also influence the migration process of a dual economy despite having considerable unemployment and underemployment in rural areas. This perspective differs from the earlier 'push' and 'pull' frameworks, which consider only the labour market conditions based on expected income differentials, higher employment opportunities, and earning probabilities in urban areas. Moreover, it added that given the imperfect job market and asymmetry of job market information in developing countries, the notion of expected earnings loses its significance in explaining rural-urban migration (Connell et al., 1976; de Haan & Roglay, 2002).

[1] Both the groups—migrants and non-migrants—are facing with the same area specific push and pull factors but one group migrates while others not.

Expansion in the scale of migration has also led to the broadening of migration literature from earlier times, based on agency, social networks, identity, and experience of migrations. Social structures, caste/kinship bonds, and contact fields among the co-residents of a cluster are among the dominant factors of migration because these networks help to minimise migration costs and information asymmetry (Bertrand et al., 2000; Manski, 1993, 2000).

While the recent theories of migration have highlighted the role of many non-economic factors, most of the empirical studies on migration in India still discuss the role of economic factors as the sole determinant for migration. In this paper, we tried to highlight the role of economic vs non-economic factors of migration by analysing aggregate and disaggregate migration trends using the Census of India and National Sample Survey Office (NSSO) data for the post-reform period. A comparative study taking a comprehensive set of factors responsible for internal migration in India may be an important extension in this direction.

The rest of the paper is as follows: In Sect. 15.2 we discuss the aggregate and disaggregate trends of migration in India to understand whether internal migration patterns have a unique direction and are homogeneous. Section 15.3 analyses economic versus non-economic reasons for migration. More specifically, Sect. 15.3.1 deals with economic factors in the case of inter-state migration, while Sect. 15.3.2 discusses the role of non-economic factors such as gender, caste, education etc. The concluding Sect. 15.4 summarises the results and discusses the limitations of the data.

15.2 Aggregate and Disaggregate Trends of Internal Migration in India

In this section, the trends of internal migration in India are presented in two parts: aggregate trends of migration and disaggregate trends of migration. This division helps to understand different patterns of internal migration, if any.

15.2.1 Aggregate Trends of Migration

The total number of migrants in India, along with the number of male and female migrants from 1961 to 2011, has been presented in Fig. 15.1. The figure shows that in recent decades, there has been a three-fold increase in the volume of total internal migration. The 2011 census recorded around 450 million persons as migrants based on the place of their last residence. This constitutes about 37% of the total population of the country. More interestingly, the figure shows an increase number of migrants reported in census 2001, which was around 309 million. Figure 15.1 confirms the increasing trends in the case of internal migration in India, which took impetus after

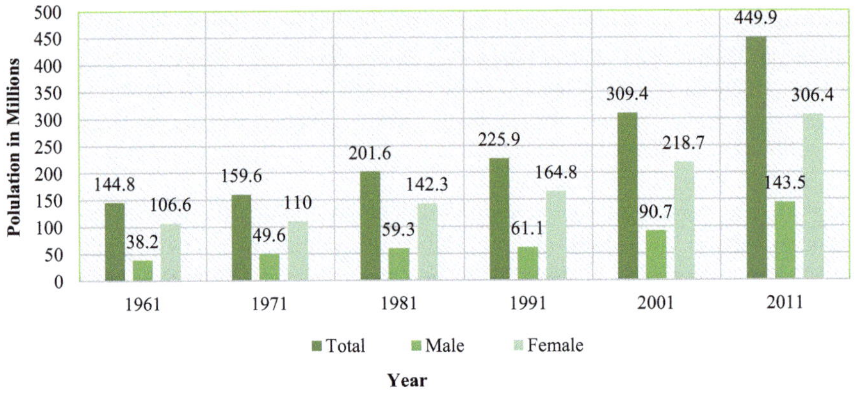

Fig. 15.1 Trends of internal migration in India, 1961–2011. *Source* Calculated from Census of India, Migration Tables

reforms in 1991 in the case of total, male and female migrants. In general, female migrates more as compared to male migrants in India due to 'marriage' migration (Premi, 1980; Srivastava & Sasikumar, 2003). Moreover, a division of the entire period into pre- and post-reform periods indicates that internal migration in India was low in the pre-reform period and increased in the post-reform period. The low internal migration in the pre-reform period has been explained by the fact India is traditional, which is predominated by agriculture, strong community ties, lack of education, the rigidity of the caste system, diversity of language, culture, and food habits, etc. (Chatterjee & Bose, 1977; Davis, 1951; Premi, 1990; Zachariah, 1963, 1964).

15.2.2 Disaggregate Trends of Migration

The aggregate figures of migration presented in Fig. 15.1 may hide many interesting facts which can be observed by looking into the migration numbers at the disaggregated level. This has been seen in terms of disaggregate numbers into two different categories—based on regions (such as rural and urban) and distances (such as intra- and inter-state). The disaggregated migration numbers have been presented in Figs. 15.2a and 15.2b using census data. Figure 15.2a shows the percentage distribution of internal male migrants categorised in terms of regions and distances. Figure 15.2b presents the same for female migrants. Over the years while the share of rural-to-rural migration has declined, the share of rural-to-urban migration has increased (for females). Interestingly, urban-to-urban migration shows an emerging phenomenon signalling the early phases of economic development in the country. This trend towards urban migration reflects the development stage of the country where rapid urbanisation attracts a large number of individuals from rural areas

(Brueckner & Lall, 2015; Zelinsky, 1971). Moreover, the figures show that for both male and female migrants' migration is limited at the intra-state level i.e., most of the migrations are happening within the states. Inter-state migration (migration from one state to another) is still very limited in the case of both male and female migrants.

In order to confirm these, disaggregate trends of internal migration presented in the above paragraph based on census data, Table 15.1 presents the percentage distribution of migrants by regions using three rounds of NSSO data covering the period from 1993 to 2008. Similarly, Fig. 15.3a and Fig. 15.3b present the percentage distribution of migrants using two rounds (49th and 64th) of NSSO data for male migrants and female migrants, respectively, covering the same period, 1993 to 2008. Similar to the case of disaggregate trend derived from census data, the results using NSSO data also reveal that while the percentage share of rural-to-rural migration continues to be high (but declining), the percentage share of rural-to-urban and urban-to-urban migration has increased during this period (see Table 15.1). More importantly, Figs. 15.3a and 15.3b show that for both males and females, inter-state migration has recorded an

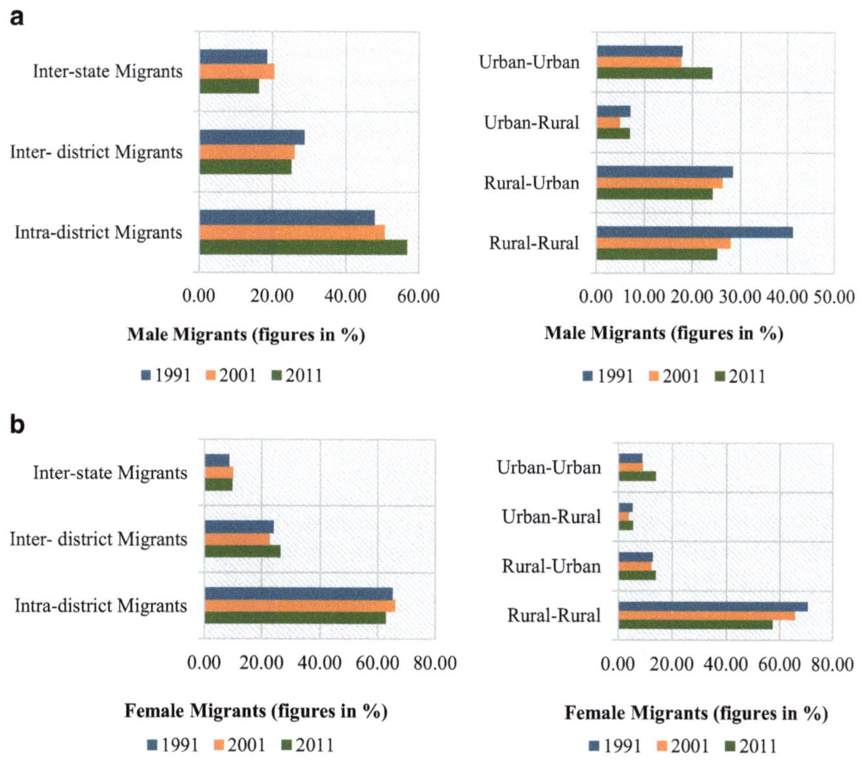

Fig. 15.2 (a) Percentage distribution of male migrants by type of migration, 1991–2011, (b) Percentage distribution of female migrants by type of migration, 1991–2011. *Source* Calculated from Census of India, Migration Tables

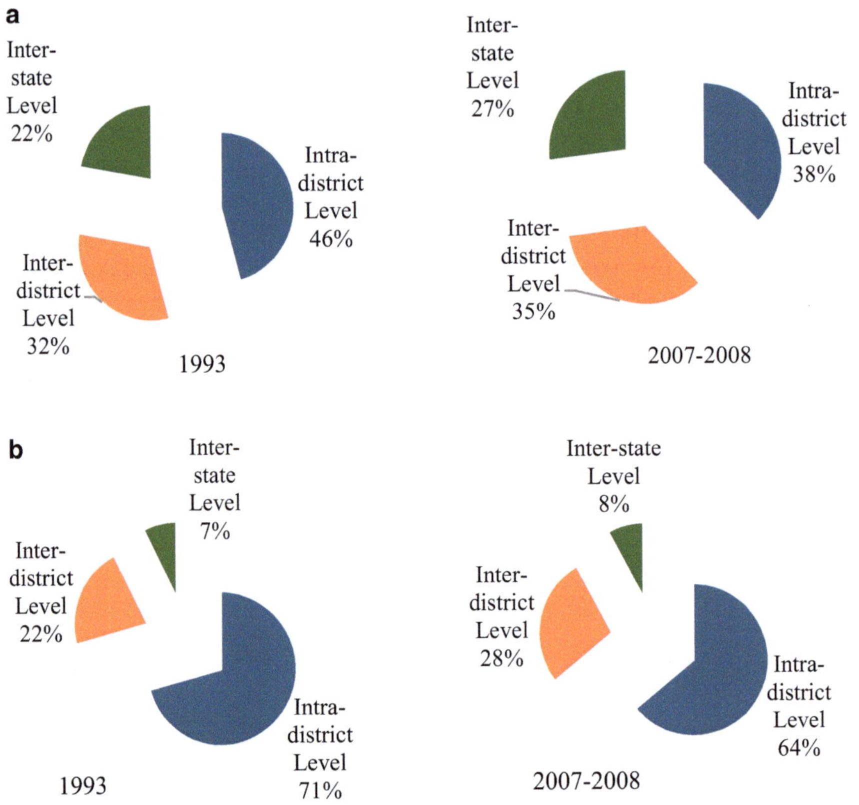

Fig. 15.3 (a) Percentage distribution of male migrants by distance of migration, 1993–2008, (b) Percentage distribution of female migrants by distance of migration, 1993–2008. *Source* Calculated from Unit Level data of NSS 49th, and 64th Rounds

increasing trend. While male inter-state migration has increased from 22% to 27%, female inter-state migration has increased from 7% to 8% from 1993 to 2008.

Therefore, it is clear from the above discussion using both census and NSSO data that although India's migration process has been influenced by recent economic changes, it is still limited to 'short distance' (within-state) migration.[2] The finding that inter-state (across-state) migration is low compared to intra-state (within-state) compels us to reconsider the role of economic factors in internal migration. If migration is influenced only by economic factors such as per capita income differences and the wage gap between regions, then inter-state migration is expected to be higher than intra-state migration because economic differences are expected to be low within a state and high across the states. To gain deeper insights into this phenomenon, the

[2] We refer migration within the district as 'short-distance' migration, and migration across state boundaries as 'long-distance' migration.

Table 15.1 Percentage distribution of migrants by region, 1993–2008

Migration streams	Total			Male			Female		
	Jan-June 1993 (49th)	July 1999-June 2000 (55th)	July 2007-June 2008 (64th)	Jan-June 1993 (49th)	July 1999-June 2000 (55th)	July 2007-June 2008 (64th)	Jan-June 1993 (49th)	July 1999-June 2000 (55th)	July 2007-June 2008 (64th)
Rural to Rural	63.33	61.74	61.74	33.47	32.7	27.19	71.9	70.19	70.01
Urban to Rural	6.41	6.5	5.65	10.98	10.79	8.94	5.1	5.26	4.87
Rural to Urban	18.73	18.86	19.47	34.58	34.16	39.03	14.17	14.41	14.79
Urban to Urban	11.53	12.89	13.14	20.97	22.35	24.84	8.82	10.14	10.34

Source Calculated from Unit Level data of NSS 49th, 55th, and 64th Rounds next section deals with whether there is any evidence that non-economic factors can explain the observed differences between inter-state and intra-state migration.

15.3 Role of Economic *vs* Non-Economic Factors in Internal Migration in India

To examine the economic and non-economic factors of internal migration, this section is divided into two parts. The first section (Sect. 15. 3.1) focuses the role of economic factors while the second section (Sect. 15.3.2) delves the role of non-economic factors influencing internal migration patterns.

15.3.1 Role of Economic Factors in Migration

Here, an exclusive focus has been given on one of the most important streams of migration i.e., inter-state migration, because economic variables such as per capita income (per capita gross state domestic product) are available only at the state level. Moreover, inter-state migration is important because it works as the engine of economic growth and urbanisation by supplying labour to the labour-scarce states from the states where labour is abundant. Literature on inter-state migration suggests that this kind of migration is heavily influenced by factors like regional disparities in per capita income, urbanization, etc. (Bhagat & Mohanty, 2009; Srivastava & Sasikumar, 2003), and inequalities in fiscal variables across states (Chakraborty & Garg, 2018). Therefore, inter-state migration is normally accepted as migration for economic reasons, and there is a belief that non-economic factors play an insignificant role. However, recent empirical studies have challenged this position and shown the significance of non-economic reasons. This section first presents evidence of the correlation between inter-state migration and economic factors like per capita income and urbanisation across states.

In India, the process of economic reform has given opportunities to the potential states to reap benefits of the changing economic environment, such as industrialisation, telecommunication and transportation, health and education enhancement, etc., resulting in large-scale urbanisation which enhances urban-centric migration in the country. During the post-reform period, some states developed while others languished behind. Hence, there is a possibility of having a positive relationship between inter-state migration and increasing per capita income differences and urbanisation between states. One measure that captures the dynamics of inter-state migration well is net inter-state migration flow.[3] Net inter-state migration flow of

---

[3] Net migration flow is defined as difference between In- and Out-migration with respect to the particular state in population. Positive net migration flow symbols in-migrating (migrant receiving) state and *vice-versa.*

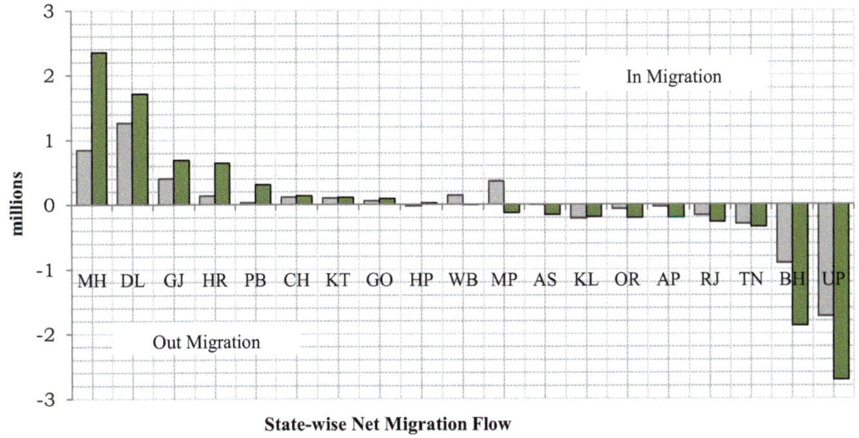

Fig. 15.4 Net inter-state migration flow of major Indian states during 1991–2001 and 2001–2011. *Source* Calculated from the Census of India (2001, 2011)

the Indian states has been presented in Fig. 15.4 for the periods 1991–2001 and 2001–2011, respectively, using census data. The figure demonstrates that while Delhi was the largest net inter-state in-migrating (migrant-receiving) state between 1991 and 2001, Maharashtra became the highest net inter-state in-migrant state between 2001 and 2011. Moreover, two net in-migrant states, Delhi and Maharashtra, have contributed more than 60% of the total inter-state in-migrants in both the decades, 1991–2001 and 2001–2011. Uttar Pradesh and Bihar were the two top net inter-state out-migrant (migrant-sending) states between 1991 and 2001 and maintained their respective positions even between 2001 and 2011, covering 75% of total inter-state out-migrants. States at the forefront of industrial development (including Maharashtra, Delhi, Gujarat, and Haryana) have remained principal destinations for inter-state migrants. In contrast, states with low levels of urbanisation (including Uttar Pradesh, Bihar, Assam, Rajasthan, and Andra Pradesh) remained the main net out-migrating states. It is important to note that the net inter-state out-migrating states are characterised by high population density, poverty, and illiteracy, which often compel individuals in these states to make migration decisions.

To understand how strong the correlation between state per capita income and inter-state migration is, a simple graphical representation has been presented between the net inter-state migration rate[4] of states with the state's gross domestic product in Fig. 15.5 for the year 2011 using census data. While all rich states in India such as Delhi, Maharashtra, Gujarat, Haryana, Goa, Punjab, etc. come out having positive net migration and lying above the red horizontal line, all the poor states such as Bihar, Uttar Pradesh, Odisha, Madhya Pradesh, etc. have negative net inter-state migration and lie below the line demarcating positive and negative range of net inter-state migration. The positive slope of the line indicates that net inter-state migration and

[4] Net migration rate is defined as net migration of a state divided by its total population.

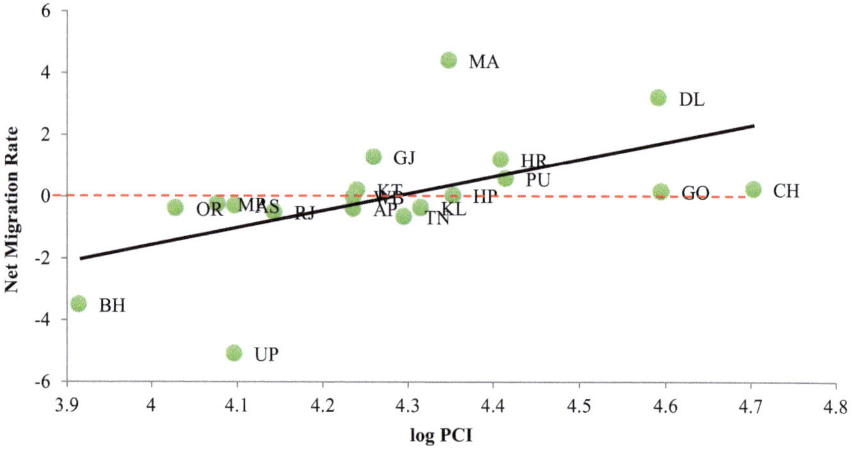

Fig. 15.5 State net migration rate vs. Per Capita income, 2011. *Source* Calculated from the Census of India, 2011

per capita income are positively correlated i.e., migration is happening in response to income differences across states in India.

Urbanisation of a region is another driver of inter-state migration. It has been already observed that there is a net transfer of population from rural-to-urban areas. To understand the direction of flows in inter-state migration towards urban areas, the analysis tried to show a correlation between inter-state migration rate and population density in the states in Fig. 15.6. The analysis considers population density as a proxy of urbanisation instead of taking the urban population to the total population as an indicator of urbanisation. This has been done with a purpose, for example, Delhi has a very high population density (11,312 persons per km^2 compared to 382 for India as a whole) with the highest level of urbanisation (97.5% compared to 31% for All-India). On the other hand, the state of Bihar also has a high-density population (1102 persons per km^2) but has one of the lowest levels of urbanisation (11%). To take care of the dichotomy in the level of population density and level of urbanisation, migration rate, and population density have been considered, and the logarithm of the state's population density has been used in Fig. 15.6 (following Bhagat & Keshri, 2020; Rees et al., 2017). A positive correlation can be observed, indicating that inter-state migration occurs from less populated states to densely populated states. It has also been observed that Delhi and Chandigarh attract a large number of migrants due to their high state gross domestic product and urbanisation. The industrialised states (including Maharashtra, Gujarat, and Haryana) make a cluster with the feature of low population density. Out-migrant states like Uttar Pradesh and Bihar represent high population density with low net migration satisfying the sender states' characteristics. In contrast, some states record lower population densities, such as Manipur, Orissa, and Rajasthan, but perform as net inter-state out-migrating states. Recently, Sikkim

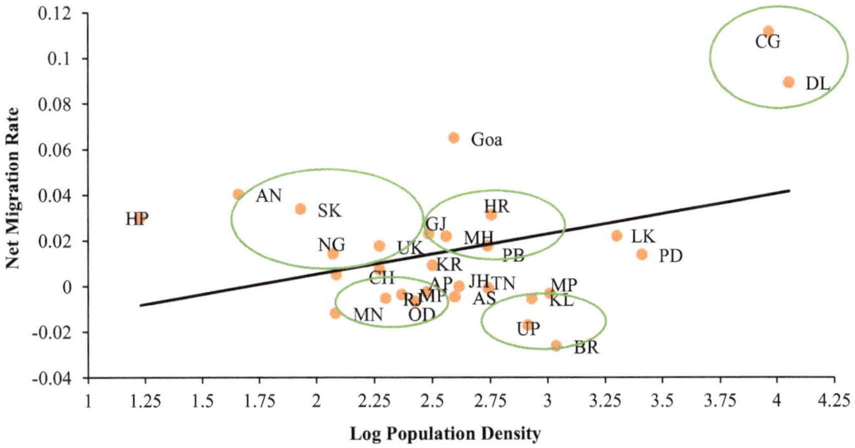

Fig. 15.6 Net Inter-state migration rate vs. population density, 2011. *Source* Calculated from the Census of India, 2011

and Uttarakhand have gained net inter-state in-migration due to their better economic performance but having very low population densities.

In summary, it can be pointed out that per capita income difference plays an important role in choosing migration decisions, while a state's population density seems to have a lower relative role in inter-state migration. Moreover, while it is clear that state per capita income difference and urbanisation play an important role in inter-state migration, these factors are insufficient to explain why inter-state migration is low compared to intra-state migration.

In recent years, empirical studies on labour migration among different regions of a country highlighted the role of administrative or institutional borders[5] (Helliwell, 1997; McCallum, 1995; Poncet, 2006). Literature suggests that state borders are the most significant barrier to internal migration in India (Ghatak & Jha, 2021; Kone et al., 2018). These studies identified less inter-state migration compared to intra-state migration due to the non-portability of entitlement benefits such as public distribution system (PDS), state public sector jobs, entry into tertiary education, etc. across the states and more inter-state migration within the group of physically contiguous states. Therefore, internal migration dynamics in India has changed not only in response to the labour market conditions but also in responding to the non-economic factors discussed above. Moreover, migration depends on 'social' ties as well as reduced access to caste-based insurance networks (Munshi & Rosenzweig, 2016).

[5] Borders are characterised by differences in laws, institutions, and cultures (Belot & Ederveen, 2012).

15.3.2 *Role of Non-Economic Factors in Migration*

From the analysis of aggregate and disaggregate (at regions and states) trends of migration discussed above, it is clear that migration decisions are selective and depend on the individual characteristics of the migrants. What are these characteristics? According to the human capital theory, education plays a vital role in determining the migratory patterns of a society and establishes the capacity to grab the available job opportunities at the destination (Sjaastad, 1962). Moreover, the caste and ethnicity of an individual is a crucial identity of the traditional society in India, which determines migration choice (Bertrand et al., 2000; Manski, 1993, 2000). Empirically, it has been argued that caste-kinship bonds and other kinds of village networks help rural job seekers to set up such urban jobs (Banerjee, 1986). In contrast, the traditional caste system in India imposes certain restrictions on the belongings in the matter of social interaction. Hence, the decision to migrate is affected by the caste system (Dubey et al., 2004). In order to discuss the non-economic factors of internal migration, the paper analyses the characteristics of migrants, such as education status (as a proxy of 'human capital') and social belongings (as a proxy of 'cast-kinship' bonds and networks).

Table 15.2 represents the percentage of work/employment-related migrants by their educational status using census data. This table provides information by region (such as rural and urban), distance (such as intra- and inter-state), and gender between 2001 and 2011. As per census 2011 data, a large portion of male work/employment-related migrants moving towards urban areas are literate but have education below a graduate degree. In contrast to male migrants, illiterate female migrants have a higher percentage of migration for work/employment-related reasons. One can relate that most of the female migrants are from a lower caste (see Fig. 15.7) and happen to be illiterate or have a lower level of education. They generally engage as domestic help or in low-status jobs to contribute to the household income (Neetha, 2004). This could be because, informal activities in the urban areas have increased in the post-reform period, attracting many low-educated and unskilled female migrants to the urban centres.

Further exploration of Table 15.2 shows some interesting features of internal migrants by considering the distance of migration. A large percentage of male and female migrants with higher education (graduation, technical degree, or diploma equal to degree or post-graduate degree) have migrated to longer distances (i.e., inter-state compared to intra-state migration). The percentage of inter-state migration has increased for female work/employment-related migration from 28.60 in 2001% to 32.70% in 2011 (see inter-state urban to urban). Thus, the percentage of migration by education status indicates that the current migration with higher education is relatively more directed towards inter-state migration, while the low-educated people populated the urban areas within the states from 2001 to 2011. This is because, after the economic liberalisation, job profiles in large cities have changed—many modern sector jobs have become available and require specialised training. In these jobs,

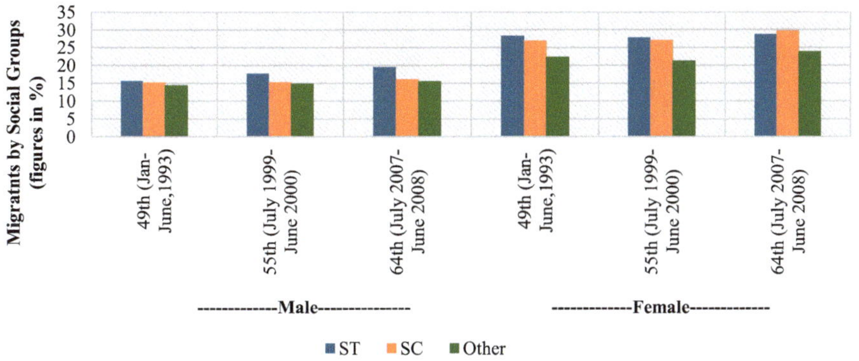

Fig. 15.7 Percentage distribution of migrants by social groups and gender. *Source* Calculated from Unit Level data of NSS 49th, 55th, and 64th Rounds

persons from large cities, those with the required training and skills, etc., get an advantage (Kundu & Mohanan, 2009).

In order to understand the role of social groups on internal migration, analysis has been done based on NSSO data.[6] Figure 15.7 presents the percentage distribution of migrants by social group and gender. The figure reveals that the migration process for both males and females are dominated by caste selectivity. It is observed that the percentage of ST migrants is higher compared to SCs and other categories. This is because the opportunity cost of migration for STs and OBCs is less. After all, they generally possess less amount of land and are involved in low-paid work. Moreover, SCs are generally involved in agricultural activities on a daily wage basis in the land of the landlords. These ensure that they will not leave the house of the landlord until they do not get a better employment opportunity in the urban areas (Banerjee, 1986).

Therefore, the non-economic factors of migration in India uncover some interesting features of internal migration. First, education plays a crucial role in migration decisions. Higher educational status often equips individuals with the skills and knowledge necessary to seek better job opportunities, leading them to migrate from rural-to-urban areas or even across states. Educated individuals are more likely to be aware of and pursue opportunities that promise better economic prospects and living standards. Second, internal migration is caste selective. This caste selectivity may be one of the most important reasons for low inter-state migration by certain castes. This is because the migration decision of an individual is not only based on economic opportunities available at the destination but also depends on the entitlement benefits available at the place of origin (Ghatak & Jha, 2021). Therefore, whenever an individual migrates, she faces a trade-off between the income gain from migration besides the risk of losing administrative benefits and benefits of social networks.

[6] Census of India records separate tables for different social groups.

Table 15.2 Percentage distribution of migrants by education status, gender, and type of migration, 2001–2011[7]

	Intra-state				Inter-state			
	Rural–Urban		Urban-Urban		Rural–Urban		Urban-Urban	
	M	F	M	F	M	F	M	F
Education level	2001							
Illiterate	10.42	26.11	5.86	16.63	14.40	39.14	10.34	20.05
Literate but below Matric/Secondary	28.23	21.31	20.37	20.77	30.87	18.40	24.50	15.66
Matric/Secondary but below graduate	29.87	22.15	30.24	23.49	28.64	16.56	26.23	20.31
Technical diploma or certificate not equal to degree	4.01	4.05	4.68	3.08	3.00	2.70	3.01	3.34
Graduate and above other than technical degree	19.21	17.28	28.13	25.29	15.19	15.49	24.48	28.60
Technical degree or diploma equal to degree or post-graduate degree	6.31	6.93	9.12	8.71	6.12	5.54	10.09	10.21
Education level	2011							
Illiterate	14.00	28.90	7.40	15.50	15.47	38.31	8.00	13.80
Literate but below Matric/Secondary	30.20	24.40	19.70	19.60	33.07	21.11	19.90	13.40
Matric/Secondary but below graduate	26.70	18.30	27.70	21.40	25.74	14.46	22.30	14.60
Technical diploma or certificate not equal to degree	3.70	3.20	4.80	3.20	2.69	2.42	2.90	2.70
Graduate and above other than technical degree	16.10	15.20	25.60	24.50	13.10	13.83	27.20	32.70
Technical degree or diploma equal to degree or post-graduate degree	5.20	5.60	10.30	10.70	6.25	6.02	15.70	18.60

Source Calculated from the Census of India Migration Tables D7, 2001 and 2011

[7] Migrants by Place of Last Residence with Duration 0–9 years reporting 'Work/Employment' as Reason for Migration.

15.4 Conclusions

Being the largest populous country in the world, the dynamics of internal migration in India is an important area of analysis. While the theoretical literature on migration highlights the important role played by non-economic factors, the existing empirical studies on internal migration in India mostly focused on economic factors such as income, wage differential, urbanisation, etc. This paper provided an overview of different trends of internal migration in India and demonstrated that non-economic factors also play an important role in internal migration in the country, especially in the post-reform period. More specifically, migration in India has significantly increased since the economic reforms. Migration trends show gender disparities, with women migrating primarily for marriage. There has been a decline in rural-to-rural migration and an increase in urban-centric migration, reflecting economic development. Most migrations occur within states, influenced by social networks and caste-kinship bonds, rather than solely economic opportunities. Education impacts migration patterns, with higher educational attainment leading to longer-distance inter-state migration, while lower-educated individuals tend to migrate within states. Therefore, analysis shows a significant impact of non-economic factors such as education, caste, state administrative borders, etc. along with economic factors such as per capita income and urbanisation.

In the context of the present paper, it is important to note the limitations of official data on migration. The low level of internal migration and restricted inter-state migration captured in the official migration data sources like census and NSSO can be explained by the limitation of the data. First, census data counts only permanent migrants and underestimates two other types of migration—commuting and circular or seasonal migration[8]—which has significantly increased in recent years.[9] It has been reported that the Indian population circulates over various distances annually for employment (Keshri & Bhagat, 2012, 2013); originating from lower castes and this form of migration has been increasing in recent times (Srivastava, 2012); is seven times higher than that of permanent and semi-permanent migration (Deshingkar et al., 2008; Sharma & Chandrasekhar, 2014). This issue can be resolved by complementing using NSSO data (captures both short-term[10] and long-term migration). Other important surveys, namely, IHDS[11] and NFHS[12] provide data on seasonal and short-term migration with remittances but don't give information on the places of origin and destination. This makes these two datasets inappropriate for the use of tracing the movement of people from one place to another. Secondly, another issue of underestimation is because both census and NSSO data capture only one origin and one destination, and hence, these datasets are unable to capture multiple changes in destination. Thirdly, the low level of internal migration in India has been

[8] These two types of migration are also known as 'short-term' migration.

[9] In contrast to Census, NSS captures both 'long-term' and 'short-term' migration.

[10] But may not fully since it is measured on place of birth (POB) and place of last residence (POLR).

[11] Indian Human Development Survey.

[12] National Family Health Survey.

explained by cultural factors such as kinship and caste systems, which often tie individuals to their places of origin (Munshi & Rosenzweig, 2016). However, reasons for migration do not capture social networks as a factor in migration decisions and therefore it is impossible to identify the role of social networks in migration using available secondary data in India. Fourthly, as pointed out earlier, higher numbers of female migrants reported 'marriage' as their reason for migration. This underestimates the economic reasons for female migration because the question of 'reasons for migration' does not allow for multiple responses and male interviewees might downplay women's work during interviews. Female migrants, especially in part-time or informal work, might not see themselves as economic contributors. This leads to women being seen as secondary earners and invisible in official statistics. Additionally, data often overlook females who worked before migration and doesn't track if 'marriage' migrants join the workforce later. This makes it hard to capture the full picture of women's migration for both work and family reasons, hindering the understanding of 'feminisation of migration' (Ghatak, 2020; Neetha, 2004; Raju, 2006; Shanthi, 2006). Lastly, the census 2011 data and NSSO[13] 2007–08 data both are very old. Unless new data is published, it is difficult to get a recent picture of internal migration in India. In conclusion, it can be highlighted that the research on internal migration demands higher quality recent data to address several dimensions of migration discussed in migration theories. Otherwise, the topic of internal migration would remain a blind spot in the literature and not be an integral part of the development process.

References

Banerjee, B. (1986). *Rural to urban migration and the urban labour market: A case study of Delhi.* Himalaya Publication House.

Belot, M., & Ederveen, S. (2012). Cultural barriers in migration between OECD countries. *Journal of Population Economics, 25*(3), 1077–1105.

Bertrand, M., Luttmer, M., & Mullainathan, S. (2000). Network effects and welfare cultures. *The Quarterly Journal of Economics, 115*, 1019–1055.

Bhagat, R. B., & Mohanty, S. (2009). Emerging pattern of urbanization and the contribution of migration in urban growth in India. *Asian Population Studies, 5*(1), 5–20.

Bhagat, R. B., & Keshri, K. (2020). Internal migration in India. In M. Bell, A. Bernard, E. Charles-Edwards, & Y. Zhu (Eds.), *Internal migration in the countries of Asia.* Springer. https://doi.org/10.1007/978-3-030-44010-7_11

Brueckner, J. K., & Lall, S. V. (2015). Cities in developing countries: Handbook of regional and urban economics. In G. Duranton, J. V. Henderson, & W. C. Strange (Eds.), *Handbook of regional and urban economics* (pp. 1399–1455). Elsevier.

Census of India. (1991). *Data highlights: Migration tables.* Office of the Registrar General and Census Commissioner.

Census of India. (2001). *Data highlights: Migration tables.* Office of the Registrar General and Census Commissioner.

[13] 70th round NSS (2013) only represents rural migration while annual Periodic Labour Force Survey (PLFS) 2020–2021 induced lockdown has information on temporary visitors.

Census of India. (2011). *Census schedule: Household*. Office of the Registrar General and Census Commissioner.

Chakraborty, P., & Garg, S. (2018). *Fiscal pressure of migration & horizontal fiscal inequality: Evidence from Indian experience* (WIDER Working Paper Series 004). World Institute for Development Economic Research (UNU-WIDER).

Chatterjee, A., & Bose, A. (1977). Demographic data on internal migration and urbanisation from census and NSS—An appraisal. In A. Bose, D. B. Gupta, & G. Raychaudhuri (Eds.), *Population statistics in India*. Vikas Publishing House Pvt. Ltd.

Connell, J., Dasgupta, B., Laishley, R., & Lipton, M. (1976). *Migration from rural areas: The evidence from village studies*. Oxford University Press.

Davis, K. (1951). *The population of India and Pakistan*. Princeton University Press.

de Haan, A., & Rogaly, B. (2002). *Labor mobility and rural society*. Frank Cass.

Deshingkar, P., Sharma, P., & Kumar, S. (2008). Circular migration in Madhya Pradesh: Changing patterns and social protection needs. *The European Journal of Development Research, 20*, 612–628.

Dubey, A., Palmer-Jones, R., & Sen, K. (2004). *Surplus labour, social structure and rural-to-urban migration: Evidence from Indian data*. Paper presented at the Conference on the 50th Anniversary of the Lewis Model.

Ghatak, S. (2020). Women's economic migration. In S. I. Rajan & M. Sumeetha (Eds.), *Handbook of internal migration in India* (pp. 372–384). Sage.

Ghatak, S., & Jha, D. (2021). Role of economic reforms on dismantling barriers to inter-state migration in India. *Migration Letters, 18*(3), 297–304.

Harris, J. R., & Todaro, M. P. (1970). Migration, unemployment and development: A two-sector analysis. *The American Economic Review, 60*(1), 126–142.

Helliwell, J. F. (1997). National borders, trade and migration. *Pacific Economic Review, 2*(3), 165–185.

Keshri, K., & Bhagat, R. B. (2012). Temporary and seasonal migration: Regional pattern, characteristics and associated factors. *Economic and Political Weekly, 47*(4), 81–88.

Keshri, K., & Bhagat, R. B. (2013). Socioeconomic determinants of temporary labour migration in India. *Asian Population Studies, 9*(2), 175–195.

Kone, Z. L., Liu, M., Mattoo, A., Ozden, C., & Sharma, S. (2018). Internal borders and migration in India. *Journal of Economic Geography, 18*(4), 729–759.

Kundu, A., & Mohanan, P. C. (2009). *Employment and inequality outcome in India* (OECD Conference Paris). OECD Paris.

Lewis, W. A. (1954). Economic development with unlimited supplies of labour. *The Manchester School, 22*(2), 139–191.

Mahapatro, S. R. (2012, June 13–16). *The changing pattern of internal migration in India: Issues and challenges*. Paper presented in European Population Conference, Stockholm, Sweden.

Manski, C. F. (1993). Identification of endogenous social effects: The reflection problem. *Review of Economic Studies, 60*, 531–542.

Manski, C. F. (2000). Economic analysis of social interactions. *Journal of Economic Perspectives, 14*(3), 115–136.

McCallum, J. (1995). National borders matter: Canada-us regional trade patterns. *The American Economic Review, 85*(3), 615–623.

Munshi, K., & Rosenzweig, M. (2016). Networks and misallocation: Insurance, migration, and the rural-urban wage gap. *American Economic Review, 106*(1), 46–98.

Nair, P. S., & Narain, V. (1985, January 24–28). *Internal migration in India: Demographic knowledge and Policy Issues*. IUSSP Seminar on Policy Formulation, Implementation and Evaluation: the case of East, South and South East Asia, contributed papers, Bombay, India.

Neetha, N. (2004). Making of female breadwinners: Migration and social networking of women domestics in Delhi. *Economic and Political Weekly, 39*(17).

Pandey, A. (2015). Anatomy of rural-urban migration in India: Socio-economic selectivity in the process of male migration based on NSS. *Man & Development, 37*, 73–92.

Poncet, S. (2006). Provincial migration dynamics in China: Borders, costs and economic motivations. *Regional Science and Urban Economics, 36*(3), 385–398.
Premi, M. K. (1980). Aspects of female Migration in India. *Economic and Political Weekly, 15*, 714–720.
Premi, M. K. (1990). India. In C. B. Nam, W. J. Serow, & D. F. Sly (Eds.), *International Handbook on Internal Migration*. Greenwood Press.
Raju, S. (2006). *Locating women in social development*. Oxford University Press.
Rees, P., Bell, M., Kupiszewski, M., Kupiszewska, D., Ueffing, P., Bernard, A., Charles-Edwards, E., & Stillwell, J. (2017). The impact of internal migration on population redistribution: An international comparison. *Population, Space and Place, 23*(6), 1–22.
Shanthi, K. (2006). *Female labour migration in India: Insights from NSSO data* (Working paper No. 4). http://www.mse.ac.in
Sharma, A., & Chandrasekhar, S. (2014). *Internal migration for education and employment among Youth in India* (Working Papers id:5682). eSocialSciences.
Sjaastad, L. A. (1962). Cost and returns of human migration. *Journal of Political Economy, 7*, 88–93.
Srivastava, R. (2012). Internal migration in India: An overview of its features, trends and policy challenges. In *National workshop on internal migration and human development: Workshop compendium* (vol. 2). Workshop papers (pp. 1–47). UNESCO and UNICEF.
Srivastava, R. S., & Sasikumar, S. K. (2003, June 22–24). *An overview of migration in India, its impacts and key issues*. Paper Presented in Regional Conference on Migration, Development and Pro-Poor Policy Choices in Asia, Dhaka, Bangladesh.
Todaro, M. P. (1969). A model of labor migration and urban unemployment in less developed countries. *American Economic Review, 59*, 138–148.
Zachariah, K. C. (1963). *Internal migration in India from the historical standpoint* (Invited Paper). 34th Session, I.S.I., Ottawa, Canada.
Zachariah, K. C. (1964). *A historical study of internal migration in the Indian Sub-Continent, 1901–1931*. Asia Publishing House.
Zelinsky, Z. (1971). The hypothesis of the mobility transition. *Geographical Review, 61*, 219–249.

Part VII
Social Sectors

Chapter 16
International Finance: Missing Link in Theory and Practice

Gargi Sanati, Anup Kumar Bhandari, and Rajesh Ramakrishnan

Abstract The field of international finance can be highly complex and challenging to navigate. One of the major issues that individuals and businesses face is the lack of comprehensive documentation that delves into the intricacies of products and processes related to the role of banks and the legal frameworks of international bodies like the International Chamber of Commerce (ICC). To truly gain a deep understanding of the practical applications of international trade, it is essential to study the process and documentation flows that pertain to these transactions. Also, trade-based money laundering is another important aspect of modern day's international trade scenario. We have touched upon each of these aspects to make this chapter an interesting and important document in connection with the overall modern international trade atmosphere. Recently, there has been some literature available that bridges the existing gap between theory and practice related to international trade and finance. These resources cover a wide range of topics, from banking theories to operational procedures relating to the methods of payment in international trade, and the use of various Letters of Credit (LCs), for example, revolving LCs, back-to-back LCs, transferable LCs, standby LCs, with their specific applications of documents and documentary compliances. Also, the significance of merchanting trade and the differences between export credit and trade credit have been discussed in the literature. Besides, different types of bank guarantees are discussed with their practical applications. Hedging of foreign exchange risk for the merchants has been discussed elaborately. On the other hand, the mechanism of interbank cover operation is discussed to elaborate the risk mitigation techniques in the banking book. Also, some empirical literature has been referred to which highlights the change in

---

G. Sanati · R. Ramakrishnan
National Institute of Bank Management (NIBM), Pune, India
e-mail: gargi@nibmindia.org

R. Ramakrishnan
e-mail: r.rajesh@nibmindia.org

A. K. Bhandari (✉)
Department of Humanities and Social Sciences, Indian Institute of Technology (IIT), Chennai, India
e-mail: anup@iitm.ac.in

D. Maiti et al. (eds.), *75 Years of Growth, Development and Productivity in India*, India Studies in Business and Economics, https://doi.org/10.1007/978-981-97-8054-9_16

operational efficiency of the banks if the credit risk and the market risk become an integral part of the efficiency measure.

Keywords International Finance · Methods of Payments · Letter of Credit Business · Export Credit or Packing Credit · Export Subsidy · Trade-based Money Laundering

16.1 Introduction

International trade and finance are two interlinked domains that rely heavily on theoretical concepts. While international trade covers topics ranging from as old as Adam Smith's theory of absolute advantage to relatively modern trade theories like the Stolper-Samuelson trade theorem and others based on imperfect competition, international finance delves into exchange rate regimes, parity conditions, derivatives products, and pricing mechanisms. However, there is a lack of comprehensive documentation that explores the intricacies of the products and processes related to the role of banks and the legal frameworks of international bodies like the International Chamber of Commerce (ICC). To truly understand the practical applications of international trade, one must study the process and documentation flows that pertain to these transactions.

Against this backdrop Sanati (2017, 2024) bridges the existing gap between the theory and practices related to international finance, covering banking theories and operational procedures relating to the methods of payment with special reference to Letters of Credit (LCs), like revolving LCs, back-to-back LCs, transferable LCs, and standby LCs, with specific applications of documents and documentary compliances. In addition Sanati (2024) discusses several other aspects of international trade, such as merchanting trade, buyers' credit, supplier's credit, and bank guarantees. She provides practical examples of their applications and how they relate to the rules and regulations of the ICC and other regulatory bodies. The book also examines the different roles of banks in financing international trade, with the use of several case studies. It provides a detailed explanation of the complexities and discrepancies involved in international trade documentation, covering all the necessary stages involved in executing an import or export deal. This includes signing the contract, managing pre-shipment credit, booking a forward contract to hedge the exchange rate risk, and ultimately closing the deal. It also provides comprehensive information about all trade finance products, including their processes, procedures, rules, regulations, risks, and ways to mitigate them.

The book provides a comprehensive discussion of the practical application of ICC rules through detailed case studies. The case studies help exporters understand what actions to take when payment is denied by an overseas party. Likewise, it explains how Indian importers can deny payment if there are documentary non-compliances. The book also scrutinizes various types of forex transactions, the regulatory framework within which they take place, and the associated risks and solutions. Furthermore, it aims to address the existing disparity in the understanding and interpretation of regulatory guidelines and the practices adopted by banks and corporate houses in implementing them.

The book at hand is an invaluable resource for anyone interested in the intricacies of trade transactions. It not only delves into the process of dealing with discrepancies that may arise but also provides a comprehensive overview of forex dealing in the front-office treasury of the dealing room. Given this backdrop, this chapter points out some important aspects of international finance that may be focused on in future research and literature. The first section of this chapter serves to introduce the reader to the topic, while Sect. 16.2 summarizes the existing literature. Section 16.3 is particularly interesting, as it aims to bridge the gap between concerned theories and practitioners' perspectives. Section 16.4 is dedicated to elaborating on empirical literature focusing on the contribution of export subsidy channelized through packing credit or pre-shipment credit for the growth of Indian exports. This is an important aspect as it sheds light on a topic that is often overlooked in mainstream discussions on international trade. Section 16.5 discusses few recent cases of trade-based money laundering, which is an important aspect of modern day's international trade scenario. Finally, in Sect. 16.6, the authors conclude the study. It is worth noting that bridging the gap between theory and practice is not only useful for students, researchers, and teachers in the fields of management, business studies, international trade, and treasury operations, but also for professionals working in the domains of export–import businesses, treasury front-office and back-office operations, bureaucrats, and public policymakers. Overall, we endeavour to highlight some of the important work in this domain which provides an opportunity to gain a deeper understanding of the complex world of international trade and finance practices.

16.2 A Brief Discussion on Existing Literature

The existing literature on international trade and finance tends to treat these two critical areas of economics and business research as separate and distinct from one another. This approach fails to recognize the intricate and interconnected relationship between international trade and international finance, which are inextricably linked and impact each other in various ways. A more comprehensive understanding of the interplay between these two domains is necessary for developing effective policies and strategies for businesses and governments operating in the global market place. Apte (2009) offers an in-depth exploration of various aspects of the global financial system. He delves into the international monetary system, discussing the functioning of domestic and offshore financial markets, exchange rate regimes, and the global monetary system. It also provides a comprehensive yet accessible discussion of modern theories of exchange rate determination and forecasting. Readers can also learn about currency derivatives such as futures and options, short-term funding, investment of cash surpluses, and centralized cash management. Furthermore, the book covers the global debt market, elucidating the concepts of syndicated credits and bond issues. It also delves into the equity market, providing insights into global depository receipts and American depository receipts (GDR-ADR). The book also discusses the financial appraisal of cross-border investment projects in detail, helping readers understand the nuances of assessing such investments. Overall, the book (Apte, 2009) is a valuable resource for anyone interested in gaining a comprehensive understanding of international finance and the global financial systems.

International finance is a complex and multifaceted field, and while much of it has been explored, there remains a large part of it that is linked to the banking sector and its operational aspects which is yet to be explored. The reason for this is that the concepts of products linked to the export–import businesses are too operational and technical, which makes it harder to examine them. Moreover, the process flow and legal aspects of non-payments are relatively unexplored areas of international trade and international finance. This presents a twofold challenge: firstly, there is a need to understand international trade and finance from a practical point of view, right from its different products, the role of the banks, and process flow. Secondly, although the determinants of export growth are quite well-researched areas, the importance of finance in terms of packing credit or pre-shipment credit on export growth has not been discussed in the literature. It may be noted that the Government of India started an important initiative in 2007–2008 by introducing a subsidy in the interest rate for the packing credit. This was done to encourage more exports and to facilitate the growth of the export sector. The impact of interest rate subsidy and access to this subsidized packing credit has been examined through some empirical works conducted by researchers like Sanati in 2019 and Sanati et al. in 2023. These studies have provided valuable insights into the impact of this initiative on the export sector and the overall economy. By exploring these aspects of international finance, we gain a better understanding of the challenges and opportunities that exist in this field and develop strategies to navigate them successfully.

As previously noted, the growth of exports and the factors influencing it are widely discussed topics within economic and financial literature; however, very few studies have investigated how access to financing affects export growth. As determinants of export growth, the primary factors that are analysed and extensively discussed in the literature pertain to macroeconomic elements; for instance, *foreign income*, *real exchange rates*, and *stages of development* (Grier & Smallwood, 2007); *demand spillover* and *domestic market supply* (Tran et al., 2012); *GDP*, *investments*, and *capital stock* (Patnaik & Chandrashekhar, 1996), among others. The role of finance as a factor influencing export growth is not the only under-researched topic; the idea of *packing credit* or *pre-shipment credit* (Reserve Bank of India [RBI], 2015) is also quite unfamiliar in the global economic and financial literature.

Sanati (2019) and Sanati et al. (2023) fill this gap in their study, which examines the availability of finance as a significant constraint for exporters in supporting the production process. Typically, an exporting company can access two primary types of financing from banks: (a) a working capital loan or short-term loan; and (b) packing credit (PC), which converts to post-shipment credit, once the goods have been shipped. However, the studies by Sanati (2019) and Sanati et al. (2023) conclude that the PC is the most preferred option for financing exports as the cost of the fund is relatively lower. PC refers to the loan or advances availed from banks by an exporter for financing the purchase, processing, manufacturing, or packaging of goods before shipment and/or working account expenses towards the rendering of services (RBI, 2013). It is mainly provided against the irrevocable LC opened in favour of the exporter or against the confirmed purchase order, and the exporter is not paid in advance to the shipment of the products (Sanati, 2017). Directorate General of Foreign Trade (DGFT), Government of India (GoI), has introduced an interest subvention scheme (2007–2014) or interest equalization scheme (2015 onwards) for PC to enable finance to reach the exporting sectors at an affordable cost (RBI, 2016a). The major objective of interest subsidy in PC is to bring down the interest cost of the fund to provide a level playing field for exporters who do not have access to the low-cost fund. Against this backdrop, Sanati (2019) examines the impact assessment of this subsidized scheme since banks usually have skewed preferences in disbursing PCs for various reasons. Further details on this study are elaborated in Sect. 16.4. Two important assumptions were the basis of her study: first, the larger the size of the firm, the more creditworthy it becomes. This positive correlation is well discussed in the literature; for example, Falkenstein (1996) suggests that since larger firms are generally more diversified in their products, geographic locations, and people, their earnings are less risky, so they are considered to be more creditworthy to a bank. Likewise, Matthies (2013) also finds an inverse relationship between firm size and credit risk. Also, it is argued that more creditworthy firms enjoy more bargaining power to have the credit disbursed at a much lower interest rate. Second, Tirole (2006, Chapter 3) shows that larger firms have more assets to lose if they fail. Sanati (2019) contributes to the existing literature by examining the availability and accessibility of finance as an important determinant of export growth in India and draws some important policy recommendations therefrom.

16.3 Bridging the Gap Between Practice and Theories

Sanati (2017, 2024) provides an in-depth analysis of different payment methods like *advance payment, open account, documentary collection, and documentary credit* and their implications for the execution of export–import business (Box 16.1). For each of the payment methods, we first have to establish a contract of sale and risk exposures vary across exporters, importers, and banks depending on the different payment methods. Also, depending on the specialized service offered, banks may bear different roles and responsibilities.

Associated with the methods of payments, we discuss the role and responsibilities of *negotiating banks, confirming banks, and paying banks* (Sanati, 2017, 2024). For example, to mitigate the non-payment possibility due to country risk, especially after the shipment happens, many Indian companies with high-value invoicing would hire the service of a confirming bank. This bank needs to be located in India and undertake payment obligations on and above the payment obligations undertaken by the issuing banks. Similarly, a paying bank is a bank that undertakes the payment obligation to the exporter after scrutinizing the documents. So, the paying bank once confirms that there are "no documentary discrepancies", it cannot call back the fund from the exporters in case the issuing bank (importer's bank) finds some discrepancies in the export documents and refuses to make the payment. So, in other words, the role of paying banks is without recourse as it already has certified that the documents are without discrepancies. Each of these banks has its own rules and documentary flow requirements. Exporters often require funds to finance their exports. These funds could be in the form of a working capital limit or pre-shipment credit. After the exporter ships the goods to the importer country, they may require the funds to pay off their existing loan. However, there is a time gap between when the exporter ships the goods and when they receive the payment. To bridge this gap, exporters often submit all the relevant export documents to a bank for negotiation. This process is known as document negotiation. During the negotiation process, the bank provides the payment to the exporter at a minimum cost (much lower than the other interest cost) with the expectation of payment receivables from the importer. The bank that negotiates the documents is called a negotiating bank. The LC issuing bank or the importer bank can nominate a bank as the negotiating bank, or they may keep the LC unrestricted without nominating any bank as the negotiating bank.

In summary, document negotiation is a common practice in international trade, which allows exporters to receive funds on time and helps to minimize the risks associated with international trade transactions in any bank as a negotiating bank. Moreover, it is important to note that there are some risk factors that banks carry while using documentary collection, following ICC guidelines. When carrying out a trade transaction, it is important to be aware of the various types of bills of exchange that can be used, such as the usance bill. This type of bill allows for payables to be settled at a future date, giving the importer some time to make the payment. However, it often comes with a pre-condition, especially for the countries with higher levels of country risk that the banks can only release the necessary documents to the importer once payment has been made.

Box 16.1

Open Account—If shipment happens before the payment to the exporter, it is known as an open account payment method. Exporter takes maximum risk in this case

Advance Payment—If payment is received by the exporter before the shipment of the goods it is known as Advance Payment.

Documentary Collection—After the shipment of the goods, the exporter collects all the relevant documents, bill of lading, insurance certificate, packing list, etc., and submits the commercial documents and financial documents (bill of exchange) to its bank, that is remittance bank which sends the documents to the importer's bank or collecting bank for the payment. Under documentary collection, bank does not take payment obligations unless Uniform rules for Collection (URC-522) instructions are violated.

Documentary Credit or Letter of Credit—Under letter of credit importer's bank or issuing bank undertakes the payment obligations on behalf of the importer under documentary compliances. Documentary credit or letter of credit is governed under Uniform Rules for Customs and Practices (UCP—600).

Source Authors' Creation

This is an important clause that the collecting bank must adhere to avoid any legal consequences as per the rules of URC-522. Although the usance bill is intended to provide some flexibility for the importer, this particular condition can nullify that purpose and cause issues if not followed.

The SWIFT message format is also discussed in detail, with a focus on the Message Types (MT) fields and their relevance. Additionally, Sanati (2017, 2024) explains the functionality of partial shipment and transhipment, as described by UCP 600 with some applications in the international trade domain. Furthermore, the concept of the normal transit period and its importance in the settlement of funds for sight bills and the 'n' day's usance bill from the date of sight is also clarified. Lastly, factoring and forfaiting concepts are depicted as a parallel financial facility to the banking sector. Overall, this comprehensive chapter provides valuable insights into the intricate workings of payment methods and their role in the successful execution of export–import business.

Sanati (2024) is the first of its kind the state of the art that describes the operational structure and functionality of different letters of credit products, for example, *Back-to-Back LC, Transferable LC, Standby LC, Instalment LC, Revolving LC, Green Clause and Red Clause LC,* and *Transit LC*. For example, theoretically, the revolving credit is the LC under which the exporter can draw bills (or bill of exchange) 'n' number of times within the face value of LC and once the amount is drawn the credit is reinstated in its original value. It means every time the exporter draws the bill, he becomes eligible to draw the full value of LC once again. Under such conditions, banks face unlimited exposure to risk. So, it is important to follow some operational guidelines appropriate for the banks issuing the revolving credit while limiting the risk exposure following the credit sanction. Likewise, standby LC invoked only in case of non-payment and the operational and documentation flow of the credit are very different than the other commercial LC. FEDAI (Foreign Exchange Dealers Association of LC) describes the safeguard measure of a bank that must be adopted to mitigate its own risk of exposure.

Box 16.2

Back-to-Back LC—The Second LC is opened with the same terms and credit mentioned in the principal LC. Mostly used in merchanting trade (where goods do not touch India's periphery) or for trade transactions where an intermediary works like a trader who knows a seller and a buyer in two different countries. The second LC is known as the back-to-back LC.

Transferable LC—A part of the credit gets transferred to a second beneficiary or exporter. There may be multiple second beneficiaries. If Tata Motors has to make a final product which is a car and Tata Motors buys raw materials from different other sub-suppliers, Tata Motors becomes the first beneficiary for a trade transaction that employs transferable LC as the payment method and the sub-suppliers become the second beneficiary.

Instalment LC—LC which requires a stipulated amount of goods to be supplied within a stipulated fixed period is known as instalment credit. For example, if the credit validity is for 6 months, then the exporter may have to ship the same value of the product every month for 6 months.

Red clause LC—It allows pre-shipment advances to be made to the exporter at the risk and expenses of the applicant. Under a red clause credit, the bank would honour the exporter's sight drafts up to a specified percentage of the total credit agreement against the production of certain preliminary documents. This credit is extended for purchasing raw materials/purchasing/and/or packing the goods. The clause letter of credit is so named as it was originally written in red ink to draw the attention of the nominated bank.

Green Clause LC—It is an extended version of red clause credit in the sense that it not only provides for advance towards purchase, processing, and packing, but also for warehousing and insurance charges at port when the goods are stored pending availability of ships/shipping space.

Transit Credit—LC is opened by a bank located in a country that is neither the exporter's country nor importer's country.

Source Authors' Creation

For each of the above-mentioned LCs, the conceptual framework depicts documentation flow, cash flow, and associated risk of the banks. Also, the role and responsibilities of the banks may vary as per the interpretation and execution of ICC guidelines by commercial banks. For example, it describes that a Standby LC may be open under Uniform Customs & Practice for Documentary Credits 600 (UCP 600) or International Standby Practices 98 (ISP 98). It explains some other important concepts, like, *third-party documents, stale documents,* and *the applications of 5% and 10% tolerance limits* with the associated documentary discrepancies in the LC business of the banks (Box 16.3). Also, we understand that the Documentary Credit Dispute Resolution Export Committee (DOCDEX) plays a very significant role in resolving cases related to documentary discrepancies and subsequent non-payment by the importer. As most of the countries differ in terms of their languages, and culture, the interpretation of the ICC guidelines may sometimes vary across countries and parties. So, the DOCDEX decision becomes mandatory for some of the cases where disputes are not otherwise resolved between the exporter and importer or exporting bank and importing bank.

Box 16.3

Third-Party Document—Most of the LCs do not allow the submission of third-party documents by the exporter. If the third-party document is allowed by the LC, the exporter can submit any document, including invoices, excluding bills of exchange, issued by anyone other than the beneficiary. Documents cannot be treated as discrepant documents under above-mentioned condition if LC allows third-party documents.

Stale Document—The exporter has to submit the relevant documents evidencing shipment to its bank within 21 days from the date of shipment but within the validity of the credit. If the exporter submits the documents after 21 days from the date of shipment but within the validity of the credit, the documents may be called as a stale document. If LC prohibits stale documents, the submission of stale documents would be treated as discrepant documents and the importer may reject the payment subsequently.

Tolerance Limit—It is not always possible to ship the goods of exact quantity, amount, and value. So, two types of tolerance limits LC may allow. First, if a ± 5% tolerance is allowed, it is allowed only in quantity. So for goods like 500 tonnes of rice exporter may supply 5% more or less quantity of the product. However, if the product is measured only by whole numbers like cars, phones, laptops, etc., this tolerance is not allowed. However, if ± 10% tolerance is allowed, it may be allowed in quantity, amount, and unit price of the product.

Bill of Lading—It is the main transport document issued by the shipper. Bill of Lading also is considered as the title of the goods, it means if anyone carries the bill of lading that gives him the right to claim the goods from the shipper. Besides it bears the evidence of the shipment and the terms and conditions are written at the back side of the bill of lading.

Waybill—It is another evidence of shipment if the goods are carried by railways, roadways, or airways. This is not a title of the goods.

Negotiable Bill of Lading—Any bill of lading which can be transferred from one party to another party by "order to" is known as a negotiable bill of lading.

Non-negotiable BL—Any bill of lading which cannot be transferred by order to from one party to another party is known as non-negotiable bill of lading.

Source Authors' Creation

Sanati (2024) delves into the issue of documentary discrepancies, one of the main challenges faced in the international trade domain. From the discussion of various caselets, we understand that inappropriate use of date and signature in transport documents may lead to documentary discrepancies and subsequent non-payment by the importer. In addition, the study elaborates on the conditions under which transport documents may be rejected for payment, providing valuable insights for industry professionals. The study also provides a comprehensive overview of different types of transport documents, such as bills of lading and ways bills. Through various case studies, the author explains the essential role of *negotiable bills of lading and non-negotiable bills of lading in the transport industry* (Box 16.3). For example, it describes the importance of converting the *receipt for shipment* documents into the appropriate bill of lading to avoid documentary discrepancies. Also, with different case studies, the book describes the conditions under which the bill of lading date may be the same as the shipment date and when the bill of lading date would differ from the shipment date. Furthermore, the study presents a detailed analysis of the advantages and shortcomings of the charter party bill in a contextual manner.

Beyond transport documents, the study also covers other essential *commercial documents, including Proforma Invoices, Packing Lists, Insurance Certificates,*

Certificate of Origin, Quality Certificates, among others. The author provides a thorough description of each document and its significance in facilitating international trade transactions. A briefs discussion on the provisions of export credit available to the Indian exporter is also covered in Sanati (2024). It explains the basic functionality of Exchange Earner Foreign Currency Accounts and Diamond Dollar Accounts. It conceptualizes advance payment against export, consignment export, counter trade agreement, export of goods by Special Economic Zones, export of services by Special Economic Zones to Domestic Tariff Area (DTA) Units, project exports, service exports, and currency export. Sanati (2024) also discusses the switch from barter trade to normal trade at the Indo-Myanmar Border, and Counter-Trade Arrangements with Romania. Export credit financing is discussed by the pre-shipment credit and various types of post-shipment credit, for example, advance against undrawn balances on export bills, advance against retention money, export on a consignment basis, post-shipment advance against duty drawback entitlement, post-shipment export credit in foreign currency, etc. This study addresses the recent development of Trade credit, that is buyer's credit and supplier's credit. Following RBI's definition of Trade credit as the credit extended to the importer, it discusses many intricacies in the process flow of trade credit. Also, beside these, this study describes in large the importance of suppliers' credit, the reason for the requirement, and the process flow. This book also explains many practical case studies associated with the buyer's credit and suppliers' credit.

Box 16.4

Pre-shipment Credit or Packing Credit—Pre-shipment/Packing Credit refers to a type of loan, advance or credit provided by a bank to an exporter. This credit is meant to finance the purchase, processing, and manufacturing of packing of goods, prior to shipment or estimated cost of working capital expenditure required for the proposed service. It is provided on the basis of the letter of credit opened in the exporter's favour or in favour of some other person by an overseas buyer or a confirmed and irrevocable order for the export of goods/services from India. The bank may waive the lodgement of export orders or letter of credit with the bank.

Post-shipment Credit—After the shipment happens, pre-shipment credit gets converted into post-shipment credit.

Trade Credit—Buyer's Credit and Suppliers' Credit both are part of the credit. The Person resident in India, having an import transaction is eligible to borrow trade credit. Recognized lenders for (a) for suppliers' credit: supplier of goods located outside India; (b) for buyers' credit: banks, financial institutions, foreign equity holder(s) located outside India, and financial institutions in IFSCs located in India.

Source Authors' Creation

The topic of discussion in the following text is the concept of merchanting trade and its process flow in the international trade domain. Merchanting trade refers to a trade transaction in which goods go from the importer to the exporter country without touching the periphery of the importing country. It is a type of trade that has gained immense popularity in recent times and is majorly operated through two payment methods, namely bank-to-back LC and transferable LC. The study of Sanati (2024) delves deeper into the merchanting trade concept and covers both the export leg and import leg of the transaction. It also explains the cash flow and documentation procedures involved in such trade. The payment methods linked to merchanting trade and the associated regulatory methods are well depicted through various case studies. It provides a comprehensive understanding of the merchanting trade process and its nuances.

The foreign exchange market and the intricacies of the market operation are the areas that have been developed over time and as of now confined within the dealing rooms of the banks. There are plenty of academic textbooks that have captured the determining factors of exchange rate variations across different currencies and how interest rate parity works in fully convertible capital account scenarios. However, it has been observed that the risk in dealing foreign exchange market with its practical intricacies is largely missed out in the academic literature. The present structure of the textbook hardly captures any concept of how the exchange rate risks are being created in the banking book and what operational structure the bank adopts to offload the exchange rate risk.

In the above context, Sanati (2024) endeavours to cover the operational structure of the foreign exchange market. Being an important segment of the treasury front-office operations, this market alone holds liquidity which is more than 7.5 trillion dollars a day. Worldwide there are no other single-market experiences such gigantic liquidity. Importantly, forex swap is the product that makes having maximum contribution in creating such liquidity. Nonetheless, this product is hardly known in mainstream economics and finance. Also, there is hardly any research in the academia relating to the forex market volatility and integration that covers the concept of forex swap, the most liquid segment of the foreign exchange market as per *Bank for International Settlements, triennial report* (2022), which says out of the 7.5 trillion USD per day the forex swap generates 3.8 trillion a day liquidity. There is only one paper by Bergljot and Ong (2010) that emphasizes the role of forex swaps in maintaining economic and financial stability during the US crisis of 2007–2008.

Starting from the forex dealing room structure we discuss the importance of two-way quotes and market-making in different market scenarios. We cover the fundamentals of value dates and settlement dates, exchange arithmetic for INR, and crosses as practiced in the quoting to the large corporates and the small or medium corporates. Sanati (2024) discusses how the merchant dealer acts in different merchant transactions following the global code of conduct. We discuss the mechanism of transferring the risk from the merchant dealers' desk to the interbank desk and the details of the interbank cover operations by the spot dealers and swap dealers. It may be interesting to know that the interbank segment of the market is a self-regulated market, and other than some global code of conduct that is practiced by the dealers worldwide no one regulates this market. This makes the operations of the dealers all the more ethical and systematic. By using different examples, we cover the dealing perspectives of the merchant and interbank segments.

Box 16.5

Base Currency—In a two-way quote, the currency which is being priced is known as base currency.

Offer Currency—In a two-way quote, the currency that is used for valuing the base currency is known as Offer currency.

Two-Way Quotes—Forex interbank market is quoted two-way price, that is, purchase price and sell price of the product or the base currency.

Market Maker—The bank that provides two-way quotes to the interbank market. If EUR/USD is 1.0834/35, then a market maker buys EUR at 1.0834 and sells EUR at 1.0835.

Market Taker—The bank that asks for two-way quotes to the interbank market without revealing its intention to buy or to sell. If EUR/USD is 1.0834/35 then a market taker buys EUR at 1.0835 and sells EUR at 1.0834.

Bid Rate—The rate at which base currency is bought by the market maker. If EUR/USD is 1.0834/35, then bid rate represents buying rate of EUR by the market maker.

Offer Rate—The rate at which base currency is sold by the market maker. If EUR/USD is 1.0834/35, then offer rate represents selling rate of EUR by the market maker.

Deal Date—The date on which the forward exchange deal is being booked by the client for any value dates.

Value Date—The date on which the cash flow (credit or debit) happens in the NOSTRO account. There are four value dates; Cash, Tom, Spot and Forward.

NOSTRO Account—If an Indian bank keeps an account in foreign currency in a foreign land, it is called a NOSTRO account.

Exchange Position—The position that is being created with every purchase and sale transaction in the foreign exchange market without having any connection to the settlement date.

Fund Position—The NOSTRO position is connected to the settlement date or the value date.

Cross Rate—A currency pair in which USD is not seen explicitly as any of the currencies in the pair.

Liquidity Gap—This measures the cash flow gap in the NOSTRO account. If a one-month forward contract is booked by the exporter invoiced in USD, the proceeds of receivables will be received by the bank's USD NOSTRO account after a month. However, to mitigate the exchange rate risk, the interbank dealer has to get into a cover operation, in which he can book a sale in the spot leg. So the NOSTRO position in the spot segment is oversold with USD and the forward segment is overbought by USD on account of the exporter's receivables. This is called a liquidity gap or liquidity mismatch.

Source Authors' Creation

Sanati (2024) discusses the concepts of Exchange Position NOSTRO position and liquidity gap (Box 16.5). The volatility of the foreign exchange market when transferred from the merchant's book to the interbank book the major risk the bank faces is the probable risk linked to the exchange rate movement. Though outright spot settlement of the NOSTRO account is possible, the same is not possible for other value dates like Cash, Tom, and forward. The liquidity gap in the NOSTRO fund is to be covered by Forex swap which is a purely interbank product.

By using different market scenarios, Sanati (2024) covers the deal blotters for different merchant deals while discussing the cover operation for spot and cash, tom, and forward settlement. Merchant dealings are discussed with examples of exchange and fund positions for different value dates. For example, she shows different deals in EUR/USD, GBP/USD, USD/JPY, USD/CHF, and USD/INR by explaining the exchange position, NOSTRO position, and the deal blotters. Besides spot deals, the above pairs are also used for the other value dates and settlement dates. Also, we show the merchant deals and interbank cover operations for cross rates, like EUR/GBP, EUR/JPY, GBP/JPY, EUR/CHF, EUR/INR, CHF/INR, GBP/INR, JPY/INR, etc. Moreover, we explain each of the transactions with the relevant deal blotters.

Lastly, we cover different types of bank guarantees, for example, *performance guarantees, advance payment guarantees, payment guarantees, retention money guarantees, bid-bond guarantees*, etc. (Box 16.6) with practical examples and the SWIFT message format. For each of the types of bank guarantees covered in this chapter, we have discussed the process flows and the documentation flows with some case study applications. This chapter also covers cases to make an easy understanding of the operations of bank guarantees. Furthermore, different rules of Uniform Rules for Demand Guarantees (URDG) have been explained through case studies. For example, under *Force Majeure or Act of God,* including war, strikes, riots, floods, and exporters are allowed to present the documents even after the expiry of the LC, within 30 calendar days from the date the bank resumes its normal business. Likewise, many scenarios are developed to describe the discrepancies and related applications of URDG rules.

Box 16.6

Performance Guarantees—If any bank or financial institution issues this kind of bond guaranteeing the performance of the seller and if the seller fails to perform, then the buyer can invoke the guarantee as collateral for any loss suffered due to non-performance or the low-quality performance of the seller.

Advance Payment Guarantees—This guarantee is issued by a bank or a financial institution to safeguard the interest of the importer in case the importer has paid to the exporter in advance and received shipment afterwards. In case the seller fails to deliver the goods then the buyer can get his money back.

Payment Guarantees—Generally, the importer applies for a payment guarantee to his bank. The importer's bank does issue a payment guarantee undertaking the payment obligation to the exporter, in case the importer fails to make payment to the exporter.

Retention Money Guarantees—in case of the establishment of a production plant or any such large project exporter may not be paid in full amount even after the successful completion of the project. It may be a condition mentioned in the project that 10% of the total invoice amount would be due for payment till the production unit or plantation unit is installed as required by the contract and runs agreeably for next year from the date of completion of the project. In this process exporter's fund gets blocked. To eliminate the problem of part payment or due payment exporter may request his bank to issue a Retention Money Guarantee in favour of the importer or the buyer. It provides a guarantee that the planation or the production unit or the machinery supplied would run as per the contract. Once the exporter's bank gives the guarantee, exporter would not be held back with his money.

Bid-bod Guarantees—If the project is large enough and there are many potential companies to bid for the project, the bid-bond guarantee may be called for. This guarantee is a tool to judge the capability of the company to complete it successfully, on winning the bid. So, a company, say ABC which requires to bid for an infrastructure project in Ethiopia and would like to win the bid, may be submitting a bid-bond guarantee to the Ethiopian government to ensure competence of the ABC company for the project. On the other hand, if bank is assured about the creditworthiness of the company ABC then they can issue a bid-bond guarantee which can be used by the company for bidding for several projects across borders.

Source Authors' Creation

16.4 Empirical Literature

However, as far as the empirical literature in this regard is concerned, apparently there are only two studies that introduce and deliberate upon the concept of packing credit or pre-shipment credit in mainstream economics and finance research. Sanati (2019) examines the PC or *pre-shipment credit* as a key determinant factor for export growth in India. PC is considered to be an important means of financing exports if advance payment is not received by the exporter before the shipment of goods. It may be noted that other types of bank loans (BL) may be an important alternative to PC. However, due to differential pricing the demand for the PC by the exporter is much higher (Fig. 16.1).

The Government of India's (GoI) scheme of interest subsidy in the form of PC is mostly to boost the export growth in India. Actually, the sanction of PC is available in bulk for any sector—for example, the engineering sector—banks are likely to have more preference towards the large exporter within this sector. In this backdrop, Sanati (2019) investigates into threefold objectives: (a) to examine the distribution pattern of PC across various exporting sectors; (b) to analyse the availability of export financing at different interest rate range; and (c) to estimate the sensitivity of export growth of India to its utilization of PC in small, medium, and large exporting sectors. It was the first of its kind which focuses on subsidized finance and its reach and utilization for export growth in India. As a prelude, the study first analyses utilization pattern of PC to its sanctioned limit, and this analysis is done in each interest rate range in pre- and post-subvention period in order to have an understanding if there is any shortfall of demand. Next, to comprehend the shift in demand in relation to the cost of funds, it shows the utilization pattern of PC across different interest rate ranges. It further examines the disbursement of PC to small, medium, and large exporters

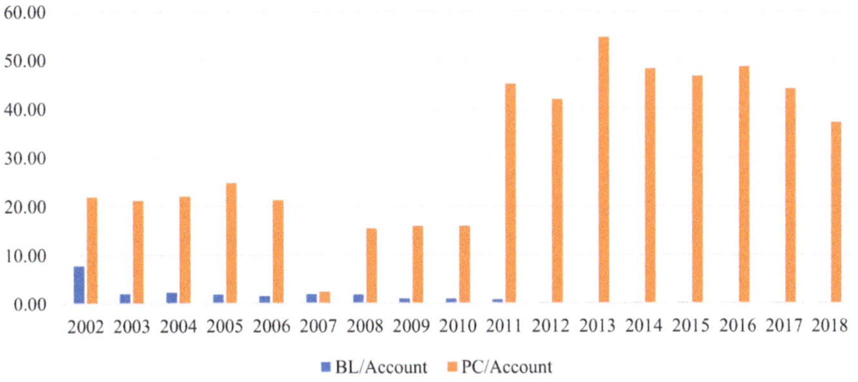

Fig. 16.1 Per account PC vs. Per account BL outstanding for exporting sector (in INR Million for 2002–2003 to 2018–2019). *Source* Authors' Own Compilation using RBI database

to examine the effectiveness of interest subsidy. Specifically, the bank prefers larger exporters over small exporters in PC disbursement due to the high credit rating of the large exporter. Sanati (2019) shows in her study that Indian commercial banks have a highly skewed preference for large borrowers in case of per capita PC disbursement, even if these large corporate are not subject to the benefit of interest subvention (Fig. 16.2).

To be specific, large and creditworthy exporters are the natural choice of the banks (for their cherry picking business strategy) to earn more profit with lesser risk. Examining the sensitivity of export contributed by the large, medium, and small groups of exporting houses (where this classification is on the basis of differential interest rate for which it is assumed that the firm with a voluminous balance sheet is likely to get credit at a lower interest rate and vice versa), it observes that small exporters

Fig. 16.2 Sectoral distribution of outstanding BL and PC per Account from 2002–2003 to 2018–2019 (amount in Million INR). *Source* Authors' Own Compilation using RBI database

hold the maximum number of PC account, although having the least outstanding amount per account, although her empirical findings contradicts this. This is so since her Arellano-Bond Dynamic panel analysis for the period 1996–1997 to 2015–2016 shows that the utilization of PC by medium and small exporters respectively are more sensitive to boost the export growth of India. It concludes that interest subvention plays a positive and significant role to boost the export growth and additional reduction in the cost of production may add to the export growth of India. Hence it recommends that the government may introduce a differential interest subsidy for different creditworthy exporters within the entitled sectors to more effectively reduce the cost of fund for more needy and sensitive exporters. Given the resource constraint, it may be ensured that large exporters are restricted from receiving the subsidised export finance. Nonetheless, her study also finds that the effect of the interest subvention scheme was dampened due to the financial crisis of 2008–2009 and concludes that the export growth could have been much worse affected if the interest subvention scheme were absent.

Since a major conclusion of the study is that, to make interest subvention more effective, important policy prescription includes that the medium and small exporters should be given more priority in the disbursement of the credit. And this may be implemented in two possible ways: (a) to incentivize the banks to disburse the PC more towards the needy sector and (b) to follow a differential pattern in interest subsidy for different creditworthy exporters within the entitled sectors. It may help in reducing the spread of the cost of borrowing PC across, and thereby establishing a competitive price in the international market. It also argues that to make the interest subvention or equalization scheme more effective, there may be an exclusion strategy as well.

On the other hand, considering uneven access to bank finances, Sanati et al. (2023) empirically examine the asymmetric contribution of the large and small exporters to India's export growth. Employing the panel threshold model of Hansen (1999), Sanati et al. (2023) examine the relative role of packing credit (PC), short-term bank loans (BLs), and other alternate bank finances on export growth for the period from 2002–2003 to 2018–2019. Their empirical estimations of threshold panel regression analyses reveal that there exists a significant impact of asymmetric utilization of available bank finances on India's export growth. This result is in line with the previous study by Sanati (2019), whereas Sanati et al. (2023) also concluded that the interest subvention has a positive and significant effect on the export growth of India. They also show that further reduction in interest costs might improve the export growth of the Indian economy. Overall, they conclude that although all the bank finances, like PC, short-term BLs, and liquidity have export-inducing effects, the relative importance of the PC is more conducive than the others as far as India's export growth is concerned. Interestingly, their non-linear threshold estimation shows that not only the small exporters are more sensitive to the usage of PC for their export, but are also more dependent on other alternative bank credits. On the contrary, the large exporters show significant reliance only on the usage of subsidized PC and do not use the other alternative bank credits. It supports the preliminary findings that Indian banks are more focused to retain their businesses with the large exporters and their lending preferences are highly skewed in the case of subsidized credit. Overall, the study by Sanati et al. (2023) concludes that, although all types of bank finances are important, the relative importance of the PC is more conducive than the others in terms of India's export growth. Therefore, their study concludes that the export promotion scheme may be more beneficial if Indian banks are incentivized with better PC disbursement schemes.

16.5 Trade-Based Money Laundering: A Few Cases

Trade-based money laundering (TBML) refers to the use of trade instruments to obfuscate illegal origins while moving value through jurisdictions. The main drivers of money laundering are corruption, drug trade, organized crime, financial fraud, etc. Although Trade-based money laundering is a relatively new phenomenon, the concept and need for money laundering are as old as the origin of money itself. It can simply be understood as the methodology adopted to obliterate the trail of money through the financial system to mask the origin which is the result of a criminal activity. Money laundering has been addressed in the UN Vienna 1988 Convention Article 3.1 describing Money Laundering as: "the conversion or transfer of property, knowing that such property is derived from any offense(s), for the purpose of concealing or disguising the illicit origin of the property or of assisting any person who is involved in such offense(s) to evade the legal consequences of his actions".[1]

International trade is a high-volume and complex system with multiple parties in a single transaction chain across different geographies subject to varied regulations. Trade transactions have two distinct flows, the first is the movement of goods and the second is the movement of documents. Banks and financial institutions are tasked with the handling of documents and the related remittances. The matching of value with the actual goods depends on certification by respective customs authorities and the movement of the goods depends on the documents issued by the carrier. The sheer volume of international trade and the costs associated with the transit results in a very small percentage of the goods being physically tallied with the stated value. Consequently, the chances of money laundering increases.

As a result of regulatory measures and tighter monitoring, the traditional methods of money laundering using smuggling or direct money transfers have become less attractive. In the recent times, the techniques used by money launderers have evolved adapting to the increased monitoring and regulation. The volume and complexity of trade instruments has made trade based money laundering a popular method to launder money. The primary methods of TBML are:

a. Over or under-invoicing of goods
b. Over or under-shipment of goods.
c. Deliberate misdescription of goods.

[1] https://www.unodc.org/unodc/en/money-laundering/overview.html.

d. Phantom shipments, carousel trade, and
e. Exploitation of regulatory loopholes.

In this section, we present a few case-based scenario analysis that describe different methods and channels through which trade-based money laundering may happen. These cases have no reference to the parties involved. We represent one case in the international context and two cases in the context of India. Although we describe the modus operandi of the case on black money peso exchange (BMPE),[2]we also describe the regulatory framework in the Indian market in the context of TBML.

16.5.1 International Context—Black Market Peso Exchange (BMPE)

One of the oldest and most popular methods of trade-based money laundering is the Black-market peso exchange scheme. This was a popular method used by South American parties to legitimately move illegal funds across international borders.

The process commences with South American drug cartels smuggling drugs across the border into the United States. Once the drugs reached the US soil, they were sold using the extensive trafficking network created by the cartels. The drugs were always sold to the end user for cash and usually in small amounts. If, for example, drugs worth USD one million were smuggled and sold, cash for more than USD one million would have been collected by the cartel representatives across the country. Thus the cartel had successfully sold their drugs and collected cash. However, the money was in the United States held in the form of cash and not accessible by the South American based cartels. One of the options was to smuggle the cash back to the cartel, but over a period of time due to the tightening of border controls, moving large volumes of paper money was not feasible.

Here an individual called the peso broker plays a central role in the movement of the funds. The peso broker purchases the dollars from the cartel at a discount and pays the cartel owner with pesos from his bank account in the South American country. This would complete the transaction for the cartel who receives cash for the drugs sold.

The peso broker is in a unique situation of holding cash in the United States while his account in the South American country is in deficit to the amount paid to the cartel. He therefore has to remit the US dollars into the South American country through the local banking channels without raising any red flags on either side of the border. An additional complication is the Banking Secrecy Act of the United States which requires additional disclosure/reporting for any cash deposit exceeding USD 10,000.

The modus operandi of the peso broker:

[2] https://www.fincen.gov/sites/default/files/advisory/advisu9.pdf.

Using his extensive network of individuals/companies' cash is legally placed into the banking system by structuring or smurfing the deposits into amounts less than USD 10,000, making sure to avoid red flags that would result in the reporting of the transactions. Once the money is in its accounts in the United States, the peso broker contacts a South American importer who needs US dollars to pay for its purchase of goods from a US exporter. The peso broker then arranges to pay the exporter in US dollars using the funds in his United States account. This would typically be structured as a third-party trade payment transaction which is a widely used structure for international trade. Once the exporter in the United States receives the funds he ships, the goods to the South American importer. On receipt of the goods, the South American importer sells the goods (often high-value items) for pesos and repays the peso broker. This completes the cash flow of the peso broker thus balancing his books with a good margin. The import leg of the transaction can be put through using instruments such as Letters of credit or Standby Letters of credit thereby lending an aura of authenticity to the transaction.

The goods imported are normally legitimate with perfect documentation to avoid any red flags. The BMPE and its variants are difficult to detect due to their simplicity and ability to comingle illicit funds with mainstream transactions.

The BMPE is a structure that can be easily replicated across geographies. In the Indian context, the importer can misuse the third-party payment or Merchant trade transaction structure to settle the import leg. The Foreign Exchange Management Act 1999, has laid out additional reporting and monitoring requirements for these types of transactions. Often the Indian leg of the transaction may be genuine, however, the overall structure may be designed to evade the authorities. It is therefore critical that the officers handling/ monitoring international trade transactions are familiar with the BMPE structures and their variants and can identify suspicious transactions thereby safeguarding the resources of the country.

In India, The Prevention of Money Laundering Act, 2002 (PMLA) is the legal weapon to combat money laundering. The PMLA is an act to prevent money laundering and it imposes obligations on banking companies, financial institutions, intermediaries, and persons carrying on designated business or profession to verify the identity of its clients, to maintain records, and to furnish information as prescribed by the act and rules thereunder.

16.5.2 Remittance Scam in the Indian Context[3]

In 2015, a massive remittance scam involving multiple high-value import remittances was unearthed. The modus operandi of the fraudsters was as below:

The fraudsters who represented themselves as major traders of commodities, opened current accounts with a few private sector banks using fake and forged documents. Over a period of time funds were deposited into these accounts across banks and then transferred into one main bank account with Bank X using several layers of transfers to erase the audit trail.

[3] This case is based on a FIU-IND judgement accessed at https://fiuindia.gov.in/pdfs/judgements/BOB_1_2018.pdf on 8th July 2024.

These fraudsters needed to transfer the money to their accounts overseas. Under the Foreign Exchange Management Act, 1999 cross-border remittances are permitted for the import of goods and services and other permitted capital and current account transactions. For the transactions representing imports, each remittance had to be matched with a corresponding proof of import, the bill of entry. The fraudsters identified the advance import remittance product wherein the importer was entitled to remit funds to the overseas supplier before receipt of goods in India.

As per extant regulations, each such remittance above the value of USD 100,000 or equivalent had to be matched with the proof of physical import issued by the customs department, i.e., with the Bill of Entry. The fraudsters layered the transactions in a manner that no individual transaction was more than USD 100,000. The banks remitted the funds as per the request of the customer. The fraudsters exploited this loophole and remitted millions of dollars to its overseas accounts under the guise of imports.

Subsequent investigations revealed the absence of any underlying trade transaction for these remittances. The accounts too were operated by the same beneficial owner. Thus, the trade instrument of advance import was exploited to send value overseas without any corresponding import of goods.

The shortcomings on the part of the bank were:

- Inadequate KYC, accounts opened with forged/fake documents.
- Lack of clarity on beneficial ownership
- Non-tracking of the pattern of remittances by the trade processing team.
- Inadequate monitoring and reporting of high-value and volume accounts.
- Lack of ongoing due diligence.

16.5.3 TBML in Diamond Transaction[4]

In the early 2000s, a three-carat diamond with an actual price of $200,000 changed hands at least four times over a two-month week period between shell companies owned by Mr. X a well-known exporter of diamonds.

The modus operandi used was carousel transactions along with round-tripping. The diamond was first sold for $1.5 million by a company owned by Mr X to a shell company in Dubai owned indirectly by Mr X. A few weeks later an Indian company owned by Mr X, shipped the diamonds back to the original company at the actual price. The diamonds were again sold back to the Dubai company for $1.2 million.

The diamonds were sold by the Dubai company to a US-based company owned by Mr X at the actual price of USD 200,000. The US-based company then finally sold the diamonds to a UAE-based company for USD 1.2 million.

Thus, Mr X and his associates used the same goods to represent several unique import–export transactions. This served as an underlying for availing of bank finance

[4] This case is based on an article accessed at https://www.bloomberg.com/news/articles/2018-08-29/fedex-d-diamonds-fueled-india-s-biggest-bank-fraud-report-says#xj4y7vzkg on 8th July 2014.

from unsuspecting lenders. The whole scheme came to light when the loans taken by the various entities on the collateral of the diamonds started defaulting.

India has been one of the early implementors of the recommendations of the Financial Action Task Force (FATF). Through the implementation of the Electronic data interchange (EDI) systems, Import Data Processing and Monitoring System (IDPMS), and Export Data Processing and Monitoring System (EDPMS), the transactional data flow has been digitized while maintaining a high level of security and data sanctity. This has reduced the scope for fraudsters to exploit the weaknesses of legacy systems and has strengthened the monitoring mechanism leading to early detection and prosecution of trade-based money laundering cases.

16.6 Conclusions

International trade and finance are two closely linked concepts that have a significant impact on the global economy. These two fields are based on a range of theoretical concepts, which have evolved and continue to shape the way businesses operate across borders. International trade covers a vast array of topics, from the classic theory of absolute advantage proposed by Adam Smith to modern theories such as the Stolper-Samuelson trade theorem. On the other hand, international finance deals with topics such as exchange rate regimes, parity conditions, and pricing mechanisms of derivative products etc.

Despite the abundance of theoretical literature on these two fields, there is a lack of comprehensive documentation that explains the intricacies of the products and processes related to the role of banks and the legal frameworks of international bodies like the International Chamber of Commerce (ICC). To truly comprehend the practical applications of international trade and finance, it is crucial to study the process and documentation flows that pertain to these transactions. These include the various legal and regulatory frameworks that govern international trade and finance, as well as the different financial instruments and products that companies use to facilitate their transactions.

In this discussion, we dive into the intricacies dealt with a few literatures in the international trade finance domain. We discuss the importance of understanding contract of sales, different LCs, the mechanism of LCs, banks' roles and responsibilities in handling documentary discrepancies, the existence of pre-shipment credit or packing credit for the exporters, and the trade credit in the form of buyer's credit and suppliers' credit for the importer, significant of merchanting trade, etc. We also discuss the importance of understanding the forex dealing room structure and the critical role of two-way quotes and market-making in various market scenarios. We describe the importance of understanding the practical aspects of risk transformation from the merchant to the interbank dealing book. The fundamental concepts of value dates and settlement dates, exchange arithmetic for INR, and crosses as applied in quoting to both large and small or medium corporates are mentioned with their importance of foreign exchange hedging. Additionally, we examine the behaviour of the merchant dealer in various merchant transactions, adhering to the global code of conduct. We also cover the mechanism of transferring risk from the merchant dealers' desk to the interbank desk, as well as the interbank cover operations by the spot dealers and swap dealers. It may interesting to know that the interbank segment of the market is self-regulated, meaning that apart from the global code of conduct practiced by dealers worldwide, no other authority regulates this market. This underscores the importance of ethical and systematic operations by the dealers. By providing different examples, we took a deep dive into the dealing perspectives of the merchant and interbank segments.

Lastly, we mentioned the brief on Trade-based money laundering and also discussed three cases in the Indian and international context. India has been an early adopter of the recommendations provided by the Financial Action Task Force (FATF). By implementing Electronic Data Interchange (EDI) systems, Import Data Processing and Monitoring System (IDPMS), and Export Data Processing and Monitoring System (EDPMS), the flow of transactional data has been digitized, while ensuring the security and integrity of the data. This has minimized the opportunities for fraudsters to take advantage of the weaknesses in traditional systems and has enhanced the monitoring process, facilitating the early identification and prosecution of trade-based money laundering cases.

In this chapter, we aim to provide a brief overview of the practical aspects of international trade and trade-related finance. We review the limited literature available on the subject, with the hope that this information will be useful to all stakeholders involved in international trade and finance. By understanding the practical applications of these theoretical concepts, individuals and organizations can make informed decisions and navigate the complexities of international trade with greater ease to all the concerned stakeholders to a large extent.

Acknowledgements The authors thankfully acknowledge the constructive suggestions and comments they received at the Workshop on 75 Years of Productivity Growth in India during March 7–9, 2024, held at the Delhi School of Economics. The usual disclaimer applies.

References

Apte, P. G. (2009). *International finance* (2nd ed.). McGraw Hill.

Bergljot, B., & Ong, L. L. (2010). *Forex swaps: Implications for financial and economic stability*. International Monetary Fund (working paper series 10/55).

Falkenstein, E. G. (1996). Preferences for stock characteristics as revealed by mutual fund portfolio holdings. *The Journal of Finance*. https://onlinelibrary.wiley.com/doi/abs/10.1111/j.1540-6261.1996.tb05204

Grier, K. B., & Smallwood, A. D. (2007). Uncertainty and export performance: Evidence from 18 countries. *Journal of Money, Credit and Banking, 39*(4), 965–979.

Hansen, B. E. (1999). Threshold effects in non-dynamic panels: Estimation, testing, and inference. *Journal of Econometrics, 93*(2), 345–368.

Matthies, A. B. (2013). *Empirical research on corporate credit ratings: A literature review* (SFB 649 Discussion Paper #2013-003). Berlin: Humboldt University. http://sfb649.wiwi.hu-berlin.de/papers/pdf/SFB649DP2013-003.pdf

Patnaik, P., & Chandrasekhar, C. P. (1996). Investment, exports and growth: A cross country analysis. *Economic and Political Weekly, 31*(1), 31–36.

Reserve Bank of India. (2013). *Master circular on rupee/foreign currency export credit & customer service to exporters* (DBOD No. DIR.BC.06/04.02.002/2012–13). Mumbai.

Reserve Bank of India. (2015). *Master circular: Rupee/foreign currency export credit and customer service to exporters*. https://www.rbi.org.in/scripts/BS_ViewMasCirculardetails.aspx?id=9852

Reserve Bank of India. (2016a). *Interest equalisation scheme on pre- and post-shipment rupee export credit*. http://pdicai.org/docs/RBI_322_12220161300112.PDF

Reserve Bank of India. (2016b). *Master direction: External commercial borrowings, trade credit, borrowing and lending in foreign currency by authorised dealers and persons other than authorised dealers* (Updated as on May 9, 2018). https://rbi.org.in/SCRIPTS/BS_ViewMasDirections.aspx?id=10204#C63

Sanati, G. (2024). *International trade finance and forex operations: Theory and applications*. Routledge.

Sanati, G. (2017). *Financing international trade: Banking theories and applications*. Sage.

Sanati, G. (2019). Access to subsidised packing credit for financing export: Who are the gainers? *Indian Economic Journal, 66*(1–2), 72–88.

Sanati, G., Bhandari, A. K., & Roy, R. P. (2023). Distinctive pay-off of packing credit and alternate bank credits for large and small exporters of India: A non-linear approach. *Global Business Review*. https://doi.org/10.1177/097215092311529

Tirole, J. (2006). *The theory of corporate finance*. Princeton University Press.

Tran, T.A.-D., Diaw, D., & Rieber, A. (2012). International demand spillovers in south-south exports: Application to Sub-Saharan Africa and Developing Asia. *Journal of Economic Integration, 27*(3), 410–436.

Gargi Sanati is an Associate Professor at NIBM, Pune, India, specializing in trade finance and forex markets and having 14 years of work experience. Her expertise encompasses Forex Trading, Macro-Finance, International Trade Finance, and ICC Guidelines. She leads the coordination and instruction of banking professionals in specialized areas such as Forex Dealing, Bourse Game, International Trade Financing, Letter of Credit Business, Data Analytics, and Econometric Methods. Additionally, she has provided consulting services to the banking industry and the Government of India. Her research has been published in esteemed national and international journals. She is the author of a book titled "International Trade Finance: Forex Operations," published by Routledge in 2024. She obtained her Ph.D. from the Centre for Development Studies, Jawaharlal Nehru University (JNU).

Anup Kumar Bhandari is currently a Professor at the Department of Humanities and Social Sciences, IIT Madras. He obtained his doctoral degree (in Quantitative Economics) from the Indian Statistical Institute. Prior to his present affiliation, he also served ICRA Ltd. as an Economist and Centre for Development Studies, Trivandrum, as an Assistant Professor. His overall research areas cover Production Economics, Productivity and Efficiency Analysis using both Stochastic Frontier Analysis (SFA) and Data Envelopment Analysis (DEA), Applied Industrial Economics, and Issues related to Indian Banking and her overall Financial Markets. He has published extensively in scholarly academic journals of international repute, of which *Journal of Productivity Analysis, Review of Development Economics, Economic Modelling, Research in International Business and Finance, Journal of Economic Asymmetries, Indian Economic Review*—to mention a few. Nevertheless, before all these, he is a passionate teacher and his teaching is widely cherished among students across various academic institutions.

Rajesh Ramakrishnan is a Chartered Accountant with over 25 years of work experience in various roles in the banking and education sector. Since 2021, he has been working at NIBM as an Adjunct Faculty and is part of the Money International Banking and Finance area group, specializing in Trade Finance and related areas. Previously, he worked at Kotak Mahindra Bank. From 2016 to 2020, he led the trade finance process team and was part of the core team implementing technological changes and process innovations. From 2012 to 2014, he served as the Regional Head of transaction banking sales for the West Zone (ROMG and Gujarat). Throughout his career, he has worked in Trade Finance operations, Trade Finance and Cash Management Sales, and Trade Finance Technology initiatives in the Transaction Banking segment.

Chapter 17
Mapping Skill, Education, and Employment in Determining Social Capital

Pooja Sharma

Abstract Education coupled with skill constitutes the backbone of innovation and economic growth. Skilled individuals not only contribute more efficiently and productively but also improve social welfare. Firstly, the linkages between education, skill, innovation, and employment have been examined in the Indian context since independence. Secondly, the indirect impact of education, skill, and employability on social capital and peace in society has been examined. It is observed that the share of the organized sector was high in the beginning, but it began to decline gradually. The labour-intensive sectors could control unemployment, but later the labour force began to grow more rapidly than the increase in employment. An augmented framework of education, peace, and social capital is presented to map the role of skills, innovation, and education in determining social capital. A thematic review of the literature is adopted to examine the objectives. It is observed that there is a two-way relationship that education as one of the components of human capital increases economic growth on one side, but at the same time exacerbates income inequality. The nexuses between education, skill, and employability consequently affect social capital by transforming the systems towards social development, political stability, and justice. The policies must promote a more ethical and inclusive education system coupled with the required skill and employability to ensure equitable access to education and knowledge base. Thus, a more just and equitable social capital would foster a more peaceful and non-violent society.

Keywords Skill · Education · Employment · Human capital · Social capital · Peace

---

P. Sharma (✉)
Daulat Ram College, University of Delhi, Delhi, India
e-mail: poojasharma@dr.du.ac.in

D. Maiti et al. (eds.), *75 Years of Growth, Development and Productivity in India*, India Studies in Business and Economics, https://doi.org/10.1007/978-981-97-8054-9_17

17.1 Introduction

Education is a crucial component of human capital. It contributes to the overall development of the individual, state, and nation and significantly improves an educated individual's productivity and employability. Employability is a set of achievements—skills, understandings, and personal attributes—that makes the youth of the country gain more employability and accomplish their goals and ambitions. Thus, along with youth, the community, the economy, and finally, the country benefit. Employability, therefore, is not just about getting a job. It is about a broader set of skills and attributes that will enable a graduate to be successful throughout their working life (The Mirriority, 2024).[1] Moreover, upskilling enhances innovation, equipping individuals with updated knowledge and technical know-how.

According to the latest Annual Status of Education Report (ASER), productivity in education has come down by about 18% between 2008 and 2018 (ASER, 2023).[2] Though overall enrolment in the 6–14 age group is at over 96%, one out of four children in class 8 does not have basic reading skills. In addition, more than 50 % of them can't solve basic mathematics. There is a wide gap in learning skills exhibited across the states in rural children. The report also revealed that infrastructure facilities such as drinking water facilities, separate girls' toilets, computer availability, etc., have deteriorated or remained stagnant over the past years.

According to the Human Development Report 2020, only five Indians in the labour force are skilled (Times of India, 2020).[3] The unemployment of educated was witnessed sharply. For graduates, the unemployment rate rose from 19.2% to 35.8%, and for post-graduates, from 21.3% to 36.2% (The Wire, 2024).[4] Amidst the catastrophe of the COVID-19 pandemic and unemployment, the Government of India (GOI) announced a New Education Policy 2020 that higher education enrolment should rise from the prevailing 27% (for the relevant age cohort of 18-23-year-olds) to nearly double to 50% by 2035. This further accentuates the challenge of creating more unemployment.

The World Bank has approved US$250 million under the Skill India Mission Operation programme (Skilling India, World Bank, June 23, 2017).[5] The SIMO programme plans to enhance skills and focus on developing high-quality training modules based on market-specific skills (Skilling India, World Bank, June 23, 2017).[6] The programme will target new labour market entrants and work to improve the quality of existing skills programmes under the framework of public-private partnerships in preparing the curriculum for training packages, which will be encouraged

---

[1] https://www.themirrority.com/data/employability#trainings.

[2] https://asercentre.org/aser-survey/.

[3] https://timesofindia.indiatimes.com/india/with-1-in-5-workers-skilled-india-ranks-129-among-162/articleshow/79769587.cms.

[4] https://thewire.in/economy/what-we-know-about-indias-post-covid-economy-recovery-and-rising-inequality.

[5] https://www.worldbank.org/en/news/feature/2017/06/23/skilling-india.

[6] https://www.worldbank.org/en/news/feature/2017/06/23/skilling-india.

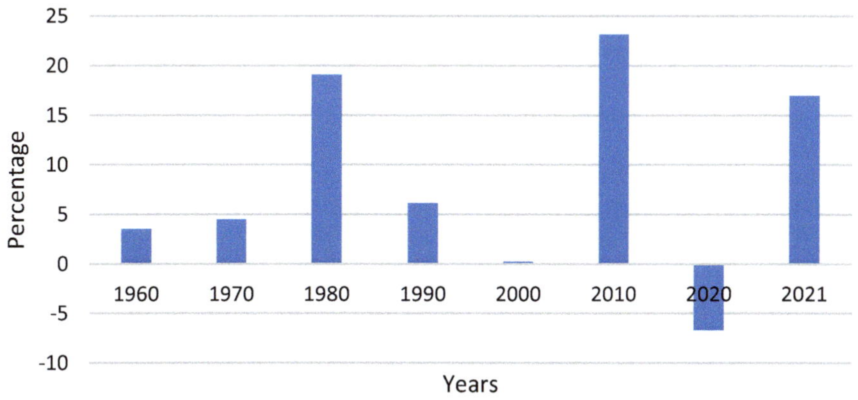

Fig. 17.1 GDP per capita annual growth rate. Source: Ministry of Finance

(Skilling India, World Bank, June 23, 2017).[7] The programme will also seek to set up a Corporate Social Responsibility (CSR) Skills Fund through which incentives will be given to the private sector to use their CSR funds for skill development activities (Skilling India, World Bank, June 23, 2017).[8]

The present study tests the interlinkages between education, skill, and innovation. Further, the study attempts to examine the role played by human capital in ensuring social capital in a country. To achieve these objectives, appropriate indicators have been selected from World Databank for the period 1990–2021. The linkages between Education, Skill, Innovation, and Employment, as well as between education, peace, social value systems, and capital are explored. The next section presents the theoretical underpinnings of the conceptual framework.

17.2 A Journey of Economic Growth, Growth of Organized Sector, and Employment in India Since Independence

In the 1950s, the government of India adopted a specific development strategy of rapid industrialization based on five-year plans. This development strategy excessively depended on raising massive resources for building state-owned enterprises. Investment in industrial goods such as steel, heavy machines, tools, power, etc. was largely a process of industrialization, opening tremendous scope for production growth. The per capita growth of GDP can be visualized in Fig. 17.1.

The growth after independence was strictly based on the public sector, as the investments in infrastructure, public health, and education could not be served by the private sector. The rate of growth of real GDP was 6% per year during 1950–1980.

[7] https://www.worldbank.org/en/news/feature/2017/06/23/skilling-india.

[8] https://www.worldbank.org/en/news/feature/2017/06/23/skilling-india.

Though the prime objective of the development strategy was rapid industrialization, however, it did not happen. It is evident from the share of industry including mining and quarrying, manufacturing and electricity, gas and water supply in real GDP that increased substantially slowly from 11% in 1950–1951 to 14% in 1980–1981, as visualized in Fig. 17.1.

Since independence, the manufacturing sector has undergone various stages of development. The preliminary industrial foundation was laid down in the 1950s since then it has travelled a journey of license between 1965 and 1980, liberalization of the 1990s, and ultimately the global competitiveness phase of today in the era of globalization. The share of the manufacturing sector in GDP is around 16 to 17% in 2014 (Confederation of India Industry, CII). The share of value-added of the manufacturing sector in GDP can be observed in Fig. 17.2.

As visualized in Fig. 17.2, the share of the organized sector in GDP was substantially high in the beginning of the path of economic growth, later, it started declining. As the country moves further on the path of economic growth, economic development takes the centre stage of all discourses and challenges. Human capital and its base become the driving force of the overall development of the economy. Education and health that constitute human capital should be the central focus of all development policies. Consequently, employment and productivity become the main concerns of targets of development policies. In this context, the organized sector is supposed to be a critical sector for fostering employment in the country. Several studies have concluded that every job created in the manufacturing sector has a multiplier effect of 2–3 jobs in the services sector (Confederation of India Industry, CII).

The issue of employment has taken different shapes across different phases of development. In the early stages of development, unemployment did not emerge as a problem as it was assumed that labour-intensive sectors would control any rise in unemployment. However, it was witnessed that the labour force grew more rapidly than the increase in employment. Consequently, unemployment increased

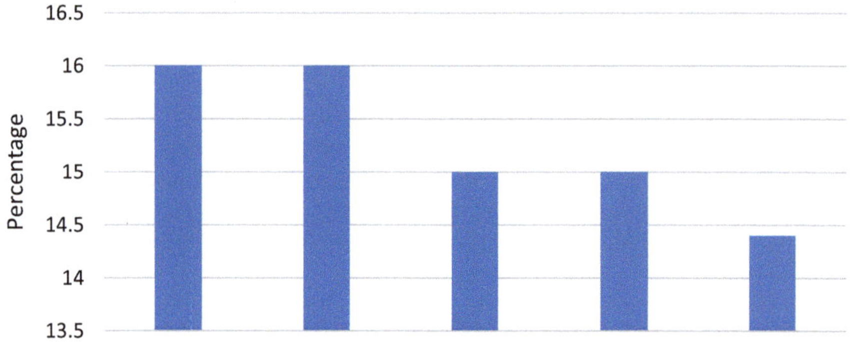

Fig. 17.2 Share of Value Added of the organized sector in GDP. *Source* Ministry of Finance

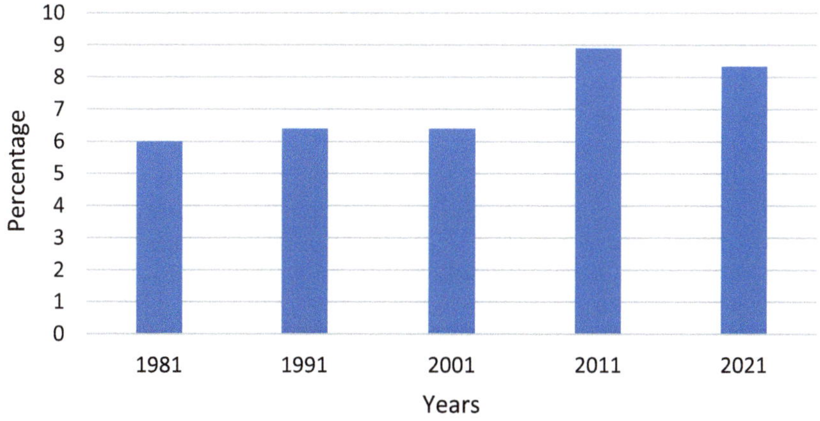

Fig. 17.3 Share of Employment of organized sector. *Source* Ministry of Finance

significantly during 1956–1972 from 5 to 10 million (Employment Trends in India, Ministry of Statistics and Programme Implementation, Mospi). According to the Quarterly Employment Survey, Labour Bureau, approximately 40.6 per cent of estimated workers were employed in the manufacturing sector. Figure 17.3 maps the share of employment in the organized sector.

As the economic growth picked up, the share of employment in manufacturing sector began to increase and significantly increased in 2011. Education is significant driver and a factor for employability and skill generation. It is a crucial component of human capital. The following section describes the journey of growth in human capital (education in specific) and its contribution in employment and economic growth since independence.

17.3 Education, Employment, and Inequality: Interlinkages and Trends

Human capital has been defined as 'resources, qualifications, skills, and knowledge that are available to and acquired by individuals to maximize their employability' (Marron, 2018). It is observed that a healthy, educated and productive labour force is instrumental in determining long-term economic success. It is not only a crucial determinant of economic growth but also contributes to the reduction of inequality. It becomes an integral part of the sustainability of any economic and social agenda. (SDG). Healy and Côté (2001) suggest that human and social capital contributes to higher income, life satisfaction and social cohesion. However, the study points out the limited scope for public policy to change the quality, stock, and distribution of human and social capital in the short term. Developing countries have made considerable progress in reducing the gap with developed countries in terms of school attainment but it is realized that long-run economic performance cannot be achieved without improving the school quality in developing countries (Knowledge, evidence and learning for development, Report 2017). Human capital is positively significantly correlated with physical capital in developing countries such as Pakistan and India (Abbas & Mujahid-Mukhtar, 2000). Examining the impact of education on income growth in India for the period 1966–1996, it is found that female education at all levels has the potential to generate economic growth (Kotásková et al., 2018). Haldar and Mallik (2010) used the impulse response function to confirm that innovation in a change in education human capital investment significantly and positively explains the movement of the changes in education human capital investment, health human capital investment, and growth of GNP per capita.

Babatunde and Adefabi (2005) investigated the long-run relationship between education and economic growth in Nigeria, concluding that a well-educated labour force appears to significantly influence economic growth both as a factor in the production function and through total factor productivity. Capital, labour, human capital, and technical progress are the four principal sources of growth of aggregate real output (Galor & Tsiddon, 1997). Bowman (1980) advocated the role of quality of human resources in fostering development, the presence of a strong association between research and development and human resources in industrial advances, and the human factor in agricultural progress and education and progress in small-scale enterprises. Hanushek and Wößmann (2007) emphasized the role of improved schooling in development strategies and in promoting economic well-being focusing on the role of educational quality.

The literacy rate is considered the most widely accepted parameter of education status in a country. A high literacy rate suggests the existence of an effective primary education system or literacy programme that has enabled a large proportion of the population to acquire the ability of using the written word in daily life and to continue learning (UNESCO, Institute for Statistics).[9] Though the literacy rate has increased six times since independence; however, India still has the world's largest population of illiterate people, around 37 per cent of the total global illiterate people (OXFAM, India).[10]

As evident in Fig. 17.4, the literacy rate since independence has been consistently rising significantly, a rise of 18.3 per cent in 1951 to 74.4 per cent in 2018 (Times of India, August 14, 2022).[11] India has come a long way from just about 2 in 10 Indians being literate in 1950, and the figure has nearly revered.

Further, the gross enrolment ratio is the ratio of total enrolment, regardless of age, to the population of the age group that officially corresponds to the level of education (World Bank, DataBank, Metadata Glossary).[12] Secondary education completes the

---

[9] https://uis.unesco.org/en/glossary-term/literacy-rate.

[10] https://www.oxfamindia.org/featuredstories/10-facts-illiteracy-india-you-must-know.

[11] https://timesofindia.indiatimes.com/india/75-years-75-literacy-indias-long-fight-against-illiteracy/articleshow/93555770.cms.

[12] https://databank.worldbank.org/metadataglossary/world-development-indicators/series/SE.SEC.ENRR.

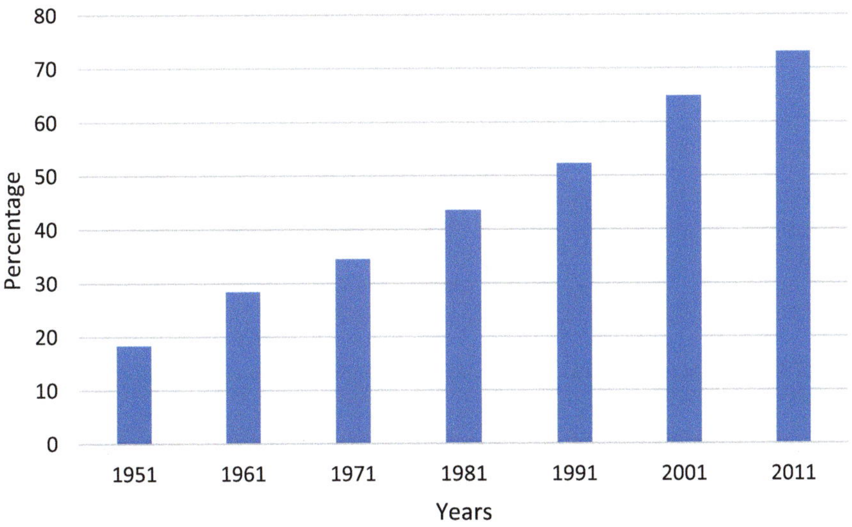

Fig. 17.4 The Literacy rate since independence. *Source* Census of India

provision of basic education that begins at the primary level and aims at laying the foundations for lifelong learning and human development, by offering more subject or skill-oriented instructions using more specialized teachers (UNESCO Institute for Statistics (UIS).[13]

In the financial year 2022, the school enrolment stood at 26.5 crores children with 19.4 lakh additional children enrolled in Primary to Higher Secondary Levels. The enrolments increased across all level such as Primary, Upper-Primary, Secondary, and Higher Secondary except for Pre-Primary level (Ministry of Finance).[14] Figure 17.5 maps the growth of enrolment in higher secondary education in millions since independence.

It is evident that the enrolment increased significantly since 1951, as observed in Fig. 17.6. There was a substantial improvement in the enrolment in the year 1990–1991. The year 1991 serves as a remarkable year that catalysed liberalization and deregulation of industry. India's annual rate of economic growth doubled and is famously referred to as 'the Hindu rate of growth', lifting 400 million people out of poverty. It was during this time that the Indian education sector experienced a breakthrough, with an aggregate enrolment of 300 million children and youth (Education World).[15] Later, with the National Education Policy 2020, the focus of the teaching pedagogy is to integrate skill-based development.

Education has served as a tool or method for economic development since independence since independence. Various steps and initiatives have been undertaken to

[13] https://uis.unesco.org/.

[14] https://pib.gov.in/PressReleaseIframePage.aspx?PRID=1894915.

[15] https://www.educationworld.in/1991-inflection-point-for-indian-education/.

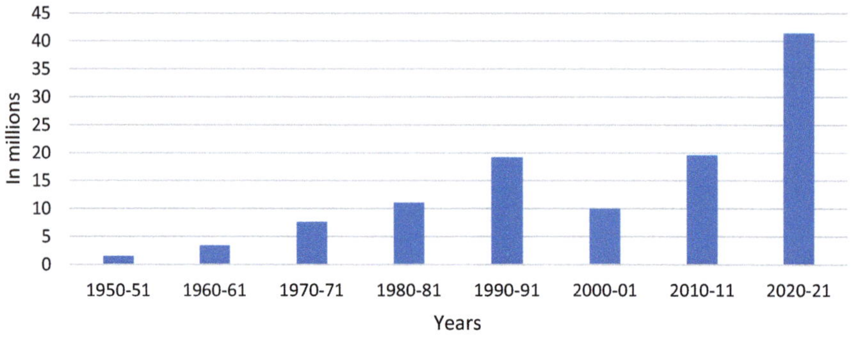

Fig. 17.5 Enrollment in higher secondary education (in millions). *Source* Department of Education, MHRD, GOI, 2000–01

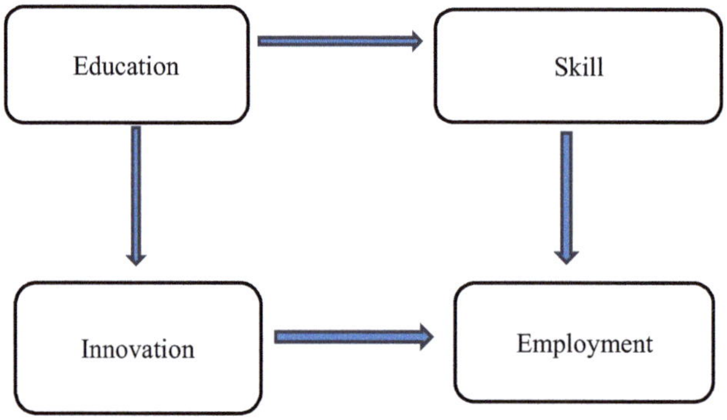

Fig. 17.6 Interlinkages between education, skill, innovation, and employment. *Source* Department of Education, MHRD, GOI, 2000–2001

democratize education ensure equal access for all citizens and achieve the Sustainable Development Goal SDG 4, incorporating 10 targets for education (Directorate General of Employment, Government of India).[16] Several factors have been responsible for developing an intricate relationship between education and employment in India. Among many factors is human capital formation, which is reflective of qualitative improvement in the people or human resource their health and skills. The second crucial factor for the relationship is the demand for skilled labour, and the demand for labour in India is expected to remain high in the coming years and require skills and qualified labour.

The employability of youth is a crucial macroeconomic concern of all the policies since independence. However, both educated and uneducated youth lack the skills necessary for acquiring employability. Various initiatives have been undertaken by government to promote more employment in the country such as Kaushal Bharat, Kushal Bharat project, the Pradhan Mantri Vikas Yojana (PMKVY), and the National

[16] https://dge.gov.in/dge/schemes_programmes.

Policy for Skill Development and Entrepreneurship 2015 (Directorate General of Employment, Government of India).[17]

Moreover, the Government has also launched several employment-oriented schemes such as the National Career Services (NCS) project, the Mahatma Gandhi National Rural Employment Guarantee Act (MGNREGA), and the Pradhan Mantri Garib Kalyan Rojgar Abhiyaan (PMGKRA) (Directorate General of Employment, Government of India).[18]

The employment generation in a country is expected to bring about income equality. Inequality in the distribution of landownership adversely affected human capital-promoting institutions (Galor et al., 2005). Eicher and Garcia-Penalosa (2001) examine how human capital accumulation influences both economic growth and income inequality. The results identify parameters that are central to the evolution of inequality during the development process. O'Neill (1993) examines the extent to which patterns of human capital convergence account for observed patterns of income inequality between countries. It is observed that among the developed countries, convergence in education levels has resulted in a reduction in income dispersion.

The income inequality decreased after independence until the early 1980s. However, it started to increase again, and since 2000 income inequality has been increasing significantly. The relationship between inequality and economic growth can be observed in the fact that in the 1990s the employment growth in India slowed significantly in rural areas. The annual growth rate in the rural areas fell to 0.67 per cent from 1993–94 to 1999–2000 (Kannan, 2022).

In this regard, the path-breaking work of Kuznets indicates that inequalities rise with economic growth up to a point and then decline, also referred to as the Kuznets Curve, an inverted U-shaped curve. However, Piketty's work on the UK and Europe concluded a U-shaped curve (Piketty, 2014). Tendulkar (2010) distinguishes inequity and inequality. In other words, even if measured inequality increases, there may not be any increase in feelings of inequity as people get inspired to move upwards. Economic inequalities co-exist with social, political, and cultural inequalities (Cammack, 2014). Caste plays a critical role in the case of India, where caste or social groups along with gender inequalities become important (Drèze & Sen, 2013).[19]

Since the 1980s, inequality in India has begun to rise, with the top 1 per cent of India's population holding 22.6 per cent of the national income and 40.1 per cent of the country's wealth in 2022–2023. It is the highest level since 1961 (Bharti et al., 2024). Education policies can help reduce economic inequality and promote social mobility by providing people with skills and knowledge (Yang & Qiu, 2016). Kijima (2006) demonstrated that the changing distribution attainment was the dominant force in increasing wage inequality among urban male workers. However, later between 1993 and 1999, it was observed that higher education widened the wage inequalities.

[17] https://dge.gov.in/dge/schemes_programmes.

[18] https://dge.gov.in/dge/schemes_programmes.

[19] http://www.igidr.ac.in/pdf/publication/WP-2018-003.pdf.

17.4 Interlinkages Between Education, Skill, Innovation, and Employment

The National Education Policy (Com, 2021) has recently been implemented in India to achieve full human potential, developing an equitable and just society. Several macroeconomic models depict the relationship between human capital and economic growth, such as the neoclassical model (Solow; growth accounting total factor productivity models) and new growth theory (Lucas; Romer). In addition, the Kuznets curve depicts an inverted U-shaped curve, stating inequality initially increases with higher economic growth and then decreases economic inequality. However, in this era, when India is caught up with 70% of the literacy rate and only 20% of employability, it is crucial to intensify productivity and quality of work. According to the World Trade Organization, the GDP can increase up to 3 to 5% in 2035 (Skill Development and Employment Opportunity, GOI).[20] Under the Skill India Mission, the Ministry of Skill Development and Entrepreneurship, in July 2015, aims to coordinate the efforts to integrate the government and private sector for skill development (Skill Development and Employment Opportunity, GOI).[21] Skills mainly comprise technical expertise, vocational skills, transferrable skills, digital skills, and other appropriate abilities required for employment and livelihood (Skill Development and Employment Opportunity, GOI).[22]

Based on the above framework, the interlinkages between education, skills, innovation, and employment are tested by deploying selected indicators for each variable. Education is measured by selecting government expenditure as a percentage of GDP and also the gross enrolment ratio from primary to tertiary as the indicators. Technical expertise, vocational skills, transferrable skills, digital skills, and other appropriate abilities are considered for capturing the skills in the country. The amount spent on research and development and the number of patents are the selected indicators for reflecting innovation. Employment is captured by the labour force participation rate.

The framework indicates that skills must be linked to employment and innovation. Similarly, education must lead to employment and innovation. It is crucial to note that skills and Education are distinct fields that may not be associated with each other, but they must be separated to ensure employability and innovation.

Suleman (2018) concluded that the social and economic processes might affect employability by reviewing the literature on employability and skills. Şentürk (2021) found a notable difference in academic achievement and twenty-first-century skills favouring the experimental group. The study suggests that the issue of graduates' employability extends beyond higher education institutions providing relevant skills. The soft skill gap was examined to comprehend the bottleneck in the availability of talent in emerging economies (Singh Dubey et al., 2022). The partnership between educational institutions and the IT industry to address this gap. This partnership will

[20] https://blog.mygov.in/skill-development-and-employment-opportunity/.

[21] https://blog.mygov.in/skill-development-and-employment-opportunity/.

[22] https://blog.mygov.in/skill-development-and-employment-opportunity/.

benefit all stakeholders. The paper also argued that although talent management is dealt with at the industry level, academia plays an important role in making this process easier and more effective by developing the desired skills in students. The educators within this discipline should recognize the importance of incorporating greater human skills aspects into their educational programmes (Pant & Baroudi, 2008).

Mason et al. (2009) found that while departmental efforts to teach and assess employability skills did not affect job market performance, educational credentials had a notable impact on wage costs. This indicates that a higher education level correlates with higher earnings potential. Firms' profitability rises when educated workers are substituted by higher-educated ones (Kampelmann et al., 2018).

Eid (2012) concluded that the long-run propensity of productivity growth to R&D performed by the higher education sector is positive and significant while it was insignificant to business R&D. The findings of Piva and Vivarelli (2009) endorse the widely recognized technology-push and demand-pull hypotheses, providing evidence for the influence of skill levels on boosting a firm's R&D investment. Adams (1999) shows that R&D affects skill bias through two channels: directly increasing demand for skilled labour in product-specific R&D and favouring equipment over structures in broader firms and industry R&D, amplifying skill bias over time. Leiponen (2005) asserts that firms lacking skills benefit less from innovation. Their research highlights how high technical skills complement R&D collaboration, emphasizing human capital's key role in fostering profitable innovation.

Cobo (2013) identifies five essential elements for fostering learning and human capital development in an innovative society: addressing the gap between formal education and societal needs, focusing on learning methods, adapting to digital advancements, emphasizing lifelong learning, and nurturing soft skills. The article emphasizes the critical role of expanded learning and skill development for the future of education.

Postholm (2009) suggests that the collaboration between teachers and researchers could serve as a model for ongoing teacher training and the education of future teachers. Borras and Edquist (2015) point out three key issues in innovation systems regarding education, training, and skills: insufficient competency levels, delays in meeting firms' competency needs, and imbalances between internal and external competency sources within firms.

17.5 Part II: Education, Peace, and Social Capital: An Augmented Framework

Several studies have examined the interlinkages between economic growth, education, and terrorism. Korotayev et al. (2021) found that per capita GDP growth in low-income countries coincides with higher education levels, reduced unemployment, decreased inequality, and improved democracy. However, economic growth doesn't necessarily lead to these improvements in middle and high-income countries. Yang and Qiu (2016) discovered that lower investment in early education by poor families results in their children attending lower-quality schools, making them less likely to pursue higher education. By simulating policy experiments for different types of government education expenditure, we find that direct subsidies to poor parents are the most efficient and effective policy for mitigating poor families' budget constraints concerning early education investment in their children. Further, the results show that more unequal societies tend to spend comparatively more on higher levels of education (Di Gioacchino & Sabani, 2009). The relationship between income inequality and average years of schooling is positive, and consistent with constant or increasing returns to additional years of schooling (Coady & Dizioli, 2018). While this positive relationship is small and not always statistically significant, we find a statistically significant negative relationship with years of schooling of younger cohorts.

Another study concluded that a curriculum response that addresses the acquisition of knowledge can build students' critical capacity for engagement with radicalization through enhanced political literacy and media literacy. We further argue this represents a genuinely educational response to Prevent, as opposed to a more restrictive securitized approach (Jerome & Elwick, 2019). Education should not be relied upon to counter extremism without additional initiatives to facilitate socioeconomic opportunities in the African sub-continent (Danzell et al., 2020).

Ide (2020) concluded that the significance of education in political socialization and the influence of terrorism discourses on promoting or suppressing specific interests have been widely recognized. Esmailzadeh (2023) underscores education's pivotal role in promoting peace and countering terrorism by nurturing critical thinking and empathy, reducing extremist influences, and fostering unity. Sas et al. (2020) propose improving education access, creating safe schools, involving all levels in anti-radicalization efforts, and aligning job markets with graduates' skills. Terrorism, driven by political, religious, or ideological motives, is a global challenge. ur Rahman (2023) highlights the essential role of primary education in fostering peace, especially in terrorism-affected areas. The study recommends providing training to primary school teachers in these regions to promote peace and development effectively.

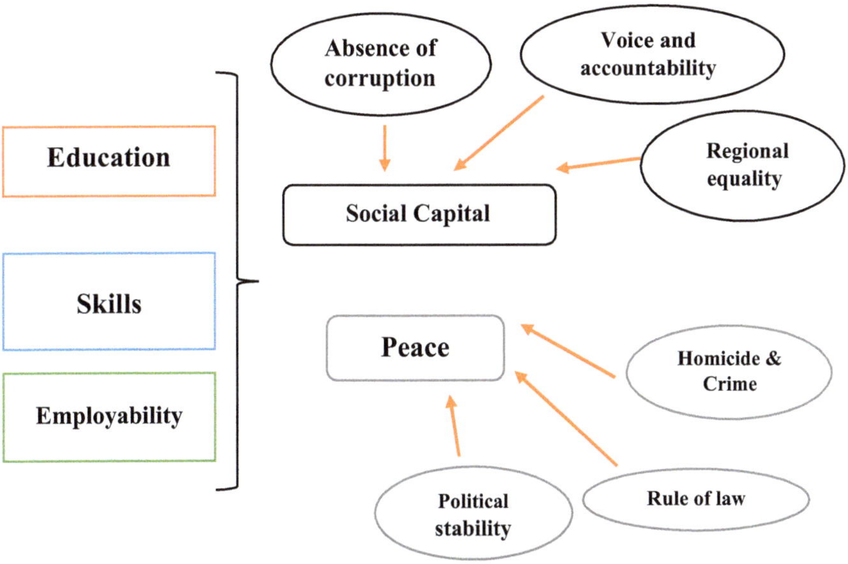

The above-augmented framework indicates the hypothesis that education, skill, and employability could affect social capital in society. Several studies have contributed in empirically testing the relationship between social capital and economic inequality. By deploying a cross-section analysis of America between 1976 and 2009, it was concluded that social capital is strongly related to socioeconomic status (Wright, 2015). The economic inequality weakens the social capital was deduced by (Costa & Kahn, 2003; Putnam, 2007; Uslaner & Brown, 2005). The social capital in the integrated framework represents the value system of the society. Therefore, the social capital in the given framework is measured by the absence of corruption, voice, and accountability and the degree of regional equality in terms of economic disparity. Peace is reflected by political stability, the frequency of homicides and criminal incidents, and the degree of rule of law.

Several studies have endorsed that under certain circumstances, education leads to peace, supported by transformation processes such as the transformation of security, political institutions, economic regeneration, and social development (Cox, 2009).[23] When education stakeholders function with the objective of inclusive education systems, differences in language, curriculum, and decentralized resources will be eliminated (UNESCO, 2011).[24] Societies with schools that promote values such as peace, tolerance, and mutual respect, would be less susceptible to conflicts, unrest, and violence (UNESCO, 2011). Further, education. However, poor quality of education that fails to deliver the necessary skills would increase the risk of conflicts (UNESCO, 2011). This is because unequal access may develop feelings of injustice, leading to violence and unrest. Thus, education can indirectly aggravate conflict

[23] Cox, M. (2009). Social capital and peace-building. *Creating and Resolving Conflict.*

[24] https://www.unicef.org/education/inclusive-education.

by triggering socioeconomic divisions, political inclusion or exclusion, and cultural diversity (Cox, 2009).[25]

17.6 Conclusion

Education constitutes a significant part of human capital. A profound knowledge base becomes necessary for a country to not only grow but also maintain peace, political stability, and non-violence. The paper investigates the interlinkages between education, skills, and employment in the Indian context after independence. The share of the organized sector in GDP was substantially high at the beginning of the path of economic growth, later, it started declining. In the early stages of development, unemployment did not emerge as a problem as it was assumed that labour-intensive sectors would control any rise in unemployment. However, it was witnessed that the labour force grew more rapidly than the increase in employment, consequently, unemployment increased. While investigating the interlinkages between education, employment, and inequality, there is a two-way relationship that education, as one of the components of human capital, increases economic growth but at the same time exacerbates income inequality.

Further, the paper investigates the nexuses between education, skill, and employability consequently affect social capital. The study concludes that education and employability have a substantial impact on peace, tolerance, and equity in society. The transformation process that entails the foundation of social development and political stability signifies security and ensures a peaceful and just society. However, unequal access to education can lead to the attribute of inequality, further inducing conflict, injustice, violence, and unrest. Thus, the policies must promote a more ethical and inclusive education system coupled with the required skill and employability to ensure equitable access to education and knowledge base. Thus, a more just and equitable social capital would foster a more peaceful and non-violent society.

References

Abbas, Q., & Mujahid-Mukhtar, E. (2000). The role of human capital in economic growth: A comparative study of Pakistan and India [with Comments]. *The Pakistan Development Review*, 451–473.

Adams, J. D. (1999). The structure of firm R&D, the factor intensity of production, and skill bias. *Review of Economics and Statistics, 81*(3), 499–510.

Babatunde, M. A., & Adefabi, R. A. (2005, November). Long run relationship between education and economic growth in Nigeria: Evidence from the Johansen's cointegration approach. In *Regional conference on education in West Africa* (pp. 1–2).

Bharti, N. K., Chancel, L., Piketty, T., & Somanchi, A. (2024). Income and Wealth Inequality in India, 1922–2023: The Rise of the Billionaire Raj.

[25] Cox, M. (2009). Social capital and peace-building. *Creating and Resolving Conflict*.

Borras, S., & Edquist, C. (2015). Education, training and skills in innovation policy. *Science and Public Policy, 42*(2), 215–227.
Bowman, M. J. (1980). On Theodore W. Schultz's contributions to economics. *The Scandinavian Journal of Economics, 82*(1), 80–107.
Cammack, P. (2014). *World development report 2015: Programming the poor*. The Multilateral Development Banks and the Global Financial Crisis (Working Papers Series, No. 7).
Coady, D., & Dizioli, A. (2018). Income inequality and education revisited: Persistence, endogeneity and heterogeneity. *Applied Economics, 50*(25), 2747–2761.
Cobo, C. (2013). Skills for innovation: Envisioning an education that prepares for the changing world. *Curriculum Journal, 24*(1), 67–85.
Com, B. (2021). National education policy 2020.
Costa, D. L., & Kahn, M. E. (2003). Understanding the American decline in social capital, 1952–1998. *Kyklos, 56*(1), 17–46.
Cox, M. (2009). Social capital and peace-building. *Creating and Resolving Conflict*.
Danzell, O. E., Yeh, Y. Y., & Pfannenstiel, M. (2020). Does education mitigate terrorism? Examining the effects of educated youth cohorts on domestic terror in Africa. *Terrorism and Political Violence, 32*(8), 1731–1752.
Di Gioacchino, D., & Sabani, L. (2009). Education policy and inequality: A political economy approach. *European Journal of Political Economy, 25*(4), 463–478.
Drèze, J., & Sen, A. (2013). *An uncertain glory: India and its contradictions*. Princeton University Press.
Eicher, T. S., & Garcıa-Penalosa, C. (2001). Inequality and growth: The dual role of human capital in development. *Journal of Development Economics, 66*(1), 173–197.
Eid, A. (2012). Higher education R&D and productivity growth: An empirical study on high-income OECD countries. *Education Economics, 20*(1), 53–68.
Esmailzadeh, Y. (2023). The role of education in promoting peace and countering terrorism. *The American Journal of Social Science and Education Innovations, 5*(04), 38–45.
Galor, O., & Tsiddon, D. (1997). The distribution of human capital and economic growth. *Journal of Economic Growth, 2*(1), 93–124.
Galor, O., Moav, O., & Vollrath, D. (2005). *Land inequality and the emergence of human capital promoting institutions* (No. 2005–03) (Working Paper).
Haldar, S. K., & Mallik, G. (2010). Does human capital cause economic growth? A case study of India. *International Journal of Economic Sciences & Applied Research, 3*(1).
Hanushek, E. A., & Wößmann, L. (2007). *The role of education quality for economic growth* (World Bank policy research working paper [4122]).
Healy, T., & Côté, S. (2001). *The well-being of nations: The role of human and social capital. Education and skills*. Organisation for Economic Cooperation and Development, 2 rue Andre Pascal, F-75775 Paris Cedex 16, France.
Ide, T. (2020). Teaching terrorism, saving the state? Education and geopolitical imaginations of terrorism in 12 violently challenged states. *Political geography, 77*, 102125.
Iuga, I., & Cioca, I. C. (2013). Analysis of correlation between the unemployment rate and gross domestic product in the European Union. *Polish Journal of Management Studies, 7*, 71–78.
Jerome, L., & Elwick, A. (2019). Identifying an educational response to the prevent policy: Student perspectives on learning about terrorism, extremism and radicalisation. *British Journal of Educational Studies, 67*(1), 97–114.
Kampelmann, S., Rycx, F., Saks, Y., & Tojerow, I. (2018). Does education raise productivity and wages equally? The moderating role of age and gender. *IZA Journal of Labor Economics, 7*(1), 1–37.
Kannan, K. P. (2022). India's elusive quest for inclusive development: An employment perspective. *The Indian Journal of Labour Economics, 65*(3), 579–623.
Kijima, Y. (2006). Why did wage inequality increase? Evidence from urban India 1983–99. *Journal of Development Economics, 81*(1), 97–117.

Korotayev, A., Vaskin, I., & Romanov, D. (2021). Terrorism and democracy: A reconsideration. *Comparative Sociology, 20*(3), 344–379.
Kotásková, S. K., Procházka, P., Smutka, L., Maitah, M., Kuzmenko, E., Kopecká, M., & Hönig, V. (2018). The impact of education on economic growth: The case of India. *Acta Universitatis Agriculturae et Silviculturae Mendelianae Brunensis, 66*(1).
Leiponen, A. (2005). Skills and innovation. *International Journal of Industrial Organization, 23*(5–6), 303–323.
Marron, M. E. (2018). *Youth unemployment: Transition from school to work* (Doctoral dissertation, California State University, Northridge).
Mason, G., Williams, G., & Cranmer, S. (2009). Employability skills initiatives in higher education: What effects do they have on graduate labour market outcomes? *Education Economics, 17*(1), 1–30.
O'Neill, D. P. (1993). *The role of human capital accumulation in determining income distribution.* The University of Iowa.
Pant, I., & Baroudi, B. (2008). Project management education: The human skills imperative. *International Journal of Project Management, 26*(2), 124–128.
Piketty, T. (2014). *Capital in the twenty-first century.* Harvard University Press.
Piva, M., & Vivarelli, M. (2009). The role of skills as a major driver of corporate R&D. *International Journal of Manpower, 30*(8), 835–852.
Postholm, M. B. (2009). Research and development work: Developing teachers as researchers or just teachers? *Educational Action Research, 17*(4), 551–565.
Putnam, R. D. (2007). E Pluribus Unum: Diversity and community in the twenty-first century. *Scandinavian Political Studies, 30*(2), 137–173.
Sas, M., Ponnet, K., Reniers, G., & Hardyns, W. (2020). The role of education in the prevention of radicalization and violent extremism in developing countries. *Sustainability, 12*(6), 2320.
Şentürk, C. (2021). Effects of the blended learning model on preservice teachers' academic achievements and twenty-first century skills. *Education and Information Technologies, 26*(1), 35–48.
Singh Dubey, R., Paul, J., & Tewari, V. (2022). The soft skills gap: A bottleneck in the talent supply in emerging economies. *The International Journal of Human Resource Management, 33*(13), 2630–2661.
Suleman, F. (2018). The employability skills of higher education graduates: Insights into conceptual frameworks and methodological options. *Higher Education, 76*, 263–278.
Tendulkar, D. S. (2010). Inequality and equity during rapid growth process. *India's Economy Performance and Challenges.* Oxford University Press, New Delhi.
ur Rahman, K. (2023). Role of primary education in promoting peace in terrorism affected areas: Primary school teachers' perspectives. *American Journal of Applied Psychology, 12*(2), 36–46.
Uslaner, E. M., & Brown, M. (2005). Inequality, trust, and civic engagement. *American Politics Research, 33*(6), 868–894.
Wright, M. (2015). Economic inequality and the social capital gap in the United States across time and space. *Political Studies, 63*(3), 642–662.
Yang, J., & Qiu, M. (2016). The impact of education on income inequality and intergenerational mobility. *China Economic Review, 37*, 110–125.

Website Links

https://www.themirrority.com/data/employability#trainings
https://asercentre.org/aser-survey/
https://timesofindia.indiatimes.com/india/with-1-in-5-workers-skilled-india-ranks-129-among-162/articleshow/79769587.cms

https://thewire.in/economy/what-we-know-about-indias-post-covid-economy-recovery-and-rising-inequality

https://www.worldbank.org/en/news/feature/2017/06/23/skilling-india

https://assets.publishing.service.gov.uk/media/5b9b87f340f0b67896977bae/K4D_HDR_The_Contribution_of_Education_to_Economic_Growth_Final.pdf

https://uis.unesco.org/en/glossary-term/literacy-rate

https://www.oxfamindia.org/featuredstories/10-facts-illiteracy-india-you-must-know

https://timesofindia.indiatimes.com/india/75-years-75-literacy-indias-long-fight-against-illiteracy/articleshow/93555770.cms

https://databank.worldbank.org/metadataglossary/world-development-indicators/series/SE.SEC.ENRR

https://uis.unesco.org/

https://pib.gov.in/PressReleaseIframePage.aspx?PRID=1894915

https://www.educationworld.in/1991-inflection-point-for-indian-education/

https://dge.gov.in/dge/schemes_programmes

http://www.igidr.ac.in/pdf/publication/WP-2018-003.pdf

https://blog.mygov.in/skill-development-and-employment-opportunity/

https://wid.world/www-site/uploads/2024/03/WorldInequalityLab_WP2024_09_Income-and-Wealth-Inequality-in-India-1922-2023_Final.pdf

https://www.unicef.org/education/inclusive-education

Chapter 18
Economic Impact of Global Warming in India: An Updated Review of Methods, Policies, and Recent Empirical Literature*

Naveen Kumar and Dibyendu Maiti

Abstract This chapter reviews empirical methodologies studying the impact of global warming on economic indicators in India. We begin with an analysis of global climate dynamics, which includes definitional debate of level and growth effects, using climate econometrics to highlight the methodological issue in temperature-GDP econometrics, and summarising methodological discussion on differentiation between weather and climate change. The chapter then evaluates India's vulnerability to climate shocks, detailing macroeconomic impacts on critical sectors such as agriculture, health, and productivity, and reviews the evolution of India's environmental policies. We further review the role of fiscal, regulatory, and monetary policies in facilitating climate adaptation and mitigation. Additionally, we explore diverse econometric approaches for estimating climate change impacts, including cross-sections and panel methods. This review highlights the urgency of coordinated international action and the need for India to implement robust climate policies to ensure sustainable economic growth and fulfil its emission reduction targets.

Keywords Temperature · India · Climate change · Adaptation · Mitigation

JEL Code Q54 · Q50 · Q58

N. Kumar (✉) · D. Maiti
Delhi School of Economics, New Delhi, India
e-mail: naveenkumar@econdse.org

D. Maiti
e-mail: dibyendu@econdse.org

D. Maiti et al. (eds.), *75 Years of Growth, Development and Productivity in India*, India Studies in Business and Economics, https://doi.org/10.1007/978-981-97-8054-9_18

18.1 Introduction

Global warming has led to an alarming rise in the intensity and frequency of extreme weather events, such as heatwaves, droughts, severe storms, and flooding (RBI, 2023). This trend, largely driven by increasing greenhouse gas emissions, has severe implications for economic growth, individual well-being, and overall happiness worldwide. Economic losses from natural disasters have surged, while the mental and physical health impacts on affected populations have worsened, contributing to higher stress levels and decreased life satisfaction (Calvin et al., 2023). Furthermore, the COVID-19 pandemic has raised the importance of robust environmental policies, highlighting how neglect can worsen crises and lead to the rise of environmental consequences. In response to these challenges, India aims to significantly cut its emission intensity by 33–35% by 2030, compared to 2005 levels, as part of its ambitious Nationally Determined Contributions (NDCs), and achieving net-zero emissions by 2070, highlighting a shift towards renewable energy and enhanced disaster resilience (MoEFCC, 2022). This commitment reflects a broader recognition of the urgent need for comprehensive climate adaptation and mitigation strategies. This chapter aims to review the environmental challenges that the country is facing, the magnitudes of their economic impacts, the mitigation strategies, and the challenges therein. Additionally, this study would explore global climate change dynamics, which includes methodological definitions of level and growth effects, review climate econometrics to analyse temperature-GDP relationships and broader sectoral impacts. This paper also reviews diverse econometric approaches for estimating climate change impacts, including cross-sections and panel methods. It is noteworthy to mention that the Environmental Kuznets Curve (EKC) hypothesis suggests that environmental degradation initially rises with economic growth but eventually declines; however, the rapid pace of industrialisation often leads to more severe environmental impacts before effective mitigation can be implemented. Therefore, India would face the challenges of sustaining growth while committing to reducing carbon content in a reasonably shorter time (Kumar & Maiti, 2024c; Maiti et al., 2024).

India's diverse topography makes it vulnerable to climate change (RBI, 2023), with rising temperatures, erratic monsoons, and extreme weather events impacting its long coastline, agriculture, and water supply (RBI, 2023). Over two-thirds of India's population resides in rural areas, relying on agriculture. This is evident that the direct impact on agricultural productivity threatens the rural economy and food security, compounded by limited resources for adaptation and mitigation. Studies show that climate change has more adverse impacts on the global economic growth of developing countries like India than others because of significant agricultural productivity declines (Kahn et al., 2021; Kumar & Maiti, 2024b). Despite resilience during past global crises, India's economic growth sustainability is questioned without sound mitigation strategies (Maiti et al., 2024) Climate change affects both the demand and supply sides of the economy, with extreme weather events disrupting supply chains and increasing costs. In contrast, regulatory shifts and changing consumer preferences demand eco-friendly products (RBI, 2023).

India's environmental legal framework has evolved significantly since the colonial era. Early efforts were focused on forest conservation and pollution control. Post-independence, legislation expanded to address water and air pollution, culminating in the comprehensive Environmental Protection Act of 1986 (Dubash & Joseph, 2016; Saryal, 2018). Institutional developments, such as establishing the Ministry of Environment and Forests, have been crucial in monitoring and enforcing environmental laws. India's climate policy has also evolved, shifting from idealism, which asserted that wealthier nations bear primary responsibility, to pragmatism with active engagement in climate actions (Dubash & Joseph, 2016; Saryal, 2018). The National Action Plan on Climate Change (NAPCC) and sector-specific strategies like the National Electricity Plan and National Green Hydrogen Mission guide India's climate efforts. Despite these efforts, India's policies are rated as "Highly Insufficient" by the Climate Action Tracker, which calls for a more ambitious measures (Dubash & Joseph, 2016; Saryal, 2018).

Figure 18.1 provides an overview of the various dimensions of the current climate crisis. Panel (a) details the rise in sea levels since 1900, highlighting significant acceleration in recent decades due to global warming, which has led to the melting of polar ice caps and the thermal expansion of seawater. This rising trend poses significant threats to coastal regions worldwide, including densely populated coastal areas in India. Panel (c) depicts the upward trend in monthly average surface temperatures globally, with a significant increase observed since the mid-twentieth century. The data for 2023 suggests the intensifying nature of global warming, which requires robust international climate policies to reduce greenhouse gas emissions. Panel (b) illustrates the contributions of various countries to global temperature change from 1850 to 2022, revealing that historically, the United States and the European Union have been the largest contributors, followed by China and India. This shows the historical responsibility of developed nations and the need for equitable climate policies that support developing countries in their transition to sustainable energy sources. Finally, panel (d) shows the decadal average number of deaths from natural disasters since 1900, indicating a decrease in recent decades, possibly due to improved disaster response and preparedness. The persistent threat of climate-related natural disasters, particularly in vulnerable regions like India, highlights the critical need for robust disaster management strategies and climate adaptation measures to protect affected populations from the increasing frequency and severity of such events.

This review significantly contributes to the literature on the impact of climate change, particularly rising temperatures, on various sectors of India's economy. The urgency of addressing the current climate shift stresses the need for extensive research to understand the implications and formulate effective policies. The chapter also traces the evolution of India's climate policy, drawing attention to its transformation from an idealistic phase to a pragmatic approach post-2010.[1] The literature review is structured around three fundamental themes. The first theme explores into global

[1] This review evaluates the economic impacts of global warming on India using a systematic literature review adhering to PRISMA guidelines. We gathered articles for our review by searching Google Scholar, Scopus, and Web of Science using keywords such as "Temperature," "India," "Climate Change," "Adaptation," and "Mitigation." Searches in Scopus, Google Scholar, and Web of

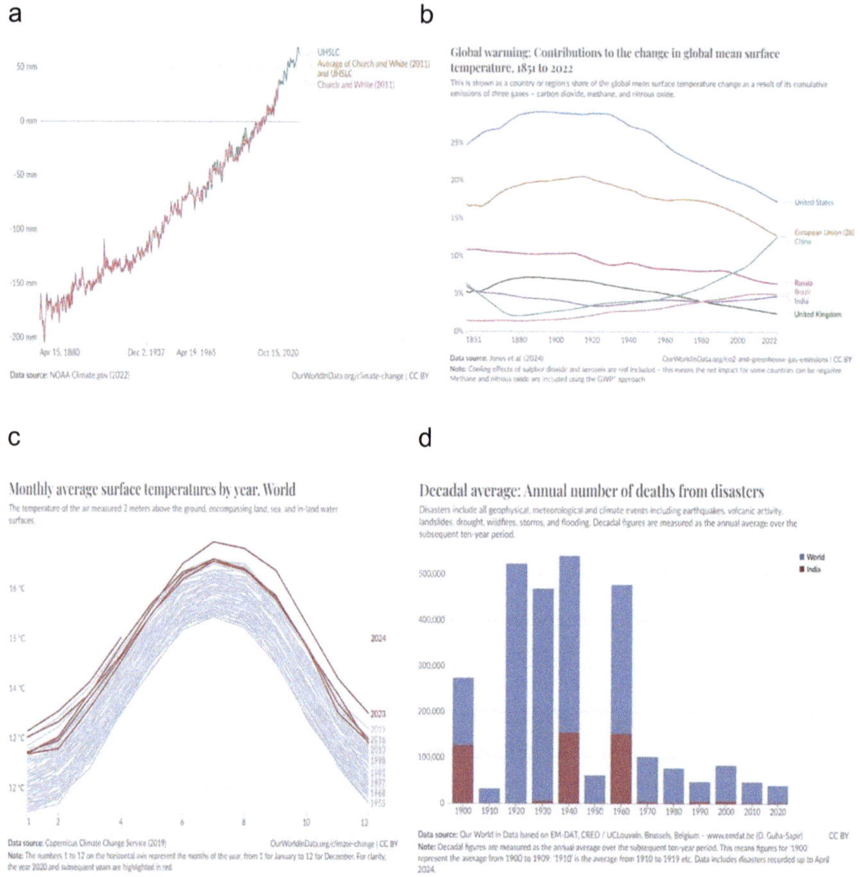

Fig. 18.1 Current shifts in climate change across globe **a** Sea level rise **b** Monthly Average surface temperature by year **c** Contribution to temperature change by countries (d) Annual number of death from natural disasters. *Source* Our World in Data (Ritchie et al., 2024)

climate change dynamics, specifically focusing on differentiating between weather and climate change (Dell et al., 2014; Frijters et al., 2020; Hsiang, 2016). The second theme focuses on temperature dynamics in India, India's exposure to climate change, the evolution of the environment, and climate policy history. In the final section of the chapter, we discuss policies for tackling climate change in India. The chapter highlights the role of fiscal policy, drawing lessons from global practices.

This chapter is organised into five main sections. It starts with global climate change dynamics, which includes subsections on weather and climate change, methodological issues, and the history of climate policy. Section 18.3 focuses on the relationship between climate change and the Indian economy, covering exposure

Science covered 1990–2023. After screening 1577 articles, more than 120 high-quality studies were selected.

to climate shocks, macroeconomic impact, sectoral impact, and the historical context of India's environmental and climate policies. In Sect. 18.4, the chapter discusses the role of fiscal, regulatory, and monetary policies in adaptation and mitigation. Finally, the chapter concludes with key observations and policy recommendations.

18.2 Global Climate Change Dynamics

The latest scientific IPCC (Calvin et al., 2023) report reveals that scientists observe unprecedented climate changes in every region and across the entire climate system,[2] with some irreversible changes already underway,[3,4]like sea level rise. Urgent and sustained reductions in carbon dioxide and greenhouse gas emissions are crucial to limit these changes.

Figure 18.2a shows the global contribution to temperature rise by various gases from 1851 to 2021, with carbon dioxide being the primary driver, showcasing the pressing need to curb CO_2 emissions. Figure 18.2b details cumulative carbon dioxide emissions by world region, revealing the historical dominance of the United States and the European Union, while recent surges in emissions from China and other regions. Figure 18.2c tracks global monthly temperature anomalies from 1850 to 2023, showing a consistent upward trend indicative of persistent global warming. Figure 18.2d illustrates the increase in global reported natural disasters by type from 1970 to 2023, linking this rise to climate change, intensifying the frequency and severity of such events. These findings suggests the critical need for coordinated global action to address the multifaceted challenges posed by climate change.

The main greenhouse gases causing climate change are carbon dioxide and methane (See Fig. 18.2). Climate scientists have shown that humans are responsible for virtually all global heating over the last 200 years (Calvin et al., 2023). Human activities like these have caused greenhouse gases that are warming the world faster than ever in at least the last 2000 years. Climate change is often misunderstood as solely involving rising temperatures, but this oversimplification overlooks the intricate interconnections within the Earth's system. Changes in one aspect can trigger cascading effects throughout the entire system. Presently, the consequences of climate change include increased intensity of occurrences of severe droughts, water scarcity, intense fires, rising sea levels, floods, polar ice melting, catastrophic storms, and declining biodiversity (Nordhaus, 2019; Pachauri et al., 2014).

Climate change poses a real threat, affecting health, food production, housing, safety, and employment, particularly for vulnerable populations. The imperative to limit global temperature rise to 1.5 °C is stressed by scientists, yet current policies point towards a 3 °C rise by the century's end. A few major emitters contribute

[2] See Fig. 18.1 which suggests extreme temperature in the recent times.

[3] Figure 18.1 shows the exceeding level of sea rise with increase in the frequency of natural disasters.

[4] Burke et al. (2015a) showed the impact of climate change on human conflicts, including interpersonal and inter-group conflict, riots, and civil wars.

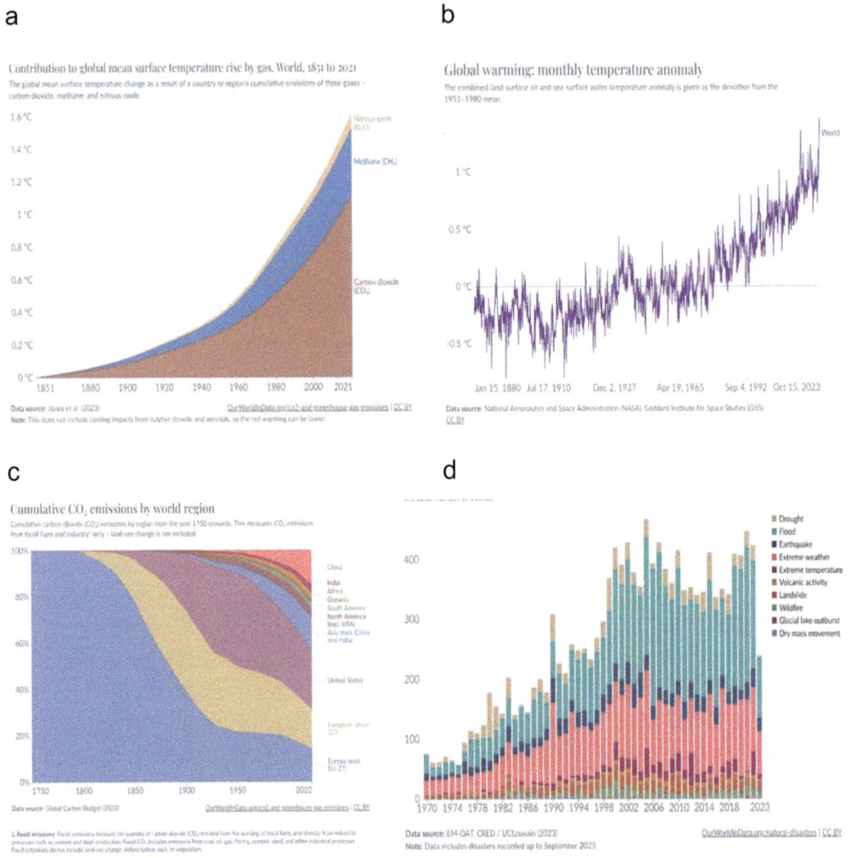

Fig. 18.2 Global climate change dynamics **a** Global-contribution to global temperature rise by gas **b** Cumulative carbon dioxide emission by world region **c** Global-monthly temperature anomalies **d** Global-reported natural disaster by type. *Source* Our World in Data (Ritchie et al., 2024)

significantly to greenhouse gas emissions, highlighting the need of the shared but differentiated responsibility for climate action. Viable solutions include transitioning to renewable energy, which demands substantial emission cuts by 2030. Adaptation measures, particularly for vulnerable communities, offer high returns on investment. While climate action requires significant financial investments, inaction is far more expensive. Fulfilling commitments, such as the $100 billion annual support to developing nations, is crucial for climate resilience and a sustainable future (Nordhaus, 2019; Calvin et al., 2023).

Choice is clear: act now or face more significant consequences later. Climate negotiations have emerged as a critical means to address the global challenge of climate change, requiring collaborative efforts from nations worldwide. These negotiations play a vital role in shaping emission reduction commitments, ensuring equitable distribution of responsibilities, securing climate finance, facilitating technology transfer, and outlining adaptation measures.

The evolution of international climate negotiations spans several crucial milestones, each reflecting the global community's increasing awareness and commitment to addressing the complex challenges posed by climate change. The UN's involvement in environmental conservation began with the inaugural Earth Summit held in Stockholm in 1972, marking the initiation of global cooperation and consensus on climate change, and resulting in the establishment of the UN Environment Programme (UNEP).

The historical trajectory of climate negotiations highlights several key milestones. The 1987 Montreal Protocol was pivotal in global environmental cooperation, addressing ozone layer depletion and showcasing early collective responsibility beyond climate change. In 1988, the establishment of the Intergovernmental Panel on Climate Change (IPCC) marked a critical step, showcasing global collaboration in assessing and responding to climate change challenges. The United Nations Framework Convention on Climate Change (UNFCCC) in 1992 set the stage for international cooperation, establishing the overall framework for intergovernmental efforts to address climate change. The subsequent Kyoto Protocol in 1997 established binding emission reduction targets for developed nations, albeit facing challenges.

The Copenhagen Accord in 2009 aimed for inclusivity but demonstrated the complexity of achieving a unified global climate agreement. This Accord signalled a global commitment to reducing emissions to hold the increase in global temperature below 2 °C, laying the groundwork for subsequent negotiations and highlighting the urgency of collective action. The Paris Agreement in 2015 was a landmark achievement, focusing on reducing greenhouse gas emissions to limit global temperature increases. It introduced the goal of limiting the temperature increase to 1.5 degrees Celsius and highlighted the importance of financing developing countries for climate change mitigation and adaptation. This agreement introduced Nationally Determined Contributions (NDCs), providing a comprehensive framework for individual countries to outline their climate action plans (RBI, 2023).

COP26 in 2021 marked another significant milestone with the Glasgow Climate Pact, showcasing the need for enhanced NDCs and a more aggressive stance towards limiting temperature rise to 1.5 degrees Celsius. Key issues addressed included coal power reduction, fossil fuel subsidy phase-out, and fulfilling the climate finance pledge of USD 100 billion. The introduction of the "Glasgow dialogue" highlighted a dynamic approach to addressing loss and damage from climate change. In 2022, COP27 reaffirmed commitments to global temperature reduction and achieved a breakthrough on the "Loss and Damage" fund. This fund, covering damage to crops, homes, and infrastructure, marked a significant step in acknowledging and addressing the tangible impacts of climate change (RBI, 2023).

Climate policy achievements showcase global commitment to combat climate change, with most nations targeting net-zero emissions by 2050. Financial commitments for climate finance have grown, starting with a notable pledge of US $100 billion annually by 2020 in COP15 and acknowledging its insufficiency in COP27 (RBI, 2023).

Cross-country variations in climate change opinions reveal significant differences between developed and developing nations, impacting global mitigation strategies. In developed countries like those in Europe and North America, there is higher awareness and support for climate policies, with many young people recognising climate threats (Fig. 18.3a) and a substantial share supporting governmental action (Fig. 18.3b). Conversely, developing regions such as parts of Africa and Southeast Asia prioritise economic concerns, which can overshadow climate policies yet still show a significant demand for increased governmental action on climate change (Fig. 18.3d). For instance, while $70 - 90\%$ of people in Europe believe their country should act on climate change (Fig. 18.3c), support is lower but still notable in developing regions. This suggests that global climate policies must be context-specific, with developed nations providing financial and technological aid to developing countries to balance development with environmental sustainability. This tailored, collaborative approach is essential for achieving global climate targets and ensuring an equitable transition to a low-carbon future.

Financial commitments towards climate finance for both adaptation and mitigation have evolved significantly, reflecting an increased understanding of the financial support required to tackle the complexities of climate challenges. The Copenhagen COP15 in 2009 marked a watershed moment when developed countries committed to providing a substantial $100 billion annually by 2020 for climate action in developing nations. At COP 27 in Sharm. El-Sheikh in 2022, it became evident that this initial pledge was insufficient to address the growing climate crises. To highlight the evolving financial requirements, experts at COP27 recognised that an annual commitment ranging from $160 billion to $340 billion would be necessary by 2030 (RBI, 2023). This figure is projected to escalate to a staggering $565 billion annually by 2050 if climate conditions continue to deteriorate. Beyond these pledges, parties have agreed to establish dedicated funding arrangements, including a specific fund for loss and damage, to support vulnerable nations better (RBI, 2023).

In addition to these commitments, the United Nations has unveiled a $3.1 billion plan to ascertain that everyone is covered by early warning systems within the next five years. This proactive measure aims to enhance countries' preparedness for hazardous weather (RBI, 2023). The positive impact of such initiatives is evident in the decline in weather-related mortality over the decades, thanks to technological advancements and improved early warning systems. These efforts have significantly reduced the incidence of death and have saved countless lives. Nationally Determined Contributions (NDCs) have played a crucial role in driving the momentum of emission reductions, setting the world on a path towards net-zero emissions (RBI, 2023). This has led to a relative decoupling of economic growth and emissions on a global scale, demonstrating that economic development can occur alongside environmental sustainability. Despite these commendable strides, the pace of climate policy implementation remains inadequate. Implementing various climate finance commitments from advanced economies has fallen short of expectations. Specifically, the extent of green financing for climate change adaptation remains about 5–10 times lower

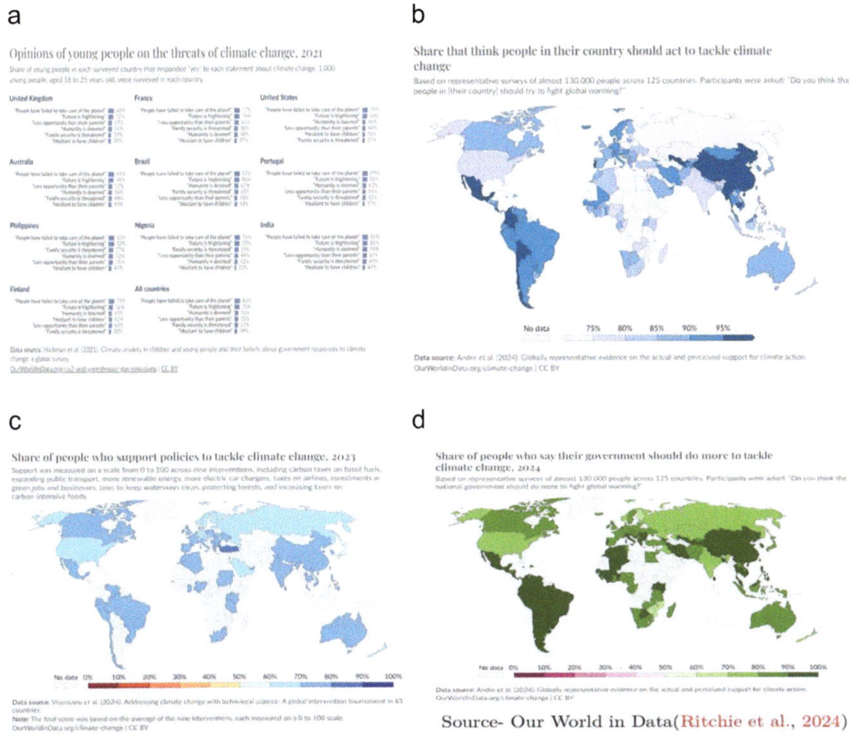

Fig. 18.3 Progress towards sustainable environment across globe **a** Opinion of young people about climate **b** Share of people who support policies to change in selected countries **c** Share that think people in their countries should act on Climate change **d** Share of people who say that their government should do more on climate change. *Source* Our World in Data (Ritchie et al., 2024)

than required (RBI, 2023). For instance, while advanced economies pledged $100 billion annually, only $83.3 billion was provided in 2020, representing a minimal 4% increase from 2019. This discrepancy highlights the significant gap between pledged and actual funding (RBI, 2023).

To further illustrate the crucial financing gap, consider that to meet the lower end of the required range by 2030, an additional $76.7 billion annually is needed beyond the current $83.3 billion. If aiming for the upper end of $340 billion by 2030, the gap widens dramatically, requiring an additional $256.7 billion each year. By 2050, meeting the $565 billion annual requirements could require nearly a sevenfold increase in current funding levels. This substantial shortfall highlights the urgent need for increased financial support to combat climate change and achieve global climate goals effectively (RBI, 2023).

Against this backdrop, in this section, we explore the distinction between weather and climate change. Subsequently, we explore the historical trajectory of global environmental regulations and climate change policies. The section concludes by addressing significant methodological challenges arising at the intersection of climate change and macroeconomic outcomes within a global context.

18.2.1 Definitional Debate: Weather vs. Climate Change

In general, weather has a more immediate impact than climate, and the effects of weather on outcomes differ significantly from the influence of climate due to various adaptation mechanisms. Weather refers to the short-term atmospheric conditions in a specific location, including variables such as temperature, humidity, precipitation, wind speed, and atmospheric pressure (Tol, 2018) . Individuals optimise their behaviour based on the climate they inhabit. Climate change stands for long-term alterations in average weather patterns over extended periods, typically spanning decades to millions of years. Unlike weather, which fluctuates rapidly, climate change involves sustained shifts in global or regional climate conditions (Hsiang, 2016; Tol, 2018). The long-term consequences of climate include changes in agriculture, dwelling types, food and clothing choices, sports activities, traded goods, and even residential choices. These cumulative impacts are reflected in average outcome differences across various locations. Given the confusion in the literature about the distinction between weather and climate, it is essential to carefully differentiate between the two before examining existing literature.

The term "weather" denotes daily atmospheric conditions, often summarised by temperature peaks and precipitation levels (Dell et al., 2014). Although weather includes multiple variables, authors commonly simplify discussions by focusing on average temperature and total precipitation. Dell et al. (2009) distinguish weather as an annual realisation of temperature and precipitation, while climate refers to their long-term distribution.

According to Auffhammer et al. (2013), "the difference between weather and climate is basically a matter of time. Weather is the condition of the atmosphere over a short period of time, while climate is the behaviour of the atmosphere over a relatively long period of time." This definition is criticised by Frijters et al. (2020) as the definition presents a challenge in deciding the duration of a long period. In the context of climate change, it meets difficulty as the concept of "average weather" emerges, blending the climate at the end of the specified period with prior climates, creating a representation that does not distinctly reflect the current climate or any specific moment in time. Tol (2018) defines climate statistically, "Climate is what you expect, while the weather is what you get" (Frijters et al., 2020). Again, Frijters et al. (2020) suggests that if authors generously interpret this definition, climate includes the entire multidimensional distribution of weather, extending beyond statistical averages. However, this definition poses challenges as it implies climate cannot be directly measured; instead, it relies on inference through climate change models fed with observed weather data (Frijters et al., 2020). The fact that climate changes are thus different from "average weather" measured over any period makes it difficult to estimate the effect of climate cleanly and separate it from the effects of weather (Frijters et al., 2020).

In their study on climate, Hsiang, (2016) propose a flexible and comprehensive definition. They describe climate as the vector of atmospheric and oceanic conditions at a given location, denoted by X_{it}, including variables like temperature (temp $_{it}$), precipitation (precip $_{it}$), and humidity (hum $_{it}$) (S. Hsiang, 2016). These variables are modelled as a vector drawn from a joint probability distribution $\psi(\Theta_{i\tau})$, where $\Theta_{i\tau}$ stands for a set of parameters characterising the climate during a time interval $\tau = [\underline{t}, \bar{t})$ at location i. $\Theta_{i\tau}$ includes key statistics that describe the distribution of X_{it}, such as location and shape parameters (Hsiang, 2016). For instance, $\theta_{i\tau}$ may include sample statistics like mean and standard deviation of rainfall for a period, whereas $\Theta_{i\tau}$ captures the population parameters (Hsiang, 2016). This differentiation between observed weather measures ($\theta_{i\tau}$) and underlying climate parameters ($\Theta_{i\tau}$) clarifies distinctions between short-term weather events and long-term climatic trends (Hsiang, 2016).

Defining weather and climate change in economics poses a complex challenge due to the intertwined nature of these systems. While weather refers to short-term atmospheric conditions and climate includes long-term trends, isolating the economic effects of climate change is difficult amidst various influencing factors (Hsiang, 2016). Additionally, temporal, and spatial variations, coupled with uncertainties in future projections and adaptation strategies, further complicate economic analysis. Despite these challenges, economists have a growing consensus on the requirement of interdisciplinary approaches to understand better and address the economic impacts of weather and climate change (Hsiang, 2016).

U.S. Environmental Protection Agency (EPA) (2024) defines weather as refers to the state of the atmosphere at any given time and place, predominantly occurring in the lower layer of the atmosphere and affecting individuals, agriculture, and ecosystems. Common weather elements include temperature, precipitation, clouds, and wind, influencing daily experiences. Extreme weather phenomena, like hurricanes, tornadoes, blizzards, and droughts, can have significant consequences. Climate represents the long-term average of weather patterns in a specific location. While weather fluctuates rapidly, climate changes gradually over decades to centuries, containing factors beyond temperature and precipitation, such as the frequency and intensity of heat waves, cold spells, storms, floods, and droughts. Distinguishing between weather and climate can be likened to selecting daily attire based on weather conditions, whereas climate determines the entire wardrobe selection for a particular region.

18.2.2 Methodological Issues and Data Constraints

The economic ramifications of climate change are profound, affecting various sectors such as agriculture, industry, and public health. Climate-induced disruptions can lead to reduced labour productivity, increased healthcare costs, and damage to infrastructure, imposing significant economic burdens on societies. Panel data techniques such as TWFE offers a robust framework for studying the relationship between climate variables and economic outcomes. Models such as fixed effects (FE), dynamic panel models, and generalised method of moments (GMM) estimators are employed to account for both cross-sectional and time-series dimensions in the data. Initial efforts focused on fixed effects models to control for unobserved heterogeneity. However, endogeneity concerns led to adopting instrumental variable (IV) estimation techniques (Tol, 2024). IV estimation involves the identification of instrumental variables that are correlated with the endogenous regressors but uncorrelated with the error term (Table 18.1).

Dell et al. (2009) found an 8.5% drop in per capita national income per 1 °C temperature increases in panels of both developed and developing countries. However, this approach does not consider the time factor that plays a critical role in the climate change literature and may be influenced by other factors like institutional quality (Acemoglu et al., 2001). A study by Dell et al. (2012), analysing 125 countries from 1950 to 2003, found that higher temperatures significantly hinder short-term economic growth in less affluent nations, with a 1 °C increase leading to a 1.3% decline in economic output. Various researchers have employed different temperature metrics to assess its impact on GDP over multiple time frames, including annual (Burke et al., 2015b; Dell et al., 2012; Acevedo et al., 2020), monthly (Pretis et al., 2018), and seasonal data (Colacito et al., 2019). Relying solely on annual temperature averages may overlook critical aspects of climate change's economic effects, such as heatwaves, prolonged cold spells, and changing precipitation patterns that can significantly affect socioeconomic systems in the short term. Therefore, seasonal data provides valuable insights into when and where interventions are most needed to mitigate the adverse effects of climate change on economic growth (Kumar & Maiti, 2024b) (Table 18.2).

One major challenge in climate econometrics is determining how to appropriately specify econometric models. Advanced models in this field incorporate various data types while accounting for unobserved factors, allowing for the differentiation between short-term and long-term climate impacts and identifying possible adaptation mechanisms (Tol, 2024; Chang et al., 2023). Recent research utilises panel models with multiple fixed effects to analyse the link between temperature fluctuations and GDP (e.g., Dell et al., 2012; Letta & Tol, 2019). These panel models include economic variables—such as GDP or its components like total factor productivity (TFP)—combined with weather data, fixed effects, and control variables that vary across both temporal and spatial dimensions. Linear and nonlinear functions are employed to effectively capture these relationships. Nordhaus (1991) suggests a feedback mechanism where increased economic growth contributes to greater greenhouse gas emissions, leading to higher global temperatures, which subsequently inhibit economic growth. A critical issue in the temperature-GDP literature is selecting the appropriate functional form, given the absence of predefined, measurable structural connections between temperature and GDP in the current econometric framework (Tol, 2024; Burke et al., 2015a, 2015b; Dell et al., 2012) (Table 18.3).

Table 18.1 Summary of functional forms of temperature-GDP relationship (Adapted from the paper by Kolstad & Moore, 2020)

Method	Functional form	Weather indicators	Typical representation of climate	Remarks	Selected papers
Linear form					
Cross-section	$(y_i = f(c_i) + \text{Controls}_i + \varepsilon_i)$	None	Direct and Nonlinear	Applies at a single time point	Mendelsohn et al. (1994)
Linear panel	$(y_{it} = \beta w_{it} + \mu_i + \theta_t + \varepsilon_{it})$	Linear	Panel fixed effects (both time and region specific)	Numerous studies use this to explore the temperature-economic growth relationship, focusing on short-term effects and temporary temperatures shocks	Colacito et al (2019), Dell et al. (2012, 2014), and Jain et al. (2020), Sandhani et al. (2023), and Deschênes and Greenstone (2007)
Long differences	$(y_{i,t} - y_{i,t-\Delta t} = f\left(w_{i,t} - w_{i,t-\Delta t}\right) + \varepsilon_i)$	Linear	Medium-run climatic variation captured through long differences	Captures medium-run climatic variations by looking at long differences	Liu et al. (2023) and Burke and Emerick (2016)
Non-linear form					
Heterogeneous marginal effects: nonlinear panel	$(y_{it} = f(w_{it}) + \mu_i + \theta_t + \varepsilon_{it})$	Non-linear	Uses fixed effects. Materials effect of weather varies with climate	Captures non-linear relationships between weather variables and GDP. Allows exploration of marginal effects of temperature changes	Burke et al. (2015a) and Deryugina and Hsiang (2017)

(continued)

Table 18.1 (continued)

Method	Functional form	Weather indicators	Typical representation of climate	Remarks	Selected papers
Partitioning variation	$(y_{it} = f(w_{it} - c_i) + g(c_i) + \text{Controls}_i + \varepsilon_{it})$	Nonlinear	Nonlinear	Separates short-time temperature deviations from long-term climate changes, considering potential adaptations and responses to long-run climatic changes	Kelly et al. (2005) and Moore and Lobell (2014)
Hybrid form					
Heterogenous marginal effects: two stage Panel	$(1^{st}$ stage: $y_{it} = \beta_i w_{it} + \mu_i + \theta_t + \varepsilon_{it})$ $(2^{nd}$ stage: $\beta_i = f(c_i) + \text{Controls}_i + \varepsilon_i)$	Linear in first stage; absent in second stage	Fixed effects in first stage; direct nonlinear in second stage	Coefficient on weather in first stage becomes LHS in stage 2	Auffhammer et al. (2013)
Hybrid model	$(y_{it} = \alpha + \beta_1 w_{it} + \beta_2 w_{it}^2 + \gamma X_{it} + \delta(w_{it} \times t) + \mu_i + \theta_t + \varepsilon_{it})$	Both linear and Nonlinear	Combines fixed effects and interaction terms	Combines the advantage of linear and non-linear models, can distinguish between short-term shocks and long-term climatic changes	Kalkuhl and Wenz (2020)
ARDL type Model	$(\Delta Y_{i,t} = \sum_{l=1}^{p_{\Delta Y}} \lambda_{l,i} \Delta Y_{i,t-l} + \sum_{l=0}^{p_T} \beta_{l,i} (T)_{i,t-l} + \sum_{l=0}^{p_{Prec}} \gamma_{l,i} (Prec)_{i,t-l} + e_{i,t})$	Both Linear and Nonlinear	ARDL type model, Captures Dynamic impact	Dynamic impact, both Short run and long run estimation, Deals with the issues of slope heterogeneity, Cross-sectional dependence, endogeneity and trends	Kahn et al. (2021) and Kumar and Maiti (2024a, b)

Notes This table is an updated version with recent empirical literature and extension of the work of Kolstad and Moore (2020) and Chang et al (2023)

Table 18.2 Temporal specification of temperature variables

Temporal specification	Description	Examples	Remarks
Annual average temperature	Captures long-term effects, but may overlook short-term extreme events	Dell et al. (2012, 2014), Sandhani et al. (2023), Kalkuhl and Wenz (2020), Burke et al. (2015b), Kumar and Maiti (2024a), and Letta and Tol (2019)	Focuses on the average annual temperature impacts on economic growth
Monthly temperature	Addresses short-term variations but may not capture long-term trends	Pretis et al. (2018) and Kumar and Maiti (2024b)	Considers within-year monthly temperature variability
Seasonal temperature	Reveals seasonal variations in temperature effects	Colacito et al. (2019) and Kumar and Maiti (2024b)	Examines the impacts of different seasonal weather variation on economic indicators
Temperature bins	Allows for non-parametric analysis, identifying critical temperature thresholds	Deschênes and Greenstone (2007), Chen et al. (2023), and Zhang et al. (2018)	Uses the frequency of temperature events (Number of Hot days etc.) falling into different temperature ranges
Daily variability	Considers intra-day fluctuations	Kotz et al. (2021)	Investigates the variability in daily temperature averaged across different time scales i.e yearly, quarterly etc.
Deviation from historical norms	Captures long-term trends and adaptations	Kahn et al. (2021)	Considers the deviation of temperature from historical averages

Notes Refer Chang et al. (2023) on detailed Review of this issue

18.2.3 Growth vs Level Effects

The recent empirical literature on the relationship between temperature and GDP displays a debate on whether temperature primarily affects the level of economic output or its growth trajectory. This disagreement is highlighted by Schlenker and Auffhammer (2018), who believed that the significant implications depend on the modelling choice, noting that growth effects compound over time, whereas level effects do not. The literature demonstrates a tendency to relate temperature to the levels of economic outcomes rather than their growth rates, as evidenced by studies conducted by Dell et al. (2012). However, alternative models proposed by Burke et al. (2015b); Hsiang and Jina (2014) suggest that temperature may influence GDP

Table 18.3 Comparison of climate econometrics models

Model type	Description	Advantages	Criticisms
Cross-sectional model	Analyses the long-term effects of climate change by comparing region's current climates. Specifies an explained variable measuring the economy, along with temperature, control variables, and an error term	Captures long-term equilibrium effects	Biased estimation due to omitted variables and challenges in controlling for endogeneity
Panel model	Utilises panel data with various fixed effects (FEs) to identify relationships between temperature change and GDP. Allows for the control of time-invariant and time-varying omitted variables	Provides causal identification and accounts for unobserved omitted variables	Relies on assumptions of exogenous climate variables
Hybrid panel model	Integrates cross-sectional, inter-annual, and decadal variations in temperature to estimate short- and long-term climate impacts. Allows for distinguishing between climate change and weather change effects	Provides accurate estimation of climate impacts and distinguishes between short- and long-term effects	Interpretation challenges compared to the panel model and required averaging overtime periods

growth beyond its immediate effects on output. Despite the empirical evidence, the theoretical foundations for favouring either growth or level specifications remain elusive in the literature, leading to further divergence in interpretations.

Models in the literature vary significantly in their functional forms for relating temperature to economic outcomes (Newell et al., 2021). For instance, Dell et al. (2012) favours linear relationships, while Burke et al. (2015b) prefers quadratic specifications. A model developed by Dell et al. (2012) implies that temperature shocks affect economic outcomes, whereas Burke et al. (2015b) quadratic specification suggests that warming may boost growth in countries with cold climates but impede growth in hot countries (Jain et al, 2020; Newell et al., 2021). Burke et al.'s (2015b) approach is characterised by its flexibility, accommodating asymmetric effects of small temperature changes relative to an optimum. This contrast highlights the complexity of the temperature-GDP relationship and the challenges in accurately predicting its future impacts (Jain et al, 2020, Newell et al., 2021).

Moreover, the empirical literature lacks a clear consensus on the interpretation of available evidence. DJO, for instance, report growth effects of lagged temperature, interpreting the coefficients on temperature lags as indicative of growth effects (Jain et al, 2020, Newell et al., 2021). However, as pointed out by other scholars, the sign reversal on temperature lags may suggest a temporary effect on GDP levels rather than sustained growth effects. BHM estimates the distributed lag models with quadratic temperature polynomials to explore the persistence of temperature effects. Yet, none of these models show statistically distinguishable cumulative temperature effects on growth. Instead, lagged temperature effects exhibit sign reversal, implying transitory effects of temperature shocks on output (Jain et al, 2020, Newell et al., 2021).

Casey et al. (2023) used a simple economic model incorporating the impacts of climate change, extending the Solow (1956) growth model to distinguish between growth vs level effect. The model developed by (Casey et al., 2023) processes for TFP (A_{it}) to incorporate both level and growth effects from climate change:

$$A_{it} = D_l(T_{it})\hat{A} \text{ and } \hat{A} = \left(1 + g + D_g(T_{it+1})\right)\hat{A}$$

where T_{it} denotes average temperature in country i in year t, and D_l and D_g are level effect and growth effect damage functions, respectively. To compare the implications of these damage functions, Casey et al. (2023) analyse a scenario of a one-time, permanent increase in temperature using a simple model. Casey et al. (2023) focus on the scenario where both damage functions exhibit weakly negative first derivatives. Two extreme cases are studied: (1) climate change solely affects the level of TFP, implying $D_g = 0$ for all temperatures (T), , and (2) climate change solely influences the growth rate of TFP, suggesting $D_l = 1$ for all temperatures (Casey et al. (2023). In the short run, economic growth consistently decelerates as capital adjusts to a lower-balanced growth path following a shock. In scenarios characterised by level effects, capital returns to its original growth rate upon reaching the new balanced path, restoring economic growth to its previous level. Conversely, in cases with growth effects, increased climate damage permanently reduces the growth rate of total factor productivity (TFP), subsequently slowing the growth rates of both capital and output indefinitely. The similarity in the short-term slowdown of output per capita under both level and growth effects complicates their differentiation in annual panel data on GDP and temperature. However, as capital dynamics diminish, the output per capita growth rate primarily hinges on TFP's growth rate (Casey et al., 2023).

After examining the impact of current temperatures on growth rates within the same year, Dell et al. (2012), Colacito et al. (2019), and Jain et al. (2020) delve into the impact of lagged temperatures. Simultaneously analysing both current and lagged temperatures allows us to discern whether higher temperatures exert a transient effect on economic activity or if there is a more enduring effect on the underlying growth rate. To explore this concept, we draw insights from discussions (Colacito et al., 2019; Dell et al., 2012; Jain et al., 2020). Dell et al. (2012), Colacito et al. (2019), and Jain et al. (2020) first present a simple model to clarify the difference between a level effect on output and a growth effect (Fig. 18.4).

Let us denote economic output as E_t, given by the equation:

$$E_t = \gamma + E_{t-1} + \theta_1 T_t + \theta_2 T_t^2 + \theta_{\text{lag}_1} T_{t-1} + \theta_{\text{lag}_2} T_{t-1}^2 + \epsilon_t \tag{18.1}$$

Here, γ represents the intercept, E_{t-1} is the lagged economic output, θ_1 and θ_2 capture the nonlinear effect of current temperature on economic output, while θ_{lag_1} and θ_{lag_2} capture the nonlinear effect of lagged temperature (Dell et al., 2012; Jain et al. 2020). Assuming $\epsilon_t = 0$ for all t, let us consider the impact of a shock in year $t = 1$ that permanently raises temperatures by 1 °C, from $T_0 = 0$ to $T_t = 1, \forall t \geq 1$ (Dell et al.,

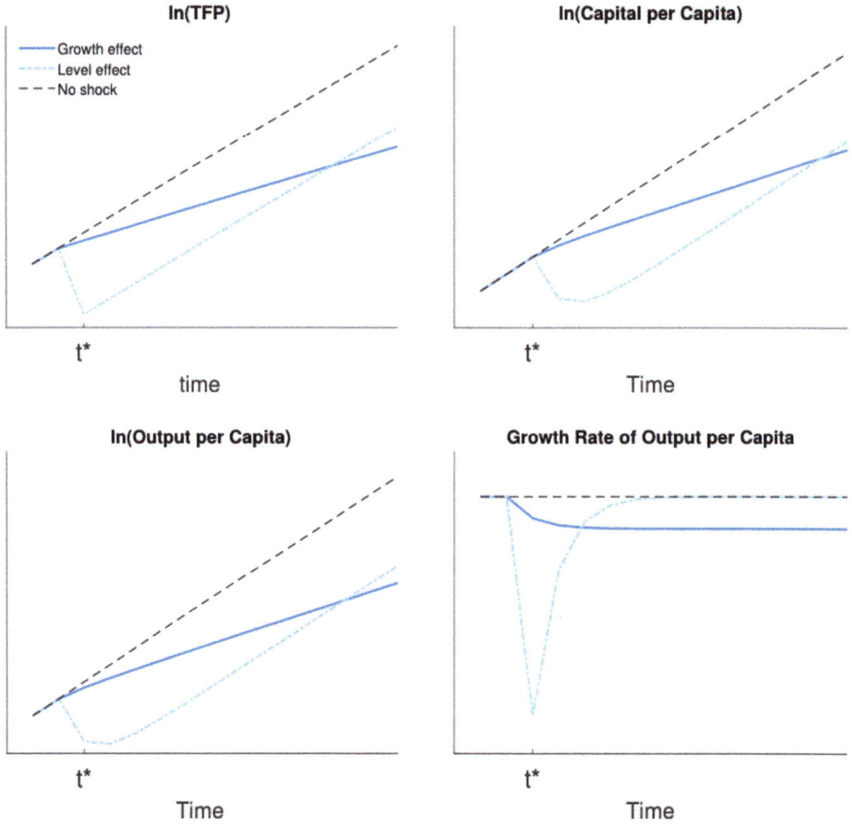

Fig. 18.4 Impact of a one-time increase in temperature (Casey et al., 2023). *Notes* This figure is taken from Casey et al. (2023) paper which demonstrates the effects of a one-time temperature increase at period t⋆. It consists of four panels: the top left shows the evolution of TFP, the top right displays the logarithm of capital per capita, the bottom left illustrates the logarithm of output per capita, and the bottom right presents the growth rate of output per capita. The graph compares three scenarios within the simple model: one with no shock (dashed black line), one with a one-time drop in the TFP level at period t⋆ (dashed-dotted light blue line), and one with a one-time drop in the TFP growth rate at period t⋆ (solid dark blue line)

2012; Jain et al., 2020). This simplified scenario captures climate change, facilitating our analysis (Dell et al., 2012; Jain et al., 2020). Given this temperature trajectory, we can use Eq. 18.1 recursively calculate the level of economic output and growth rate in each subsequent year following the temperature increase (Dell et al., 2012; Jain et al., 2020). This yields:

$$E_t = (E_0 + \theta_1 + \theta_2) + (t-1)\left[\gamma + \left(\theta_1 + \theta_2 + \theta_{\text{lag}_1} + \theta_{\text{lag}_2}\right)\right] \textit{and}$$
$$\Delta E_1 = \gamma + \theta_1 + \theta_2, \text{ and } \Delta E_t = \gamma + \left(\theta_1 + \theta_2 + \theta_{\text{lag}_1} + \theta_{\text{lag}_2}\right), \forall t \geq 2 \quad (18.2)$$

According to Dell et al. (2012), Colacito et al. (2019), and Jain et al. (2020), three cases are interesting. First, if neither contemporaneous nor lagged temperature affects economic output, i.e., $\theta_1 = \theta_2 = \theta_{\text{lag }1} = \theta_{\text{lag }2} = 0$ (Jain et al, 2020). Second, if $\theta_1 + \theta_2 + \theta_{\text{lag }1} + \theta_{\text{lag }2} = 0$, then the 1 °C increase in temperature has a permanent effect on output (as captured by the terms $\theta_1 + \theta_2$ in Eq. 18.2), but it only affects the growth rate in the first period (Jain et al., 2020). This scenario is referred to as the "level effects" case (Jain et al., 2020). Third, if $\theta_1 + \theta_2 + \theta_{\text{lag}_1} + \theta_{\text{lag}_2} \neq 0$, then the permanent 1 °C increase in temperature will affect both the level of output and the growth rate of output persistently (Colacito et al., 2019; Dell et al., 2012; Jain et al., 2020). This is known as the "growth effects" case (Colacito et al., 2019; Dell et al., 2012; Jain et al., 2020). Effects detected under a "growth effects" scenario will compound over time, leading to greater potential economic losses compared to those sustained under the "level effects" scenario (Dell et al., 2012; Jain et al., 2020).

To test whether the temperature-output relationship aligns more with level or growth effects, a group of scholars (Dell et al., 2012; Colacito et al., 2019; Jain et al., 2020) followed an integrating lagged temperature into the regression framework. Specifically, researcher like Dell et al. (2012), Colacito et al. (2019), and Jain et al. (2020) estimate a regression of the format:

$$\begin{aligned}\Delta E_{s,t} &= \phi_l T_{s,t} + \phi_2 T_{s,t}^2 + \phi_{\text{lag}_l} T_{s,t-1} + \phi_{\text{lag}_2} T_{s,t-1}^2 \\ &\quad + f\left(P_{s,t}, P_{s,t-1}\right) + \rho \Delta E_{s,t-1} + \alpha_s + \alpha_t +_{s,t}\end{aligned} \tag{18.3}$$

Here, $T_{s,t-1}$ represents temperature from the previous fiscal year, and $f\left(P_{s,t}, P_{s,t-1}\right)$ is a quadratic function of contemporaneous and lagged precipitation (Jain et al., 2020). These results highlight the distinction between the level and growth effects of climate change on economic outcomes, providing valuable insights into their respective implications for long-term economic growth discussions (Colacito et al., 2019; Dell et al., 2012; Jain et al., 2020). Overall, the disagreement in the literature draw attention to the complexity of the temperature-GDP relationship and the need for further research to understand the mechanisms at play discussions (Colacito et al., 2019; Dell et al., 2012; Jain et al., 2020).

18.3 Climate Change and Indian Economy

India's vulnerability to climate change is rooted in its diverse topography, exposing the nation to various climate risks such as rising temperatures, erratic monsoons, and extreme weather events (RBI, 2023). The distinct geographical features, including the long coastline, fertile plains, and the Thar Desert, make India uniquely susceptible to the impacts of global warming. The extensive coastline, vital for economic activities, faces escalating risks from global warming, including flooding, storm surges, and the increased frequency of cyclones. The country's reliance on monsoon rains for water supply contributes to water stress, and the increasing frequency of heat waves poses risks to health and agriculture (RBI, 2023). The direct impact of changing climate conditions on agricultural productivity poses a critical threat to both the economy and food security. Compounded by limited financial and technological resources, India faces challenges in implementing robust adaptation and mitigation measures. The high population density, with over two-thirds residing in rural areas, further complicates efforts to provide adequate infrastructure and services, intensifying the country's susceptibility to climate-induced risks (RBI, 2023).

18.3.1 Indian Exposure to Climate Shocks

In recent years, India has witnessed a disconcerting trend marked by a steady rise in temperatures and an alarming surge in the frequency of extreme weather events (RBI, 2023). As the Fig. 18.5a depicts a steady rise in annual mean temperatures from 1980 to 2020, while Fig. 18.5b illustrates temperatures consistently surpassing historical averages. Figure 18.5c highlights a surge in natural disaster frequency. Lastly, Fig. 18.5d presents India's IMF Climate Risk Profile, portraying high scores for climate driven hazard and exposure (7.5), signifying substantial risk from climate change impacts. The scores for the climate driven INFORM Risk Indicator (5.3), lack of coping capacity (4.2), and vulnerability (4.8) further suggests India's struggle in effectively addressing climate risks (RBI, 2023). These indicators show the nation's elevated susceptibility to climate hazards and the existing gaps in its ability to manage and mitigate these risks.

As the mercury soars, the nation grapples with the intensification of heatwaves, leading to adverse impacts on agriculture, water resources, and public health (RBI, 2023). This temperature surge has led to more frequent and prolonged heatwaves and contributed to alterations in precipitation patterns, triggering intense and erratic rainfall (RBI, 2023). The years 2022 and 2021 rank as the fifth and sixth warmest, respectively, with annual mean temperatures surpassing the 1981–2010 average by 0.51 and 0.44 degrees Celsius. These rising temperatures only show climate change, evident in the intensifying frequency of extreme weather events (Krishnan et al., 2020; RBI, 2023). The unseasonal rainfall, leading to floods, and severe temperature fluctuations like heatwaves have become increasingly common, affecting various regions, with states such as Maharashtra, Karnataka, Uttar Pradesh, and Madhya Pradesh experiencing frequent unseasonal rains. At the same time, Rajasthan, Haryana, Punjab, Delhi, Uttar Pradesh, and Jharkhand are most affected by heatwaves (RBI, 2023). Simultaneously, there is a noticeable seasonal and temporal volatility of temperature across states, with the winter months shrinking and periods of extended summer temperatures prevalent, contributing to widespread heat waves across Indian states (RBI, 2023).

Climate change is not just a challenge, it's a market failure due to externalities and characteristics of public goods. The costs of burning fossil fuels extend far beyond private expenses, creating a "social cost of carbon" that the market fails to address (RBI, 2023). The actions needed to reduce CO_2 emissions have public good

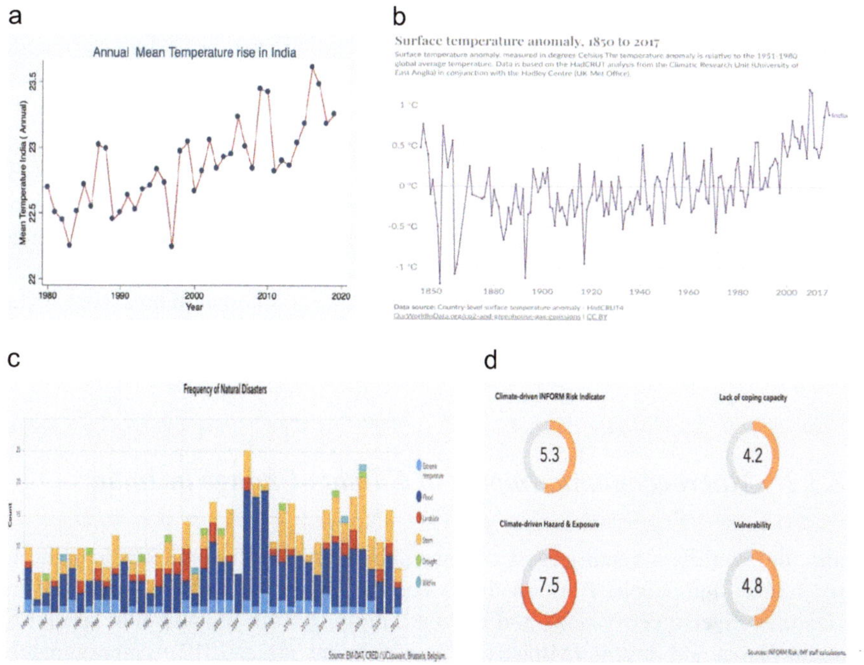

Fig. 18.5 India—temperature trends **a** India-mean temperature rise **b** India-temperature anomalies **c** India-frequency of natural disasters **d** India-IMF climate risk profile

attributes, which requires urgent and significant government intervention to prevent under-provision. The prolonged impact of climate change and the enduring presence of CO_2 in the atmosphere raises inter-generational equity concerns. It's clear that government action is not just important but vital to rectify market failures, internalise costs, and ascertain the provision of essential public goods, all while acknowledging the long-term nature of climate change challenges (RBI, 2023).

Despite its relatively low contribution to global carbon emissions and per capita carbon footprint, India faces a significant trade-off between economic growth and climate change mitigation/adaptation. When comparing the share of global cumulative CO_2 emissions, India's share is less than that of the United States and China, the leading contributors. Even when comparing per capita carbon dioxide, India's emissions are lower than the global average. However, the path of CO_2 emissions tells a different story-in 2020, India emitted less than the United States and China. This stark contrast between India's low emissions and the severity of its climate change impact highlights the need for immediate action.

The "Polluter Pays Principle" and "Common but Differentiated Responsibility principles" in international climate talks are vital for climate justice. While both developed and developing nations share the responsibility, the burden must lean heavily towards the developed world, considering historical and per capita emissions (RBI, 2023). However, this does not grant developing nations unrestricted emission allowances. They must leverage green growth opportunities, unlike the early industrial era (RBI, 2023). Despite being the most populous nation, India's per capita carbon emissions stand at 1.8 tonnes, significantly lower than the US's 14.7 tonnes. India has committed to substantial emissions reduction, aiming for net zero by 2070, largely through aggressive renewable energy plans (RBI, 2023). The discourse on climate change remains top-down, exemplified by India's 2070 net-zero target (RBI, 2023). This urgency stems from the climate emergency and the current availability of low-cost green alternatives that don't compromise economic growth. Climate change demands a global effort but also requires substantial funding, with the onus primarily on the developed world for climate justice. In essence, every nation must contribute, but the financial responsibility must disproportionately rest on the global north (RBI, 2023).

18.3.2 Macroeconomic Impact of Climate Change in India

India, the world's seventh-largest country and second-most populous, is home to over 1.36 billion people. Positioned between the Himalayas and the Indian Ocean, it features diverse ecosystems and cultures, ranging from mountainous terrain to coastal plains and deserts (Ministry of Environment India, 2012). Approximately 43% of the population relies on agriculture, constituting 16% of the GDP in 2019, while the services sector contributes 49.4% and industry contributes 24.8%. The key challenges facing the Indian government involve ensuring equitable and environmentally sustainable growth, promoting high-quality jobs, and addressing environmental issues such as land degradation, poor air quality, and unsustainable groundwater use (RBI, 2023).

Model-based simulations and cross-country studies indicate that rising temperatures adversely impact India more severely than Europe or the United States. Kahn et al. (2021) project that under a business-as-usual scenario, India's per capita GDP could decline by 9.9% to 13.4% by 2100, approximately twice the estimated losses for the European Union, which range from 4.7% to 6.7%. In a district-level analysis across South Asia, Mani et al. (2018) utilised data on average temperature, precipitation, and household surveys to assess the effects of climatic changes on living standards. Their findings show that increases in average temperatures are associated with decreases in living standards in India, Pakistan, Sri Lanka, and Bangladesh compared to a business-as-usual scenario. Especially, Nepal and Afghanistan, which experience colder temperatures, did not exhibit negative impacts. The study also revealed that the relationship between temperature and consumption follows a U-shaped pattern across all South Asian countries (Table 18.4).

Kumar and Maiti (2024b) aimed to investigate the dynamic causal impact of temperature on India's long-term economic growth across different states and sectors. It finds three potential pathways through which temperature changes affect economic growth: labour, capital, and ecosystem services. By applying the CS-ARDL model, the study addresses the limitations of existing research and provides more accurate

Table 18.4 Summary of climate econometrics studies

Author	Dependent variable	Independent variable	Countries	Sample	Conclusion
Jain et al. (2020)	(GSDP) at factor cost	Linear temperature and precipitation	India	1980–2015	Short-run negative impact of temp on economic growth rate but no evidence of long-run damage
Burke et al. (2015b)	GDP Per capita	Non-Linear Temperature	166 countries	1960–2010	Economic productivity is nonlinear in temperature for all countries, with productivity peaking at an annual average temperature of 13 °C
Dell et al. (2012)	GDP Per capita	Temperature	125 countries	1950–2003	Temperature shocks have significant negative effects on the GDP growth of poor countries.
Colacito et al. (2019)	Nominal GSDP	Average temperature, precipitation, and snowfall	US	1957–2012	1°F increase in average summer temperature was associated with a reduction in the annual growth rate of US state-level output of 0.15 to 0.25 percentage points
Kahn et al. (2021)	(GSDP) at factor cost	Linear temperature and precipitation	India	1980–2015	Show that the marginal effects of temperature shocks find that persistent deviations of temperature from its historical norm adversely affect per-capita real output growth, whereas changes in precipitation do not yield statistically significant effects. Moreover, the marginal impact of temperature shocks differs across climatic zones and income groups
Kumar and Maiti (2024b)	(GSDP) growth rate	Linear temperature	India	1980–2019	Long term impact with CS-ARDL model, Decline in GDP by 3.89 percentage points

estimates of the economic impact of climate change in India. The findings suggest that India's GDP growth rates are significantly affected by temperature changes and that tailored adaptation strategies are necessary to mitigate these effects. Furthermore, the study projects substantial GDP growth losses under different emission scenarios, emphasising the importance of proactive climate action. In the next section, we review papers on the impact of temperature and climate-related variables on the sectoral impact.

18.3.3 Sectoral Impact

This review concentrates on panel estimates derived from weather variations and reviews the diverse impacts of weather fluctuations on economic activity, spanning agriculture, labour productivity, health, and energy. Rigorous econometric evidence highlights the multifaceted effects of weather-temperature and precipitation. Economies with limited resources emerge as particularly susceptible to adverse weather effects, accentuating the vulnerability to poverty (Dell et al., 2012; Kumar & Maiti, 2024a; Letta & Tol, 2019). Specific demographic groups, particularly children and the elderly, exhibit increased sensitivity to health-related dimensions affected by weather variations. This review allows for meticulously analysing the intricate linkages between weather and the Indian economy like Dell et al. (2014).

18.3.3.1 Agriculture

The vulnerability of developing countries, particularly India, to the impacts of climate change on agriculture is a topic of increasing concern. Agriculture is uniquely susceptible to the direct impact of climate variations compared to other sectors, and its impact is adverse in developing countries, which are anticipated to have the most severe consequences of climate change (Pachauri et al., 2014). India, characterised by limited per capita arable land and substantial reliance on agriculture, faces amplified vulnerability to the impacts of climate change (Mendelsohn et al., 2006; Nelson et al., 2009; Stern, 2007). Their constrained technological and financial capacities for climate change mitigation and adaptation further worsens this situation. The confluence of biotic and abiotic stresses, worsened by climate change, poses unprecedented challenges to Indian food production systems. However, the persistent challenge of meeting the food demands of a growing population remains formidable.

Three principal approaches-bio-physical crop modelling, the Ricardian or hedonic approach, and the panel data approach-are employed to estimate the impacts of climate change on agriculture. The crop modelling approach assesses temperature impacts on crops through controlled experiments. However, it tends to exaggerate negative and underestimate positive effects, lacking consideration for farmers' responses and adaptation to climate change (Aggarwal & Sinha, 1993). The Ricardian approach posits that land value reflects the present value of future profits or rent in a perfectly competitive market. Assuming constant conditions, farmers maximise profits by allocating land based on declining crop fertility and climate. Similar to the hedonic price method, this approach attributes regional land value or productivity differences to climate variations. Ricardian studies involve regressing land value or net revenue per hectare on climate normal and controls. However, a limitation arises from the assumption of minimal variation in crop choices and production technology over time, irrespective of climate change. Mendelsohn et al. (2010) found that farmland values in Mexico are sensitive to climate using the Ricardian approach. Deschênes and Greenstone (2007) used a panel data approach in the context of US Agriculture and found the negative impact of climate. Deschênes and Greenstone (2007) used yearly changes in temperature and rainfall to affect farming profits, employing actual weather data instead of climate averages. Unlike the Ricardian method, Deschênes and Greenstone (2007) look at yearly figures for land value or revenue per hectare. Applying panel data allows us to consider unchanging factors like soil and elevation and see the short-term effects of farmer adjustments. Spatial fixed effects help absorb location-specific factors impacting agriculture, offering a more comprehensive understanding of the economic impact of climate change on the sector (Birthal et al., 2014).

Guiteras (2009) studied the impact of climate change on Indian agriculture using a 40-year district-level panel data set. Incorporating within-year adaptations by farmers, the study estimated that climate change between 2010 and 2039 could reduce major crop yields by 4.5 to 9%. In the long run (2070–2099), the projected impact is more severe, with yields potentially decreasing by 25% or more. Fishman (2016) investigated the impact of intra-seasonal rainfall variability on major crops over four decades, incorporating district-level data on weather, irrigation, and yields. The study focused on climate change adaptation, emphasising irrigation expansion. Various precipitation measures and "growing season degree-days" for temperature are utilised. Results show irrigated yields outperform rain-fed yields, particularly for rainy season crops, but irrigation is less effective against higher temperatures. Krishnamurthy (2012), using quantile regressions to assess climate change effects on rice and wheat yields. Unlike traditional approaches, (Krishnamurthy, 2012) method considered changes in the entire yield distribution, revealing a significant decline in wheat yield and varied effects on rice yields based on productivity levels and warming influences. Recent papers have also studied the impact of climate change on crop yield (Birthal et al., 2014; Gupta et al., 2014, 2017; Pattanayak & Kumar, 2021; Verma et al., 2020). Amale et al. (2023) found that delayed monsoon decreases crop yield.

Pattanayak et al. (2021) studied climate change's effects on agricultural productivity in Indian districts. Using data from national surveys, it analyses the relationship between Total Factor Productivity (TFP) and climate for two time periods. Findings reveal a 4.5% reduction in productivity with a 1 °C temperature increase. Projections using climate sensitivity and downscaled climate data suggest declining TFP in all states by 2050, with the later period showing more adverse impacts. The results showed increasing climate sensitivity in Indian agriculture over time. Birthal et al. (2021) studied the impact of climatic hazards on agricultural growth in India from 1970 to 2018. The findings reveal that droughts and heat waves have significant negative effects, especially in poorer and agrarian states. However, adaptation measures like irrigation and crop diversification can partially offset these impacts, although their effectiveness decreases with more frequent hazards. Integrating animal husbandry and adjusting fertiliser use also offers sustainable adaptation benefits across various climatic challenges. Kumar and Khanna (2023) find limited adaptation to rising temperatures for rice and wheat. Wheat and maize show small but statistically significant adaptations to changes in precipitation. The effects are asymmetric, with a 1 °C temperature increase reducing rice and wheat productivity by 23% and 9% at lower productivity levels, compared to 6% and 5% at higher levels.

Food security depends on the food production process, and climate change will affect it by influencing food availability, access, supply stability, and price volatility. The impact extends to the availability of food, access to it, supply stability, and price fluctuations. Rice and wheat, crucial staples for many Indians, are expected to see considerable yield declines due to climate changes. The effects on pulse production are also anticipated to be substantial (Gupta et al., 2017). Climate change's repercussions on food production extend beyond crops, affecting other components of agricultural systems, particularly livestock production. Carpena (2019) investigated the impact of droughts on food expenditure and macro-nutrient consumption in rural Indian households. The research revealed a statistically significant and negative effect on household nutrition using random year-to-year variation in dry shocks (rainfall deviation below its long-run mean). A median dry shock leads to a 1% reduction in monthly per capita food spending and upto a 1.4% decrease in calorie, protein, and fat consumption. Droughts affect the quantity and quality of diets, with households relying more on cereals and less on vegetables, fruits, pulses, and animal-sourced foods. The study suggests that a decline in income, rather than higher food prices, is the primary reason for reduced food consumption during droughts.

Birthal and Hazrana (2019) used a panel of district-level data to study the effectiveness of crop diversification in mitigating the harmful effects of climatic shocks on the performance of agriculture in a dynamic setting. Taraz (2017) found that farmers adjust their irrigation investments and their crop portfolios in response to the medium-run rainfall variation.

18.3.3.2 Productivity

This section provides an overview of recent economic studies examining the causal impact of temperature on productivity. Kumar and Maiti (2024a) have shown that the productivity loss can be decomposed into three terms, i.e. loss of productivity due to ecological damage, damage in labour, and capital efficiencies, respectively. Now, we discuss papers that have studied aggregate productivity, labour productivity, capital productivity, and labour supply in the Indian context. Elevated temperatures affect factory workers by reducing productivity and increasing absenteeism. Somanathan et al. (2021) gathered data from workers in cloth weaving, garment sewing, and steel product manufacturing, finding decreased output on hot days and increased absenteeism with current and past temperatures. Climate control in the workplace eliminates productivity declines but not absenteeism, suggesting continued heat exposure at home and outdoors. Analysing a 15 year national panel of manufacturing plants reveals a 2.1% annual output decline for every 1 °C temperature increase. This decline is primarily driven by reduced labour output elasticity due to temperature. The study finds that heat stress contributes to declines in non-agricultural GDP during high temperatures, impacting productivity, and overall well-being. Using three years of daily data from 274 workers in 86 places of a big welding company in India, Gupta and Somanathan (2023) found if it gets 1 °C hotter, workers without climate control are 3.4% more likely to miss work. But for those with climate control, missing work is 2.5% less likely. This happens when it's hotter than 22 °C for those without climate control and hotter than 28 °C for those with climate control.

Colmer (2021) studied the impact of temperature-driven changes in agricultural productivity and revealed that rising temperatures significantly reduce agricultural production, affecting employment and wages for agricultural workers. Colmer (2021) found that the temperature is a more influential factor than rainfall.[5] Despite adverse effects, there is evidence of labour reallocation across sectors, particularly in manufacturing and services, demonstrating the adaptability of local labour markets. Colmer (2021) evidence of labour reallocation across sectors in response to temperature-driven changes in agricultural productivity. Workers move into both the manufacturing and services sectors, indicating the ability of non-agricultural sectors to absorb displaced workers. This suggests that labour reallocation within local labour markets, rather than across districts, is crucial for managing the economic consequences of temperature-driven changes in agricultural productivity. Moreover, it exploits variations in the effects of temperature across different labour regulation environments and finds that regulated firms exhibit a differential response to temperature increases compared to unregulated firms. Liu et al. (2023) investigated the impact of rising temperatures on labour reallocation within local labour markets in developing economies. Focusing on India, the study examined the relationship between climate variations and structural transformation. Using a district-level panel dataset spanning six decades, the research found that increasing temperatures inhibit structural transformation, leading to a rise in agricultural labour and a decline in non-agricultural engagement. This effect is more pronounced over a longer time frame, indicating challenges adapting to sustained higher temperatures. The study attributed these findings to local demand effects, where declining farm

[5] Agricultural productivity shocks influence labor allocation in a two-sector economy. Two mechanisms are discussed: the "labour pull" effect, where increased productivity attracts labour to agriculture due to higher wages, and the "local demand" effect, where rising agricultural incomes stimulate demand for local goods, pulling labour away from agriculture. Liquidity constraints, including migration costs, play a role, with positive productivity shocks potentially easing constraints and promoting rural–urban migration. Additionally, sectoral linkages suggest that lower agricultural prices, resulting from productivity growth, could drive labour reallocation by increasing demand in sectors using agricultural output. For details, see Emerick (2018); Asher et al. (2024); Shanmugan & Baria (2019), Gendered perspective (Afridi et al., 2022; Mahajan, 2017; Maitra & Tagat, 2019).

incomes reduce demand for non-agricultural goods and services. The mechanism underlying these findings revolves around local demand effects. The paper posits that declining farm incomes resulting from lower agricultural productivity reduce the demand for local non-agricultural goods and services. Consequently, there is a contraction in non-agricultural labour demand, leading to increased agricultural labour engagement (Liu et al., 2023). Other potential mechanisms, such as differential labour productivity losses and liquidity and mobility costs, exist but reveal weak evidence supporting their significant role in the observed labour reallocation patterns. Saxena (2023) investigated the impact of climate change on labour adaptation in India, emphasising the inadequacy of mitigation strategies alone. Focusing on sectoral reallocation, migration, and trade, the study explores how rising temperatures affect labour behaviour across agriculture, manufacturing, and services sectors at the district level. The concept of "food problem" in low-income countries is introduced, suggesting that climate-induced agricultural productivity declines worsen adaptation challenges. Empirical findings revealed that extreme temperatures intensify the labour share in agriculture, underscoring the worsening "food problem." Despite the improved market access, inefficiencies in agricultural markets hinder mitigation efforts. Gender-specific responses are noted, with women adapting more through sectoral reallocation, particularly in the service sector. Saxena (2023) contributed to spatial climate change literature by bringing macroeconomic discussions on non-homothetic preferences and the policy debate on climate impact in India. Neog (2022) studied the multifaceted impact of weather anomalies on labour adaptation in rural India, emphasizing the often-overlooked strategy of worker commuting as a response to temperature shocks. Employing individual-level panel data from the Village Dynamics in South Asia dataset for 2010–2014, the research revealed that negative temperature shocks prompt labour out-migration and longer-distance commutes, adversely affecting non-agricultural earnings. Heterogeneous responses, particularly age-related, highlight the need for targeted policy interventions. The study also delves into the influence of temperature anomalies on the non-agricultural sector, demonstrating a negative impact on earnings but no effect on sector participation. By bridging short-run estimates to potential long-term effects, the paper identified evidence of both adaptation and intensification effects, with climate uncertainty influencing the adaptability of different regions. Theoretical underpinnings suggest that temperature shocks impact labour markets through two channels—labour push effects and local demand effects. Other literature in the context of India has also studied the impact of climate change on teacher absence (Léonard, 2019), lower student cognitive performance (Sircar, 2022), loss in human capital (Balakrishnan & Tsaneva, 2021; Dasgupta & Karandikar, 2021; Garg et al., 2020; Singh et al., 2022), differences in the gender pay gap (Mahajan, 2017), sleep (Minor et al., 2022), and gendered labour outcomes (Afridi et al., 2022; Maitra & Tagat, 2024).

18.3.3.3 Industries Output

Climate change manifest through shifts in mean temperature, precipitation patterns, and the frequency of extreme weather events, Pachauri et al. (2014) presented a multifaceted challenge to labour-intensive sectors, particularly the manufacturing and service industries. The manufacturing and service industries, reliant on labour-intensive processes, are not only directly impacted by the health effects on workers within their sectors but also face reduced productivity stemming from climate-induced challenges in the primary sector. Sectors with climate-dependent activities, such as food, brewery, textiles, and natural resource-based industries, witness double-edged repercussions through both labour productivity declines and broader economic impacts. Industries intertwined with climate-dependent primary economic activities, such as those reliant on food, brewery, textiles, and natural resources (timber, pulp, and fishery), confront a dual blow, a direct hit on labour productivity and broader economic reverberations. Moreover, climate change influences consumer preferences, altering the demand for goods and services. Temperature changes, for instance, can shift preferences, impacting industries like wool production. The manufacturing industry experiences market effects through changing consumer tastes and preferences, which calls for climate adaptation and green innovation. Industries facing increased weather-related risks, such as construction and perishable goods production, incur elevated risk premiums, impacting production costs and complicating access to financial loans (Kumar & Yalew, 2012). Increased occupational health risks, triggered by climate-related uncertainties, lead to demands for higher wages, reducing the gross profit of manufacturing industries. Simultaneously, non-agricultural industries, particularly those employing unskilled labour, may benefit from an influx of affordable labour due to rural–urban migration prompted by declining agricultural productivity caused by climate change. In the construction sector, climate variations lead to delays, increased costs, and reputational challenges. In the food and brewery industries, dependencies on agriculture expose vulnerability to climate change. Livestock production faces challenges due to altered forage and higher temperatures. As a primary determinant, agriculture significantly impacts farm income and food security. Warmer years reduce export growth rates, particularly affecting poor countries. The wine and sugar industries exemplify climate sensitive crop impacts. Grape cultivation faces potential shifts in viticulture regions, impacting wine production. Sugar cane production, reliant on climate variables, suffers from climate shocks, impacting economies. Timber, fishery, and mining industries reflect on the bio-physical relationship with climate. Timber industry assessments present mixed findings. Fishery requires adaptive policies for sustainable production. Mining and quarrying operations face challenges from water scarcity and extreme events, impacting labour and financial dynamics. (For a detailed review, see Kumar and Yalew (2012)).

In the context of India, Somanathan et al. (2021) suggests a decline in non-agricultural GDP in India with elevated temperatures. According to Jain et al. (2020), higher temperatures negatively affect the secondary sector, but the impact is smaller and not statistically significant. Microdata research indicates a significant negative effect on manufacturing. In the tertiary sector, higher temperatures are associated with a 1.2 percentage point reduction in growth rates, statistically significant at the 90% confidence level. Sectoral linkages in the Indian economy may contribute to these results.

18.3.3.4 Health, Mortality, and Crime

Weather can directly impact an agent's health through shocks like extreme temperatures, affecting the cardiovascular and respiratory systems. The indirect mechanism involves weather affecting productivity, which is crucial in rural areas dependent on agriculture. Few studies have also established the relationship between temperature and mortality (Burgess et al., 2014, 2017; Fu et al., 2018; Mazdiyasni et al., 2017; Son et al., 2019). Agents seek to minimise damage to their utility by purchasing health-improving goods or reallocating resources between periods. Mitigation involves acquiring health goods, potentially including medicine or services, and adjusting consumption or borrowing to smooth marginal utility over time. Burgess et al. (2017) found a significant difference in the impact of ambient temperatures on mortality in human populations. Analysing district-level weather and mortality data from 1957 to 2000 in India, the study revealed that hot days substantially increase mortality in rural areas, driven by effects on agriculture and productivity. Interestingly, despite being economically poorer, urban India exhibits mortality responses similar to those of the United States. The expansion of bank branches in rural India is identified as a mitigating factor. The research implies potential life expectancy reductions in rural India due to climate change. Expensive air-conditioning is effective but limited to high-income cities, which contrasts with widely used, less effective evaporative coolers in many Indian households. Overall, heat adaptation has reduced heat-related deaths by 21%, generating a $32 billion annual welfare gain, with evaporative coolers contributing two-thirds of these benefits.

Blakeslee and Fishman (2018) studied the relationship between weather, income, and crime in contemporary developing countries, focusing on India. Analysing data from 1971 to 2000, it identifies strong causal links between weather shocks and crime, primarily influenced by agricultural income shocks. Negative rainfall and positive temperature shocks during the main agricultural season leads to increase in property crime rates. The findings highlight more substantial effects of weather shocks on property crimes than non-property crimes, aligning with economic models income mechanisms. Comparing weather shocks and crime with their impact on agricultural production reveals a consistent connection. High temperatures demonstrate larger-than-expected effects, possibly due to psychological responses. The study also noted a consistent relationship between crime and weather over time, with negative rainfall consistently associated with a 5% increase in crime and temperature shocks remaining stable at about 4%. The expansion of irrigation does not seem to mitigate these impacts, suggesting the enduring vulnerability of a segment of society susceptible to weather-induced income shocks and prone to criminal adaptation. Blakeslee et al. (2021) examined the potential rise in crime due to climate change in developing countries, focusing on Karnataka, India. Using a unique dataset from Karnataka, the study distinguished between economically and psychologically driven impacts of weather on crime. Elevated daily temperatures are linked to increased violent crime, while daily rainfall is associated with a decline in crime. Seasonal weather variation, crucial for agricultural incomes, impacts both crime types, showcasing the economic aspect. The study also pays special attention to violence against socially vulnerable groups, demonstrating that daily temperature increases lead to higher violence against women and marginalised communities. Contrary to expectations that economic development might mitigate climate-induced crime, the findings suggest a persistent influence of non-economic factors. While structural transformation may reduce economically driven impacts, non-economic impacts remain unaffected.

18.3.3.5 Energy

The extensive literature on how temperature affects energy consumption—especially in residential settings—highlights its critical role in electricity system design, a relevance that has intensified due to potential climate change. Residential energy demand is sensitive to temperature variations and is influenced by preferences for heating and cooling. The impact of an "unusually warm day" on energy demand depends on factors such as the season, geographic location, and the existing stock of heating and cooling equipment. Auffhammer and Mansur (2014) provide a comprehensive review of the relationship between climate and the energy sector, focusing on feedback effects. Their study examines how temperature changes influence energy consumption across residential, commercial, and industrial sectors. They address both intensive behavioural changes—alterations in the usage patterns of existing capital like air conditioners—and extensive behavioural changes, such as adjustments in capital stock. The authors discuss the potential impacts of climate change on energy expenditures, fuel source choices, and building characteristics, emphasising the importance of understanding both short-term and long-term adaptations. They outline three methodological approaches to studying consumer adaptation to climate change: analysing changes in household consumption in randomly assigned climates, examining cross-sectional climatic variations, and assessing temporal variations through panel data in response to weather shocks.

Gupta (2012) explored the potential impact of global warming on electricity demand in Delhi, India, using a semi-parametric variable coefficient approach. It aimed to quantify the effects of temperature changes on daily electricity demand over a 10-year period and simulate the impact of future temperature increases (Gupta, 2012). The study addressed the U-shaped non-linear temperature-electricity curve, where rising temperatures initially decrease demand due to lower heating requirements but eventually increase demand with higher cooling needs (Gupta, 2012). The study addresses the non-linear temperature-electricity curve, and highlight the unique challenges faced by developing countries. It acknowledges the shift in the temperature-electricity relationship over time due to economic changes and compensates for power outages by adjusting observed electricity consumption (Gupta, 2012).

India's electricity demand, influenced by climate changes, is intricately linked to income growth, especially in the context of adjustments in cooling and heating practices. Analysing data from 28 Indian states over 2005–2009, Gupta (2016) predicted a 6.7% and 8.5% increase in electricity demand by 2030, with 4% and 6% annual GDP growth, respectively, compared to a climate-stable scenario. Harish et al. (2020) examined the changes in electricity demand in response to weather shocks in Delhi and across India, utilising a semi-parametric model for a nuanced understanding of temperature response. On average, aggregate electricity demand in India increases by 11% or more at temperatures exceeding 30 °C, with variations among states. Delhi experiences a surge of 30% or more at such temperatures (Harish et al., 2020). Analysing household-level data reveals limited temperature responses among low-income consumers, especially in slums, highlighting the challenges of climate change adaptation in impoverished communities (Harish et al.,). The findings suggested that increasing affluence will lead to a significant rise in electricity demand for cooling (Harish et al., 2020).

18.3.3.6 Other Sectors

Social scientists are increasingly turning to subjective well-being measures, alongside traditional "objective" indicators like gross domestic product, crime rates, and statistics, to assess welfare. Recently, a handful of studies have revisited the impact of weather on subjective well-being. Household preferences for specific climates stem from various factors, influencing domestic heating and cooling needs, calorific requirements, clothing choices, and outdoor leisure activities. Sociological, psychological, and physiological research indicates that certain climates contribute to health and well-being. Rehdanz and Maddison (2005) examined cross-country averages for subjective well-being using 185 observations from 67 countries and found higher temperatures in the coldest month and lower temperatures in the hottest month increase significantly subjective well-being. Examining data from the World Values Survey across 79 countries Maddison and Rehdanz (2011) investigated the impact of climate on average life satisfaction and their findings showed that countries experiencing a higher number of degree months tend to have significantly lower levels of life satisfaction.

Pailler and Tsaneva (2018) examined how climate variations impact mental health in rural India. Higher temperatures in the preceding year are associated with adverse effects on well-being, particularly in terms of depression, cognition, and coping skills. The impact is linked to hot temperatures during the agricultural season, possibly due to reduced agricultural production. Pailler and Tsaneva (2018) also showed that poverty reduction programmes, such as India's National Rural Employment Guarantee Scheme, may mitigate the effects of weather shocks on psychological well-being. Given the established association between poor mental health, low productivity, and increased healthcare expenditures, particularly in developing countries like India, understanding the repercussions of climate on psychological well-being becomes crucial. Aggarwal (2021) delved into how climate shocks impact the real monthly per capita consumption expenditure of Indian households (1988–2012). The analysis finds increased consumption inequality across sectors due to climatic shocks, urging consideration in climate policy for sustainable development in India (Aggarwal, 2021).

18.3.4 Environmental and Climate Policy of India: History

The evolution of India's environmental legal framework began during the colonial era with significant early efforts focused on forest conservation and pollution control. The Indian Forest Act of 1865 marked one of the earliest legislative measures aimed at regulating forest exploitation and conserving forest resources, primarily to secure a steady supply of timber for British industries and railways. Another notable early legislation was the Shore Nuisance (Bombay and Kolaba) Act of 1853, which addressed water pollution in coastal areas, focusing on preventing the discharge of pollutants into the coastal waters affecting public health and hygiene. The Oriental Gas Company Act of 1857 further advanced water pollution control by penalising companies responsible for polluting water bodies. Complementing these efforts, the Indian Easement Act of 1882 protected riparian rights, providing legal recourse for those affected by upstream water pollution and ensuring downstream water quality. A pivotal development in the evolution of India's environmental governance was the Government of India Act of 1935. This act established a federal structure, delineating responsibilities between central and state governments. This division of powers laid the groundwork for a more structured approach to environmental regulation, enabling both levels of government to legislate on environmental matters. In the early twentieth century, efforts to combat air pollution began to take shape with the Bengal Smoke Nuisance Act of 1905 and the Bombay Smoke Nuisance Act of 1912. These laws targeted the smoke emitted by factories, particularly in urban areas, recognising the adverse health effects of industrial air pollution. The Bengal Act provided for the inspection of industrial premises and imposed fines for violations of smoke emission standards, while the Bombay Act authorised local authorities to take action against polluters, setting a precedent for urban air quality management. Wildlife protection also gained legislative attention during this period. The Elephants' Preservation Act of 1879 was among the earliest efforts to protect wildlife, prohibiting the killing of elephants except under specific licences, thereby addressing the decline in elephant populations due to hunting and habitat loss. Similarly, the Wild Birds and Animals Protection Act of 1912 extended protection to a broader range of wildlife, safeguarding various species during their breeding seasons to maintain ecological balance and biodiversity.

India's commitment to environmental protection continued to grow after gaining independence in 1947. The legislative framework expanded, reflecting the country's progressive stance. The Factories Act of 1948 was a comprehensive piece of legislation regulating labour and industrial conditions, including provisions for waste disposal to address industrial pollution. This act mandated the installation of treatment facilities and safe disposal practices for industrial waste, reflecting the government's commitment to worker safety and environmental health. The River Boards Act of 1956 further aimed to regulate and develop interstate rivers and river valleys, allowing for the creation of river boards to advise on pollution control and integrated development of river basins. The 1970s marked a significant turning point with the introduction of comprehensive environmental legislation. The Water (Prevention and Control of Pollution) Act of 1974 established central and state pollution control boards to regulate and monitor water quality. Adopting a command-and-control approach, the act set effluent standards and authorised the boards to take action against polluters, including fines and imprisonment. This act aimed to prevent and control water pollution by regulating the discharge of pollutants into water bodies. The Water (Prevention and Control of Pollution) Cess Act of 1977 introduced a tax on water consumption by industries and local authorities, generating revenue to support the activities of the pollution control boards and incentivising industries to minimise water use and invest in pollution control measures. The Air (Prevention and Control of Pollution) Act of 1981 extended similar regulatory measures to air pollution, influenced by India's commitments made at the 1972 United Nations Conference on the Human Environment. This legislation required industries to obtain consent from state pollution control boards to operate within designated air pollution control areas, establishing ambient air quality standards and empowering the boards to take action against violators, thereby creating a comprehensive framework for air quality management across the nation. The catastrophic Bhopal gas tragedy of 1984, which resulted in thousands of deaths and injuries due to a gas leak, significantly influenced the enactment of the Environmental Protection Act (EPA) of 1986. This comprehensive "umbrella" legislation consolidated various environmental laws under a single framework and granted extensive powers to the central government to protect and improve environmental quality, prevent and control pollution, and manage hazardous substances. The EPA established nationwide standards for air and water quality, coordinating actions across different regulatory bodies and providing a robust legal basis for environmental governance. Institutional developments paralleled these legislative advancements. In 1980, the Department of Environment (DoE) was established following recommendations from the N.D. Tiwari Committee to coordinate national environmental policies and resource management. In 1985, the DoE was upgraded to the Ministry of Environment and Forests (MoEF), which became the central agency responsible for implementing environmental and forestry programmes. The central and state pollution control boards, initially created under the Water Act, played crucial roles in monitoring pollution and enforcing environmental laws, setting ambient and emission standards for air and water quality.

The evolution of climate policy in India since the 1970s is deeply rooted in the country's commitment to addressing environmental challenges and promoting sustainable development. In the early years of independence, there was no formal environmental policy, but environmental preservation was considered in the national planning procedure and forest strategy. India's legal frameworks played a crucial role in responding to environmental challenges, evolving significantly since the Stockholm Declaration in 1972. The adoption of the Stockholm Declaration in 1972 was a watershed moment, highlighting the importance of environmental preservation in national development and significantly influencing India's environmental policy landscape. M.C. Mehta, an Indian lawyer, significantly influenced environmental legislation in 1985 by arguing that the "right to life" under Article 21 of the Indian Constitution includes the "right to a healthy environment." Mehta's argument granted every Indian citizen the right to petition the Supreme Court of India or a State High Court for environmental law enforcement (Dubash & Joseph, 2016; Saryal, 2018). The environmental policy landscape in India has transformed profoundly since the early years of independence. The establishment of the National Council for Environmental Policy and Planning in 1972 reflected the growing realisation that the development process must incorporate stronger environmental considerations. Key environmental laws, including the Wildlife (Protection) Act of 1972, aimed at safeguarding wildlife and combating illegal activities (Dubash & Joseph, 2016; Saryal, 2018). The Water (Prevention and Control of Pollution) Act of 1974 addressed water quality preservation, and the Forest (Conservation) Act of 1980 focused on conserving forests and preventing non-forest activities without Central Government approval. The Air (Prevention and Control of Pollution) Act of 1981 looked to reduce air pollution through federal and state committees, while the Environment (Protection) Act of 1986 comprehensively safeguarded and improved the environment. The Public Liability Insurance Act of 1991, amended in 1992, warranted the compensation for individuals affected by disasters involving hazardous materials.

In the post-1990s era, India saw a significant evolution in its environmental policy landscape, marked by the introduction of key legislative measures. The National Environmental Tribunal Act (1995, Amended in 2010) established a framework for legal recourse, emphasising compensation for harm caused by activities involving hazardous substances. The subsequent enactment of the National Environment Appellate Authority Act (1997) addressed appeals related to precautions mandated by the Environmental Protection Act, ensuring a fair hearing process. The Biomedical Waste (Management and Handling) Rules (1998) streamlined healthcare waste management, reflecting a more organised approach. The Environment (Siting for Industrial Projects) Rules (1999) provided guidelines for industrial plant locations, emphasising safety and environmental considerations (Dubash & Joseph, 2016; Saryal, 2018). The Municipal Solid Wastes (Management and Handling) Rules (2000) mandated proper waste management by local authorities, addressing urban environmental sustainability. Simultaneously, the Noise Pollution (Regulation and Control) Rules (2000, Amended in 2010) regulated loudspeaker use during cultural or religious activities, preventing noise pollution. The Ozone-Depleting Substances (Regulation and Control) Rules (2000) prohibited substances harmful to the ozone layer, aligning with international conservation efforts. The Energy Conservation Act (2001) promoted energy efficiency and waste reduction, setting guidelines for consumer energy use. The Batteries (Management and Handling) Rules (2001) regulated lead-acid battery collection and recycling, preventing environmental pollution. The Biological Diversity Act (2002) implemented the Convention on Biological Diversity, highlighting conservation and traditional knowledge. The Scheduled Tribes and Other Traditional Forest Dwellers (Recognition of Forest Rights) Act (2006) recognised forest-dwelling communities' rights, addressing historical injustices. In 2010, the National Green Tribunal Act established a tribunal for legal remedies in pollution cases, aligning with the constitutional right to a healthy environment. Collectively, these interventions showcase India's dynamic and proactive approach to diverse environmental challenges, highlighting sustainability and accountability.

In the post-2010 era, India has undergone notable changes in its environmental laws and policies, showcasing a commitment to sustainable development. The introduction of the National Green Tribunal (NGT) in 2010 stands out as a significant development (Dubash & Joseph, 2016; Saryal, 2018). It provides a dedicated platform for addressing environmental disputes and ensuring timely resolutions, in alignment with citizens' right to a healthy environment under Article 21 of the constitution. The Hazardous Wastes Management Regulations of 2016 represented a crucial step towards improving the management of hazardous waste. This amendment to the Hazardous and Other Wastes (Management & Transboundary Movement) Rules set clear guidelines for the handling and disposal of hazardous waste, defining it as any substance posing a threat to human health or the environment. The Compensatory Afforestation Fund (CAF) Act of 2016 focused on mitigating the adverse effects of diverting forest land for non-forest purposes. The establishment of the Compensatory Afforestation Fund Management and Planning Authority (CAMPA) aimed to ascertain transparent and efficient fund utilisation. This act allocated 90% of funds to states, providing financial support for projects like catchment area management, wildlife protection, and conflict resolution between people and wildlife. In 2018, the Coastal Regulation Zone (CRZ) Notification was introduced, following the recommendations of the Shailesh Nayak Committee. This notification classified different coastal zones and implemented regulations to address natural calamities associated with global warming while promoting sustainable coastal development. It aimed to safeguard the welfare of coastal communities, particularly fishers, and preserve wildlife. The Wildlife (Protection) Amendment Bill of 2021, presented before the Lok Sabha, showcased India's commitment to biodiversity conservation. Aligned with the Convention on International Trade in Endangered Species of Wild Fauna and Flora (CITES), this bill sought to increase legal protection for a broader range of species (Dubash & Joseph, 2016; Saryal, 2018). It reflected India's dedication to global environmental cooperation and efforts to combat illegal trade in endangered wildlife (Dubash & Joseph, 2016; Saryal, 2018).

Dubash and Joseph (2016) suggested a more deliberate and tailored approach to institutionalising India's climate response is crucial. This involves a facilitative approach, robust analytical capacity, and institutional structures at multiple levels, along with a high-level strategy group for effective coordination and accountability in climate institutions. Saryal (2018) found two distinct phases in India's climate policy. Initially characterised by idealism and ideology, India asserted that climate change mitigation was primarily the responsibility of wealthier nations. The current pragmatic phase reflects a departure from this stance, with India actively engaging in concrete actions both domestically and on the international stage.

Initially, India's policy was idealistic, shaped by the success of the Montreal Protocol in 1987. Believing that developed nations should take responsibility for mitigation and financial liability, India considered climate change a non-issue, relying on principles like "common but differentiated responsibility," "per capita emission," "equity," and "environmental justice" (Dubash & Joseph, 2016; Saryal, 2018). These principles were outlined in the agreement among developing countries at the New Delhi Conference in 1990, emphasising that developed nations bear the primary responsibility for greenhouse gas emissions. During the Intergovernmental Negotiating Committee (INC) sessions from 1991 to 1992, India advocated for "per capita equity" and opposed international review of national policies, reflecting a cautious stance. The UNFCCC adopted in 1992 acknowledged developed countries' historical role in climate change, yet it did not impose binding obligations on developing nations (Dubash & Joseph, 2016; Saryal, 2018). India's policy revolved around equity-based narratives, emphasising the developed world's responsibility and incorporating the "Polluter Pays Principle." The Kyoto Protocol ratified by India in 2002 allowed the country, as a developing nation, to delay the immediate reduction of greenhouse gas emissions. Hosting COP-8 in 2002, India resisted pressure to intensify efforts, citing its minimal contribution to global emissions. In subsequent conferences, India maintained its stance, highlighting that developing countries lack resources to combat climate change. Concerns about developed countries' attempts to separate environmental and trade issues persisted, reflecting India's apprehensions about re-colonisation and dependence on foreign capital (Dubash & Joseph, 2016; Saryal, 2018).

In the period after 2007, there has been a noticeable shift in India's climate change policy, marked by pragmatic steps. The establishment of the Prime Minister's Council on Climate Change in 2007 and the proposal by Prime Minister Manmohan Singh, known as the "Singh Convergence Principle" (SCP), demonstrated this pragmatism (Dubash & Joseph, 2016; Saryal, 2018). The SCP asserted that India's per capita emissions would not exceed those of industrialised countries, creating a sensible approach that required developed nations to reduce their emissions first. While India's climate policy continued to address climate change from an equity perspective, post-2007, there was an observable change in the rhetoric and signs of willingness to be part of the solution (Dubash & Joseph, 2016; Saryal, 2018). The adoption of the National Action Plan on Climate Change and the "co-benefit approach," linking energy security and climate action, reflected a pragmatic shift. The co-benefit approach aimed to identify measures promoting development objectives while also yielding co-benefits for effective climate change action (Dubash & Joseph, 2016; Saryal, 2018).

India's climate policy has evolved significantly post-2014, marked by the reconstitution of the Prime Minister's Council on Climate Change to enhance effectiveness. Despite this, major political parties have largely side-lined climate change in their agendas, focusing instead on short-term economic gains over long-term sustainability. This omission is evident in vague manifesto commitments that lack specific, measurable actions. For instance, proposed programmes often do not outline clear directives for reducing carbon emissions. For instance, proposed programmes often do not outline clear directives for reducing carbon emissions (Dasgupta, 2024).

Environmental crises, like those highlighted by activists in Ladakh, draw attention to the urgent need for robust climate action integrated into national policies (Dubash & Joseph, 2016; Saryal, 2018). The National Action Plan on Climate Change (NAPCC) is the guiding framework for India's climate efforts, supported by sector-specific strategies like the National Electricity Plan 2023, the National Green Hydrogen Mission, and the Energy Conservation (Amendment) Act, 2022. The National Action Plan on Climate Change (NAPCC) is the guiding framework for India's climate efforts, supported by sector-specific strategies like the National Electricity Plan 2023, the National Green Hydrogen Mission, and the Energy Conservation (Amendment) Act, 2022 (Dasgupta, 2024). Despite these efforts, India's policies are rated as "Highly Insufficient" by the Climate Action Tracker, indicating the need for more ambitious measures.[6]

The National Clean Air Programme (NCAP), launched in 2019, aims to reduce particulate matter pollution by 20–30% in 132 cities by 2024. At the 2021 COP26 summit, India pledged to achieve net-zero emissions by 2070. The Environmental Impact Assessment (EIA) Notification of 2006, though controversially revised in 2020 to expedite industrial clearances, remains central to environmental governance. Judicial activism, especially through Public Interest Litigations (PILs), has significantly influenced environmental policies, with landmark Supreme Court rulings such as the 1996 directive mandating compressed natural gas (CNG) for Delhi's public transport. In international negotiations, India emphasises "common but differentiated responsibilities," advocating for developed nations to lead mitigation efforts while supporting developing countries through finance and technology. Recent initiatives, including the LiFE Mission (Lifestyle for Environment) promoting sustainable consumption, the Green Credit Programme incentivising eco-friendly practices, and PM-PRANAM targeting reduced synthetic fertilizer use, reflect a shift towards innovative, citizen-centric climate action.

A positive development is the Supreme Court ruling in March 2024, which affirmed that Indians have the right to be free from the adverse effects of climate change, invoking Articles 21 and 14 of the Constitution. This ruling enhances accountability and legal scrutiny of government climate actions. The challenge now is to bridge the gap between electoral politics and climate policy. Media and civil society play crucial roles in advocating for environmental sustainability. While expressing commitment to global climate action, India maintained its traditional aversion to external influence. This stance was evident before COP-21, where India stressed that its Intended Nationally Determined Contributions (INDCs) should be determined nationally. India's revised approach highlights two key facets: persistent questioning

[6] For more information on specific policy documents, refer to the National Electricity Plan 2023 at https://powermin.gov.in/en/content/national-electricity-plan, the National Green Hydrogen Mission at https://mnre.gov.in/national-green-hydrogen-mission, and the Energy Conservation (Amendment) Act, 2022 at https://powermin.gov.in/sites/default/files/webform/notices/The_Energy_Conservation_Amendment_Act_2022.pdf.

of developed states' moral responsibility and the introduction of a new role as a guardian of Nature. India combines arguments of historical responsibility and equity with the invocation of cultural elements that treat Nature as sacred.

18.3.5 Progress and Future Impact of Climate Change on the Indian Economy

Climate change poses a significant threat to India's economic stability and growth, as highlighted by projections and scenarios depicted in the provided graphs. The future impact of climate shocks on India paints a potentially grim picture if decisive actions are not taken to mitigate the effects. Figure 18.6(a) illustrates the potential GDP gains if India undertakes vigorous climate action. The "Delayed Transition (Disorderly Scenario)" and the "Net Zero 2050 (Orderly Scenario)" show that proactive investments in green technology, renewable energy, and sustainable practices can increase economic growth. These scenarios show the benefits of a well-planned transition to a low-carbon economy. However, the more probable and concerning outlook is depicted in Fig. 18.6(b), which outlines GDP losses under different scenarios should current policies persist. The "Current Policies (Hot house world scenario)" and the "Net Zero 2050 (Orderly Scenario)" both indicate varying degrees of economic decline, with the former predicting more severe losses due to inadequate climate action. This scenario underscores the physical risks of ongoing climate change, such as more frequent and severe extreme weather events, which disrupt economic activities, damage infrastructure, and reduce productivity. The gravity of these projections is further highlighted by Fig. 18.6(c), which presents GDP losses due to climate change under various Shared Socioeconomic Pathways (SSPs). The SSP scenarios (SSP126, SSP245, SSP370, SSP585) offer different trajectories based on levels of climate action and socioeconomic development. All scenarios predict a decline in GDP growth rates, with the most severe losses occurring under higher emission pathways (SSP370 and SSP585). The table shows how climate change could affect India's economy in the future. It predicts that by 2050, India's GDP might decrease between 1.91% and 9.87% due to climate change, depending on different situations and policies.

In the short term, India is already experiencing the consequences of climate change. The increasing frequency of extreme weather events such as floods, droughts, and heatwaves have immediate impacts, including infrastructure damage, agricultural losses, and health crises. These events strain public resources and disrupt economic activities, leading to immediate economic setbacks. Long-term consequences are even more alarming. Persistent climate impacts are projected to result in continued economic decline, increased costs for adaptation and mitigation, and significant social upheavals. For instance, rising sea levels and more intense weather patterns may force

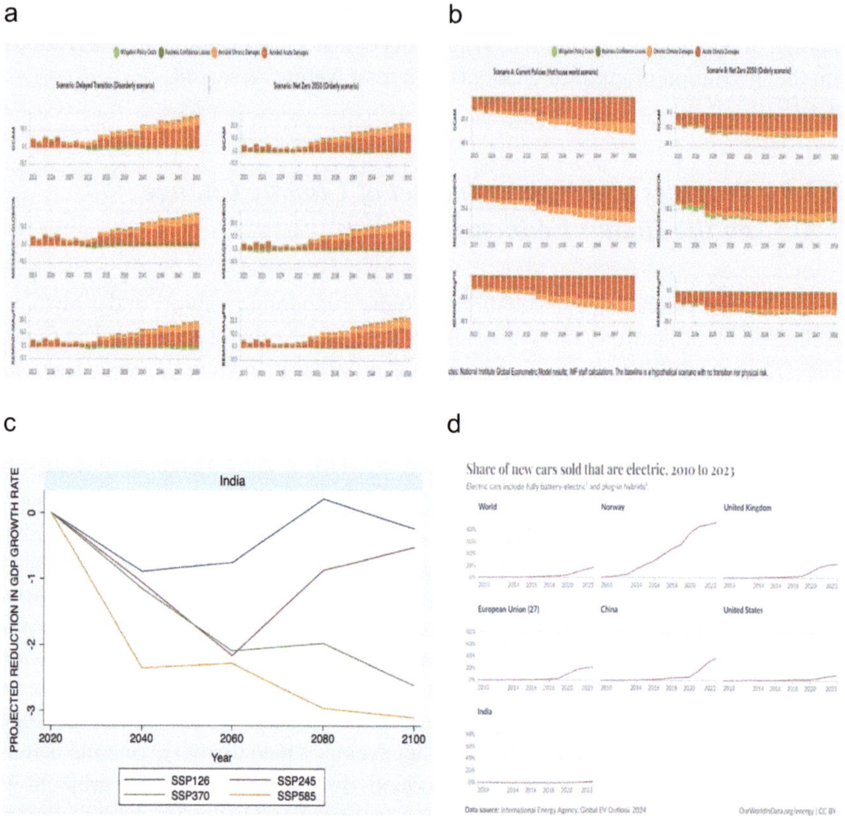

Fig. 18.6 Future impact of climate shocks in India **a** India-GDP gain if taken climate actions (NIGEM) **b** India-GDP losses under different scenarios (NIGEM) **c** India-GDP losses due to climate change (Kumar & Maiti, 2024b) **d** India-progress in adoption of electric vehicles

large-scale migration, disrupt communities, and lead to loss of livelihoods. The cumulative economic burden from these impacts could severely undermine India's development trajectory. The progress in the adoption of electric vehicles (EVs), as shown in Fig. 18.6(d), provides a glimmer of hope for mitigating future climate impacts. The increased share of EVs in the market signifies a shift towards reducing carbon emissions from the transportation sector. However, this progress is insufficient to meet India's ambitious net-zero target by 2070. Achieving this target will require a substantial acceleration in adopting clean technologies, significant improvements in energy efficiency, and comprehensive policy measures to support these transitions. India's net-zero targets by 2070 is critical in mitigating climate change impacts. This target entails transitioning to renewable energy sources, enhancing energy efficiency, and drastically reducing greenhouse gas emissions.

Meeting this target is crucial for mitigating the long-term economic impacts of climate change and ensuring sustainable development.

Table 18.5 shows the severe economic impacts of climate change on India and the world. The NGFS, NiGEM (2024) study indicates that stringent policies (below 2 °C) could limit India's GDP loss to 1.91% by 2030 and 3.80% by 2050. Without stronger action, current policies could result in a 9.87% GDP loss by 2050, highlighting the need for better mitigation. The OECD (2015) and Dellink et al. (2019) studied project a wide range of GDP declines (1.9% – 12.5% by 2060), showing the uncertainty and potential severity of impacts. Kahn et al. (2021) forecasted a 13.39% GDP decline for India by 2100 under high emissions (RCP 8.5), stressing the dire consequences of not limiting warming. Kiley (2021) estimated GDP declines upto 3.66%, indicating significant impacts from temperature increases. Swiss Re (2021) showed that meeting the Paris targets could limit India's GDP losses to 0.8% – 5.7%, but severe warming could cause a 35.1% decline, underscoring the risks of inaction. Kumar and Maiti (2024b) predict a catastrophic 25.0% GDP decline for India by 2100 under high emissions (RCP 8.5). These estimates paint a gloomy picture for India, which is facing substantial economic losses without strong climate action. To mitigate these impacts, India must adopt stringent policies, invest in sustainable technologies, and enhance adaptive capacities to ensure sustainable development and reduce vulnerabilities.

18.4 Adaptation and Mitigation—Role of Fiscal, Regulatory, and Monetary Policy

Climate change is the most profound market failure in history,[7] which calls for urgent global action and collaboration. Developed nations, particularly affluent ones, must lead by adopting ambitious emissions reduction targets, effective market mechanisms, and supporting anti-deforestation programmes. The urgency emanates from the disproportionate vulnerability of poor nations to climate change impacts juxtaposed against the historical emissions culpability of rich nations. The costs of this plan are small compared to the risks it prevents. Properly executed, it can eliminate the need for massive future spending on adaptation (Stern, 2007).

International climate agreements call for a shift to a low-carbon economy, a massive change unlikely to be driven by market mechanisms alone due to inherent market failures. Policy action is crucial, with a focus on energy and carbon pricing policies. However, high emissions, fossil fuel dominance, and low-carbon prices suggest the need for additional complementary policies (Krogstrup & Oman, 2019). Achieving a net-zero economy for India demands a profound "deep decarbonisation" strategy covering power, transportation, industry, construction, agriculture, and lifestyle changes. India's Mission LiFE focuses on sustainable living to reduce carbon footprints. Despite the gradual adoption of greener practices, the vast scale of the transition requires immediate and comprehensive policy interventions. The

[7] The problem of greenhouse gas emissions is linked to several market failures, like a lack of information on emission reduction, network effects, and insufficient incentives for innovation.

Table 18.5 Estimated economic impacts of climate change on GDP for India and the world

Authors	Time horizon	Outcome	India estimated negative impact	World estimated negative impact
NGFS-NIGEM (2024)	2030	GDP (Below 2 °C)	1.91%	1.67%
NGFS-NIGEM (2024)	2050	GDP (Below 2 °C)	3.80%	3.02%
NGFS-NIGEM (2024)	2030	GDP (NDC)	3,16%	2.14%
NGFS-NIGEM (2024)	2050	GDP (NDC)	9.08%	5.74%
NGFS-NIGEM (2024)	2030	GDP (Current Policies)	2.86%	1.63%
NGFS-NIGEM (2024)	2050	GDP (Current Policies)	9.87%	6.05%
OECD (2015)	2060	GDP (ECS 1.5 °C–4.5 °C)	1.9% to 8.4%	–
OECD (2015)	2060	GDP (ECS 1 °C–6°C)	1.2% to 12.5%	–
LoPalo et al. (2019)	Near-term	Consumption-equivalent losses (business-as-usual)	29% per year for 20 years	–
LoPalo et al. (2019)	Near-term	Consumption-equivalent losses (3.5 °C increase)	10% per year for 20 years	–
Kahn et al. (2021)	2100	GDP (RCP 2.6)	3.69%	1.57%
Kahn et al. (2021)	2100	GDP (RCP 8.5)	13.39%	9.96%
Kiley (2024)	2100	Quadratic Marginal Impact	1.30% to 3.66%	–
Kiley (2024)	2100	Linear/low Income Marginal Impact	1.2% to 3.37%	–
Swiss Re (2021)	Paris target	GDP (Well below 2 °C increase)	0.8% to 5.7%	0.5% to 4.2%
Swiss Re (2021)	2.0 °C increase	GDP	2.0% to 17.4%	1.3% to 11.0%
Swiss Re (2021)	2.6 °C increase	GDP	3.2% to 27.0%	1.7% to 13.9%
Swiss Re (2021)	3.2 °C increase	GDP	4.0% to 35.1%	2.2% to 18.1%
Swiss Re (2021)	3.2 °C increase (severe case)	GDP	4.0% to 35.1%	2.2% to 18.1%
Kumar and Maiti (2024b)	2100	GDP (RCP 2.6)	5.0%	–
Kumar and Maiti (2024b)	2100	GDP (RCP 8.5)	25.0%	–

NDC: Nationally Determined Contributions; ECS: Equilibrium Climate Sensitivity; Business-as-usual scenario assumes no significant policy changes to mitigate climate change; SDP: State Domestic Product; RCP: Representative Concentration Pathway existing low-carbon development strategy must be dynamic, reflecting international experiences and prompt actions for net-zero success.

According to RBI (2023), addressing the carbon challenge involves replacing 40% of emissions with renewable, 15% through EVs, while 45% from hard-to-abate sectors require attention due to technology limitations or prohibitive costs. A balanced policy intervention, integrating fiscal, technology, regulatory, trade, and monetary levers, could reduce emissions from 3.9 to 0.9 gigatonnes by 2030. Mitigation efforts must also consider substantial resources for adaptation and disaster management, presenting challenges in financial planning (RBI, 2023). Access to technology and minerals is another dimension, with an increasing reliance on new technologies requiring substantial R&D investment (RBI, 2023). Geo-economic fragmentation raises uncertainty about resource access. Each sector faces challenges hindering the green transition's pace, which demands a multi-pronged policy approach with incentives and enforcement (RBI, 2023).

Figures 18.7(a–d) provide critical insights into global progress towards a sustainable environment. Figure 18.7(a) highlights financial support trends through the Green Climate Fund, underscoring the gap between current funding and the $100 billion annual goal. Figures 18.7(b) and (c) illustrate global commitments to net-zero emissions and carbon trading systems, with a significant portion of the world yet to pledge or implement comprehensive strategies. Figure 18.7(d) showcases the adoption of carbon taxes, revealing a slow and uneven uptake critical for driving emissions reductions.

Against this backdrop, this section explores policy choices for India's greener future, covering fiscal, regulatory, and monetary aspects. We also briefly discuss the case for policy action and review the literature on how macroeconomic and financial policies can contribute to climate mitigation and adaptation.

18.4.1 Fiscal Policy

Climate change is framed as a negative externality, with market prices not reflecting the true social cost of carbon, leading to significant negative externalities from greenhouse gas emissions. Furthermore, climate change mitigation is considered a public good,[8] implying non-market interdependence[9] and complexities beyond emissions' effect on future climate (Krogstrup & Oman, 2019).

[8] Climate change mitigation as a public good, emphasizing its value through the prism of the Social Value of Mitigation Actions (SVMA). This conceptual approach considers the broad interdependence between human activities and natural systems, encompassing non-market interactions and co-benefits of mitigation. Both the externality and SVMA perspectives point to markets under providing mitigation, failing to consider externalities and co-benefits, resulting in the over-emission of GHGs or under-provision of mitigation investments.

[9] Government failures further complicate the situation. Common pool problems at national and local government levels, along with collective action issues and capture by powerful interest groups, impede climate mitigation actions. Political agendas influenced by those benefiting from the status

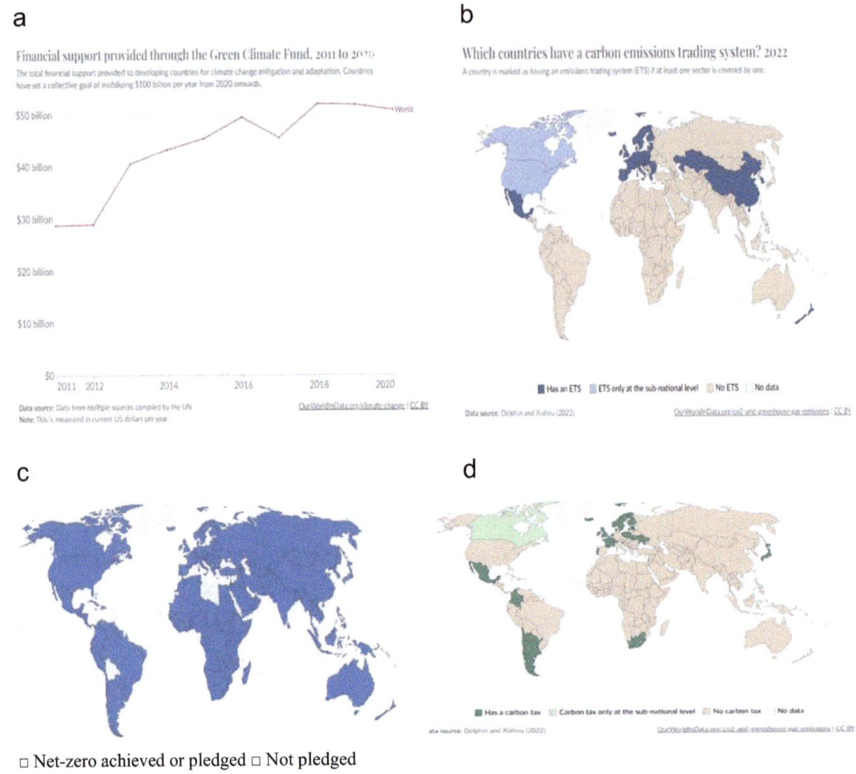

Fig. 18.7 Progress towards sustainable environment across globe **a** Green climate fund pledges. **b** Which countries have set net-zero emission targets? **c** Which countries have set carbon emission targets? **d** Which countries have adopted carbon tax. *Source* Our World in Data (Ritchie et al., 2024)

Market failures, such as externalities from carbon-intensive goods and the under-provision of mitigation, which requires a policy intervention. Weitzman (1974) discussed the choice of policy instruments for regulating a market where government intervention is required due to market failure. The central question is whether a price (tax) or quantity (permit) instrument leads to the best welfare outcome, measured as net social surplus. The decision must be made before uncertainties are resolved (RBI, 2023). When costs are certain, both price and quantity controls can achieve the same outcomes. However, when costs are uncertain, fixing marginal cost through a price instrument leads to uncertain production levels, and fixing the level of production with a quantity instrument leads to uncertain marginal costs (RBI, 2023). Weitzman (1974) result suggests that price instruments are favoured when marginal benefits are relatively flat, and quantity instruments are favoured when marginal costs are relatively flat (RBI, 2023).

quo may stifle efforts for change. Time inconsistency and an inability to commit due to democratic election cycles further constrain governments in making long-term commitments to climate action.

Fiscal policy can be a powerful tool for addressing climate change by creating economic incentives and disincentives that guide behaviour towards more sustainable practices. To achieve the net-zero goal by moving from industries that harm the environment to eco-friendly ones, we need structural change in resource allocation and invest more, and the government's money plans (fiscal policy) are crucial. This involves using tools like taxes and subsidies to support green efforts. It's important because, on the one hand, the government gives a lot of money to support harmful fossil fuels, but on the other hand, they spend a good amount on protecting the environment (RBI, 2023). This balancing act is necessary because climate change can hurt our finances in the long run (RBI, 2023). Fiscal tools can be categorised into three main groups: price policies (including taxation and subsidies), spending and investment, and public guarantees (Krogstrup & Oman, 2019).

Carbon pricing is really important for dealing with climate change. Having the right pricing system is key for it to work well. This means considering all the environmental costs linked to carbon emissions, like climate change, local air pollution, traffic problems, accidents, and road damage. There are two main ways to do carbon pricing: through taxes or cap-and-trade schemes (RBI, 2023). Carbon taxes are a form of environmental taxation. The basic idea is to assign a monetary value to the amount of carbon dioxide (CO_2) and other greenhouse gases emitted when fossil fuels are consumed. These taxes aim to internalise the external costs associated with climate change and environmental degradation caused by carbon emissions. The primary purpose of carbon taxes is to incentivise businesses and individuals to reduce their carbon footprint and transition towards cleaner, more sustainable energy sources. They incentivise a shift to cleaner energy sources, as seen in effective implementations in Finland, Sweden, and Norway. However, achieving a 2 °C limit may require a swift increase in tax rates to $75 per tonne by 2030. In India, a 50 per tonne clean energy cess on coal was introduced in 2015. Particularly, carbon taxes can be regressive, impacting social welfare and increasing income inequality. Carbon taxes on fossil fuels can have distributional consequences, often being regressive and potentially reducing social welfare while increasing income inequality (RBI, 2023). To address this, revenue recycling, car-marking tax revenues for citizen welfare schemes, can enhance public support for carbon taxation. The impact of carbon taxes also depends on the utilisation of tax proceeds. Three potential ways to use tax revenue include providing a lump sum dividend to households, implementing a corporate tax rate cut, or reducing income tax. The last option, as seen in Finland, may be a preferred policy tool to mitigate the adverse impact of a carbon tax, improving progressivity, income, and employment (RBI, 2023).

An Emission Trading Scheme (ETS) is a policy tool that creates a market for greenhouse gas emissions permits. Governments set an overall cap on emissions, and companies can buy or trade permits. In the event of a company exceeding its emission limit, it must procure additional permits from others (RBI, 2023). This framework incentivises companies to explore cost-efficient methods of pollution reduction. Similar to a carbon tax, an Emission Trading Scheme (ETS) presents both challenges and benefits. Implementing a new carbon pricing mechanism like ETS may require a restructuring of the existing carbon tax and subsidy framework (RBI, 2023).

Several Emerging Market Economies (EMEs) have already embraced carbon pricing mechanisms, accounting for a substantial portion of global greenhouse gas emissions. These mechanisms include ETS or carbon taxes, with the goal of curbing emissions and advancing sustainable practices. Mexico, for instance, conducted several pilot programmes before the operationalisation of its ETS market in 2020. China implemented a national ETS market in 2021 following trials in eight provinces (RBI, 2023). The introduction of ETS provides a transformational alternative to traditional command-and-control policies, which are often criticised for being expensive, inflexible, and reliant on imposing costly penalties (RBI, 2023). ETS, on the other hand, is anticipated to offer emissions reduction certainty without significantly altering existing carbon tax or subsidy structures. The adoption of carbon pricing mechanisms, such as a carbon tax or an ETS, is a critical component of India's strategy to address climate change and achieve its decarbonisation goals (RBI, 2023). Sovereign green bonds (SGBs), akin to traditional government securities but with a unique "use of proceeds" clause, earmark funds exclusively for green investments. SGBs offer advantages such as lower refinancing risk and a "green premium" due to increased transparency (RBI, 2023). Fiscal measures are crucial for promoting clean technologies, including increased budgetary allocation for R&D and compensating losses during the transition. Investing in climate-resilient infrastructure and earmarked resources for post-disaster loss management are vital components of a sound fiscal policy (RBI, 2023).

18.4.2 Monetary Policy

Monetary policy, traditionally associated with short-term stabilisation, is now being reconsidered in the context of long-term climate change mitigation. While fiscal authorities usually handle long-term policies, some argue for integrating climate considerations into the central bank's balance sheet as part of the initial defence against climate risks. Climate change and mitigation policies can influence supply shocks, business cycles, risk, and volatility, affecting various economic aspects. While most central banks are cautious about directly integrating climate concerns into their monetary policy, the ECB and BoE stand out for explicitly incorporating climate change considerations. The impact of emission reduction through a carbon tax is estimated to be four times greater than that achievable through green quantitative easing (Abiry et al., 2022). In spite of this, green QE is recognised as a valuable complementary policy instrument. The evolving dynamics of monetary policy transmission, influenced by climate change, may impede the credit and interest rate channels, particularly for sectors facing adverse climate-induced risks (RBI, 2023).

Climate change could alter how monetary policy works. Sectors facing climate risks might see higher costs and reduced borrowing channels. One key tool, Quantitative Easing (QE), was used after the financial crisis, and it involves large-scale asset purchases (RBI, 2023). When central banks engage in the purchase of corporate debt, they reduce the risk premium, enhancing corporations' ability to finance their activities at lower costs. Asset purchases typically follow the principle of "market neutrality," where bonds are acquired in proportion to their outstanding quantity in the market to minimise the impact on relative borrowing costs across sectors (RBI, 2023). However, the market neutrality principle can be suboptimal, creating a pro-carbon bias by favouring large firms in carbon-intensive industries. For example, over 70% of the European Central Bank's (ECB) corporate bond holdings were associated with sectors having a high or very high impact on nature (RBI, 2023). The ECB initiated the process of decarbonising its corporate bond holdings in October 2022, with a focus on issuers with a higher climate score. This score considers backwards-looking emissions, forward-looking targets, and climate disclosure. Similarly, the Bank of England (BoE) began greening its corporate bond portfolio in November 2021, setting an intermediate target of reducing the weighted average carbon intensity by 25% by 2025(RBI, 2023).Some central banks have introduced new monetary policy tools to provide low-cost funds to financial institutions, directing them towards private firms involved in clean energy, energy conservation, and carbon reduction technologies (RBI, 2023). The Bank of Japan (BoJ) and the People's Bank of China (PBoC) have implemented such measures, supporting climate change responses with 0% interest loans and carbon emission reduction facilities, respectively (RBI, 2023).

The European Central Bank (ECB) and the Reserve Bank of India are considering policy changes to address climate risks in their operations. The ECB plans to restrict collateral from high carbon entities, aiming to improve with better climate data. The ECB's move towards green collateral aligns with global efforts to incorporate environmental considerations into financial systems. The disclosure requirements on climate-related assets as collateral are anticipated to be in place by 2026. This trend is notable globally, with central banks increasingly adopting policies that reflect climate considerations in their operations (RBI, 2023).

Furthermore, the adoption of Central Bank Digital Currency (CBDC) is explored for its potential environmental benefits. CBDCs can be more environmentally friendly than traditional cashless methods, reducing energy consumption in payment processes. Designed with Environmental, Social, and Governance (ESG) objectives, CBDCs could offer instantaneous, final payments while minimising reliance on energy-intensive infrastructure (RBI, 2023). The transition to CBDCs could contribute to lower energy consumption compared to existing payment systems, aligning with sustainable practices (RBI, 2023).

18.4.3 Regulatory Policy

The regulatory policy for climate change mitigation goes beyond traditional elements, aiming to bolster industries against climate events, guarantee financial stability, and position them as key contributors to financing technologies that drive a low-carbon economy. Initially voluntary, corporate social responsibility (CSR) has become a mandatory compliance tool, legislated by the government, acting as a catalyst for the green transition by guiding corporations towards activities with positive externalities. As financial regulators, central banks possess tools to influence investments and credit allocation for sustainability goals. They can enforce regulations on banks, requiring them to disclose climate-related risks and mispricing of assets and sharp price corrections in the future, incorporate environmental factors into risk management, and maintain a minimum Green Asset Ratio (GAR) (RBI, 2023). These measures prevent misallocation of assets and encourage financial institutions to invest in sustainable projects, reducing reliance on carbon-intensive sectors. Green finance, crucial for achieving climate goals, encompasses funding for green investments and policies promoting mitigation or adaptation. The estimated cumulative expenditure for adapting to climate change in India by 2030 is 85.6 lakh crore (RBI, 2023). Central banks, acting as financial regulators, employ policy instruments to influence investment decisions, focusing resources on sustainability targets through disclosure requirements, environmental risk management, and green asset ratios (RBI, 2023) A taxonomy of green finance aids funding institutions in analysing climate risks, facilitating increased funding for environmentally friendly projects. Especially, regulatory measures related to green bonds in India gained significance. SEBI issued guidelines defining purposes for raising funds through "green debt security" and introducing sub-categories like blue and yellow bonds (RBI, 2023).

Macroprudential regulation seeks to mitigate systemic risks by expanding stress testing frameworks to include the potential impact of climate-related events on banks' balance sheets (RBI, 2023). Discussion revolves around adjusting risk weights and introducing an "environment coefficient" to incentivise banks to allocate more loans to green sectors. The green supporting factor (GSF) is a tool that makes it easier for banks to invest in environmentally friendly projects by lowering capital requirements. However, it has a drawback—green investments may still be risky. Banks can also face problems if their ratings drop due to investing in risky environmental assets, affecting their profitability (RBI, 2023).

18.4.4 Climate Change Adaptation

Climate change adaptation[10] involves making adjustments to the impacts of climate change to minimise harm and leverage opportunities for both humans and natural systems. It includes strategies in infrastructure, institutions, behaviour, and nature-based solutions. Developing countries, facing increased vulnerability, especially in sectors like food and water, require effective adaptation planning. Mitigation aims to reduce the severity of climate change by lowering the emission of greenhouse gases (RBI, 2023).

[10] The Intergovernmental Panel on Climate Change (IPCC) defines climate change adaptation as the process of adjustment to actual or expected climate and its effects to moderate harm or take advantage of beneficial opportunities.

India's climate change adaptation policies are primarily driven by the National Action Plan for Climate Change (NAPCC), launched in 2008, comprising missions focused on critical sectors like agriculture, water, and the Himalayan ecosystem. These initiatives aim to enhance adaptive capacity and reduce vulnerability. State-specific strategies outlined in State Action Plans on Climate Change (SAPCCs) complement national efforts. Particularly, the agricultural sector receives emphasis through initiatives like the National Mission for Sustainable Agriculture (NMSA), promoting integrated farming systems and efficient water management. These targeted policies emphasise India's commitment to building resilience in the face of climate change (RBI, 2023).

18.5 Conclusion and Policy Recommendation

This chapter has provided an in-depth analysis of the economic impacts of climate change in India, particularly focusing on the effects of rising temperatures and extreme weather events. The discussion began with an overview of global climate dynamics, addressing methodological issues related to climate data collection and modelling. It then moved to an examination of India's vulnerability to climate shocks, detailing the macroeconomic impacts on key sectors such as agriculture, water resources, and coastal regions. The evolution of India's environmental policies was also reviewed, alongside an assessment of the role of fiscal, regulatory, and monetary policies in supporting climate adaptation and mitigation.

The review lays a robust foundation for understanding climate change at both global and regional scales by providing a theoretical review of climate change modelling and delving into historical policy measures. Furthermore, the examination of temperature impacts on various sectors, from agriculture to non-agricultural GDP and human health, adds granularity to our understanding. The study highlights the intricate relationship between temperature rise and sectors like manufacturing, services, agriculture, and energy, elucidating the vulnerability of labour-intensive industries. The chapter also traces the evolution of India's climate policy, capturing its transformation from an idealistic phase to a pragmatic approach. This historical perspective provides critical insights into the proactive measures and policy shifts, contributing to the broader discourse on climate governance. In essence, this chapter goes beyond being a mere update; it represents an effort to systematically review the implications of temperature fluctuations on India's diverse economic sectors. While this study offers an updated review, several limitations must be acknowledged. The study mainly focuses on temperature impacts, which may overlook other climate variables such as precipitation and extreme weather events. Moreover, the adaptation measures discussed are primarily driven by national and state-level policies, potentially missing out on grassroots-level initiatives and localised impacts. Moreover, while the study covers a broad range of impacts, some sectors and indirect effects may not have been fully explored. Future research should explore other climate variables and their effects, localised impacts, and grassroots-level adaptation measures. It also calls for more granular studies on the vulnerability of labour-intensive industries and the effectiveness of current climate policies and adaptation strategies.

Acknowledgments The author gratefully acknowledges the editorial guidance of Professor K. L. Krishna, whose timely correspondence and meticulous corrections were invaluable. Further gratitude is extended to Professor Bishwanath Goldar. The author also thanks the anonymous reviewer for useful comments. Appreciation is due to the organisers and participants of the workshop "Growth, Development and Productivity: 75 Years of Indian Experiences" (CDE/DSE, March 2024) for their stimulating discussions and constructive feedback. This paper solely focuses on the impact of temperature on the Indian economy. Usual disclaimers apply.

References

Abiry, R., Ferdinandusse, M., Ludwig, A., & Nerlich, C. (2022). *Climate change mitigation: How effective is green quantitative easing?* (No. 2701). ECB Working Paper.

Acemoglu, D., Johnson, S., & Robinson, J. A. (2001). The colonial origins of comparative development: An empirical investigation. *American Economic Review, 91*(5), 1369–1401.

Acevedo, S., Mrkaic, M., Novta, N., Pugacheva, E., & Topalova, P. (2020). The effects of weather shocks on economic activity: What are the channels of impact? *Journal of Macroeconomics, 65*, Article 103207.

Afridi, F., Mahajan, K., & Sangwan, N. (2022). The gendered effects of droughts: Production shocks and labor response in agriculture. *Labour Economics, 78*, Article 102227.

Aggarwal, P. K., & Sinha, S. K. (1993). Effect of probable increase in carbon dioxide and temperature on wheat yields in India. *Journal of Agricultural Meteorology, 48*(5), 811–814.

Aggarwal, R. (2021). Impacts of climate shocks on household consumption and inequality in India. *Environment and Development Economics, 26*(5–6), 488–511.

Amale, H. S., Birthal, P. S., & Negi, D. S. (2023). Delayed monsoon, irrigation and crop yields. *Agricultural Economics, 54*(1), 77–94.

Asher, S., Campion, A., Gollin, D., & Novosad, P. (2024). *The long-run development impacts of agricultural productivity gains: Evidence from irrigation canals in India.*

Auffhammer, M., Hsiang, S. M., Schlenker, W., & Sobel, A. (2013). Using weather data and climate model output in economic analyses of climate change. *Review of Environmental Economics and Policy.*

Auffhammer, M., & Mansur, E. T. (2014). Measuring climatic impacts on energy consumption: A review of the empirical literature. *Energy Economics, 46*, 522–530.

Balakrishnan, U., & Tsaneva, M. (2021). Air pollution and academic performance: Evidence from India. *World Development, 146*, Article 105553.

Birthal, P. S., & Hazrana, J. (2019). Crop diversification and resilience of agriculture to climatic shocks: Evidence from India. *Agricultural Systems, 173*, 345–354.

Birthal, P. S., Hazrana, J., & Negi, D. S. (2021). Impacts of climatic hazards on agricultural growth in India. *Climate and Development, 13*(10), 895–908.

Birthal, P. S., Khan, T., Negi, D. S., & Agarwal, S. (2014). Impact of climate change on yields of major food crops in India: Implications for food security. *Agricultural Economics Research Review, 27*(2), 145–155.

Blakeslee, D., Chaurey, R., Fishman, R., Malghan, D., & Malik, S. (2021). In the heat of the moment: Economic and non-economic drivers of the weather-crime relationship. *Journal of Economic Behavior & Organization, 192*, 832–856.

Blakeslee, D. S., & Fishman, R. (2018). Weather shocks, agriculture, and crime: Evidence from India. *Journal of Human Resources, 53*(3), 750–782.

Burgess, R., Deschenes, O., Donaldson, D., & Greenstone, M. (2014). *The unequal effects of weather and climate change: Evidence from mortality in India.* Massachusetts Institute of Technology, Department of Economics. Manuscript.

Burgess, R., Deschenes, O., Donaldson, D., & Greenstone, M. (2017). Weather, climate change and death in India. *University of Chicago*, 577–617.

Burke, M., & Emerick, K. (2016). Adaptation to climate change: Evidence from US agriculture. *American Economic Journal: Economic Policy, 8*(3), 106–140.

Burke, M., Hsiang, S. M., & Miguel, E. (2015a). Climate and conflict. *Annual Review of Economics, 7*(1), 577–617.

Burke, M., Hsiang, S. M., & Miguel, E. (2015b). Global non-linear effect of temperature on economic production. *Nature, 527*(7577), 235–239.

Calvin, K., Dasgupta, D., Krinner, G., Mukherji, A., Thorne, P. W., Trisos, C., Hauser, M., et al. (2023). IPCC, 2023: Climate change 2023: Synthesis report, summary for policymakers. Contribution of Working Groups I, II and III to the Sixth Assessment Report of the Intergovernmental Panel on Climate Change [Core Writing Team, H. Lee, & V. Romero, Eds.]. IPCC, Geneva, Switzerland. *IPCC, 2023: Climate Change 2023: Synthesis Report. Contribution of Working Groups I, II and III to the Sixth Assessment Report of the Intergovernmental Panel on Climate Change* [Core Writing Team, H. Lee & J. Romero, Eds.] (pp. 1–34). IPCC, Geneva, Switzerland.

Carpena, F. (2019). How do droughts impact household food consumption and nutritional intake? A study of rural India. *World Development, 122*, 349–369.

Casey, G., Fried, S., & Goode, E. (2023). Projecting the impact of rising temperatures: The role of macroeconomic dynamics. *IMF Economic Review, 71*(3), 688–718.

Chen, F., Zhang, X., & Chen, Z. (2023). Behind climate change: Extreme heat and health cost. *Structural Change and Economic Dynamics, 64*, 101–110.

Chang, J. J., Mi, Z., & Wei, Y. M. (2023). Temperature and GDP: A review of climate econometrics analysis. *Structural Change and Economic Dynamics, 66*, 383–392.

Colacito, R., Hoffmann, B., & Phan, T. (2019). Temperature and growth: A panel analysis of the United States. *Journal of Money, Credit and Banking, 51*(2–3), 313–368.

Colmer, J. (2021). Temperature, labor reallocation, and industrial production: Evidence from India. *American Economic Journal: Applied Economics, 13*(4), 101–124.

Dasgupta, A., & Karandikar, A. (2021). *Gender-gap in learning outcomes under rainfall shocks: The role of gender norms* (Ashoka University Economics Discussion Paper, p. 70).

Dasgupta, O. (2024). Climate change: A passing cloud in Indian politics. *The Hindu.* https://www.thehindu.com/opinion/lead/climate-change-a-passing-cloud-in-indian-politics/article68201128.ece. Accessed 2 July 2024.

Dellink, R., Lanzi, E., & Chateau, J. (2019). The sectoral and regional economic consequences of climate change to 2060. *Environmental and Resource Economics, 72*, 309–363. https://doi.org/10.1007/s10640-017-0197-5

Dell, M., Jones, B. F., & Olken, B. A. (2009). Temperature and income: Reconciling new cross-sectional and panel estimates. *American Economic Review, 99*(2), 198–204.

Dell, M., Jones, B. F., & Olken, B. A. (2012). Temperature shocks and economic growth: Evidence from the last half century. *American Economic Journal: Macroeconomics, 4*(3), 66–95.

Dell, M., Jones, B. F., & Olken, B. A. (2014). What do we learn from the weather? The new climate-economy literature. *Journal of Economic Literature, 52*(3), 740–798.

Deryugina, T., & Hsiang, S. (2017). *The marginal product of climate* (No. w24072). National Bureau of Economic Research.

Deschênes, O., & Greenstone, M. (2007). The economic impacts of climate change: Evidence from agricultural output and random fluctuations in weather. *American Economic Review, 97*(1), 354–385.

Dubash, N. K., & Joseph, N. B. (2016). Evolution of institutions for climate policy in India. *Economic and Political Weekly*, 44–54.

Emerick, K. (2018). Agricultural productivity and the sectoral reallocation of labor in rural India. *Journal of Development Economics, 135*, 488–503.

Fishman, R. (2016). More uneven distributions overturn benefits of higher precipitation for crop yields. *Environmental Research Letters, 11*(2), Article 024004.

Frijters, P., Lalji, C., & Pakrashi, D. (2020). Daily weather only has small effects on wellbeing in the US. *Journal of Economic Behavior & Organization, 176*, 747–762.

Fu, S. H., Gasparrini, A., Rodriguez, P. S., & Jha, P. (2018). Mortality attributable to hot and cold ambient temperatures in India: A nationally representative case-crossover study. *PLoS Medicine, 15*(7), Article e1002619.

Garg, T., Jagnani, M., & Taraz, V. (2020). Temperature and human capital in India. *Journal of the Association of Environmental and Resource Economists, 7*(6), 1113–1150.

Guiteras, R. (2009). *The impact of climate change on Indian agriculture* (pp. 1–54). Department of Economics, University of Maryland.

Gupta, E. (2012). Global warming and electricity demand in the rapidly growing city of Delhi: A semi-parametric variable coefficient approach. *Energy Economics, 34*(5), 1407–1421.

Gupta, E. (2016). The effect of development on the climate sensitivity of electricity demand in India. *Climate Change Economics, 7*(02), 1650003.

Gupta, R., & Somanathan, E. (2023). *Hot days and worker absence in the formal sector: Evidence from India.* Available at SSRN 4636875.

Gupta, R., Somanathan, E., & Dey, S. (2017). Global warming and local air pollution have reduced wheat yields in India. *Climatic Change, 140*(3), 593–604.

Gupta, S., Sen, P., & Srinivasan, S. (2014). Impact of climate change on the Indian economy: Evidence from food grain yields. *Climate Change Economics, 5*(02), 1450001.

Harish, S., Singh, N., & Tongia, R. (2020). Impact of temperature on electricity demand: Evidence from Delhi and Indian states. *Energy Policy, 140*, Article 111445.

Hsiang, S. (2016). Climate econometrics. *Annual Review of Resource Economics, 8*(1), 43–75.

Hsiang, S. M., & Jina, A. S. (2014). *The causal effect of environmental catastrophe on long-run economic growth: Evidence from 6,700 cyclones* (No. w20352). National Bureau of Economic Research.

Jain, A., O'Sullivan, R., & Taraz, V. (2020). Temperature and economic activity: Evidence from India. *Journal of Environmental Economics and Policy, 9*(4), 430–446.

Kahn, M. E., Mohaddes, K., Ng, R. N., Pesaran, M. H., Raissi, M., & Yang, J. C. (2021). Long-term macroeconomic effects of climate change: A cross-country analysis. *Energy Economics, 104*, Article 105624.

Kalkuhl, M., & Wenz, L. (2020). The impact of climate conditions on economic production. Evidence from a global panel of regions. *Journal of Environmental Economics and Management, 103*, 102360.

Kelly, D. L., Kolstad, C. D., & Mitchell, G. T. (2005). Adjustment costs from environmental change. *Journal of Environmental Economics and Management, 50*(3), 468–495.

Kiley, M. T. (2024). Growth at risk from climate change. *Economic Inquiry, 62*(3), 1134–1151.

Kolstad, C. D., & Moore, F. C. (2020). Estimating the economic impacts of climate change using weather observations. *Review of Environmental Economics and Policy, 14*, 1–24.

Kotz, M., Wenz, L., Stechemesser, A., Kalkuhl, M., & Levermann, A. (2021). Day-to-day temperature variability reduces economic growth. *Nature Climate Change, 11*(4), 319–325.

Krishnamurthy, C. K. B. (2012). *The distributional impacts of climate change on Indian agriculture: A quantile regression approach* (No. 2012–069).

Krishnan, R., Sanjay, J., Gnanaseelan, C., Mujumdar, M., Kulkarni, A., & Chakraborty, S. (2020). *Assessment of climate change over the Indian region: a report of the ministry of earth sciences (MOES), government of India* (p. 226). Springer Nature.

Krogstrup, S., & Oman, W. (2019). Macroeconomic and financial policies for climate change mitigation: A review of the literature.

Kumar, N., & Maiti, D. (2024a). Long-run macroeconomic impact of climate change on total factor productivity—Evidence from emerging economies. *Structural Change and Economic Dynamics, 68*, 204–223.

Kumar, N., & Maiti, D. (2024b). *The dynamic causal impact of climate change on economic activity- a disaggregated panel analysis of India* (Tech. Rep.).
Kumar, N., & Maiti, D. (2024c). Viksit Bharat 2047: Balancing uneven growth, climate change, and energy challenges. *Jindal Journal of Public Policy, 8*(I), 1–13. https://doi.org/10.54945/jjpp.v8i1.247
Kumar, S., & Khanna, M. (2023). Distributional heterogeneity in climate change impacts and adaptation: Evidence from Indian agriculture. *Agricultural Economics, 54*(2), 147–160.
Kumar, S., & Yalew, A. W. (2012). Economic impacts of climate change on secondary activities: A literature review. *Low Carbon Economy, 3*(02), 39–48.
Léonard, C. (2019). *Temperature and teacher absence: Evidence from 4,085 schools in India.*
Letta, M., & Tol, R. S. (2019). Weather, climate and total factor productivity. *Environmental and Resource Economics, 73*(1), 283–305.
Liu, M., Shamdasani, Y., & Taraz, V. (2023). Climate change and labor reallocation: Evidence from six decades of the Indian Census. *American Economic Journal: Economic Policy, 15*(2), 395–423.
LoPalo, M., Kuruc, K., Budolfson, M., & Spears, D. (2019). Quantifying India's climate vulnerability. In *India Policy Forum* (Vol. 15, No. 1, pp. 107–148). National Council of Applied Economic Research.
India. Ministry of Environment, & United Nations Framework Convention on Climate Change (Organization). (2012). *India, Second National Communication to the United Nations Framework Convention on Climate Change.* Ministry of Environment and Forests, Government of India.
Maddison, D., & Rehdanz, K. (2011). The impact of climate on life satisfaction. *Ecological Economics, 70*(12), 2437–2445.
Mahajan, K. (2017). Rainfall shocks and the gender wage gap: Evidence from Indian agriculture. *World Development, 91*, 156–172.
Maiti, D., Kumar, N., Jha, D., & Sarkar, S. (2024). Post-COVID recovery and long-run forecasting of Indian GDP with Factor-Augmented Error Correction Model (FECM). *Computational Economics, 63*(3), 1095–1120.
Maitra, P., & Tagat, A. (2024). Labor supply responses to rainfall shocks. *Review of Development Economics, 28*(3), 851–887.
Mani, M., Bandyopadhyay, S., Chonabayashi, S., & Markandya, A. (2018). *South Asia's hotspots: The impact of temperature and precipitation changes on living standards.* World Bank Publications.
Mazdiyasni, O., AghaKouchak, A., Davis, S. J., Madadgar, S., Mehran, A., Ragno, E., Niknejad, M., et al. (2017). Increasing probability of mortality during Indian heat waves. *Science Advances, 3*(6), e1700066.
Mendelsohn, R., Arellano-Gonzalez, J., & Christensen, P. (2010). A Ricardian analysis of Mexican farms. *Environment and Development Economics, 15*(2), 153–171.
Mendelsohn, R., Dinar, A., & Williams, L. (2006). The distributional impact of climate change on rich and poor countries. *Environment and Development Economics, 11*(2), 159–178.
Mendelsohn, R., Nordhaus, W. D., & Shaw, D. (1994). The impact of global warming on agriculture: a Ricardian analysis. *The American Economic Review*, 753–771.
Minor, K., Bjerre-Nielsen, A., Jonasdottir, S. S., Lehmann, S., & Obradovich, N. (2022). Rising temperatures erode human sleep globally. *One Earth, 5*(5), 534–549.
MoEFCC. (2022). *India's long-term low-carbon development strategy.* https://unfccc.int/sites/default/files/resource/IndiaLTLEDS.pdf (Ministry of Environment, Forest and Climate Change, Government of India).
Moore, F. C., & Lobell, D. B. (2014). Adaptation potential of European agriculture in response to climate change. *Nature Climate Change, 4*(7), 610–614.
Nelson, G. C., Rosegrant, M. W., Koo, J., Robertson, R., Sulser, T., Zhu, T., Lee, D., et al. (2009). *Climate change: Impact on agriculture and costs of adaptation* (Vol. 21). Intl Food Policy Res Inst.

Neog, B. J. (2022). Temperature shocks and rural labour markets: Evidence from India. *Climatic Change, 171*(1), 16.

Newell, R. G., Prest, B. C., & Sexton, S. E. (2021). The GDP-temperature relationship: Implications for climate change damages. *Journal of Environmental Economics and Management, 108*, Article 102445.

NGFS-NIGEM. (2024). *NGFS GDP losses and benefits*. https://climatedata.imf.org/

Nordhaus, W. (2019). Climate change: The ultimate challenge for economics. *American Economic Review, 109*(6), 1991–2014.

Nordhaus, W. D. (1991). To slow or not to slow: The economics of the greenhouse effect. *The Economic Journal, 101*(407), 920–937.

OECD. (2015). *The economic consequences of climate change*. Paris: OECD. https://www.oecd.org/en/publications/2015/11/the-economic-consequences-of-climate-change_g1g558e1.html

Pachauri, R. K., Allen, M. R., Barros, V. R., Broome, J., Cramer, W., Christ, R., van Ypserle, J. P., et al. (2014). *Climate change 2014: Synthesis report. Contribution of Working Groups I, II and III to the fifth assessment report of the Intergovernmental Panel on Climate Change* (p. 151). IPCC.

Pailler, S., & Tsaneva, M. (2018). The effects of climate variability on psychological well-being in India. *World Development, 106*, 15–26.

Pattanayak, A., & Kumar, K. K. (2021). Does weather sensitivity of rice yield vary across subregions of a country? Evidence from Eastern and Southern India. *Journal of the Asia Pacific Economy, 26*(1), 51–72.

Pattanayak, A., Kumar, K. K., & Anneboina, L. R. (2021). Distributional impacts of climate change on agricultural total factor productivity in India. *Journal of the Asia Pacific Economy, 26*(2), 381–401.

Pretis, F., Schwarz, M., Tang, K., Haustein, K., & Allen, M. R. (2018). Uncertain impacts on economic growth when stabilizing global temperatures at 1.5 C or 2 C warming. *Philosophical Transactions of the Royal Society A: Mathematical, Physical and Engineering Sciences, 376*(2119), 20160460.

RBI. (2023). *Report on currency and finance*. Author. https://rbidocs.rbi.org.in/rdocs/Publications/PDFs/RCF03052023395FAF37181E40188BAD3AFA59BF3907.PDF

Rehdanz, K., & Maddison, D. (2005). Climate and happiness. *Ecological Economics, 52*(1), 111–125.

Ritchie, H., Rosado, P., & Samborska, V. (2024). *Climate change. Our world in data*. https://ourworldindata.org/climate-change

Sandhani, M., Pattanayak, A., & Kavi Kumar, K. S. (2023). Weather shocks and economic growth in India. *Journal of Environmental Economics and Policy, 12*(2), 97–123.

Saryal, R. (2018). Climate change policy of India: Modifying the environment. *South Asia Research, 38*(1), 1–19.

Saxena, R. (2023). *Structural transformation and climate change in India*.

Schlenker, W., & Auffhammer, M. (2018). The cost of a warming climate. *Nature, 557*(7706), 498–499.

Shanmugan, K., & Baria, B. P. (2019). Agricultural labour productivity and its determinants in India. *The Indian Journal of Labour Economics, 62*, 431–449.

Singh, D., Gupta, I., & Dey, S. (2022). *Effect of air pollution on cognitive performance in India* (Tech. Rep.). Institute of Economic Growth.

Sircar, S. (2022). *A weather eye on employment and education* (Doctoral dissertation, Indian Statistical Institute, Kolkata).

Solow, R. M. (1956). A contribution to the theory of economic growth. *The Quarterly Journal of Economics, 70*(1), 65–94.

Somanathan, E., Somanathan, R., Sudarshan, A., & Tewari, M. (2021). The impact of temperature on productivity and labor supply: Evidence from Indian manufacturing. *Journal of Political Economy, 129*(6), 1797–1827.

Son, J. Y., Liu, J. C., & Bell, M. L. (2019). Temperature-related mortality: A systematic review and investigation of effect modifiers. *Environmental Research Letters, 14*(7), Article 073004.

Stern, S. N. (2007). Climate change, ethics and the economics of the global deal. *Combatting Climate Change: A CEPR Collection.*

Swiss Re. (2021). *The economics of climate change: No action not an option.*

Taraz, V. (2017). Adaptation to climate change: Historical evidence from the Indian monsoon. *Environment and Development Economics, 22*(5), 517–545.

Tol, R. S. (2018). The economic impacts of climate change. *Review of environmental economics and policy.*

Tol, R. S. (2024). A meta-analysis of the total economic impact of climate change. *Energy Policy, 185*, Article 113922.

U.S. Environmental Protection Agency (EPA). (2024). *Weather and climate indicators.* Retrieved 21 February 2024, from https://www.epa.gov/climate-indicators/weather-climate

Verma, S., Gupta, S., & Sen, P. (2020). *Does climate change make foodgrain yields more unpredictable? Evidence from India* (No. 8161). CESifo Working Paper.

Weitzman, M. L. (1974). Prices vs. quantities. *The Review of Economic Studies, 41*(4), 477–491.

Zhang, P., Deschenes, O., Meng, K., & Zhang, J. (2018). Temperature effects on productivity and factor reallocation: Evidence from a half million Chinese manufacturing plants. *Journal of Environmental Economics and Management, 88*, 1–17.

Part VIII
Industrialisation

Chapter 19
National Accounts and Productivity Measurement: Challenges in Time Series Analysis

T. C. A. Anant

Abstract The India Productivity Report (2022) (Krishna, K. L., et al. [2022]. India productivity report. RBI. https://rbi.org.in/Scripts/PublicationReportDetails.aspx?UrlPage=&ID=1217.) has a comprehensive introduction and review of productivity measurement and research both in India and globally. This study—which reflects the work of the India KLEMS project—also forms the basis of the KLEMS data now housed at RBI (KLEMS Database, RBI. https://rbi.org.in/Scripts/KLEMS.aspx.). This database is increasingly being used by many researchers working on the Indian economy. It draws upon National Accounts, Household and Establishment Surveys of the NSS and the Population Census to construct a time series of Capital (K), Labour (L), Energy (E), Material (M) and Services(S). This allows users to do time-series analyses on India Economy since 1981. However, since the source datasets have seen changes over the years due to improvements in measurement techniques, it creates challenges for time-series analysts. In this paper, we will examine the developments in National Accounts after 1981, focusing on issues of estimation of value-added in the Informal Sector, Trade and Construction and examine their implications for productivity studies (Some puzzles in productivity growth have been highlighted by Prof Goldar in his presentation at the Indian Econometric Conference, 2024, Keynote paper.).

Keywords National accounts · CSO · Productivity estimates · Informal sector

19.1 National Accounts: A Brief Background

Indian National Accounts measurement has its roots in the recommendations of the National Income Committee set up by the Government of India in 1949 under the chairmanship of Prof. PC Mahalanobis. Based on the recommendations of this committee, India started preparing annual national accounts—the first regular series

T. C. A. Anant (✉)
Institute for Studies in Industrial Development, ISID, New Delhi, India
e-mail: tca.anant@gmail.com

D. Maiti et al. (eds.), *75 Years of Growth, Development and Productivity in India*, India Studies in Business and Economics, https://doi.org/10.1007/978-981-97-8054-9_19

started with the base year of 1948–1949 (released in 1956). This series was then periodically revised to different base years—in 1961 (released in 1967), 1971 (1978), 1981 (1988), 1993 (1999), 1999 (2006), 2004 (2010) and 2011 (2015).[1] The base revision exercise reflects a complete overhaul of the estimation method, reflecting the availability of new data and changes in methodology.

There are two types of methodological changes—those on account of newer or different data and those due to major changes in the core System of National Accounts (SNA) methodology. The SNA is an internationally agreed-upon standard set of recommendations on how to compile measures of economic activity. The base system was released in 1953 and has had three major revisions—in 1968, 1993 and 2008.[2] Each of these revisions substantially overhauled the computation and presentation of national accounts. These revisions were incorporated into the Indian system of national accounts in the revisions of 1971, 1999 and 2011.

In our discussion, we examine the changes introduced in these different revisions of national accounts, starting with the 1981 series, which focused on manufacturing, trade and construction.

19.2 Institutional Sectors in National Accounts

Prior to 2011–2012, national accounts presented accounts separately for the Public and Private Sectors. The Public Sector comprised both departmental and non-departmental enterprises, with the latter comprising PSUs, while the former included Railways, Posts and Ordnance Factories. The Private Sector was presented as Organized and Unorganized. What is Organized or Unorganized differs in different segments of the economy.

In Manufacturing, the Organized sector was equated principally with the coverage of the Factories Act and the estimates derived from the Annual Survey of Industries. The Unorganized sector was described residually (as in, whatever was not covered under the Organized sector) and measured by NSS Surveys of Unorganized Manufacturing. In the Services segment, Private Organized usually[3] referred to the Private Corporate Sector, with data being sourced from the RBI's studies on Company finances.

The estimates for value-added in the registered manufacturing sector in the base year of each series were made using ASI data. In the 1981, 1993 and 2004–2005 series, a combination of IIP and ASI data was typically used for estimating value-added for the years following the base year. This was because there would be a time lag before the ASI data became available, so early estimates would typically be based

[1] The figures in parenthesis are the year of release of the revised series.

[2] For an overview of changes and links to historical documents see https://unstats.un.org/unsd/nationalaccount/HistoricSNA.asp.

[3] One Notable exception is Transportation, where prior to the 2011–2012 revision, there is no private organized segment in Road Transport.

on IIP data. In the 1999 revision, a decision was made to use IIP data exclusively. The revision in 2004–2005 reverted to the earlier practice.

In the 2011–2012 revision, a new institution classification framework was put in place. Data was released separately for Financial (Public and Private) corporations, non-financial (Public and Private) corporations and General Government and Household sectors. While data for the General Government, Financial and non-financial Public corporations and the Household sector were as in the earlier series, data for the Private Corporate Segment was compiled using the MCA database. The Private Corporate estimates also include quasi-corporate enterprises (non-corporate entities but with complete accounts). Estimates for these are compiled from NSS establishment surveys. In manufacturing, quasi-corporate estimates include both non-corporate establishments, which are covered in the ASI, as well as Unincorporated enterprises (with complete books of accounts), which are covered in the NSS survey.

The shift in institutional classification has introduced a measure of non-comparability with the past data. There are two major reasons for this. The RBI's surveys of company finances were a non-random sample of public limited companies, whereas the MCA database covers all companies (both listed and unlisted). Further, in the manufacturing sector, shifting from ASI to MCA implied a change from an establishment-based approach to an enterprise-based one. A manufacturing enterprise could also include non-manufacturing establishments—for instance, value-added from repairs and sales outlets of manufacturing companies.[4] As a consequence, there will be a structural break in the time series of manufacturing GVA in 2011–2012.

19.3 Informal or Unorganized Sector

The informal sector, as per 1993 SNA as well as 2008 SNA, essentially refers to productive units within the household sector which are not constituted as separate legal entities independent of the households and for which no complete sets of accounts are available. In cases where accounts are available, these entities, as per SNA, would be classified as quasi-corporate. The measurement of value-added in the informal sector differs according to the different activities in which it is located. In the agricultural sector, added value is estimated through the production approach. In the manufacturing and service sectors, value-added, informal units are estimated using the benchmark-indicator procedure. This is an approach to generate time-series data from cross-sectional estimates. The benchmark estimate based on a comprehensive cross-sectional estimate is projected using time-series indicators that are more readily available. Typically, growth rates in the indicators are projected onto the benchmark to generate time-series estimates over the years between benchmark estimates. In

[4] The inclusion is justified from the view point of improving aggregate national accounts estimates. They have a side effect of overstating the growth in manufacturing GVA post 2011.

assessing time series' constructed in this manner, the gap between benchmark estimates and the stability of the relationship between the benchmark and the indicator series are major concerns.

GVA estimates are initially prepared for the base year of the national accounts series using the estimated labour input, calculated from Employment Surveys/ Population Census and the value-added per worker (VAPW) and calculated from establishment surveys. The establishment surveys had varying coverage over the years. Thus, we see that Unorganized Manufacturing was covered in the 45th, 51st, 56th and 62nd rounds of the NSS; Trade was covered in the 46th round, while all unincorporated enterprises were covered in the 55th and 67th rounds.[5] It is important to note that none of these surveys covered construction, for which a different approach has been adopted in all national accounts. The varying coverage in some cases led to long gaps between revisions of benchmark estimates. This has led to significant drift in the estimates in different sectors[6]—for example, in trade (as we will see below).

For Unorganized Manufacturing, the indicators used for projecting value-added in non-benchmark years were based on the IIP; for both retail and wholesale Trade, an indicator of Gross Trading Income (GTI) was used; for other services, an indicator based on projected labour input was used. These different indicators have had different implications which are discussed below.

19.4 Using IIP as an Indicator

For growth in manufacturing, IIP is used as an indicator in early estimates, as the ASI estimates were available after a long gap. The 2004–2005 base was dispensed with ASI altogether for reasons of the delay. Using IIP as an indicator to measure value-added has probably contributed to underestimating the growth in value-added. The index has been criticized for not being able to track changes in a dynamic sector.[7] The dampened growth in IIP can also be seen by comparing IIP to a comparable index based on the ASI. This is done in the attached graph, which takes data from three IIP series' (base years 1993–1994, 2004–2005, and 2011–2012)[8] and compares them to the ASI. To construct a comparable index using ASI data, the value of output from the ASI is taken, measured at constant prices (using WPI) and expressed as an index

---

[5] It is only from the 67th round (July 2010 to June 2011) that a comprehensive survey of unincorporated enterprises in manufacturing, trade and other services (excluding construction) was put in place as part of the regular programme. The survey was repeated in the 73rd round (2015–2016), and now is conducted annually as the Annual Survey of Unincorporated Sector Enterprises (ASUSE).

[6] Drift here refers to the introduction of a systematic bias due to the poor correlation between growth in the benchmark and the indicator used for projecting value-added.

[7] See for instance Rajesh, R., & Kumar, N. (2012, July–August). A critical assessment of the index of industrial production data in India. *The Journal of Income and Wealth, 34*(2).

[8] The 1999 revision of IIP was abandoned due to the long delay.

for comparable base years. The graph shows that after a few years, the divergence between IIP and ASI has become quite marked.[9]

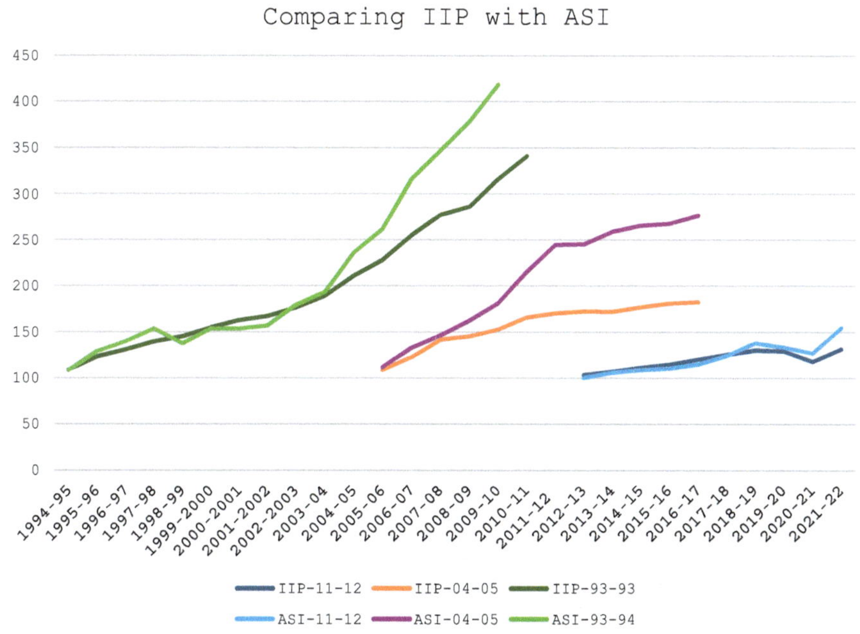

In fact, comparisons of the IIP growth in overlapping years of different revisions also bring out this feature (seen in the following table). Thus, the use of the IIP as an indicator has meant that there has been a generic underestimation of growth in informal manufacturing across different base years.

Year	IIP 2011–2012	IIP 2004–2005	IIP 1993–1993
2005–2006		8.6	8.0
2006–2007		12.9	11.9
2007–2008		15.5	8.7
2008–2009		2.5	3.2
2009–2010		5.3	10.5
2010–2011		8.2	7.8
2013–2014	3.3	–0.1	
2014–2015	4.0	2.8	
2015–2016	3.3	2.4	
2016–2017	4.6	0.7	

[9] Discussed in an earlier article ('There's plenty that ails India's index of industrial production'. (2024, February 15). *Mint*. https://www.livemint.com/opinion/online-views/theres-plenty-that-ails-india-s-index-of-industrial-production-11707916942675.html).

19.5 Workforce Estimation for National Accounts

Estimates of the workforce are used to calculate benchmark estimates of value-added in both Unorganized Manufacturing and Services. Projected growth in the labour force is used as an indicator for estimating growth in value-added for other services after the benchmark year. In this section, we review the changes in approaches to measuring labour input across different base years of National accounts starting from 1980 till the 2011–2012 base year. We also examine the implications of these changes in the estimate of value-added.

In the 1981 series (and also in earlier series') of National Accounts, the workforce was estimated from the population census and growth was projected using growth between 1971 and 1981 censuses. As population growth has been slowing, this introduced a small bias in the estimates.

A departure from this approach was first adopted in the 1993 revision in response to the concern that the census under-reports female workforce participation. Therefore, the Advisory Committee of National Accounts recommended estimating the workforce using the Workforce Participation Rate (WPR) estimated from NSS EUS surveys along with census population estimates. Further, growth after the benchmark year was projected using the change between the NSS estimates of the 43rd and 50th rounds. This approach was continued in the 1999–2000 and 2004–2005 revisions. Estimates of the workforce for the informal sector were obtained by netting out estimates of formal employment from the ASI (for Manufacturing) and from the Directorate General of Employment and Training (DGET) (for non-manufacturing Organized employment). In 2004–2005, the organized employment was estimated from the EUS survey rather than the data of DGET. In the 2011–2012 revision, this approach was further modified to use a concept of effective labour that combined EUS estimates with productivity measures derived from the Unorganized enterprise survey.[10]

19.6 Estimates of Value-Added in Construction

Value-added in construction has followed the same methodology through the different base years. Essentially, value-added estimates from construction activity are prepared separately for *pucca* construction and *kutcha* construction. In the case of the former, the estimates are prepared using the commodity flow approach, and the value of all pucca construction undertaken with the use of construction materials such as cement, steel, bricks, timber, fixtures etc., is determined. The 2011–2012 revision continued this practice—only the list of materials was increased to separately include

[10] Anant, T. C. A. (2020). Informal sector in national accounts estimation: Importance of workforce and productivity. In S. Aggarwal, D. Das, & R. Banga (Eds.), *Accelerators of India's growth—Industry, trade and employment*. India Studies in Business and Economics. Springer. https://doi.org/10.1007/978-981-32-9397-7_11.

Bitumen and Bitumen products and Glass and Glass products. The estimates of labour-intensive kutcha construction are prepared using an expenditure approach. The rates and ratios applied to the inputs to derive value-added have also remained quite stable over the years.

A limitation of the approach noted in Sources and Methods (1989) remains valid today. "*The proportions of GVA to value of output for various types of construction works are not based on satisfactory data. Because of the wide diversity in the types of construction, even within the broad groups of pucca and kutcha construction, the proportions of GVA to the total value of construction for different types are likely to vary. It is desirable that the different types of construction are classified into homogeneous groups and the proportion of value added for each group is worked out on a more satisfactory basis*". This fixed proportions model for estimating value-added in construction leaves little space for any productivity improvements.

19.7 Estimates of Value-Added in Trade

The segment related to Trade, Hotels and Restaurants had seen major discrepancies in the 2011–2012 revision of national accounts. Trade has been subject to diverse treatment in different NSS rounds pertaining to unorganized enterprises, as we noted earlier. There was no sample survey of unorganized trade available for the 2004–05 revision as the 63rd round Establishment Survey did not cover trading enterprises. Thus, the estimates for the 1999–2000 base year continued through 2004–05. As noted in the Sources and Methods (2007), even in 1999–2000, the estimates of VAPW were calculated from the "'*all enterprises' category available in informal sector survey conducted during 55th round (1999–00) of NSS, since no separate trade survey has been undertaken by the NSSO after 53rd round*". The estimates were projected in subsequent years using gross trading income (GTI) as an indicator.

The GTI is based on the value of marketable surplus in commodity-producing sectors in agriculture, livestock, fishing, forestry, mining and manufacturing and value of imports. The index essentially tracks the growth in the volume of tradable goods in the economy. The Sub-Committee on Unorganized Sector (2015–2016) pointed out in its report[11] that "*the index tracked the growth in volume of tradable goods, in the economy, derived from current estimates of production in agriculture, manufacturing and mining. This is a reasonable assumption in short intervals of time. However, when projections are extended over long periods of time, errors build up. This is because in addition to physical volume, value added also depends on levels of intermediation between the producers and consumers, changes in underlying quality of goods, changes in marketing practices for instance bundling higher quality value added services with goods like warranties,* etc.". The volume of production used in the GTI includes production for export. The level and form of intermediation in domestic

[11] Report of the Sub Committee on Unorganised Manufacturing and Services Sectors for Compilation of National Accounts Statistics with Base Year 2011–2012, Govt. of India, MOSPI.

sales and exports are very different. The rising volume of exports (particularly in mining) has meant that domestic value-added could have been over-estimated. These issues get picked up in focused surveys as they gather information on all value-added aspects. In the 1993 revision, it was noted that this method underestimated value-added in Trade by about 10%. Similarly, the 1999–2000 revision noted a small underestimation of about 1%. However, in 2011–2012, it was observed that the estimate of Trade had been over-estimated by a massive 55.87%; the 2011–2012 series suggested an alternative indicator to GTI based on sales tax collections to track growth in value-added in years after the base year.[12]

19.8 Computation of Back Series of National Accounts

Time series analysis using national accounts data relies on a linked (or back) series generated after each revision. There are essentially two methods available for the compilation of a linked series. First, the splicing method, or second, by reworking the previous estimates as per the current series methodology. Reworking the estimates becomes challenging as we go further back in time because both the structure and availability of data evolve. In splicing time series, the major issue is in maintaining either growth rates or additivity. When we splice the series, if we maintain growth rates at the component level and in the aggregate, then we lose additivity, i.e. the components will not add up to the aggregate. On the other hand, if the aggregate is derived as a sum of the components, the growth rates of the aggregates in the linked series will be different from those in the earlier series. In the back series generated for the 2004–2005 revision and the 2011–2012 revision, a common approach of reworking the immediate past was combined with splicing older data to maintain growth rates at component and aggregate levels. A consequence of this approach has led to the following:

(a) a **Drift** in the estimates. Thus we see, for instance, GDP at Factor Cost of 1980 at 1980–1981 prices was Rs 1,22,427 Crores in the 1981 series, which changed to Rs 1,32,520 Crores(1993 Series), Rs 1,36,838 Crores (2004–2005 series) and Rs 1,33,745 Crores (2011–2012) series.
(b) **Compositional change.** The share of unregistered Manufacturing in total Manufacturing value-added in 1980–1981 varies significantly—it rises from 46.3% in the 1980–1981 series to 49.6% in the 2004–2005 series and then has a sharp decline to 18.6% in the 2011–2012 series. The last figure is in part because Organized Manufacturing now includes both the quasi-corporate segment from NSS surveys and also non-manufacturing activities of manufacturing enterprises.[13]

[12] This would have been adapted to GST after the introduction of GST subsuming sales tax, but details of the conversion are not public.

[13] Discussed in an earlier article—'The Old GDP Series Overstate Sectoral Growth' Financial Express (2018): https://www.financialexpress.com/opinion/the-old-gdp-series-overstated-sectoral-growth-heres-how/1411231/.

19.9 Concluding Remarks

In our discussion we have noted that revisions in national accounts have introduced structural breaks in value-added time series at both sectoral levels and in the aggregate. For users of time-series data, this poses significant challenges in interpretation, particularly for productivity measurement. Since productivity is measured essentially as a residual (after accounting for growth in inputs), it is a challenge to disentangle the effects of true productivity change from those on account of measurement-induced biases. In the construction sector, for instance, low productivity growth is built in essentially because of the Leontief type (fixed coefficient) value-added function with constant returns to scale being used. In other sectors (particularly Trade and Manufacturing), part of the Total Factor Productivity (TFP) growth may well be spurious on account of the measurement bias in the earlier series. One should note that these problems of inter-temporal comparability are likely to occur in all cases where development and technological change have led to improvements in both coverage and quality of statistical data.

References

Government of India, Ministry of Statistics and Program Implementation

Back Series Estimation Base 2011–2012 Methodology. https://www.mospi.gov.in/sites/default/files/publication_reports/Methodology_back_series_base_2011_12_9jan19.pdf

Back-Series of National Accounts (Base 2011–2012) contains data. https://www.mospi.gov.in/publication/back-series-national-accounts-base-2011-12

Brochure on the Series of National Accounts Statistics (Base Year 1993–1994). https://www.mospi.gov.in/sites/default/files/publication_reports/brochure1_9june04.pdf

Changes in Methodology and Data Sources in the New Series of National Accounts (Base Year 2011–2012). https://www.mospi.gov.in/sites/default/files/publication_reports/Changes%20in%20Methodology%20and%20Data%20Sources%20in%20the%20New%20Series%20of%20National%20Accounts_Base%20year%202011-12.pdf

National Accounts Old Series 1980–1981. https://www.mospi.gov.in/publication/national-accounts-statistics-old-series-1980-81

National Accounts Old Series 1993–1994. https://www.mospi.gov.in/publication/national-accounts-statistics-old-series-1993-94

National Accounts Sources and Methods 1989. https://www.mospi.gov.in/publication/national-accounts-statistics-sources-and-methods-1989

National Accounts Sources and Methods 2007. https://www.mospi.gov.in/publication/national-accounts-statistics-sources-and-methods-2007

National Accounts Sources and Methods 2012. https://www.mospi.gov.in/sites/default/files/publication_reports/sources_method_2012%20%281%29.pdf

National Accounts Statistics—Back Series 2007 (Base year 1999–2000). https://www.mospi.gov.in/publication/national-accounts-statistics-back-series-2007-1950-51-1999-2000

National Accounts Statistics—Back Series 2011 (Base year 2004–2005). https://www.mospi.gov.in/sites/default/files/reports_and_publication/cso_national_accounts/national_account_statistics/back_series_2011/Notes%20on%20Methodology%2028.09.2011.pdf and data https://www.mospi.gov.in/publication/national-accounts-statistics-back-series-2011

Report of the Sub Committee on Unorganised Manufacturing & Services Sectors for Compilation of National Accounts Statistics with Base Year 2011–2012. https://www.mospi.gov.in/sites/default/files/publication_reports/Report_Subcommi_Unorga_MSS_2mar15.pdf

Other Sources

Anant, T. C. A. (2018). The old GDP series overstate sectoral growth. *Financial Express*. https://www.financialexpress.com/opinion/the-old-gdp-series-overstated-sectoral-growth-heres-how/1411231/

Anant, T. C. A. (2020). Informal sector in national accounts estimation: Importance of workforce and productivity. In S. Aggarwal, D. Das, & R. Banga (Eds.), *Accelerators of India's growth—Industry, trade and employment*. India Studies in Business and Economics. Springer. https://doi.org/10.1007/978-981-32-9397-7_11

Anant, T. C. A. (2024, February 15). There's plenty that ails India's index of industrial production. *Mint*. https://www.livemint.com/opinion/online-views/theres-plenty-that-ails-india-s-index-of-industrial-production-11707916942675.html

KLEMS Database. RBI. https://rbi.org.in/Scripts/KLEMS.aspx

Kolli, R. (2011). Measuring the trade sector in the national accounts of India. *The Review of Income and Wealth, 57*(s1). Special Issue: The Informal Economy in Developing Countries: Analysis and Measurement.

Krishna, K. L., et al. (2022). India productivity report. RBI. https://rbi.org.in/Scripts/PublicationReportDetails.aspx?UrlPage=&ID=1217

Rajesh, R., & Kumar, N. (2012, July–August). A critical assessment of the index of industrial production data in India. *The Journal of Income and Wealth, 34*(2).

Chapter 20
75 Years of India's Industrial Policy and Performance and Prospects for a Manufacturing-Led Transformation

Nagesh Kumar

Abstract Rapid job-creating economic growth through manufacturing-led transformation is imperative for India to realize its development aspirations of building a developed economy by 2047 and to address the challenge of employment creation. Industrial policy and emphasis on the real economy is a global trend in the context of the fractured trading system. As global companies restructure their supply chains on China +1 lines, India can potentially leverage its geopolitical and demographic sweet spots to build manufacturing capacities to feed growing domestic and global demand and tap the opportunities presented by the digital and green industrial revolutions.

To tap these opportunities, a strategic approach is needed to harness the potential of manufacturing, for which many useful lessons are available from the experiences of East Asian countries. In that context, India should build on PLI to a more proactive targeting approach to investment promotion that would help to attract better quality investments meeting its development needs. India also needs to make the regional and global trade rules supportive of its ambitious manufacturing-led transformation. Finally, to be effective, the different elements of industrial policy as outlined above need to be pursued in a coordinated manner through a high-powered institutional architecture for a coordinated implementation of industrial policy. An updated Industrial Policy Resolution providing a framework for accelerated growth of the manufacturing sector, generating jobs and prosperity in an inclusive and balanced manner, and a roadmap for achieving it is also desirable.

Keywords Industrial Policy · Industrialization · Innovation · Manufacturing Sector · MSMEs · PLI

N. Kumar (✉)
Institute for Studies in Industrial Development (ISID), New Delhi, India
e-mail: nkumar@isid.org.in

D. Maiti et al. (eds.), *75 Years of Growth, Development and Productivity in India*, India Studies in Business and Economics, https://doi.org/10.1007/978-981-97-8054-9_20

20.1 Introduction

The Indian economy has emerged from the pandemic as the fastest-growing large economy that is the fifth largest globally besides many other impressive achievements to celebrate the 75 years of its Independence. However, several challenges remain including pervasive informality and persisting poverty linked with declining employment elasticity of economic growth (see Kumar, 2022). Jobless growth is a major challenge in the context of a country passing through a youth bulge phase in its demographic transition. The job creation is linked to structural transformation and the failure to industrialize the economy and harness the direct and indirect job-creating potential of manufacturing. Therefore, manufacturing needs to drive the next phase of India's transformation to create an adequate number of decent jobs and to realise the developed country vision for 2047.

Against that backdrop, this paper reviews the evolution of India's industrial policy and performance over the 75 years, India's potential for manufacturing-led growth and strategic interventions that would be important for realizing this potential. The discussion is organized as follows. Section 20.2 summarizes the evolution of India's approach towards the manufacturing sector over 75 years against the backdrop of the changing external context for industrial policy. Section 20.3 reviews the evolving industrial structure, trade, FDI, and innovation landscape. The fourth section of the paper examines the prospects of a manufacturing-led transformation in India. The paper concludes with a policy agenda for harnessing India's manufacturing potential to foster inclusive and sustainable prosperity for all its people and realisation of its developed country vision.

20.2 Job-Creation and the Changing Context of Industrial Policy

Realization of the developed country status needs to be underpinned by inclusive and sustainable prosperity for all citizens through the creation of decent job opportunities for India's youthful workforce. The inability to create an adequate number of decent jobs in the past has led to nearly 86% of India's workforce getting locked in the informal sector without adequate social protection and remaining vulnerable to any shocks. The issue of decent job creation is linked with structural transformation, where workers move over time from low-productivity activities (such as agriculture) to higher-productivity sectors (such as industry and services). India has witnessed the transformation of an agricultural-dominated economy into a services-dominated one bypassing the industry. While the service sector has delivered robust growth rates, it has not been able to absorb workers especially the unskilled and semi-skilled ones, proportionately. As a result, agriculture continues to sustain as much as 46% of India's workforce with barely a 15% share of GDP. This services-oriented structural transformation, as it has been termed, has been able to absorb only 26%

of the workforce in services. The manufacturing sector has been bypassed with its share in GDP stagnating at around 16% in contrast to an average of 30% in the East Asian countries. The neglect of manufacturing to underpin the structural transformation in India has cost the country dearly in terms of creating decent jobs directly, and indirectly through its extensive backward and forward linkages (Kumar, 2018). Not only has the share of manufacturing stagnated in India, but there is also evidence of some deindustrialization taking place (see Amirapu & Subramanian, 2015; Dasgupta & Singh, 2006; Felipe et al., 2014; Rodrik, 2015; Kumar, 2018).

History corroborates that few countries, if at all, have attained prosperity without industrialization (Kaldor, 1967). Kaldor (1967) has also argued persuasively that the growth of manufacturing will not only drive economic growth but will also enhance the productivity of the economy overall with increasing returns to scale which could be dynamic in nature. An expanded manufacturing sector could also help to make India's balance of payments (BoP) more sustainable—which tends to periodically get into stress—by substituting imports or expanding exports. Therefore, faster job-creating rapid economic growth through industry-oriented structural transformation is the key to inclusive and sustainable prosperity of India for the realization of India's Vision 2047 of a developed country.

20.2.1 Rationale and Rise of Industrial Policy

In achieving a manufacturing-led economic transformation, India could learn from the experiences of the industrialized and East Asian countries in fostering competitive manufacturing capacities through extensive state interventions. The developmental role of the State in these countries and the aspects of strategic interventions deployed are collectively called industrial policy. The case for state intervention in industrial development has continued to be made in the theoretical literature at regular intervals. The argument for infant industry protection had been around for a very long time since List (1909) and was used to justify high tariff barriers imposed in the US in its period of industrialization, as documented by Chang (2002). Infant industry protection, later on, was used to justify the incorporation of a chapter on trade and development in the General Agreement on Tariffs and Trade in the 1960s. The literature on the Developmental State has documented extensive state intervention for industrialization employed in East Asian countries (Johnson, 1982). Strategic Trade Theory has also justified state intervention that can be welfare-enhancing shifting profits from international to domestic firms under certain conditions (Brander & Spencer, 1985). More recently the New Structural Economics has justified state intervention for building industrial capabilities (Lin, 2012).

After becoming a bad word in the heydays of globalization, industrial policy is back in fashion across the world. A widely circulated IMF paper *The Return of the Policy that shall not be named: Principles of Industrial Policy,* issued in 2019, recognized the 'strong commonalities in policies pursued by the Asian Miracles, and one cannot ignore the preeminent role of industrial policy in their development' (Cherif &

Hasanov, 2019). Over the past few years, there has been a deluge of evidence and debates on the relevance of industrial policy tools employed with varying degrees of success by traditional and late industrialisers (*The Economist*, 2022). An extensive new review of evidence and experiences has concluded that 'there is a generic and powerful economic case for industrial policy and that the usual critiques rely on practical rather principled objections' and that the debate on industrial policy should be focused not on 'the whether' but on 'the how' (Juhasz et al., 2023).

Governments around the world are adopting the so-called industrial policies that incentivize domestic manufacturing to create jobs and reshoring of value chains. For instance, in the US, once the greatest champion of free markets and globalization, the Biden Administration has defined its industrial policy recently with the $280 billion CHIPS and Science Act, the $737 billion Inflation Reduction Act, and the $550 billion Infrastructure Investment and Jobs Act. These Acts will foster local manufacturing and innovation of semiconductors chips, electric mobility, and other new technology products through hundreds of billions of dollars in subsidies and tax breaks. Therefore, the New Washington Consensus is not about liberalization and free markets any more. It is about industrial policy. The European Union is also following the US playbook in incentivizing the manufacturing sector (Kumar, 2024). In that context, the Make-in-India programme announced by the Indian Government in 2014 which seeks to tap the potential of manufacturing for India's development, is timely and is a part of a global trend.

20.2.2 Evolution of Industrial Policy in India

India's policy approach towards manufacturing has evolved over the past seven decades. Three distinct phases are notable in this evolution (see ISID, 2025 for more details).

20.2.2.1 Import-Substituting Industrialization: Mid-1960s-1991

Recognizing the strategic importance of a strong industrial base for self-reliance, India pursued import-substituting industrialization (ISI) from the mid-1960s until the reforms of 1991. The policy included high tariffs (up to 350%), import licensing, industrial licensing (or approvals), a rather strict foreign direct investment (FDI) regime, and a softer intellectual property protection regime that did not recognize product patents in pharmaceuticals. The public sector was expected to serve as the 'commanding heights' of the economy and several strategic sectors were reserved for exclusive development by state-owned enterprises. Several products were also reserved for exclusive production by MSMEs.

The industrial policy helped build a diversified industrial base by the end of the 1980s, one that produced virtually all items of consumption in India. During this time, manufacturing's share of GDP nearly doubled from around 9% to nearly

17%. India's overall dependence on imports dropped dramatically even for heavy machinery and capital goods. However, high tariffs and quantitative restrictions on imports, and industrial licensing led to the creation of virtual monopolies resulting in high prices, poor quality, and limited variety for Indian consumers. Poor attention paid to innovation led to technological obsolescence and international competitiveness suffered.

Given the poor competitiveness, many of the Indian companies could not stay in business when exposed to foreign competition after 1991. Many of them entered joint ventures with multinational enterprises (MNEs) to update their technology or were acquired by them. This underscored a crucial difference between India's experience with industrial policy and those of the East Asian countries such as South Korea. Indian policy targeted import-substituting industrialization in a closed economy context and did not particularly seek international competitiveness. The East Asian countries, on the other hand, focused on building internationally competitive industries. They constantly leveraged rivalries between domestic champions and pushed them into international markets through export incentives and performance requirements.

This is not to say, however, that the import-substituting industrialization strategy failed completely in India. India's success in generic pharmaceuticals, information and communication technology (ICT) software, and building a vertically integrated automobile industry with global leadership in two-wheelers and compact cars can be attributed to the strategic interventions of the time (see Nayyar & Nayyar, 2024). Some of today's leading Indian enterprises with significant global footprints, including Hindalco Industries, Tata Motors, Tata Global Beverages, Mahindra & Mahindra, Bajaj Auto, Ashok Leyland, TVS Motors, and Hero Motors, also have their origins in the import-substituting industrialization era. The diversified industrial base that India enjoys is an important legacy of the import-substituting industrialization policy.

20.2.2.2 Reforms of 1991: Liberalization and Global Economic Integration

Economic reforms adopted since 1991 have removed the industrial licensing system and have liberalized the FDI policy. Tariff rates have been gradually reduced to align broadly with those in the Southeast Asian countries, the rupee's exchange rate began to be floated on the market, and quantitative restrictions on imports have been phased out.

India's FDI policy has been consistently moved towards greater liberalization and facilitation, to leverage the resources of multinational corporations (MNCs) including capital, technology, and access to markets. Policy reforms adopted have included the creation of a system of automatic clearance of FDI proposals fulfilling the conditions laid down, such as the ownership levels of 49%, 74%, and 100% foreign equity and opening of new sectors such as mining, banking, insurance, telecommunications, construction and management of ports, harbours, roads and highways, airlines, and defence equipment, to foreign-owned companies subject to sectoral caps. The dividend balancing and the related export obligation conditions on foreign investors, which applied to 22 consumer goods industries, were withdrawn in 2000. In September 2012, India allowed FDI in multi-brand retail and in civil aviation. Sectoral caps have been constantly revised upwards over the years. Foreign ownership up to 100% is permitted now in most manufacturing sectors—in some sectors even on an automatic basis—except for defence equipment where it is limited to 74%, multi-brand retail to 51%, digital media to 26%, broadcasting content to 49%, newspapers to 26%, and scheduled air transport to 49%.[1] India had also entered into 88 Double Taxation Avoidance Treaties, and Bilateral Investment Promotion and Protection Agreement (BIPAs) with 86 countries by 2020. India adopted a new patent law consistent with the WTO's Agreement on Trade-Related Intellectual Property Rights (TRIPS). India also liberalized the entry of portfolio foreign investment flows.

The reforms and liberalization have led to a lot of restructuring of Indian industry. Besides liberalized imports of goods not made in the country, local producers began to outsource production to cheaper sources in other countries, especially China, in a trend sometimes referred to as the 'hollowing out' of Indian manufacturing leading to premature deindustrialization (Kumar, 2018 for evidence). Consequently, the share of imports in final consumption rose sharply in many sectors, such as electronics, electrical equipment, and telecommunication equipment, but also labour-intensive, household electric goods, such as toasters, wall clocks, electric irons, refrigerators, and televisions, among others. The current account balance was kept in check by the rising export of services, while rising inflows of FDI and portfolio investments helped to close the remaining deficit. Manufacturing's share of GDP came down from a peak of 17% in 1997 and has stagnated at around 14–16%, compared to around 30% in the East Asian countries. As the manufacturing sector struggled, India's economic growth was sustained by the services sector, which now accounts for 56% of the GDP.

20.2.2.3 Revival of Industrial Policy Since 2014

The imperative of job creation has pushed the National Democratic Alliance (NDA) Government to implement Make-in-India to harness the potential of manufacturing. As part of the Make-in-India programme, the Government amended the general financial rules (GFRs) to prescribe purchase preference for local suppliers in all procurements undertaken by procuring entities with a minimum of 50% local content and 20% as the margin of purchase preference in October 2017.[2] The big reforms brought in include the Insolvency and Bankruptcy Code, 2016 which provided a consolidated framework governing insolvency and bankruptcy proceedings for companies. The Goods and Services Tax (GST) introduced in 2017 made India a single market.

[1] https://www.investindia.gov.in/foreign-direct-investment.

[2] http://dipp.nic.in/whats-new/public-procurement-preference-make-india-order-2017.

Besides these big-picture reforms, the government also has focused on improving the ease-of-doing-business (EODB) in India through the abolition of obsolete regulations and processes that hindered industrial investments. The FDI ownership limits in several sectors—such as railways, defence manufacturing, insurance, and medical devices—were increased and an investment promotion and facilitation agency, *Invest India* was established. Import tariffs were raised in select sectors to give some infant industry protection, and the government also identified six industrial corridors across the country for development. The corporate tax rates were also brought down in 2019/2020 from 35% to just 22% and 15% for the new companies. Indian companies now have to pay a lower statutory tax rate than companies in some other emerging economies such as Brazil, Argentina, and Mexico, adding to India's competitiveness in terms of attracting investments. The government has also focused on improving the logistics infrastructure in the country through the US$1.2 trillion National Master Plan for Multi-modal Connectivity launched in 2021.

As a result of these steps, India's place in the World Bank's EODB rankings moved up sharply from 142 in 2014 to 63 in 2019 (the World Bank abandoned the rankings in 2021). India has started to attract greater magnitudes of FDI inflows which crossed a record figure of $81 billion in 2021–2022. Make-in-India was reinforced in a big manner by the production-linked incentives (PLI) scheme introduced in 2020 as a part of the *AatmaNirbhar Bharat* package announced to revive the economy in the aftermath of the COVID-19 pandemic. The PLI scheme provides a 4–6% incentive to boost local production (or substitute imports) and exports for 14 select sectors. These include sunrise and green manufacturing products such as solar photovoltaic cells and modules, advanced chemistry batteries, active pharmaceutical ingredients, large-scale electronics, medical devices, speciality steels, and telecom and networking equipment. To create a full ecosystem of electronics, the government launched a $10 billion Semiconductor Mission in 2022 to foster the manufacture of semiconductor chips and displays. Also in 2022, the government announced a $2.3 billion Green Hydrogen Mission to make India a leading manufacturer and exporter of green hydrogen.

20.3 Emerging Trends in Industrial Structure and Performance

The industrial policy pursued over the past seven and a half decades has helped to develop a diversified industrial base with growing complexity and sophistication. In what follows, the industrial structure, trends, and patterns are reviewed briefly.

Rising Global Share: India produced approximately 3.1% of the world's total manufacturing value-added (MVA) in 2022, a share that has grown consistently from 0.72% in 1970. The 3.1 share in global manufacturing makes India the fifth most important centre of manufacturing globally, behind China, the US, Japan, and Germany (Fig. 20.1). However, India's manufacturing share is only a fraction of

India's share in global manufacturing value added

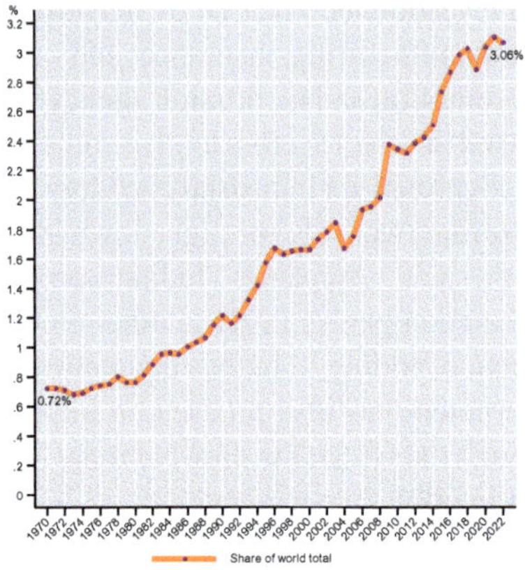

Biggest manufacturing countries in the world

□□ China - 28.7%
□□ United States - 16.8%
□□ Japan - 7.5%
□□ Germany - 5.3%
□□ India - 3.1%
□□ South Korea - 3%
□□ Italy - 2.1%
□□ France - 1.9%
□□ United Kingdom - 1.8%
□□ Indonesia - 1.6%

Fig. 20.1 India's share and rank in global manufacturing. *Source* ISID (2025)

28.7% share of China's and 16.8% of the US. While the share of global manufacturing is commensurate with India's fifth place in global GDP rankings, it needs to move up to the third rank in tune with the expected position of the country in GDP rankings by 2027–2028.

Changing Industrial Structure: Manufacturing in India till 1980–1981 was dominated by the textiles sector accounting for 16% of GVA. Other important sectors were basic metals (11.1%), chemicals (10.5%), food products (6.2%), machinery and equipment (6.3%), electrical equipment (5.2%), and motor vehicles (3.5%). Over time the relative importance of textiles has gradually come down to under 5% by 2021–2022. While food products (7.8%), chemicals (11.2%), basic metals (10.1%), and machinery and equipment (6.2%) have maintained or improved their salience, pharmaceuticals (8.2%) and motor vehicles (7.3%) have emerged as important sectors of manufacturing in India (Fig. 20.2).

Changing Industry Structure by Technology-Intensity of Products: If the entire manufacturing industry in India is classified into four categories based on technology intensity, using the OECD classification, namely High Technology (HT), Medium to High technology (MHT), Medium to Low Technology (MLT) and Low Technology (LT), a major transformation is visible in terms of emergence of HT at the cost of LT, in terms of key performance variables such as Gross Value Added (GVA), Wages, Employment, and Capital Investment. In terms of GVA, the largest contributor was MHT followed by MLT, LT, and HT in 2021–2022. In terms of wages, the MHT sector contributed the highest followed by LT, MLT, and HT. In the case of employment, the LT sector had the highest while the HT, the lowest shares. Finally, in terms of the size of capital investment in total manufacturing, the share of MLT was the highest followed by MHT, LT, and HT (see Fig. 20.3). Even though their share in GVA has declined from 31.1% to 21.9%, the low technology (LT) sectors are key providers of

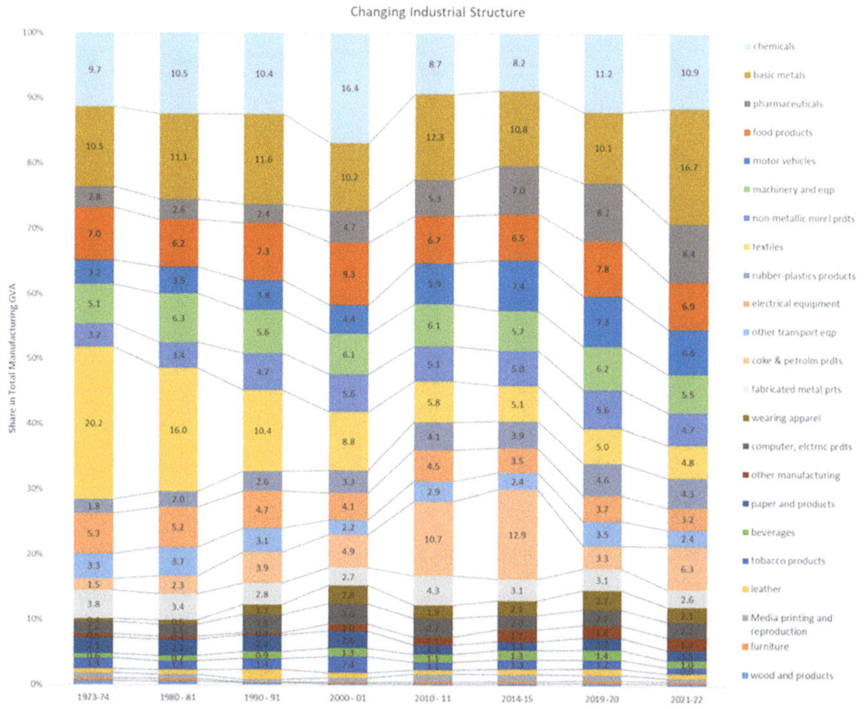

Fig. 20.2 India's changing industrial structure, 1970s to 2021–2022. *Source* ISID based on the Annual Surveys of Industries database

jobs accounting for 41.5% of total employment in manufacturing. The key LT job providers include textiles, wearing apparel and dressing, dyeing, and articles of fur and food products n.e.c.

Productivity Trends in International Comparative Perspective:
In the 2000s, total factor productivity (TFP) on average made a 17.4% contribution to India's GDP growth. This is comparable with averages seen in China as well as other emerging economies. In 2011–2019, TFP contribution was relatively higher at 26%, reflecting reliance on innovation to sustain growth. Mostly, India's growth has been driven by capital accumulation, which accounts for over 60% of GDP growth. The addition of workers into the economy and their upskilling has been a small driver, accounting for as much as 18% of growth in 2000–2007 which has declined to 9% during 2011–2019 (Fig. 20.4). The −7.6% GDP growth in 2020 corresponded with a labour quantity contribution of −7.2% and −2.9%TFP growth. Most of the growth in 2021 is contributed by labour quantity. Furthermore, in a recent study decomposing the sources of India's economic growth based on KLEMS Database, Krishna et al. (2022) found that nearly one-third of India's GDP growth was contributed by the growth of total factor productivity and more than two-thirds contributed by capital accumulation and employment growth. As much as 40% of growth of total factor

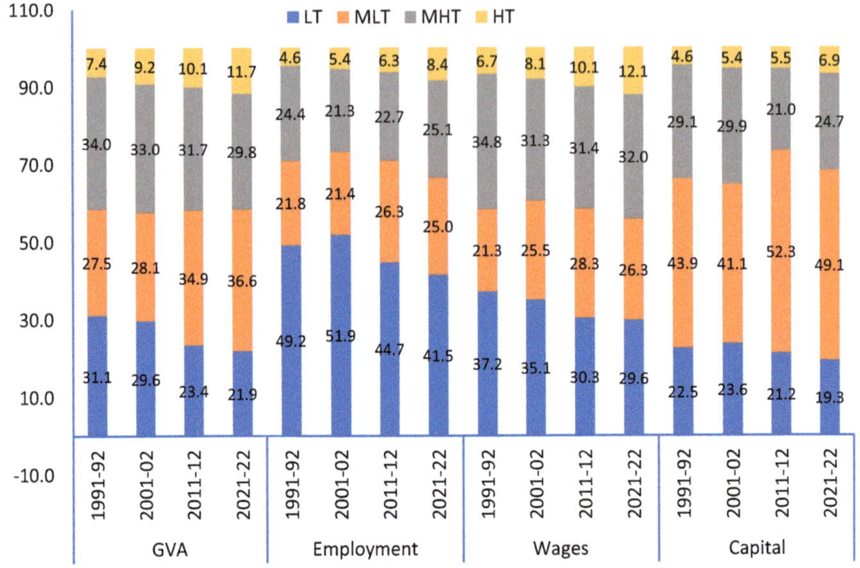

***Notes*:** **High Technology (HT):** Aircraft and spacecraft, pharmaceuticals, medical, precision and optical instruments, TV, Radio transmitters, receivers, sound or video recording apparatus and associated goods, and electronic valves, tubes, and electrical, n.e.c.; **Medium-High Technology (MHT):** chemicals excluding pharmaceuticals, machinery and equipment, n.e.c, Office, accounting, and computing machinery, electrical machinery and apparatus, radio, and apparatus, motor vehicles, trailers & other transport equipment; **Medium–Low-Technology (MLT):** coke, refined petroleum products, and nuclear fuel, rubber and plastics products, other non-metallic mineral products, basic metals, fabricated metal products; **Low Technology (LT):** food products and beverages, tobacco products, textiles, dressing and dyeing of fur, Tanning and dressing of leather, wood and wood products, paper and paper products, Publishing, printing, and reproduction of recorded media, furniture & recycling

Fig. 20.3 Changes in industrial composition by technology intensity (1991–1992 and 2021–2022) (in %). *Notes* **High Technology (HT):** Aircraft and spacecraft, pharmaceuticals, medical, precision and optical instruments, TV, Radio transmitters, receivers, sound or video recording apparatus and associated goods, and electronic valves, tubes, and electrical, n.e.c.; **Medium–High Technology (MHT):** chemicals excluding pharmaceuticals, machinery and equipment, n.e.c, Office, accounting, and computing machinery, electrical machinery and apparatus, radio, and apparatus, motor vehicles, trailers and other transport equipment; **Medium–Low Technology (MLT):** coke, refined petroleum products, nuclear fuel, rubber and plastics products, other non-metallic mineral products, basic metals, and fabricated metal products; **Low Technology (LT):** food products and beverages, tobacco products, textiles, dressing and dyeing of fur, Tanning and dressing of leather, wood and wood products, paper and paper products, Publishing, printing, and reproduction of recorded media, furniture, and recycling. *Source* ISID based on the Annual Surveys of Industries database; see Rijesh (2024) for details

productivity was contributed by the manufacturing sector while the rest came from inter-industry resource allocation.

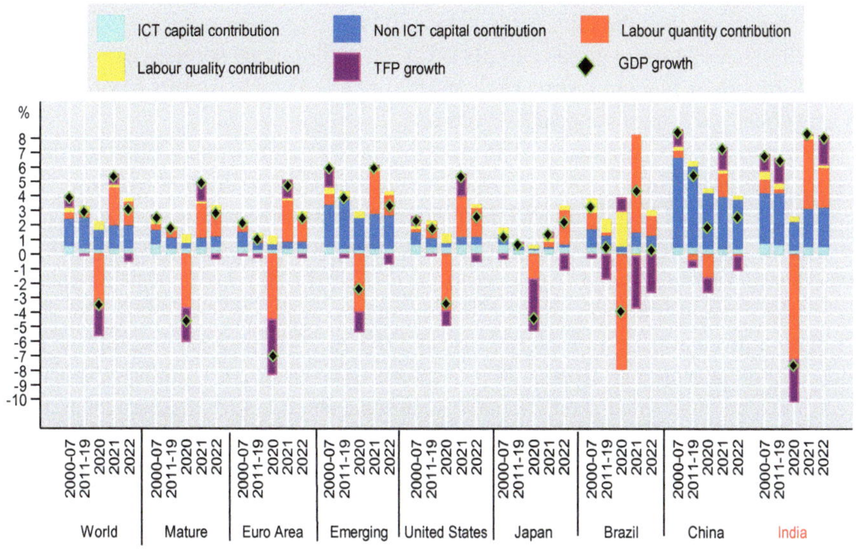

Notes: Data for 2022 are forecasts; All growth rates are calculated as log differences. Growth rates for 2000-2007 and 2011-2019 are the averages of yearly growth rates; Regional aggregates are weighted using shares in nominal PPP converted GDP; Growth rates for China, as well as the regional aggregates which include China, are based on TCB alternative estimates of Chinese GDP growth.
ICT capital contribution (contribution of capital services provided by ICT assets to GDP growth), Non-ICT capital contribution (contribution of capital services provided by Non-ICT assets to GDP growth), total capital contribution (contribution of total capital services to GDP growth).

Fig. 20.4 Average percentage point contributions of factors to GDP growth, major regions, and selected countries, 2000–2022. *Notes*: Data for 2022 are forecasts; All growth rates are calculated as log differences. Growth rates for 2000–2007 and 2011–2019 are the averages of yearly growth rates; Regional aggregates are weighted using shares in nominal PPP converted GDP; Growth rates for China, as well as the regional aggregates which include China, are based on TCB alternative estimates of Chinese GDP growth. ICT capital contribution (contribution of capital services provided by ICT assets to GDP growth), Non-ICT capital contribution (contribution of capital services provided by Non-ICT assets to GDP growth), and total capital contribution (contribution of total capital services to GDP growth). *Source* ISID based on The Conference Board, Total Economy Database, Summary Tables, April 2022. https://www.conference-board.org/data/economydatabase/

20.3.1 Landscape of International Trade

India's share in global exports has increased from 0.52% to 1.81% between 1990 and 2022. While it would appear to be an impressive 350% increase in about 3 decades, some other countries especially China have gained much more from globalization increasing its share in global exports from 1.79% to 14.36%. China was able to exploit the opportunities presented by hyper-globalization and capture a greater share of rapidly expanding global trade at the cost of others by quickly enhancing its manufacturing capacity (Kumar, 2024). With the economic reforms of 1991, India's trade openness has increased from a trade-to-GDP ratio of 20.7% in the 1990s to 49.4% in 2022 (having peaked at 55.7% in 2011/2012), currently higher than China's

37.4%, but lower than the OECD (56.4% in 2021).[3] Exporting products worth USD 638 billion in 2021 (total goods exports USD 398 billion, total services exports USD 241 billion), India has an exporter rank of 11th out of 133, with exports having grown by an annual 8.7% over the past five years.[4]

Changing Exports Structure. The changing industrial structure is reflected on the export structure of India which has become increasingly diversified over the years (Fig. 20.5). Refined petroleum and petroleum products have emerged to be the most important export item accounting for 13.9% of exports, followed by apparel and textiles (9.7%), chemicals (8.9%), and iron and steel (6%). Exports of machinery also make a rising share of exports (7.2% compared with 3.9% in 2000). The share of pharma product exports increased from 3.0% in 2001 to 5.3% in 2021. Transport equipment increased from 2.3% of exports to 6.0% in 2021. India's exports of electronics and electrical products have seen their share nearly double since 2001, 4.2% of the total, data for more recent years 2022–2024 will reveal their share rising dramatically with India rapidly emerging as the hub of mobile phone assembling.

The increasing diversification of India's export basket in favour of relatively technology-intensive goods such as machinery, chemicals, pharmaceuticals, and electronics has helped the country move up by 10 ranks in terms of the Harvard Growth Lab's Economic Complexity Index (ECI) ranking between 2011 and 2021.[5] India's export structure is considered to be more complex for its income level.

A comparison of India's global market share across 11 product sectors (agriculture, textiles, stone, minerals, metals, chemicals, vehicles, machinery, electronics, services, and other) with that of select economies, however, suggests that the pattern of India's export growth has been somewhat less impressive. Global market share in textile exports has stagnated, while electronics and machinery, with a global market share of 0.6% and 0.88%, respectively, in 2021, are yet to take-off. In comparison, China has entered all major, high-productivity sectors, seeing much more dynamism in textiles, electronics, and machinery. Thailand has witnessed export growth in machinery, while Malaysia's export growth in recent years has been driven by electronics. Bangladesh has seen increasing global presence in textile exports though its other sectors have stagnated, while Vietnam has exhibited dynamism in textiles and electronics (ISID, 2025).

India's Participation in Value Chains: Liberalization of FDI and trade regimes have also helped to enhance India's participation in global value chains (GVCs). A country's or country sector's total GVC participation in gross exports is measured as the sum of forward and backward participation. Forward participation is domestic value-added in foreign exports as a share of gross exports, by foreign exporting country. Backward participation is the foreign value-added share of gross exports, by value-added origin country, indicating value-added of intermediates inputs or 'tasks'

---

[3] World Development Indicators, World Bank (2023), https://data.worldbank.org/indicator/NE.TRD.GNFS.ZS.

[4] Exporting products worth USD 3.70 trillion (USD 3.36 trillion in merchandise products), China's exporter rank was 1st in 2021. https://atlas.cid.harvard.edu/countries/104/export-basket.

[5] The Atlas of Economic Complexity, https://atlas.cid.harvard.edu/rankings.

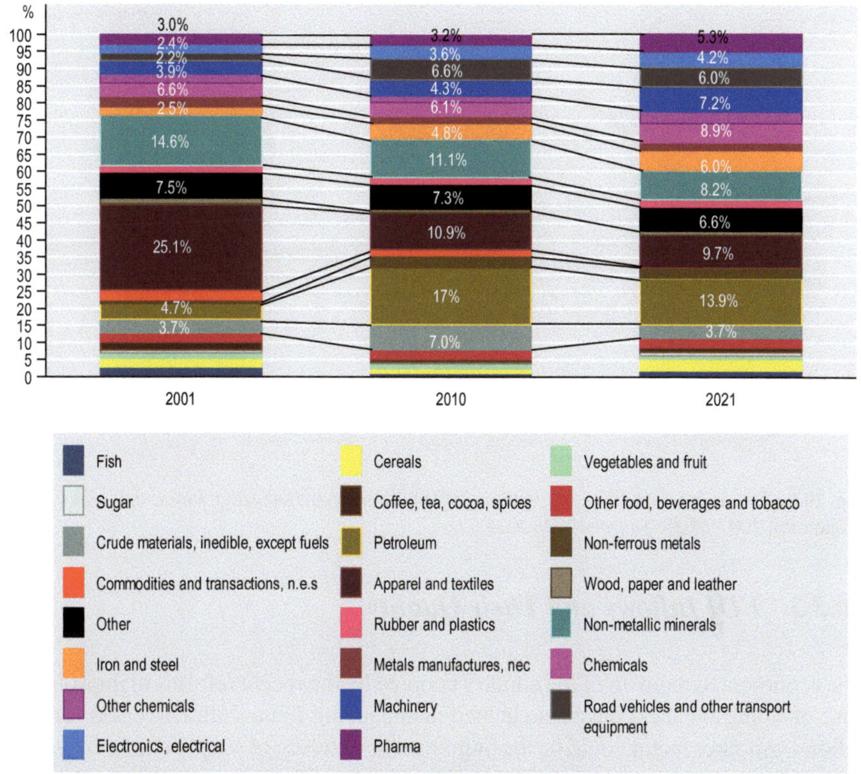

Notes: Based on classification of product groups and composition by UNCTAD Standard International Trade Classification (SITC) Revision 3 2- digit codes, https://unctadstat.unctad.org/en/Classifications/DimSitcRev3Products_DsibSpecialGroupings_Hierarchy.pdf. Some product codes have been aggregated.
Source: ISID based on UN Comtrade database, https://comtrade.un.org/

Fig. 20.5 Structure of India's merchandize exports, 2001–2021. *Notes* Based on classification of product groups and composition by UNCTAD Standard International Trade Classification (SITC) Revision 3 2-digit codes, https://unctadstat.unctad.org/en/Classifications/DimSitcRev3Products_DsibSpecialGroupings_Hierarchy.pdf. Some product codes have been aggregated. *Source* ISID based on UN Comtrade database, https://comtrade.un.org/

that are imported and enter into the production of goods and services to be exported. For manufacturing exports, China's GVC-related trade is the largest among all Asian economies, followed by South Korea and Japan (Fig. 20.6) (Chawla & Kumar, 2023). Though India has much lower GVC-related trade, its trade through value chains is comparable with Malaysia and Thailand. In recent years, Vietnam has emerged as an important GVC participant, due to its higher backward participation, though its forward participation remains lower. Indonesia, the Philippines, and Bangladesh have lower GVC participation compared to India.

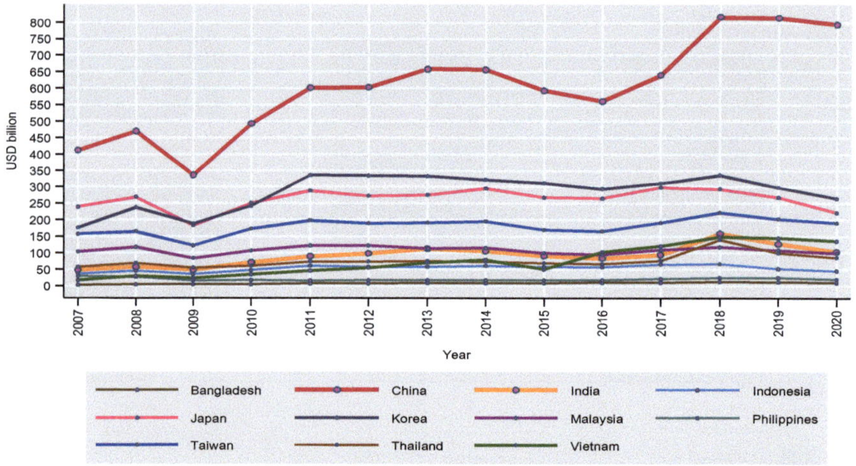

Fig. 20.6 Trends in total GVC participation (USD billion), manufacturing, India, and Select Asian economies, 2007–2020. *Source* ISID (2025)

20.3.2 FDI Inflows and Their Quality

The economic dynamism of the country coupled by the recent reforms to improve the ease-of-doing-business have also helped in enhancing India's attractiveness for FDI inflows. Another factor could be the ongoing restructuring of supply chains by global companies as a part of their de-risking strategies. In the surveys conducted of the Japanese investors by the Japanese Bank of International Cooperation (JBIC, 2022), India moved to the top rank among the promising medium-term business destination countries with China moving to second place and the US in third. India received support from Japanese investors in a wide range of industries including automobiles, electrical equipment, and electronics.

With FDI inflows of US$49.3 billion received in 2022, India was the fourth most attractive host country among emerging countries after China (including Hong Kong), Singapore, and Brazil (Fig. 20.7). However, FDI inflows in India are yet to reach the pre-pandemic peak of $64 billion (2020) (UNCTAD, 2023). Figure 20.8 shows that India's share in FDI inflows globally as well as regionally has risen over time. Many influential commentators including Martin Wolf (2023) of the *Financial Times,* expect India to become an important magnet for FDI in the coming years given its economic potential especially in view of the interest generated by the Make-in-India/PLI schemes and the ongoing friend-shoring as a part of de-risking of supply chains by MNCs, as is clear from trends in greenfield projects. India was the top destination among emerging countries for greenfield investment opportunities and for international project financing deals (UNCTAD, 2023). The share of FDI inflows in gross fixed capital formation (GFKF) is an indicator of its importance as an investible resource. The FDI to GFKF ratio for India has been rather low but has been rising steadily as is apparent from Fig. 20.9. In 2019–2021, India's annual average FDI

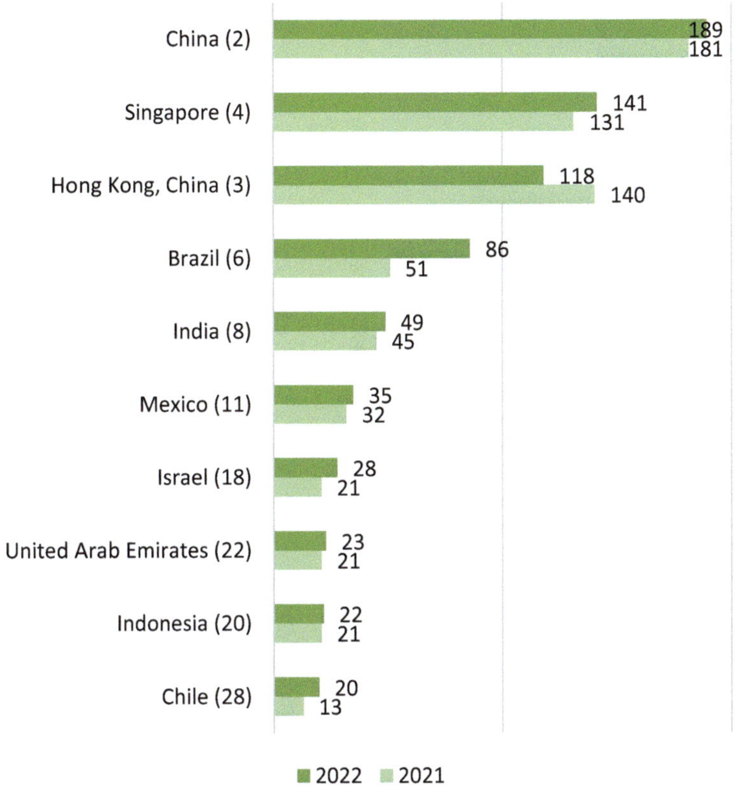

Fig. 20.7 FDI inflows, top emerging countries among 20 host economies, 2021 and 2022 (Billions of dollars). *Source* ISID adapted from UNCTAD, *World Investment Report 2023,* https://unctad.org/system/files/official-document/wir2023_en.pdf, Fig. 1.4

inflows as percentage of gross fixed capital formation (GFCF) at 6.7% compare favourably with that of developing Asia (5.8%), developing economies (6.6%) and worldwide (5.8%). However, due to global slow down and uncertainty surrounding the elections, FDI inflows to India declined in India in 2023 (UNCTAD, 2024) (Fig. 20.9).

20.3.3 Quality of FDI Inflows

While governments try to attract increasing magnitudes of FDI inflows, the recent literature has also pointed out that all inflows do not benefit their host countries in a similar manner and that there is a great variation in the extent of capital, entrepreneurship, technology, and market access or GVC integration (see Kumar, 2002). For instance, it matters whether FDI is going to the modern technology-intensive sectors

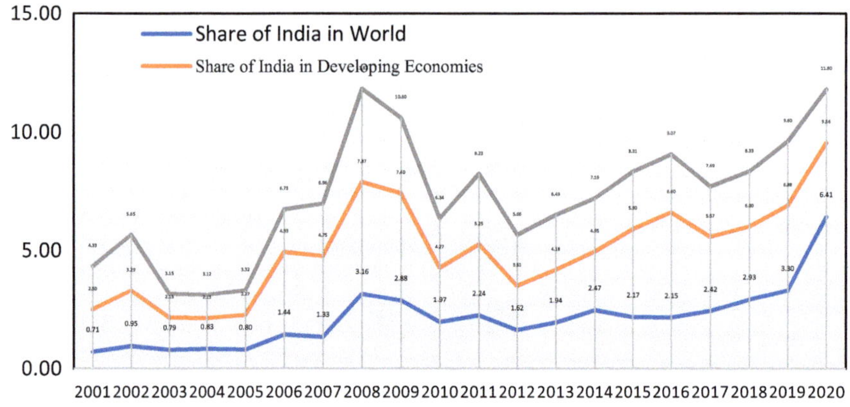

Fig. 20.8 India's share in global and regional FDI inflows. *Source* ISID based on UNCTAD data

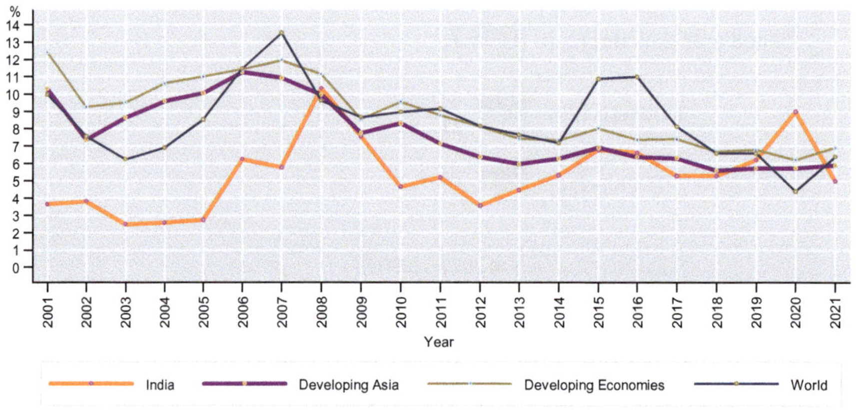

Fig. 20.9 FDI inflows as percentage of GFCF, India, developing Asia, developing economies, and worldwide, 2001–2021. *Source* ISID based on UNCTAD, *World Investment Report 2022*

that help to build productive capabilities or to conventional sectors crowding out domestic investments. Manufacturing accounted for about 36% of cumulative inflows in the 2000–2023 period, with construction and energy accounting for 17%, and services accounting for nearly 50% share.[6] Among the manufacturing subsectors, FDI stock is distributed between food processing, transport equipment, machinery, metals and metal products, electrical and electronics, chemicals and pharma products, and miscellaneous manufacturing. In China, on the other hand, the bulk of FDI inflows have been directed by the government policy to manufacturing (of the export-oriented type), and very little has gone to services (Yongding, 2006). The PLI

[6] See India, DPIIT (2023) FDI Factsheet, June 2023. https://dpiit.gov.in/sites/default/files/FDI_factsheet_June_23.pdf.

scheme may help in attracting greater FDI inflows to modern technology-intensive manufacturing sectors.

FDI inflows have a two-way relationship with economic growth—FDI inflows could contribute to growth by augmenting the capital stock and infusion of new technology but high growth rates may also attract more FDI inflows. Therefore, the FDI–growth relationship is subject to causality bias. What is the nature of the relationship in India? A study that examined the direction of causation between FDI and growth empirically for a sample of 107 countries, found the relationship for India to be neutral as the direction of causation was not pronounced. It means that FDI inflows received by India have been of mixed type, some enhancing growth, others attracted by it (Kumar & Pradhan, 2005). Another exercise analysing the impact of FDI on domestic investment also did not find a statistically significant effect, suggesting that FDI inflows received by India have been of mixed type combining some inflows crowding in domestic investments while others crowding them out, with no predominant pattern emerging (Kumar and Pradhan, op cit). In the case of East Asian countries such as South Korea and Thailand, the relationship clearly indicated FDI crowding in domestic investments. Therefore, the quality of FDI in India concerning its impact on growth and domestic investment leaves scope for improvement. Similarly, unlike the East Asian countries, India has not been able to exploit the potential of FDI for export-oriented production with the bulk of FDI inflows in India being market-seeking, coming for tapping the domestic market.

20.3.4 Landscape of Innovative Activity

The innovative activity of enterprises is a critical factor in determining their competitiveness and growth and their collective innovative activity reflects on the growth prospects of the country. Therefore, most governments around the world tend to incentivise the R&D activity of their enterprises.

In terms of innovative or R&D activity, India has lagged behind the global average and its peers. India invests nearly 0.7% of its GDP in R&D which is similar to South Africa (0.62%), higher than Indonesia (0.28%), lower than Malaysia (1.04%), and 2.9 times less than the world average (1.93%) (Fig. 20.10). Researchers per million inhabitants in India stood at 252 in 2018, which is higher than Sub-Saharan Africa (96), but small compared to emerging economies, such as Malaysia (2,184) and China (1,584), and the world (1,341). While other countries like South Korea and China have rapidly expanded the proportion of GDP devoted to R&D activity, in India this proportion has come down from 0.9% in 2008 to 0.7% in 2020. In China's case, it has increased from 0.9% to 2.4% between 2000 and 2020. India needs to increase R&D activity to upwards of 2% of GDP, as in the leading innovative nations. In terms of a composite indicator of innovative activity, namely, the WIPO (2023)'s *Global Innovation Index (GII) 2022,* however, India has moved up to occupy 40th rank globally, up from 81st in 2015 out of 132 economies. China now occupying

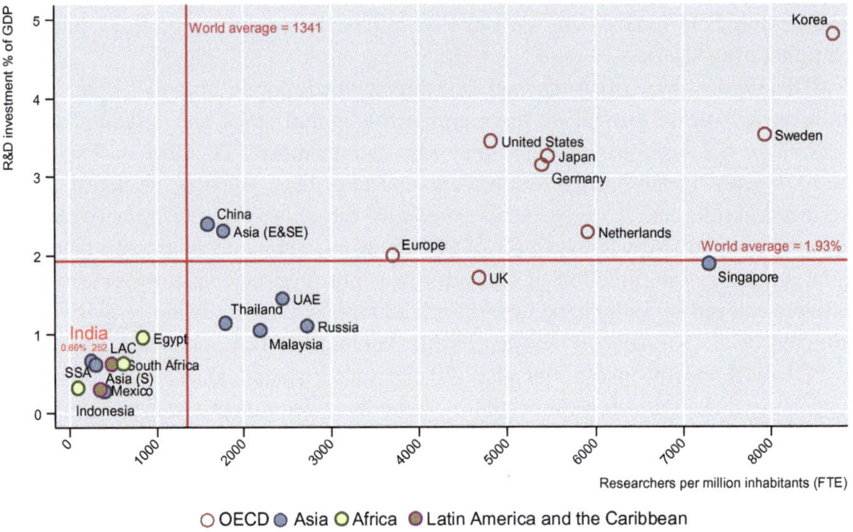

Note: R&D: Research and development.

Fig. 20.10 R&D as a share of GDP (%), researchers per million inhabitants, selected countries and world average, 2020 or the latest year available. *Note* R&D: Research and development. *Source* ISID (2025) based on UNESCO (2021), Institute for Statistics Database, http://data.uis.unesco.org

12th rank in GII, ahead of Japan at 13th, shows that it is possible to move up the innovation ladder with sustained effort.

Another issue of concern about innovative activity is that over 60% of India's national R&D expenditure is spent in the public-funded research organizations like the Council for Scientific and Industrial Research (CSIR), Indian Council of Medical Research (ICMR), Indian Council of Agricultural Research (ICAR), and higher education institutions. The share of in-house R&D activity by industry or the private sector in national R&D activity is under 40% compared to 62.9% globally. It suggests that Indian enterprises, even the most profitable ones, have not gotten into an R&D culture, not to talk of innovative rivalry (Forbes, 2023). The relative neglect of R&D activity by business enterprises is an issue of concern. This neglect has cost them dearly in terms of their competitiveness. The success of the current thrust on manufacturing through Make-in-India and PLI would be critically dependent on enhancing the innovative activity of the industry.

A recent national survey undertaken by UNIDO and the Indian Government's Department of Science and Technology of manufacturing innovation found only 16.32% of the firms to be innovation-active (engaged during the survey period in any innovation activity) (DST-UNIDO, 2023). The Survey found innovation levels to be highest among large firms (56%), followed by medium firms (39%), small firms (30%), and micro-enterprises (15%). The Survey found that of the firms reporting innovations, 83% had increased turnover, 80% opened new market opportunities,

77% responded to market pressures, and 71% responded to cost pressures. Therefore, innovative activity delivers value to the firms.

20.3.5 FDI in R&D

Multinational corporations (MNCs) are increasingly looking at India as a base for R&D activity. Normally the MNC affiliates may be less inclined to undertake R&D activity for their technological needs given their privileged access to their parent's laboratories. However, globalization of R&D activity has become an important trend as MNCs do relocate some of their R&D activity away from their home bases to take advantage of the abundant low-cost talent available in some countries and to absorb some knowledge spillovers from national innovation systems in other countries (Kumar, 2001), Kumar and Agarwal (2005). Such R&D activity is termed as the home-base augmenting R&D and is different from R&D undertaken by MNC affiliates to adapt their products for their host markets. India has emerged as an important location for such home-base augmenting R&D centres or the so-called Global Capability Centres (GCCs), established by MNCs. According to NASSCOM (2023), in 2023, there were over 1,580 Global Capability Centres (GCCs) operated by MNCs in India with 2740+ units, registering a 65% growth since 2015. Engineering, Research, and Development (ER&D) seemed to be the predominant focus of GCCs in India with 1,440 ER&D GCCs. Besides employment and income generation and boosting exports of services from the country, R&D centres operated by MNCs, given their much better technology capabilities, are expected to enhance the innovation ecosystem of the country. According to NASSCOM, GCCs have engaged 1.66 million talent and had a market size of US$ 46 billion in FY2023 (NASSCOM, op. cit.). Their R&D activity in India could lead to some important knowledge spillovers for the domestic economy through movement of technical staff who may carry with them advanced skills accumulated while working in the GCCs.

20.3.6 Preparedness for Industrial Revolution 4.0

The rise of new technologies such as artificial intelligence (AI), blockchain, cloud computing, big data analytics, machine learning (ML), internet of things (IoT), 3-D printing, collectively referred to as Industrial Revolution 4.0 (IR4.0) or digital revolution has a lot of opportunities as well as important challenges for developing countries such as India (ISID, 2021). Hence, they are attracting the attention of policymakers across the world. Some of the defining features of IR4.0, include their widespread applications across different fields of agriculture, industry, and services. They could bring potentially hugely disruptive consequences including extensive job losses and potential restructuring of value chains. They can also have a very substantial potential for inclusive development and societal transformation. The rapid evolution of IR4.0 technologies, almost on a real-time basis, provides a big advantage to the first movers. Countries like India, therefore, need to move very fast to tap their potential if they wish not to be left behind.

India's readiness in terms of leveraging IR4.0 is quite advanced due to its leadership in ICT and BPO capabilities and its demographic and skills advantage. India was found by UNCTAD to be the 'greatest outperformer' in terms of the frontier technology readiness index with a rank of 43 which was 65 positions higher than its rank according to per capita incomes. India has been classified among the countries with high levels of Opportunities but low levels of Skills in terms of IR4.0 indicators of readiness, along with a number of much richer countries such as China, Thailand, and Mexico (UNCTAD, 2022: 18). Another assessment put India among the top 10 countries in terms of having a robust technology and research platform and substantial public/private investments for AI preparedness by another assessment (Fig. 20.11) (Kumar, 2023a).

The landscape of IR4.0 adoption by the Indian industry is highly uneven. There are islands of excellence such as Tata Steel have been nominated by the World Economic Forum (WEF) as a member of the Global Lighthouse Network (GLN) in recognition of its excellence in the adoption of IR4.0 technologies, among other Indian companies, there is a serious risk of MSMEs getting left behind, which requires a policy response (Kumar, 2023a).

India has successfully deployed new digital technology to foster inclusive governance and development. Among the most visible applications include *Aadhaar*, the digital identity for nearly 1.3 billion people covering 99% of India's population. *Aadhaar* has also served as an identity marker for 500 million Jan Dhan bank accounts facilitating direct benefit transfers (DBT). Universal Payments Interface (UPI), a

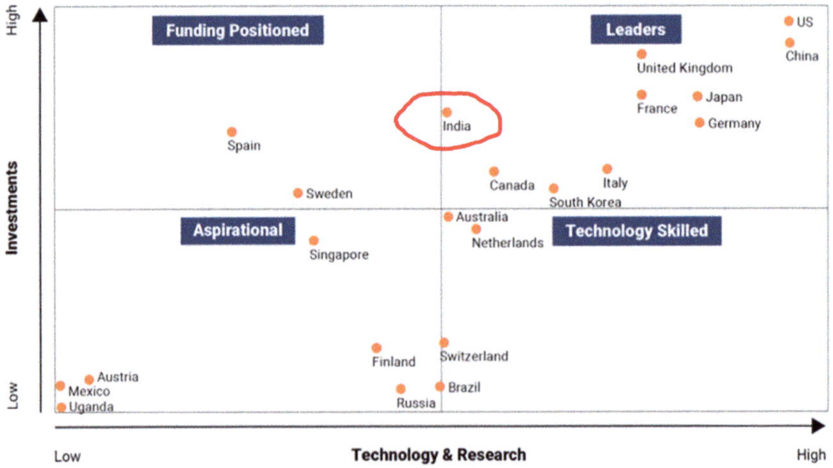

Fig. 20.11 AI preparedness in terms of technology and investments. *Source* https://www.brookings.edu/blog/techtank/2022/01/12/how-countries-are-leveraging-computing-power-to-achieve-their-national-artificial-intelligence-strategies/#cancel

highly successful mobile app-based digital payments interface that accounts for over 60% of all digital transactions in the country. UPI has become a stunning international success with 50 countries all across the world adopting it for digital payments. Government e-Marketplace (GeM), the government e-procurement system launched in 2017 has linked more than 4 million suppliers including MSMEs and women entrepreneurs. The digital platform TReDS facilitates MSMEs by financing their receivables. The National Agriculture Market or e-NAM, an online trading platform for agricultural commodities in India for farmers, traders, and buyers. The Open Network for Digital Commerce (ONDC) has begun to provide an e-commerce platform for MSMEs, akin to Amazon that charges no commission.[7]

20.4 Opportunities for Manufacturing-Led Transformation

The *India Industrial Development Report (IIDR) 2024–25* prepared by ISID (ISID, 2025) has reviewed the manufacturing opportunities available to India, including Making-for-India and Making-for-the-World, in labour-intensive, skill-intensive, resource-intensive, and strategic and defence industries besides opportunities presented by the green industrialisation and digital revolution. In particular, IIDR has identified the following sectors having great opportunities for further development for feeding the domestic market as well as exports:

- Labour-intensive sectors such as textiles and garments, leather goods, food processing, gems and jewellery, toys, and furniture, for their job-creating potential;
- Skill-intensive industries such as pharmaceuticals, vaccines, medical devices, chemicals, automotive and auto components, metal products, electrical and non-electrical machinery, and electronics and telecom equipment, for their rapidly rising demand within and outside the country;
- Green industries such as Solar PV cells and modules, wind turbines, advanced chemistry batteries, electric vehicles, green hydrogen, and electrolysers, making it, among others, for sustainability considerations and expanding markets; and
- New strategic and sunrise industries including semiconductors, defence industrialization, ship-building, and assembly of civilian aircraft.

These opportunities have the potential to more than double the manufacturing value-added from US$ 717 billion in 2024 to $1.45 trillion by 2030, out of the $7.5 trillion GDP, creating in that process, millions of direct and indirect jobs. India's emergence as one of the largest assemblers and exporters of smartphones in the past few years, creating hundreds of thousands of jobs, points to the opportunities as the policies are driving billions of dollars of investments into solar PV cells and modules, electrolysers for green hydrogen, and semiconductors, and pharmaceutical APIs, among others.

[7] See Kumar (2023a) for a more detailed analysis.

20.5 Industrial Policy for a Manufacturing-Led Transformation

The experiences of the East Asian countries provide valuable lessons for building industrial capacities. These lessons include incentivization of manufacturing sector including through pioneer industry investments, giving privileged access to domestic market through tariffs and non-tariff barriers, FDI promotion including through a proactive targeting of desirable investments. In recent years, Indian government has offered incentives for localization of production under the Production-Linked Incentives (PLI) scheme offered to 14 sectors. The Indian government has also raised tariffs on some products to give protection to local manufacturing. The other important lesson from the East Asian and European experiences is directed financing to manufacturing through national development banks. ISID (2023) has made a case for a new national industrial development bank to offer term-loans to manufacturing projects, in particular, to MSMEs as larger firms may have easier access to cheaper funding sources abroad. Management of a competitive exchange rate is another important element of the industrial strategy pursued by the East Asian countries.

A successful manufacturing strategy will need to be supported by an active innovation policy which fosters R&D activity of enterprises in product and process development and innovative rivalry. It becomes even more critical in the context of the new technology revolution and green industrialization where technology frontier is still moving forward and early emphasis on innovative activity could help in building leadership position, as in the EV batteries. R&D activity is closely linked with the education and skills development. Adopting a second-tier patent system viz. Utility Models or Petty Patents may foster innovative activity of MSMEs that is of a generally incremental nature. Given its youthful population and projections of dependency ratio still declining for another two decades, India has the potential to play an important role as the talent capital of the world. This would however require major investments in enhancing and strengthening education and skill development infrastructure in the country with greater emphasis on new technologies.

India also needs to close the gaps in the industrial infrastructure and logistics to reduce the overall cost of trade. This would also require investments in not only the domestic transport infrastructure such as highways and railways corridors and ports but also in transport and trade facilitation at the borders. The industrial corridors passing through lagging regions may also help in bringing them up and help in reducing interregional inequalities.

Besides harnessing the potential of new green industries such as solar PVs, wind turbines, electric vehicles, batteries, and storage solutions, the decarbonization of conventional industry such as steel, aluminium, fertilizer, and cement is also critical not only to achieve the net zero goals taken by the country under the United Nations Framework Convention on Climate Change (UNFCCC), but also to comply with the requirements of importers. Some countries like the European Union and the UK are already adopting Carbon Border Adjustment Mechanism (CBAM) which would impose carbon taxes on imports not meeting the emission requirements. Hence, supporting decarbonization of the traditional and hard-to-abate sectors through finance and technology would be important going forward.

Finally, India should engage its trade partners in negotiations at the bilateral, regional, and multilateral levels to obtain preferential market access for its products, especially in this age of trade wars and supply chain restructuring. India's opportunity to get integrated with the supply chains of global companies will be facilitated by its participation in a broader regional trading arrangement. Although India has free trade arrangements with key regional players such as Japan, the Republic of Korea, the ASEAN, and Australia, its inability to be a part of a regional agreement with cumulative rules of origin may affect its attractiveness for value chain integration adversely. From that point of view, India should consider joining either the Regional Comprehensive Economic Partnership of East Asia (RCEP), the Comprehensive and Progressive Agreement for Trans-Pacific Partnership (CPTPP), or the incipient trade agreement under the Indo-Pacific Economic Framework (IPEF). Being part of the regional arrangement would certainly be an advantage for supply chain integration (Kumar, 2024).

A key lesson from the experiences of the East Asian countries is the criticality of pursuing different elements of industrial policy such as investment facilitation, trade policy, innovation policy, exchange rate management, financing, and credit in a coordinated manner. To ensure that all different elements of industrial policy are coordinated, it is important to have a high-powered industrial policy secretariat with powers to call upon different arms of the government to come together at a single platform and coordinate their actions. The coordination should also extend to India's development assistance policy focused on countries in the Global South. It may also be helpful to adopt a new updated industrial policy resolution for the changed domestic and external context to provide a framework and clarity of objectives and targets to investors and other stakeholders (see ISID, 2025 for a detailed discussion).

20.6 Concluding Remarks

To sum up therefore, rapid job-creating economic growth through manufacturing-led transformation is imperative for India to realize its development aspirations of building a developed economy by 2047 and to address the challenge of employment creation. Industrial policy and emphasis on the real economy is a global trend in the context of the fractured trading system. As global companies restructure their supply chains on China +1 lines, India can potentially leverage its geopolitical and demographic sweet spots to build manufacturing capacities to feed growing domestic and global demand and tap the opportunities presented by the digital and green industrial revolutions.

To tap these opportunities, a strategic approach is needed to harness the potential of manufacturing, for which many useful lessons are available from the experiences of East Asian countries. In that context, India should build on PLI to a more proactive targeting approach to investment promotion that would help to attract better quality investments meeting its development needs. India also needs to make the regional and global trade rules supportive of its ambitious manufacturing-led transformation. Finally, to be effective, the different elements of industrial policy as outlined above need to be pursued in a coordinated manner through a high-powered institutional architecture for a coordinated implementation of industrial policy. An updated Industrial Policy Resolution providing a framework for accelerated growth of the manufacturing sector, generating jobs and prosperity in an inclusive and balanced manner, and a roadmap for achieving it is also desirable.

References

Amirapu, A., & Subramanian, A. (2015). *Manufacturing or services? An Indian illustration of a development dilemma, WP 409*. Centre for Global Development.

Arun Kumar, R. (2023). *Impact of import liberalisation on employment in manufacturing industries in India* (ISID Working Paper No. 265).

Brander, J. A., & Spencer, B. J. (1985). Export subsidies and international market share rivalry. *Journal of International Economics, 18*(1985), 83–100.

Chang, H.-J. (2002). *Kicking away the ladder: Development strategy in historical perspective.* Anthem.

Chawla, I., & Kumar, N. (2023). *FDI, international trade and Global Value Chains (GVCs): Trends and patterns in India's GVC participation* (Working Paper No. 267). Institute for Studies in Industrial Development. https://isid.org.in/wpcontent/uploads/2023/05/WP267.pdf

Cheriff, R., & Hasanov, F. (2019). *The return of the policy that shall not be named: Principles of industrial policy* (IMF WP/19/74).

Dasgupta, S., & Singh, A. (2006). *Manufacturing, services and premature deindustrialization in developing countries* (RP# 2006/49), Helsinki: UNU/WIDER.

DST-UNIDO. (2023). *National Manufacturing Innovation Survey (NMIS) 2021–22.* Department of Science and Technology, Government of India.

The Economist. (2022, January 10). Many countries are seeing a revival of industrial policy: A previously discredited approach has found new believers. *The Economist.* https://www.economist.com/special-report/2022/01/10/many-countries-are-seeing-a-revival-of-industrial-policy

Felipe, J., Mehta, A., & Rhee, C. (2014). *Manufacturing matters...but it's jobs that count* (Economics Working Paper 420). Manila: Asian Development Bank.

Forbes, N. (2023, December). *Towards innovations-driven industrial transformation of India.* Naushad Forbes ISID Policy Briefs #23-08.

ISID. (2021, December). *Harnessing industry 4.0 for India's development: Opportunities and challenges* (ISID Policy Briefs 21-04).

ISID. (2023). *Financing India's industrial transformation: Some policy lessons from international and national experiences.* Institute for Studies in Industrial Development.

ISID. (2025). *India industrial development report 2024–25: Towards a manufacturing-led transformation.* Institute for Studies in Industrial Development (ISID), and Academic Foundation.

JBIC. (2022). *Survey report on overseas business operations by Japanese manufacturing companies 34th survey.* Strategic Research Department. https://www.jbic.go.jp

Johnson, C. (1982). *MITI and the Japanese miracle.* Stanford University Press.

Juhasz, R., Lane, N., & Rodrik, D. (2023). *The new economics of industrial policy* (NBER Working Paper 31538). http://www.nber.org/papers/w31538

Kaldor, N. (1967). *Strategic factors in economic development.* New York State School of Industrial and Labour Relations, Cornell University.

Krishna, K. L., et al. (2022, July 30). Sources of India's post-reform economic growth: An analysis based on India KLEMS database. *Economic and Political Weekly, 57*(31).
Kumar, N. (2001). Determinants of location of overseas R&D activity of multinational enterprises: The case of US and Japanese corporations. *Research Policy, 30*, 159–174.
Kumar, N. (2002). *Globalization and the quality of foreign direct investment*. Oxford University Press.
Kumar, N. (2018). Reversing the pre-mature de-industrialization for job-creation: Lessons for 'Make-in-India' from experiences of industrialized and East Asian countries. In A. Ghosh Dastidar, et al. (Eds.), *Economic theory and policy amidst global discontent: Essays in Honour of Deepak Nayyar* (pp. 389–415). Routledge.
Kumar, N. (2022). Indian Economy@75: Achievements, gaps and aspirations for the Indian centenary. *The Indian Economic Journal.*https://doi.org/10.1177/00194662221105552
Kumar, N. (2023a). Unlocking India's potential in Industrial Revolution 4.0: National innovation system, demography, and inclusive development. *Indian Public Policy Review, 4*(3), 67–87. https://ippr.in/index.php/ippr/article/view/196
Kumar, N. (2023b, Spring). India's evolving industrial policy is critical for realizing its development vision. *ProMarket*, 54–59. Stigler Center, Chicago Booth. https://www.promarket.org/2023/03/21/indias-evolving-industrial-policy-is-critical-for-realizing-its-developmental-vision/
Kumar, N. (2024). Manufacturing-led transformation for realizing India's 2047 vision in the context of a fractured trading system: Challenges, opportunities and strategic interventions. *Indian Economic Review*. https://link.springer.com/article/10.1007/s41775-024-00220-4
Kumar, N., & Agarwal, A. (2005). Liberalization, outward orientation and in-house R&D activity of multinational and local firms: A quantitative exploration for Indian manufacturing. *Research Policy, 34*(4), 441–460.
Kumar, N., & Pradhan, J. (2005). Foreign direct investment, externalities and economic growth in developing countries: Some empirical explorations. In E. M. Graham (Ed.), *Multinationals and foreign investment in economic development* (pp. 42–84). Palgrave.
Lin, J. Y. (2012). *New structural economics: A framework for rethinking development*. The World Bank.
List, F. (1909). *The national system of political economy*. Longmans Green & Co.
NASSCOM. (2023). *GCC 4.0: India redefining the globalization blueprint*. NASSCOM.
Nayyar, D., & Nayyar, G. (2024, Springer). Made in India: Industrial policy in a changing world. *Journal of Industry, Competition and Trade, 24*(1), 1–27.
Rijesh, R. (2024). Trade, labour reallocation and productivity growth in the Indian manufacturing sector. *Indian Economic Review, 59*(Suppl 1), 327–353. https://doi.org/10.1007/s41775-024-00210-6
Rodrik, D. (2015). *Premature deindustrialization* (WP #20935). National Bureau of Economic Research.
WIPO. (2023). *Global innovation index 2022*. World Intellectual Property Organization.
Yongding, Y. (2006). The experience of FDI recipients: The case of China. In S. Urata, C. Siow, & F. Kimura (Eds.), *Multinationals and economic growth in East Asia* (pp. 423–452). Routledge.
Wolf, M. (2023). Quoted in *Business Standard*. https://www.business-standard.com/economy/news/india-could-become-a-magnet-for-foreign-direct-investment-martin-wolf-123070800479_1.html
UNCTAD. (2022). *Technology and innovation report 2022: Forging ahead at the digital frontiers*. UNCTAD, https://unctad.org/page/technology-and-innovation-report-2021#:~:text=The%20Technology%20and%20Innovation%20Report,also%20could%20accentuate%20initial%20inequalities
UNCTAD. (2023). *World investment report 2023*. UN.
UNCTAD. (2024). *World investment report 2024*. UN.

Part IX
Trade and Capital Inflows

Chapter 21
International Trade and Uneven Gains: What Do Theory and Structure of India's Foreign Trade Tell Us?

Rajat Acharyya and Shrimoyee Ganguly

Abstract The Gains from Trade theorem, based on the Ricardian doctrine of comparative advantage, constitutes one of the core propositions in international trade theory. But while it postulates that the trading nations will experience welfare gains at the aggregate when they specialize according to their comparative advantage, it does not suggest that all economic agents within a trading nation will gain. This chapter reviews the theoretical discourses and country experiences regarding such uneven gains from trade that have been pushing policy makers towards trade-policy reversals and raising concerns for future of globalization. We build an analytical model of politically optimum trade liberalization based on inequality driven discontents regarding trade liberalization to show that the politically optimum choice of tariff rate is larger than economic optimum rates. Finally, we review India's trade-policy paradigm before and after the 1991 Crisis, and discuss changing structure and increasing skill composition of our exports as potential sources of uneven gains and income inequality.

Keywords Uneven gains · Wage inequality · Globalization discontents · Skill composition of exports · GVC trade

JEL Codes F11 · F14 · F16

R. Acharyya (✉)
Department of Economics, Jadavpur University, Kolkata, India
e-mail: rajat.acharyya@gmail.com

S. Ganguly
Centre for Quantitative Economics and Data Science, BIT Mesra, Ranchi, India
e-mail: shrimoyee@bitmesra.ac.in

D. Maiti et al. (eds.), *75 Years of Growth, Development and Productivity in India*, India Studies in Business and Economics, https://doi.org/10.1007/978-981-97-8054-9_21

21.1 Introduction

The most celebrated idea in international economics, and in entire economics discipline in general according to Paul Samuelson, is David Ricardo's doctrine of comparative advantage driving trade between dissimilar countries. Ever since the introduction of this doctrine by him in his 1817 book, it has been widely recognized as the fundamental building block for the theory of international trade. The core wisdom of the Ricardian doctrine is that even countries that have technological superiority and absolute advantage—in the terminology of Adam Smith—in producing all the goods, should produce only a subset according to their comparative advantages and import the rest from the countries having comparative advantages in those goods. That is, countries should specialize and this will maximize their real incomes. Thus, not only there will be scope for a country with all-round superiority to exchange goods with an all-round inferior country, contrary to the no-trade prediction of Adam Smith, but such exchange or trade according to comparative advantages will be gainful for both. This Gains from Trade theorem constitutes one of the fundamental theorems in international trade theory. But it rests on several assumptions, some of which may seem to be bit restrictive, including perfectly competitive markets and markets correctly signalling the cost of production. More important, however, is that GFT does not mean that every economic agent gains from international trade. It merely states that the trading nation will experience real income and welfare gains *at the aggregate*. In fact, trade creates winners and losers within the trading nations. That is, trade may lead to uneven gains for economic agents of a trading nation.[1] This chapter reviews the theoretical discourses on such uneven gains from trade *within a trading nation* and ramifications for such uneven gains on trade-policy reversals and future of globalization. It also discusses India's trade-policy paradigm and changing structure of trade as potential sources of uneven gains and income inequality.

Consideration of the redistribution effect of trade and uneven gains therefrom holds significance for three reasons. First is its growth implications. The relatively richer income classes such as capitalists, landlords and skilled workers have higher marginal propensity to save than poorer income classes such as landless agricultural workers, unskilled factory workers and those working in the informal sector. Thus, if trade redistributes incomes in favour of the former group, then aggregate savings increases, which leads to larger investment, capital formation and hence growth (see Kaldor (1957) and Corden (1971) for such an argument). Second, in case of such a type of redistribution of income, trade may lead to larger incidence of poverty since most of the poor belong to the latter group of unskilled and low-skilled workers. Thus, trade-led growth and absolute position of the poor may be conflicting with each other

---

[1] Gains from trade are also uneven across trading nations. David Ricardo (1817) himself discussed that the relative size of trading nations matters for the distribution of aggregate gains from trade among them. Subsequently, uneven distribution of gains across trading nations, and possibility of welfare losses through both export-led and import-led growths, have been well-discussed in theoretical discourses as well as in empirical observations through the writings of Prebisch (1950), Singer (1950), Emmanuel (1972), Bhagwati (1958), Johnson (1967), Brecher and Alejandro (1977) and more recently by Acharyya and Marjit (2023).

at least in the short run. By this aggregate savings effect, redistribution of income in favour of the rich is desirable for growth but that accentuates income inequality and hurts the poor,[2] whereas a redistribution of income in favour of the unskilled and low-skilled workers improve their absolute positions and lowers income inequality, but lowers the growth rate as well. As we will elaborate in a subsequent section, the celebrated Stolper-Samuelson theorem in the context of Heckscher-Ohlin pattern of trade, and subsequent generalizations by Ronald Jones in his price magnification effects (Jones, 1965, 1971), point out that the nature of the redistribution of income due to freer trade is determined by the pattern of comparative advantage and trade itself.

Third is the trade-policy choice in a democracy. Economic agents, *rich and poor alike*, value their relative positions more than absolute positions. We envy others outside our peer groups, and as such even when our absolute positions improve in terms of income gains we cannot feel happy if our relative positions vis-à-vis such persons do not improve as well. Just as globally optimum environmental regulations and pollution abatement measures cannot be implemented because national interests precede global (or, regional or even bilateral) interests, conflicting individual interests precede group interests, and conflicting group interests precede national interests. Even altruism has its limits. Among many causes of conflicting individual or group interests, relative incomes are most important. Thus, income redistribution effect of any policy, be it trade or domestic policy, matters per se, regardless of in whose favour national income is redistributed. This dimension makes redistribution effect of trade more important and relevant than the overall gains from trade for incumbent governments as well as political parties contesting elections in democracies, since losers from freer trade will be the dissenting voices favouring and supporting for anti-trade parties. In democracies, the incumbent government is concerned more with maximizing political support and *minimizing political risks.* The political support comes only from the potential winning groups. Thus, the political risks of being overthrown from power emerge from creating more losers than winners from a policy change. Further, since the reality is that we envy others, even a Pareto Superior move through transfers may not get sufficient political support. This is because transfers compensate losers for their income losses but does not protect their relative income positions.

Rest of the chapter is organized as follows. In Sect. 21.2, we discuss on theoretical discourses on the effects of trade liberalization on within-country income and wage inequality. Section 21.3 documents the empirical evidences and discontents about globalization. We also build an analytical model of politically optimum trade liberalization. In Sect. 21.4, we examine the changing structure of Indian trade and its ramifications for growth and income inequality. Finally, Sect. 21.5 concludes the paper.

---

[2] In the long run, however, output and income growth can sustain redistribution policies in favour of the poor and lower the incidence of poverty.

21.2 Theoretical Discourses on Income Inequality

21.2.1 *Trade Liberalization and Income Redistribution: Conventional Wisdoms*

In the context of Heckscher-Ohlin-Samuelson model of trade with two goods and two factors, the seminal work of Stolper and Samuelson (1941) established that a tariff on the imported good hurts the abundant factor and benefits the scarcer factor of the economy. This celebrated Stolper-Samuelson theorem was subsequently generalized by Jones (1965): A tariff that raises the domestic relative price of the imported (and the import-competing) good, leads to a *real* income gain for the factor intensively used in production of it and *real* income loss for the factor of production intensively used in the production of the export good. Conversely, and more relevant in our context, a trade liberalization makes the factor intensively used in the import-competing good unambiguously worse-off and the other factor unambiguously better-off. This so-called price magnification effect essentially delinks the nature of income distribution effect of a tariff (or, conversely, trade liberalization) from the Heckscher-Ohlin pattern of trade. To reflect upon this price magnification effect, consider a small open economy that produces an agricultural export good (X) and an import-competing manufacturing good (Y) using unskilled labour (L) and capital (K). With exchange rate normalized to unity and an ad valorem tariff at the rate $0 < t < 1$ imposed on imports of Y, perfect competition in all domestic markets gives us the following zero-profit conditions:

$$P_X^W = a_{LX} w + a_{KX} r \tag{21.1}$$

$$(1+t)P_Y^W = a_{LY} w + a_{KY} r \tag{21.2}$$

where r is the rate of return to capital, w is the unskilled wage rate and P_j^W, $j = X, Y$ are the world prices of the two goods that the small country faces as given. Under CRS production technology, a_{hj}, $h = L, K$; $j = X, Y$, is the per unit requirement of factor-h in producing good j, which depends on the relevant factor-price ratio as below:

$$a_{hj} = a_{hj}(w/r),\ \frac{\partial a_{Kj}}{\partial (w/r)} > 0,\ \frac{\partial a_{Lj}}{\partial (w/r)} < 0, j = X, Y \tag{21.3a}$$

Note that each input earns the same return irrespective of which sector X or Y, it is engaged in. In other words, the factor prices are common in both the sectors under the assumption of homogeneity and perfect mobility of the inputs across the two sectors.

Suppose, the agricultural good is relatively more unskilled labour intensive than capital compared to the manufacturing good, which implies:

$$\frac{a_{LX}}{a_{KX}} > \frac{a_{LY}}{a_{KY}} \quad (21.3b)$$

This assumption will be crucial in determining the price magnification effect and how the two groups of unskilled workers and capitalists fare in response to a tariff cut.

The important point to note here is that the two factor prices are determined by the exogenously given world commodity prices and the tariff rate, regardless of the economy's endowment of labour and capital as long as both the traded goods are produced after trade opens up.[3] This is known as the factor-price insensitivity theorem in the trade literature.

Similar mechanism will ensure that all capital owners will earn the same rate of return across the two sectors. Now consider a ceteris paribus reduction in the tariff rate t. This lowers the domestic-currency price of the import-competing good by the proportion $\hat{P}_Y = \gamma\hat{t} + \hat{P}_Y^W = \gamma\hat{t}$, where $\gamma = \frac{t}{1+t}$. With the domestic-currency price of the agricultural export X being unchanged, producers find it comparatively more profitable to invest resources towards the X sector rather than in the Y sector. And resources released from the contracting import-competing sector Y makes such a shift in the composition of aggregate output feasible.

But since by (21.3b), Y is more capital-intensive so it will release more capital than labour for every unit of its output contraction. On the other hand, for every unit of expansion of good X, it will require proportionately larger amount of labour than capital. So reallocation of labour and capital would generate a situation of excess demand for the unskilled labour and excess supply of capital, and thereby would push up the unskilled wage and lower the rate of return to capital. Algebraically, following Jones (1965), totally differentiating the zero-profit conditions we can write:

$$\hat{P}_X^W = 0 = \theta_{LX}\hat{w} + \theta_{KX}\hat{r} \quad (21.4)$$

$$\hat{P}_Y = \gamma\hat{t} = \theta_{LY}\hat{w} + \theta_{KY}\hat{r} \quad (21.5)$$

Now subtracting (21.5) from (21.4), we get:

$$\hat{w} = -\frac{\theta_{KX}}{|\theta|}\gamma\hat{t},\ \hat{r} = \frac{\theta_{LX}}{|\theta|}\gamma\hat{t} \quad (21.6)$$

where θ_{ij} is the cost share of input i in per unit price of good j and $|\theta|$ is the determinant of cost share matrix and is positive under the assumption in (21.3b); $\gamma \equiv \frac{t}{1+t}$.

However, the Stolper-Samuelson theorem and the price magnification effect as Jones (1965) tells us more than these changes in absolute factor incomes. Since

---

[3] This result also holds with n > 2 number of commodities and m > 2 number of domestically available factors for $m = n$ and $m < n$ (see Feenstra (2006) and Samuelson (1953)). Domestic demand for the two goods do not matter as well as long as all the goods are traded.

$|\theta| = \theta_{LX} - \theta_{KX} > 0$, the rate of return to capital falls more than proportionate to the fall in the tariff-inclusive domestic price of good Y. Hence from (21.4) to (21.6), it follows that:

$$\hat{w} > \hat{P}_X = 0 > \hat{P}_Y > \hat{r} \tag{21.7}$$

Thus, if the import-competing good is relatively capital intensive, the workers not only have higher wages but also have higher real wage or income, whereas the capital owners experience real income losses, regardless of what fractions of their respective incomes they spend on the two goods. In general, the factor intensively used in the import-competing good (which is also the scarcer factor of the economy if the Heckscher-Ohlin trade pattern holds)—capital in this instance—is unambiguously worse-off; and the factor used in the export sector (which is also the abundant factor if the Heckscher-Ohlin trade pattern holds)—labour in this instance—is unambiguously better-off. The excluded-middle property of the price magnification effect also indicates a polarisation of the two groups of income earners in the economy in supporting or contesting trade liberalization.

However, in many instances, some goods may require certain specific types of inputs as well as skills that may not be required to produce the other goods. For example, the production of computers requires the skills of hardware engineers and high-technology intensive inputs like semi-conductors, which is not of much use in production of textiles or leather manufacture. Similarly, land is an essential primary input required in cotton production, which is not so necessary in providing IT-enabled and skill-based services. Thus, factors may have *sector-specific* use. On the other hand, some homogeneous factors of production commonly used in more than one sectors may be immobile, at least in the short run, across such sectors. In either case, freer trade redistributes factor incomes in a different way than stated above in the context of HOS production structure. To illustrate, following Jones (1971), suppose the agricultural good X is produced by unskilled labour (L) and land (T) while the import-competing manufacturing good (Y) is produced by unskilled labour and capital (K). So unskilled labour is the common (and homogeneous) input shared by the two sectors and land and capital are specific to X and Y, respectively. Suppose, unskilled labour is fully mobile. The zero-profit conditions now are rewritten as:

$$P_X^W = a_{LX}w + a_{TX}R \tag{21.8}$$

$$(1+t)P_Y^W = a_{LY}w + a_{KY}r \tag{21.9}$$

$$a_{ij} = a_{ij}(w, r, R) \tag{21.10}$$

Note that now the factor-price insensitivity theorem and the one-to-one correspondence between commodity prices and factor prices do not hold. The three factor prices cannot be determined solely by the exogenously given world prices of X and Y. The three factor-market clearing conditions given below will now be required to close the model and solve the factor prices and the output levels (along with input-intensities) *simultaneously*:

$$\overline{L} = a_{LX}X + a_{LY}Y \tag{21.11}$$

$$\overline{K} = a_{KY}Y \tag{21.12}$$

$$\overline{T} = a_{TX}X \tag{21.13}$$

where R is the rate of return to land, and all other variables are as defined earlier.

Now as a tariff reduction causes a scale contraction of Y, it lowers both the rate of return to capital and the unskilled wage at the initial output level of X. But, while the laid off workers move to sector X, capital has no alternative use, and thus its rate of return falls more than the unskilled wage. This induces producers of Y to adopt relatively more capital-intensive technique, as a result of which the initial excess supply of capital due to scale contraction gets absorbed in the Y sector itself. On the other hand, at the initial rate of return to land, lower unskilled wage induces producers of X to shift to a relatively less land-intensive technique of production. As a result, for every unit produced it releases some amount of land which enables a scale expansion of X, thereby absorbing all the unskilled workers displaced from the import-competing sector Y.

Algebraically, changes in the three factor prices can be worked out as:

$$\hat{w} = \frac{\lambda_{LY}\sigma_Y\theta_{TX}}{(\lambda_{LX}\sigma_X\theta_{KY} + \lambda_{LY}\sigma_Y\theta_{TX})}\gamma\hat{t} < 0 \tag{21.14}$$

$$\hat{R} = -\frac{\lambda_{LY}\sigma_Y\theta_{LX}}{(\lambda_{LX}\sigma_X\theta_{KY} + \lambda_{LY}\sigma_Y\theta_{TX})}\gamma\hat{t} > 0 \tag{21.15}$$

$$\hat{r} = \left\{1 - \frac{\theta_{LY}}{\theta_{KY}}\frac{\lambda_{LY}\sigma_Y\theta_{TX}}{(\lambda_{LX}\sigma_X\theta_{KY} + \lambda_{LY}\sigma_Y\theta_{TX})}\right\}\frac{\gamma\hat{t}}{\theta_{KY}} < 0 \tag{21.16}$$

where σ_j is the absolute value of the factor-substitution elasticity in production of good j; λ_{ij} is the share of sector-j in total employment of factor-i.

From (21.14) it follows that the fall in the unskilled wage is less than proportionate to the fall in the tariff-inclusive domestic price of imports:

$$\hat{w} - \hat{P}_Y = -\left[1 - \frac{\lambda_{LY}\sigma_Y\theta_{TX}}{(\lambda_{LX}\sigma_X\theta_{KY} + \lambda_{LY}\sigma_Y\theta_{TX})}\right]\gamma\hat{t} > 0$$

Accordingly, the rate of return must fall more than proportionate to the fall in the tariff-inclusive domestic price of imports: $\hat{r} < \hat{P}_Y < 0$. Combining all these, we arrive at the following price magnification effect:

$$\hat{R} > \hat{P}_X = 0 > \hat{w} > \hat{P}_Y > \hat{r} \tag{21.17}$$

Thus, while the real income of the landowners rise and that of the capitalists go down unambiguously, such a definite statement about the *real wage to unskilled labour* cannot be made. Thus, workers—the mobile factor—may gain or lose depending on what proportions of their incomes they spend to consume the two goods X and Y. At the one extreme, if it be the case that they consume only X, then the unskilled workers are unambiguously worse-off as their real wage (with respect to price of good X) falls. At the other extreme, if they consume only good Y, then they are better off as their real wage (with respect to price of good) increases.

Thus, unlike the HOS case of the same (and mobile) set of factors of production used in the production of all the goods, the interest groups will be less polarized after a policy shock like trade liberalization. Interests of owners of factors of production specific to the export and import-competing goods—landlords and capitalists in this instance—will still be polarized, but interests of unskilled workers—the commonly used mobile factor—will now be aligned with either of them.

21.2.2 Trade Liberalization and Wage Inequality: Going Beyond Standard Trade Theories

What one may derive from the above discussions is that the HOS and its specific-factor variant suggests that freer trade between developed and developing countries should lower the wage gap (and the wage inequality) between the skilled and unskilled workers in the developing countries but raise the same in the developed countries. The reason is simple as laid out in Acharyya (2017). To understand, recall the capital used in the import-competing Y sector and imagine it to be skilled labour against the unskilled labour that is used in the export sector. By the factor-abundance argument of HO theorem, developed countries being relatively skill abundant export skill-intensive goods and services, whereas the unskilled-labour-abundant developing countries by and large export unskilled labour intensive goods and services. With such pattern of trade, price of the skill-intensive good relative to the price of unskilled labour intensive good should fall in the developing country due to lowering tariff rates on the imports and thereby increasingly engaging itself in trade with its developed trading partner. By the price magnification effect stated in (21.7), the skilled wage relative to unskilled wage should decline in the developing country. The opposite should happen in the developed country. That is, freer trade should lead to asymmetric changes in the relative price of the skill-intensive good, and subsequently to *asymmetric* changes in the wage gap through the price magnification effect.[4]

However, contrary to this theoretical prediction, skill premium or the wage gap has been found to be growing the world over by a large number of studies over the

[4] Similar result would follow in the specific factor case, with skilled labour and unskilled labour being specific to the import-competing and export sectors, whereas capital being commonly used.

last three decades. For example, as documented in Marjit and Acharyya (2003) and subsequently in Acharyya (2017), the skill premium has increased for Latin American countries like Chile, Mexico, Uruguay and Costa Rica (Beyer et al., 1999; Pederson, 1998; Robbins, 1995a, 1995b) and in high income developed countries like Australia, Japan, Canada, UK, Germany and the United States (Freeman & Katz, 1994; Katz et al., 1992; Lawrence, 1994; Leamer, 2000). In case of the Asian countries, the wage gap has moved both ways: though for countries like Korea, Singapore and Taiwan, which are in more advanced stages of development, the wage gap has narrowed down, for China, Sri Lanka and India, the wage gap has widened (ILO, 2018; Rodrigo, 1988; Robbins, 1995b; Shariff & Gamber, 1999; Sharma, 2022; Wood, 1997). For India, it has been observed recently by an ILO (2018) study that workers in the lowest-skilled occupation in India earned 40% below the average wage earnings 1993–94 to 2011–12. In contrast, workers in the high-skilled occupations earned between 1.9 and 4.3 times higher than average wage earnings during the same period.

There is a general consensus among economists that the root cause of such widely observed widening of skilled–unskilled wage gap in the developing countries is driven by an increase in the demand for skilled labour relative to that of the unskilled labour. However, researchers are divided in their opinions over the cause of such rising demand for skill. Theoretical discourses bring out two dogmatic positions being held in this debate: some argue that it is the advent of information technology in the rich nations in the 1970s and 1980s and changes in production structures that it has caused in the developing countries (Bound & Johnson, 1992; Krugman, 2000; Lawrence, 1994); while another group talks about significant and sustained episodes of liberalization of trade regimes across the globe beginning in the 1980s (Feenstra & Hanson 1996; Jones & Engerman, 1996; Leamer, 2000; Robbins, 1995a, 1995b; Wood, 1997) being the reason.[5]

Generalizing and extending the basic HOS and SF models of trade by incorporating observed trade patterns and labour market characteristics of the developing countries, trade theorists have extensively discussed three major sources of trade liberalization accentuating wage inequality over the last three decades: diverse trade pattern, particularly exports of skill-based goods and services by some developing countries such as Brazil, China, India, Mexico and some of the east Asian countries; segmented labour markets, or coexistence of formal and informal labour markets; and changing composition of export baskets in terms of better quality goods. The analytical structured of the specific-factor model as discussed in Sect. 21.2.1 can be extended suitably to illustrate how these three major sources of trade liberalization policy adopted by a developing country accentuates wage inequality. In the following sub-section, we begin with the case of a diverse trade pattern.

[5] Explanations for the two-sided growing wage gap, i.e. rising wage inequality in both the skill abundant and unskilled-labour abundant trading partners, have been given in terms of countries commonly producing "middle" goods either in the fragmented vertical stages of production, or in a multi-commodity setting of the HOS model (Davis, 1996; Feenstra & Hansen, 1996; Marjit & Acharyya, 2003; Zhu & Trefler, 2005).

21.2.2.1 Diverse Trade Pattern

Suppose, in addition to the agricultural export good X and the import-competing manufacturing good Y, the small developing economy also produces a skill-based good Z which is entirely exported. It requires skilled labour (S) and along with it shares the same capital (K) as the Y sector uses. So while land (T) is specific to the X sector, now skill is specific to Z. It is basically a three commodity-four factor general equilibrium structure, wherein, the economy is producing less traded goods than the number of factors it is endowed with. Free entry and exit of firms in the Z sector ensure they break-even and operate by the following price-average cost condition:

$$P_Z^W = a_{SZ}w_S + a_{KZ}r \tag{21.18}$$

where P_Z^W is the per unit price of Z as given from the world market in domestic currency with the nominal value of the exchange rate is normalised to unity. w_S is the skilled wage that is fully flexible and adjusts to clear the perfectly competitive skilled labour market. With the supply of skilled workers $\overline{S}$ being exogenously given, the full employment condition that also solves for the output of the Z good, is given as:

$$\overline{S} = a_{SZ}Z \tag{21.19}$$

The remaining structure of the model is the same as that specified in Sect. 21.2.1.

Now to see how wage inequality between skilled and unskilled labour is affected, recall the price magnification effect that trade liberalization policy had led to in the (X, Y) nugget as specified in (21.17). Since the skill-based export good Z shares the same capital with the manufacturing good Y, the fall in its rate of return will lower unit costs of producing Z and induce profit maximising producers there to raise output. This will raise the demand for skilled labour and with it the skilled wage. The consequent rise in the w_S/r ratio induces a technique effect whereby producers of Z shift to a relatively less skill-intensive technique of production and thereby releases some amount of skilled labour which then makes way for expansion in output of Z. Thus, the skilled–unskilled wage gap unambiguously worsens. With a similar production structure, Marjit and Beladi (1998) arrived at a similar result of worsening wage gap following an increased in the world price of the unskilled-labour produced export good (X, in the present context).

21.2.2.2 Segmented labour markets and Informalization[6]

The existence of segmented labour markets, a typical feature of developing and less-developed countries, adds further dimensions to the effect of trade liberalization on wage inequality. In India and in many Latin American countries, formal and informal

[6] This Section and the following Sect. 21.2.2.3 draw from Ganguly and Acharyya (2021).

unskilled-labour markets coexist with more than 80% of the work-force employed in informal sectors. Evidences from such countries reveal that import liberalization contributes to increase in wage inequality through displacement of workers from the formal to the informal segments, a phenomenon known as informalization (Bogliaccini (2013), Brady et al. (2011), Marjit (2003), Marjit and Kar (2011), Marjit et al. (2007)). When the formal and informal sectors are connected by the use of common inputs, and if a trade policy induces more intensive use of such a factor in one sector, its scarcity may imply a trade-off between the production of the traded goods among these sectors. If it be so that such changes in output composition leads to contraction of the formal sector and consequent fall in the relative demand for unskilled workers and job losses therein, these displaced workers, however, may not be absorbed back if unemployment already exists due to rigidity of wages. Thus, opening up trade barriers may increase the pool of unemployed in the short run. Informal sectors may absorb a part of the displaced workers but only for a significant drop in the informal wage. If the skilled wage rises as before, wage inequality will be accentuated in three dimensions: between skilled and unskilled informal workers, between skilled and the formal unskilled workers and also, most interesting to observe, among the unskilled workers themselves, i.e. between formal and informal workers.

To get a clearer picture, let us revisit the three-sector four factor production structure used in 21.2.2.1 to explain implications on wage inequality under a diverse trade pattern.[7] But, now let the production of Y be organized in the formal sector and production of X in the informal sector of the economy. This assumption is made in parity with what we typically observe in many developing countries. The import-competing manufacturing sectors mostly consist of medium and large enterprises that hire unskilled workers on the basis of formal contracts. On the other hand, agricultural production activities (as well as many low-skill-intensive exports like leather and leather manufacture) are mostly informal in nature. The distinction between formal and informal sectors also follows the standard literature (Kar et al. (2019), Marjit (2003), Marjit and Kar (2011)). The unskilled workers in the formal Y sector are paid a minimum, and fixed, wage, $\overline{w}$, whereas those engaged in the informal X sector are paid the competitive market-determined wage (without any floor), w. The three relevant zero-profit conditions are reproduced below with appropriate modifications:

$$P_X^W = a_{LX}w + a_{TX}R \tag{21.20}$$

$$(1+t)P_Y^W = a_{LY}\overline{w} + a_{KY}r \tag{21.21}$$

$$P_Z^W = a_{SZ}w_S + a_{KZ}r \tag{21.22}$$

The other equations depicting the per unit input requirements and full employment of factors, remain as used in Sect. 21.2.2. From the above zero-profit conditions, one may note that given the fixed unskilled wage in the formal Y sector, the rate of return

[7] See also Ganguly and Acharyya (2021).

to capital (r) will be directly determined by the tariff rate for any given world price of Y. Since this same capital is also used in the Z sector, this value of r will then determine the wage to skilled labour in the Z sector. However, unlike the skilled wage and the rate of return to capital, the informal unskilled wage and the return to the land specific to the informal X sector cannot be determined independent of the resources available for production of goods X and Y. This follows from the specific-factor structure of the (X, Y) subsystem. Thus, trade liberalization will affect the informal unskilled wage and correspondingly the rate of return to land through reallocation of unskilled workers across formal and informal sectors.

Now, consider a ceteris paribus reduction in the tariff rate. With fixed formal wage this lowers the rate of return to capital by stroke of the pen:

$$\hat{r} = \frac{1}{\theta_{KY}}\gamma\hat{t} < 0 \tag{21.23}$$

Increased foreign competition as a consequence of tariff reduction forces the import-competing industry to contract, which lowers the demand for both unskilled labour and capital. With the unskilled money wage being fixed in this formal sector, the entire burden of adjustments fall on capital and through a fall in its rate of return the domestic producers of Y break-even again at the lower tariff-inclusive domestic price. As a reduction of tariff lowers the capital cost of producing Z good, producers then expand the production level and the demand for skilled workers and their wage thus rises:

$$\hat{w}_S = -\frac{\theta_{KZ}}{\theta_{SZ}\theta_{KY}}\gamma\hat{t} \tag{21.24}$$

Now, turning to the effect on unskilled informal wage, as the demand for unskilled workers fall in the contracting import-competing Y sector, the workers thus displaced move into the informal X sector, which causes the marginal productivity of labour to diminish given the fixed amount of land to work with there. The unskilled wage in the informal sector thus declines on this account. Second, a substitution of unskilled workers by capital per unit production of Y in face of lower r (and fixed formal wage), which further reinforces the displacement of unskilled workers and decline in the informal unskilled wage.[8]

Algebraically, the extent of worsening wage inequality can be worked out as:

[8] Note, we assume that those who cannot get employment in the formal sector are absorbed in the informal sector through competitive forces and consequent fall in the informal unskilled wage. This assumption has been largely motivated by the analyses of Carruth and Oswald (1981), Rauch (1991), Agenor and Montiel (1996), Marjit (2003), Marjit (2000), Marjit and Kar (2011) and Kar et al. (2019). On the contrary, some researchers observe that all unskilled workers displaced from the formal sectors may not be fully absorbed in informal sectors the short run for various reasons (Fields (1990), Rogers and Swinnerton (2004) and Swinnerton (1996)). In such a case, some unemployment may still exist. See also Ganguly and Acharyya (2021).

$$\hat{w}_S - \hat{w} = -\left(\frac{\theta_{KZ}\lambda_{LX}\sigma_X + \theta_{SZ}\theta_{TX}\lambda_{LY}\sigma_Y}{\lambda_{LX}\sigma_X\theta_{SZ}\theta_{KY}}\right)\gamma\hat{t} \tag{21.25}$$

So tariff reduction unambiguously lowers the informal unskilled wage through informalization. Wage inequality thus worsens in all the three dimensions: between skilled workers and formal unskilled workers, which is captured through the rise in skilled wage (given by 28); among the unskilled workers themselves, that is, between formal and informal unskilled workers, which is captured through the decline in the informal wage along with the increase in the share of the informal sector in total employment of unskilled workers, and finally, between skilled and informal unskilled workers, captured through $\theta_{KZ}^2\gamma_{KZ}^2$.

21.2.2.3 Export Quality and Wage Inequality

Recent evidences better export performances of countries highlight the importance of the export-quality (Baldwin and Harrigan (2011), Dongwen et al. (2016), Fan et al. (2018), Galera and Fraga (2022), Gambero and Garcia-Ramos (2015), Hallak (2006), Manova and Zhang (2012), Mukerji (2021)). This quality dimension of exports is also one primary explanation of the export-supply–import-demand misalignment problem faced by the developing countries currently. While on the one hand buyers in the richer countries prefer to spend a larger proportion of their income on high quality products (Hallak, 2006), on the other hand, the export baskets of the developing countries consist mostly of low-quality goods. This dimension of misalignment has been severely constraining the exports of the developing countries rates to the advanced richer countries. In such a context, export-promoting trade liberalization policies in the developing countries must target at improving quality of export goods rather than at making their low-quality exports cheaper.

However, both theory and recent evidences reveal that producing higher-quality varieties of export products require more intensive use of domestic inputs like skill and capital other than imported high-quality inputs (Acharyya & Jones, 2001; Brambilla & Porto, 2016; Brambilla et al., 2012; Falvey & Kierzkowski, 1987; Flam & Helpman, 1987; Ganguly & Acharyya, 2021). Thus, quality upgrading induced by export-promotion strategies like tariff reductions may cause other traded sectors to squeeze in the face of scarcity of these resources. The demand for unskilled labour, which is needed in those sectors but not directly used in quality upgrading, would decrease in the process, which would lower the unskilled wage and thereby accentuate wage inequality. Thus, in a broader context, a policy conflict between quality upgrading and containing wage inequality may be apparent, making it difficult for policy makers, particularly in democracies like India, to focus solely on quality-upgrading trade promoting strategies. The large body of literature on trade and wage inequality mentioned earlier has not accounted for quality variations in skill-based exports induced by such policies as a plausible source and cause of the observed increase in wage inequality. But to the extent to which quality variations per se accentuate wage inequality, the effects of a tariff reduction on wage inequality will be an underestimation if quality variations induced by it are not considered. This has been recently emphasized in Ganguly and Acharyya (2021).

To illustrate, suppose the skill-based export Z defined in Sect. 21.2.2.2 is quality-differentiated, whose qualities are observable and indexed by $Q \in [0, \overline{Q}]$.[9] Suppose also that per unit requirement of S and K increases at an increasing rate with quality upgrading, with reflect diminishing returns to each factor:

$$a_{iz} = a_{iz}(Q),\ a'_{iz}(Q) > 0,\ a''_{iz}(Q) > 0, i = K,\ S \tag{21.26}$$

The relative skill intensity of higher-quality varieties of export good Z defined as,$s_Z = a_{SZ}(Q)/a_{KZ}(Q)$,is increasing or decreasing with quality upgrading according to the technological requirements. In particular, if quality upgrading of Z requires relatively more capital than skilled labour per unit, then s_Z is decreasing in higher qualities.

Given these technological requirements, and foreign buyers' willingness to pay increasing with higher qualities—$P_Z^{W'}(Q) > 0,\ P_Z^{W''}(Q) > 0$—the zero-profit condition for Z can be rewritten as:

$$P_Z^W(Q) = a_{SZ}(Q)w_S + a_{KZ}(Q)r \tag{21.27}$$

On the other hand, the profit maximising export-quality Q^0 of export good Z is given by the following marginal condition:

$$P_Z^{W'}(Q^0) = a'_{Kz}(Q^0)r + a'_{sz}(Q^0)w_s \tag{21.28}$$

The full employment conditions of capital and skilled labour will change as we incorporate the introduction of quality dimension of Z, in the following way:

$$\tilde{K}(Q) \equiv \overline{K} - a_{KZ}(Q)Z = a_{KY}Y \tag{21.29}$$

$$\overline{S} = a_{SZ}(Q)Z \tag{21.30}$$

where $\tilde{K}(Q)$ is the availability of capital for production of Y which is its total stock $(\overline{K})$ less what is required in production of Z for any given quality of it.

Now recall that as ad valorem tariff rate determines the rate of return to capital (from 21.26), this in turn will determine the skilled wage as earlier, but now for any given level of quality Q—and corresponding world price of Z_from the relevant zero-profit condition in (21.27). On the other hand, for any given skilled wage and rate of return to capital, producers of Z choose the quality level Q that satisfies the marginal condition in (21.28). Since, by the zero-profit condition rate of return to

[9] Note that the observable quality rules out any information externality and associated moral hazard and adverse selection problems.

capital and the skilled wage are inversely related,[10] so the profit maximizing quality level may be obtained from (21.35) as:

$$\hat{Q} = \frac{P_Z^W}{\delta Q^2}\theta_{KZ}(\gamma_{KZ} - \gamma_{SZ})\hat{r} \tag{21.31}$$

where $\delta \equiv \left(P_Z^{W''}(Q) - w_S a''_{SZ}(Q) - r a''_{KZ}(Q)\right) < 0$ by the second order condition for profit maximization; $\gamma_{iZ} = \frac{\partial a_{iZ}}{\partial Q}\frac{Q}{a_{iZ}} > 0, i = K, S$, denote the quality-elasticity of per unit requirements of input i in production of Z.

Now, turning to the effect on wage inequality, the informal unskilled wage will now decline on two counts. First, at the initial quality levels, tariff reduction unambiguously lowers the informal unskilled wage through informalization of unskilled workers from the contracting formal Y sector to the informal X sector as explained in the previous Sect. 21.2.2.2. In addition to this initial change, tariff reduction induced quality variations affects the unskilled informal wage further through reallocation of capital across Z and Y sectors. To see this, note that capital requirement in Z sector changes in two ways. First, if quality is upgraded, it lowers output of Z since higher quality requires more skilled labour which is specific to this sector and the extent of such output contraction is given by $\hat{Z} = -\gamma_{SZ}\hat{Q}$. Thus, on this account, less capital is required. Second, capital requirement per unit of output of good Z rises if quality is upgraded, and the extent of such additional capital requirement is given by $\hat{a}_{KZ} = \gamma_{KZ}\hat{Q}$. So, if $\gamma_{SZ} < \gamma_{KZ}$, the condition for which quality is upgraded, then overall capital requirement in Z production will rise. The reverse reasoning shows that if $\gamma_{SZ} > \gamma_{KZ}$, as tariff reduction downgrades quality, larger capital requirement due to expansion of output of Z dominates smaller capital requirement per unit due to quality degradation. Thus, in either case, the overall capital requirement in Z sector rises in all cases regardless whether it induces quality upgrading or downgrading:

$$\hat{K}_Z = \lambda_{KZ}(\gamma_{KZ} - \gamma_{SZ})^2\gamma\hat{t} > 0 \tag{21.32}$$

where λ_{KZ} is the share of sector Z in total employment of capital.

Thus, export-quality variation lowers capital availability for production of Y and lowers its output. This causes larger informalization, and pushes down the informal wage *further*. Algebraically, the overall fall in the informal wage is given by[11]:

$$\hat{w} = \frac{1}{A}\frac{\lambda_{KY}\sigma_Y}{\theta_{KY}}\gamma\hat{t} - \frac{1}{A}\lambda_{KZ}(\gamma_{KZ} - \gamma_{SZ})\hat{Q} \tag{21.33}$$

$$\textit{where } A = \lambda_{KY}\sigma_Y + \lambda_{KY}\frac{\lambda_{LX}}{\lambda_{LY}}\frac{\sigma_X}{\theta_{KX}} > 0$$

[10] By envelope theorem, the skilled wage will be invariant with respect to the quality variation.

[11] See Ganguly and Acharyya (2021) for algebraic details.

The first term in the parenthesis is the initial effect of tariff reduction, whereas the second term captures the induced effect through quality variation.

Thus, wage inequality worsens even more on all counts: between skilled and informal unskilled workers ($\hat{w}_S - \hat{w} > 0$); between skilled and formal unskilled workers and between formal and informal unskilled workers, the latter due to informalization. What this implies is that that when we account for quality variations of skill-based exports, the wage inequality worsens by a larger extent than when such quality variations are not accounted for. And this is regardless of the direction of such quality variations. This brings out the relevance of accounting for product quality variations induced by export promotion strategies like tariff reduction, in measuring the magnitude of changes in wage inequality. Figure 21.1, reproduced from Ganguly and Acharyya (2021), illustrates this. The inverse relationship between the skilled–unskilled wage ratio and the tariff rate is denoted by the $\overline{\omega}$-curves for any given $K_Z(Q)$ that corresponds to a given quality. Higher $\overline{\omega}$-curves correspond to larger $K_Z(Q)$ amounts *for any given tariff rate* since a rise in the amount of capital used in Z will lower the unskilled informal wage and raise the wage inequality.

When tariff is lowered from t_0 to t_1, the wage inequality accentuates at initial quality levels, from $\overline{\omega}_0$ to $\overline{\omega}_1'$ (corresponding to movement from point *a* to point *b*) along the initial $\hat{Q}_2 = \frac{P^W_{Z2}}{\delta Q_2^2}\frac{\theta^1_{KZ}}{\theta^1_{SZ}}\left(1 + \frac{\mu_S}{\theta^2_{KZ}}\right)\varphi\hat{s}$ curve. But lower tariff raises Q if $\gamma_{SZ} < \gamma_{KZ}$ and lowers it if $\gamma_{SZ} > \gamma_{KZ}$, either of which uses up more capital and thus raises $\overline{\omega}$ further to $\overline{\omega}_1$ (corresponding to movement from point *b* to point *c* on a higher $\overline{\omega}$ curve). Therefore, accounting for export-quality variations induced by a tariff reduction, the total change in wage inequality should be measured by the movement from *a* to *c* along the steeper bold curve.

Thus, the effect of a tariff reduction on wage inequality would be an underestimation when induced quality variations are not accounted for.

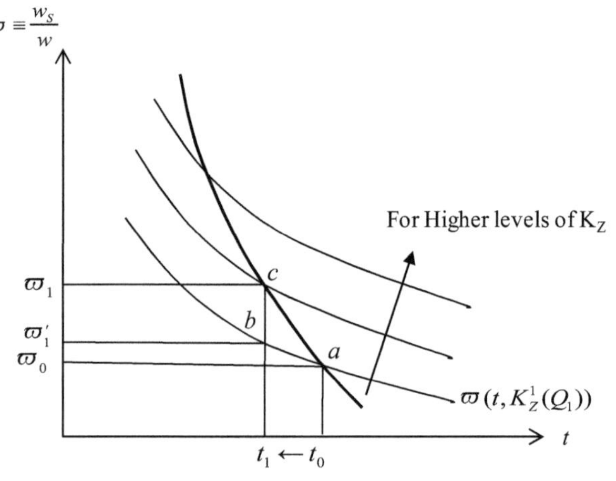

Fig. 21.1 Tariff reduction and wage inequality. *Source* Ganguly and Acharyya (2021)

21.2.3 Uneven Gains from Global Value Chains and Input Trade

Trade in intermediate goods can also explain the observed phenomenon of growing wage inequality. This is important to understand because fragmentation of production processes, location of different production stages in different countries and connecting such production stages in different country-locations through trade in intermediate and semi-finished goods have been the dominant feature of global trade over the last two decades. A single finished product now results from manufacturing and assembly in multiple countries, with each stage generating and adding value to the end product. The emerging production process is known as the global value chains (GVCs). GVCs has also caused a lot of capital inflows, foreign direct investment and transfer of technical know-how from the developed to the developing countries through outsourcing of different production stages or processes. However, gains from GVCs have been uneven across participating nations. The developing countries being typically engaged in the low-value addition lower-stages, gain much less than the more technologically advanced developed countries, and some of the relatively advanced developing countries, like China and Mexico, and, to some extent and in some specific sectors, India. Gains have been uneven also within nations favouring the more skilled workers (see Hollweg (2019), for example).

Three theoretical analyses deserve attention in this context. First, given continuum of vertical stages with a higher stage being relatively more skill-labour intensive, Feenstra and Hanson (1996) show that outsourcing of some intermediate stages of production in the value chain by USA to Mexico raises wage inequality in both the countries. The reversal of the local skill-intensities of these intermediate stages in the two countries drives the result. Second is Marjit and Acharyya (2006), who demonstrate that a tariff reduction by a large developing country on its imports of an intermediate good from a developed country may raise the wage gap in both the countries. Their result is driven by two key factors: the domestic prices of the traded intermediate good move in different directions in the two countries; and different factor-intensity ranking of this good relative to the final goods produced and exported by these two countries. Third is Acharyya and Dutta (2024), who examine impacts of transport cost and global demand shocks on within-country wage inequality in the context of two sets of large number of small countries participating in input trade and global value chain with two discrete stages of production of a manufacturing good. They used the specific-factor production structure for the purpose. A set of upstream countries $m = 1,2,\ldots,M$, specializes in the lower stage of production of the manufacturing good Y, and produces the semi-finished (or, intermediate) good, I; and a set of downstream countries $h = 1,2,\ldots,H$, specializes in the final stage and produces the final consumption good Y using the imported intermediate good. Both the stages require skilled labour (S) and unskilled labour (L), with the higher stage being more skill-intensive. Both set of countries also produce a numeraire good, say food grain (F)—which cannot be fragmented and thus must be produced at the same location and hence in the same country—using land (T) and unskilled labour. The analytical structure of the model can be described by the following set of zero-profit conditions and factor-market clearing conditions in representative m and$h$ countries:

$$1 = a_{LF}W^m + a_{TY}R^m \tag{21.34}$$

$$P_I^W = a_{LI}W^m + a_{SI}W_S^m \tag{21.35}$$

$$1 = a_{LF}W^h + a_{TY}R^h \tag{21.36}$$

$$P_Y^W = a_{IY}P_I^W + a_{LY}W^h + a_{SY}W_S^h \tag{21.37}$$

$$T^m = a_{TF}X_F^m, \;\; T^h = a_{TF}X_F^h \tag{21.38}$$

$$S^m = a_{SI}X_I^m, \;\; S^h = a_{SY}X_Y^h \tag{21.39}$$

$$L^m = a_{LF}X_F^m + a_{LI}X_I^m, \;\; L^h = a_{LF}X_F^h + a_{LY}X_Y^h \tag{21.40}$$

where R^m is the rate of return to land in the country-m, W^m and W_S^m are respectively the unskilled and skilled wage rate in the country-m. R^h, W^h and W_S^h are respectively return to land, unskilled labour and skilled labour rate in country-h.

Finally, there are the world market clearing conditions:

$$\frac{\alpha}{1-\alpha}P_Y^W = \frac{X_F^W}{X_Y^W} \tag{21.41}$$

$$a_{IY}X_Y^W = X_I^W \tag{21.42}$$

where $X_F^W = \sum X_F^h + \sum X_F^m; X_Y^W = \sum X_Y^h; X_I^W = \sum X_I^m X_I^W = \Sigma X_I^m.$

Note that the world relative demand for food as specified in the left hand side in (21.41) follows from the identical and homothetic tastes in both sets of countries which are represented by the following aggregate utility function for each country: $U = C_F^{\alpha}C_Y^{1-\alpha}$. In such a context, Acharyya and Dutta (2024) show that a shift in consumers' taste towards the consumption of the manufactured good and away from food, resulting in larger activities along the global value chain, accentuates wage inequality between skilled and unskilled workers in both these set of countries. But the results are somewhat asymmetrical if an increase in activity along the GVCs take place via fall in transport cost. Wage inequality declines in the m-set of countries specializing in the lower stage of production. Uneven gains for them, however, may arise again when a large endowment shock affects the relative world price of the manufactured good, regardless of in which set of countries such a shock originates.

21.3 Globalization Discontents and Political Economy

21.3.1 Country Experiences and Globalization Discontents

Recent political and economic discourses regarding costs and benefits of globalization based on country experiences since the present era of globalization began during 1980s, reflect a general and growing discontent regarding globalization and, therefore, cast doubts regarding its future self. And the discontents and conflicts have intensified more over the last one decade, primarily because of growing income inequalities not only across trading nations but also within the trading nations. While the theoretical discourses discussed above suggest that trade liberalization may redistribute incomes unfavourably for the less skilled and the poor, the country-specific evidences have not been very encouraging either as mentioned above. The recent world-wide pandemic has worsened the situation further. First, skilled workers working in less contact-intensive sectors, such as financial services, banking and insurance, education and other ITeS, and thus having the scope of working-from-home, were hit far less by the pandemic than factory workers and less skilled workers engaged in contact-intensive production of goods and services (such as nursing) whose miseries reached unprecedented levels due to shut down of such activities during the lockdown. Second, countries that rely relatively more on the rest of the world than others for a larger proportion of their consumption needs as well as for import of intermediate goods, have been relatively worse-off. The glaring example is inter-dependence of countries in the global value chains. Asymmetry in capability of participating in virtual trade, such as ITeS trade, is another example. This has caused a digital-divide across the globe and resulted in more pronounced uneven gains from trade during and after the 2020-pandemic.

The cross-country evidences regarding growing within-country income inequality since the 1980s, which is considered as the beginning of the present era of globalization, have emerged from a large number of researches. One of the earliest comprehensive evidence was put forward by Cornia and Kiiski (2001) in their UNU-WIDER Discussion Paper. For a sample of 77 countries accounting for 82% of world population and 95% of world GDP at PPP, they observed worsening intra-country income inequality in 45 of those countries, and improvement in income distribution in only 9 small or medium-sized countries during 1980–2000. Those 45 countries together accounted for 77% of the world GDP. Thus, income inequality grew among the global population holding together 77% of world GDP. Subsequent empirical studies have revealed more or less similar trends. For example, the IMF study in 2014 documents that inequality in the personal distribution of income has increased in most economies in the world during 1980–2010, including more than one-third of advanced economies and half of emerging Europe. Inequality also rose in most economies in Asia and the Pacific, in Middle East and in North Africa. Two observations are in order at this point. First, this IMF study used Gini coefficient for *disposable incomes*—that is, market incomes minus direct taxes plus cash transfers—as the measure of inequality, which reflects both the inequality of market-determined incomes as well as the distributional impact of income taxes and public transfers. Second, with world trade increasing quite significantly during these three decades (1980–2010), role of trade globalization causing widespread and growing intra-country income inequality, as documented by these two studies as well as by many others, cannot be ruled out.

Other inequality measures show similar trends. For example, Thomas Piketty (2014) has observed that the income shares of the richest one-per cent of the population have increased substantially in English-speaking advanced economies, as well as in emerging economies such as Brazil, China and India. Based on this, Piketty made two postulates. First, ceteris paribus, whenever the difference between the returns on capital (r) and the output growth rate (g) increases, the share of capital in national income increases. Second, since capital income tends to be more unequally distributed than labour income, *an increase of the capital share would likely lead to increased overall income inequality*.

On the contrary, however, Goes (2016) has found that increases in income inequality in 19 advanced economies to be largely uncorrelated with changes in $(r-g)$. On the other hand, Acemoglu and Robinson (2015), Francese and Mulas-Granados (2015), Dabla-Norris et al. (2015), Goes (2016), Mare (2016) and Greenwood et al. (2016) argued that the rising inequality of labour income rather than distribution of national income in favour of capital income has been the primary driver of recent trends of within-country income inequality.

21.3.2 De-Globalization Trends?

Growing within-country income inequality, whether due to a rise in share of capital in national income following output growth, or due to unequal distribution of labour income, has led to growing concerns across the globe and discontents for globalization. Protectionist trends are making their way back slowly, although in piecemeal fashion, in many developing countries with voices for such policies becoming louder as the discontents regarding globalization grow. In fact, there has been a persistent slowdown in world trade after the global financial crisis (2008–2009). In sharp contrast to world trade-GDP ratio surging from 38% to 61% during 1985 and 2008, global trade slowed down with world trade-GDP ratio declining to 56% in 2019, just before the outbreak of the COVID-19 pandemic that disrupted global supply chains as well as economic activities and livelihood throughout the world. Events like United Kingdom leaving the European Union after Brexit causing declines in the trade between them, the abandonment of the Trans-Pacific Partnership by the United States, the China-US trade war and the disabling of the World Trade Organisation's dispute settlement system having far-reaching global impacts, have not helped world trade grow either. All these have given rise to an idea that de-globalisation is underway (Irwin, 2020).

At the same time, this de-globalisation hypothesis is contested by many (see Antras, 2021; Arslan et al., 2019; Baldwin, 2022). They attribute the global slowdown of trade-GDP ratio primarily to the slowing down of the Chinese economy in recent past. The slowdown has triggered a vicious cycle for China, where people not being sure about their future income are saving more, which has brought down consumption. This in turn has forced the firms to pause further investment and capacity expansion as the demand has slowed down. There has also been a sharp inversion in China's trade-GDP ratio. By its sheer size, effect of this accounts for at least one-third of the slowdown in the world trade/GDP ratio. Moreover, China's slowing economy has been adversely affecting the exports of its trading partners on two counts. First is through lower import demand of China. Second is through fall in Chinese exports of intermediate goods that constraints production and export capacity of final goods produced by its trade partners. Glaring example is the heavy dependence of India in China for imports of parts and components for electrical and electronic goods.

21.3.3 Discontents, Voting and Politically Optimum Trade Liberalization

As we have mentioned earlier, choice of trade policies and policy reforms in democratic developing countries are often constrained by political resistance and apprehension of loss of political support (Acharyya (2023), Baldwin [2006], Cassing and Hilman [1985], Francois and Nelson [2014], Nelson [2009]). Adverse distributional consequences of policy reforms for a larger number of interest groups are the primary sources of such political resistance. Such politically constrained policy reforms emanate from the political risks that an incumbent democratic government faces due to exclusion of some interest groups from benefits of the reforms. A democratic government aspiring to return to power through election after completion of its current term in the office, would be concerned with maximization of political support by minimizing political risks from policy reforms. This idea has been the basis of pioneering political-support maximizing theory of Cassing and Hilman [1985]; and of a very recent formalization of choice of tariff reforms in presence of political resistances from beneficiaries of government expenditures financed by tariff revenue by Acharyya (2023). The idea in Acharyya (2023) is that in developing countries tariff revenues are often a significant proportion of total tax revenue, which finances government's different welfare schemes for the poor, including direct and indirect cash transfer schemes. Thus, tariff reforms may adversely affect such employments in the public sector (or in government projects) by lowering revenues earned, and correspondingly political resistance from workers employed in such sectors can reinforce the political resistance due to redistribution of incomes brought about by tariff reforms.

Similar idea can be used to formalize the discontent from globalization and slowing down of tariff reforms in terms of voting by economic agents based on their relative positions. Suppose, the government in a democratic country chooses trade policy, say, a tariff rate, by maximizing political support (PS) gathered from different factor-income earners. The income-earners value their *relative* positions and thus extend their support for a policy choice according to whether it improves their relative position or not. This is the building bloc of our argument here. Thus, political support for choice of a tariff rate depends on the income inequality that it results in. The incumbent government also targets to gather political support by providing income subsidies to the largest income class given that the *aggregate political support depends on the size of income classes* (as in case of voting) and hence on the relative position of the larger income class.[12]

In absence of any income or wage tax *to begin with*, the scope of income subsidy is, however, limited by the revenue earned from the choice of tariff rate. In sum, the government chooses the tariff rate t and income subsidy γ to maximize political-support subject to the tariff revenue earned:Max $PS(t, \gamma)$ s.t. $\gamma = tp^W M/V$

where V is the size of the largest income class.

Note that, here, the balanced budget essentially means that the tariff revenue is redistributed by the government only to the larger income class given the objective of gathering maximum political support, instead of to *all* income earners as in the standard trade model.

The politically optimum choice of tariff rate can be obtained graphically with the help of iso-political-support curves. To simplify the matters, suppose there are only two income classes—skilled workers and unskilled workers—and that the number of unskilled workers are larger than that of skilled workers, $L > S$. This latter assumption captures the endowment pattern of the developing countries. Thus, $V = L$. On the other hand, the arguments below can be suitably modified, without changing the main results *qualitatively*, by incorporating other factors like capital (and/or, land) and assigning ownership of such factors to the skilled workers. Consistent with empirical observations and theoretical constructs mentioned above, suppose a tariff reduction raises W_s/W. Thus, from a reduction in tariff the government gets political support from skilled workers but loses that from unskilled workers. But larger number of unskilled workers means a tariff reduction lowers (aggregate) political support: $\frac{\partial PS}{\partial t} > 0$.

On the other hand, an increase in income subsidy to unskilled workers, who by assumption is the larger income class, gets political support from them but loses the same from skilled workers. Overall, an increase in income subsidy raises (aggregate) political support: $\frac{\partial PS}{\partial \gamma} > 0$. Thus, the iso-political-support curves are negatively sloped in (t, γ) space: $\left.\frac{d\gamma}{dt}\right|_{ps} = -\frac{\partial PS/\partial t}{\partial PS/\partial \gamma} < 0$

[12] Varshney (2002) argued that the poor do not vote as economic classes but according to which religious groups they belong to. This observation is particularly relevant for policies targeting polarization on such basis.

Fig. 21.2 Iso-political-support curves

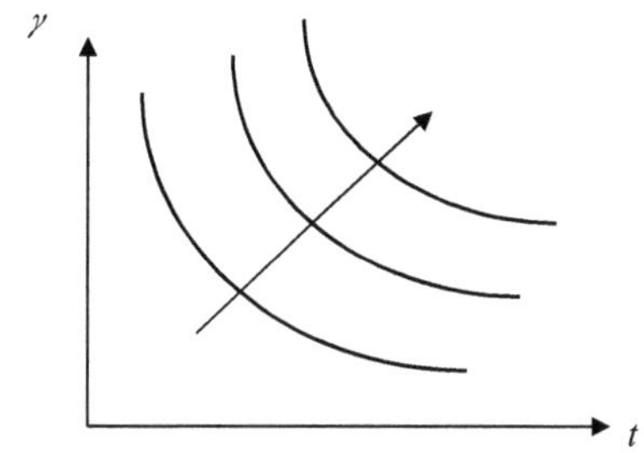

Figure 21.2 depicts such curves. Evidently, higher iso-political-support curve indicate larger political support for the government policies (t, γ).

Now, it is straightforward that the tariff revenue and hence the budget constraint $\gamma = tp^W M/L$ is hump-shaped for an import demand function for which import demand elasticity rises with the rise in tariff-inclusive price. In this context, note that TR = 0 for $t = 0$ and for $t = t_P$, whereas TR > 0 for $0 < t < t_P$. The maximum revenue and hence the maximum income subsidy that the government can provide is realized at $t = t_R$. Hence, given that the iso-political-support curves are negatively sloped, the political support maximizing tariff rate is strictly positive and in fact larger than t_R. Further, in a standard HOS model, economic optimum tariff is smaller than the revenue-maximizing tariff (see Acharyya (2022)). Thus, the political-support maximizing tariff is larger than both these tariff rates (Fig. 21.3).

The politically optimum choice of tariff rate would have been similarly larger than both economic optimum and revenue-maximizing rates even if we consider taxing skilled wage as an additional source of revenue for the government to finance subsidies, as shown in Fig. 21.4. Suppose the government taxes the skilled workers α fraction of their wage-incomes. Thus, the revenue curve is now the scaled-up one as indicated by the broken curve. However, since skilled wage increases as tariff is lowered, consistent with the empirical observations, the total revenue curve is non-parallel to the tariff-revenue curve.

Fig. 21.3 Political-support maximizing tariff rate

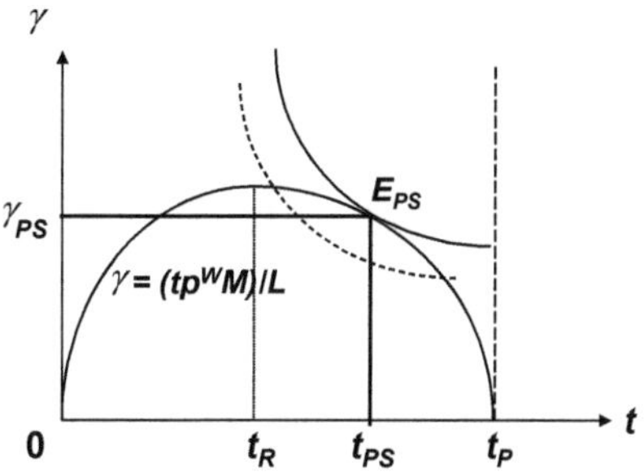

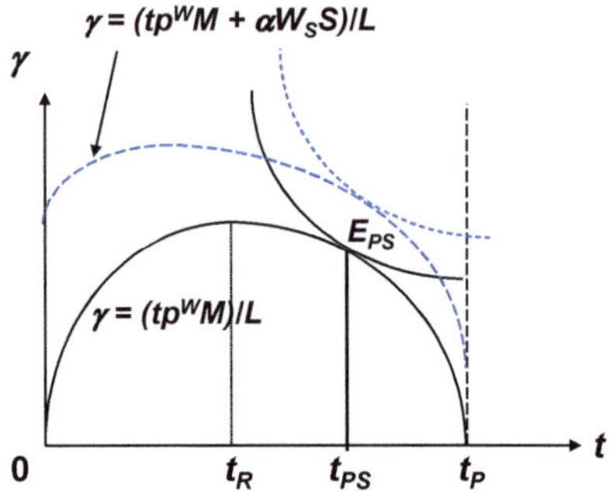

Fig. 21.4 Wage-Tax and the tariff rate

21.4 Changing Structure of India's Exports: A Potential Source of Income Inequality?

21.4.1 India's Trade-Policy Paradigm and Trends in Its Exports

Post-independence, trade-policy paradigm of India was characterized largely by import-substituting and inward-looking industrialization. The idea of self-reliance in production of final goods and infant-industry argument also played their parts for such an inward-looking development strategy. On the other hand, there was a general scepticism regarding export-led growth as a development strategy, which got momentum from writings of development and trade theorists like Arthur Lewis, Ragner Nurkse, Rosenstein-Rodan, Albert Hirschman, Jagdish Bhagwati, Harry G. Johnson and Diaz-Alejandro during 1950s to 1970s. Writings of Prebisch (1950), Singer (1950), Emmanuel (1972) and Bacha (1978) on unequal share of gains from trade for the developing countries added further fuel to such scepticism.

Tariffs and non-tariff barriers were also necessitated by an over-valued pegged exchange rate of the Indian Rupee vis-à-vis US Dollar (along with an exchange control), that was put in place to lower the domestic currency price of imported inputs and capital goods (including POL) needed for domestic production of manufacturing goods and industrialization.[13] Insulating the domestic economy from external price shocks, particularly the oil price shock, feeding into the price inflation, was another thing that had been in the minds of the policy makers.

But, for obvious reasons, growing trade and balance of payments deficits, inefficiencies in production and rent-seeking lobbying activities evolved under the over-valued pegged exchange rate regime and inward-looking development strategy under trade protection. There were misallocation of scarce resources resulting in higher-cost of export productions relative to the competitors in the world market. Large and protected domestic markets also took away incentives for innovation, either for cost innovation that could have a volume effect on exports and gains in the intensive

[13] See Acharyya (2012) for a detailed argument.

margin, or for product-innovation that could lead to gains from trade at the extensive margin.

The balance of payments crisis culminating in 1991 finally changed the entire perspective of trade, investment and exchange rate policies. A paradigm shift was observed that focussed on removing market inefficiencies, on laissez faire and market principles, and, of course, on the export-led growth strategy. Beginning of an outward-oriented development strategy was even earlier (in 1985, approximately), but the Crisis in 1991 accelerated the pace of trade reforms.

These two distinct phases are reflected in Fig. 21.5. Exports of goods and services as a percentage of India's GDP remained stagnated at 6–7% during 1970–1986, but thereafter started rising steadily and attaining the level of approximately 22% of GDP in 2022. Trade as a percentage of GDP, which is the sum of exports and imports in goods and services as a percentage of GDP and is considered as a crude measure of trade openness, also had a similar trend, but it had increased faster than exports during 1994–2010. The faster rate of growth in total trade than exports meant a faster rate of growth in imports than exports. After the exchange rate reforms during 1991–1993, trade liberalizing measures were initiated in the year 1994 with conversion of import quotas and other non-tariff barkers into equivalent tariffs (known as tariffication), followed by successive reduction of tariff rates till 2001 as part of commitment for accession to WTO as a member. So, growth in imports was expected. But, this did not result in commensurate increase in India's exports as the theory of GFT would suggest. This is partly, if not largely, due to the production rigidities and labour market inflexibilities prohibiting efficient reallocation of resources from the erstwhile-protected inefficient domestic import-competing industries to export sectors. This mismatch between the export and import growth is reflected in the worsening trade and current account balances during 2002–2012 in particular.

Of the total merchandise exports, manufacturing exports have constituted on the average 70% during the last two decades. But, over the last one decade, the share of goods trade in total exports of goods and services itself has fallen quite significantly (see Fig. 21.6). So there has been a structural shift from goods exports to service exports, which is also commensurate with the rising share of services in India's GDP from 38% in 1995 to 48% in 2022.

Growth of service sector and service exports has further been reflected in India emerging as a net exporter of services after 2008. The value of export surplus has increased steadily since then (Fig. 21.7).[14]

21.4.2 Structure and Skill Composition of Exports

India's export basket is well diversified as it exports a wide range of goods, from low-skill-intensive manufacturing goods, such as leather manufacture, textiles, cotton

[14] Rodrik (2006) observed that India's growth has been primarily driven by service exports.

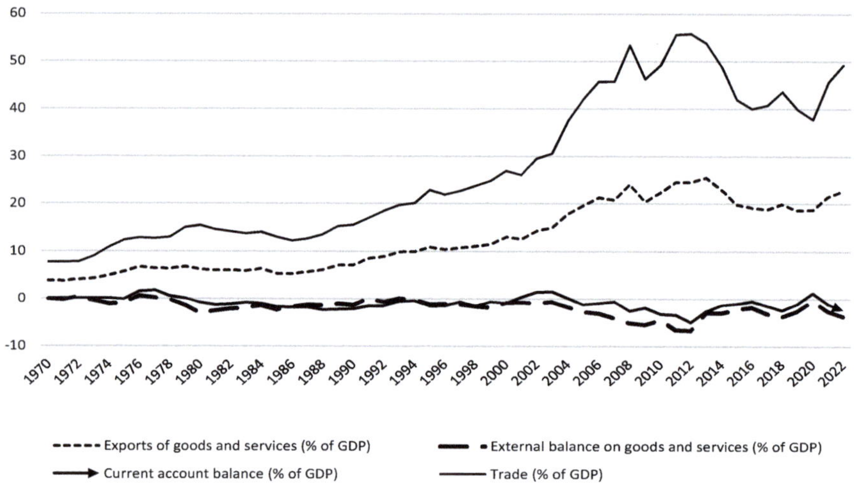

Fig. 21.5 Trends in India's trade. *Source* Authors' Compilation from World Development Indicator data

Fig. 21.6 Share of goods exports in total exports. *Source* Authors' Compilation from UNCTAD Stat

fabrics, to skill-intensive and R&D intensive products such as chemicals, pharmaceutical products and scientific instruments. But, the revealed comparative advantage (RCA) values of export items at SITC 3-digit level reveal that India's comparative advantage still lies in traditional items such as tea, spices, rice, cotton, iron ore and concentrates, organic chemicals, synthetic organic colouring materials, leather manufacture, textiles yarn, clothing and apparels, pearls and precious stones, Jewellery,

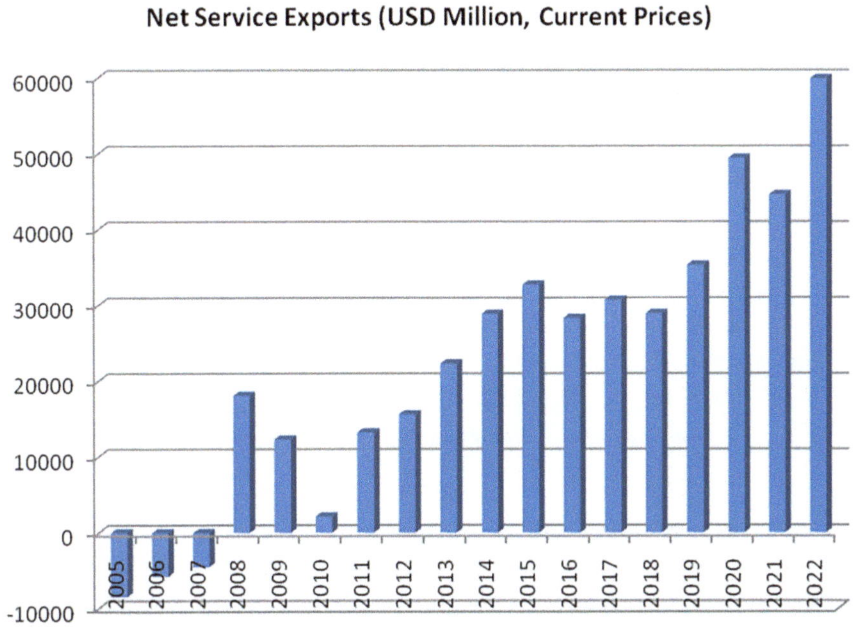

Fig. 21.7 Net service exports

etc. However, most of these items have a declining trend. The four panels in Fig. 21.8 document trends in RCA values over the period 1995–2022 for sample of products (for which RCA values in 1995 were significantly high) under four categories: Food and live animals; crude materials; chemicals and manufactured goods.

For example, RCA values for rice, tea, spices, cotton fabrics, textile yarn and leather manufacture have declined to large extents during 1995–2009, and thereafter have remained stable at low values. For organic chemicals, on the other hand, RCA values changed in an almost inverted-U manner: increasing during 1995–2005 and declining thereafter over the next one decade. But, exports of the synthetic organic colouring matters reveal increasing comparative advantage during the entire period, from RCA value of 6 in 1995 to the value 12 in 2020.

Among exports of machinery and transport equipments, only motorcycles and cycles and vapour generating boilers show a steady trend of RCA. But, India's exports do not reveal any comparative advantage in automatic data-processing machines, telecommunication equipment, parts and accessories for office machines and automatic data-processing machines; optical instruments and apparatus, other scientific instruments including watches and clocks as well as electrical machinery and apparatus.

One of the plausible reasons for declining trends in RCA values in most of our major export items, and not being able to gain any comparative advantage in non-traditional manufacturing items and in exports of machinery and transport equipment is misalignment of our export baskets with the changing world demand. This is

a

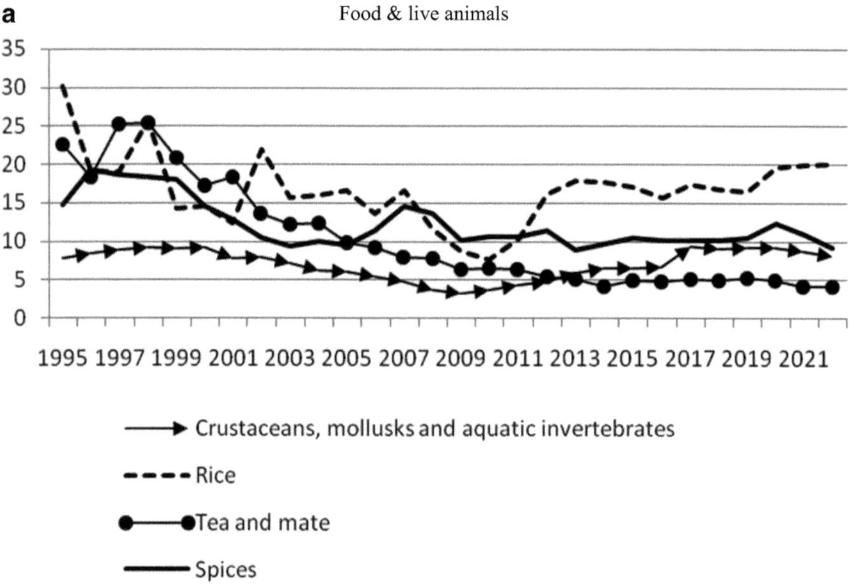

b

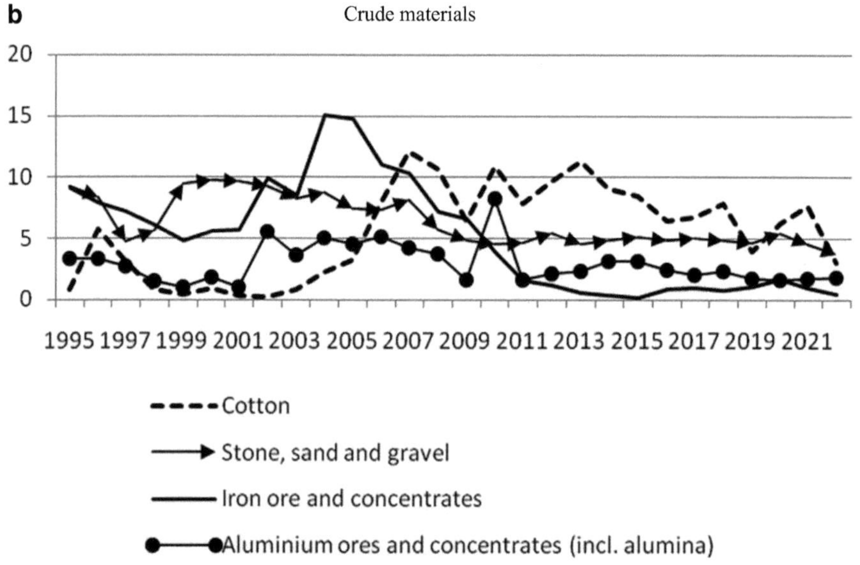

Fig. 21.8 Trends in RCA of selected export items. *Source* Author's compilation from UNCTAD Stat

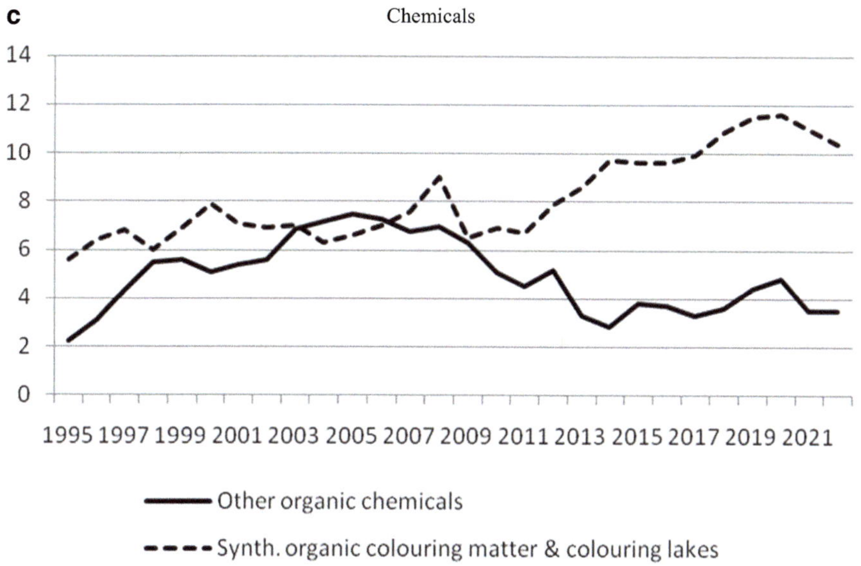

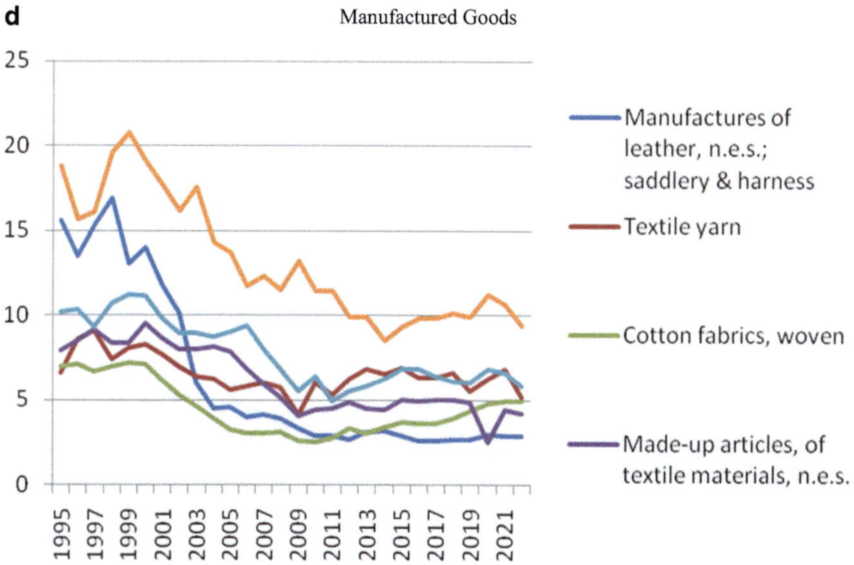

Fig. 21.8 (continued)

partly due to a shift in world demand towards goods in which we do not traditionally have any comparative advantage, such as office machines, automatic data-processing machines and telecommunication equipment. For example, as observed in Acharyya (2024), using the UNCTAD data, India's export structure diverges significantly from the world average. It is also partly due to the fact that in many cases, particularly for manufacturing goods, machineries and transport equipment, we produce lower quality varieties than the advanced countries would like to import. Though in theory, comparative advantage is a bilateral concept, a country can penetrate an export market only when it is better than its rivals in terms of costs and/or product quality. These are the dimensions in which India often loses out to China, one of its competitor in the world market for a large number of goods. On the one hand, large scale production capacities enable Chinese firms to attain economies of scale and bring down thereby production costs significantly. On the other hand, there has been some remarkable improvement in quality of many of its manufactured export goods relative to the Indian goods during last two decades, as documented in Acharyya and Ganguly (2023) drawing from the cross-country estimates of export-quality index at the aggregate as well as at the SITC 2-digit and 3-digit levels.

However, notwithstanding low RCA values, growth in high-technology exports (HTX) has been quite significant during the last three decades, resulting in its share in India's manufacturing exports growing steadily from 4% in 1990 to more than 10% in 2021 (see Fig. 21.9). According to the World Bank classification, high-technology intensive products are also intensive in R&D. This means, these goods also indirectly uses a lot of skilled labour per unit of its production.

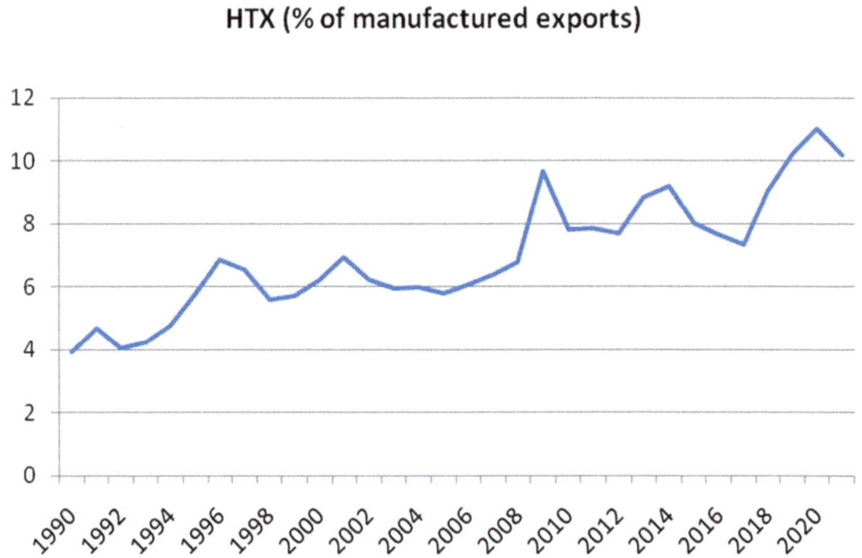

Fig. 21.9 Share of HTX in manufacturing Exports. *Source* Authors' compilation using WDI data

Further, as documented in Acharyya (2024), there has been a shift in the composition of exports towards high and medium skill intensive (and technology intensive) during 2005–2020. The share of the low-skill labour intensive and resource intensive manufactures, which constituted more than 50% of India's manufacturing exports during 1990s, declined monotonically to 20% in 2020.

On the other hand, of the total service exports, telecommunications, computer and information services and other business services constitute the largest shares. They together account for 70% of India's total service exports. While telecommunications service exports include business network services, teleconferencing, mobile telecommunications services, Internet backbone services and online access services, the computer services consist of hardware and software related services and data-processing services. On the other hand, other business services are comprised of research and development, professional and management consulting and technical, trade-related and other business services. As the Fig. 21.10 depicts, share of these two categories of service exports in total service exports have a similar trend during 2005–2022, with share of other business services falling behind that of telecommunications, computer and information services 2007–2016 and thereafter surging ahead.

All these facts and figures point out towards increasing skill composition of India's exports, whether it be manufactured exports or service exports, which raises the relative demand for skilled workers and consequently may have worsened the wage inequality between skilled and unskilled workers in the short run.

As our earlier theoretical discussion has suggested, global value chains can also have some far-reaching implications for wage inequality. However, data tells us that India has been only a fringe player, accounting for only $241 billion or 1.5% of

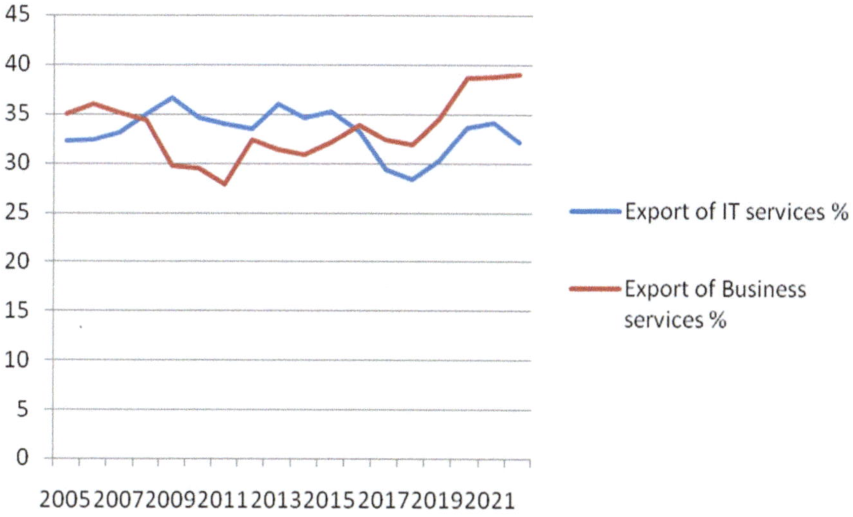

Fig. 21.10 Composition of India's service exports. *Source* Authors' compilation using UNCTAD Stat

global GVC exports in 2017, which was much lower than India's share in global exports of goods and services. Out of India's total merchandise exports, only 10% are network products like electronics, computers, telecommunication equipment and vehicles, which are primarily GVC driven (Veeramani & Dhir, 2019). Despite its nearness to Factory Asia, India is yet to integrate itself to such regional supply chains. India's GVC participation has been mainly through forward participation (domestic value added in exports of intermediate goods, as a share of gross exports) rather than backward participation (foreign value added as a share of gross exports) as noted by Banga (2022). Share of backward linkages has declined from 35% in 2012 to 23% in 2016. That means India is relatively more engaged in upstream production activities that involves providing materials required to create a product, including raw material processing, drilling and exploration in the oil industry, renting machinery and equipments, basic and fabricated metals, textiles and agriculture products (Mitra et al., 2020). Such forward linkages in the manufacturing sector is mostly unskilled-labour intensive as opposed to backward linkages which are relatively more skilled labour intensive. So while the final commodity composition of exports being biased towards capital- and skill-intensive products for India, thereby accounting for demand driven rise in skilled–unskilled wage gap as discussed above, such an imminent threat to wage inequality cannot be seen as coming from India's manufacturing GVC trade. Linking this to the ongoing debate on the distributional effects of GVC participation with two opposing views, it may be argued that it largely depends on whether such participation is based on unskilled labour intensive upstream production activities or more of downstream skill-based production and distribution activities. Nevertheless, for India, the call of the hour is to boost its GVC-driven trade participation through policies that facilitate technological upgrading and spillovers from FDI and 'servicification' of Indian manufacturing and increasing backward linkages and foreign value added shares. This is important because raising the use of services inputs, for example, ITeS, will boost export intensity of firms and sustain GVC survival (Goldar et al., 2017). The consequent development goal fallouts in terms of accentuating wage inequality levels in the economy, need to be controlled and corrected through effective concurrent policies. Subsidizing the low-skilled factor owners may be one of the short-run policies. But in the long run, raising basic and technical skills of the vast majority of workers for a smooth employment transition to the skill-intensive sectors is of utmost importance.

21.5 Conclusion

This chapter discusses theoretical discourses and empirical observations regarding uneven distribution of gains from trade *within a trading nation* and ramifications for such uneven gains on trade-policy reversals and future of globalization. A benchmark political-support model has been developed to examine the politically optimum trade liberalization in this context. The chapter also reviews trends and structure of India's exports. The increasing skill composition of exports, be it goods exports or service exports, has the potential of worsening the wage inequality between skilled and unskilled workers.

References

Acemoglu, D., & Robinson, J. A. (2014). *The rise and decline of general laws of capitalism* (NBER Working Paper 20766).

Acharyya, R. (2024). *Forthcoming.* India's foreign trade: Prospects and challenges in the globalized world. In B. Chatterjee & J. Sasmal, (Eds.), *Indian economy after 75 years of independence: Success, challenges and emerging issues.* Routledge, India.

Acharyya, R. (2023). Discontent and political resistance to tariff reform. In K. Gupta & J. Dwibedi, eds. *International trade, economic development and national welfare: Essays in memory of Sarbajit Chaudhuri.* Routledge, India.

Acharyya, R. (2017). International trade and widening wage gap: A general equilibrium approach. In Bandyopadhyay, S., Andre Torre, Paulo Casaca & Tomaz Ponce Dentinho (Eds.), *Regional cooperation in South Asia: Socio-economic, spatial, ecological and institutional aspects, Chapter 2.* Springer.

Acharyya, R. (2012). India's trade and exchange rate policies: Understanding the BOP crisis and the reforms thereafter. In C. Ghate, ed, *Oxford handbook on Indian Economy*, OUP (UK).

Acharyya, R. (2011). A note on quantitative trade restrictions, income effects and wage inequality. *Economic Modelling, 28*(6), 2628–2633.

Acharyya, R. , & A. Dutta. (2024). Forthcoming. "Value chain in discrete stages, input trade, and distribution of incomes. In S. Marjit, & B. Mondal, (Eds.), *International trade, resource mobility and adjustments in a changing world.* Springer.

Acharyya, R., & Ganguly, S. (2023). Export quality and income Distribution. In the Book Series: Kenneth Reinert, (Ed.), *Cambridge elements in international economics*, Cambridge University Press.

Acharyya, R., & Jones, R. W. (2001). Export quality and income distribution in a small dependent economy. *International Review of Economics and Finance, 10*, 337–351.

Acharyya, R., & Marjit, S. (2023). Why trade when you can transfer technology? Revisiting Smith and Ricardo. *Review of International Economics, 31*(4), 1508–1527.

Agenor, P. R., & Montiel, P. (1996). *Development macroeconomics.* Princeton University Press.

Aizenman, J., Lee, M., & Park, D. (2012). *The relationship between structural change and inequality: A conceptual overview with special reference to developing Asia*, Working Papers DP-2012–13, Economic Research Institute for ASEAN and East Asia (ERIA).

Antràs, P. (2021). *De-Globalisation? Global value chains in the post-COVID-19 age.* ECB Forum: "Central Banks in a Shifting World" Conference Proceedings.

Arslan, Y., Contreras, J., Patel, N., & Shu, C. (2019). *Globalisation and deglobalisation in emerging market economies: Facts and trends.* BIS Paper No. 100a.

Bacha, E. (1978). An interpretation of unequal exchange from Prebisch-Singer to Emmanuel. *Journal of Development Economics, 5*(4), 319–330.

Baldwin, R. (2022). *Globotics and macroeconomics: Globalization and automation of service sector.* NBER Working Paper # 30317, http://www.nber.org/papers/w30317

Baldwin, R. (2006). Multilateralizing regionalism: Spaghetti bowls as building blocs on the path to global free trade. *The World Economy, 29*(11), 1451–1518.

Baldwin, R., & Harrigan, J. (2011). Zeros, quality, and space: Trade theory and trade evidence. *American Economic Journal: Microeconomics, 3*(2).

Banga, K. (2022). Impact of global value chains on total factor productivity: The case of Indian manufacturing. *Review of Development Economics, 26*(2), 704–735.

Beyer, H., Rojas, P., & Vergara, R. (1999). Trade liberalization and wage inequality. *Journal of Development Economics, 59*, 103–123.

Bhagwati, J. N. (1958). Immiserizing growth: A geometric note. *Review of Economic Studies, 25*, 201–205.

Bogliaccini, J. A. (2013). Trade liberalization, de-industrialisation, and inequality: Evidence from middle-income Latin American Countries. *Latin American Research Review 48*(2), 79–105.

Bound, J., & George, J. (1992). Changes in the structure of wages in the 1980's: An evaluation of alternative explanations. *American Economic Review, 82-#3*, 371–392.

Brady, D., Kaya, Y., & Gereffi, G. (2011). Stagnating industrial employment in Latin America. *Work and Occupations, 38*(2), 179–220.

Brambilla, I., Lederman, D., & Porto, G. (2012). Exports, export destinations, and skills. *American Economic Review, 102*(7), December.

Brambilla, I., & Porto. G. (2016). High-income export destinations, quality and wages. *Journal of International Economics, 98*98(C), 21–35.

Brecher, R., & Diaz-Alejandro, C. (1977). Tariffs, foreign capital and immiserizing growth. *Journal of International Economics, 7*(4), 317–322.

Carruth, A. A., & Oswald, A. J. (1981). The determination of union and non-union wage rates. *European Economic Review, 16*, 285–302.

Cassing, J. H., & Hillman, A. L. (1985). Political influence motives and the choice between tariffs and quotas. *Journal of International Economics, 19*, 279–290.

Chakraborty, B. S., & Sarkar, A. (2009). *Trade and wage inequality with endogenous skill formation*, paper presented at the International Conference on Globalization, Agglomeration and Inclusive Growth, Jadavpur University.

Corden, M. (1971). *The theory of protection*. Clarendon Press.

Cornia, G. A., & Kiiski, S. (2001). Trends in income distribution in the post-World War II period: evicence and interpretation. In G. A. Cornia (Ed.), *Inequality, growth and poverty in the era liberalization and globalization*. UNU-WIDER.

Dabla-Norris, E., Kochhar, K., Suphaphiphat, N., Ricka, F., & Tsounta, E. (2015). *Causes and consequences of income inequality: A global perspective*. IMF Strategy, Policy, and Review Department, IMF Staff Discussion Note 15/13.

Davis, D. (1996). *Trade liberalization and income distribution*. NBER Working Paper No. 5693.

Dongwen, T., Hu, N., Wang, X., & Huang, L. (2016). Trade margins, quality upgrading, and China's agri-food export growth. *China Agricultural Economic Review, 8*(2), 277–298.

Emmanuel, A. (1972). *Unequal exchange: A study of the imperialism of trade*. Translation by B. Pearce. Monthly Review Press.

Falvey, R. E., & Kierzkowski, H. (1987). Product quality, intra-industry trade and (im)perfect competition. In H. Kierzkowski (Ed.), *Protection and competition in international trade: Essays in Honor of W. M. Corden* (pp. 143–161). Blackwell.

Fan, H., Li, Y. A., & Yeaple, S. R. (2018). On the relationship between quality and productivity: Evidence from China's accession to the WTO. *Journal of International Economics, 110*(C), 28–49.

Flam, H., & Helpman, E. (1987). Vertical product differentiation and North-South trade. *The American Economic Review, 77*, 810–822.

Feenstra, R. (2006).*Advanced international trade: Theory and evidence*, New Age International Publishers.

Feenstra, R. C., & Hanson, G. H. (1996). Foreign investment, outsourcing and relative wages. In R. Feenstra, G. Grossman, & D. Irwin (Eds.), *Political economy of trade policies: Essays in Honor of J. N. Bhagwati*. MIT Press.

Fields, G. (1990). Labour market modeling and the urban informal sector: Theory and evidence. In D. Turnham (Ed.), *The informal sector and evidence revisited*. OECD, Paris.

Francese, M., & Mulas-Granados, C. (2015). *Functional income distribution and its role in explaining inequality*. IMF Working Paper #2015/244.

Francois, J., & Nelson, D. R. (2014). Political support for trade policy in the European Union. *European Journal of Political Economy, 36*, 243–253.

Freeman, R., & Katz, L. (1994). Rising Wage Inequality: The United States vs. Other Advanced Countries. In R. Freeman (Ed.), *Working under different rules*. Russell Sage Foundation, NY.

Galera, G., & Fraga, G. J. (2022). Product quality and export probability: Evidence from a large developing country. *The Journal of International Trade & Economic Development, 32*(3).

Gambero, G. F., & Garcia-Ramos, M. (2015). Revisiting the quality of exports. *Journal of Economic Structures, 4*(1), 1–17.

Ganguly, S., & Acharyya, R. (2021). Trade liberalization, export quality, and three dimensions of wage inequality. *Review of Development Economics, 25*(4), 1–23.

Goes, C. (2016). *Testing piketty's hypothesis on the drivers of income inequality: Evidence from panel VARs with heterogeneous dynamics*. IMF Working Paper # WP/16/160.

Goldar, B., Banga, R., & Banga, K. (2017). India's linkages into global value chains: The role of imported services. *India Policy Forum, 14*(1), 107–172.

Greenwood, J., Guner, N., Kocharkov, G., & Santoseremy, C. (2016). Technology and the changing family: A unified model of marriage, divorce, educational attainment and married female labor-force participation. *American Economic Journal: Macroeconomics, 8*(1) (January 2016), 1–41.

Hallak, J. C. (2006). Product quality and the direction of trade. *Journal of International Economics, 68*(1), 238–265.

Henn, C., Papageorgiou, C. & Spatafora, N. (2013). *Export quality in developing countries*. IMF Working Paper 13/108.

Hollweg, C. H. (2019). Global value chains and employment in developing economies. *Global Value Chain Development Report 2019*, 63–81. https://doi.org/10.30875/6b9727ab-en

International Labour Organization (2018). *India Waged Report: Wage policies for decent work and inclusive growth.*

Irwin, D. A. (2020). The pandemic adds momentum to the deglobalization trend. *Peterson Institute for International Economics*. Available from: https://www.piie.com/blogs/realtime-economic-issues-watch/pandemic-adds-momentum-deglobalization-trend

Johnson, H. G. (1967). Economic expansion and international trade. *Manchester School of Economic and Social Studies, 23*, 95–112.

Jones, R. W. (1965). The structure of simple general equilibrium. *Journal of Political Economy, 73*, 557–572.

Jones, R. W. (1971). A three factor model in trade, theory and history. In J. N. Bhagwati et al. (Eds.), *Trade, balance of payments and growth*, North Holland.

Jones, R. W., & Engerman, S. L. (1996). Trade, technology and wages. A tale of two countries. *American Economic Review, 86*, 35–40.

Jones, R. W., & Marjit, S. (1992). International trade and endogenous production structures. In R. Riezman & W. Neuefiend (Eds.), *Economic theory and international trade*. Springer-Verlag.

Kaldor, N. (1957). A model of economic growth. *The Economic Journal., 67*(263), 591–624.

Kar, S., Mandal, B., Marjit, S., & Mukherjee, V. (2019). Seeking rent in the informal sector. *Annals of Public and Cooperative Economics, 91*(1).

Katz, L., Loveman, G. W., & Blanchflower, D. G. (1992). *A comparison of changes in the structure of wages in four OECD countries*. NBER.

Krugman, P. R. (2000). Technology, trade and factor prices. *Journal of International Economics, 50*, 51–71.

Lawrence, R. Z. (1994). *Trade, multinationals and labour*. NBER Working Paper 4836.

Leamer, E. (2000) What's the use of factor contents? *Journal of International Economics, 50*, 51–71.

Mare, R. D. (2016). Educational homogamy in two gilded ages: Evidence from Inter-generational Social Mobility Data. *The ANNALS of the American Academy of Political and Social Science, 663*(1), 117–139.

Manova, K., & Zhang, Z. (2012). *Multi-product firms and product quality*. NBER Working paper, 18637.

Marjit, S. (2003). Economic reform and informal wage—A general equilibrium analysis. *Journal of Development Economics, 72*, 371–378.
Marjit, S., & Acharyya, R. (2003). *International trade, wage inequality and the developing economy.* Physica/Springer Verlag.
Marjit, S., & Beladi, H. (1998). *Trade and wage inequality in developing countries.* Mimeo, Centre for Studies in Social Sciences, Calcutta.
Marjit, S., & Kar, S. (2005). Emigration and wage inequality. *Economics Letters, 88*(1), 141–145.
Marjit, S., & Kar, S. (2011). *The outsiders: Economic reform and informal labour in a developing country.* Oxford University Press.
Marjit, S., Kar, S., & Beladi, H. (2007). Trade reform and informal wages. *Review of Development Economics, 11*(2), 313–320.
Marjit, S., Pant, M., & Huria, S. (2019). Unskilled immigration, technical progress, and Wages—Role of the household sector. *Review of International Economics, 28*(1), 1–17.
Mitra, S., Gupta, A. S., & Sanganeria, A. (2020). *Drivers and benefits of enhancing participation in global value chains: Lessons for India,* South Asia Working Paper Series No. 79, Asian Development Bank.
Mukerji, P. (2021). A panel study of factor accumulation and export quality. *Journal of Risk and Financial Management, 14*(9), 1–53.
Nelson, D. R. (2009). The political economy of protection. In K. A. Reinert, R. Rajan, A. J. Glass, & L. S. Davis (Eds.), *Princeton encyclopedia of international economics* (pp. 916–924). Princeton University Press.
Pedersen, K. (1998). Comment on trade and employment in Latin America. In O. Memedovic et. al. (Eds.), *Globalization of labour markets.* Challenges, Adjustments and Policy Response in the European Union and Less Developed Countries. Kluwer Academic Publishers.
Pi, J., & Zhang, P. (2018). Skill-biased technological change and wage inequality in developing countries. *International Review of Economics & Finance, 56*, 347–362.
Piketty, T. (2014). *Capital in the twenty-first century.* Harvard University Press.
Prebisch, R. (1950). The economic development of Latin America and its principal problems', reprinted in *Economic Bulletin for Latin America, 7*(1), 1962.
Rauch, J. (1991). Modelling the informal sector formally. *Journal of Development Economics, 35*, 33–47.
Ricardo, David. (1971 [1817]). *The principles of political economy and taxation.* Penguin.
Robbins, D. (1995a). *Earnings dispersion in chile after trade liberalization.* Working Paper, Harvard Institute for International Development.
Robbins, D. (1995b). *Trade, trade liberalization and inequality in Latin America and East Asia.* Synthesis of Seven Country Studies. Working Paper, Harvard Institute of International Development.
Rodrigo, C. (1988). *Employment, wages and income distribution in Sri Lanka.* ILO/ARTEP, New Delhi.
Rodrik, D. (2006). What's so special about China's exports? *China and the World Economy, 14*(5), 1–19.
Rogers, C. A., & Swinnerton, K. A. (2004). *A model of informal sector labour markets.* Unpublished manuscript.
Ruffin, R. J. (2003). Oligopoly and trade: What, how much, and for whom? *Journal of International Economics, 60*(2), 315–335. https://doi.org/10.1016/S0022-1996(02)00050-8
Ruffin, R. J. (2009). *Monopolistic competition.* Reinert, Princeton University Press.
Samuelson, P. (1953). Prices of goods and factors in general equilibrium. *Review of Economic Studies, 21*(1), 1–20.
Shariff, A., & Gumber, A. (1999). Employment and wages in India. Pre and post reforms. *Indian Journal of Labour Economics, 42*, 195–216.
Sharma, S. (2022). Trends in employment and wages of female and male workers in India: A task-content-of-occupations approach. *Asian Development Review, 39*(1), 169–199.

Singer, H. (1950). U.S. Foreign investment in underdeveloped areas: The distribution of gains between investing and borrowing ountries. *American Economic Review, Papers and Proceedings, 40*, 473–485.

Stolper, W., & Samuelson, P. A. (1941). Protection and real wages. *Review of Economic Studies, 9*, 58–73.

Swinnerton, K. A. (1996). Minimum wages in an equilibrium search model with diminishing returns to labor in production. *Journal of Labor Economics, 14*(2), 340–355.

Varshney, A. (2002). *Poverty eradication and democracy in the developing world*, Background Paper, Human Development Report, United Nations.

Veeramani, C., & Dhir, G. (2019). *Dynamics and determinants of fragmentation trade: Asian countries in comparative and long-term perspective*, Working Paper No. 2019–040, Indira Gandhi Institute of Development Research.

Wood, A. (1997). Openness and wage inequality in developing countries: The Latin American challenge to East Asian conventional wisdom. *The World Bank Economic Review, 11*(1), 33–57.

Yabuuchi, S., & Chaudhuri, S. (2008). Foreign capital and skilled-unskilled wage inequality in a developing economy with non-traded goods. In S. Marjit & E. Yu (Eds.), *Contemporary and emerging issues in trade theory and policy, Chapter 12.* Emerald Group Publishing Limited.

Xu, B. (2003). Trade liberalization, wage inequality and endogeneously determined non-traded goods. *Journal of International Economics, 60*(2), 417–431.

Zhu, S., & Trefler, D. (2005). Trade and inequality in developing countries: A general equilibrium analysis. *Journal of International Economics, 65*(1), 21–48.

Rajat Acharyya is a professor of economics at Jadavpur University, Kolkata, and a former dean of the Faculty of Arts at Jadavpur University. He is currently the Director (Additional Charge) of the UGC-Malavya Mission Teachers Training Centre, JU. Professor Acharyya received his M.Sc. (Economics) degree from Calcutta University in 1990 and his Ph.D. (Economics) degree from Jadavpur University in 1996. He was a Ford Foundation post-doctoral fellow at Rochester University, New York, during 1997-98, and a Visiting Scholar at the University of Kent at Canterbury, UK (during 2008-2010) and at Utrecht University (2010), Netherlands. Professor Acharyya has so far written six monographs and textbooks, edited six volumes and published more than 70 articles in journals like Economics Letters, Economic Modeling, European Journal of Political Economy, The World Economy, Journal of International Trade and Economic Development, Review of International Economics, International Review of Economics and Finance, Journal of Asian Economics, Bulletin of Economic Research, Environment and Development Economics, Journal of Policy Reform, Journal of Post Keynesian Economics. His recent books include International Economics: Theory and Policy (Second Edition), OUP, 2022; Export Quality and Income Distribution (co-authored with Shrimoyee Ganguly), Cambridge University Press, UK, 2023. Prof. Acharyya was awarded the EXIM Bank International Trade Research Award in 1997; Global Development Network (Washington D.C.) Research Medal in 2003; the Mahalanobis Memorial Medal in 2006; Best University Teacher Award, GoWB in 2016; and Panchanan Chakravarty Memorial Best Teacher of Economics Award, Bangiya Arthiniti Parishad, 2023.

Shrimoyee Ganguly is currently employed as an Assistant Professor in Economics at the Centre for Quantitative Economics and Data Science, Birla Institute of Technology Mesra, Ranchi. Prior to this, she was a Lecturer at the Department of Economics, Ramaiah University of Applied Sciences, Bangalore. She defended her Ph.D. thesis titled "Essays on Export Quality, Employment and Wage Inequality: Role of Trade, Fiscal and Monetary Policies" in 2023. She has been a UGC NET JRF (2018-2022). She did her bachelor (Hons. First Class Second, 2015), Master (First Class Third, 2017) in Economics and received her M.Phil degree in 2019 from Jadavpur University, Kolkata. Her research interests are international trade policy, product quality, labour market, monetary policy, infrastructure development, and export promotion. She teaches subjects of Microeconomics, International Economics, Game Theory, Growth and Development Economics.

Chapter 22
Trade, FDI, and Growth: Policies, Trends, Patterns, and Econometric Evidence from India

C. Veeramani

Keywords India · FDI · Trade · Global value chains · Economic growth · Employment

22.1 Introduction

Recent global events like the COVID-19 pandemic, the US-China trade war, and rising geopolitical tensions have reignited debate on the benefits of global integration through trade and Foreign Direct Investment (FDI) for economic growth. Some advocate for reduced reliance on foreign products, arguing it strengthens national resilience and stimulates domestic growth. Consequently, protectionist policies aimed at curbing imports have been implemented by certain countries.[1]

However, mainstream economic theory challenges the protectionist narrative. Trade and investment barriers are often associated with diminished productivity, increased firm monopoly power, and ultimately, lower economic efficiency and welfare.

Greater international integration holds significant potential for developing countries like India, especially in the post-pandemic landscape. The "plus-one strategy" employed by multinational corporations (MNCs) presents an opportunity for diversifying global supply chains. This, coupled with rising wages in China, incentivizes MNCs to relocate operations to other parts of Asia, potentially including India.

C. Veeramani (✉)
Centre for Development Studies (CDS), Thiruvananthapuram, India
e-mail: veeramani@cds.edu

[1] Populist political campaigns have also emerged, such as "Make America Great Again," "Atmanirbhar Bharat Abhiyan" (self-reliant India movement), and "100% Made in Italy."

D. Maiti et al. (eds.), *75 Years of Growth, Development and Productivity in India*, India Studies in Business and Economics, https://doi.org/10.1007/978-981-97-8054-9_22

India has the potential to leverage this realignment of GVCs by becoming a major assembly hub for manufactured exports. This could generate millions of jobs for low-skilled labour, accelerating the Lewisian transformation by transferring surplus agricultural labour to high-productivity positions in modern sectors. Export growth through GVC participation presents a viable strategy for creating gainful and productive employment opportunities for India's growing youth population.

According to the McKinsey Global Institute (2020), India needs to create 90 million non-farm jobs between 2023 and 2030. This is essential to absorb new workforce entrants (60 million) and facilitate the transition of 30 million individuals from agriculture to non-farm sectors. Achieving this ambitious target necessitates an annual GDP growth rate of 8.0–8.5% over the next decade.

However, the increasing debt burden across households, firms, and the government suggests that relying solely on the domestic market is unlikely to drive India's medium-term growth (Chatterjee, 2020). In contrast, India possesses significant unexploited export potential in low-skill manufacturing and global value chain (GVC)-intensive industries (Athukorala, 2014; Chatterjee, 2020; Veeramani & Dhir, 2016). This potential encompasses network product industries, including electronics, machinery, and computers, as well as traditional labour-intensive sectors such as apparel and footwear. To capitalize on these opportunities, India must implement comprehensive reforms in trade policies, foreign direct investment (FDI), and factor markets.

This study contributes to the existing discourse on trade and FDI in India by (i) examining the policy changes with respect to trade, FDI, and factor markets since the post-1991 reforms; (ii) evaluating the impact of these policy shifts on key economic indicators, drawing on evidence from existing research; (iii) analysing recent trends and patterns in trade and FDI; and (iv) providing new econometric evidence on the relationship between trade, FDI, and sectoral growth performance in India.

Subsequent sections explore these contributions in detail. Section II provides an overview of trade and FDI policy changes since 1991. Section III summarizes existing research on the impact of these policies on productivity, economic growth, exports, and FDI. Section IV discusses recent trends and patterns in trade and FDI and utilizes econometric analysis to assess their impact on sectoral growth in India. Finally, Section V offers concluding remarks.

22.2 Overview of Trade and FDI Policies

22.2.1 Trade Openness with Respect to Goods and Services

India has implemented substantial trade liberalization measures, including tariff reductions, the elimination of quantitative import restrictions, and exchange rate liberalization. Quantitative restrictions (QRs) imposed on capital and intermediate goods imports were largely eliminated in 1992. However, the import ban on consumer

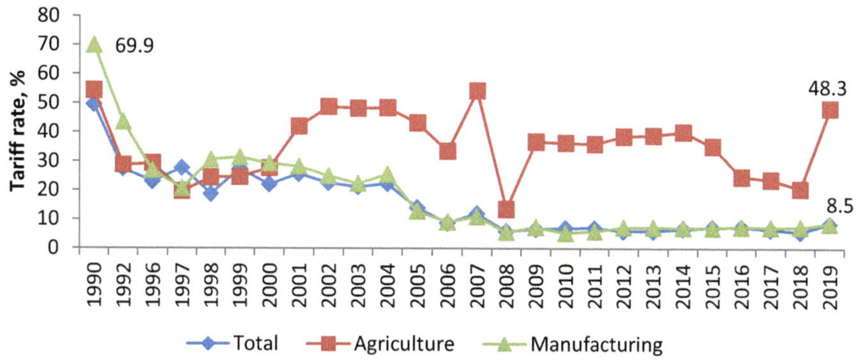

Fig. 22.1 Import Tariff Rates, MFN (Imported weighted averages). *Source* Plotted using data from UNCTAD- TRAINS and WTO-IDB (accessed using WITS, World Bank)

goods persisted until the late 1990s. Import-weighted tariff rates in the manufacturing sector have witnessed a dramatic decline, falling from approximately 70% in 1990 to a mere 6% by 2008 (Fig. 22.1). This trend was mirrored by a decrease in simple average tariff rates, which fell from 84 to 9% during the same period (Fig. 22.2). A rigorous quantitative analysis by Pursell et al. (2008) suggests that by the mid-2000s, India had transformed into one of the world's economies with the lowest levels of protection and the most open industrial sectors.[2]

This transformation is further corroborated by the significant rise in exports as a share of GDP, increasing steadily from less than 9% in 1991 to nearly 25% in 2012 (Fig. 22.3). Import openness (imports as a percentage of GDP) also witnessed a substantial increase, rising from less than 9% in 1991 to around 30% in 2012.

The trajectory of trade liberalization in India, however, appears to have undergone a partial reversal since the late 2000s. This is evident in the gradual rise of average import tariffs within the manufacturing sector, increasing from approximately 5.3% in 2010 to 8.5% in 2019 (Fig. 22.1). This trend is further substantiated by data indicating tariff hikes on a significant portion of imports. Since 2014, over 60% of total imports (measured at the HS 6-digit level) have been subjected to increased tariffs, impacting over 3,200 out of 5,300 products (Fig. 22.4). Notably, a substantial number of products (approximately 2,460) witnessed tariff increases in 2018 alone. Furthermore, the period between 2012 and 2019 coincides with a decline in the share of exports relative to GDP, dropping from around 25% to less than 19% (Fig. 22.3). Import openness also experienced a similar decline, falling from 30% of GDP to 21% during the same timeframe. Notably, the decreasing trade-to-GDP ratio for India since 2012 diverges from the global trend, as the world experienced a slight improvement during this period (Fig. 22.3). This suggests that India's declining trade openness is not driven by external pressures.

[2] However, the agricultural sector experienced a less pronounced decline in tariff rates following the initial reduction in the early 1990s.

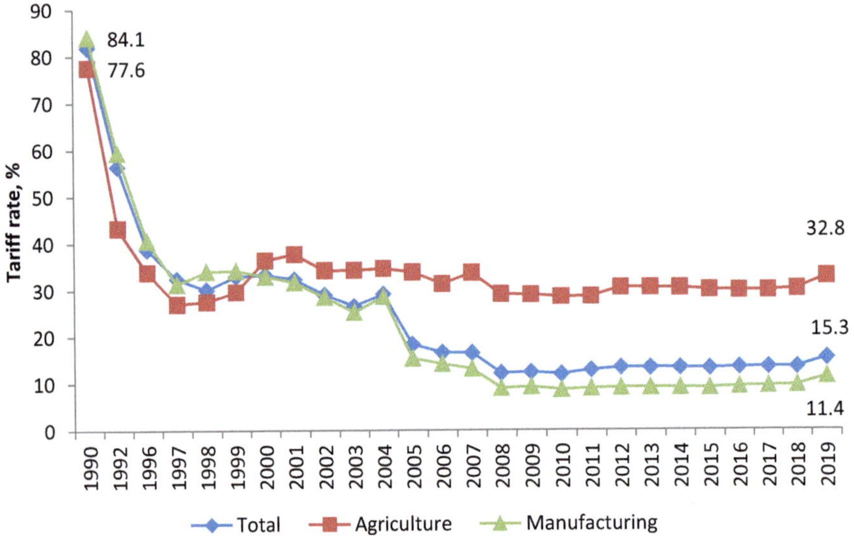

Fig. 22.2 Import Tariff Rates, MFN (Simple averages). *Source* Plotted using data from UNCTAD-TRAINS and WTO-IDB (accessed using WITS, World Bank)

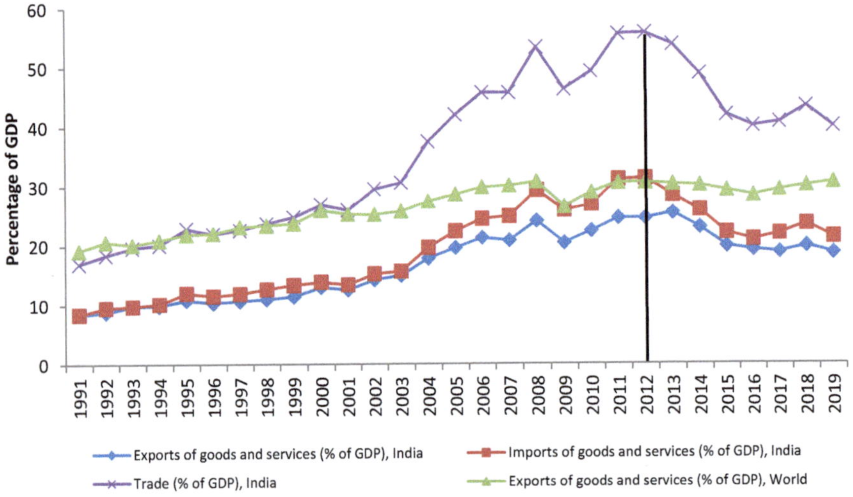

Fig. 22.3 India's Trade Oppennes—Exports, Imports, and Total Trade as percentage of GDP. *Source* World Development Indicators, World Bank

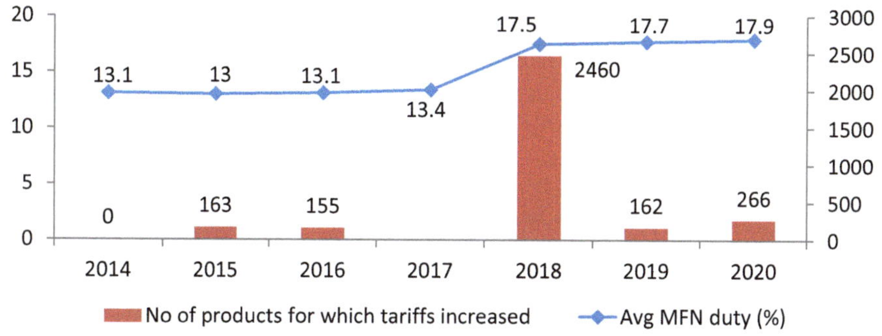

Fig. 22.4 Recent Increase in India's Import Tariff Rates. *Source* BACI dataset, CEPII and Subramanian and Chatterjee (2020)

To facilitate a cross-country comparison, Fig. 22.5 illustrates the import tariff rates for India, China, and Vietnam from 1996 to 2018. An examination of the data reveals that India's average tariff rates have consistently remained higher than China's throughout the period. Notably, between 2005 and 2008, India's tariff rates briefly approached Vietnam's levels. However, this trend proved short-lived, as India's tariffs began to diverge significantly from those of China and Vietnam in 2008. Conversely, Vietnam's tariff rates converged towards China's levels during the same period.

Several empirical studies have documented the positive effect of tariff reduction on India's industrial productivity. A decline in trade openness could potentially undermine the benefits reaped through increased global integration.

Open international markets for diverse services are crucial in today's modern and increasingly digitalized economy. They facilitate access to essential resources like information, expertise, technology, and capital. Notably, intermediate services

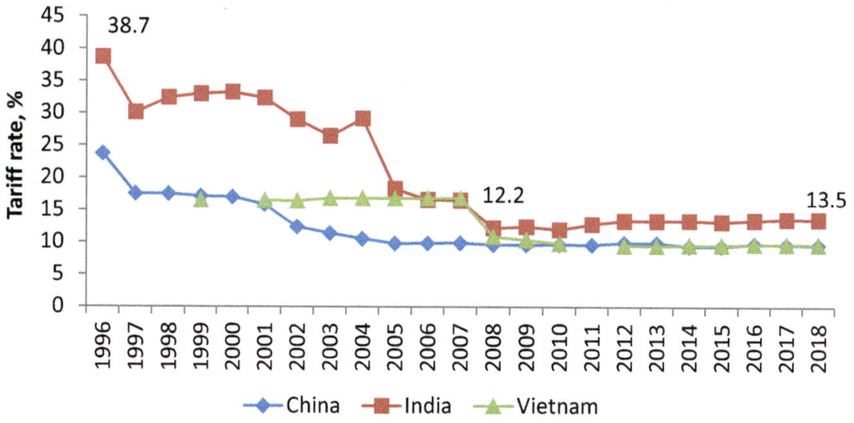

Fig. 22.5 Comparison of tariff rates, India, China, and Vietnam, MFN (Simple Averages). *Source* Plotted using data from UNCTAD- TRAINS and WTO-IDB (accessed using WITS, World Bank

offer cost-reduction and quality enhancement for final products, playing a vital role in modern manufacturing. Providing seamless access to cutting-edge service inputs can significantly improve the competitiveness of the manufacturing sector. However, significant obstacles continue to hinder global services trade. According to the OECD (2020, p. 3), "the trade cost equivalent of services trade barriers considerably exceeds the average tariff on traded goods."

The OECD's Services Trade Restrictiveness Index (STRI) measures regulatory barriers in different countries, ranging from 0 (least restrictive) to 1 (most restrictive). Notably, India exhibits the highest STRI scores in sectors like rail freight transport, legal services, accounting, and architecture. Compared to China, India's STRI remains higher in all sectors except for courier, motion pictures, broadcasting, sound recording, and telecom. A comparative analysis of India's STRI with other countries underscores the significant potential for further reforms aimed at liberalizing several of India's service sectors.

India has entered into a total of 13 Free Trade Agreements (FTAs) over the years, with only three—those involving Mauritius, the UAE, and Australia—signed within the last three years. The remainder have been in force for over a decade. FTAs are primarily pursued to reduce trade barriers, foster greater market access and generate gains from trade through trade creation rather than trade diversion.

A crucial question for policymakers concerns the selection of partner countries for FTAs. Trade theory suggests that contrary to partnering with nations possessing similar endowments, engaging in FTAs with countries having dissimilar relative endowments aligns with the principle of comparative advantage, yielding greater benefits in terms of trade creation. Previous studies indicate that India has not fully reaped the expected benefits from its prior trade agreements. This shortfall may be attributed to the fact that these agreements were mostly signed with nations possessing factor endowments broadly similar to those of India, thereby limiting the potential for trade creation.

To maximize its gains from FTAs, India should select partners from among the developed countries. This approach, in line with the Heckscher-Ohlin model of trade, posits that India, being a labour-abundant nation, can derive significant benefits from engaging in trade with capital-abundant countries that have a comparative advantage in capital and technology-intensive goods.

In this context, a noticeable shift is evident in India's recent pursuit of FTAs, with a deliberate focus on agreements with advanced countries. FTAs were signed with the UAE and Australia in 2022, followed by an FTA with the European Free Trade Association countries—Switzerland, Norway, Iceland, and Liechtenstein—in 2024. Negotiations are currently in progress for FTAs with the UK, the EU, and Canada. This strategic shift underscores an emphasis on trade complementarities and the potential for trade creation. The envisaged high trade complementarity with advanced economies suggests that recent FTAs may foster trade creation and significantly enhance India's prospects in labour-intensive exports.

22.2.2 *Openness with Respect to Inward FDI*

FDI plays a crucial role in injecting long-term capital into an economy, significantly contributing to technology transfer, fostering development in strategic sectors, stimulating innovation, intensifying competition, and generating employment opportunities. India's FDI policy is governed by regulations specific to each sector, encompassing investment caps, eligibility criteria, and prohibited sectors. Investors can navigate two routes: (i) the automatic route, permitting approval-free investment up to a pre-determined threshold and (ii) the government approval route, mandating prior approval for investments exceeding the automatic route limit or falling in restricted sectors.

Since 1991, the Indian government has implemented a series of progressive measures to liberalize its economy, fostering an environment conducive to attracting inbound FDI. Foreign investors have been granted permission to invest up to 100% equity under the automatic route in manufacturing, mining, and most service sectors. Notably, in 2019, the government permitted 100% FDI under the automatic route for coal mining. Additionally, the FDI limit in defence manufacturing under the automatic route was increased from 49 to 74% in May 2020.

The OECD's FDI Regulatory Restrictiveness Index indicates a substantial decline in India's restrictiveness, from 0.33 in 2010 to 0.21 in 2020 (Fig. 22.6). Notably, India exhibits a less restrictive FDI policy compared to China, as evidenced by its lower overall FDI Restrictiveness Index. Additionally, India's score surpasses other developing Asian economies like Thailand, the Philippines, Malaysia, and Indonesia.

As depicted in Fig. 22.6, India has comprehensively liberalized FDI across various sectors. The post-2014/2015 decline in both the consolidated FDI restrictiveness index and sector-specific indices underscores the government's significant efforts to

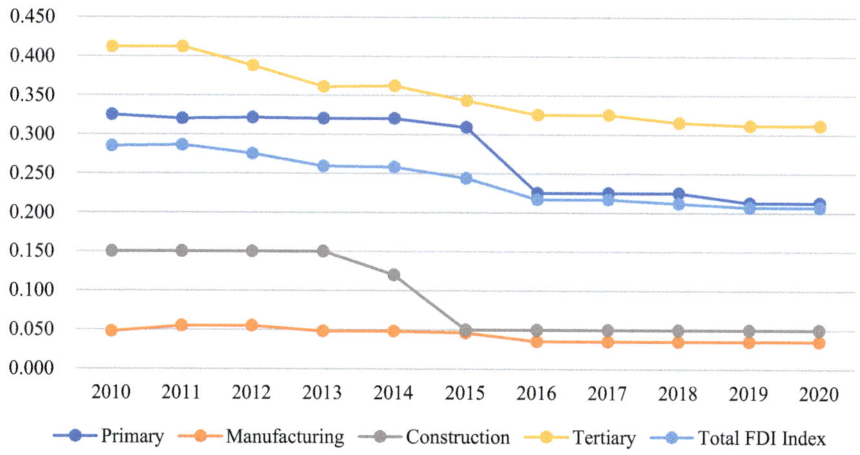

Fig. 22.6 Sector-wise FDI Restrictiveness Index: 2010–2020. *Source* Dataset: OECD FDI Regulatory Restrictiveness Index

liberalize FDI norms in sectors such as telecom, defence, education, civil aviation, pharmaceuticals, food product retail trading, and insurance. Most sectors permit 100% FDI through the automatic route, eliminating the need for prior government approval.

Certain sectors, such as multi-brand retail, print media, private banking, and insurance, still have limitations on FDI equity caps or approval routes. These sectors offer potential for further liberalization in the future.

Table 22.1 compares India's FDI restrictiveness index with China, Vietnam, and OECD averages. The index has declined significantly across all countries since 1997, reflecting broader trends in global FDI liberalization. Notably, India's restrictiveness is lower than China's, indicating a relatively more open FDI regime. However, India maintains stricter FDI policies in sectors like agriculture, retail, and some professional services, despite its comparative advantage in these areas. Conversely, China exhibits higher restrictiveness in media, broadcasting, and telecommunications sectors.

India has made significant strides in liberalizing its FDI regime. While further progress is necessary in specific sectors, the country's overall FDI policy framework demonstrably stands as more open compared to China's. Continued reforms hold the potential to unlock the full potential of FDI and propel India's economic growth and development.

22.2.3 Reforms in Factor Markets and Bankruptcy Laws

Until approximately 2010, India's trade and industrial policies were predominantly focused on product market liberalization. This was reflected in initiatives such as industrial delicensing, privatization, liberalization of FDI, removal of quantitative restrictions on imports, and reductions in import tariffs. These measures significantly lowered entry barriers for businesses. However, exit barriers for non-viable enterprises remained largely unaddressed until recent years, primarily due to rigid labour and bankruptcy laws.

These exit barriers have hampered the efficient reallocation of resources within and across industries, thereby obstructing the entry of new firms. While liberalizing product markets is crucial, its effectiveness in sustaining export growth is contingent upon a nation's ability to specialize according to the principle of comparative advantage. Specialization, in turn, requires the absence of exit barriers and the presence of flexible factor markets. Rigidities in these markets obstruct resource reallocation, impeding both inter-industry and intra-industry specialization, thus undermining export growth based on comparative advantage. Recognizing this, recent policy reforms—including bankruptcy reforms and the introduction of four new labour codes in 2020—reflect an understanding of the need for simultaneous reforms in factor markets and bankruptcy laws to achieve optimal outcomes.

A considerable body of scholarly discourse highlights the impact of India's rigid labour laws in creating substantial exit barriers. These barriers discourage large firms

Table 22.1 FDI Restrictiveness Index for India, China, and Viet Nam

Sector/Industry	1997				2019			
	China	India	Viet Nam	OECD average	China	India	Viet Nam	OECD average
Agriculture	0.83	1.00	0.82	0.12	0.19	0.44	0.08	0.06
Forestry	0.55	0.20	0.82	0.08	0.05	0.00	0.12	0.04
Fisheries	0.75	0.60	0.62	0.30	1.00	0.35	0.02	0.24
Mining & Quarrying	0.53	0.15	0.62	0.09	0.14	0.06	0.02	0.03
Manufacturing	0.38	0.24	0.62	0.05	0.07	0.04	0.03	0.02
Food and other	0.29	0.26	0.62	0.05	0.05	0.10	0.05	0.02
Oil ref. & Chemicals	0.29	0.32	0.62	0.05	0.06	0.08	0.02	0.02
Metals, machinery, and other minerals	0.44	0.15	0.62	0.05	0.08	0.00	0.02	0.02
Electric, Electronics, and other instruments	0.25	0.11	0.62	0.05	0.06	0.00	0.02	0.02
Transport equipment	0.63	0.35	0.62	0.06	0.12	0.00	0.02	0.02
Electricity	0.68	0.15	0.31	0.16	0.09	0.06	0.01	0.11
Construction	0.39	0.25	0.62	0.05	0.17	0.05	0.02	0.02
Distribution	0.76	0.60	0.62	0.05	0.08	0.28	0.13	0.02
Wholesale	0.75	0.20	0.62	0.05	0.08	0.00	0.05	0.02
Retail	0.78	1.00	0.62	0.06	0.08	0.57	0.21	0.02
Transport	0.78	0.45	0.93	0.36	0.40	0.09	0.53	0.21
Surface	0.78	0.20	0.87	0.13	0.05	0.00	0.35	0.04
Maritime	0.79	0.20	1.00	0.37	0.39	0.00	0.66	0.25
Air	0.78	0.95	0.93	0.59	0.75	0.28	0.58	0.34
Hotels and restaurants	0.35	0.35	0.62	0.05	0.05	0.00	0.06	0.02
Media	1.00	1.00	0.62	0.24	0.99	0.28	0.41	0.16
Radio and TV broadcasting	1.00	1.00	0.62	0.31	1.00	0.21	0.35	0.23
Other media	1.00	1.00	0.62	0.18	0.97	0.35	0.47	0.09
Communications	1.00	0.70	0.62	0.18	0.73	0.18	0.58	0.08
Fixed telecoms	1.00	0.70	0.62	0.19	0.75	0.18	0.58	0.09
Mobile telecoms	1.00	0.70	0.62	0.18	0.72	0.18	0.58	0.07
Financial services	0.81	0.55	0.79	0.14	0.24	0.26	0.12	0.03
Banking	0.63	0.70	0.87	0.16	0.05	0.41	0.27	0.04
Insurance	0.95	0.70	0.62	0.13	0.42	0.36	0.02	0.02

(continued)

Table 22.1 (continued)

Sector/Industry	1997				2019			
	China	India	Viet Nam	OECD average	China	India	Viet Nam	OECD average
Other finance	0.85	0.26	0.87	0.13	0.25	0.02	0.06	0.04
Business services	0.55	0.66	0.59	0.11	0.23	0.56	0.05	0.06
Legal	0.65	1.00	0.50	0.17	0.75	1.00	0.08	0.11
Accounting and audit	0.50	1.00	0.62	0.13	0.05	1.00	0.08	0.09
Architectural	0.50	0.20	0.62	0.07	0.05	0.00	0.02	0.02
Engineering	0.55	0.45	0.62	0.07	0.05	0.25	0.02	0.02
Real estate investment	0.50	1.00	0.87	0.26	0.11	0.95	0.24	0.16
Total	0.63	0.48	0.67	0.13	0.24	0.21	0.13	0.06

Source OECD

from engaging in labour-intensive activities and adopting technologies suited to such endeavours (see Aghion et al., 2008; Besley & Burgess, 2004; Gupta et al., 2009; Hasan et al, 2007; Kochhar et al., 2006; Krueger, 2010; Mitra & Ural, 2008; Panagariya, 2007). Other constraints on labour-intensive manufacturing in India include inadequate physical infrastructure—especially in power, roads, and ports—as well as cumbersome land acquisition procedures.

India's merchandise export composition has exhibited a distinct trend over time, characterized by a decline in the share of labour-intensive industries. This decline underscores the prevailing bias against labour-intensive manufacturing despite India's abundant labour force. The share of labour-intensive industries in total non-oil exports has nearly halved, falling from 30.7% in 2000 to 16.3% in 2018. Conversely, capital-intensive commodities have grown rapidly within India's export basket (Kochhar et al., 2006; Panagariya, 2007; Veeramani, 2012; Veeramani & Aerath, 2020). Such patterns of specialization are anomalous for a labour-abundant country. India's limited participation in global value chains (GVCs), especially compared to East and Southeast Asian nations, can be attributed to these idiosyncrasies in its specialization patterns (Athukorala, 2014; Veeramani & Dhir, 2017).

To address these challenges and promote labour-intensive manufacturing, several Indian states have recently initiated substantial labour market reforms. Since 2014, sixteen states have raised the threshold of the Industrial Dispute Act from 100 to 300 workers. Additionally, all but one of the 24 states have reformed the Factories Act post-2014, raising the threshold for defining a factory from 10 to 20 workers (with power) and from 20 to 40 workers (without power). In parallel, all states have raised the threshold of the Contract Labour Act from 20 to 50 and introduced Fixed Term Employment (FTE) post-2014.

Bankruptcy laws delineate a structured process for enterprises experiencing financial distress to pursue resolution or exit strategies. These legal frameworks govern the mechanisms by which businesses, unable to meet their financial obligations, can undergo restructuring or orderly liquidation. Reforms in bankruptcy laws are essential for establishing a predictable and transparent environment that benefits both creditors and debtors. Such reforms facilitate the expeditious resolution of insolvency cases, foster a business-friendly climate, and encourage entrepreneurship by mitigating the fear of failure.

This legal framework is crucial for the process of resource reallocation based on comparative advantage, as it enables investors to divest from failing investments within a stipulated timeframe, thus avoiding protracted legal disputes and reallocating funds to more profitable endeavours. However, prior to the introduction of the Insolvency and Bankruptcy Code (IBC) in 2016, the Indian corporate insolvency resolution framework was plagued by deficiencies in laws, procedures, implementation, and the capacity of supporting institutions. The absence of a cohesive and effective mechanism for corporate insolvency resolution resulted in suboptimal economic and legal outcomes.

The IBC 2016 represents a contemporary and comprehensive legal framework providing a straightforward solution to insolvency resolution challenges within the current Indian context (Sengupta et al., 2018). It substantially differs from the intricate web of pre-existing Indian laws addressing corporate insolvency, both in principle and in the design of the resolution framework. The IBC 2016 aims to achieve objectives such as swift resolution, enhanced recovery rates, and increased levels of debt financing from diverse sources.

In conjunction with reforms in the aforementioned domains, efforts to enhance resource mobility through improvements in the Ease of Doing Business, the initiation of the National Logistics Policy in 2022, the implementation of ambitious projects such as PM Gati Shakti to augment connectivity, and the maintenance of a liberal FDI policy have collectively mitigated rigidity in factor markets. These measures have fostered an environment conducive to promoting specialization and allocative efficiency.

The World Bank's Logistics Performance Index (LPI) indicates a notable improvement for India, reflecting a rise of six places from a global rank of 44 in 2018 to 38 in 2023. India has instituted various trade facilitation measures in recent years. A prime example is the introduction of the Single Window Interface for Trade (SWIFT) in 2016, which incorporates integrated risk assessment, automated routing, consolidation of nine distinct documents into an integrated declaration, and online clearance procedures. Currently, approximately 50 government agencies participate in the SWIFT initiative. The Indian Customs and Central Excise Electronic Gateway (ICEGATE) serves as the national portal offering e-filing services for importers and exporters. This platform enables the electronic filing of bills of entry or import goods declarations, shipping bills or export goods declarations, e-payment of customs duties, electronic signing of all customs documents, and online submission of supporting documents.

Additionally, the implementation of initiatives such as the National Single Window System (NSWS), which provides a centralized digital platform for all central and state approvals for businesses, combined with the decriminalization and reduction of compliance burdens, represents affirmative measures aimed at fortifying the business environment in the country.

Future reforms should prioritize addressing the rigidity in the land market to enhance factor market flexibility even further. Streamlining land acquisition processes, clarifying land ownership rights, and implementing transparent land use policies are crucial steps towards reducing barriers to entry for businesses and facilitating efficient resource allocation. Moreover, incentivizing land consolidation and facilitating land leasing arrangements can unlock untapped potential for agricultural and industrial development, fostering a more dynamic and competitive economic landscape.

22.3 Impact of the Policy Changes: Evidence from Previous Studies

In the context of India's trade and FDI liberalization initiatives, a substantial body of research has investigated the impact of these reforms on various economic indicators, including trade performance, industrial productivity, employment, and other outcomes. This section provides a concise review of several key studies within this field.

22.3.1 Productivity and Growth

Several studies have examined the relationship between tariff reduction initiatives since the early 1990s and their impact on industrial productivity and overall economic growth in India. Much of the early research centred on comparing the growth rates of total factor productivity (TFP) within India's organized manufacturing sector across the pre- and post-reform periods (see Goldar, 2012 for a comprehensive survey). These studies present conflicting findings: some studies indicate a deceleration in TFP growth during the 1990s relative to the 1980s (Balakrishnan et al., 2000; Goldar, 2004; Srivastava et al., 2001). Conversely, others demonstrate an opposite trend with a higher TFP growth rate in the 1990s (Bollard et al., 2013; Krishna & Mitra, 1998; Ray, 2002; Sivadasan, 2009; Topalova & Khandelwal, 2011; TSL, 2003; Unel, 2003).

Goldar and Kumari (2003) employed regression analysis using data on tariff and non-tariff barriers across two-digit industries to assess the impact of trade reforms on productivity. Their findings suggest that lowering effective protection for industries leads to positive growth in productivity. However, the authors attribute the observed deceleration in TFP growth during the first decade following the reforms to gestation lags in investment projects. They further argue that when adjusted for capacity utilization, the estimated TFP growth in the 1990s is comparable to that observed in the 1980s. Additionally, Virmani (2005) and Hashim et al. (2011) posit the possibility of a J-curve relationship between trade liberalization and productivity, implying an initial decline followed by a gradual rise in productivity.

The majority of the studies reviewed above utilized either industry-level data from the Annual Survey of Industries (ASI) or firm-level data from the Centre for Monitoring Indian Economy (CMIE). Notably, Sivadasan (2009) pioneered the use of plant-level data for the early reform period (1986–1994) through repeated cross-sections. He observed a significant increase in productivity in 1994–1995 compared to 1987–1990, attributed to reductions in final goods tariffs and FDI liberalization.

Subsequent studies by Harrison et al. (2013) and Bollard et al. (2013) employed plant-level data for the formal manufacturing sector. The analysis suggests that import tariff reduction fosters productivity growth through two primary channels. Firstly, input tariff reduction, which involves lowering tariffs on intermediate inputs used in an industry, increases the accessibility of foreign inputs, leading to enhanced productivity. Secondly, output tariff reduction, which decreases tariffs on finished goods produced by an industry, intensifies competitive pressures, motivating domestic firms to optimize their efficiency and improve productivity.

Interestingly, the study demonstrates that the beneficial effect on productivity is greater through input tariff reduction. Specifically, it is estimated that the decline in input tariffs contributed roughly 22% to the overall rise in industrial productivity, whereas output tariff reduction only accounted for approximately 3%. Bollard et al. (2013), who analysed a broader timeframe (1980–2007), observed a substantial rise in aggregate productivity growth exceeding 5% annually, starting in the early 1990s.

Nataraj (2011) expanded the research scope by analysing the impact of both output and input tariff reduction on productivity growth in manufacturing enterprises across formal and informal sectors (1989–2000). While the overall effect of trade liberalization is positive, the study revealed distinct channels for productivity gains in each sector. Output tariff reduction led to increased average productivity within the informal sector, while input tariff reduction played a more significant role in elevating average productivity in the formal sector.

Furthermore, Parameswaran (2009) identified a positive influence of import-induced technology spillovers on firm-level productivity. Similarly, studies by Goldberg et al. (2010) and Goldar (2015) demonstrated that utilizing imported inputs contributes to improved productivity among Indian firms. Collectively, this evidence strengthens the argument that tariff reduction has positively impacted the productivity of India's industrial sectors.

Consistent with the findings on productivity, several studies have demonstrated the positive effect of India's trade and FDI liberalization policies on GDP growth performance. While Virmani (1997), Rodrik and Subramanian (2005), and Kohli (2006a, 2006b) acknowledged an initial acceleration in India's GDP growth during the 1980s, predating the reforms of the early 1990s, they attributed it to "pro-business" reforms initiated in the early 1980s.

However, Srinivasan (2003) and Panagariya (2004, 2008) offered a contrasting perspective, arguing that the higher growth in the 1980s largely stemmed from unsustainable increases in public expenditure and foreign borrowing. They contended that the growth process since the 1990s, driven by substantial economic reforms, was more sustainable. Notably, Marelli and Signorelli (2011) employed an econometric analysis to provide robust evidence for the positive effect of trade openness and FDI on India's economic growth, controlling for other key variables.

Several studies have examined the impact of the recent reforms in labour laws on employment and output. Recent investigations, including those conducted by the Ministry of Finance (2019) and Goldar (2023), have specifically analysed the effects of labour reforms implemented by the state of Rajasthan. Goldar's (2023) estimations indicate employment gains ranging from 7 to 10%, while the Ministry of Finance suggests a more conservative estimate of approximately 5%.

Goldar (2023) extends the analysis to six states—Andhra Pradesh, Haryana, Jharkhand, Maharashtra, Rajasthan, and Uttar Pradesh—over the period from 2014 to 2017. The findings indicate a positive contribution of labour reforms in all these states. Such reforms have the potential to provide a substantial impetus to specialization based on comparative advantage, foster greater integration of Indian industries into global value chains (GVCs), and facilitate export growth.

Given the evidence presented, it is advisable to raise the threshold of the Industrial Dispute Act to encompass establishments with 1,000 or more workers. This adjustment could further enhance the positive outcomes observed from labour market reforms.

22.3.2 Export Performance

In addition to its direct contribution to GDP, exports help economic growth through a number of other channels such as learning from exporting, exploitation of economies of scale, knowledge spillovers from foreign market participation, etc. Similarly, imports of intermediate and capital goods are an important channel through which domestic firms can acquire the benefits of foreign technology and improve their overall efficiency.

Prior to 1991, India's import substitution policies led to an overvalued exchange rate, creating a bias against exports. Economic reforms initiated in 1991 aimed to rectify this by establishing a more realistic exchange rate and fostering export-oriented growth. This section deals with the studies that analyse India's export performance in the post-reform period, analysing its response to the reform measures and identifying key challenges.

Following the exchange rate reforms and import tariff reduction, the overall growth rate of Indian exports exceeded that of world exports (Veeramani, 2007). This contrasted with the pre-reform period, when India's export growth lagged behind the global average. The first decade (1993–1994 to 2001–2002) saw a moderate 8% annual growth in dollar export earnings. During 2000–2011, exports enjoyed robust growth, with goods and services expanding at 21% and 24% annually, respectively. However, the period from 2012 to 2019 witnessed stagnation in goods exports (0%

annual growth) and a significant decline in services exports (5.9% annual growth) (Dev & Veeramani, 2021; Ministry of Finance, 2020; Veeramani & Aerath, 2020).

Veeramani (2012) and Panagariya (2008) observed that the fastest-growing export segments were capital-intensive, while traditional labour-intensive industries exhibited sluggish performance. The share of unskilled labour-intensive industries in non-oil merchandise exports declined from 30.7% in 2000 to 16.3% in 2018 (Ministry of Finance, 2020).

India's share of global merchandise exports increased from 0.6% in 1991 to 1.7% in 2018 (Ministry of Finance, 2020). However, it remains significantly lower than China's 12.8% share. Veeramani et al. (2018) attribute this gap primarily to India's lack of specialization (intensive margin) in specific products or industries. While India has diversified its exports across products and markets (extensive margin), its comparative advantage in labour-intensive activities is underutilized leading to low intensive margin.

In contrast, China exhibits a strong presence in both intensive and extensive margins. India's low intensive margin is linked to limited participation in Global Value Chains (GVCs) and a bias towards capital and skill-intensive industries. This is incongruous with India's abundant labour resources. To achieve faster export growth, India needs to leverage its comparative advantage by focusing on labour-intensive activities and actively participating in GVCs.

Several studies attribute India's limited specialization in labour-intensive industries to rigid labour laws that create substantial exit barriers for firms, discouraging them from entering these sectors (Kochhar et al., 2006; Krueger, 2010; Panagariya, 2008). The Industrial Disputes Act (IDA) of 1948 mandates prior government consent for retrenchment or closure of firms employing 100 or more regular workers.

An OECD study compared India's labour market regulations to other countries and concluded that they are stricter than those in Brazil, Chile, China, and most OECD nations. This regulatory environment incentivizes firms to choose skill and capital-intensive product lines that rely more on white-collar workers (not classified as "workmen" under the IDA) and therefore face less stringent employment protection. Additionally, econometric studies by Hasan et al. (2007) and Aghion et al. (2008) among others suggest that labour market rigidities have impeded employment, firm performance, and overall industrial growth in India.

While India's export performance has improved since the 1991 reforms, it faces significant challenges. The lack of specialization in labour-intensive industries, fuelled by rigid labour regulations, hinders India's potential to unlock its comparative advantage and achieve faster export growth. Addressing these challenges through policy reforms and fostering greater participation in GVCs are crucial for India to enhance its global trade competitiveness.

22.3.3 *Exports and Jobs*

Veeramani and Exim Bank of India (2016, 2023) utilize Input–Output (IO) analysis to estimate the number of jobs supported by India's merchandise and services exports from 1995 to 2018, providing both aggregate and sector-level time series data. A key advantage of IO analysis is its ability to capture not only the direct employment effect within exporting sectors but also the indirect employment effects arising from these sectors' backward linkages with other domestic sectors.

The estimates reveal a steady increase in the total number of jobs supported by Indian exports, rising from 35.7 million in 1995 to 73.9 million in 2008. This upward trend was temporarily interrupted by the global financial crisis, leading to a decline in export-related jobs to 65.1 million and 70.1 million in 2009 and 2010, respectively. However, with the resumption of export growth, the number of jobs associated with exports climbed to 75.1 million in 2011 and peaked at 75.6 million in 2012. Subsequently, as export growth slowed down after 2012, the number of export-related jobs gradually declined to 58.2 million in 2018.

The manufacturing sector contributes the largest share of export-related jobs, followed by services and agriculture. In 2017–2018, exports supported approximately 43.4 million jobs for males and 14.7 million jobs for females. Additionally, 37.5% of the total export-related jobs belonged to categories with relatively higher educational qualifications: 21.4% for workers with secondary and higher secondary education, and 16.1% for diploma holders, graduates, and post-graduates. Notably, 76% of the export-related jobs for workers with secondary and higher secondary education can be attributed to manufactured exports, whereas over half of the jobs for diploma holders, graduates, and post-graduates originate from the services sector.

These findings suggest that an export-oriented growth strategy, compared to one focused solely on the domestic market, can potentially create greater employment opportunities for women workers and for individuals with educational qualifications above the middle school level.

22.3.4 *Participation in Global Value Chains (GVCs)*

Global value chains (GVCs) have become a defining feature of the contemporary international economy. Reduced trade barriers and technological advancements have facilitated the fragmentation of production processes across diverse geographical locations. This has led to a significant shift in the nature and pattern of global trade, with countries specializing in specific stages of production rather than solely focusing on final goods. Consequently, trade in parts and components (P&C) has witnessed significant growth, exceeding that of final goods, as intermediate products traverse national borders throughout the production cycle (Athukorala, 2012; Baldwin & Lopez-Gonzalez, 2015; Feenstra, 1998; Hummels et al., 2001).

This phenomenon of international fragmentation, characterized by interconnected production processes and sequential, vertical trading across numerous countries, has been described through various terms such as "trade in value added," "fragmentation trade," "trade in middle products," "task trade," and "vertical specialization trade."

Despite the global trend, India's participation in GVCs, particularly within labour-intensive sectors, has remained limited (Athukorala, 2014; Ministry of Finance, 2020; Veeramani & Dhir, 2019). However, India's backward participation (utilizing imported inputs for export production) has exhibited gradual progress since the early 2000s.

To quantify India's level of engagement in GVCs, Veeramani and Dhir (2019) employed the backward value-added (BVAX) ratio. This metric measures the amount of foreign value-added incorporated within a unit of exports. Higher BVAX ratios generally signify greater participation in GVCs (Johnson & Noguera, 2012). Their study revealed a consistent increase in India's BVAX ratio from 0.14 in 1999–2000 to 0.35 in 2012–2013, indicating a growing involvement in GVCs. Nevertheless, India's participation remains significantly lower compared to China and other East and Southeast Asian economies.

Furthermore, Veeramani and Dhir (2022) demonstrate a positive correlation between increased BVAX ratio (greater GVC participation) and growth in domestic value-added (DVA) and employment generation. Similarly, the Ministry of Finance (2020) acknowledges this positive association. Greater openness towards trade and foreign direct investment (FDI) can facilitate deeper engagement in GVCs, thereby promoting domestic output and employment expansion in India.

22.3.5 Impact of FDI on Exports. Productivity and Growth

The impact of FDI on India's economic growth and exports has been a subject of considerable research, with findings varying across studies. Empirical research on the impact of FDI on India's gross domestic product (GDP) growth presents a mixed picture. Pradhan (2002) and Agrawal (2005) fail to find statistically significant evidence of a positive relationship between inward FDI and GDP growth. Conversely, Chakraborty and Nunnenkamp (2008) using a panel co-integration method and Dash and Parida (2013) employing a vector error correction (VEC) model, report a positive impact of FDI on growth.

Bhattarai and Negi (2020) offer a microeconomic perspective, highlighting the positive contributions of FDI on various firm-level factors such as sales, profits, employment, and wages in India from 2004 to 2018. They suggest that foreign capital acts as a complement to domestic capital, providing essential technology and innovation for domestic firm expansion.

Studies by Aggarwal (2002), Sharma (2003), and UNCTAD (2003) do not find a direct causal link between foreign equity share and India's overall export performance. These studies neglect the potential for positive spillover effects from multinational corporations (MNCs) to domestic firms, which could eventually enhance their export capabilities (Kathuria, 2002).

Joseph and Reddy (2009) and Franco and Sasidharan (2010) demonstrate that FDI can positively impact the export performance of Indian firms through horizontal and vertical export spillover channels. Notably, firms with higher R&D capabilities tend to benefit more significantly from FDI spillovers compared to non-R&D firms (Franco & Sasidharan, 2010).

In a broader context, the investment motives of multinational corporations in foreign countries can be categorized into three main types of FDI: (i) domestic market-seeking, also known as horizontal FDI; (ii) export-promoting FDI, also referred to as vertical FDI; and (iii) resource-seeking FDI. Previous studies reveal that FDI inflows into India have predominantly aligned with domestic market-seeking objectives rather than export-promoting intentions (Aggarwal, 2002; Sharma, 2003; UNCTAD, 2003). In contrast, countries like China have successfully attracted a significant amount of FDI geared towards promoting exports. This success is attributed to policies that involve maintaining low-import tariff rates for intermediate inputs and actively fostering participation in GVCs. India, by contrast, has faced difficulties in attracting export-promoting FDI, largely owing to its industries' limited integration into GVCs in the past.

While the direct impact of FDI on India's exports may not be pronounced, studies indicate that FDI has played a pivotal role in India's economic development through alternative channels, including (i) augmenting domestic investment by complementing indigenous capital, (ii) facilitating technology transfer to domestic enterprises, and (iii) generating positive productivity and export spillovers to domestic companies. To substantially enhance FDI's contribution to India's export growth, policy reforms must be implemented to strengthen the nation's integration into GVCs.

To leverage FDI's potential for enhancing export growth, policy reforms aimed at strengthening India's participation in GVCs are crucial. As long as this integration remains limited, inward FDI in India is likely to remain primarily focused on serving the domestic market.

22.4 Trade, FDI, and Growth: Recent Trends, Patterns, and Econometric Evidence

22.4.1 Recent Trends and Patterns

Figure 22.7 compares average annual growth rates of GDP, trade, and FDI during the pre-reform period (1970–1971 to 1990–1991) and the post-reform period (1991–1992 to 2019–2020). Real GDP growth in India accelerated significantly during the post-reform era, averaging 6.8% per annum compared to 4.3% in the pre-reform era. This improvement in GDP growth coincided with a marked increase in the growth rates of exports, imports, and FDI.

Total exports grew at a rate of 9.8% per annum during the post-reforms period, exceeding the pre-reform rate of 5.8%. Similarly, total imports witnessed a higher growth rate of 11.2% post-reforms compared to 7.7% pre-reforms. The most notable change is observed in FDI, which grew at a remarkable 21.3% per annum post-reforms compared to 7.5% pre-reforms. These trends strongly suggest that India's economic liberalization since 1991, characterized by increased import openness and FDI inflows, has positively impacted both export growth and overall GDP.

During the initial two decades of reforms, India's share in global exports of goods and services displayed steady growth, rising from 0.5% in 1991 to 2.3% in 2013. However, this trend subsequently witnessed a relative decline, falling to 2% in 2015 and slowly recovering to 2.2% in 2019. This relative decline post-2013 implies that India's export growth lagged behind global export growth, contrasting with the pre-2013 period. In contrast, India's world market share in services exports maintained its growth trajectory after a brief dip in 2014, reaching 3.5% in 2019. However, the country's share in merchandise exports remained largely stagnant at around 1.7% after 2011. The notable growth in both import and export market share during the second decade of reforms (2001–2012) suggests a complementary relationship between export and import growth. Imposing restrictions on imports may therefore negatively impact not only consumer welfare but also export growth.

Despite some improvement post-reforms, India's share in global merchandise exports remains considerably lower than China's (Fig. 22.8). In 2019, India's share stood at 1.7%, compared to China's dominant 13.2%. Even Vietnam, a much smaller economy, holds a 1.4% share. This comparison highlights India's significant potential

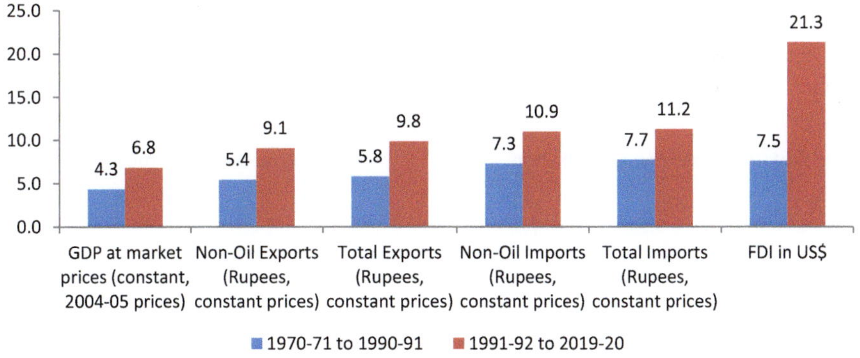

Fig. 22.7 Average Annual Growth Rates of GDP, Trade, and FDI: Comparison of Pre and Post Reforms Period. *Source* Handbook of Statistics, Reserve Bank of India. *Note* GDP data as per 2011–2012 base year (new series) has been changed to 2004–2005 base year (old series) using the ratio of GDP for 2013–2014 in the new series to that in the old series so that growth rates in the two series are the same. Trade values (in current Rupees) have been converted to constant prices using the GDP deflator

for increased merchandise exports. Regarding services exports, the gap between India and China is smaller, although China still holds a higher share (Fig. 22.8).

Figure 22.9 provides indicators of actual FDI inflows, highlighting India's superior performance compared to China since 2008 in terms of inward FDI flows as a percentage of gross fixed capital formation (GFCF) or as a percentage of GDP. Analysing the sector composition of cumulative inward FDI flows from April 2000 to March 2021 reveals that financial, banking, and business services; computer software and hardware; and construction have attracted the bulk of inward FDI.

India's share in global FDI inflows has increased considerably since the early 2000s, reaching 3.3% in 2019 compared to China's 9.2% (Fig. 22.10). Comparing Fig. 22.10 with Fig. 22.8 reveals some key points. Firstly, the disparity between India and China is significantly smaller in FDI compared to merchandise exports. Secondly, while China's world market share in merchandise exports is far greater

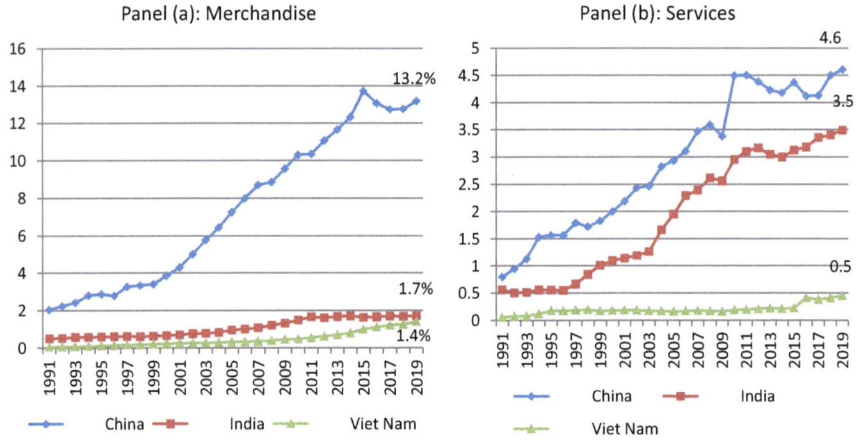

Fig. 22.8 Share in World Exports, India, China, and Viet Nam. *Source* Plotted using data from WTO

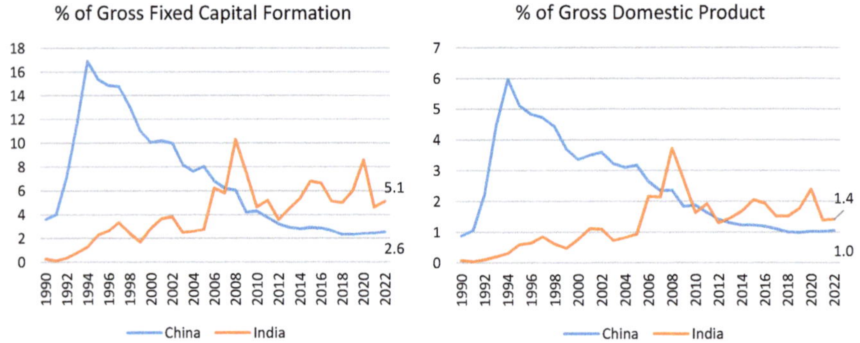

Fig. 22.9 Inward Foreign Direct Investment Inflows, India and China. *Source* UNCTAD

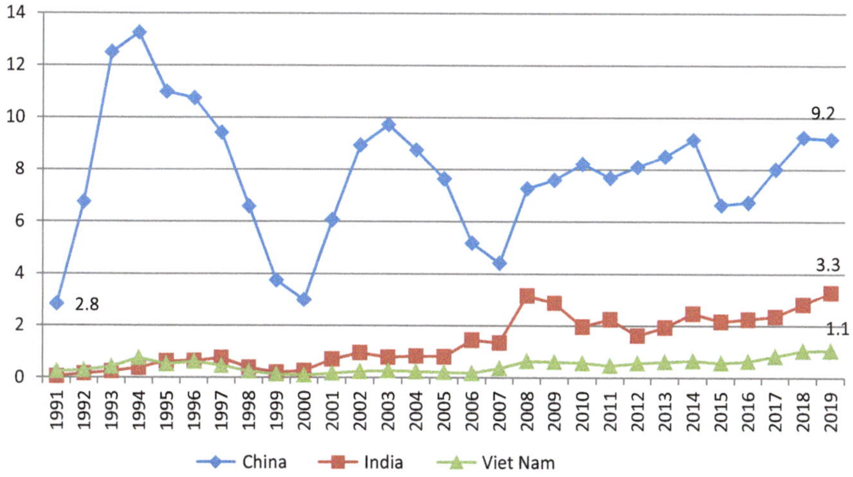

Fig. 22.10 Inward FDI flows as percentage of total world. *Source* Plotted using data from UNCTAD

than its share of inward FDI, the opposite holds true for India. These observations suggest that India, despite attracting substantial FDI, has not seen a corresponding rise in export performance. This indicates that a significant portion of India's inward FDI is "domestic market seeking" rather than "export promoting." In contrast, FDI played a critical role in boosting export growth for China and Vietnam. India's low participation in GVCs could be a major reason why its inward FDI primarily focuses on the domestic market rather than export promotion. Furthermore, India's high trade protection may incentivize "tariff jumping" type FDI, solely focused on capturing the domestic market.

22.4.2 Econometric Analysis

This study employs Indian sectoral panel data from 1999–2000 to 2014–2015 to estimate a system of equations within a simultaneous equations framework

$$\begin{aligned} ln(VA_{i,t}) = {} & \beta_0 + \beta_1 ln(K_{i,t}) + \beta_2 ln(E_{i,t}) + \beta_3 ln(FDI_{i,t}) \\ & + \beta_4(LS_{i,t}) + \beta_5(EI_{i,t}) + \beta_5(EI_{i,t}) + \beta_6(IO_{i,t}) \\ & + \beta_7(Mdummy) + \gamma_t(Yeardummies) + v_{i,t} \end{aligned} \tag{22.1}$$

$$\begin{aligned} ln(E_{i,t}) = {} & \alpha_0 + \alpha_1 ln(E_{i,t-1}) + \alpha_2 ln(VA_{i,t}) \\ & + \alpha_3(FDIopen_{i,t}) + \alpha_4(LS_{i,t}) + \alpha_5(EI_{i,t}) + \alpha_6(IO_{i,t}) \\ & + \alpha_7(Mdummy) + \theta_t(Yeardummies) + e_{i,t} \end{aligned} \tag{22.2}$$

where the variables are defined as follows:

$VA_{i,t}$ = Value added in sector i and year t at constant 2011–2012 prices (in Crores of Rupees)
$K_{i,t}$ = Capital stock in sector i and year t at constant 2011–2012 prices (in Crores of ₹)
$E_{i,t}$ = Number of persons employed in sector i and year t (in 1000s)
$FDI_{i,t}$ = Inflows of foreign direct investment in sector i and year t at constant 2011–2012 prices (in Crores of Rupees)
$LS_{i,t}$ = Labour income share in value added in sector i and year t
$EI_{i,t}$ = Export intensity (ratio of exports to employment) in sector i and year t
$IO_{i,t}$ = Import openness of sector i and year t. Import openness is measured using two alternative indicators; (i) ratio of imports to apparent consumption; apparent consumption defined as ($\text{output}_{i,t} + \text{imports}_{i,t} - \text{exports}_{i,t}$) and (ii) import weighted average tariff rates in sector i and year t.
$FDIopen_{i,t}$ = Openness with respect to FDI, defined as the ratio of FDI inflows to gross output of sector i and year t.
Mdummy = Manufacturing sector dummy which takes value 1 for all manufacturing sectors *i* and 0 otherwise

The variables $K_{i,t}$ and $E_{i,t}$, representing capital and labour inputs, are expected to show positive coefficients in the value-added function (Eq. 22.1). In addition to these inputs, the value-added function also includes FDI inflows, which is expected to yield a positive coefficient.

Studies show that India's economic growth is primarily driven by the service sector, with less emphasis on manufacturing (e.g. Kochhar et al., 2006; Panagariya, 2008). Furthermore, these studies posit a bias against labour-intensive sectors within the overall growth trajectory. The fastest-growing segments, across both manufacturing and services, tend to be capital and skill-intensive rather than labour-intensive.

To account for this unique growth pattern, Eq. (22.1) incorporates the variable $LS_{i,t}$ representing the labour income share within value added. This variable serves as a proxy for sectoral labour intensity. Drawing upon prior research, we anticipate a negative coefficient for $LS_{i,t}$ in Eq. (22.1). Additionally, a dummy variable (*Mdummy*) for the manufacturing sector is included, with the expectation of a negative coefficient. This aligns with the observation that service sectors have been the primary driver of Indian growth.

To assess the influence of trade openness, both Eqs. (22.1) and (22.2) incorporate measures of export intensity ($EI_{i,t}$) and import openness ($IO_{i,t}$). The variable ($EI_{i,t}$) is anticipated to exhibit a positive coefficient in both equations. This is based on the expectation that a more export-oriented sector would experience an increase in both value added and employment. Import openness can also influence value added and employment positively. This effect can be attributed to two primary mechanisms: (1) efficiency gains arising from heightened competition from foreign firms and (2) the utilization of imported intermediate inputs. As previously mentioned, two alternative indicators are employed to capture the degree of import openness.

The outcome-based indicator, represented by the ratio of imports to apparent consumption, is expected to yield a positive coefficient. This is because a higher ratio signifies greater openness. Conversely, the policy-based measure, reflected by the average tariff rate, is anticipated to demonstrate a negative coefficient. This aligns with the understanding that higher tariffs imply lower trade openness.

India's organized manufacturing sector is characterized by its high degree of labour market rigidity. This characteristic suggests potential persistence in sectoral employment levels. To account for this, a lagged value of employment is incorporated as an explanatory variable in Eq. (22.2). The dependent variable in Eq. (22.1) (value added) is included as a regressor in Eq. (22.2). This reflects the well-established influence of sectoral value added on sectoral employment levels. A positive coefficient for the variable $VA_{i,t}$ in Eq. (22.2) is anticipated.

Furthermore, Eq. (22.2) includes the variable $LS_{i,t}$, representing the labour income share within value added. This variable serves as a proxy for sectoral labour intensity. We expect a positive coefficient for $LS_{i,t}$ as labour-intensive sectors are typically associated with higher employment generation. As an alternative measure of labour intensity, the ratio of capital stock to labour ($K_{i,t}/E_{i,t}$) is also considered for inclusion in Eq. (22.2).

Equations (22.1) and (22.2) incorporate year dummies to control for year-specific shocks. As these equations are simultaneously determined, we employ the three-stage least squares (3SLS) econometric approach for estimation. The 3SLS approach, which combines elements of seemingly unrelated regressions (SUR) and two-stage least squares (2SLS), yields instrumental variable estimates that account for the potential covariance between the disturbances in the two equations.

Sectoral data on value-added, employment, capital stock, gross output, and labour income share within value added were sourced from the India-KLEMS database (September 2020 release) [Reserve Bank of India, 2020]. This database utilizes the International Standard Industrial Classification (ISIC Rev 3.1) and encompasses all primary, secondary, and tertiary sectors, comprising 27 sectors in total.

Data on sectoral exports and imports were obtained from a combination of sources: the Exim Bank (2016) and India's input–output (IO) tables and Supply Use tables published by the Central Statistical Organization (CSO). Foreign direct investment (FDI) data at the sectoral level was acquired from the Ministry of Commerce and Industry, Government of India. Sector classifications in the trade and FDI data were harmonized with those employed in the India-KLEMS database.

Table 22.2 presents the baseline 3SLS results for Eq. (22.1). All variables, except the import openness measure (ratio of imports to apparent consumption), exhibit statistically significant coefficients consistent with theoretical expectations. Table 22.3 replicates the specification in Table 22.2, except the analysis is restricted to the manufacturing sector. Notably, the import openness measure now yields the anticipated positive and statistically significant coefficient in both Eqs. (22.1 and 22.2).

Table 22.4 utilizes the imported weighted tariff rate as the measure of import openness. This table reveals highly significant coefficients with expected signs for

Table 22.2 3-SLS regression results, all sectors

Dep. Variable: $\ln(VA_{i,t})$	Equation 22.1			
	Coeff	Std. Err	Z	P > z
$ln(K_{i,t})$	0.401***	0.029	13.9	0
$ln(E_{i,t})$	0.384***	0.028	13.9	0
$ln(FDI_{i,t})$	0.065***	0.012	5.6	0
$(LS_{i,t})$	−2.015***	0.212	−9.5	0
$(EI_{i,t})$	0.772***	0.110	7.1	0
$IO_{i,t}$: Ratio of imports to apparent consumption	0.011	0.107	0.1	0.92
Mdummy	−0.868***	0.061	−14.3	0
Constant	3.870***	0.388	10.0	0
Observations	340			
Dep. Variable: $ln(E_{i,t})$	Equation 22.2			
$ln(E_{i,t-1})$	0.988***	0.003	335.9	0
$ln(VA_{i,t})$	0.021***	0.004	4.9	0
$(FDIopen_{i,t})$	0.005***	0.001	5.8	0
$(LS_{i,t})$	0.096***	0.019	5.0	0
$(EI_{i,t})$	0.018**	0.008	2.1	0.032
$IO_{i,t}$: Ratio of imports to apparent consumption	0.015*	0.008	1.9	0.057
Mdummy	0.012*	0.007	1.8	0.074
Constant	−0.148***	0.041	−3.6	0
Observations	340			

Notes (i) All regression equations include year dummies; (ii) ***$p < 0.01$, **$p < 0.05$, *$p < 0.1$; (iii) R^2 values are not reported as it does not have the usual interpretation in 3SLS

the trade openness indicators (export intensity and import tariff rate) and the foreign direct investment (FDI) measures.

Having established the influence of trade and foreign direct investment (FDI) variables on sectoral value added and employment, we now shift our focus to analyse the determinants of sectoral exports and imports. To this end, we estimate the following simultaneous equations using the 3SLS method.

$$\begin{aligned} ln(X_{i,t}) = \beta_0 + \beta_1 ln(VA_{i,t}) + \beta_2(FDIopen_{i,t}) + \beta_3(IO_{i,t}) \\ + \beta_4(LS_{i,t}) + \beta_5 ln(REER_t) + \beta_6(Mdummy) \\ + \gamma_t(Yeardummies) + v_{i,t} \end{aligned} \quad (22.3)$$

Table 22.3 3SLS regression results, manufacturing sectors

Dep. Variable: $ln(VA_{i,t})$	Equation 22.1			
	Coef	Std. Err	z	P > z
$ln(K_{i,t})$	0.579***	0.041	14.1	0
$ln(E_{i,t})$	0.321***	0.029	10.9	0
$ln(FDI_{i,t})$	0.073***	0.014	5.4	0
$(LS_{i,t})$	−4.146***	0.242	−17.2	0
$(EI_{i,t})$	0.272***	0.077	3.5	0
$IO_{i,t}$: Ratio of imports to apparent consumption	0.556***	0.105	5.3	0
Constant	1.865***	0.369	5.1	0
Observations	200			
Dep. Variable: $ln(E_{i,t})$	***Dep. Variable:***			
$ln(E_{i,t-1})$	0.989***	0.004	258.6	0
$ln(VA_{i,t})$	0.015***	0.005	3.1	0.002
$(FDIopen_{i,t})$	0.004***	0.001	3.7	0
$(LS_{i,t})$	0.051	0.037	1.4	0.171
$(EI_{i,t})$	0.012	0.008	1.5	0.146
$IO_{i,t}$: Ratio of imports to apparent consumption	0.037***	0.011	3.3	0.001
Constant	−0.072*	0.043	−1.7	0.095
Observations	200			

Notes (i) All regression equations include year dummies; (ii) ***$p < 0.01$, **$p < 0.05$, *$p < 0.1$; (iii) R^2 values are not reported as it does not have the usual interpretation in 3SLS

$$\begin{aligned} ln(IM_{i,t}) = \alpha_0 + \alpha_1 ln(K) + \alpha_2(LS_{i,t}) + \alpha_3(EI_{i,t}) \\ + \alpha_4(IO_{i,t}) + \alpha_5(FDIopen_{i,t}) + \alpha_6 ln(REER_t) \\ + \alpha_7(Mdummy) + \theta_t(Yeardummies) + e_{i,t} \end{aligned} \tag{22.4}$$

where the variables are defined as follows:

$X_{i,t}$, $IM_{i,t}$ = Value of exports and imports, respectively, in sector i and year t at constant 2011–2012 prices (in Crores of Rupees)[3]

$REER_t$ = 36 country real effective exchange rate of Indian Rupee.[4] An increase in the value of REER implies depreciation of Indian Rupee vis-a-viz the foreign currencies.

[3] Nominal values of exports are deflated using sector-level gross output deflator obtained from India-KLEMS database.

[4] Data on REER is taken from the Handbook of Statistics on Indian Economy, Reserve Bank of India.

Table 22.4 3SLS regression results, all sectors

Dep. Variable: $\boldsymbol{ln(VA_{i,t})}$	Equation 22.1			
	Coef	Std. Err	z	P > z
$ln(K_{i,t})$	0.437***	0.040	10.9	0
$ln(E_{i,t})$	0.393***	0.031	12.7	0
$ln(FDI_{i,t})$	0.089***	0.013	6.8	0
$(LS_{i,t})$	−4.016***	0.232	−17.3	0
$(EI_{i,t})$	0.357***	0.089	4.0	0
$IO_{i,t}$: Import-weighted tariff rate	−0.116***	0.042	−2.8	0.005
Mdummy	−0.679***	0.098	−7.0	0
Constant	3.990***	0.420	9.5	0
Observations	219			
Dep. Variable: $ln(E_{i,t})$	Equation 22.2			
$ln(E_{i,t-1})$	1.000***	0.003	344.0	0
$ln(VA_{i,t})$	−0.001	0.004	−0.2	0.832
$(FDIopen_{i,t})$	0.005***	0.001	4.0	0
$K_{i,t}/EI_{i,t}$	0.0005***	0.000	−2.8	0.005
$(EI_{i,t})$	0.019**	0.009	2.1	0.036
$IO_{i,t}$: Import-weighted tariff rate	−0.009***	0.004	−2.5	0.012
Mdummy	0.021**	0.009	2.4	0.018
Constant	0.056	0.042	1.3	0.181
Observations	219			

Notes (i) All regression equations include year dummies; (ii) ***$p < 0.01$, **$p < 0.05$, * $p < 0.1$; (iii) R^2 values are not reported as it does not have the usual interpretation in 3SLS

All the other variables are as defined earlier. A positive coefficient is anticipated for $VA_{i,t}$, in Eq. (22.3) reflecting the positive influence of domestic supply capacity on exports. Openness to FDI and imports may also contribute positively to export volumes. Given India's comparative advantage in exporting labour-intensive products, a positive coefficient is expected for $LS_{i,t}$ in Eq. (22.3). Depreciation of the Rupee (higher REER) is expected to yield a positive coefficient, indicating improved price competitiveness of Indian exports.

Turning to the determinants of imports (Eq. 22.4), the variable *Kt* is included to capture the positive effect of domestic investment on imports for industrial use. Higher capital stock is likely to lead to increased demand for imported equipment and machinery. Participation in global value chains may imply a positive association between export intensity (*EIi,t*) and the value of imports, as exporting firms may need to import intermediate inputs. Lower tariff rates and greater openness to FDI may also positively influence the value of imports. Reflecting India's comparative disadvantage in capital-intensive goods, we expect a negative coefficient for labour income share ($LS_{i,t}$) in Eq. (22.4), indicating a propensity to import such products. Depreciation of the Rupee (higher REER) is expected to show a negative coefficient, as it makes imports relatively more expensive.

Table 22.5 presents the 3SLS results for Eqs. (22.3) and (22.4). Most coefficients exhibit statistically significant effects and align with theoretical expectations. These findings suggest a complementary relationship between imports and exports. Notably, the real effective exchange rate (REER) has a statistically significant impact on the import equation but not on the export equation.

Table 22.6 utilizes import-weighted tariff rates as the measure of import openness. As anticipated, this variable exhibits the expected negative coefficient in both the export and import equations. This finding suggests that tariff reductions stimulate not only imports but also exports.

Foreign direct investment (FDI) appears to promote imports but not exports in Table 22.5. This observation aligns with the perspective that a significant portion of FDI in India caters to the domestic market rather than fostering exports.

Table 22.5 3SLS regression results, all sectors

Dep. Variable: $ln(X_{i,t})$	Equation 22.3			
	Coef	Std. Err	Z	P > z
$ln(VA_{i,t})$	1.187***	0.082	14.5	0
$(FDIopen_{i,t})$	0.092***	0.031	3.0	0.003
$IO_{i,t}$: Ratio of imports to apparent consumption	3.066***	0.270	11.4	0
$(LS_{i,t})$	−1.643***	0.433	−3.8	0
$ln(REER_t)$	−0.613	2.240	−0.3	0.785
Mdummy	1.165***	0.192	6.1	0
Constant	−1.582	10.190	−0.2	0.877
Observations	297			
Dep. Variable: $ln(IM_{i,t})$	Equation 22.4			
$ln(K)$	0.701***	0.045	15.5	0
$(LS_{i,t})$	−4.511***	0.291	−15.5	0
$EI_{i,t}$	−0.092	0.158	−0.6	0.563
$IO_{i,t}$: Ratio of imports to apparent consumption	5.052***	0.173	29.3	0
$FDIopen_{i,t}$	0.004	0.020	0.2	0.854
$ln(REER_t)$	3.655***	1.419	2.6	0.01
Mdummy	0.376***	0.103	3.6	0
Constant	−15.020	6.489	−2.3	0.021
Observations	297			

Table 22.6 3SLS regression results, all sectors

Dep. Variable: $\boldsymbol{ln(X_{i,t})}$	Equation 22.3			
	Coef	Std. Err	z	P > z
$ln(VA_{i,t})$	1.543***	0.092	16.7	0
$(FDIopen_{i,t})$	0.024	0.039	0.6	0.538
$IO_{i,t}$: Import-weighted tariff rate	−0.358***	0.123	−2.9	0.004
$(LS_{i,t})$	2.304***	0.537	4.3	0
$ln(REER_t)$	−2.886	2.542	−1.1	0.256
Mdummy	1.927***	0.341	5.7	0
Constant	4.674	11.556	0.4	0.686
Observations	228			
Dep. Variable: $\boldsymbol{ln(IM_{i,t})}$	Equation 22.4			
$ln(K)$	0.718***	0.095	7.6	0
$(LS_{i,t})$	−2.042***	0.558	−3.7	0
$EI_{i,t}$	−0.685***	0.217	−3.2	0.002
$IO_{i,t}$: Import-weighted tariff rate	−0.620***	0.133	−4.7	0
$FDIopen_{i,t}$	0.127***	0.042	3.0	0.003
$ln(REER_t)$	0.105	2.669	0.0	0.969
Mdummy	−1.660***	0.342	−4.9	0
Constant	5.087	12.204	0.4	0.677
Observations	228			

Finally, we estimate all four aforementioned equations simultaneously within a single model framework. Table 22.7 presents the results. Notably, the majority of the previously observed relationships remain consistent. However, for specific variables like the real effective exchange rate (REER), Table 22.7 yields more robust findings. Employing the alternative measure of import openness (tariff rates) in the model estimation of Table 22.7 leads to stronger results. Similarly, restricting the sample to solely encompass the manufacturing sectors preserves the validity of the previously observed relationships.

22.5 Conclusions

This paper has investigated the impacts of trade openness and foreign direct investment (FDI) on India's economic growth since the economic reforms initiated in 1991. The analysis reveals both positive and concerning trends.

Table 22.7 3SLS Regression Results, All sectors

Dep. Variable: $\boldsymbol{ln(VA_{i,t})}$	Equation 22.1			
	Coef	Std. Err	z	P > z
$ln(K_{i,t})$	0.379***	0.035	11.0	0
$ln(E_{i,t})$	0.364***	0.031	11.9	0
$(LS_{i,t})$	−2.516***	0.219	−11.5	0
$(EI_{i,t})$	0.713***	0.091	7.9	0
$IO_{i,t}$: Ratio of imports to apparent consumption	0.087	0.099	0.9	0.377
$ln(FDI_{i,t})$	0.118***	0.013	9.2	0
Mdummy	−0.851***	0.059	−14.3	0
Constant	3.862***	0.373	10.3	0
Observations	277			
Dep. Variable: $ln(E_{i,t})$	Equation 22.2			
$ln(VA_{i,t})$	0.014***	0.005	2.9	0.003
$ln(E_{i,t-1})$	0.999***	0.003	349.5	0
$(EI_{i,t})$	0.023**	0.010	2.3	0.019
$IO_{i,t}$: Ratio of imports to apparent consumption	0.020**	0.009	2.3	0.019
$(FDIopen_{i,t})$	0.006***	0.001	6.1	0
$(K_{i,t})/(E_{i,t})$	0.000	0.000	1.2	0.231
Mdummy	0.000	0.007	−0.1	0.958
Constant	−0.111**	0.046	−2.4	0.015
Observations	277			
Dep. Variable: $\boldsymbol{ln(X_{i,t})}$	Equation 22.3			
$ln(VA_{i,t})$	1.577***	0.094	16.7	0
$(FDIopen_{i,t})$	0.006	0.030	0.2	0.838
$IO_{i,t}$: Ratio of imports to apparent consumption	3.296***	0.266	12.4	0
$(LS_{i,t})$	−1.594***	0.427	−3.7	0
$ln(REER_t)$	−6.555**	2.807	−2.3	0.02
Mdummy	1.682***	0.201	8.4	0
Constant	21.559*	12.839	1.7	0.093
Observations	277			
Dep. Variable: $\boldsymbol{ln(IM_{i,t})}$	Equation 22.4			
$EI_{i,t}$	0.038	0.147	0.3	0.796

(continued)

Table 22.7 (continued)

$(LS_{i,t})$	−4.376***	0.268	−16.3	0
$ln(K)$	0.759***	0.045	17.0	0
$IO_{i,t}$: Ratio of imports to apparent consumption	4.939***	0.158	31.3	0
$FDIopen_{i,t}$	0.031*	0.018	1.7	0.081
$ln(REER_t)$	2.062	1.646	1.3	0.21
Mdummy	0.452***	0.095	4.7	0
Constant	−8.383	7.586	−1.1	0.269
Observations	277			

On the positive side, trade liberalization has played a significant role in fostering economic activity in India. Following the reforms, the country witnessed remarkable growth in both exports and imports alongside a significant acceleration in real GDP growth. This suggests that increased openness has contributed positively to India's economic landscape.

However, concerning trends emerge when examining India's performance in global trade. While the initial years following the reforms saw promising growth in India's share of global merchandise exports, this trend has stagnated, significantly lagging behind competitor nations like China. Conversely, India has experienced a surge in FDI inflows, particularly in the financial and service sectors. This raises concerns about the nature of FDI received, as a significant portion appears to be directed towards the domestic market rather than promoting export-oriented activities.

A comparison with China revealed India's progress in export diversification but highlighted its lag in specialization and global value chain (GVC) participation. A complementary relationship exists between India's export and import growth, suggesting that import restrictions could harm both consumer welfare and export potential.

An econometric analysis focusing on the effects of trade openness and FDI on sector-level value added and employment (1999–2000 to 2014–2015) revealed positive effects of both on these indicators. Importantly, the analysis found that import openness positively affects export performance, suggesting that lowering tariffs stimulates both imports and exports. However, the analysis also revealed that FDI appears to promote imports more than exports, reflecting India's inclination towards domestic market-seeking FDI rather than export promotion. This trend aligns with India's low participation in GVCs. Furthermore, the analysis shed light on the bias against labour-intensive sectors in India's growth trajectory, as evidenced by the negative coefficient for the labour income share variable.

In light of these findings, several policy reforms are recommended. Firstly, reforms are needed to enhance GVC integration and leverage FDI for export-led growth and job creation, emphasizing capitalizing on India's comparative advantages for faster export expansion. Secondly, focusing on export growth through specialization (intensive margin) can improve India's competitiveness in the global market for merchandise exports. Lastly, addressing the existing bias against labour-intensive sectors is crucial to ensure inclusive and sustainable economic growth in India.

References

Aggarwal, A. (2002). Liberalisation, multinational enterprises and export performance: Evidence from Indian Manufacturing. *Journal of Development Studies, 38*(3).

Agrawal, P. (2005). Foreign direct investment in south Asia: Impact on economic growth and local investment. In Edward M. Graham (Ed.), *Multinationals and foreign investment in economic development* (pp. 94–118) Springer.

Aghion, P., Burgess, R., Redding, S. J., & Zilibotti, F. (2008). The unequal effects of liberalization: Evidence from dismantling the License Raj in India. *American Economic Review, 98*(4), 1397–1412.

Athukorala, P. (2012). Asian trade flows: Trends, patterns and prospects. *Japan and the World Economy, 24*(2), 150–162.

Athukorala, P. (2014). *How India fits into global production sharing: Experience, prospects and policy options.* India Policy Forum (2013/14) (Vol. 10, pp. 57–116). Sage Publications.

Balakrishnan, P., Pushpangadan, K., & Babu, S. M. (2000). Trade liberalization and productivity growth in manufacturing: Evidence from firm level data. *Economics & Political Weekly, 35*(41), 3679–3682.

Baldwin, R., & Lopez-Gonzalez, J. (2015). Supply-chain trade: A portrait of global patterns and several testable hypotheses. *The World Economy, 38*(11), 1682–1721.

Besley, T., & Burgess, R. (2004). Can labor regulation hinder economic performance? Evidence from India. *The Quarterly Journal of Economics, 119*(1), 91–134.

Bhattarai, K., & Negi, V. (2020). FDI and economic performance of firms in India. *Studies in Microeconomics, 8*(1), 2020.

Bollard, A., Klenow, P. J., & Sharma, G. (2013). India's mysterious manufacturing miracle. *Review of Economic Dynamics, 16*(1), 59–85.

Chakraborty, C., & Nunnenkamp, P. (2008). *Economic reforms, FDI, and economic growth in India: A sector level analysis.* World Development.

Chatterjee, S. (2023). India's inward (re)turn: is it warranted? Will it work? *Indian Economic Review, 58*(Suppl 1), 35–59. https://doi.org/10.1007/s41775-023-00156-1

Dash, R. K., & Parida, P. C. (2013). FDI, services trade and economic growth in India: Empirical evidence on causal links. *Empirical Economics, 45*(1), 217–238. *36*(7), 1192–1212.

Dev, M., & Veeramani, C. (2021). Exports: A post-Covid opportunity. *Business Standard*, January 7. https://www.business-standard.com/article/opinion/exports-a-post-covid-opportunity-121010700058_1.html

Feenstra, R. C. (1998). Integration of trade and disintegration of production in the global economy. *The Journal of Economic Perspectives, 12*(4), 31–50.

Franco, C., & Sasidharan, S. (2010). MNEs, technological efforts and channels of export spillover: An analysis of Indian manufacturing industries. *Economic Systems, 34*(3), 270–288.

Goldar, B., & Kumari, A. (2003). Import liberalization and productivity growth in Indian manufacturing industries in the 1990s. *The Developing Economies, 41*(4), 436–460.

Goldar, B. (2004). Indian manufacturing: productivity trends in pre-and post-reform periods. *Economic and Political Weekly*, November 20, 5033–5043.

Goldar, B. (2012). Productivity in Indian manufacturing in the post-reform period: A review of studies. In V. Kathuria, S. N. Rajesh Raj, & K. Sen (Eds.), *Productivity in Indian manufacturing: Measurement, methods and analysis.* Routledge.

Goldar, B. (2015). Productivity in Indian manufacturing (1999–2011): Accounting for imported materials input. *Economic & Political Weekly, 50*(35), 104–111.

Goldar, B. (2023). *Labour reforms and employment in manufacturing plants in India: An analysis using a difference-in-difference research design* (April 6). Available at SSRN: https://ssrn.com/abstract=4390183 or https://doi.org/10.2139/ssrn.4390183

Goldberg, P. K., Khandelwal, A. K., Pavnick, N., & Topalova, P. (2010). Imported intermediate inputs and domestic product growth: Evidence from India. *Quarterly Journal of Economics, 125*(4), 1727–1767.

Gupta, P., Hasan, R., & Kumar, U. (2009). Big reforms but small payoffs: Explaining the weak record of growth in Indian manufacturing. *India Policy Forum, 2008–09*(5), 59–108.

Harrison, A. E., Martin, L. A., & Nataraj, S. (2013). Learning versus stealing: How important are market-share reallocations to India's productivity growth? *The World Bank Economic Review, 27*(2), 202–228.

Hasan, R., Mitra, D., & Ramaswamy, K. V. (2007). Trade reforms, labor regulations, and labor-demand elasticities: Empirical evidence from India. *The Review of Economics and Statistics, 89*(3), 466–481.

Hashim, D. A., Kumar, A., & Virmani, A. (2011). J-Curve hypothesis of productivity and output growth: A case study of Indian manufacturing in the post reforms period. *Indian Economic Review, 46*(1), 1–21.

Hummels, D., Ishii, J., & Yi, K. M. (2001). The nature and growth of vertical specialization in world trade. *Journal of International Economics, 54*(1), 75–96.

Johnson, R. C., & Noguera, G. (2012). Accounting for intermediates: Production sharing and trade in value added. *Journal of International Economics, 86*(2), 224–236.

Joseph, T. J., & Reddy, V. N. (2009). FDI spillovers and export performance of Indian manufacturing firms after liberalisation. *Economic and Political Weekly*, 97–105.

Kathuria, V. (2002). Liberalisation, FDI, and productivity spillovers-an analysis of Indian manufacturing firms. *Oxford Economic Papers, 54*, 688–718.

Kochhar, K., Kumar, U., Rajan, R., Subramanian, A., & Tokatlidis, I. (2006). India's pattern of development: What happened, what follows? *Journal of Monetary Economics, 53*(5), 981–1019.

Kohli, A. (2006a). Politics of economic growth in India, 1980–2005—Part I: the 1980s. *Economic and Political Weekly*, April 1, 1251–1259.

Kohli, A. (2006b). Politics of economic growth in India, 1980–2005—Part II: the 1990s and beyond. *Economic and Political Weekly*, April 8, 1361–1370.

Krishna, P., & Mitra, D. (1998). Trade Liberalization, market discipline and productivity growth: New evidence from India. *Journal of Development Economics, 56*, 447–462.

Krueger, A. O. (2010). India's trade with the world: Retrospect and prospect. In S. Acharya & R. Mohan (Eds.), *India's economy: Performance and challenges* (pp. 399–429). Oxford University Press.

Marelli, E., & Signorelli, M. (2011). China and India: Openness, trade and effects on economic growth. *The European Journal of Comparative Economics, 8*(1), 129–154.

McKinsey Global Institute. (2020). *India's turning point: An economic agenda to spur growth and jobs*, August. https://www.mckinsey.com/featured-insights/india/indias-turning-point-an-economic-agenda-to-spur-growth-and-jobs

Ministry of Finance. (2019). *Nourishing Dwarfs to become Giants: Reorienting policies for MSME Growth*, Chapter 3, in Economic Survey 2018–19, Government of India.

Ministry of Finance. (2020). *Creating jobs and growth by specializing to exports in network products*, Chapter 5, in Economic Survey 2019–20, Government of India.

Mitra, D., & Ural, B. P. (2008). Indian manufacturing: A slow sector in a rapidly growing economy. *The Journal of International Trade and Economic Development, 17*(4), 525–559.

Nataraj, S. (2011). The impact of trade liberalization on productivity: Evidence from India's formal and informal manufacturing sectors. *Journal of International Economics, 85*(2), 292–301.

OECD. (2020). *OECD Services trade restrictiveness index: Policy trends up to 2020*, January. https://www.oecd.org/trade/topics/services-trade/documents/oecd-stri-policy-trends-up-to-2020.pdf

Panagariya, A. (2004). India in the 1980s and 1990s: A triumph of reforms. *Economic and Political Weekly, 39*(25), 2581–2594.

Panagariya, A. (2007). Why India lags behind China and how it can bridge the gap. *World Economy, 30*(2), 229–248.

Panagariya, A. (2008). *India: The emerging giant*. Oxford University Press.

Parameswaran, M. (2009). International trade, R&D spillovers and productivity: Evidence from Indian manufacturing industry. *Journal of Development Studies, 45*(8), 1249–1266.

Pradhan, J. P. (2002). Foreign direct investment and economic growth in India: A production function analysis. *Indian Journal of Economics, 82*(327), 582–586.

Pursell, G., Kishor, N., & Gupta, K. (2008). Manufacturing protection in India since independence. In R. Jha (Ed.), *The Indian economy sixty years after independence*. Palgrave Macmillan.

Ray, S. C. (2002). Did India's economic reforms improve efficiency and productivity? A nonparametric analysis of the initial evidence from manufacturing. *Indian Economic Review*, 23–57.

Rodrik, D., & Subramanian, A. (2005). From "Hindu Growth" to productivity surge: The mystery of the Indian growth transition. *IMF Staff Papers, 52*(2).

Sengupta, R., Sharma, A., & Thomas, S. (2018). Evolution of the insolvency framework for non-financial firms in India. In S. Mahendra Dev (Ed.), *India development report*. Oxford University Press.

Sharma, K. (2003). Factors determining India's export performance. *Journal of Asian Economics, 14*(3), 435–446.

Sivadasan, J. (2009). Barriers to competition and productivity: Evidence from India. *The BE Journal of Economic Analysis & Policy, 9*(1), Article 42.

Srinivasan T N. (2003). *Indian Economic reforms: A stocktaking* (Working Paper No. 190). Stanford Center for International Development (October)

Srivastava, V., Gupta, P., & Datta, A. (2001). *The impact of India's economic reforms on industrial productivity, efficiency and competitiveness: A panel study of Indian companies, 1980–97, Report*. National Council of Applied Economic Research, New Delhi.

Tata Services Limited (TSL). (2003). *Reforms and productivity trends in Indian manufacturing sector*. Department of Economics and Statistics Tata Services Limited. Mumbai.

Topalova, P., & Khandelwal, A. (2011). Trade liberalization and firm productivity: The case of India. *The Review of Economics and Statistics, 93*(3), 995–1009.

UNCTAD. (2003). *World investment report 2003: FDI policies for development: National and international perspectives*. UNCTAD.

Unel, B. (2003). *Productivity trends in India's manufacturing sectors in the last two decades* (IMF Working Paper no. WP/03/22).

Veeramani, C. (2007). Sources of India's export growth in pre- and post-reform periods. *Economic & Political Weekly, 42*(25), 23–29 June, 2419–2427.

Veeramani, C. (2012). Anatomy of India's merchandise export growth, 1993–94 to 2010–11. *Economic and Political Weekly, 47*(1), 94–102.

Veeramani, C., & Dhir, G. (2016). India's export of unskilled labor-intensive products: A comparative analysis. In C. Veeramani, & R. Nagaraj (Eds.), *International trade and industrial development in India: Emerging trends, patterns and issues*. Orient Blackswan.

Veeramani and Exim Bank of India. (2016). *Inter-linkages between exports and employment in India* (EXIM Bank Occasional Paper 179).

Veeramani, C., & Dhir, G. (2017). Make What in India? In S. Mahendra Dev (Ed.), *India Development Report 2017*. Oxford University Press.

Veeramani, C., Lakshmi, A., & Prachi, G. (2018). Intensive and extensive margins of exports: What can India learn from China? *The World Economy, 41*(5), Wiley.

Veeramani, C., & Dhir, G. (2019). *Reaping gains from global production sharing: Domestic value addition and job creation by Indian export* (IGIDR Working Paper No WP-2019-024), Indira Gandhi Institute of Development Research, Mumbai.

Veeramani, C., & Aerath, L. (2020). Emerging trends and patterns of India's Trade Flowsin A comparative Asian perspective. In S. Chand Aggarwal, D. Kusum Das, R. Banga (Eds.), *Accelerators of India's growth-industry, trade and employment: Festschrift in Honor of Bishwanath Goldar*. Springer.
Veeramani, C., & Dhir, G. (2022). Do developing countries gain by participating in global value chains? Evidence from India. *Review of World Economics, 158*, 1011–1042.
Veeramani and Exim Bank of India. (2023). *Inter-linkages between exports and employment in India: An update*. EXIM Bank of India.
Virmani, A. (1997, August 9). India: Crises, reform and growth. *Economic and Political Weekly*.
Virmani, A. (2005). *Policy regimes, growth and poverty in India: lessons of government failure and entrepreneurial success* (ICRIER Working Paper) (No. 170, pp. 1–133).

Chapter 23
Assessing the Productivity of Indian Ports

Prabir De and Arpit Barman

Abstract Ports are the lifeline of Indian economy. More than 90% of India's merchandise trade by volume is transported via ocean routes. Not only does it handle trade, but ports are also planned to serve the country's strategic needs. However, low productivity and inefficiency of ports in India have been identified as major constraints affecting India's trade. Why is productivity of port so important? A productive and efficient port has often been a prerequisite for successful growth strategies, particularly those driven by exports. By sharp contrast, a poorly functioning or inefficient port can hinder growth. This chapter analyses the TFP growth (TFPG) of the Indian ports. One of the conclusions is that major ports in India have witnessed significant productivity strides post-inauguration of the Sagarmala project.

Keywords Indian ports · Port performance · Total factor productivity · TFPG · Efficiency

JEL codes O4 · R40

23.1 Introduction

Ports are the lifeline of Indian economy and have been playing a critical role in India's international trade. More than 90% of India's merchandise trade (by volume) is transported via ocean routes. Not only does it handle trade, ports are also planned to serve the country's strategic needs. At the time of independence, India was left with five major ports, and today India has 13 major and over 200 notified non-major

Authors are grateful to Professors K L Krishna, Biswanath Goldar and Dibyendu Maiti for their useful comments. Usual disclaimers apply.

P. De (✉) · A. Barman
Research and Information System for Developing Countries (RIS), New Delhi, India
e-mail: prabirde@ris.org.in

D. Maiti et al. (eds.), *75 Years of Growth, Development and Productivity in India*, India Studies in Business and Economics, https://doi.org/10.1007/978-981-97-8054-9_23

ports, which are the key nodes in global supply chains and crucial to the growth of the economy.[1]

The last decade and half were the watershed phase of the Indian economy, where ports were identified as key growth enabler. While the Indian economic size has grown to US$ 3 trillion in 2022 from US$ 1.5 trillion in 2010, total port cargo in India in the same period has increased from 885 million tonnes in 2010–11 to 1410 million tonnes in 2022–23. Notwithstanding the rise of Indian economy, ports remain a slow-starter, and the accentuation of structural constraints has been one of the factors contributing to as low as 4% growth in cargo during 2010 to 2022. One of the common constraints identified in De (2006, 2009), Monteiro (2010), Gaur et al. (2011), Mandal et al. (2016), Sinha and Bagodi (2019), Mitra et al. (2021) and Nanyam and Jha (2023) is low productivity and inefficiency of Indian ports. In other words, efficient and productive port has been identified as a key contributor to overall port competitiveness and international trade costs.[2]

Why is productivity of port important? A productive and efficient port has often been a prerequisite for successful growth strategies, particularly those driven by exports. By sharp contrast, a poorly functioning or inefficient port can hinder growth. India's growth slowdown in the past was identified as an outcome of the sharp decline of the total factor productivity (TFP).[3] Several studies have shown that benefits of early reforms and liberalization were partly wiped out by the inefficiency of ports in India.[4] Therefore, to add further impetus to the maritime sector and scale up the development, India has subsequently introduced the National Maritime Development Programme (NMDP),[5] Sagarmala, Maritime India Vision 2030 and Maritime Amrit Kaal Vision 2047. Needless to add, boosting performance and productivity of India's maritime sector is remained one of the prime objectives of these initiatives.[6] For example, enhancing efficiency through technology and innovation is one of the stated objectives of the MAKV 2047.[7] This grand plan underscores the need for technology advancement, innovation and transformation with the aim to bring in efficiency in operation, cost optimization and ease of doing business. Therefore, there is an in-built need to study the trends in productivity of the Indian ports, which would help us not only to understand inter-port productivity relations but also to better implement the strategic plans such as the MAKV 2047.

---

[1] Refer, for example, Sahai (1986), which discussed the role that was played by ports after Independence in India.

[2] Improved efficiency of ports has a positive impact on country's export performance. Goldar and Paul (2018) argued that improved port efficiency enhances competitiveness of India's manufactured exports enabling Indian manufacturing firms to export more.

[3] Refer, for example, Ahluwalia (1991), Virmani (2004) Goldar (2022), Goldar et al. (2023), RBI (2021), etc.

[4] Refer, for example, De (2009). Also refer, Virmani and Hashim (2011) who argued that the fall in productivity in the post-reform era was the result of technological obsolescence and the gradual adoption of new technology, and the slow effect of learning by doing.

[5] Refer, https://pib.gov.in/newsite/PrintRelease.aspx?relid=133484.

[6] Refer, Appendix 1 which presents the broad contour of India's major port development initiatives.

[7] Refer, for example, https://shipmin.gov.in/.

How has been the productivity growth across the major ports of India so far? How do we measure the productivity of the ports of India? Globally, the empirical evidences suggest that a country's or a region's economic growth in the long run is supported by sustained growth in the TFP.[8] Labour and capital significantly improve total factor productivity. However, there are other factors that affect productivity such as innovation and technological efficiency. On the other hand, performance has a significant impact on TFP. Building upon De (2006, 2009), this chapter aims to assess TFP growth (also known as TFPG) of the Indian port sector. This study has three research objectives: first, to assess the performance of major ports of India; second, to analyse the trends in productivity of major ports of India over time; and third, to look at factors such as performance responsible for variation in the TFPG across ports.

Rest of the chapter is organized as follows. Section 23.2 presents methodology and data. Section 23.3 thereafter presents an overview of Indian major ports. Empirical results are briefed in Section 23.4, followed by conclusions and policy implications in Section 23.5.

23.2 Methodology and Data

Productivity is a measurement of the overall efficiency of production. It describes the complex interlinked relationship between the output and inputs used in the production process. Productivity is often considered as a residual once we account for the growth in output due to the growth in inputs of labour and capital. The TFP compares total outputs relative to the total inputs used in the production of an output. Since both outputs and inputs are usually expressed in terms of volume of indices, the indicator measures the TFPG. TFP cannot be explained using the growth in other observable inputs, since firm level inputs are measurable and not the residuals. In analysing the residual growth, the underlying dynamics in the economy that may influence the output growth are ignored by the traditional estimation methods of TFP such as the Solow residual. In this study, we are interested in understanding total factor productivity in the sense of 'unexplained residual' from the contributions of labour and capital and also other factor such as the port performance.

Production, which can be simply defined as a process by which inputs are combined, transformed, and turned into outputs, is a fundamental concept in economic theory. Productivity and efficiency are the two most important but different concepts in measuring performance. The productivity of a producer can be loosely defined as the ratio of output(s) to input(s). This definition is easily and very obviously capable of explaining any situation where there is a single output and single

[8] Refer, for example, Solow (1956); Griliches and Jorgenson (1967); Kendrick and vaccara (1980); Klenow and Rodriguez-Clare (1997); Hall and Jones (1999); van Ark et al. (2000); Dieppe (2021); etc.

input. As production has multiple outputs and inputs, it is more common to refer to TFP; a productivity measure involving all factors of production (Coelli et al., 1998).

Efficiency can be defined as relative productivity over time or space, or both. For instance, it can be divided into intra- and inter-firm efficiency measures. The former involves measuring the use of the firm's own production potential by computing the productivity level over time relative to a firm-specific Production Frontier, which refers to the set of maximum outputs given the different level of inputs. In contrast, the latter measures the performance of a particular firm relative to its best counterpart(s) available in the industry (Lansink et al., 2001). Efficiency can be defined as technical efficiency and includes output- and input-oriented technical efficiencies, i.e., the producer can either improve output given the same input (output-oriented) or reduce the input given the same output (input-oriented,) by improving technology. The production frontier reflects the current state of technology in the industry.

23.2.1 The TFP Model

The TFP is a measure of technological change in industry. There are two related approaches to the measurement of TFP: the production function approach and the growth accounting approach using some fixed shares. In our study, we use the first approach explicitly in terms of a Cobb–Douglas production function. The econometric approach to estimation of TFP demands that we must specify the form of the function. In a single commodity two factor world, it looks like:

$$Y_t = A_t L_t^{\alpha} K_t^{\beta} \tag{23.1}$$

where Y_t, L_t and K_t are output (in our case port traffic), labour input and capital input used in the production process at time t, respectively. A_t is the technology parameter which conceals within it all the myths about the invisible that governs the shift in production function. Here, α is the output elasticity of labour, β is that of capital and the sum of these two elasticities (α+β) is one, which simply means constant returns to scale (CRS). In other words, returns to scale are equal to ($\alpha + \beta$), implying that the Cobb–Douglas production function is homogeneous of degree ($\alpha + \beta$). The form of A_t can be defined in many ways, but we consider the simplest one, i.e. Equation (23.2).

$$A_t = A_0 e^{\lambda t} \tag{23.2}$$

The Eq. (23.2) implies that technology progresses at a constant exponential rate of λ. Putting this value into (1), we get:

$$Y_t = A_0 e^{\lambda t} L_t^{\alpha} K_t^{\beta} \tag{23.3}$$

Taking logarithm on both sides gives us the final estimable equation.

$$LnY_t = LnA_0 + \lambda t + \alpha LnL_t + \beta LnK_t + \varepsilon_t \tag{23.4}$$

To derive the TFP estimates in our particular case, we incorporate time coefficients into the Eq. (23.4), and we get:

$$LnY_t = LnA_0 + \lambda t + \alpha LnL_t + \beta LnK_t + D_1 t_1 + \varepsilon_t \tag{23.5}$$

$$LnY_t = LnA_0 + \lambda t + \alpha LnL_t + \beta LnK_t + D_1 t_1 + D_2 t_2 + \varepsilon_t \tag{23.6}$$

where the time dummy in Eq. (23.5) is for the whole period (2000 to 2022), and the additional time dummy in Eq. (23.6) is for the period 2015 to 2022. Purpose of putting an additional dummy in Eq. (23.6) is basically to test the impact of the Sagarmala project initiated in India in 2014.

What is important is that Eq. (23.4) helps us to estimate the technology parameter (λ), the labour elasticity (α) and the capital elasticity (β) if we have the time-series data on Y, K and L. The determination of λ helps to understand the contribution of technological change to the growth of output in the Indian port sector. However, the meaning of λ must be clearly understood before extending it too far as is very common in the existing literature. Here, λ is disembodied, exogenous and Hicks-neutral technological progress. 'Disembodied' technological change means that it is not embodied into the factor inputs (labour and/or capital) but it takes place like 'manna from heaven' in the forms of better methods, organization and management of production that improve efficiency of input use. 'Exogenous' here means that it is independent of the variables utilized in the growth model. Therefore, we are left only with 'time' as the only factor. Quite contrary to this, the entire endogenous growth literature has been based on various internal (in a sense man-made) factors of production which govern, or which have strong influence on productivity, efficiency and technological change. On the whole, this λ fails to take into account the entire range of external factors on which the port has no direct control and social, economic and political infrastructure facilities like education, transport, R&D, energy, openness, governance and the like.

After estimating the TFP ($EstTFP_{it}$), we then aim to analyse the likely determinants of the TFP. In other words, how the TFP is affected by port's internal as well as external factors with the following equation:

$$EstTFP_{it} = \alpha_0 + \beta TFP_{i(t-1)} + \gamma(X_{it}) + \varepsilon_t \tag{23.9}$$

where $TFP_{i(t\text{-}1)}$ are the lag values of $EstTFP_{it}$ and X_{it} is the function of the following variables:

$$X_{it} = f(PPI_{it}, II_{it}, LO_{it}) \tag{23.10}$$

where II is the state-level Infrastructure Index and *LO* is the Law and Order situation of respective states in which the ports are located. We want to understand the significant determinants from internal and external sides that can influence a port's TFP. Here, *PPI* (Port Performance Index)[9] is purely a port's internal indicator, whereas the *II* and *LO* are some external indicators of the port. Note that for the analysis of TFP with internal and external factors, we have utilized 3 models; model 1 comprises of internal and external factors without the lag value of TFP, time and port dummies; model 2 comprises of all the factors except the lag value of TFP and model 3 is inclusive of all the factors. Lag of TFP also helps us to check the issue of endogeneity.

23.2.2 Data

In view of aforesaid discussion, we have chosen the period of our analysis is 2000 to 2022 we have selected the period between 2000 to 2022 for our analysis. A period of 23 years is supposed to be reasonable enough for our purpose to check the extent of the impact of new technology on the productivity of the factors of production in Indian port sector. However, technological issues like import of technical know-how and/or techniques are basically embodied in our analysis and not directly dealt with.

It may be admitted here that the measurement of the stock of capital always poses some conceptual problems. For our purpose, we have followed the Perpetual Inventory Accumulation (PIA) method. Most researchers who have dealt with capital stock in Indian industries (and also elsewhere) have preferred to use the gross fixed capital stock (GFCS), perpetuated from the base year and converted into real terms with the help of capital formation deflators. In fact, there are conflicting views about the measurement of capital in general and in Indian industry particularly. One basic and pioneering work on capital stock in Indian industries is by Hashim and Dadi (1973). Some of the other important works using this method are Roychoudhury (1977) and Ahluwalia (1991).

The major source of our data relating to traffic, capital and labour of Indian ports is various issues of *Basic Ports Statistics of India*, published by the Ministry of Ports, Shipping and Waterways (MoPSW). While tabulating port-wise capital, we have considered year-wise capital employed (expenditure). Year-wise capital data were converted into real terms with the help of capital formation deflator. Similarly, port performance indicator data are obtained from the various issues of Basic Ports Statistics of India. Unlike the TFPG analysis based on the KLEMS database,[10] our estimation is based on MoPSW's own database, mostly drawn from the *Basic Ports Statistics of India.*

---

[9] PPI has been calculated using eight performance indicators which are port's internal factors, computed based on the PCA. See Appendix 2 for more information.

[10] The industry-level TFP growth estimates are based on the gross output function framework, and these estimates were drawn from the India KLEMS database.

Finally, the data for external factors have been taken from multiple sources. The state-wise LO variable is represented by crime variable, which is the percentage share of murder (under Sect. 302 of IPC) with the total murder at all India. The data is collected from *National Crime Records Bureau of India.* Infrastructure Index comprises of four variables: (a) Per Capita Availability of Power (in kilowatt hours) collected from Central Electricity Authority of India; (b) ratio of state-wise length of national highway (km) to state area (in km^2), collected from the Ministry of Road Transports and Highway; (c) ratio of state-wise railway route (km) to state area (in km^2), collected from Ministry of Railways; and (d) state-wise telephones per 100 population, collected from the Telecom Regulatory Authority of India.

23.3 Overview of Indian Ports

India has six major ports in the west coast (Kandla or Deendayal, Mumbai, Jawaharlal Nehru, Mormugao, New Mangalore or Mangaluru, Kochi or Cochin) and seven major ports in east coast (Tuticorin or V.O.Chidambaranar, Chennai, Kamarajar or Ennore, Visakhapatnam or Vizag, Paradip, Kolkata or SMP (Kolkata Dock System) and Haldia or SMP (Haldia Dock Complex)) along its 7517 km long coastline and with vast network of navigable waterways. Four of the major ports, that is, Kolkata, Mumbai, Chennai and Mormugao are more than 100 years old. Cochin and Vizag ports are more than 50 years old. The ports of Deendayal, V.O. Chidambaranar, New Mangalore and Paradip came into existence after independence. Jawaharlal Nehru port became operational only after 1989. Ennore (Kamarjar) port is the first corporate port of India under the public sector, established in 1999.

Indian major ports have witnessed a sharp rise in its cargo throughput during the period 2010–11 and 2021–22 (Table 23.1). With an annual CAGR of 4%, total cargo of all major ports increased from 570.09 million tonnes (MT) in 2010–11 to 720.05 MT in 2021–22, and the growth in cargo has been increasing steadily since the 2000s. Out of the total cargo handled by major ports, it is the overseas cargo (export and import cargo) accounted for 76.2% (548.73 MT), which recorded an increase of 4.5% in 2021–22 compared to 2020–21.[11] Port-wise analysis of the traffic growth indicates that Kamarajar recorded the highest growth of 49.6% in 2021–22, followed by Jawaharlal Nehru (17.3%) and Mumbai (12.3%) in 2021–22, compared to 2020–21.[12] Among the major ports, Deendayal handled the highest cargo (127.10 MT) in 2021–22, followed by Paradip (116.13 MT) and Jawaharlal Nehru (76 MT) (Table 23.1). Deendayal port (located in Gujarat) has consistently occupied the top rank among the major ports of India since 2010–11, thus showing a remarkable strength in the Indian port sector. Another interesting development is ports located in bigger urban clusters like Kolkata, Chennai or Mumbai have witnessed negative

[11] Refer, https://shipmin.gov.in/sites/default/files/MoPSW%20achievemnts%20and%20initiatives%20of%20FY%202023-24_0.pdf.

[12] Ibid.

or very marginal growth in traffic over time, thereby indicating cargo diffusion in the geographic space.

Containerization started in India in 1973 in a limited way with the creation of interim container handling facilities at Mumbai and Cochin ports. Since then, container traffic has steadily increased over the years in tune with the increasing use of containers in international trade (Government of India, 2022). Presented in Table 23.1, Jawaharlal Nehru port continues to function as a major container port in India, followed by Chennai (30.93 MT) and V.O Chidambaranar (15.91 MT). The share of Jawaharlal Nehru port in total container traffic in 2021–22 stood at 50.6% (in TEUs) and 41.3% (in tonnage), thus making it the premier container port in India.

Port capacity of the major ports have increased significantly from 670.13 MT in 2010–11 to 1597.59 MT in 2021–22, but mostly concentrated in Paradip (289.2 MT), Deendayal (267.1 MT) and Jawaharlal Nehru (141.4 MT). Port capacity utilization has drastically declined from 85% in 2000–01 to 45% in 2021–22. India has also been witnessing under-utilization of port capacity.

Table 23.1 presents one of the key performance indicators of the major ports of India and provides comparison for the years 2010–11 and 2021–22. The average Turnaround Time (TRT), the time spent a ship spends entering, unloading, loading and exiting the port, has significantly improved in the last two decades, reducing to half from around 4 days (101.7 h) to roughly 2 days (53.34 h). Jawaharlal Nehru has the lowest TRT time of roughly 1 day (28.04 h), followed by Kamarajar and New Mangalore having close to 2 days. Ports like Paradip, Mormugao, Deendayal, Kolkata and Mumbai have managed to improve the TRT between 2000–01 and 2021–22.

To conclude, there has been a steady increase in handling of cargo at Indian ports over the last two decades. However, to sustain the momentum of exports and improve competitiveness, the country would need adequate and efficient ports and maritime services. This also raises the question as to how effectively India's major ports, which handle 76% of overseas cargo, can efficiently handle the trade. The TFP analyses will, therefore, help us to understand the productivity of each of these major ports.

23.4 Estimation and Results

In this section, we present the results of the estimation of production functions including Cobb–Douglas for three time periods: pre-Sagarmala (2000–01 to 2013–14), post-Sagarmala (2014–15 to 2021–22) and the whole period (2000–01 to 2021–22), respectively. To estimate the Cobb–Douglas production function, we use Fixed Effect (FE), Random Effect (RE) and Pooled OLS. To check which model (FEM or REM) is preferred, we first run the Hausman tests.[13] From the Hausman tests, we infer that when observations are taken for the whole period and pre-Sagarmala, we

[13] Diagnostic tests results are available on request from authors. For all time periods and both the production functions, the models suffer from heteroskedasticity and first order autocorrelation as per the results of modified Wald Tests and Wooldridge tests, respectively. Therefore, we use robust

Table 23.1 Profile of major ports of India

Major ports	Cargo handled			Container traffic			Port capacity		Turnaround time	
	2010–11	2021–22	CAGR	2010–11	2021–22	CAGR	2010–11	2021–22	2010–11	2021–22
	MT	MT	(%)	MT	MT	(%)	MT	MT	Hours	Hours
Kolkata	35 (6.1)	15.30 (2.1)	−7.9	6.22 (5.4)	8.44 (5)	3.1	67.05	92.77	149.04	82.8
Haldia	12.54 (2.2)	42.88 (5.9)	13.1	2.84 (2.5)	3.35 (2)	1.7			106.8	51.19
Paradip	56.04 (9.8)	116.13 (16.1)	7.6	0.07 (0.06)	0.18 (0.1)	10.3	76.5	289.75	185.52	53.16
Visakhapatnam	68.04 (11.9)	69.30 (9.6)	0.2	2.57 (2.5)	8.58 (5.10	12.8	64.93	134.18	140.16	73.83
Kamarajar	11.01 (1.9)	38.74 (5.3)	13.4		9.27 (5.5)		31	91	66.72	46.38
Chennai	61.46 (10.8)	48.56 (6.7)	−2.3	29.42 (25.8)	30.93 (18.5)	0.5	79.72	135	104.64	53.19
V.O. Chidambaranar	25.73 (4.5)	34.12 (4.7)	2.9	8.17 (7.2)	15.91 (9.5)	6.9	27.04	111.46	96	48.54
Cochin	17.87 (3.1)	34.55 (4.8)	6.8	4.42 (3.9)	10.28 (6.1)	8.8	40.98	78.6	52.8	45.87
New Mangalore	31.55 (5.5)	39.30 (5.4)	2.2	0.57 (0.4)	2.31 (1.4)	15.1	45.57	108.96	64.8	47.99
Mormugao	50.06 (8.7)	18.46 (2.5)	−9.5	0.22 (0.2)	0.18 (0.1)	−1.8	41.9	63.4	250.32	63.94
J.L. Nehru	64.32 (11.2)	76.00 (10.5)	1.7	56.43 (49.4)	69.09 (41.3)	2.0	64	141.37	63.36	28.04
Mumbai	54.59 (9.6)	59.89 (8.3)	0.9	0.65 (0.6)	0.24 (0.1)	−9.6	44.53	84	119.04	57.99
Deendayal	81.88 (14.7)	127.10 (17.6)	4.5	2.59 (2.3)	8.62 (5.1)	12.8	86.91	267.1	141.6	59.99
All Ports	**570.09**	**720.05**	**2.4**	**114.16**	**167.38**	**3.9**	**670.13**	**1597.59**	**126.96**	**53.34**

Note Port capacity of Kolkata and Haldia are combined, MT- Million Tonnes. Figures in brackets are share of individual ports (%) in all major ports
Source Authors' compilation from various editions of *Basic Ports Statistics of India*, MoPSW

conclude that there are systematic differences in coefficients of FEM and REM ($p < 0.05$). Thus, the FEM for estimation gives us efficient and consistent estimates. However, in case of post-Sagarmala, we infer from Huasman tests that there are no systematic differences in coefficients of FEM and REM ($p > 0.05$). So, the REM for estimation gives us efficient and consistent estimates. Lastly, applying the Breusch Pangan Lagrange Multiplier test we conclude that there is presence of unobserved effect in all time periods across all the production functions, thus the statistical result from pooled OLS gives the different result from the RE estimation. Pair-wise correlation matrix indicates that Y (cargo handled), L (labour) and K (capital) are not correlated. However, Y/L is positively correlated with K/L for all three periods.[14] The TFPG estimates show robust since estimated coefficients of Ln(K/L) show positive, statistically significant coefficient and less than unity.

Table 23.2 presents the estimates of production function parameters for Cobb–Douglas production function. The term statistically significant is used to indicate that the coefficient is significantly different from zero and is of the sign indicated at 5% level of significance of a two-tailed test. We infer that Pooled OLS estimation provides the best results for the whole period and pre-Sagarmala timeline. The labour coefficients are positive and statistically significant when applying Pooled OLS estimation in all the three production functions. Although, in case of post-Sagarmala timeline, Cobb–Douglas production function estimation using the Pooled OLS provides positive coefficient estimates for labour, rest of the estimation by FE and RE. When estimating the log of capital some important observations need to be noted. First, when the whole period is factor in, the pooled OLS estimation has statistically significant coefficients. Second, the coefficient of LnK is positive. Third, the coefficients of LnK are statistically insignificant pre-Sagarmala. However, in case of post-Sagarmala, the coefficient of LnK estimated using Pooled OLS in Cobb–Douglas and is statistically significant and positive.

To what follows is that labour input had positive impact on the port traffic in the whole period as well as the pre-Sagarmala phase, whereas the capital input led to impact port traffic in post-Sagarmala.

Thereafter, we predict the TFP and TFPG using Pooled OLS estimation based on the Cobb–Douglas production function. Note that in Cobb–Douglas production function, the sum of the estimates of coefficients of LnL and LnK measure the degree of homogeneity of the production function and accordingly the returns to scale. Here we infer that for all the three periods the Decreasing Returns to Scale is observed (Homogeneity < 1).

Table 23.3 provides the estimated values of TFP and TFPG using Cobb–Douglas production function based on the pooled time-series cross-section data. From the Table 23.3 one can conclude that on an average the TFP growth has accelerated post-Sagarmala period (2014–15 to 2021–22), compared to pre-Sagarmala period

---

cluster variance (Robust Standard Error) for estimating the p-values of various models to check for significance of independent variables.

[14] Refer, Appendix 3 for pair-wise correlation.

Table 23.2 Estimates of Cobb–Douglas production function parameters

Dependent Variable: Ln(Y)				Dependent Variable: Ln(Y/L)			
	RE	FE	OLS		OLS	RE	FE
2000–01 to 2021–22							
LnL	−0.228	−0.338	0.182***	Ln(K/L)	0.418***	0.212***	0.149***
	(0.210)	(0.203)	(0.019)		(0.048)	(0.055)	(0.041)
LnK	0.009	0.008	0.008				
	(0.007)	(0.007)	(0.008)				
Constant	18.942***	19.811***	15.221***	Constant	3.176***	6.835***	7.734***
	(1.831)	(1.665)	(0.201)		(0.602)	(0.705)	(0.538)
N	188	188	188	N	188	188	188
R-squared		0.184	0.292	R-squared	0.55		0.063
2000–01 to 2013–14							
LnL	−0.037	−0.322	0.221***	Ln(K/L)	0.445***	0.109	0.0485
	(0.231)	(0.441)	(0.02)		(0.065)	(0.073)	(0.051)
LnK	0.002	0.003	0.004				
	(0.003)	(0.003)	(0.008)				
Constant	17.459***	19.746***	14.816***	Constant	2.619***	7.791***	8.653***
	(1.931)	(3.516)	(0.207)		(0.817)	(0.825)	(0.659)
N	116	116	116	N	116	116	116
R-squared		0.073	0.399	R-squared	0.534		0.014
2014–15 to 2021–22							
LnL	−0.156**	−0.189**	0.064	Ln(K/L)	0.388***	0.0760*	0.0533
	(0.077)	(0.077)	(0.045)		(0.0692)	(0.0396)	(0.0367)
LnK	0.027	0.027	0.11**				
	(0.019)	(0.019)	(0.050)				
Constant	18.181***	18.419***	14.707***	Constant	4.719***	9.245***	9.660***
	(0.779)	(0.681)	(1.128)		(0.954)	(0.633)	(0.499)
N	72	72	72	N	72	72	72
R-squared		0.181	0.09	R-squared	0.355		0.03

Note Models follow cross-section time-series panel for 13 major ports. Robust standard errors in parentheses. ***p < 0.01, ** p < 0.05, * p < 0.1

(2000–01 to 2013–14).[15] In case of pre-Sagarmala period, Port of Deendayal (DPA) (1.77), Jawaharlal Nehru Port (JNPA) (1.57) and Vizag Port (VPA) (1.54) had the highest average TFP among all major ports. In post-Sagarmala period, Paradip (PPA) (2.44), Deendayal (DPA) (2.16) and Jawaharlal Nehru (JNPA) (1.55) had the highest average TFP. Overall (period 2000–01 to 2021–22), DPA (1.94), PPA (1.66) and JNPA (1.56) have been the top three productive ports.

[15] Also refer Appendix 4 for the trend of the TFP and TFPG across major ports.

Table 23.3 Predicted average TFP and TFPG

Major ports	2000–01 to 2013–14		2014–15 to 2021–22		2000–01 to 2021–22	
	TFP	TFPG (%)	TFP	TFPG (%)	TFP	TFPG (%)
ChPA	1.26	−1.01	0.84	−2.08	1.21	−0.45
CoPA	0.47	−2.44	0.75	−2.56	0.53	0.96
DPA	1.77	−1.84	2.16	29.63	1.94	0.30
JNPA	1.57	2.08	1.55	−1.41	1.56	2.04
KPL	0.89	0.36	0.80	0.20	0.94	3.73
MbPA	0.96	−3.22	1.09	7.27	1.02	−0.21
MoPA	1.05	2.17	0.55	3.04	0.82	6.01
NMPA	1.02	−2.12	1.05	3.49	1.03	−0.76
PPA	1.16	5.84	2.44	7.61	1.66	6.76
SMP (HDC)	1.04	1.80	0.79	−0.97	0.96	3.04
SMP(KDS)	0.34	1.57	0.35	−4.00	0.34	1.09
VOCA	0.63	3.24	0.93	6.02	0.72	2.81
VPA	1.54	−4.71	1.38	3.69	1.51	−1.95
Coefficient of Variation (CV)	0.40		0.54		0.42	

The TFPG rates have shown significant rise in post-inauguration of Sagarmala project. In case of pre-Sagarmala period, seven ports had positive average TFPG with highest growth experienced in Paradip port (PPA) (5.84%) and V.O. Chidambaram Port (VOCA) (3.24%). In post-Sagarmala period, eight ports had positive average TFPG with highest growth experiences by DPA (staggering 29.4%), followed by PPA (7.61%). When considering the whole period, nine ports had positive average TFPG with DPA (1.96) had the highest productivity levels, followed by PPA (1.66). One can infer from the TFP trends the Paradip Port has shown consistent rise in productivity from 2000 to 2022.

It can be said that although some Indian major ports such as Paradip, Jawaharlal Nehru and Deendayal have shown improvement in productivity levels post implementation of Sagarmala project, other ports such SMP Haldia and SMP Kolkata have not shown any improvement in productivity levels post-Sagarmala. Therefore, there seems to be an increase in divergence among major ports in terms of productivity level (as measured by CV) post-Sagarmala. Nonetheless, the acceleration of TFPG after the implementation of Sagarmala project suggests that investments in infrastructure development have yielded positive results.

At the end, we determine the factors that affect the TFP—port's internal and external factors. As discussed extensively we know that internal factors (represented the Port Performance Index) affect the TFP. To assess the effects of some external factors, we have taken Infrastructure Index (II), Law and Order (LO) (denoted by crime rate) and lagged values of the TFP. The Infrastructure Index has been computed

Table 23.4 Determinants of TFP

Variable	Model 1	Model 2	Model 3
LnTFP$_{(t-1)}$			0.603***
			(0.005)
LnPPI	0.162**	0.139**	0.063
	(0.046)	(0.045)	(0.112)
LnII	−0.070	0.151	0.014
	(0.583)	(0.463)	(0.924)
LnLO	−0.209***	0.053	−0.015
	(0.000)	(0.861)	(0.927)
Constant	0.752***	−0.256	0.025
	(0.008)	(0.785)	(0.964)
Year dummy	No	Yes	Yes
Port dummy	No	Yes	Yes
R-square	0.300	0.902	0.937
No. of observations	50	50	50
Method	OLS	OLS	OLS

Note Dependent variable: Log (TFP$_t$), p-values (in bracket) ***$p < 0.01$, ** $p < 0.05$, * $p < 0.1$
Source Authors' own

using the PCA.[16] As discussed in Sect. 23.2, the predicted value of TFP is analysed using three types of models. Cross-section pooled data are taken for four time periods: 2010–11, 2015–16, 2020–21 and 2021–22. The regression results are presented in Table 23.4. Following observations are worth noting.

First, we use robust standard errors to check the heteroskedasticity. In Model 1, coefficient of PPI and LO were significantly different from zero. Thus, we can infer that, *ceterius paribus,* 1% improvement in PPI may lead to increase the TFP by 0.16%. Similarly, *ceterius paribus,* 1% reduction in crime rate (represented by LO) may lead to increase the TFP by 0.21%. The caveat is low R-square value in model 1 indicates that the OLS does not have a good fit. In case of Model 2, the estimated coefficient of II is positive but statistically insignificant. In fact, the coefficient of the LO is statistically insignificant and the sign is positive. Nonetheless, PPI has come out positive and statistically significant in Model 1 and Model 2. However, the Model 3 resolves the signs of the coefficient of each variable. In this model, the past values of TFP have significant and positive impact on current TFP.

[16] Due to space constraints, we avoid presenting the weights and state-wise Infrastructure Index scores and rank, which are available on request.

23.5 Conclusions and Policy Implications

Based on the Cobb–Douglas production function, this study shows that Indian major ports witnessed deceleration of TFPG in pre-Sagarmala. However, it is important to note that there has been acceleration in TFPG in post-Sagarmala. Deendayal, Jawaharlal Nehru and Paradip are the top productive ports in the country. These are the ports also came out with top performing ports consistently since 2010–11. Therefore, Indian ports have witnessed significant strides in TFPG in post-Sagarmala period.

It can be further inferred that although some Indian major ports such as Paradip, Jawaharlal Nehru and Deendayal have shown improvement in productivity levels post implementation of Sagarmala project, other ports such as Haldia and Kolkata have not witnessed any improvement in productivity levels. Therefore, there seems to be an increase in divergence among major ports in terms of productivity level in post-Sagarmala period.

This study also presents the major determinants of the TFP particularly those which are linked to port's internal and external economies. Import of port performance, law and order situation, where the port is located, may lead to increase in the TFP. This study also suggests that past values of TFP have significant and positive impact on current TFP in the major ports of India.

Ports are the lifeline of Indian economy. Since India's Independence, ports have been playing a key role in India's trade and economic integration. Outcomes of this study indicate that boosting of productivity of ports must be taken up as a priority objective of the Government of India. Besides, Government may attempt to undo the divergences of productivity through augmenting higher capital and technology to those ports which are falling behind. Port authorities should continue prioritizing investments in port infrastructure, including berths, cargo handling equipment and connectivity to hinterland, to sustain this momentum.

While some ports like Deendayal (DPA), Paradip (PPA) and Jawaharlal Nehru (JNPA) have shown consistent improvement in productivity, other ports need targeted interventions to improve their performance. Policies should focus on addressing the specific bottlenecks faced by these ports, such as infrastructure limitations, inefficient processes or skill gaps.

Policies should be undertaken to encourage the adoption of advanced technologies like automation and artificial intelligence (AI), to further enhance productivity in ports. Also, AI and automation will further improve the port analytics by providing real time data of some of the key port indicators, which will allow for live tracking of key performance indicators, thus improving policy-making decisions. Lastly, a separate port-wise plan for technology upgradation shall be monitored closely. Port authorities should prioritize skill development and training programmes for port workers to ensure they have the necessary competencies to operate modern equipment and handle increasingly complex cargo.

Appendix 1

See Table 23.5.

Table 23.5 India's maritime development programme

Initiative	Primary objectives
National Maritime Development Programme (NMDP) (2005–2012)	• To modernize port infrastructure through adding new cargo handling facilities, construction/upgradation of berths, deepening of channels, rail/road connectivity projects, equipment upgradation/modernization schemes and other related schemes for creation of backup facilities • To benchmark the performance of ports to international standards
Sagarmala (2015–2023)	• To reduce logistics cost for both domestic and export–import cargo with minimal infrastructure investment • To implement projects for port modernization, port connectivity, port-led industrialization, coastal community development and coastal shipping and IWT
India Maritime Vision 2030 (Introduced in 2021)	• MIV 2030 emphasizes on boosting performance and productivity of India's maritime sector • To strengthen India's position in the global maritime sector, MIV 2030 identifies over 150 initiatives across various maritime sub-sectors like ports, shipping and waterways. These initiatives particularly focus on operational efficiency improvement, port-driven industrialization and creating safe and sustainable world-class ports to address the growing trade volume needs, as well as reducing logistics cost through better evacuation and cost effective processes
Maritime Amrit Kaal Vision 2047 (Introduced in 2023)	• The Amrit Kaal Vision 2047 builds on the Maritime India Vision 2030 and aims to develop world-class ports and promote inland water transport, coastal shipping and a sustainable maritime sector • It encompasses aspirations in logistics, infrastructure and shipping, supporting India's 'Blue Economy' for enhancing ports, shipping and waterways by 2047

Source Authors' own based on several secondary sources

Appendix 2: PPI Scores and Ranks

Major ports	2021–22		2020–21		2015–16		2010–11		2005–06		2000–01	
	S	R	S	R	S	R	S	R	S	R	S	R
SMP (KDS)	−0.81	13	−0.48	13	1.39	12	0.42	13	0.49	5	−0.38	11
SMP (HDC)	0.18	11	1.02	10	2.24	8	1.95	7	1.18	1	2.59	1
PPA	1.77	2	2.59	1	3.37	3	2.74	3	0.07	9	1.89	3
VPA	0.31	9	1.33	8	2.53	5	2.10	5	0.12	8	1.61	5
KPL	1.79	1	1.96	3	5.69	1	2.52	4	−1.62	13	*	*
ChPTA	0.23	10	0.78	11	1.16	13	1.30	10	0.25	7	0.46	10
VOCA	0.84	5	1.46	6	2.44	6	1.59	9	0.06	10	1.36	7
CoPA	0.72	7	1.20	9	1.55	11	0.55	12	0.29	6	0.83	9
NMPA	0.73	6	1.36	7	1.87	10	1.63	8	−0.28	11	1.89	4
MoPA	0.51	8	1.51	5	2.34	7	3.02	2	0.88	3	1.54	6
JNPA	1.61	3	2.12	2	3.76	2	3.31	1	−0.59	12	2.06	2
MbPA	0.01	12	0.64	12	2.15	9	1.16	11	0.70	4	−0.50	12
DPA	0.99	4	1.83	4	2.73	4	2.05	6	0.95	2	1.32	8
CV	**1.09**		**0.58**		**0.47**		**0.47**		**3.84**		**0.78**	

Note CV is Coefficient of Variation, * Port was not established, S is Score and R is Rank. Performance indicators: Ship Turn-Round Time (TRT) is the duration of the vessel's stay in port and is calculated from the time of arrival to the time of departure; Pre-Berthing Waiting Time (PBWT) is the time a ship has to wait before getting entry into a berth; Percentage of Idle Time at Berth to Time at Working Berth (PITTWB) is the ratio of total idle time to total working time while a ship is in the port; Output per Ship Berth Day (OSBD) means total tonnage handled, or distributed over the total number of ship berth days; Berth Throughput Rate (BTR) means total cargo handled by a berth in a port; Berth Occupancy Rate (BOR) is the time that a berth is occupied by ships; Operating Surplus per tonnes of Cargo Handled (PTOS) derives from total operating surplus divided by total tonnage of cargo handled by the port; Rate of Return on Turnover (RRT) derives from operating surplus divided by operating income of a port

Sources Based on the PCA, construction of the PPI follows De (2009). Data was sourced from the Government of India (2024)

Appendix 3: Pair-Wise Correlation Matrix

2000–2022 (Whole Period)

Variables	(1)	(2)	(3)
(1) Y	1.000		
(2) L	0.008	1.000	
(3) K	0.044	−0.001	1.000

Variables	(1)	(2)
(1) y/l	1.000	
(2) k/l	0.363	1.000

2000–14 (Pre-Sagarmala)

Variables	(1)	(2)	(3)
(1) Y	1.000		
(2) L	0.141	1.000	
(3) K	0.004	0.042	1.000

Variables	(1)	(2)
(1) y/l	1.000	
(2) k/l	0.437	1.000

2015–22 (Post-Sagarmala)

Variables	(1)	(2)	(3)
(1) Y	1.000		
(2) L	0.121	1.000	
(3) K	0.075	−0.136	1.000

Variables	(1)	(2)
(1) y/l	1.000	
(2) k/l	0.590	1.000

Appendix 4: Trends in TFP and TFPG for the Period 2000–2022

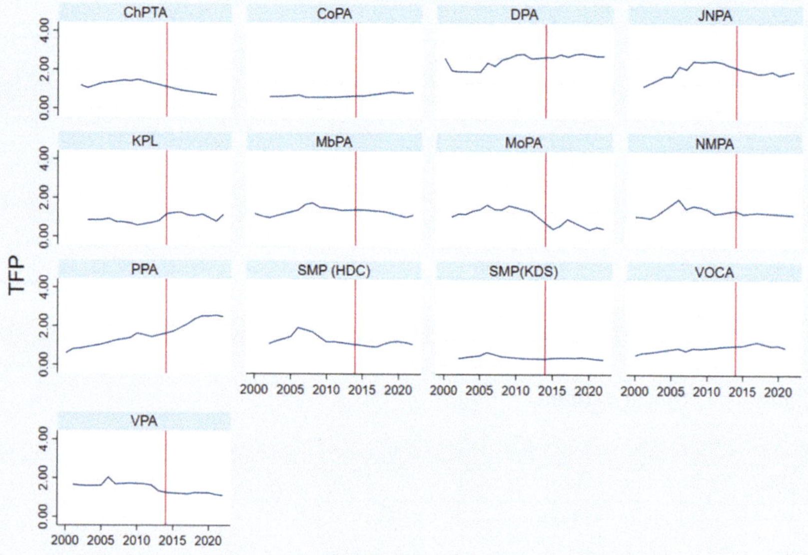

Trends In Total Factor Productivity of Ports for the whole period (2000-22)

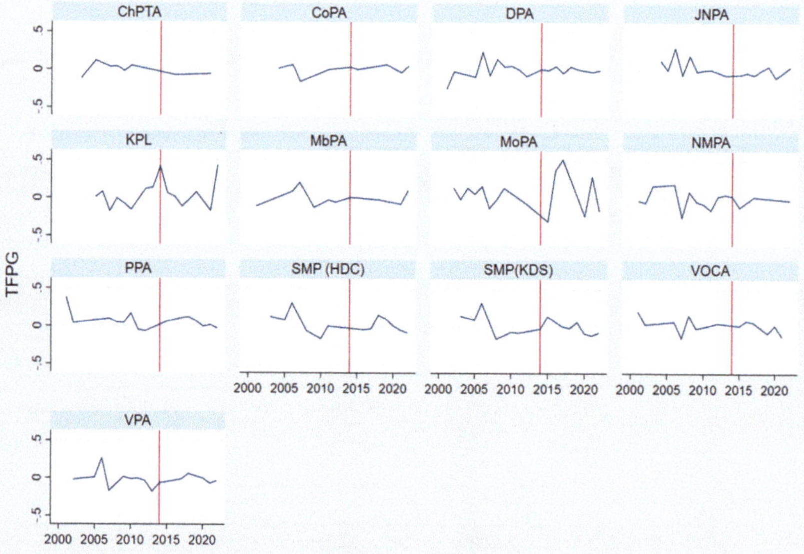

Trends in Growth in Total Factor Porductivity of the Ports

Source Authors' own

References

Ahluwalia, I. J. (1991). *Productivity and growth in Indian manufacturing sector*. Oxford University Press.

Choudhury, U. D. R. (1977). Changes in distribution of household income, consumption and wealth in rural areas. *Economic and Political Weekly*, 1709–1713.

Coelli, T., Prasad Rao, D. S., & Battese, G. E. (1998). *An introduction to efficiency and productivity analysis*. Kluwer Academic Publishers.

De, P. (2006). Total factor productivity growth: Indian ports in the era of globalisation. *Maritime Economics & Logistics, 8*, 366–386.

De, P. (2009). *Globalisation and the changing face of port infrastructure: The Indian perspective*. Peter Lang.

Dieppe, A. (Ed.). (2021). *Global productivity: Trends, drivers, and policies*. World Bank Publications.

Gaur, P., Shivani, P., & Tarun, S. (2011). Ports face inadequate capacity, efficiency and competitiveness in a developing country: Case of India. *Maritime Policy & Management, 38*(3), 293–314.

Goldar, B. (1989). Determinants of India's Export performance in engineering products, 1960–79. *Developing Economies, 27*(1), 3–18.

Goldar, B., & Paul, M. (2018). *Impact of port infrastructure development and operational efficiency of ports on export performance: A study of manufactured product exports from India*, ISID, New Delhi.

Goldar, B. (2022). Did trade liberalization boost total factor productivity growth in manufacturing in India in the 1990s? *International Productivity Monitor, 43*, 110–139.

Goldar, B., Chattopadhyay, S. K., Nath, S., Sengupta, S., & Das, P. C. (2023). Determinants of total factor productivity growth in India. *Theoretical Economics Letters, 13*, 683–718.

Government of India (2022). *Basic Port Statistics of India*. Delhi: Ministry of Ports, Shipping & Waterways, Transport Research Wing.

Government of India (2024). *Basic Port Statistics of India*. Delhi: Ministry of Ports, Shipping & Waterways, Transport Research Wing.

Griliches, Z., & Jorgenson, D. W. (1966). Sources of measured productivity change: Capital input. *The American Economic Review, 56*, 50–61.

Hall, R. E., & Jones, C. I. (1999). Why do some countries produce so much more output per worker than others? *The Quarterly Journal of Economics, 114*(1), 83–116.

Hashim, B. R., & Dadi, M. M. (1973). *Capital output relations in Indian manufacturing, 1946–1964*. Maharaja Sayajirao University of Baroda.

Hicks, J. R. (1932). Marginal productivity and the principle of variation. *Economica, 35*, 79–88.

Klenow, P. J., & Rodriguez-Clare, A. (1997). The neoclassical revival in growth economics: Has it gone too far? *NBER Macroeconomics Annual, 12*, 73–103.

Kendrick, J. W., & Vaccara, B. N. (1980). *Introduction to "new developments in productivity measurement*. In *New developments in productivity measurement* (pp. 1–14). University of Chicago Press.

Lansink, A. O., Silva, E., & Stefanou, S. (2001). Inter-firm and intra-firm efficiency measures. *Journal of Productivity Analysis, 15*, 185–199.

Mitra, S., Banerjee, P., Atul, S., Mayank, P., & Dhruv, G. (2021). *Reforming port processes in India for logistics efficiency*. Asia Development Bank (ADB).

Mandal, A., Roy, S., & chowdhury, and Jhumoor Biswas,. (2016). Performance analysis of major ports in India: A quantitative approach. *International Journal of Business Performance Management, 17*(3), 345–364.

MoPSW (2021). *Maritime India Vision 2030*, Ministry of Ports, Shipping and Waterways, Government of India, New Delhi.

MoPSW (2024). *Maritime Amrit Kaal Vision 2047*, Ministry of Ports, Shipping and Waterways, Government of India, New Delhi.

MoRTH (2015). *Manual on Port Statistics.* Transport Reach Wing, Ministry of Road Transport & Highways, Government of India.

Monteiro, J. G. R. (2010). Measuring productivity and efficiency of major ports of India. *Economic and Political Weekly, 2010*, 325–331.

Nanyam, V. P. S. N., & Jha, N. K. (2023). Modeling challenges affecting the performance of major ports of India. *The Asian Journal of Shipping and Logistics, 39*(3), 26–38.

Reserve Bank of India (2021). *Measuring productivity at the industry level—The India KLEMS Database*, Mumbai.

Sahai, B. (1986). *The ports of India.* Ministry of information and broadcasting. Government of India.

Sinha, D., & Bagodi, V. (2019). A causal review of dynamics in Indian ports. *IIM Kozhikode Society & Management Review, 8*(1), 60–73.

Solow, R. M. (1957). Technical change and the aggregate production function. *The Review of Economics and Statistics, 39*, 312–320.

Van Ark, H. H. (2000). *Economic growth and labour productivity in Europe: Half a century of East-West comparisons.*

Virmani, A. (2004). *Sources of India's economic growth: trends in total factor productivity.* ICRIER, New Delhi.

Virmani, A., & Hashim, M. D. A. (2011) *J-curve of productivity and growth: Indian manufacturing post-liberalization.* International Monetary Fund (IMF), Washington, D.C.

Prabir De is a Professor at the Research and Information System for Developing Countries (RIS), New Delhi. He is also the Adjunct Fellow of the National Maritime Foundation (NMF), New Delhi. He works in the field of international economics and has research interests in international trade and development. He has been conducting policy research for the Government of India and several national and international organisations, including UN agencies and multilateral development banks. He did his Masters in economics from Calcutta University and PhD in economics from Jadavpur University, Kolkata. He has contributed several research papers in international journals and written books on trade and development.

Arpit Barman is currently working with the National Investment and Infrastructure Fund Limited (NIIFL), New Delhi. Before joining the NIIFL, he worked as a Research Assistant at Research and Information System for Developing Countries (RIS), New Delhi. He did his Master in economics from Dr. B.R. Ambedkar University, Delhi, and he has over two years of experience in policy research. His broad areas of interest comprise econometrics, macroeconomics, financial economics and health, education and welfare. He has co-authored several publications on topics such as multidimensional well-being framework and economics of early childhood nutrition.

MIX
Papier aus verantwortungsvollen Quellen
Paper from responsible sources
FSC® C105338

If you have any concerns about our products,
you can contact us on
ProductSafety@springernature.com

In case Publisher is established outside the EU,
the EU authorized representative is:
Springer Nature Customer Service Center GmbH
Europaplatz 3, 69115 Heidelberg, Germany

Printed by Libri Plureos GmbH
in Hamburg, Germany